W9-ATA-011

The Life Span

Human Development for Helping Professionals

Patricia C. Broderick
West Chester University

Pamela Blewitt
Villanova University

Merrill
Prentice Hall

Upper Saddle River, New Jersey
Columbus, Ohio

Library of Congress Cataloging-in-Publication Data

Broderick, Patricia C.
    The life span: human development for helping professionals / Patricia C. Broderick and Pamela
Blewitt.—1st ed.
      p. cm.
    Includes bibliographical references and index.
    ISBN 0-13-014425-8 (hc.)
      1. Developmental psychology.   I. Blewitt, Pamela. II. Title.

BF713 .B755 2003
155—dc21

2002070101

Vice President and Publisher: Jeffery W. Johnston
Executive Editor: Kevin M. Davis
Editorial Assistant: Autumn Crisp
Production Editor: Mary Harlan
Production Coordination: Rebecca Giusti, Clarinda Publication Services
Design Coordinator: Diane C. Lorenzo
Photo Coordinator: Kathy Kirtland
Cover Design: Thomas Borah
Cover Image: FPG International
Text Design and Illustrations: Clarinda Publication Services
Production Manager: Laura Messerly
Director of Marketing: Ann Castel Davis
Marketing Manager: Amy June
Marketing Coordinator: Tyra Cooper

This book was set in Berkeley by The Clarinda Company. It was printed and bound by Courier Kendallville, Inc. The cover was printed by Phoenix Color Corp.

Photo Credits: Bill Anderson/Photo Researchers, Inc.: p. 86; Scott T. Baxter/Getty Images, Inc./PhotoDisc, Inc: pp. 287, 449; CNRI/Phototake NYC: fig. 2.2A; CNRI/Science Photo Library/Photo Researchers, Inc.: fig. 2.2B; Scott Cunningham/Merrill: pp. 4, 152, 211, 326, 403; Richard Drew/AP/Wide World Photos: p. 462; Laimute E. Druskis/PH College: pp. 183, 278; John Paul Endress/Silver Burdett Ginn: p. 197; ExxonMobil Corporation: p. 379; Myrleen Ferguson/PhotoEdit: p. 297; Leroy Francis/Photo Researchers, Inc.: p. 43; Tony Freeman/ PhotoEdit: p. 65; William Hamilton/Johns Hopkins University/Mary Ainsworth: p. 135; Michal Heron/PH College: pp. 428, 497; Richard Hutchings/PhotoEdit: p. 218; Infantest Corporation: p. 91; Frank La Bua/PH College: p. 164; Lynchburg Police Department: p. 474; Anthony Magnacca/Merrill: pp. 28, 176, 213, 242, 359; Steve Mason/Getty Images, Inc./PhotoDisc, Inc.: pp. 419, 516; Doug Menuez/ Getty Images, Inc./PhotoDisc, Inc.: pp. 53, 363, 387; Ryan McVay/Getty Images, Inc./PhotoDisc, Inc.: pp. 303, 424; Mrs. Robin Palmer: p. 127; PH College: p. 487; Christine Pemberton/Omni-Photo Communications, Inc.: p. 508; Rhoda Sidney/PH College: p. 471; Skjold Photographs/ PH College: p. 414; Teri Leigh Stratford/PH College: pp. 112, 134; SW Productions/Getty Images, Inc./PhotoDisc, Inc.: pp. 171, 259, 315; Anne Vega/Merrill: p. 240; Tom Watson/Merrill: p. 237; Karl Weatherly/Getty Images, Inc./PhotoDisc, Inc.: p. 329; David Young-Wolff/ PhotoEdit: p. 348; Shirley Zeiberg/PH College: pp. 253, 337.

Pearson Education Ltd.
Pearson Education Australia Pty. Limited
Pearson Education Singapore Pte. Ltd.
Pearson Education North Asia Ltd.
Pearson Education Canada, Ltd.
Pearson Educación de Mexico, S.A. de C.V.
Pearson Education—Japan
Pearson Education Malaysia Pte. Ltd.
Pearson Education, *Upper Saddle River, New Jersey*

10 9 8 7 6 5 4 3 2
ISBN: 0-13-014425-8

For the children—
especially Evan and Meredith, Michelle and Christopher

Preface

CONCEPTUAL FRAMEWORK OF THIS BOOK

The study of human development over the life span reveals the fascinating story of human beings and how they change over time. The story is both universal and uniquely personal, because it speaks to us about ourselves and the people who are important to us in our lives. Besides being intrinsically interesting, knowledge about development has obvious relevance for professionals engaged in counseling, social work, and other helping fields. We believe that in order to understand our clients and the nature of their problems, we must see clients in context. One important context is clients' developmental history. As helping professionals, we must take into account the threads of continuity and change in people's lives that bring them to their present point in development. This text provides the background and the tools to enable professionals to view their clients from a developmental perspective.

This text also reflects the contemporary view that life span development is a process deeply embedded within and inseparable from the context of family, social network, and culture. People do not progress through life in isolation; rather their developmental course influences and is influenced by other people and systems. Some of these influences are related to the cultural differences that exist in a world of increasing diversity. We recognize the importance of these factors in understanding human development and emphasize cultural and systemic influences on human growth and change throughout the book.

Knowledge about development increases every day, making it exceptionally difficult to summarize this dynamic field. Presumably, every author needs to make some choices about what to include in a book of this nature. This particular text is configured to emphasize selected theories and research that have useful applications for helping professionals. The main purpose of this book is to provide students in the helping professions with information that can be translated into professional "best practice" applications.

Throughout this text, we also emphasize the role of clinicians as reflective practitioners. Reflective practice involves "active, persistent, and careful consideration of any belief or supposed form of knowledge in light of the grounds that support it and the further conclusions to which it leads" (Dewey, 1933/1998, p. 9). Our primary vehicle for accomplishing this goal is twofold: (1) encouraging the reader to reflect on personal experience and assumptions about development and (2) communicating the value of research-based knowledge as a means of understanding human development. Our particular orientation intentionally emphasizes the significance of developmental research to the work of the professional helper. We attempt to integrate various lines of developmental research into a useful whole that has practical value for helpers in applied settings. In so doing, this book bears witness to the enormous amount of work done by developmental researchers, particularly in the last several decades. Without their groundbreaking efforts, clinicians' own work to improve people's lives would be greatly impoverished. It has been a challenge and an honor to record their contributions in this book.

COVERAGE AND ORGANIZATION

The opening chapters establish the theme of the text and introduce broad issues in development. Chapter 1 begins with an examination of the role of developmental knowledge in reflective practice. Students are introduced to theoretical models and issues that appear and reappear throughout the text. They are encouraged to reflect on their own theoretical assumptions about development and on the impact those assumptions could have in clinical practice. Boxed features help students understand how developmental processes are studied scientifically and how scientifically established information can be useful in practice. Chapter 2 takes a close look at the role of genetics in behavioral development, describing basic hereditary mechanisms by which any genetic influences must operate and examining alternative scientific strategies for assessing the contribution of genetics to behavior. Aspects of prenatal development and the multiple influences on prenatal development are also considered.

The remaining chapters follow a chronological sequence, covering a full range of critical topics in physical, cognitive, and social development. In Chapters 3 through 5, the infancy and preschool periods are the focus. Among the topics covered are early brain development and many aspects of early cognitive growth, such as the development of representational thought and memory, children's early "theory of mind" or naïve psychology, the early understanding of symbols and of language, and more. Coverage of early social development includes the emergence of emotions, emotion regulation, attachment processes, early self-development, temperament, and the role of parental disciplinary style in the growth of self-regulation. Chapters 6, 7, and 8 examine important developments in middle childhood and in the transition to adolescence, including the growth of logical thinking, the expanding capacity to process and remember information, perspective-taking skills and friendship development, influences on the developing self-concept, developments in moral thinking, influences on the emergence of prosocial and antisocial behavior, sex-role development, and peer relationships. Adolescence is the subject of Chapters 9 and 10, covering pubertal change, advances in logical and metacognitive skill, identity development, and the influences of peers, parents, school, and culture on adolescent behavior. Chapters 11 and 12 describe the young adult period, or what has been called "emerging adulthood," and includes a close look at the way thinking changes as adulthood looms and at the progress of work and career and of intimate relationships. Chapters 13 and 14 are focused on changes in physical, cognitive, and social functioning during middle and late adulthood, respectively. These chapters examine the many kinds of change that adults experience and the maintenance of well-being in the face of loss. Among the key developmental tasks discussed are marriage and its discontents, the experience of child rearing, the role of wisdom, stereotypes about aging, coping with death and bereavement, and many more.

FEATURES AND HIGHLIGHTS

- **Depth of coverage:** Because the book is designed for graduate students, most topics, especially those that have special relevance to helping professionals, are covered in greater depth than in a typical life span text.
- **Writing style:** The writing style is conversational in tone and is aimed at making even complex material accessible. To avoid sexist language use and yet still have the luxury of using the singular pronouns "she" and "he," the feminine pronoun is used in odd-numbered chapters and the masculine pronoun in even-numbered chapters.

- **Culture and gender:** In every chapter, cross-cultural and cross-gender issues are discussed wherever relevant developmental research is available.
- **Boxed features:** In many chapters, boxes highlight special topics. These may be the biographies of influential theorists or detailed examinations of issues such as infant day care, children's credibility as eyewitnesses, developmental psychopathology, the kinds of decision-making errors that adult clients often make, cross-cultural differences in funeral rituals, and many others.
- **Applications:** Application sections in each chapter offer information and suggestions for how helping professionals might apply what they have learned in a clinical setting.
- **Case studies and case study discussion questions:** Case studies and questions at the end of each chapter are another set of pedagogical tools for helping students think about the clinical implications of the developmental facts and theories they have learned.
- **Journal questions:** Journal questions at the end of each chapter help students reflect on the issues they have read about, encouraging them to consider the relevance of those issues in their own development.
- **Important terms:** Throughout the text, new or technical terms are printed in bold italics and defined. At the end of each chapter, a list of these key terms is provided as a study tool.
- **Chapter summaries:** Every chapter ends with a summary of the major topics covered in that chapter, providing yet another study tool for students and a planning tool for instructors.
- **Test bank:** A test bank for instructors accompanies the text. For each chapter, the test bank includes a chapter outline, a set of learning objectives, and 30 potential test questions, both multiple-choice and essay style. Multiple-choice questions assess comprehension of basic content knowledge and ability to apply knowledge to problem solving.

ACKNOWLEDGMENTS

Over the years spent working on this book, I have relied on the encouragement and kindness of many people. My family members, friends, and colleagues showed their support and expressed their interest ("Is the book done yet?") in innumerable ways that have earned my deepest appreciation. I would like to express special gratitude to Nicole Small for her invaluable assistance in many of the day-to-day details, to Bob Kerns for his generous advice, and to Gary Bundy and Naijian Zhang for sharing their insights with me. I would also like to acknowledge my graduate students at West Chester University, who have put up with me as I enthused about these ideas in class and whose interest in the topic of human development often rivals my own. Finally, sincere appreciation goes to my parents, who have inspired me in so many ways; to Pam Blewitt, whose friendship made this collaboration deeply satisfying; and to my husband, Bob Broderick, for being the most supportive of partners.

P. C. Broderick

My husband, children, sisters, and friends have been a continuing source of support throughout the long hours of research and writing that have gone into this text. I especially want to thank my husband, Tom Toppino, for recognizing the value of this enterprise and for sacrificing his time and ease to take on my responsibilities when deadlines loomed. My children, sisters, and good friends have encouraged and rallied me when the last chapter seemed a long way off, and they've joined in the celebrations, sometimes even arranging them, when milestones have been reached. Thank you all for being there. I also want to express deep appreciation to my coauthor and friend, Trish Broderick, for realizing that a developmental psychology text for helping professionals was really needed and for inviting me to join her on this remarkable journey.

P. Blewitt

We both wish to thank Kevin Davis at Merrill Education, who has been dedicated to the success of this project right from the start. Many others, especially Autumn Crisp, Christina Tawney, Rebecca Giusti, Mary Harlan, Kathy Kirtland, and Carol Sykes, have helped us with their expertise, patience, and support, for which we are very grateful.

We also wish to thank the following reviewers: David Andrews, Indiana State University; Michael R. Carns, Southwest Texas State University; Harry Daniels, University of Florida; Moira A. Fallon, University of Portland; Lois Flagstad, University of Nebraska at Kearney; Scott E. Hall, University of Dayton; Vonda Jump, Utah State University; Lynn F. Katz, University of Pittsburgh; Eugenie Joan Looby, Mississippi State University; Suzanne Morin, Shippensburg University; Linda W. Morse, Mississippi State University; Jane E. Myers, University of North Carolina at Greensboro; Jo-Ann Lipford Sanders, Heidelberg College; and Peggy P. Whiting, Winthrop University.

Contents

Organizing Themes in Development

INTRODUCTION

What importance do difficulties in getting along with others have for a 6-year-old youngster? Is she just "passing through a stage"? How much freedom should be given to adolescents? What implications do social problems with friends and coworkers suggest for a 22-year-old male? How significant is it for a married couple to experience increased conflicts following the births of their children? Does divorce cause lasting emotional damage to the children involved in a family breakup? What kind of day care experience is best for young children? Do we normally lose many intellectual abilities as we age? What factors enable a person to overcome early unfavorable circumstances and become a successful, healthy adult?

These intriguing questions represent a sampling of the kinds of topics that form the core of the developmentalist's study. *Life span development,* which can be defined as the study of human development from conception to death, is not a remote or esoteric body of knowledge. Rather, it has much to offer the helping professional both personally and professionally. The study of development allows helpers to understand more completely clients' concerns that are rooted in shared human experience. It provides a knowledge base built upon research and serves as a useful tool for decision making. It encourages a way of thinking about client problems from a developmental perspective. Studying development also facilitates counselors' personal growth by providing a foundation for reflecting on their own lives.

The field of counseling has been intimately tied to that of human development from its historical beginnings (Whiteley, 1984). The preamble from the code of ethics of the American Counseling Association states that its members are "dedicated to the enhancement of human development throughout the lifespan." Steenbarger (1991) noted that the field is unique because it builds upon developmental metatheory for its basic tenets and assumptions. Mosher (1995) further emphasized the connection by stating that helping professionals' reliance on developmental literature can be attributed to the fact that *the facilitation of human growth and development is the primary purpose of therapeutic practice.*

REFLECTION AND ACTION

Despite strong support for a comprehensive academic grounding in scientific developmental knowledge for the helping professional (Van Hesteren & Ivey, 1990), there has been a somewhat uneasy alliance between practitioners, such as mental health professionals, and those with a more empirical bent, such as behavioral scientists. The clinical fields have depended on research from developmental psychology to inform their practice. Yet in the past, overreliance on traditional experimental methodologies sometimes resulted in researchers' neglect of important issues that could not be studied using these rigorous methods (Hetherington, 1998). Consequently, there was a tendency for clinicians to perceive some behavioral science literature as irrelevant to real-world concerns (Turner, 1986). Clearly, the gap between science and practice is not unique to the mental health professions. Medicine, education, and law have all struggled with the problems involved in preparing students to grapple with the complex demands of the workplace. Contemporary debate on this issue has led to the development of serious alternative paradigms for the training of practitioners.

One of the most promising of these alternatives for counselors is the concept of *reflective practice,* which is receiving considerable interest and attention. The idea of "reflectivity" derives from Dewey's (1933/1998) view of education, which emphasized careful consideration of one's beliefs and forms of knowledge as a precursor to practice. Donald Schon (1987), a modern pioneer in the field of reflective practice, describes the problem this way:

> In the varied topography of professional practice, there is a high, hard ground overlooking a swamp. On the high ground, manageable problems lend themselves to solution through the application of research-based theory and technique. In the swampy lowland, messy confusing problems defy technical solutions. The irony of this situation is that the problems of the high ground tend to be relatively unimportant to individuals or society at large, however great their technical interest may be, while in the swamp lie the problems of greatest human concern. (p. 3)

The Gap Between Science and Practice

Traditionally, the modern, university-based educational process has been driven by the belief that problems can be solved best by applying objective, technical, or scientific information amassed from laboratory investigations. Implicit in this assumption is that human nature operates according to universal principles that, if known and understood, will enable us to predict behavior. For example, if I understand the principles of conditioning and reinforcement, I can apply a contingency contract to modify my client's inappropriate behavior. Postmodern critics have pointed out the many difficulties associated with this approach. Sometimes a "problem" behavior is related to, or maintained by, neurological, systemic, or cultural conditions. Sometimes the very existence of a "problem" may be a cultural construction. Unless a problem is viewed within its larger context, a problem-solving strategy may prove ineffective.

Most of the situations helpers face are confusing, complex, ill-defined, and often unresponsive to the application of a specific set of scientific principles. Thus, the training of helping professionals often involves a "dual curriculum." The first is more formal and may be presented as a conglomeration of research-based facts, whereas the second, often learned in a practicum or field placement, covers the curriculum of "what is really done" when working with clients. The antidote to this dichotomous pedagogy, Schon (1987) and his followers suggest, is reflective practice. This is a creative method of thinking about practice in which the helper masters the knowledge and skills base pertinent to the profession but is encouraged to go beyond rote technical applications to generate new kinds of understanding and strategies of action. Rather than relying solely on objective technical applications to determine ways of operating in a given situation, the reflective practitioner constructs solutions to problems by engaging in personal hypothesis generating and hypothesis testing.

How can one use the knowledge of developmental science in a meaningful and reflective way? What place does it have in the process of reflective construction? Consideration of another important line of research, namely, that of characteristics of expert problem solvers, will help us answer this question. Research studies on expert-novice differences in many areas such as teaching, science, and athletics all support the contention that experts have a great store of knowledge and skill in a particular area. Expertise is domain specific. When compared to novices in any given field, experts possess well-organized and integrated stores of information that they draw upon, almost automatically, when faced with novel challenges. Since this knowledge is well practiced, truly a "working body" of information, retrieval is relatively easy (Anderson, 1993). Progress in problem solving is closely self-monitored. Problems are analyzed and broken down into smaller units, which can be handled more efficiently.

If we apply this information to the reflective practice model, we can see some connections. One core condition of reflective practice is that practitioners use theory as a "partial lens through which to consider a problem" (Nelson & Neufelt, 1998). Practitioners also use another partial lens: their professional and other life experience. In reflective practice, theory-driven hypotheses about client and system problems are generated and tested for goodness of fit. A rich supply of problem-solving strategies depends upon a deep understanding and thorough grounding in fundamental knowledge germane to the field. Notice that there is a sequence to reflective practice. Schon (1987), for example, argues against putting the cart before the horse. He states that true reflectivity depends upon the ability to "recognize and apply standard rules, facts and operations; *then* to reason from general rules to problematic cases in ways characteristic of the profession; and *only then* to develop and test new forms of understanding and action where familiar categories and ways of thinking fail" (p. 40). In other words, background knowledge is important, but it is most useful in a dynamic interaction with contextual applications (Hoshman & Polkinghorne, 1992). A working knowledge of human development supplies the clinician with a firm base from which to proceed.

Given the relevance of background knowledge to expertise in helping and to reflective practice, we hope we have made a sufficiently convincing case for the study of developmental science. However, it is obvious that students approaching this study are not "blank slates." You already have many ideas and theories about the ways that people grow and change. These implicit theories have been constructed over time, partly from personal experience, observation, and your own cultural "take" on situations. Dweck and her colleagues have demonstrated that reliably different interpretations of situations can be predicted based upon individual differences in people's implicit beliefs about certain human attributes, such as intelligence or personality (see Levy, Stoessner, & Dweck, 1998). Take the case of intelligence. If you happen to hold the implicit belief that a person's intellectual capacity can change and improve over time, you might be more inclined to take a skill-building approach to some presenting problem involving knowledge or ability. However, if you espouse the belief that a person's intelligence is fixed and not amenable to incremental improvement, possibly because of genetic inheritance, you might be more likely to encourage a client to cope with and adjust to cognitive limitations. For helping professionals, the implicit theoretical lens that shapes their worldview can have important implications for their clients.

We are often reluctant to give up our personal theories even in the face of evidence that these theories are incorrect (Gardner, 1991; Kuhn, 1991). The best antidote to misapplication of our personal views is self-monitoring: being aware of what our theories are and recognizing that they are only one of a set of possibilities. (See Chapter 8 for a more extensive discussion of this issue.) Before we discuss some specific beliefs about the nature of development, take a few minutes to consider what you think about the questions posed in Box 1.1.

Helping professionals need to understand the needs of clients of different ages.

THE BIG PICTURE: MODELS AND METAPHORS

Now that you have examined some of your own developmental assumptions, let's consider some of the broad models of development that a counselor may bring to bear on client problems. Later, we will examine how these models may differentially affect the counseling process. Like counselors, researchers in developmental psychology bring to their studies theoretical assumptions and beliefs that direct their research and influence how they interpret their findings. Every theorist develops a theory that is consistent with her own cultural background and experience. No one operates in a vacuum. Throughout this text, you will be introduced to many theories of development, some broad and sweeping in their coverage of whole areas of development, such as Freud's theory of personality development (see Chapters 7 and 8) or Piaget's theory of cognitive development (see Chapters 3, 6, and 9), and some are narrower in scope, focusing on a particular issue, such as Bowlby's attachment theory (see Chapters 4 and 12). Some theories that are very useful for counselors' understanding of human behavior, such as Rogers's person-centered theory or Adler's individual psychology, are not included here, because they are not technically theories of development. Those theories that describe systematic, age-related changes in behavior or functioning are considered.

It is useful to begin by considering three classes into which many developmental theories can be grouped: stage models, incremental models, and multidimensional models. You may find that your own assumptions fit with one of these classifications more than with the others.

Stage Models

Imagine a girl when she is 4 months old and then again when she is 4 years old. If your sense is that these two versions of the same child are fundamentally different *in kind,* with different intellectual capacities, different emotional structure, or different ways of perceiving others, you may be a stage theorist. A ***stage*** is a period of time, perhaps several years,

Box 1.1 Questionnaire

Examine Your Beliefs About Development

Rate yourself using the forced-choice format for each of the following items.

1. Physical characteristics such as eye color, height, and weight are primarily inherited.

   ❑   ❑   ❑   ❑
   Strongly Disagree   Moderately Disagree   Moderately Agree   Strongly Agree

2. Intelligence is primarily inherited.

   ❑   ❑   ❑   ❑
   Strongly Disagree   Moderately Disagree   Moderately Agree   Strongly Agree

3. Personality is primarily inherited.

   ❑   ❑   ❑   ❑
   Strongly Disagree   Moderately Disagree   Moderately Agree   Strongly Agree

4. Events in the first three years of life have permanent effects on a person's psychological development.

   ❑   ❑   ❑   ❑
   Strongly Disagree   Moderately Disagree   Moderately Agree   Strongly Agree

5. People's personalities do not change very much over their lifetimes.

   ❑   ❑   ❑   ❑
   Strongly Disagree   Moderately Disagree   Moderately Agree   Strongly Agree

6. People all go through the same stages in their lives.

   ❑   ❑   ❑   ❑
   Strongly Disagree   Moderately Disagree   Moderately Agree   Strongly Agree

7. Parents have a somewhat limited impact on their children's development.

   ❑   ❑   ❑   ❑
   Strongly Disagree   Moderately Disagree   Moderately Agree   Strongly Agree

8. The cultural context in which the individual lives has a primary effect upon the psychological development of that person.

   ❑   ❑   ❑   ❑
   Strongly Disagree   Moderately Disagree   Moderately Agree   Strongly Agree

9. Common sense is a better guide to child rearing than is scientific knowledge.

   ❑   ❑   ❑   ❑
   Strongly Disagree   Moderately Disagree   Moderately Agree   Strongly Agree

during which a person's activities (at least in one broad domain) have certain characteristics in common. For example, we could say that in language development, the 4-month-old girl is in a preverbal stage: among other things, her communications share in common the fact that they do not include talking. As a person moves to a different stage, the common characteristics of behavior change. In other words, a person's activities have similar qualities within stages but different qualities across stages. Also, after long periods of stability, qualitative shifts in behavior seem to happen relatively quickly. For example, the change from not talking to talking seems abrupt. It tends to happen between 12 and 18 months of age, and once it starts, language use seems to advance very rapidly. A 4-year-old is someone who communicates primarily by talking; she is clearly in a verbal stage.

The preverbal to verbal example illustrates two features of stage theories. First, they posit important qualitative differences in behavior and/or mental processes from one stage to another. Second, they imply periods of relative stability (within stages) and periods of rapid change (between stages). Development is metaphorically like a staircase. Each stage shift lifts a person to a new plateau for some period of time, and then there is another steep rise to another plateau.

Another quality of some stage theories is also suggested by the example of preverbal and verbal stages. Frequently, the "common characteristics" of a person's activities at one stage are defined as much by their contrast with other stages as by their own particular qualities. For example, the preverbal stage can be defined as the stage before talking begins.

Sigmund Freud's theory of personality development was among the first to include a description of stages (e.g., Freud, 1905/1989; 1949/1969). Freud's theory no longer takes center stage in the interpretations favored by most counselors or by developmental researchers. First, there is little evidence for the specific proposals in Freud's theory. Second, his theory has been criticized for incorporating the gender biases of early twentieth-century Austrian culture. Yet, some of Freud's broad insights are routinely accepted and incorporated into other theories, such as his emphasis on the importance of family relationships in development, his notion that some behavior is unconsciously motivated, and his view that internal conflicts can play a primary role in social functioning. Several more current and popular theories, like Erik Erikson's, were originally framed either as extensions of or specifically to contrast with Freud's ideas. For these reasons, it is important to understand Freud's theory. Also, his ideas have permeated popular culture, and they influence many of our assumptions about people's behavior. If we are to make our own implicit assumptions about development explicit, we must understand where they originated and how well the theories that spawned them stand up in the light of scientific investigation.

Freud's Personality Theory

Sigmund Freud's theory both describes the complex functioning of the adult personality and offers an explanation of the processes and progress of its development throughout childhood. As with many stage theories, to understand any given stage it helps to understand Freud's view of the fully developed adult.

Id, Ego, and Superego. According to Freud, the adult personality functions as if there were actually three personalities, or aspects of personality, all potentially in conflict with one another. The first, the *id,* is the biological self, the source of all psychic energy. Babies are born with an id; the other two aspects of personality develop later. The id blindly pursues the fulfillment of physical needs or "instincts," such as the hunger drive and the sex drive. It is irrational, driven by the *pleasure principle,* that is, by the pursuit of gratification. Its function is to keep the individual, and the species, alive, although Freud also proposed that there are inborn aggressive, destructive instincts served by the id.

The *ego* begins to develop as cognitive and physical skills emerge. In Freud's view, some psychic energy is invested in these skills, and a rational, realistic self begins to take shape. The id still presses for fulfillment of bodily needs, but the rational ego seeks to meet these needs in sensible ways that take into account all aspects of a situation. For example, if you were hungry, and you saw a child with an ice cream cone, your id might press you to grab the cone away from the child—an instance of blind, immediate pleasure seeking. Of course, stealing ice cream from a child might satisfy your hunger quickly, but it could have negative consequences if someone else saw you do it or if the child reported you to authorities. Unlike your id, your ego would operate on the *reality principle,* garnering your understanding of the world and of behavioral consequences to devise a more sensible and self-protective approach, such as waiting until you arrive at the ice cream store yourself and paying for an ice cream cone.

The *superego* is the last of the three aspects of personality to emerge. Psychic energy is invested in this "internalized parent" during the preschool period as children begin to feel guilty if they behave in ways that are inconsistent with parental restrictions. With the superego in place, the ego must now take account not only of instinctual pressures from the id, and of external realities, but also of the superego's constraints. It must meet the needs of the id without upsetting the superego in order to avoid the unpleasant anxiety of guilt. In this view, when you choose against stealing a child's ice cream cone to meet your immediate hunger, your ego is taking account not only of the realistic problems of getting caught but also of the unpleasant feelings that would be generated by the superego.

The Psychosexual Stages. In Freud's view, the complexities of the relationships and conflicts that arise among the id, the ego, and the superego are the result of the individual's experiences during five developmental stages (and especially during the first three). Freud called these *psychosexual stages* because he believed that changes in the id and its energy levels initiated each new stage. The term "sexual" here applies to all biological instincts or drives and their satisfaction, and it can be broadly defined as "sensual."

The first psychosexual stage, called the *oral stage,* corresponds to the first year of life, when Freud believed that a disproportionate amount of id energy is invested in drives satisfied through the mouth. Eating, drinking, and even nonnutritive sucking might provide more pleasure in this phase of life than at any other. The baby's experiences with feeding and the degree to which oral pleasure is promoted or prevented by parenting practices could influence how much energy is invested in these activities in the future. For example, suppose that a mother in the early twentieth century believed the parenting advice of "experts" who claimed that nonnutritive sucking is bad for babies. To prevent her baby from sucking his thumb, the mother might tie the baby's hands to the sides of the crib at night—a practice recommended by the same "experts"! Freudian theory would predict that such extreme denial of oral pleasure could cause an *oral fixation:* the boy might grow up to need oral pleasures more than most adults, perhaps leading to overeating, to being especially talkative, or to being a chain smoker. The grown man might also exhibit his fixation in more subtle ways, maintaining behaviors or feelings in adulthood that are particularly characteristic of babies, such as crying easily or experiencing overwhelming feelings of helplessness. According to Freud, fixations at any stage could be the result of either denial of a child's needs, as in this example, or overindulgence of those needs. Specific defense mechanisms, such as "reaction formation" or "repression," can also be associated with the conflicts that arise at a particular stage.

The second psychosexual stage, called the *anal stage,* is said to begin in the second year of life, caused by a shift in the energy of the id, a shift that is presumably the result of normal biological changes. Now the anal area of the body is the focus of greatest pleasure, and as control over the anal sphincter develops, the child especially enjoys both holding on and letting go. In this stage, Freud hypothesized that parenting practices, especially either overcontrolling or overindulgent practices associated with toilet training, could have long-lasting effects on personality development. Popular use of the term *anal personality* is a reference to some of Freud's predictions about the effects of an *anal fixation,* which can include being withholding (of material or emotional resources) and being compulsively cautious about keeping things clean and in order. Freud also suggested that an anal fixation might lead an adult to be overly messy and disorganized, a person who "lets go" too easily.

Freud proposed that in the third stage, the **phallic stage,** id energy shifts again, this time to be focused primarily in the genital region. Freud's theory has been criticized for its male-dominated focus, which is illustrated by this stage name. From age 3 to about 5, children's special pleasure comes from fondling the genitals. Vague sexual urges embroil children in complex emotional and motivational conundrums that include wanting to be physically closer to the opposite-sexed parent and fearing the fallout from competing with the same-sexed parent (the Oedipus and Electra complexes described in Chapter 8). It is during this stage that children begin to feel the full force of parental discipline. Feelings of guilt emerge, and the superego develops. The child's resolution of the difficult emotional turmoil of the phallic stage establishes how she will later cope with postpubertal sexual needs and depends, as always, on how parents deal with the child at this stage. For example, excessively strong, punitive action when children are caught masturbating or when children compete jealously for the preferred parent's affections could produce excessively strong internalized prohibitions against sexual behavior or against asserting oneself in adulthood. Conversely, seductive, indulgent behavior on the part of the parent might lead to self-centered vanity or flirtatiousness.

Freud called his final two stages the **latency stage** and the **genital stage.** *Latency* begins at about age 5, when the turmoil of the phallic period recedes and the id's energy is not especially linked to any particular pleasure or body part. The child's nascent personality continues to evolve following the patterns laid down in the first three stages but with the potential conflicts among the three aspects of personality largely latent and unexpressed. Turmoil emerges anew at puberty, the beginning of the *genital stage,* when the changes of puberty mean that id energy is especially invested in adult sexual impulses, and the child seeks ways of meeting these powerful new needs. The psychosexual stages are summarized in Table 1.1.

Freud's Theory as a Stage Model.   The psychosexual stages have all of the characteristics of a stage model. First, the child is qualitatively different across stages, primarily as a function of shifting motivational qualities or "id energy." For example, the 2-year-old is obsessed with anal functioning, the 4-year-old with sexual feelings. Second, the stages are fairly long, and the periods of transition relatively rapid. For example, the anal stage lasts for about 2 years, the phallic stage for about 3 years, but the transition between them appears to occur quickly. Finally, the stages are defined in part by the contrasts among them. The latency stage in particular is defined primarily in *not* being characterized by the passions of the earlier three.

Notice, however, that despite these clearcut stages with different motivations and different sets of possible outcomes for personality development, there are similarities across stages, which is typical of other stage theories as well. For example, Freud saw parenting experiences as critical for personality development in each stage. (He also argued that parenting effects are, at each stage, limited by the inborn biological qualities of a particular child's id.) The point is that the qualitative discontinuities that stage theories emphasize in human development are usually combined with functional similarities across stages in the processes by which development is said to proceed.

Let's consider more briefly two other important stage theories to illustrate this point.

Erikson's Personality Theory

Erik Erikson was a student of Freud's who later proposed his own theory of personality development (e.g., Erikson, 1950/1963). Like many "neo-Freudians," Erikson deemphasized the id as the driving force behind all behavior, and he emphasized the more rational processes of the ego. His theory is focused on explaining the psychosocial aspects

TABLE 1.1

Freud's Psychosexual Stages of Development

Stage	Approximate Age	Description
Oral	Birth to 1 year	Mouth is the source of greatest pleasure. Too much or too little oral satisfaction can cause an "oral fixation," leading to traits that actively (smoking) or symbolically (overdependency) are oral or infantile.
Anal	1 to 3 years	Anal area is the source of greatest pleasure. Harsh or overly indulgent toilet training can cause an "anal fixation," leading to later adult traits that recall this stage, such as being greedy or messy.
Phallic	3 to 5 or 6 years	Genitalia are the source of greatest pleasure. Sexual desire directed toward the opposite-sexed parent makes the same-sexed parent a rival. Fear of angering the same-sexed parent is resolved by identifying with that parent, which explains how children acquire both sex-typed behaviors and moral values. If a child has trouble resolving the emotional upheaval of this stage through identification, sex role development may be deviant and/or moral character may be weak.
Latency	6 years to puberty	Relatively quiescent period of personality development. Sexual desires are repressed after the turmoil of the last stage. Energy is directed into work and play. There is continued consolidation of traits laid down in the first three stages.
Genital	Puberty through adulthood	At puberty, adult sexual needs become the most important motivators of behavior. The individual seeks to fulfill needs and expend energy in socially acceptable activities, such as work, and through marriage with a partner who will substitute for the early object of desire, the opposite-sexed parent.

of behavior: attitudes and feelings toward the self and toward others. Erikson described eight *psychosocial stages.* The first five correspond to the age periods laid out in Freud's psychosexual stages, but the last three are adult life stages, reflecting Erikson's view that personal identity and interpersonal attitudes are continually evolving from birth to death.

The "Eight Stages of Man." In each stage, the individual faces a different "crisis" or developmental task (see Chapter 9 for a detailed discussion of Erikson's concept of "crisis"). The crisis is initiated, on the one hand, by changing characteristics of the person—biological maturation or decline, cognitive changes, advancing (or deteriorating) motor skills—and, on the other hand, by corresponding changes in others' attitudes, behaviors, and expectations. As in all stage theories, people qualitatively change from stage to stage, and so do the crises or tasks that they confront. In the first stage, infants must resolve the crisis of **trust versus mistrust.** Infants, in their relative helplessness, are "incorporative." They "take in" what is offered, including not only nourishment but stimulation, information, affection, and attention. If infants' needs for such input are met by responsive caregivers, babies begin to trust others, to feel valued and valuable, and to view the world as a safe place. If caregivers are not consistently responsive, infants will fail to establish basic trust or to feel valuable, carrying "mistrust" with them into the next stage of development, when the 1- to 3-year-old toddler faces the crisis of **autonomy versus shame and doubt.** Mistrust in others and self will make it more difficult to successfully achieve a sense of autonomy.

The new stage is initiated by the child's maturing muscular control and emerging cognitive and language skills. Unlike helpless infants, toddlers can learn not only to control their elimination but also to feed and dress themselves, to express their desires with some precision, and to move around the environment without help. The new capacities bring a strong need to practice and perfect the skills that make children feel in control of their own destinies. Caregivers must be sensitive to the child's need for independence and yet must exercise enough control to keep the child safe and to help the child learn self-control. Failure to strike the right balance may rob children of feelings of autonomy—a sense that "I can do it myself"—and can promote instead either shame or self-doubt.

These first two stages illustrate features of all of Erikson's stages (see Table 1.2 for a description of all eight stages). First, others' sensitivity and responsiveness to the individual's needs create a context for positive psychosocial development. Second, attitudes

TABLE 1.2

Erikson's Psychosocial Stages of Development

Stage or Psychosocial "Crisis"	Approximate Age	Significant Events	Positive Outcome or Virtue Developed	Negative Outcome
Trust vs. Mistrust	Birth to 1 year	Child develops a sense that the world is a safe and reliable place because of sensitive caregiving.	Hope	Fear & mistrust of others
Autonomy vs. Shame & doubt	1 to 3 years	Child develops a sense of independence tied to use of new mental and motor skills.	Willpower	Self-doubt
Initiative vs. Guilt	3 to 5 or 6 years	Child tries to behave in ways that involve more "grown-up" responsibility and experiment with "grown-up" roles.	Purpose	Guilt over thought & action
Industry vs. Inferiority	6 to 12 years	Child needs to learn important academic skills and compare favorably with peers in school.	Competence	Lack of competence
Identity vs. Role confusion	12 to 20 years	Adolescent must move toward adulthood by making choices about values, vocational goals, etc.	Fidelity	Inability to establish sense of self
Intimacy vs. Isolation	Young Adulthood	Adult becomes willing to share identity with other and to commit to affiliations and partnerships.	Love	Fear of intimacy, distantiation
Generativity vs. Stagnation	Middle Adulthood	Adult wishes to make a contribution to the next generation, to produce, mentor, create something of lasting value, as in the rearing of children or community service or expert work.	Care	Self-absorption
Ego integrity vs. Despair	Late Adulthood	Adult comes to terms with life's successes, failures, and missed opportunities and realizes the dignity of own life.	Wisdom	Regret

toward self and toward others emerge together. For example, developing trust in others also means valuing (or trusting) the self. Third, every psychosocial crisis or task involves finding the right balance between positive and negative feelings, with the positive outweighing the negative. Finally, the successful resolution of a crisis at one stage helps smooth the way for successful resolutions of future crises. Unsuccessful resolution at an earlier stage may stall progress and make maladaptive behavior more likely.

Erikson's personality theory is often more appealing to helping professionals than Freud's theory. Erikson's emphasis on the psychosocial aspects of personality focuses attention on precisely the issues that counselors feel they are most often called on to address: feelings and attitudes about self and about others. Also, Erikson assumed that the child or adult is an active, self-organizing individual, who needs only the right social context to move in a positive direction. Further, Erikson was himself an optimistic therapist who believed that poorly resolved crises *could* be resolved more adequately in later stages if the right conditions prevailed. Also, Erikson was sensitive to cultural differences in behavioral development. Finally, developmental researchers frequently find Eriksonian interpretations of behavior useful. Studies of attachment, self-concept, self-esteem, and adolescent identity, among other topics addressed in subsequent chapters, have produced results compatible with some of Erikson's ideas. (See Chapter 4, Box 4.3, for a biographical sketch of Erikson.)

Piaget's Cognitive Development Theory

Jean Piaget's influential theory outlines stages in the development of cognition, especially logical thinking (e.g., Inhelder & Piaget; 1955/1958, 1964; Piaget, 1952, 1954). He assumed that normal adults are capable of thinking logically about both concrete and abstract contents but that this capacity evolves in four stages through childhood. Briefly, the first **sensorimotor stage,** lasting for about two years, is characterized by an absence of representational thought. Although babies are busy taking in the sensory world, organizing it on the basis of inborn reflexes or patterns, and then responding to their sensations, Piaget believed that they cannot yet symbolically represent their experiences, and so they cannot really reflect on them. This means that young infants do not form mental images or store memories symbolically, and they do not plan their behavior or intentionally act. These capacities emerge between 18 and 24 months, launching the next stage.

Piaget's second, third, and fourth stages roughly correspond to the preschool, elementary school, and the adolescent/adult years. These stages are named for the kinds of thinking that Piaget believed possible for these age groups. He characterized the preschooler as a thinking person in the **preoperational stage,** with *preoperational* meaning "unable to think logically." Piaget believed that the deficiencies in preschoolers' thinking account for problems they have understanding both the world and other people. For example, 3-year-old Tommy can play some simple board games, like "Candy Land," proficiently, but he fails to understand that you might want to win when you play him. He focuses his attention on his own goals—that he wants to win—and cannot at the same time think about or make sense of a different goal—yours!

By about age 7, thinking has advanced in complexity, and children enter the **concrete operational stage.** Operational means "logical." Children's thinking now seems more rational, more like adults'. They can begin to understand and use logical processes, such as addition and subtraction, but they are still limited in some respects. In particular, they find it difficult to think logically about material that is not somehow anchored in the concrete, real world. For example, they can understand that "$2 + 6 = 8$," because the logical relationships among numbers can be illustrated with concrete things in the real world. But if we ask children of elementary school age to understand the relationships among more abstract concepts, such as the *x*s and *y*s of algebra, they usually falter. When the material children must think about is this abstract, elementary-school-aged children seem flummoxed, apparently because they need concrete reference points to make sense of a situation.

By age 11 or 12, children are more successful at logically organizing abstract material, and they have entered Piaget's *formal operational stage.* New cognitive horizons open up as a result. Adolescents become capable of logically planning their futures (the world of the possible, not the real), for example, or of imagining ideal (abstract) political or economic systems. See Table 1.3 for a summary of Piaget's stages.

Piaget's theory is another classic stage model. Cognitive abilities are qualitatively different across stages. Each stage is fairly long and is at least partly defined by contrast to other stages. For example, the preoperational stage is a time when children can think, unlike babies at the previous stage, but their thinking is not yet logical, as it will be in subsequent stages. Finally, despite the qualitative differences across stages, there are functional similarities or continuities from stage to stage in the ways in which children's cognitive development proceeds. At each stage, developmental progress depends on children assimilating experiences (that is, shaping experiences to fit) with their current ways of understanding, and at the same time, accommodating (that is, adjusting) their old ways of understanding, at least a little, to what is new in an experience.

Piaget's ideas about cognitive development were first translated into English in the 1960s, and they swept American developmental researchers off their feet. His theory filled the need for an explanation that acknowledged complex qualitative changes in children's abilities over time, and it launched an era of unprecedented research on all aspects of children's intellectual functioning that continues today. Although some of the specifics of Piaget's theory have been challenged by research findings, many researchers, educators, and helping professionals still find the broad outlines of this theory very useful for

TABLE 1.3

Piaget's Cognitive Stages of Development

Stage	Approximate Age	Description
Sensorimotor	Birth to 2 years	Through 6 substages, the source of infants' organized actions gradually shifts. At first, all organized behavior is reflexive—automatically triggered by particular stimuli. By the end of this stage, behavior is guided more by representational thought.
Preoperational thought	2 to 6 or 7 years	Early representational thought tends to be slow. Thought is "centered," usually focused on one salient piece of information, or aspect of an event, at a time. As a result, thinking is usually not yet logical.
Concrete operational thought	7 to 11 or 12 years	Thinking has gradually become more rapid and efficient, allowing children to now "decenter," or think about more than one thing at a time. This also allows them to discover logical relationships between/among pieces of information. Their logical thinking is best about information that can be demonstrated in the concrete world.
Formal operational thought	12 years through adulthood	Logical thinking extends now to "formal" or abstract material. Young adolescents can think logically about hypothetical situations, for example.

organizing their thinking about the kinds of understandings that children of different ages can bring to a problem or social situation.

Incremental Models

Unlike stage theories, some models characterize development as **incremental,** metaphorically resembling not a staircase but a steadily rising mountainside. Again, picture a 4-month-old girl, and the same girl when she is 4 years old. If you tend to "see" her evolving in small steps from a smiling, attentive infant (at least occasionally!) to a smiling, eager toddler, to a smiling, mischievous preschooler, always noting in your observations threads of sameness as well as differences, your own theoretical assumptions about development may be more compatible with one of these incremental models. Like stage models, they can be very different in the types and breadth of behaviors they attempt to explain. They also differ in the kinds of processes they assume to underlie psychological change, such as the kinds of processes involved in learning. But they all agree that developmental change is *not* marked by major, sweeping reorganizations that affect many behaviors at once, as in stage theories. Rather, change is steady and specific to particular behaviors or mental activities. Social learning theory and most information processing theories are among the many incremental models available to explain development.

Learning Theories

Learning theories, in what is called the **behaviorist tradition,** have a distinguished history in American psychology, having been the most widely accepted class of theories for a significant part of the 20th century. Such theories at one time explained all behavioral change as a function of chains of specific environmental events, such as those that occur in **classical** and **operant conditioning.** In these processes, change in behavior takes place because environmental events are paired with certain behaviors. For example, suppose a child initially approaches a dog with curiosity and interest, but the dog barks loudly, causing the child to automatically startle and pull back. The next time the dog appears, the child may automatically startle and pull back, even though the dog is quiet. Just the sight of the dog now triggers the same response as loud barking; the child has learned a new response because the formerly neutral event (sight of dog) has been paired with an event (loud barking) that automatically causes a startle. Perhaps the startle reaction is also accompanied by feelings of fear. If so, the child has learned to fear this dog, and will likely *generalize* that fear to other, similar dogs. When a neutral event or stimulus is associated with a stimulus that causes an automatic response, the neutral stimulus can become a **conditioned stimulus,** meaning that it can cause the person to make the same automatic response in the future. This is *classical conditioning.*

Operant conditioning is different. First, a person just happens to perform some behavior. The behavior is an **operant,** an accidental or random action. Immediately after the operant occurs, there is a "reinforcing event," or **reinforcement,** something that is experienced by the person as pleasurable or rewarding. For example, suppose that a young child happens to babble "da" just as a dog appears in the child's line of sight, and the child's mother excitedly claps and kisses the child. (She has mistakenly assumed that the child has tried to say "dog.") The mother's reaction serves as a reinforcement for the child, who will repeat the "da" sound the next time a dog comes into view. In *operant conditioning,* the child learns to produce a formerly random behavior or *operant* (e.g., "da") in response to a cue (e.g., the appearance of a dog) because the behavior was previously reinforced in that situation.

Social learning theories, which have focused specifically on how children acquire personality characteristics and social skills, consider conditioning processes part of the story, but they also emphasize "observational learning," or **modeling.** In this kind of learning, one person (the learner) observes another (the model) performing some behavior, and just from close observation, learns to do it too. The observer may or may not imitate the modeled behavior, immediately or in the future, depending on many factors, such as whether the observer expects a reward for the behavior, whether the model is perceived as nurturing or competent, and even whether the observer believes that the performance will meet the observer's own performance standards. Current versions of social learning theory emphasize many similar cognitive, self-regulated determiners of performance and suggest that they too are often learned from models (e.g., Bandura, 1974, 1999).

Whatever the learning processes that are emphasized in a particular learning theory, the story of development is one in which behaviors or beliefs or feelings change in response to specific experiences, one experience at a time. Broader changes can occur by *generalization.* If new events are experienced that are very similar to events in the original learning context, the learned behaviors may be extended to these new events. For example, the child who learns to say "da" when a particular dog appears may do the same when other dogs appear, or even in the presence of other four-legged animals. Or a child who observes a model sharing candy with a friend may later share toys with a sibling. But these extensions of learned activities are narrow in scope compared to the sweeping changes hypothesized by stage theorists. Overall, development is the product of many independent changes in many different behaviors and/or mental processes.

Information Processing Theories

Not all **information processing theories** can be strictly classified as incremental theories, but many can. Like learning theories, these do not hypothesize broad stages, but emphasize incremental changes in narrow domains of behavior or thought. These theories tend to liken human cognitive functioning to computer processing of information. The mind works on information—attending to it, holding it in a temporary store or "working memory," putting it into long-term storage, using strategies to organize it or to draw conclusions from it, and so on. How the information is processed depends on general characteristics of the human computer, such as how much information can be accessed, or made available for our attention, at one time. And these characteristics can change to some degree over time. For example, children's attentional capacity increases gradually with age. Yet most changes with age are quite specific to particular domains of knowledge, such as changes in the way that certain kinds of problems are solved. Furthermore, the individual changes in processing that occur in different knowledge domains are not stage-like; they do not extend beyond the particular situation or problem space in which they occur. For example, Siegler and his colleagues (e.g., Crowley & Siegler, 1993; Siegler, 1996; Siegler & Shrager, 1984) describe changes in the ways that children do arithmetic, read, solve problems of various kinds, and perform many other tasks and skills. Siegler analyzes very particular changes in the kinds of strategies that children use when they attempt these tasks. While there can be similarities across tasks in the ways that strategies change (e.g., they become more automatic with practice, they generalize to similar problems, etc.), usually the specific strategies used in one kind of task do not apply to another, and changes are not coordinated across tasks. To illustrate, a kindergartner trying to solve an addition problem might use the strategy of "counting from one": ". . . this typically involves putting up fingers on one hand to represent the first addend, putting up fingers on the other hand to represent the second addend, and then counting the raised fingers on both hands" (Siegler, 1998, p. 93). This strategy is characteristic of early addition efforts, but would play no role in tasks such as reading or spelling. Overall, then, cognitive development in this kind of model is like social development in social learning theories: it results from the accrual of independent changes in many different domains of thought and skill.

Multidimensional Models

Modern theorists are becoming more and more ambitious in their efforts to explain and describe the enormous complexity of interrelated causal processes in development. In this third class of models, theorists consider development to be the result of the relationships among many causal components. These **multidimensional models** generally apply to all domains of development from the cognitive to the social. They suggest that there are layers, or levels, of interacting causes for behavioral change: physical/molecular, biological, psychological, social, and cultural. What happens at one level both causes and is caused by what happens at other levels. That is, the relationships among causes are reciprocal. For example, increased testosterone levels at puberty (biological change) might help influence a boy to pursue an aggressive sport, like wrestling. If his success at wrestling gives him more status among his male friends (social change), his experience of increased social dominance may reciprocally influence his biological functioning. Specifically, it may lead to additional increases in his testosterone levels (Cacioppo & Berntson, 1992).

These models also describe many kinds of change: qualitative, transforming changes, both great (stagelike) and small (such as strategy changes within a particular problem-solving domain), as well as continuous, incremental variations that can even be reversible (such as learning and then forgetting new information) (e.g., Overton, 1998). Theories with the characteristics described in this section can be called "multidimensional," but writers use many other names as well, calling them **transactional models** (Sameroff and Chandler, 1975), **relational models** (Lerner, 1998), **systems models** (Thelen & Smith, 1998), and so on.

Think again about a girl who is 4 months old, and then later 4 years old. Do you perceive so many changes that she is transformed into a different sort of creature, and yet, at the same time, do you see enduring qualities that characterize her at both ages? Does your sense of the forces that have changed her include influences such as her family, community, and culture? Do you also recognize that she has played a significant role in her own change and in modifying those other forces? If so, your implicit assumptions about development may be more consistent with multidimensional models than with either stage or continuity theories alone.

Multidimensional models can be described metaphorically as like a vine growing through a thick forest (Kagan, 1994). In doing so, the vine is propelled by its own inner processes, but its path, even its form, is in part created by the forest it inhabits. There is continuous growth, but there are changes in structure too—in its form and direction—as the vine wends its way through the forest. Finally, its presence in the forest changes the forest itself, affecting the growth of the trees and other plants, which reciprocally influence the growth of the vine. One example of a multidimensional model will help to flesh out the typical characteristics of these theories.

Bronfenbrenner's Bioecological Model

Bronfenbrenner and his colleagues (e.g., Bronfenbrenner & Ceci, 1994; Bronfenbrenner & Morris, 1998) have described all developments—including personality and cognitive change—as a function of **proximal processes**. These are reciprocal interactions between an ". . . active, evolving biopsychological human organism and the persons, objects and symbols in its immediate external environment" (Bronfenbrenner & Morris, 1998, p. 996). In other words, proximal processes refer to a person's immediate interactions with people or with the physical environment or with informational sources (such as books or movies). These proximal processes are modified by more **distal processes.** Some of these are within the organism—such as genes. Others are outside the immediate environment—such as features of the educational system or of the broader culture. Proximal processes are truly interactive: the organism influences and is influenced by the immediate environment.

The quality and effectiveness of the immediate environment—its responsiveness to the individual's particular needs and characteristics and the opportunities it provides—depend on the larger context. For example, parental monitoring of children's homework benefits children's academic performance. But monitoring is more effective if parents are knowledgeable about the child's work. A parent who insists that his child do her algebra homework may have less effect if the parent cannot be a resource who guides and explains the work. Thus, the parent's own educational background affects the usefulness of the monitoring (Bronfenbrenner & Ceci, 1994).

An individual's characteristics also influence the effectiveness of the environment. For example, *motivations* affect the impact of learning opportunities in a given context. A man interested in gambling may learn to reason in very complex ways about horses and their relative probability of winning at the track, but he may not display such complex reasoning in other contexts (Ceci & Liker, 1986). Other important individual qualities include **demand characteristics,** behavioral tendencies that often either encourage or discourage certain kinds of reactions from others. A child who is shy and inhibited, a trait that appears to have some biological roots (Kagan, 1998), may often fail to elicit attention from others, and may receive less support when she needs it, than a child who is open and outgoing (Bell & Chapman, 1986; see Chapters 4 and 5).

Changes in the organism can be emergent, stagelike qualitative changes, such as a shift from preoperational to concrete operational thought, or they can be more continuous, graded changes, such as shifts in academic interest or involvement in athletics. Both kinds of change are the result of proximal processes, influenced by more distal internal and external causes. And once changes occur, the individual brings new resources to these proximal processes. For example, when a child begins to demonstrate concrete operational thought, she will be given different tasks to do at home or at school than before, and she will learn things from those experiences that she would not have learned earlier.

In earlier versions of his theory, Bronfenbrenner characterized in detail the many levels of environment that influence a person's development (see Figure 1.1). He referred to the immediate environment, where proximal processes are played out, as the **microsystem.** Babies interact primarily with family members, but as children get older other microsystems, such as the school, the neighborhood, or a local playground and its inhabitants, become part of their lives. Relations among these microsystems—referred to as the **mesosystem**—modify each of them. For example, a child's interactions with teachers affect interactions with parents. The next level of the environment, the **exosystem,** includes settings that children may not directly interact with but that influence the child nonetheless. For example, a teacher's family life will influence the teacher and thereby the child. Or a child's socioeconomic status influences where her family lives, affecting the school the child will attend, and thus affecting the kinds of experiences the child has with teachers. Finally, there is the **macrosystem,** including the customs and character of the larger culture that help shape the microsystems. For example, cultural attitudes and laws

FIGURE 1.1

Bronfenbrenner's Bioecological Model

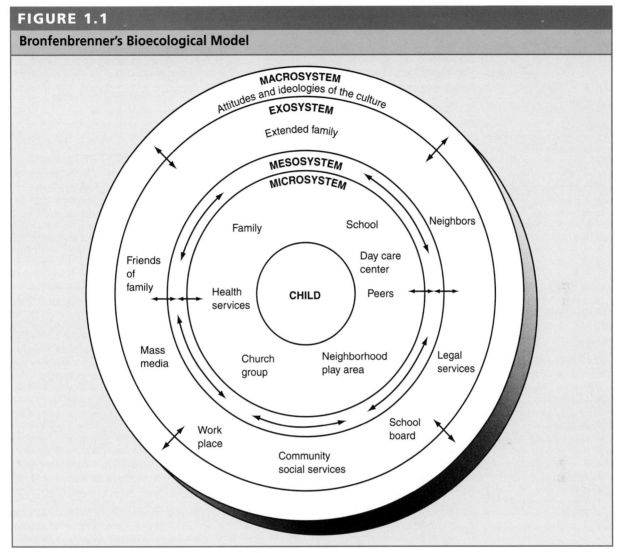

Source: *Early Childhood Development: A Multicultural Perspective,* 2nd ed., by Jeffrey Trawick-Smith, © 2000. Reprinted by permission of Pearson Education, Inc., Upper Saddle River, NJ..

regarding the education of exceptional students influence the operation of a school and therefore a child's interactions with teachers.

The environment, then, is like ". . . a set of nested structures, each inside the next, like a set of Russian dolls . . . " (Bronfenbrenner, 1979). In newer versions of his theory, Bronfenbrenner gives equal attention to the nested internal levels of the organism. As we have seen, a person brings to proximal processes a set of dispositions, resources (preexisting abilities, experiences, knowledge, and skills), and demand characteristics. These, in turn, are influenced by biological and physical levels of functioning that include the genes. Bronfenbrenner now also emphasizes, as other multidimensional theorists do, the bidirectional effects of each level on the adjacent levels. For example, proximal psychological processes playing out in the immediate context are both influenced by, and influencing, physiological processes (Bronfenbrenner & Morris, 1998; Ceci, Rosenblum, deBruyn, & Lee, 1997).

APPLYING MODELS AND METAPHORS

We have described three major theoretical approaches to development. Favoring one of these paradigms can influence the way counselors assess and interpret client concerns. Let's consider how various theoretical orientations to development might apply to a counseling situation:

Juliana is a 26-year-old Latina female who was raised in an intact, middle-class family. Her father is a teacher and her mother a housewife who occasionally worked in a neighborhood preschool as a teacher's aide. Juliana was the second child in the family, which included an older brother and a younger sister. She attended parochial schools from kindergarten through twelfth grade, where she worked very hard to achieve average and sometimes above average grades. During her early years in school, Juliana had reading difficulties and received remedial instruction. At home, her parents stressed the value of education and kept a close watch on the children. The children were well-behaved, respectful, and devoted to the family. Most of their spare time was spent with their close relatives, who lived nearby. Despite Juliana's interest in dating during high school, her parents did not permit her to spend time with boyfriends. They told her that she needed to concentrate on her schoolwork so that she could be a nurse when she grew up. After graduation, Juliana entered a small local college and enrolled in a program designed to prepare her for a career in nursing. She lived at home and commuted to school on a daily basis. Life proceeded as it had for most of her high school years. Her course work, however, became increasingly more difficult for her. She also felt isolated from most of her classmates, many of whom were working and living on their own. She tried to participate in some of the college's social events, but without much satisfaction or success. In order to pass her science courses, Juliana had to spend most of her time studying. By the middle of her academic program, it was clear that she was in danger of failing. She felt frustrated and angry. At this point, she became romantically involved with Bill, a young Anglo man who worked at the college. She dropped out of school and moved in with him, hoping their relationship would lead to marriage. Her family was shocked and upset with her decision and put pressure on her to come home. Eventually, the relationship with Bill ended, and Juliana, unwilling to return home, moved in with a group of young students who were looking for someone to share the rent. She found a low-wage job, changed her style of dress to look more like the younger students, and quickly became involved in a series of other romantic relationships. Juliana grew increasingly despondent about her inability to maintain a relationship that would lead to marriage and a family. In addition, she felt some distress about not completing her college degree. She enrolled in a night-school program at a local community college to retake her science courses. Once again, she experienced confusion, problems fitting in, and academic difficulty. She went to the college counseling center to ask for help.

Take a minute to think about how you would respond to Juliana. Do any of your views about development enter into your appraisal of her situation? If you tend to be a stage theorist, you might consider Juliana's problems to be based on Erikson's crisis of intimacy in early adulthood (see Table 1.1). She does seem to have difficulties with intimacy, and she is just at the age when these issues are supposed to become central to psychosocial development. But a rigid assumption of age/stage correspondence could prevent you from considering other possibilities, such as an unresolved identity crisis.

If you tend to be an incremental theorist, perhaps favoring social learning explanations, you might perceive Juliana's situation quite differently. You may see Juliana as having problems in her intimate relationships that are similar to her difficulties with school. In both domains, she is apparently "delayed," perhaps because she has had insufficient opportunities to learn social and academic skills or perhaps because she has been reinforced for behaviors that are ineffective in more challenging contexts. Although this may be a useful way of construing Juliana's dilemma, any stage issues contributing to her distress may be missed. Also, there could be factors in her social environment, such as cultural expectations, that might not be considered.

If you take a more multidimensional approach, you will try to remain alert to multiple influences, both proximal and distal, on Juliana's development. The roles of her biological status, her individual capabilities, her stage of development, her earlier experiences, her family, and her culture will all be considered as possible influences and points of intervention. The danger could be that the complexity of the interacting factors is so great that you may find it difficult to sort out the most effective place to begin. In particular, macrosystem influences, such as cultural expectations about appropriate roles for women, may be quite resistant to intervention.

Counselors with different developmental assumptions are likely to choose different approaches and strategies in their work with Juliana. In a sense, any set of theoretical biases is like a set of blinders. It will focus your attention on some aspects of the situation and reduce the visibility of other aspects. Knowing your own biases can help you avoid the pitfalls of overreliance on one way of viewing development.

MAJOR ISSUES IN DEVELOPMENT

A number of core issues or dilemmas are usually addressed by the kinds of models we have described. Traditionally, these issues have been framed as "either/or" possibilities. Which is more important in causing developmental change, nature (heredity) or nurture (environment)? Are some developments restricted to certain "critical periods" in the life cycle, or is any developmental change possible at any time given the appropriate opportunities? Are there important continuities across the life span, or is everything in flux? Do people actively influence the course and nature of their own development, or are they passive products of other forces? As with most things, close examination of any of these issues reveals that taking an extreme position on any of them does not fit the available data. The best answer to all of the questions just posed may be, "Both!"

Nature Versus Nurture

How did you respond to the first three items of the questionnaire in Box 1.1? Did you say that physical traits are primarily inherited? Did you say that intelligence or personality are inherited? Your opinions on these matters are likely to be influenced by your cultural background. For example, Americans have traditionally seen intelligence as mostly hereditary, but Japanese tend to disregard the notion of "native ability" and to consider intellectual achievements a function of opportunity and hard work (Stevenson, Chen, & Lee, 1993). Alternatively, Americans usually view personality and social adjustment as a result of environmental experiences, especially parents' nurturance and socialization practices, but Japanese usually see these qualities as mostly unalterable, native traits.

Developmental researchers usually acknowledge that both nature and nurture influence most traits, but they tend to emphasize the importance of one over the other. For example, work in the **behavior genetics** tradition (see Chapter 2) is based on the assumption that many psychological traits are dependent on the genes one inherits. Behavior geneticists also ask whether the environment influences the outcome of genetic inheritance, but a strong focus on genetic causes nonetheless informs their work.

At the opposite extreme, researchers concerned with socialization processes, such as those working in the social learning theory tradition, assume that heredity affects some aspects of behavior as well as our responsiveness to some features of the environment, but they focus their research primarily on the impact of the environment on learning and behavioral change.

Most research traditions focus on one kind of cause of behavior, either hereditary or environmental, partly because a research enterprise that examines multiple causes at the same time tends to be a massive undertaking. So, based on personal interest, theoretical bias, and practical limitations, developmental researchers often systematically investigate one kind of cause, setting aside examination of other causes of behavior. Interestingly, what these limited research approaches have accomplished is to establish impressive bodies of evidence, *both* for the importance of genes *and* for the importance of the environment!

Consider the example of intelligence. We can formulate two extreme theories about intelligence: "heredity causes intelligence" or "environment causes intelligence." To test a theory, we must generate predictions from it (see Box 1.2: *Understanding the Scientific Process*), so let's begin with the first theory. If "heredity causes intelligence," we can predict that if two organisms demonstrating high levels of intelligence produce offspring together, the offspring should also show high levels of intelligence, because they inherit the genes of the parents. Conversely, if two organisms of low intelligence mate, they should produce offspring with low intelligence. To test these predictions, a researcher could not conduct experiments with humans because controlling who breeds with whom is outside the province (thank goodness!) of scientists. (See Box 1.3: *Testing Scientific Theories,* to understand the nature of experiments.) So breeding experiments have been done with other mammalian species, such as rats and mice. Henderson (1972) tested mouse "intelligence" by assessing learning ability in a number of ways, such as measuring the number of trials a mouse needed to learn to run through a maze without making errors. He allowed the "maze-bright" mice to breed together and the "maze-dull" mice to breed together. When the offspring reached maturity, they too were given the various measures of mouse "intelligence." Sure enough, maze-bright parents produced maze-bright offspring, and maze-dull parents had maze-dull offspring. Breeding experiments like these have been done with many species, and the results are usually the same, strongly supporting the theory that heredity causes intelligence.

With humans, the theory has been tested using correlational studies (see Box 1.3: *Testing Scientific Theories,* to understand the nature of correlational studies), most often by studying the degree of similarity between identical twins, who share exactly the same heredity (see Chapter 2). Sure enough, as the theory predicts, identical twins are more alike in intelligence than other siblings with whom they are raised. (Ordinary siblings usually have about half of their genes in common.) Identical twins even tend to be alike in intelligence when they have been raised in different households. So, the theory that heredity causes intelligence is supported by evidence with humans.

Now, let's consider the second theory, that "environment causes intelligence." This theory predicts that if we improve the environment (usually interpreted to mean making it more stimulating, providing more learning opportunities and more varied activities and materials with which to interact), we should see increases in intelligence. Conversely, if we make the environment less stimulating, we should see decreases in intelligence. Both kinds of environmental manipulation have been done in animal studies. In one classic study, Cooper and Zubeck (1958) reared offspring of maze-bright and of maze-dull rats in ordinary cage environments or in less stimulating (deprived) or in more stimulating (enriched) environments. While the offspring of maze-bright parents were maze-bright if raised in the ordinary cage environment or in the enriched environment, they were maze-dull if raised in the deprived environment. And the offspring of maze-dull parents were maze-dull when raised in the ordinary or the deprived environments, but they were maze-bright if raised in

Box 1.2 Understanding the Scientific Process

We have argued that information gained from scientific research on development is important for clinical practitioners to know. Yet, practitioners often do not find research findings helpful or relevant to the problems they face with their clients. What is going on here? Is scientific work of practical value or not? It can be, but only if the practitioner understands the scientific process.

Most of us are enculturated to believe that the sciences provide answers to life's conundrums, and sometimes they do. For example, at one time the causes of diseases such as tuberculosis or polio were a mystery, but biological research has now established that microorganisms are the culprits. The path that biologists followed to achieve this insight was a laborious and time-consuming one, with many wrong turns or apparent missteps. Adequate scientific answers almost always are found at the end of similarly circuitous routes. As a result, practitioners closely allied to any scientific field sometimes find that the best scientific information of today can change tomorrow. In addition, scientists may offer competing answers to the same question until enough work has been done on a phenomenon to establish one answer, or some amalgam of previous answers, as valid. It is not unusual for practitioners faced with competing scientific "answers" to begin to wonder, "What good is science?"

Let's address this question by first looking at the nature of the scientific process. Then we will examine how practitioners can effectively use science to achieve their goals.

Psychology as the Study of Human Behavior

The study of human behavior and its associated mental processes—motivations, cognitions, emotions, and so on—is a topic of great interest to most of us, and it is the subject of many disciplines besides the social sciences. Most of the humanities, such as literature, history, and philosophy, are focused primarily on human behavior. What differentiates these different disciplines are the *methods* that they use to gain understanding. For example, the study of *literature* is in part the study of human behavior as seen through the eyes of great writers of fiction. Through their literary work, writers share with us their observations and beliefs about human motivation, morality, social functioning, and so on. *History* examines the unfolding of human behavior in past events, lining up the facts that can be uncovered about the actions of real people in earlier times and speculating about the connections between these actions and their underlying causes. *Philosophers* usually focus their attention on human behavior as well, but their preferred method is rational analysis. For example, a particular philosopher may take human language as her subject matter and attempt to analyze its sources and its implications for the operation of the human mind. The social sciences are like these other disciplines in their subject matter, human behavior, but they use different methods—the methods of science.

The Three Steps in Scientific Investigation

Across different scientific disciplines—psychology, biology, physics, or any other science—the subject matter changes, but the general methods are the same. Some specific techniques may vary, adapted to the particulars of the topics under scrutiny, but three broad steps are alike for all sciences: ***description, explanation,*** and ***verification.***

Description

Description is a research step aimed at answering factual questions about a phenomenon, questions such as who, what, when, where, and with whom. Suppose we were interested in understanding the phenomenon of juvenile delinquency. We would begin our scientific exploration by seeking answers to questions such as the following: *Who* engages in juvenile delinquency? (What are the usual ages, gender, socioeconomic status, family characteristics, intellectual characteristics, academic performance, social skills, personality characteristics, and so on, of children identified as delinquent?) *What* kinds of behaviors usually characterize delinquency? (Are most delinquents truants, or nonviolent thieves, or violent murderers, or other kinds of perpetrators?) *Where* and *when* are delinquent acts most likely to occur? *With whom* are delinquents likely to associate and to commit their evil deeds?

Explanation

With an arsenal of facts gained from descriptive research, we are ready to take the next step, *explanation.* At this point, we frame a *theory* or set of *hypotheses* about *how* the facts are related to each other and *why* they occur. Our other theoretical commitments are likely to influence us here. For example, we may tend to make stage assumptions, or we may be more apt to formulate continuity theories. Our theories may be broad

(continued)

Box 1.2   **Continued**

in scope, attempting to integrate all the data we've collected, or they may be simple hypotheses, focused on particular aspects of the facts. In formulating a theory, we should meet certain criteria. First, the theory must be *comprehensive,* that is, either it must take into account all of the known facts (for a broad theory) or at least it should not be inconsistent with any of the known facts (for a more simple, focused hypothesis). Second, it must be presented with sufficient clarity that we can make *verifiable predictions* from it.

A note of caution here: It is important to recognize that by definition, a theory or hypothesis is an *inference* rather than an observed fact. Statements about causes are always inferences, because causal relationships cannot be directly observed. We can obtain evidence for them—as you will see in the next step—but we cannot actually *prove* them without a doubt.

Verification

The gathering of evidence for our theories, or *verification,* is the third step in scientific method. Verification processes provide a means of judging theories *objectively,* on the basis of factual support, rather than *subjectively,* on the basis of how appealing they might be or how well they might fit our biases. At this point again, the scientist turns to research. It is not good enough for a theory to be effective at *post hoc* explanation, that is, comprehensively explaining the facts we already have. To be really convincing, a theory must generate predictions about events or behaviors that have not yet been observed. Research is designed to test those predictions. If they come true, there is evidence to support the theory. If the predictions fail to come true, there is evidence against the theory. Albert Einstein's theory of relativity revolutionized physics, posing relationships among known facts and suggesting causal processes not previously proposed. It was appealing because it helped explain some findings that had not fit with previous theories. But, like any scientific theory, Einstein's view had to pass the litmus test: could it predict events not previously observed? Despite the abstractness of his principles, the theory did succeed in generating a few predictions about concrete events that had not yet been observed, and these predictions did come true. Thus, Einstein's idea now has the status of being not just a creative explanation of known data, but a theory with supporting evidence.

Suppose, however, that we formulate a theory that sounds good, but its predictions do not come true. Or,

as more often happens, some of its predictions come true, and some do not. Or, even more disconcerting, the predictions of our theory come true, but so do the predictions of a very different theory to explain the same phenomenon! This is a situation that drives many students of a science, and allied practitioners, to distraction: scientists providing more than one answer to the same question! (See the section "Nature versus Nurture" for an example.)

There is a scientific approach to resolving such dilemmas. The next step is to go back to the explanation process, taking the new data we have gained from our verification efforts to craft a new, or at least a modified, theory. Then we move forward again to the verification process. Science advances in this fashion, taking the evidence (both pro and con) gathered from testing one theory to help develop a better one, then subjecting the new theory to the same rigorous tests, until eventually we have a theory that encompasses all the known facts and can generate valid predictions.

In our everyday lives, all of us sometimes operate a little like scientists. Suppose there is a phenomenon that concerns us. Perhaps a close friend begins to behave erratically, laughing or grunting inappropriately during conversations, having animated discussions with no one at all, acting irritable or becoming strangely silent. Our first step in confronting this problem is somewhat comparable to the scientist's *description* process: we try to gather more facts about our friend's behavior from coworkers, family, and friends, and we make more observations of our own. Our second step is similar to the scientist's *explanation* process: we try to develop a coherent theory that will explain how these facts fit together and why they are happening at all. Perhaps we hypothesize a schizophrenic breakdown or the onset of a degenerative brain disorder. At this point, however, our approach to our friend's behavior will probably lose its resemblance to the scientific process. Scientists would put all action on hold, make predictions from their theories, and proceed to test the predictions in carefully designed studies (see Box 1.3: *Testing Scientific Theories*). In our everyday lives, however, we are more likely to jump into practical application, such as urging the family to seek medical help. We rarely have the time or the resources to actually verify our theories in systematic ways. We simply act on them and hope that we've made the right guesses. Scientists advance more slowly to action, avoiding practical application until theories are strongly supported by evidence.

Box 1.2   Continued

Helping professionals, too, use a process closely akin to scientific method if they follow the tenets of reflective practice. First, as in the scientist's description process, they gather all the information they can about a client and the client's problem. This part of reflective practice includes examining theories and information available from scientific work that might be relevant, as well as considering both standard practices for dealing with similar problems and the practitioner's own experiences. From all of this information, the practitioner formulates hypotheses about the client and about the most

appropriate clinical strategy (as in the scientist's explanation process) and then "tests" these hypotheses (as in the scientist's verification process). However, for the practitioner, testing hypotheses occurs in the practice itself, so that, unlike the scientist, clinical professionals apply and adjust their hypotheses in the context of practice. In sum, scientifically generated knowledge informs clinical practice not by providing *answers* but by providing *options* for the development of hypotheses that can be tested in application and by suggesting strategies for handling problems.

Box 1.3   Testing Theories Scientifically

To understand how scientific research is done, particularly in the social sciences, let's consider examples of research done to test a hypothesis that was popular among developmental scientists about fifty years ago. The hypothesis was that a baby's dependency is substantially caused by parental nurturance. When parents respond to their infant's cries or give their babies attention of any kind, they are reinforcing help-seeking behavior, or "dependency." So, for example, a baby who gets a lot of attention for crying will become more of a crybaby. No one suggested that babies should be ignored, but the implications of this theory were that nonessential caregiving should be sparse if one hoped that the baby would learn to tolerate waiting and eventually learn to do things for itself. The idea was consistent with some common ideas about appropriate baby care, such as the warning that running to a baby every time it cries will "spoil" the child.

The proposal that "nurturance causes infant dependency" is a simple theory or hypothesis. "Nurturance" is the single postulated cause, or *causal variable,* and "infant dependency" is what is said to be affected by the cause, or the *outcome variable.* Some theories are much more complex, posing more than one cause, suggesting interactions among causes, or speculating about effects on more than one outcome variable. But regardless of how complex a theory becomes, it can be verified only by testing its predictions. There are two general techniques for testing the predictions of any theory: *experiments* and *correlational studies.* These techniques can be as complex as the theories that inspire them, but no matter how complex they become they are only extensions of the basic experimental or correlational procedures that we will now describe.

Experiments

An experiment is a study in which the researcher purposely changes (or manipulates) the causal variable in order to observe or measure the effects of the manipulation on the outcome variable. In a good experiment, the researcher also takes care that nothing else systematically changes at the same time as the causal variable. This ensures that if the outcome variable does seem to be affected, only the postulated causal variable could be responsible. When a scientist succeeds in eliminating alternative explanations for the changes in the outcome variable, we say that the researcher has exercised *control* over other, possible causes.

When proposed causes of human behavior are put to experimental test, psychologists and other social scientists use certain standard procedures, adapted to the study of people. To test the hypothesis that "nurturance causes infant dependency," Rheingold (1956) conducted an experiment with babies in an orphanage who ordinarily did not get any attention beyond essential physical care. Her plan was to increase the babies' nurturance (manipulate the causal variable) and later determine whether the babies' dependency had also increased (observe/measure the outcome variable). However, Rheingold needed to be sure that no other changes in the babies' lives could account for any observed change in the babies' dependency. If Rheingold were studying inanimate objects, she might have been able to make certain that nothing else changed at the same time that she changed the causal variable. But with human infants, it was not possible to simply keep everything else from changing. In most

(continued)

Box 1.3   Continued

studies with humans, researchers simply do not have that much power. For example, the babies' nurturance was increased for a 6-week period. But during this period the babies changed in age as well, a process that could not be stopped. There may also have been other, less obvious changes in the babies' experiences. For example, the orphanage could have contracted to buy baby formula from a different vendor, so that the taste and quality of the babies' food could have changed. Rheingold exercised control over all of these alternative explanations of the outcome not by preventing them from changing, but by using a *control group.*

The control group was a second group of babies from the same orphanage nursery who experienced all of the "unstoppable" changes that the first group of babies (the experimental group) experienced: they got older in the 6 weeks of the study, and if anything else in the nursery changed, such as the baby formula, it changed for them, too. However, Rheingold did not increase the amount of nurturance that the control group babies received. In the end, the babies in the experimental group, for whom nurturance was increased, showed increased dependency, just as predicted, but the babies in the control group showed no change in their dependency. Because the control group babies experienced everything that the experimental group babies experienced except for increased nurturance, *only* the increased nurturance could have been the cause of greater dependency in the experimental group babies.

Experiments with humans usually "control" causes other than the postulated causal variable by incorporating control groups to which the experimental group can be compared. The experimental group is defined as the group for which the causal variable is purposely changed. The control group is a group like the experimental group in every way except that the causal variable is not purposely changed. Chemists and other scientists who study the inanimate, physical world need not use control group procedures, but psychologists need this technique because, either for practical or for ethical reasons, they cannot necessarily prevent other possible causes from changing during the course of an experiment.

Correlational Studies

Sometimes, both in psychology and in other sciences, predictions cannot be tested using experiments. Remember, in an experiment, the researcher purposely

changes the causal variable. But what if the researcher does not have the power to change the causal variable? In some sciences, such as astronomy, this is usually the case. Suppose an astronomer hypothesizes that "meteor showers cause temperature increases in the outer atmosphere of planet X" (a hypothesis invented by a textbook author who knows little about astronomy). To do an experiment, the astronomer would have to manipulate the occurrence of meteor showers (the causal variable) and then observe or measure atmospheric temperature (the outcome variable) to see whether it also changes. But astronomers cannot (at least at the present time) manipulate the occurrence of meteor showers, so such an experiment could not be done. The alternative, in such a case, is to do a *correlational study,* a technique in which both the causal variable and the outcome variable are measured or observed, and nothing is actually manipulated by the researcher. The research question is, do the two variables change together in the ways predicted by the hypothesis? In this astronomical example, the prediction is that the more intense a naturally occurring meteor shower is, the greater will be the temperature increase in planet X's atmosphere.

A correlational study can determine whether changes in the causal variable are matched by predicted changes in the outcome variable. What a correlational study *cannot* do is tell us whether the changes in the causal variable actually determined the matching changes in the outcome variable. For example, an astronomer would not know if some other variable might also have changed when the meteor shower occurred. If it did, the other variable might actually have caused the increased temperature of planet X's atmosphere. Only experiments, with proper controls, can tell us whether the postulated causal variable is the real cause. But when the predictions of a theory come true in a correlational study, it is still evidence *for* the theory that made the prediction, because the results are consistent with the theory. And, when the predictions do not come true, it is still evidence *against* the theory, because the results are inconsistent with the theory.

Correlational studies are usually done in the social sciences when experiments are either impractical or unethical. Consider again the hypothesis that "nurturance causes infant dependency." Rheingold was able to purposely change the nurturance of babies in an orphanage because they were getting very little nurtur-

Box 1.3   Continued

ance already, and no one considered it unethical to increase their nurturance for a while. But if Rheingold had wanted to change the nurturance of babies being cared for by their own parents, it is unlikely that the parents would have considered that reasonable. Parents have their own ideas about how much nurturance their babies should get. For this reason, when Ainsworth and her colleagues (e.g., Ainsworth, Bell, & Stayton, 1972; Ainsworth, Blehar, Waters, & Wall, 1978) wanted to look at the relationship between parental nurturance and infant dependency, they did a correlational study. They asked parents only to allow them to watch the nurturing process. Over a period of many months, they observed and measured mothers' nurturance of their infants (the causal variable in this hypothesis) and also measured infants' dependency (the outcome variable in this hypothesis). The hypothesis predicts that the more nurturance that mothers give their babies, the more dependent the babies become. This would be a **positive correlation:** the two variables would change in the same direction, either both increasing or both decreasing. Surprisingly, given Rheingold's findings, the prediction did not come true. In fact, the results were just the opposite. At 8 months old, the infants whose mothers had provided the most nurturance until then were the ones who were the most independent! So, Ainsworth and her colleagues found a **negative correlation:** the two variables (nurturance and dependency) changed together but in *opposite* directions, so that as one increased, the other decreased. Ainsworth's correlational study provided evidence *against* the hypothesis that "nurturance causes infant dependency."

When theories are tested, contradictory findings like Rheingold's and Ainsworth's are typical. No single study, either experiment or correlational study, is ever a sufficient test of a theory. Theories become more convincing as the stockpile of supporting evidence grows. If the evidence is contradictory, it's time to go back to the drawing board and consider how to change or replace this theory in order to explain all of the new findings. As you will see in Chapter 4, the studies of nurturance and dependency just described have led most researchers to prefer a more complex explanation of their relationship, now referred to as "attachment theory."

A Special Case: Studying Age Effects

Suppose we have a theory that some behavior or skill changes with age, for example, "In adulthood, aging causes declines in intelligence." We can use only correlational studies to test hypotheses where age is the causal variable, because age is not something that a researcher can directly change or manipulate. So age is observed, and the outcome variable (such as intelligence in this hypothesis) is observed or measured. However, age can be observed in three different ways, and each method has its own advantages and disadvantages.

Cross-Sectional Studies

In **cross-sectional studies,** different ages are represented by different groups of people. For example, a group of 20-year-olds might represent young adults, a group of 40-year-olds might represent middle-aged adults, and a group of 70-year-olds might represent older adults. Then all the subjects would be measured for the outcome variable (such as intelligence). When age and intelligence have been examined in this way, typically intelligence scores have declined with age as our sample hypothesis predicts.

But in cross-sectional studies, what look like the effects of age could be the result of **cohort** differences. Participants in each age group belong to a *cohort:* they were born in the same historical period, and they grew up at about the same time. People in different age groups belong to different cohorts. When it appears that age is causing some change, such as a decline in intelligence, the change could be the result of other differences among the cohorts. For example, educational approaches and opportunities may have changed dramatically from the time that today's 70-year-olds were kids to the time that today's 40-year-olds were kids, and these changes in education may be the cause of their differences in measured intelligence. Age may have nothing to do with it!

Longitudinal Studies

Some researchers study age and its effects by doing **longitudinal** research. Only one group of subjects, all the same age, participates. They are measured several times as they get older. For example, in place of the cross-sectional study we just described, we could do a longitudinal study testing the intelligence of one group of participants several times throughout their lives, starting when they were all 20 years old.

This kind of design eliminates cohort differences because only one cohort is included. In longitudinal

(continued)

Box 1.3   **Continued**

studies of intelligence, no declines are usually found until after age 50 or 60, and many individuals show increasing scores through much of adulthood, indicating that the steady declines in intelligence often observed in cross-sectional studies are due to cohort effects (see Chapter 13).

But longitudinal studies have their own disadvantages. First, they can take so long that the original researchers are retired or dead before the studies are completed! Second, age is not the only thing that could be causing the observed changes. Cultural changes could also be a cause of what look like age changes. For example, medical care and nutrition improved dramatically after World War II. If subjects in our imaginary longitudinal study have benefitted from such improvements, they may actually enjoy greater mental alertness as older adults than they did when they were young, helping them to perform better in a testing situation even though other elements of intelligence have not actually improved and may even have declined as a function of age.

Take heart, however, because there is a way to combine the advantages of both cross-sectional and longitudinal studies that helps to isolate the effects of age.

Sequential Studies

A *sequential* study is like a cross-sectional study in that more than one cohort is included, and it is like a longitudinal study in that each cohort is measured at more than one age. Suppose again that we want to know if intelligence changes with age. We might include three cohorts in our study. Let's say one cohort, born in 1930, is measured at age 60 and again at 70; the second cohort, born in 1940, is measured at ages 50 and 60; and the last cohort, born in 1950, is measured at ages 40 and 50. All subjects are measured in the years 1990 and 2000. Our study will be 10 years long, but we will have information on whether intelligence increases or decreases over each 10-year age period from age 40 to age 70. The subjects who were born first may not have intelligence scores as high as those born later, but we are examining increases or decreases with age, not absolute scores. And cultural changes will be uniform for all cohorts because they are all being measured at the same times. Cultural changes could still explain results if all groups change the same way from the first to the second testing, but if there are improvements in some cohorts and declines in others, these differences cannot be explained by cultural change and are more likely the result of age.

the enriched environment! Clearly, the environment strongly influenced the "intellectual" functioning of these rats (see Figure 1.2).

To test the predictions of this theory with humans, some researchers have enriched the environments of children growing up in unstimulating contexts. For example, another classic study was reported by Skodak and Skeels (1949). Skeels removed a group of babies from an orphanage nursery and put them in the care of mildly retarded teenage girls housed in an institution for the mentally retarded. The girls enthusiastically "mothered" the children for 18 months, providing the kind of stimulation they had been missing in the orphanage: talking to the babies, playing with them, taking them for walks, reading to them. The "adopted" children's intelligence test scores showed dramatic increases after 18 months. A control group of children who had been left in the relatively unstimulating orphanage nursery showed significant decreases in intelligence test scores over the same period. The beneficial effects of enriching environments on the intellectual functioning of human children have been reported by many more recent researchers. For example, poor children who participated in a special day care program—the Carolina Abecedarian Project—from infancy until kindergarten, performed better on intelligence test scores throughout elementary school than a comparable group of children who did not participate in the program (Campbell & Ramey, 1994). So, predictions of the theory that environment causes intelligence have been validated both in animal and in human research.

It looks like intelligence is caused *both* by heredity and by the environment. And similar sets of findings could be presented to argue that both causes operate in the production

FIGURE 1.2

Environmental Effects on "Maze-bright" and "Maze-dull" Rats (Cooper & Zubeck, 1958).

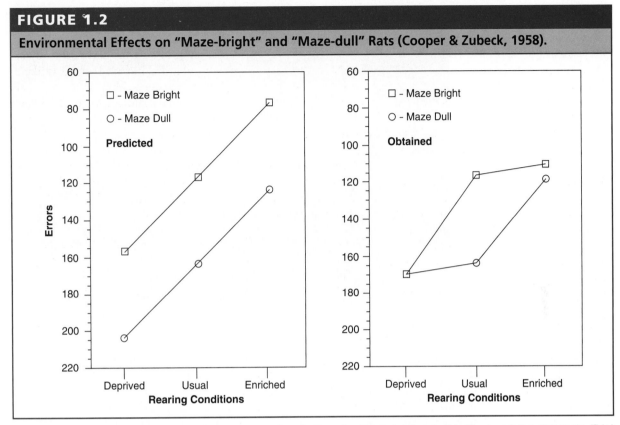

Source: Wahlstein, D., & Gottlieb, G. (1997). The invalid separation of effects of nature and nurture. In R. V. Sternberg & E. L. Grigorenko (Eds.) *Intelligence, heredity, and environment* (p. 175). New York: Cambridge University Press. Reprinted with permission of the publisher.

of physical traits and of personality traits. What theorists and researchers face now is the difficult task of specifying how the two sets of causes work together: Do they have separate effects that "add up," for example, or do they qualitatively modify each other, creating together, in unique combinations, unique outcomes? Modern multidimensional theories generally make the latter assumption. They are responding to the growing body of evidence that heredity and environment are interdependent: the same genes operate differently in different environments, and the same environments are experienced differently by individuals with different genetic characteristics. Developmental outcomes are always a function of interplay between genes and environment, and the operation of one cannot even be described adequately without reference to the other.

One last set of examples from animal and from human research should help illustrate the complexity of the interdependence we are describing. First, consider an example from animal research. A species of parasitic wasp lays its eggs in other "host" insects, either a fly or a butterfly. The genetic endowment of the eggs is the same regardless of where the eggs are laid, but the environments in which the eggs are developing are clearly different. Some physical traits of the offspring wasps are different depending on the environment. For example, if the offspring mature in the butterfly, they grow wings; but if they mature in the fly, they do not grow wings (Gottlieb, 1992). The same genes lead to different outcomes, depending on the characteristics of the context in which they operate.

Now, consider a final example from human research. Identical twins are generally quite similar in height whether raised together or apart, indicating that height is "very heritable." Yet, in some cultures, heights have changed greatly from one generation to the

Enriched and stimulating environments provide long-term benefits for children's functioning.

next—too quickly for genetic changes to be significant. To illustrate, Angoff (1988) found that the average height of young men in Japan had increased by three and a half inches in the three decades following World War II. Only environmental variation, such as improved nutrition, could be responsible for such rapid height changes in a population, an illustration of the same genes (or gene pool in this case) producing different effects in different contexts. We will have more to say about this topic in Chapter 2.

Critical Periods Versus Unlimited Plasticity

The issue here is whether some developments, such as first language learning, must take place within a certain time frame, called a ***critical period,*** or whether the organism is able to develop or learn any new skill at any time with the right opportunities. There is little doubt that there are some behavioral developments that usually take place within a particular period of time. Language acquisition is in many ways nearly complete by the age of 5 or 6, for example. But is it possible to acquire a language at another point in the life cycle if this usual time is somehow "missed?" Pinker (1994) reviewed several findings that led him to conclude that although language can be learned at other times, it is never learned as well or as effortlessly as it would have been in the critical period from about 1 to 5 years. One interesting example from Pinker's review concerns the learning of sign language by deaf individuals. American Sign Language (ASL) is a "real" symbolic language, with a complex grammar. Often, however, American deaf children are not given the opportunity to learn ASL in their early years, sometimes because of a belief that deaf children should learn to read lips and speak English (the "oralist" tradition). As a result, many deaf children simply do not learn any language. When these individuals have been introduced to ASL in late childhood or adolescence, they have failed to acquire the same degree of facility with the grammar that children who learn ASL as preschoolers achieve.

If findings like these mean that a critical period has been missed, what could be the cause of such time-dependent learning? It is usually assumed that the end of a critical period is due to brain changes that make learning more difficult after the change. An alternative explanation is that the environmental conditions that are likely to exist during the critical period are especially favorable. And, as with the other dilemmas discussed in this section, the explanation is likely to be complex. Sensitivity to new learning opportunities probably does vary across the life span as a function of changes in the nervous system. But how effectively an individual can learn new skills may be just as much a function of the availability and nature of the opportunities presented, which may need to be different depending on the developmental period in which the opportunities occur. For example, total immersion in a language may be just the right arrangement for a preschooler who knows no other communicative system. An older learner, even deaf children or adults who have learned no formal language early in life, may always filter a new language through previously established symbol systems, however informal or idiosyncratic their symbol systems may be. If so, for an older child or adult, total immersion may be less effective than a learning environment that can make correspondences between the new language and the old one. In later chapters, we will examine this issue as it relates to several developments, such as the emergence of sexual identity (Chapter 8) and the formation of bonds between mothers and infants (Chapter 4). In each case, the evidence indicates that some features of a critical period exist alongside continuing plasticity.

Continuity Versus Change

This question actually presents itself in two different ways. First, there is the issue of whether characteristics that emerge early in life, perhaps even at birth, sometimes persist, relatively unchanged, throughout life. For example, does a shy, inhibited child usually become a shy, inhibited adult? If so, it would appear that some qualities, once established, are intractable, unaffected by the flux of experience in an individual's life. However, if trait persistence does exist, it could actually be a product of dynamic interactions (the proximal processes described by Bronfenbrenner) that have the effect of maintaining a trait that *could* change. Suppose, for example, that a shy, inhibited youngster is protected by parents from any risk taking, or from having to be sociable, with explanations such as "He's too shy to say 'Hello.'" The child may then miss opportunities to develop social skills and strategies that could help him to become more sociable and less inhibited. Multidimensional models predict that traits can exhibit both continuity and discontinuity, depending on the multiple, interacting forces in play.

A second manifestation of this dilemma is the issue of whether early events or experiences can have more or less permanent, continuous effects on an individual's development. These could be normal, expected events, such as parents providing warm responsive care in infancy, or they could be unexpected, "off-time," or nonnormative events such as loss of a job or the untimely death of a parent. In either case, the question is whether or not salient experiences of relatively short duration can have long-term impacts. Freud's stage theory is centered on the notion that early events do have continuous effects. For example, Freud considered an "oral" fixation in adulthood to be the long-term effect of unsatisfactory or inappropriate oral experiences in the first year of life, which permanently modify the balance of id energies. Multidimensional models, however, usually suggest that early events have long-term effects only if the initial fallout is continuously maintained by proximal processes (e.g., Sameroff, 1989). Suppose an infant's mother suffers from a postpartum depression that dissipates when the baby is 8 weeks old. Many depressed mothers provide their babies with less stimulation, less responsive care, and less affection, on average, than nondepressed mothers (e.g., Fleming, Ruble, Flett, & Schaul, 1988). These are characteristics of infant care that could impact the child's intellectual and/or social development; but in this case, as long as the mother's caregiving improves after her depression ends, there are not likely to be long-term effects on the infant.

Activity Versus Passivity

Another question that has been the focus of theorizing by developmentalists concerns whether human development is intrinsically an active or a passive process. Is the course of a person's development primarily shaped by external forces over which the individual has limited control? Or are human beings active "masters of their fate," defining, selecting, and shaping their lives' trajectories? If you espouse the first, or "passive," view, you might construe individuals to be highly malleable and receptive to outside intervention, sometimes described as a *mechanistic view* of the human being. Implicit in this paradigm is the notion that development can ultimately, at least in principle, be reduced to a chainlike sequence of events. Alter a link on the chain, and you can have some effect on the person's subsequent development. Early behavioral approaches to teaching, learning, and counseling held this view of the organism.

The alternative, "active," view characterizes *organismic theories* of development (e.g., Piaget, 1970; Werner, 1948/1973), which depict human beings as active initiators of their own development. In other words, psychological determinants of growth and change reside within individuals, who are actively involved in constructing their worlds. If you espouse this perspective, you might believe that human beings are not as amenable to change from outside forces and are not easily coerced by external agents. Teachers and counselors working from this perspective might focus less on directive approaches and more on facilitating personal expression and meaning making, as traditional humanistic approaches to education and therapy have done. From this perspective, people are more than the sum total of their environmental inputs; they need to be "discovered instead of shaped" (Hamer & Copeland, 1998).

To illustrate the opposing sides of this dilemma, consider the example of a 1-month-old infant. For many years, infants were viewed as passive organisms who were "socialized" by parents or other caretakers (Gewirtz & Boyd, 1977). Parents were cautioned by child-rearing experts to establish strict schedules for feeding, napping, and so on, to mold the baby's behavior to acceptable standards. Then, evidence began to emerge that infants have a great effect on their caregivers (Bell, 1971; Tronick, Als, & Brazelton, 1980). Can the newborn actually be controlling the parent rather than the other way around? Just recall how quickly an adult caregiver responds to a newborn baby's cry! This new perspective changed experts' advice and led them to advise parents to "take their cue" from what the baby seemed to need or want.

Even though it would be incorrect to assume that contemporary developmentalists take either extreme position, the pendulum has clearly come to rest more on the "active" side of the continuum. For example, modern multidimensional theories describe developing individuals as *self-organizing,* filtering incoming information through their own existing mental constructs and influencing the environment's inputs with their actions and reactions. A similar position is taken in the writings of educational and clinical constructivists (Guterman, 1994; Mahoney, 1993, 1995). *Constructivism,* while not a single, unified theory, is rooted in older psychological theories such as Piaget's. The key assumption in all constructivist approaches is that individuals are not just passive receptors of information who acquire knowledge via external manipulations. Instead, people actively construct their knowledge by interpreting information in light of prior learning, by actively restructuring prior knowledge, or by co-constructing knowledge in interactions with others (Moshman, 1982). *Social constructivism,* a variation of cognitive constructivism, emphasizes that knowledge is constructed within the context of social relationships with others and stresses the influence of such variables as gender, class, and culture on the development of beliefs (Lyddon, 1990).

Consider the example of a class of students taking a multiple-choice exam. Frequently, students' answers will differ not because they have not studied the material but because they interpret the questions in idiosyncratic ways. They have actively built their knowledge of course content on the foundations of earlier associations that may or may not have been consonant with the meanings of the test maker. Similarly, many interpersonal conflicts that provide the raw material for therapy are often the result of idiosyncratic "meaning making" by each of the parties involved. This phenomenon, constructivists tell us, describes the human condition. Recent developments in therapy such as the use of narratives and therapeutic metaphors capitalize on this constructivist process. By questioning, offering interpretations, and explaining, a therapist can alter the client's frame of reference, help change meaning, and encourage revision of previously held beliefs (see Haley, 1976).

APPLICATIONS

In this chapter, we have discussed the importance of the study of development and introduced you to some of the worldviews and issues central to the field. The value of developmental knowledge to practitioners of the helping professions cannot be underestimated, as is underscored by a consensus growing out of a number of different theoretical orientations. Some of these include the emerging field of *applied developmental science,* which has begun to synthesize and apply the findings of developmental psychology to the solution of real-world problems (Fisher & Lerner, 1993). The field of *developmental psychopathology,* another new and influential subspecialty, has applied a developmental focus to the study of abnormal behavior and dysfunction (e.g., Cicchetti, 1984; Sroufe & Rutter, 1984). Writers in this area have used the results of longitudinal analyses to understand trajectories of risk and resilience in human development. Clinically oriented writers have also applied specific developmental theories such as Piaget's theory of cognitive development (Ivey, 1986), Freud's psychosexual stage theory (Garcia, 1995), and Kohlberg's moral development theory (Hayes, 1994) to the counseling process.

These developmental approaches to counseling and therapy, for the most part, have encouraged clinicians to take into account the developmental features of client functioning as a critical part of assessing and treating problems. Finally, Noam (1992, 1998), who takes a developmental and constructivist approach to the study of disorders, has developed a therapeutic approach called *clinical-developmental psychology,* which also blends developmental knowledge with clinical practice.

Despite the fact that researchers and clinicians are still just beginning to collaborate, these approaches share a number of commonalities: a sensitivity to the fact that persons grow and change over time and that their capacities and concerns also shift over the life course; an appreciation for the knowledge that scientific studies of developmental change can provide for clinicians; and a commitment to the application of this knowledge to improving the lives of individuals, families, and society as a whole. Instead of asking clinicians to choose a therapeutic approach from a set of treatment modalities, each with its own bounded theoretical tradition, Noam (1998) argues for a developmental viewpoint in training programs, which can help new clinicians organize the vast amount of information they need to master. "Developmental psychology and developmental psychopathology need to become 'basic sciences' for the mental health field" (Rolf, Masten, Cichetti, Neuchterlein, & Weintraub, 1990). Use of developmental knowledge as a kind of metatheory helps counselors to integrate the problems presented by the "person-in-situation" and can help reduce the confusion often felt by helpers exposed to a heterogeneous array of treatments for isolated problems.

Noam suggests that, in this age of short-term treatments, the goal is often to "jump start" those normal developmental processes that can promote healthy functioning. What is needed is a developmental template that the helper can use to facilitate this process. For example, if part of the client's difficulty involves relatively immature thinking about the self in relationship with others, knowledge of the typical sequence of social-cognitive development may be useful in assessing the problem. Strategies can be tried that encourage the growth of perspective-taking skills along the lines of typical development. Not only is this approach useful in addressing immediate difficulties, but it also has the secondary benefit of anticipating what clients will need at later points in their growth.

Knowledge of developmental science helps clinicians in other ways as well. The helper must be able to distinguish normal developmental perturbations from real deviations in development in order to intervene wisely. A prime example of this occurs in adolescence, which Freud described as a period of "normal psychopathology." Understanding some of the issues typical of this time of life can inform a clinician's guidance, advocacy, and support. Moreover, using a developmental focus can allow the helper to consider ways to support developmental transitions (Lerner, 1996) to later life stages by taking steps to promote a caring network.

Tavris (1998) makes the point that helpers who are unaware of current developmental knowledge may even be practicing unethically. She recounts the story of one mother who consulted a therapist because of her young daughter's extraordinary shyness. Rather than recognizing the child as temperamentally inhibited (see Chapter 4), the therapist diagnosed the little girl as suffering from "repressed rage syndrome" due to the mother's work outside the home. Ignorance of the developmental roots of various other behavioral symptoms may cause clinicians to misidentify problems and apply ineffective, and potentially harmful, solutions.

It helps to bear in mind that the various theoretical models or metaphors for developmental growth that we have presented should not be applied rigidly. Steenbarger (1991) cautions against thinking about developmental progress as movement through a fixed set of stages that are the same for all people. Obviously, this view can be excessively rigid and can lead to interpretations of problems in which the complexities of person-environment interactions go unrecognized. Nonetheless, radical constructivist views that abandon all sense of developmental stage progressions may prove unwieldy for the helper who needs to construct a developmental map of the client. What is the answer? As usual, an informed middle ground may be the best alternative. Stages of psychosocial development are not entirely dependent upon chronological age and maturational attainments. However, they are not independent of these achievements either. The skilled clinician must consider a number of possibilities at the same time and, like the reflective thinker described earlier, work to find the best fit.

With respect to the traditional dilemmas in development, it is most consistent with *current* research that helpers refrain from taking an "either-or" position in favor of a "both-and" stance. Above all, awareness of the interacting contributions of genetics and environment can allow helpers to take a more reasoned and accurate view of problems. The current trend toward "over-biologizing" (Tavris, 1998) many kinds of physical and psychological conditions can lead people to the false belief that our genes control our behavior. In fact, they may produce tendencies for people to respond to environments in certain ways. One more example of the nature-nurture interaction may be of use here. Cadoret, Yates, Troughton, Wordsworth, and Stewart (1995) studied rates of conduct disorder in a sample of adopted children. They used the biological parents' rates of drug abuse or antisocial personality disorder as a measure of genetic risk and the adoptive families' levels of psychiatric and family problems as a measure of environmental risk. The adopted children most likely to develop conduct disorder were those who had high-risk

Box 1.4   Qualitative Research Methods

Qualitative research methods afford the developmentalist another, less traditional way of doing research. *Qualitative research* has been defined as "any kind of research that produces findings not arrived at by means of statistical procedures or other means of quantification" (Strauss & Corbin, 1990, p. 17). This definition appears to allow for many types of methodologies and techniques and may seem somewhat ambiguous. One way to clarify the concept is to view qualitative research as a way of answering questions not readily answerable by quantitative methods. For example, qualitative studies can be aimed at providing rich descriptive information about some concept or experience that is not well understood. Rather than using tests or other assessment instruments, the qualitative researcher may choose to interview the participants, make observations, or gather life histories. Although one of the purposes of this kind of research is to build theory, the actual data are not analyzed and tested as in more traditional methods. Instead, the data are the "voices" of the participants, who are allowed to speak for themselves. The data are not categorized according to any predetermined scheme but are allowed to evolve in novel ways. Consider, for example, the question of how middle-aged men cope over time with the death of a spouse when adolescent children are still in the home. A researcher may legitimately choose to study this topic using standardized questionnaires or interviews in an effort to categorize the fathers according to various established typologies of coping behavior. In contrast, a qualitative analysis would probably involve extensive, ongoing interviews without a predetermined typology or way of categorizing the fathers and would allow a "theory" of fathers' coping styles to build over the course of the project.

Daniel Levinson's (1996) study of the stages of a woman's life represents a good example of a qualitative research project. Using methods he called biographical interviewing and biographical reconstruction, he studied 45 women in order to learn about "the nature of

women's development and about specific life issues relating to friendship, work, love, marriage, motherhood, good times and bad times, the stuff life is made of" (pp. 7–8). Levinson's intensive work with these participants resulted in complex, descriptive narratives that provided a framework for a theoretical construction about women's life trajectories.

Qualitative research approaches differ from more traditional methodologies in a number of ways. First, the data, as we have indicated, consist primarily of the words and actions of participants instead of numerical scores of frequencies. Second, the design of a study may change as the study progresses and the "data" are collected and considered. Third, a qualitative researcher may appear to be less objective than the more traditional researcher and may write about the study in a narrative style. Sometimes the data are reported in the first person. Fourth, no hypothesis is used to guide the study. However, a research question identifies the topic of the project, as in "how do middle-aged men, with adolescent children, cope with the death of a spouse?" Other differences exist as well, but these are some of the primary ones. Despite these differences, qualitative and traditional (quantitative) research methods share some similar features. Both approaches can be descriptive and have theory building as their goal (see Box 1.1: *Understanding the Scientific Process*). Most importantly, perhaps, both maintain their own rigorous standards for reliability and validity (Lincoln & Guba, 1985).

Qualitative and quantitative methods can enhance each other by approaching a problem from more than one direction. Recently, a consortium of editors of developmental psychology journals endorsed the importance of qualitative methods and encouraged researchers to use them in their research projects. The editors stated that quantitative tools alone "cannot reveal the complex processes that likely give rise to normal and abnormal behavior among different children and adolescents" (Azar, 1999, pp. 20–21).

biological parents *in addition to* chronic stress in their adopted families. Clearly, individuals are most vulnerable when they experience both genetic and environmental risk factors. Rather than construe genetics as deterministic, the identification of the genetic risk should signal the need for various kinds of environmental interventions. More than ever, clinicians need to be aware of the fact that overdependence on biological explanation is just as inaccurate as overly idealistic claims about environmental influence.

In this chapter, we have introduced you to some of the classic paradigms and issues in the field of human development and have specified ways in which knowledge of development is fundamental to practitioners. We now suggest a few general guidelines for the application of developmental research to the work of the helping professional. Perhaps the most important place to start is with the term "theory." This term is used differently in science than it is in everyday language. In science, a theory represents a synthesis of hypotheses that have been tested and supported by careful research, such as the theory of relativity or evolution. In everyday use, a theory can mean one's personal opinion, such as one's opinion about the best way to educate or counsel children or one's guess about what causes marriages to fail. Scientific theories are not immutable; they can evolve or be disproved with the accumulation of evidence. Although evaluating theories in light of evidence is by no means the only way we learn about life, this approach offers many strengths that set it apart from everyday speculation. Consequently, skilled clinicians should keep themselves well informed about current research findings, but they must also avoid overgeneralizing from single studies.

In addition, they must be cautious about the sources of information they accept. As with any scientific endeavor, knowledge builds relatively slowly and is buttressed by repeated observations of similar results. A simplistic approach to developmental issues will typically miss the mark by ignoring the complexities of interacting factors, including contextual and historical influences. Additionally, the kinds of direct causal connections between experiences and outcomes that would make prediction much easier for therapists and consultants are, unfortunately, almost impossible to obtain.

Finally, if we are to pursue the best possible outcomes for our clients, we need to be committed to advancing our professional knowledge. While we will try in this book to present the best available information that applies to helpers, it is important to be aware that the field of developmental science is itself continually developing. Helpers and others need to keep an open mind and continually work to accommodate new information as they practice reflection in action.

SUMMARY

Reflection and Practice

1. The fields of counseling and of human development have long been linked. Counselors are "dedicated to the enhancement of human development," and researchers in human development provide counselors with theories and data that can contribute to therapeutic practice. In the approach to counseling called *reflective practice,* developmental research and theory are among the resources counselors use to generate hypotheses about appropriate problem solutions, which the counselor will then test and revise in practice. The more extensive and well-organized the counselor's knowledge of basic developmental issues, the more able the counselor will be to retrieve developmental information that is useful to problem solving.

The Big Picture: Models and Metaphors

2. Theories of human development fall into three broad classes: stage models, incremental models, and multidimensional models. In *stage models,* a person's activities share some common characteristics during the period of time called a *stage*. These common characteristics change qualitatively as the person moves from one stage to another. Thus, the period within a stage is a time of relative stability, which ends in a period of rapid change (stage shift), which leads to another relatively stable time. Among the more well-known stage theories are Freud's and Erikson's classic theories of personality development and Piaget's theory of cognitive development.

3. In Freud's theory of *psychosexual stages,* personality develops in childhood through five periods: the oral, the anal, the phallic, the latency, and, finally, the genital stages. A child moves from one stage to another as the biological self, or *id,* changes. In each stage, the child's experiences of need fulfillment, such as the satisfaction of oral needs in the first stage, play a critical role in the formation and further development of the other aspects of personality—the *ego* and the *superego.* Although there is little evidence to support Freud's developmental theory, it has influenced other theories, and Freud's ideas are so widely known that they are a part of our culture.

4. In Erikson's eight *psychosocial stages* of development, personal identity and interpersonal attitudes are expanded and reworked throughout the life span. At each stage, changes in the individual's needs or abilities and/or changes in societal expectations create new challenges or *crises.* As each crisis is faced, a new aspect of self-concept emerges, along with feelings or attitudes toward others. If others are sensitive and responsive to the individual's needs during a given stage, positive feelings will result. If the individual's needs are not adequately met, predominantly negative feelings toward self or others may be the consequence. Erikson's emphasis on explaining the development of feelings about self and other has been appealing to counselors, and many of his ideas are compatible with findings from developmental research on issues such as attachment formation and the development of self-esteem.

5. Piaget's *cognitive developmental theory* describes changes in children's logical thinking skills through four stages. Infants in the *sensorimotor stage* do not yet have the capacity for representational thought. Children in the stage of *preoperational thought,* from 2 to 7, can think, but their thinking is not yet logical. In the *concrete operational stage,* 7- to 11-year-olds think logically, but they do so most effectively if what they are thinking about can be directly related to the concrete, real world. By the *formal operational stage,* however, the young adolescent begins to be able to think logically about abstract contents. This is the most advanced stage of logical thinking in Piaget's view. Piaget's theory has generated volumes of research. Although many details of his theory are no longer considered correct, his general characterizations of children's abilities at different ages are widely seen as useful descriptions.

6. *Incremental models* of development come in many different forms, but they all characterize behavioral change as a gradual, step-by-step process. *Learning theories,* for example, emphasize that behavior changes as children learn responses through the processes of *classical* and *operant conditioning. Social learning theories* stress one more learning process: *modeling,* or observational learning. All learning theories portray any change in behavior as a result of specific experiences, affecting specific behaviors. Development results from many independent changes in many different behaviors or mental processes.

7. Among incremental models are many *information processing theories.* As the mind attends to, analyzes, and stores information, there are gradual changes in the amount of information stored, in the availability of strategies to process information or solve problems, in the links established between or among pieces of information, and perhaps in the size of one's attentional capacity. Most of these changes are limited to whatever kind of information is being processed, so that, for example, acquiring a new strategy for adding or subtracting numbers does not affect the strategies a child might use in reading. Thus, development involves the accrual of small changes within specific domains of knowledge rather than broad, sweeping changes that affect many domains at once.

8. *Multidimensional models* are broad in scope, explaining both cognitive and social developments. Changes in behavior are the result of causes both within the organism and in the environment. These causes mutually influence one another as well as

behavior. One example of such a theory is Bronfenbrenner's *bioecological model,* in which all developments are seen as the result of *proximal processes*—reciprocal interactions between an active organism and its immediate environment. More distal processes modify proximal processes and include aspects of the organism, such as genetic functioning, and aspects of the environment, such as family structure or cultural institutions. Proximal processes, such as a child's particular interactions with peers or adults, also influence distal processes, such as the child's internal physiological functioning or the dynamic structure of the child's family.

Applying Models and Metaphors

9. In counseling practice, applying a particular developmental model to the assessment of a client's needs can help a counselor to organize what the counselor knows about a client and to gain insight into how to intervene. But our theories also provide a set of blinders, focusing our attention on some aspects of a situation and reducing the visibility of other aspects. Maintaining an awareness of our own theoretical biases can help us avoid the problems of a narrowed perspective.

Major Issues in Development

10. Among the core issues or "either/or" dilemmas that developmental theorists often address is the *nature versus nurture controversy.* Which are the more important causes of developmental change, genetic or environmental processes? While specific theories often focus our attention on the importance of just one type of cause, research has established that for most behavioral developments, genetic and environmental processes interact, mutually affecting each other and the behavior in question. Modern multidimensional theories take into account the complexity of this interdependency.

11. Another core issue in development, *critical periods versus plasticity,* addresses the question of whether some behaviors can develop only at certain crucial times in the life span or whether behaviors can change at any time. Some have argued, for example, that learning language is best accomplished in the preschool years. If critical periods exist, a further question (which may have different answers depending on the behavior) concerns whether developmental changes in the brain could be the source of time-limited opportunities for learning or whether favorable environmental conditions are simply more likely to exist in some developmental periods than in others.

12. A third core issue in development, whether there is *continuity vs. change,* has two manifestations. First, we can ask whether early characteristics, once established, can persist unchanged throughout life or whether the flux of experience eventually causes changes in all characteristics. Second, we can ask whether or not early experiences can have continuous or relatively permanent, long-term effects on a person's development, regardless of later experiences. Different theories offer different answers to these questions. Modern multidimensional theories take the position that continuity of either type is likely only if ongoing proximal processes support that continuity. For example, the death of a mother in the preschool years might continuously influence a child's development if no one in the child's immediate environment takes over the mother's role or if there are constant reminders in the child's experience of her loss.

13. A final core issue concerns the degree to which the developing person is an active agent in his or her own developmental processes. On one side of the *activity versus passivity* debate, theorists argue that human beings help shape their own lives. Individuals are to some important extent *self-organizing,* actively participating in the *construction* of their own knowledge and experience. On the other side of the debate, theorists suggest that experience is the primary determiner of knowledge, behavior,

and developmental change. Modern theorists tend to accept the notion of an active organism, but do not discount the importance of experience in the construction of behavior and knowledge.

Case Study

Charles, a 5-year-old black youngster, lives with his mother, Valerie, and his maternal grandparents in a high-rise apartment in an urban area. Valerie's mother works regularly as a member of a small housecleaning business. Valerie's father is unemployed because of an injury. Valerie was 16 when she gave birth to her son. At that time, she was a sophomore at the local public school but had never been very interested in school work and was a marginal student academically. Valerie did enjoy participating in some of the extracurricular activities, such as the chorus and the musical productions, provided by her public school. Her teachers felt that she was quite talented in these areas. When she became pregnant, she dropped out of high school and all related activities to take care of her infant son. Charles's father, Howard, was uninvolved in the pregnancy and has had virtually no contact with his son for the past five years. Recently, Valerie learned that Howard has been convicted of burglary and is awaiting sentencing. She does not want her son to have any contact with his father.

After learning that she was pregnant, Valerie concealed the news from her family for several months, fearing their disapproval. Her parents are very religious and hold strong views against premarital sex. Consequently, Valerie did not receive any prenatal medical care until she was five months pregnant. Charles was born three weeks premature and weighed only 4 pounds, 2 ounces. He had to remain in the hospital for four weeks after birth because of his immature respiratory system. Fortunately, Charles's health improved, and he has had only the typical childhood illnesses since that time.

Valerie has three older siblings who no longer live at home. One of her brothers does live nearby and regularly visits the family. Valerie's unemployed father serves as a babysitter for Charles during the day. The family looked for a nursery school for Charles in their neighborhood, but they were unable to find one that they could afford. Consequently, Charles remains inside the apartment during the day with TV and toys to occupy his time. His grandfather is concerned about his safety and does not allow him to play outside very often. Occasionally, his grandfather will take Charles to a neighborhood playground where he can interact with other children his age.

Valerie has worked sporadically for the last two years, mostly as a cashier for a local grocery store. She comes home feeling tired and likes to have some time to go out or to talk with her friends on the telephone after work. At 5 years old, Charles is now a very active child who is often hard to handle. Most of the time Valerie ignores his misbehavior because she is preoccupied with getting herself ready for work or is engaged in other activities. When she does ask Charles to do something and he refuses, she gets irritated and screams at him. Charles's grandparents are more patient with him, but they, too, are frustrated by his noncompliance. They worry that he will be a problem when he goes to school next year, because he does not seem to be able to sit still and listen for any length of time.

Charles's grandfather is a deacon in their church, and religion figures very prominently in the life of the family. They all attend church services regularly, and Valerie sings in the choir. She enjoys this opportunity to express her musical talents in the company of people her own age. Although Valerie has dated occasionally since Charles's birth, she has had no serious relationships. Primarily because of her parents' encouragement, she is contemplating enrolling in a local night school program to complete her high school education.

Discussion Questions

1. Consider Charles's development with regard to the following issues or concepts: contributions of nature; contributions of nurture; proximal processes; distal processes.
2. Can you predict outcomes? Consider issues of continuity and change.
3. What are the strengths and weaknesses of each of the family members?
4. What environmental modifications would be helpful to promote healthy developmental outcomes? Be specific about each family member.

 Journal Questions

1. The long-standing debate on the value of empirically based knowledge versus applied knowledge can be applied to a course such as this. Empirically based knowledge is often explanatory, providing explanations that answer the question "Why does this happen?" Applied knowledge provides solutions and answers the question "What should I do about this?" As a professional counselor, and as an educated person, what are your views on this debate?
2. What do you hope to gain from this course? What are your specific learning goals?

Key Terms

life span development
reflective practice
stage
id
ego
superego
pleasure principle
reality principle
Freud's psychosexual
    stages
oral stage
oral fixation
anal stage
anal personality
anal fixation
phallic stage
latency stage
genital stage
Erikson's psychosocial
    stages
trust versus mistrust

autonomy versus shame
    and doubt
Piaget's cognitive
    development
sensorimotor stage
preoperational stage
concrete operational stage
formal operational stage
incremental models
behaviorist tradition
classical conditioning
operant conditioning
conditioned stimulus
operant
reinforcement
social learning theories
modeling
generalization
information processing
    theories
multidimensional models

transactional models
relational models
systems models
Bronfenbrenner's
    bioecological model
proximal processes
distal processes
demand characteristics
microsystem
mesosystem
exosystem
macrosystem
behavior genetics
description
explanation
verification
causal variable
outcome variable
experiments
correlational studies

control group
positive correlation
negative correlation
cross-sectional studies
cohort
longitudinal
sequential
critical period
mechanistic view
organismic theories
self-organizing
constructivism
social constructivism
applied developmental
    science
developmental
    psychopathology
clinical-developmental
    psychology
qualitative research

Heredity, Environment, and the Beginnings of Human Life

THE NATURE/NURTURE ILLUSION

Look at the image in Figure 2.1. Do you see a haggard old woman or a pretty young girl? If the figure that you focus on is the old woman, the other parts of the image fade into the background or become the "ground." If you change your focus, the young girl will become the "figure" and the rest background. It is virtually impossible to maintain both perspectives simultaneously. This image has been used by Gestalt psychologists to illustrate a perceptual phenomenon known as figure-ground, but we introduce it here because it provides a useful model for understanding the nature-nurture debate. No one would dispute that both heredity and environment influence human development, but when we focus on information about one of these contributors, the other seems to fade into the background. Evidence from both sides is compelling, and the clinician may be persuaded to attend to one side of the argument to the exclusion of the other. The challenge is to guard against taking such a one-sided perspective, which allows for consideration of only half of the story. In this chapter, we will review the major contemporary approaches to the nature-nurture debate. We begin with an overview of genetic mechanisms, then we examine the role of genetics in behavior and the nature of gene-environment interactions. Finally, we consider clinical applications.

MECHANISMS OF GENETIC INFLUENCE: HOW DO GENES WORK?

Is television watching inherited? Do genes cause young teens to take up smoking or to abuse other drugs or to shoplift? If you follow science reporting in the popular press, or even dip into a scientific journal on human development, you are likely to find articles that seem to link heredity to human behaviors of every description. The genetics of behavior is a "hot" issue in science today. But to understand the real implications of research reports on heredity for science or practice, it is important to have basic knowledge of hereditary mechanisms and what they can and cannot do. In this section, we will provide an overview of the biological structures and processes that contribute to intergenerational inheritance. Then we will examine the most current approaches to investigating the relationship between genes and behavior.

FIGURE 2.1
Gestalt Illusion

Source: Boring, E. G. (1930). A new ambiguous figure. *American Journal of Psychology 42*, 444. From *American Journal of Psychology.* Copyright 1930 by the Board of Trustees of the University of Illinois. Used with permission of the University of Illinois.

Biological Inheritance

Chromosomes and DNA

Whether it comes from the inside of your mouth or from the cartilage in your thumb bone, each cell in your body has a nucleus, and inside that nucleus are 46 tiny structures called **chromosomes.** Chromosomes are the source of biological inheritance. They come in pairs—23 of them. Twenty-two of these pairs are matched and are called **autosomes.** In autosome pairs, the two chromosomes look and function alike. In the 23rd pair, the chromosomes are alike in females but not in males and are called the **sex chromosomes.**

During certain stages in the life cycle of a cell, the chromosomes are easily visible under a microscope. Figure 2.2 is an example of a **karyotype,** a display of the actual chromosomes from human body cells, photographed under a microscope and laid out in matching pairs. Notice the 23rd pair is matched in the female example but not in the male example.

Chromosomes are strands of a complex organic substance called **deoxyribonucleic acid** or **DNA,** which is constructed from 4 simple molecules or bases, adenine, thymine, guanine, and cytosine. Genes make up only about 3% of chromosomal DNA. The function of the remaining 97%, called **intergenic DNA** is not well understood. DNA has the

FIGURE 2.2

Human Karyotypes

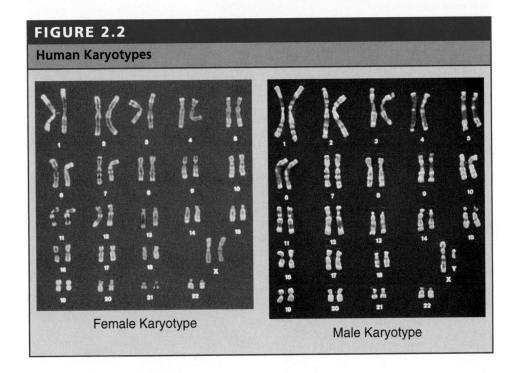

Female Karyotype   Male Karyotype

remarkable property of self-replication, which means that chromosomes can reproduce themselves. In this complex chemical process, the helical strands of DNA separate, and each becomes a template for a new DNA molecule. At first, the duplicate chromosomes remain joined at one location, called the **centromere.** In the karyotypes shown in Figure 2.2, the chromosomes were photographed after they had duplicated, but they remained joined at the centromere. When a cell begins to divide, the chromosomes line up in the middle of the nucleus, as if there were an invisible axis running through the center of the cell. (See Figure 2.3.) The duplicates then pull apart along that axis and migrate to opposite ends of the original cell. Two new cells now form, each of which contains one full set of 46 chromosomes. This kind of cell division, called **mitosis,** produces two new cells identical to the original cell. Nearly all body cells undergo mitosis, making growth possible.

Intergenerational Transmission of Chromosomes

Where do the chromosomes in a human body come from in the first place? They are passed on at conception. One member of each chromosome pair comes from the mother and one member comes from the father. This intergenerational transport begins in special cells, called **germ cells,** located only in the ovaries of females and in the testes of males. Germ cells undergo a special kind of cell division, called **meiosis.** Meiosis begins like mitosis, with the duplication of chromosomes. When germ cells prepare to divide, each duplicated chromosome matches up with the other chromosome in its pair. (See Figure 2.4.) So, for example, the chromosomes in pair number 12 line up together. When the cell begins to divide, the duplicate chromosomes do *not* pull apart at the centromere—they remain attached. One chromosome in each pair migrates to one side of the cell; the other member of the pair migrates to the other side. When two new cells are formed, each one contains only 23 chromosomes, one member of each pair. Each of the 23 is duplicated, but the duplicates remain attached, until each of these new cells begins to divide *again*. Now the

FIGURE 2.3

Cell Dividing by Mitosis (Only two of the 23 pairs of chromosomes—pairs #3 and #20—are depicted for illustration.)

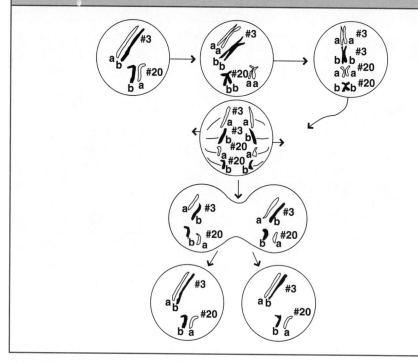

FIGURE 2.4

Cell Dividing by Meiosis (Only two of the 23 pairs of chromosomes—pairs #3 and #20—are depicted for illustration.)

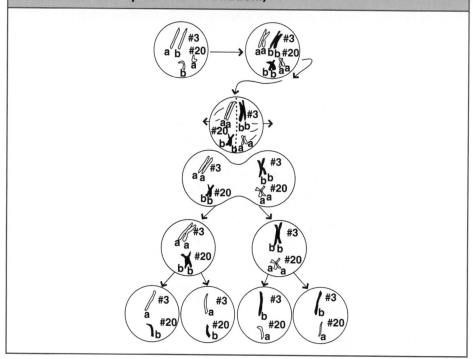

duplicated chromosomes line up, single file, in the middle of the cell, just as they would for mitosis, and as the cell divides, the duplicates pull apart. The important outcome of this multistage process is that the four new cells that are formed each will contain only 23 chromosomes, one member of each pair.

What happens to these four new cells now depends on whether they were produced in an ovary or a testis. In an ovary, three of the new cells disintegrate, and the fourth becomes an **ovum** or egg. In males, all four new cells form tails and become **sperm.** Thus, all ova and sperm contain only 23 chromosomes each. When an ovum is released into a woman's fallopian tube, if a sperm fertilizes the ovum, the two cells merge to form one cell with one nucleus. This fertilized ovum is called a **zygote,** and its nucleus contains 46 chromosomes, 23 pairs. The mother and the father of this newly conceived human each contributed one member of each of the chromosome pairs.

Once formed, the zygote immediately begins to divide by mitosis. Soon there are two cells, which quickly divide to produce four new cells, and so on. The cell divisions continue in quick succession, and before long there is a cluster of cells, each one containing a duplicate set of the original 46 chromosomes, half inherited from the mother and half from the father. As the cluster forms, the growing organism migrates down the mother's fallopian tube, into the uterus, and may succeed in **implanting** itself, that is, becoming attached to the uterine lining. The progress of intrauterine growth and development is summarized in Figure 2.5: *Fetal Development.*

How Genes Influence Traits

Genes and Their Functions

Now that you know how chromosomes are passed on from generation to generation, let's consider how they function. Chromosomes, as we have said, are strands of DNA. **Genes** are functional units or sections of DNA. Altogether, in one individual's 46 chromosomes, there are approximately 30,000 genes (International Human Genome Sequencing Consortium, 2001). For each member of a pair of chromosomes, the number and location of genes are the same. Thus, genes come in matched pairs also.

Genes provide a blueprint or code to the cell for how to produce **proteins** and **enzymes.** Proteins are the building blocks of the body; for example, melanin, the pigment that affects the color of your eyes, is a protein. Enzymes are protein-like substances that facilitate chemical reactions, such as those involved in metabolizing food; for example, **lactase** is an enzyme necessary for digesting milk. The body is built from proteins, and the proteins are built following the code provided by genes. However, most genes do not

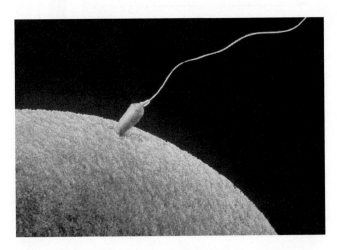

The moment of conception: sperm and ovum unite to create a new organism.

FIGURE 2.5

Fetal Development

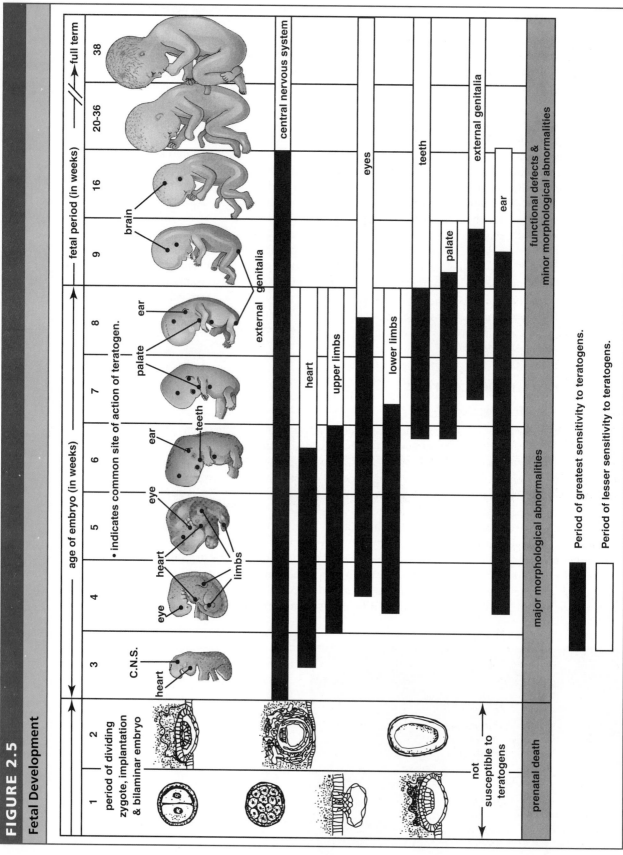

Period of greatest sensitivity to teratogens.

Period of lesser sensitivity to teratogens.

Source: Moore, K. L., & Persaud, T. V. N. (1984). Before we are born: Basic embryology and birth defects 3rd ed. (p. 118). Philadelphia: Saunders. Reprinted by permission.

function full time. When a gene is "on," its code is transcribed by other substances that provide the cell with the code, and the cell manufactures the coded product. How and when a gene's code will be transcribed and used by the cell is determined by **regulator** genes, possibly located on the long stretches of intergenic DNA, and by the cellular environment.

Gene Alleles and Their Relationships

What significance is there to having matched pairs of genes, one from each parent? One important effect is that it increases hereditary diversity. The genes at matching locations on a pair of chromosomes often are identical, coding for exactly the same protein, but they can also be slightly different forms of the same gene, providing somewhat different messages to the cell. These slightly different varieties of genes at the same location or locus on the chromosome are called **alleles.** For eye color, for example, an individual (call him Tom) might inherit from one parent an allele that would usually produce brown eyes but inherit an allele for blue eyes from the other parent. (Both alleles provide the cell with a blueprint for melanin production, but the brown eye allele dictates that it be produced in larger quantities.) These two alleles represent Tom's **genotype** for eye color. But his actual, expressed eye color, or **phenotype**, is brown.

This example illustrates two characteristics of our genetic endowment. First, two alleles of the same gene can have a **dominant-recessive** relationship, with the first being expressed and the second being suppressed. Second, as a result, not all of a person's genes actually influence the body or behavior. Tom, for example, is a **carrier** of the unexpressed trait, because recessive genes can "surface" in the phenotype of an individual's offspring. If a child receives two recessive alleles, one from each parent, the child will have the recessive trait. For instance, in Table 2.1, a mother and a father both have curly hair. Each of the parents has one dominant gene allele for curly hair and one recessive allele for straight hair. On the average, three out of four children born to these parents will inherit at least one curly hair allele. Even if they also inherit a straight hair allele, they will have curly hair. But one child out of four, on average, will inherit two straight hair alleles, one from each parent. Without a curly hair allele to suppress the effects of the straight hair allele, such a child will have straight hair, probably much to the surprise of the parents, who were unaware that they were carriers of the straight-hair trait! Table 2.2 lists several traits that seem to be heavily influenced by a single gene location where alleles of the gene usually

TABLE 2.1

Intergenerational Transmission of Recessive Traits (by parents who are carriers)

		Mother	Father	
Genotype:		Cc	Cc	
Phenotype:		Curly Hair	Curly Hair	

	Child$_1$	Child$_2$	Child$_3$	Child$_4$
Genotype:	CC	Cc	Cc	cc
Phenotype:	Curly Hair	Curly Hair	Curly Hair	Straight Hair*

*On average, one child in four will have the recessive trait if both parents are carriers.
Note: C stands for the dominant curly hair allele; c stands for the recessive straight hair allele.

TABLE 2.2

Dominant and Recessive Traits Linked to Single Pairs of Genes

Dominant Trait	Recessive Trait
Curly hair	Straight hair
Dark hair	Blonde or red hair
Dimpled cheeks	No dimples
Immunity to poison ivy	Susceptibility to poison ivy
Thick lips	Thin lips
Roman nose	Straight nose
Farsightedness	Normal vision
Type A blood	Type O blood
Type B blood	Type O blood

have a dominant-recessive relationship, so that to get the recessive trait, a person must inherit two recessive alleles.

Two different alleles will not necessarily have a dominant-recessive relationship. Sometimes, alleles exhibit **codominance,** producing a blended outcome. For example, Type A blood is the result of one gene allele; Type B blood is the result of a different allele. If a child inherits a Type A allele from one parent and a Type B allele from the other parent, the outcome will be a blend—Type AB blood.

Some traits, such as eye color, the curliness of hair, and blood type are heavily influenced by gene alleles at a single gene location. But most traits are affected by the products of many different gene pairs. Often these pairs are located on different chromosomes. Such **polygenic** trait determination makes the prediction of traits from one generation to another very difficult and suggests that any one pair of gene alleles has only a modest influence on phenotypic outcomes. Height, skin color, and a host of other physical traits are polygenic, and most genetic influences on intelligence, personality, psychopathology, and behavior appear to be of this kind as well.

The Inheritance of Sex

So far, we have seen that pairs of genes, single pairs or multiple pairs, located on chromosomes, are the source of hereditary influences for most traits. But the hereditary explanation for an individual's sex, whether male or female, is linked to the entire 23rd pair of chromosomes: the *sex chromosomes*. In females, this is a matched pair of elongated chromosomes called **X chromosomes**. But in males, this pair is mismatched; one is an X chromosome, and the other is a shorter **Y chromosome**. Because females have only X chromosomes, when they produce eggs each ovum contains an X chromosome as its representative of the 23rd pair. But because males have an X and a Y chromosome, half of the sperm they produce contain an X chromosome, and the other half contain a Y chromosome. At the time of conception, if a sperm containing an X chromosome fertilizes the ovum, the resulting child will be female: she will have an X chromosome from each parent. However, if a sperm containing a Y chromosome fertilizes the ovum, the child will be male, with an X chromosome from his mother and a Y chromosome from his father. (See

FIGURE 2.6

Sex Chromosome Transmission

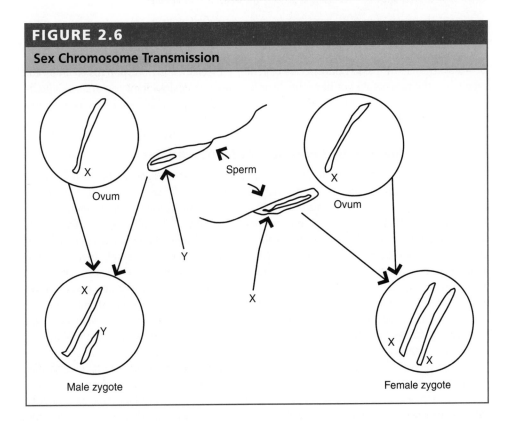

Figure 2.6.) Given that the biological determiner of a child's sex is the sperm that wins the race to the egg, it is ironic that in many cultures of the world, women are held responsible for the sex of their offspring. In some patriarchal societies where sons are more highly valued than daughters, women have in the past been punished, divorced, or even put to death for failing to produce a son.

The development of female characteristics is the natural or default process in human fetal development. Development of male characteristics typically depends on the presence of a gene located on the Y chromosome. This gene leads to the development of testes, which produce male hormones called **androgens,** primarily **testosterone.** When androgens are released in adequate quantities and at appropriate time intervals, other male reproductive organs develop and some aspects of brain development appear to be affected. As Ward (1992) described the process, "if these hormones are not present in adequate amounts or over the correct temporal intervals, the natural tendency to retain female characteristics prevails" (p. 158), which is what happens in individuals with two X chromosomes.

Given that sperm containing X chromosomes and sperm containing Y chromosomes are produced in equal numbers, it seems reasonable to expect that male and female zygotes would be conceived with equal frequency. However, male conceptions far outnumber female conceptions, with some estimates of the ratio (e.g., Shettles, 1961; Zaslow & Hayes, 1986) being as high as 140 to 100! Yet, male *births* only slightly outnumber female births, because males are less likely to survive the prenatal period than females. More males than females are spontaneously aborted early in pregnancy, often before a woman knows that she is pregnant, and more are miscarried later in pregnancy. As you will see in the next section, the vulnerability of males is at least partly a function of their susceptibility to hereditary diseases, and that vulnerability continues into childhood.

Hereditary Diseases

Some disorders, such as sickle-cell anemia, Huntington's chorea, muscular dystrophy, and Down syndrome are passed on through hereditary mechanisms from parents to children, even when the parents do not have the disorders themselves. Problems can arise as a function of normal hereditary processes or because something goes haywire in the production of ova or sperm. Here are some examples.

Disorders Influenced by Recessive, Defective Alleles

In sickle-cell anemia, the red blood cells are abnormally shaped, more like a half moon than the usual, round shape. The abnormal cells are not as efficient as normal cells in carrying oxygen to the tissues; victims of this disorder have breathing problems and a host of other difficulties that typically lead to organ malfunctions and, usually, to death by adolescence. A recessive gene allele causes the malformed blood cells. If one normal gene allele is present, it will be dominant, and the individual will not have sickle-cell anemia. Many hereditary disorders are caused by such recessive, defective alleles, and it is estimated that most people are carriers of three to five such alleles. Yet, most of these illnesses are rare, because to get them an individual has to be unlucky enough to have both parents be carriers of the same defective allele and then to be the one in four (on average) offspring to get the recessive alleles from both parents (refer again to Figure 2.5, explaining the inheritance of recessive traits). Table 2.3 lists some examples of these illnesses.

Some recessive, defective genes are more common in some ethnic or geographic groups than in others. The sickle-cell anemia gene, for example, is more common among people of African descent. For some of these disorders, tests are available that can identify carriers. Prospective parents who have family members with the disorder or who come

TABLE 2.3	
Some Disorders Caused by Recessive Gene Alleles	
Disorder	**Description**
Cystic fibrosis	Inadequate mucus production; breathing & digestive problems; early death.
Phenylketonuria (PKU)	Metabolism of phenylalanines in food is insufficient; gradually compromises the nervous system, causing mental retardation.
Sickle-cell anemia	Blood cells have an unusual "sickle" shape; causes heart and kidney problems.
Tay-Sachs disease	Enzyme disease; causes degeneration of the nervous system and death in the first few years of life.
Thalassemia	Blood cells abnormal; low energy, paleness, poor resistance to infection.
Hemophilia*	Blood-clotting factor not produced; vulnerable to death by bleeding.
Duchenne's muscular dystrophy*	Wasting of muscles produces gradual weakness, eventual death.

*Disorders that are X-linked and are therefore expressed primarily or exclusively in males.

from groups with a higher than average incidence of the disorder may choose to be tested to help them determine the probable risk for their own offspring. **Genetic counselors** help screen candidates for such testing, as well as provide information and support to prospective parents, helping them to understand and cope with the choices that confront them—choices about testing, childbearing, and parenting (Shiloh, 1996).

Disorders Influenced by Dominant, Defective Alleles

Some genetic disorders are caused by dominant gene alleles, so that only one defective gene need be present. There are no carriers of such disorders—anyone who has the defective gene will have the problem it causes, because a dominant gene allele is always expressed in the phenotype. Suppose that such an illness causes an early death, before puberty. Then, the defective, dominant gene that causes the illness will die with the victim, because no offspring are produced. When these alleles occur in some future generation, it must be through **mutation,** a change in the chemical structure of an existing gene. Sometimes mutations occur spontaneously, and sometimes they are due to environmental influences, like exposure to radiation or toxic chemicals (Strachan & Read, 2000). For example, **progeria** is a fatal disorder that causes rapid aging, so that by late childhood its victims are dying of "old age." Progeria sufferers do not survive long enough to reproduce. When the disease occurs, it is caused by a genetic mutation, so that while it is precipitated by a genetic defect, it does not run in families.

Some disorders caused by dominant, defective alleles do not kill their victims in childhood, and thus can be passed on from one generation to another. When one parent has the disease, each child has a 50% chance of inheriting the dominant, defective gene from that parent. Some of these disorders are quite mild in their effects, such as farsightedness. Others unleash lethal effects late in life. Among the most famous is **Huntington's chorea,** which causes the nervous system to deteriorate, usually beginning between 30 and 40 years of age. Symptoms include uncontrolled movements and increasingly disordered psychological functioning, eventually ending in death. In recent years, the gene responsible for Huntington's chorea has been identified, and a test is now available that will allow early detection, before symptoms appear. Unfortunately, there is no cure, and the offspring of victims face a difficult set of dilemmas, including whether or not to have the test and, if they choose to do so and find they have the gene, how to plan for the future. Again, genetic counselors may play a critical role in this process (Morell, 1993; Shiloh, 1996).

Disorders of Polygenic Origin

As with most normal characteristics, many inherited disorders seem to be related to multiple pairs of genes, such that some combination of defective alleles at several chromosomal sites predispose the victim to the illness. Like all polygenic traits, these disorders run in families, but they cannot be predicted with the precision of disorders caused by genes at a single chromosomal location. Most forms of muscular dystrophy are polygenically determined. Polygenic influences have also been implicated in diabetes, clubfoot, some forms of Alzheimer's disease, and multiple sclerosis, to name just a few. As we noted earlier, genetic effects on behavioral traits are usually polygenic. This appears to be true for many mental illnesses and behavioral disorders as well, such as alcoholism, criminality, schizophrenia, and clinical depression (e.g., Charney, Nestler, & Bunney, 1999; DeAngelis, 1997; Heath et al., 1997; Plomin, Owen, & McGuffin, 1994).

Disorders Caused by Chromosomal Abnormalities

Occasionally, a zygote will form containing too many chromosomes, or too few. Such zygotes often do not survive. When they do, the individuals usually have multiple physical or mental problems. Among the most well known of these disorders is **Down syndrome** (also called **Trisomy 21**), caused by an extra copy of chromosome number 21. Children with Down syndrome experience some degree of mental retardation, although educational interventions can have a big impact on the severity of intellectual impairment. In addition, they are likely to have several distinctive characteristics, such as a flattening of facial features, poor muscle tone, and heart problems.

The causes of chromosomal abnormalities are not well understood. Either the mother or the father could be the source, and ordinarily, the older the parent, the more likely that an ovum or sperm will contain a chromosomal abnormality. Oddly enough, however, with Down syndrome, the increased risk with parental age only holds for mothers. Older fathers are at less risk than younger fathers to produce sperm carrying an extra chromosome number 21 (Merewood, 1991)!

Sex-Linked Disorders

Males are more susceptible to some genetic disorders than females, which helps account for males being less viable both before and after birth. The problem for males is the mismatched sex chromosomes. The smaller Y chromosome does not carry all of the genes that the longer X chromosome does. There are a slew of **X-linked, recessive disorders,** such as hemophilia, baldness, color blindness, night blindness, Duchenne's muscular dystrophy, and so on, and males are much more likely to suffer from these disorders than are females. To understand why, consider color blindness. Normal color vision is influenced by a gene on the X chromosome that is ordinarily dominant over any defective allele. Thus, even if a girl (who has two X chromosomes) has on one X chromosome a defective allele that could cause color blindness, she will not be color-blind as long as she has a normal color-vision allele on her other X chromosome. If she happens to inherit defective alleles from both parents, then she will be color-blind. In other words, *for females only*, color blindness, and all of the other X-linked recessive disorders, function like all inherited diseases caused by recessive, defective gene alleles. *For males*, the process is different. If a boy inherits a defective gene allele for color vision on the X chromosome, which comes from his mother, he will be color-blind, because his Y chromosome, inherited from his father, bears no matching gene. This is true for all the X-linked recessive diseases. The result is that females tend to be carriers, and males are more likely to be victims.

Males are also more vulnerable to any breakage or dysfunction of the X chromosome. For example, *fragile X syndrome* is more problematic in males than females. In this condition, an X chromosome is constricted at one end and may break. Boys with one fragile X chromosome are usually mentally retarded and have a variety of behavioral problems. Girls with one fragile X chromosome are much less likely to have such difficulties, apparently because having another, normal X chromosome provides protection, although about a third of girls with one fragile X do have some symptoms.

FOCUS ON GENETICS: ITS INFLUENCE ON BEHAVIOR

Having examined some of the mechanisms of genetic influence on physical traits, we are ready to tackle the questions of whether and how genetics can influence behavior and its development. Could it really be true that complex, culturally dependent activities, such as television watching, are hereditary, as one recent scientific article implied (Plomin, Corley, DeFries, & Fulker, 1990)? If genes code for protein and enzyme production, how can they be responsible for behavior?

The influence of genetics on behavior is indirect. Genes impact the development and functioning of the nervous system, its structures and its chemical processes. The nervous system, interacting with other body systems *and* with the environment, generates behavior.

Like most physical traits, however, it is rare that behavior or behavioral effects can be traced to the impact of a single gene or pair of gene alleles. As we have already noted, most influences on behavior appear to be polygenic. Take intellectual functioning, for example. A number of genes, if they are defective, can influence the development of mental retardation. In many cases, the defective genes seem to result in an important cell product being missing. For example, in the disorder called *phenylketonuria (PKU),* children are missing an important enzyme. Without the enzyme, an amino acid in food, called phenylalanine, cannot be metabolized. Unless the victim's diet is severely restricted, phenylalanine soon accumulates in the body and causes mental retardation (Strickberger, 1985). Thus, a single missing cell product disrupts intellectual functioning. But no single cell product is responsible for intelligence; rather, normal functioning is the result of the combined impact of a large number of genes and their products (e.g., Helmuth, 2001).

It's easy to be confused by popular-press reports of genetic advances. Newspaper headlines routinely broadcast "discoveries" of new links between genes and behavior. But what do we really know? To figure this out, it helps to understand that there are two main scientific approaches to this question: molecular genetics and behavior genetics.

Molecular Genetics and Behavior

The study of what genes do and how their products influence the body and behavior is called *molecular genetics.* Molecular geneticists study the cascade of biochemical changes that occur in the transmission and translation of DNA information to cells, a process called *gene expression.* This science is rapidly progressing, but in reality, little is yet known about the impact of specific genes on complex behavior such as social inhibition, to ordinary variations in motor coordination, or to extraordinary needs for sensory stimulation. There is great hope that the *Human Genome Project* will begin to unravel such mysteries. This project is a massive effort in molecular genetics that has involved thousands of scientists around the world for over 15 years. They have successfully mapped the locations of genes on human chromosomes, and they hope to discover each gene's functions over the next decade or so, which will help induce greater progress in the study of genetic influences on behavior and development (Grodin & Laurie, 2000; International Human Genome Sequencing Consortium, 2001; McGuffin, Riley, & Plomin, 2001; Peltonen & McKusick, 2001).

Behavior Genetics

Molecular genetics addresses questions such as where are genes located, how do they turn on and off, what is their structure, how do they function, what are their products, and what do those products do to influence physical and behavioral traits. But we can ask a different question about heredity: *what proportion of any behavior is due to genetics?* This question is the domain of *quantitative genetics*, which when applied to behavior is called *behavior genetics* (Plomin et al., 1994; Plomin & Rutter, 1998) or *quantitative developmental behavioral genetics* (Plomin, 1986).

Most of the available research on genetics and behavior comes from the behavior genetics tradition. Behavior geneticists are the scientists who have implicated heredity in such complex activities as television watching, work attitudes, cigarette smoking, and criminality. Their research tools are not microscopes and petri dishes, but the tools that all behavioral scientists use to measure individual differences in behavior: interviews, questionnaires, standardized tests, and observational techniques. They apply these measures to special populations of people, such as twins and adoptees. Their goal is to identify behavioral variations that run in families and to figure out how much of the similarity among family members is due to shared nature (genes) as opposed to shared nurture (environment).

Behavior genetics relies on the assumption that with the right methods, the influence of genes can be separated from the influence of environment and that the contribution of each can be measured. In a twin study, for example, scores on a behavioral trait are obtained both for **identical twins (monozygotic)** and for **fraternal twins (dizygotic)**. Identical twins come from a single zygote and have exactly the same genes. Fraternal twins develop from two separate zygotes, and, like any two siblings, on the average they share about 50% of their genes. The underlying assumption in a twin study is that the environment is as similar for fraternal twins as it is for identical twins. Thus, if identical twins are more alike on a trait than fraternal twins, the greater similarity must be due to their shared genes—that is, to **heritability.** Some twin studies have been done with twins who have been raised apart, in many cases separated in infancy and raised by different families. In these special circumstances, the environments of twins may be quite different, but again the assumption is that the similarities or differences in environments will be about the same, on average, both for identical and for fraternal twins. Therefore, if identical twins are more alike than fraternal twins on some trait, heritability of the trait is responsible.

Adoption studies capitalize on the fact that adoptees share genes (50%), but not environments, with a biological parent and that they share environments, but not genes, with adoptive parents or siblings. If adoptees are more like their biological parents than their adoptive parents or siblings on some trait, it is assumed that heritability of the trait is the only explanation.

Twin and adoption studies have produced evidence of heritability for behavioral traits from intelligence to personality characteristics to, yes, television viewing (e.g., Plomin et al., 1990). Such studies have also provided evidence for differences in the heritability of behavioral characteristics that, on the surface, seem quite similar. For example, some antisocial behaviors appear to be more heritable than others. When antisocial behavior is accompanied by other problems, including early-onset hyperactivity and poor peer relationships, heredity seems to play a larger role than it does for other antisocial behavior that does not include these additional factors. Also, some kinds of crime, such as petty theft, appear to be more heritable than others, such as violent crime (Rutter, 1997; Silberg, Meyer, Pickles, Simonoff, Eaves, Hewitt, Maes, & Rutter, 1996).

When behavior geneticists estimate the proportion of a trait that is affected by genes, they also produce estimates of the influence of the environment, both **nonshared** and **shared environment** (e.g., Hetherington, Reiss, & Plomin, 1994; Rutter, 1997). The degree to which identical twins tend to differ on some trait is considered a measure of the role of *nonshared environment,* that is, different environmental input. Because identical twins have exactly the same genes, when they differ on a characteristic, such as propensity for violent behavior, then their differences must be due to experiences that were not the same for both. Perhaps their parents treated them differently, or they became members of different crowds in high school. Alternatively, similarities between twins that go beyond estimates of genetic influence can be attributed to *shared environment,* that is, to having similar experiences. For example, behavior geneticists estimate a moderate effect of shared environment, like growing up in the same household, on children's intelligence.

Genetic Influences on Environments

Behavior geneticists have proposed that some environmental influences on behavior are themselves affected by a person's genes. There are three kinds of effects that genes can have on the environments that a developing individual experiences: **passive, evocative,** and *active* (Scarr & McCartney, 1983). First, *passive* effects are due to children and their parents sharing genes. Parents' genes affect the kind of environment that they create for their children. For example, suppose that parents have genes that contribute to musical talent. Because of their own musical interest and skill, such parents are likely to provide their children with exposure to music, opportunities for music education, and experiences with music that help to cultivate their children's own musical proclivities. When the genes of a parent lead to environmental experiences that are compatible with a child's own hereditary tendencies, the child's genes are a passive source of environmental influence.

Evocative gene influences on environment are important when an individual's genes affect his behavior, which in turn affects the reactions of others. Recently, for example, researchers have reported that adoptive children whose *biological parents* have a history of antisocial behavior frequently have *adoptive parents* who use negative, hostile forms of control with their adopted child. Apparently, children who are at genetic risk for the development of antisocial behavior may act in ways that tend to evoke negative parental behaviors, which in turn, researchers have found, tend to increase the antisocial behavior of the children (O'Connor, Deater-Deckard, Fulker, Rutter, & Plomin (1998).

Active gene influences could be in play when people choose their own environments, companions, and activities. As children get older and are less constrained by their parents' choices, behavior geneticists argue that **niche picking** increases: people choose environments that are compatible with their interests (Scarr, 1992; Scarr & McCartney, 1983). These environments then provide support for and probably strengthen those interests. For example, a musically talented adolescent may choose friends with the same interests, and the social environment they create together encourages each member's continuing pursuit of music. Another example is provided by long-term studies of antisocial children. As adults they tend to put themselves into high-risk environments, often by partnering with or marrying individuals who engage in criminal and addictive behavior. These companions and the environments they create then support the likelihood of continuing antisocial behavior (Champion, Goodall, & Rutter, 1995; Plomin, DeFries, Craig, & McGuffin, 2003; Quinton, Pickles, Maughan, & Rutter, 1993).

Niche picking:
As children get older, they choose environments and companions that are compatible with their interests.

The description of passive, evocative, and active genetic effects on environments is consistent with the notion that children and adults play a role in shaping their own experiences. Recall from Chapter 1 that modern developmental theories, especially multidimensional models of development, posit that there are layers, or levels, of interacting causes of behavior. What happens at one level both causes and is caused by what happens at other levels. There is little disagreement among modern developmental scientists about the bidirectional character of effects. What is often disputed, however, is the degree to which the individual's influence on his or her own environment can be traced specifically to the mediating effects of genes. Behavior geneticists have sometimes described the role of genes as if they had a direct line to behavior and, through behavior, to the environment. But many interacting causal layers of functioning exist between the physical/molecular level at which genes operate and the level of the social environment. Can behavior geneticists actually specify the impact of genes, per se, on behavior and the environment? At the present, we have clear evidence that genes are important, and we even have some information about which ones are important. What has yet to be deciphered is how specific genes express themselves behaviorally. In the next section, we will examine the relationships between genes and environment, with a critical eye to the contribution of the behavior genetics approach.

SHIFTING FOCUS TO THE INTERACTION OF GENETICS AND ENVIRONMENT

Behavior geneticists have made us aware that genes really do matter for the expression of behavior, but critics have argued that the approaches employed by behavioral genetics researchers can be misleading. Sometimes the tendency to emphasize the importance of genes can lead to an oversimplified understanding of their effects. Is nature really the prime mover in a person's development? Or is there a contemporary counterpoint to the behavior genetics position?

Criticisms of Behavior Genetics

Outmoded Model

Many scientists have rebutted behavior genetics arguments, claiming that they represent an outmoded view of gene action. In the early 1970s, researchers who studied prenatal development (Gottlieb, 1970) began investigating the importance of environmental or exogenous experience in initiating and channeling development. Their approach reflected a significant shift from a unidirectional model (genes directing development) to a reciprocal view (gene activity affects and is affected by other levels of the system). It is now generally accepted among molecular biologists that genes do not by themselves produce finished products such as nerve cells, blue eyes, or behavioral patterns such as obsessive-compulsive disorder. In fact, Johnson (1998) reported that the use of the term "innate" has been dropped from use or even banned in some scientific writings of geneticists and ethologists. This is so because of the widespread recognition that the term is inaccurate. Nothing exists in the natural world that is purely genetic, with the exception of the genes themselves. Development always occurs within an environmental milieu.

So what do we know about how genes operate? In an earlier section we discussed how DNA reproduces itself through the basic processes of replication during cell division. But how does the DNA inside each cell's nucleus actually influence the organism's growth and functioning? The process that starts a complex chain of biochemical events that ultimately account for genetic expression or influence is called *transcription.* When DNA strands separate, one of the strands acts like a template for the synthesis of a new, single strand of *ribonucleic acid,* or **RNA.** Although there are several types of RNA, messenger RNA (mRNA) is the type that reads out the coded information from a gene to specify how particular proteins will be synthesized. Transcription can be activated by processes both within the cell itself as well as outside it. For example, hormones in the blood are absorbed into the cell nucleus, activating its DNA and influencing protein production (Gorbman, Dickoff, Vigna, Clark, & Ralph, 1983). Proteins, as we have noted, are the body's building blocks. They make up a variety of substances that affect the functioning of the brain, including some hormones that influence both the brain and other internal organs, neurotransmitters that relay messages between neurons, and enzymes that synthesize or erase neurotransmitters (see Chapter 3). These substances are extremely important for the brain's efficient functioning. However, they do not, in and of themselves, directly cause particular behavioral manifestations. Rather, they produce tendencies or predispositions to react in certain ways.

For example, someone with a genetic predisposition to depression may be more sensitive to environmental stressors than someone without this predisposition. However, even this predisposition does not determine a person's destiny. Many people with this specific genetic makeup do not get depressed, while many without this genetic legacy do suffer from the disease.

What could be the genetic contribution, if any exists, to a complex, culturally dependent behavior such as television viewing? First, it is clear that no gene or set of genes causes television viewing directly. At most, what may be genetically influenced in television viewing are behavioral dispositions that make a passive, solitary, rapidly visual activity particularly appealing. We can all speculate about what such dispositions could be. Perhaps, for example, being exceedingly inhibited makes the solitary nature of television viewing especially attractive. Perhaps poor muscle coordination makes more active forms of personal amusement *less* attractive to some individuals. Perhaps there are people whose brains ordinarily are understimulated because they screen out too much stimulation; for such individuals, the rapid visual changes characteristic of much TV programming could be attractive if they help maintain a normal level of brain stimulation. Obviously, TV viewing can be appealing for many reasons, and behavioral dispositions that might run in families could influence just how appealing. As we have seen, if these behavioral dispositions are genetically affected, they are probably polygenic.

The environment also affects long stretches of DNA (over 97%) that have been described as noncoded genes. Many of these genes serve to regulate the action of other genes situated close to them on the DNA strand. These regulator genes give instructions about how and when the coded genes are to function. But how do they know when to operate? Who regulates the regulators? The action of the regulator genes may be responsive to the hormones we previously mentioned, *which are themselves* influenced by environmental conditions such as nutrition, stress, light, and so forth. Thus, genes and environment operate from the very beginning in an intricate pattern of **coaction.**

Several examples serve to illustrate this point. At the cellular level, it is important to note that each cell has the potential to develop into any part of the body. Despite this fact, cells do not develop randomly but rather in coaction with their surrounding environments. For example, cells located in the anterior portion of an embryo develop into parts of the head, whereas cells located in the embryo's lateral portion develop into parts of the back, and so on. Something in the cell's chemical environment or in some other level of the developing system, although not yet fully understood, interacts with genetic material to direct the cell's developmental outcome.

Let's consider another example from the higher, postnatal level of development of rat pups that are exposed to enriched environmental stimulation after birth. When compared to pups reared in social isolation, the enriched pups have more differentiated neuronal connections (Renner & Rosenzweig, 1987) and greater amounts of DNA in the brain. At even higher levels of development or those involving whole behavioral systems, the genetic-environmental coaction principle also holds true. Cierpal and McCarty (1987) discovered that a particular hypertensive rat strain, which is considered the animal model for hypertension in humans, will not develop hypertension unless reared by hypertensive mothers! Interestingly, genetically nonhypertensive rats will *not* develop hypertension if reared by hypertensive mothers. The expression of hypertension appears to depend upon some combination of elements in hypertensive mother and hypertensive pup. Despite the fact that hypertensive rat pups have the genetic programming for hypertension, its functional expression is not inevitable.

Perhaps you are thinking that these results from animal studies do not apply to humans. However, biologists claim that there is no evidence at the molecular level to suggest that human prenatal development proceeds very differently from that of other animal species (Wahlstein & Gottlieb, 1997). In addition, the overwhelming majority of genes recognized as important for healthy human brain functioning are shared with many other vertebrate species. Nonetheless, evidence is also accumulating from human infancy research to support the principle of coaction. Edelman (1987) notes that the pattern of brain development (neuronal connections) laid down early in the infant's life is partly due to the quality of environmental stimulation. An example is provided by Dawson and her colleagues (1997), who found that infants of depressed mothers demonstrated greater increases in frontal lobe activity during the experience of negative emotions as measured by electroencephalograms (EEGs) than did infants of nondepressed mothers when they experienced negative emotions. The authors speculate that this may show a pattern of selective brain activation that is triggered essentially by differences in the context of development.

Methodology

A second major criticism of the behavior genetics approach relates to the methods employed in this kind of research. In particular, behavior genetics is based on an additive model: phenotype = genes + experience. Yet, as we have just seen, the contributions of genes and environment do not just add up. Rather they interact in complex ways. In some environments genes play a major role in affecting behaviors; in other environments the genes have less influence on outcomes (Gottlieb, 1992).

The use of twin studies by behavior geneticists has also come under attack. Recall that we posed several questions about genes causing behaviors such as TV watching. Much of the recent publicity in this area comes from the work of researchers who study the relationships of identical twins separated at birth and reunited in adulthood. These studies have demonstrated that a variety of behavioral and personality characteristics are highly correlated in monozygotic twin pairs. For example, traits such as extraversion, leadership, alienation, religious conviction, and so on, appear to be highly heritable. Researchers who administer tests of intelligence or personality to these twin pairs use the correlations between scores to determine heritability as a measure of genetic contribution. However, for most traits, the heritability is roughly 50%, which leaves another 50% contribution, presumably from the environment. Furthermore, there may be confounding nature-nurture effects even for the twins who are separated at birth. For the participants in the large "Minnesota Twin Study" (Bouchard, Lykken, McGue, Segal, & Tellegen, 1990), for example, the average age of separation was 5 months, the average age at reunion was 30 years, and the average age at testing was more that 10 years after reunion! Both before and after separation, then, there was plenty of time for shared environments to have had some influence on observed behavior similarities.

Another striking criticism of many twin studies is that some ignore the important environmental influences shared by twins prenatally. In animal studies, many features of the uterine environment, such as temperature, gravity, chemical composition (Yoshinaga & Mori, 1989), location (Crews, 1994), stress and nutrition (Morgane, Austin-LaFrance, Bronzino, Tonkiss, Diaz-Cintra, Cintra, Kemper, & Galler, 1993) have been shown to make important contributions to later development.

It is important to note, however, that recent advances have given a "new look" to behavior genetics, one that is marked by a more integrative approach to genetic and environmental influences. Many of the original criticisms of behavior genetics stemmed from an overemphasis on genetic influences. More recent work pays equal attention to genetic and social/environmental factors, as demonstrated by increased efforts to understand the contribution of **genotype-environment interaction** on behavior (see Reiss, Neiderhiser, Hetherington, & Plomin, 2000). Genotype-environment interactions refer to the ways genes express themselves, for good or for ill, within particular environmental circumstances and sounds much like the coaction we have been discussing.

An interesting and complex picture of genetic influences on behavior is emerging from these investigations. For example, genes appear to exert their influence on behavior at all stages of the life span. Some influence behavior early in life, while others, such as genetic influences on maternal attachment or antisocial behavior, appear in adolescence or adulthood (see Lyons, True, Eisen, Goldberg, Meyer, Faraone, Eaves, & Tsuang, 1995). Contrary to what many people think, genetic influences on certain behaviors can be stronger at later points in the life course than at earlier points. Consider intelligence, for example. Genetic influences increase rather than decrease as children approach adolescence (Plomin, Fulker, Corley, & DeFries, 1997). Most importantly, genetic influences can never be fully disentangled from environmental influences, as we have indicated repeatedly. Indeed, the nature of the question about what influences development has changed. Despite the fact that an oversimplified view of the nature–nurture controversy is still remarkably tenacious, the either–or dualism implied in this position is truly out of date. To ask which of the two, nature or nurture, is more important is a little like asking which element is more important in salt, sodium or chlorine. LeDoux (2002) captures the essence of this shift in reference to brain development.

> No one today seriously proposes that the brain is a blank slate at birth, waiting to be written on by experience, or alternatively, that it is a genetically predetermined, unchangeable repository of tendencies to act, think, and feel a particular way. Instead, it is widely believed that brain circuits come about through a particular combination of genetic and nongenetic influences, and the debate now hinges less on the dichotomy than on the manner in which nature and nurture contribute to brain construction. The dichotomy, in fact, begins to dissolve when it is realized that, regarding questions of mind and behavior, nature and nurture are really two ways of doing the same thing—wiring up synapses—and both are needed to get the job done. (pp. 65–66)

Developmental Systems: A Multidimensional Perspective

The new generation of behavior genetics research has elements in common with an alternative way of conceptualizing the nature-nurture relationship, the **epigenetic model,** which is a type of *multidimensional* or *systems theory*. Epigenetic approaches to development assume that development is the result of interacting genetic and environmental elements and that these interactions are complex. Ongoing developmental changes have effects that are bidirectional, with influences on both the environment and the biological system (Gordon & Lemons, 1997). A common metaphor for this approach to development has been that of the "epigenetic landscape" (Waddington, 1942; see Figure 2.7), which is the appealing visual image of a metaphorical ball traversing a landscape of ridges and furrows as it wends its way down a developmental path. Implicit in this model is the concept of ***canalization,*** or the "channeling of behavior and the correlated decrease in plasticity over the course of ontogenesis (which can) be explained by the individual's particular developmental history" (Gottlieb, 1991, p. 4). In other words, as development akin to the rolling ball proceeds down the pathway, behaviors unfold that guide the ball in certain directions, determining in turn which new pathways become available.

Many researchers (Parker & Gibson, 1979; Scarr-Salapatek, 1976), including Waddington himself (1942, 1957), have interpreted canalization as largely genetic. In such a view, the ball is fated to roll down certain pathways, as predetermined by the genes directing the movement. Normal development is buffered by the genes against extreme deviations such that a normal range of environmental conditions will produce essentially the same outcomes. So far, this interpretation resembles the "nature" paradigm described in the earlier section, and it has been criticized for overemphasizing genetic determinism (Gottlieb, 1991). The "rolling ball" metaphor has also been criticized for oversimplifying developmental processes, because it presents the individual as one wholly integrated system progressing down one epigenetic landscape. Cairns (1991) offers this critique: "Development has multiple facets, and the description of particular features may be distorted by assuming a single trajectory for the whole and all of its parts. In buying too much too cheaply, metaphors substitute simple images for the hard-won gains of empirical science. It is a misguided economy" (p. 24). We should take pains, these authors suggest, to understand gene-environment influences on the unfolding of particular systems of development, not on the development of the individual as a whole.

Overall, both sides appear to be reaching a rapprochement. What is important to remember is that genetic influences should not be disregarded because they appear to be

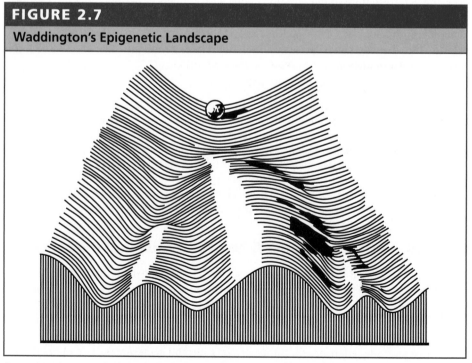

FIGURE 2.7

Waddington's Epigenetic Landscape

Source: Waddington, C. H. (1957). *The strategy of the genes* (p. 29). London: Allen & Unwin.

uncontrollable, nor should they be construed to exert their influence only before birth. If genes are the "push" that nature provides, then environment is the "pull" that makes their expression possible. Viewed from this perspective, the environment becomes even more important as a possible elicitor or suppressor of genetic expression.

Gottlieb (1991) provides an example of this coaction in the development of acoustical recognition in animals. He demonstrated that animals need to be exposed to certain behaviors of their own species in order to develop normally. Typically, wood ducklings and mallard ducklings show a preference for the maternal calls of their own species. Across species, maternal calls differ in several critical acoustic dimensions. However, the ducklings' own vocalizations share some of the acoustic features of their own mothers' calls. Gottlieb hypothesized that the early experience of the newly hatched duckling, that is, hearing its own and its siblings' calls, helps establish the duckling's preference for maternal vocalizations. In other words, if ducklings were raised in incubators and were prevented from hearing either their own or their siblings' calls, they would be as likely to respond to the social signals of other species as those of their own species. This is exactly what happened in the experiment. When ducklings were prevented from hearing their own species-specific calls, they did not show their selective response and were likely to respond to the maternal calls of other species. (This is a little like toddlers responding in a similar way to any adult who calls their names.) For ducklings, early exposure to the calls of their own species inoculates them against the possibility of extraspecific responsivity.

In this elegant experiment, Gottlieb (1991) demonstrated that environmental experience plays an important canalizing role in the development of this particular kind of behavior. He proposed that "canalization can take place not only at the genetic level, but at *all levels of the developing system,* including the developing organism's usually occurring experiences" (p. 5).

In humans, similar processes appear to be at work. Reiss and Neiderhiser (2000), summarizing evidence from their studies of adolescent social relationships, suggest that for some children, qualities, such as irritability, that appear to have a heritable component, evoke negative reactions from other members of their social worlds. In response, the social environment for these youngsters becomes hostile, further supporting the expression of genetically influenced tendencies toward irritability. These authors propose that heritable tendencies can be modified by environmental circumstances that do not support their expression. Speaking about adolescents, they hypothesize that

> most, *but not all,* parents, peers, teachers, and best friends react adversely to a difficult child. The "off-diagonal" responders—the ones who do not respond to provocations—may hold the key to the powerful suppression achieved by positive social environments on adverse genetic influences. Those environments that do not respond adversely may interrupt a fundamental mechanism of socially-mediated gene expression as effectively, and more selectively and safely, than pharmacological agents that are currently used to block the transcription of DNA into RNA. (p. 365)

Clearly, the interplay of genes and environment must be considered in any comprehensive theory of development. In the next section, we begin a description of developmental change from conception onward, a process that at every stage is a function of bidirectional and complexly interacting genetic and environmental influences.

HEALTHY PRENATAL DEVELOPMENT

The amazing story of human prenatal development is one of orderly and continuous progress from a single fertilized cell to a highly differentiated organism with many interconnected and efficiently functioning systems. The principle of coaction operates at every level of this developmental drama—with genes and environment in constant communication. Typically the 9-month gestational period is divided into three parts, which reflect the kind of development taking place at each specific period of time. The *period of the ovum* spans the first three weeks of pregnancy, from the time of fertilization through implantation into the uterine lining to the development of the *neural tube,* the rudimentary beginnings of the central nervous system. The *period of the embryo* lasts from the fourth week through the eighth week of gestation. During this time, most of the body's organ systems and structures are forming. Nature has determined that this progression move in a "head-to-tail" (called *cephalo-caudal*) as well as "near-to-far" (called *proximo-distal*) direction. Thus, the head forms before the legs, and the most vital inner organs form before the extremities. The *period of the fetus,* lasting from the ninth week until birth, characterizes a time of rapid growth and further differentiation. The reproductive system forms, gains in body weight occur, and the brain and nervous system continue to develop. Refer again to Figure 2.5 for more information.

Genetic Interventions

What can be done to promote a healthy start? From the helper's point of view, there is much that can be done, even before the baby is born. Interventions can address either of the major players, genes or environment. Recent advances in genetic research promise revolutionary treatments based upon the detection of genes or disease-causing mutations within the genes that are involved in inherited disorders, birth defects, or other medical conditions. It is hoped that the genetic map that is the work-in-progress of the Human Genome Project will eventually provide a guide for identifying where specific disease genes are located so that interventions can be applied.

What are the benefits that can come from this kind of information? First, we will be able to diagnose more reliably those conditions that are presently inferred from clinical evaluations. It is possible to detect the genetic markers for disorders in advance of the presence of the symptoms both in the person with the disease and in the person who is a carrier of the disease. Understanding the genetic contribution to disease is also a first step in the possible development of vaccines. Recently, researchers investigating diabetes discovered that a certain gene in mice (called GAD) influences the production of a protein (called glutamate acid decarboxylase) that, when circulating in the body, triggers an immune system response that kills cells involved in insulin production (Yoon, Yoon, Lim, Huang, Kang, Pryn, Hirasawa, Sherwin, & Jun, 1999). This knowledge may, in time, result in the production of a vaccine that could desensitize the body to the presence of the GAD gene and protect the insulin-producing cells. These innovative treatments hold more promise for physical rather than for behavioral disorders, given the extraordinary complexity of the polygenetic influences associated with the latter.

In addition to diagnosis, screening, and the development of vaccines, researchers are currently using genetic research to develop methods that would replace or correct defective genes. This kind of gene therapy, although still very experimental, holds out the hope for a cure for genetically caused diseases. Two possible approaches are under investigation: *somatic cell therapy,* which involves insertion of healthy genes into appropriate tissue, and *germline gene therapy,* which involves altering the sperm or egg cells so as to pass on healthy genes to future generations (Gelehrter & Collins, 1990).

Most of these methods, however, are still in the experimental stage and are prohibitively expensive. Clinical trials have met with more failures than successes at this point. Since this field is so new, very little is known about the possible side effects of genetic manipulations. Interventions such as these also raise many serious ethical questions about the appropriateness of treatment and who should be able to get it. Certainly these are questions that helpers will be asked to help their clients deal with as genetic treatment options become more commonplace in the future. At this time, however, let us consider the kinds of cost-effective, environmental approaches that have been well established to help the most people. What can be done to promote healthy practices during the prenatal period? To answer this question, it is important to understand the mechanisms through which development can go awry.

Environmental Influences on Prenatal Development

Teratogens

Many agents and circumstances can cause harm to the developing fetus. Public health efforts have made great strides in alerting the general population to the risks faced by the developing fetus during pregnancy. Despite what appears to be a relatively recent concern, it is interesting to note that even the ancient Greeks, like Hippocrates who wrote 2,500 years ago, recognized that ingestion of certain drugs particularly during the early stages of pregnancy could weaken the fetus and cause it to be misshapen. Those substances or agents, which produce fetal deformities when taken or absorbed by the mother during pregnancy, are called **teratogens.** The fetus is surrounded by a **placenta,** which allows nutrients from the mother's blood to pass into the baby's blood and allows waste to be removed by the mother's blood, but which otherwise keeps the two circulatory systems separate. *Teratogens* can cross the placental barrier. They include some drugs and other chemicals, certain disease organisms, and radioactivity. The name comes from the Greek and literally means "monstrosity making." The list of known teratogens is quite lengthy, so we have presented in Table 2.4 a summary of the main characteristics of a few of the most well-researched agents. A few principles are helpful to understand in guiding your thinking about the operation of these causes of birth defects. Generally, the potential for harm is impossible to determine with absolute precision. Rather, what happens to the developing organism depends upon several conditions (Wilson, 1973).

The first principle is that the kind of damage done is related to the stage of development during which the mother is exposed to the teratogen. If, for example, exposure to some harmful substance occurs during the fourth or fifth week of gestation when the major organ systems are being laid down, the result may be major structural malformation. If the mother is exposed to the same teratogen during the last month of her pregnancy, possible neurobehavioral rather than gross structural deficits may occur. Rubella, or German measles contracted during the first trimester of pregnancy can produce blindness, deafness, heart defects, and mental retardation. However, if the infection occurs during the second trimester, less severe problems involving vision and hearing may result. It is important to note that although prenatal development can be divided into trimesters or periods (e.g., ovum, embryo, fetus) for convenience sake, development is orderly and continuous throughout gestation. "At any time in the total span of development, these ongoing processes can be subtly deflected, severely perturbed, or abruptly halted, resulting in death or abnormal development" (Stratton, Howe, & Battaglia, 1996, p. 37).

A second principle is that not all developing organisms will be susceptible to teratogenic effects. Both the mother's and the baby's genes play a role in sensitivity or resistance to a teratogen. A teratogen that is harmful to one individual may produce different outcomes or no outcome in another individual. These differences appear to be related to specific characteristics such as metabolism rates or variations in placental structure. Streissguth and Dehaene (1993) report that monozygotic (identical) twins, who are alike genetically, show more similar patterns of alcohol-related birth defects than dizygotic (fraternal) twins, who share only about one half of their genes. These data suggest that

TABLE 2.4

Selected Teratogens

Legal and Illegal Drugs	Effects on Fetus	Safe Dosage	References
Alcohol	Great variability in outcome. May include: distinct facial structure, cardiac, skeletal, & urogenital abnormalities; dental abnormalities, growth deficiencies, metacognitive deficits, attentional problems, social perception problems, language deficits, & other learning problems.	No safe dosage during pregnancy	Stressiguth, A. P., Aase, J. M., Clarren, S. K., Randels, S. P., LaDue, R. A., & Smith, D. F. (1991). Fetal alcohol syndrome in adolescents and adults. *Journal of the American Medical Association, 265*, 1961–1967.
Tobacco	Low birth weight due to constricted blood flow and reduced nutrition; prematurity; respiratory problems, cleft palate; learning problems, hyperactivity.	No safe dosage during pregnancy	Floyd, R. L., Rimer, B. K., Giovino, G. A., Mullen, P. D., & Sullivan, S. E. (1993). A review of smoking in pregnancy: Effects on pregnancy outcomes and cessation efforts. *Annual Review of Public Health, 14*, 379–411.
Cocaine	Prematurity or stillbirth, low birth weight; drug withdrawal after birth including irritability, restlessness, tremors; medically and psychologically fragile; higher rates of later learning problems and ADHD.	No safe dosage during pregnancy	Bateman, D., Ng, S., Hansen, C., & Heagarty, M. (1993). The effects of interuterine cocaine exposure in newborns. *American Journal of Public Health, 83*, 190–194.
Marijuana	Less well studied; some data to link its use to neurological effects; low birth weight, learning problems, etc.	No safe dosage during pregnancy	Dahl, R. E., Scher, M. S., Williamson, D. E., Robles, N., & Day, N. (1995). A longitudinal study of prenatal marijuana use: Effects on sleep and arousal at age 3 years. *Archives of Pediatric and Adolescent Medicine, 149*, 145–150.
Infections			
AIDS	Transmitted through contact with maternal blood via the placenta or at delivery. Causes damage to immune system, facial abnormalities, growth problems, brain disorders, developmental delays; usually fatal.		Nozyce, M., Hittelman, J., Muenz, L., Durako, S. J., Fischer, M., & Willoughby, A. (1994). Effect of perinatally acquired human immunodeficiency virus infection on neurodevelopment during the first two years of life. *Pediatrics, 94*, 883–891.
Environmental Hazards			
Lead	Prematurity, low birth weight, brain damage, mental retardation, physical deformities.		Dye-White, E. (1986). Environmental hazards in the work setting: Their effect on women of child-bearing age. *American Association of Occupational Health and Nursing Journal, 43*, 76–78.
PCBs (Polychlorinated biphenyls)	Low birth weight, cognitive impairments.		Jacobson, J. L., Jacobson, S. W., Padgett, R. J., Brumitt, G. A., & Billings, R. L. (1992). Effects of prenatal PCB exposure or cognitive processing efficiency and sustained attention. *Dev. Psych., 28*, 297–306.

genes play a role in moderating the influence of alcohol on the developing fetus. Other researchers (Sonderegger, 1992) have found that male fetuses are more susceptible than female fetuses to the effects of teratogens.

A third principle is that adverse outcomes also depend upon dosage amount. Larger amounts of a teratogenic agent over longer periods of time generally have more potent effects than smaller doses over a shorter period of time. For example, babies who are exposed to alcohol prenatally may be born with *fetal alcohol syndrome (FAS),* which is identifiable in its victims by virtue of their unique facial configuration (small head, widely spaced eyes, flattened nose, and so on). In addition to the facial characteristics, children with FAS may also suffer from mental retardation and behavior problems. Children exposed to smaller amounts of alcohol prenatally do not necessarily have to meet the diagnostic criteria of FAS to exhibit deficits. Such children are said to exhibit *fetal alcohol effects (FAE).* Recent research has identified significant learning impairments in children who had been prenatally exposed to alcohol but who did not have the physical features or growth deficiencies of FAS children. The researchers concluded that the absence of physical symptoms or structural malformations does not rule out serious cognitive limitations from prenatal alcohol exposure (Mattson, Riley, Gramling, Delis, & Jones, 1998).

The possible toxic effects of a teratogen such as alcohol can be construed to range along a continuum from no observable effect to one that is lethal to the embryo or fetus. If the amount of alcohol ingested by the mother exceeds that of the *no observable effect level,* the fetus will experience some functional impairment (*lowest observable adverse effect level*) but may sustain structural malformations only as dosage is increased. This hypothetical dose-response relationship presumes that the effects of alcohol ingestion on the fetus are always more potent than they are on the mother. In other words, the fetus may have crossed the toxic threshold even if the mother experiences few or very mild alcohol-related effects (Stratton et al., 1996). Consequently, as the Surgeon General has warned, there is no safe level of alcohol consumption during pregnancy.

A final principle regarding the effects of teratogens is that their negative effects can be amplified if the fetus or infant is exposed to more than one risk factor. For example, mothers who take cocaine typically use other drugs such as alcohol, marijuana, tobacco, and heroin and have poorer nutrition. They may also experience more poverty and stress during and after pregnancy than other women. Drug effects are therefore confounded by, and can be amplified by, the effects of the maternal lifestyle, and the results of these interacting risk factors are not yet well understood (Lester, Freier, & LaGasse, 1995). Generally, babies born to cocaine-abusing mothers are at increased risk for poor developmental outcomes. Bendersky and Lewis (1998) found that infants exposed to cocaine use prenatally showed less enjoyment during playful interactions with their mothers and had more difficulty calming themselves after they sustained a period of maternal nonresponsiveness. The result was still significant when other variables (such as abuse of other drugs, bad environmental conditions) were controlled. This evidence points to cocaine's negative impact on regulation of arousal, which can have an impact on the child's social interactions. Needless to say, the presence of other deleterious factors, such as nonresponsive parenting, can only exacerbate the situation. Thus, babies who were prenatally exposed to cocaine benefit from a stabilizing environment, and their postnatal risks are reduced.

Nutrition

Teratogens are problematic because they *add* something to the ordinary fetal environment, intruding on the developing system and driving it off course. But what happens when contextual factors that *belong* in the ordinary fetal environment are missing or in short supply?

A rapidly growing body of evidence reveals that when food sources are short on protein and/or essential vitamins and minerals during prenatal and early postnatal development, an infant's physical, social-emotional, and intellectual development can be compromised (Eysenck & Schoenthaler, 1997). For example, Rush, Stein, and Susser (1980) provided nutritional supplements to pregnant women whose socioeconomic circumstances indicated that they were likely to experience inadequate diets. At age 1, the babies whose mothers received a protein supplement during pregnancy performed better on measures of play behavior and perceptual habituation (which is correlated with later intelligence) than those whose mothers received a high-calorie liquid or no supplement at all (Rush, Stein, & Susser, 1980).

Are there longer-term behavioral consequences of prenatal nutrition? Some research does reveal enduring effects. For example, in a study of Guatemalan village populations, pregnant women and later their children received either daily protein supplements or supplements consisting of a low-calorie drink (a placebo). Children who had received protein supplements both pre- and postnatally were generally larger than those who received the placebo, and there were cognitive and behavioral effects as well. Follow-ups of the children at age 4 indicated that differences in social and cognitive functioning could be traced to the amount and/or kind of supplement they had received. But the longer-term follow-ups were perhaps the most interesting: the children who received the protein supplements both prenatally and for two years postnatally continued to show benefits in adolescence, long after the supplements had been discontinued, performing better on a variety of cognitive measures, such as reading achievement, vocabulary comprehension, and number skills, with children in the lowest socioeconomic groups benefiting most. Thus, some advantages of good early nutrition seem to be long-range (Barrett, Radke-Yarrow, & Klein, 1983; Pollitt, Gorman, Engle, Martorell, & Rivera, 1993; Townsend, Klein, Irwin, Owens, Yarbrough, & Engle, 1982).

It is not surprising that *prenatal* nutrition has such effects, given what we have learned about the effects of *postnatal* nutrition on children's functioning. We have known for decades that children who suffer severe protein and calorie shortages at any age may develop **kwashiorkor,** characterized by stunted growth, a protuberant belly, and extreme apathy (Williams, 1933). Researchers have determined that therapeutic diets can eliminate the apathy of kwashiorkor, but cognitive impairments are likely to persist (e.g., Yatkin & McClaren, 1970). Other research indicates that much less severe nutritional deficits may have impacts on children's cognitive functioning. An intriguing study of changes in the food supplied to New York City schools provides a strong illustration (Schoenthaler, Doraz, & Wakefield, 1986). In a three-stage process, from 1978 to 1983, many food additives and foods high in sugar (sucrose) were eliminated from school meals, so that children's consumption of "empty calories" was reduced, and, presumably, their intake of foods with a higher nutrient-to-calorie ratio increased. With each stage of this process, average achievement test scores increased in New York City schools, with improvements occurring primarily among the children who were performing worst academically.

Findings such as these suggest that children whose prenatal and postnatal environments are short on protein and other essential nutrients may not achieve the levels of behavioral functioning that they could have with adequate diets. But the long-range impact of early diet, like the effects of teratogens, depends in part on the presence or absence of other risk factors. Recall that in the Guatemala study, children for whom protein supplements made the most difference were from the poorest homes. Although these children may have been the most nutritionally deprived, most participants in this study experienced protein-poor diets. Other aspects of being poor apparently made the dietary inadequacies more problematic. Poor children, for example, are likely to have limited access to education and health care; they may have more than average exposure to

Children whose prenatal or postnatal environments are nutritionally deficient may suffer long-term cognitive deficits.

unsanitary conditions and infectious agents; they may be more subject to unresponsive care or even abuse than other children, and so on. When children are *not* exposed to multiple risk factors, long-range effects of prenatal or postnatal malnutrition are less apparent. For example, studies of economically advantaged children subjected to early malnutrition due to illness or to the privations of war have not found long-term cognitive or behavioral deficits (Hart, 1993; Pollit, Golub, Gorman, Grantham-McGregor, Levitsky, Schurch, Strupp, & Wachs, 1996; Stein, Susser, Saenger, & Marolla, 1975). Apparently, social, educational, and medical advantages help to moderate the effects of early food deprivation. As we will see in later chapters, any single developmental risk factor, either biological or environmental, often has its effects lessened by other more benign influences. It is in combination that risk factors do the most harm. One heartening consequence is that when we intervene to reduce one risk factor, such as malnutrition, we may actually modify the impact of other negative influences on development as well.

Stress

Stress seems to be the affliction of our modern age, and coping with stress has become a cottage industry. It is routine to hear experts tell us that we should avoid stress. Buoyed by research on the relationship of stress and health, employers commonly sponsor "stress-management" seminars. Stores are full of stress-relieving vitamins and relaxation-enhancing gadgets. If stress has an important part to play in the health of an adult, what is its impact on the well-being of the unborn child? In order to answer that question, we need to look at what we know about the effects of stress on the body in general.

Stress is an unavoidable part of life, and despite its negative connotation, it is not all bad. The happy anticipation of a new baby is for many couples a form of positive stress, or **eustress** as defined by Selye (1980). This can be contrasted to **distress,** which refers to the kinds of frustrations, conflicts, pressures, and negative events that people experience in their lives either intermittently or chronically. The body has a characteristic way of handling these stressors, which involves three stages: the **alarm phase,** during which the activity of the sympathetic nervous system and adrenal glands increases in preparation for flight or fight; the **resistance phase,** during which the body is moderately aroused, the parasympathetic system takes over, and the body continues to resist the effects of the stressor; and finally, the **exhaustion phase,** which occurs if the struggle persists to the point that the body's resources are depleted. Depression, illness, or even death can occur after severe, prolonged stress.

The actual physical response of the body to stress involves what is called the **hypothalamic-pituitary-adrenal axis (HPA axis),** which works something like this. When a person experiences or anticipates stress, the amygdala, or one part of the brain that controls emotions, detects the danger and immediately informs the hypothalamus, a small centrally located region in the midbrain (see Chapter 3 for information on brain structure). Next, the hypothalamus communicates the danger message to the pituitary gland, which is positioned directly below it. The message is read by the pituitary as a sign to release **adrenocorticotropic hormone**, or **ACTH**, into the bloodstream. ACTH makes its way to the adrenal glands, situated atop the kidneys, which receive the message to release **epinephrine, norepinephrine**, and **cortisol**. Some of these so-called stress hormones (particularly cortisol) then travel back to the brain and bind to receptors on the amygdala and the hippocampus.

So far, so good. Hormones such as epinephrine and norepinephrine prepare the body to resist the stressor by sending a burst of energy to those parts of the body necessary for fighting or fleeing (e.g., heart, lungs) while diverting energy from less necessary systems (e.g., digestion, reproduction). Cortisol acts to increase blood glucose levels and to suppress the immune response. Under normal conditions, the returning cortisol tells the hippocampus to alert the HPA axis to slow down its attack because all is well. The problems start when stress is prolonged and a communication gap develops between the hippocampus's messages to "cease and desist" and the amygdala's "fire away" message. Ultimately, the hippocampus becomes unable to shut down the stress response effectively, and the individual's stress-response system may become chronically activated, putting a great deal of wear and tear on the body. The capability of the immune system to fight infection and ward off disease is compromised. Growth hormone is suppressed. Long-term negative effects on cardiovascular and nervous system functioning result. Some studies have found damaged or shrunken nerve cells in the hippocampus of humans and animals exposed to traumatic or social stressors. For example, McEwen and Sapolsky (1995) reported that the hippocampi of veterans with post-traumatic stress disorder (PTSD) were 25% smaller than those of a control group, causing those veterans significant problems in memory formation and retrieval despite the fact that they had otherwise normal brains. It is not yet clear whether such effects are due to an excess of cortisol, pumped in from the agitated adrenals, or to a highly sensitized cortisol-response system, but it is clear from studies such as these that a negative relationship exists between excessive stress and memory functions.

All of this leads us back to our discussion of early fetal development. The increased levels of stress hormones secreted by the pregnant mother under stress can cross the placental barrier and eventually affect the developing child in a number of ways. First, these hormones will contribute to the shaping of the infant's own neuroendocrine system, which will greatly influence responsivity to stimulation, activity rhythms, and ability to modulate and regulate behavior. The relationships between maternal stress and neonatal hyperactivity and irritability have been well documented (Levine, 1969). Second, heightened levels of maternal epinephrine decrease blood flow to the uterus and, ultimately, to the placenta. Consequently, oxygen flow to the fetus is reduced (Nathanielz, 1992). Third, evidence from animal studies suggests that sexual orientation may be altered by severe maternal stress during pregnancy. The timing of the stress and the release of stress hormones interfere with fetal testosterone production and affect the sexual orientation of male offspring (Ward, 1992). Finally, as we have seen, hormones influence the expression of the genes and work in coaction with them to direct development. The impact of the stress hormones on the developing brain can be lasting and profound, as in the case of damage to the cells of the hippocampus. The stress experienced by mothers can actually alter the environment in which their unborn children develop and can lead the children to be hyper-reactive to stress later on (Lederman, 1996). Although the precise relationship between prenatal exposure to stress and later psychopathology is still being investigated, many researchers agree that early exposure can produce lasting biological changes (Benes, 1994; Chrousos & Gold, 1999). We should remember, however, that postnatal environmental factors, such as positive child-rearing experiences, can modify the effects of early deleterious exposure (Meyer, Chrousos & Gold, 2001).

APPLICATIONS

In this chapter we have summarized information that is important for understanding how human life begins and develops. Those time-honored players, nature and nurture, take center stage as the story unfolds. What is the point of this theoretical debate for someone in the helping professions? It is far from an "ivory-tower" issue, as we have noted before. A bias in either of the possible directions, toward nature or nurture, can powerfully affect attitudes and expectations about behavior. These attitudes and expectations will be communicated directly or indirectly to clients, parents, and others who come to us for help. For example, a tendency to view genetics as the powerful "quarterback" (Scarr & McCartney, 1983) of the nature-nurture team may tip the balance in favor of reliance on oversimplified genetic explanations for academic, social, or emotional difficulties. It may predispose the helper to minimize environmental influences and to suggest medical or psychopharmacological remedies as the routine way of handling problems. It could discourage a helper (and the helper's clients) from working on a problem, because the problem is framed as virtually impossible to change, a belief that is clearly unsupported by the evidence we have presented. One of the author's students told her about a fifth-grade youngster she was counseling in the schools. This young girl had made repeated visits to the counselor (as well as to the principal!) for a number of behavioral missteps during the school year. Sarah (not her real name) usually got into trouble for acting out, talking during class, and so on, and understandably exasperated her well-meaning teacher. Attempting to explain her side of the story to the counselor, Sarah blurted out, "What they don't understand, Mrs. Johnson, is that people like you were born to follow the rules and I was not. It's all GENETIC!" Imagine how powerfully this explanation has permeated our culture if even grade school students use it to make attributions for causality.

A bias in the other direction, toward nurture, could predispose a helper to hold unrealistically high expectations for what can be changed. It may encourage a comparably simplistic, molecular approach to problem solving in situations that are complicated and multilayered. Also, it could promote a kind of intolerance for diverse expressions of human behavior and personality by attempting to change behavior deemed inappropriate. In some ways, the emphasis on nurture may place too much responsibility on the individual, or perhaps on parents of children, to produce outcomes that may not be possible given the "niche-picking" tendencies of their offspring. Seligman (1993) has described the collision between helpers' cherished beliefs in self-improvement and advances in biological psychiatry. Just peruse the self-help section of your local bookstore, and you will be bombarded with texts that promise recipes for changing everything from weight to shyness to unruly children. The proliferation of quick-fix advice found in books, magazines, TV, and radio feeds the notion that physical, behavioral, emotional, intellectual, and social change is a combination of the "right" strategy and some good, old-fashioned willpower. Seligman cautions that an ideology that holds that all human problems are the result of poor environmental conditions is "seriously incomplete" (p. 7).

Sometimes emphasizing one side over the other is correct when the weight of the evidence supports that choice. However, this tendency to "either/or" thinking can distort understanding of other issues beyond nature and nurture, such as "either/or" thinking about gender differences (Hare-Mustin & Maracek, 1988). One's fundamental underlying biases should always be examined reflectively. In other words, when as a helper, you always see the young girl (in Figure 2.1) rather than the old woman or vice versa, your perspective needs to be realigned.

We can also learn from the available scientific information presented in this chapter that certain practices really do promote healthy prenatal development and some put the fetus's well-being at substantial risk. One of the most well-established recommendations offered to pregnant women is to eat a healthy diet that includes a variety of foods. To prevent the risk of brain and spinal birth defects, foods high in folic acid should be eaten regularly and supplemented by a multivitamin. Since alcohol is such a powerful teratogen, its consumption during pregnancy should be completely eliminated. Drugs, both legal and illegal, and cigarettes should be avoided as well because of their potential to damage the fetus. The spouses or partners of pregnant women should also avoid dangerous substances, both to provide support for their partners and to reduce the availability of the substance in the home. If a woman must take prescription medication for preexisting conditions such as epilepsy, bipolar disorder, cancer, or thyroid dysfunction, she should inform her physician, if possible, when she is considering a pregnancy and certainly if she suspects she is pregnant. No over-the-counter medication should be taken without the advice of a physician. Even the innocuous aspirin tablet, if taken in excess during the last trimester, can prolong labor and cause excessive bleeding. Stress, particularly if chronic and serious, can be detrimental to a healthy pregnancy. Every effort should be made to provide social support and to reduce ongoing interpersonal conflict during this time. Fathers and extended family members are likely support-system candidates. When they are not available, the helper must use creative means to provide for contacts (support groups, church members, agency contacts, etc.) who will lend a listening ear and a helping hand to mothers-to-be who are experiencing the emotional upheaval of pregnancy. Finally, good medical care is one of the most important elements in a healthy pregnancy and delivery. Research has shown that it is significantly associated with fewer birth complications and lower rates of infant mortality (Kotch, Blakely, Brown, & Wong, 1992).

The above recommendations represent some of the best, albeit commonsense, advice for having a healthy baby. Following these guidelines is, in no small way, an investment in the future. For some populations, primarily women who live in poverty, who abuse drugs and alcohol, who are unmarried or teenagers, or who live in highly stressful circumstances, the best-practice standards will be more difficult to meet. Frequently, these are precisely the women that helping professionals will encounter. The escalation of social problems spawned by drugs, poverty, and diseases such as AIDS combined with diminishing social services and restrictions on welfare present formidable obstacles to the task at hand.

Teen pregnancy represents a particular challenge to the helper because the normal tasks of adolescent development (see Chapters 9, 10, and 11) are overlaid on the issues of pregnancy and parenthood. While rates of teenage births have stabilized or have declined slightly in recent years (National Campaign to Prevent Teen Pregnancy, 1999), the numbers are still unacceptably high. Studies have demonstrated that children of teenage mothers are likely to face a grim future that includes poverty, academic failure, high rates of family violence, unemployment, contact with the criminal justice system, and the likelihood of becoming teenage parents themselves. Pregnant teens experience more health problems, have higher rates of birth complications due to poor prenatal care, and tend to drop out of school, risking under- or unemployment in the future (Furstenberg, Brooks-Gunn & Chase-Lansdale, 1989; Hayes, 1987). For a multifaceted and cyclical problem such as this, interventions need to be embedded in the social and cultural system of the teenager, and most effective programs address concerns of parenthood and adolescent development together. Although evidence is somewhat scanty, the best approaches appear to involve coordination of school and clinic services. In other words, programs that target multiple issues, providing support and information on birth control, pregnancy, and child care, academic and vocational education, and the social and emotional concerns of the teenager hold out the promise of greater success than do programs that address single issues alone (Cowen et al., 1996). Programs for pregnant teens should also provide coordinated services for the new mothers, their babies, and the grandmothers who often play a central role in the caretaking functions. In order to break the repetitive cycle of early pregnancy, children of teenage mothers should be the target of preventive efforts as they approach adolescence themselves (Chase-Lansdale & Brooks-Gunn, 1994).

SUMMARY

The Nature/Nurture Illusion

1. Both heredity and environment influence human development, but when we focus our attention on one of these causes the other seems to fade into the background. It is an especially important challenge for the helper to avoid taking a one-sided perspective.

Mechanisms of Genetic Influence: How Do Genes Work?

2. Understanding how genetic processes work is important if we hope to evaluate claims about the role heredity plays in development. Each human has 23 pairs of *chromosomes* in each of his body cells. Chromosomes are composed of *deoxyribonucleic acid (DNA)*. Chromosomes divide during normal cell division (*mitosis*), and each new cell then contains a duplicate set of the original 46 chromosomes.

3. Specialized germ cells in ovaries and testes can undergo *meiosis*, a multistage cell division. The resulting cells, *ova* (eggs) in females and *sperm* in males, contain only one member of each chromosome pair, or 23 chromosomes altogether. When a sperm fertilizes an ovum, the resulting *zygote* contains 46 chromosomes. Thus, mother's ovum and father's sperm each contribute one member of every chromosome pair to their offspring.

4. *Genes* are the functional units of DNA. Human cells, by following blueprints provided by the genes, produce *proteins*, the building blocks of the body, and *enzymes*, which facilitate chemical reactions. Genes, like chromosomes, come in matched pairs, one from the mother, one from the father. Matching genes can have slightly different forms, called *alleles*, presenting cells with slightly different blueprints to follow. Different alleles of the same gene can have a *dominant-recessive relationship* such that one has a larger influence on the *phenotype*. In this situation, a person is a *carrier* of an unexpressed trait, which can be passed on to the next generation. Sometimes two different alleles have a *codominance* relationship and together produce a blended trait.

5. Most frequently, our traits are affected by many pairs of genes at many chromosomal sites. Such polygenic influences probably characterize most behavioral traits, such as intelligence and personality.

6. Whether one is male or female is affected by a whole pair of chromosomes: the XX pair in females and the XY pair in males. Mothers pass one of their X chromosomes on to their offspring, but fathers can pass along either an X or a Y, determining the sex of a child.

7. Hereditary diseases can occur either as a function of defective genes or because an ovum or a sperm contains the wrong number of chromosomes. Some disorders are caused by a single pair of genes. In this case, defective gene alleles can be recessive, so that a victim must have two of them to have the disorder, or a defective allele can be dominant, causing the disorder in anyone who has one of the defective genes. Many hereditary diseases, including many mental illnesses and behavioral disorders, are polygenic. Finally, some hereditary disorders result when a zygote forms containing too many chromosomes or too few. Often, the age of the parent at conception has some effect on the likelihood of such a problem. The genetic counselor can help parents and prospective parents who may be at risk of passing on hereditary diseases. The counselor's role includes helping clients to understand the benefits and risks of screening procedures and to understand and cope with the choices that confront them about testing, childbearing, and parenting.

8. Sex-linked disorders are more likely to affect males than females. They are caused by defective, recessive alleles on the X chromosome at a site that is unmatched by the smaller Y chromosome. For these diseases, a female must have two defective alleles to be a victim, but a male need only have one defective allele on his X chromosome.

Focus on Genetics: Its Influence on Behavior

9. There are two scientific approaches to understanding the role of genetics in behavior. The first is *molecular genetics,* which addresses questions such as where are genes located and what is the specific function and product of each gene. The second approach is *behavior genetics.* Its goal is to determine *heritability,* meaning the proportion of any behavior or trait that can be attributed to genetics. Behavior geneticists also estimate the degree of *environmental influence on behaviors.* They assess the degree to which both *nonshared* environments (dissimilar experiences) and *shared environments* (similar experiences) affect behavioral outcomes. Behavior geneticists rely heavily on studies of twins and of adoptees to estimate the contributions of heredity to behavior.

10. Some behavior geneticists have described several ways in which genes can even influence the environments we experience. *Passive* genetic effects occur when the genes of a parent affect the environment the parent provides for a child. *Evocative* genetic effects occur when a person's genes influence his behavior, which in turn affects how others react. When genes influence an individual's choice of environments, companions, or activities, the gene effects are called *active.*

Shifting Focus to the Interaction of Genetics and Environment

11. Some biologists argue that behavior genetics is based on an outmoded view of gene action. They point out that no development exists in the natural world that is purely genetic. Environment always reciprocally interacts with gene activity in an intricate pattern called *coaction.* Coaction can be seen in the development of cells and at each level of functioning, from the molecular to the behavioral.

12. Two methodological criticisms have been leveled at the behavior genetics approach. First, its calculations are based on the assumption that phenotype is the sum of genetic and environmental influences. But this assumption violates the observation that genes behave differently in different environments and that the same environment

has different effects in combination with different genes. Second, the interpretation of findings from twin studies is controversial. For example, some similarities attributed to shared genes may actually be a function of shared environment, such as the shared uterine environment.

13. Current *epigenetic models* take into account the complexity of gene-environment inter-actions and provide an alternative to behavior genetics. In these systems approaches, ongoing developmental changes are seen as influencing both the environment and the biological system. Both genetics and environment can *canalize* behavior, guiding it in certain directions and determining which new pathways for development become available.

Healthy Prenatal Development

14. During normal prenatal development, the first three weeks is the period of the ovum, when implantation occurs and the neural tube forms. The period of the embryo, from the 4th through the 8th weeks, is when most organ systems form, with development moving in cephalo-caudal and proximo-distal directions. From 9 weeks until birth is the period of the fetus, when the reproductive system forms and all other systems continue to mature.

15. Counseling interventions to promote healthy development can be targeted at either genetic or environmental influences. Most interventions targeted at changing or influ-encing gene function are experimental, but as they become available, counselors will help clients evaluate the ethics and feasibility of these options for themselves and their offspring.

16. Counselors can affect environmental influences on prenatal development more effec-tively than we can affect genetic influences. Helping parents understand *teratogens* and their influences on fetal development is important. These environmental agents, including many disease organisms and drugs, can have varying effects on the devel-oping fetus, depending on when they are introduced, the mother's and baby's genes, and the amount of exposure or "dosage" the fetus experiences. For example, the effects of prenatal exposure to alcohol can range from subtle learning and behavior problems to *fetal alcohol syndrome,* which includes physical abnormalities, mental retardation, and behavioral problems. The number of risk factors to which a child is exposed, both prenatally and postnatally, can also influence how severe the long-term effects of teratogens will be.

17. It is also important for parents and parents-to-be to understand the significance of prenatal nutrition. A number of studies demonstrate that adequate protein, vitamins, and minerals in the prenatal and immediate postnatal diet can have long-term benefits for children's social and cognitive development. These findings suggest that inade-quate prenatal nutrition has negative effects on cognitive and behavioral functioning, just as inadequate postnatal nutrition does. But like other risk factors, poor pre- or postnatal nutrition is more problematic the more risks a child experiences. Children who have experienced early food deprivation but who otherwise are socially, educa-tionally, and medically advantaged show no long-term effects of poor pre- or postna-tal nutrition.

18. The environment can be a source of prolonged stress for a pregnant woman, another factor that can have effects on the developing fetus. Stress experienced by the mother activates a complex set of responses involving parts of her brain and the endocrine glands—the *hypothalamic-pituitary-adrenal axis.* Part of the reaction includes a process for returning to normal, but continued exposure to stress sometimes interferes with the brain's ability to shut down the stress response. There can be long-term negative

effects for the fetus as well as for the mother. Hormones involved in the stress reaction cross the placenta from mother to fetus and can affect the infant's own developing neuroendocrine system, increasing neonatal hyperactivity and irritability.

Case Study

Jennifer and Jianshe Li have been married for 10 years. Jennifer is a white, 37-year-old woman who is an associate in a law firm in a medium-sized, Midwestern city. Her husband, Jianshe, a 36-year-old Chinese-American man, is a software developer employed by a large locally based company. The couple met while they were in graduate school and married shortly thereafter. They have no children. They own a home in one of the newly developed suburban areas just outside the city. Jennifer was adopted as an infant and maintains close ties with her adoptive parents. She is their only child. There has been no contact between Jennifer and her biological parents, and she has never attempted to learn their names or find out where they live. Jianshe's parents, two brothers, and one sister live on the West Coast, and all the family members try to get together for visits several times a year. Jennifer and Jianshe are active in a few local community organizations. They enjoy the company of many friends and often spend what leisure time they have hiking and camping.

The Lis have been unsuccessful in conceiving a child even though they have tried for the past four years. Both husband and wife have undergone testing. Jennifer has had infertility treatment for the past three years but without success. The treatments have been lengthy, expensive, and emotionally stressful. Approximately a year ago, Jennifer began to experience some mild symptoms of dizziness and dimmed vision. At first, she disregarded the symptoms, attributing them to overwork. However, they persisted for several weeks, and she consulted her physician. He thought that they might be a side effect of the medication she had been taking to increase fertility. Jennifer's treatment protocol was changed, and shortly afterward, much to the couple's delight, Jennifer became pregnant.

Unfortunately, the symptoms she had experienced earlier began to worsen, and she noticed some mild tremors in her arms and legs as well. Jennifer's physician referred her to a specialist, who tentatively diagnosed a progressive disease of the central nervous system that has a suspected genetic link and is marked by an unpredictable course. The Lis were devastated by the news. They were very concerned about the risks of the pregnancy to Jennifer's health. They also worried about the possible transmission of the disease to the new baby whom they had wanted for such a long time. In great distress, they sought counseling to help them deal with some of these concerns.

Discussion Questions

1. As a counselor, what are some of the issues you would need to be prepared to discuss with this couple? What information or training do you think you would need in order to deal effectively with this family?
2. List the possible problems faced by this couple as well as the supports available to them. What are the options available to Jennifer and Jianshe?
3. As a genetic counselor, how would you help them in the decision-making process?

To use as a resource:

Patenaude, A. F., Guttmacher, A. E., & Collins, F. S. (2002). Genetic testing and psychology: New roles, new responsibilities. *American Psychologist, 57,* 271–282.

Shiloh, S. (1996). Genetic counseling: A developing area of interest for psychologists. *Professional Psychology: Research and Practice, 27,* 475–486.

Journal Questions

1. Consider one feature of your own development (a trait, talent, behavior). Discuss the development of this feature using the idea of nature-nurture *coaction*. How has this particular feature of your personality influenced other people?
2. Interview your mother or father, if possible, about your prenatal developmental period. What can you learn about this important period of your development?
3. How has increased knowledge about prenatal development changed the behaviors of pregnant women? Are there any beliefs specific to your particular cultural background that shaped the way your mother viewed her pregnancy or acted during her pregnancy? Ask a member of a different culture about the ways that culture views pregnancy.

Key Terms

chromosomes
autosomes
sex chromosomes
karyotype
deoxyribonucleic acid
    (DNA)
intergenic DNA
centromere
mitosis
germ cells
meiosis
ovum
sperm
zygote
implantation
genes
proteins
enzymes
lactase
regulator genes
alleles
genotype
phenotype
dominant-recessive

carrier
codominance
polygenic
X chromosome
Y chromosome
androgens
testosterone
genetic counselors
mutation
progeria
Huntington's chorea
Down syndrome
    (Trisomy 21)
X-linked recessive
    disorders
fragile X syndrome
phenylketonuria (PKU)
molecular genetics
gene expression
Human Genome Project
behavior genetics
identical, or monozygotic,
    twins

fraternal, or dizygotic,
    twins
heritability
nonshared environment
shared environment
passive gene effects
evocative gene effects
active gene effects
niche picking
transcription
ribonucleic acid (RNA)
coaction
genotype-environment
    interaction
epigenetic model
canalization
period of the ovum
neural tube
period of the embryo
cephalo-caudal
proximo-distal
period of the fetus
somatic cell therapy

germline gene therapy
teratogens
placenta
fetal alcohol syndrome
    (FAS)
fetal alcohol effects (FAE)
no observable effect level
lowest observable adverse
    effect level
kwashiorkor
eustress
distress
alarm phase
resistance phase
exhaustion phase
hypothalamic-pituitary-
    adrenal axis (HPA axis)
adrenocorticotropic
    hormone (ACTH)
epinephrine
norepinephrine
cortisol

3

Neural and Cognitive Developments in the Early Years

Is there any value for helping professionals in learning the details of infant and preschool development? Of course, some clinicians work primarily with infants, preschoolers, and their parents, and the benefits to them are clear. But what about helpers for whom the majority of clients will be older children, adolescents, and adults? As you have already seen, developments at these later ages cannot be divorced from earlier events. Skills, abilities, and tendencies that develop in the early years of life establish trajectories that influence the progress and direction of later developments. To put it simply, who a person will become is at least partially channeled even before birth. Pre- and postnatal brain development are particularly important elements of developmental knowledge.

Consider this analogy: any discussion of specific counseling techniques would be incomplete without first understanding the fundamental principles of the counseling theory from which they are derived. It is difficult to imagine that helpers could be expected to develop, for example, a cognitive-behavioral treatment plan for depressed adolescents without first understanding how cognitive-behavioral therapy is supposed to work. Imagine, as well, a helper who is expected to embark on a therapeutic relationship with a young adult client without ever hearing about the concept of empathy. These counselors might muddle through, but how effective would they be?

While this analogy may be a stretch, trying to understand how people develop without understanding how their brains work is similar. You might not miss the obvious physical and behavioral changes your clients exhibit, but part of the mystery behind them would elude you. The new millenium began following a decade of intensive brain research, aided by new technologies. It is important to understand how far scientists have come in unraveling the complexities of this most mysterious part of human beings. Helpers of all theoretical bents stand to understand better how their clients *think and feel and learn* if they give some attention to the workings of this marvelous internal organ, the brain. In this chapter, we describe prenatal brain development. We then go on to look at the emergence of perceptual, motor, and cognitive skills in early childhood. In the next two chapters, we will consider parallel developments in the social and emotional life of the young child.

THE BRAIN

Early Prenatal Brain Development

When you were just a two-week-old embryo, your very existence still unknown to your parents, cells from the embryo's upper surface (see Chapter 2) began to form a sheet that rearranged itself by turning inward and curling into a *neural tube.* This phenomenon, called *neurulation,* signaled the beginning of your central nervous system's development. Once formed, this structure was covered over by another sheet of cells, to become your skin, and was moved inside you so that the rest of your body could develop around it. Around the 25th day of your gestational life, your neural tube began to take on a pronounced curved shape. At the top of your "C-shaped" embryonic self, three distinct bulges appeared, which eventually became your hindbrain, midbrain, and forebrain. (See Figure 3.1: *Stages of Brain Development.*)

Within the primitive neural tube, important events were occurring. Cells from the interior surface of the neural tube reproduced to form *neurons,* or nerve cells, that would become the building blocks of your brain. From about the 40th day, or 5th week, of gestation, your neurons began to increase at a staggering rate—one quarter of a million per minute for nine months—to create the 100 billion neurons that make up a baby's brain at birth. At least half would be destroyed later either because they were not necessary or were not used. We will have more to say about this loss of neurons later.

Your neurons began to migrate outward from their place of birth rather like filaments extending from the neural tube to various sites in your still incomplete brain. Supporting cells called *glia,* stretching from the inside of the neural tube to its outside, provided a type of scaffolding for your neurons, guiding them as they ventured out on their way to their final destinations. Those neurons that developed first migrated only a short distance from your neural tube and were destined to become the *hindbrain.* Those that developed later, traveled a little farther and ultimately formed the *midbrain.* Those that developed last migrated the farthest to populate the *cerebral cortex* of the *forebrain.* This development always progressed from the inside out, so that cells traveling the farthest had to migrate through several other already formed layers in order to reach their proper location. To build the six layers of your cortex, a neuron with genetically influenced knowledge of its ultimate address had to move through the bottom layers that had been already built up before it could get to the outside layer. (See Box 3.1: *The Major Structures of the Brain* and Figures 3.2 and 3.3.)

Scientists have discovered that neurons sometimes need to find their destinations (for example, on the part of the cortex specialized for vision) before that part of the cortex develops. It's a little like traveling in outer space. Or as Davis (1997) has suggested, "It's a bit like an arrow reaching the space where the bull's-eye will be before anyone has even set up the target" (pp. 54–55). Certain cells behave like signposts, providing the traveling neurons with way stations as they progress on their journey. Neurons may also respond to the presence of certain chemicals that guide their movements in a particular direction.

About the 4th month of your prenatal life, your brain's basic structures were formed. Your neurons migrated in an orderly way and clustered with similar cells into distinct sections or regions in your brain, such as in the cerebral cortex or in the specific *nuclei.* The term *nucleus* here refers to a cluster of cells creating a structure, rather than to the kind of nucleus that is found in a single cell. An example is the *caudate nucleus,* part of the *basal ganglia* in the brain's interior. Like-minded neurons that clustered in these areas or structures were destined to handle certain kinds of information. Figure 3.3 presents a picture of the major functional areas of the cerebral cortex.

FIGURE 3.1

Stages of Brain Development

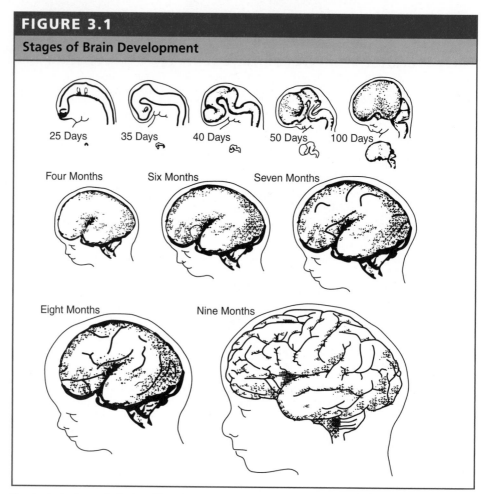

The developing human brain viewed from the side in a succession of embryonic and fetal stages. The small figures beneath the first five embryonic stages are in proper relative proportion to the last five figures.
Source: Cowan, W. M. The development of the brain. In Llinas, R. R. (Ed.) *The workings of the brain* (p. 41). *Scientific American* (Sept. 1979) p. 166. Illustration by Tom Prentiss. Reproduced by permission of the illustrator.

One important current debate concerns just how this specialization occurs and what directs it. Do the neurons possess a "protomap" (Rakic, 1988) that tells them where to locate and what to do? Or are the functions of neurons somehow influenced by the environmental input they receive (O'Leary, 1989)? This issue is still controversial and extraordinarily complicated to research. However, most available evidence supports the view that cortical differentiation is primarily influenced by the kinds of environmental inputs the cortex receives. In other words, the geography of the cortex is not rigidly built in but responds to activity and experiences by making changes in its structural organization. This principle was demonstrated by researchers who transplanted part of the visual cortex of an animal to its parietal lobe (O'Leary & Stanfield, 1989). The transplanted neurons began to process somatosensory rather than visual information. Studies such as these have shown that the brain is amazingly malleable and demonstrates great ***plasticity,*** particularly during early stages of development. In time, however, most cells become specialized for their activity, and it is harder to reverse their operation.

Box 3.1   The Major Structures of the Brain

The human brain is composed of three main parts, forebrain, midbrain, and hindbrain, which reflect the evolutionary history of this amazing organ. The oldest part, or hindbrain, evolved more than five hundred million years ago and "carries our evolution inside us" (Ornstein & Thompson, 1984). This particular part of the brain has been called the reptilian brain because it is the most primitive and even looks like a reptile's brain. Refer to Figure 3.2 for a depiction of the brain structures described here.

The main parts of the hindbrain, the *medulla,* the *pons,* the *cerebellum,* and the *reticular formation,* regulate *autonomic functions* that are outside our conscious control. The medulla contains nuclei that regulate functions that are basic for survival, such as heart rate, blood pressure, and respiration. Damage to this area of the brain can be fatal. The pons, situated above the medulla, is involved in the regulation of the sleep-wake cycle. Individuals with sleep disturbances can sometimes have abnormal activity in this area. The medulla and the pons are also especially sensitive to an overdose of drugs or alcohol. Drug effects on these structures can cause suffocation and death. The pons transmits nerve impulses to the cerebellum, a structure that looks like a smaller version of the brain itself. The cerebellum is involved in the planning, coordination, and smoothness of complex motor activities such as hitting a tennis ball or dancing.

Within the *brainstem* (medulla, pons, and midbrain) is a bundle of neural tissue called the reticular formation. This structure acts together with specific nuclei to form the *reticular activating system,* that part of the brain that alerts the higher structures to "pay attention" to incoming stimuli. This system also filters out the extraneous stimuli that we perceive at any point in time. For example, it is possible for workers who share an office to tune out the speech, music, or general background hum going on around them when they are involved in important telephone conversations. However, they can easily "perk up" and attend if a coworker calls their name.

The midbrain, the next highest structure on the evolutionary scale, consists of several small structures (*superior colliculi, inferior colliculi,* and *substantia nigra*) that are involved in vision, hearing, and consciousness. The midbrain is also a part of the reticular activating system. These parts of the brain receive sensory input from the eyes and ears and are instrumental in controlling eye movement.

The forebrain is, by far, the dominant part of the brain and is the part that most clearly differentiates us as human. Its most recognizable aspect is the *cerebrum,* which comprises two thirds of the total mass. A crevice, or fissure, divides the cerebrum into two halves, like the halves of a walnut. Information is transferred between the two halves by a network of fibers comprising the *corpus callosum.* These halves are referred to as the left and right hemispheres. Research on *hemispheric specialization* pioneered by Sperry (1964) demonstrated that the left hemisphere controls functioning of the right side of the body and vice versa. Language functions such as vocabulary knowledge and speech are usually localized in the left hemisphere, and visual-spatial skills are localized on the right. Recently, this research was introduced to lay readers through a rash of popular books about left brain–right brain differences. Overall, many of these publications have distorted the facts and oversimplified the findings. Generally the hemispheres work together, sharing information via the corpus callosum and cooperating with each other in the execution of most tasks (Geschwind, 1990). There is no reliable evidence that underlying modes of thinking, personality traits, or cultural differences can be traced to left-right hemispheric lateralization.

Each hemisphere of the cerebral cortex can be further divided into lobes, or areas of functional specialization (see Figure 3.3). The *occipital lobe,* located at the back of the head, handles visual information. The *temporal lobe,* found on the sides of each hemisphere, is responsible for auditory processing. At the top of each hemisphere, behind a fissure called the *central sulcus,* is the *parietal lobe.* This area is responsible for the processing of somatosensory information such as touch, temperature, and pain. Finally, the *frontal lobe,* situated at the top front part of each hemisphere, controls voluntary muscle movements and higher-level cognitive functions such as planning, goal setting, and decision making. A great deal of the cortex, approximately three quarters, is not so clearly specified for primary involvement in vision, hearing, sensory, or motor functions. This area is called *association area,* and its job is to integrate information coming from the various primary cortical areas. It appears to be important for complex cognitive functioning.

Completing the forebrain are the structures of the *limbic system (hippocampus, amygdala,* and *septum),*

(continued)

Box 3.1 **Continued**

the *thalamus,* and the *hypothalamus.* Along with the thalamus, these structures work to produce feelings such as pleasure, pain, anger, sexuality, fear, and affection. Often referred to as the "emotional brain," the limbic system works in concert with other parts of the brain, such as the frontal lobes, to help us think and reason. We will have more to say about the workings of the emotional brain and its ties to several emotional disorders in a later chapter. (See Box 4.1 in Chapter 4.)

The structures of the limbic system have direct connections with neurons from the olfactory bulb, which is responsible for our sense of smell. It has been noted that pheromones, a particular kind of hormonal substance secreted by animals and humans, can trigger particular reactions that affect emotional responsivity below the level of conscious awareness. While the evidence is still suggestive, there is some support for the belief that humans can sense sexual signals by means of pheromones (Grammer, 1993). Other parts of the limbic system, most notably the hippocampus, are very important in the process of learning and the formation of memory.

The thalamus is a primary way station for handling neural communication, something like "information central." It receives information from the sense of sight, hearing, touch, taste, and the limbic system and sends these messages to their appropriate destinations. For example, the thalamus projects visual information, received via the optic nerve, to the occipital lobe. The hypothalamus is divided into groups of neurons called nuclei, which help sort out the information.

Consequently, the thalamus behaves like an efficient switchboard operator in a large company, who takes incoming calls and connects the caller with the proper office. A study by Andreason and colleagues (1994) reveals that the thalamus is much smaller in the brains of schizophrenic patients than in those of normal individuals, suggesting that an unregulated flood of stimulation may be overwhelming and lead to disorganized thinking.

The hypothalamus, situated below the thalamus, is a small but important structure that regulates hunger, thirst, body temperature, and breathing rate. Lesions in areas of the hypothalamus have been found to produce eating abnormalities in animals, including obesity (Leibowitz, Hammer, & Chang, 1981) or starvation (Anand & Brobeck, 1951). It is also important in the regulation of emotional responses. Recall our discussion of the stress response from Chapter 2. The hypothalamus functions as an intermediary, translating the emotional messages received from the cortex and the amygdala into a command to the *endocrine system* to release stress hormones in preparation for fight or flight. The hypothalamus is involved in the expression of sexual behavior as well. Although results are still inconclusive, LeVay (1991) found that the size of one of the hypothalamic nuclei is twice as large in heterosexual men as in homosexual men. This evidence has been seen as an indicator of a biological basis for sexual orientation. As we can see, the size of the various brain structures as well as the brain's patterns of neural connections and levels of neurotransmitters all play a part in shaping the individual's personality and behavior.

Structure and Function of Neurons

The neurons in your brain are one of nature's most fantastic accomplishments. Although neurons come in various sizes and shapes, a typical neuron is composed of a cell body with a long extension, or *axon,* which is like a cable attached to a piece of electronic equipment. The axon itself can be quite long relative to the size of the cell's other structures because it needs to connect or "wire" various parts of the brain, such as the visual thalamus to the visual cortex. At the end of the axon are the *axon terminals,* which contain tiny sacs of chemical substances called *neurotransmitters,* such as serotonin. Growing out from the cell body are smaller projections, called *dendrites,* resembling little branches, which send or receive messages or transmissions from other neurons. The unique structure of the neuron equips it to do its job very effectively. (See Figure 3.4: *Structure of a Neuron.*)

So how do brain cells "talk" to each other? Even though we speak of wiring or connecting, each neuron does not actually make physical contact with other neurons but

FIGURE 3.2

The Major Structures of the Brain

Hindbrain, Midbrain, and Forebrain
This is a picture of the brain from the left side. Beneath the cortex are three parts of the brain: the hindbrain, the midbrain, and the forebrain. The hindbrain controls some basic processes necessary for life. The midbrain is a relay station to the brain. The forebrain is where complex thoughts, motives, and emotions are stored and processed.

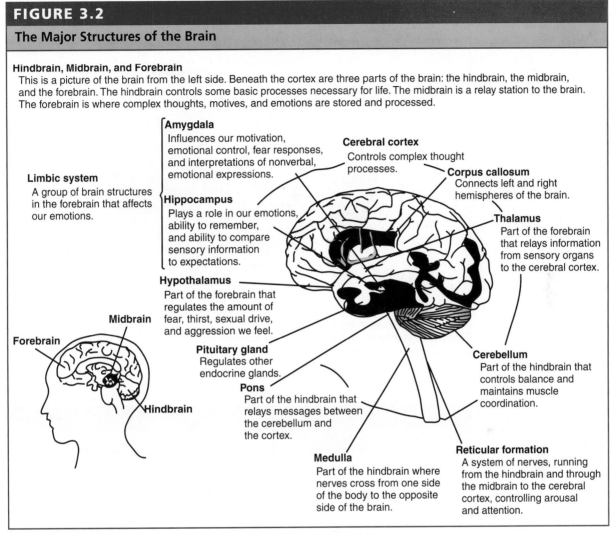

Amygdala
Influences our motivation, emotional control, fear responses, and interpretations of nonverbal, emotional expressions.

Cerebral cortex
Controls complex thought processes.

Corpus callosum
Connects left and right hemispheres of the brain.

Limbic system
A group of brain structures in the forebrain that affects our emotions.

Hippocampus
Plays a role in our emotions, ability to remember, and ability to compare sensory information to expectations.

Thalamus
Part of the forebrain that relays information from sensory organs to the cerebral cortex.

Hypothalamus
Part of the forebrain that regulates the amount of fear, thirst, sexual drive, and aggression we feel.

Midbrain

Forebrain

Pituitary gland
Regulates other endocrine glands.

Hindbrain

Pons
Part of the hindbrain that relays messages between the cerebellum and the cortex.

Cerebellum
Part of the hindbrain that controls balance and maintains muscle coordination.

Medulla
Part of the hindbrain where nerves cross from one side of the body to the opposite side of the brain.

Reticular formation
A system of nerves, running from the hindbrain and through the midbrain to the cerebral cortex, controlling arousal and attention.

Source: Psychology by L. Uba and K. Huang, ©1999. Reprinted by permission of Pearson Education, Inc., Upper Saddle River, N.J.

remains separate. Communication is a process of sending and receiving electrochemical messages. Simply put, when a neuron responds to some excitation, or when it "fires," the electrical impulse, or message, travels down the axon to the axon terminals. The sacs in the axon terminals containing neurotransmitters burst and release their contents into the space between the neurons called the **synaptic gap**. This chemical message, once picked up by the dendrites, the cell body, or axon of the neighboring neuron, is read by that cell as a message to "fire" or "stop firing." The speed of these messages is increased when glial cells wrap themselves around the axon, thus facilitating conduction. This phenomenon, called **myelination,** begins prenatally for neurons in the sensorimotor areas of the brain but happens later in other areas. The myelination of some areas of the frontal cortex is not complete until adolescence or even later (Michel & Moore, 1995).

Neurons are not "wired together" randomly. Rather, they are joined via their synaptic connections into groups called **circuits.** Circuits are part of larger organizations of neurons,

FIGURE 3.3
The Cerebral Cortex

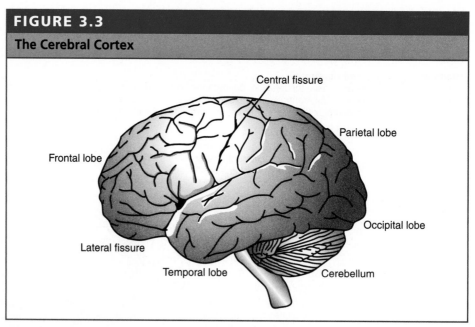

Source: From *Psychology,* Fourth Edition, by Henry Gleitman. Copyright © 1995, 1991, 1986, 1981 by W. W. Norton & Company, Inc. Used by permission of W. W. Norton & Company, Inc.

FIGURE 3.4
Structure of a Neuron

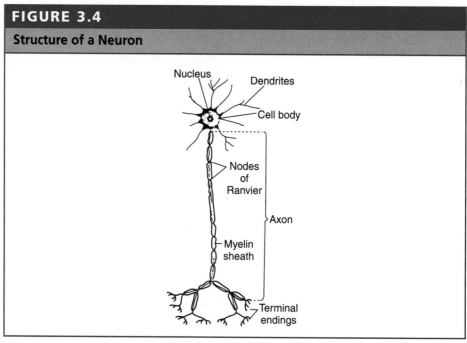

Source: From *Psychology,* Fourth Edition, by Henry Gleitman. Copyright © 1995, 1991, 1986, 1981 by W. W. Norton & Company, Inc. Used by permission of W. W. Norton & Company, Inc.

called systems, such as the visual and olfactory systems. Two main types of neurons populate these systems, **projection neurons,** which have axons that extend far away from the cell body, and **interneurons,** which branch out closer to the local area (see Katz & Shatz, 1996). The intricate neural fireworks described earlier are going on all the time in your brain. Perhaps as you read this chapter, you are also listening to music and drinking a cup of coffee. Or you may be distracted by thoughts of a telephone conversation that you had earlier. The neuronal circuitry in your brain is processing all these stimuli, allowing for your experiences to be perceived and comprehended.

Later Prenatal Brain Development

To return to your prenatal life story, your neurons began to fire spontaneously around the fourth month of gestation. This happened despite a lack of sensory input. Even though your eyes were not completely formed, the neurons that would later process visual information began firing as though they were preparing for the work they would do in a few months' time. By the end of the second and beginning of the third trimesters, your sense organs had developed sufficiently to respond to perceptual stimulation from outside your mother's womb. Sounds were heard by 15 weeks. Not only did you learn to recognize the sound of your mother's voice, but you became familiar as well with the rhythms and patterns of your native language. DeCasper and colleagues (1994) conducted an interesting study in which they directed pregnant women to recite a child's nursery rhyme out loud each day from the 33rd to the 37th week of pregnancy. During the 38th week, the women were asked to listen to a recording of either the familiar rhyme or an unfamiliar one while their fetuses' heart rates were being measured. The fetal heart rates dropped for the group who heard the familiar rhyme, signifying attention, but did not change for the group who heard the unfamiliar one. This result suggests that the fetus can attend to and discriminate the cadence of the rhyme. Studies such as this one should not be misinterpreted to mean that the fetus can "learn" as the term is commonly used. No one has suggested that the fetus can understand the poem. However, what this and other similar studies do indicate is an early responsivity to experience that begins to shape the contours of the brain by establishing patterns of neural or synaptic connections.

By your 25th week, you could open and close your eyes. You could see light then rather like the way you see things now when you turn toward a bright light with your eyes closed. At this point in development a fetus turns her head toward a light source. Sensory experience is critical for healthy brain development, and vision provides a good example of this principle. The interplay between neurons and visual experience was documented dramatically by Wiesel and Hubel (1965), who, in a series of experiments with kittens for which they won the Nobel prize, showed that early visual deprivation has permanently deleterious effects. They sewed shut one of each kitten's eyes at birth so that only one eye was exposed to visual input. Several weeks later when the eyes were reopened, the kittens were found to be permanently blinded in the eye that had been deprived of stimulation. No amount of intervention or aggressive treatment could repair the damage. The neurons needed visual stimulation in order to make the proper connections for sight; in the absence of stimulation, the connections were never made, and blindness resulted. The existence of a **critical period** for visual development was established. This research prompted surgeons to remove infant cataracts very shortly after birth so that permanent damage to sight could be avoided, instead of waiting several years.

Sensory systems, such as the auditory and visual systems, influence each other so that their eventual development is a function of their interrelationships. The integration of these systems seems to serve the baby well in making sense of her world. So, for example, when a 4-month-old sees an object she also has some sense of how it feels. (See the discussion of *intermodal perception* later in this chapter.)

The amount of stimulation is also important. A series of recent studies lends support to the idea that there is an optimal range of sensory input that is necessary for proper development. Too much stimulation or too little can cause disturbances in the sensory systems at birth. Moreover, from birth and perhaps even before, babies partially control how much or how little sensory stimulation they experience. Lewkowicz and Turkewitz (1980, 1981) showed that young infants attend to high- or low-arousing visual and auditory stimuli depending upon their own level of arousal. For example, if they are hungry they pay less attention to highly arousing external stimuli. Scientists continue to examine the interaction between the amount of stimulation, the timing of the stimulation, and the arousal level of the individual, which together influence the way sensory systems develop.

Postnatal Brain Development

After your birth, your neurons continued to reproduce at a rapid pace, finally slowing down around 12 months of age (Huttenlocher, 1994). Except for those pruned or lost, the neurons you formed as an embryo will survive until you die. For many years it was assumed that nerve cells do not reproduce after early infancy. Recent research, however, has documented the duplication of neurons in the hippocampus of adults, thus shedding new light on this issue and raising new questions about typical brain development (Kempermann & Gage, 1999). Nonetheless, it still appears that most brain growth after birth is due not to the creation of more neurons but to the formation of **synapses,** new connections among neurons. The growth spurt in synapses reflects the vast amount of learning that typically occurred for you and for most babies in the early months of postnatal life. Some areas of your developing brain experienced periods of rapid synaptic growth after birth, such as in the visual and auditory cortices, which increased dramatically between 3 and 4 months. In contrast, the synapses in your prefrontal cortex developed more slowly and reached their maximum density around 12 months. As you will see in the following sections, infants make rapid strides in cognitive development at the end of the first year, at about the time when prefrontal synapses have reached their peak density.

The growth of these connections was the product of both internal and external factors. Certain chemical substances within your brain, such as **nerve growth factor,** were absorbed by the neurons and aided in the production of synapses. Your own prenatal actions, such as turning, sucking your thumb, and kicking, as well as the other sensory stimulation you experienced, such as sound, light, and pressure, all contributed to synaptic development. However, as we noted above, the major work of **synaptogenesis,** the generation of synapses, took place after birth, when much more sensory stimulation became available.

You arrived in the world with many more neurons than you would ever need. Over the next twelve years or so, through a process known as **neural pruning,** many neurons would die off, and many synaptic connections would be selectively discarded. Some of these neurons migrated incorrectly and failed to make the proper connections, rendering them useless. Some of the synaptic connections were never established or were rarely used, so they ultimately disappeared as well. What counts most after birth is not the sheer number of neurons, but the number and strength of the interconnections. Those branching points of contact that remained to constitute your brain would be a unique reflection of your genetics, the conditions of your prenatal period, the nutrition you received, and your postnatal experience and environment. This rich network of connections makes for your thinking, feeling brain, and its structure depends heavily upon what happens to you both before and after your birth.

You may be wondering how to account for the simultaneous processes of synaptogenesis and pruning, which seem to be acting at cross-purposes. What is the point of making new synaptic connections if many will just be culled eventually? Greenough and Black (1992) offer an explanation for the apparent contradiction. They argue that **synaptic overproduction** occurs when it is highly likely that nature will provide the appropriate experience to structure the development of a particular system. For example, many animal species, as well as humans, go through a predictable sequence of activities designed to provide information for the brain to use in the development of vision. These include opening eyes, reaching for and grasping objects, and so on. This type of development depends upon environmental input that is **experience-expectant** because it is experience that is part of the evolutionary history of the organism and that occurs reliably in most situations. Hence, it is "expected." Lack of such experience results in developmental abnormalities, as we saw in the kitten experiments performed by Hubel and Wiesel. The timing of this particular kind of experience for nervous system growth is typically very important; that is, there is a *critical period* for such experience-expectant development. Nature may provide for an overabundance of synapses because it then can select only those that work best, pruning out the rest. This process may "fine-tune" the quality of a system and could be critical to species survival.

In contrast to overproducing synapses in anticipation of later experience, some synaptic growth occurs as a direct result of exposure to more individualized kinds of environmental events. This type of neural growth is called **experience-dependent.** The quality of the synaptic growth "depends" upon variations in environmental opportunities. Consider the differences in synaptic development between children raised by parents who speak two different languages in their home and children raised by those who speak only one. Or imagine the synaptic growth of an infant raised in impoverished conditions with very little verbal interaction from adults, and very little chance to explore the environment, as compared to that of an infant reared in an environment rich in adult attention and opportunities for engagement with interesting objects. Experience-dependent processes do not seem to be limited to sensitive periods but can occur throughout the life span. Connections that remain active become stabilized, whereas those that are not used die out. This type of experientially responsive synaptic growth and the concomitant changes in brain structure it induces have been linked to learning and the formation of some kinds of memory.

Sensory and Motor Development

From what you have just read, it should be obvious that babies have a number of emerging competencies at birth, which enable them to begin to interact with the world and with their caregivers. This understanding, however, is of fairly recent origin. Only a few decades ago, newborns were considered almost blind and deaf, virtual "blank slates" waiting for the first environmental imprint. Some of this thinking persists in the often-expressed idea that nurture begins after birth or in the lack of appreciation for the *temperament* differences found among newborns (see Chapter 4). Nonetheless, it is true that the major work of cognitive, emotional, and sensorimotor development will occur over the baby's early years. During the first 12 months of life, the sensory and motor systems that functioned in a rudimentary way prenatally develop greatly and become more smoothly integrated. Table 3.1 provides examples of major milestones in sensory and motor development.

Sometimes, communication between the motor systems and the sensory systems (touch, sight, hearing, balance, and movement) does not develop in a coordinated way.

TABLE 3.1

Major Milestones in Motor, Visual, and Auditoy Development

Age	Motor Development		Visual Development	Auditory Development
	Gross Motor	Fine Motor		
1 Month	Lifts head.	Holds things placed in hands.	Visual acuity: 20/600; scans edges of figures and visual objects.	Alert to sounds; prefers sound of mother's voice.
2 Months			Visual acuity: 20/300; shows preference for faces over objects; discriminates basic colors.	
3 Months			Faces (especially mother's face) perceived as attractive; scans interiors of faces and objects.	Locates where sounds come from.
4 Months	Sits with support; rolls over from front to back.	Visually guided reaching.	Visual acuity: 20/160; smooth tracking of slowly moving objects; development of *stereopsis*, or ability to perceive depth based upon information from both left and right eyes.	
5 Months				
6 Months				Coordination of vision and hearing; turns eyes to nearby sounds smoothly.
7 Months	Sits without support.	Transfers objects from hand to hand; plays with simple toys.	Visual acuity: 20/80.	
8 Months				

Difficulties such as extreme hypersensitivity or hyposensitivity to sensations such as bright lights, loud sounds, pain, certain textures, or human touch; motor clumsiness; balance problems; fidgeting; and poor eye-hand coordination, to name some of the most common, may be part of a disorder called ***sensory integration dysfunction.*** Recognition of this problem is becoming more frequent, and interventions, such as those performed by occupational therapists, can be done to ameliorate the symptoms (Greenspan & Weider, 1997). Even in normal children, sensory and cognitive development is somewhat uneven, with certain abilities, such as vision, developing faster than others, such as problem solving. Scientists have begun to link these sequences of sensorimotor and cognitive development to actual brain changes. For example, Fischer (1987) has provided evidence for a

TABLE 3.1
Continued

Age	Motor Development		Visual Development	Auditory Development
	Gross Motor	Fine Motor		
9 Months	Crawls.	Pincer grasp.	Interprets others' facial expressions.	
10 Months	Stands holding on; drops and throws things.			
11 Months				
12 Months	Walks holding on.	Scribbles with crayon.	Visual acuity: 20/20.	
12–18 Months	Walks alone.			
18–23 Months		Draws lines; constructs simple tower; drinks from cup using one hand.		
2–3 Years	Runs, jumps, climbs; balance improves; kicks ball forward. Stands on one foot briefly.	Pours milk; dressing and feeding improves; builds towers of 6 blocks; turns pages in book.	Oldest age at which surgical correction of crossed eyes for depth perception can be successful.	
3–4 Years	Walks up stairs alternating feet; walks on tiptoes; throwing improves; buttons clothing; eats with spoon and fork.	Completes simple puzzles; uses art materials, scissors; more careful in execution of art and drawing projects.	Continued integration of visual-motor systems.	
4–5 Years	Ties knots; dresses and undresses easily.	More skillful with scissors.		

convergence between Piaget's stages of sensorimotor development (see the next sections of this chapter) and the sequence of synaptic bursts that occur over the first year of life.

COGNITIVE DEVELOPMENT

If you had to guess, would you say that more intellectual growth occurs in the first few years of life or in the transition from childhood to adulthood? John Flavell, a noted cognitive researcher, has argued that "The brief span from young infancy to young childhood is marked by a momentous transformation of the cognitive system unparalleled by any other period of life" (Flavell, Miller, & Miller, 1993). In this section, we look first at how Jean Piaget described the vast changes that occur in these early years. Then, we examine a few of the many intellectual changes that take place from earliest infancy through the preschool years, with an eye to evaluating how well Piaget's theory accounts for these changes. And finally, we take a look at another major theory of cognitive development, that of Lev S. Vygotsky, whose ideas and findings were compatible with Piaget's in many ways but who added a special emphasis on the importance of culture and social experience to the story of intellectual change in childhood.

Piaget's Constructivist Theory

Debbie, age 10, and Mark, age 4, are overheard discussing their mother's pregnancy. Their parents have read them children's books about how babies are conceived and born, and the topic has been discussed openly in the family. The children have the following conversation:

> DEBBIE: "Do you know how the baby got there?"
> MARK: "Sure. Mommy got a duck."
> DEBBIE: "A duck?"
> MARK: "Yeah, they just get a duck or rabbit and it grows a little more and it turns into a baby."
> DEBBIE: "A duck will turn into a baby?"
> MARK: "Sure. They give them some food, people food, and they grow into a baby."
> DEBBIE: "Where did you get that idea?"
> MARK: "I saw it in a book and Mommy and Daddy told me."

Piaget was one of the first theorists to propose that children actively construct their knowledge.

DEBBIE: "They told you that ducks turn into babies?"

MARK: "Yeah!" (As reported by P. A. Cowan, 1978, adapted from Bernstein & Cowan, 1975).

This anecdote illustrates a fundamental feature of learning, knowing, and understanding according to Piaget's theory: that the human mind *constructs* its knowledge. When infants and children are presented with new stimuli or pieces of information, what is learned or stored is not just a "true" reflection of what comes from the environment. That is, new information is not simply written on a blank slate, as John Locke and other empiricists assumed. Rather, children learn by a process of **adaptation**. First, they interpret new stimulation in ways that fit with what they already know, sometimes distorting it as a result. This aspect of adaptation is called **assimilation**. As the new information is assimilated, the child's existing knowledge may be modified somewhat, providing a better match or fit to what is new. The latter process is called **accommodation**. Assimilation and accommodation are complementary activities involved in every interaction with the environment. In order to accommodate (learn), children must be able to assimilate. In other words, they cannot learn something that they cannot make some sense out of already. And assimilation often means that new information is distorted or changed so that sense *can* be made of it! A child's understandings are gradually changed as a result of interactions with the environment, although what a child will learn in any single step is always shaped by what the child already knows, and the new "understanding" may not be a completely accurate reflection of reality. In Mark's case, his parents' explanations, which apparently included comparing human reproduction to ducks laying eggs, far outstripped Mark's knowledge structures, and Mark's assimilation and accommodation of his parents' elaborate explanations produced a charmingly naive linear progression: ducks turn into people.

Piaget spent a lifetime doing intensive research on the development of knowledge; he wrote dozens of books on his findings and hundreds of articles (see Box 3.2: *Biographical Sketch: Jean Piaget*). His own ideas evolved and changed as new work was completed, discussed, and challenged by scientists around the world. Since his death, developmental researchers have followed up on his pioneering work, and, naturally, the field has moved on. Not all of his ideas have been corroborated, but in a remarkable number of areas, his research has been the starting point for more expanded, clarifying work, and his theoretical explanations have informed newer theories.

The idea that knowledge is *constructed* by the developing child (and adult!) is a Piagetian view that has become an underlying assumption of much of the current research on cognitive development and educational practice (e.g., APA, 1995). This constructivist stance takes the child to be an active participant in the learning process, constantly seeking out and trying to make sense of new information. In other words, children are **intrinsically motivated** to learn—another idea that is widely accepted by modern developmental scientists. Piaget also considered a child's active exploration to be *organized* and *organizing*. When children assimilate new information to what they already know they are fitting the new information into an organized way of thinking—some sort of knowledge structure. And when they accommodate their knowledge structures to fit what is new in the environment, the organization is changing. (We will have more to say about knowledge structures in later chapters.) That mental activity is organized and that the organization evolves in response to the environment are further Piagetian notions that seem to be taken for granted by many modern researchers.

Thus, many widely accepted assumptions about cognitive development are derived from Piaget. But some of his fundamental ideas are particularly controversial. Among these is the idea that cognitive development can be characterized by stages (see Chapter 1).

Box 3.2   Biographical Sketch: Jean Piaget

Jean Piaget (1896–1980) was remarkably precocious as a child, publishing his first scholarly paper at the age of 10. At 14, after producing a series of scientific reports, he was offered a position as curator of a museum of natural history—an offer promptly withdrawn when his age was discovered! Piaget completed a bachelor's degree by age 18 and a Ph.D. by 22, despite spending a year away from school when he suffered a nervous breakdown (which he later attributed to his study of philosophy). His early education, research, and writing ranged widely from biological science (his first published article reported his observations of an albino sparrow), to mathematics and logic, to experimental psychology, to psychoanalysis, to psychopathology. He even wrote a philosophical novel! He found a way to integrate many of his interests when he was hired by Henri Simon, an early developer of IQ tests, to standardize an English test with French children. Piaget soon lost interest in the task he was assigned—asking children test questions, recording their responses, and specifying whether they were right or wrong for the purposes of quantifying intelligence. But he was intrigued by the qualitative features of children's answers. Even children's wrong answers often seemed to reveal an underlying structure or pattern of thought. While studying psychopathology, Piaget had learned to conduct clinical interviews with mental patients. Now,

he began to combine clinical interview techniques with the use of standardized questions in an effort to reveal the nature of children's knowledge and reasoning. After publishing several articles on his findings, Piaget was invited to become the director of studies in the Institute Jean Jacques Rousseau in Geneva, a center for scientific child study and teacher training. At the age of 25, his life's work had begun. Until his death at 84, Piaget wrote prolifically on the development of children's knowledge, reporting an endless stream of studies, and constructing a wide-ranging, coherent theory. His empirical methods combined observations of children's hands-on problem solving with the probing, clinical interview technique that he pioneered in Simon's laboratory. He originated a remarkable array of problem tasks that are easy for adults to solve but not for children, revealing what appeared to be astonishing age changes in our reasoning about the world. As Piaget put it, "Just as the tadpole already breathes, though with different organs from those of the frog, so the child acts like the adult, but employing a mentality whose structure varies according to the stages of its development" (1970, p. 153).

It is rare today to find any subject in cognitive development, from perception to mathematical reasoning to memory to social perspective taking, for which Piaget did not pose key questions and design provocative,

Although Piaget saw cognitive change as the result of small, gradual reorganizations of knowledge structures, he described periods of time in which all of a child's mental structures can be expected to have some organizational properties in common. For example, the infancy and preschool periods covered in this chapter were divided by Piaget into two stages, the **sensorimotor stage** (from birth to about age 2) and the **preoperational stage** (between ages 2 and 7). Each of these stages was further divided into substages. The notion of stages implies that children's understandings within a stage (or a substage) about many different things will have some general similarities. So, for example, in the early preoperational stage, whether we are examining a child's understanding of number or causality, we should be able to detect some similarities in the ways in which children organize their thinking about these concepts. Although Piaget did find many such similarities, more recent research, using different kinds of tasks, often finds less support for the notion of overarching stages. In particular, newer work suggests that infants and preschoolers sometimes show signs of understandings that Piaget believed to be possible only for much older children. And children's progress in understanding concepts from different domains of knowledge is not always organized or structured in the same ways at the same time. In fact, an important addition to cognitive developmental work since Piaget is the idea that progress is often **domain specific.** That is, development can proceed at different rates in different domains. Domains that have been studied in detail include number concepts, morality, biological versus physical realities, and so on. For example, if

Box 3.2   Continued

ingenious research tasks. Given the breadth, depth, and complexity of Piaget's work, it is not surprising that others often oversimplify it in their effort to understand. For example, Piaget has been described as a nativist by some, as an empiricist by others. In fact, Piaget was a true interactionist. He, like modern systems theorists, viewed development as taking place at the proximal interface between the organism and the environment. Biological and psychological systems affect how the knower acts on the environment, and the environment "feeds" the knower. What the environment provides is absorbed and changed by the organism, but the environment also shapes and changes the organism's knowledge.

Educators have been especially affected by Piaget's work, although again, they have sometimes misinterpreted its implications. Piaget saw schooling as an opportunity to provide children with food for their naturally occurring "mental digestion." He warned teachers, however, that children will either memorize new information by rote or ignore it if it is beyond their current level of understanding. But if information is at least partially comprehensible to them or moderately novel, children will actively and eagerly explore and absorb it. Unfortunately, educators have sometimes misinterpreted Piaget's emphasis on children's active exploration as a recommendation that children simply be provided with lots of interesting and fun "stuff" and then left on

their own to learn. Instead, Piaget encouraged educators to plan the presentation of learning opportunities carefully, being especially sensitive to children's current level of functioning in introducing tasks and allowing children to actively explore and discover but recognizing that an orchestrated, if flexible, presentation of tasks aimed at the child's level of understanding can promote development (e.g., 1970).

Interestingly, although Piaget recognized the advantage of teachers' carefully crafting a program of learning opportunities to optimize a child's progress, he was somewhat exasperated by what he referred to as "the American question": "How can we speed up children's development?" He once remarked that kittens have been found to go through some developments in three months that take human babies nine to twelve months to achieve. But "the kitten is not going to go much further. The child has taken longer, but he is capable of going further so it seems to me that the nine months were not for nothing" (as quoted in Elkind, 1968). Respect and appreciation of the human child's cognitive pace is perhaps symptomatic of what made Piaget so successful in uncovering the mysteries of cognitive development in general: an enormous empathy for children.

(Biographical sources: Brainerd, 1996; P. A. Cowan, 1978; Elkind, 1968; Flavell, 1963).

---

we want to learn about children's understanding of causality, we may need to look at it within particular domains of knowledge. Children's understanding of physical causality (e.g., how objects move) may progress differently from their understanding of human or animal agency (e.g., how animate organisms move). We should note that Piaget, in his later years, continued to revise his theory. Recent translations of his later work show that he put less emphasis on stages and more on the dynamic quality of repeated assimilation and accommodation in the context of feedback from the environment (e.g., Piaget, 1975/1985).

Nonetheless, most developmental scientists, clinicians, and educators still find Piaget's stage divisions to be useful for many purposes. On the whole, for example, infants' understandings of many different concepts are more similar to one another's than to those of a 5-year-old. For this reason, in this chapter and in other discussions of cognitive development in this book, we will use Piaget's stage divisions as an aid in describing children's cognitive progress.

Infant Cognition: The Sensorimotor Stage

Infants' cognitive functioning seems more mysterious than that of older children and adults because infants do not talk. We cannot ask them to describe what they can see or how many objects are in front of them or to tell us their solutions to a problem. Most efforts to probe cognition at all other age levels depend on giving verbal instructions, and they usually also require at least some verbal responses from study participants.

How then can we understand what a baby knows, thinks, or even feels? Piaget's research with infants, done primarily with his own three children, focused on detailed analyses of babies' motor interactions with the environment. A newborn's reflexive responses to sensory stimuli—like *looking* and *following* when a visual stimulus moves across the visual field, *head turning* in the direction of a sound, *grasping* at a touch to the palm, and *sucking* at a touch to the lips—were examined under many different stimulus conditions. Piaget carefully noted how these sensorimotor patterns functioned and, especially, how they changed with time and experience. From such observations, Piaget inferred what babies might actually understand or be capable of learning.

Today, additional techniques have been added to the infant research repertoire. Among these, for example, is the **habituation paradigm,** which takes advantage of a baby's tendency to *orient* to new stimulation and to *habituate* to repeated or old stimulation. Suppose, for example, that a baby is propped up in an infant seat in a darkened room in front of a large, blank video screen. Suddenly, a picture of a green circle flashes on the screen. The baby is likely to produce an **orienting response** to this new stimulus. She will look longer at the picture than she had at the blank screen. She will suck more vigorously on the pacifier in her mouth, and her blood pressure and her heart rate are likely to decrease from their previous base rate. If the green circle is repeatedly presented, however, after a time the baby will seem to grow bored with the stimulus. Perhaps it now seems familiar, even "old." We call this response **habituation,** and it is indicated by lower looking times, less vigorous sucking, and a return to base rate for heartbeat and blood pressure. With the help of video cameras and computers, all of these subtle response changes can be closely monitored. Now, suppose we flash a new picture on the screen, a picture of a *yellow* circle. We are looking for a **dishabituation** response, that is, a renewed orienting response, which we will take to mean that the baby has noticed the difference between the first circle and the second, and her interest is renewed. If the baby is a newborn, we will be disappointed. Newborns show no sign of being able to tell the difference between green and yellow: they do not dishabituate to yellow after becoming habituated to green. But if the baby is 3 months old, she probably *will* dishabituate to the yellow stimulus, indicating to us that she can discriminate between the two colors. Thus, we have learned that babies cannot perceive differences between green and yellow when they are born but that by 3 months they can do so.

Research using the habituation paradigm has provided us with much of what we know about the infant's *perceptual* abilities, especially what they can see and hear (described above and in Table 3.1). But researchers are also using habituation methods to make inferences about what babies can understand and how they think, as you will see below. Modern researchers do not always agree about what inferences to draw from such data (e.g., Haith & Benson, 1998), but their work has certainly stimulated a great deal of interest in looking more closely at infant development, and it has led to several challenges of Piaget's ideas. Let's consider now two interesting and important cognitive developments in infancy, combining data from both older and newer approaches.

Understanding Objects

There would be little that you and I would understand about the physical or social world if we did not have a fundamental understanding that there are objects (including human objects, such as ourselves!) with substance and constancy, occupying locations in a spatial field. To become attached to a parent and to begin the process of healthy emotional development, a baby must have some conception of the parent as a permanent, substantive

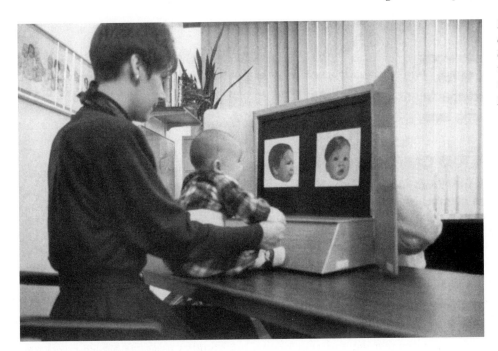

Researchers have learned a great deal about infant cognition and perception using methods that measure habituation or preference.

object in her world (see Chapter 4 for an account of the infant's ability to conceptualize the parent as a separate being).

What must infants understand to "know" about objects—that is, to have an ***object concept?*** First, they need to know that objects have properties that can stimulate all of their senses: vision, hearing, taste, smell, and touch. For example, what they feel in their mouths as they suck a pacifier is the same as what they see when Mom or Dad holds the pacifier up in front of them. When can they make such connections? It appears that they have some capacity to do so as early as the first month of life. Meltzoff and Borton (1979) gave 1-month-olds an opportunity to suck on either a smooth pacifier or a bumpy one, without letting the infants see the pacifiers. Then, the researchers used a technique known as the ***preferential looking paradigm*** to explore whether the babies had learned anything about the visual characteristics of the pacifiers that they had sucked on but had never seen. The babies looked at a split video screen. On one side was a picture of the smooth pacifier, on the other side a picture of the bumpy pacifier. A camera recorded the infants' eye movements. The babies spent more time looking at whichever pacifier they had previously sucked—suggesting that they were capable of recognizing the appearance of the pacifier from their tactile experience of it. Findings like this one indicate that the senses are already somewhat related very early in infancy, perhaps at birth, and that when babies perceive an object in one way, they can construct some notion of the object's other perceptual characteristics. This quality of ***intersensory integration*** (also referred to as crossmodal matching or ***intermodal perception***) is not surprising given what we now know about prenatal brain development—that the development of one sensory system is influenced by the development of other systems (see the discussion of the brain, earlier in this chapter). Piaget (1954), without the benefit of today's research methods, assumed that intersensory integration appears later in infancy, after babies have learned to coordinate their reflexive responses to stimulation. For example, not until about 6 weeks do babies reach up to grasp an object that they are sucking; and not until 4 to 6 months do they smoothly coordinate grasping and looking, allowing easy exploration of objects through visually guided reaching. Surely, these motor coordinations enrich a baby's understanding of objects as "packages" of perceptual characteristics, but such understanding is initiated earlier than Piaget realized.

What else must infants know to have an understanding of objects? Piaget pointed out that adults realize that objects have a separate existence from the perceiver. Think for a moment about something that is out of sight, like the sink in your bathroom. Despite your inability to see the sink at this moment, you realize that it still exists. Your perceptual processes or actions on the object are not necessary to its continuation. This quality of objects is referred to as ***object permanence:*** they exist apart from the perceiver.

It can be argued that to understand the permanence of objects, a child must have at least a rudimentary capacity to keep the object in mind when it is not present. To put it another way, the child must have a *mental representation* of the object, like your mental image of the bathroom sink. The capacity to think about things or events that are not currently stimulating our senses is called ***representational thought.*** Thus, if we could find out when a baby understands object permanence, we would not only know something about her object concept, but we would also know that she was capable of representational thought. Piaget invented the ***hidden object test*** to assess object permanence. An interesting object, like a small toy, is placed in front of a baby, within her reach. As the baby watches, we cover the object with a cloth, so that it is out of sight. What we want to know is, will the baby search for the object under the cloth, or does the baby act as if the object's disappearance means that the object no longer exists? Studies using the hidden object test, beginning with Piaget's own studies, have consistently found that infants younger than 8 to 12 months fail to search for the object, even though they have the motor skills they need to succeed much earlier (e.g., they engage in visually guided reaching by about 4 months, and they can sit without support by about 6 months). Piaget concluded that understanding object permanence has its rudimentary beginnings late in the first year of life and gradually improves thereafter. It may also be that representational thought—the ability to form mental representations, such as images—is a skill that begins to develop only in the late months of the first year of life. This representational ability evolves and improves through the second year of life, until, by the end of the sensorimotor period, children not only think about objects but can mentally plan their actions, solve simple problems "all in their heads," remember past experiences, and so on. In other words, they have developed a broad capacity for thinking.

In recent years, studies using procedures such as the habituation paradigm have indicated that babies may have some understanding of object permanence, and therefore, perhaps, some representational thinking skills, much earlier in infancy. In one famous study, Baillargeon (1987) worked with infants only 4 months old, too young to do the hidden object test. Babies sat in front of an apparatus that consisted of a board attached by a hinge to a table top. The board lay flat on the table and gradually swung on its hinge up and away from the watching baby until it was again flat on the table (see Figure 3.5). Babies watched the action of the board repeated until they had habituated. Then the researchers placed a box on the table, so that if the board swung up and away from the baby, it would eventually be stopped by the box, although the baby could no longer see the box at that point. Then, babies saw either what you would expect—the board stopping part way through its descent because of the box being in the way—or an impossible event, with the board continuing to swing smoothly down to the table (because the researchers had sneakily removed the box). Babies looked longer and harder at the impossible event, dishabituating, even though it was more like the event they had previously seen. It seemed as if they were surprised that the box, no longer visible, had not stopped the board's movement. Because the babies acted as if they believed the box was still there, even though they could not see it, Baillargeon argued that even 4-month-olds understand

FIGURE 3.5

Baillargeon's Habituation Study of Infant Object Permanence

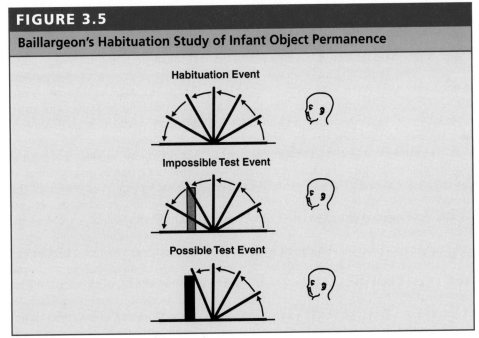

Source: Baillargeon, R. (1987). Object permanence in 3½- and 4½-month-old infants. *Developmental Psychology, 23,* 656. Copyright © 1987 by the American Psychological Association. Adapted with permission.

object permanence, calling into question Piaget's views that object permanence and representational thinking begin to emerge only late in the first year of life.

Findings such as Baillargeon's have created lively controversy about just when representational thinking begins and have even raised the possibility that it might be characteristic of human babies from birth (see discussions by Haith & Benson, 1998, and Mandler, 1998). Nonetheless, most research supports the general idea that thinking, and conceptual developments that are dependent on thinking, such as object permanence, gradually emerge and improve through the first and second years of life and beyond. In the next section, we will see that studies of infant memory and of babies' abilities to plan their actions indicate the same kind of gradual development.

Infant Memory

New research on infant memory is becoming available at a very rapid rate, stimulated by the availability of methods such as the habituation and preferential looking paradigms and by the special interest of researchers who favor information processing theories of cognitive development (see Chapter 1). Storage of information, duration of storage, retrieval of stored information—these are the centerpieces of cognitive functioning from the point of view of scientists who think about the human cognitive system as akin in some ways to a computer processor. Their special interest has provided us with a much better picture today of what infants can learn and remember than we had even a decade ago. What follows is only a sampling of what we are discovering about infant memory, that is, the ability to learn and to store information.

First, memory is not just one mental function. There are different kinds of memory. Here we will describe two: *recognition* and *recall.* Recognition memory is the ability to differentiate between experiences that are new and experiences that we have had before. When you see a face across a room and say to yourself, "I've seen that person before," you are demonstrating recognition. Piaget (1952) guessed from the way that babies use their reflexes that at least a primitive form of recognition is possible in earliest infancy. Babies will suck anything that touches their lips, but if they are hungry, they only continue to suck objects that have become associated with nourishment, like nipples. Thus, they show a kind of motor recognition of the nipple through their sucking.

Today's researchers typically use the habituation paradigm to assess infant recognition. When babies habituate to a stimulus that is repeatedly presented, they are showing us that the stimulus is becoming familiar. Since even newborns will habituate to at least some repeatedly presented stimuli, we are now confident that newborns are capable of recognition. Operant conditioning has also demonstrated that recognition skills are present from birth. For example, a 3-day-old infant will learn to suck harder for the reward of hearing its own mother's voice (rather than a stranger's voice), indicating that the baby recognizes the mother's voice (e.g., DeCasper & Fifer, 1980). The newborn's recognition of the mother's voice seems to be a result of opportunities to hear her voice before birth, suggesting that the capacity for recognition is already in place before birth (DeCasper & Prescott, 1984; DeCasper & Spence, 1986).

Recognition improves throughout infancy. In many instances, recognition in the newborn period fades after a few minutes or even seconds, although some studies have found much longer durations (e.g., DeCasper & Spence, 1986). If infants are 3 months old or older when they are exposed to a stimulus, they sometimes recognize it after several months of nonexposure, especially if it is a moving stimulus (e.g., Bahrick & Pickens, 1995).

Not only does the duration of recognition increase with age, but the speed with which babies habituate increases. Younger babies need more exposures to a stimulus than older babies before they show signs of recognition. But there are also individual differences among babies of the same age. Interestingly, how quickly babies habituate to a new stimulus is one of the few measures of infant functioning that has been found to correlate with later intelligence test performance. Apparently, recognition speed is an early indicator of the efficiency with which a child may later process information (Bornstein & Sigman, 1986; Fagan, 1990).

In contrast to the early and rapid development of recognition memory, recall seems to emerge later in infancy. Recall is the ability to bring to mind an experience that has happened in the past. It is different from recognition because the to-be-remembered experience is not presently occurring, but must be mentally represented. In other words, thinking that involves mental representation, such as forming mental images, is necessary for recall. One indicator of recall is *deferred imitation,* in which children observe the actions of another on one occasion, and then imitate those actions sometime later. In order to do so, the child must be able to recall the observed actions. Based on observations of his own children's behavior, Piaget believed that deferred imitation begins around the middle of the baby's second year. At 16 months, for example, his daughter, Jacqueline, watched a visiting boy have a temper tantrum, screaming and stamping his feet in a playpen. The next day, Jacqueline did the same, only she was smiling and her foot stamping was gentle. She was not actually having a temper tantrum, but was imitating her little friend's fascinating performance (Piaget, 1962). More recent research demonstrates that infants from about 9 months of age will recall, and later imitate, actions that they have witnessed. For example, Meltzoff (1988) showed babies an interesting box, then demonstrated that pushing a button on the box would produce a beep. The next day, the babies were given the opportunity to play with the box themselves for the first time. Nine-month-old babies who had watched the button pushing the previous day were much more likely to push the button themselves than were babies who had not previously observed the action. On the whole, available research suggests that deferred imitation can begin late in the first year but that it does improve dramatically over the next year, both in duration and in the complexity of what can be recalled. For example, 11-month-old babies will imitate a simple sequence of actions a few minutes after observing them; but 20-month-olds can do so as long as 2 weeks later (Bauer & Mandler, 1989; 1990). Deferred imitation is, of course, what makes *observational learning,* or *modeling,* possible. Once children can mentally represent and thus recall the actions of others, they have a cognitive skill that is critical for social learning. A toddler who has watched his big sister painting pictures might on his own open a jar of paint, dip a paintbrush into it, and then sweep the paintbrush across some available surface. His proficiency at each of these actions will be limited, but the sequence will be executed more or less correctly because he recalls his big sister's past actions.

Searching for a hidden object, which begins at about 8 months of age, can be seen as a sign not only that a child believes in the object's permanence but that the child *recalls* the object. A particularly important sign of such recall is the beginning of *separation anxiety.* When parents leave a young baby with another caregiver, the baby typically does not seem to miss the absent parents or to mourn their loss while they are gone. When they are out of sight, they seem to be out of mind. But in the second half of the first year, at about 8 months for most babies, leaving a child with another caregiver may be more difficult. The baby may continue for some time to watch for the missing parents, to cry or fuss, and to generally act distressed. Bouts of separation anxiety are usually of fairly short duration at first, but tend to increase in length, suggesting that the child's ability to recall the parents is increasing in duration. An 18- to 24-month-old left with a babysitter might show signs of anxiety repeatedly throughout the parents' absence. Of course, many factors contribute to separation anxiety: the familiarity of the alternate caregiver and of the surroundings, the quality of the infant's relationship to the parents, the infant's temperament (see Chapter 4), and so on. But the consistency with which babies around the world begin showing separation distress at about 8 months is attributable to the development of the basic cognitive skills of recall and object permanence (Kagan, Kearsley, & Zelazo, 1978; McBride & DiCero, 1990).

Having and Inferring Intentions

If we intentionally act, choosing to pick up a fork rather than a spoon, searching through a closet for just the right outfit to wear, or planning a presentation at work, we are thinking about what we do before we do it. Very little conscious effort may be involved in some intentional acts, but at least some thought is required. Like many other cognitive skills, the ability to intend to do something has important consequences not just for intellectual performance but for social interactions as well. A child who can choose whether or not to cry to call for attention, for example, is likely to be treated differently than one who can only reflexively cry in response to discomfort. Obviously, the development of intentional action is related to the development of self-control and decision making, which we will discuss at greater length in future chapters.

Having Intentions. When does intentional action begin? Piaget (1952) assumed that infants' earliest behaviors are entirely unintentional and are typically based on reflexive responses to incoming stimulation and on the need to act, that is, to repetitively exercise one's reflexes. By 4 to 8 months, infants' behaviors have expanded as a result of constant differentiation and integration of the original reflexes, according to Piaget, and now a baby has a large repertoire of behavioral responses to stimuli. If one of these behaviors accidentally produces an interesting event, a child is likely to notice the effect and repeat the action, as if she is hoping to repeat the effect. Piaget called this **making interesting sights last.** He did not consider it to be intentional behavior, but a precursor of intentional behavior. In fact, it appears to be simple operant conditioning. After a behavior occurs, there is a reinforcing event, and the behavior is likely to be repeated. But there is a twist. Piaget described infants as appearing somewhat reflective, as if they had noticed the connection between their action and the outcome, and they were *trying* to make it happen again. Rovee-Collier (1990) has reported a similar sequence of events in infants as young as 3 months old. When a mobile hanging over a baby's crib is tied to a baby's foot, the child will soon learn to shake her foot to make the mobile move. At some point, the baby appears to notice the connection, as if she were having an insight, and the baby shakes her foot more vigorously afterward.

From these first inklings of intentional behavior, infants move to more clearly intentional action in that magical time, the last few months of the first year. By 8 to 12 months, Piaget reported that babies will engage in **means-end behavior:** they will divert their attention from a goal, such as grasping a toy, in order to produce another action that will help achieve the goal. For example, a baby might try to grasp a rattle that is behind a clear Plexiglas screen. When her hand touches the screen, the baby redirects her attention to the screen, perhaps pushing it aside, before focusing again on the rattle. Younger babies simply keep reaching for the rattle and failing. Their behavior seems more controlled by the stimulus of the rattle than by their own plans. Thus, again, it appears that a behavior that requires mental representation, planning, begins in the 8- to 12-month period. Recent studies also indicate that infants may do some fairly complex sizing up of such situations. Willatts (1989) found that 9-month-olds would put aside a barrier and then pull a cloth to get an out-of-reach toy resting on the cloth. But when the toy was not on the cloth, babies tended to simply play with the barrier, as though they realized there was no point in pulling on the cloth.

More sophisticated intentional control of behavior emerges in the second year. Whereas a 10-month-old will typically use only previously practiced actions as means to an end, 12- to 18-month-olds begin to actively invent new variations on their actions to fit the situation, trying out one variation after another. By 24 months, toddlers' control of their mental representations is advanced enough that they will mentally invent new means to an end. Rather than trying this and trying that, sometimes they solve a problem by quietly studying the situation first, and producing a useful means to an end on the first try.

The beginning of intentional behavior by the end of the first year is evident in babies' communicative behaviors. When a younger baby repeats an action that has attracted attention in the past, such as patting mommy's cheek, the child may be doing no more than "making interesting sights last." But by 8 to 12 months, most babies are using some of their behaviors, including some vocalizations, not just to attract attention, but as a communicative means to an end. For example, a typical 12-month-old might make a wailing sound while intently looking at her father. When he looks in her direction, she extends her hand in an urgent reach, apparently indicating a toy that she would like retrieved. It is difficult not to interpret such complex means-end behavior as intentional communication (Golinkoff, 1983).

Inferring Others' Intentions. As babies are developing intentions of their own, what do they understand about the intentions of others? Researchers make a distinction between a child's understanding of human **agency** and of human **intention.** *Agency* refers to the ability to act without an external trigger. People and animals have agency, because they can act without being pushed or "launched" by some other force, whereas objects require launching. *Intention* is an internal mental state, such as a plan or a desire, that is the source of an action. Infants begin to understand agency by the end of the first year. Just trying to get other people to do things for her, like the baby described in the last paragraph, suggests that a baby has some sense that others are agents. Understanding that other people have intentions, desires, feelings, and so on, and inferring what those intentions might be, appear to be much more difficult achievements. As you will see in the discussion of the preoperational stage, understanding intentions is part of developing a ***theory of mind,*** and it is a complex and long-term process.

Yet, as with other cognitive skills, there appear to be preliminary developments in the understanding of intentions by the end of the first year. Using an habituation task, Woodward (1998) has found some apparent awareness of the goal-directedness (intentionality) of human action even in babies as young as 6 months. In her study, babies saw an actor's arm reach for one of two toys that were side-by-side on a platform. Say, for example, that the arm reached for the toy on the left. The sequence was repeated until the babies habituated. Then, the position of the toys was switched, so that the toy that had been on the left was now on the right. The babies now witnessed one of two events. In the first event, the actor reached for the same toy as before, but the actor's arm had to reach in a different direction (to the right in our example) because the toys had been switched. In other words, the actor's *goal* remained the same—to pick up the same toy. In the second event, the actor reached for a new toy that was now in the original location (on the left in our example). Babies dishabituated more to the second event, as though they were surprised by the change in goal. The change in the *direction of movement* in the first event did not seem to be experienced as particularly new or important. Rather, it was the change in *goal* that the babies noticed. The same study done with an inanimate rod "reaching" toward the toys did not produce the same results. The babies seemed to expect goal-directedness from humans, but they did not expect it from an inanimate rod. The results of Woodward's study suggest that while full understanding of human intentions may take a long time, babies appear to have a rudimentary sense that there are significant differences between humans and other objects as early as 6 months.

Preschoolers' Cognition: The Preoperational Stage

By the age of 2, children have moved beyond the limits of sensorimotor activity to become thinkers. Instead of responding to the world primarily by connecting sensation to action, constantly exercising and adapting reflexive patterns of behavior, children can engage the world on the plane of thought. As we have seen, they understand that objects exist apart from their own perceptions and actions; they can call to mind previously experienced events; they can plan and execute complex behaviors, even behaviors they have not tried before; and they know that humans, unlike objects, are agents of action whose behavior is goal-directed. While there are precursors to most or all of these skills even in early infancy, and scientists argue about when the earliest representations actually occur, the flowering of thinking in the second year of life is indisputable. Among the abilities that toddlers' thinking permits is the use of ***symbols*** (Piaget, 1962). *Symbols* are stand-ins for other things. Words are symbols; so are the props used in pretend play when they stand for something else, the way a broom stands for a horse when a child gallops around "riding" the broom. To use and understand such symbols, children must be able to mentally represent the things being symbolized. As babies' representational skills grow, especially over the second year, language skill and pretend play begin to blossom.

In this section, we will highlight some of the cognitive developments of the preschool years that are launched as the infancy period ends. You will find that Piaget, while celebrating the accomplishments of what he called the "preoperational" or prelogical years, also identified many limitations of children's early thought. You will also learn that in recent years developmental scientists have focused heavily on exploring the limitations that Piaget identified. Sometimes, the new data suggest that preschoolers possess greater skill than Piaget may have realized, and some of the newer findings have helped us to specify step-by-step changes in some of the abilities that Piaget first described.

Understanding Numbers

Piaget (1952) launched the systematic study of children's number skills by inventing the *number conservation task.* A set of discrete items, let's say five candies, is laid out in a neatly spaced line. Below the first set is a second set, laid out the same way, with the candies in each row matched one to one. A child is asked if the two rows have the same number or whether one or the other has more candies. Typically, 3- and 4-year-olds recognize that the two rows have the same number of candies. But when the researcher then changes the appearance of the second row by spreading out the candies, preschoolers usually think that the number has changed along with the appearance of the row. Most frequently, they say that the longer row now has more candy. Even if they count the candies and report that each has five, they believe that the longer row has more. Do they really believe that? They seem to: if you ask them which row they would rather have to eat, they will choose the longer row!

Endless debate has swirled around the meaning of preschoolers' failure on this number conservation task. Piaget felt that children were revealing some fundamental characteristics of preoperational thought. Most importantly, preoperational thought tends to be *centered* or focused on one salient feature of an experience or event at a time. In a sense, young thinkers can only think about one thing at a time. In the number conservation task, when they look at the rows of candies, preschoolers focus on the differences in length, but they ignore the differences in density. If they noticed both, especially the transformations that occurred in both as the second row was reconfigured, they might recognize that as the length of the row increased, the density of the row decreased, so that the number of candies stayed the same despite the increased length. Because their thought is centered, Piaget argued, preoperational children tend to link observations in serial order, rather than discovering and representing the more complex relationships among them. In the number conservation task, even when children notice both the change in length and the change in density of the second row, they observe these changes serially, and they do not recognize the reciprocal relationship between them. All in all, the contents of preoperational thought tend to be limited to the most salient perceptual characteristics. Young children have trouble recognizing "underlying realities" (Flavell, Miller, & Miller, 1993). For example, children fail to realize that the number of candies is conserved even when they are moved around, because they do not take into account all the relevant observations at one time. As a result, young children do not discover the relationships among the facts, and they draw conclusions that to adults are quite illogical.

Piaget argued that as children interact with the world and practice representing the events they observe, their thinking becomes more efficient, and eventually they are able to *decenter,* that is, to take into account multiple pieces of information simultaneously. As a result, important relationships among their observations can be discovered and represented, and their thinking becomes more logical and sensible from an adult's point of view. Piaget found that improvements in children's thinking moved forward rapidly in the years from 5 to 7, so that most children were successful on tasks such as number conservation by about age 7.

Newer research on children's understanding of number emphasizes how much preschoolers *do* know about numbers, even though they still fail Piaget's number conservation task. Even newborns appear to discriminate differences between small numbers; they will habituate to displays of two items, but then dishabituate to a display of three items (Antell & Keating, 1983). In exploring the number skills of preschoolers, Gelman and her colleagues (e.g., Gelman & Gallistel, 1978; see Gelman, 1982; Gelman & Williams, 1998) found that 2- to 3-year-olds have at least implicit understanding of many fundamental counting principles. For example, they know that counting requires the "one-to-one" principle: one number for one item. Such young children sometimes do mistakenly recount items, but they seem to realize that recounting is not really acceptable. Between 3 and 5 years, children can count the same set of items in versatile order, starting once with the item on the left, another time with the item on the right, and so forth. Gelman calls this the "order-irrelevance principle." She has even found that children as young as 3 can sometimes remain focused on number despite changes in the length and density of rows. In a series of studies using "magic number games," Gelman showed children two plates, each with a row of toy mice, two on one plate, three on the other. Some children saw two rows of equal length but of unequal density; others saw rows of unequal length but equal density. First, the children were trained to pick the "winner" plate (the one with three mice) by giving them lots of trials and telling them whether they were right or wrong. Once they had learned to pick the correct plate without error, the researcher surreptitiously changed the appearance of the plates. For example, if the rows of mice had been of equal length, they were changed to be of equal density. Children tended to register surprise when the changed plates were revealed, but they still correctly picked the winners. Thus it was clear that they had learned to select the correct plate on the basis of number, not on the basis of length or density differences. It appears that under the right circumstances, young children can pay attention to "underlying realities," although their ability to do so is quite fragile and easily disrupted: the same children who succeeded in the magic number games still failed Piaget's classic number conservation tasks.

Gelman's magic number games are characteristic of many of the tasks that modern researchers have designed to explore the apparent limitations of preschoolers' thinking. They are different from Piaget's tasks in that they provide simple instructions, and they often do not require verbal responses or explanations. They also establish different criteria for granting children some knowledge or skill. Piaget's criteria were conservative. He wanted children to demonstrate that they had complete mastery of a skill or concept, such as the concept of number, such that it could not be disrupted by countersuggestions or by superficial transformation, before he granted that the skill was present. He often required that children be able to give sensible explanations of their right answers before he credited them with true understanding (Haith & Benson, 1998). Modern researchers tend to make minimal demands on children and to grant them the presence of a skill even when children's success can be easily disrupted by increased demands. The data are not in dispute, but the interpretation of the data is. One approach to resolving the dispute is to assume that concepts such as number are understood by children in ever-increasing depth and breadth. Specifying the levels of understanding and the experiences that help children to advance from one level to another is what researchers must aim to discover (Bidell & Fischer, 1997; Blewitt, 1994; Haith & Benson, 1998).

At this time, many of Piaget's characterizations of the limitations of preoperational thought remain useful. As Flavell has argued (e.g., Flavell, Miller, & Miller, 1993), for example, preschoolers do seem to make appearance-based conclusions, and they often miss the deeper significance of events. Also, their thinking often does seem especially affected by singular, salient dimensions of a situation. However, most researchers recognize that such limitations aptly describe young children's abilities sometimes, but not always. Specifying the conditions that govern these limitations is more and more a focus of research.

Understanding the Mind

Piaget (1926; Piaget & Inhelder, 1956) pioneered the investigation of children's understanding of other people's mental processes by studying perspective-taking skills in preschoolers. In his "three mountains task," a three-dimensional model of three mountains was shown to children from several different angles. Children then had to select a picture of how the scene looked to them, as well as a picture of how it looked to another observer on a different side of the display. Until about age 7, children tended to select the same picture both times, suggesting that they believed that other observers shared their perspective. Piaget believed children's poor perspective-taking skills reflected **preoperational egocentrism.** Because preschoolers can only think about one thing at a time, they are centered on their own perspective and have no awareness of the possibility of a different perspective.

Egocentrism is often evident in young children's encounters with others. A young girl may suggest that Daddy should be given a dollhouse for his birthday; she assumes that he wants what she wants. When parents eagerly ask for information about what happened in nursery school, their son fails to respond, as if he cannot fathom what it is the parents do not know; if he knows what happened today, surely they do too. During a telephone conversation, when her grandmother asks a toddler what she's going to wear to her birthday party, the child responds "This!" and points to the dress she is wearing, as if her grandmother can see what she can see. These are all typical examples of a failure to take another person's perspective.

Today, researchers see such behaviors as reflecting aspects of a child's theory of mind or "naive psychology," that is, the child's understanding of psychological processes. Such understanding is ultimately critical for developing satisfactory relationships with others. We have already seen that in the first year of infancy children begin to have a sense that humans are agents of action and that others' (and perhaps their own) behaviors can be goal directed. Among the earliest signs that children have some notion of the existence of mental states is their use of "mental" words. Words for emotions or desires, such as *need, feel, want,* tend to occur as early as age 2, and words such as *think, forget, remember* that describe cognitive functions are often used by age 3 (Huttenlocher & Smiley, 1990; Ruffman, Slade, & Crowe, 2002). What concepts underlie these words we do not really know. It is likely that they are not the same as an adult's, but clearly the young preschooler is beginning to assign some meaning to these words.

Thus, in the early preschool years, children have a sense that they and others have mental states, such as thoughts, desires, feelings, and plans. Piaget's perspective-taking work focused on what children infer those states to be, and he found that preschoolers usually assume that others' mental states match their own. Newer work has expanded the focus of research to address questions such as what do children understand about how people acquire information, when do they understand that mental states may or may not match reality, and do children correctly impute to others some mental states before other mental states. There is some dispute about the answers to these questions (see Flavell & Miller, 1998), but available findings do indicate that children very gradually build such understandings. Two- and 3-year-olds often seem oblivious to what others know and how they know it, although they show some signs of making progress on these issues. For example, as early as age 2, a child can understand that if she is looking at a picture of a cat and you are standing opposite her, looking at the back of the picture, you will not be able to see the cat. In other words, the child can figure out *that* you see or do not see something under these conditions. However, suppose we place the picture of the cat on a table, face up, so that the child can see it right-side-up and you see it upside-down. At age 2, the child cannot understand that you have a different perspective on the cat, and she assumes that you also see it right-side-up. By age 3, in this simple situation, the child will be able to attribute a different visual perspective to you. She still will not be able to compute any kind of complex perspective difference, such as Piaget's three mountains task requires, but she can understand that someone else might see the same picture differently from herself (e.g., Masangkay, McCluskey, McIntyre, Sims-Knight, Vaughn, & Flavell, 1974).

Understanding that people *know* different things is more difficult for the young child. Until 4 or 5 years, most children attribute the same knowledge to others that they have themselves, as research using **false belief tasks** illustrates. In such tasks, one person has correct knowledge of a situation, but another person (or the same person at another time) has incorrect knowledge, or a "false belief." Suppose a child is aware that a box of candy has been removed from its original location and is now hidden in a cabinet. The child is asked where a second person, let's call him Sam, will look for the candy. Even though the child knows Sam was not present for the hiding, the child does not attribute a false belief to Sam but assumes that Sam will search in the appropriate hiding place, as if Sam must know what the child knows (e.g., Wimmer & Perner, 1983; see Wellman, 1990; Wellman, Cross, & Watson, 2001). In fact, until age 4 or 5 children have trouble realizing that they themselves have not always known what they know now (Gopnik & Astington, 1988). If they open a candy box expecting to find candy and are surprised to find something else instead, say pencils, they will later say that they knew before they opened the box that the pencils were there.

The trouble young children have figuring out what other people know, or need to know, is reflected in their attempts to communicate and can be responsible for both the charm and sometimes the spectacular failure of their efforts. Here are some samples from children's attempts to describe their favorite recipes:

> "Skabbetti:" First you decide what it will be tonight—sausages or meatballs. When your father tells you which one, then you cook. (p. 1)
>
> "Popcorn:" Put the popcorn seeds in the popcorn bowl and plug it in the plug hold—and get the toaster out of the way. . . . If your brother takes the lid off, popcorn go zinging all over the kitchen . . . POW! POW! POW! (p. 45)
>
> "Banilla Cake:" 1 cake stuff; 2 eggs (But on "Sesame Street" they put 8 eggs in a cake. I always watch "Love American Style" after "Sesame Street"); a drop of milk; 7 of those little silver baseballs for on the top. Put every single thing you have into a mother-size pan—a little one wouldn't do. . . . Put it in the oven department of the stove. Make it as hot as a coffee pot. Pretty soon it will come popping right out! Eat it when the news comes on. (p. 34)

(From Martel, 1974)

Most research on children's theory of mind indicates that, on the one hand, preschoolers are less egocentric than Piaget inferred based on his very complex perspective-taking task, but that on the other hand, he was on target in assuming that taking another's perspective and understanding the limits of one's own perspective are difficult, and sometimes impossible, tasks for young children. The implications for children's social development are far reaching. For example, when toddlers want to grab a dog's tail or to chase a ball into the street, they do not understand that the adults who restrain them *want* something different. Disciplinary action by others is frustrating to a 2-year-old not just because she does not get what she wants, but because she does not understand that others do not share her desires. Three-year-olds do better understanding that others may have different desires or preferences. They might accept, for example, that their parents like coffee even though they themselves do not. But when two people have different beliefs, even 3- and 4-year-olds are often mystified (Flavell, Mumme, Green, & Flavell, 1992). For example, 3-year-olds found it difficult to comprehend that a girl in a story could think a toothbrush was hers when another child thought it was his!

Finally, when children are personally involved, taking another's perspective seems especially difficult. Apparently the salience of one's own perspective, especially in an emotionally charged situation, can undermine the child's fragile understanding of the differences between her own mental state and that of another person. For example, one

6-year-old girl, who in many situations was quite capable of understanding that others have different feelings and motives than she, was furious whenever she lost a board game or any other competition, calling her competitor "mean." Her own desire to win was so overwhelmingly salient that she assumed that it was shared by others, and that any interference with her success was simply mean-spiritedness!

How do young children overcome their problems with perspective taking and build a more realistic theory of mind? Piaget credited two processes: first, the gradual improvement in a child's ability to hold in mind multiple ideas at the same time (decentering), and second, the continual give and take of social interaction in which a child repeatedly confronts feedback from other people indicating that others do not always share the child's feelings, desires, or knowledge. Children find it difficult to assimilate such feedback, but gradually they accommodate their views of others until they can conceive of independent mental states. Modern theorists have proposed several other explanations, but many, like Piaget, consider experience in social interaction to be a key factor (see Flavell & Miller, 1998; for changes in perspective-taking skill in older children, see Chapter 6).

Understanding Symbolic Artifacts

When and how do children make sense of the many symbols that humans use to communicate? A symbol, remember, stands for something other than itself. In the next section we will look at the development of language, or linguistic symbols, which are quite arbitrary (e.g., the word "elephant" bears no resemblance to the real thing that it symbolizes), but first let's consider more analogical symbols, such as pictures or maps or scale models, which DeLoache (1999; DeLoache, Miller, & Pierrovtsakos, 1998) calls **symbolic artifacts.** Since these kinds of symbols are quite often similar to the things they represent, one might think that children would find them easier to interpret than words, but in fact the reverse may be true. DeLoache suggests that young children have difficulty with symbolic artifacts because of their dual nature: they are both concrete objects themselves *and* symbols for other things. To understand a symbolic artifact, a child must mentally represent the same thing in two ways at once, and as we have already seen, young children often have difficulty holding more than one idea in mind simultaneously. Perhaps as a result, children often understand less about things such as pictures or models than adults may think. For example, research on children's understanding of pictures indicates that if a picture is realistic, like a photograph, 9-month-olds attempt to pick up the object in the picture. Eighteen-month-olds are indifferent to whether a picture is right-side-up or upside-down, and even 2-year-olds often cannot pick which picture represents a real object.

Young preschoolers have similar trouble with television (e.g., Troseth & DeLoache, 1996). When children younger than 2½ watch a doll being hidden in a room on a video screen, the children will not be able to figure out where the doll is when they search for it in the real room. These children *are* able to respond directly to what they see on the screen. For example, they can follow the action and imitate what the actors do. However, they have trouble understanding that what they are watching symbolizes something that is happening somewhere else, other than on the screen. Curiously, children's performance improves if the edges of the video screen are covered and children believe that they are witnessing a scene through a window into a room. Then, even a 2-year-old will be able to find a doll hidden in a room after watching the hiding "through the window"! In this situation, the child does not have to perceive the screen events as symbolic of something happening elsewhere.

Children have even more trouble with scale models. DeLoache (1987) showed children a scale model of a room. She hid a miniature doll in the scale model and explained to the children that a full-size model of the doll was hidden in the full-size room.

Typically, not until age 3 could children use what they knew about the location of the miniature doll in the model to help them find the full-size doll in the real room. Even though 2-year-olds recognized the similarity between the rooms, they could not use one as a symbol for the other. This point was vividly revealed when researchers convinced 2-year-olds that the scale model was actually the larger room in a shrunken state (DeLoache, Miller, & Rosengren, 1997). In this situation the children did not see the scale model as a symbol of the large room. After witnessing the hiding of the miniature doll in the "shrunken" room, the children were then further duped into thinking that the scale model had been re-enlarged into its full size. Now they had no trouble locating the "enlarged" hidden doll!

DeLoache (1999) points out that recognizing the problems that children can have understanding symbolic artifacts has important practical implications. For example, anatomically accurate dolls are often used to question children about their experiences when sexual abuse is suspected. Such dolls are scale models of humans, and our assumption that the symbolic use of the doll is understandable to young preschoolers is highly questionable.

Understanding Language

Language development is a remarkable achievement of almost all young children, made even more notable by the fact that many aspects of language learning are nearly complete by the end of the preoperational stage. Volumes can, and have, been written summarizing the research on language acquisition. Here we will provide only a sampling of what is entailed when preschoolers master language.

Phonology. First, when children learn language they are learning its **phonology,** that is, the sound system of the language. Every language uses only a subset of the sounds that humans can use for language. Babies are beginning to learn something about what sounds are important for their language even before they are born. For example, soon after birth young infants show a preference for listening to voices speaking the native language of their mothers, apparently because they have heard their mothers while in the womb (Locke, 1993). One group of researchers found that by 6 months babies exposed to just one language show signs of sharpening their ability to discriminate distinctions that are important in that language, but have begun to lose the ability to perceive distinctions that are unimportant. Japanese babies, for example, start to lose the ability to distinguish "l" sounds from "r" sounds by this time (Kuhl, Williams, Lacerda, Stevens, & Lindblom, 1992). Babies begin **babbling** at about 6 months, repeating consonant-vowel-consonant sequences such as "bababa" or "doodoodoo." At first these babblings include most possible language sounds, but by 9 months they are limited to the sounds permissible in the baby's native language. Thus, phonological development begins before birth, and there are measurable advances long before babies begin to talk. Yet the full sound system may not be mastered for many years. Most adults find it difficult to understand the speech of a 2-year-old, although doting parents, tuned in to the toddler's phonological errors, can usually translate. The problem often is that 2-year-olds have not learned how, where, or when to use some of the sound distinctions that are important for their native tongue. For example, in English, we take advantage of **voicing,** using our vocal chords to make some consonant sounds but not others. The difference between the "d" sound and the "t" sound is only that the "d" is voiced and the "t" is not. A toddler may not yet have caught the importance of this distinction, and when she means to say "toy" she may say "doy." Children master most sound distinctions like these by age 3, but may continue to struggle with other aspects of phonology, such as making the "th" sound in the right places, for much longer.

Semantics. Second, when children learn language they are learning which words and word parts express what meanings. This is referred to as the ***semantic system*** of a language. Progress in producing words begins by the end of the first year, as already noted, and moves slowly for a time. In the first six months of word use, many words are produced only in limited contexts, as though tied to particular cues. For example, a child might say "daw" only when she sees the family's cocker spaniel, and then only if the dog barks.

At about the time that children can produce about 50 words, they typically go into a new phase of vocabulary learning called the ***vocabulary spurt:*** suddenly, at about 18 to 24 months, toddlers begin learning words very rapidly, expanding their productive vocabulary from 50 to about 500 words in just a few months. Their comprehension vocabulary appears to be even larger. It seems as if the child has had a sudden insight into the fact that anything can be labeled and thus communicated through words. Some have suggested that the vocabulary spurt marks the end of the sensorimotor period and is made possible by a fully functioning representational capacity; words are now truly being used as symbols for concepts and ideas, rather than being triggered by contextual cues. By age 5, the typical child may understand 15,000 words, so that an average of 9 or 10 words have been added every day for three years! The rapidity with which young children add new words to functional vocabulary after only one or two exposures is described as ***fast mapping.***

Using words as symbols may actually be a bit simpler in one respect than the use of artifactual symbols, in that words are not things themselves: they function only to represent meanings. Using them correctly probably does not require representing them in two ways at once, as children must do with artifactual symbols. Rather, a word may at first be perceived by children as more like a part of the concept to which it refers. Understanding that words are *arbitrary* symbols actually seems to be much more difficult for children than using them to make meaning. Although toddlers and preschoolers rapidly acquire vocabulary, even at age 5 children may still fail to realize that labels are arbitrary and conventionally determined. For example, if we propose to change our words around and call things by different names, like calling a dog a "cat" and vice versa, a 5-year-old is likely to object that it cannot be done. The child seems to feel that the word, in a sense, "belongs" to the thing it symbolizes and cannot be shifted (Homer, Brockmeier, Kamawar, & Olsen, 2001).

Syntax. Third, learning language requires learning to produce sentences that make sense. The aspect of language that specifies how to link words into meaningful sentences is called the ***syntactic system*** or ***grammar.*** Words must be ordered in a sentence in just the right way to communicate what we mean to someone else. Linguists have found that proper ordering of words and word parts (such as prefixes and suffixes in English) is governed by a complex set of rules. One of the most baffling things about children's language acquisition is that they learn these rules with little difficulty, despite the fact that no one teaches them.

Beginning with two-word strings at about the time of the vocabulary spurt, children quickly progress, until by age 5 they can produce most sentence structures. To give you a sense of how complex the rules are that children implicitly know, consider the following "tag questions":

That boy kicked the dog, didn't he?

The ceiling leaks all the time, doesn't it?

You and I are getting along well, aren't we?

Making the right question tag at the end of the sentence requires knowledge of several rules, including how to add an auxiliary (such as "did" or "does") to a verb and how to negate a verb, for starters. To make proper tag questions requires so many rules that children are slow to learn this particular sentence form (Brown & Hanlon, 1970). Nonetheless, most children can produce tag questions effortlessly by age 5.

Pragmatics. Finally, children must learn the *pragmatics* of language use, that is, how to use language effectively to communicate. Knowing how to put together a proper sentence, or knowing the labels for things, is not enough. One must be able to craft a *narrative,* a story or event description, that conveys the full sense of an experience or gets at the point of an event while taking into account what the listener needs to hear to understand. Different listeners have different needs—say a little sister versus a grandfather—and there are different conventions of address that are acceptable in different situations. All of these kinds of language-use issues must be learned in addition to the mechanics of language. Preschoolers begin to construct narratives, usually with the help of others, by about 2 or 3 years old. Initially, their narratives are sketchy and largely uninformative. A child telling about an all-day trip to the zoo, for example, might only mention that "we went" and indicate one salient experience: "We saw a lion." A listener counting on the narrative to learn where, when, and what is likely to be quite disappointed. Some aspects of developing pragmatic skill are dependent on cognitive developments in perspective taking, which helps to account for the inadequacy of children's early narratives (Cameron & Wang, 1999; Uccelli, Hemphill, Pan, & Snow, 1999).

Pragmatic skill also requires making appropriate adjustments in speech depending on the listener. Most children gradually learn *code switching,* shifting from using, say, slang with friends to using more polite forms with teachers. They also learn, eventually, to distinguish between what people really mean and the literal meaning of their words. Everyday expressions such as "What do ya' know" or "That's cool" are not to be taken literally in most social exchanges. And many such expressions require similar idiomatic responses. For example, a greeting like "What's happening?" is today usually followed by "Nothing much!"

How Language Is Learned. Language consists of so many complex systems, and it is learned so early, that it is difficult to explain how children manage the task. Some psycholinguists have proposed that language is learned by special genetically programmed procedures that are unique to language learning (e.g., Chomsky, 1968; Pinker, 1994). Others contend that the general analytic capacity of the human brain is such that even complex language rules can be worked out without any innate knowledge or special language acquisition procedures (e.g., Karmiloff-Smith, 1992; 2000). Regardless of which view is correct, experience with one's native language must be critically important. Recognizing the importance of experience raises two questions: first, how much exposure to language is necessary, and second, are there particular language experiences that can facilitate the process of learning?

Researchers have really only scratched the surface in addressing these questions. Two domains in which both the quantity and the quality of experience have been linked to quality of learning are semantic development, specifically in the learning of vocabulary, and pragmatic development, specifically in the production of narratives.

Although most 5-year-olds know enough vocabulary to communicate about everyday things, there are large individual differences among children in the size of their vocabularies. In recent years, it has become clear that vocabulary size is a key predictor of later literacy and success in school; it has also become clear that children's vocabulary is related to home and preschool environment (e.g., Cunningham, Stanovich, & West, 1994; Weizman & Snow, 2001). The amount and kind of language experience children have with adults, in parent-child conversations and in joint book reading, are linked with children's vocabulary. In one study, researchers made monthly visits for over two years to the homes of children whose families were either poor and on welfare, lower middle class (mostly in blue-color occupations), or upper middle class with at least one professional parent (Hart & Risley, 1992; 1995). All of the parents were actively involved with their children, playing with them, expressing affection, providing them with toys, and so on. But there were marked differences in how much the three groups of parents talked to their children right from the start. (Children were about 9 months old at the beginning of the study.) In a 100-hour week, a toddler in a professional family might hear 215,000 words on the average; in a lower-middle-class family children heard about 125,000 words; and in the poorest homes about 62,000. All of the children learned to talk on schedule, but the differences in parental input were correlated with children's vocabulary measures by age 3; children who heard the most language performed best. The content of parents' conversations with their youngsters also differed. Those who spoke with their children most tended to ask more questions and elaborated more on topics of conversation. Parents who spoke with their children the least tended to utter more prohibitions. Even when the researchers looked within a single socioeconomic group, so that social class was not a factor, children whose parents talked with them more had the most advanced vocabularies. From this and many other studies, it appears that, regardless of social class, the quantity and quality of parent-child conversation can be a significant factor in vocabulary expansion.

Children's narrative skills may also be tied to the kinds of language opportunities that parents and other caregivers provide. Consider how different the narrative skills of two 5-year-olds in the same classroom proved to be. Both children were retelling a story they were told about a boy's trip to a grocery store. Both children were clearly familiar with all of the details of the story, having successfully acted it out with dolls and other props.

> FIRST CHILD: John went to the grocery store. He got a cake for his grandmother's birth-
> day party. And he paid the clerk and ran home.
> SECOND CHILD: He got cake and he ran home. (Feagans & Farran, 1981, p. 723)

Several studies have found that narrative skill differences like these are connected to the way that mothers converse with their children. If they engage in lengthy discussions about children's past experiences, providing lots of details and encouraging children to do so also, their children's narratives tend to be more adequate and informative (e.g., Reese & Fivush, 1993). An interesting twist is that mothers who engage their children in this kind of high-quality narrative practice also have children who remember past events in their own lives better (Tessler & Nelson, 1994). K. Nelson (1993b; 1996) has proposed that narrative practice is a key ingredient in the development of autobiographical memories. We are all familiar with the phenomenon of **infantile amnesia,** the difficulty we have remembering events in our lives earlier than about our third or fourth year. There are probably many factors that contribute, but perhaps one is that our early experiences occur before we have much mastery of language. Nelson argues that it is the mastery of *narrative* language that is particularly important. When we tell our own life experiences in conversation with others, we also learn to encode stories in language form, a form that is well suited for later recall. In a way, talking out loud about our experiences teaches us not just how to tell stories but how to remember them as well. As you will see in the next section, Nelson's view of how autobiographical memory develops is consistent with the ideas of a highly influential psychologist and educator, Lev Vygotsky, who was a contemporary of Piaget and who emphasized the importance of social experience in many aspects of cognitive development.

Vygotsky's Sociocultural Theory

As we have seen, it would be virtually impossible to consider the topic of cognitive development in children without considering Piaget's contributions. His ideas have been so widely adopted that they provide the foundation for many of our beliefs about child development, and they inform our notions of developmentally appropriate practice in profound ways. As Elkind (1968) noted, he is the "giant in the nursery." However, another theorist also lays claim to widespread influence in the area of cognitive development and has attracted much contemporary attention. His name was Lev S. Vygotsky. (See Box 3.3: *Biographical Sketch: Lev S. Vygotsky.*) Frequently, Vygotsky's ideas are presented as a counterpoint to those of Piaget, as if the two theorists were in opposing camps. While Vygotsky did criticize some of Piaget's ideas, the criticisms need to be understood in context. Both men understood that the advancement of scientific thinking depended upon the kind of dialectic that a mutual critique of ideas provides. Even though Piaget himself was slow to respond to Vygotsky's criticisms, he applauded the work of the young Russian scholar and

Box 3.3   Biographical Sketch: Lev S. Vygotsky

Lev Semenovich Vygotsky was born in 1896 in the small Russian village of Orscha in the province of Belorussia. His parents were both well-educated, middle-class individuals of Jewish descent. Vygotsky's father, a manager for a local bank, actively supported educational causes such as the development of the local public library. Vygotsky's experience with the Russian school system began when he reached junior high school age. Prior to this time, his parents had paid for him to be educated by a private tutor.

Vygotsky was clearly an extraordinary student from a very early age. Like Piaget, he began to write while he was still a young man: his essay on Hamlet was written when he was 18 and was later published. He loved to study and had wide academic interests, which included the philosophy of history, literature, art, and poetry. When he entered the University of Moscow in 1913, he was a student in the medical school. During his first semester there, he decided to transfer to the law school. As if this were not challenging enough, Vygotsky simultaneously enrolled in Shaniavsky University in order to study history and philosophy with some of Russia's most brilliant professors of that time.

Upon graduation from Moscow University in 1917, he secured a position teaching literature in a secondary school in the province of Gomel, where his parents lived. He worked in this capacity from 1918 to early 1924, when he left the school to join the faculty of a nearby teachers' college. He also worked to complete the requirements for his doctoral degree, which was granted from Moscow University in 1925.

One of Vygotsky's responsibilities at the college was to give lectures in the area of psychology. While presenting a lecture to professionals at the Second Psychoneurological Congress in Leningrad in early 1924, he attracted the attention of a young man named Alexander Luria. Luria was the academic secretary at the Moscow Institute of Psychology and would go on to become quite famous in the area of neuropsychology. Luria was so impressed with Vygotsky that he prevailed upon his director to hire him. Toward the end of 1924, Vygotsky moved with his wife to Moscow to take this appointment.

During his career at the Institute, he studied the development of human mental functioning. Many of his ideas were not available to scientists and educators in the West until quite recently because of the general ban on dissemination of information as well as problems involved in translation. Since the release of his ideas, Vygotsky has enjoyed great popularity in the West, particularly with those involved in education. During his lifetime, Vygotsky carried out many experiments on children using qualitative methods similar to those used by Piaget. His thinking was influenced by Piaget, and he actively tried to initiate a dialogue with him about certain points of disagreement. A full-fledged dialogue never developed, possibly because of the barriers of language and ideology. However, Piaget was aware of Vygotsky's ideas. In 1962, Piaget stated that he respected Vygotsky's position and noted their areas of agreement.

While at the Institute, Vygotsky wrote prodigiously and traveled extensively to oversee work in clinics with children and adults suffering from neurological disorders. Throughout much of his adult life, Vygotsky himself was in poor health. Toward the end of his life, colleagues such as Luria helped him conduct research projects, because Vygotsky was too weak to leave Moscow. His promising life was cut short in 1934, when he succumbed to an attack of tuberculosis. In Vygotsky, we have another example of a truly great mind whose ideas have inspired the work of many students of cognitive development.

actually came to agree with him in certain areas, such as the usefulness of egocentric speech (van der Veer, 1996; see below). The celebrated differences between the two more often than not reflect Vygotsky's differing emphases rather than any outright rejection of major Piagetian constructs. Readers need to be careful not to misinterpret the philosophy of either theorist by oversimplifying their ideas or by construing their positions as concrete "either-or" sets of beliefs. Let's examine some of the ideas for which Vygotsky is best known and consider how these two theorists compare.

Vygotsky, as did Piaget, found the question of how thinking develops in human beings an intriguing one. However, he did not identify a progression of stages that the individual child traverses on her way to logical, abstract thought. Nor did he emphasize the importance of the individual's construction of knowledge in the cognitive developmental process. Instead, he focused on themes that provide a different perspective on development. Vygotsky is arguably best known for his emphasis on the critical role that the culture or society into which one is born plays in the transmission of knowledge. Hence, his theory is called "sociocultural." He also stressed that human thinking was mediated by the tools humans use (Wertsch, 1991).

It seems quite understandable that he would take this point of view, embedded as he was in his own cultural context. Vygotsky was a Marxist who had been powerfully influenced by the writings of Marx and Engels. He was accustomed to the concept of a dalectic, that logical advancement comes from mutual examination of ideas, generating point and counterpoint and, ultimately, perhaps, a more adequate synthesis of ideas. He was grounded in the idea that society could be improved by the collective efforts of its members. Marxist philosophy also emphasized human mastery of the physical world by means of the use and production of tools (Marx & Engels, 1846/1972). Vygotsky took this concept and applied it to psychological development, reasoning that cognitive growth also resulted from continuous expansion in the use and scope of *tools.* Tools, or *signs* as Vygotsky came to refer to them, meant anything that people used to help them think and learn, such as numbering or writing systems. The most important tool for Vygotsky was language.

Let's consider the simple example of a vocabulary word, "television." Vygotsky pointed out that the child does not independently construct a definition for such a word but rather learns the meaning that her culture has ascribed to it. Understanding this shared meaning enables the child to use the "tool" to communicate. But the word can be used not only in its literal sense. It can be transformed to create a new tool or sign, like "telemarketing," which incorporates part of the original idea but is qualitatively different. Such new signs are the products of cultural and historical *mediation.* That is, the signs are shaped and developed by others. Vygotsky claimed that a child's use of such tools or signs actually transforms thinking and shapes it into new kinds of thought. The idea of *mediated learning,* so central to Vygotsky's theory, is very reminiscent of Piaget's concepts of assimilation and accommodation (van Geert, 1998), although Piaget tended to emphasize the development of thinking within the child, whereas Vygotsky's focus was squarely on the "child-in-context." In his view, because children acquire and use tools that are the products of others' thinking, "the mind is no longer to be located entirely inside the head" (Cole & Wertsch, 1996, p. 253) but is part of a collective experience. We have already learned that multidimensional models of development, such as Bronfenbrenner's, recognize the powerful influence of the individual's environment on her development. Vygotsky went a step further. He believed that the individual could never really be separated from her environment or culture.

Another theme in Vygotsky's work is that progress or improvement in thinking is both possible and desirable. The press toward more advanced levels of thinking not only pulls the individual forward but improves the society as well. Vygotsky placed great importance on the transmission of formal knowledge, because he believed that learning culturally defined concepts, which he referred to as **scientific concepts,** presented the learner with an internal organizational system for ideas and allowed the learner to utilize the ideas more efficiently (Vygotsky, 1934). But how do these cognitive advances occur? Vygotsky believed that more advanced thinkers or more capable members of a culture provide novice learners with *scaffolding* that enables the novices to reach higher levels of thinking. *Scaffolding* serves as a temporary prop until the child has mastered a task. Interestingly, Vygotsky did not apply his ideas to specific kinds of educational practice despite the obvious parallels to teaching and the widespread popularity of his ideas among educators (van der Veer & Valsiner, 1994). He did discuss education in the broad sense of the term and highlighted the important role of society in providing the tools that form the basis for thinking.

In educational circles, the concept of *scaffolding* has been interpreted as learning that occurs when a more cognitively advanced individual (a teacher or peer) guides a learner with prompts, cues, and other supports to reach a point where the learner can manifest in actuality what had previously only been her potential. The notion that children have a **zone of proximal development** is one of Vygotsky's most influential ideas. It describes the situation in which a learner is able to grasp a concept or perform some skill only with support or scaffolding from someone else. She would not yet be capable of the task on her own, but she can do it with assistance. Obviously, this does not mean simply telling a child an answer to a question! It means, instead, that a parent or teacher assesses the child's thinking, provides judicious support and appropriate cognitive tools, and in so doing, propels the child's development forward. Let's consider an application of this concept presented by Tharp and Gallimore (1988):

> A 6-year-old child has lost a toy and asks her father for help. The father asks where she last saw the toy: the child says, "I can't remember." He asks a series of questions: "Did you have it in your room? Outside? Next door?" To each question, the child answers, "No." When he says, "In the car?" she says, "I think so" and goes to retrieve the toy." (p. 14)

In this case, the father scaffolded the child's thinking and, in the process, helped her develop a way of remembering where her toy was. It should be noted that neither father nor daughter knew the answer to the question, "Where is the toy?" However, by encouraging the child to consider the right questions, her father was able to help his daughter to remember. The joint effort was possible because both shared certain kinds of information, such as knowledge of which toy was missing and what the layout of the house was. And both focused attention on a common goal, finding the toy. This process has been called intersubjectivity. From a Vygotskian point of view, the scaffolding occurred in the intermental space between parent and child.

Vygotsky's ideas have had a major impact on education in large measure because of their applicability to the teaching/learning process. Piaget was also sensitive to the role of outside influence on the developing learner. The frequent characterizations of Piaget as concerned *only* with individual cognitive development and of Vygotsky as concerned *only* with social influences on learning are both inaccurate. Piaget noted that the relationships between the individual and her social environment are essential to cognitive development (Piaget, 1977), as we have seen in his view of the development of perspective taking. Piaget's view of the role of teachers in cognitive development is also similar to Vygotsky's (see Box 3.2). For his part, Vygotsky posited two kinds of **developmental lines** that accounted for cognitive development, one that was "socio-historical" or cultural, and one that was "natural," coming from within the infant, much like Piaget's stage of sensorimotor development (Vygotsky, 1931). Despite differences in their emphases, both Piaget and Vygotsky can be described as concerned with the interpenetration of the individual mind and society in the formation of thought.

One difference between Piaget's and Vygotsky's ideas concerns the role of *egocentric speech* in cognitive development. While Piaget originally stated that the *egocentric speech* of the child (talking aloud to the self, with no apparent communicative function) serves no useful purpose and simply disappears with the growth of more mature language use, Vygotsky had a different idea. To him and his colleague, Alexander Luria, egocentric speech serves an eminently useful purpose in human development (Vygotsky & Luria, 1930). It was construed as the precursor to problem solving, planning ability, and self-control. From this perspective, egocentric or *private speech* eventually becomes internalized or transformed into *inner speech,* the kind of internal dialogue that facilitates thinking. If you happen to be someone who talks to yourself as you think something through, you are probably in very good company.

Vygotsky identified three stages in the movement of private speech to inner speech. First, the child of about 3 years of age engages in running commentaries about his actions, intentions, objects of interest, and the like whether anyone is nearby to listen or not. Very often, young children manifest a kind of "parallel" conversation, playing side by side without really interacting. Children also talk themselves through problems such as "Where is my toy?" Despite the fact that they may pose the statement as a question, they act as though they do not really expect anyone to answer it. Vygotsky believed that this speech was actually directing their thoughts and keeping them focused on the task at hand.

As children reach about 6 years of age, this private speech becomes more subdued and idiosyncratic, often capturing only the general sense of the idea. Children may subvocalize the dialogue or only move their lips. Finally, around the age of 8, children truly internalize the dialogue, and it is no longer audible. Vygotsky claimed that egocentric speech "went underground" and became inner speech, which was maintained for its self-regulatory properties. Research has demonstrated that the use of private speech enhances children's attention and involvement when faced with a difficult task (Berk & Spulh, 1995). Also, as we have seen, internalized narrative speech is thought to play a role in the development of autobiographical memory (K. Nelson, 1993b, 1996). Meichenbaum and Goodman (1971), using Vygotsky's analysis of the benefits of inner speech, pioneered the use of self-talk, or the enhancement of inner speech, to facilitate impulse control in children. Many schools of therapy, particularly cognitive-behavioral approaches, owe a debt to Vygotsky for his elucidation of the inner speech concept.

APPLICATIONS

The theories of Piaget and Vygotsky present the helper with some useful ideas for working with young children in a counseling relationship. It is certainly the case that helpers need to take into account the cognitive developmental level of their clients along with their level of social and emotional functioning for any helping to be effective. Very often, the shape of a symptom will change depending upon the child's cognitive skills. For example, sadness or depression in an adolescent subsequent to a family breakup may take the form of crying, ruminating, or writing long, self-absorbed diary entries. For a preschooler who lacks such verbal and introspective capacities, reaction to the same problem might take the shape of regressive behavior (wetting the bed, having tantrums) or pronounced social difficulties (biting, hitting). Ability to profit from therapeutic techniques also depends upon cognitive level. While a mature adolescent may be intrigued by the notion of the "unconscious," a younger child lacks the understanding of mental states needed to comprehend such a concept. Counseling interventions need to match the client's level of understanding.

Young children are naturally egocentric. They typically lack the cognitive ability to consider other points of view, including those of their parents, siblings, and teachers. A helper may encounter parents who state that they are angry with their infant for crying because they perceive it as a mark of the child's disobedience or disrespect. A babysitter might punish a 15-month-old for not being toilet trained. A preschool teacher might express concern that a 3-year-old is selfish because she won't share a special toy with her playmates. In all these cases, the adults fail to recognize the nature of the young child's thinking, and they attribute to the child abilities that she has not yet mastered. In a way, this reflects egocentrism on the part of the adults. Frequently, these misinterpretations are made because of lack of knowledge, which can be handled by providing information to the adults about child development. Sometimes these cognitive biases also indicate deep frustration, high stress levels, or limited empathy on the part of the adults. In these cases, support and understanding should be made available to the caretaker, and measures should be taken to protect the child from a potentially neglectful or abusive situation.

In general, helpers dealing with the normal range of child behavior should advocate a measure of patience to caretakers while trying to help them understand the way the child sees the world (Kazdin, 1988). Understanding the cognitive limitations of the young child need not prevent parents and other caregivers from attempting to teach youngsters to share, to control their behaviors, or to act appropriately. However, this teaching should take the form of scaffolding, gently guiding the child through questioning, repetition, and practice to a point where she has mastered the skill or new idea.

In any interaction with the young child, the helper's language should be geared to the child's level of understanding. In the case of preschool children, this means that language should be as simplified and concrete as possible. Too much abstraction or complexity will tax the developing language abilities of a young child. Since children of this age are still constructing their understanding of cause-and-effect relationships, helpers should not assume that preschoolers can easily grasp the connection between actions and consequences except at a very simple level. Saying to a youngster, "Since you hit Jimmy at day care yesterday, you won't be able to go to the playground tomorrow" will probably be ineffective if it is intended to teach the child about the consequences of his acts. Young children's sense of time is not well developed, and their memory for event sequences is rather poor. Tying tomorrow's consequences to yesterday's behavior is really asking a child to construct or detect an underlying organization or logical connection. The child has a better chance of remembering and understanding the sequence if misbehavior is linked with immediate consequences.

One of the most useful guidelines for helpers from Piaget's work is the idea that learning results from the dynamic interaction between assimilative and accommodative processes. Since much, if not all, of what transpires in counseling and therapy comes under the broad rubric of learning, these ideas can be readily translated into applications for therapeutic work with children and even adults. Piaget's ideas suggest that the helper should find ways to relate new information or insight to a client's current knowledge structures. In other words, if new knowledge, ideas, or information is too discrepant or if the individual lacks the context or experience to understand it, the new information will be ignored or discounted. On the other hand, if the new information is too similar to what the individual already knows, it will be assimilated into existing knowledge structures without any learning or cognitive change at all. To maximize learning, the counselor needs to understand how clients are thinking and what meanings they have already made. Interventions or examples that build on previous knowledge allow the client the best chance of incorporating the new information into useful working knowledge.

With young children, learning new things takes time. From studies of brain development we have seen that initial connections are somewhat fragile. The new connections involved in learning need to be reinforced regularly for them to be firmly established.

Adults are sometimes dismayed by the number of times children need to hear an idea or message repeated before they can understand it. Yet, this is the essence of cognitive development. Mature thinking is constructed bit by bit, each part building on the previous one and helping to shape the next.

One of the particularly interesting legacies of Vygotskian theory for practice is his emphasis on culture in cognitive development. In this view, our ideas, including our ideas about children's development, are conditioned and shaped by our culture. It should be stressed, however, that culture is not monolithic. Within any kind of cultural group, be it ethnic, socioeconomic, gender-based, religious, or the culture of our family homes, individual differences still flourish. Indeed individuals may be more similar in beliefs, values, and practices to members of another cultural group than they are to those with whom they share a similar cultural heritage (Greenfield & Suzuki, 1998). It has been frequently stated, for example, that Eurocentric cultures place more importance on the value of individualism than do Asian cultures, which hold more communitarian ideals. Certain assumptions, such as these about individualism and collectivism, need to be refined, clarified, and carefully evaluated in order to avoid dualistic overgeneralizations. Recent meta-analyses of cultural differences in orientations to individualism and collectivism found that Latinos, African Americans, and European Americans do not differ significantly in their levels of individualism, as defined in these studies, nor are European Americans less collectivist in orientation than Japanese and Koreans (see Oyserman, Coon, & Kemmelmeier, 2002).

Nonetheless, members of distinct cultural groups can differ systematically in certain beliefs and values (Greenfield, 1994). Therefore, when the cultural orientation of a family is different from that of the helper, professionals need to recognize and appreciate that different developmental goals can and do exist. For example, Japanese parents generally place great value on the interdependence of family members and their mutual responsibilities toward each other. This value is expressed concretely in the sleeping arrangements parents make for their infants. In the United States, infants generally sleep in a room separated from their parents (Morelli, Rogoff, Oppenheim, & Goldsmith, 1992), whereas in Japan, children routinely sleep with their parents until age 5 or 6 (Caudill & Plath, 1966). In fact, co-sleeping is the most frequently used sleeping arrangement for children in many non-Western cultures worldwide (Konner & Worthman, 1980). Unless this and other practices, such as co-bathing and care of young children by siblings, are understood contextually, the risk of misinterpreting them as harmful is a real one. Clinicians need to be able to separate culturally different child-rearing practices from those that are truly abusive or neglectful. While each cultural practice has its own costs and benefits, understanding the cultural underpinnings of different child-rearing approaches can provide us with helpful information that can reduce our own culture-bound ways of thinking. To use the sleeping example, researchers have reported that childhood problems such as **SIDS** (Sudden Infant Death Syndrome), sleep disturbances, and thumbsucking are all reduced in cultures that practice co-sleeping (Greenfield & Suzuki, 1998). Knowledge about the outcomes of such variations in practice may allow helpers to consider a fuller range of options for child care. Our communication with parents will be more helpful and compassionate if we understand, as Vygotsky pointed out, that our own ideas and values are mediated by the culture in which we live. (See Table 3.2.)

One final area of application needs to be addressed. How can our knowledge of cognitive and brain development be used to enhance the abilities of young children? This is a particularly important question for infants and young children who have been exposed to conditions that pose some risk, such as constitutional handicaps, poor family circumstances, and poverty. A wealth of information exists to support the

TABLE 3.2

Contrasting Cultural Models of Parent-Child Relations

	Developmental Goals	
	Independence	**Interdependence**
Developmental trajectory	From dependent to independent self	From asocial to socially responsible self
Children's relations to parents	Personal choice concerning relationship to parents	Obligations to parents
Communication	Verbal emphasis	Nonverbal emphasis (empathy, observation, participation)
	Autonomous self-expression by child	Child comprehension, mother speaks for child
	Frequent parental questions to child	Frequent parental directives to child
	Frequent praise	Infrequent praise
	Child negotiation	Harmony, respect, obedience
Parenting style	Authoritative: controlling, demanding, warm, rational	Rigorous and responsible teaching, high involvement, physical closeness
Parents helping children	A matter of personal choice except under extreme need	A moral obligation under all circumstances

Source: Greenfield, P. M. & Suzuki, L. K. Cultural human development. In W. Damon et al. *Handbook of Child Psychology vol. 4* (5th ed., pp. 1059–1109). Copyright © 1998. This material is used by permission of John Wiley & Sons, Inc.

effectiveness of home and clinic-based early intervention programs for such children. Research of this sort is fueling a movement in favor of universal publicly funded preschool programs in the United States. Such findings have already influenced some aspects of public policy, resulting, for example, in passage of Public Law 99–457, which mandates early intervention services for children with developmental disabilities and their families. Summarizing the existing knowledge in this area, Zigler (1994) documented three essential components of effective early intervention approaches: outreach to families; center-based, enriched preschool experiences; and transition services to ease adaptation to elementary school. These solutions seem to work for two main reasons. Early and consistent stimulation promotes cognitive development in children and, in turn, enhances readiness for school and later school performance (e.g., Campbell, Pungello, Miller-Johnson, Burchinal, and Ramey, 2001). In addition, parental participation and education increases parenting competence and changes misinformed attitudes and expectations to ones that are more child-centered and developmentally appropriate.

Early intervention programs, however, are not a panacea for all social ills. While they can reduce risk factors and enhance protective ones, they cannot eliminate all the problems facing children born in difficult situations. Speaking about the research on Head Start, the most familiar early intervention program for disadvantaged children, Zigler and Styfco (1994) provide this realistic appraisal:

> The empirical literature delivers good news and bad news. The bad news is that neither Head Start nor any preschool program can inoculate children against the ravages of poverty. Early intervention simply cannot overpower the effects of poor living conditions, inadequate nutrition and health care, negative role models, and substandard schools. But good programs can prepare children for school and possibly help them deliver better coping and adaptation skills that will enable better life outcomes, albeit not perfect ones. (p. 129)

Taking good care of our children in their earliest stages of development is an investment in their future physical, cognitive, and mental health.

SUMMARY

The Brain

1. The embryo begins to form a *neural tube* at about 2 weeks of gestation. By the 5th week, neurons are being produced at a remarkable rate, such that by birth there are 100 billion of them. Until about 4 months of gestation much of brain development involves *neuron* migration. The first neurons produced at the interior surface of the neural tube migrate the shortest distance and form the *hindbrain*. Later developing neurons travel farther to form the *midbrain*, and the last neurons to be produced travel furthest and form the *forebrain* or *cerebrum* and its *cortex*. Neurons in different parts of the brain later specialize for certain functions. Specialization is at least partially influenced by the context or environment of the cell. Neurons from one part of the cortex will respecialize if transplanted to another part of the cortex.

2. A neuron has one long extension called an *axon,* and may have many shorter extensions called *dendrites*. Electrical impulses begin when dendrites or cell bodies pick up a message from another cell. The impulse then passes through the axon to the *axon terminals,* where chemicals called neurotransmitters are released into the gap—or *synapse*—between neurons. The neurotransmitters carry the message to the next cell, causing it to "fire" or to "stop firing." *Myelination,* formation of an insulating substance around axons, promotes efficient conduction of electrical impulses. Myelination occurs prenatally and throughout childhood and adolescence. Neurons begin firing

spontaneously at about 4 months of gestation. Before birth, sensory neurons are beginning to be functional. A fetus will turn toward a light source by 25 weeks of gestation, and she can begin to recognize some aspects of sounds, like her mother's voice, in the later weeks of pregnancy. Availability of appropriate stimulation appears to be critical in the late prenatal and early postnatal period for normal sensory functioning to develop. There is an optimal range of stimulation—too much as well as too little may be problematic. Different sensory systems influence one another's development.

3. Rapid neuron reproduction continues after birth until the end of the first year. Although some neurons can reproduce even in adulthood, most nerve cell reproduction seems to end in infancy. The formation of synapses is ongoing throughout childhood and adolescence, and perhaps even into adulthood, and seems to be linked to cognitive advances. Many more synapses are formed than will be needed, and brain development postnatally involves synapse formation and *neural pruning. Experience-expectant* synapses are formed in anticipation of typical experiences. Experience shapes the pruning process—synapses that are used remain, and those that are not may be "discarded." *Experience-dependent* synapses are formed as a result of exposure to certain kinds of experience and may be pruned if they do not remain active.

4. Sensory and motor systems are laid down at a rudimentary level in human prenatal development but become integrated in complex ways in the first two years of life, partly as a function of experience. Some degree of *sensory integration dysfunction* may occur in some children. Hyper- and hyposensitivity to some kinds of stimulation, motor clumsiness, and poor eye-hand coordination are among the resulting difficulties.

Cognitive Development

5. In Piaget's theory, the mind constructs knowledge through *adaptation*. First, children interpret new information coming in from the environment in ways that fit what they already know or can do, called *assimilation*. They also show *accommodation*, with existing knowledge somewhat changed to create a better "fit" to what is new. Thus, children's understandings change only a little at a time, and the child may distort completely new information as she tries to assimilate it to her current knowledge structures. Piaget saw children as active learners, *intrinsically motivated* to seek out and understand new information. He believed that at any age their knowledge is organized or structured and that its organization changes over time as adaptation occurs. For some periods of time, called *stages,* a child's mental structures can be expected to have organizational properties in common. That is, within stages there are similarities in the ways children organize their thinking across a variety of concepts.

6. Modern research indicates that cognitive development is often *domain specific,* so that understandings in different domains of knowledge are not always organized in similar ways. The idea that children's cognitive development progresses in stages may not be strictly accurate. Yet, Piaget's stage divisions are broadly useful for organizing our thinking about children, their understandings, and their limitations at different ages.

7. Piaget studied infants' cognition in the *sensorimotor stage* (ages 0 to 2) by making inferences from babies' motor interactions with the environment. Today, researchers have available some additional tools, such as the *habituation* and the *preferential looking paradigms*. Modern research techniques produce findings that challenge some of Piaget's ideas about infants.

8. The *object concept* requires knowing first, that objects can stimulate multiple senses and second, that objects are permanent. Piaget assumed that infants develop the first understanding at about 2 to 4 months, as they coordinate their reflexive motor responses to stimulation. The second understanding requires representational

thought, and Piaget assumed it began between 8 and 12 months, when babies will search for a hidden object. Newer research, however, indicates earlier understandings of both aspects of the object concept. *Intersensory integration* is apparently possible in the first weeks of life, so that very young babies in some sense "know" that objects can be the source of many different forms of sensation. And with use of the habituation paradigm, some early signs of object permanence have been observed in 4-month-olds.

9. Despite these findings, most memory research indicates that representational thought in infants begins in earnest in the last part of the first year. *Recognition* ability, which requires only that a stimulus can be identified as familiar, is present by birth. However, the earliest indicator of *recall,* which requires representational thought, occurs at about 8 or 9 months. Two indicators of recall are *deferred imitation* and *separation anxiety*.

10. Intentional or planful action has precursors in early infancy, such as *making interesting sights last,* but *means-end behavior,* which seems to require some degree of representational thought, begins in the last part of the first year, when babies' communicative behaviors also begin to appear intentional. In the last few months of the first year, infants also begin to attribute to others *agency,* the ability to act without an external trigger. Understanding that other people have intentions, part of a *theory of mind,* seems to require a long developmental process beginning in the second half of the first year.

11. By age 2, children are in Piaget's stage of *preoperational* (meaning prelogical) *thought.* In his studies of preschoolers' skills, including understanding of numbers and of perspective taking, Piaget identified what he believed to be important limitations on early representational thought, limitations that are overcome by the end of this stage. Preoperational thought is *centered,* focused on one salient experience or event at a time. Because they cannot keep in mind all the relevant facts in a situation at one time, young children have trouble identifying the logical relationships among such facts, as indicated by children's early failure at *number conservation.* Since Piaget's work, researchers have developed simpler tasks and have been able to specify some of the early skills that children *do* have. Regarding number understanding, for example, Gelman found that young children's counting skills include adherence to the "one-to-one" principle and to the "order-irrelevance" principle and that in very simple situations they can even recognize that number stays the same when objects are rearranged.

12. Piaget pioneered the study of children's *theory of mind* with his perspective-taking tasks. Preschoolers find perspective taking difficult and usually assume that others have the same perspective that they do. Piaget argued that young children are *egocentric,* centered on their own perspective and therefore unaware of the possibility of another perspective. Newer work supports this idea, but identifies a gradual progression of perspective-taking skill in early childhood. Even 2-year-olds realize that others do not always see what they can see. By age 3, children can sometimes attribute a different visual perspective on the same object to another viewer. Between ages 4 and 5, children begin to realize that others sometimes know different things, as illustrated by their ability to recognize, in *false belief tasks,* that another person may be misinformed even when the child is not. These understandings are fragile, and when a situation is emotionally charged, even older children often fall back on the assumption that another's perspective must be like their own. In addition to growth in the ability to hold in mind multiple pieces of information, advances in perspective taking are generally seen as an outgrowth of experience with social interaction.

13. Preschool children can use and understand symbols, but research with *symbolic artifacts* indicates that their symbolic skills progress gradually. For example, before age 3

they cannot treat a video presentation or a toy model as both the concrete objects that they are *and* as symbols for other things.

14. Young children seem to have less difficulty understanding the use of words as symbols, perhaps because words are not objects in themselves—they are used only to represent other things. At first, children seem to construe words as one property of the concepts to which they refer. Language acquisition is a complex process that requires learning several systems.

15. Children begin to learn the *phonology* of their native language even before birth. By 6 months, babies have begun to lose the ability to discriminate sounds that are not important in their native language, and by 9 months their *babbling* is limited to only the sounds of their native language. Learning how, when, and where to use those sounds can take several years.

16. The *semantic system* includes the words and word parts that carry meaning. First words appear by the end of the first year, and a *vocabulary spurt* begins by 18 to 24 months. For many years, children learn new words at a rapid pace, *fast mapping* 9 or 10 new words a day.

17. Learning the *syntactic system* of a language requires learning the rules for creating meaningful sentences. Children begin to produce two-word utterances about the time of the vocabulary spurt, and can produce most sentence structures by the time they are 5.

18. *Pragmatics* involves using language effectively to communicate: learning to construct well-organized, clear *narratives, code-switching,* and learning to distinguish actual meaning from literal meaning.

19. Because of the complexity of language learning, some theorists argue that aspects of language learning must be innate. But all theorists recognize that language experience has to affect the language learning process in some ways. Two that have been identified are the importance of language experience to vocabulary acquisition and to the development of narrative skill. How much language is addressed to children in conversation and book reading is important for vocabulary growth. And the kinds of narrative exchanges young children have with adults affect their narrative skill.

20. Vygotsky's theory of cognitive development is focused on the role of culture and society in children's intellectual growth. One theme is that often novice learners grasp a concept or perform a skill only when others provide *scaffolding*. When understanding or performance requires scaffolding, it is said to be in the child's *zone of proximal development*.

21. Vygotsky especially emphasized language as a *tool* through which others convey formal knowledge, or *scientific concepts*. Language mediates learning in children and is one of the primary means by which culture and society help children's thinking to advance. Preschool children eventually come to use language as a way to mediate their own thinking. The private speech of 3-year-olds eventually becomes the *inner speech* of 8-year-olds. Internalization of speech is linked to attentional control, autobiographical memory, and impulse control.

Case Study

Shady Grove Preschool is located in an old suburban neighborhood adjacent to a large metropolitan area. It serves infants, toddlers, and preschoolers from families with diverse cultural and ethnic backgrounds who have lower- to upper-middle-class income levels. The director of the facility, Mrs. Anthony, has decided to implement a new component, monthly group discussion sessions for parents. She has employed a counselor to facilitate the discussions and to field questions about child development from the parents who come to the sessions.

At the first meeting, the participants, primarily a group of mothers, begin with introductions and questions of a general nature. "How do I know when my toddler is ready for toilet training?" "How can I get my 6-month-old to sleep through the night?" Then the discussion becomes more animated. One mother, Mrs. Winger, a white woman, starts to raise concerns about the educational program at the school. Her son, Brad, who is 4½, is a precocious child who enjoys learning. "I can't understand why they don't teach the children how to use computers in this school," she says. "These children need to get a head start on technological education because they will be competing with so many other students in schools for good colleges and, eventually, good jobs. We need to give them every advantage that we can."

Mrs. Winger is quick to add that she does not believe the children should be stressed. However, she clearly feels the days when children spend their time in preschool playing in a sandbox, drawing, and building with blocks should be over. She mentions that she has been reading some new information in parenting magazines about children's brain development, and she cautions the group against letting opportunities for the children's brain development to pass them by.

Mrs. Ramirez, a Latina, has a different concern. Her daughter, Tina, is 2½, and her 8-month-old son, Nicky, is in the infant program. "Tina is so jealous of her baby brother," says Mrs. Ramirez, "that she can't stand when I pay attention to him. She whines and cries when I play with him, even if I let her watch TV when I'm doing it. She won't let him touch anything that is hers. Her father gets very upset with her behavior, too. We've talked to her about being a big girl and about sharing with her brother. We can't believe that she is so selfish." After a pause she notes, sadly, "My sister's children are the same ages and they seem to get along much better. We're too embarrassed to take her to family gatherings now, because she doesn't know how to behave and only draws attention to herself. My parents insist that we are spoiling her."

Discussion Questions

1. What are the underlying assumptions about child development in Mrs. Winger's comments? What is your assessment of her concerns based upon what you know? How would you respond to her concerns?
2. Consider Mrs. Ramirez's statements. What are her beliefs about child development? How would you go about helping her resolve her problem? How have her assumptions about development affected her family relationships?
3. If you were the counselor in this situation, how would you plan a series of parent discussion sessions? What topics would you consider most important to cover? How could you present this information?
4. What is your position on accelerating development? Do you think that children can learn more than they are typically expected to? Should they be encouraged to do so?

 Journal Questions

1. "Culture" is a broad concept. Identify an idea, belief, or value that you learned as a child that came from the culture of your family, one that came from the culture of your community or neighborhood, one that came from your broader cultural/ethnic background, and one that came from your religious culture.
2. Discuss why it might be easier to talk to people of your own culture(s) from the perspective of Vygotsky's notion of intersubjectivity. Give an example from your experience.

Key Terms

neural tube
neurulation
neurons
glia
hindbrain
midbrain
cerebral cortex
forebrain
nucleus
medulla
pons
cerebellum
reticular formation
autonomic functions
brainstem
reticular activating system
superior colliculi
inferior colliculi
substantia nigra
cerebrum
corpus callosum
hemispheric specialization
occipital lobe
temporal lobe
central sulcus
parietal lobe
frontal lobe
association area
limbic system
hippocampus

amygdala
septum
thalamus
hypothalamus
endocrine system
plasticity
axon
axon terminals
neurotransmitters
dendrites
synaptic gap
myelination
circuits
projection neuron
interneuron
critical period
synapses
nerve growth factor
synaptogenesis
neural pruning
synaptic overproduction
experience-expectant
experience-dependent
sensory integration
    dysfunction
adaptation
assimilation
accommodation
intrinsically motivated
sensorimotor stage

preoperational stage
domain specific
habituation paradigm
orienting response
habituation
dishabituation
object concept
preferential looking
    paradigm
intersensory integration or
    intermodal perception
object permanence
representational thought
hidden object test
recognition
recall
deferred imitation
observational learning or
    modeling
separation anxiety
making interesting sights
    last
means-end behavior
agency
intention
theory of mind
symbols
number conservation task
centered thought

decentered thought
preoperational
    egocentrism
false belief tasks
symbolic artifacts
phonology
babbling
voicing
semantic system
vocabulary spurt
fast mapping
syntactic system or
    grammar
pragmatics
narrative
code switching
infantile amnesia
tools or signs
mediation
mediated learning
scientific concepts
scaffolding
zone of proximal
    development
developmental lines
egocentric or private
    speech
inner speech
SIDS

Emotional Development in the Early Years

In the course of their daily work, most clinicians encounter an array of human problems. Despite their different presenting features, all concerns—a young child's difficulty adjusting to school, a teenager's uncertainty about the future, a couple's recurring arguments about money, a widower's difficulty living alone—have a common aspect: they all, to a greater or lesser degree, involve human emotion. You probably could identify the emotional responses that would most likely be manifested by the hypothetical individuals in the previous examples. The child might feel lonely; the teenager, anxious; the couple, angry; and the older person, sad. And depending upon your particular theoretical orientation, you could probably suggest ways to help each individual. Yet, simply identifying the emotions and proposing techniques, as good a starting point as that may be, reveals nothing about the person's emotional development, nor does it provide you any insight as to whether your techniques might work. Are these clients' reactions appropriate or even adaptive in light of their situations? How concerned should you be about their symptoms? What were the precursors that led to their particular level of emotional adjustment or maladjustment? What coping styles have they developed over time and how useful are they? Unless we understand the process of emotional development in its normative context, we may only view our clients' emotions clinically, as if we were looking at their snapshots, detached from context and earlier experience. Their problems might be seen as manifestations of individual differences (for example, depressed versus anxious) rather than as reflections of their development, and their diagnoses might imply only possession of a set of clinical criteria. Overall, our understanding of clients would be impoverished.

The study of emotional development is a critical link to a better understanding of emotional problems whenever they appear during the life span. Sroufe (1996) states that "emotional development is the foundation for the study of individual adaptation and psychopathology. Pursuing these fields without being fully grounded in emotional development is analogous to trying to do research in genetics without being grounded in biology" (p. xii). Perhaps being an interpreter of emotional messages and a forger of affective change in a therapeutic context (Strupp, 1988) is also impossible without a fundamental working knowledge of emotional development. In this chapter, we review the beginnings of emotional development, the processes involved in early bonding, and the implications of these events for later well-being.

THEORIES OF EMOTIONS: THE STATE OF THE ART

Before we can address the topic of emotional development, we need to concern ourselves briefly with the question of what emotions are. This fundamental dilemma has occupied the time, attention, and brainpower of many gifted writers in the fields of philosophy, psychology and psychiatry, biology, and the neurosciences. However, there are still many unanswered questions and some major controversies in this area. For example, theorists disagree about whether emotions are best defined as physiological states, action tendencies, subjectively perceived experiences, or some combination of the above. A clear, comprehensive, universally accepted theory of the nature of emotions, the way emotions develop, the function of emotionally related brain structures, and the role of emotions in psychotherapy and mental health (Greenberg & Safran, 1989) has not yet been fully constructed.

One central question is whether there is a biological or evolutionary reason for emotions in humans. The consensus on this issue is that there is. Emotions are built into our nature for their survival value (Ortoney & Turner, 1992). Less agreement is found on what constitutes the set of basic human emotions. While most researchers agree that babies possess an emotional repertoire, opinions differ on the number, nature, and names of the emotions babies display. This is partly because different researchers emphasize different aspects of the question. Some writers have focused on the physical, particularly facial, manifestations of emotions (Ekman & Oster, 1979; Izard 1991), others on the neurological underpinnings (Damasio, 1994; Panksepp, 1982), while still others have centered their attention on the emergence of changes in kinds of emotional expression over the first few years of life (Sroufe, 1996). Despite these differences, studies of emotional development are beginning to converge with brain science to enrich our understanding of this vitally important aspect of human nature.

Functions of Emotions

Emotions exist to serve many purposes for human beings. It would be hard to disagree that they provide us with a trusty arsenal of survival skills. The fear response that alerts us to a dangerous situation signals us to fight back or escape in order to protect ourselves. The urge to engage in sexual relations propagates the species. The disgust we experience when we encounter decaying material protects us from exposure to potentially toxic bacteria. The affection elicited by a baby's smiling face promotes the caregiving needed to ensure his continued survival. Emotional responses have ancient, evolutionary significance.

Examples of the role emotions play in survival demonstrate how powerful emotions are as motivators of behavior. The force of conscience provides another clear example of the motivational properties of emotion. Conscience is like a thermostat balanced for feeling good. If we do something we consider morally or ethically wrong, we may experience shame or guilt. These feelings prod us to make restitution or to change our errant ways.

Emotions also serve as a major means of communication. An infant's distressed facial expression and piercing cry after receiving an inoculation serve as preemptory commands to the caretaker: "Help me! I'm in pain." When counselors speak of nonverbal communication, an essential component is always the emotional message conveyed through the face, posture, and gestures (Ekman & Friesen, 1969). The view of emotion-as-communication underscores the basic social significance of the emotions and captures an essential quality of the attachment relationship, to be discussed later in this chapter. Emotions are the stepping-stones that infants use to develop reciprocity with caregivers, ultimately leading to the capacity for emotion management.

The role of emotions in cognitive functions has received notice as well. Contrary to that age-old warning to keep your feelings out of your logical decision making, Damasio (1994) has provided compelling evidence that the absence of emotion clearly impairs rather than enhances cognition. Damasio observed patients with damage to the frontal lobe region and noted that they shared a syndrome that he called the **Phineas Gage matrix.** This syndrome consists of cognitive dysfunctions such as poor planning, inadequate decision making, inability to take another's perspective, and problems in sustaining employment. These cognitive limitations go hand in hand with emotional problems such as shallow affect, lack of an enriched emotional life, lack of passion and initiative, and a diminished sense of pleasure and pain. Far from enabling us to be more "rational," the absence of emotion in our intellectual functioning leaves us sadly lacking in resourcefulness.

Last, but certainly not least, emotions have a role to play in overall mental health and wellness. Research originally done by Salovey and Mayer (1990) and popularized by Coleman (1995) has emphasized the importance of so-called *emotional intelligence* (or emotional IQ), defined as the ability to perceive emotions, to identify and understand their meaning, to integrate them with other kinds of cognition, and to manage them. Despite recent claims found in the popular press that people with high emotional IQs have strong advantages in life over those not so well endowed, the scientific research in this area is in its infancy and cannot support such claims at the present time (Mayer & Cobb, 2000; Pfeiffer, 2001). Nonetheless, available data indicate a modest yet reliable correlation between emotional intelligence and certain positive life outcomes. Counselors very often deal with problems in emotional recognition and management. These can range from emotional underexpression, as in the case of affectively constricted or autistic individuals, to overexpression or poor regulation, as in the case of individuals who are chronically angry or anxious. The key to well-being is a healthy balance between emotional awareness, emotional acceptance, and emotional expression. So where does it all start? Let's begin our developmental story with a review of the evidence for innate emotional states.

Basic Emotions: Do They Exist?

Charles Darwin, writing in 1872, viewed certain emotions as innate and universal among humans and primates, rather like primitive instincts. He believed that facial expressions communicated the underlying emotions and that these emotions were present because they were necessary for survival. Modern evidence supporting the position that emotions are inborn and universal comes from three main sources: cross-cultural research, investigations of infant and child facial expressions, and physiological studies.

There is consistent evidence (Ekman, 1994; Ekman & Friesen, 1971) that people across a wide variety of cultures, including societies without exposure to Western ideas, fundamentally agree on what constitute expressions of basic emotions such as fear, sadness, happiness, anger, and surprise. Some disagreement currently surrounds the distinction between the emotions of contempt and disgust. The standard methodology used in cross-cultural research involves asking participants from different cultures to view pictures of facial expressions and then to identify the emotions depicted in the photographs. In reviewing studies conducted during the past 50 years, Ekman (1992) concluded that certain facial expressions are interpreted as the same emotions regardless of cultural context. From American cities to the highlands of New Guinea, both industrialized and nonindustrialized peoples derive the same meanings from certain characteristic facial expressions.

Drawing on this Darwinian tradition, Izard (1992), to help determine basic emotions, focused his attention on babies and their ways of communicating emotional messages. He reasoned that infants have little time to learn social conventions and therefore will exhibit only those emotional responses that are inborn. Izard developed coding schemes that enable researchers and clinicians to identify different emotions based upon the position of the facial musculature (Izard, 1979; Izard, Dougherty, & Hembree, 1983). Generally, research done with infants and children using these coding approaches has also supported the existence of basic emotions. Infants display predictable facial expressions in certain circumstances, implying, according to Izard, the underlying presence of a comparable feeling. For example, when an infant is presented with a new and interesting picture, he will show the facial response of interest. When interacting pleasantly with a beloved caretaker, the infant's face conveys happiness or joy.

A third line of evidence for the biological basis of emotions comes from brain research. As mentioned in Box 4.1: *The Emotional Brain*, specific brain systems or circuits, governing the expression of certain emotional states, appear to be prewired but responsive to experience. While there is diversity in the language used to describe them and some disagreement on the number of circuits, at this point researchers are generally agreed about the neural executive systems that mediate fear, expectancy, panic, and rage or anger (Gray, 1990; Panksepp, 1992). These subcortical circuits register the feeling components of experience. They have reciprocal associations with cortical areas that involve higher-order thinking and decision making. They can also come under the control of conditioning processes. Several writers have hypothesized that chemical substances such as drugs and alcohol become addictive because they have rewarding emotional effects, creating high levels of euphoria or an "emotional high" (DuPont, 1997). Cues associated with these substances may come to elicit physiological responses even in the absence of the original substance.

Theories and Sequence of Emotional Development

So infants do have some basic emotional systems in place at birth. Witness a group of crying newborns in a hospital nursery for evidence of this! However, the range of their emotional expression increases dramatically over the first two years of life. At birth or close to it, infants display distress (crying), contentment (smiling), disgust (avoiding bitter tastes or unpleasant odors), and interest (staring at faces and objects) (Izard & Malatesta, 1987). Anger, surprise, fear, and sadness begin to emerge from 2 months to approximately 6 months of age. So-called social emotions, such as pride, shame, embarrassment, and guilt, depend upon self-recognition and higher levels of cognitive functioning (M. Lewis & Brooks-Gunn, 1979). These social emotions, which emerge during the last half of the second year of life, will be discussed in Chapter 5. Not all researchers agree about the particulars of early emotional development. Disagreements center on which emotions emerge first and on what early emotional expressions mean. The central ideas of two of the main researchers in this field, Izard and Sroufe, will be reviewed next.

Izard's Differential Emotions Theory

Izard (1991) concluded that infant expressive behaviors are components of basic emotions. In other words, babies' faces are mirrors of the felt emotions within them. Izard's theory, called ***differential emotions theory,*** construes emotions to be the direct product of the underlying neural processes related to each of the emotional expressions. For example, a sad expression implies the operation of the neural circuitry associated with sadness. If a baby looks sad, he is sad. In Izard's view, emotions are based on evolution rather than learning and do not require cognitive components, such as appraisal or intent, in order to exist. Emotions emerge in infancy and early childhood in a form that is comparable to the emotions experienced by adults. In Izard's theory, socialization or learning plays a role in

Box 4.1   The Emotional Brain

Are you a person who is used to going to bed early at night and who is typically more alert and energetic early in the morning? If so, you may have occasionally had the difficult experience of trying to keep yourself awake late at night to study for a test. Or perhaps you are a right-handed person who once had your writing hand in a cast and needed to maneuver with your left hand. In either of these cases, you would have been "fighting" your body's natural inclinations, either to sleep according to its accustomed cycles or to write using a preferred hand. It's not easy. Moreover, it's more time-consuming and labor-intensive than it would be otherwise. Some current writers in the neurosciences make the same point when talking about the brain. If we do not understand and accept how our brains work, they claim, we may be operating at cross-purposes. That is, we may be fighting against our biology when we employ clinical and educational strategies that do not make sense from the perspective of *brain-behavior relationships*. Even though it seems fair to say that most clinicians are interested more in people than in the science of brain function, it is also fair to say that we stand to profit immensely from some understanding of what science has to offer in this area.

Probably this is of greatest importance to clinicians in the area of emotions. For what human problem or concern does not, in some way, touch on our feelings? Since our brains process emotions, it is worth our time to try to understand the biology involved. What areas of the brain are responsible for handling emotional messages? What causes emotions to get out of control? What is the relationship between thinking and emotion? Recently, researchers have addressed these questions and have provided some intriguing, although admittedly incomplete, answers. Allowing brain science to inform our psychological theories of emotion will guide us to choose theories that are compatible with biological processes and that will be more effective therapeutically. Furthermore, knowledge of the brain can open up possibilities for new understanding about how emotions operate (LeDoux, 1995). Let us examine some of this new information about the emotional brain so that we can make better informed decisions as reflective practitioners.

Historically, the study of emotion has not received the kind of attention from researchers that, for example, learning or memory has been given (Neisser, 1967). Perhaps this happened because researchers had difficulty defining emotions. Perhaps researchers had a bias against "soft, subjective" topics in favor of those considered more objective and, therefore, more appropriate to science. The somewhat artificial split between "cognition" and "emotion" resulted in the common perception that information processing involved only higher-order thinking capacities separate from emotion. This perception existed despite the fact that higher-order cognitive processing is *just one kind* of information processing that the brain is able to accomplish. In any case, the study of emotions, so central to human experience and so critical to helpers, was largely left out of the cognitive revolution that started around the middle of the twentieth century. In the words of LeDoux (1996), cognitive scientists seemed to view people as "souls on ice" (p. 22). Clinicians were further distanced from an appreciation of the emotional brain because traditional academic training separated students of social science and of science into different tracks, thus leaving students with clinical interests ill-prepared in the biological sciences (deCatanzaro, 1999).

This is not to say that there has been no interest in emotions. Early theorists such as William James, Carl Lange, Walter Cannon, Philip Bard, and others provided theories of emotions that held sway for many years. These theorists tended to disagree about the directionality of emotional responses and the primacy of body or brain. James believed that environmental events lead to bodily changes and behaviors, which people then interpret as particular emotions. Cannon and Bard argued that external stimuli had to be detected and evaluated by the rational brain before conscious feelings and bodily changes could be produced (see deCatanzaro, 1999, for a review of classic theories). From the biological camp, the most influential ideas came from James Papez (1937), who identified the structures of the limbic circuit, and Robert MacLean (1952, 1970), who proposed that the limbic system was the *visceral brain,* or the site of emotions. MacLean, building on the earlier work of Papez, concluded that the brain had evolved over millions of years to its present tripartite, or "three-brains-in-one," state. His *triune brain* included the (1) reptilian, (2) paleomammalian, or limbic, and (3) mammalian brains, each with its own particular structures and functions. All three were thought to exist in man and in other advanced animal species. Lower-level mammals had both paleomammalian and reptilian brains, while lower-level species had only the latter.

According to MacLean's theory, each "brain" was distinct, represented successively higher levels of cortical

Box 4.1 Continued

functioning, and arrived on the scene at a different time in history. The limbic brain was composed of evolutionarily "old" cortex or brain matter that was present in species that were phylogenetically older than humans. The functions served by this system—fight, flight, feeding, mating, and so on—were necessary for the survival of the species. Many early studies of anatomy supported the ties between limbic structures and emotional responses, so that the limbic system as the processor and repository of emotions was dogma for many years.

Beginning in the 1970s, however, researchers began to uncover evidence that poked holes in MacLean's theory. First, it was shown that species that are very primitive (and old in the evolutionary sense) have brain structures that function as the cerebral cortex does in more advanced species (Northcutt & Kaas, 1995). This cast doubt on the evolution of a triune brain. Furthermore, some parts of the limbic system do not deal with emotions at all, while parts of the cerebral cortex do. Rather than consider the limbic system as the all-purpose emotional power plant, researchers such as LeDoux (1996) claim that there are several discrete emotional systems or circuits in the brain designed to take care of different problems that have faced humans and animals over the course of evolution. For example, the brain system that helps us deal with fearful situations appears to be distinct from the one that enables us to feel pleasure. Therefore, if we want to understand the emotions (and the disorders linked to them), we probably need to consider these systems as separate but interacting. We also need to consider the relationships of these emotional systems, or modules, to the higher cortical areas.

LeDoux's ideas have been supported by evidence for several different emotional "circuits," seven to be precise, identified by scientists such as Panksepp (1982; 1992). These circuits operate semiautomatically when triggered, producing the emotional responses of seeking, rage, fear, lust, nurturance, sorrow, and play.

We can find some specific answers to the question of how the brain processes emotion by considering LeDoux's illuminating work on the fear circuit. Conventional wisdom used to be that the cerebral cortex receives sensory input first before conveying such input to the limbic structures for an emotional "reading" (Schacter & Singer, 1962). Thus, the cortex was perceived as the broker of all brain activity. It had a hand in all the action, able to exert its rational control over all thinking and feeling. Much to the surprise of many

researchers, LeDoux identified a neural "back alley" through which information about a fearful stimulus travels directly from the sensory systems through the thalamus to the amygdala, bypassing the cortex altogether. Information traveling via this "low road" pathway leads to quicker, more powerful, and longer lasting, but also less rational, responses than information processed first via the cortex.

Let us consider what this means. Given this state of biological affairs, it is possible for people to experience an emotional response, such as fear, and to start to react in typical flight-or-fight ways before the more rational cortex has even registered the event. Emotions such as fear are present in humans for some adaptive purpose; they have helped us survive. LeDoux's findings suggest that we have a *biological preparedness* to respond emotionally to at least some harmful stimuli. It is far easier to learn to fear snakes, for example, than it is to fear shrubbery!

Imagine that one sunny summer afternoon you are swimming alone in the ocean, off the coast of your beach resort. Out of the corner of your eye, you spot a gray triangular shape rising above the water not too far away. Your body responds in characteristically defensive ways. Your hair stands on end, your stomach tightens, your heart races, and so on. The threat is transmitted to your brain's emotional centers almost instantaneously so that your body can ready itself against the danger. Now, suppose the putative shark fin turns out to be only a piece of debris. Upon closer observation, your cortex distinguishes the difference and allows you to adjust your response to one that is more appropriate. Your initial emotional reaction is only a split second ahead of your rational response. Nature has apparently given us an early warning emotional system to provide us with a survival advantage. It is the cortex's job to decide whether the response is warranted or not. Thus, high-road and low-road processing, involving both reason and emotion, work in concert.

The glitch is that low-road emotional processing could be responsible for persistent emotional responses that we don't understand. This can happen through *conditioning*, or the pairing of emotional responses to stimuli that were once neutral. LeDoux believes that phobias, panic, post-traumatic stress disorder, and anxiety all arise from the operation of the brain's fear system. As helpers know, these problems and reactions can persist despite the absence of real threat. Another tricky

(continued)

Box 4.1   Continued

part is that these fears do not extinguish by themselves; probably active new learning or extinction training is needed for their control. They appear to lay in wait until, under stressful conditions, they rear their ugly heads again and affect our responses.

Since emotional memories seem to be indelibly fixed in the neural circuits, the best chance we have to change things therapeutically is to help the more rational cortex gain control over emotional centers through new learning. LeDoux states that therapy rewires the brain pathways to facilitate a kind of emotional control but never completely erases the amygdala's memory. Thus, the therapeutic process is fairly daunting from a biological perspective. He notes:

> It is well known that the connections from the cortical areas to the amygdala are far weaker than the connections from the amygdala to the cortex. This may explain why it is so easy for emotional information to invade our conscious thoughts, but so hard for us to gain conscious control over our emotions. (1996, p. 265)

LeDoux suggests that psychotherapy may be a long process "because of this asymmetry in connections between the cortex and the amygdala" (p. 265).

emotional expression, mainly to expand or facilitate the individual's capacity to regulate the innate forms of emotions.

Sroufe's Developmental Position

In contrast, Sroufe (1996) takes the position that emotions are not fully formed at birth but that they develop from undifferentiated responses into more differentiated ones and finally into an integrated emotional repertoire. This principle is called **orthogenetic:** as behavior becomes differentiated or elaborated, it also becomes hierarchically organized or controlled by higher levels of functioning. Early infant emotional expressions are considered precursors or forerunners of more mature emotions. Emotions start in this fashion, Sroufe reasons, because infants lack the cognitive ability needed to ascribe meaning to emotional experiences. An example of this notion is that the generalized distress of the early infant period can be reliably differentiated into either fear or anger roughly at 6 months, only after the infant can recognize a threat. At this later time, the infant's facial expressions can be interpreted more reliably as communicating anger or fear.

EARLY CAREGIVER-INFANT INTERACTIONS AND EMOTIONAL DEVELOPMENT

As we have already seen, it is hard to argue with the idea that emotions provide for human beings' continued survival. Given our long period of dependence, human infants, for obvious reasons, cannot do much to ensure survival on their own. In order to grow and thrive, babies depend upon the nurturance of adult caregivers who can "read" their emotional expressions and attend to their physical and emotional needs. As it turns out, babies are masters in the art of eliciting the care and attention they need from adults. Among the tools of their art are their physical characteristics, which entice adults to care for them. Characteristics such as small body size, large eyes, and large head size relative to the total body size have been called **releasers** because they appeal to the nurturant proclivities of caregivers (Fullard & Reiling, 1976). Just think of the people you know who cannot pass an infant they see without smiling and gazing at the baby, perhaps even engaging in a bit of "baby talk" for good measure.

Infant behaviors also serve the function of eliciting care as well as positive attention. Crying and clinging typically bring or keep caregivers close by. Infants have been shown to display more "greeting" or communicative responses to people than to objects and appear more contented and relaxed when they see people (Brazelton, Koslowski, & Main, 1974). With the onset of the social smile around 5 weeks of age, babies lavish many more smiles on their primary caregivers than on others. Mothers, most often the primary caretakers, and their infants engage in increasingly longer mutual gaze interactions. By the age of 3 months, actual turn taking can be observed. The mother's responses and movements are in synchrony with those of her infant (Condon & Sander, 1974).

All these behaviors facilitate the creation of a social and communicative bond between infant and caregiver, ensuring that needs as basic as food, shelter, and safety are met. They also are important for the development of the infant's emotional health. Let us recall our earlier discussion of experience-expectant and experience-dependent brain development (see Chapter 3). The newborn's development is only partially laid down at birth and depends upon certain types of environmental input in order to continue normally. Like all other aspects of brain development, the development of emotions depends upon the interaction of genetics and environment. The specific, facilitative environmental circumstances needed for healthy emotional development to occur include supportive, responsive caregiving. As we will see later in the chapter, the attachments that result between infants and caregivers allow feelings of security and trust to flourish in infants. Responsive caregiving also helps infants to develop emotional regulation.

Emotional Regulation

Emotional regulation is one of the cornerstones of emotional well-being and positive adjustment throughout the life span. How do we learn to manage the power of our emotions? At birth, like a thermostat with an unreliable shut-off valve, the emotions of the newborn are poorly regulated. Emotional states can range from contentment to intense distress within minutes. Typically, adult caregivers serve the critical function of helping to manage affect or to modulate affective expression while scaffolding the infant's own developing self-regulation. With older infants, the caretaker's emotional expressions can teach

Caregivers' emotional messages influence babies' willingness to crawl over the edge of the visual cliff.

the child how to make sense of the world when dealing with emotionally charged situations. Experiments by Campos and his colleagues (1983) demonstrate that 10-month-old infants who are able to crawl over a "visual cliff" (a glass-covered surface that looks like a sharp "drop-off") actively seek out their mothers' responses before proceeding to crawl over the "cliff." Infants whose mothers respond with fearful facial or vocal expressions do not advance, whereas those whose mothers respond with smiles or encouragement proceed to cross the surface without fear. Interestingly, infants use the emotional information provided by caregivers to help them interpret situations that are ambiguous to them.

However, a baby is not totally dependent upon his caregivers to manage emotional experiences. Nature also provides some inborn coping strategies, both other-directed and self-directed, that help a baby develop and regulate his emotions. Imagine, for example, an infant who gazes, smiles, and coos at his mother and receives smiles, attention, and verbalizations in return. The infant's emotional state is likely to remain positive, opening the way for further social engagement. Now imagine the infant who smiles at his mother but gets no response. The infant's needs (to establish contact, maintain security and proximity, experience positive emotions, and control distress) are frustrated. Such frustration usually leads to a negative emotional state and allows us to observe how infants respond to frustration. The dynamics of social engagement and frustration, distress, and coping are stunningly apparent in a research technique called the **"still-face" paradigm** (Tronick, Als, & Brazelton, 1980). The infant, usually around 3 months of age, is placed in an infant seat directly in front of his mother. The mother is instructed to interact in a normally pleasant and playful way with her child. The mother responds to her infant's emotional displays, and a synchronous "dance" between her and her child develops. Then the mother is instructed to change her behavior, either by remaining completely nonresponsive or by acting in an emotionally withdrawn fashion. When the infant recognizes this change, he will initiate his **other-directed coping behaviors,** using facial expressions, movements, and verbalizations that seem designed to get his mother to resume the previous interactive style. The baby's distress heightens if the mother still fails to engage, and the infant resorts to **self-directed coping behaviors** that seem designed for self-comfort. Babies look away or may even self-stimulate by rocking, sucking, and so on. Interestingly, this effect is observed if the mother is unresponsive only for a few seconds. The baby's negative mood persists even when the mother resumes contact. Babies look at their mothers less for several minutes after this experience (Tronick, 1989).

It is important to note that normal mother-infant interactions are not all positive. Tronick has reported that only about 30% of the face-to-face interactions during the first year of life are positive in the sense that the baby is calm and alert and able to be responsive to the mother in interactions that are mutually coordinated. Coordinated sequences involve frequent shifts from positive emotional states to negative emotional states and then back to positive states. It takes the sensitivity of the patient caregiver to gently prod the baby toward longer periods of positive affect, resulting in fewer and briefer periods of negative emotion. The key, as we shall see, seems to be the ability to move the derailed interaction back onto a positive track. Under normal circumstances, the caregiver-baby interaction gets repaired because of efforts of the caregiver. This positive movement or **interactive repair** allows the infant to come to depend upon his caregiver for help as well as to shape his own sense of effectiveness as a social agent. Ultimately, the infant's other-directed coping strategies, which he learns are effective in the context of sensitive caregiving, enhance communication and promote engagement with the external environment. Essentially, the effect of this reciprocal process is to help babies learn to be content most of the time. Note that the caregiver provides the "experience dependent" environment in which the baby's coping strategies play out. Once again, the interplay of native and environmental factors is required for a successful outcome.

Infants of Depressed Mothers

Infants of depressed mothers are a group at particular risk because this synchrony is chronically interrupted. Depressed caretakers typically show less positive affect than nondepressed caretakers. They look away from their babies more often and display more anger, intrusiveness, and poorly timed responses. In short, they thwart their babies' efforts to establish predictable contact, leading to more negative emotional periods for the infant and increased levels of self-directed coping. A baby needs help regulating his emotions and learning the predictability that characterizes well-coordinated interactions. Unfortunately, the depressed caregiver is unable to provide the kind of help that is needed. For infants of depressed mothers, interactions frequently go unrepaired, and the infant resorts to a style of affective coping marked by escaping and turning away. Both future social relationships and cognitive development can be negatively affected.

Physiological studies have documented differences in the brain activity of infants of depressed and nondepressed mothers. For example, Field and her colleagues (1995) reported asymmetrical electrical activity in the right frontal area of 3- to 4-month-old infants of depressed mothers. This pattern of heightened right frontal activation and lowered left frontal activation is consistent with the patterns observed in extremely fearful and inhibited children and in chronically depressed adults, suggesting the experience of more negative than positive emotions. The authors point out that this physiological marker may be a useful indicator of infants who are at risk of emotional problems and who might profit from early intervention. In addition, infants of depressed mothers showed elevated heart rates and cortisol levels, both symptomatic of stress (Field, 1989).

Does all this mean that depressed mothers *pass on* their depression? The longitudinal studies needed to answer this question are not available. As with other questions, experts take somewhat different stands. Field and colleagues (1988) hold the view that a mother's depression does predispose her child to more depressed affect. Their position is supported by findings that infants' depressed behaviors generalize to other nondepressed adults, indicating a style of relating characterized by negative affect. Some infants of depressed mothers may become sensitive to others' emotional states by virtue of their experience, making them more socially adept and skilled at obtaining social support. Nonetheless, it is fair to say that infants exposed to chronically depressed and/or nonresponsive caregivers are at risk for increased interactive failure. This group of caregivers need treatment aimed at reducing their depression and teaching effective parenting skills.

Neurobiology of Early Social Bonding

One exciting new area of research focuses on the underlying neurophysiology associated with the formation and expression of emotional relationships (see Box 4.1). We know from research on adults that the brain's right hemisphere is specialized for recognizing and interpreting nonverbal communication (Borod, Koff, & Buck, 1986). Although research support is still tentative at this point, the right hemisphere appears to be more mature than the left hemisphere in infancy (Tucker, 1986). Thus, nature may have equipped the infant with a sensitive period for the development of social attachments based upon the brain's developmental trajectory. Tucker reasons that the more rapid development of the left hemisphere in the second year of life is manifested outwardly by the toddler's achievements in motor and language skills. Tucker also interprets the toddler's increasing autonomy as a shift away from the right-hemisphere-mediated attention to emotional and social contexts that characterize the first year of life. We need to be careful, however, not to think exclusively in terms of hemispheric specialization. As we have seen, cortical brain functions interact with subcortical structures in an integrated way.

Schore (1994), for example, cites the importance of the right hemisphere in his discussion of the biological roots of emotional development, but he emphasizes the relationship between cortical and subcortical regions. He reports evidence from animal and some human studies that identifies the right orbitofrontal region, located in the internal region of the right frontal lobe, as the primary brain region involved in social bonding. This area is enlarged in humans and has dense connections to the brain's emotional centers, the limbic system, hypothalamus, and brain stem. He posits that the development and reorganization of this brain area over the first two years of life are critically dependent upon the caregiver's rhythmic, sensitive responses, which help to regulate the infant's uneven hormonal, autonomic, and behavioral states.

Working at the neurochemical level, Panksepp and his colleagues (1978) have hypothesized that the brain's opiate system plays a special role in the formation of social attachments. Studying puppies and other animal species, these researchers have found that low doses of opiates can effectively reduce the specific kinds of distress caused by social separation, while they are ineffective with other kinds of pain. These researchers reason that normal social interaction and the formation of affective social bonds activate the brain's own opiate system. Externally delivered opiates apparently mimic the normal operation of the brain's internal opiate system. In essence, narcotics may function like a social relationship. These authors speculate that problems as diverse as drug addiction and autism are human responses to the perception of social isolation and may be related at the neurological level to the brain's opiate system.

ATTACHMENT: EARLY SOCIAL RELATIONSHIPS

Human infants are emotionally and behaviorally equipped to elicit responsive care and stimulation from adults. Adults, in turn, are prepared by nature to stimulate and nurture infants. The social interactions that result help an infant to expand his emotional repertoire, and they support the development of his capacity for emotion regulation. But early interpersonal interactions may have a much broader impact on the infant's development. Theorists such as John Bowlby (1969/1982; 1973; 1980) and Erik Erikson (1950/1963) have proposed that the relationships that an infant has with one or a few caregivers during the first year of life provide him with a working model of himself and of others. (See Box 4.2: *A Biographical Sketch: John Bowlby* and Box 4.3: *A Biographical Sketch: Erik H. Erikson.*) These emerging models play an important role in determining how secure and optimistic a child will later feel about venturing forth to explore the broader world. Thus, early relationships are said to lay the groundwork for future interactions with others, for the child's self-concept, and even for his outlook on life.

For Erikson, the characteristics of early caregiving enable a child to form his first feelings about others. When care is timely, sensitive to the infant's needs, and consistently available, he begins to establish **basic trust,** seeing others as dependable and trustworthy. As his rudimentary view of others takes shape, it influences how he begins to see himself. If others can be trusted to provide for his needs, then his needs must be important and he must be a worthy recipient of care. Feeling trust and feeling worthy emerge together, two sides of the same coin. These early attitudes toward others and toward the self create a sense of hope or optimism that experiences beyond the caregiving relationship will also be positive and are therefore worth pursuing.

Bowlby described the infant's connection with the primary caregiver (usually the mother) as his first attachment relationship. Bowlby's theory of how it changes and what it means for the child's psychosocial life is called **attachment theory.** In Bowlby's description,

Box 4.2   A Biographical Sketch: John Bowlby

In the 1950s, 7-year-old Marianne was hospitalized for a tonsillectomy. The small-town hospital where the surgery was performed had very strict policies governing visitors to its child patients: one hour in the afternoon, maximum of two visitors. Marianne's experiences with doctors had generally been positive up until then. In addition, her mother was a nurse, so Marianne was warmly disposed to women dressed in white from head to foot and smelling wonderfully clean, and she was, blessedly, old enough to understand what was happening to her. The first afternoon and evening, preoperatively, were a pleasant adventure, and Marianne was able to sleep without distress despite the separation from her family. But the next day, after the early morning surgery, the pain struck, and Marianne wanted her mother's cool hand and soothing voice. The hours until her mother's first visit were endless, and the end of the visit was agony. The release into her parents' care the next afternoon was a respite from hell.

Through the middle 1900s, restricted visitation to child hospital patients was standard policy, based on concerns about infection and about disruptions to medical routines. Today, parents not only are allowed complete access to their children in most hospitals but are encouraged to stay with their children continuously and to be part of the healing and helping process. Many hospitals provide cots and even rooms for showering and changing to encourage parental involvement. It was John Bowlby's groundbreaking theorizing and research on the sometimes devastating emotional costs of mother-child separations, especially during hospitalizations, that initiated a major shift in thinking about the relative benefits of separating children from their families.

John Bowlby (1907–1990) and Mary D. Salter Ainsworth (1913–1999) were jointly responsible for a revolution in the way that parent-child relationships are perceived by researchers and clinicians. Bowlby began his professional life in England as a psychoanalyst who worked with children. In the 1930s, Bowlby's clinical work was supervised by Melanie Klein, who invented psychoanalytic play therapy. Bowlby was inclined to look for a relationship between his young patients' behavior and the kind of parenting they were receiving, but Klein discouraged his family-oriented approach, arguing that the child's "object" relations (interpersonal beliefs and behaviors) were a function of fantasy, not experience in relationships. Bowlby, however, was convinced that early relationships play a large role in per-

sonality and behavioral development. He discovered in the work of *ethologists,* biologists who do careful observations of animal behavior in natural environments, that animals such as ducks and geese are inclined to become devoted followers of whatever they first see moving – usually their mothers, but sometimes a different animal, such as a human researcher. Such bonding, when it works "the way nature intended," promotes the survival of ducklings and goslings by keeping them close to a protective adult. Eventually, Bowlby integrated ideas from ethology, from systems theory, from cognitive development (including the work of Piaget), and from psychoanalysis into attachment theory, arguing that some human infant behaviors, for example clinging and sucking, help to keep the mother close, while others, for example smiling, naturally elicit maternal caregiving. Such behaviors initiate the development of an attachment system that promotes the infant's survival and creates a feeling of security. That system changes and consolidates over time as the child's skills develop. Early clinging and sucking are later replaced by other attachment behaviors, such as protesting when mother leaves or joyfully greeting her when she returns, but the system's evolutionary function remains the same. The attachment system is enhanced and developed by the responses of the environment (i.e., of the caregiver) and helps the child to develop a working model of the self (e.g., I am valuable, worthy of care) and of others (e.g., others are reliable and caring).

Bowlby's theoretical work was enhanced and enriched by research into the importance of early relationships on children's behavior. For example, he and his colleagues studied the effects of hospitalization and institutionalization on 15- to 30-month-olds using the careful, detailed observational style of ethology. They documented a series of stages of distress and withdrawal that helped create the impetus for change in hospital visitation policies described above (see also Box 4.5: *Infant Day Care: Is There an Attachment Risk?*). But the research that captured the attention of both the scientific and the clinical community was Ainsworth's studies of mothers and babies in their own homes.

Ainsworth, who earned a Ph.D. in psychology at the University of Toronto, submerged her own career to follow her husband to London. There she answered Bowlby's newspaper ad seeking researchers. His views

(continued)

Box 4.2   Continued

of the importance of early relationships were consistent with many of her own ideas, and Ainsworth became an eager student and associate. When her husband's career took her to Uganda, she launched a study of local mothers caring for their unweaned infants. She became convinced from her observations that Bowlby was right: babies actively help create an attachment system that protects them and provides a foundation for later developments. She also believed that the 28 Ganda babies she studied were forming attachments of different qualities, and she looked for relationships between the infants' attachment quality and the mothers' sensitivity and responsiveness. When her husband moved again, this time to Baltimore, Ainsworth took a position at Johns Hopkins University. Eventually, she launched a more detailed and intensive study of 26 mother-infant dyads. After 18 home visits over the course of each baby's first year, she invented the "strange situation test" to assess the infants' feelings of security when they were 1 year old. That test is now the preeminent means for assessing attachment quality and has been used in dozens of studies since, by researchers around the world eager to test the tenets of attachment theory and to explore the precursors and consequences of an infant's first attachments. Ainsworth's careful research both enhanced the credibility of Bowlby's views and demonstrated that interpersonal relationships, and not just individual behaviors, could be meaningfully investigated using scientific techniques. (Source: Karen, 1998).

Box 4.3   A Biographical Sketch: Erik H. Erikson

The parents of a 4-year-old boy named Peter brought him to Erik Erikson for treatment of a frightening problem that appeared to be emotionally based. Peter retained his feces for up to a week at a time, and his colon had become enlarged. As he learned more about Peter, Erikson came to see his problem as a reaction to the way others had dealt with normal, stage appropriate behavior. Before the problem began, Peter had entered what Erikson described as the developmental stage of initiative versus guilt, when it is common for children to intrude themselves on others in a rather aggressive way—such as trying to take over the conversation at the dinner table or, as in Peter's case, being physically aggressive and bossy with adults (see Table 1.2 in Chapter 1). Peter's aggressive style was tolerated amiably by his nanny, but his mother was disturbed by it and by the nanny's tolerance, so she fired the nanny. Peter's anal retention problem started soon afterward. Eventually, Erikson helped Peter to see that his problem was related to his distress at losing his beloved nanny. Peter, Erikson felt, was identifying with the nanny, who had told Peter that she was going to have a baby of her own, and he was trying to hold on to her by retaining his feces.

Erikson's work with Peter reflects the Freudian roots of his perspective. He saw Peter's 4-year-old aggressiveness with his nanny as having sexual overtones, a normal process for a child in Freud's phallic stage. When Peter's aggressiveness led to the painful loss of the beloved nanny, he regressed to using behaviors more typical of the anal stage: holding on to his feces. But Erikson's interpretation also reveals his innovative, psychosocial perspective, which went well beyond his Freudian training. Preschoolers need to express their bold new sense of initiative. Adults can be accepting of this need, even as they impose some constraints so that children will learn to behave in socially acceptable ways. In the process, children will learn to curb their own behavior, controlled by their own feelings of guilt. But when constraints are imposed in an abrupt, disapproving, unsupportive way, or when they are excessive, children's appropriate exuberance can be stifled, leading a child to be overly restrained and guilty about normal behavior. Just as in infancy, when children must form basic trust, the warmth, sensitivity, and understanding of responsive adults is an important ingredient in the development of positive feelings about self and/or others.

Erik H. Erikson (1902–1994) was the son of Danish parents; his mother was Jewish, his father, Protestant. His parents separated before he was born, and he was raised in Germany by his mother and stepfather. His undistinguished youth seems an unlikely beginning for a great developmental theorist. He was something of a misfit as a young boy. His ethnicity as a Jew coupled with his Gentile appearance caused him to experience social rejection from both his Jewish and his Gentile peers. As a young man, Erik, born Erik Homberger, changed his surname to Erikson—a clear attempt to construct his own identity. He was not much of a

Box 4.3   Continued

student, and after high school, uncertain of his goals or interests, he wandered through Europe rather than attend college. He studied art for a while, wandered again, and eventually accepted an offer to teach children at a school where Anna Freud, daughter of Sigmund, was a cofounder. Thus began his life's work as a child clinician. He studied psychoanalysis with Anna Freud, and when he and his wife, Joan, fled Europe in 1933 with the rise of Hitler, he became the first child analyst in Boston. In his career as a therapist and developmental theorist, he held faculty appointments at Yale, in the University of California system, and finally at Harvard, despite the fact that he had earned no degrees beyond high school. In his scholarly work he not only contributed to research and theory on normal personality development, including the formerly uncharted area of adult life stages, he pioneered exploration into cross-cultural variations in development, observing the life experiences of Sioux Indians in South Dakota and of Yurok Indians in California. Although Erikson extended his work to include adult developmental issues, he seems to have had a special concern for the vulnerability of children. In his writing on child rearing, he urged parents to recognize that the most fundamental requirement of good parenting is to provide a sense of security, to give children the benefit of calm, reliable care, starting in earliest infancy. (Sources: Coles, 1970; Crain, 1992).

infant and caregiver participate in an attachment system that has evolved to serve the purpose of keeping the infant safe and assuring his survival. As we have already noted, both the infant and the adult bring to the system a set of biologically prepared behaviors. These behaviors change as the infant's repertoire of abilities changes, partly as a function of interactions with others. Early in infancy, as we have seen, infant cries and clinging bring a caregiver. Later, instead of clinging, the toddler may keep an eye on one particular adult, often the mother, keeping track of her whereabouts in case of need. Instead of crying, the toddler may call to the caregiver or communicate by reaching or pointing. When the baby does cry, the caregiver may respond differently to different cries, assessing the level and kind of need from variations in the sound, apparently recognizing that crying can serve multiple purposes for the older baby (see R. A. Thompson & Leger, 1999). Thus, the system broadens to include and accommodate the infant's more advanced physical and cognitive abilities, but it still serves the purpose of making the child secure.

In the context of this attachment system, an affectional bond develops between infant and caregiver. Bowlby argued that as a result of cognitive and emotional developments in the infancy period, the baby's connection to the caregiver emerges in stages, with a full-fledged attachment likely by about 7 or 8 months. Schaffer and Emerson (1964) followed the development of a group of infants through their first 18 months and found a sequence of attachment stages consistent with those Bowlby has described. In the first 2 months, infants signal their needs, producing behaviors such as clinging, smiling, and crying. Although we now know that even newborns have some ability to recognize their mothers' voices (e.g., DeCasper & Fifer, 1980), they show little sign of discriminating among potential caregivers or of having a social preference, so that babies cannot yet be seen as attached to anyone. Next, between about 2 and 7 or 8 months, infants gradually show stronger and stronger preferences for particular caregivers, as when a baby smiles more brightly or is more readily soothed by Mom or Dad than by Grandma or Uncle Bill. Usually by 8 months, babies behave in ways that signal a strong preference for one caregiver, most often the mother. The chief indicator of attachment is that an infant will protest being separated from the mother and will greet her happily when she returns. Along with this *separation anxiety* (see Chapter 3 for a full description) may come *stranger anxiety:* an increased tendency to be wary of strangers and to seek the comfort and protection of the primary caregiver when a stranger is present. Note that infants can recognize familiar faces and voices much earlier than 7 or 8 months, and they may show some wariness with strangers, but a more intense reaction is common once other indicators of the first attachment emerge. Finally, Schaffer and Emerson observed that soon after babies show signs of their first emotional attachment, many of them are forming other attachments as well, with their fathers, with regular babysitters, with older siblings, and with other family members. By 18 months, most of the babies in their study were attached to more than one person.

Attachment is a system, not a particular set of behaviors. The system serves three purposes: it maintains proximity between infant and caregiver (called **proximity maintenance**), providing the potential for ongoing protection (called **secure base**); it creates a haven for the infant when distressed (called **safe haven**); and it maintains an emotional bond between infant and caregiver. Behaviors as diverse as smiling and crying all serve attachment functions, and as already noted, the particular behaviors serving these functions can change over time and circumstance. When helpers reflect on problems faced by children and families, attachment theory indicates that the proper unit of analysis is at the level of relationships. That is, a behavior (e.g., crying or clinging) must be interpreted within its social context in order to understand its significance.

Let's consider the notion of *safe haven* more specifically, for it is here that attachments serve the important function of stress management. Think back, for a moment, to the earlier discussion of emotion regulation. The infant has limited ability to regulate his episodes of physiological distress. Threats such as hunger, pain, fatigue, loneliness, or overstimulation can produce periods of dysregulation or heightened arousal. Some infants are more easily aroused than others because of temperamental differences in autonomic reactivity. For all infants, and especially for these more sensitive and vulnerable ones, the stressfulness of physical or emotional discomfort activates the attachment system. By crying, clinging, or showing distress in some other way, the infant signals his need for his caregiver to step in to help manage stress. Distress, triggered from within the infant or from without, activates the attachment system. The helpless infant needs a caregiver to deactivate his escalating discomfort. With time, sensitive caregiving episodes become associated with relief and love for the caregiver. The caregiver scaffolds the child's own developing capacity to regulate his emotions and helps build the tolerance necessary for healthy emotional control.

Around 8 months of age most babies will show separation anxiety accompanied by wariness of strangers.

Bowlby, like Erikson, assumed that the quality of care that an infant receives will affect the nature and the eventual impact of his attachments. With responsive, sensitive care, infants come to see their primary attachment figure as a source of security, a *secure base* from which to explore the world (Ainsworth, Blehar, Waters, & Wall, 1978). They correspondingly feel confidence in themselves and in their ability to negotiate that world. The infant learns that his signals of distress are heard by others—that they are adaptive in helping him to get needs for care and attention met. He also learns that the very expression of these needs is legitimate in that others take them seriously.

More broadly, the nature or quality of the infant's first attachments affects his expectations and behaviors in other relationships, "providing implicit decision rules for relating to others that may, for better or worse, help to confirm and perpetuate intuitive expectations about oneself" (R. A. Thompson, 1998, p. 36). In sum, early experience with a primary caregiver helps the child form his first representations of the self, of others, and of relationships. Bowlby referred to these representations as **working models**—prototypes of social functioning that affect the child's expectations and behaviors in future relationships.

Bowlby's attachment theory prompted developmental researchers to explore babies' earliest relationships, seeking a better understanding of how the first attachments develop and how important they really are for psychosocial development. In the following sections, we take a look at what this research has revealed and what it might mean for the helping professions.

Attachment Quality

Using a measurement technique called the **strange situation test,** Mary Ainsworth and her colleagues found that infants form different kinds of attachments to their primary caregivers (Ainsworth et al., 1978). For the test, 12-month-olds and their mothers were brought to a room (the strange situation) where the child experienced a series of eight 3-minute episodes, each one introducing changes in the social situation, some of which

Researchers use the strange situation task to investigate the nature of infants' attachments to caregivers and the ways that infants cope with the stress of separation.

were likely to be stressful to an infant. The stress component was important, given that attachment theory assumes that infants cannot handle stress on their own. At first the mother and baby were left alone in the room; in subsequent episodes, the mother and a stranger (one of the researchers) entered and left the room in various combinations. The baby's reactions to all of these events were carefully recorded, particularly his tendency to explore the room and the toys and his reactions to his mother and the stranger. The researchers paid special attention to the baby's response to his mother when she returned after an absence.

Ainsworth and her colleagues identified three patterns of infant response, now considered indicative of three different kinds of infant attachment to an adult caregiver. In subsequent research a fourth category of attachment has been identified (Main & Solomon, 1990). It is important to note that all of these patterns do represent attachments, as all babies seem to have needs for proximity maintenance and safe haven. The style of the attachment, however, varies. The following list includes descriptions of all four types of attachment patterns.*

Securely Attached

Most babies are found to be *securely attached* (originally described as the "B" category). They show distress on separation from the mother, often crying and trying to go after her, but they greet her happily on her return, usually reaching up to be held, sometimes molding their bodies to the mother as they seek comfort. Once reassured by her presence and her gestures, they tend to go off and explore the room. Ainsworth argued that babies in this category can use mother as a secure base from which to explore the world; perhaps they are showing the beginnings of optimism or hope, as Erikson suggested. They may also have learned to tolerate more separation because they have confidence in the mother's availability if they need her. Sixty-five percent of the 1-year-olds in the Ainsworth et al. (1978) study showed this response pattern, and in most subsequent research the majority of babies fit this description (R. A. Thompson, 1998).

Anxious Ambivalent—Insecurely Attached

Babies in this and the remaining two categories are considered to be attached, in that they show signs of having a special pattern of behavior *vis a vis* their mothers, but their attachments seem insecure, often laced with high levels of anxiety, as though the infant cannot quite achieve a sense of security and ease even when mother is available. *Anxious ambivalent* babies (originally called "C" babies, comprising about 10% of many samples) often seem stressed even in the initial episode (e.g., sometimes failing to explore at all), and they are quite distressed when separated from their mothers. It is their reunion behavior, however, that distinguishes them as insecurely attached. They may act angry, alternately approaching and resisting the mother, or they may respond listlessly to her efforts to comfort. They seem preoccupied with their mothers and rarely return to exploration after a separation.

Avoidant—Insecurely Attached

Avoidant babies, about 20% of most samples, typically fail to cry when separated from their mothers. They actively avoid or ignore her when she returns, sometimes combining proximity seeking and moving away, but mostly turning away. In contrast to babies in other categories, these children often appear unemotional during the episodes of

---

*Terminology varies somewhat throughout the literature. For example, ambivalent babies are also called *resistant*. There are places in the literature where avoidant, ambivalent, and disorganized/disoriented babies may be called insecure or anxious. We reserve the term *anxious* to refer to ambivalent babies.

separation and reunion. However, Spangler and Grossman (1993) found that their heart rates are elevated as much as other babies' during separations from their mothers. Unlike other infants, when they are attending to toys instead of mother as they typically do, avoidant babies do not show the heart rate drop that normally accompanies concentration and interest. Mary Main has suggested that, in response to the stress of the strange situation test, avoidant babies may direct their attention to toys as a way of defending themselves against anxiety, whereas other babies direct their attention to mother for that purpose (Main, 1996; Spangler & Grossman, 1993).

Disorganized/Disoriented—Insecurely Attached

The category *disorganized/disoriented* (referred to as "D" babies) was first described by Main and Solomon (1990), who examined strange situation videotapes from several studies, focusing on babies who had previously been difficult to classify. These infants produced contradictory behaviors, showing both an inclination to approach the mother when stressed and a tendency to avoid her when she approached! Their resulting array of behaviors could be quite unusual:

> rocking on hands and knees with face averted after an abortive approach (toward mother); freezing all movement, arms in air, with a trance-like expression; moving away from the parent to lean head on wall when frightened; and rising to greet the parent then falling prone. (Main, 1996, p. 239)

Maternal Care and Attachment Quality: Linking Mother's Sensitivity to Infant Security

Where do attachment types or styles originate? As we have indicated, attachment theory suggests that caregiving during the baby's first year is the key, and Ainsworth's early study strongly supported that claim (Ainsworth et al., 1978). All 26 babies and mothers in her study had been observed in their homes at regular intervals from the time of birth. The middle-class mothers were their infants' primary caregivers, and they did not work outside the home. Yet, they did not all provide the same quality of care. Infants who became *securely attached* had mothers who responded promptly and consistently to crying during the first year, who handled the infant with sensitivity, who held the baby tenderly and often, and whose face-to-face interactions were responsive to the baby's signals. In other words, they showed many of the features that both Bowlby and Erikson proposed to be important for infant care to create security or trust.

Babies who became insecurely attached had mothers who seemed insensitive to their infants in one way or another. The mothers of *ambivalent* babies were affectionate but were often awkward in holding. They were inconsistent in their responsiveness to crying. And in face-to-face interactions, they often failed to respond to their babies' signals. For example, in a game of peek-a-boo, an infant might begin to seem overstimulated and turn his gaze away. A responsive mother would be likely to wait until the baby reengaged before saying or doing anything, whereas an unresponsive mother might try to force the reengagement by vocalizing or jiggling the baby.

The mothers of *avoidant* babies seemed to actively avoid holding their babies. They were more often rejecting and angry, and they showed less warmth and affection than other mothers. Babies in the *disorganized-disoriented* category of attachment were not identified in Ainsworth's study. Main (e.g., 1996; Main & Hesse, 1990) has proposed that the mothers of these infants have subjected their children to neglect or maltreatment, so that they are themselves frightening to their babies. For this reason, when such a baby is stressed in the strange situation procedure, he "suffer(s) a collapse of behavioral strategy" (Main, 1996, p. 239). He does not feel safe approaching his mother, but he also cannot use

Box 4.4   Developmental Psychopathology

The new discipline of developmental psychopathology offers clinicians a unique perspective, because its focus is on the shared boundary of three important fields for helpers: abnormal, clinical, and developmental psychology. In order to appreciate its unique contribution, it is important to understand how it differs from these other disciplines, which have traditionally provided the foundation for much of therapeutic practice. In contrast to abnormal psychology's focus on the characteristic features of clinical disorders, developmental psychopathologists investigate the origins of disordered behaviors that may appear at any time throughout the life span. Unlike researchers in clinical psychology, researchers in this discipline do not emphasize treatment techniques or diagnostic assessments, per se. Nor do they focus exclusively on the traditional areas of interest to developmentalists. Instead, researchers search for the linkages between normal development and the factors that cause that development to go awry. They ask questions about why certain individuals fail to meet developmental expectations, how they adapt to those circumstances, and what purposes their particular patterns of adaptation serve. Developmental psychopathologists search for the roots of disordered behavior with the assumption that these problems might be better prevented and better treated if they were better understood developmentally. One might say that this field attempts to apply the power of advances in genetics, biochemistry, physiology, social and cul-

tural studies, and cognitive and affective development to the problems human beings face at any point in their lifetimes. The Institute of Medicine (IOM) included developmental psychopathology as one of four core areas of research at the forefront of prevention and intervention (1994).

At the center of this approach is the assumption that the course of human development follows a lawful coherence. The pattern of a person's adaptation shows continuity even if his specific behavioral traits do not. For example, a maltreated child might deal with a stressful social situation by sucking his thumb, avoiding eye contact with other people, or even crying. That same individual as an adult may adapt or cope with social stress by avoiding social situations, taking a low-threat job, or drinking before a social engagement. The specific behaviors change, but the underlying pattern of avoidant coping does not. Note another key principle of this approach. A "problem" behavior makes sense when we consider its adaptive function. The disturbed or dysfunctional behavior works at least at some level. It is one way, albeit an unhealthy one, to solve a problem that a person faces. Sometimes, as in the case of infants, it may be the only way available.

Developmental psychopathologists believe that studying individuals at the extremes of disordered behavior can enlighten us about the processes that have operated to produce those outcomes. As we have explained in earlier chapters, development can be viewed

the avoidant baby's strategy of shifting attention away from the mother, because the mother must be watched. Some recent studies have found that maltreated children do typically show the disorganized attachment pattern (e.g., Cicchetti, Toth, & Lynch, 1995), and that babies of depressed mothers are also at risk of falling into this category (Lyons-Ruth, Connell, Grunebaum, & Botein, 1990; Lyons-Ruth, Repacholi, McLeod, & Silva, 1991), although Main's interpretation of the underlying dynamics needs further corroboration.

Ainsworth's initial research linking mother care to infant security was striking in the strength of the correlations she reported. Her work excited the research community and attracted the attention of clinicians, especially those interested in developmental psychopathology (see Box 4.4: *Developmental Psychopathology*). More recent studies have sometimes replicated her finding of a strong connection between mother care and infant-mother attachment, but not always. De Wolff and van IJzendoorn (1997) examined more than 60 studies done since Ainsworth et al.'s (1978) pioneering work, all of which measured the quality of maternal care and of infant attachment security. The average correlation was significant but much more moderate than initially thought. De Wolff and van IJzendoorn concluded that "maternal sensitivity is an important condition of attachment security" but that other influences must also be important.

Box 4.4   Continued

as a series of progressively higher-order integrations of functioning in various areas (social, cognitive, moral, etc.). As individuals generally become more capable of higher levels of functioning, more complex levels of psychopathology can also develop. Much like the qualitative shifts described by Piaget that transform thinking into new forms, psychopathology can also be transformed as people move through life.

The field of developmental psychopathology emphasizes the diversity that is possible in human development, incorporating some key principles from multidimensional or systems theories (see Chapter 1). The *principle of multifinality* holds that individual pathways of development may result in a wide range of possible outcomes. For example, children exhibiting conduct-disordered behavior in the elementary school years may as adults display a number of disorders including antisocial personality, depression, substance abuse, and so on. A complementary *principle of equifinality* specifies that many early developmental pathways can produce similar outcomes. For example, Sroufe (1989) has demonstrated two pathways, one primarily biological and one primarily related to parenting style, that lead to attention deficit hyperactivity disorder (ADHD). Using these ideas from general systems theory allows for the study of multiple subgroups and multiple pathways to disorders. Most importantly, it allows for a more realistic look at the problems people face (Cicchetti & Toth, 1994).

Several key implications for clinicians present themselves. First, interventions and treatments need to be developmentally appropriate in order to be effective. Treatment approaches for children should not be based upon adult models of psychopathology. Second, periods throughout the life span marked by disequilibrium or disorganization with resultant reorganization may be considered points at which individuals might be most receptive to change. Developmental psychopathologists suggest that at these "sensitive" periods, interventions may be most effective because the individual can incorporate treatment into new levels of cognitive, emotional, and behavioral organization. Thus, the issue of timing of interventions is one of great interest to this field. In addition, the wide variety of possible pathways and outcomes involved in the development of psychopathology is an argument for the use of multiple means of intervention and treatment. However, interventions should be carefully considered and based upon a thoughtful assessment of a person's developmental level and his quality of adaptation, as well as the availability of external supports. Since this field is relatively new, much more research is needed to establish these principles with greater certainty. However, this discipline's ideas and research findings hold out great promise for helpers. We discuss this approach more in subsequent chapters.

Beyond Maternal Caregiving: Other Influences on Relationship Quality

Many attachment theorists and researchers now take a multidimensional approach to attachment, seeking to understand how factors in addition to early caregiving might impact on the attachment system that Bowlby described. Among the influences that appear to interact with caregiving to predict attachment outcomes are infant characteristics such as temperament, cultural context, family variables such as socioeconomic status, and so on.

Infant Temperament

A visit to a newborn nursery provides convincing demonstrations that different babies have different emotional and behavioral characteristics, or *temperaments,* from the time they are born. Ahmed and Joseph, born at the same hospital on the same day, challenge the staff in different ways. Ahmed has been sleeping in fairly long stretches, averaging 3 hours, with about 40 minutes of wakefulness between naps. When he is awake, he is often quiet, although like any newborn he cries when he's hungry or uncomfortable. When the nurses pick him up he calms quickly, and his breastfeeding mother says he sucks on the nipple peacefully, with moderate force. Joseph sleeps more irregularly; at 1 day old he has had two sleep periods of about 3 hours each, and many others that have ranged from 10 to 30 minutes. When he awakens, he cries lustily and is not easy to sooth. He also seems to be in constant motion, and his mother finds him squirmy and erratic in his breastfeeding attempts.

Different researchers have identified somewhat different infant traits, but they often include *fearfulness or reactivity* (the infant's proneness to cry or pull away from new stimuli), *irritability or negative emotionality* (the infant's tendency to react with fussiness to negative or frustrating events), *activity level* (the intensity and quantity of movement), *positive affect* (smiling and laughing, especially to social stimuli), *attention-persistence* (duration of orienting or looking), and *rhythmicity* (predictability of sleep, feeding, elimination, and so on). (See reviews by Kagan, 1998, and by Rothbart & Bates, 1998, for the many ways of conceptualizing such traits.)

The cataloging of infant temperament traits raises a number of intriguing questions. Are these traits stable over time, predicting personality characteristics of older children and adults? Where do temperament traits come from? How is infant temperament related to parents' caregiving? (This question has several component parts: Do infant traits affect the sensitivity and responsiveness of parents' caregiving? Can caregiving affect temperament? Are babies with different temperamental traits affected differently by sensitive versus insensitive caregiving?) And, finally, does temperament play a role in the development of attachment security?

Lively debate has raged around each of these questions. We will save the first question, whether infant temperament is continuous with later personality characteristics, for later chapters. For now, we will focus on characterizing infant temperament, identifying its relationship to parental caregiving, and understanding its role in attachment security.

Where Do Temperament Traits Come From? They are often assumed to be biologically based reactivity patterns. Researchers have found that some temperamental characteristics among infants are correlated with physiological differences. The most famous attempts to connect temperament to biology are studies done by Jerome Kagan and his colleagues on children who as infants are "high reactive" or "low reactive" (e.g., Kagan 1997, 1998; Kagan, Arcus, Snidman, & Rimm, 1995; Kagan, Arcus, Snidman, Yufeng, Hendler, & Greene, 1994). High reactive 4-month-olds produce frequent vigorous limb activity, have high levels of muscle tension, and react irritably (e.g., crying) to sensory stimulation, such as new smells or sounds. Low reactive infants, of course, score unusually low on these kinds of measures. Early reactivity is related to later measures of *behavioral inhibition,* or shyness. For example, by 7 to 9 months, when stranger anxiety tends to peak, high reactive infants often show more extreme avoidance or distress than most other infants. These infants also tend to have relatively high heart rates before birth and in some contexts after birth. Kagan has proposed that the behavioral and physiological characteristics of high reactive infants may indicate a lower than average threshold of excitability in parts of the limbic system of the brain—the amygdala and many of its associated structures.

Most infant temperament characteristics have not been examined as intensively as high reactivity. It is not clear whether physiological correlates exist for other traits, but researchers such as Kagan suggest babies may be born with a push from nature to react to environmental conditions in somewhat different ways.

How Is Infant Temperament Related to Parents' Caregiving? In the landmark New York Longitudinal Study, psychiatrists Alexander Thomas and Stella Chess (1977) found that they could categorize 3-month-olds in their large sample into four "temperament

TABLE 4.1

The New York Longitudinal Study: Behavioral Traits Assessed in Infancy and Their Characteristic Levels in Babies with Easy and Difficult Temperaments

Trait	Description	Level of Trait in Two Temperament Styles
1. Activity Level	Frequency and speed of movement	*Easy*: Low *Difficult*: High
2. Rhythmicity	Biological regularity, as in sleep-wake cycles and frequency of hunger	*Easy*: High regularity *Difficult*: Low regularity
3. Approach/withdrawal	Child's immediate reaction to new experience: acceptance or rejection	*Easy*: Approaches, acceptance *Difficult*: Withdraws, rejection
4. Adaptability	When child does withdraw, does adaptation take a short, moderate, or long time?	*Easy*: Short period of adaptation *Difficult*: Long period of adaptation
5. Threshold	Minimum strength of stimulus required for child to attend or react	*Easy*: High *Difficult*: Low
6. Intensity	Energy the child expends in expressing mood	*Easy*: Low *Difficult*: High
7. Mood	Predominance of positive vs. neutral or negative mood expression	*Easy*: More positive *Difficult*: More negative
8. Distractibility	Ease with which child's attention is drawn away from an ongoing activity by a new stimulus	*Easy*: Low *Difficult*: High
9. Attention span and persistence	Length of uninterrupted attention to a single activity, and spontaneous return to a task after interruption	*Easy*: Long *Difficult*: Short

Sources: Chess, S., & Hassibi, M. (1978). *Principles and practice of child psychiatry.* New York: Plenum; Chess, S., & Thomas, A. (1987). *Origins and evolution of behavior.* Cambridge, MA: Harvard University Press.

types" (using a set of 9 temperament traits; see Table 4.1). **Difficult babies** (about 10%), compared to the others, were more fearful, more irritable, and more active, displayed less positive affect, were more irregular, and so on—a mix of traits that made them difficult and challenging to parent. Joseph, in the above example, might fit this category. **Easy babies** (about 40%) were more placid, less active, more positive, and more regular in their rhythms than most, and thus easier to care for. Ahmed seems to fit this description. **Slow-to-warm-up babies** (about 15%) were like easy babies in many ways, but they were like difficult babies in their fearfulness, showing more wariness in new situations than most other babies. The last category (about 35%) were more variable in their traits and did not fit well into any of the more extreme groups.

Over the course of many years, Thomas and Chess (1977) tracked the personalities and adjustment of the babies they had first observed at 3 months. Fortunately, they also followed the parents' experience with their children, and they found that on the whole, parents too could be categorized. Some were generally accepting of the particular characteristics of their infants. They either happened to have a baby whose emotional and behavioral reactions were consistent with their own propensities and expectations, or they responsively adjusted their caregiving to match the infants' qualities. In either case, these parents provided care that was a "good fit" for their babies. Other parents were jarred by having a baby that did not match their expectations, something that was most likely to happen with a difficult or slow-to-warm-up infant. These parents often felt stymied and angry, sometimes blaming themselves and their poor caregiving skills for their infants' irritability and resistance. They felt disappointed, discouraged, and guilty when the baby did not fit their expectations or did not adjust to their demands. Not surprisingly, parents of babies with easy temperaments were more likely to be able to create a good fit between their caregiving and the child's characteristics, although some parents did not. For example, parents who were active, feisty people might find a placid, inactive baby hard to tolerate.

In time, some of the children showed signs of socioemotional problems. The majority of these had displayed a difficult temperament in infancy. In fact, 70% of the difficult babies eventually had some adjustment problems, ranging from learning difficulties to stealing to phobias. What differentiated the 70% with later problems from the 30% who seemed well adjusted, however, was the "goodness of fit" that the parents were able to achieve between their caregiving and the child's needs. If the parents were consistent and patient, difficult babies often became less irritable and more adaptable in time, and they were less likely to have adjustment problems as they got older.

Easy babies were not often represented in the group with later adjustment problems. Even when their parents had trouble accepting their characteristics, they usually were able to cope effectively. But when they did have later problems, caregiving seemed to be a critical ingredient—there was usually a poor fit between parental demands and the child's temperament.

The picture that emerges from the Thomas and Chess study is complex. First, it suggests that infant temperament may show some persistence into childhood and beyond. Second, it provides some indication that infant temperament affects caregiving. For example, infant temperament can make it easier or harder for a parent to be a responsive, sensitive caregiver. Third, it indicates that caregiving can change or at least moderate temperamental qualities. A parent's care influences the impact of early temperament on later adjustment. A child with difficult temperamental traits appears to be at risk for later adjustment problems, but the right caregiving can make that child much less vulnerable. Finally, it suggests that some children, especially those with easy temperaments, can tolerate a wider range of caregiving responsiveness without developing emotional or behavioral problems later. It is also important to note that parenting quality is only one of many factors that influence children's socioemotional development. Examples of others are peer networks and the quality of schooling. Some factors, such as socioeconomic status, have direct effects on the parents and their levels of stress, indirectly influencing their parenting quality.

Does Temperament Play a Role in the Development of Attachment Relationships?
Thomas and Chess did not look at children's attachment security, but the **"goodness of fit" model** suggests that temperament and caregiving should similarly interact in determining the quality of a child's attachment relationships. This has proved to be a particularly contentious issue both for researchers and clinicians. Some have argued strongly that what appears to be attachment security or insecurity could be *nothing but* a manifestation of infant temperament (see Karen, 1998). For example, in the strange situation test, easy babies who experience no stress in new situations might look avoidant; difficult, irritable infants might look ambivalent. Some attachment findings, but not all, are consistent with this general idea. For example, Stevenson-Hinde and Marshall (1999) found that insecurely attached infants are likely to be at the extremes of behavioral inhibition, with avoidant babies low on behavioral inhibition and ambivalent babies high on behavioral inhibition.

Others have argued that what appear to be biologically based temperamental differences among infants could be *nothing but* a reflection of the sensitivity of care the infant has experienced. For example, mothers who are inconsistent and unresponsive to infant cues may *create* babies who find social interactions stressful and frustrating. Soon their infants begin to look more irritable and negative than other babies (see Karen, 1998).

Neither of these extreme views accounts for the full complement of research findings, however. A multidimensional view, such as Thomas and Chess's "goodness of fit" model, seems to best explain the available evidence: temperament and sensitivity of care (both also influenced by other variables) interact at several levels to produce attachment security.

Three studies from this rapidly growing literature illustrate the kinds of interactions there may be. In the first study, 9-month-olds' "proneness to distress," defined as a baby's tendency to exhibit negative emotions (e.g., crying, fussing), was inversely related to mothers' warmth, support, and positive emotional tone (Mangelsdorf, Gunnar, Kestenbaum, Lang, & Andreas, 1990). More supportive, emotionally positive mothers tended to have babies who were more placid—less prone to distress. Less supportive, more depressive mothers had fussier babies. These data do not tell us who influenced whom, but they make clear that by 9 months the behavior of the mother and of the infant are coordinated. It is very likely that infant fussiness and mother's emotional tone have influenced one another. At 13 months, the babies' strange situation test performance was related both to their proneness to distress and to their mothers' personalities. Babies who were high on proneness to distress *and* whose mothers had "constrained" personalities (rigid, fearful of risk taking) were most likely to be insecurely attached. Babies low on proneness to distress were more likely to be securely attached, even when their mothers had "constrained" personalities. "Goodness of fit" seems to be key here. As the researchers argue,

> The prone-to-distress infant most likely taxes the caregiver more, requiring that the caregiver has better emotional supports and a personality better suited for taking care of a demanding child. In addition, the prone-to-distress infant may also be more vulnerable to nonoptimal care. (Mangelsdorf et al., 1990, p. 821)

A second study suggests that maternal caregiving predicts whether infants will be securely or insecurely attached. However, infant temperament predicts the *type* of insecure attachment that develops and even the tone of the secure attachment. Kochanska (1998) measured infants' *fearfulness* (comparable to Kagan's *behavioral inhibition*) and mothers' responsiveness when the babies were 8 to 10 months and when they were 13 to 15 months. Attachment security in the strange situation was assessed at the later time as well. Maternal responsiveness was linked to whether babies would be securely or insecurely attached. But for insecurely attached infants, fearfulness predicted the *type* of insecurity. More-fearful infants tended to be ambivalent; less-fearful babies were more often avoidant. Even the tone of secure attachment behavior was related to the babies' fearfulness, with more-fearful babies more highly aroused in the separation and reunion episodes.

Finally, a third study is important because it goes beyond *suggesting* that caregiving affects infants' attachment security, which is all that correlational research can do. Van den Boom (1994) was able to demonstrate that caregiving actually plays a *causal* role in attachment security, especially with children at the more difficult temperamental extreme. In a large sample of low-income families, van den Boom identified a group of 100 1- to 2-week-olds who were assessed as highly "irritable." The author assigned half of the infants to a treatment condition in which their mothers were trained to be more sensitive and responsive. The remaining infant-mother pairs simply had to fend for themselves. The mothers in both groups tended to be frustrated by their fussy babies, and, without intervention, their caregiving was often insensitive and unresponsive. By 12 months, 72% of the infants whose mothers had received *no* training were insecurely attached. But after being given caregiving support and training, the mothers in the intervention group treated their babies more sensitively and were more responsive to their needs. Sixty-eight percent of *their* infants were securely attached by 12 months! This study demonstrates experimentally that sensitive caregiving does make a difference in security of attachment.

Class and Culture

Van den Boom's (1994) study also underscores the need to look beyond both the infant and the caregiver to understand infant attachments. About 72% of the babies in her non-intervention group developed insecure attachments to their mothers, as compared to about 30% of infants in most other studies. Part of the difference, of course, is probably due to the difficult temperaments of the babies in van den Boom's sample, but social class probably also contributed to the poor outcomes. Indeed, van den Boom selected lower-class dyads because previous research indicated that greater numbers of insecure attachments (presumably linked to poor quality care) are found in lower economic groups (NICHD, 1997; see R. A. Thompson, 1998). It hardly seems likely that poorer families love their children less. But the caregiving environment can be impacted by the stresses confronting families who have inadequate, or barely adequate, education, housing, and income (McLoyd, 1990). Vaughn, Egeland, Sroufe, and Waters (1979) measured attachment security both at 12 months and at 18 months in 100 babies from lower-income families. Ten of the babies who were securely attached at first had become insecurely attached by 18 months. The mothers of those babies were more likely than other mothers to report significant increases in their life stresses during the intervening 6 months. Apparently, the attachment relationship can be vulnerable to events that may distract, depress, or preoccupy the mother or otherwise upset family life. This dynamic does not operate only in low-income families. Studies that have investigated the relationship between job stress and parenting have found that work hassles are linked to greater parental irritability, more emotional withdrawal, and less attention focused on children in play sessions. (See Perry-Jenkins, Repetti, & Crouter, 2000.)

The broader culture is also a factor in understanding how attachment relationships evolve. The distribution of attachment patterns varies from one country to another, and even from one subculture to another in the United States. For example, some studies of Japanese and Israeli infants have found fewer avoidant attachments and more ambivalent attachments than in the United States (e.g., Sagi et al., 1995; Takahashi, 1986, 1990), while studies of German samples (e.g., Grossman, Grossman, Huber, & Wartner, 1981) find more avoidant infants, sometimes more than in the securely attached category! These differences are yet to be adequately explained. They may partly reflect how stressful the strange situation test is for infants with differing amounts of separation experience. For example, Japanese infants rarely are parted from their mothers, while German infants are strongly encouraged to be independent. Such findings do underscore the fact that cultural context must contribute in some meaningful way to the kinds of attachments that are likely to develop. If different degrees of dependency are valued (or devalued) in different ways in different cultures, perhaps the working models of self and other that Bowlby believes are spawned from attachment relationships have different meanings and consequences in different cultures as well.

Variations in Attachment Relationships

Mothers and Fathers

Infants form attachments to familiar caregivers. Mother is usually the primary caregiver, and so infant-mother attachments tend to be the first to form, but we have already noted that soon babies become attached to their fathers, their babysitters, and other significant caregivers in their lives. The existence of multiple attachments raises several questions: Is attachment quality uniform across caregivers? In other words, once attached to the primary caregiver, do babies extend the same kind of attachment to others? Or does each relationship produce its own attachment pattern? Fox, Kimmerly, and Schafer (1991) compared attachment quality for mothers and fathers in 11 studies and found substantial similarities. If an infant was securely attached to one parent, he was unlikely to be insecurely attached to the other parent, although many exceptions were found. There are several ways to explain this tendency toward consistency. First, we might be seeing the impact of an infant's forming a working model of self and other from his primary attachment relationship and then extending that model to other attachments, as Bowlby described. Or, second, each early attachment may develop as a function of the attachment figure's caregiving sensitivity. If so, then mothers and fathers must often be similar in their handling of their infants. Belsky and Volling (1987) did find that both mothers and fathers tend to be highly involved and responsive (or not), so this remains a possible explanation. However, it should be noted that Belsky, Gilstrap, and Rovine (1984) found on the average that mothers were more positive and more responsive than fathers. There are also some studies that indicate discordance (inconsistency) between infants' maternal attachments and their attachments to nonfamily caregivers (e.g., Goossens & van IJzendoorn, 1990; Sagi, Lamb, Lewkowicz, Shoham, Dvir, & Estes, 1985), which could mean that quality of caregiving in each relationship is what is important, rather than that infants are generalizing from their primary attachment figure to others. (See Box 4.5: *Infant Day Care: Is There an Attachment Risk?*)

Stability and Change

Not only do infants sometimes form different kinds of attachments to different caregivers but they also may change their attachment status across time with the same caregiver. Secure attachments are less likely to change than insecure attachments (R. A. Thompson, 1998), although it appears that the insecure attachments of maltreated infants may be highly stable (Schneider-Rosen, Braunwald, Carlson, & Cicchetti, 1985). As we have seen, children from lower socioeconomic groups are more likely to shift from secure to insecure, or vice versa, than children from higher-income groups. Changes in family stressors, presumably causing changes in caregiving quality, are usually associated with these shifts.

That the security of infants' attachments can change raises yet another question. When does attachment security stabilize, or does it? The shifts we are describing have usually been observed in the second year of a child's life. Might later changes in caregiving quality lead to similar changes, or are there limits to when a child's security can be renegotiated? One reasonable working hypothesis is that children's attachment security can change after the infancy-toddler period if caregiving quality changes substantially, but that the longer a particular attachment status is in place, the more entrenched it is likely to become and the more it will influence other relationships, especially as children begin to mentally represent constructs of self and other, assign meanings to their experiences, and relate present events to past ones.

Research with children whose early attachments are seriously distorted or even nonexistent—what is now called ***reactive attachment disorder***—suggest that attachment security may be established, or refurbished, in later childhood. Children with this disorder have been seriously deprived of opportunities to interact with a responsive attachment figure in their early years. For example, prior to the collapse of the Soviet government in Romania in 1990, large numbers of Romanian children were being warehoused in orphanages that were notably inadequate. Caregivers were very few, and they frequently changed. Infants and toddlers received almost no attention, so they had little opportunity to form attachments. Americans began adopting these children after their plight was publicized,

Box 4.5   Infant Day Care: Is There an Attachment Risk?

John Bowlby (e.g., 1973) brought attention to the damage that could be done to young children's relationships if they were separated from attachment figures for long periods of time. For example, when hospitalized children are denied regular access to their mothers, their emotional distress is intense, and it progresses through a worrisome series of stages, beginning with typical separation protest such as crying and searching for the lost parent followed by "despair," which is marked by listlessness, loss of appetite, and reduced emotional vitality. Finally, after many days or weeks, the child seems to become detached, treating the mother with indifference when she visits, or attending only to the "treats" that mother brings (e.g., Robertson & Robertson, 1989).

Extrapolating from the effects of long-term separations, Bowlby also expressed concern about shorter-term separations, such as the daily breaks in maternal care that babies experience when their mothers are employed and leave their children with relatives or nonfamilial caregivers for many hours a day. Given that attachment quality is significantly related to sensitive, responsive caregiving, could regular interruptions of that caregiving impede the development of secure attachments? And when there is a change in child care arrangements—when beloved nannies or day care teachers leave—does the disruption of the child's attachment to that caregiver also disrupt the child's sense of security? Bowlby felt that although there might not be definitive answers to these questions, the potential risks associated with forming insecure attachments were great enough that parents should be encouraged to avoid regular substitute care for children under age 3.

Research over the last several decades has begun to address the questions that Bowlby raised, and a sense of the scope and nature of the risks in infant day care is beginning to emerge. The following points capture the primary conclusions that can be drawn thus far about the relationship between substitute care and infant-mother attachments. These points are largely drawn from a study of more than 1,100 babies, sponsored by the National Institutes of Child Health and Development (NICHD, 1997), which has helped to clarify the findings from many earlier studies (see reviews and/or analyses of multiple sets of data by Belsky & Rovine, 1988; Clarke-Stewart, 1989; Lamb & Sternberg, 1990; Scarr, 1998; and R. A. Thompson, 1998).

1. It appears that the *majority* of infants who experience nonparental care on a regular basis still form secure attachments to their parents; there is little disagreement among studies or their authors on this point.
2. There is, nonetheless, an increase in the risk of insecure attachments for infants in day care as compared to infants in full-time home care.
3. The increased risk of insecure attachments for infants in care exists *only* when these infants are exposed to *low levels of maternal sensitivity and responsiveness*. In

providing researchers an opportunity to assess their attachment prognosis, that is, their ability to form secure attachments in the post-infancy period. Because these children had almost no opportunity to interact with adults in infancy, attachment theory would argue that they had formed distorted and impoverished working models of themselves, of others, and of relationships from their early experiences.

Chisholm (1998) followed Romanian adoptees for three years. Despite their lack of early attachments, most were able to form secure attachments with their adoptive parents, although the rate of insecure attachments was higher than in a sample of American children being raised by their own parents. Researchers also found some cases of children who seemed to form no bond at all with their adoptive parents, regardless of the sensitivity and responsiveness of the parents (DeAngelis, 1997). Overall, such findings suggest that initial attachments *can be*, and often are, formed after the infancy period, but the process is more difficult and may not be successful in some cases.

The Importance of Early Attachments

Secure early attachments are said to pave the way for later psychosocial developments. Erikson and Bowlby portrayed the trusting, secure infant as one who is fortified with

Box 4.5   **Continued**

other words, when mothers are providing insensitive care themselves, infants in day care are even more likely than infants in full-time home care to develop insecure attachments. Another way to say this is that when mothers are sensitive and responsive to their infants, substitute care does not interfere with the formation of a secure infant-mother attachment.

4. Risk of insecure attachment is further increased when substitute child care is of poor quality or involves many hours per week or when there is more than one substitute care arrangement. Research that preceded the NICHD study suggested that at least some of these factors alone might negatively affect the quality of infant-mother attachments, but the NICHD study strongly indicates that these factors have their effects only when mothers are providing insensitive care.

Overall, mothers and babies can, and usually do, form secure attachments, even if mothers work outside the home during the first year, as long as mother provides her infant with quality care when she is with the baby. Substitute care can, however, exacerbate the negative effects of poor maternal care. Fortunately, employed mothers are about as likely as unemployed mothers to provide sensitive care to their babies, despite the stresses of balancing family responsibilities and work (e.g., Schubert, Bradley-Johnson, & Nuttal, 1980). Some research even indicates that employed

mothers might be more positive in their caregiving (e.g., Crockenberg & Litman, 1991). However, at least one study suggests that very early return to work (before the baby is 12 weeks old) might put a mother at risk of being a less sensitive caregiver than she might otherwise have been (Clark, Hyde, Essex, and Klein, 1997). Mothers who returned to work at 6 weeks postpartum were less sensitive to their 4-month-old babies than mothers who returned to work at 12 weeks, especially if the mothers were exposed to other risk factors, such as depressive symptoms or a baby with a difficult temperament. Very early return to work may make it somewhat more difficult for a mother to learn to read her baby's cues (Brazelton, 1986); and/or it may just be harder to feel effective and competent as a caregiver when a mother begins work in her infant's first weeks, because the baby has not yet become very socially responsive. Sensitive caregiving appears to be easier when mothers feel competent (Donovan, Leavitt, & Walsh, 1990; Teti & Gelfand, 1991).

On the whole, mothers' use of substitute caregivers does not put the mother-infant attachment relationship in jeopardy. But clearly, parents are well advised to proceed cautiously in making decisions about alternative care arrangements for their infants. Substitute care is a risk factor when it combines with poor maternal care, and other risk factors, such as poor-quality day care, make the danger greater.

---

positive attitudes toward self and toward others. He enters new relationships with an expectation that his needs will be respected and with a willingness to respect the needs of others. His security helps him face new challenges; he trusts in the future. Steinberg and Avenevoli (2000) identify two functions that context, such as that of a parent-child relationship, can play in the development of wellness or psychopathology. First, the context works to *elicit* a particular pattern of behavior, cognition, and emotion, as in the case of a secure or insecure attachment. But it also functions to *maintain* the established patterns by providing the circumstances that allow the specific patterns to be repeated. Modifying the context, through prevention or intervention, reduces opportunities for negative patterns to be repeated and weakens the chances that they will persist over time.

Neither Erikson nor Bowlby saw the positive outlook of the secure child as immutable. While secure children play a role in making their positive expectations come true by their choice of partners and through their own responses to others (Sroufe, 1996), they are not all powerful. If later experiences, especially with caregivers, violate their expectations, their burgeoning ideas about self and others could be modified, incorporating more negative expectations. In sum, early attachment is said to launch processes that can have long-term consequences; but the quality of care that the child continues to receive can either strengthen or redirect those processes.

Does early attachment quality predict later psychosocial functioning? Sroufe, Egeland, and their colleagues followed a large sample of Minneapolis children, beginning with two assessments of attachment status in the strange situation at 12 and at 18 months (e.g., Vaughn et al., 1979). Children whose attachment status was stable from the first to the second assessment were later evaluated on a variety of interpersonal and cognitive dimensions, and differences were found between the insecurely and securely attached children on many measures. For example, when the children were 4 years old, 40 of them participated in a summer nursery school program at the University of Minnesota (Sroufe, Fox, & Pancake, 1983). Teachers, who knew nothing about the earlier attachment ratings, ranked the children each day on characteristics related to autonomy, such as attention seeking, extreme reliance on the teacher, involvement with teachers at the expense of peers, and so on. The children who had been securely attached as toddlers were more often seen by teachers as direct and appropriate in their dependency behaviors, seeking help when they realistically needed it but functioning independently in other situations. Insecurely attached children were more likely to act helpless, to act out for attention, or in some cases to passively avoid seeking help when they genuinely needed it.

In assessments at later ages, the children in the Minneapolis project showed other continuities as well. In a summer camp at age 10, for example, securely attached children tended to be more self-confident, to have more friends, to have better social skills, and so on. Many studies, though not all, have found similar continuities (see R. A. Thompson, 1998, for a review of these findings).

If infant-mother attachments predict later developments, what about father-infant attachments? When infants are securely attached to both parents they seem to have the best outcomes; if they are securely attached to one parent, but not the other, their outcomes are better than if they are insecurely attached to both (e.g., Belsky, Garduque, & Hrncir, 1984; Main et al., 1985; Suess, Grossman, & Sroufe, 1992). Thus, a secure attachment relationship with a second parent adds a protective factor, perhaps helping to safeguard a child from the negative influence of an insecure attachment. Several investigators have also suggested that because fathers and mothers tend to interact differently with their infants, the attachment relationship with each parent may affect different aspects of the child's psychosocial development. For example, in American families, mothers spend more time with infants in quiet, ritualized routines such as peek-a-boo games, where synchrony of eye contact, vocalizations, and facial expressions are key factors. Fathers tend to engage in more energetic, stimulating games (such as whirling the baby through the air); they are more unpredictable and exciting (MacDonald & Parke, 1986; Pecheux & Labrell, 1994). Of course, though there tend to be differences in the types of interactions infants have with each parent, there is much overlap, especially when fathers are highly involved in infant care. Whether infant attachments to mother versus father affect different aspects of later social functioning is yet to be determined. One study is suggestive, however. Pecheux and Lebrell (1994) found that 18-month-olds were more playful and more inclined to smile with a stranger if their fathers were present when the new person approached than if their mothers were present.

Overall, there is little doubt that infant attachment relationships are predictive of some later behaviors. What is presently uncertain is, how important are early attachments in producing such outcome differences? More specifically, does the early attachment actually have long-term effects, or could the more recent and current caregiving environment be responsible for the apparent continuities? In the Minneapolis study, for example, some children who had been securely attached as infants were having behavior problems by age 4. The quality of parenting during the preschool period helped account for this change. Mothers of these children were less supportive when engaging their children in educational tasks at age 3. They provided less encouragement and were less effective teachers than mothers whose children did not develop later behavior problems. Also, children who had been insecurely attached as infants but who were well adjusted at 4 years tended to have mothers who were supportive and effective in their interactions with their preschoolers (Erickson, Sroufe, & Egeland, 1985). It seems that the role of early attachments in later development can be diminished, and perhaps even eliminated, when parental acceptance, support, and responsiveness changes substantially, either rising to the challenges of the child's new developmental stage or failing to do so (see also Easterbrooks & Goldberg, 1990; Youngblade & Belsky, 1992). The importance of ongoing quality parenting for children's socioemotional development will be taken up again in Chapter 5.

What, then, is the value of getting a "good start" with a secure infant attachment? It may be that the primary influence of infant attachments is their tendency to perpetuate themselves. Once a relationship pattern between parent and child is established, it tends to be repeated; when it is, the older child's behavior is consistent with predictions from the early attachment. In his first relationships, a baby may well form an incipient "working model" of what to expect from interactions. That model affects his behavior and expectations in the future, but the model is in progress and will be *reworked* in the context of new interactions, just as Erikson and Bowlby proposed.

Working Models of Attachment

As we have just seen, what may be most important about infant attachments is that they influence the internal working model of relationships that children begin to construct. Researchers studying adult romantic relationships describe the concept of the internal working model of attachment as providing a template for adult social relationships. Investigators have recently begun to study the nature and development of these models, or representations. We will examine some of this work in later chapters, as we discuss the development of self-concept and relationship capacity beyond the infancy period, but one aspect of this research bears directly on the formation of infant attachments, and we will touch on this work here.

Main and her colleagues (Main, Kaplan, & Cassidy, 1985) evaluated mothers' and fathers' models of attachment using a structured interview procedure called the **Adult Attachment Inventory (AAI)** (see Chapter 12 for a full discussion). Parents described their memories of the parenting they had received and their beliefs about whether that parenting influenced their own personalities. The "security" of their attachment representations (categorized using a procedure devised by Main & Goldwyn, 1985–1994) was related to the quality of attachment they had established with their own infants.

"Secure-autonomous" parents valued relationships and believed that their own personalities were influenced by them. They could talk openly and objectively about their early experiences, good or bad. Their ideas were coherent and showed signs of previous reflection. Not all of these adults recalled their early experiences as positive; some had even been abused. But by whatever means, these adults had apparently come to terms with their early experiences and had faith in the power of relationships. These parents tended to have secure attachments with their own infants.

"Insecure" parents showed several patterns. In one, attachment relationships were not readily recalled, not valued, and not seen as influential. Infants tended to have avoidant attachments with parents who showed this "dismissive" pattern. Another group of parents ("preoccupied/entangled") were preoccupied with their own parents, often still struggling to please, and they seemed confused, angry, or especially passive. Their infants' attachments to them were typically ambivalent. Finally, an "unresolved/disorganized" pattern characterized parents who made irrational and inconsistent comments, especially when discussing traumatic experiences. For example, they might talk about a dead parent as if he were alive. Infants whose parents showed this pattern tended to be disorganized/disoriented in the strange situation test.

A substantial correspondence between parents' and infants' attachment classifications has been found in other studies as well (see van IJzendoorn, 1995). As Main (1996) points out, this correspondence could be affected by many factors, including similarities in temperament between parent and infant. But the match in parent-infant security measures may indicate that parents' working models of attachment can influence their infant caregiving, thereby affecting their babies' attachment security. Perhaps, for example, parents whose concepts of relationship are more coherent, or who have come to terms with past relationships, are more likely to behave consistently and sensitively with their infants, fostering a secure attachment.

Parenting Practices Versus Relationship Quality in Infant Development

It should be clear from this overview of theory and research on infant attachments that focusing attention on relationship quality in infant-caregiver interactions has proven to be a highly productive enterprise. As Mary Ainsworth noted in her earliest observations of mother-infant dyads, the specifics of parenting practices may not be very important in the long run. For example, breastfeeding versus bottle feeding does not seem to be critical for later emotional adjustment. Rather, it is the relationship context within which such practices occur that is significant. Some parenting practices may be more conducive to, or consistent with, responsive caregiving. Breastfeeding, for example, *requires* that a mother hold her baby close during feeding, providing the "contact comfort" infants find soothing. When babies are bottle fed, they *can* be held and soothed just as effectively, but it is also possible to "prop" a bottle or to hold a baby away from the caregiver's body when feeding, thus failing to provide contact comfort. So, both breast and bottle feeding *can* be practiced in a way that provides close, comforting interactions, but breastfeeding is more conducive to such interactions.

It should also be noted that while both breastfeeding and bottle feeding can be done sensitively and responsively, breastfeeding has some advantages for healthy physical and cognitive development that bottle feeding does not (American Academy of Pediatrics, 1997; Rogan & Gladen, 1993). In comparison to baby formulas, breast milk is more digestible and more adequately balanced for infant nutrition. It contains antibodies that the mother carries, and it is sterile, a particularly important benefit in countries with water that may contain disease organisms. Breast milk even carries growth hormones and other substances that may affect long-term development. The World Health Organization now recommends exclusive breastfeeding for the first six months and breastfeeding with solid food supplements through the second year (UNICEF, 1995).

Ainsworth's observations of an Ugandan baby and his mother (as described in Karen, 1998) help to illustrate, however, that feeding by breast is not the critical factor in the formation of secure attachments. Muhamidi's mother kept him close most of the time, as is the custom in Ugandan families. She slept with him and breastfed him on demand. Yet by 8 months, Muhamidi seemed insecure. Not yet having invented the strange situation test, Ainsworth depended on a variety of observations to make this classification, most notably that over time he seemed to lose his vitality, to become sadder and duller. Unlike other babies whose mothers used similar infant care practices, he did not tolerate his mother's absence even when left with an older sibling. Muhamidi's mother seemed anxious and overtaxed by the demands of her large family, and Ainsworth observed that despite her nearly constant availability, the mother's caregiving responses were somewhat brusque and did not necessarily match Muhamidi's needs. For example, on one visit, she responded to Muhamidi's crying by putting him "immediately to breast, without stopping to wipe his nose, which was streaming, or to wipe his face, which was muddy" (Ainsworth, 1967, p. 144).

A student of social and personality development in the mid-1900s would probably have read extensive discussions about the relative importance of particular child-rearing practices such as breastfeeding versus bottle feeding. The current trend, spawned by attachment theory, is to emphasize the overall quality of infant-caregiver relationships instead. This approach seems to be bringing us much closer to an understanding of the role of infancy in later socioemotional development.

APPLICATIONS

What are we to make of this information on attachment? Clearly, if it is as important as it appears, a host of practical applications present themselves, from mandated parenting interventions to supports for working mothers. On the one hand, there is a great temptation to go overboard and to diagnose all problems as attachment related. On the other hand, there are voices telling us that parents matter little if at all to the future success of their children (Harris, 1998). So what is a counselor to do? Our advice is to take a position informed by research. No one has demonstrated that relatively infrequent incidents of caretaker unavailability will harm a child for life, nor are chronic interactive failures the single pathway to a depressive future. *However, it would be incorrect to assume that early interactive patterns have no influence at all on later emotional and social development.* As Tronick (1989) observed:

> The pathways leading to the varieties of normalcy and psychopathology derive from the divergent experiences infants have with success, reparation of failure, and the transformation of negative emotions to positive emotions. Typically, there is no single traumatic juncture or special moment separating these pathways, only the slowly accumulating interactive and affective experiences with different people and events in different contexts that shape the regulatory processes and representations of the infant over time. (p. 117)

If we conceptualize the infant as constructing a framework for interacting with the world, using both the tools provided by nature and the materials available in daily experience, it is difficult to imagine that the earliest affective experiences with a primary caregiver would not help to lay the foundation for later models of social relationships. Outcomes, however, are rarely the result of one early relationship. Although mothers are most often primary caretakers, fathers, siblings, grandparents, and others are also significant. It is important to resist the assumption that all the responsibility for social and emotional development rests solely on the mother's shoulders. Future outcomes also involve co-occurring and later-occurring experiences that build on and reshape prior configurations.

Van IJzendoorn and Bakermans-Kranenburg (1997) provide a promising model that describes how this may work. They propose a modification on the model of intergenerational transmission of attachment—that is, from parents' own early attachment experiences to their parenting behavior to their infant's attachment classification. As we have seen, the available research does not support such strict linear progression. In fact, Bowlby (1988) and traditional object relations theorists (Klein, 1921/1945; Mahler, Pine, & Bergman, 1975; Winnicott, 1965) have held that therapists (or intimate partners and friends) can serve to realign or reconstruct an originally problematic early relationship by becoming another "secure base."

Van IJzendoorn and Bakermans-Kranenburg's multidimensional model of intergenerational transmission reflects the effects of context and later experience on the attachment classification of the infant. A parent's own early attachment experiences are modified (for good or for ill) by later attachment relationships with others, which together determine the parent's attachment representation or mental model of close relationships. So one's memories of past experiences are never totally pure but are reconstructed, at least in part, on the basis of current attachments. These authors conclude that parents operate more on their current belief systems about the past than on what actually may have happened. The parent's mental model of attachment is further influenced by the present social context. A supportive spouse, for example, might ameliorate the effects of earlier negative experiences. A difficult divorce might complicate earlier positive attachment representations. These factors combine to influence actual parenting behavior. These behaviors are further modified by the temperament of the child. Having an extremely fussy or irritable baby may increase the amount of time spent in poorly coordinated communication sequences and may ultimately come to affect the baby's emotional regulation and the quality of attachment.

Most researchers agree that early affective experiences between infant and caretaker are predispositional rather than strictly deterministic (Bruer, 1999). Even if the first few years are not "forever," they lay the groundwork for subsequent development. Attachment classification can be remarkably stable through adolescence provided that the environment is also relatively stable. A growing body of evidence implicates disruptive experiences in the child's or adolescent's life, such as loss of a parent, divorce, economic hardship, abuse, serious illness of the child or the parent, to name a few, in discontinuity of attachment (van IJzendoorn & Bakermans-Kranenburg, 1997). An implication we can draw from this is the importance of prevention and early intervention. As Steinberg and Avenevoli (2000) point out, "over time the psychologically rich get richer and the psychologically poor get poorer" (p. 71). Addressing problematic parent-infant relationships can redirect the developmental pathways in healthy ways early on. Providing continuing supports for good parent-child relationships can sustain them over time.

Attachment theory has been the source of an enormous amount of research interest over the past few years, including research on attachments in early and late adulthood (see

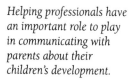

Helping professionals have an important role to play in communicating with parents about their children's development.

Chapter 12). The theory provides many useful ideas for clinicians. First, the concept of attachment as a constellation of behaviors in a goal-corrected partnership is particularly significant in helping us understand problems and motivations for behavior. This perspective emphasizes the fundamentally social nature of human development. It reminds us that all human growth and human problems occur in some relational context. Second, attachment theory provides clinicians with a new way to view behavior that might, at first glance, seem puzzling. Since the principal goal of attachment is to maintain proximity, either physical or psychological, seemingly contradictory behaviors can be interpreted as means to this end. Even avoidant behaviors, for example, can serve to maintain some distant relationship while minimizing psychological threat to the self. As Greenberg and Speltz (1988) have pointed out, noncompliant child behaviors can be interpreted as bids for more attention (or closer attachment). Presumably, all behaviors are functional in that they serve to help individuals adapt to present circumstances. Their adaptiveness may be more or less well suited to any given situation or context. For the infant who needs to reduce the risk of rejection, avoidant behaviors or withdrawal may be an effective method for adapting to negative circumstances. However, this pattern of withdrawal from close relationships, particularly when under stress, can be counterproductive in the context of close adult relationships. Even though the behavior isn't suited to the new context, it certainly can be understood.

The concept of an internal working model is contemporary in its resemblance to a cognitive schema. It puts the emphasis squarely on the importance of the individual's mental representation of the relationship rather than on any particular behavior observed within that relationship. It highlights the importance of individual meaning. Efforts to change parenting behaviors, such as teaching parents to respond sensitively to crying infants, can be very successful (van den Boom, 1999), and they seem to have a remarkably positive effect on the attachment security of infants (van den Boom, 1988; 1994). However, if a parent's working model of relationships is founded on insecure attachments, the parent might not be able to generate appropriately responsive parenting behaviors when the infant reaches a new stage of development and has new needs. Suppose that a mother is enmeshed in her own attachment conflicts, for example, or she is dismissive of her own earlier negative experiences. Despite having learned to respond sensitively to her infant's needs, when her infant becomes a toddler and needs more autonomy, the parent may be unable to respond appropriately. The enmeshed parent may be threatened by her child's new needs; the dismissive parent may prefer to ignore them. We must await future research to determine whether the changes in attachment security brought about by behavioral interventions in infancy are durable without interventions designed to alter a parent's own representations of relationships as well.

Finally, attachment theory comes as close as any psychological theory to blending developmental and clinical orientations. It highlights the truth that not only do we grow from relationships but we suffer from them too. Noam and Fischer (1996) make the excellent observation that, inasmuch as we are all dependent upon one another, we have all experienced injuries in relationships and are beset by specific interpersonal vulnerabilities as a result of our attachment histories. He believes that developmentalists need to incorporate into their work the "periods of regression and fragmentation" that characterize development and that coexist with capacities for integration and growth. He adds that clinicians

> need to, and have begun to, account for the adaptive nature of psychopathology, including attempts to solve complex problems, through the detour of symptom formation. Traditional medical models of mental health need to be supplanted by truly developmental, interpersonal accounts that allow for dynamic interweaving of problems and strengths. (Noam & Fischer, 1996, pp. xii–xiii)

SUMMARY

Theories of Emotions: The State of the Art

1. Although theorists do not all agree about how to define or characterize basic emotions, they do agree that emotions have "survival value." Emotions are powerful motivators of behavior, and spontaneous emotional expressions help us to communicate with one another. For infants, this communicative function helps to initiate reciprocal interaction with a caregiver. Emotions enhance cognitive functioning such as planning and social perspective taking. And they play a role in mental health and wellness. More positive life outcomes are associated with higher levels of *emotional intelligence*.

2. The biological basis of basic emotions has been demonstrated in three lines of research. First, across cultures people agree about what expressions signal fear, sadness, happiness, anger, and surprise. Second, young infants' facial expressions appear to display basic emotions. Third, researchers have identified some specific brain systems or circuits governing the expression of some emotions.

3. Izard's *differential emotions theory* argues that infant emotional expressions are innate, a product of evolution. Learning only facilitates an individual's capacity to regulate emotions. In Sroufe's more *orthogenetic* theory, early emotional expressions are precursors of more mature emotions, and the later emotions depend on cognitive developments. Emotions are differentiated over time and come under the control of higher levels of functioning.

Early Caregiver-Infant Interactions and Emotional Development

4. Human infants depend on caregivers for survival. Caregivers must read an infant's signals and meet his physical and emotional needs. Infant physical characteristics, such as large head and large eyes, and infant behaviors, such as crying and smiling, are *releasers* of adult caregiving. The caregiving relationship fosters feelings of security in infants and helps infants to regulate their emotions.

5. Infants have some inborn strategies for coping with emotional arousal. When mothers are asked to be unresponsive to children's cues, in the *still-face paradigm,* young babies at first initiate *other-directed coping behaviors,* actions designed to reengage the caregiver. If these don't work, babies initiate *self-directed coping behaviors,* such as looking away and self-stimulating. When caregiver-infant interactions go off-track, caregivers often respond positively to infants' other-directed coping behaviors, and they initiate *interactive repair* procedures. Gradually the infant comes to depend upon his caregiver for help in emotion control and begins to experience himself as an effective social agent.

6. Depressed mothers are less responsive than nondepressed mothers to infants' other-directed coping behaviors, and their infants more often turn to self-directed coping behaviors. Chronic experiences like this may affect brain development and influence future social relationships.

7. Several lines of research suggest connections between brain development and the importance of social interaction for infant emotional development. First, the brain's right hemisphere, which is specialized for interpreting nonverbal communication in adults, appears to be more mature in early infancy than the left hemisphere. Second, the right orbitofrontal region, located in the interior of the right frontal lobe, may be the primary brain region involved in social bonding, and a caregiver's rhythmic, sensitive responses may influence the development of this region in infancy. Finally, social interaction and social bonding may activate the brain's internal opiate system, helping to explain why caregiver responsiveness is so effective in regulating infants' distress.

Attachment: Early Social Relationships

8. Theorists such as Bowlby and Erikson have proposed that the infant's first relationships with caregivers provide him with *working models* of the self, of others, and of relationships. Erikson argued that consistent, sensitive care helps the infant establish *basic trust* in others and feelings of worthiness, both of which contribute to optimism about future relationships. In Bowlby's *attachment theory,* biologically prepared behaviors bring infant and mother into a close relationship, or attachment system, that emerges in stages such that by 7 or 8 months the infant has a strong affectional bond to the primary caregiver, which leads to both *separation anxiety* and *stranger anxiety*. The attachment system serves the purpose of *proximity maintenance* and provides a *secure base* and *safe haven*.

9. Using the *strange situation test* to measure the quality of infant-mother attachments, Ainsworth and her colleagues identified three different types of attachment quality. *Securely attached* infants explore a new situation when mother is present, are distressed if she leaves, and are comforted and happy when she returns. They appear to use their mothers as a secure base. *Anxious ambivalent* babies are insecurely attached. They are most clearly different from other babies in their response to their mothers' return from an absence. They may alternately approach and resist the mother, or may respond listlessly to her, rather than taking ready comfort. *Avoidant* babies are also insecurely attached. They actually avoid or ignore their mothers when they return after an absence, although their heart rates reveal that they are stressed in her absence. Main and others have identified a fourth attachment category, another insecurely attached group called *disorganized/disoriented*. These babies react to their mothers in contradictory ways, engaging in an odd array of behaviors.

10. Maternal caregiving in the first year of life is correlated with infants' attachment quality at 12 months. The mothers of securely attached babies provide consistent, sensitive care to their infants. Mothers of insecurely attached babies are more likely to be insensitive in one way or another, and the mothers of disorganized/disoriented babies can be abusive. Across many different studies, the correlation between mother care and infant attachment quality is moderate, indicating that other influences must also be important.

11. Infant *temperament* may be one influence on attachment quality. Babies have different emotional and behavioral characteristics. Such traits make up infant temperament, and for at least one of these traits, *reactivity,* physiological correlates have been identified, such as high heart rates before birth. Some babies have *difficult* temperaments: they are highly reactive and irritable and have a number of other traits that make them more difficult than average babies to care for. *Easy* babies have a combination of traits that make them easy to care for. A longitudinal study by Thomas and Chess included babies with different temperaments and indicates that temperament can persist beyond infancy and that it can affect caregiving, making it easier or harder for a parent to be responsive and sensitive. But this study also found that parents who adjust to their infants' temperament, creating *goodness of fit* between their caregiving and the needs of a particular infant, can moderate their child's temperament and influence the impact of early temperament on later adjustment.

12. Temperament and caregiving seem to interact to affect security of attachment. For example, some caregivers may react to the frustrations of caring for a difficult baby by becoming less sensitive and responsive to their baby's needs. Their unresponsive caregiving may then contribute to an insecure attachment.

13. Across social classes and across cultures, there are differences in the proportion of infants who are categorized as securely or insecurely attached. Larger numbers of insecure infant attachments are found in lower-income families. It appears that

increases in life stress are related to less responsive care and to increases in insecure attachments. Across cultures, different values, rearing practices, and expectations of infants may influence attachment security.

14. Attachment quality can change over time if caregiving quality changes. It is also possible for children with *reactive attachment disorder,* who have been deprived of adequate adult care as infants, to later form secure attachments. Early attachment launches processes that can have long-term consequences; but the quality of care a child continues to receive can either strengthen or redirect those processes.

15. Early attachment quality has been found to predict later psychosocial functioning, including dependency, self-confidence, and social skills. Moreover, if children have secure attachments with both parents, their later functioning is more positive than if they have a secure attachment with only one parent. However, it is unclear whether the early attachment quality is the *cause* of later psychosocial adjustment or whether the ongoing quality of the parents' caregiving is the key predictor. The primary influence of early infant attachments may be their tendency to perpetuate themselves. Once a pattern is established between parent and child, it tends to be repeated. However, it can be changed, and if it is, the child's working model of relationships, of self, and of others can also change.

16. Methods for assessing attachment security in adults have been devised, such as the *Adult Attachment Inventory.* In some studies, parents' own attachment quality has been predictive of the quality of attachment they establish with their own infants.

17. The specifics of infant care—such as bottle feeding versus breastfeeding—may be less important to child outcomes than the sensitivity of caregiving. Focusing on the quality of infant-caregiver relations, rather than the specifics of parenting practices, seems to provide a better understanding of later socioemotional development.

Case Study

Angela is a White 17-year-old girl who is also the mother of a baby named Adam, now 11 months of age. Both Angela and her baby live with Angela's mother, Sarah, in a small rented house in a semirural community in the Midwest. Sarah, a single mother herself, works as a waitress in a local restaurant. Sarah has another child, David, who is 13. Angela's father abandoned the family when she was 7 years old. Wayne, Angela's boyfriend and Adam's father, has also become estranged primarily because Sarah refuses to allow him in her house. She is angry that Angela became pregnant and views Wayne as incapable of, and uninterested in, taking on his share of the responsibility.

During her pregnancy, Angela continued to attend classes at her high school. She dropped out, however, when she was seven months pregnant. She had grown increasingly depressed about the prospect of caring for an infant, and she found dealing with schoolwork and her pregnancy overwhelming. Following Adam's birth, Angela tried hard to be a good mother to her son. She took on most of the caretaking responsibilities by herself, which gave her some measure of satisfaction. However, she also felt deeply ambivalent. Above all, she resented the restrictions that the baby placed on her life. Adam's frequent crying for no apparent reason was particularly frustrating. According to Angela, Adam cried even when he was not hungry or wet. Sometimes she handled Adam roughly, when he wouldn't quiet down after a feeding or around bedtime. At other times, Angela was upset that Adam didn't seem to smile enough at her when she wanted to play with him. Sometimes, Adam paid no attention to her when she wanted interaction. At these times, she would raise her voice and hold his face in her hands to make him look at her. She was beginning to feel that she was not a very good mother to her son after all.

Sarah and Angela's already strained relationship grew more hostile as Adam approached his first birthday. Angela felt that her mother wasn't interested in helping her. Angela always idealized her father and believed that it was her mother's frequent outbursts of anger that led to her father's leaving home.

For her part, Sarah believed that her daughter wasn't doing enough to help herself. Angela chose not to go back to school, even though she could have access to school-based child care services. All through Angela's high school years, Sarah had expected her daughter to find a steady job after graduation and to contribute to the family financially. Instead, Sarah found herself in the role of financial provider for another child. She was very angry and hurt that Angela didn't seem to appreciate all she had done for her over the years. Whenever the mother and daughter had an argument, Angela would say that she felt her mother never really cared about her. What was even worse for Sarah was that Angela had begun seeing Wayne again, without her mother's permission. She made it clear to Angela that she and the baby would need to move out if she ever got pregnant again.

Discussion Questions

1. Comment on the quality of the attachment relationship between Angela and Adam and between Sarah and Angela. Do you think that Adam is at risk for developmental problems? Discuss.
2. Using the model of intergenerational transmission of attachment presented in this chapter, discuss the transmission sequence as it applies in this case.
3. What kinds of interventions could you suggest to help the members of this family?

Journal Questions

1. Present five adjectives that describe your early childhood relationship to each parent.
   A. Why did you choose these adjectives?
   B. To which parent did you feel the closest?
   C. What did you do as a child when you were upset, hurt, or ill?
   D. What do you remember about any separation that you experienced as a child?
2. How would your parents describe your temperament as a young child? In what ways is it the same now and in what ways is it different?

Key Terms

Phineas Gage matrix
emotional intelligence
differential emotions
   theory
orthogenetic principle
releasers
still-face paradigm
other-directed coping
   behaviors
self-directed coping
   behaviors
interactive repair

basic trust
attachment theory
ethologists
separation anxiety
stranger anxiety
proximity maintenance
secure base
safe haven
working model
strange situation test
securely attached

anxious ambivalent
avoidant
disorganized/disoriented
principle of multifinality
principle of equifinality
temperament
fearfulness or reactivity
irritability or negative
   emotionality
activity level
positive affect

attention-persistence
rhythmicity
behavioral inhibition
difficult babies
easy babies
slow-to-warm-up babies
"goodness of fit" model
reactive attachment
   disorder
Adult Attachment
   Inventory (AAI)

CHAPTER 5

The Emerging Self and Socialization in the Early Years

"Mirror, mirror on the wall, who is the real me, after all?" Philosophers, poets, wicked stepmothers, and regular human beings have pondered versions of this question since the time the ancient Greeks advised, "Know thyself." The search for self embodies within it many of the profound questions at the heart of the human condition: What is the nature of human consciousness? Are we the same or different across situations? How do people come to understand and accept who they are? Modern cultures, as we have noted, are not the first to express interest in these matters. Nonetheless, critics have raised concerns that the level of attention directed toward the self has increased in recent decades. Note the amount of press devoted to the ideas of self-concept, self-esteem, self-enhancement, and self-actualization, and you might agree that we have become downright self-centered!

Those of us in the helping professions are no exception to this trend. Even a cursory review of the professional literature in counseling reveals an intense interest in topics related to the self. Therapeutic approaches that emphasize self-development are very common. Educational institutions struggle to incorporate self-development into their more traditional academic objectives. The popular press is saturated with advice about self-concept and self-esteem. All together, the pieces add up to a crazy quilt, part folklore, part research, part anecdote, and part good intention. Our task in this chapter is to unscramble some of this information and present the self in its developmental context.

Helpers need to understand the research findings in this critically important area lest they assume that all of our popular, contemporary notions about self-development are valid. For example, the postmodern focus on individualism might convey the idea that the self is truly independent and autonomous when, in fact, it is largely a product of social interaction. Bowlby (e.g., 1969/1982) suggested that working models of the self develop in concert with working models of attachment figures. Erikson (1950/1963) developed the idea that when others respond sensitively to their needs, children develop concepts of themselves as worthy of respect. Cultural groups differ in their emphasis on an autonomous self. So self-development, despite our Western predilection for thinking of the self as independent, occurs in interaction with others and is influenced by culture and context. In this chapter, we will describe the earliest roots of self-development and emphasize the importance of parenting to this process. As we will see, the role of caretakers is of major significance in the development of many of the processes related to the self.

THE SELF-SYSTEM: TRADITIONAL CONCEPTIONS

The self and its development are complicated, abstract topics. Writers still grapple with the question of what constitutes a self. In their search for answers, theorists and researchers need to account for the fact that selves are multifaceted and possess elements of both stability and change. If you have ever said that you are not the same person that you were some time ago, you can understand this point. Recently, writers have begun to use the term *self-system* to replace "self," because the latter seems too unidimensional (see Damon & Hart, 1988). The self-system includes aspects related to the self, such as self-concept, self-regulation, and self-esteem.

We will begin our look at the nature of the self-system with a brief description of the classic work of James, Cooley, and Mead. William James (1890) made a distinction between the "I" and the "Me," a distinction that is still used productively in contemporary research about the self. That part of the self called *"I"* refers to the *self-as-subject,* as active agent, or as the knower. It is that part of the self that experiences a sense of subjective self-awareness. The part called "Me" is that part of the self that is the object of self or others' observations, or in other words, the part that is known. One might think of the *"Me"* part of the self as the *self-concept.*

Implicit in James's traditional construction of selfhood is the idea that the self is multidimensional. Freud (1956) once wrote that a person could be construed as a whole "cast of characters." Interestingly, this view of the multiplicity of selves was rejected by a number of influential writers in the first half of the 20th century. Gergen (1971) described the emphasis placed on the importance of maintaining a unified, coherent self by important therapists and scholars such as Horney (1950), Jung (1928), Maslow (1954), and Rogers (1951). Considerable recent evidence, however, has not supported the view of the unified self but has demonstrated that individuals vary across situations, that they may possess conflicting self-ideas that speak with different voices at different times, and that the self-concept differentiates with maturity. A basic feature of the self, then, is that it incorporates both the private and the more public sides of our nature, accommodating our ability to keep our own counsel and still be known to others by virtue of our interactions with them.

Recently, writers have developed alternative ways of categorizing the classic "I-Me" distinction. Among these are M. Lewis's (1994) *subjective* and *objective self-awareness,* Case's (1991) *implicit* and *explicit self,* and Neisser's (1993) *ecological* and *remembered self.* All the newer contrasts share the original distinction between the self as knower and the self as known. Furthermore, there is consensus between classic and contemporary theorists that the "I" self emerges first.

What specifically does the "I" comprise? James proposed that this is the side of the self that experiences *continuity* over time. Even though we all grow and change, we know we embody core elements of the same "self" throughout our lifetime. The "I" also recognizes the *distinctiveness* of the self as a person compared to other persons. You know where you end and the person sitting next to you begins. Finally, the "I" reflects *agency* or is that part of the self that engages in self-directed activity, self-control, and contemplation of the "me." With time, these elements will be explored and further consolidated in the adolescent search for identity.

The "me" includes all those attributes that are used to define the self and that make up the self-concept. In James's typology, these are the "material self," the "social self," and the "spiritual self," ranked in that order of importance from lowest to highest. The material self encompasses a person's physical characteristics and material possessions. The social self includes her social standing, her reputation, and those personal characteristics that were recognized by others, such as gregariousness or stubbornness. The spiritual self, viewed by

James as the most precious, incorporates her qualities of character, beliefs, and personal values.

Self-concept, as defined here, is distinct from **self-esteem.** The former is a description of personal attributes. The latter is one's evaluation of these attributes, or the positive or negative *valence* associated with those attributes. Valence refers to the affective value of a characteristic, either good, bad, or neutral. James believed that self-esteem is more than just the measure of accomplishments. Rather, he believed that it depends upon the number of successes we enjoy relative to our aspirations, or, in his terminology, *pretensions.* Pretensions are goals that we choose to meet for ourselves because of their personal importance. For example, if it is highly important to you to be popular and socially active, the lack of a date for an important New Year's Eve party can be a real blow to your self-esteem. However, if you really care more about earning enough money to become rich at an early age, you might consider working overtime on New Year's Eve to be highly congruent with your aspirations. Your dateless condition is less damaging to your self-esteem. Failures or even successes in areas that are relatively unimportant to us may be discounted and will have less effect on self-esteem.

If James provided ideas about the structure of the self that resonate with contemporary theorizing, Charles Cooley (1902) introduced a developmental perspective that describes how interactions with others help construct the self-system. Using his now-famous metaphor of the "**looking-glass self,**" Cooley described the process of self-development as one that originates from observing the reflected appraisals of others, primarily attachment figures. Cooley hypothesized that this process consists of three steps. As we interact with others, we first imagine how we must appear to the other person on a certain dimension, such as intelligence. Then, we interpret or imagine how that other person evaluates us on that certain dimension. Finally, we experience some emotional response to that perceived evaluation. The resulting interpretation and its affective valence constitute a building block for constructing self-knowledge. So it is that our self-representations are shaped and given affective valences by the significant people in our life.

Let's consider a simplified example of a young child's display of affection for a parent. A 4-year-old girl approaches her father to give him a hug. The father, preoccupied with a pressing business matter, looks annoyed by the interruption. He gives her a quick hug and returns to his work. If this type of sequence is repeated on a regular basis across various situations, the child may come to develop a "self-idea" that she is bothersome and not important enough to interrupt her father's work. She may begin to construct a vague impression of herself as unappealing or possibly too emotionally expressive or dependent. Because the child perceives her father's response as impatient and irritated, her interpretation of the event includes a self-appraisal—presumably that she is irritating—that is incorporated into her self-system. The youngster comes to regard herself in certain ways by looking at the mirror of her parent's view of her, warped as that mirror might be. The emotional valence associated with this aspect of the child's self-image is negative. This self-representation may serve as a standard for her behavior in social interactions (e.g., in her willingness to express her need for attention and affection from others) and inform her sense of right and wrong.

Now imagine this same little girl in another family. She interrupts her father to give him a hug, and he beams, expressing evident satisfaction in his daughter's affectionate nature. This child's self-concept is likely to include a positively valenced sense of being emotionally expressive. The same child and the same behavior could lead to different social responses in different families, setting the child's developing sense of self, relationships, and morality on a different pathway. Thus early attachment and parenting interactions have been viewed as instrumental in the development of individual differences in self-concept (Sroufe, 1996).

While the development of the self is obviously influenced by many factors and is extraordinarily complex, Cooley believed that it was largely the product of social influences. Recent researchers have investigated the possibility that the sequence Cooley proposed can also operate in reverse order, namely that a positive appraisal of oneself can generate positive interpretations of others' appraisals.

George Herbert Mead (1934) expanded on Cooley's work, enlarging the scope of influence to include the role of language and society in shaping the self-system. He held that the self-idea, or self-concept, becomes internalized or "generalized" through repeated interactions with others of the same cultural group. The individual adopts the perspective of others who share the same societal perspective, producing a kind of *ecological self* (Neisser, 1993). An example of this phenomenon is provided by Markus and Kitayama (1991), who found cultural differences in preferred ways of viewing the self. In their study, Japanese were more likely to describe themselves by emphasizing their affiliations, such as family membership, whereas Americans used self-descriptors that emphasized their individuality. Children not only adopt descriptive information about the self from their cultural milieu, they also incorporate those standards, rules, and goals that their family and their culture have determined to be appropriate ways of behaving and thinking (Stipek, Recchia, & McClintic, 1992). Note the parallels between Mead's approach and Vygotsky's (see Chapter 3).

These classic formulations of the self as multidimensional, as influenced by the reflected appraisals of significant others, and as shaped by the cultural milieu, provide a foundation for current thinking about the self-system. You may have noticed that conceptions of self and of morality overlap in these models. Damon and Hart (1992) have noted:

> Children cannot know themselves without some sense of the other. Nor can they forge their self-identities without an awareness of their own values. Moreover, at all developmental periods, social activities derive from—and in turn shape—judgments about the self, other, and morality. In these and many other ways, self-understanding, social interaction, and morality are intertwined in a developing psychological system that grows and changes throughout the life span. (p. 421)

Self-understanding is one of the key building blocks of personality, social, and moral development. How does this mysterious self begin? In the next section, we will review the earliest stages of developing self-awareness.

THE EARLY DEVELOPMENT OF THE SELF-SYSTEM

The Beginnings of the "I" and the "Me"

Settling on a time that marks the beginning of the self is a difficult task, because various aspects of the self emerge at different rates and may be identified differently depending upon one's theoretical viewpoint. A child's ability to describe herself as "smart" or "funny" will not be apparent until several years after birth. Does this mean there is no sense of self until the time when she can recognize and articulate her personal characteristics? Most contemporary developmentalists would disagree with this idea. In general, the development of self is viewed as a gradually unfolding process, beginning at birth and lasting throughout life. Even adults continue to grow and change, thus experiencing self-development. However, the adult sense of self is far more differentiated than that of the infant, or even that of the articulate preschooler. What are the competencies of the infant that make self-development possible? How do these competencies interact with the social relationships that ultimately give birth to the self as a manifestation of personal consciousness?

Precursors of Self-Awareness in Infancy—the "Pre-Self"

We might say that the newborn's capacities for rudimentary information processing and social bonding provide the building material out of which the self is born. For example, one early competency is the infant's capacity for imitation. As soon as a few days after birth, babies can imitate the facial gestures of adults (Meltzoff, 1990). When a baby imitates an adult opening and closing his mouth, she is detecting, at least at a behavioral level, similarity between herself and the adult model. Meltzoff argues that such early imitative skills are precursors of the older child's ability to draw parallels between her own and another person's mind or feelings.

As we saw in Chapter 4, from birth through the first half year of life, the infant is primarily engaged in the business of regulating physiological and emotional states, largely in the context of infant-caregiver interactions. Young infants have limited power to regulate a caregiver's responses, and so it is primarily the caregiver's responsibility to scaffold interactions, providing the sensitive care that allows for the establishment of routines. Meltzoff (1990) argues that from the regularity and reliability of caregiver-infant interactions babies extract notions of "self invariance" and "other invariance," which precede self-awareness. We might say that the infant comes to possess a *pre-self,* composed of early inklings of the permanence of her body, its separateness from others, and the rhythms of interpersonal connections.

Gradually, over the second half year, the infant assumes more control in signaling the caregiver to provide for her needs. The regularity with which the caregiver is available and sensitive or unavailable and insensitive is stored in memory in what Stern (1985) calls *representations of interactions* (or **RIGs**). These are "procedural" representations, preverbal, unconscious, and a kind of sensorimotor memory. They are patterns generalized from the repetitive nature of caregiver-infant interactions.

When the infant's attempts to exert some control over caregiver contingencies are successful, she is thought to experience a budding sense of mastery or self-efficacy (Bandura, 1990). She takes pleasure in expressing the agentic "I." Imagine the lesson learned by an infant who, when she coos and babbles, regularly attracts the smile and responsive vocalizations of her caregivers. This baby's world, in some small way, begins to come under her control. She might encode the message, "When I am upset or need attention, my parent responds and takes care of me." Again, the infant does not represent these ideas linguistically, but rather encodes these kinds of organized sequences as procedural models or patterns of the self-in-relationship. Affective responses, such as feelings of love and relief, also become associated with these memories. The infant's self-system is under construction.

As the infant approaches the end of the first year, other cognitive and affective developments point to an increasing sense of self as separate from the caretaker. We saw in Chapter 4 that by about 8 to 10 months infants display separation anxiety, signaling the formation of an attachment to the primary caregiver. For example, they might show distress even at an impending separation from an attachment figure, perhaps by looking anxiously at the door when the babysitter arrives. Many babies cry and cling to a departing caregiver. These behaviors serve to maintain proximity, and they demonstrate the infant's recognition that the caregiver is separate from herself.

Attachment theorists like Bowlby assume that the attachment between infant and caregiver gives rise to a sense of security and optimism in an infant, what Erikson described as a burgeoning trust in others and an early sense of self-worth. From this perspective, when the 1-year-old begins to use the caregiver as a secure base from which to explore the environment, we are seeing the emergence of a kind of preliminary sense of self-worth. Once again, the infant's self-development evolves from her experience in relationships.

We also saw in the last chapter that late in the first year, caregivers' facial expressions influence infants' reactions to situations, such as their willingness to cross a visual cliff (Campos et al., 1983; Klinnert, 1984). *Social referencing*—the baby's adjustment of reactions depending on feedback provided by a caregiver—also implies recognition of the separateness of the other. This phenomenon is thought to be a source of information for the self-system, providing the baby with a context in which she begins to differentiate experience of the self from experience of the other and from the combined experience of the "we" (Emde & Buchsbaum, 1990). Social referencing demonstrates how transactional the self-development process really is. The child uses the caregiver's emotions to discern meaning in events and to intuit information about the self.

Campos and his colleagues (1989) have suggested that when caregivers communicate consistent emotional signals about environmental events, certain pervasive emotional dispositions are created. These processes can have far-reaching effects: "Can I trust other people? Is it safe to take risks?" These emotional dispositions constitute a part of the "value system" of a family or a culture. Furthermore, these authors note that emotional signaling by caregivers may affect the process of emotional regulation and emotional self-knowledge well beyond infancy. For example, a child growing up in an emotional climate marked by parental anger and blame might "read" and internalize the parents' emotional messages as shame and guilt, concluding that she is shameful (Zahn-Waxler & Kochanska, 1990).

The Emergence of Self-Awareness and Self-Concept

Certain cognitive advances in the second year seem to play important roles in the development of the self-system. For example, the toddler's capacity for establishing joint reference with another supports the early development of a theory of mind. Imagine that the father of a 15-month-old girl tries to get the toddler to look at a kitten that has just walked into the room. The father points to the kitten, looks at the child, smiles broadly and says, "cat." This sequence is repeated until the child, following the direction of her father's gaze, spies the cat and looks back at him with a big grin. She and her father are sharing the same point of reference. Jointly attending to the pet, in this case, may encourage a beginning understanding of "mind," of private experience that is sometimes shared. The toddler's sense of herself as a separate person is enhanced. Note, as well, that the affective part of the experience can also be shared. The toddler and her caregiver both delight in the kitten's appearance.

A benchmark event occurs in self-development roughly around the age of 18 months, perhaps supported by an emerging capacity for mental representation (see Chapter 3). Up to this time, human infants do not show *self-recognition* when they view themselves in a mirror. Self-recognition is typically manifested by the observer's display of self-directed behavior upon viewing her reflection. Reasoning that self-directed behavior signals the presence of objective self-awareness, Lewis and his colleagues used a mirror recognition technique to study infants and children (e.g., Lewis & Michalson, 1983). The researchers placed the children in front of a mirror after marking their faces with a spot of rouge. Toddlers over about 15 months old showed mark-directed behavior, such as touching their faces, averting their gaze, and then turning back to look again. No children younger than 15 months had this reaction, and all children in the 24-month-old group displayed it. Children over 15 months were also able to distinguish their own images from those of age mates on videotapes. Such consistent age related findings suggest that self-recognition is universally acquired during the second half of the second year of life.

This toddler recognizes that the image in the mirror is her own reflection, a milestone in self-recognition.

The timing of self-recognition is highly reliable. For children whose development is delayed, as in the case of children with Down syndrome, self-recognition occurs whenever they achieve a developmental level of approximately two years (Kopp & Wyer, 1994). Comparison studies of maltreated and nonmaltreated children show no differences in the timing of self-recognition (Schneider-Rosen & Cicchetti, 1984, 1991). These studies also suggest that self-evaluation, or self-esteem, begins to emerge along with self-recognition. Maltreated children show considerably more negative or neutral affect when seeing their faces in the mirror than do nonmaltreated children, who display more positive affect.

Self-recognition is a clear signal that a child has begun to formulate a conscious concept of self. Roughly after the child's second birthday, an increase in language skills makes possible further elaboration of the self-concept or "Me-self." Children begin to describe themselves as "a boy" or "a girl" or as "big" or "little," and they begin to use appropriate personal pronouns to refer to themselves. These achievements mark a watershed in the development of the self-concept, and caregivers make important contributions by virtue of the labels they apply to children. Parental statements such as "You are a big girl" can now be stored in a child's semantic memory as part of her self-knowledge (e.g., K. Nelson, 1993a). Caregivers' descriptions can be neutral and objective (such as the child's name or personal pronoun) or evaluative and subjective (such as "pretty" or "good"), and these appear not to be differentiated by young children according to their objectivity or subjectivity. Stipek and her associates (1990) reported that toddlers appear to believe both objective and subjective claims about themselves, apparently because the claims come from an authoritative source. In other words, young children cannot discount the negative part of the parental evaluation "*bad* girl" as due to parental bias or temporary bad mood. A study by Beeghly and Cicchetti (1994) found that when self-description begins, maltreated children use fewer words to describe their feelings than do nonmaltreated children, despite comparable performance on measures of receptive language ability. The authors conclude that these results, together with the less-positive affective responses maltreated children display on the self-recognition task, are early indicators of poor self-esteem and of the influence of caregivers' words and deeds on children's earliest self-evaluations.

As toddlers become preschoolers, their self-concepts become more and more differentiated and complex. For example, as early as 3 years of age, children can correctly identify their race, ethnicity, and skin color (Katz & Zalk, 1974). In general, children from minority groups tend to develop racial awareness faster than do nonminorities. A study by Feinman and Entwhistle (1976) demonstrated that young African American children outperform other children in their ability to discriminate colors of faces, suggesting the early influence of race on perception. Ramsey and Myers (1990) also found that race is one of the primary dimensions children refer to when describing people.

Unfortunately, many early studies of preschool children found evidence for a pro-white bias among children from minority groups (see Banks, 1976; Beuf, 1977; Spencer, 1982). Typically, these studies involved questioning young children about their preferences for, and identification with, dolls that represent their own ethnic or racial group and that represent the majority culture. Overall, young children tended to perceive a white doll as possessing more positive attributes, and some researchers have interpreted these findings to be early predictors of identity formation problems or misidentification among minority group children. However, more recent studies of African American children have found that a pro-white bias may coexist with high levels of personal self-esteem (Powell, 1985). Spencer and Markstrom-Adams (1990), after reviewing this body of work, conclude that these dissonant results reflect the child's cognitive awareness of social stereotypes, but not necessarily a self-esteem deficit. In other words, young children from minority groups may be somewhat more attuned to society's valuing of white culture without necessarily devaluing themselves or their cultural heritage.

Consistent with their level of cognitive development, preschoolers generally describe themselves in concrete, physical terms, such as "little" or "strong," whereas older children and adolescents employ more abstract words. As children mature, they become more skilled at identifying various aspects of themselves. For example, a 7-year-old might describe herself as helpful, a good soccer player, and smart in reading but not in math. As we shall see in a later chapter, the self-concept continues to become more differentiated with age.

In summary, the self-system begins to develop in earliest infancy. There are many precursors to a conscious concept of self in the first year, a kind of procedural knowledge of the self in action and interaction, or "pre-self." But awareness of self as a distinct entity begins with self-recognition in the second year and is followed by explicit self-description in the third year. Self-evaluation or self-esteem is evident as soon as toddlers show signs of self-recognition. See Table 5.1 for a summary of the early phases of self-development.

Throughout infancy and beyond, the self-system is a joint construction of child, caregiver, and cultural/family milieu. We have described some ways in which caregiver-infant interactions seem to contribute to the development of the self. Later in this chapter, we will discuss in greater detail how parenting in the toddler and preschool years contributes to child outcomes, including the development of the self-system.

Roots of Self-Control and Self-Regulation

Up to now, we have described the emerging "I" and "me." Now we turn our attention to another important dimension of the developing self-system, **self-control** and **self-regulation.** *Self-control* refers to two things: first, the child's ability to *stop herself* from performing a proscribed act, as when a toddler can pull her hand back from the cookie jar

TABLE 5.1

Phases of Self-Development

Age	Developing Aspects of Self	Manifestations
0–6 months	Pre-self	Beginnings of "self invariance" and "other invariance" embedded in infant-caregiver interactions
6–12 months	Intentional or Agentic Self or "I"	Intentional signaling of caregiver; social referencing; shared referents; beginning self-efficacy; using caregiver as secure base (beginning self-worth and trust)
12–24 months	Objective Self or "Me"	Self-recognition; early self-control; early self-esteem (feelings of autonomy)
24–60 months	Self-Monitoring Self	Self-description; self-conscious emotions; self-regulation

after being told "No cookies before dinner"; and second, her ability to *make herself* perform an act that she may not feel much like doing, such as giving Aunt Matilda a required kiss on the cheek. According to Kopp (1982), *self-regulation* is a more advanced and flexible version of self-control:

> the ability to comply with a request, to initiate and cease activities according to situational demands, to modulate the intensity, frequency, and duration of verbal and motor acts in social and educational settings, to postpone acting upon a desired object or goal, and to generate socially approved behavior in the absence of external monitors. (pp. 199–200)

Counselors regularly deal with problems involving self-regulation in one form or another. The preschooler who throws tantrums in school, the rebellious adolescent who runs away from home, the young adult who repeatedly loses jobs because she fails to show up on time, all may be examples of difficulties in this area. While many other factors contribute to such adjustment problems, they all reflect some lack of compliance with specific requests or rules.

Obviously, achieving self-regulation is a rather formidable task for a mischievous toddler or even for a sophisticated high-schooler! And even though this may sound like the accomplishment that many parents of tempestuous 2-year-olds long for, it is not realistic to expect a child to be able to master her behavior and emotions in every circumstance. The movement from dyadic emotion regulation to self-regulation of behavior and emotion, permitting harmonious interchange with the social environment, is a painstaking and long-term process.

The Importance of Emotion Regulation

It is absolutely essential to recognize that *emotion* regulation underlies any ability to control behaviors. In fact, the earliest developmental task of infancy is to establish physiological balance, or control over fluctuating levels of arousal. The affective tension that the infant experiences when her homeostatic "set point" has been altered through hunger, pain, or too much stimulation motivates her to return to a more balanced state. Unable to manage this on her own, the infant signals the caregiver, whose soothing attentions function as critical ingredients in the development of the affect-regulation system. When the toddler or preschooler experiences periods of high arousal or distress, the sensitive caregiver steps in once again to help the child regain some affective control or to shore up the boundaries of the self. As we have emphasized in Chapter 4, good caregiving in infancy and beyond involves scaffolding the child's developing ability to regulate both emotional and behavioral expression.

The Early Progress of Behavior Regulation

How does *behavior* regulation come into being? It depends on two major cognitive and emotional advances that emerge in tandem with objective self-awareness or self-recognition: first, representational thought, and second, emotional response to wrongdoing.

Recall from our discussion of Piagetian theory that children around 18 months of age can use a symbol to stand in for an object. Toddlers hear, understand, and store structures such as "Don't jump on the furniture," which might be a manifestation of a broader value that property should not be damaged, or "Share your candy with your sister," a version of "Do unto others." This cognitive machinery allows children to construct internalized representations of *standards for everyday behavior* (Kopp & Wyer, 1994). These standards or rules might differ somewhat according to the child's family and culture, but every cultural group maintains them and provides sanctions for their violation (M. Lewis, 1993).

Along with the basic capacity for mental representation, many other cognitive skills contribute to the learning of standards: ability to focus attention, comprehension of caregiver requests, procedural knowledge of rules, and generalization of rules across situations. As these abilities are sharpened in the second year, toddlers begin the process of internalizing rules and prohibitions (Emde, Biringen, Clyman, & Oppenheim, 1991). Obviously, an infant cannot comply with social conventions precisely because she has no comprehension of them. A baby may be prevented from engaging in some activity by external parental displays of control, as when a mother whisks her adventurous 10-month-old away from the edge of a swimming pool. But a 2-year-old who has the requisite level of cognitive maturity to understand and remember some rules, as well as the motivation to comply, begins to show signs of inhibiting her own behavior in such situations.

The growth of emotions, often linked to violations of standards for everyday behavior, appears to begin late in the second year. Called the **self-conscious emotions,** shame, embarrassment, guilt, and pride take their place in the child's emotional repertoire after objective self-awareness, or self-recognition, has been attained (M. Lewis & Michalson, 1983). These emotions are different from the emotions of infancy because they require the ability to consider the self as separate from others and as the subject of others' judgments. Between the ages of 2 and 3, young children often display emotional responses to their wrongdoing and mistakes, suggesting that they have begun to evaluate themselves in ways that they expect to be evaluated by others (Kagan, 1981). At 18 months, a child might take notice of her rule violation but without any discernable emotional response. Consider for example, the toddler who spills milk on the floor. She may say "Uh oh!" and giggle or point to the spill without much concern. Later, rule breaking becomes associated with some negative affect. This same youngster at 3 may experience a sense of embarrassment, evaluate herself as "bad," and try to hide the evidence.

The capacity for emotional response to wrongdoing is an important milestone, long considered to be the beginning of conscience development (Sears, Maccoby, & Levin, 1957). While not yet a reflection of full-fledged conscience, the child's emotional responses to rule violations are linked to what she perceives her parents' reactions might be, and these perceptions serve to shape her developing sense of morality (Emde, Johnson, & Easterbrooks, 1987).

Self-regulation is made possible by the progress of emotion regulation, which begins in infancy, and by cognitive and emotional advances that begin in the child's second year. But like all aspects of self-development, the progress of self-regulation is deeply embedded in the social experiences of the child. Parenting style and parenting practices are particularly important contributors, as we shall see in the next section, on socialization.

EARLY SOCIALIZATION: PARENTING AND THE DEVELOPMENT OF THE SELF-SYSTEM

Theorists from Cooley (1902) to Bowlby (e.g., 1969/1982) and Erikson (1950/1963) have assumed that many parts of the self-system, such as self-concept, self-esteem, and self-regulation, grow out of our social interactions with the significant people in our lives, from infancy onward. According to Bowlby, for example, the caregiver-infant relationship helps the baby to begin the construction of a working model of the self, of others, and of relationships. As we saw in the last chapter, the available data *do* suggest that our earliest relationships create a trajectory for the development of self-concept and self-esteem. For example, when babies are securely attached to their mothers, they tend to be appropriately independent as 4-year-olds and to be self-confident and socially skilled as 10-year-olds (e.g., Sroufe, Fox, et al., 1983; see Thompson, 1998, for a review).

We know that early caregiving quality can make an important contribution to the quality of babies' attachments. Infants are likely to become securely attached to caregivers who respond promptly and consistently to crying, who react appropriately to babies' facial expressions, eye contact and other signals, who handle their infants sensitively, and who hold them often during the first year, providing the contact comfort that helps infants modulate their emotions. Such caregiving requires patience and a child-centered approach that can be difficult for any parent sometimes, but is especially challenging if the baby has a difficult temperament (irritable, active, difficult to soothe, and so on) or other special needs or if the parent is stressed or depressed. But the effort and self-sacrifice required for parents to create a "good fit," as Thomas and Chess (1977) described it, between their caregiving and a baby's needs does appear to contribute to attachment quality and to the direction that self-knowledge and self-evaluation will take. This process continues after infancy, as the description of self-development in the last section indicates. In this section, we will take a close look at parent-child relationships in the toddler and preschool years. We will focus especially on the characteristics of parenting that may be most conducive to helping young children to develop positive self-esteem and adaptive self-regulatory mechanisms.

As the infant becomes a toddler, gaining cognitive, communicative, and motor skills, there are new challenges for parents trying to be sensitive and responsive, to create a "good fit" between their care and the child's needs. *First*, caregivers are faced with the need to grant some autonomy to the child. As toddlers become capable of doing more on their own, they are motivated to practice and expand their growing competencies. The strong dependency that characterizes young babies is gradually replaced by a capacity and need for independent action. Erikson theorized that toddlers' emerging feelings of worth are benefited when they can use their growing skills to function at least somewhat autonomously, whether it is by feeding themselves or by buttoning their own buttons, or more subtly, by saying "NO!"—that is, refusing to do what someone else requires (see Table 1.1 in Chapter 1). Thus, although the earliest feelings of worth grow out of an infant's trust in others to meet all her needs, those feelings of worth grow in the toddler years when the child begins to experience self-sufficiency, or autonomy, a sense that "I can do it myself."

Second, also because the child's behavioral and cognitive skills are growing, the caregiver must begin to *socialize* the child, limiting some behaviors and demanding others, so that the child will be safe ("No, you cannot climb on the counter") and so that she will learn the standards of her culture and behave in ways that are conventionally acceptable ("You must wear clothes"). Socialization pressure requires *discipline,* when parents limit or demand behavior by exerting or requiring control. Parents generally impose more discipline on the child as they perceive her to be more and more capable of self-control. When parents tell a child to do, or not to do, something, they are depending on the child's ability to initiate or to stop her own actions. As we saw earlier, the only way to make an infant do, or not do, something is to rely on physically moving or restraining the child. Parents do a lot of that with infants, but they rely more and more on controlling by request or command during early childhood, apparently recognizing that the requisite abilities (such as representational and comprehension skills) are developing.

Thus, caregiver-child relationships are reorganized in the post-infancy period, with the additions of children's autonomy seeking, on the one hand, and parents' imposition of discipline, on the other hand. What are the important features of this more complex relationship between parent and child? What role does the parent-child relationship play in the child's developing self-system? Let's begin by examining what research indicates are the most important dimensions or features of a parent's behavior in this relationship.

The Dimensions of Parenting Style

Studies of parenting after infancy have a long history and have produced many complicated findings. Remarkably, researchers from very different theoretical traditions have repeatedly identified two major dimensions or aspects of parents' behavior that seem to characterize the quality of parenting. These can be thought of as the primary contributors to what is called *parenting style* (for reviews see Baumrind, 1989, 1993; Darling & Steinberg, 1993; Maccoby & Martin, 1983; Parke & Buriel, 1998).

The Warmth Dimension—Parental Responsiveness

In the post-infancy period, parents continue to create an emotional climate for their children. Contributing to a positive climate is the parent's responsiveness: listening to the child, being involved and interested in the child's activities, accepting the child, making positive attributions toward the child, being "tuned in" and supportive (e.g., Baumrind, 1989). In essence, high levels of warmth with toddlers and older children are comparable to high levels of responsive, sensitive care with infants. But some of the child's needs have changed. With toddlers, as we have seen, autonomy needs begin to be important, and responsive parents accept these needs, acquiescing when possible to their children's reasonable demands for autonomy (Baumrind, 1993). So, when 25-month-old Amanda begins to insist that she can dress herself, her mother tries to accommodate her by setting aside extra time for the morning dressing ritual. She also ignores the inconvenience and the sometimes strange-looking outcomes and gives Amanda positive messages about the process: "You're getting to be such a big girl to put on your own clothes!" Her attitude is **child centered,** setting aside parental needs (for time, convenience, and coordinated outfits) to meet Amanda's developmental needs.

Some parents create a more negative emotional climate. Their behavior is often *parent centered:* they show little responsiveness to their children's concerns and are unlikely to do things just to meet those concerns. They may even make hostile attributions when children's needs are out of line with their own. When 20-month-old Jessie wants to feed herself her morning cereal, for example, at first her mother ignores her, and when Jessie insists, her mother attends to her demands by making negative attributions, such as "You'll just make a mess" and "Why do you always make things so hard in the morning?" When Jessie accidentally spills the milk, her mother responds in frustration, "I told you that you couldn't do it yourself!"

We have seen that sensitive, responsive mother care in infancy promotes secure attachments. Likewise, mothers' warmth and responsiveness with their toddlers help maintain secure attachments and increase the likelihood that toddlers will be cooperative when mothers place demands on them (e.g., Emde, Biringen, et al., 1991; Lay, Waters, & Parke, 1989; NICHD, 1998). In one study, for example, toddlers' compliance with their mothers was observed in toy cleanup tasks and in a situation where mothers designated some attractive toys as "off limits." The most enthusiastically compliant toddlers were those who were securely attached to their mothers (according to a separate assessment), and whose mothers maintained a warm, positive emotional climate throughout the sessions (Kochanska, 1995; Kochanska, Aksan, & Koenig, 1995).

The Control Dimension—Parental Demandingness

The second major dimension of parenting style is parental demandingness. If parental responsiveness means that parents sometimes acquiesce to their children's demands, parental demandingness leads parents to impose discipline. Demanding parents require their children to curb some of their behaviors and insist that they perform other behaviors that are suitable to their level of maturity (sometimes called *maturity demands*). Demanding parents impose standards and rules and enforce them. Interestingly, this dimension of parenting can be either child centered or parent centered. If the parent's concern is the development of self-control necessary for children to feel secure, to behave in ways that gain social acceptance, and to become skillful at social give and take, then discipline has a child focus. If the parents' concerns—for example, for quiet, or convenience, or orderliness, and so on—are primary, then discipline has a parent focus. Of course, parents' disciplinary motives may sometimes combine both kinds of concerns, and the same parents may shift their focus depending on the given situation. For example, Hastings and Grusec (1998) found that parents expressed more parent-centered concerns (such as wanting to be in control) when disciplining their children in public, but more child-centered concerns (such as teaching a child not to give up easily) in private interactions.

Four Parenting Styles

We can describe four basic *parenting styles,* or constellations of parenting characteristics, by combining and crossing the positive and negative poles of parental responsiveness and demandingness (see Table 5.2: *Parenting Dimensions and Parenting Styles*) (Maccoby & Martin, 1983). As you will see, these styles are often predictive of child characteristics (e.g., Baumrind, 1989, 1993).

The Authoritative Style

Parents with an authoritative style are both highly responsive and highly demanding. So, they create a positive emotional climate for their children, promoting autonomy and supporting assertiveness and individuality. At the same time these parents accept responsibility for socializing their children by expecting mature behavior and setting and enforcing clear standards. Other qualities also tend to be part of this constellation: these parents are often openly affectionate; they encourage two-way communication with their children (that is, they genuinely listen and pay attention as well as talking themselves). Their communications about expectations and standards are usually clear and come with explanations that go beyond "You do it because I said so" to statements that help children make sense of their parents' demands.

The Authoritarian Style

Authoritarian parents are low on responsiveness, but highly demanding. Thus they do not create a positive emotional climate and do not encourage children's individualistic strivings or assertiveness, but they do tend to exercise considerable control, making maturity

TABLE 5.2

Parenting Dimensions and Parenting Styles

	Parental Warmth:	
	Accepting **Responsive** **Child-Centered**	**Rejecting** **Unresponsive** **Parent-Centered**
Parental Demandingness:		
Demanding Controlling	*Authoritative Style*	*Authoritarian Style*
Undemanding Not Controlling	*Permissive Style*	*Neglecting-Uninvolved Style*

Source: Maccoby, E. E., & Martin, J. A. Socialization in the context of the family. In P. H. Mussin & E. M. Hetherington, *Handbook of child psychology* vol. 4 (4th ed., pp. 1–101). Copyright © 1983. This material is adapted by permission of John Wiley & Sons, Inc.

demands and requiring conformity to rules. In addition, other qualities tend to be characteristic of authoritarian parents. First, authoritarian parents usually communicate less effectively with their children than authoritative parents; their communications are more one-sided ("I say what will happen; you listen"); they express less affection; and their control tends to be more restrictive, meaning that they tend to restrict their children's emotional expressiveness and other self-assertive behaviors. They also are more likely to exercise control by using power assertion (see *Parenting Practices: Methods of Control*, below) and are less likely to provide explanations that go beyond "Because I said so."

Parents who create a positive emotional climate promote autonomy and elicit cooperation from their children.

The Permissive Style

Permissive parents are moderately to highly responsive to their children, but low on demandingness. Thus, they exercise less control than other parents, putting fewer maturity demands on their children, especially with regard to expressions of anger and aggressive behavior. They are more nurturing and affectionate than authoritarian parents, but usually not as nurturant as authoritative parents.

The Neglecting-Uninvolved Style

Some parents are both low on responsiveness and low on demandingness, so that they actually invest little time or attention in a child and are largely parent centered in their concerns. Like permissive parents, these parents seem to neglect their responsibility to socialize the child, but they also express less affection and are not likely to be responsive to their children's needs, perhaps even expressing hostility or making negative attributions to their children. When they do impose limits on their children, they tend to use power assertive techniques and little explanation.

Parenting Style and Child Outcomes

Through the long history of research on parenting, small but significant correlations have been found between parenting style, on the one hand, and children's typical behaviors, on the other. Briefly, *authoritative* parenting has been associated with many positive outcomes in young children: adaptability, competence and achievement, good social skills and peer acceptance, and low levels of antisocial or aggressive behavior. Of particular interest to us in this chapter, authoritative parenting seems to promote positive self-development, especially high self-esteem and the capacity for self-regulation.

The children of *authoritarian* parents are more likely to be irritable and conflicted, showing signs of both anxiety and anger. They are conforming (self-controlled) with authority figures, but are not socially skillful and are susceptible to being bullied (e.g., Ladd & Ladd, 1998). Not surprisingly, they tend to have low self-esteem, and although they exhibit self-control with authorities, they may not be as well self-regulated when not being observed, so that they are unlikely to get caught.

Permissive parents are more likely to have children who exhibit uncontrolled, impulsive behavior and low levels of self-reliance. They are low on cognitive competence and social agency, and high on aggression, especially in family interactions. In some studies they have had high self-esteem, apparently when parents' exhibit high levels of warmth, but many studies suggest that warmth combined with demandingness is more certain to be associated with self-esteem (see Maccoby & Martin, 1983).

Finally, the children of *neglecting/uninvolved* parents are likely to be impulsive, to show high levels of both **externalizing problems** (e.g., aggressiveness) and **internalizing problems** (e.g., depression), and to have low self-esteem.

Be cautious in interpreting these relationships between parenting style and child outcomes. The strength of the associations is modest, cueing us that many factors interact with parenting and modify its effects. Researchers have begun to identify a multiplicity of interacting factors, which we will discuss in a later section of this chapter. (See Collins, Maccoby, Steinberg, Hetherington, and Bornstein, 2000, for further discussion.)

Parenting Practices: Methods of Control

Thus far, we have looked at *parenting style*—parents' combined responsiveness and demandingness—as a source of children's behavior and self-development. Another aspect of parenting concerns the **method of control** parents choose when they attempt to exercise control. Researchers have identified three categories of control method: **power assertion, love withdrawal,** and **induction.** *Power assertion* can involve physical punishment or the threat of physical punishment, ranging from mild (e.g., a calm whack on a diapered bottom), to harsh (e.g., screaming in rage; a beating); *or* it can involve withdrawal of privileges, from mild forms (such as time-out procedures with toddlers, see Box 5.1: *Effective Ways to Use Time-Out*), to severe denial (e.g., withholding meals). Power assertion is usually effective for the immediate control of behavior: children often show self-control when they feel threatened. But there can be unwanted side effects: harsh or severe power assertion has been linked to high levels of anger and anxiety in children, and children whose parents use harsh, punitive practices tend to be more aggressive than other children (e.g., Baumrind, 2001; Strassberg, Pettit, Gregory, & Bates, 1994; Straus & Gelles, 1990; Straus & Yodanis, 1996).

If a child is accustomed to power assertive control, what happens when the threat is removed (e.g., Mom or Dad is not present or not likely to find out)? Does the child engage in self-regulation? In other words, will she regulate her own behavior because she is committed to an internalized set of standards? There are conflicting data on this issue. On the whole, power assertion does not seem to be particularly effective in promoting self-regulation. Interestingly, milder forms of power assertion are more effective than harsher forms. But the picture is complex and cannot be fully understood without considering other factors, such as child temperament, culture, and overall parenting style. We will return to this issue later. (See *Parenting and the Developing Self-System*, below).

Love withdrawal, such as a parent's withdrawing attention or affection, expressing disappointment or disillusionment with a child, turning away from a child, cutting off verbal or emotional contact, or enforcing separations, is rarely used alone by parents, but when it is used, it seems to generate high anxiety and is more effective in eliciting immediate compliance than any other method. As with power assertion, there is little evidence that the compliance that love withdrawal generates is anything but short term (Maccoby & Martin, 1983).

Induction refers to parents' use of explanation: giving reasons for rules ("If everybody touched the paintings they would soon be very dirty from fingerprints") and appealing to children's desires to be grown-up ("Big girls don't take toys away from babies"). "Other-oriented" explanations seem to be especially powerful in promoting empathy ("When you hit people, it hurts them and makes them sad"). Using induction seems to be the most effective way to promote the internalization of rules, so that children regulate their own behavior by the standards they have learned whether or not authorities are present and whether or not immediate consequences are likely.

Many studies have found that the same parents may use one practice on some occasions and another in other situations, and sometimes parents use multiple practices in the same disciplinary episode (e.g., Hastings & Grusec, 1998; Kuczynski, 1984). But most parents favor using one type of practice more than the others, and when they do, their primary practice is somewhat predictive of certain child outcomes. But, much as we found with rearing practices in infancy, such as breast versus bottle feeding, *particular* practices may be less important than the overall quality of the parent-child relationship. For toddlers and older children, the meaning that the child attributes to parents' practices is likely to be important and appears to be tied to the emotional climate established by parenting style (Darling & Steinberg, 1993). In particular, when parents are warm and responsive, their children are more likely to comply with parental demands (e.g., NICHD, 1998). Parenting style, then, affects how effective a parenting practice will be with a child (Darling & Steinberg, 1993). As it happens, certain practices tend to be combined with certain parenting styles. Authoritative parents, for example, are often characterized by

Box 5.1 **Effective Ways to Use Time-Out**

In many Dennis the Menace cartoons, Dennis sits in a pint-sized chair, hugging his teddy bear, facing into a corner, banished for some infraction. Dennis's parents use **time-out** as a disciplinary procedure: during a short span of time, Dennis is required to discontinue his involvement in ongoing activities to quietly sit somewhere apart. The technique involves mild power assertion and is suitable for use with toddlers and preschoolers. There is no pain involved, but time-out gets the attention of young children. Requiring a child to sit in a corner is one approach, but you can choose any place that separates the child from the action, while keeping her in a safe place that is within calling distance. Do not choose a spot where the child might be overwhelmed by feelings of isolation. The purpose of time-out is to eliminate the rewards of misbehavior, not to frighten a child. Indeed, it will work even if the "place apart" is in the midst of things. For example, in one day care center, the time-out chair is in the middle of a busy classroom so that the teachers can keep an eye on the offender. For the children, just being confined to the chair is sufficiently aversive to be effective.

J. E. Hamilton (1993) offers a number of pointers for using time-out effectively. To start, it helps to choose just two or three target behaviors that need to be changed. Reserve time-out for behaviors that are important to control because of safety, such as climbing on the kitchen counter, or because they are antisocial and hurtful, such as hitting or biting. Explain to the child which behaviors will lead to time-out, why they are unacceptable, and what alternative behaviors would be acceptable. It works best if children know the rules in advance so that what will lead to time-out is clear. (Don't forget to provide some positive attention for those more acceptable behaviors.) Don't use time-out for behaviors that have not been previously identified as inappropriate, and when the time-out is over, follow up with a reminder of your reasons for restricting this behavior. Remember, mild power assertion combined with induction can be very effective. Although Dennis the Menace is allowed to have a teddy bear in time-out, it is more consistent to eliminate access to toys, television, and attention from others.

Don't expect everything to go smoothly right from the start. At first a child may refuse to stay in time-out, or she may repeat the offending behavior just to test your resolve. If the child won't stay in time-out, make it very brief—a minute or so—and hold the child in place, turning your face away to create the condition of no attention. Then make eye contact and praise the child for staying in time-out. Stick it out—it will pay off. Time-out needs only to be long enough to get the point across. The younger the child, the less time is appropriate. One rule of thumb is one or two minutes for each year of age, so that the maximum time-out for a 2-year-old would be four minutes. Longer times are likely to become so aversive that they could defeat the purpose of simply getting the child's attention and creating an opportunity for her to think over her behavior.

Time-out, like most effective discipline, requires putting aside what you are doing to attend to the misbehavior when it happens. It can be inconvenient, but *immediacy* is important to help young children make the right connection between their behavior and its consequences. Similarly, *consistency* is essential. When a parent's responses are unreliable, it is difficult for a child to learn what the rules are. Just how consistent can a parent be? There are going to be times when you simply cannot follow up on a misbehavior. But most times you can, if you make it a priority and if you are careful to use time-out for just a few important behaviors. Suppose, for example, that you are teaching your 4-year-old, Jenny, not to hit her baby brother. In the middle of your grocery shopping, sure enough, Jenny hauls off and whacks him. Immediately, tell Jenny what's wrong with this picture: "Jenny, you know that hitting is not okay. It hurts and it makes people cry, and we don't hit in our family, ever! You have to go to time-out for that." Pick up the baby, grab Jenny's hand, leave the cart, and head for the car. In the car, put Jenny in the back seat and sit in the front with the baby. Say clearly, "You are in time-out," and face forward for the designated time. At the end, explain the rule again, tell Jenny that time-out is over, and head back to the shopping cart. In other words, if at all possible, improvise. (No car? Stand silently on the sidewalk for the time-out period.) There are bound to be situations that make immediate and full follow-through impossible. You could have been in the middle of checking out your groceries, for example. But if your usual response is swift and sure, your efforts will pay off.

extensive use of induction, regardless of what other practices they might sometimes use. And as we have seen, the children of authoritative parents are likely to show higher levels of competence, self-esteem, and self-regulation than children exposed to other parenting styles. But what might happen if parents who show most of the qualities of an authoritative style—especially high responsiveness and high demandingness—were to use primarily power assertion to enforce their demands? In the next section, we will consider how parenting style interacts with practice for different children and in different cultural contexts, focusing on what we are learning about how these factors interact in the early phases of self-development, during the toddler and early preschool years. We will revisit these issues in later chapters when we describe self-regulatory and moral development in older children and adolescents.

Moderators of Parenting and Parenting Effectiveness

Authoritative parents seem to get the best results from their children, but are their behaviors really having any influence? Both developmentalists (e.g., Scarr, 1993) and popular writers (e.g., J. R. Harris, 1998) have asked whether we are wrong to assume that correlations between parenting and child outcomes imply that parenting style and practice are actually causing children's behavior. In other words, several other possibilities exist. *First,* the shared biological inheritance of parents and children might account for both the parental and the child characteristics measured in these studies (Scarr, 1993; 1997). For example, the same genetic endowment that makes parents affectionate and responsive might produce children who are cooperative and good-natured. *Second,* children's predispositions and temperaments may actually cause parents' behaviors rather than vice versa. For example, perhaps children who are "naturally" sunny and compliant could elicit authoritative parenting, but hostile, negative children might elicit more authoritarian or neglectful parenting behaviors.

Overall, although controversy persists on these issues, most researchers and clinicians take a multidimensional approach to the question of direction of effects in children's social development (e.g., R. Q. Bell & Chapman, 1986; W. A. Collins et al., 2000; Kochanska, 1993; Lytton, 1990). That means that multiple causes are thought to be interacting, mutually modifying one another. As in Bronfenbrenner's bioecological model, proximal processes—reciprocal interactions between the child and the people and things that surround the child—as well as distal processes, such as genes and culture, are all playing a role (e.g., Bronfenbrenner & Ceci, 1994; see Chapter 1). In this section, we will consider two important factors in the multidimensional mix: the child's temperament and the broader cultural environment.

The Child's Temperament, Parenting, and Child Outcomes

Recall that in infancy, both parents and infants contribute to the quality of the caregiving relationship. It is harder for mothers to be sensitive and responsive to a baby with a difficult temperament, for example. But when mothers *are* highly responsive during infancy, the "good fit" they create between their caregiving and the baby's needs supports the development of a secure attachment even for babies with difficult temperaments. When mothers are not able to create a good fit, the type of insecure attachment that emerges often seems to be at least partly influenced by the baby's temperament (e.g., Kochanska, 1998).

With toddlers and preschoolers, temperament and other child characteristics continue to contribute to the quality of the parent-child relationship. Children's typical behaviors can affect both parenting style and the particular disciplinary practices that parents are most likely to use.

Bell and Chapman (1986) reviewed 14 studies that demonstrated the influence of children on parents. Many of these studies were at least partly experimental, with adults (usually parents) reacting to, or interacting with, children who were not their own, in situations created by the researchers. The studies examined adults' responses to children's dependence/independence behaviors, their tendencies to be aggressive or to withdraw, and their responsiveness to adults (e.g., tendencies to smile, chat, imitate, and so on). For example, in one of these studies, Marcus (1975, 1976) showed parents videotapes of a child actor solving a puzzle. The child in the film behaved either dependently (e.g., seeking help, like, "Would this piece go better here or here?") or independently. The adults' reactions were more directive with the dependent than with the independent child. Stevens-Long (1973) examined parents' reactions to unrelated children's aggressive, uncooperative behavior or to anxious, withdrawn behavior. The adults were more likely to command or ignore the more aggressive children, but to verbally help or reward the more depressive children. Bell and Harper (1977) found that adults used more power assertive behaviors with socially unresponsive girls and more inductive behaviors with girls who were highly responsive. All of these studies demonstrate that adults' reactions are moderated by the characteristics or behaviors of the particular child with whom they are interacting.

Studies such as these, along with research on parents with their own children, have begun to paint a picture of a complex interactive system between parent and child. The child's characteristics are likely to affect the parent's behavior, and the parent's style and practices affect the child's behavior. But *whether* the child affects the parent's practices and beliefs depends on the parents' initial attitudes toward child rearing, which, as we saw in the last chapter, are probably influenced by the parents' own relationship histories and their working models of attachment. And *how* parenting affects the child depends on the child's temperament, abilities, and vulnerabilities! The following study of aggressiveness in toddlers provides a good illustration of some of these interactive complexities.

Child Temperament, Parents' Negativity, and Toddlers' Aggressiveness. In a study by K. H. Rubin and his colleagues (1998), 2-year-olds who frequently expressed negative

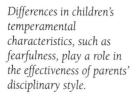

Differences in children's temperamental characteristics, such as fearfulness, play a role in the effectiveness of parents' disciplinary style.

emotion, especially anger, and low levels of behavioral and emotional self-control were considered to show "emotion dysregulation," one feature of a difficult temperament in toddlers. These children were not wary when a stranger approached them with new and unusual toys, and they showed strong frustration and distress when they could not get a toy out of a container or when asked to wait briefly before drawing with a new set of crayons. Other studies have found a connection between difficult temperaments in young children and aggressive, disruptive behavior (e.g., Zahn-Waxler, Iannotti, Cummings, & Denham, 1990; see Lytton, 1990), but the correlations are low, suggesting that other factors are also important. In this study, the researchers found that the link between difficult temperament and aggressive behavior depended on parents' reactions to their children's temperaments. Those boys who showed emotion dysregulation, *and who also had mothers who responded with negative control* (such as being physically intrusive) *and with hostile emotion* (such as frowning, criticizing, yelling) were the children who were at high risk to be aggressive with peers. *When mothers showed high levels of warmth* (positive tone, praise, verbal affection, and so on), *boys with difficult temperaments were not likely to be aggressive.* Note that mothers' negative control and hostile emotion did not predict aggressive behavior in children who did not have difficult temperaments, or in girls, so that *both* child characteristics *and* mothers' behaviors played important roles in children's aggressive behavior.

The Cultural Context, Parenting, and Child Outcomes

Just as children's characteristics can affect parenting and outcomes, cultural factors, such as the race, ethnicity, and socioeconomic class of the family, can moderate parenting practices *and* may even alter their effects. In particular, the constellations of parenting behaviors that "go together" seem to be somewhat different across cultures. For example, European American parents who are warm and responsive also tend to use gentle parenting practices—offering suggestions, making polite requests, distracting a child, using induction, and so on. But Harwood, Schoelmerich, Schulze, and Gonzalez (1999) found another pattern of associations between parents' warmth and parenting practices in Puerto Rican American mothers as they interacted with their 12- to 15-month-olds. They found no differences between the two ethnic groups on maternal warmth: both European American and Puerto Rican American mothers tended to be affectionate and committed to providing a supportive emotional climate for their toddlers. But the Puerto Rican mothers were more directive and more likely to issue commands. Consistent with other research on European Americans, the Anglo mothers were more likely to let their toddlers try to do things for themselves and were more likely to make suggestions than to issue commands. These differences in mothers' behavior were consistent with their long-term goals. Puerto Rican mothers were more concerned about "sociocentric" outcomes, focusing more on wanting children to recognize their obligations and their connectedness to others. In this study, Anglo mothers were perceived as emphasizing "individualization" as a long-term socialization goal, valuing assertiveness and self-reliance. Clearly, to the extent that parenting goals differ across cultural groups, parenting practices are likely to differ as well.

As we have noted, authoritarian disciplinary practices that involve physical punishments such as hitting and spanking have been associated with externalizing, aggressive child outcomes. Yet relatively few studies have investigated the effects of such practices in different cultural settings. Although consistent links have been found for actual physical abuse and problematic child outcomes for *both* European and African American families (Deater-Deckard, Dodge, Bates, & Pettit, 1995), less is known about the effects of disciplinary practices that would not be considered abusive among diverse groups of people.

Box 5.2   Popular Views of Parenting: What Should We Believe?

Child rearing "experts" abound in today's society, each touting his or her own set of certainties about how to raise good or happy or successful kids. Popular beliefs about effective parenting have varied from one historical era to another, and, like today, even within each era there has been wide divergence among the kinds of advice that parents could confront. Consider these two wildly different suggestions. The first is from an *Infant Care* bulletin published by the U.S. Department of Labor in 1914, a tract heavily influenced by animal studies of associationism. It seems insensitive to the emotional needs of both the child and the parent, emphasizing routine over all else.

> A properly trained baby is not allowed to learn bad habits. . . . It is a regrettable fact that the few minutes of play that the father has when he gets home at night, which is often almost the only time he has with the child, may result in nervous disturbance of the baby and upset his regular habits . . . much of the play that is indulged in is more or less harmful." (as quoted in Lomax, Kagan, & Rosenkrantz, 1978, p. 130)

In contrast, the second example, from a *Parents Magazine* article in 1950, is based on a misinterpretation of Freudian ideas and seems remarkably overindulgent of children's emotional excesses, with no regard for control. As described in Lomax et al.:

> mothers were told that they must learn to face and accept all types of emotional outbursts on the part of their children, so that the children would not become fearful of their own feelings. . . . "we should feel suspicious of ourselves when we react strongly to something as absurdly simple, for example, as a child calling us names." (p. 66)

Ironically, as Lomax et al. note, Freud actually expected that parents *would* set limits on their children's antisocial behaviors.

Today, some self-styled "experts" advocate a "return" to authoritarian parenting from earliest childhood, reacting to what they perceive as overly permissive trends (Bolotin, 1999). These "traditionalists" encourage parents not to be child centered. John Rosemond, for example, exhorts parents to make their marriage the focus of attention. Children, he argues, acquire self-esteem from successfully facing hardship and frustration. Give them a lot of responsibility for household chores, and punish all disobedience with unpleasant, memorable consequences. He has expressed disdain for parents who place a high priority on having a "warm and fuzzy" relationship with their children (Rosemond, 1991). Gary and Anne Marie Ezzo, a former pastor and his wife, advocate "biblical principles" for families, among which they include: expecting immediate obedience to first-time directions or commands; feeding babies on a schedule and expecting them to sleep through the night when they are 8 weeks old; potty training by 18 to 24 months, with children accountable

Recent research attention to disciplinary practices of African American families is one more example of the search for contextual influences on parenting. Thus far, results from some studies indicate that the use of physical discipline, such as hitting and spanking, is not associated with more aggressive behavior in African American children in the same way that it is in European American children (Baumrind, 1993; Deater-Deckard, Dodge, Bates, & Pettit, 1996). Other studies have found, however, that mothers' use of physical discipline was related to children's aggressiveness in both European American and African American samples; in other words, race did not moderate the relationship between physical discipline and aggressive behavior (Nix, Pinderhughes, Dodge, Bates, Pettit, & McFayden-Ketchum, 1999). While the results are inconclusive at the present time, some explanations for this inconsistency have been submitted. It may be that the meanings children attach to the discipline their parents use may make all the difference. So, for example, some children might interpret their parents' high levels of control and use of physical discipline as an expression of caring and protectiveness.

The way that these practices affect children may depend in part on how clearly they are connected to parents' positive feelings for, and concerns about, their children (Darling & Steinberg, 1993; Dix, 1991). We will have much more to say about the interaction of culture and parenting practices in chapters on middle childhood and adolescence.

Box 5.2   Continued

for their own cleanup of toilet "accidents" by 30 months; and the use of corporal punishment, starting with hand swatting or squeezing in infancy and moving to spanking with something that creates "a sting" by 18 months (Ezzo & Buckman, 1995; 1999). What is especially notable in the advice of these and other "traditionalists" is their lack of concern for what researchers describe as the "warmth factor" (see text): parental responsiveness to children's needs, high levels of expressed affection, and willingness to listen and explain. Their emphasis is clearly on the "control factor" alone: take care of the child's need for discipline and all else will follow. They also ignore data indicating that mild power assertion is often more effective than severe forms and that the children of parents who use physical punishment tend to be physically aggressive themselves.

What is a parent to do, and how can a counselor help guide inexperienced or dissatisfied parents as they struggle to sort through the confusing array of advice? The most valuable guidance a counselor can offer is advice informed by research. From research reviewed in this and other chapters on social development, it is clear that parents have an abiding influence on their children's development, although outcomes are the product of many interacting factors, including temperament differences among children and family and cultural context. It is also clear that *both* parental warmth

and control are important. Awareness of such information can help parents evaluate the suggestions they encounter. For example, is it true, as Rosemond argues, that self-esteem is a product of accomplishments that include overcoming hardship? It sounds sensible, but the data indicate that the picture is much more complex. Parents' responsiveness and sensitivity to children's individual and developmental needs are core elements of successful parenting. Making children do things that are too difficult for them is insensitive—in such a case, hardship seems unlikely to lead to anything but frustration and a sense of defeat or abandonment for the child. Rigid age formulas are therefore a risky business. For example, many 2-year-olds may be ready to potty train quickly, but some are not. Many 8-week-olds probably cannot sleep through the night, because they get too hungry and/or because their neurological systems are too immature to maintain such a routine.

But when parental demands are embedded in a context of warmth, so that they are appropriately keyed to the child's emerging skills, and when children feel safe expressing their own feelings and concerns, high levels of demandingness do indeed seem to be associated with feelings of competence and self-confidence. Authoritative, not authoritarian, parenting has the best track record.

PARENTING AND THE DEVELOPING SELF-SYSTEM

You can see that research on parenting supports the many theories of self-development that emphasize the importance of social interactive experiences in the development of the self-system. Parenting style especially has been found to correlate with children's self-esteem—how worthy and competent children feel—and it appears to be linked to self-confidence in social interaction. In particular, children whose parents are child centered, responsive, and warm tend to show high levels of self-esteem, and they are likely to be skillful in social interaction, as evidenced by peer acceptance and teacher ratings of social competence. These findings suggest that Erikson (1950/1963) may have been on the right track when he argued that after initial feelings of worth are laid down in late infancy, these feelings will be reworked by the child as she changes. For example, as toddlers become more capable of self-sufficiency, they acquire needs, such as autonomy and control needs, that sensitive, responsive caregivers accommodate. If a toddler's needs are met in a positive, affirming way, the child will go beyond having global feelings of worth and will acquire more differentiated feelings of competency.

Parenting appears to contribute to other aspects of the developing self-system as well. In particular, parenting style and practice are related to children's self-regulation, including the child's ability to "generate socially approved behavior in the absence of external monitors" (Kopp, 1982, p. 200). This last ability is assumed to be a function of **internalization,** the process by which children adopt adults' standards and rules as their own. Internalization, in turn, is associated with the development of **conscience,** feelings of discomfort or distress when the violation of a rule is contemplated or carried out. Internalization and conscience formation are both aspects of the broader topic of moral development and will be discussed again in later chapters as we look at the course of moral development in older children, adolescents, and adults.

At this point, let's take a closer look at the complex connections among early parenting, the beginnings of self-regulation, and the associated processes of internalization and conscience formation. We have already noted that children can begin to learn self-control when they can understand and remember adults' behavioral commands—when statements such as "No cookies before dinner" have meaning for them—certainly during their second year. At about age 2, children often begin to show signs of emotional distress if a standard is violated (e.g., Cole, Barrett, & Zahn-Waxler, 1992; Hoffman, 1970; Stipek, Gralinkski, & Kopp, 1990) and soon after they can show strong reactions if they are tempted to break a prohibition (Emde & Buchsbaum, 1990). At the same time, toddlers begin to offer comfort to others in distress (e.g., Zahn-Waxler & Radke-Yarrow, 1982).

Two aspects of parenting seem to promote these processes (Kochanska, 1995). *First,* parents' warmth and responsiveness facilitate compliance (self-control) and promote the development of concern for others (Maccoby & Martin, 1983). Sensitive, responsive parents seem to establish a cooperative, mutually responsive relationship with their toddlers—an ongoing secure attachment—and toddlers tend to be eager to maintain such relationships. *Second,* children's anxiety or emotional arousal seems to play a role in their willingness to comply and in the internalization of standards. Hoffman (1983) proposed that a parent's discipline causes a child to feel **anxious arousal.** He proposed that *mild* arousal helps the child pay attention but is not really upsetting. When a child is aroused enough to take notice, but not to be especially fearful, she is likely to notice, to try to understand, and to remember the parent's "socialization message." She may attribute her own compliance with the rule to her acceptance of it, which is a step toward internalization of the rule. But if the child experiences *intense* arousal during a disciplinary episode, she may pay more attention to concerns other than the socialization message. She might notice, and later remember, how scared she is, for example, or her parent's loud and angry voice, and then attribute her compliance to these factors rather than to the standard or rule that could have been learned. Hoffman's ideas help explain why mild power assertion is more effective for long-term internalization of rules than harsh power assertion. His views are also consistent with findings that induction—parents' use of explanation and reasoning—is helpful for internalization. Children are more likely to remember and accept rules they can understand.

If anxious arousal is an important ingredient in how children respond to their parents' discipline, individual differences among children in how easily their anxiety is aroused should also be important (Kochanska, 1993). In other words, temperament differences among toddlers should influence the early development of conscience. For fearful children, even gentle discipline that deemphasizes power and emphasizes requests and reasoning should be sufficiently arousing to produce optimal effects. But what about children who are not easily aroused—who seem almost fearless? Do they need harsh discipline to be sufficiently aroused to pay attention? To find out, Kochanska (1995) studied 2-year-olds' **committed compliance,** that is, their eager and enthusiastic willingness to go along with their mothers' requests. Committed compliance in 2-year-olds is predictive of measures of internalization and conscience in the later preschool period (Kochanska, Aksan, et al., 1995). Kochanska found that toddlers' fearfulness is indeed an important ingredient in the effectiveness of mothers' discipline. Highly fearful children, as expected, showed the most committed compliance if their mothers used *gentle* discipline. *Harsh* discipline was not as effective. However, *neither gentle nor harsh discipline was more effective in promoting compliance for the most fearless toddlers!* For them, only the security of their attachment to their mothers made a difference. Securely attached, fearless toddlers tended to show committed compliance, but insecurely attached, fearless toddlers were much less likely to do so. We can begin to see why correlations between parenting behaviors and child outcomes tend to be moderate. Parenting clearly is important, but it works somewhat differently with different children.

To clarify Kochanska's findings, imagine a 2-year-old, Joel, who tends to be more fearful than the other children in his play group. For example, he holds back and ducks his head when a supervising adult offers him a turn to ride the new "race car" at the neighborhood playground, even though many of the other children are clamoring for a turn. When Joel's mother encourages him gently to participate in a cleanup session, explaining how much help it would be, he is quite cooperative. She tells an observer that she never "yells" at him because he gets so upset that it is counterproductive. José's mother, on the other hand, says that her son seems unphased by yelling. José does not seem to be afraid of anything. He can't wait for his turn to ride the new race car, and the fact that the supervising adult is a stranger is of no concern to him. Fortunately, José and his mother seem to share a warm relationship, and José, too, cooperates enthusiastically when his mother asks him to help with the cleanup. Andrew, another toddler in the play group, seems a lot like José in his fearlessness. He is panting to ride the race car and to try all the toys in the playground, and he marches right up to the supervising adult, asking for help. But there seems to be very little warmth between him and his mother, and when she asks him to help out with cleanup, he ignores her. Even when she gives him a shove and speaks sharply to him, he only half-heartedly moves to pick up a toy and abandons the cleanup effort almost immediately.

In sum, parenting influences the development of the self-system in early childhood. Which aspects of parenting will be influential depends in part on the particular child. For the development of self-regulation, the quality of attachment, grounded in warm, responsive caregiving, may be all-important for some children. For others, particular parenting practices (methods of control) also play an important role.

APPLICATIONS

The stages of infancy and early childhood have long been viewed as important ones for later socioemotional development and have merited significant attention from researchers and clinicians alike. It is clearly impossible to summarize what is known about social and affective development in infancy and early childhood in a few chapters because of the sheer volume of studies on these topics. Another reason is that writers with different theoretical bents have addressed similar topics in diverse ways. For example, many developmental psychologists have examined self-development by looking at its cognitive roots. Among more clinically oriented writers, the emphasis has been directed toward the self's affective development and dysfunction. For example, writers such as A. Miller (1981), Winnicott (1965), and Kernberg (1976) applied psychodynamic perspectives to the problem of the "false self," or the self that is not confident of its own needs and wishes but that functions to meet the demands of others. Thus, the very same topic can seem quite different when viewed from each of these different perspectives. Sometimes different developmental phenomena are segmented into distinct content areas (cognition, emotion, moral development, etc.) or chronological stages (infancy, early childhood, etc.) and seem disconnected. For example, discussions of parenting style often focus on the preschool years, even though parenting style is a critical aspect of development for school age and older children as well.

It is no surprise that students of development are often dismayed by the overwhelming complexity of the subject. They may gain knowledge of stages of development, but too often these stages seem dissociated, and they are left with a less than cohesive picture. Perhaps nowhere more than in the area of socioemotional development are we compelled to think in a more integrative fashion. Since it is the goal of this book to provide a working knowledge of development for helpers, it is worthwhile to attempt a linkage among theories of early attachment, self-development, and parenting. Crittenden's (1994, 1997) insightful theoretical formulation is a good starting point for helpers because it knits together these three topics and attempts to explain the roots of early behavior problems.

In Crittenden's view, attachment classifications are linked to operant conditioning processes. Securely attached infants and toddlers receive predictable, soothing care when their physiological needs, fear, aggression, excitement, or anxiety threaten to overwhelm their capacity for homeostatic regulation. These children learn that expressions of their positive as well as their negative feelings (anxiety, distress, and anger) are acceptable because they will be tolerated by a caregiver who accepts and helps them. In other words, they are positively reinforced for expressing both positive and negative feelings.

We have pointed out several times that secure attachment provides a healthy affect regulation system for the infant. When the vulnerable infant experiences fatigue, hunger, loneliness, fear, or other stressors, she lacks the emotional maturity to modulate these feelings all alone. Her emotions become unregulated, and she depends upon the caregiver for soothing. Let's consider an example that might apply to adult students. Imagine a time when you were close to despair because of all the work you had to do. You had a number of responsibilities to complete at your job, you had family obligations to attend to, and your professors were being unreasonably demanding about their assignments! On top of everything, you felt tired and on the verge of getting your annual cold. Your level of crankiness increased significantly, suggesting that you were starting to lose some emotional control. Now imagine that some loving person in your life approached you, and instead of telling you to "grow up," was able to see through the irritability to the anxieties underneath. This person offered to help shoulder some of your burdens. Emotionally you experienced what amounts to a sigh of relief. You were able to function much better with the support, and your sense of yourself as a valuable and loved person increased greatly. In this supportive context, you would probably be even more receptive to constructive suggestions about how you might schedule your time to improve your situation.

Although this example is not a strict analogy to early experience, young children have special need for caregiver support to help them regulate their emotions and internalize positively valenced self-understanding. Crittendon believes that secure reciprocity with a caregiver allows the infant to be open to both cognitive and affective experiences, gradually building procedural models of the self as competent to communicate with the caretaker, able to manage affect with the caretaker's reliable help, and able to accept and express both positive and negative parts of the self. Essentially, the positive message the secure child encodes is that she is a valuable, competent, and loved person. Crittendon believes that these repeated dyadic patterns of attachment are encoded as procedural memories that serve as precursors to the mature self.

In contrast, insecure-avoidant infants who learn that displays of distress elicit rejection, punishment, or withdrawal become conditioned to inhibition of affect. These infants are, in fact, punished for their emotional displays, so these children come to actively avoid or block out perceptions that arouse their feelings because of the aversive consequences.

Crittendon and DiLalla (1988) have reported that even very young children who have been severely abused actively block out information about their own feelings and demonstrate false affect, that is, affect that is superficially positive and incongruent with true feelings. Consistent with the general assumption of attachment theory, this pattern of avoidance is adaptive for an early nonresponsive caregiving environment but may have significantly negative consequences for later functioning. A highly defended or "false self" may result from the inhibition of affect because the child distorts or mistrusts the evidence of her feelings. This situation effectively reduces the information that the young child can access in constructing the self. The message the child encodes is that feeling anger or distress is not acceptable and should be avoided because the expression of these feelings distances the caregiver, emotionally if not physically. The child views the self as able to communicate with caregivers only if her own emotional needs are kept in check. Positive aspects of the self may be expressed, but negative aspects, such as emotional neediness, need to be repressed.

Insecure-anxious infants learn that their displays of distress elicit unpredictable results, sometimes positive and sometimes negative. They essentially lack a method of communicating with the caregiver that works reliably. Consequently, they experience the "anxiety of unresolvable arousal in which desire for the attachment figure, distress at her absence, and aggression toward her are all felt concurrently" (Crittendon, 1994, p. 93).

Children's sense of themselves as valuable and worthy of care is strongly shaped by the responsiveness of adults throughout the early years of development.

Their model of themselves becomes one of incompetence with respect to communicating with a caregiver. Ultimately these children learn they can trust neither their affect nor their cognitions. However, they may learn that escalation of affect often works best in getting their caregivers' attention. These children might develop highly coercive strategies (for example, aggressiveness, tantrums, etc.) and very coy behaviors (disarming manipulation) to maintain proximity.

We can conceive of a developmental extension of early attachment patterns to the child's functioning in the preschool years. Specific behaviors, characterized as attachment-related in infancy and toddlerhood, simply take on other forms as the child matures, yet they serve the same attachment-related purposes. Hence, the earlier observed differences in patterns of attachment are linked to different ways of regulating feeling states and different views of the self in early childhood.

Secure children, in the context of developmentally appropriate parenting, tend to display instrumental competence. They develop skills in coping and learn to integrate positive and negative affect. Avoidant children who have learned that emotional expression can be dangerous take on the responsibility of their own emotion regulation without seeking caregiver help. They function defensively to keep the caregiver "close but not too close" (Crittendon, 1994, p. 95). In order to cope with this style of parenting, they learn a style of relating that involves repressing emotions that might anger or distance their more authoritarian caregivers. Negative affect (feelings of distress, sadness, anger) is not well integrated into the self-system, and a false self develops that is biased in favor of its "good" parts and against its more shameful ones. These avoidant or defended children may appear self-reliant to their parents, who may not be very responsive to their children's feelings anyway. In extreme circumstances, these children may demonstrate what Bowlby called *compulsive caregiving.* This is the pattern of taking emotional care of a caregiver. A pattern of *compulsive self-sufficiency* represents an opposite yet equally unhealthy result. These children are at risk because they appear so self-possessed. A closer look reveals their self-evaluations to be based on others' negative appraisals, including shaming for their expressions of dependency or needs for closeness.

Ambivalently attached infants may develop a coercive pattern in the preschool years characterized by the transformation of the alternating anger and passivity observed in infancy into aggressive and coy behavior. Most frequently observed in the context of inconsistent or neglectful parenting, this pattern can be viewed as an attempt to control the caregivers, to gain their attention, and thus to maintain psychological proximity. Positive and negative affect are not integrated successfully into the self-system, and feelings are acted out rather than verbalized. The self incorporates messages that reflect its ineffectiveness in communicating its needs to caregivers. Their aggressive behavior threatens the caregiver ("You must listen to me!") while their coy behavior disarms ("Please don't get angry at me"). This pattern has been hypothesized to represent the child's attempts to cope with an unpredictable and inconsistent parental environment. As Crittendon notes, "It is easy to see that, by splitting their affective displays, children are failing to display all their feelings. Consequently, aggressive children may be presumed to feel fearful and vulnerable whereas disarming children may be presumed to feel angry" (p. 106).

Not all coercive child behavior problems are due to insecure attachments, however. Sometimes children discover that this approach works well in getting them what they want. Patterson (1982; see also Reid, Patterson, & Snyder, 2002), who studied the development of defiance in children, maintains that an intermittent (or inconsistent) schedule of reinforcement sustains the coercive child's behavior problems. A pattern of negative reinforcement follows the child's display of intense negativity or some misbehavior. For example, a parent might tell her 4-year-old to go upstairs because it is time to go to bed. The little boy, detesting this interruption of his play time, begins to whine. The parent repeats her command several more times only to be met by continued resistance. The parent's patience begins to thin and she escalates into threats, which, according to Patterson's research, are usually not carried out. Instead, the parent appeases the child out of guilt or exasperation. This response reinforces the child's coercive interaction style, which with time and repetition can become the predominant mode of communication. Ironically, Patterson believes that coercive children do not really want parents to give in. Instead, they crave the predictability that derives from knowing what their limits are and the security of knowing that parents will enforce them. Coercive children, however, need help developing a communication style that expresses their needs more directly so that caregivers will understand and respond appropriately.

It would be incorrect to assume that the quality of the early attachment relationship will automatically be transformed into a complementary pattern of parent-child relationships in early childhood. That is, it is not necessarily the case that every securely attached baby becomes a securely attached preschooler, and so forth. But, as our discussion of parenting style in the toddler and preschool years illustrates, the elements of sensitive parenting that characterize the infancy period are not much different from those that are right for preschoolers. The specific parenting behaviors might change, but the underlying requirement to be psychologically available and sensitive to the child's developmental needs and capabilities remains the same. And for the most part, messages about the self-in-relationship that the child has internalized become the foundation for more mature interactions.

How can we interpret this information for use in our practice? Cicchetti and Toth (1994) believe that the negative adolescent and adult self-views that undergird many psychological disorders stem from insults to the self experienced during childhood. Consequently, clinicians need to apply primary prevention strategies to strengthen early parent-child relationships. When these relationships are marked by features of insecure attachment, the helper should take steps to educate parents about their children's emotional needs and make efforts to address ways to increase parents' psychological availability. Particularly with parents of infants, the helper should take care to emphasize the importance of reducing infant distress and promoting homeostatic balance. Sometimes new parents receive the advice to allow babies to cry for long periods of time in order to avoid spoiling them. This misinformation should be clarified in light of developmental research.

For mothers who are themselves depressed or under stress, provision of therapy, promotion of paternal or support system involvement, or enrollment of the child in day care might allow the child some exposure to more positive social influences and buffer the effects of adverse mother-child interactions. Techniques such as massage therapy for mothers and infants have been shown to alleviate stress in mothers and reduce infant fussiness caused by colic and sleep disturbances (Field, 1998). Counseling that helps parents come to terms with their own problematic attachment histories and that aims to reduce marital stress can induce greater empathy and sensitivity for children as well. Overall, attachment-based interventions with parents have shown great success (Cicchetti & Toth, 1994) possibly because these interventions allow for healthy modifications of working models at critical points in the child's development.

As children get older, they should be provided with experiences that allow for the growth of mastery, autonomy, and self-efficacy. Parent education and discussion groups can be helpful forums for parents to gain support for their strengths and to learn about the developmental needs of toddlers and preschoolers. Parents sometimes construe insensitive parenting to mean actions that are mean or rejecting. But intrusive interference, such as picking the child up to give her a hug when she is absorbed in an activity, or arbitrary restriction of a child's mobility, may also be insensitive to the child's needs if done repeatedly. Of particular relevance to self-concept development is educating parents about the implications of their language when conversing with their children. Insulting or insensitive remarks, particularly those intended to shame the child, should be avoided lest they become part of the young child's self-concept.

The growth of a healthy self-system depends upon an environment that provides the child with love and limits appropriate to her developmental level. When the proximal environment is distorted, as is the environment of defended and coercive children, youngsters will make adaptations. However, their adaptations will come with a cost to the development of a child's true self. Fostering the growth of the authentic self in infancy and early childhood sets the child on a developmental pathway that will support healthy functioning at every stage thereafter.

SUMMARY

The Self-System: Traditional Conceptions

1. Some traditional theorists viewed the self-system as multidimensional. William James, for example, distinguished between the *self-as-subject,* as active agent or "I", and the *self-concept,* the object of our own observations and evaluations, or the "me." The "I" is continuously experienced, is distinguished from others, and is an agent of action. The "me" consists of personal attributes, the material (or physical), social, and spiritual characteristics of self. Self-esteem, the evaluation of one's attributes, can be good, bad, or neutral. The valence assigned to one's own attributes depends on the number of successes we enjoy relative to our aspirations.

2. James Cooley introduced a developmental perspective into theorizing about the self. Self-representations are constructed from our interactions with others, especially caregivers. We build a "looking-glass self" that reflects our view of how others see us.

3. George Herbert Mead added that language and society contribute to shaping the self-system. There are culturally determined differences in people's preferred ways of viewing themselves. For example, Japanese emphasize affiliations in their self-descriptions, whereas Americans emphasize more individualistic qualities.

The Early Development of the Self-System

4. The *pre-self* that develops in infancy begins with early inklings of one's body permanence and separateness from others that are derived from the regularity and reliability of infant-caregiver interactions. Procedural representations of interactions are established and may promote a budding sense of mastery by the second half of the first year, if babies' behavior "controls" caregiving responses. A sense of self as self-in-relationship begins to emerge. By the end of the first year, separation distress signals the baby's deepening understanding that the other is separate. Additional indicators include the baby's tendency to explore more readily in the presence of a familiar caregiver. If the caregiver provides a secure base, the baby in a sense has the "self-worth" or confidence to explore. Social referencing also implies recognition of separateness. All of these indicators of a growing sense of the self as separate emerge from and depend on the baby's relationship to others.

5. Toddlers in the second year engage in joint reference, suggesting the earliest inkling that some separate experiences are shared—the first sign of a sense of mind. *Self-recognition* is demonstrated as early as 15 months in tests of mirror recognition. It is a strong indicator that children are forming a self-concept, or a "me." After the second birthday, children begin to use self-descriptive words. Self-evaluation or self-esteem advances with self-recognition, with abused children showing signs of poorer

self-esteem than nonmaltreated children from the beginnings of mirror recognition. Gradually, more differentiated self-descriptions emerge, with preschoolers describing more concrete characteristics, such as "little," and older children beginning to refer to more abstract, less obvious qualities, such as "funny."

6. *Self-control* and *self-regulation* are dependent on the development of the *emotion* regulation that begins in infancy. The attentions of a caregiver when an infant is aroused (e.g., hungry) help the baby to return to a more comfortable emotional state. The interaction process gives a baby outside assistance with affective control. The caregiving relationship is the context in which the infant's own capacity for emotion regulation develops.

7. *Behavior* regulation begins in the second year when toddlers achieve objective self-recognition. The simultaneous emergence of symbolic or representational thought and other cognitive skills allow the child to begin learning and storing rules or standards of conduct. By late in the second year, *self-conscious emotions* emerge, such as embarrassment or guilt, emotions that require awareness of self and of others' judgments. Between 2 and 3, children show some such emotions when they realize they have broken a rule or made a mistake. Once these capacities are in place, self-regulation can begin. How its development proceeds depends on many factors, especially socialization processes.

Early Socialization: Parenting and the Development of the Self-System

8. As the infant becomes a toddler, her needs shift from total dependency to growing independence, and the parent-child relationship reorganizes such that sensitive responsive caregiving begins to include efforts to *socialize* the child—to shape or control the child's autonomous action, so that she remains safe and behaves in culturally appropriate ways. *Discipline* begins.

9. Two dimensions of *parenting style,* parents' approach to caring for and disciplining their children, are important. First is *warmth* or *parental responsiveness,* which includes affection, acceptance, involvement and interest, and so on. Second is *control* or *parental demandingness,* the degree to which parents impose and enforce standards of conduct.

10. Four parenting styles can be described, crossing the positive and negative poles of the two dimensions. *Authoritative parents* are high on warmth and on demandingness. *Authoritarian parents* are low on warmth but high on demandingness. *Permissive parents* are high or moderate on warmth but low on demandingness, and *neglecting* or *uninvolved parents* are low on both dimensions. Authoritative parenting is associated with the most positive outcomes in child development, including adaptability, competence, good social relations, low levels of antisocial behavior, high self-esteem, and good self-regulation. The correlations between parenting styles and outcomes are significant but moderate, indicating that such outcomes are also influenced by other factors, not just parenting style.

11. Parents use a variety of *methods of control. Power assertion,* which involves either physical punishment or withdrawal of privileges, tends to be effective for immediate control of behavior, but may not have longer-term benefits, and harsher forms can have some negative side effects, such as increased aggressiveness in children. *Love withdrawal* generates high anxiety and elicits immediate compliance, but seems to have few effects on long-term self-regulation. *Induction,* providing explanations and emphasizing benefits to the child and to others, seems most effective for promoting internalization of rules and longer-term self-regulation.

12. Are parenting practices actually having an effect, or are there other reasons why parenting is correlated with child outcomes? For example, could it be that the correlation is the result of shared inheritance of traits between parents and children? Data support a multidimensional approach. Parenting, genetics, child temperament, and other factors all contribute to child outcomes.

13. Parenting practices are partly the result of child characteristics, such as temperament traits. For example, adults are more directive with dependent than with independent children. Also, the effectiveness of different parenting practices is partly a function of a child's temperament. For example, toddler boys with difficult temperaments respond with high levels of aggressiveness when parents use physically intrusive control methods, whereas boys with easy temperaments do not.

14. The broader cultural context seems to have an influence on parenting practices and may have an impact on their effectiveness. For example, Puerto Rican American mothers emphasize "sociocentric" goals with their young children, while European American mothers focus more on "individualization." Some parenting practices may have different meaning, and therefore different outcomes, depending on ethnicity and culture. For example, some evidence suggests that physical punishment is less clearly associated with increased child aggressiveness in African American children than it is in European American children.

Parenting and the Developing Self-System

15. Parenting affects the developing self-system in many ways. Children's self-esteem is related to their parents' warmth and responsiveness. Children's self-regulation is associated with parenting style and practice. A child's ability to monitor her own behavior even in the absence of authority figures is considered a function of *internalization,* that is, the degree to which she has adopted standards and rules as her own. Internalization is associated with *conscience,* feeling distress when one violates a rule.

16. Children are more cooperative and compliant when they share a warm, responsive relationship with a parent. Their compliance can also be related to *anxious arousal.* Hoffman argued that mild arousal can help children to pay attention to a rule, but doesn't make them so anxious that they pay attention only to how afraid they are. This is consistent with the finding that mild power assertion practices are more likely to lead to children's internalization of rules and long-term compliance than strong or severe power assertion practices. Further, Hoffman's ideas help explain why children who have fearful temperaments respond best to gentle discipline, but children who are fearless are unfazed by either gentle or harsh disciplinary practices. The most important determiner of compliance for fearless children is the warmth of their relationship to the parent.

Case Study

Terry and Bill, married for 5 years, are a Black couple who live in a small suburban community. Terry graduated from high school and worked as a receptionist before her marriage to Bill, a telephone company manager. Because both of them believed that mothers should stay at home with young children, Terry quit her job when she had her first child, who is now an intense and active 4-year-old daughter named Dawn. Both parents were very attentive to their daughter and enjoyed caring for and playing with her when she was a baby. As Dawn got older, she became more active and assertive. When Dawn fussed, resisted, or showed frustration, Terry was patient and affectionate with her. She was able to coax Dawn out of her bad temper by making up little games that Dawn enjoyed. Both Terry and Bill liked Dawn's spirited personality. Because her parents wanted her to have access to play-mates, Dawn attended a church-related program for toddlers and preschoolers three morn-ings a week.

When Dawn was 3 years old, Terry gave birth to the couple's second child, a son named Darren. Soon after the baby's birth, the family learned that Darren had a congenital heart problem that would require ongoing medical treatment and a specific regimen of care at home. Darren was an irritable baby. He fussed for long periods of time and was very dif-ficult for Terry to soothe. Because of Darren's need for medical care and the limitations of Bill's medical insurance, the couple soon found themselves in financial difficulty. Bill began to take on overtime work at the phone company to subsidize some of the bills and was away from the home several nights a week and part of each weekend.

Terry found the care of two demanding young children and the worries about money to be increasingly more stressful. She was always tired and seemed to have less patience with her family. When she once had the leisure time to read to Dawn, to take her for walks, and to help her master tasks that proved frustrating, Terry now had to shift her attention to the care of her medically fragile infant. Because Dawn looked so grown-up compared to the vulnerable newborn, Terry began to perceive her daughter as able to do many things for herself. When Dawn demonstrated her neediness by clinging or whining, Terry became abrupt and demanded that Dawn stop. Many battles revolved around Terry's new rule that Dawn have a nap or "quiet time" each afternoon so that mother and baby could get some rest.

One day, Dawn's preschool teacher, Mrs. Adams, asked to speak with Terry. Mrs. Adams noted that Dawn's behavior was becoming a problem in the morning preschool ses-sions. Dawn had begun throwing toys when she became upset and often refused to coop-erate in group activities. Terry was greatly embarrassed to hear about her daughter's misbe-havior. Dawn was the only Black child in the small class, and her mother wondered if this was part of the problem. When Terry got home, she put her tearful, clinging daughter in her room for "time-out" for being "bad at school." She loved Dawn, but she could not tol-erate this kind of behavior, especially when Darren needed so much of her time. She began to wonder if she and Bill had spoiled their daughter. Terry feared that Dawn would have problems when it came time for her to enter kindergarten if they didn't take a strong stand with her now.

Discussion Questions

1. Explain Dawn's behavior from an attachment point of view. How would you describe Dawn's attachment history?
2. Describe Terry's parenting style. Has the style changed? What suggestions would you make to Terry and Bill about handling this problem?
3. What are some of the contextual influences on Dawn's behavior?

 ## Journal Questions

1. How would you describe your parents' parenting style?
2. What kinds of discipline were used in your family? What would you advise other par-ents about disciplining their children?
3. What do you believe is the relationship between your early self-development and your later self-esteem?

Key Terms

self-system
"I" or self-as-subject
"me" or self-concept
self-esteem
"looking-glass self"
pre-self
representations of
    interactions (RIGs)
social referencing
self-recognition
self-control
self-regulation

self-conscious emotions
socialize
discipline
warmth dimension
    (parental
    responsiveness)
child centered
parent centered
control dimension
    (parental
    demandingness)
maturity demands

parenting styles
authoritative style
authoritarian style
permissive style
neglecting-uninvolved
    style
externalizing problems
internalizing problems
method of control
power assertion
love withdrawal
induction

time-out
internalization
conscience
anxious arousal
committed compliance
compulsive caregiving
compulsive self-sufficiency

Realms of Cognitive Development in Middle Childhood

In the preceding chapters, we have described some of the major developmental tasks and achievements of infants and preschool children. The pace of developmental progress is quite remarkable during those periods, and much of the foundation for later achievements is laid down. Consider, for example, the qualitative difference between the skills of a new-born and those of his 6-year-old sibling. Development has been so rapid during this first six years that it is not uncommon for parents with a newborn second child to view their older child as having grown up, almost overnight, because of physical size, motor skills, and verbal ability. However, children in middle childhood, the years spanning the elementary school period, are still far from grown up. Their growth takes on new forms in this stage, metamorphosing into ever more highly differentiated patterns of cognitive, emotional, and social functioning.

For children at the start of the middle years, school and its peer group structure represent a new frontier. The movement into the school years ushers in a whole new set of developmental challenges for children. Youngsters at this age must spend longer periods of time away from home and adjust to more rigorous schedules. They must learn to control their behavior, monitor their attention, and acquire more formal and more complicated academic competencies than had been formerly attained. They must make friends and learn to navigate the schoolyard, with its greater demands for athletic prowess, social skill, and cooperative negotiation of conflicts. They must also learn the rules of the group and when to abide by them. They must learn what it means to be male or female, not to mention what it means to be themselves. So many challenges await them.

However, children at elementary school age are also more adept at almost every task when compared to their preschool-aged siblings. Observing the eagerness and energy young children exhibit in the early school years makes it easy to understand the capacity for industry that Erikson described (see Chapter 1). For most children, the challenges of school and peer group will be mastered gradually, and in many different ways. Armed with foundational skills in language, mobility, self/other understanding, and self-control, the youngster is now poised to assume membership in a larger social network.

Clearly, the years of elementary school, as the years to follow, are marked by ups and downs. These normal fluctuations create opportunities for helpers to provide support or guidance for children, their families, and their teachers. What are the cognitive, emotional, and social needs of children at this stage? What approaches are most helpful given children's developmental level? In the next two chapters, we will attempt to provide you with information that will be useful when working with children at this point in their development. Your understanding of cognitive development, the focus of this chapter, will enable you to understand children's ways of construing the world, helping you appreciate their academic needs as well as the intellectual bases for their friendships, gender roles, moral understanding, and conflicts.

PHYSICAL AND BRAIN-RELATED CHANGES

During the first two years of a child's life, physical growth is very rapid. As the child moves closer to the school years, growth slows down a bit, becoming steadier and more even. However, not all youngsters grow and mature at the same rate. A look at a typical 2nd-grade classroom will make this point obvious. Children come in all shapes and sizes, and these differences are relevant to what children think about themselves and how they are perceived and accepted by other members of their social network.

Motor development improves greatly over the preschool to school years. Elementary school children make great strides in motor coordination. At 6, most children can ride a bike, skate, climb trees, and jump rope with ease. The development of gross motor coordination is followed by refinements in fine motor development. By 8 or 9, most children have mastered the fine motor coordination needed to write, draw, and use tools. Eye-hand coordination also improves, as demonstrated by legions of youngsters on the T-ball or softball fields. Improvements in coordination are benefited by maturing of the corpus callosum, which provides a network of connecting fibers between the right and the left hemispheres.

Changes in the brain underlie these achievements and the cognitive advances that we will describe later in this chapter (e.g., Janowsky & Carper, 1996). The part of the brain that is involved in alertness and consciousness, called the reticular formation, myelinates throughout childhood and into adolescence. This ongoing process coupled with increased synaptogenesis in the frontal lobe area results in increases in attention, concentration, and planning abilities. Roughly by age 7 or 8, frontal lobe maturation has also contributed to children's increasing ability to inhibit inappropriate responses and block out extraneous stimuli (Siegler, 1998). It is hard to imagine a child successfully negotiating the years of formal schooling without the capacity to sustain attention and to show increased control over thinking and behavior. Certain association areas of the cortex that are involved in cross-modal processing of information are not myelinated until around age 8. These areas are instrumental in the development of higher-order thinking skills.

Changes in the brain's development and functioning also influence the acquisition of basic academic skills. Recent advances in technology have provided new information about how the brain works and what may go wrong when children can't learn. For example, in the area of mathematics, we know that adults generally perform calculations by relying heavily upon previous rote learning and retrieval of number facts from verbal memory, a left-hemisphere function. Children, on the other hand, rely more heavily on concept formation, strategy use, and reasoning, utilizing right-hemisphere capacities. Once the number facts and basic arithmetic procedures have been learned, they become "automatic" and are carried out by left-hemisphere systems. In essence, arithmetic procedures that begin as novel, conceptual, and visual-spatial for the child eventually become routine for the adult (Rourke & Conway, 1997). This developmental trajectory can result in mathematical learning problems for children whose right-hemisphere functions are immature or compromised.

Studies of reading using brain imaging technology have illustrated the neural circuitry at work in the reading process. T. Roberts and Kraft (1987) demonstrated that among younger students (6- to 8-year-olds), reading activity is primarily centered in the left hemisphere. For older students, (10- to 12-year-olds), reading activity is more evenly distributed between left and right hemispheres, demonstrating the effects of brain maturation, practice, and more strategic, planned approaches to reading.

Increased knowledge about brain development and functioning has contributed to our understanding not only of the normal cognitive achievements and limitations we will describe in this chapter but also of the specific learning difficulties some children experience in the school years. In general, clinicians need to remember that there is a *significant amount of unevenness in brain development among all children at this age* (Berninger & Hart, 1992). Even for normal children, relatively poor performance in isolated skills, such as problems with letter or number recognition or letter reversals in writing, is quite common. And despite the cognitive achievements of school age children, brain maturation is far from complete. Myelination continues, particularly in the frontal lobes, until at least the early 20s (Nathan, 1969).

COGNITIVE DEVELOPMENT

When children leave the preschool years behind, they begin to seem much more "savvy" to adults. They can be given fairly complex responsibilities ("Take out the dog before you go to school, and don't forget to lock the door after you leave"). They can participate in discussions of local or world events, and they often appreciate humor that would have been lost on them earlier. The cognitive developments that underlie these new capacities have been described and studied from several different theoretical traditions. We will first present Piaget's characterization of cognitive change in middle childhood.

Piaget's Stage of Concrete Operations

Since the days of Christopher Columbus, we have been teaching children that the earth is round. Of course, it *looks* flat, especially if you live somewhere in the midwestern United States, such as Minnesota. How do children reconcile what they are told with what they perceive? When Vosniadou and Brewer (1992) asked Minnesota school children in grades one through five about this apparent contradiction, they got some surprising answers. Figure 6.1 illustrates a few of them. Some children said the earth was a flat disc—like a coin. Some thought it was a ball that has a flat surface within it and a domed sky overhead. Others saw the earth as spherical but with a flattened side where people live. The researchers found that the older the child, the more likely he was to represent the earth as the sphere that scientists believe it to be. But even in fifth grade, 40% of the children still had some other idea of what it meant for the earth to be round.

The inventive solutions of the Minnesota kids in the round earth study remind us of what Jean Piaget considered the fundamental characteristics of learning and cognitive change. As we saw in Chapter 3, he stressed that knowledge is not just stamped in by experience or teaching; it is *constructed*. Children *assimilate* new information, meaning that they change it, interpreting it in ways that fit in with what they already know or with the way their thinking is structured; they also *accommodate* their existing knowledge structures, adjusting them somewhat. If new information is presented in ways that do not match children's current understandings, their resulting understanding probably will not be completely consistent with reality or with the information that adults mean to convey. Gradually, as new experiences are assimilated and accommodated, better approximations of reality are achieved.

You'll recall that despite the gradual construction process that Piaget described, in which knowledge structures are continually changing, he considered there to be *stages of*

FIGURE 6.1

Children's Images of a Round Earth

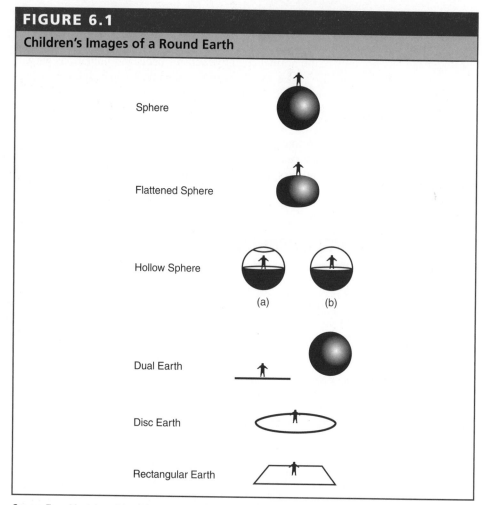

Sphere

Flattened Sphere

Hollow Sphere

(a)   (b)

Dual Earth

Disc Earth

Rectangular Earth

Source: From Mental models of the earth: A study of conceptual change in childhood by S. Vosniadou and N. F. Brewer in *Cognitive Psychology*, Volume 24, p. 549, copyright 1992, Elsevier Science (USA), reproduced by permission of the publisher.

thought development, so that within a relatively broad period of time, children's thinking about many different things has some similar organizational properties. We have already discussed some of the characteristics that Piaget attributed to the *sensorimotor* (0 to 2 years) and *preoperational* (2 to 6 or 7 years) stages (see Chapter 3). In this chapter, we will be considering his view of children's thinking in the **concrete operational stage,** the period spanning the elementary school years from about age 6 to 12.

To understand how Piaget described the thinking of young school-aged children, recall the limitations of the younger, preoperational thinker. Generally, preschoolers focus on one salient dimension of a situation at a time, and so they often miss the important relationships among aspects of a situation. Logical thinking is difficult to characterize, but it certainly includes the ability to recognize and take into account *all* of the relevant information in a problem situation and then to identify how those pieces of relevant information are related to each other. Consider the following simple problem in deductive logic: "All glippies are annoying. George is a glippy. Is George annoying?" To answer correctly, you must take into account a number of pieces of information—that there are glippies, that they are annoying, that there is an individual named George, and that George is a glippy.

The important relationship you are then in a position to identify is between George and the glippies: he's one of them. From there you can infer that George is, indeed, annoying.

As we saw in Chapter 3, in very simple situations, even preschoolers can sometimes take into account more than one piece of information at a time. For example, sometimes they can solve very simple deductive inference problems (e.g., Blewitt, 1989; C. L. Smith, 1979). But more often, their thinking is *centered,* making it seem quite illogical. Remember the number conservation problems that Piaget invented? Let's consider another kind of conservation problem, in which children must infer that an object remains the same weight even if you change its shape. Imagine two balls of clay of identical size and shape. If we put them on a balance scale, we find their weight to be equal. Now, suppose we roll one ball into the shape of a snake so that it is long and thin. Despite its different appearance we have not adjusted its weight, so it will still be equivalent in weight to the other ball of clay. Preschoolers typically predict, however, that the weight will now be different—they often say it will be lighter than before because it's so skinny, or they might say it will be heavier because it's longer. They focus on one salient dimension and predict weight differences between the ball and the snake based on that dimension. But if they took into account both length and width, they might recognize that the changes in the two dimensions have compensated for each other, and so the weight is the same as before, even though it is differently distributed.

When children are in the *concrete operational* stage, they usually answer conservation questions correctly. They may look at the snake and say "it looks lighter than before" but they can logically conclude that it remains the same weight as the ball. Piaget argued that their logic is dependent on being able to see and understand the relationship between length and width changes—that one perfectly compensates for the other. Because they can *decenter* (think about more than one dimension of the situation at once), they can discover the relationships among those dimensions.

The compensatory relationship between the length and width of the clay snake is a kind of **reversible relationship.** In essence, one change reverses the effects of the other change. Piaget thought that being able to recognize reversible relationships is especially important for solving many kinds of logical problems, allowing children a deeper understanding of the world around them. For example, before he achieves concrete operations, a young child might learn the following two number facts: "2 + 1 = 3" and "3 − 1 = 2". But only when he recognizes reversible relationships is he likely to realize that the second fact is the inverse of the first and therefore that they are logically connected. If the first fact is true, then the second fact must be true. To put it differently, knowing the first fact allows the child to deduce the second one if he can think reversibly. When children's thinking becomes efficient enough to decenter, and thus to identify reversible relationships, children can begin to draw logical conclusions in many situations. This is the hallmark of the concrete operational child.

Piaget also identified limits to concrete operations. School-aged children seem to be most capable when the problems they are solving relate to concrete contents, and they seem to expect their solutions to map onto the real world in a straightforward way. But when a problem is disconnected from familiar, realistic content, these children have a difficult time identifying the relevant aspects of the problem and finding how those aspects are related to each other. In a classic example, Osherson and Markman (1975) asked children to say whether certain statements were true, false, or "can't tell." The experimenter made statements such as "The (poker) chip in my hand is either green or it's not green." Sometimes the poker chip was visible; other times the chip was hidden in the experimenter's fist. If the chip were hidden, children in the elementary school years would usually say "can't tell," asking to see the chip to judge the statements. But the statement's truth was not determined by the actual color of the chip; it was determined by the linguistic elements in the sentence and the relationships between them (e.g., "either/or"). No check with the concrete world was necessary or even helpful. A chip, any chip, is either green or it's not. In other words, the abstract, formal properties of the statement, not concrete objects, were the contents of importance. Concrete operational children find it difficult to think logically about abstract contents, and they seek out concrete or realistic equivalents to think about in order to solve a problem.

Children's tendency to "hug the ground of empirical reality" (Flavell, Miller, & Miller, 1993, p. 139) is especially obvious when they need to think logically about their own thinking. Suppose for a moment that you are a child who believes that you're more likely to hit a home run playing baseball if you wear your lucky socks. To test this theory scientifically, you would need to weigh the evidence, pro and con. But before you could do this effectively, you would need to recognize that your belief about your lucky socks is really an assumption or a theory, only one of many possible theories. As such, it could be wrong. Since you already believe your theory, it will seem like a fact to you. You would need to apply careful logical thinking *to your own thought processes*, first to distinguish your belief from true facts or observations and then to see the relationship between your theory and those facts. However, if you are 8 or 9 years old, you have trouble thinking logically about anything abstract, and theories (or thoughts) are certainly abstract. So, logically evaluating any of your own beliefs or theories is not likely to be easy for you.

What we are describing is a form of egocentrism that emerges in middle childhood. The term *egocentrism* refers to some failure to recognize your own subjectivity. You fail to see things realistically because you are, in a sense, trapped in your own perspective. Preschool children often exhibit what Piaget called *preoperational egocentrism* (see Chapter 3): they have trouble recognizing that their own mental experiences are private and may not be shared by others. By about 5 years, children's *theory of mind* includes knowing that people can have mental experiences that are not all the same from one person to another. So, their preoperational egocentrism recedes, and their ability to take another person's perspective begins to improve. (As you will see later in this chapter, perspective-taking skills increase in complexity and subtlety throughout childhood and adolescence.) But in middle childhood, difficulty thinking logically about abstract contents makes elementary school–aged children vulnerable to another form of egocentrism: failure to distinguish between their own assumptions or theories and objective fact (see Elkind, 1981; Looft, 1972).

As a result, researchers have found that although elementary school–aged children can think scientifically sometimes, identifying simple theories and checking them against evidence, they make a muddle of it if they already *believe* a certain theory (e.g., Kuhn, 1989; Schauble, 1991). It is easy to understand why elementary school children might have difficulty believing that the earth is really round, since they can't observe it. Children get better at evaluating their own theories as they move into adolescence and become capable of what Piaget called *formal operational thought*—logical thought about abstract contents. As you will see in Chapter 9, adolescents often extend their logical thought processes to many kinds of highly abstract contents, including their own thinking (although even adolescents and adults find this kind of abstract thinking a challenge and may fall into the same egocentric traps as concrete thinkers).

Even though middle childhood has its cognitive limitations, Piaget was on to something in identifying it as a time when children can be expected to think logically. In every culture in the world, adults seem to recognize that somewhere between ages 5 and 7 children become more sensible, reliable problem solvers. In societies with formal schooling, kids are sent to school to work at serious tasks that will prepare them to take their place in the community of adults. In societies without formal schooling, children are given real work to do by age 6 or 7, tasks that are essential to the community (such as watching the younger children, planting, or shepherding).

Piaget's description of the concrete operational child as a logical thinker about concrete contents has proved a useful one, and it seems to capture the typical cognitive characteristics of middle childhood quite well. However, as we saw in Chapter 3, newer work makes it clear that there are at best fuzzy boundaries between the stages Piaget proposed. How advanced a child's thinking will be and what kinds of content a child can think logically about depend on many factors. One important factor is the amount of prior experience a child has had with the ***domain of knowledge*** (or particular subject matter) that he is thinking about. If a child has a lot of knowledge about a particular domain, say dinosaurs or chess, his ability to think logically about problems within that domain may be more advanced than in other content areas (e.g., Chi, Hutchinson, & Robin, 1989). Of course, the child may appear more logical simply because he has seen other problems of the same sort more often and can remember effective solutions, so his better problem solving may have less to do with more advanced thinking than with memory for past experiences (see the section in this chapter on memory development) (e.g., J. R. Anderson, 1980). But it also seems to be the case that a child or adult with a lot of domain knowledge is better at identifying the important features of a problem within that domain and at identifying the relationships among those important features (Flavell, Miller, & Miller, 1993). Thus, logical thinking may be at least somewhat ***domain specific*** (that is, applicable to a particular area of knowledge) rather than strictly domain general and determined by one's stage of development, as Piaget's theory implies. For a kid who loves experimenting with chemistry sets, reasoning about chemistry may advance more quickly than for a child whose passion is music.

In the next sections, we will consider some other ways of characterizing children's cognitive abilities in the middle years, especially the *information processing approach,* and

These children's interest in and experience with their hobby may help them think more logically about problems in this domain.

we will examine what we have learned about some abilities, combining research from the Piagetian, information processing, and other research traditions.

An Alternative Perspective: The Information Processing Approach

Many interesting studies of middle childhood cognition—especially memory and problem solving—have been done by researchers in the information processing tradition. Information processing theories compare cognitive functioning to a computer's processing of information (see Chapter 1). The structural organization of the cognitive system is thought to be the same throughout development. A typical example of the kinds of structural components through which information is thought to "flow" during cognitive processing is presented in Figure 6.2. In this view, there are no qualitative, stage-like changes that characterize most of a child's thinking or processing. There are some changes with time, however, mostly in the amount and efficiency with which information can be processed. With increasing age, children can work with more information at once, and the strategies that children use to organize, understand, or remember information may also change. However, children apply different processing strategies to different specific contents, such as math, reading, and spatial concepts, so that strategies are not usually considered to be the result of broad cognitive skills that are applied across different domains. Instead, strategies appear to be largely domain specific. Information processing researchers focus heavily on what children do with information of particular kinds: what they pay attention to, how they encode it, what and how much information they store, what other information they link it with, how they retrieve it. In other words, information processing theories are focused on the mechanics of thinking. Thus, whereas a Piagetian researcher

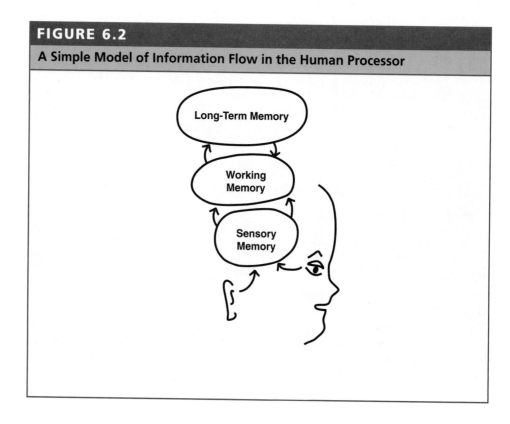

FIGURE 6.2

A Simple Model of Information Flow in the Human Processor

might try to demonstrate that one cognitive achievement, perhaps in math, is related to another, perhaps in social perspective taking, in order to illustrate the global effects of some underlying stage characteristic, an information processing researcher typically tries to track the specific information handling that underlies a child's increasing mastery of a single domain.

The influence of both Piagetian and information processing approaches has fueled a rapid increase in our understanding of cognitive development, and it is not surprising that some theorists have attempted to marry the best components of both approaches. Typically known as *neoPiagetians,* these theorists explain Piaget's stages, or revise the stages, using many information processing concepts (Case, 1985, 1992; Fischer, 1980; Halford, 1993; and others). For example, Case (1985) specifies four stages comparable to Piaget's, but explains the transition from one to another partly in terms of increases in the capacity of *working memory,* the part of the cognitive machinery that holds information we are actively thinking about at the moment (see Figure 6.2, and below).

Let's now take a look at some of what we have learned about elementary school children's cognitive abilities.

Achievements of the Concrete Operational Child

Memory and Attention

Imagine a child who has just had his annual medical examination. With his parent's consent, an interviewer asks a set of questions to explore what he remembers about the experience. Some are open-ended questions, such as "Can you tell me what happened when you went to the doctor?" Others are specific yes-no questions, such as "Did she look in your nose?" A subset of the yes-no questions are strange or silly, such as "Did the doctor cut your hair?"

As you might expect, elementary school–aged children usually answer such questions more accurately than preschoolers do. If you wait for several weeks and then ask about the doctor's exam again, a 3-year-old will forget more of what he could originally remember than a 7-year-old will. In one study, by 12 weeks after the checkup, 3-year-olds' responses to the silly questions were at chance levels of accuracy (meaning that they were saying "yes" to about half of the silly questions), but 7-year-olds averaged about 90% accuracy, despite the delay. The older children's answers had also remained relatively consistent over time, so that if they answered "yes" to a question right after the exam they tended to do so on repeated tests at later times (Gordon, Ornstein, Clubb, Nida, & Baker-Ward, 1991, as cited in Ceci & Bruck, 1998).

Almost all aspects of memory seem to improve with age, at least up through young adulthood. As you will see, developmental changes in memory are affected by many characteristics of cognitive functioning and development. In this section, we will consider several contributors to memory improvement in the school years and beyond. But before we do, let's briefly define some of the terminology that is commonly used in discussions of memory. Many of these terms were first introduced by information processing theorists, and some are included in the information processing flow model depicted in Figure 6.2.

Memory Terminology. First, we can describe memory as consisting of different memory stores. *Sensory memory* refers to a brief retention of sensory experience. For about one third of a second, when we first see a scene, we store most of the sensory information that has come in, almost as though our eyes have taken a snapshot of the whole scene. A similar phenomenon occurs with hearing. Interestingly, sensory memory does not seem to change much with age. Not much research has been done on sensory memory in very young children, but studies comparing 5-year-olds with adults indicate that children's sensory memory is just as good as adults' (e.g., Morrison, Holmes, & Haith, 1974). *Working memory,* also called "short-term store," is usually described as the thinking part of our cognitive system. Here we execute problem-solving strategies, make inferences, and transfer information into **long-term memory,** the almost unlimited store of knowledge. The information we pay attention to in working memory comes from our immediate sensory experience *and* from long-term memory. For example, suppose you are watching a movie about an African adventure, and an array of color and movement suddenly fills the screen. Your working memory combines the sensory data coming from the screen with information drawn from long-term memory to create a meaningful interpretation: it's a charging zebra. Or suppose your supervisor reminds you that your counseling approach to a client's new problem is similar to one that was not very successful in the past. Your thinking about the strategy (in working memory) includes elements of the supervisor's input with stored memories of prior interactions.

Unlike long-term memory, working memory is thought to have a limited capacity. We can pay attention to, and think about, a limited number of meaningful units of information at one time, and material is lost from working memory in 15 to 30 seconds unless we engage in **rehearsal** (i.e., unless we actually keep working with it, making an effort to pay attention, such as repeating it to ourselves). Generally, it seems that in order for sensory information to get into long-term memory, it must be attended to in working memory. For example, you may hear the music playing as the zebra on the screen charges, but unless you pay attention to it, you are not likely to remember it later. Or if you're mulling over another problem while your supervisor gives you feedback, you will be unlikely to profit from the comments. So, learning seems to require real work or effort. If you find you have to go back and reread a section of this chapter to get it into memory, you are making the kind of mental effort that characterizes working memory and accounts for successful learning.

Learning, or acquiring knowledge, involves the **storage** of information. **Retrieval** is what we usually mean by remembering, that is, getting information out of storage so we can use it. In Chapter 3, we talked about two kinds of remembering or retrieval: *recognition* and **recall.** *Recognition* happens when the information to be remembered is immediately available to your senses. For example, you see your least favorite teacher from high school crossing the street in front of you, and you realize that you're experiencing someone who is familiar. Your sensory image elicits information about the teacher stored in long-term memory. We saw in Chapter 3 that some ability for recognition seems to be present from birth, and generally young children's recognition skills are very good, especially for *visual-spatial* information, such as memory for pictures. (Try playing the visual memory game "Concentration" with a 4-year-old. You might not win!) Recognition of *verbally* presented information shows more long-term developmental improvement (Schneider & Bjorklund, 1998).

Recall is more work. The to-be-remembered information is not present, and you must somehow draw it out of long-term memory and *re*-present it to yourself, as when you must answer an essay question on an exam. Or, as we described in the opening of this section, a researcher asks a child to remember what he experienced when he went to the doctor. When a child has problems with recall, it could be because he did not attend to the information in the first place because he did not store the information in long-term memory despite having paid attention to it, or because the child does not have adequate strategies for finding the stored information. Clearly, recall is a multifaceted process.

One feature of human memory is that we can store different kinds of information or knowledge. Knowledge about facts and events, called **declarative knowledge,** is of two kinds. The first kind is **semantic,** which includes factual information ("the earth is round"), rules ("red lights mean stop"), and concepts ("an elephant is a large, gray animal"). The second kind is **episodic,** which refers to our knowledge of the events that we have experienced. When researchers ask children to recall their visit to a doctor's office or when your supervisor asks you to describe a counseling session, they are asking about episodic knowledge. Episodic knowledge is organized around time and space—what happened in what order, where, and when. After we've had several experiences with one kind of event, such as being examined by a doctor, we begin to form a schematic representation of the typical features of the event and the order in which they happen. This is called a **script.**

In addition to declarative knowledge, we have **nondeclarative** knowledge, knowledge that we cannot adequately put into words and that may not even enter our awareness. For example, you may *know* how to shift the gears in a standard transmission vehicle, but you might have a difficult time *explaining* how to do it. Many physical skills are based on this kind of unconscious, nondeclarative knowledge, which we usually call **procedural.** You may remember that we have used the term *procedural knowledge* to describe what infants "know" about how to do things or what to expect from interpersonal interactions (see Chapter 5). Early working models of attachment are probably a kind of procedural knowledge. Much of what infants and toddlers know seems to be nondeclarative rather than declarative.

Now that we have a vocabulary of memory terms, let's take a look at how memory seems to work in middle childhood, and specifically at what improves with age.

What Improves with Development? With age, *working memory* seems to expand. Like Piaget, most observers, regardless of theoretical orientation, have noted that older children usually pay attention to more pieces of information at one time than younger children. **Digit span tests** provide the standard demonstration of this change in working memory capacity. You may recognize them as a typical part of most intelligence tests. A series of digits are presented to the test participant, who must immediately say the numbers back in the same order. A child of 2 years can usually produce about a two-digit string; by the time he is 7, he will probably be able to remember a five-digit string. Adults, on average, can remember about a seven-digit string (hence, the standard telephone number) (Dempster, 1981). But what actually accounts for these increases in memory capacity? There could literally be, somehow, more "room" in the older child's working memory. But many other cognitive changes seem to contribute and may actually be more important. We will consider several of these.

The *first* cognitive change that contributes to memory improvement is that children can process information more quickly as they get older. Piaget attributed the *decentering* skill of school-aged children (their ability to pay attention to more than one thing at a time) to the speeding up of mental activities with practice, and modern research does support the idea that practice can accelerate information processing. In addition, speed of processing can increase with physical maturation—that is, simply as a function of age (Kail, 1991). The upshot is that as children get older, they can do more with more information at one time.

The *second* cognitive change that affects memory improvement is that as children get older their knowledge about many things increases: they expand their **knowledge base.** Consider the study of children's recall of a medical examination mentioned earlier. One reason that a 7-year-old might have recalled more accurately than a 3-year-old is that the older child probably knew more about medical exams. By 7, a child has formulated a script of the typical medical exam. When an interviewer asks questions about a particular exam, even many weeks after it happened, the 7-year-old may not actually remember whether the doctor cut his hair, for example, but he knows that doctors don't do that sort of thing in medical exams, and so he answers correctly. In general, older children know more about most events, and so they are more likely than younger children to be able to *reconstruct* accurately what probably happened in any given situation.

It should be noted that prior knowledge can also lead to false memories. For example, in a number of studies, children have been shown videos or pictures of people playing roles such as that of a doctor or a nurse. Sometimes the gender of the adult is consistent with traditional expectations—such as a man playing the role of doctor—and sometimes the person's gender and occupation are not traditionally consistent—such as a man playing the role of nurse (e.g., see Bigler & Liben, 1992). Children's preexisting beliefs about gender and work roles—that is, their gender stereotypes—influence what they will later remember about what they saw. In one particularly interesting study, Signorella and Liben (1984) found that elementary school children with strong gender stereotypes were more likely than children with less stereotyped beliefs to misremember who had played what role in the pictures they had seen when gender and occupation were not traditionally matched. So, for example, if they had seen a woman doctor, the children with strong stereotypes would be likely to remember that it was a man they had seen instead, or that the woman had been a nurse. (See Box 6.1: *Children's Eyewitness Testimony* for other examples of how false memories can be induced.)

In addition to prior knowledge affecting your ability to reconstruct what you've experienced, the more you know about a particular subject, or *domain of knowledge,* the more easily you can learn new information in that domain and the better you will remember it later. If knowledge in most domains expands with age, then learning and retrieval of information in most domains should get better with age. But age is not what is most important—knowledge is. Suppose, for example, that we show an 8-year-old child a chess board with chess pieces arranged as if in the middle of a chess game. Later, we ask the child to reconstruct the placement of all the pieces on an empty board—that is, to recall the layout of the pieces. If the child happens to be an "expert" chess player—someone who plays in competitions and is highly knowledgeable about the game—his performance on this recall task will be much better than that of an average adult "novice," who knows how to play but who does not have extensive knowledge of the game. In other words, when children are more expert than adults in a domain of knowledge, they can remember more new information from that domain than adults can (e.g., Chi, 1978; Chi & Koeske, 1983). We will see later that other domains of knowledge, such as knowledge about others' perspectives and feelings, improve at this age and enhance social relationships.

Many studies suggest that as we amass knowledge of a subject, new information in that domain is understood more quickly and more completely. Some researchers describe the formation of a rich web of well-organized connections among the pieces of information in long-term store. For example, a counselor's concept of "therapy" might be part of a detailed web of stored information such as the one presented in Figure 6.3. We fit new information into this web, allowing us to later retrieve it through many routes and making it more accessible than if there were fewer connections. The processing speed for new information increases, and the depth of understanding is greater. All aspects of memory seem to be positively affected. Of course, ordinarily, the older you are, the more knowledgeable you are, and so the better you are at remembering, particularly in your area of expertise.

One advantage of a rich web of knowledge is that it allows **chunking** of information in working memory. *Chunking* is a process whereby we link several pieces of information together into a single meaningful unit. For example, suppose you were given the following series of numbers in a digit span test: 149217761929. You might notice that you could divide the series into three chunks that represent famous dates in American history: 1492, 1776, and 1929. If so, you would be able to remember all the digits, because you converted them to just three pieces of information, which would not exceed your working

Box 6.1 Children's Eyewitness Testimony

The following is an experience reported by Bill, a 4-year-old:

> My brother Colin was trying to get Blowtorch (an action figure) from me, and I wouldn't let him take it from me, so he pushed me into the woodpile where the mousetrap was. And then my finger got caught in it. And then we went to the hospital, and my mommy, daddy, and Colin (older brother) drove me there, to the hospital in our van, because it was far away. And the doctor put a bandage on this finger (indicating). (Ceci, Loftus, Leichtman, & Bruck, 1994, quoted in Ceci & Bruck, 1998, p. 749)

Bill appeared to have a clear memory of this scary event, and he was confident even about details such as where his father was at the time of the accident. But the experience Bill could describe so convincingly never happened! It was a false memory, induced by a researcher who had read brief descriptions of a set of pictures to Bill each week for 9 weeks. The description for one of the pictures had said, "Got finger caught in a mousetrap and had to go to the hospital to get the trap off." The researcher then said, "Think real hard and tell me if this ever happened to you. Do you remember going to the hospital with a mousetrap on your finger?" In the first session, Bill said he had not had such an experience. By the tenth session, as you have seen, he seemed convinced that he had.

Preschoolers can have some difficulty with *reality monitoring,* distinguishing fantasies from realities. Young children *can* tell the difference between what is real and what is not and between what it feels like to only imagine something versus to actually experience it (e.g., Flavell, Flavell, & Green, 1987), but they have more difficulty with these distinctions than older children or adults (e.g., Foley, Harris, & Hermann, 1994; Parker, 1995). In particular, if they imagine an event, they are somewhat prone to say later that it actually happened. One charming and usually harmless example occurs when a child becomes devoted to an imaginary friend. But a young child's problems with reality monitoring can make him more susceptible to suggestion than older children or adults, a serious concern when children serve as eyewitnesses. Some interviewers and therapists in child sexual abuse cases, for example, use a professional technique called *guided imagery* as an aid to memory. A child might be asked to pretend that an event occurred, then create a mental picture of the event and its details (Ceci & Bruck, 1998). Unfortunately, if an adult encourages a child to construct a fantasy about what *might* have happened, the child may eventually come to believe that it *did* happen, even if it did not.

In considering whether children should serve as eyewitnesses, the key issue is, how valid can children's reports be expected to be? In the late 1600s, children's testimony at the witch trials in Salem, Massachusetts, led to the execution of 20 defendants. Young girls testified convincingly that they had seen defendants doing fantastic things, like flying on broomsticks. Some of the testimony was later recanted, and the whole episode created such a negative view of children's testimony that for three centuries child witnesses were not often seen in American court proceedings. Only in the 1980s did many states end restrictions on children serving as witnesses (see Ceci & Bruck, 1998).

Modern memory research has helped increase the acceptance of children's testimony in America. Many studies indicate that what children remember *can* be accurate, although the number of details a child will recall and with what accuracy improves with age (see text). But at any age, a witness's memory for observed events could be incomplete or distorted or simply wrong, sometimes as a result of exposure to suggestion. And the younger the child, the more susceptible he is likely to be to suggestion (e.g., Ceci, Bruck, & Battin, 2000).

We have seen that preschoolers' difficulties with reality monitoring can be a source of suggestibility, and there are several other sources as well, many of which children might encounter in the course of being interviewed by parents, police, social workers, therapists, and other court officials. When interviewers are biased, they may guide children's testimony, planting suggestions without realizing that they are doing so. So, for example, if an interviewer is already convinced that a child has been abused, she may encourage a child's admission of abuse by asking leading questions, such as "Where did he kiss you?" instead of "What did he do?" The interviewer might also ask the same question repeatedly if the child's initial answers are not consistent with the interviewer's belief. Studies of interview transcripts indicate that even the most well meaning and concerned interviewers, including parents, use many such tactics to try to get at what they believe, or fear, is the truth (Ceci & Bruck, 1998). Unfortunately, they may be planting suggestions that can lead the child to reconstruct his memory of an event.

(continued)

Box 6.1   **Continued**

A study by Pettit, Fegan, and Howie (1990) is just one of many that illustrates how effective such suggestions can be with young children. Two actors visited a preschool classroom. They pretended to be park rangers and talked to the children about helping a bird find a nest for her eggs. In the middle of the discussion, one "ranger" knocked a cake off of the top of a piano "by accident." The cake was smashed, and there was silence for a few moments in the classroom, creating a rather distinctive event. Two weeks later, each of the children in the class was interviewed about the incident. Before the children were questioned, the researchers gave some of the interviewers an accurate account of what had happened. Others were provided with false information, and a third group was given no information at all. An interviewer's instructions were to find out what had happened from each child, but without asking leading questions. Despite the instructions, the interviewers did ask leading questions—30% of the time—and half of these were misleading. Naturally, the interviewers who had false beliefs about the event asked the most misleading questions. And the children were often misled, agreeing with 41% of the misinformation suggested to them. Apparently, interviewers biased by false beliefs can unwittingly maneuver children into providing false information.

Elementary school–aged children are clearly less suggestible than preschoolers (Ceci, Bruck, & Battin, 2000). For example, their reality monitoring is more adequate, and they are less affected by leading questions. But even older children and adults are not immune to suggestion (e.g., Ackil & Zaragoza, 1995; Loftus, 1979). Fortunately, witnesses of all ages can provide more accurate information if they are interviewed under conditions designed to minimize suggestion. A sweeping review of research on children's eyewitness testimony by Ceci and Bruck (1998) reveals a number of characteristics that may reduce the influence of suggestion in interviews. Of course, interviewers should avoid leading questions, as we have seen, and they should keep both the repetition of questions and of interviews to a minimum. The interviewer's tone should also be neutral, rather than urgent, aggressive, or accusatory. For example, an accusatory tone may be set by statements such as "Are you afraid to tell? You'll feel better once you've told." In one study, when interviewers made such comments, even children who previously indicated no recall of an event sometimes agreed with questions that incorrectly suggested abuse (see Goodman & Clarke-Stewart, 1991).

Interviewers should not use inducements such as telling children that they can help their friends by making disclosures. In one criminal investigation, for example, investigators said things to children such as "Boy, I'd hate having to tell your friends that you didn't want to help them" and "All the other friends I talked to told me everything that happened . . . You don't want to be left out do you?" (quoted in Ceci & Bruck, 1998, p. 745). Such pressure might have the effect of encouraging children to produce responses even when they do not recall the events in question. Another interview strategy to be avoided involves **stereotype induction,** that is, slanting the interviewee's view of an individual. Sometimes interviewers will encourage children to make revelations by indicating that the alleged perpetrator is a bad person or does bad things. But in studies where this strategy was implemented, young children were found to produce incorrect, negative recollections of such an individual's behavior more often than children who were not exposed to the induction (e.g., Leichtman & Ceci, 1995; Lepore & Sesco, 1994).

As Ceci and Bruck (1998) emphasize, interviewers are motivated by concern about the welfare of the child; ". . . no interviewer sets out with the intention of tainting a child's memory . . ." (p. 730). But even with the best of intentions, an interviewer can elicit questionable testimony. An understanding of the ways in which memory is constructed and reconstructed can help investigators to make eyewitness testimony, especially in children, more trustworthy.

memory capacity. The more extensive the webs of information in your long-term memory, the more likely you are to find ways to chunk information meaningfully in working memory. When expert chess players look at a chess board set up as if in the middle of a chess game, they see meaningfully related chunks consisting of four or five chess pieces each, allowing them to, in effect, rehearse the positions of 20 to 25 individual pieces without exceeding their working memory capacity. Novices see only individual pieces, allowing them to rehearse the positions of only about 5 to 7 pieces (Chase & Simon, 1973).

FIGURE 6.3

A Conceptual Web for the Term "Therapy"

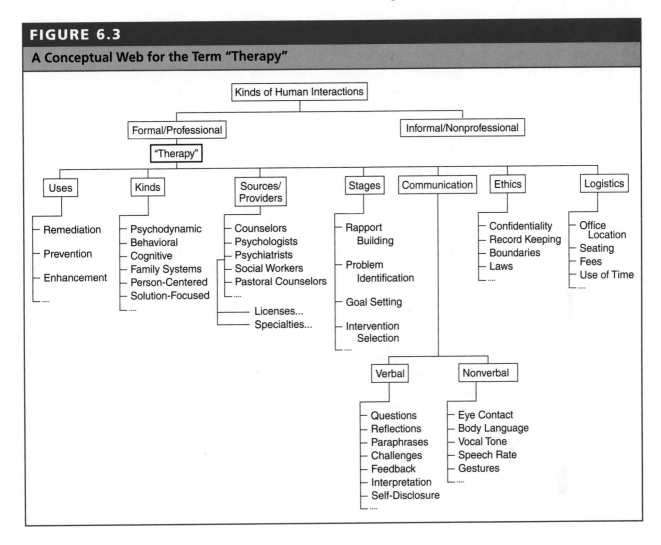

A *third* cognitive change that contributes to memory improvement with age is advanced logical thinking. If older children can think more logically than younger children, they may have a better understanding of at least some of their experiences, and understanding better helps them to remember more about the experience later. Piaget's own research on memory improvement with age focused heavily on the contribution of logical development (see Piaget & Inhelder, 1973). In a typical study, he showed children from ages 3 to 7 an array of sticks, arranged in serial order by size. One week later, children were asked to draw what they had seen as a test of their recall. They were also given an opportunity to put a series of sticks in order according to size. This seriation task is a lot like the conservation of number task: it looks simple, but children are not usually completely successful at it until about age 7. In other words, it seems to require the logical thinking of the concrete operational stage. What Piaget found was that if children did not have the logical thinking skills needed to seriate sticks themselves, they typically could not remember the serial pattern they had been shown a week earlier; but children who could seriate the sticks (mostly 6- and 7-year-olds) showed better memory for the serial pattern. Remarkably, though, when the children's memory was tested again at least 6 months later, many of the younger children were now more accurate in their memory drawings than they had been originally, depicting some aspects of the serial order. These findings have often been replicated, indicating that children's memory for some experiences can actually improve over time! How could this happen?

The key here seems to be that memory is often *reconstructive*. That is, when we recall an experience, we integrate "what we currently experience, what we already know, and what we infer" (Kuhn, 2000, p. 22). We have already seen that older children may use what they *know* about doctor's examinations in general to reconstruct a particular doctor's examination, thus recalling it more accurately than a younger child. It also appears that if a child's logical understanding of an event improves from the time he first experiences it to the time his memory is tested, he may reconstruct it more accurately than he could have earlier. As the children in Piaget's study got older, they could understand seriation better, and so when they "remembered" the original stick array, they often *inferred* that the sticks had been arranged according to size.

A *fourth* cognitive change that can benefit memory with age is greater facility with language, especially improvements in **narrative skill,** the ability to tell a coherent story. Clearly, one way in which we mentally represent information is in words. As children's vocabularies grow and their skill in describing events develops, their ability to store information about experiences in coherent verbal form also improves (e.g., Tessler & Nelson, 1994). As we saw in Chapter 3, recent research suggests that this aspect of memory improvement is enhanced by narrative interactions with adults. When by asking questions and by constructing narratives together about shared events, parents encourage their children to talk out loud about their experiences, children are better storytellers and show better memory for autobiographical events. On the whole, language skills such as these improve with age and experience, and so older children's memory for events can generally be expected to be better than younger children's (e.g., Nelson, 1993b; 1996).

A *fifth* cognitive change that can facilitate memory improvement with age is learning to use **memory strategies.** Strategies are "potentially conscious activities a person may voluntarily carry out" in order to remember something (Flavell, Miller, & Miller, 1993, p. 235). Imagine that we asked you to remember all the names of the children in your class when you were in the fifth grade. After you finished groaning, you would probably take a strategic approach to this retrieval task—that is, your retrieval would follow some plan. Maybe you would try to remember all the girls and then all the boys; or maybe all your good friends and then all your enemies; or maybe all the popular kids, then the less popular ones; or maybe you would start with the tallest kids and work your way to the shortest. Generally, adults do approach memory tasks strategically, and when they do, they remember more than if their approach is haphazard. There are a host of strategies that we can call on, both for encoding new material that we expect to have to remember later and for retrieving information that is already stored. People who are really good at remembering names and phone numbers and other details of experience are generally well practiced at applying strategies.

But what about children? Preschoolers are usually considered nonstrategic in their memory efforts. An interesting example is provided by a study of 3- to 8-year-olds who were shown rows of boxes that contained either toy animals or household objects. Boxes with animals had a picture of a cage on top; boxes with household objects had a picture of a house. Children had to remember the locations of either the animals or the household objects. The researchers carefully observed the children's actions during a study period, and found that the younger children tended to open all the boxes, whereas the oldest children were more strategic, opening only the boxes with the items that they would have to remember later. In other words, older children *selectively attended* to the locations that they had to learn about. Younger children did not seem able to use selective attention to help them with the memory task (see P. H. Miller, 1994).

Selectively attending to one thing and not to another is very difficult for preschoolers, and so it is not a skill that 3- or 4-year-olds are likely to deploy to aid memory. But sometimes preschoolers seem to use other skills in ways that we might call "pre-strategic." When they know that they will be asked to remember something later, sometimes they do things differently than they might otherwise. For example, 4-year-olds were given a set of toys to play with. Some children were told that later they would be asked to remember what some of the toys were. These children tended to play with the toys less and to name them more than children who were not given such instructions (Baker-Ward, Ornstein, & Holden, 1984). So, in other words, they seemed to act in ways that would help them remember.

Systematic use of strategies is much more likely in middle childhood. If you give a group of third-graders the job of learning the names of all the states and their capitals, you will probably see them using *rehearsal*—repeating the names over and over. There are a variety of more complex strategies, but children usually do not use them spontaneously until the late elementary school years or even adolescence. For example, to help with the task of learning the states and their capitals, a child could use an **organization** strategy—sorting the items to be learned on some meaningful basis, such as grouping the names by region. Or he might use an **elaboration** strategy—finding or creating some kind of meaningful link between items. To help remember that Baton Rouge is the capital of Louisiana, he might make up a sentence like "Louise saw a bat," or he might create a mental picture, visualizing a girl named Louise with a bat on her head. At about 9 or 10, children will use organization strategies spontaneously and to good effect; not until adolescence are they likely to use elaboration without prompting. Strategies that are particularly useful for learning textual material, such as underlining and summarizing main ideas or key points, also emerge late, during adolescence (see Schneider & Bjorklund, 1998).

Developmental progress in children's use of memory strategies is a bumpy affair. On the one hand, children might at first use a strategy quite sporadically, often showing a **production deficiency,** meaning that they might fail to use it even in situations where it is ordinarily helpful. On the other hand, sometimes children use a strategy, but it does not seem to boost memory; then they are said to have a **utilization deficiency.** Although strategies usually do aid memory performance, when a child first uses a strategy spontaneously, it may be so much work that it takes up a lot of time and attention, minimizing its effectiveness for improving memory. Yet children still may use the strategy. As Siegler (1998) has argued, it's as though children intuitively understand the "law of practice"—that practice improves efficiency in the long run—even if there is no immediate profit!

We have been describing the development of children's spontaneous use of memory strategies, but it should be noted that effective use of strategies can be taught. Children whose parents or teachers instruct them on how to use a strategy are likely to use it on the tasks where they were taught to do so (e.g., Kurtz, Scheider, et al., 1990). However, they typically do not generalize the use of a strategy to new situations.

The discussion of memory strategies leads us to a *sixth*, and final, cognitive change that seems to affect memory. It is the development of **metacognition,** "cognition about cognition," (Flavell, Miller, et al., 1993), or thinking about our own mental processes and their effects. Preschoolers have some awareness of mental processes. Four- to 5-year-olds have a *theory of mind* that includes understanding that their own thoughts, beliefs, and desires often differ from those of other people, as we have noted. They also have some beginning skills at judging what they know. For example, if we show a 4- or 5-year-old a classmate's picture, even if the child cannot spontaneously recall the classmate's name, he will be able to accurately judge whether he would know the name if he heard it (e.g., Cultice, Somerville, & Wellman, 1983). This kind of self-monitoring and understanding of what you can and cannot accomplish cognitively, and how, improves dramatically across the elementary school years. In a classic study, Kreutzer, Leonard, and Flavell (1975) found that fifth-graders understood that remembering the gist of a story is easier than remembering it word for word; only half of kindergartners understood this point. Kindergartners understood some things about memory, such as the value of writing things down if you want to remember them, but not until fifth grade did children realize that there are differences in memory ability from one person to another or from one situation to another. Many researchers have found that while preschoolers are usually overly optimistic about how much they are likely to remember about some material, such as a list of words, older children's estimates are usually much more realistic. This kind of self-knowledge continues to improve past middle childhood, as adolescents produce increasingly accurate depictions of what strategies and approaches are likely to enhance memory in given situations (Schneider & Pressley, 1997). Many theorists have argued that metacognitive awareness at least partially accounts for the increasingly effective use of strategies that develops through middle childhood into adolescence.

One aspect of memory improvement is learning to monitor your own memory and to allocate study time. This is one metacognitive skill that shows little development through elementary school, at least with challenging material. For example, most studies find that elementary school-aged children don't often spontaneously use *self-testing* when they study. Interestingly, one of the better ways to help children in this age range use memory strategies more effectively is to train them to explicitly monitor what they have learned through techniques such as self-testing (e.g., Paris, Newman, & McVey, 1982). In other words, teaching children to keep track of *what* they have learned seems to be an important element in teaching them *how* to learn.

So metacognitive development involves improvement in three kinds of knowledge: declarative, or knowledge about facts, rules, or oneself as a learner; procedural, or knowledge about how to apply rules and strategies effectively; and conditional, or knowledge of when to apply the rules or strategies (Schraw & Moshman, 1995). Consider ten-year-old Amelia, who, having missed a day of school, calls a classmate to get her homework assignments. She knows that she must repeat the page numbers or write them down in order to remember them. She also knows how to organize her homework for each of the various assignments, for example, by showing all computations when solving math problems. She might even understand that she should do her science homework first because it takes the most time, and she may be able to judge when she has studied her spelling words sufficiently. Metacognition is the cornerstone of many clinical and educational practices that are collectively known as **self-instruction** or **self-monitoring** (Meichenbaum, 1986) and a major part of cognitive therapies for children and youth (Kendall, 1993). The general goal of such practices is to effect some behavior change (such as control of impulsivity or improvement in test-taking skills) by attending to, regulating, and sometimes changing cognitions.

This review of memory improvement through middle childhood has, of necessity, touched on many aspects of cognitive development, including advances in processing speed, growth of knowledge, development of logical thinking and language skills, growth of selective attention and other strategic skills, and metacognitive developments. It is clear that "to study memories is to study much of . . . cognition and cognitive development" (Kuhn, 2000, p. 22). But memory is more than the product of the cognitive system. It is also influenced by affective and social developments. To illustrate the role of affective characteristics, consider the point that was made about the importance of domain knowledge in how well children learn new information in that domain. Indeed, a child will remember new information better than an adult if the child is an expert in that knowledge domain and the adult is not. But how does a child become an expert in some subject, such as chess, or dinosaurs, or baseball? Although it helps to be a competent learner, exceptional intelligence does not appear to be the determining factor. What is critical is the child's motivation. Expertise comes from long-lasting attention and practice, not typically from genius (e.g., Means & Voss, 1985; Schneider, 1993).

To illustrate the role of social factors in memory, consider that adult interactions with children seem to figure critically into the development of memory skill. As we have seen, teaching children strategies for learning new material improves children's memory performance. Encouraging children to narrate their experiences helps them to develop better autobiographical memories. In other words, scaffolding by adults, in the Vygotskian sense (see Chapter 3), contributes substantially to memory development.

Number and Math Skills

In the early preschool years, the typical child has several number skills. For example, he can count, he knows there is a one-to-one relationship between number word and item when he counts, and he understands that the order in which items are counted is irrelevant (e.g., Gelman, 1982; see Chapter 3). By late preschool, he has informal arithmetic skills such as adding and subtracting small numbers by using counting strategies, like the *counting all* strategy. For example, given two red blocks and three green ones, he will probably count all the blocks to find out the sum. As children in elementary school are introduced to more formal arithmetic, with its written numbers and standard, step-wise

Children spontaneously develop strategies for solving problems including math problems.

processes (or algorithms) for computation and recording, they continue to use their informal strategies. They also devise more and more strategies, some invented, some derived from what they are taught (e.g., Siegler, 1987). For example, given a simple addition problem such as 3 + 4, they might use a strategy called **counting on,** starting with the first number and counting four more numbers from there. Soon, this strategy is likely to be modified so that the child usually "counts on" from the larger number. And as children are exposed repeatedly to addition and subtraction facts, they begin to use a **retrieval strategy,** pulling the answer from memory. Some researchers in the information processing traditions have closely followed young school children's progress in discovering and utilizing these strategies. They have found some interesting trends that seem to occur across cultures. First, most children use most of the strategies, sometimes using one, sometimes another. Second, children often use a particular strategy on problems where it is especially effective, and more efficient strategies gradually become more predominant. Third, however, even older school children sometimes use less efficient strategies (Ginsburg, Klein, & Starkey, 1998; Siegler, 1998). Thus, it appears that cognitive development moves gradually toward greater efficiency but that less efficient strategies are not entirely abandoned. "Bumpy" progress in strategy use seems to characterize the development of many skills, as we have seen already in memory development.

When children assimilate the rules they are taught to their own limited understanding of mathematics, they sometimes invent strategies that produce errors. In the information processing tradition, flawed strategies are referred to as "bugs." An example would be a boy who does not yet truly understand the base 10 system, but who thinks that one should always subtract the smaller from the larger number. When he is given the problem

$$\begin{array}{r} 21 \\ -\ 5 \\ \hline \end{array}$$

he subtracts the 1 from the 5 and comes up with 24 (Ginsburg, 1989).

In the Piagetian tradition, some research specifically explores developmental changes in what children understand about what they are taught about mathematics. Children's progress in understanding the base 10 system provides a good illustration of the extent to which their mathematical knowledge is constructed (e.g., C. Kamii, 1986; M. Kamii, 1990). If we ask a first-grader to count a set of 13 blocks and then write down the answer, he will probably be able to comply. But if we circle the "3" and then ask, "Does this part of your 13 have anything to do with how many blocks there are?" a first-grader might say, "No." He thinks that only the whole number 13 tells about the number of blocks.

When he's in second grade, he might say that the "3" represents a certain three chips; when in third grade, he may talk about ones and tens, but is likely to say that the "1" in 13 represents one single item, not ten. By fourth and fifth grades, about half of children recognize that the "1" represents a 10 (example from M. Kamii, 1990). Thus, although a child typically hears about the base 10 system from first grade onward, he seems to assimilate it to concepts that are not correct and only gradually constructs its true meaning. Findings such as these on children's understanding of math concepts are a reminder of an important tenet of Piaget's view of education: teaching children facts or algorithms is not sufficient for developing the kind of understanding they will need to truly advance in a subject, as was the case in the round earth study. Teachers need also to probe children's comprehension, asking questions such as "Does the '3' have anything to do with how many blocks there are?" Such questions both aid teachers in evaluating what kinds of supports a child might need in order to understand better and may help children begin to recognize inconsistencies in the meanings they have constructed. This kind of probing can also help teachers establish adequate placements for their students. Care should also be taken in choosing curricular materials and in structuring assessments of students' learning. Without practice and elaboration, advanced or accelerated programs of study may outstrip the abilities of many children and lead them to shallow or rote memorization of facts instead of deep conceptual understanding.

While the development of math concepts seems to follow a similar progression in most children across cultures, research in the Vygotskian tradition (see Chapter 3) indicates that social context can moderate the speed of mathematical development and the kinds of strategies that emerge. First, the kinds of practical problems that children face in living seem to affect the kinds of informal strategies they invent, as well as their understanding of mathematical principles. For example, some poor urban children in Brazil sell candy on the streets to make a living. Saxe (1991) compared the math skills of candy sellers to children who did not sell candy. The sellers had little formal schooling, but some of the nonsellers were receiving a formal education. Age affected the math skills that the children exhibited, but so did their experience selling candy. For example, 5- to 7-year-olds typically could not add or subtract currency, whether they were sellers or nonsellers. But by 11 or 12 years many of the sellers had invented strategies that allowed them to count up large numbers of bills, usually by organizing them into sets. One 11-year-old, for example, "began with a 10,000-unit bill. Then he added three 1,000-unit bills; and, finally the remaining 200- and 100-unit bills, to reach the correct total of 17,300" (quoted from Ginsburg et al., 1998, p. 423). Nonsellers typically did not have such strategies. Nonsellers with formal education also had more trouble with some advanced math concepts, such as proportions, than sellers did. Relations expressed in proportions are more abstract than the simple adding, subtracting, multiplying, and dividing of numbers, and children generally seem to do better with them as they approach adolescence (Piaget's stage of formal operations). This was generally true of the children in Saxe's study as well, but the sellers seemed to apply their abstract thinking to the proportion problems that arose from their selling activities sooner than the nonsellers were able to do so.

A second way in which social context is important to math development is that opportunities in early childhood to manipulate countable materials, to learn counting words, to work with shapes, and to verbally interact with adults about numbers seem to be contextual experiences that affect early informal mathematical development, which in turn affects how well children will learn formal mathematics when they reach school age. A number of studies have found that the parents of children from lower socioeconomic groups, especially the very poor, provide fewer and less complex number activities, especially activities that encourage talking and reasoning about numbers, than middle-class parents (e.g., Klein & Starkey, 1995; Saxe, Guberman, & Gearhart, 1987). Such activities might include counting fingers or coins, finding television channels, or spontaneous number games such as practicing number recognition in an elevator: a parent tells the child the number of their floor, and the child pushes the button with the right number. More complex number activities that tend to show the greatest social class differences include demonstrating money equivalences, such as between five pennies and a nickel, and doing addition and subtraction with fingers or coins. Not surprisingly, with less experience of such activities, poor children tend to lag behind middle-class children in their basic, informal mathematical abilities even though they typically acquire some basic skills, such as some counting, and the ability to represent quantities by holding up appropriate numbers of fingers (e.g., Jordan, Huttenlocher, & Levine, 1994).

A third influence of social context comes from the kind of mathematical language that children are taught. In English, the base 10 structure of the numerical system is not as clearly laid out in our number words as it is in some other languages, especially Asian languages such as Chinese, Korean, and Japanese. In these languages, there are fewer arbitrary number words to learn, and after ten, number names clearly specify the number of tens.

For example, the equivalent of eleven would be "one-one," of twelve would be "one-two," and so on. The equivalent of twenty-one would be "two-one." Several studies indicate that number names are learned earlier by preschool children learning Asian languages compared to American children learning English (e.g., K. F. Miller & Stigler, 1987), and that the regular system of Asian languages may facilitate understanding of the base 10 system in elementary school (Fuson & Kwon, 1992).

Clearly, studies of mathematical development inspired by several different theoretical traditions are beginning to paint a picture of how children learn mathematics. In their review of the research, Ginsburg et al. (1998) draw a number of conclusions, including that mathematical development begins in infancy and that an informal mathematics is constructed before middle childhood, "guided by biology, physical environment, and culture" (p. 427). How children understand the formal mathematical system taught in school depends on their cognitive level, the informal mathematics that they bring with them, and a range of social supports. And, as Ginsburg et al. put it, "understanding is *connecting* [italics added] . . . not simply correct calculation or correct verbal statements, [but] . . . a complex web of connections among different aspects of mathematical knowledge" (p. 428). Children assimilate what they are taught in school to their existing knowledge, using the thinking abilities that they currently have. Thus they actively construct that web of connections.

Problem-Solving Progress in Middle Childhood

Dozens of times a day children are faced with problem-solving tasks, from the mundane to the more esoteric: should I wear my heavy coat or a lightweight jacket, what's the fastest way to walk to Ailani's new house, should I tell my parents about the argument I had with my teacher, how should I organize my science report, what are the important facts to remember in this social studies unit? Development of problem-solving skills involves several kinds of change with age, many of which we have described already: *first,* children devise and use an increasing range of strategies as they get older; *second,* they usually have more resources, such as domain knowledge and logical thinking skills, to allot to a task with age; *third,* they tend to plan better as they get older, aided by better attentional control, growing metacognitive knowledge, and increases in working memory capacity. These and other typical cognitive changes are influenced or modified by social transactions—in the family, in the classroom, and in other familiar contexts. In this section, we will focus primarily on the influence of one kind of social transaction on learning and problem solving in elementary school children: peer interaction. Specifically, we will examine the benefits and liabilities of **cooperative learning environments,** that is, classroom or other organizations that encourage children to work in pairs or in groups to solve academic problems and to improve their understanding of concepts or skills.

Before we consider how children working together make progress toward a problem solution, let's take a look at how problem solving proceeds when children work with an adult. First, when a parent or teacher guides a child through a problem, researchers have found that the adult usually works to maintain the child's interest and to keep the child focused on the goal of the task. Second, the adult's behavior tends to be *contingent* on the child's performance in several ways. In particular, an adult usually keeps track of what the child can and cannot do and then tends to tailor instruction or suggestion to the child's "region of sensitivity"—one step beyond the level where the child is currently performing. Wood, Bruner, and Ross (1976) called this kind of adult behavior *scaffolding,* and research in the Vygotskian tradition has demonstrated that when an adult provides such scaffolding, children perform at a higher level than they would if they were solving problems by themselves. You will recall that Vygotsky (1978) called this region of improved

Children's learning can be enhanced by cooperative learning activities when they are carefully planned and scaffolded by adults.

performance with adult help the *zone of proximal development* (see Chapter 3). Third, an adult is likely to engage a child in a discussion of possible strategies, encouraging the child both to consider why and how steps should be taken and to make decisions. As Piagetian educators have argued (e.g., M. Kamii, 1990), when adults ask challenging questions and elicit children's active involvement in discussion and planning, children's learning and performance is enhanced (e.g., Gauvain, 1992; Lacasa & Villuendas, 1990; McLane, 1987; Rogoff & Gauvain, 1986). Finally, as children's performance advances, adults do less themselves, encouraging children to do more of the problem solving.

Adult tutoring in the style we just described helps children learn more effectively than they would on their own. What are the characteristics of children's efforts to learn collaboratively with peers, and how effective are such efforts likely to be? A number of factors linked to age are important. On the whole, the younger the child, the less likely a collaborative arrangement will be as effective as working with an adult or more effective than working alone. Preschoolers and young elementary school children have limited ability to control their own attention and to stay on task. When they work with peers, not surprisingly, the partners have difficulty coordinating their attention (Azmitia, 1996). Further, an important determiner of effective collaborative problem solving is the opportunity to communicate your ideas and to discuss the ideas of your collaborator. Yet, the limited language skills of younger children make good communication difficult when not supported by an adult facilitator. Finally, young children do not often behave contingently in a collaborative setting. Perhaps limited by their immature perspective-taking skills (see the next section of this chapter), they fail either to evaluate the needs of their partner or to adjust their behaviors to those needs. So, for example, if one partner is more expert than another, the more expert partner may simply tell the other what to do without explaining his reasons or asking helpful questions (e.g., Ellis & Rogoff, 1986). Or one partner may do all of the actual reasoning and problem solving while the other does the "manual labor," such as drawing the pictures or typing the paper (e.g., Hawkins, 1987, as cited in Rogoff, 1998). In addition, even when one partner knows more than another, the less-skilled partner may be less willing to accept his peer's claims than he would an adult's.

Peer collaboration seems to be most effective—more effective than children working alone—when decision making is shared, with all partners actively involved in discussion, planning, negotiating, and attempting solutions (e.g., Azmitia & Hesser, 1993; Duran & Gauvain, 1993; Gauvain & Rogoff, 1989; Light, Littleton, Messer, & Joiner, 1994). Researchers have found that several factors foster such active participation. Encouraging children to talk over what they do seems to help (e.g., Teasley, 1995). Also, when children feel more comfortable with their partners, they talk more even if one partner is more expert. So, for example, partners are more active if they are of a similar age (Duran & Gauvain, 1993) or if one is the older sibling of the other (e.g., Azmitia & Hesser, 1993). In addition, when adults provide feedback along the way on the effectiveness of children's solutions, peer collaborations work better than when no feedback is given (Ellis, Klahr, & Siegler, 1993). Adult feedback probably helps keep the discussion on course. For example, if one partner, who happens to be wrong, is more persuasive or domineering than the others, feedback can help to balance his influence and keep the discussion going. Alternatively, when one partner's arguments are correct, his peers may be more willing to give him credence if adult feedback is available. Without feedback, the most advanced partner is likely to make no progress, and, at best, his initial level of expertise will serve as the cap for the group (Siegler, 1998). Overall, it appears that children need support in learning to collaborate effectively. Just telling children to work together is not good enough. Adults who want to encourage cooperative learning need to take into account many factors in providing support: children's age, their roles in their social groups, their personal relationships, their motivation levels, and their relative expertise (Rogoff, 1998). Fortunately, some research indicates that when children have practice collaborating they tend to get better at it, especially when adults provide suggestions, establish rules, and monitor progress (e.g., Socha & Socha, 1994; see Rogoff, 1998). Similarly, if children are encouraged to discuss how well their group is working and what improvements could be made, their collaborations tend to improve (Yager, Johnson, Johnson, & Snider, 1986). In essence, cooperative learning among peers requires active scaffolding by an adult.

It should be noted that cooperative learning is more easily facilitated in some climates than in others. In cultures where group goals in schools are emphasized over individual needs, as in Japan, children's experiences in and out of school are more likely to prepare them for collaborative learning than in schools where individual accomplishment tends to be more important (Hatano, 1994). For example, Toma (1991a; 1991b; as cited in Rogoff, 1998) observed that a common feature in Japanese classrooms is training in how to address one's classmates in a discussion. A list of phrasings—what to say and how to say it—is often posted on a classroom wall. One such list suggested that children express agreement by saying, "I agree with (name's) opinion. This is because. . . . " To help children request clarification, the list proposed saying, "Did you mean to say. . . . " Most of us, not only children, could probably benefit from such a list!

SOCIAL COGNITION

Just as children's knowledge about the physical world and about logical-mathematical concepts becomes more sophisticated with time, so does their understanding of the social world. This latter domain, generally referred to as *social cognition,* has been of great interest to developmentalists for many years. Although the field of social cognition is broad and encompasses many aspects of cognition, it focuses primarily on *the ways people think about other people and how they reason about social relationships.*

Much of what you have already learned has provided the foundation for, and can be subsumed within, social cognition. As you will recall from earlier chapters, infants and toddlers learn a great deal about social relationships within the context of the attachments they form. The discriminations infants make between objects and people, their diligent attention to caregivers, their capacity for imitation and social referencing, and their early attempts at communication presage knowledge about people and human psychology. Toddlers try to change the behaviors of others, empathize with others' distress, and use emotion words indicating that they have explicit knowledge of others' mental states (Zahn-Waxler, Radke-Yarrow, Wagner, & Chapman, 1992). These skills suggest that infants and young children are in the process of learning about social interactions almost from birth.

Studies of the young child's *theory of mind* focus on aspects of social cognition, addressing questions such as "When does the child come to understand that the other has a mind?" and "How does the child use information about mental states to understand people and social relationships?" We have already seen that by their fifth birthday most children realize that others often have different thoughts and beliefs from their own. For example, they now succeed on *false belief tasks* in which they must anticipate that a person who has not had the opportunity to see an object moved from its original hiding place to a new location might have a false belief about the object's whereabouts (e.g., Wimmer & Perner, 1983; see Chapter 3). Success on false belief tasks has been related to reciprocal communication with peers (Slomkowski & Dunn, 1989) and to the ability to communicate about internal mental states with friends (Hughes & Dunn, 1998). Researchers are thus finding links between early cognitive social understanding and children's social relationships.

Social cognitive research with school-age children typically deals with the quality of children's understanding of the nature of other peoples' thoughts, feelings, and desires. Studies have examined theories of children's friendships, methods of conflict resolution, and the developing understanding of social rules and interactions that are central facets of both.

No one has to convince a counselor that the dynamics of social relationships are important ones to understand. Although not every social relationship can be considered a friendship, it can be argued that the special relationships we have with friends teach us about human relationships in general. During the middle years, friendships take on enormous importance for children, and social relationships continue to make a significant contribution to personal wellness from childhood through old age. The difficulties many children experience in making and keeping friends can consume much of the counselor's time because of the far-reaching consequences of poor peer relationships and inadequate conflict resolution skills on emotional well-being, academic achievement, and behavior. What is important for counselors to understand is that the skills of friendship are not just behavioral but are *heavily dependent upon cognitive development*. Conversely, problems in social relations may be heavily influenced by limitations in social cognitive skills. In this section, we will introduce some major theoretical approaches to friendship development that have a basis in cognitive developmental theory. In Chapter 7, the research on larger peer group interaction and peer group status will be reviewed.

Perspective Taking and Social Relationships

The idea that satisfactory social relationships are important in the overall picture of adjustment enjoys unanimous support from developmentalists of every theoretical persuasion. Social relationships are necessary for the child to gain experience in learning about others' points of view (Piaget, 1932/1965). They contribute to the child's sense of security and connectedness (Berndt, 1982), and foster the development of the self-concept (Mead,

1934). These three benefits are not as separate as they may seem but are, instead, three highly interconnected outcomes of positive social contact.

Recall for a moment what has been presented in earlier chapters about the development of the self. *Self-concept* has been defined by symbolic interactionist thinkers such as Mead as the individual's perception of himself that develops from the collective accumulation of social experiences. It is as if the individual proceeds through life viewing himself in the "looking glass" of other people's eyes. But remember as well that this process is not simply a passive reception of information. Rather, it involves the complicated consideration of the perspectives of other people. Mead believed that in order to define oneself, a person needs to put himself, metaphorically, in another person's shoes and then consider his own actions in the light of that alternative perspective. This uniquely human operation, which lies at the heart of self-recognition and self-knowledge, has been called *perspective taking,* and no relationship survives for very long without it.

The cognitively complex skill of perspective taking develops gradually as children mature, much in the same way that other cognitive abilities change and improve. You have already read that very young children are considered *egocentric* insofar as they are embedded in their own perspective. In Piaget's view, the ability to *decenter,* meaning in this case the ability to recognize and hold in mind more than one perspective, is enhanced by repeated interactions with others. When children decenter, they understand that others have minds that are different from theirs and that minds may be coordinated in the service of mutual understanding and problem solving. Implicit in this level of awareness is the cognitive ability to engage in relationships marked by intimacy and mutuality and to solve problems in ways that consider the interests of all parties.

How does such an immensely desirable skill as perspective taking develop and improve? Some of the earliest ideas on the subject stem from Piaget's writing. He believed that about the time children enter elementary school in industrialized cultures, they are forced to consider other children's viewpoints to survive the normal give and take of the classroom community structure. Before then, children may have been able to rely on parents' or other family members' willingness to meet their egocentric needs and to understand their egocentric communication. Peers are typically less willing and able to do so. The child in elementary school, or even before, is forced to clarify his thoughts and adopt better communication skills in order to be accepted by peers. The major and minor conflicts that accompany this process are viewed as essential to a developing awareness of perspectives other than one's own (Flavell, 1963; Piaget, 1928).

This achievement does not mean, however, that children are now free of egocentrism altogether, as we saw earlier in this chapter. Every developmental stage has its own form of this quintessentially human weakness. Even adults are not exempt because specific forms of egocentric thinking appear to be a normal by-product of cognitive advances.

> The transition from one form of egocentrism to another takes place in a dialectical fashion in such a manner that the cognitive structures that free a child from a lower form of egocentrism are the same structures that entangle him in a higher egocentric form. (Looft, 1972, p. 77)

In fact, Looft, paraphrasing Piaget, describes egocentrism as the "central problem in the history of human affairs" (p. 73). Despite the fact that seeing the world and relationships egocentrically is an inevitable part of the human condition, maturity reduces this tendency to some degree. Friendships play a particularly significant role in this process.

Perspective Taking and Friendship Development

In one of the early theories of friendship development, Sullivan (1953) reiterated the Piagetian perspective that children need interpersonal contact in order to reduce egocentrism and promote altruism. While very young children, in the "childhood era" according to Sullivan, primarily depend upon parents for reflected appraisals of themselves, children's dependence upon playmates becomes more important as they enter the "juvenile period" around age 4. However socialized some interactive behaviors (such as sharing, conformity, and expressions of sympathy) may appear at this age, these behaviors are not yet truly altruistic but are demonstrated for the egocentric purpose of gaining acceptance or building popularity in the larger peer group. A major transformation occurs around age 8, when children enter the stage Sullivan called "preadolescence." During this period, children's needs for increased interpersonal intimacy are met through the establishment of an intense, focused interest in same-sex age-mates or "chums." These relationships teach preadolescents that the needs and perspectives of other persons must be considered as carefully as their own. Seeing one's preadolescent self reflected back in the context of a chumship permits the validation of one's thoughts, feelings, and beliefs as well as a more realistic appraisal of oneself. Thus, the egocentrism of the juvenile period diminishes as the child learns to see the world through the eyes of a friend. Because the transition through early adolescence is not without its stresses and strains, attachment to a close friend or chum can function as a *secure base,* permitting the young person to navigate the many changes inherent in the adolescent transition without feeling totally isolated. Let's try to understand more about the primary cognitive ingredient needed for successful friendship development, perspective taking.

Many writers have documented children's maturing ability to take the perspective of their friends and to communicate this understanding in increasingly more sophisticated ways (Flavell, Botkin, Fry, Wright, & Jarvis, 1968). Possibly the most elegantly developed theory linking perspective taking with actual friendship development has been provided by Robert Selman (1980). Building on a Piagetian framework, Selman identified five stages in the development of perspective taking, beginning at preschool age and continuing though adolescence. Each level of perspective-taking skill is linked to a different level of friendship or shared experience, as well as to a different level of conflict resolution. Table 6.1 depicts the tight interconnections among one's ability to understand others

TABLE 6.1

Selman's Stages of Friendship and Levels of Perspective-Taking Skills

Stage	Forms of Shared Experience	Social Perspective Taking	Interpersonal Negotiation Strategies
0	Unreflective imitation or enmeshment	Undifferentiated/Egocentrism	Physical force; impulsive fight or flight
1	Unreflective sharing of expressive enthusiasm	Differentiated/Subjective	One-way, unilateral power: orders or obedience
2	Reflective sharing of similar perceptions or experiences	Reciprocal/Self-reflective	Cooperative exchange; Reciprocity: persuasion or deference
3	Empathic sharing of beliefs and values	Mutual/Third person	Mutual compromise
4	Interdependent sharing of vulnerabilities and self	Intimate/In-depth/Societal (generalized other)	Collaborative integration of relationship dynamics (commitment)

Source: Adapted with permission from Robert L. Selman, Caroline L. Watts, and Lynn Hickey Schultz. *Fostering friendship: Pair therapy for treatment and prevention.* (New York: Aldine de Gruyter). Copyright © 1997 by Walter de Gruyter, Inc., New York.

(perspective taking), one's needs for intimacy in relationship (friendship), one's skill in balancing personal needs without sacrificing the relationship (autonomy), and one's ability to solve conflicts (conflict resolution).

Think for a moment about your own close friendships. Regardless of how overtly agreeable or conflictual these relationships may be, there is always a tension between "what is good for me versus what is good for us" (Barr, 1997, p. 32). No friendship is immune to this underlying dynamic, which surfaces from time to time over the course of the relationship. In order to sustain friendships, friends must be able to coordinate both individuals' needs and resolve the inevitable conflicts that arise in ways that are mutually agreeable. Any imbalance, such as too much coercion from one partner and too little assertiveness from the other, can undermine the friendship in the long run. In other words, ineffective management of the dysynchrony between the needs of the individual and the needs of the pair puts the friendship at risk. Healthy friendships are marked by mutual give and take, allowing both partners to feel affirmed, understood, and respected.

If all this seems too good to be true, let us hasten to say that friendships, even in adulthood, are true "works in progress," which require mutual coordination of perspectives and ongoing balancing of needs. Imagine how short-lived a friendship would be if you typically perceived your friend's momentary insensitivity or inability to participate in some shared activity as a personal insult directed toward you. Your understanding that he might be overextended and thus under stress can help you take a more empathic perspective, despite your own disappointment. Children find this harder to do because they are essentially practicing their perspective taking and other friendship skills. Hurts, betrayals, and conflicts will almost inevitably accompany their friendship development as they struggle to learn to compromise, compete, and cooperate in a civil way. Without this sometimes painful experience, however, children may not learn the intimacy and autonomy strategies they need to reap the benefits of satisfying friendships throughout their lifetimes. Counselors who are knowledgeable about the nature of friendship development are in a unique position to facilitate children's progress in this area.

Although disagreements can be painful, they can help children learn to take another's perspective.

Selman's Stages of Friendship Development

Selman (1980) provides a stagewise description of the development of children's friendship skills. As with other stage theories, the age ranges are just rough approximations. What is most important is the sequence and nature of the developmental change. Stage 0, or the "Undifferentiated/Egocentrism" stage, is typically manifested in preschool children before about age 5, when perspective-taking capacity is quite limited. Youngsters at Stage 0 have little appreciation for the thoughts and feelings of either themselves or others. Friendship is defined in very concrete terms, without understanding of the other person's psychology. For example, a preschool child might define a friend as someone who lives next to you, who gives you gifts, who shares toys with you, or who likes you. Young children typically establish friendships with children who are like themselves in concrete ways, such as age, gender, race, and ethnicity (see Rubin & Coplan, 1992). Conflicts between friends are not perceived as disagreements that occur between two parties with two different and legitimate points of view but are viewed as struggles to get one's own way. Lacking much ability to consider another's perspective, children typically resort to "flight" ("Go away!") or "fight" ("I'll get you!") strategies to resolve conflicts as they seek to preserve their interests.

In Stage 1, the "Differentiated/Subjective" stage, children from about 5 to about 9 come to understand that others have viewpoints that are different from their own, but they are generally not able to coordinate these perspectives simultaneously. In other words, they can't maintain their own perspective and that of someone else at the same time. So even though they understand that their peers have different points of view, they still may act as though their own perspective or that of an "authority" is correct. They are able to understand, for example, that they can be the subject of another's thoughts, but they generally do not have the capacity to judge how their behavior is being evaluated by that other person. Dyami, for example, might understand that his friend Kono has a viewpoint or a perspective on him, but Dyami has little insight into what Kono's view of him is really like. We might say that interpersonal perspective at this age is unilateral or one-way. Yet during this period children do become better able to infer the thoughts and feelings of others, especially when they are encouraged to reflect on them. The child's understanding of physical experience, however, is another thing altogether. In the behavioral realm, two-way reciprocity ("You hit me and I hit you back") is readily understood.

On the psychological level, friendship is still largely a one-way proposition. The child at Stage 1 may understand his own psychological perspective but may fail to do the same for his friend. In other words, friendships may be defined by the behavioral and psychological rewards they provide for the individual child and not in terms of the mutual satisfaction afforded both members of the dyad. Eight-year-old Pavla might describe a friend as someone who helps her with her homework, doesn't fight with her, and doesn't walk away from her when she's upset. Notice the mix of behavioral (homework help) and psychological (social support) characteristics that are directed toward the benefit of one person. Conflicts are also viewed as one-way propositions. The responsibility to resolve a conflict is in the hands of the person who was perceived to have initiated it. There is little understanding of problem solving by mutual consensus.

At Stage 2, the "Reciprocal/Self-reflective" stage, older children master a critical developmental task. Between late childhood and early adolescence (8 to 12), they become more cognizant of the perspectives of others and learn to put themselves in another's place as a way of evaluating intentions and actions. Children can now actually assume the psychological position of another and reflect on their own behavior and motivation as perceived by someone else. Eleven-year-old Keisha, who doesn't really want to go swimming at her friend Amber's house because she'd prefer to spend the afternoon watching TV, might agree to go anyway. Keisha, seeing Amber as a person who is rather easily hurt, reasons that if she declined the invitation, Amber might think that Keisha didn't like her or that she didn't want to be her friend. This more sophisticated level of perspective-taking ability reflects two-way reciprocity ("I think; you think").

At this stage, children can grasp more highly differentiated patterns of motivations and emotions and make finer discriminations between thoughts and feelings. They can conceive of the fact that people, including themselves, can experience conflicting motives and feelings and can feel one thing but act in a completely different way. In our earlier example, Keisha wants to spend some time alone but she also wants to preserve her friendship with Amber. She may simultaneously feel liking and impatience toward her friend. She may decide to go swimming and cover up her true feelings of disinterest in the activity. Conflict resolution between children at this stage reflects the growing awareness that both parties must give a little in order to reach a solution.

At Stage 3, the "Mutual/Third-person" stage, adolescents of 10 to 15 learn to view each other's perspectives simultaneously and mutually. Rather than simply viewing each other's perspective in a back and forth approach ("first me, then you"), adolescents can mentally step back to take the perspective of a "third-party observer" even as they themselves remain a member of the pair. What this allows is a more detached view of the proceedings, somewhat like the way a disinterested spectator might construe a social interaction. Egocentrism is further reduced insofar as the adolescent can view the interchange between himself and his friend and reflect on it from the outside looking in.

Friendship at this stage is characterized by mutual support and shared intimacy and not seen just as a means of obtaining what either party desires as an individual. Consequently, conflict resolution strategies are marked by more attention to the mutuality of the relationship. There is an awareness that problems do not always reside within one of the participants but that they are the responsibility of both parties to address. Harmonious resolution of the conflicts that are inevitable in relationships is perceived to strengthen both parties' commitment to that relationship. Adolescents at this stage are more capable of understanding that a friendship could break down because "it just didn't work out between us" rather than because "she wasn't nice to me."

Finally, at Stage 4, the "Intimate/In-Depth/Societal" stage, older adolescents and adults learn to adopt the perspective of the larger society. Perspective-taking ability becomes more abstract and complex. Now the individual can assume the perspective of people beyond the limits of the dyad, namely that of a larger social group. This achievement makes possible the understanding of cultural and other group differences and the increasing appreciation of relativity—that no one person's or one group's perspective is necessarily the only correct one regardless of how deeply valued it might be. Relationships are marked by the individual's increasing ability to balance his needs for intimacy and autonomy while still preserving the friendship. With each new level of perspective-taking skill, understanding of friendship improves, interpersonal values are clarified, and social and conflict resolution skills are refined.

A Framework for Friendship

Perspective taking is an important part of social relatedness, but it is not the only determinant. We should now consider how the understanding of others' perspectives is integrated with other skills and tied to actual success in making and keeping friends. Is there a comprehensive way to look at the nature of friendship competence in children? The following friendship framework, which integrates a number of ingredients, has been proposed by Selman and his associates (Selman, Levitt, & Schultz, 1997) as one possible comprehensive model. We have chosen to describe this model in some depth because it represents a good example of a theoretical framework that lends itself to clinical applications that are developmentally sensitive. An understanding of the elements of this model can help you assess relative strengths and weaknesses in a child's social relatedness and help you choose relevant interventions.

As always, nature and nurture provide the backdrop for the child's social functioning. For example, one child's predisposition toward shyness or another child's day-to-day experience of parental discord can have some effect on the children's capacities to enter and sustain social relationships with others. In certain situations, the effects of nature or nurture are so pronounced that they make independent contributions to social functioning, as in the case of a child who lacks friends because he lives in an isolated environment. These effects are represented by dotted lines leading directly to friendship outcomes from "Nature" and "Nurture" in Figure 6.4.

What is more typical, however, is that the effects of nature and nurture are integrated with a third area of influence called ***psychosocial development.*** This has been defined as "the internal psychological processes of interpersonal understanding, skills, and values that comprise an individual's capacity for interpersonal relationships, including friendships" (Selman, Levitt, & Schultz, 1997, p. 35). ***Friendship understanding*** refers to a

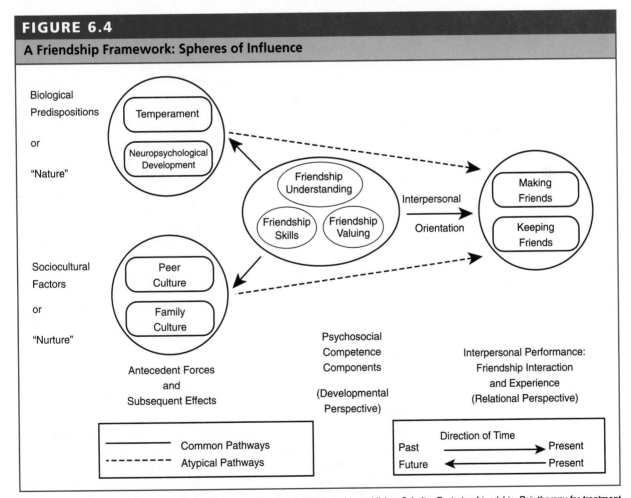

FIGURE 6.4

A Friendship Framework: Spheres of Influence

Source: Reprinted with permission from Robert L. Selman, Caroline L. Watts, and Lynn Hickey Schultz. *Fostering friendship: Pair therapy for treatment and prevention.* (New York: Aldine de Gruyter). Copyright © 1997 by Walter de Gruyter, Inc., New York.

child's changing knowledge of what friendship implies. **Friendship skills** are behavioral skills, such as appropriate assertiveness, good communication, and conflict resolution, that maintain and enhance friendships. **Friendship valuing** describes the emotional attachment or investment that the child makes in a friendship. *Each of these three components is influenced and informed by developmental changes in the child's perspective-taking ability.* In other words, competence in these three areas will be delimited by a child's cognitive understanding of interpersonal relationships.

To work effectively, clinicians need to appreciate what can be reasonably expected from children at each stage of their development. Teaching appropriate social skills, such as making eye contact and communicating effectively, may be irrelevant for children whose level of friendship understanding is very egocentric or for a child who is not particularly interested in being friendly toward another member of his class. On the other hand, learning how to solve conflicts effectively may be very helpful for a child who is invested in a friendship. All three dimensions need to be considered therapeutically so that interventions can get targeted accurately.

There is one other important element in this model, linking the child's psychosocial competencies to his interpersonal performance (see Figure 6.4). This bridge is the child's **interpersonal orientation,** or the way the child characteristically interacts on a social level. The most mature interpersonal style is characterized by a flexible balance between intimacy and autonomy strivings. Less effective orientations, as identified by Selman, are "*other-transforming*" and "*self-transforming*" social interaction styles.

A child with an *other-transforming* style characteristically tries to dominate or coerce a friend into meeting his needs. He acts to change or transform the other and can be bullying, aggressive, or manipulative. A child with a *self-transforming* style typically gives in so as to reduce the level of tension. He changes his own behaviors or feelings in order to conform. Selman and Schultz (1990) found that very young children or socially immature older children tend to behave in these extreme ways. Such children are both more labile than other children, sometimes moving from victim to victimizer position depending on the relationship, and more rigid, refusing to compromise their position once established, even at the risk of losing the friendship.

What does it mean for a child to be bossy, impulsive, stubborn, passive, or shy? On its face, each label might prescribe a certain kind of intervention: self-control training for the impulsive child, assertiveness training for the shy one, and so forth. Selman's theoretical model gives us the means to go beyond this level of understanding to unpack the fundamental psychosocial competencies that the child depends upon to engage in any social interaction. From this perspective, the bully and the victim can be functioning at the same developmental level of friendship knowledge, skills, and valuing, only using different personal orientations. Assessment of the fundamental properties that underlie friendship expression can be a helpful means of addressing interpersonal problems.

APPLICATIONS

Work with children in the middle years is enhanced when clinicians understand children's abilities, needs, and limitations. These years are marked by major advances in reasoning, in memory, and in the comprehension of many domains, including social relationships. From infancy, the child has been navigating the social world, moving from early attachment relationships to the gradually enlarging network of peers in the school setting. Certainly, there are some fundamental linkages between the early relationships we have discussed in previous chapters and children's later social interactions. For example, caregivers' encouraging preschool children to take notice of others' perspectives has been related to empathy, good social problem solving, and perspective taking at school age (Dixon & Moore, 1990). Success in relating to others rests upon having a positive internal working model for social responding, having access to peers in settings that promote mutual respect, and knowing how to resolve conflicts, among other things. And, as we have seen in this chapter, cognitive developments contribute importantly to children's social success in the middle years.

Children in the school years need to be successful in the classroom as well as on the playground. Much progress has been made in understanding the ways children process, store, and retrieve information because of the explosion of research in the area of cognitive psychology. What should helpers take from the discussion of cognitive development to help them understand the nature of children's learning? Noting a few general implications may be useful.

As you have learned, knowledge acquisition is a constructive process, built on the foundation of prior learning and experience. Children benefit from instruction that organizes information, relates it to previously learned material, and stresses its meaningfulness. Too many children, critics have noted, are taught in ways that reflect an emphasis on rote memorization of facts without any fundamental understanding of concepts. Good instructional practice involves, among other things, five basic elements: gaining the child's attention and motivation; activating what the child already knows about the material to be taught; presenting the new material in ways that capitalize on multiple sensory modalities (visual, auditory, tactile-kinesthetic); providing adequate, meaningful, and interesting practice to ensure retention; and giving task-specific feedback that scaffolds the child's progress.

An important instructional goal should be teaching children *how* to learn and to problem solve, both on their own and in groups. When adults teach children how to use memory strategies such as chunking, for example, children retain more information. Children can also be encouraged to encode information both visually and verbally to capitalize on the way the mind processes material. They also benefit from learning to identify and reflect upon the kinds of problem-solving strategies they use. Use of strategic questions, such as the self-monitoring questions presented in Table 6.2, can help children develop metacognitive awareness and self-regulation, which in turn helps them to use their problem-solving and memory strategies more effectively.

Students can also benefit from the use of techniques such as cooperative learning, if teachers offer children opportunities to learn how to work effectively together. Encouraging children to talk over their ideas and providing them with techniques for doing so seems to be helpful. Keeping track of their progress and giving them feedback is

TABLE 6.2

Sample Self-Monitoring Questions

1. Why am I trying to learn this information? What is the purpose of this exercise or assignment?
2. What do I already know about this subject?
3. Do I already know any strategies that will help me learn this?
4. What is my plan of action?
5. Do I understand the steps I need to take?
6. How should I get help if I need it?
7. How should I correct my mistakes?
8. Am I accomplishing my goals? Am I being successful?
9. How will I know when I've accomplished my goals?

also important. Cooperative methods should also incorporate some form of individual accountability as well as group recognition for goals achieved (Slavin, 1995).

One very important implication of cognitive research relates to the normal unevenness in development. Theories of development have suffered, to some degree, from their emphasis on stages, because this emphasis leads to perceptions of development in terms of static, monolithic levels. In the real world, children as well as adults are much more variable. Despite the common conception that Piaget emphasized stagewise development, he also recognized that variation in skill exists within stages. Specifically, he found that logical skills were applied to some contents (such as understanding conservation of number) before other contents (such as understanding conservation of weight). This variation he called **décalage.** This kind of variability in skill level is clearly evident in any classroom. Some may excel in reading and language arts yet find math a chore. Others may be gifted athletes who have difficulty remembering facts in social studies. Isn't such unevenness characteristic of adults as well? Most people's panorama of abilities reflects a mix of relative strengths and weaknesses. If this is true for adults, how much more typical of children, whose skills are still developing?

Unevenness in development is particularly relevant to the area of special education and the concept of disability. Some authors, notably Sternberg and Grigorenko (1999), contend that virtually everyone has a disability in something. The difference is that society determines what constitutes "disability" and identifies a select group as "disabled." Within schools, weaknesses in analytical ability, an important skill for success in most academic subject areas, may be considered particularly problematic. Yet, most contemporary theories of intelligence recognize the fact that intelligence is characterized by many kinds of skills (e.g., Gardner, 1983; Sternberg, 1985). Despite this, our curricula and instructional practices do not always address, nor assess, the myriad ways that human beings act intelligently.

In Sternberg's (1985) theoretical formulation, traditional analytic ability is just one part of the whole picture of intelligence. He includes creative and practical aspects of intelligence in the mix and recommends that teachers provide opportunities for students to manifest these other abilities, *as a supplement to more traditional forms of teaching and assessment.* For example, developing skits, creating poetry or pictures, designing experiments, establishing classroom government, or running a school store are all activities that tap creative and practical intelligence, which may be areas of relative strength for students with different learning styles.

Because concrete operational children can reason more logically than preschoolers and have more highly developed metacognitive skills, a number of counseling techniques have capitalized on their emerging cognitive competencies. Therapies designed to teach problem-solving and conflict-resolution skills have figured prominently in the counseling literature for many years and have been widely applied at the elementary school level. We should note, however, that while cognitive approaches have been highly successful with adults and adolescents, about twice as effective as they are with children (Durlak, Fuhrman, & Lampman, 1991), most of the outcome studies in this area have been done on older groups. Therapies that presume high levels of metacognitive development may strain the capabilities of young clients and even some adolescents. For example, Sigelman and Mansfield (1992) have demonstrated that children often have difficulty understanding what it is about their behavior that causes problems for other people in the first place! It is important to recognize that many cognitive approaches may not be appropriate for young children, given the metacognitive requirements of the interventions, without some modification. Mpofu and Crystal (2001) call for "child-versions" of cognitive therapies, which are less dependent on high levels of self-reflection and which incorporate teaching of discrete social skills (for example, "Use your words to tell Jordan about the problem" rather than "What do you plan to do instead of hitting Steven when he bugs you?"). In general, clinicians should try to assess the child's metacognitive skills when choosing therapeutic or psychoeducational strategies and then modify the strategies to suit the child's level of understanding.

At the heart of many therapeutic approaches, we believe, is a fundamental focus on teaching children how to get along with one another, which requires perspective taking. We stress the importance of learning to relate to others in elementary school, but it is clearly not a task just for children. Knowing how to get along with others is essential for people of all ages. Recent descriptions of *emotional intelligence* (e.g., Coleman, 1995, 1998) stress the lifelong value of having good "people skills" even in the adult world of work. Some define therapy as the process of building an awareness of how our actions affect other people, the very essence of perspective taking (see Pittman, 1998).

Children in the school years begin this kind of learning in earnest. Because they spend such large amounts of time in school, teachers and peers exert a strong influence on the development of social competence. Counselors often play a role by providing developmental guidance activities, social skills training programs, and other kinds of cognitive, affective, and behavioral interventions.

Selman's (Selman et al., 1997a) friendship framework can be a useful and somewhat unusual guide to developing interventions, because it addresses the fundamental friendship relationship and makes practice applications that are developmentally and theoretically based. His therapeutic technique, called **pair therapy,** has been applied to both preventive and remedial work with children and adolescents. While a comprehensive review of this approach is beyond the scope of this text, it is helpful to describe some of its basic ideas.

Children's social skills can be seen as involving both **competence** and **performance.** *Competence* refers to the child's level of perspective-taking ability, and *performance* refers to the child's actual use of skills for getting along with others. Selman's research indicates that adequate competence (perspective taking) is necessary but not sufficient for good performance (social functioning). In other words, children never have high-level social skills without a commensurate level of perspective taking. However, socially unskilled children may either lack interpersonal understanding or possess it without being able to act on it. Pair therapy was designed to help both kinds of poor performers: those with low competence and low performance as well as those with high competence and low performance. This kind of therapeutic approach has been adapted for use in primary prevention efforts in schools that are intended to foster good social relationships among the whole student community. Similar approaches have also been applied at the middle and high school levels in programs to reduce racism and promote intercultural understanding (Schultz, Barr, & Selman, 2000). Table 6.3 presents a comparison of two related interventions, one for therapeutic purposes (pair therapy) and one for prevention (pairing for prevention). We will have more to say about prevention and the newly evolving science that supports it in Chapter 8.

In pair therapy, two children with equally ineffective social styles, such as a controlling child and a fearful one, are paired. Both participants meet regularly with a helper whose job it is to encourage both children to be effectively assertive and empathic. The therapeutic material is what the children bring to the time they spend together. What they decide to do together, how they decide to do it, where it happens, and so on, all become grist for the therapeutic mill. Adult helpers provide a watchful eye and a knowledge of development that facilitates the pair's movement from egocentric, unilateral understanding toward more cooperative modes of interaction. The helper must ensure the physical and emotional safety of both children while allowing for their direct experience of conflict and their increasingly more advanced efforts at resolving it collaboratively. The shy child, for example, must be helped to learn ways to articulate his needs, and the more controlling child must learn to accommodate the other instead of overwhelming him. In general, this approach provides practice in the real-life experience of friendship. The counselor functions to guide the pair

TABLE 6.3

Pair Therapy and Pairing for Prevention

	Pair Therapy	Pairing for Prevention
Context of treatment	Child Guidance Clinic/Day Treatment/ Residential Treatment Program/In-patient Hospitalization (if long-term)	School-Based (during or after school); Community Center/Settlement House/Girls and Boys Clubs.
Clients	Children and adolescents with severe emotional and behavior problems. Range of psychiatric diagnoses, including cognitive and communicative disorders. Very limited peer interactions. Family trauma.	"At-risk" students with conduct and/or academic problems: may have close friends; from low-income, inner-city households; likely exposure to, and/or involvement in societal health/welfare risks. Limited social supports.
General goals	Foster personality and social development. Increase capacity to make and maintain friendships: coordinate social perspectives, communicate more effectively, resolve interpersonal conflicts, manage emotions.	Same goals as therapy but with focus on interpersonal development as vehicle for increasing capacity to make mature decisions with respect to risks. Pairs provides protective factor against risky behaviors.
Theory guiding treatment and evaluation	Primarily Psychological: Orthogenetic and Structural-Developmental Model: Intimacy and Autonomy as functional social management processes organized according to developmental level of perspective coordination.	Primarily Psychosocial Risk-Taking Model: Takes into account sociocultural and biological antecedents, and psychosocial dimensions (knowledge, management, and personal meaning) of risk taking behavior. Incorporates Structural Developmental Model.
Overall treatment plan	Often in conjunction with individual psychotherapy, adjunct therapies (i.e., speech, family), and/or a therapeutic milieu.	May be only special service student receives.
Training level of providers	Supervised clinicians or residential staff, with some understanding of individual psychodynamics.	Supervised Master's level students with some understanding of psychosocial development and the social system within which they are providing service.
Time frame of treatment/ research focus	Long-term treatment/longitudinal study of interpersonal development (1–4 years). Process oriented basic research of both the individual and the dyad. Major focus on assessment methods: interviews and observations to assess ego development.	Focus on major transitions (Elementary to Middle School; Middle School to High School) Outcome and Process Oriented research. Focus on both individual assessment and program evaluation. Additional reliance on ethnography.
Evaluation/ Research	In-depth micro and macro level assessment of affective, cognitive, motivational and dynamic dimensions of evolving pair relationship (non-experimental).	Qualitative evaluation of process of change in pair's knowledge, management and personal meaning of risk, and quantitative assessment of risk outcome in treatment group compared to control group (experimental). Additional qualitative and quantitative analysis of participant's view of prevention.

Source: Watts, C. L., Nakkula, M. J., & Barr, D. (1997). Person-in-pairs, pairs-in-program: Pair therapy in different institutional contexts. In R. L. Selman, C. L. Watts, & L. H. Schultz. (Eds.) *Fostering friendship: Pair therapy for treatment and prevention.* New York: Aldine de Gruyter. Copyright © 1997 by Walter de Gruyter, Inc., New York. Reprinted with permission.

toward a more even-handed balance of control and decision-making functions and nurtures them toward experiences of mutual sharing and cooperation. Within this context, children learn the tools of friendship, which include the development of a sense of personal responsibility, motivation to make the friendship work, and the ability to understand firsthand the impact of one's words and actions on another person.

SUMMARY

Physical and Brain-Related Changes

1. Changes in the brain underlie motor developments in middle childhood. First gross motor coordination, then fine motor coordination and eye-hand coordination benefit from continued myelination of the corpus callosum, connecting the left and right cortical hemispheres, as well as other brain maturation processes.

2. Brain maturation also contributes to cognitive development. Myelination of the reticular formation and synaptogenesis in the frontal lobe contribute to improved attention, concentration, and planning. The primary localization of certain intellectual processes, such as math and reading skills, seems to shift during middle childhood, as the brain matures and as skills become more practiced.

Cognitive Development

3. In Piaget's theory, children at the *concrete operational stage* (6 to 12 years) can *decenter,* or think about more than one dimension or aspect of a situation at one time. This allows them the possibility of recognizing or constructing the relationships among the dimensions, which is important for logical thinking. Understanding *reversible relationships,* when one change reverses the effects of another, or one change compensates for the effects of another, is especially important. Recognizing the nature of the relationships among features of an event makes it possible for children to infer underlying realities.

4. At the concrete operational stage, children's thinking is most logical when they are solving problems that relate to real, concrete events. They find it difficult to think logically about abstract contents, like their own thought processes. They are subject to a form of *egocentrism,* such that they find it difficult to distinguish between their own theories or assumptions and objective fact.

5. Logical thinking can be to some degree *domain specific*. When children have a great deal of experience with a specific *domain of knowledge,* they are more likely to think logically about problems in that domain.

6. In the information processing approach, cognition is compared to the functioning of a computer. The organization of the cognitive system stays the same across age, but there are age changes in the amount and efficiency of information flow. With increasing age, children can hold more information in working memory at one time, and they may change the strategies they use to operate on the information. Also, the same child is likely to use different strategies on different contents, so that there are no stage-similar ways of dealing with information across domains. *NeoPiagetians* are theorists who try to integrate concepts from Piaget's theory and from information processing theory to explain cognitive development.

7. Two kinds of remembering or *retrieval* are called *recognition* (realizing that information being experienced now is familiar) and *recall* (drawing information out of long-term memory and representing it to yourself). Our memories can store *declarative knowledge,* both *semantic* (about facts and concepts) and *episodic* (about events we have experienced). A schematic representation of a frequently experienced event is called a

script. We also store *nondeclarative knowledge,* which is hard to verbalize and is often referred to as *procedural,* which is "knowing how" rather than "knowing that." Infants' and toddlers' knowledge is largely nondeclarative.

8. *Working memory* increases in capacity with age, as indicated on digit span tests. This seems related to accelerated information processing, perhaps due to practice, perhaps to maturation, or to both.

9. Children's *knowledge base* increases with age, and that helps children *reconstruct* events. They "remember" more accurately because they can infer what must have happened. An expanded knowledge base also helps children learn new information more easily, perhaps because they can fit the new information into a rich web of well-organized connections. Having an expanded knowledge base also benefits *chunking* in working memory.

10. Advances in logical thinking can help children improve their memories. The better the child understands the original experience, the more likely he is to reconstruct it accurately.

11. Increasing facility with language helps children store memories for events in coherent verbal form and seems to improve later retrieval of those events.

12. Children also improve in the use of *memory strategies* with age from preschool through middle school. *Rehearsal* is an early strategy, with more effective strategies such as *organization* coming later. Children's progress in strategy use is "bumpy." They may exhibit either *production deficiencies* or *utilization deficiencies.*

13. Children gradually improve their understanding of their own cognitive processes (*metacognition*), including memory abilities, as they approach the end of middle childhood, partly accounting for improvements in strategy use with age.

14. Memory is also influenced by affective and social developments, like motivation to learn and the amount of *scaffolding* available from adults.

15. Preschool children acquire informal mathematical skills, such as adopting simple counting strategies for adding and subtracting small numbers. In elementary school, they continue to invent their own strategies as well as adopting the formal algorithms and strategies they are taught. Gradually, more efficient strategies win out over less efficient strategies, though again development, is "bumpy."

16. Children assimilate formal rules to their own concepts, and often misunderstand. Teachers can encourage mathematical development by exploring their students' understanding rather than accepting rote learning of procedures.

17. There are a number of examples of how social and cultural context contributes to some variations in children's acquisition of math concepts.

18. Adults work to keep children focused during problem solving. They respond to a child contingently, tailor instruction to the child's level, ask challenging questions, and elicit the child's active involvement. When children collaborate with other children, the process may be less effective in fostering learning. It works best when all partners are actively involved and when adults provide feedback.

Social Cognition

19. Learning about social interactions and acquiring a theory of mind begins in early childhood and is heavily dependent on cognitive developments. For example, children's *perspective taking* improves as they acquire the ability to think about their own mental experiences and those of another person at the same time.

20. Theorists such as Sullivan and Selman built on Piaget's ideas and linked the gradual improvement in perspective taking with changes in the nature of friendships over age. In Selman's five-stage theory, improvements in perspective taking affect an individual's

friendship understanding, influence his *friendship valuing,* and affect the social and conflict resolution skills (*friendship skills*) he develops.

21. In Selman's view, a mature *interpersonal orientation* balances intimacy and autonomy strivings. Less effective orientations may be "other-transforming" or "self-transforming," and are more characteristic of very young children and of socially immature older children. Both a bully and a victim may be functioning at a similar developmental level with regard to perspective-taking skill. Assessing the properties of understanding that underlie relationship skill is a helpful approach to addressing social problems.

Case Study

Alex, the second child of Ernest and Isabel Palacio, a Cuban-American couple, is a fourth-grader at J.F. Kennedy Elementary School. He has one older sister, Paula, who is in fifth grade, and a younger brother, Thomas, who is 4 years old. Until recently, Alex appeared to be a happy child and a good student in school. Although somewhat reserved, he interacted well with peers, was athletic, and was popular among his classmates. During the year Alex was in third grade, the Palacio's marriage was seriously affected by Ernest's close relationship with a female coworker. Despite an attempt at counseling, the couple could not resolve their differences. During the summer before his fourth-grade year, Alex's parents separated. The children continued to live with their mother but maintained a relationship with their father, seeing him every weekend in the apartment he rented nearby.

Both parents tried hard to make this arrangement work for the sake of their children, to whom both were devoted. The fourth-grade school year began fairly smoothly for Alex, who was happy to see his friends again after the summer vacation. His teacher, Mr. Williams, was regarded as tough but usually fair, and Alex seemed to make a good initial adjustment to his class. Ernest continued his employment with an advertising agency and paid for many of the family's living costs. However, the expense of maintaining two residences quickly became burdensome. Isabel, formerly employed as a part-time library aide, needed to find a position that provided a larger income. She began a job as a secretary shortly after the children began school in September.

In December, Isabel fell ill and needed to be hospitalized. Primary care of the children fell to Isabel's mother, the children's grandmother. Ernest took over as much of the care-taking as his work schedule would permit, but he feared that if he took off too much time for family responsibilities, his job would be in jeopardy. Because of these changes in the family, all three children needed to adjust. It became much more difficult for an adult to transport the children after school to music lessons and games, so they had to drop out of some of their activities. As Isabel recuperated, she needed much more rest and general peace and quiet. She could no longer take the children on trips or allow groups of her children's friends to have sleep-overs in her home.

Toward the middle of his fourth-grade year, Alex's grades started to slip, and he began to act up. Alex grew apathetic and sullen in class. His teacher, Mr. Williams, was a relatively young teacher in the school district. His first two years of teaching had been spent in the eighth grade of the district middle school. He liked teaching older students and reluctantly accepted the fourth grade because of his lack of seniority in the system. Mr. Williams, despite his youth, was a fairly traditional teacher. He believed in giving lots of homework and in placing high expectations for performance on his students. He ran a very disciplined classroom that was based on a system of winning and losing points for behavior. Because Alex did not participate actively in classroom exercises or turn in homework, he continually "lost points."

On one particularly difficult day, Alex and one of his friends got into an argument. Alex accused his friend of picking on him and teasing him in the lunchroom. Mr. Williams tried to intervene by taking both boys out into the hallway and listening to each version of the problem. When the disagreement got louder, Mr. Williams told both boys that they would "just have to work it out." He told them he would take away points and was sending them both to the principal's office. Alex became very agitated and said to his teacher "sometimes I feel like throwing my chair at you."

Mr. Williams began to see Alex as a threat and recommended to the principal that the incident be handled as a disciplinary matter. It was the teacher's belief that Alex should be suspended and then referred for special education evaluation by the school psychologist because of his "aggressiveness." He insisted that Alex not be returned to his classroom.

Discussion Questions

1. How would you assess the problem?
2. What are the different perspectives involved in this conflict?
3. What actions would you take and what recommendations would you make as a counselor in this situation?

 Journal Questions

1. If you can remember struggling with some subject or concept in school, describe the impact of this experience on your sense of competence and industry. If you were counseling a student in this situation, what advice would you have for his parent? His teachers?
2. Describe what your friendships were like in elementary school. Did you have a "best friend"? What characteristics did he or she possess?
3. Compare and contrast how you solved conflicts as a child in grade school and how you solve them now. How would you assess your level of perspective taking?
4. Using the "Friendship Framework" presented in this chapter, reflect upon each element in light of one particular relationship that you have experienced or are experiencing. (For example, what is your primary interpersonal orientation, other- or self-transforming?)

Key Terms

concrete operational stage
reversible relationship
egocentrism
formal operational
    thought
domain of knowledge
domain specific
neoPiagetians
working memory
sensory memory
long-term memory
rehearsal
storage
retrieval

recognition
recall
declarative knowledge
semantic
episodic
script
nondeclarative knowledge
procedural
digit span tests
knowledge base
chunking
reality monitoring
guided imagery
stereotype induction

narrative skill
memory strategies
organization
elaboration
production deficiency
utilization deficiency
metacognition
self-instruction
self-monitoring
counting all strategy
counting on strategy
retrieval strategy
cooperative learning
    environments

social cognition
perspective taking
psychosocial development
friendship understanding
friendship skills
friendship valuing
interpersonal orientation
other-transforming
self-transforming
décalage
pair therapy
competence vs.
    performance

Self and Moral Development in Middle Childhood Through Early Adolescence

Honesty, Dependability, Kindness, Fairness, Respect, Self-Control, Truthfulness, and Diligence. Rare is the adult who would *not* agree that any one of these traits is desirable for children to attain. The advantage is very basic: behaving in accordance with these values makes the world a better place for everyone. Certainly, individuals or groups might disagree on the particulars, such as what "being fair" may mean in a given situation. But it is truly difficult to imagine any sizable group of parents, teachers, or clinicians who would promote the opposite values: meanness, laziness, dishonesty, irresponsibility, or disrespect, to name a few.

Not too long ago in this country, there was considerable agreement that inculcating these values, virtues, or behavioral habits was perhaps the most important responsibility that adults have relative to their children. The public schools had as their express purpose the creation of good citizens—people who, for the most part, valued and practiced these virtues. Consider the advice educator Charles Davis presented in 1852 in a lecture to parents and teachers on their duties toward children:

> Education is the system of training which develops in their right direction and in their proper proportions our physical, intellectual, and moral natures. . . . The moral nature of the pupils will be, with the teacher, a subject of earnest and constant solicitude. What are the first things to be done? To establish his [the teacher's] authority over his school—to ensure the obedience of his scholars—to win their confidence—to gain their respect, and to call into exercise their warmest affections. (pp. 6–8)

Hiram Orcutt, writing in a famous manual to parents in 1874, advises thus:

> The child must establish a character of integrity and to be trained to habits of honesty, benevolence and industry or he will be lost to himself and to society. . . . We may not expect benevolence to spring up spontaneously in the heart of the child. . . . Without knowledge and experience, the child cannot appreciate the rights and wants of others, nor his own duty in regard to them. (pp. 72–73)

If this seems a bit quaint and outdated to you, consider the fact that even today there is evidence for broad consensus among parents in this country about what they consider is fundamental for children in order for them to achieve their life goals. When David R. Shaffer and his students asked young parents what they considered to be the most important aspect of a child's social development, most placed morality at the top of their lists (Shaffer, 2000). They apparently felt that acquiring a moral sense and living by its dictates were critical for self-development and central to successful adult functioning.

Perhaps this consensus is being shaped by our experience of the culture we share at the beginning of this new millennium. We are benumbed by the repetitious refrain that comes from all manner of media reporting on a world marred by violence, aggressiveness, hopelessness, underachievement, and declining moral standards. Overall, violent crime rose 600% from 1953 to the early 1980s (Skogan, 1983). Although arrests of youth for violent offenses such as murder and burglary have declined somewhat since 1990, juvenile arrests for drug-related offenses have increased, and the rate of school violence is alarmingly high (Osofsky & Osofsky, 2001). During the 1990s, approximately 8% of school students were threatened or injured with a weapon on school property annually (see Centers for Disease Control and Prevention, CDC, 1998), and the chance of being murdered was four times greater for adolescents in the United States than it was for their peers in 21 industrialized nations (Goldstein, 1992).

However, it is not only dramatic, highly aggressive criminal behavior that is increasing; "garden variety" problems are more widespread as well. Incidence of cheating on tests rose, up from 38% in 1969 to 68% in 1997 (CDC, 1998). In a study of New England middle school students, Kikuchi (1988) reported that two out of three boys and one out of two girls believed that it was permissible for a man to force sex on a woman if the couple had been dating at least six months. Achenbach and Howell (1993) surveyed teachers and parents over a 13-year period (1976 to 1989) to discern whether children's behavior was actually deteriorating. Results clearly supported a decline in behavioral standards over the longitudinal study as reflected in increased destruction of property, sullenness, stealing, noncompliance, underachievement, and chronic though minor physical problems.

What is happening to the healthy self-development we wish for our children? As you might have already guessed, the problem is complex and most certainly has many influential antecedents. Whatever answers researchers have made available, however, have profound significance for practice, given counselors' investment in their clients' healthy social and emotional development. In this chapter and the next, we will introduce the topics that are fundamental to understanding social and emotional development in middle and late childhood and provide some guidelines and suggestions for interventions. We pick up the discussion with the topic of the self.

SELF-CONCEPT

The Development of Self-Concept

Imagine that you live across the street from an empty lot. One day, you notice that workers have placed piles of building materials, bricks, lumber, and bags of concrete on the property. After some time, the frame of a large, box-like house takes the place of the piles of materials. From your vantage point, you can see the empty beginnings of where rooms will be. With more time, the internal structure becomes clear. Walls are assembled; doors and stairways connect the parts. Each section of the new house—living, dining, bedroom, and storage areas—has multiple divisions that provide useful space dedicated to some purpose. The disparate piles have been transformed into a coherent structure, and the once simple structure has become increasingly complex. Finishing touches are made, and ongoing renovations will undoubtedly accompany the life of the home.

This image is offered to provide a rough approximation of how the self-concept might develop from early childhood through adolescence and adulthood. It is important to recognize that self-concept or self-knowledge is very much like any other kind of knowledge, for the self is a cognitive construction. Therefore, knowledge of the self will be constrained by the child's general level of cognitive development and will most likely progress unevenly. As Harter (1999) has pointed out in her description of general cognitive-developmental stages, "decalage is accepted as the rule, rather than the exception; therefore, it is expected that the particular level of development at which one is functioning will vary across different domains of knowledge" (p. 30) as we noted in Chapter 6.

In addition, remember that the self-concept is multidimensional, like a house with various rooms (see Chapter 5). In many homes, rooms are added on after the initial construction. In contrast to this somewhat static analogy, the self-system is dynamic and changes throughout development. Generally, the child's self-concept proceeds from a rather undifferentiated state or simple structure to a much more organized and coherent structure in adulthood through a process of stage-like changes. Let us consider some of the developments in self-knowledge that occur as children mature.

The preschool child's rendering of herself is something like the lot filled with building materials. Self-descriptors such as "big," "girl," and "nice" are separate, uncoordinated elements in the child's self-portrait because she is cognitively unable to integrate these elements into an organized whole. We know from our discussion of cognitive development (see Chapter 3) that young children's ability to hold in mind several ideas at the same time and to integrate these in some meaningful way is quite underdeveloped. Furthermore, preschool youngsters find accommodating opposing characteristics, such as being "nice" and "mean" (Fischer, Hand, Watson, Van Parys, & Tucker, 1984), or opposing emotional states, such as "happy" and "sad" (P. L. Harris, 1983), to be especially difficult. Nor do young children make much use of perspective taking at this age, as we saw in Chapter 6. In failing to do so, they show limited ability to use the behaviors or perspectives of others as guides for evaluating their own conduct or performance. Stated in other words, they do not use information gleaned from observing others as a way of assessing their competencies. Consequently, the young child's self-evaluations may not conform to reality but may be overly positive. Four-year-old Jamar might insist he has won the round of miniature golf despite hitting the ball outside the lane every time!

Gradually, the early elementary school–age youngster begins to organize the characteristics of the "Me-self" into sets of categories that display some coherence. For example, the child might relate being good at drawing, at coloring, and at cutting as an indication that she is good at art. However, the child still does not accommodate sets of characteristics with opposing features (e.g., nice versus mean, Fischer et al., 1984). Given her tendency to perceive personal qualities as good and to discount the subtlety of coexisting negative attributes, the child's thinking about herself may still have an all-or-nothing quality that is often unrealistically positive. There is little discrepancy between the "real" and the "ideal" selves. Gradual improvements in perspective-taking ability, however, allow the child to begin to evaluate her own behavior according to others' standards. The child's anticipation of another person's reaction, be it as a reward or a punishment, becomes internalized (Harter, 1998). As others' rules or standards become internalized, they become adopted as self-regulatory guidelines and form the basis for the "looking-glass self."

Between middle childhood and early adolescence, the individual becomes capable of integrating opposing characteristics and begins to form more abstract "trait-like" concepts to describe herself. Self-assessments, such as "being smart," are bolstered by feedback from a wide variety of outside influences across many kinds of situations, and these assessments become more resistant to modification. Self-esteem tends to decline a bit during middle childhood and early adolescence because children recognize, often for the first time, how they fall short in comparison to others. Struggles to integrate abstract representations of the self characterize the period of adolescence as the young person works on defining a unique identity.

The Structure of Self-Concept

Although we continue to use the term "self-concept," it is not a unidimensional construct, as we noted in Chapter 5. One's overall sense of self is a composite of several related, but not necessarily overlapping, elements that are evaluated by the individual to determine self-esteem. Although technically separate constructs, self-concept and self-esteem, or our feelings about ourselves, are closely intertwined. Shavelson, Hubner, and Stanton (1976) proposed a highly influential theoretical view of the self that has received recent research confirmation (Byrne & Shavelson, 1996; Marsh, 1990). In this model (see Figure 7.1), children's general self-concept can be divided into two main domains: academic and nonacademic self-concepts. *Academic self-concept* is further divided into specific school subject areas such as math, science, English, and social studies. More recently, developmentalists have proposed the addition of other components such as artistic self-concept (Marsh & Roche, 1996; Vispoel, 1995).

The *nonacademic self-concept* is divided into social, emotional, and physical self-concepts. The last domain is further subdivided into physical ability and physical appearance. Other contemporary theories of the self (Marsh & Hattie, 1996; Harter, 1993; Markus, 1977; L'Ecuyer, 1992) also emphasize multidimensional and hierarchically arranged self-structures. Despite this general consensus, however, many researchers have retained the notion of global self-esteem within their frameworks. This appears to reflect the view that a global sense of self coexists with, and serves to shape, self-appraisals in specific domains.

By grade school, children can articulate their own assessments of their specific competencies as well as a generalized overall perception of themselves (Harter & Pike, 1984). Using her measures with individuals of different ages, Harter (1985, 1988) has found that

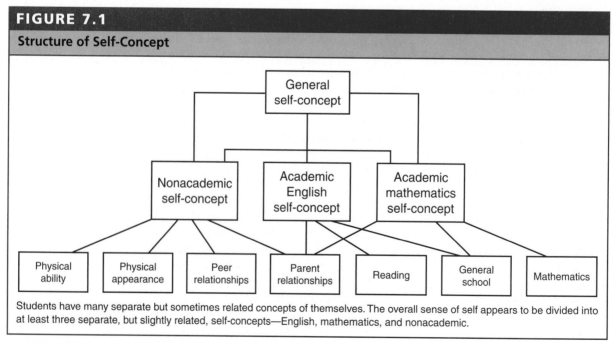

FIGURE 7.1

Structure of Self-Concept

Students have many separate but sometimes related concepts of themselves. The overall sense of self appears to be divided into at least three separate, but slightly related, self-concepts—English, mathematics, and nonacademic.

Source: From "Self-Concept: Its Multifaceted, Hierarchical Structure," by H. W. Marsh and R. J. Shavelson, 1985, *Educational Psychologist, 20,* p. 114. Copyright © 1985 Lawrence Erlbaum Associates, Inc. Adapted with permission of the publisher and the authors.

TABLE 7.1

Domains of Self-Concept across the Life Span

Early Childhood	Middle to Late Childhood	Adolescence	College Years	Early Through Middle Adulthood	Late Adulthood
Cognitive competence	Scholastic competence	Scholastic competence	Scholastic competence		
			Intellectual ability	Intelligence	Cognitive abilities
			Creativity		
		Job competence	Job competence	Job competence	Job competence
Physical competence	Athletic competence	Athletic competence	Athletic competence	Athletic competence	
Physical appearance	Physical appearance	Physical appearance	Physical appearance	Physical appearance	Physical appearance
Peer acceptance	Peer acceptance	Peer acceptance	Peer acceptance	Sociability	
		Close friendship	Close friendship	Close friendship	Relationships with friends
		Romantic relationships	Romantic relationships	Intimate relationships	Family relationships
			Relationships with parents		
Behavioral conduct	Behavioral conduct	Conduct/morality	Morality	Morality	Morality
			Sense of humor	Sense of humor	
				Nurturance	Nurturance
				Household management	Personal, household management
				Adequacy as a provider	Adequacy as a provider
					Leisure activities
					Health status
					Life satisfaction
					Reminiscence
	Global self-worth	Global self-worth	Global self-worth	Global self-worth	Global self-worth

Source: Harter, S. (1990). *The construction of the self: A developmental perspective.* New York: Guilford Press.

different domains of self-concept emerge at different points in the life span (see Table 7.1). The number of dimensions of the self that can be appraised, however, increases dramatically from early childhood through adolescence and adulthood. In middle childhood, the dimensions of importance include academic or scholastic competence, athletic competence, physical appearance, peer acceptance, and behavioral conduct.

Is any one domain more important than the others to a child's overall sense of self-esteem? Evidence from many studies reported by Harter (1990) clearly documents the powerful association between physical appearance and overall self-esteem (typical correlations are between .70 and .80) for older children, adolescents, college-age students, and adults. The strength of this association holds up for special student populations such as learning disabled and academically talented groups as well. This somewhat disconcerting reality may be due to the fact that physical attractiveness is such an omnipresent, recognizable aspect of the self. It is also true that more attractive individuals receive more positive attention from others (Maccoby & Martin, 1983), receive more affection in infancy (Langlois, Ritter, Casey, & Savin, 1995), have more good qualities ascribed to them (Dion,

Berscheid & Walster, 1972), and are generally more successful in life (Hatfield & Sprecher, 1986). Thus, physically attractive individuals may be getting a consistently larger number of positive reflected appraisals with which to construct the self than their less attractive counterparts.

It also appears that cultural emphasis on rigid and often unobtainable standards of beauty, particularly for females, contributes to observed differences in self-esteem for males and females, which we will discuss in a later section of this chapter. Beginning around early adolescence, girls report more dissatisfaction with their appearance and their bodies than do boys of the same age (Allgood-Merten, Lewinsohn, & Hops, 1990).

Influences on the Development of Self-Concept

We have already presented the earliest influences on the developing self of the infant, toddler, and preschooler (see Chapter 5). What can we add to the story of self-concept development that applies to older children? Are the same processes at work? And what can we say about the nature of self-esteem, that evaluative dimension which colors our self-appraisals? As you might suspect, the traditional positions of James (1890) and Cooley (1902) have much to offer contemporary researchers looking for explanations. Recall that William James believed that self-esteem was dependent upon the ratio of our successes to our aspirations. Harter (1990) found support for James's position. Children's, as well as adolescents' and adults', global self-esteem is heavily dependent upon competence in areas of personal importance. Individuals of all ages are more able to discount weak performance if it occurs in unimportant areas. For example, if it is very important to Ashley (and to her peers and parents) to be athletically competitive, relatively weak performance in this area is likely to lower her overall self-regard. On the other hand, if Sharon's goal is to be a stellar student, a weak athletic showing is likely to have less punishing consequences to her global sense of self.

In general, Harter found that the greater the discrepancy between adequacy in some domain and importance of that domain, the greater the negative impact on self-esteem. This helps to explain why some students who display low levels of competence in certain domains may still have high self-esteem overall. Evidence suggests, however, that this reality is not well understood and may even contradict conventional wisdom. Consider a survey of teachers, school administrators, and school counselors in which approximately 60% of the respondents believed poor academic performance was the major cause of low self-esteem among students (Scott, Murray, Mertens, & Dustin, 1996). This belief fails to acknowledge the diversity of attributes that are important to children (e.g., social relationships) as well as the fact that academic success may not be highly valued by everyone. Interestingly, in the same study, 69% of counselors compared to 35% of administrators believed that the self-esteem of underachieving students could be improved by more unconditional validation, a strategy we will examine more thoroughly later in the chapter.

Overall self-esteem seems to depend, at least in part, on a complicated, idiosyncratic calculation of perceived pluses and minuses factored against personally significant competencies. Large discrepancies, such as discrepancies between real and ideal selves as children reach adolescence, are associated with depression and anxiety (Higgins, 1991; Markus & Nurius, 1986). However, even low levels of competency in areas deemed of little personal value may not negatively alter one's general feelings about the self. High levels of competency in socially unacceptable but personally desirable behaviors (e.g., fighting, delinquent activities) may even enhance self-esteem for some youth (Brynner, O'Malley, & Bachman, 1981; Cairns & Cairns, 1994).

How do children appraise their competencies in the first place? For a child at school age and beyond, there are obviously some concrete standards of performance, such as getting good grades or being selected for a sports team, that can be used to infer competency. Cooley also emphasized the importance of social influences on appraisals of competence. In other words, he believed that self-perceptions can be based on the internalization of approval or disapproval of others in the social network. But the role of the social network involves more than just providing an accumulation of comments or responses from others that become part of the self-concept. The self-system assimilates and accommodates evaluative data from internal ("How am I doing in reading compared to math?") and external ("How does my reading performance compare with that of my classmates?") sources in ways that involve comparison (Marsh, 1994).

The process, called *social comparison* (Festinger, 1954), means that people observe the performance of others and use it as a basis for evaluating their own abilities and accomplishments. When they do this and how they do it vary somewhat depending upon context and level of global self-esteem. Social comparison processes are particularly active in situations that are novel or ambiguous or when more objective standards of performance are unavailable. It is fairly obvious that classrooms provide a wealth of material for this ongoing process. Generally, children tend to make comparisons with other children who resemble them in some important ways (Suls & Miller, 1977). Most people are motivated to maintain moderately positive beliefs about themselves, called the *self-enhancing bias* (Taylor & Brown, 1988), which is considered a good thing in most cases.

The processes involved in social comparison work somewhat differently for individuals who are lower in self-esteem. When self-esteem is low, children may prefer situations that are rich in positive reinforcement. For example, R. E. Smith and Smoll (1990) reported that children with lower levels of self-esteem responded most favorably to coaches and instructors who were highly encouraging and least favorably to those who were least supportive. Children with high or moderate levels of self-esteem showed less variation in their responsiveness to adult reinforcement styles. Researchers (Pyszczynski, Greenberg, & LaPrelle, 1985) have also noted that children will make *"downward" social comparisons* by comparing themselves to less competent or less successful peers when

As children grow, social comparison processes contribute to the construction of the self-concept.

their own self-esteem is at stake. Such comparisons protect the child from negative self-evaluations. Children and adults with lower levels of self-esteem are more susceptible to the kinds of external cues that carry evaluative messages and are more reactive to social feedback (Campbell, 1990). They are reluctant to call attention to themselves and are more cautious and self-protective. Possibly they feel they have more to lose if they experience negative evaluations from others. This contrasts with individuals with high self-esteem, who demonstrate more self-enhancement strategies and are more likely to call attention to themselves (J. D. Campbell & Lavallee, 1993).

Are children's self-perceptions congruent with the appraisals of others? In other words, do the reflected appraisals of others account for some of the substance of the child's self-structure? A study of third- and sixth-grade children carried out by D. A. Cole, Maxwell, and Martin (1997) found that the relationships between self-appraisals and others' appraisals were stronger for older students than they were for younger students. The authors hypothesized that older students were more motivated to engage in social comparison processes and more actively used the comparisons as a way of measuring their own performance. As children mature, they appear to put more stock in how peers see them. Can it be that we are what our friends believe we are? The importance of peers' appraisals in shaping self-concept, particularly as children approach adolescence, seems intuitively reasonable. Despite peers' important contribution to self-concept, however, this study also reported that the appraisals of parents and teachers contributed independently to the process.

What message can we draw from research in the tradition of James and Cooley? Harter (1993) concludes that the two theorists' positions operate in an additive way to explain the variation in self-esteem found in older children and adolescents. In other words, both competence and support contribute to the final product. The higher the level of competence in important domains *and* the greater the level of social support, the higher the level of self-esteem is overall (see Figure 7.4).

Gender, Racial, and Ethnic Differences

Gender

Much recent attention has been paid to the apparent decrease in self-esteem experienced by females around the time of their entrance to middle school. This phenomenon has been called the "loss of voice" by Gilligan and her colleagues (Brown & Gilligan, 1992), who purport that a girl experiences a gradual silencing of an authentic, imperious, and often willful self in order to identify with certain culturally prescribed roles of women as self-sacrificial and pleasing to others. Speaking one's mind, at least for women in certain contexts, can be threatening to the relationships that are such an important part of their lives. These authors argue that suppressing one's voice becomes the only possible way of maintaining important connections to others. In time, they conclude, women become disassociated from their true selves and may lose touch with their own opinions and feelings. Comparably negative claims of gender bias or silencing have been directed toward schools for "shortchanging" girls by giving them less attention than boys and for attributing their academic failure to lack of ability rather than to lack of effort (Ornstein, 1994; Sadker & Sadker, 1991). Popular accounts of these reports have contributed to the notion that the self-esteem of girls plunges precipitously around the early adolescent period while that of boys remains robust (Daley, 1991).

What actually happens to girls' views of themselves in late childhood and early adolescence? Are these gender differences in self-regard real and universal? One group of researchers looked carefully at the data from two large studies of global self-esteem, which included a combined total of 155,121 participants (Kling, Hyde, Showers, & Buswell, 1999). Results from this analysis provided evidence for a small but consistent gender effect, with males showing higher self-esteem. The level of difference is relatively small, however, compared to gender differences in aggressive behavior (Hyde, 1984) and activity level (Eaton & Enns, 1986). The authors concluded that the idea of "plummeting" self-esteem is overstated. Despite what might be an initial decline in early adolescence relative to boys, girls' self-esteem does not plunge dramatically during adolescence, never to rebound.

This small but stable gender difference in self-esteem should be taken seriously. However, Kling and her colleagues propose that inflating the significance of the ***self-esteem slide*** may create a self-fulfilling prophecy. Adults who believe that girls have lower self-esteem than boys may convey this impression to girls in subtle but powerful ways. Girls may internalize this message and alter their self-appraisals accordingly. In addition, championing the self-esteem deficits of girls may lead some to conclude that boys do not have self-esteem problems. Clearly, there are gender role strains for boys as well. For example, Kilmartin (1994) reported that boys who were not athletically inclined suffer greatly in social status and self-esteem relative to their peers.

Race and Ethnicity

For many years it was assumed that the self-esteem of minority group children would be lower than that of White children because of their minority status in North American culture. This interpretation was based on Cooley's idea of reflected appraisals and social comparison processes. Members of oppressed groups, for example, would be more likely than members of nonoppressed groups to internalize the discriminatory appraisals of others in constructing their sense of self (Cartwright, 1950). Similarly, social comparisons would be more negative when oppressed minorities held themselves to the standards of the majority culture (Gerth & Mills, 1953). Classic doll studies, in which investigators asked children to state their preference for dolls or pictures representing different racial groups, supported these interpretations (M. L. Clark, 1982). Preference for white dolls over black or brown ones was reported for all children, including those from African American (Spenser, 1970) and Native American groups (Aboud, 1977). These findings were interpreted to mean that children from oppressed minorities suffered from low self-esteem, due to the negative status accorded their racial background and their internalization of pejorative attitudes.

Current research has challenged these interpretations by demonstrating a slight but relatively consistent self-esteem advantage for Black Americans, the minority group most extensively studied, over White Americans. Several explanations have been proposed to account for this phenomenon. Crocker and Major (1989) posit that, in order to maintain their self-esteem, members of historically marginalized groups engage in three complementary processes. They attribute negative feedback directed toward themselves to the prejudice that exists in society. They make social comparisons to members of their own group rather than to members of the advantaged majority. Finally, they tend to enhance the importance of self-concept domains in which members of their group excel, while discounting the importance of domains in which their members do not excel.

Gray-Little and Hafdahl (2000) have attempted to summarize the existing data on this subject and have concluded that Blacks and other minority groups demonstrate a higher level of ethnocentrism than do Whites. In other words, racial identification is a more salient component of self-concept for members of these groups (see also Chapter 9).

Strong ethnic or racial identity appears to enhance self-esteem for children and adolescents who are part of a minority group.

African Americans, in particular, benefit from this emphasis on their desirable distinctiveness within the larger society (Judd, Park, Ryan, Bauer & Kraus, 1995). In fact, studies have found that strong racial or ethnic identity correlates positively with level of global self-esteem (Goodstein & Ponterotto, 1997; Phinney, 1990).

It is important to realize, however, that these results cannot be generalized to members of all minority groups, nor even to all members within a single minority. Gray-Little and Hafdahl (2000) make the important point that race is a complex construct, confounded with socioeconomic status, culture, gender, and other important variables. Using race as a dividing criterion to compare groups is appealing because it seems so simple, but it may mask great within-group variability.

THE MORAL SELF

One important ingredient in self-development is the acquisition of values. Colby and Damon (1992) found that adults who lead exemplary lives tend to have very clear beliefs about what is right, and they consider those beliefs to be a central feature of their own identities. Their self-esteem hinges on acting in responsible ways, consistent with their beliefs. Even for children in the middle years, behavioral conduct is an important self-concept domain that is linked to global self-esteem. Generally, moral beliefs are increasingly central to self-definition as children get older, influencing them to act in responsible ways, but as Damon points out,

> the development of the self can take many paths, and persons vary widely in the extent to which they look to their commitments and convictions in defining their personal identities. . . . For some . . . morality may always remain peripheral to who they think they are. (1995, p. 141)

In this section, we will examine some theories and research on how the moral self develops and why for some it is more compelling than for others.

Let's begin by specifying what we mean by a moral sense, or morality. First, it is a capacity to make judgments about what is right versus what is wrong, and second, it is preferring to act in ways that are judged to be "right." In other words, morality involves both an "evaluative orientation" toward actions and events (Damon, 1988) and a sense of obligation or commitment to behave in ways that are consistent with what is right. Early on, this sense of obligation is partly influenced by rewards or punishments from parents, teachers, and other adults. Gradually, a slate of standards and principles—a ***conscience***—is internalized (see discussion of self-regulation in Chapters 4 and 5) and becomes the primary guide to action, so that a moral adult could even behave in ways that are disapproved by others if she judged the behavior to be right.

It is also important to recognize that moral development and religious experience are not the same thing. Religions do, of course, address issues of morality, and they prescribe standards of conduct. But moral development is part of normal self-development in all individuals, regardless of whether they are practitioners of a religious faith or whether they receive formal religious training.

As we noted in the introduction to this chapter, it is not surprising that parents regard the development of morality as a critical concern. Even though there are cultural and historical variations in the specifics of what is construed as moral, the meaning of morality generally includes some social interactive principles or propensities that are necessary to the successful functioning of all societies and of individuals within society (see Damon, 1988; Turiel, 1998). First, *concern for others* is important, as well as a willingness to act on that concern by sharing, forgiving, and other acts of benevolence. Second, a *sense of justice and fairness,* including a willingness to take into account the rights and needs of all parties, is part of a moral sense. Third, *trustworthiness,* defined primarily as honesty in dealings with others, is critical to most discussions of morality. Finally, *self-control* is essential. To live by standards requires a capacity and willingness to inhibit one's own selfish or aggressive impulses under some circumstances, that is, to avoid misbehavior. This is one aspect of self-control. Also, to be a useful member of society, or even to fully develop one's talents or abilities, requires effort and persistence regardless of discomfort or difficulty. This is a second aspect of self-control—a willingness to do things that are not much fun, such as work and practicing skills, even when play is more enticing. For example, there may be no exciting way to learn multiplication tables. Hard work and self-control are necessary to achieve long-term goals at any point in the life span. Research on the development of morality has largely focused on this set of fundamentals: concern for others, justice, trustworthiness or honesty, and self-control.

Elements of Morality

Morality requires a complex interweaving of three elements—emotions, cognitions, and behaviors—which do not always work together in perfect harmony. Consider the following true-life experience. Several decades ago, in a blue-collar city neighborhood, 10-year-old Carmen headed for a local grocery store to buy some items for her mother. Her family never saw her alive again. But some other folks later did see her. They were motorists, driving at high speeds on an inner city expressway, heading home in the evening rush hour. They remembered seeing a girl who looked like Carmen, running naked along the edge of the expressway with a man following her. Apparently, she had escaped from his car when he parked along the side of the road. But none of the motorists stopped, and the man caught the girl. Her raped and beaten body was later found in a remote location.

In the days and weeks following Carmen's disappearance, first one motorist and then another either phoned police anonymously or came forward openly to describe what she or he had seen, although none had reported the incident when it happened. The city's inhabitants were horrified both by the crime and by the failure of the witnesses to help or to come forward immediately, but none were more distressed than the witnesses themselves. Their moral emotions—empathy and sympathy for the girl and her family, shame and guilt at their own failure to come to the girl's aid—were experienced by many as overwhelming. And these feelings were in many cases triggered from the beginning, when they first saw the naked child. Why did their behavior not match their feelings? Many witnesses reported confusion and disbelief when they passed the strange scene, and though they felt concern for the girl and guilt at their own inaction, they reasoned that there must be a sensible explanation, one that would make them feel foolish if they made the extraordinary effort to stop. Others indicated that it was impossible to process the events—so unexpected and atypical of their ordinary experience—in the split-second of decision making, and they had only "put it all together" when they heard about Carmen's disappearance on the news. Others thought that someone else would take care of it—after all, hundreds of motorists were passing the same spot—or that the risks of helping were too great.

Most adults believe that their behavior is usually consistent with their beliefs and/or feelings. But the witnesses to Carmen's plight illustrate that even adults with strong moral feelings do not always think clearly about moral issues or behave in ways that are consistent with their moral sense. Some of the earliest research on children's moral development indicated that children are particularly prone to such inconsistencies. Hartshorne and May (1928–1930) observed 10,000 children between the ages of 8 and 16 in a wide variety of situations where they had opportunities to lie, cheat, or steal. For example, children could raise their scores on a test by sneaking a look at an answer key, cheat on a test of strength, pilfer some change, or tell lies that would place them in a good light. In every situation, the researchers had devised techniques to surreptitiously detect cheating, lying, or stealing. They found that children's knowledge of moral standards did not coordinate with how likely they were to cheat or to help others to cheat. They also found that children's honesty varied from one situation to another. Some children cheated in academic tasks, for example, but not on tests of athletic skill. Hartshorne and May concluded that moral conduct is usually determined by the particular situation and is not coordinated with moral reasoning

Children's knowledge of moral standards is no guarantee of moral behavior, but synchrony among moral values, emotions, and behavior tends to increase with age.

or training. However, more recent research, with more adequate measures of children's emotions and cognitions, indicates that emotions, cognitions, and actions do tend to become more synchronized with age and that their interrelations are influenced by many factors, including training. Before we consider these many factors, let's take a brief look at some classic theories of moral development with which you may be familiar, theories that emphasize either emotions or cognitions as the most important source of moral behavior. How do these theories fare in light of modern research?

Some Classic Theories of Moral Development

Freud's Psychoanalytic Theory

In Freud's (1935/1960) psychoanalytic theory of moral development, the behavior of very young children is driven by the inborn impulses of the *id,* which are completely self-serving desires for sustenance and release, such as hunger or the need to defecate. The *superego,* which emerges in the preschool period, is the source of moral emotions, such as pride in good behavior and shame or guilt about bad behavior, and once a child has a superego, it is these emotions that impel moral functioning, like an internalized system of rewards and punishments. Freud argued that the superego develops when a complex set of id-driven motives and emotions come into conflict with parental authority. Specifically, beginning at about age 3, vague sexual desire for the opposite-sexed parent puts the young child in competition with the same-sexed parent, who is much more powerful than the child and thus a frightening competitor. The child's solution to this no-win situation is to identify with the same-sexed parent. **Identification** with the (imagined) aggressor is a solution for two reasons. First, by trying to be like the angry parent, a child wins the parent's approval and affection. Second, by pretending to be the parent, the child attains some vicarious satisfaction of her or his sexual longing for the other parent. The critical element of this situation for moral development is the identification process itself. *Identification* includes both imitation of the parent's behaviors and, most importantly, internalization of the parent's standards and values, creating the child's superego.

As we will see in the next chapter, the identification process described by Freud is an explanation of both moral development and sex role development in young children. Unfortunately, research fails to support its predictions. With regard to moral development, attributing moral emotions to the emergence of the superego, sometime between ages 3 and 5, is not consistent with findings that many toddlers show signs of empathy and shame as early as 18 to 24 months, beginning when they demonstrate self-recognition while looking in a mirror (e.g., Lewis & Michalson, 1983; see Chapter 5). By age 3, sympathy, pride, and guilt appear to be part of the emotional repertoire as well (e.g., Stipek, Recchia, & McClintic, 1992; see Chapter 4). In addition, even toddlers perform prosocial actions based on empathy, and sometimes they seem anxious to comply with a parent's rules, even if the parent is not around. Such early signs of conscience development undermine the psychoanalytic view that early behavior is driven only by selfish impulses (e.g., Kochanska, Casey, & Fukumoto, 1995; Kochanska, Tjebkes, & Forman, 1998; Turiel, 1998). Finally, and perhaps most importantly, Freud argued that children develop a conscience because they identify with a parent whom they fear. Yet, as we saw in Chapter 5, parents who intimidate their children are least successful in fostering the development of conscience. Rather, warmth, affection, and support are more likely to be characteristic of parents whose children exhibit signs of mature conscience formation—self-control in the absence of authority figures (e.g., Kochanska & Murray, 2000). We should note that psychoanalysts since Freud have increasingly explained conscience formation as linked to the bond between child and parent, that is, more as a function of the strength of attachment and the need to keep the parent close than as a function of fear (e.g., Emde, Biringen, et al., 1991).

The Cognitive Theories of Piaget and Kohlberg

While Freud focused on the impetus that emotions provide to moral behavior, cognitive theorists have emphasized the importance of changes in logical thinking as a source of moral development. To understand how children think about rules and standards of conduct, Piaget (1932/1965) presented children with moral dilemmas and asked them to both judge the behavior of the protagonists and explain what should be done. He also played marbles with children and asked them to describe and explain the rules of the game. Piaget proposed that preschoolers are **premoral** in the sense that they seem unconcerned about established rules or standards, making up their own as they go along in a game of marbles, for example, and having little regard even for their own rules. At about age 5, Piaget described children's morality as **heteronomous.** They regard rules as immutable, existing outside the self, and requiring strict adherence. So, 5-year-old Jasmine might argue that a rule should never be broken, even if some greater good might prevail or even if all the participants in a game agree to the change. When her older sister crosses the street without waiting for a "walk" signal, rushing to help a neighborhood toddler who has wandered into the street, Jasmine might insist that her sister should have waited for the signal no matter what. She might also judge that a boy who broke 15 cups trying to help his mother get ready for a party deserves more punishment than one who broke one cup while actually misbehaving. In heteronomous morality, the letter of the law must be followed, and failure to do so requires punishment. In fact, Jasmine might believe in **immanent justice,** expecting that misbehavior will eventually be punished, even if no one knows about it, as though some higher authority is always watching.

Piaget argued that heteronomy is based on the child's experiences in relationships with parents and other authority figures, where rules seem to come from above and must be obeyed. But in middle childhood, both experience with the give and take of peer relationships and advances in perspective-taking skill help children to see the rules of behavior differently. As children have more experience in egalitarian relationships with their peers, their moral thinking becomes more **autonomous,** meaning that children begin to understand that rules are based on social agreements and that they can be changed. Advancements in perspective-taking skills, which also are benefited by interactions with peers, help a child to understand that rules and standards are not just a function of authoritarian dictates but that they promote fair play and cooperation, serving to establish justice. They can also be set aside for some greater good or changed through negotiation. So, by about 9 or 10, Jasmine could support her sister's violation of their parents' rule about not crossing the street, recognizing the greater importance of protecting a younger child. Also, she would probably be more consistently well behaved than she was earlier, because, in Piaget's view, she has a better understanding of the value of rules and standards for social interaction.

Kohlberg (e.g., 1976, 1984) further investigated children's moral reasoning from late childhood into the adolescent and early adult years. His theory goes beyond Piaget's, offering a fine-grained analysis of changes in the older child's, adolescent's, and adult's reasoning about moral issues (see Table 7.2 for a comparison of ages and stages in Piaget's and Kohlberg's theories). Unlike Piaget's dilemmas, which focused on everyday challenges familiar in the lives of children, Kohlberg's stories were outside ordinary experience and raised broad philosophical issues. Perhaps the most famous of these is the story of Heinz, whose wife is very ill and will die without a certain medicine, which Heinz cannot afford. The druggist who makes the product refuses to sell it, though Heinz offers all the money

TABLE 7.2

Piaget's and Kohlberg's Stages in Moral Development

Approximate Ages	Piaget's Stages	Kohlberg's Stages
Preschool	*Premoral Period* Child is unconcerned about rules; makes up her own rules.	
		Preconventional Level
5 to 8 or 9 years	*Heteronomous Morality* Child is a *moral realist:* Rules are determined by authorities; are unalterable, moral absolutes; must be obeyed. Violations always punished.	*Stage 1: Punishment and obedience orientation* Child obeys to avoid punishment and because authority is assumed to be superior or right. Rules are interpreted literally; no judgment is involved.
8 or 9 to 11 or 12 years	*Autonomous Morality* Social rules are arbitrary, and promote cooperation, equality, and reciprocity; therefore, they serve justice. They can be changed by agreement or violated for a higher purpose.	*Stage 2: Concrete, individualistic orientation* Child follows rules to serve own interests. Others' interests may also need to be served, so follow the principle of fair exchange, e.g., "You scratch my back, I scratch yours."
		Conventional Level
13 to 16 years		*Stage 3: Social-relational perspective* Shared feelings and needs are more important than self-interest. Helpfulness, generosity, and forgiveness are idealized.
Late adolescents/ young adults		*Stage 4: Member-of-society perspective* The social order is most important now. Behaviors that contribute to functioning of social system are most valued, e.g., obeying laws, hard work.
		Postconventional Level
Some adults		*Stage 5: Prior rights and social contract* The social contract now is most valued. Specific laws are not most valued, but the process that they serve is, e.g., democratic principles, individual rights.
Some adults		*Stage 6: Universal ethical principles* Certain abstract moral principles are valued over anything else, e.g., above specific laws. Social order is also highly valued, unless it violates highest moral principles. (Theoretical; Kohlberg's subjects did not achieve this stage.)

Sources: Damon (1983); Kohlberg (1981); Piaget (1935/1965) Damon, W. (1988). *The moral child: Nurturing children's natural moral growth.* New York: Free Press; Kohlberg, L. (1984). *Essays on moral development: The psychology of moral development.* San Francisco: Harper & Row; Piaget, J. (1932/1965). *The moral judgment of the child.* New York: Free Press.

he has managed to raise—about half of the retail cost—which would more than cover the druggist's expenses. The druggist argues that he discovered the drug and plans to make money from it. In desperation, Heinz breaks into the druggist's establishment and steals the medicine.

Kohlberg was not interested in whether participants judged Heinz's behavior to be right or wrong, assuming that reasonable people might disagree. He focused instead on the reasons they gave for their judgments. He found there to be three levels of moral reasoning, each characterized by two stages. At the first level, elementary school children usually show **preconventional morality,** roughly corresponding to Piaget's heteronomous level, in which what is right is what avoids punishment, what conforms to the dictates of authority, or what serves one's personal interests. Then, young adolescents move to **conventional morality,** more consistent with Piaget's autonomous level, in which what is right depends on others' approval or on the need to maintain social order. Finally, by adulthood, some people move to **postconventional morality,** in which right is defined by universal principles or by standards of justice, not by the particular rule in question (see Table 7.2 for further elaboration of the stages within each level).

Although individuals at different levels of moral reasoning might come to the same conclusion about what is "right," their explanations reveal that they come to their decisions by different routes. Compare the "pro-stealing" decisions of Jay and Jesse when given the "Heinz" dilemma to resolve. Jay, a preconventional thinker, bases his choice on personal need:

> Heinz should take the drug, because the druggist won't really suffer, and Heinz needs to save his wife.

Jesse, a conventional thinker, bases her decision on the importance of others' agreement or approval:

> Heinz should take the drug, because nobody would blame him for wanting to keep his wife alive. They might blame him if he didn't.

There is some research support for the general trends in moral reasoning suggested in the work of Piaget and of Kohlberg. Consistent with Piaget's view, for example, when young children judge moral culpability they usually pay more attention to consequences (e.g., the number of cups broken by a child who is helping his mother prepare for a party), whereas older children pay more attention to intentions (e.g., whether the child was helping or misbehaving). Consistent with Kohlberg's view, young people around the world progress through the levels of moral reasoning—preconventional, conventional, and postconventional—in the same, invariant order (e.g., Colby, Kohlberg, Gibbs, & Lieberman, 1983; Colby & Kohlberg, 1987), although even many adults do not progress beyond the conventional level of reasoning. Perhaps most important, the role of perspective taking and peer interactions in the growth of moral reasoning skills, emphasized both by Piaget and by Kohlberg, has been supported. For example, advances in perspective-taking skills such as those described in Chapter 5 generally precede, although they do not guarantee, advances in moral reasoning (e.g., Tomlinson-Keasey & Keasey, 1974; Walker, 1980). Also, when children discuss moral issues with their peers they are more likely to think carefully about the ideas and to advance in their reasoning than when they discuss those issues with adults (e.g., Kruger, 1992; Kruger & Tomasello, 1986). Perhaps challenges from a peer may seem less threatening and create less defensiveness than challenges from adults (Walker & Taylor, 1991).

Limitations of Classic Cognitive Theories. Despite the support that these cognitive approaches to explaining moral development have received, their usefulness is limited in

Box 7.1 **Morality as an Educational Goal**

In 1917, W. J. Hutchins published the *Children's Code of Morals for Elementary Schools,* emphasizing "ten laws of right living": self-control, good health, kindness, sportsmanship, self-reliance, duty, reliability, truth, good workmanship, and teamwork. Hutchins's code was a widely used educational resource, supporting a character education movement that spanned the first three decades of the 1900s. This was a time of enormous change in the United States, marked by technological advances, population shifts that included immigration surges, and social and moral upheavals. Educators expressed concern about family breakups, increased political corruption and crime, media cynicism, and the decline of religion. Modern movie portrayals of speakeasies, crime syndicates, and loose morals in the "Roaring Twenties" probably capture some of the issues that Americans feared were having a detrimental influence on the youth of the day. Educators implemented character education by suffusing daily school activities with lessons in right living and by initiating student clubs where moral behavior could be practiced (see Leming, 1997; McClellan, 1992).

As we saw in our discussion of moral development (this chapter), a massive study by Hartshorne and May, published in the late 1920s, led those researchers to conclude that moral training had little impact on children's moral behavior. These rather disconcerting results may have dampened educators' fervor for organized programs of character education. However, some features of these programs continue even today to be typical of most schools in the United States, such as student clubs and activity groups and "conduct" grades on report cards.

In the mid-1960s, there was a new surge of educational interest in what was now deemed "moral education," fueled by theory and research on moral reasoning and by renewed social interest. Several approaches to moral education became available to teachers, but the two most influential were Kohlberg's (1966) own prescription for translating his cognitive developmental model of moral reasoning into educational practice and a "values clarification approach" to moral education by Raths, Harmin, and Simon (1966). Although the latter approach provided a more detailed formula for teachers and students to follow and was probably more widely used, both approaches focused on encouraging students to examine their own thinking about morality and to come to their own conclusions. Teachers were to act as facilitators, but they were not to impose any code or value system on students. Kohlberg's approach heavily emphasized peer discussions of moral dilemmas as a technique; "values clarification" provided a valuing process for students to follow as they critically examined the values they had learned thus far.

Many criticisms were leveled at these and other similar approaches to moral education. There is some limited evidence that peer discussions, skillfully facilitated by teachers, can help children and adolescents advance beyond their current level of moral reasoning (using Kohlbergian measures, e.g., Berkowitz & Gibbs, 1983). But teachers found the facilitation of such discussions difficult, and they worried about some of their efforts ending in children rationalizing unacceptable behavior (Leming, 1986, 1997).

Support for the "moral education" movement had waned by the 1980s. But a new surge of interest in character education has emerged in the last decade or so, fueled again by social concern with what appear to be declining morals. Parents and community leaders are looking to schools to develop systematic approaches to character development, hoping to counter rising crime and violence, increasing conduct problems in the schools, and apparently widespread malaise and disaffection even among our most affluent and privileged young people (see text, this chapter and Chapter 11). Like the character education programs of the early 1900s, newer programs focus on what their authors regard as widely accepted, even universal, standards of conduct. They often have two integrated goals: helping children understand why these standards are important and encouraging behavior consistent with these standards. Clearly, the current programs are more prescriptive than those developed in the 1960s and 1970s, but they are usually aimed at general standards that most people would agree are important (Glanzer, 1998).

Schools often develop their own character education plans, but there are many packaged programs available to teachers. Some of the latter have been the subject of systematic outcome research; many have not. Let's consider briefly one program that incorporates some of the values targeted by most other programs and that uses a broad range of teaching strategies (from Leming, 1997).

Titled the "Child Development Project," (Developmental Studies Center, 1996), this program has the advantage of having been the focus of several evaluation studies. Designed for kindergarten through sixth grade, the program has as one goal to integrate ethical

(continued)

Box 7.1   Continued

development with all aspects of social and intellectual development. To establish four core values (fairness, concern and respect for others, helpfulness, and responsibility), teachers use five techniques: focusing children's attention on prosocial examples of conduct; applying cooperative learning techniques; using examples from literature as well as real-life incidents to encourage a focus on others' needs and rights; involving children in helping activities; encouraging self-control and moral reasoning by using an authoritative disciplinary style. There's more: the program is implemented schoolwide and includes a home program as well. A number of studies have compared children in the Child Development Project to a comparison group, using interview, questionnaire, and behavioral data. Leming (1997) summarizes the results as follows:

> statistically significant program effects have been detected for the following variables: a) self-esteem, b) sensitivity and consideration of others' needs, c) spontaneous prosocial behavior, d) interpersonal harmoniousness, e) preference for democratic values, and f) conflict resolution skills. (p. 18)

(See Leming, 1997, for a comparison of ten programs, including this one.)

It appears that character education that has clear goals and specifies sound techniques for implementing those goals can be effective in encouraging some aspects of moral thinking, feeling, and behavior. Critics have raised concerns about at least some programs, worrying that children may be indoctrinated, drilled in specific behaviors rather than being encouraged to engage "in deep, critical reflection about certain ways of being" (Kohn, 1997). Indeed, if character education is based on drill and coercion, teachers can be expected to be no more effective in fostering the internalization of values than parents who use authoritarian techniques. But many character educators recognize such dangers. They encourage schools to include reasoning, emotions, and behavior in their notion of "character." They also foster the notion that character education must begin with the "character" of the school itself, which should be a caring community that shows respect toward all individuals and provides adult models of character (Character Education Partnership, 1995; see Lickona, 1998). Supporters also argue that many values are indeed shared across diverse religious, ethnic, geographic, and political communities and that if educators are careful to focus on these, character education makes sense (e.g., Benninga & Wynne, 1998; Damon, 1988, 1996; Etzioni, 1998; Glanzer, 1998; Lickona, 1998).

several ways. First, young children have a greater capacity for moral reasoning than Piaget's theory indicates. For example, although young children judge people's actions by their physical consequences (such as how many cups are broken) more than older children do, still they are capable of focusing on the intentions behind behavior if those intentions are made salient (e.g., S. A. Nelson, 1980; M. Siegel & Peterson, 1998; Zelazo, Helwig, & Lau, 1996). In one study, even preschoolers could tell the difference between intentional lying and unintentional mistakes, and they judged real liars more harshly than bunglers (M. Siegel and Peterson, 1998).

Another important challenge to Piaget's theory is the finding that young children do not necessarily treat all rules and standards as equally important just because they are specified by parents or other authority figures. Moral philosophers point out that some standards, called **moral rules,** address fundamental moral issues of justice, welfare, and rights, such as rules about stealing, hurting others, or sharing. Other standards, called **conventional rules,** are more arbitrary and variable from one culture to another and are a function of social agreement, such as rules about appropriate dress, forms of address, and table manners. Finally, there are areas of functioning that individuals or families might have standards about—such as choices of friends or recreational activities or participation in family life—which are not governed by formal social rules in Western societies. We'll call these **personal rules** (see Turiel, 1998). Piaget assumed that young children treat all rules as "handed down from above," that is, as determined by authority figures. But researchers have found that even by age 3, children are more likely to judge violations of moral rules as more serious than violations of conventional rules (e.g., Smetana & Braeges, 1990). And by ages 4 or 5 they believe that such moral rules should be obeyed despite what authority figures might say (e.g., Crane & Tisak, 1995; Smetana, Schlagman, & Adams, 1993; Tisak, 1993). For example, at 5, Jasmine believed it would be wrong to steal even if there were no laws against it and even if a friend's mother said it was okay. As children get older, they make clearer and clearer distinctions between moral and conventional rules, so that by age 9 or 10 children accurately categorize even unfamiliar rules (Davidson, Turiel, & Black, 1983). Turiel (1978) reexamined data from Hartshorne and May's (1928–1930) classic study of children's honesty and found that the participants were much more likely to cheat in academic tasks than they were to steal when given an easy opportunity. He argued that children probably saw the academic tasks as governed by conventional rules whereas stealing more clearly violates a moral rule.

By adolescence, children assume that their parents have a right to regulate and enforce moral behavior; they usually accept parents' regulation of conventional behavior as well, although there is more conflict with their parents in this domain than in the moral arena. Finally, with regard to personal issues such as appearance, spending, and friendship choices, adolescents balk at parental regulation, often arguing that parents have no legitimate authority in this domain (Smetana, 1988; Smetana & Asquith, 1994). Interestingly, Arnett (1999) has recently argued that parents may push for their right to control personal behavior more as a function of how they judge that behavior (e.g., in some instances they may see it as crossing over into the moral domain) than because they are reluctant to grant their children personal freedom. So, in other words, parents and adolescents may differ in how they categorize rules and regulations. We will address this issue again in Chapter 10.

Like Piaget's theory, Kohlberg's view seems to have some important limitations. When moral issues beyond the legalistic ones studied by Kohlberg are examined, both adults' and children's reasoning seems to include factors not described by Kohlberg. Gilligan (e.g., 1977; 1982) has argued that moral development follows different trajectories for males and females. She views Kohlberg's legalistic moral dilemmas and his approach to scoring people's reasoning as biased toward representing a more typically masculine approach to morality. Her concern is that Kohlberg's theory and the research it inspires tends to disregard the "different voice" women use in their approach to moral decision making. Males, she argues, are more likely to use a justice focus (sometimes called the "*morality of justice*") while females are more likely to use a caring focus ("*morality of caring*").

In her own research on moral reasoning, Gilligan (1977; Gilligan & Attanucci, 1988) included more practical dilemmas that are representative of the complex problems real people face, such as struggling with how to deal with an unplanned pregnancy. Although she found no significant differences in moral orientation (care versus justice) between males and females, she did report some tendency in her data for men to focus on issues of justice and for women to focus on caring issues. However, her major finding has been that *both* women and men are concerned about *both* justice and caring and that together these concerns contribute to mature moral reasoning. Perhaps the most valuable contribution of Gilligan's critique of Kohlberg's work is that she raised awareness of the need to study real-life moral problem solving and addressed the role that concerns about caring play in moral judgments. (Gilligan's ideas and related research on gender and moral reasoning are revisited in Chapter 8 in the discussion of gender development and in Chapter 11 in the discussion of relativistic thinking.)

Damon (1988) has studied children's thinking about real-life dilemmas in a child's world and has found that children consider matters of fairness even at ages when Kohlberg's scheme would assume they would not. For example, in studies of sharing and distributive justice, preschoolers and young school-age children rarely justify acts of sharing on the basis of concern about punishment, as one might expect if they were at Kohlberg's preconventional stage. Rather, they talk about fairness, and if their actions do not quite measure up to what we might consider fair, they at least seem to feel a need to somehow explain why their selfish choices might actually be fair. Consider the following exchange between a 4-year-old and a researcher, when the child is asked if she would share some poker chips with an imaginary friend. The child initially decides to keep seven of nine chips, including all the blue ones and some of the white ones, and gives her friend "Jenny" two white ones:

> You would keep all the blues for yourself? *Yes, because I like blue. And then I'd play with them.* Let's pretend Jenny said, "I like blue." Would you give her any blue? *Never, because I have a blue dress at home.* So you wouldn't give her any blue at all. Is it fair to do it this way? *Ah ha, I've got it. I'd give her two (more) of the white—I'd give her those because she's younger than me, and I get four because I'm four.* (Damon, 1988, pp. 37–38)

Even though the child's reasoning cannot disguise her blatant self-interest, she seems to feel an obligation to share (she gives away some white ones), and she wants to believe that she is being fair. Older elementary school children, still at a preconventional level of reasoning in Kohlberg's scheme, often try to balance a complex set of concerns in deciding what is fair, concerns not captured by Kohlberg's descriptions. As Damon (1988) indicates, children can now also take into account hard work, poverty, talent, and issues of equality when trying to assess the best ways of distributing property or remuneration. Consider the reasoning of an older elementary school child who is asked how children in a hypothetical classroom should distribute their earnings from sales of some of their artwork:

> What if Rebecca made more stuff? Should she get more money? *Oh, about seven more pennies. It depends on what she made—if she made something easy or hard.* What if she made something hard? *About ten cents more.* What about Peter, who made the best stuff? *Well, maybe he should. But since she (Rebecca) made more, she may have some good ones (too), so then maybe he can get around five cents more.* What about Billy, who doesn't get any allowance? *He should only get about three cents more, because—if he got a lot more, he might even have more than anybody adding up their allowance.* What about these others? *No, because they don't have such a big reason.* (Damon, 1988, p. 42)

Children's moral considerations can be far more complex and wide ranging than Kohlberg's scheme conveys.

Another limitation of Kohlberg's work seems to be his assumption that moral reasoning is the prime determiner of children's moral behavior. As we have seen, moral reasoning is only imperfectly coordinated with action. Yet counselors who work with parents and teachers are often most concerned with encouraging children's moral behavior. In the next section, we will examine the many factors that influence children's *prosocial* or *antisocial* behavior.

Children's Prosocial Behavior

When a child voluntarily acts in ways that seem intended to benefit someone else, we credit her with **prosocial behavior** or **altruism.** While prosocial behaviors are observed even in toddlers, they tend to increase with age, from preschool to grade school ages and continuing into adolescence (Eisenberg & Fabes, 1998). Altruistic tendencies are different from one child to another, and individual differences tend to be somewhat stable across age. In other words, a child who shows prosocial inclinations as a preschooler is somewhat more likely than other children to produce prosocial behavior in grade school.

Sharing, comforting a friend, helping a neighbor carry her groceries, collecting canned goods for victims of a flood—all are examples of simple prosocial behaviors that we might see from a child. You can probably see that while behaviors such as these benefit others, they can be motivated in many ways and could even provide some social reward to the benefactor. Sharing, for example, can help a child maintain a pleasant interaction.

When 15-month-old Nadia went trick-or-treating for the first time, as soon as an indulgent neighbor would put a treat in her bag, Nadia would reach into the bag and offer the neighbor a treat as well. She seemed to be sharing, literally, for the fun of the social exchange. When a child successfully comforts a crying friend she might be trying to regain her playmate's company. Or when she participates in an organized effort to provide relief to flood victims she may be hoping for positive attention from teachers or parents. For developmentalists, labeling an action altruistic or prosocial only specifies that it benefits someone other than the perpetrator, not that unselfish motives are necessarily involved. Let's consider what factors have been found to influence the development of prosocial action in children, with an eye toward understanding how counselors and other adults might be able to promote children's prosocial tendencies.

Emotions as a Source of Helping Behavior

In many cases, our emotional reactions to others' distress can be an important source of helping behavior, and the emotion of *empathy* may be the "linchpin" (Hoffman, 1982; Kagan, 1984). *Empathy* can be thought of as "feeling with" another person—recognizing her emotional condition and experiencing what she is assumed to be feeling. Hoffman (1982) argued that children have a biological predisposition toward empathy, the earliest hint of which may be the contagious crying of some infants, that is, their tendency to cry when they hear other babies crying. *Sympathy,* an emotion related to empathy, involves "feeling for" another, that is, having concern for the other person, but not necessarily sharing the feelings of the other. Both empathy and sympathy seem to propel some prosocial acts from the time that toddlers begin to clearly differentiate self from other (e.g., Miller, Eisenberg, Fabes, & Shell, 1996; Zahn-Waxler, Cole, Welsh, & Fox, 1995; Zahn-Waxler, Robinson, & Emde, 1992; see Chapter 5). Note, too, that children's empathic responses are also associated with their tendencies to inhibit antisocial behavior, as we will see in the next section. Toddlers' early helping behavior may be the result of their empathic feelings, but they still have little capacity to take another's point of view. Hoffman, for example, described the charmingly egocentric effort of a 13-month-old who sought out his own mother to comfort a crying toddler, even though the other child's mother was readily available.

While empathy and sympathy are evident in young children, their tendency to lead to effective prosocial action increases substantially with age, especially after the preschool years. Children's improving perspective-taking skills are an important ingredient. One reason appears to be that better role-taking ability can help a child to understand how another is feeling and thereby increase the child's own empathic response (Roberts & Strayer, 1996). Also, increased understanding of another's emotions and thoughts should help a child assess what kind of prosocial action, if any, is likely to be beneficial.

In late childhood, the scope of empathy expands, probably influenced by increasing abilities to think about abstractions. Whereas younger children can empathize with particular people whom they observe, older children and adolescents can empathize with whole groups of people who are living in unfortunate circumstances, such as all those suffering from a famine, or from the abrogation of their rights, and so on (Hoffman, 1982).

Clearly, as important as prosocial emotions may be for altruistic behavior, other influences interact with those emotions in complex ways. These include not only advances in cognitive abilities such as perspective taking and abstract thinking, but also individual temperamental and personality characteristics, parenting practices, and peer experiences. Also, prosocial behavior involves more than helping another in need. Behavior such as Nadia's spontaneous sharing of her Halloween treats often occurs in the absence of any apparent need on the part of the other and therefore seems not to rest on emotions like empathy or sympathy. Let's take a look at some of the other factors that can influence prosocial action.

Cognitive Contributions to Prosocial Behavior

Let's first consider how reasoning about other people's needs (called **needs-based reasoning**) changes with age, and then we will look at its relation to children's prosocial behavior. In needs-based reasoning, one must weigh one's own personal needs against those of others. For example, Eisenberg and her colleagues have posed moral dilemmas to children in which a child's needs are in competition with the needs of another. In one story, a child, on her way to a party, comes upon another child who has fallen and broken her leg. The first child must decide whether to continue on to the party, which is very important to her, or to find the parents of the injured child. (Compare this dilemma, focused on caring and concern, to Kohlberg's problems in social justice, like the story of Heinz and the druggist.) Eisenberg has found that preschoolers tend to be **hedonistic**—concerned for their own needs. By early elementary school, many children express recognition that another person's need is a good reason for helping—they are **needs oriented**—but they often do not express sympathy, nor do they talk about feeling guilty for not helping. By later elementary school, children begin to express a recognition that helping is what is required or socially approved. At the next stage, in late elementary school or adolescence, expressions of sympathy for others, guilt about inaction, and to some minimal degree, reference to duty, become part of the reasoning process. Finally, some adolescents begin talking of the relationship of helping to one's self-respect and of being consistent with one's values. For these youngsters, it appears, moral values are becoming a core aspect of their self-concept (e.g., Eisenberg, Lennon & Roth, 1983).

We have seen in our discussion of the cognitive theories of moral development that moral reasoning is somewhat related to moral behavior. If the kind of moral reasoning that is assessed is similar to the kind of moral behavior, there is a stronger (but still moderate) relationship between reasoning and behavior. This is particularly true of needs-based reasoning and altruistic behavior. In middle childhood and adolescence, more advanced levels of needs-based reasoning tend to be associated with certain kinds of prosocial behavior. Specifically, if the behavior requires some real personal sacrifice, such as volunteering some free time after school, kids whose moral reasoning is more advanced are more likely to participate. Prosocial behaviors that incur little or no cost, such as helping a teacher to pick up the papers she has just dropped, are likely to occur regardless of a child's moral reasoning (e.g., Eisenberg, Shell, Pasternack, Lennon, Beller, & Mathy, 1987).

Interestingly, moral reasoning, which is likely to be benefited by interaction with peers (Tesson, Lewko, & Bigelow, 1987), tends to be more advanced in popular children with good social skills, at least for boys. Bear and Rys (1994) found that boys who tended to be aggressive and to have poor peer relations were also low in needs-oriented reasoning. One explanation may be that children with poor social skills have fewer opportunities for positive peer interactions, contributing to a lag in the development of their moral-reasoning skills. A number of intervention programs, designed to promote children's moral functioning, including prosocial behavior and self-control, are focused on using peer discussions. For example, Gibbs (1987) describes a technique using small-group discussions aimed at encouraging empathic responding in delinquents. Actual problem incidents are recreated and discussed, and both peers and adults provide feedback to a participant about their own emotional reactions to the incident and to the participant's attitudes and emotions. Many violence prevention programs incorporate components designed to foster empathy development. We will have more to say about prevention in the next chapter.

Personality factors, like sociability, are linked to prosocial behavior in children.

Another interesting observation is that for younger children whose moral reasoning may be "needs oriented" but at the most primitive level, their tendency to engage in prosocial behavior is especially dependent on their prosocial emotions—empathy and sympathy. With children at more advanced levels of prosocial reasoning, reasoning is better matched to prosocial action regardless of how strong their prosocial emotions are (Miller, Eisenberg, Fabes, et al., 1996; see also Eisenberg & Fabes, 1998). These findings demonstrate that different children can follow different paths to prosocial conduct, suggesting that counselors and other helpers should be able to gain inroads in moral development via more than one route.

Temperament, Personality, and Prosocial Behavior

As we saw earlier, children who are prosocial in one situation are somewhat more likely than other children to be prosocial in other situations. Also, there is some consistency in the tendency to behave altruistically from early childhood through later childhood. These kinds of observations imply that temperamental or personality variables that are relatively stable across place and time might foster an "altruistic personality" (Eisenberg & Fabes, 1998). What might these characteristics be?

First, children's relative sociability or shyness might be an influence. Children who score low on social anxiety (behavioral inhibition or shyness) are a little more likely to help others than children who score high on this trait, especially when no one has requested their help, when assisting another requires initiating a social interaction, or when helping involves a stranger (e.g., Eisenberg, Pasternack, Cameron, & Tryon, 1984; Stanhope, Bell, & Parker-Cohen, 1987; Suda & Fouts, 1980).

Second, as we saw in our discussion of moral reasoning, socially competent children who are popular with peers tend to show greater levels of empathy and of prosocial behavior (Adams, 1983; Eisenberg et al., 1996). It is difficult to sort out which is cause and which is effect in this relationship, but it seems likely that social competence and prosocial behavior are mutually causal, with several other intervening influences involved as well.

Children who are empathic, for example, may do better at perspective taking, making them more appealing social partners, and may have closer friendships. The opportunities this creates for peer interaction help boost their perspective-taking skills, which in turn benefits their moral reasoning and empathy, and so on.

Another of these feedback loops may underlie a different link between personality and altruism: older children and adolescents with a positive global self-concept generally tend to be more prosocial than other children (e.g., Larrieu & Mussen, 1986). Feeling competent and secure may help a child both to focus her attention on others and to believe that her help will be effective. But helping others also is likely to foster feelings of competency and self worth (Damon, 1988, 1995; Yates & Youniss, 1996).

On the other side of the coin, assertiveness is another personality variable tied to prosocial behavior. This characteristic helps to illustrate that even though there is some tendency for individual children to be prosocial in many situations, there is also a great deal of situation-specific altruism. Assertive children, who will, for example, defend their possessions, are likely to be prosocial in situations where no one has asked them to help, probably because offering assistance is, at least in part, an assertive act. Children who are not assertive are usually prosocial when it is requested of them, not when they must take the social initiative themselves. Their prosocial behavior seems to be based more on compliance than that of assertive children. It should be noted also that children whose behavior goes beyond assertiveness to being domineering are actually less likely than other children to behave altruistically, regardless of the situation (see Eisenberg & Fabes, 1998).

Parents, Peers, and Prosocial Behavior

In Chapter 5 we began an examination of parenting behaviors and of the development of self-control, compliance, prosocial behavior, and conscience in infants and preschoolers. We observed that these aspects of moral development are on the whole most effectively launched when parents are authoritative in their style: on the one hand, warm, responsive and sensitive in their caregiving and, on the other hand, demanding, requiring that children live up to standards and values appropriate to their level of maturity (see Maccoby & Martin, 1983; Baumrind, 1989, 1993). The methods of control that seem to foster internalization of those standards and values in the long run involve mild *power assertion*, sufficient only to capture the child's attention but not to arouse a lot of anxiety, and *induction* (explaining why it is important to share, for example). It should be noted that parents who are demanding without warmth and sensitivity (the authoritarian style) may actually interfere with prosocial development. At least for toddlers, this parenting style has been associated with reductions in children's empathic responding (J. L. Robinson et al., 1994). Extremes of negative parenting, resulting in child abuse, seem to suppress prosocial responding to others' distress and promote more negative responding, such as aggression (e.g., Main & George, 1985).

In middle childhood, the same conclusions about what elements of parenting are most effective in promoting prosocial behavior (and inhibiting antisocial behavior) still apply. There are also a number of other specific characteristics of parenting that seem to foster children's altruism. First, when parents have strong prosocial values, their elementary school–aged children are more likely to be seen by peers as prosocial (Hoffman, 1975). Similarly, adults who show unusual prosocial tendencies, such as "rescuers" of Nazi victims in Europe during World War II, frequently report having had parents who strongly valued caring and helping behaviors (Oliner & Oliner, 1988).

Second, adult modeling of prosocial behavior seems to influence children's altruism. On the whole, models who are perceived by children as competent, models who have long-term, nurturant relationships with children, and models who express happiness after prosocial behavior (rather than receiving tangible rewards for their behavior) tend to foster children's prosocial behavior (see Eisenberg & Fabes, 1998).

Finally, providing children with opportunities for prosocial action seems to help encourage a commitment to altruistic action. Eisenberg and Fabes (1998) call this "the foot in the door effect." For example, Eisenberg, Cialdini, et al. (1987) found that starting in middle childhood, children who are encouraged to donate in one context are more likely to engage in helping behavior later in another context. This was mostly true for children who valued being consistent. It may be that once children begin to form a stable self-concept, they are more likely to value consistency, and that practicing prosocial behavior then fosters further prosocial activities as children seek to maintain a coherent self-concept. But there are probably other benefits to practice in some contexts, such as gaining increased feelings of competence and obtaining social approval (Eisenberg & Fabes, 1998).

Children's Antisocial Behavior

Jason, at 3 years of age, is a high-energy youngster who is active and playful. Most days, he engages in regular bouts of toy grabbing, aggressive play, and fighting. His behavior definitely has an impulsive quality to it: strike now and think later! Two years later at age 5, Jason is still going strong. He communicates his strong-willed temperament in frequent temper tantrums over household rules. His developing language ability permits him to be more argumentative with parents and peers than he had been earlier. Problems with disobedience occur at home and at school. Jason frequently refuses to go to bed on time, pick up his toys, or take a bath. In an occasional squabble with a preschool classmate, Jason may throw something or hit the other child. His teacher finds him a challenge to her patience and her classroom management skills.

Stop for a moment and reflect on 5-year-old Jason's behavior. How would you evaluate this youngster? Do you consider his behavior normal or problematic? If you perceive a problem, what would you do to help? Now consider him at age 8. He is in the third grade. His aggressive behaviors have persisted. He is not well liked by classmates and has difficulty fitting into the social fabric of the class. His academic performance is marginal. Jason has begun to steal toys and money from his classmates and has been caught vandalizing property belonging to one of his neighbors. How would you assess Jason's problems now? Are you more concerned about him? What would you advise?

Pathways of Antisocial Behavior

The development of antisocial behavior differs in some significant ways from the prosocial pathways we have been describing. Earlier chapters have detailed the kinds of positive support children need to develop well. This chapter adds to that picture by including the importance of healthy self-concept, self-control, and the achievement of competence and character as functions of a moral self in middle childhood. Just as we know a great deal about what is good for children's development, a wealth of recent research has illuminated our understanding of what might lead certain children toward more antisocial outcomes. This knowledge base is, admittedly, incomplete, but it is far from being merely suggestive. In this section, we will describe some of the findings that can lead us to a clearer understanding of the dynamics typically present in the lives of children like Jason.

Antisocial behavior is somewhat difficult to define, although it is usually characterized by the presence of aggression or the intent to harm another person. Recent formulations have recognized that antisocial behavior in adolescence and adults may also include such acts as risky sexual activity, substance abuse, defiance, cheating, lying, and vandalism (Jessor, Donovan, & Costa, 1991). Antisocial behavior can be both *overt,* such as hitting, and *covert,* such as cheating. Clinicians may identify youth who behave in antisocial ways as oppositional-defiant or conduct-disordered.

What sets the child's life course in this direction? One way to conceptualize this is to think of several possible developmental pathways that can eventually lead to antisocial outcomes in adolescence and adulthood. One pathway, which we might think of as the *early-starter model* (Moffitt, 1993b), has a life-course trajectory that is characterized by the presence of oppositional behavior that begins early, persists and diversifies over time, and becomes increasingly more serious. A second pathway for late starters, whose experience with delinquent activities begins at adolescence, is less likely to result in adult criminality. This pattern, called *adolescent-onset* antisocial behavior, although serious, seems to be more reflective of a difficult or exaggerated reaction to the adolescent period. Both pathways are more complicated than they seem, and others have identified variations on these two pathways (e.g., Loeber et al., 1993). However, early- and late-starter patterns remain among the best understood. We will expand on these topics in Chapter 10.

What might we predict from Jason's behavior? In general, there is strong evidence for the continuity of antisocial behavior from early childhood through adulthood (L. N. Robins, 1978). People diagnosed as having *antisocial personality disorder* as adults almost always report histories of conduct problems in childhood and adolescence. Roughly two thirds of 3-year-olds who display extreme problems with impulsivity and defiance continue to show these behaviors at age 8, and these early problems are related to further difficulties in school (S. B. Campbell, 1987). Children diagnosed with *oppositional defiant disorder (ODD)* or *conduct disorder* in early adolescence have typically shown these problems since childhood (Lahey, Loeber, Quay, Frick, & Grimm, 1992).

On the other hand, oppositional behaviors such as those depicted in Jason's case are relatively normal for young children of 4 and 5 (Achenbach & Edelbrock, 1983). Sometimes caregivers fail to appreciate the normal variations that occur in activity level and willfulness. The important thing to remember is that in the less extreme cases these oppositional behaviors tend to recede around age 8. The developmental course that is problematic is one in which these behaviors are maintained into elementary school, then enlarged and expanded upon in more delinquent ways. Like a storm that gathers strength as it moves along, early antisocial behaviors in certain cases are compounded by related problems in classrooms and peer groups that often trap youngsters in a downward spiral.

Influences on the Development of Antisocial Behavior

What sets this early trajectory in motion? It appears that there are a number of possible factors that, if present, point to the likelihood of antisocial outcomes. These factors are internal as well as external and operate in synergistic fashion, potentiating each other. If present without benefit of counterbalancing positive influences, the negative factors may be experienced as chronic and cumulative stressors, which place the individual at increasing risk for maladaptive outcomes (Garmezy & Masten, 1994). It is very important to remember, however, that the simple presence of risk factors in a child's life is not straightforwardly deterministic. Although the evidence for continuity of antisocial behavior is strong, there is also evidence for discontinuity, such as when a teacher, coach, or other adult steps in to help a child at a critical juncture or when a family moves out of poverty. Other environmental events, such as effective treatment and prevention programs (see Chapter 8 for more about prevention) can also turn a child's life around. Children who function well despite environmental risks, or who might even grow from them, are called *resilient.*

Physiological and Neuropsychological Influences. Certain physiological and neuropsychological characteristics have been identified as markers of risk for aggression and antisocial behavior. Children who had "difficult" temperaments as babies have been found to have significantly more behavior problems at age 3 than other children (Bates, Maslin, & Frankel, 1985), but only those preschool children with difficult infant temperaments who *also* had inadequate parenting appear to be at risk for maladaptive behavior in late childhood (e.g., Coon, Carey, Corley, & Fulker, 1992). Some research supports the relation of hormones, specifically testosterone, to heightened aggressiveness, although it is difficult to specify direction of effect. In other words, do hormones lead to aggression or does aggression increase hormone levels? Arguing for an interactionist position, Archer (1994) reported that testosterone levels were positively related to aggression and competitiveness but also that success in competitive activities, such as winning a fight, itself led to increased levels of testosterone. Neuropsychological risk factors, such as deficits in attention accompanied by impulsivity, have been associated with the development of conduct problems as well (Hinshaw, 1987). In general, difficulties with inhibition of behavioral responses that coexist with high activity levels appear to set the stage for conflictual behavior management situations at home and school. In time, the child whose behavior frequently provokes parents, teachers, and peers and who receives a steady diet of negative feedback from them ultimately defines herself as deviant (Coie & Dodge, 1998). Finally, weaknesses in verbal skills and problem-solving abilities, which have been tied to such factors as prenatal teratogens, early deprivation, or heritability, reduce the child's ability to cope with problems verbally, to understand consequences, or to take others' perspectives (Moffitt & Lynam, 1994). Instead, such weaknesses encourage reliance on physical means of conflict resolution.

Environmental Influences. Environmental factors can be divided into those operating at a more distal level (e.g., socioeconomic variables) and those exerting a more proximal influence (e.g., parenting practices). These factors interact with a child's internal characteristics to place some children at greater risk for developing antisocial patterns. As we mentioned earlier, these risks operate cumulatively, incrementally increasing the likelihood of maladaptation.

Distal influences such as poverty, substandard housing, low levels of parental education, large family size, inadequate educational opportunities, exposure to violence, and frequent residential moves exert great stress on family resources and are related to less than optimal conditions for child rearing (M. Rutter & Giller, 1983). Such conditions also heighten the risk of physical abuse, which is clearly related to later aggressive behavior (Cicchetti, 1989).

More proximal influences include the characteristics of the parent-child relationship. Much of the current research on the early antecedents of antisocial behavior focuses on parent-child socialization practices. Patterson's influential model of **coercive family interaction** describes how children learn to act aggressively (see Figure 7.2). Based upon the concept of negative reinforcement, Patterson and his associates have shown that young children learn to escape aversive consequences (such as turning off the TV) by whining, complaining, having tantrums, and so on, which cause parents to give up their demands for compliance (Snyder & Patterson, 1995). As soon as parents or caregivers cooperate with the child by backing off, the child reinforces the adults by stopping the unpleasant behavior (whining or crying). Sooner or later, these parents learn that the best way to escape or avoid the unpleasant situation their children create is by giving in to their children's demands. Thus, aggressive children reinforce parental cessation of demands by providing their parents with some short-lived peace and quiet. In such coercive interaction sequences, fairly typical in families of antisocial children, children are trained in the effectiveness of aggressive noncompliance and learn powerful parent-control strategies.

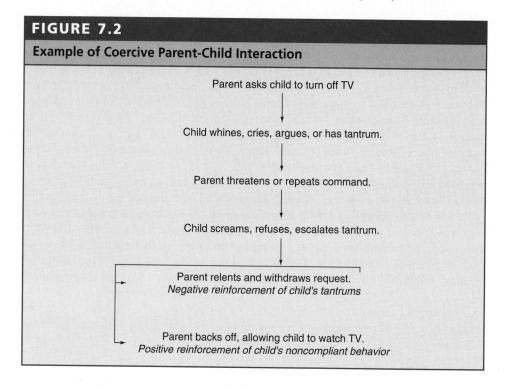

FIGURE 7.2

Example of Coercive Parent-Child Interaction

Parent asks child to turn off TV

Child whines, cries, argues, or has tantrum.

Parent threatens or repeats command.

Child screams, refuses, escalates tantrum.

Parent relents and withdraws request.
Negative reinforcement of child's tantrums

Parent backs off, allowing child to watch TV.
Positive reinforcement of child's noncompliant behavior

Social-Cognitive Influences. Certain thinking styles also characterize aggressive individuals. Dodge's work adds tremendously to our understanding of the *social information-processing* of antisocial youth (see Crick & Dodge, 1994, for a review). Idiosyncratic ways of processing social information characterize each step of the model (see Figure 7.3), resulting in the likelihood of aggression. Let's imagine Jason waiting in line for a drink at the school water fountain. Two other youngsters, involved in a clandestine game of tag in the hallway, bump into him and knock his backpack to the floor. How might he respond?

Dodge's model suggests a typical sequence of mental activity for aggressive children. First, the child *encodes* cues selectively, focusing on situational cues that suggest threatening content. This tendency may develop as a response to harsh discipline, which enhances the hypervigilance needed to protect oneself from ever present threats to personal security (Dodge, Bates, & Pettit, 1990). Jason might attend more to the boy's body coming close and bumping him rather than to the smiles on the other boys' faces.

The child next *interprets* or attributes meaning to the cues. A biased interpretive style, called **hostile attributional bias,** characterizes aggressive individuals who tend to perceive threats even in neutral situations (de Castro, Veerman, Koops, Bosche, & Monshouwer, 2002). For example, Jason might conclude that the boys knocked the backpack off intentionally because they dislike him. The next step is to *clarify goals*. In Jason's emotionally aroused state, the primary goal might be to "get even" with the other boys for the perceived insult. For aggressive children, schemas or mental guides for social interaction may be organized around aggression. In other words, these individuals use aggressive schemas to make sense of or to "figure out" what has transpired socially. Because the situation is likely to be viewed through the lens of perceived hostility and because more socially acceptable responses have not been practiced, the likelihood of aggressive responding is high.

Jason next proceeds to *access a behavioral response* from his repertoire. Then he *evaluates* the response and *enacts* the behavior. Jason, still rather impulsive, is quick to respond in anger. He may start to punch the other boy for the perceived violation. For a child like Jason who is impulsive, who has experienced the benefits of aggression, or who

FIGURE 7.3

Social Information-Processing Model

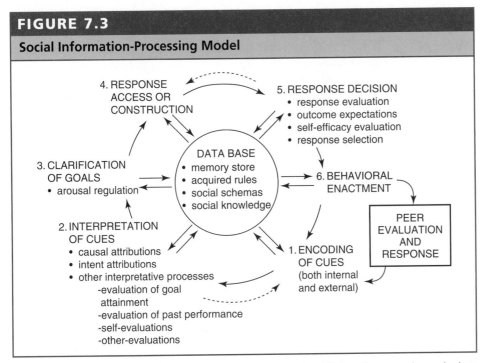

4. RESPONSE ACCESS OR CONSTRUCTION

5. RESPONSE DECISION
- response evaluation
- outcome expectations
- self-efficacy evaluation
- response selection

3. CLARIFICATION OF GOALS
- arousal regulation

DATA BASE
- memory store
- acquired rules
- social schemas
- social knowledge

6. BEHAVIORAL ENACTMENT

PEER EVALUATION AND RESPONSE

2. INTERPRETATION OF CUES
- causal attributions
- intent attributions
- other interpretative processes
  - evaluation of goal attainment
  - evaluation of past performance
  - self-evaluations
  - other-evaluations

1. ENCODING OF CUES (both internal and external)

Source: Crick, N. R. & Dodge, K. A. (1994). A review and reformulation of social information-processing mechanisms in children's social adjustment. *Psychological Bulletin, 115,* 74–101. Copyright © 1994 by the American Psychological Association. Reprinted with permission.

has learned that aggression is a preferred means of problem solving, aggressive responding may become natural. Underdeveloped self-control and weaknesses in verbally expressive means of problem solving add to the tendency to aggress.

Dodge's model emphasizes the role of cognitive processes, such as attention to cues and interpretation of events, in children's antisocial behavior. Other factors, both

Many aggressive, antisocial children have a hostile attributional bias. They assume negative intentions on the part of others and are often primed to want to "get even."

emotional and cognitive, have been found to be associated with aggressive behavior, and some of these factors work in concert. Emotions such as empathy, sympathy, and guilt seem to be important. In particular, empathy is linked to the inhibition, or control, of aggression (see Miller & Eisenberg, 1988). Presumably, when someone initiates an aggressive act, the ability to empathize with the distress of the target person can help inhibit continued aggression in that situation, and the anticipation of a target's distress may inhibit future episodes of aggressive behavior. A focus on the other, rather than the self, seems to be a key element of self-control in these situations.

As we saw in our discussion of prosocial behavior, empathy is the ability to share the feelings of another, and it becomes more effective as a motivator of behavior as children get older. We also indicated that empathy seems to have both an emotional component that involves feeling *with* another and a cognitive aspect, understanding of the other, that results from role-taking or perspective-taking skill. Cohen and Strayer (1996) found that *both* the affective and the cognitive sides of young adolescents' empathic abilities are deficient in young people with conduct disorders, especially in those with strong aggressive tendencies, compared to youngsters without serious behavior problems (see also Chalmers & Townsend, 1990; Chandler, 1973; Feschbach & Feschbach, 1982). As the researchers point out:

> it is empathy-related emotionality that is at issue . . . it does not appear that CD [conduct-disordered] youth are unemotional, callous, or indifferent . . . they tended to report higher levels of personal distress than NCD [non-conduct-disordered] youth [when presented with vignettes portraying other people's problems], suggesting the possibility that [they] may be more egocentrically distressed when involved in emotional situations. This self-focused emotion may compete with empathy with another person's emotions and needs. (p. 995)

There may be many reasons why self-focused emotion could overshadow empathic responses. One possibility is that negative or harsh parenting leaves a child with inadequate opportunities to experience empathy from others, to observe models of empathic behavior, and to discuss or learn from parents' explanations about people's emotional needs and reactions (Cohen & Strayer, 1996). Children who are abused by their parents have been found to show less empathy in response to peer distress than nonabused children. Abused children more often respond to others' problems with fear or anger (Main & George, 1985). We have also seen that children's own characteristics (such as a difficult temperament) may elicit coercive, negative parenting. Parenting that lacks warmth may in turn limit empathic development (e.g., J. L. Robinson et al., 1994) and can foster aggressive behavior (e.g., Rubin et al., 1998). Similarly, children whose behavior is aggressive, especially those who are also argumentative and disruptive, often experience peer rejection (Coie, Dodge, & Kupersmidt, 1990), which may further constrain their opportunities to learn adequate perspective-taking skills.

Clearly, many processes influence children's antisocial and aggressive behavior. These processes produce children who fail to make normal strides in their ability to regulate their own emotional responses, especially anger, and whose concern for self is not adequately balanced by concern for, and understanding of, other people.

APPLICATIONS

In this chapter, we have examined the nature of self-concept, self-esteem, and moral behavior. What are some ways that counselors can foster the development of a healthy sense of self, one that is high in esteem and also high in consideration for others' needs? Some might argue that we should start with self-esteem; however, this approach is more complicated than we might think. Consider this hypothetical situation.

You have been feeling tired and listless with an array of flu-like symptoms. You pay a visit to your family physician, who notes that your blood pressure is high and recommends medication. Your mother, who has had a persistent headache, goes to the same physician. Her diagnosis is high blood pressure requiring medication. Your neighbor visits this physician after an energetic tennis match leaves him with a sharp pain in his serving arm. His diagnosis? High blood pressure to be treated with medication. Does this sound a bit absurd? Could it possibly be that high blood pressure is the cause of all these ills?

In some way, our fascination with self-esteem has led some of us down a similar path of faulty logic. As Baumeister and Bowden (1994) point out:

> the modern growth of selfhood has included a love affair with it. Whereas, for centuries, morality and self-interest were regarded as mortal enemies, the modern individual has increasingly linked the self to positive values. Finding oneself, knowing oneself, cultivating oneself, and benefiting oneself are seen not only as moral rights, but even, increasingly, as moral duties. (p. 144)

Nowhere is this trend more evident than in the pursuit of self-esteem. As we stated in Chapter 5, self-esteem has been touted as the holy grail of mental health. Low self-esteem has been implicated as a key element in a wide variety of problems manifested by children, adolescents, and adults, including low academic motivation and diminished achievement (Carlson & Lewis, 1993), increasing abuse of drugs and alcohol (Kaplan, 1980), teenage pregnancy (Herold, Goodwin, & Lero, 1979), gang violence (E. Anderson, 1994), spousal abuse (Gondolf, 1985), hate crimes (Levin & McDevitt, 1993) and even murder (Kirschner, 1992). Identifying low self-esteem as a correlate of mental health problems does not necessarily provide evidence of a causal relationship, as any student of statistics can point out. However, many preventive and remedial efforts are sometimes structured "as if" low self-esteem caused the problems directly. As a result, interventions are focused on changing affect. The premise is that if children feel better about themselves, they will then do better. Their general mental health will improve, and they will behave in prosocial ways.

This self-enhancement approach (Caslyn & Kenny, 1977) is well intentioned. Obviously, no one would argue that children should hold negative views of themselves! Abundant research has demonstrated that negative self-views are a feature of depression (Beck, 1963; C. Peterson, Maier, & Seligman, 1993) and that dwelling on one's negative attributes both prolongs and amplifies the depressive state (Nolen-Hoeksema, Morrow, & Fredrickson, 1993). But it is something different to assume that high self-esteem automatically causes positive outcomes. Dryfoos (1990), in a review of 20 years of research, reports that there is no compelling evidence that high self-esteem is a necessary precursor for competence. In fact, much evidence points in the other direction, namely that competent performance results in feelings of high self-esteem. In recent years the emphasis has clearly shifted toward a "skills-first" approach, that is, toward enhancing competencies that indirectly bolster self-esteem. From this perspective, feeling good becomes a "delicious by-product" of doing well (Seligman, 1995)

This sea change appears not only to have resulted from the failure of research evidence to support positive, enduring effects of self-esteem manipulations. It also derives from a closer look at what has been called the "dark side" of self-esteem. A number of influential writers have pointed out the potential negative effects of inflating self-esteem unrealistically. Baumeister, Smart, and Boden (1996) review the evidence from many studies on the relationship between self-esteem and aggression. Surprisingly, they find no evidence for the assumption that low self-esteem is a cause of violence despite the widely held belief that low-self esteem is an important precursor to antisocial behavior. Instead, they marshall impressive evidence to support the opposite position—that aggressors are most likely to have inflated, albeit unstable, self-esteem, to believe themselves to be superior to others, and to be narcissistic and assertive. Cairns and Cairns (1994) reporting on the Carolina Longitudinal Study found something similar. At-risk youngsters held overly positive, inflated views of their behaviors and abilities as compared to the assessments of parents and teachers.

This is not to suggest that high self-esteem causes violence any more than low self-esteem does. What the evidence supports is that the combination of inflated, tentative self-esteem with a threat to the person's ego may result in aggression. In other words, a person's encounter with an external negative appraisal from another (criticism, failure, mockery, or contradiction) creates dissonance and anxiety if that person holds and wants to maintain unrealistically favorable views of herself. Baumeister et al. (1996) found in reviewing the evidence that it was primarily those individuals who would not "back down" from their grandiose self-views who were most likely to aggress.

These findings have important clinical implications if we are in the business of promoting the development of moral, prosocial, well-adjusted individuals. As Baumeister and his colleagues conclude,

> If low self-esteem were really the cause of violence, it would be therapeutically prudent to make every effort to convince rapists, murderers, wife beaters, professional hit men, tyrants, torturers, and others that they are superior beings. From our reading of the empirical literature, however, these people are often violent precisely because they already believe themselves to be superior beings. It would therefore be more effective to direct therapeutic efforts elsewhere (e.g., at cultivating self-control) . . . and *sic* it would be better to try instilling modesty and humility. (p. 29)

All of this, again, is not intended to suggest that self-esteem enhancement inevitably leads to antisocial outcomes. Rather it is intended to warn against the unreflective application of a universal approach for every situation. The larger question for helpers seems to be how to best support prosocial development in its broad sense without inadvertently doing harm. We will conclude this section with a brief summary of recommendations from Damon (1995) and Harter (1999) that apply to the issues of morality and self-esteem.

Harter provides a helpful model for making decisions about intervention based on the work of James (cognitive appraisal of self-concept) and Cooley (social determinants of self-concept) that applies to children as well as adolescents and adults. Overall, a key principle is to assess the specific antecedents of the problem rather than to provide the same strategy for everyone. If the problem is caused by dissonance between perceived and real competence, counselors may attempt to address self-concept problems by helping to reduce the discrepancy. Very often, this may involve supporting skill development to enhance performance in certain areas, such as in academic subjects or social interaction. Alternatively, children, as well as older individuals, can be helped to value components of their self-concepts in which they excel, such as academics, while reducing the importance of areas where they are less successful, such as athletics. Her suggestion is "to spend more psychological time in those life niches where favorable self-appraisals are more common" (p. 317). Remember, however, that working to reduce the importance of some components, such as behavioral conduct for an acting-out child, is *not* a good idea! In this case, the careful creation of a discrepancy may be what is called for.

Harter also recommends working toward a generally realistic appraisal of competencies. Bringing the self-perceptions of those who overrate their competencies more in line with external appraisers helps to reduce the potential for highly inflated self-esteem. For underraters, the task is more difficult, particularly since higher-order schemas, such as global self-esteem, are harder to change. Hattie (1992) believes that these kinds of self-views develop from early attachment experiences and provide durable working models of the self. One example of this might be the low global self-esteem and feelings of

FIGURE 7.4

Additive Effects of Competence and Social Support on Self-Esteem

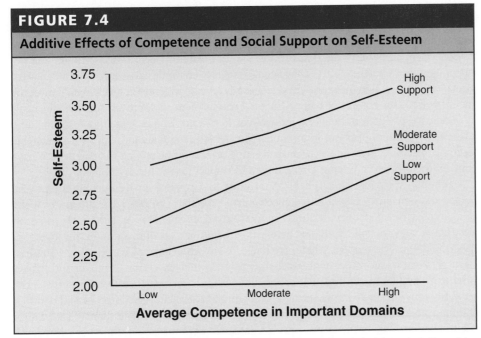

Source: Harter, S. (1993). Causes and consequences of low self-esteem in children and adolescents. In Baumeister, R. (Ed.), *Self-esteem: The puzzle of low self-regard.* New York: Plenum Press. Reprinted by permission.

unworthiness of victims of severe early childhood abuse or neglect. Despite the relative intractability of such schemas, Harter argues that these self-representations may be more open to revision at critical developmental periods (e.g., transition to new school, adolescence, within intimate relationships) when the need for psychological reorganization occurs. Use of reframing strategies that encourage the person to revise beliefs about the possibility of changing her self-schema and that increase perceptions of personal control and self-efficacy may also be useful (Seligman, 1995). For older adolescents and adults, help in understanding the root causes of the negative self-schema (e.g., early abuse) may provide more cognitive control over these beliefs. Needless to say, change may be extraordinarily difficult in certain cases when the self-views are deeply negative and entrenched.

Interventions that address the provision of realistically positive social support are important as well. Initially, care should be taken to assess whether the lack of perceived support, either from parents, teachers, or peers, is realistic. If individuals underestimate the level of support they actually receive from others, attempts to bring this discrepancy in line will promote more positive self-evaluations. If the social support is truly lacking, attempts to provide parent education, family therapy, or peer group intervention may be appropriate. But no one's "looking glass" is ever totally, continuously reinforcing. As children mature, efforts to reduce reliance on external standards and sources of feedback should be made. Children can be helped to take personal responsibility for their actions and to choose more learning or internally motivated goals (Pintrich, 2000). They can also be discouraged from excessive competition and overreliance on social comparison. These approaches can have positive effects on the internalization of personal standards.

Moving beyond the self-concept focus, Damon (1995) takes a somewhat broader look at failures in prosocial development, or the moral self, that he considers all too common in our day. Although comprehensive coverage of his advice is beyond the scope of this section, some of his suggestions for parents, schools, and communities committed to the prosocial or moral needs of children are reported here.

First, parents are advised to practice authoritative ways of parenting as the best way of inculcating prosocial values and behavioral standards. Damon repeatedly calls our attention to a very common error, that of the "false dichotomy," which is the overemphasis on one aspect of an issue to the detriment of another. Parents need to be nurturant *and* demanding, quite a balancing act! They need to avoid overemphasizing either child-centered, empathic goals (which make the child feel good) or parent-centered goals (which meet the parental needs for control or convenience). A more balanced approach supports the goals of socializing children to be moral individuals. For example, a certain amount of empathy makes for warm, supportive communication, which facilitates induction. A reasonable degree of parent-centeredness (such as insisting on a bedtime so that the parents can have time for themselves) promotes concern for and respect for the needs of others.

Schooling provides an excellent opportunity to support the development of prosocial values and behavior. "Like a broad-spectrum vaccine that can block the growth of many dangerous viruses at once, a child's wholehearted engagement in schooling can stop destructive and wasteful activities before they begin to consume a child's life" (Damon, 1995, p. 195). The emphasis here, we stress, is on wholehearted engagement. Children need personal relationships with teachers who hold high intellectual, moral, and behavioral expectations in settings that are small enough to permit these relationships. They need rigorous and meaningful learning experiences that encourage diligence and depth of thinking, and they need high standards for behavior that actually hold them to account for their behavior. This is the crux of developmentally appropriate education at every level, given that most children excel when opportunities to develop competence and character are provided within a supportive environment.

Finally, community organizations such as YMCA, sports leagues, and so on, composed of members who live and work in the communities they serve, have a critical part to play. The most successful ones provide a source of care and mentoring to children and require them to abide by strict rules and regulations. In this way, they provide a healthy dose of adjunct parenting by helping youth to internalize values and standards. Opportunities for children to provide meaningful service to others sharpen their sense of purpose and competence and reduce the demoralization that grows from excessive self-centeredness. Finally, Damon and many others (see Tannen, 1999) have called for an end to the kinds of false-dichotomy debates in society that polarize people and paralyze efforts to change. Despite our diversity, we will provide a more powerful environment for moral development if we communicate some shared values to all our children through our words and deeds. Children learn the important messages best when homes, schools, and communities speak with one voice.

Summary

Self-Concept

1. Although preschoolers can describe themselves, they have difficulty coordinating the different aspects of themselves. Also, they do not accommodate the opposition of some traits, such as "nice" and "mean," and they usually see themselves in an overly positive light. By middle childhood, the me-self is becoming a more organized structure, although children still tend to emphasize the positive. Gradually, more trait-like concepts of self emerge, social comparison begins building on perspective-taking skills, and self-esteem tends to decline a bit.

2. During middle childhood and beyond, the self-concept can be divided into multiple domains, such as academic and nonacademic, and each of these can be further

differentiated. A global sense of self and self-esteem may coexist with these more differentiated assessments of self. Appearance is particularly associated with overall self-esteem, especially for girls.

3. Global self-esteem depends on competence in areas of importance to the individual, as William James suggested. In evaluating their own competencies, children may use concrete standards (e.g., making a team), but they are also influenced by social processes, as suggested by Cooley. They internalize the assessments of others, and they engage in *social comparison,* evaluating their own abilities and accomplishments against those of others who resemble them in some important way. They tend to be motivated by a *self-enhancing bias,* sometimes making *"downward" social comparisons* when their self-esteem is at stake. Children's self-appraisals come more and more into congruence with others' appraisals as they get older.

4. There is a small but stable gender difference in self-esteem favoring males in late childhood and early adolescence, sometimes called the *self-esteem slide.*

5. Older views that marginalized groups would have lower self-esteem than mainstream groups due to the internalization of discriminatory appraisals are not supported by current research. African Americans, for example, have a slight self-esteem advantage over White Americans. In general, strong racial or ethnic identity correlates positively with level of global self-esteem, although findings vary from group to group and from individual to individual.

The Moral Self

6. The meaning of morality varies across individuals, groups, and cultures, but generally includes fundamental principles necessary to successful functioning of society: *concern for others, a sense of justice and fairness, trustworthiness* or *honesty,* and *self-control.*

7. Emotions, cognitions, and behaviors are all part of morality, and are not always well coordinated.

8. In Freud's psychoanalytic theory, conscience emerges between ages 3 and 5, when children identify with the same-sexed parent. In the process, children internalize the same-sexed parent's values and rules, forming a *superego.* Much evidence is inconsistent with this view. For example, moral emotions and prosocial behavior begin as early as toddlerhood.

9. Piaget and Kohlberg propose cognitive theories, arguing that moral development is influenced by developmental changes in logical thinking and emerges in a series of stages. While there is some clear support for these views, there are inconsistent findings. For example, Piaget assumed that preschoolers treat all rules as inviolable, determined by authorities. But even 3-year-olds judge violations of *moral rules,* such as rules about stealing, more seriously than violations of *conventional rules,* such as how one should dress.

10. *Altruism* may be motivated in many ways. Emotional reactions, such as *empathy* and *sympathy,* are important motivators. Even toddlers show signs that empathy can propel prosocial action such as sharing or comforting, but such emotions are much more effective motivators after the preschool years, as perspective-taking ability improves.

11. *Needs-based reasoning* can also affect prosocial behavior and shows predictable developments with age. It also tends to be more advanced in popular children with good social skills, especially boys. Also, younger children whose moral reasoning is needs oriented are not as likely as older children to engage in prosocial behavior unless they also experience prosocial emotions. For older children whose reasoning is needs oriented, the presence of such emotions is not so important.

12. Personality characteristics also affect tendencies toward prosocial behavior—characteristics such as sociability, social competence, positive self-concept, and assertiveness.

13. Parents who use an authoritative parenting style with high levels of warmth and demandingness seem to promote prosocial behavior. Also, when parents have strong prosocial values their children are likely to follow suit. Providing children with opportunities to practice prosocial behavior increases further prosocial behavior, referred to as the "foot in the door effect."

14. Antisocial behavior can develop along several different pathways. The *early-starter* pathway becomes increasingly more serious over time. The *adolescent-onset* pathway is less likely to have long-lasting consequences. Early oppositional behaviors often recede by age 8 or so; it is when they continue into elementary school that they predict later deliquent behavior.

15. Internal risk factors for long-term antisocial behavior include difficult temperaments, attention deficits, impulsivity, high activity level, and weakness in verbal skill and problem-solving ability. Environmental risk factors include low socioeconomic status, physical abuse, authoritarian parenting, and a tendency for parents to reinforce aggressive behavior by withdrawing demands. Dodge also describes the idiosyncratic ways in which antisocial children process social information, a social-cognitive process that helps establish a trajectory of increasing antisocial feelings and behavior.

Case Study

Kevin Miller, a White fifth-grade student at Greentree Elementary School, is in the principal's office with his parents. Mr. Dolan, the school principal, has just informed Mr. and Mrs. Miller that Kevin's fifth-grade trip privilege will be revoked because of an accumulation of disciplinary offenses. Kevin's behavior in fifth grade has become progressively more disruptive. This time, he has managed to create enough problems for his teachers to prevent his participation in the end-of-the-year event, which was planned as a reward for the students' effort and achievement.

Kevin is a very intelligent and physically attractive youngster with particular interests and abilities in sports and computer games. In second grade, he was identified as a candidate for the school's gifted student program, yet he invests little energy in schoolwork. He tells his teachers that he finds the assignments boring and can find no reason to involve himself in the learning process. He does little studying, but he manages to get by with a C+ average. In class, he talks to other students when he should be working, makes disrespectful comments to his teachers, and basically tries to get away with doing what he pleases most of the time.

Kevin relishes his position of power in the group. Many students in the class look up to Kevin because of his engaging bravado. They like him because he is often funny and provides a diversion from class work. Other students find him a nuisance who distracts the teachers from their instruction. Students know that if they work with Kevin on a group project, they may have a good time, but it will come with a price: getting in trouble with their teachers.

Kevin's parents have a long history of conferencing with the school principal and counselor. Over the years, problems have increased from some concerns about his attention span in the early grades to more serious issues. In fourth grade, Kevin was caught cheating on a test proctored by a substitute teacher. Kevin claimed that he was falsely accused because the teacher "didn't like him." At the beginning of fifth grade, Kevin responded to his English teacher, who was trying to get him to focus on a classroom writing assignment, with a profane comment. When confronted about his behavior, Kevin was convinced that he did not do anything seriously wrong. His explanation was that he was joking, and he suggested that the adults should "lighten up."

Kevin's parents believe it is their job to stand up for their only son and support him, even though they are unhappy about his frequent problems at school. The Millers describe their son as "lively and creative" and "smarter than they are" in some areas, such as computer literacy. Encouraged by the school counselor, they initiated private counseling for Kevin at the end of fourth grade. Kevin has seen his counselor sporadically for almost a year. Both parents believe that Kevin is a good boy whose irrepressible spirit and intellect get him into trouble with those who misunderstand him.

Faced with this new consequence, Kevin is quite upset. He was looking forward to the class trip and believes that the punishment is extreme. The Millers understand the principal's reasoning, but they also disagree with the punishment. They indicate that they will request a meeting with the superintendent in order to have the decision changed. They express the view that most kids behave like Kevin sometimes. From their perspective, Kevin should be allowed to express himself and to have the autonomy to make choices about what he does. They emphasize his persistence and interest in activities that engage his attention. They come close to faulting Kevin's teachers for failing to motivate him.

The district superintendent, after considering the case, decides that depriving Kevin of the trip would jeopardize any relationship teachers would be able to develop with him in the future. Kevin's consequence is changed to an in-school suspension; he is allowed to participate in the class trip.

Discussion Questions

1. What are the issues involved in Kevin's case? What assessment can you make of his moral development and his self-concept?
2. If you were his counselor, what would you recommend in order to promote healthy development?

 ## Journal Questions

1. Give an example of a moral principle you learned as a child. How and when did you learn it? Provide an example from your own experience of an inconsistency between your level of moral reasoning and your behavior.
2. If you can remember struggling with some subject or concept in school, describe the impact of that experience on your sense of competence and industry. How have you resolved this struggle?
3. Rate your level of self-esteem on a scale of 1 (low) to 10 (high) in the following areas: Academic, Physical Appearance, Social (friendship relationships), Athletic, and Career Success. Now rate each on a scale of 1 (not important) to 10 (very important) in terms of their significance to you. Where are the biggest discrepancies? How do these discrepancies affect your overall self-esteem?
4. How did your peers contribute to your understanding of yourself? Explain.

Key Terms

academic self-concept
nonacademic self-concept
social comparison
self-enhancing bias
"downward" social
    comparisons
self-esteem slide
conscience
identification
premoral stage
heteronomous stage

immanent justice
autonomous stage
preconventional morality
conventional morality
postconventional morality
moral rules
conventional rules
personal rules
morality of justice
morality of caring

prosocial behavior or
    altruism
empathy
sympathy
needs-based reasoning
hedonistic
needs oriented
antisocial behavior
early-starter model
adolescent-onset

antisocial personality
    disorder
oppositional defiant
    disorder (ODD)
conduct disorder
resilient
coercive family interaction
social information-
    processing
hostile attributional bias

Gender and Peer Relationships in Middle Childhood Through Early Adolescence

It's recess time for the third-graders at Columbus Elementary. Four girls take turns jumping rope, while other small clusters of girls are playing hopscotch or sitting and talking. One pair whispers conspiratorially, occasionally giggling and glancing up at the girls playing jump rope. One girl skips across the grass alone and then sits on a swing, occasionally watching three friends play a climbing game on the modern jungle gym. The game has something to do with the plot of a TV show they saw the night before. A crew of boys is playing a variant of tag, in which whoever is "it" must not only catch someone else (who will then become "it") but must also dodge the assaults of players who risk being caught in order to race past and punch the boy who is "it" in the back or arms. A boy watching on the sidelines suddenly jumps into the tag game, punching the player who is "it." The others gather round, shoving and yelling at the intruder. When he says, "I can play if I want to," one boy shouts more loudly than the rest, "Let him play, but he's *gotta* be it." In the remaining ten minutes of recess, the intruder catches three different boys, but the captives are forcibly freed by their compatriots, and the intruder never escapes being "it" despite his bitter protests. Moments before the recess ends, he stomps off in a rage, shouting epithets at the others.

As the third-graders move off the playground, recess begins for the higher grades. Soon a group of sixth-graders, seven boys and one girl, is playing basketball on the paved court; another larger group, all boys, is playing soccer on a grassy field. Most of the sixth-grade girls are standing around in circles, talking.

We could watch a large assembly of elementary school children on any playground—the roof of a private Manhattan school, the small, fenced yard of a crumbling Chicago public school, or, as in this example, the ample playing fields, paved courts, and wood-chipped, well-equipped play area of a sprawling school in an affluent Seattle suburb. Despite the constraints of the setting, some key elements of the children's behavior would be strikingly similar. Most of the girls would be playing or talking in clusters of two or three, separately from the boys. The boys would be playing in larger groups, and often their play would consist of some mostly good-natured roughhousing. Some children would probably be alone. They might stand apart, or they might push their way into a group where they are not welcome and then find themselves in conflict with others. Occasionally, a child of one sex might play comfortably with a group of the opposite sex, but generally she or he will be a quiet, peripheral member of the group. More often than not, this child will be a girl. Sometimes, groups of boys will interfere with the play of a cluster of girls, most often to chase them or to upset their game. The girls might chase the boys back, always with their girlfriends along for support.

These patterns will be familiar to anyone who has ever participated in, or observed, a children's recess. In this chapter, we will examine two major features of child development that contribute to these patterns. The first is sex role development in childhood and early adolescence, including the formation of a gender identity and the acquisition of gender-related behaviors. (We will discuss the emergence of sexual orientation in Chapter 9.) The second is the formation and influence of peer relations in the lives of children and young adolescents, including both the degree to which children are able to establish satisfying relationships with their peers and the degree and kind of influence that peer groups wield. Sex role development and peer relations have traditionally been separate disciplines in the developmental sciences, and to some degree we will discuss them separately here. But, as you will see, it is becoming more and more clear not only that peer interactions differ as a function of gender but that peer processes may be very important in shaping gendered behavior.

For counselors and other helpers, understanding the processes of sex role development can be a key element in providing valid supports to children and adults as they struggle with identity issues, self-acceptance, and self-esteem. Many coping difficulties, both externalizing and internalizing problems, are more typical of either one gender or the other in our society, or they have different features and implications depending on the sex of the client.

It has also become increasingly obvious that a major function of counselors, especially those who work with children and adolescents, is to identify and intervene with individuals whose peer relationships are distorted. Many developments—including perspective taking, as we have already seen, and sex role development, as we will see in this chapter—are now recognized to be at least partly a function of peer group interaction. Victims, bullies, and social isolates in the world of childhood are at risk for long-term social problems. Among the more spectacular examples are the child perpetrators of major community catastrophies, such as those at Columbine High School in 1998, whose actions appear to have been at least partly a function of peer relations gone awry (Greenfield & Juvonen, 1999).

SEX ROLE DEVELOPMENT

Descriptions of sex-related phenomena, such as gender-typed behavior or sexual orientation, can elicit strong feelings and can have significant political, religious, or personal implications. One focus of some of these feelings has been the denotation of words such as "sex" and "gender." Some authors argue that the term "sex" should be reserved for biologically determined processes and that "gender" should be used for any socially influenced characteristics. Yet, we found this formula difficult to apply because biological and environmental causes play interactive roles in all of human development (see Chapter 2). Other authors argue that "sex" should be used when the reference is based on objective characteristics of males versus females (e.g., "members of both *sexes* were included in the study"), whereas "gender" should be used when making references based on judgments or inferences about males and females (e.g., "the feminine *gender* role includes being responsible for meal preparation") (e.g., Deaux, 1993). Yet, whether references are objectively based or a function of judgment or inference is not easily determined either. For example, in our culture we dichotomize sex, recognizing only the male and female categories, but some cultures recognize other categories as well, and some people in our own culture believe that we should see gender as existing more on a continuum than as two clearly separate categories. Therefore, inference and judgment influence even what are considered objective criteria for the categorization of individuals as male or female (or other).

Frankly, we found all of the criteria that have been proposed for differentiating use of the terms "sex" and "gender" too difficult to apply consistently. What we have done instead is to treat the terms as interchangeable, except where one word is used in a uniform, conventional way through much of the literature, as in the phrase "gender identity."

Let's now take a look at the development of cognitive, social, and behavioral phenomena related to one's sex. The first part of our discussion of sex role development deals with the development of gender identity. The second part centers on gender differences in behavior. We will consider some of the processes that might account for these phenomena, and later we will examine how a helping professional could use this information to benefit his clients.

Gender Identity

Augustina was the youngest girl in a family of nine children. Her parents had emigrated from Italy to the United States before she was born in 1913. When she was an elderly woman, one of Augustina's memories of herself as a young child was that she had firmly believed she would be a man when she grew up. She remembered that sometime in her preschool years she was aware of being a girl, but she was excited about the prospect of becoming like her oldest brothers, whom she saw as confident, swaggering, well-dressed young men to whom her mother deferred and who could stand toe to toe with her imposing father. (In the cultural tradition of her family, men were more privileged and powerful than women.) She could also remember a feeling of bitter disappointment that hung with her for many months after she realized, some time later, that she was destined to remain female and that she would inevitably become a woman.

Augustina's early **gender identity,** her awareness of her own gender assignment and understanding of its meaning, illustrates some elements in the progress of gender identity for young children, although fortunately most kids do not associate negative feelings with the process but seem to wholeheartedly accept their status. The first step in the process is learning to categorize oneself as male or female. By late in their first year, babies seem to be able to make *perceptual distinctions* between the sexes. They can distinguish pictures of men from pictures of women (Leinbach & Fagot, 1993), they can distinguish the voices of men from those of women (even when the voices are matched for pitch) (D. L. Miller, 1983), and they even seem to recognize that male voices go with male faces and female voices with female faces (Poulin-Dubois, Serbin, Kenyon, & Derbyshire, 1994).

Children show some skill at labeling males and females and at understanding labels such as "mommy" and "daddy" (for woman and man) or "girl" and "boy" by early in their third year (e.g., Huston, 1983; Leinbach & Fagot, 1986, 1993). At age 2, they do not usually know the label for themselves, but soon after, by age $2\frac{1}{2}$ to 3, most children can label themselves correctly and identify others who fit into the same category as they do themselves (see Maccoby, 1998).

As Augustina's experience illustrates, however, knowing your gender category today may not mean that you understand that it will stay that way forever. A second step in the process of identity formation is understanding **gender stability,** that over time, one's gender category stays the same: boys grow into men, girls grow into women. A third step appears to be recognizing that gender category membership is permanent, that it could *never* change, even if one's behavior or appearance were changed to resemble the other gender. This is called **gender constancy** (see Slaby & Frey, 1975). Most children seem to have *gender stability* by 3 to 4 years old—a girl knows she was a girl yesterday and expects to be one again tomorrow. But even older preschoolers may not understand *gender constancy.* For this, children must realize that even if major surface changes were made—in hairstyle, dress, and/or behavior—the sex of the individual would not also change.

Controversy swirls around the question of when gender constancy develops. In some studies, preschoolers who are shown pictures of, say, a boy dressed up like a girl, with a long-haired wig and a dress, often express the belief that the boy has changed into a girl (e.g., DeLisi & Gallagher, 1991; Kohlberg, 1966). In other studies, even some 3-year-olds seem to have a pretty clear sense of gender constancy (e.g., Bem, 1989; A. Johnson & Ames, 1994; Leonard & Archer, 1989; Martin & Little, 1990). But it is safe to say that until about the time of school entry, a child's understanding of this concept can be fragile, and he can show uncertainty about the permanence of gender categories.

What influences affect the formation of a gender identity? How do children come to make gender a part of their self-concept? Like every other important behavioral development, many factors appear to contribute: social, cognitive, and biological.

The Role of Social Processes in Gender Identity

When babies are born, adults assign them to gender categories based on their genital characteristics. From the first, young children hear themselves described as male or female. They are told, "You're a big *girl* to help Daddy like that," "Mommy loves her sweet *boy*," or "You don't want to be a mean *girl* who makes her friend cry!" Children are literally surrounded by verbal reminders of their assigned gender. It's not surprising, then, that between 2 and 3, at the same time that they are learning other labels for themselves such as "naughty" or "nice" (see Chapter 5), children have learned their own gender label.

Research with **gender atypical** children suggests that social assignment to a gender category is a powerful determiner of gender identity. *Gender atypical* children have either ambiguous genitalia or genitalia that are inconsistent with their sex chromosomes. In one example, biologically male children, with one X and one Y chromosome, have suffered surgical damage to their genitals during infancy, sometimes as a result of a botched circumcision. Faced with this difficult situation, some parents have raised these children as girls from infancy onward. In one recently reported example, a boy was reassigned by his family as a "girl" at age 7 months (Bradley, Oliver, Chernick, & Zucker, 1998). Physicians provided treatments with female hormones at puberty so that female secondary sexual characteristics would develop, such as enlarged breasts. At the most recent follow-up, in early adulthood, the young woman still accepted her female identity and was comfortable with her female role. (Note that the results in this case do not necessarily indicate that such a solution will be the right one in all cases. See the discussion, below, of another boy whose penis was ablated in infancy, and the very different outcome he experienced.)

Another gender atypical problem is a condition called **congenital adrenal hyperplasia (CAH)**, in which biological females with two X chromosomes are exposed to high levels of androgens (male hormones) during prenatal and postnatal development. The overproduction of androgens by their own adrenal glands is caused by a defective gene. The upshot is that although CAH females usually have the internal organs of a girl, their external genitalia may be masculinized. They may, for example, have an enlarged clitoris that looks like a penis, and they have sometimes been misidentified at birth as boys. When these girls are properly diagnosed, a set of medical interventions can minimize the overproduction of androgens postnatally, and the genitalia can be surgically altered to resemble those of a girl. But John Money and his colleagues, who have done extensive studies of children with CAH, report that if the diagnosis is not made before the age of $2\frac{1}{2}$ to 3, a child's gender identity can be very difficult to alter, and physicians have often advised parents to continue raising their child as a boy (which requires intervention at puberty to provide further masculinizing hormones) (Money & Dalery, 1977; Money & Erhardt, 1972; Erhardt & Baker, 1974).

When CAH females are raised as boys, their gender identity is inconsistent with their biological sex, and yet they can accept their gender assignment. Of course, their social assignment to the status of male may not be the only factor that supports their acceptance of a male identity. Their exposure to androgens appears to have a masculinizing effect on their behavior as well as on their genitalia, and this biologically generated difference in behavior may make a male identity a comfortable "fit" for some CAH females.

Indeed, as you will see shortly, research with gender atypical children not only demonstrates that social assignment is a powerful influence on gender identity but also provides hints that biological factors can modify or enhance that influence. Once again, nature and nurture operate in tandem.

The Role of Cognition in Gender Identity

Forming a concept of oneself as either a boy or a girl is a cognitive task. Some theorists have argued that one's gender identity changes partly as a function of general developments in cognitive ability, especially logical thinking (e.g., Kohlberg, 1966). As we have seen, when children first categorize themselves as boys or girls, they may have done little more than learn a label. Their understanding of the implications of that label is limited. Gradually, they begin to recognize that there is stability to their category membership and, finally, that their category membership is constant, based on underlying properties that do not change when superficial perceptual characteristics alter. In a sense, gender is something that is *conserved* (at least under normal circumstances), much like number is conserved when candies in a pile are made to look different by spreading them out in a row. We have seen (Chapter 3) that a full understanding of number conservation typically is achieved between 5 and 7 years and seems to be based on the development of logical thinking. Gender constancy may also be dependent on the logical thinking skills that emerge as children reach middle childhood.

While developments in logical thinking may be important, there are other cognitive factors that can influence the progress of gender identity, such as being given accurate information about how gender is decided. As we pointed out earlier, adults assign babies to a gender category based on their genitalia. But unless young children are explicitly taught about the importance of genitals to gender assignment, they are likely to be unaware of the typical genital differences between the sexes. References to gender categorization are pervasive in our society, and they are a large part of children's daily experiences. Not only do children frequently hear themselves being categorized, but many references to other people contain gender labels, such as, "This *man* will help us find the toy department." However, most of these references are *not* based on observation of people's genitals. They depend on people's other physical attributes, such as size and shape, and on more superficial characteristics, such as clothing and hair style. It's not really surprising, then, that young children are sometimes oblivious to the genital basis for gender assignment or that they might initially assume that gender categories are determined by superficial properties.

Researcher Sandra Bem (1989) tells the story of her son, Jeremy, who *was* informed about genital differences between boys and girls and about the importance of genitalia in gender assignment. One day, he chose to go off to nursery school wearing barrettes in his hair. When another little boy repeatedly insisted that Jeremy must be a girl because he was wearing barrettes, Jeremy just as vehemently insisted that he was a boy, because "wearing barrettes doesn't matter; being a boy means having a penis and testicles." Jeremy was even provoked enough at one point to pull down his pants to demonstrate. The other boy was not impressed. He said, "Everybody has a penis; only girls wear barrettes."

A study by Bem (1989) illustrates that when children do have knowledge of the genital basis of gender assignment, as Jeremy did, they are fortified with information that may help them to avoid some confusion about gender constancy. She presented 3- to 5-year-olds with two large photographs of nude toddlers. One was a boy (Gaw), and one a girl (Khwan) (see Figure 8.1). Bem gave the pictured toddlers Thai names so that most North American youngsters would be unfamiliar with the names and would not associate them with gender. Children were asked to say whether a pictured toddler was a boy or a girl, and then were asked to explain how they knew. If no genital information was offered, the researcher probed by asking questions such as "Can you point to anything about Gaw's body that makes Gaw a boy?" Nearly half of the children showed no awareness of the relevance of genitalia for specifying sex. The children who *did* know about genitals also seemed to have a better grasp of gender constancy. When they were shown pictures of Gaw or Khwan with cross-gendered clothes or hairstyles, they asserted that their genders had not changed.

It appears, then, that when adults provide appropriate scaffolding, giving children accurate information about how gender is assigned, children's understanding of their own gender identity is more advanced.

The Role of Biology in Gender Identity

If children are assigned to a gender based on their genitalia and if genitals are usually a product of underlying biological processes (such as the functioning of XX or XY chromosome pairs, see Chapter 2), then biology plays at least an indirect role in gender identity. But does biology have any other influence, beyond affecting the genitalia? That has proven

FIGURE 8.1

Photographs Used to Measure Gender Constancy in Bem's (1989) Study

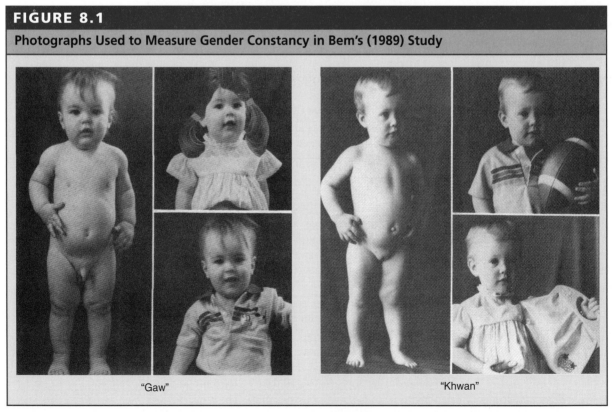

"Gaw"   "Khwan"

Source: Bem, S. L. (1989). Genital knowledge and gender constancy in preschool children. *Child Development, 60,* pp. 653, 654. Reprinted by permission of Blackwell Publisher, Inc.

a difficult question to answer, but there are some indicators that "feeling like a male" or "feeling like a female" may to some degree be related to factors other than social assignment to a gender category, and these factors could be biological.

Again, research on gender atypical individuals provides some clues. Consider the case of a biological male, one of identical twins, who suffered surgical damage to his penis in infancy (Diamond & Sigmundson, 1997; Money & Tucker, 1975). As with the child we described earlier (Bradley et al., 1998), the parents raised this twin as a girl. By the time the twins were 5 years old, the "girl" seemed to accept her female gender assignment, and was observed to behave in more "feminine" ways than her twin brother. It seemed a clear indication of the importance of social assignment for gender identity. Yet by age 10, unlike the child described by Bradley et al., the girl twin was feeling like she was not a girl. And by age 14, she had taken a stand: she refused hormone treatments that feminized her appearance. Male hormone treatments were begun, and surgical reconstruction of the penis was undertaken. By the time he was 25, the former girl was a married man, comfortable with his male identity.

The case of the identical twin is no more than suggestive that biology can outdo social influences in affecting gender identity. By puberty, this child had a somewhat masculinized appearance, despite the female hormones she had been getting. Because of her appearance, she experienced substantial hazing from her peers, a social factor that could have been important in creating her gender uncertainty and distress. Further, we cannot say how effective her own family had been in accepting her status as a girl and thus how unambiguous her socialization experiences had been. However, cases such as these raise the possibility that biology can exert an influence on how "male" or "female" one feels, or at least on how comfortable one is with a particular gender assignment. We should note that the results of this case appear to be quite different from the one reported earlier (Bradley et al., 1998). Clearly, in individual cases outcomes are difficult to predict, creating considerable ambiguity for helpers who must advise parents faced with difficult questions of how to assign gender to an infant.

Another kind of gender atypicality affects individuals with an XY chromosome pair who have a defective gene, causing their external genitalia to look much like a girl's at birth. This is a rare disorder that occurs with unusual frequency in the Dominican Republic, where such children are raised as girls. Yet at puberty, when their bodies become more masculine in appearance and the genitals begin to develop more normally, most of these individuals accept reassignment to a male identity with apparently no difficulty, despite their early socialization as girls (e.g., Imperato-McGinley, Peterson, Gautier, & Sturla, 1979; see Collaer & Hines, 1995). Again, questions can be raised about just how unambiguously such children are treated before puberty, given that the culture has a lot of experience with these "girls who turn into boys," but there is room to speculate here about whether biological factors contribute to how easily a gender assignment, or reassignment, is adopted. Socialization may not be as powerful as it was once thought to be in the development of gender identity.

Gender and Behavior

Many of us believe that males and females have at least some different behavioral tendencies, and some people believe that there are major differences in the distribution of personality traits between the sexes. Such beliefs about sex differences are called **gender stereotypes.** Researchers have found evidence for some of the differences that people believe in, but other stereotypes seem to be based on expectations that have no basis in fact. In this section, we will first take a look at some of the sex differences that have been found, especially in children. Then, we'll consider some of the theoretical explanations that have been proposed for sex differences. That is, when they actually exist, how do they develop?

Sex Differences in Behavior, Personality, and Preference

In 1974, Maccoby and Jacklin did a careful review of the scientific literature on sex differences. They surprised most observers by concluding that there were only four behaviors, skills, or tendencies that clearly differed for males and females: physical aggression, language skills, math skills, and spatial skills. Even in these domains, some behaviors differed across the life span (e.g., aggression) and others only during certain developmental periods, such as after puberty (e.g., math skills). Since 1974, researchers have acquired a new analytic tool for assessing the effects of variables such as sex. It's called *meta-analysis,* in which the results from a large number of studies on the same question—such as, "are there sex differences in physical aggression?"—can be combined to produce an average estimate of the difference in a population (G. Glass, 1976).

The results of many meta-analyses are now available, and the list of "real" sex differences has lengthened. (See Table 8.1: *A Sampling of Sex Differences.*) In addition, our knowledge of sex differences is now more fine tuned. With regard to math, for example, we know that boys tend to do better than girls in *problem solving* after puberty but that girls tend to do better than boys on *computations* in elementary school and early adolescence (Hyde, Fennema, & Lamon, 1990). We also have been collecting data for long enough, and in enough circumstances, that we know that these differences can change historically, and they can vary from one situation to another. For example, historical change has affected math skills, such that differences between boys and girls are smaller now than they were three or four decades ago (e.g., Feingold, 1988). An example of situational variation has been found for children's tendency to be adult oriented, that is, to want to have adults nearby. When both boys and girls are present, girls are more adult oriented than boys. But when girls are with girls, they are no more adult oriented than boys are with boys (Greeno, 1989).

It is just as interesting to note the differences that have *not* been found as those that have. Among the common sex stereotypes, for example, are that females are more sociable, more dependent, and more prosocial than males and that males are more competent at analytical tasks. Although occasional studies have reported findings that are consistent with these expectations, in most studies such differences are not found. Similarly, arguments that males and females differ in moral reasoning have received a great deal of popular and scientific attention in recent years. As we mentioned in Chapter 7, Gilligan (e.g., 1977, 1982) proposed that whereas males are more likely to focus on issues of justice or fairness in their moral reasoning, females are more concerned with issues of interpersonal responsibility and compassion. But the evidence indicates that children show no differences in their tendencies to focus on such issues (Garrod & Beal, 1993) and that both men and women raise both kinds of issues when they solve moral problems or judge moral maturity (e.g., Walker & Pitts, 1998). Occasionally, adolescent and adult females have been found to raise more concerns about people's needs than adolescent or adult males in addressing real-life dilemmas, but people of both genders raise such concerns quite frequently (Walker, 1984, 1995; Wark & Krebs, 1996).

When sex differences are consistently found, they usually turn out to be small in size. Figure 8.2 illustrates the considerable overlap between males and females on those traits that show some sex difference. Some researchers have argued strongly that gender differences are too small to be important in development, especially since the *average* difference *between* genders is much smaller than the *range* of differences *within* each gender (Thorne, 1994).

TABLE 8.1

A Sampling of Gender Differences

Trait or Quality	More Typical of	Time of Onset
Developmental vulnerability (learning disabilities, illness, accidents, etc.)	Boys	Prebirth
Activity level	Boys	Infant
Happy, excited mood	Boys	Infant/toddler
Risk taking	Boys	Infant/toddler
Physical aggression	Boys	Toddler
Competitive play	Boys	Preschool
Controlling "egoistic" discourse style	Boys	Preschool
Dominance seeking; clear group hierarchy	Boys	Preschool
Spatial skill: Mental rotation	Boys	Middle childhood
Antisocial aggressive disorders	Boys	Middle childhood
Satisfaction with one's gender assignment	Boys	Middle childhood
Math problem solving	Boys	After puberty
Homosexuality, bisexuality	Boys	Adolescence
Preference for gender-typed toys	Both	Toddler
Preference for same-gender playmates	Both	Toddler
Quiet, clam mood	Girls	Infant
Language onset (vocabulary)	Girls	Toddler
Collaborative discourse style	Girls	Preschool
Verbal achievement (spelling, language tests)	Girls	Middle childhood
Emotional expressiveness	Girls	Middle childhood
Relational aggression (refusing friendship, exclusion from group)	Girls	Middle childhood
Depression	Girls	Adolescence
Social sensitivity	Girls	Adulthood

Key: Prebirth—Conception to birth; Infant—0 to 1 year; Toddler—1 to 3 years; Preschool—3 to 6 years; Middle childhood—6 to puberty; Adolescence—Puberty to 18; Adulthood—18 onward

Sources: Maccoby, E. E. (1998) *The two sexes: Growing up apart, coming together.* Cambridge, MA: Harvard University Press; Ruble, D. N., & Martin, C. L. (1998). Gender development. In W. Damon (Series Ed.) & N. Eisenberg (Vol. Ed.) *Handbook of child psychology vol. 3* (5th ed., pp. 933–1016); Shaffer, D. R. (2000). *Social and personality development.* Belmont, CA: Wadsworth/Thomson.

However, average individual differences between the sexes may not be the important story in gender role development. More and more, developmentalists are recognizing that although boys and girls do not behave much differently in laboratory measures of personality or on individual abilities, they do spend their time differently. Specifically, girls spend their time interacting primarily with girls, and boys spend their time mostly with boys. In settings where there are both males and females of similar ages available, such as schools and playgrounds, and where there is freedom to choose one's companions, this

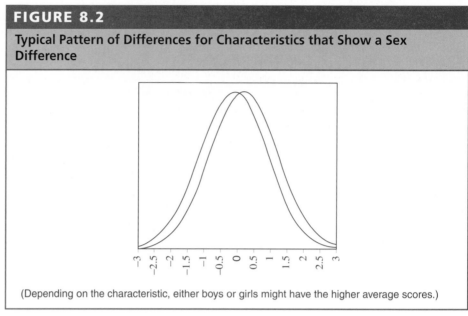

FIGURE 8.2

Typical Pattern of Differences for Characteristics that Show a Sex Difference

(Depending on the characteristic, either boys or girls might have the higher average scores.)

Source: Maccoby, E. E. (1998). *The two sexes: Growing up apart, coming together,* Figure 6, p. 80: Based on Eagley, 1995: *American Psychologist,* 50; pp. 145–158. Reprinted by permission of Harvard University Press.

sex segregation process begins by about 2½ for girls and by about 3 for boys (e.g., La Freniere, Strayer, & Gauthier, 1984), and it increases with age (Maccoby & Jacklin, 1987). Sex segregation characterizes children around the world, in both industrialized and nonindustrialized societies (e.g., Omark, Omark, & Edelman, 1973; Whiting and Edwards, 1988). When children are about 4, the time they spend with same-sex peers is triple the time they spend with other-sex peers. By the time children are 6, they spend 11 times more time with same-sex peers! During elementary school, sex segregation intensifies, and it

As children mature, they spend increasingly greater amounts of time in sex-segregated peer groups.

begins to ease off only after puberty, when, drawn together by sexual interest, children begin to participate more readily in mixed-gender activities. During middle childhood, mixed-gender interactions, called **borderwork,** tend to be quite limited (Thorne, 1986, 1994). In fact, there seem to be unwritten "rules" that govern when it is acceptable for boys and girls to engage in mixed-gender interactions. Allen Sroufe and his colleagues (Sroufe, Bennett, Englund, Urban, & Shulman, 1993) observed 10- and 11-year-olds at a summer camp, for example, and identified a set of six rules that seemed to determine when children would cross the boundaries of their single-sex groups (see Table 8.2).

When children segregate by gender, other behaviors also tend to diverge. For example, suppose that Carissa and Duane, both 6 years old, are equally active when they play alone on the playground. They climb on the jungle gym with about average vigor for children their age, and they are more inclined to skip and jog from place to place than either to walk or to run full tilt. When Carissa plays with her girlfriends, her activity level stays about the same. But when Duane plays with a group of boys, he is notably more active than when he plays alone: he moves more vigorously on the jungle gym or runs with greater intensity. "Boys are stimulated to high levels of activity by other boys" (Maccoby, 1998).

Children do somewhat different things in their same-sex groups. Perhaps most notable is that boys' play in groups is more physical and more aggressive than girls' play. (This is true in all primate species, across cultures, and from the earliest ages that youngsters play together, Ruble & Martin, 1998). When Carissa and her friends ride the wheeled vehicles in the play yard of their after-school child care center, they ride around carefully to avoid hitting each other. But when Duane and his friends are in the drivers' seats, their favorite thing to do is ram into each other—the harder the better (e.g., S. Dunn & Morgan, 1987).

TABLE 8.2

Rules Governing Mixed-Gender Interaction, or "Borderwork"

Rule:	The contact is accidental.
Example:	You're not looking where you are going and you bump into someone.
Rule:	The contact is incidental.
Example:	You go to get some lemonade and wait while two children of the other gender get some. (There should be no conversation.)
Rule:	The contact is in the guise of some clear and necessary purpose.
Example:	You may say, "Pass the lemonade," to persons of the other gender at the next table. No interest in them is expressed.
Rule:	An adult compels you to have contact.
Example:	"Go get that map from X and Y and bring it to me."
Rule:	You are accompanied by someone of your own gender.
Example:	Two girls may talk to two boys, though physical closeness with your own partner must be maintained and intimacy with the others is disallowed.
Rule:	The interaction or contact is accompanied by disavowal.
Example:	You say someone is ugly or hurl some other insult or (more commonly for boys) push or throw something at them as you pass by.

Source: Sroufe, L. A., Bennett, C., England, M., et al. (1993). The significance of gender. *Child Development, 64,* p. 456. Reprinted by permission of Blackwell Publishers, Inc.

Good-natured physical roughness is called **rough and tumble play,** an almost exclusive property of boys' play with boys. Maccoby (1998) indicates that most boys are not consistently aggressive across situations. That is, physical aggressiveness is not so much a personality trait that you see when a child is in any situation—with adults, girls, or boys—although it can be for some children. More typically, it emerges when boys are with boys. Thus, it becomes an important defining feature of boys' social groups, which differ in specific ways from girls' social groups. Boys often use rough and tumble play to help establish dominance hierarchies within their groups, with more dominant boys less likely to back down and less often aggressed against. Generally, boys play in larger groups than do girls, who are more likely to play in twos and threes, and the boys' groups are more clearly structured hierarchically. Although girls' groups usually have their more and less dominant members, the rankings are not very stable, and leadership does not depend on toughness as much as on other leadership qualities, such as social skill (Maccoby, 1998; Martin & Fabes, 2001).

Girls' and boys' groups differ on other dimensions as well. Boys compete with each other more than girls do. As preschoolers they compete for resources, such as attractive toys, and in middle childhood they compete in structured games. Girls' interactions tend to be more cooperative and to involve much more turn taking. These characteristics of gendered groups are integrally related to the kinds of activities that bring boys and girls together. In particular, boys seem to spend time with other boys who have shared interests, especially starting in middle childhood, and they are more likely than girls to be interested in sports and games and in adventure. For example, when boys pretend, their play tends to involve heroic or warlike themes (e.g., Flannery & Watson, 1993).

Girls often seem to get together just to be together, and their choice of companions is based more on personality (Erwin, 1985). On the whole, they tend to have broader interests than boys, and they are more interested in boys' activities than boys are in girls' activities. But they do have stronger tendencies than boys to like play that enacts family or school experiences, and increasingly from preschool onward, girls' pretend play themes have to do with adornment and beauty—being models or brides, doing glamorous or romantic things (Maccoby, 1998).

As you can see, girls' groups and boys' groups have different cultures to which the members, regardless of their individual characteristics, must adapt. A good example of this difference is the degree to which they use **collaborative** versus **domineering discourse** techniques (Leaper, 1991). In collaborative speech, more often used in girls' groups, children's responses are keyed to what someone else has said, expressing agreement, making further suggestions, often in the form of a question rather than declarative or imperative sentences, which seems to soften the suggestion. For example, Carissa might say to a friend as they plan a game, "You want to be the mommy. Why don't we both be the mommy sometimes?" In domineering speech, more typical of boys' groups, commands and restrictions are common, as when Duane says, "Don't move that block; build the road there!" It is important to note that both boys and girls will use both kinds of discourse. It is the predominance of one type over the other that differs between their groups (e.g., Sachs, 1987). On the whole, girls' discourse strategies are more "conflict mitigating" and boys strategies are more "egoistic"—threatening, demanding, interrupting, or ignoring of another's remarks (Maccoby, 1998).

Where do sex differences in behavior come from? There are theories that emphasize the importance of biology, of cognitive processes, and of socialization pressures. Clearly, all three, as always, are important. As you will see, some theorists are emphasizing the interaction of the three as children spend time in same-gender peer groups. It seems that gender segregation in childhood, perhaps the most pervasive sex difference, may be both an outcome of some sex differences and a source of others.

The Role of Biology in Generating Sex Differences

We know that genetic differences between males and females normally play a role in the differential development of reproductive organs. For a male, who has an X and a Y chromosome, a gene on the Y chromosome influences the gonads to develop into testes (see Chapter 2). Without that gene, the gonads develop into ovaries. Testes then produce masculinizing hormones (mostly androgens), which influence the development of the remaining male genitalia. Without the quantities of androgens that testes produce, other female parts gradually develop. Do masculinizing hormones also affect the developing nervous system, thus influencing postnatal behavior? In animals, there is evidence that prenatal hormones do affect neural structures (e.g., Arnold & Gorski, 1984), and in both animals and humans, there appear to be effects on early behavior. For example, male rats whose exposure to prenatal androgens is delayed not only show a slight demasculinization of their genitalia but they also show more feminized play behaviors as pups (e.g., I. L. Ward, 1992; I. L. Ward & Stehm, 1991).

In humans, girls with CAH who are overexposed to prenatal (and sometimes postnatal) androgens have been found to exhibit more ***tomboyism***—playing with boys and preferring boys' toys and activities—than non-CAH girls (e.g., Ehrhardt, Epstein, & Money, 1968; Berenbaum & Hines, 1992; Berenbaum & Snyder, 1995). Findings such as these are open to several interpretations. For one, parents of girls with CAH may have doubts about their daughters' sexual identity that could affect their daughters' behavior; for another, these girls have many unusual experiences, such as genital surgeries and ongoing medical treatments, that could affect their behavioral development; and so on (see Collaer & Hines, 1995). However, the somewhat masculinized behaviors of CAH girls may also indicate a role for prenatal (and/or postnatal) hormones in some of the typical behavioral differences found between boys and girls.

At puberty, hormonal changes, and hormonal differences, between boys and girls may also cause some behavioral differences that emerge at about that time. For example, although depressive symptoms increase for both girls and boys after puberty, they increase more for girls; boys show more increases in aggressive, delinquent behaviors than girls (see Table 8.1 and Chapter 9). Could these differences in problem behavior be linked to hormones? It is a sensible question to ask, and some connections have been identified. For example, there is a link between boys' androgen levels and their aggressiveness (Buchanan, Eccles, & Becker, 1992). But one difficulty in interpreting such connections is that while androgens may increase aggressiveness, one's experiences, such as family conflict, may change hormone levels (e.g., Steinberg, 1988). In particular, for males, aggression and dominance seeking can increase testosterone, an androgen (see Cacioppo & Berntson, 1992). So whether hormone levels cause or result from behavior and experience during and after puberty is not clear.

Research on brain structures and functioning has sometimes supported the idea that brain differences may underlie some gender differences, but many of the findings are controversial. Among the differences for which there is some evidence is greater lateralization in males than in females, that is, greater differentiation in the functioning of the two hemispheres of the brain, with language functions more clearly governed by the left hemisphere in males (Bryden, 1988; Halpern, 1992). Even in children as young as 16 months, patterns of brain activation appear to be more lateralized for word comprehension in boys than in girls (as measured by magnetic resonance imaging, or MRI) (Molfese, 1990). If females are less lateralized, using more of both hemispheres for language functions, it could account for the female advantage in language. But this, and other brain differences, if they exist, could as easily be the result of different experiences. That is, when behavioral differences develop, they may *cause* differences in brain function rather than being the result of such differences. Given what we have learned about brain development (see Chapter 3), it seems likely that the causal links work both ways.

The Role of Cognition in Generating Sex Differences

When Ben was 5 years old, he loved to sit with his mother early in the morning while she dressed for work. He especially enjoyed watching her comb her hair and tie it back with a ribbon. One day he asked if he could have a ribbon in his own hair. His mother, who tried to encourage nonsexist ideas in her children, tied a ribbon in Ben's hair, and he spent some happy moments admiring himself in the mirror. But soon he grew still, staring at his image, and he finally asked, "Do boys wear ribbons in their hair?" to which his mother responded, "Not usually." Ben grasped the ribbon and tore it off his head, pulling strands of hair along with it. Then, bursting into tears, he ran from the room. Despite his mother's neutrality, Ben was angry and humiliated that he had done a "girl" thing. Several cognitive theories of gender differences have been proposed to explain behaviors such as Ben's. We will examine them next.

Cognitive-Developmental Theories. Cognitive-developmental theorists such as Kohlberg (1966) have argued that when children acquire an understanding of the constancy of gender identity, partly as a function of advances in their logical thinking skills, they are *intrinsically motivated* to learn all they can about what it means to be male or female, and they are eager to behave in gender-appropriate ways. In other words, children actively seek to make their behavior consistent with their gender identity, whether or not they experience social pressure to do so. The anecdote about Ben seems to illustrate the power of such a cognitively based motivational system. There is also research evidence to support a cognitive basis for at least some of children's gendered behaviors, although contrary to Kohlberg's notion, a full understanding of gender constancy does not seem to be required. Rather, establishing basic gender identity (i.e., learning one's own gender category) seems to be sufficient to foster a drive to learn about gendered behavior and a tendency to make gender-typical choices (e.g., Weinraub, Clemens, Sockloff, Ethridge, Gracely, & Myers, 1984). Once gender stability is established, children are increasingly likely to make gender-based choices over what may be more attractive choices, as Ben did (e.g, Frey & Ruble, 1992).

Cognitive-developmental theories also suggest that when children achieve gender constancy, their thinking about gender differences should become more "flexible" and less stereotyped. They now understand that superficial characteristics can change without changing one's underlying gender category. Therefore, children should be able to see that sex role stereotypes, such as girls wearing dresses and boys wearing pants, are social conventions, not moral imperatives and not requirements for maintaining one's gender identity. Indeed, children's thinking about gender does tend to become more flexible in middle childhood, after gender constancy is achieved, although in early adolescence, there is some tendency for kids to become more rigid in their thinking about what's permissible for people of different genders (Huston, 1983; Ruble & Martin, 1998). The *gender intensification hypothesis* suggests that one way young teens cope with the demands of establishing an adult identity is to fall back on stereotyped notions of masculinity or femininity (Hill & Lynch, 1983; see Chapter 9 on the development of identity in adolescence).

Gender Schema Theories. Cognitive theorists in the information processing tradition emphasize the role of *gender schemas* in influencing the behavior of children and adults (S. L. Bem, 1981; Markus, Crane, Bernstein, & Siladi, 1982). A gender schema is a network of expectations and beliefs about male and female characteristics. Schemas affect what we pay attention to, what we interpret, and what we remember about events. So, for example, if elementary school children hear stories or see pictures of men or women engaged in cross-sex behaviors—such as a woman doing carpentry work—they are likely to remember the pictures later in ways more consistent with their gender schemas. In this example, they might later remember that they heard about, or saw, a *man* working as a carpenter (e.g., Liben & Signorella, 1980; 1993; Welch-Ross & Schmidt, 1996).

These theories posit that the gender schema children have for their own sex affects what behaviors they choose to learn about and what behaviors they choose for themselves, but the theories do not account for the exact mechanisms by which schemas are constructed. Social experiences and available role models presumably affect sex differences by affecting what children know or believe about what is gender appropriate. But, according to cognitive theorists, it is the schemas, not the social experiences directly, that motivate children to adopt sex-typed behavior. Research on schema theory has provided mixed support (Fagot, 1985; Fagot & Leinbach, 1989). Specifically, linkages between cognitive schemas and actual behavior have not been well established.

Children's Knowledge of Gender Stereotypes. In general, cognitive theorists assume that the acquisition of knowledge about sex stereotypes influences the feminization and masculinization of children's behavior, regardless of whether others reward or otherwise pressure children to adopt gender-typed behavior. From this perspective, it is important to learn what children know about sex stereotypes and when they know it if we want to understand the development of sex differences. Research indicates that by age 3, most children know something about gender-related preferences for toys and activities. For example, they expect girls to enjoy playing with dolls and to be more likely to cry, and they expect boys to enjoy playing with trucks and to be more likely to be rough or "mean" (Ruble & Martin, 1998). By school entry, about age 5 or 6, knowledge of gendered activities and occupations is very extensive (Liben, Bigler, & Krogh, 2002; Signorella, Bigler, & Liben, 1993). In middle childhood, children become more aware of psychological stereotypes, such as expecting boys to be more competent, and they begin to expect that a person with one gender-typical trait or behavior will have others as well. By age 10, children are aware of differences in the ways males and females are evaluated in their culture. In particular, they recognize that females and many female-typical behaviors are devalued (Intons-Peterson, 1988). Of course, such awareness may help explain why females show a greater susceptibility to depression beginning in early adolescence than males do.

However, knowledge of stereotypes does not necessarily lead to conduct in keeping with those stereotypes. Similarly, individuals may vary in their behavior (both consistent with and inconsistent with stereotypes) depending upon context (Bandura, 1986). For example, female officers in the armed services may behave in stereotypically masculine ways while on duty but may act in more stereotypically feminine ways outside of work. A young boy may play house with his sister at home but never do so with other boys at school.

Research also indicates that factors other than gender knowledge affect some sex differences. For example, cognitive theories explain children's preferences for same-sex playmates as a function of the human tendency to value members of one's own in-group over members of an out-group. Once children identify themselves as male or female, they should quickly begin the gender segregation process. But even though boys tend to learn their own gender category a bit earlier than girls do, girls show same-sex playmate preferences earlier than boys do. As Maccoby (1998) suggested, knowledge of one's own gender identity may be a necessary but not a sufficient condition for gender segregation. In the next section, we will examine some of the social influences that may directly affect the development of sex differences, including children's preferences for same-sex playmates.

The Role of Parenting Processes in Generating Sex Differences

A number of theories, in many different traditions, have argued that parenting practices have a special role to play in the development of sex differences.

Freud's Psychoanalytic Theory. One of the oldest social influence theories of sex role development is Freud's psychoanalytic theory (e.g., 1935/1960; see Chapter 1). Freud argued that at about age 3, children begin to have vague sexual needs. These needs create a family triangle that plays out somewhat differently for boys versus girls. Boys are buffeted by a tempest of motives and emotions called an **Oedipus complex.** First, they direct their sexual urges toward their mothers, because they are most strongly attached to their mothers as primary caretakers. Then, this desire for the mother, to usurp her time, to be physically close to her, puts a boy in competition with his father for her affections. The boy fears that his more powerful father will retaliate with a physical punishment that fits the crime—castration. Finally, the boy is so terrified by the prospect of his father's retaliation that he redirects his energy into pleasing his father by identifying with him. This *identification* process involves both imitation and internalization. Identification explains why boys adopt sex-typed behaviors: they are acting like their fathers. It also explains how boys form a *superego,* a kind of conscience: they internalize their fathers' values (see Chapter 7).

In Freud's theory, girls go through a similar process called the **Electra complex.** They direct their initial sexual desires toward their fathers, even though they too are more strongly attached to their mothers. That is because they experience **penis envy,** a desire to have what they naively assume is the greater genital pleasure that must come with having the external genitalia of a male. Then they find themselves in competition with their mothers, although their fear of their mothers' displeasure is not so great as a boy's because they assume that somehow they have already been castrated. They do not understand that their genitalia are simply more internal than are a boy's. Eventually, they identify with their mothers to make peace, although because they do not fear castration, they do not identify as closely with their mothers as boys do with their fathers. Thus, girls too become gender typed in their behavior and form a superego. However, neither process is as intense for a girl as it is for a boy. This was Freud's way of explaining why women are "morally inferior" to men, a belief that was endemic to the time and place in which Freud himself was enculturated.

Although many aspects of Freud's tale of sexual desire, competition, and fear in young children have become deeply embedded in our culture, efforts to validate the theory have been unsuccessful. For example, one prediction we can make from Freud's theory is that traditional family structure—mother as primary caregiver, father as her sexual partner and a strong presence in the home—should be necessary for children to experience normal sex role development. Yet, sex role development is not impeded in children who come from single-parent homes, nor even in children who come from homes where both parents are of one sex (e.g., Bailey, Bobrow, Wolfe, & Mikach, 1995; Golombok & Tasker, 1996; C. J. Patterson, 1992).

There is also little evidence that children model themselves after a single identification figure. Rather, research indicates that children will model themselves after others whom they perceive to be like themselves (e.g., same gender) (Bussey & Bandura 1984), as the cognitive theorists predict, and whom they perceive as competent. It also helps if the model is not scary or punitive, but rather is perceived as nurturant (Bandura, 1977; see Ruble & Martin, 1998).

Social Learning Theories. Social learning theorists argue that many parents and other adults influence children's sex-typed behaviors, both by modeling such behaviors and by differential treatment of boys and girls that teaches them to behave in sex-appropriate ways.

What evidence is there that adults actually do behave differently toward children based on gender? First, we should note that in many ways, boys and girls are not treated differently. Meta-analyses indicate no differences in how much parents interact with their sons and daughters, in how much parents encourage them to achieve, in how much parents encourage dependency or help-seeking, in how much warmth or responsiveness parents show, or in how effectively parents communicate or reason with them (e.g., Lytton & Romney, 1991).

However, there are *some* important differences in parental behaviors. Mothers talk more, use more supportive speech, and talk more about emotions with their daughters (e.g., Dunn, Bretherton, & Munn, 1987; Leaper, Anderson, & Sanders, 1998). Many parents place more pressure on preschool boys than girls not to cry or express feelings (Block, 1978). There are other parental differences as well, with fathers more likely than mothers to have different expectations of their sons than their daughters (Siegal, 1987). They are more likely to be disapproving of cross-sex behavior in their sons than in their daughters, more likely to roughhouse with their sons, and more likely to be negative or confrontational with them (Maccoby, 1998). Indeed, Katz and Walsh (1991) suggest that children come to see men as "the custodians of gender-role norms" (p. 349). In Western societies, boys typically experience stronger pressure to conform to gender-stereotypic behavior than do girls, because the sanctions when boys deviate from such norms are more severe than they are for girls (Sandnabba & Alhberg, 1999).

Other differences in adult socialization practices with boys versus girls may be particularly important in laying the groundwork for later sex differences in psychopathology. Keenan and Shaw (1997) reviewed a number of findings that are consistent with such a conclusion. They report that preschool girls, in contrast to boys, are more often reinforced by their parents for compliant behavior and more often ignored for attempts to direct interaction in free-play situations (Kerig, Cowan, & Cowan, 1993). Parents also socialize children to deal with conflict in different ways. Girls are more frequently encouraged to yield to peers in conflict situations, for example, by giving up a desired toy (Ross, Tesla, Kenyon, & Lollis, 1990). Girls are also taught, to a greater degree than boys, to take others' perspectives and feelings into account in situations involving conflict (Smetana, 1989). Preschool teachers have sometimes been found to react more negatively to girls than to boys for high levels of activity, including activity levels during play, and more positively to girls than to boys for dependency behaviors (Fagot, 1984). In sum, these authors conclude that there is evidence to suggest that early socialization experiences help channel the development of internalizing behaviors in girls and externalizing behaviors in boys.

To what extent are adults' behaviors causes of sex differences in children, as social learning theorists would argue, and to what extent are they *responses* to already existing sex differences? As we have seen so many times, the causal processes here seem to be reciprocal. For example, parents make more attempts to "down-regulate" boys' emotional responses in the preschool years (Block, 1978), but boys are also slower to develop self-regulatory skills than are girls. It seems likely that parents are influenced in part by the fact that boys have more impulsive emotional outbursts *and* in part by their desire to teach boys not to display weakness (Maccoby, 1998). Another example is that parents talk more to their daughters than to their sons. This may influence girls' language development, but earlier growth of vocabulary in girls may help influence parents' behavior as well.

The Role of Peer Interactions in Generating Sex Differences

We have already emphasized how intensive the sex segregation process is, beginning as early as 2½, and becoming by middle childhood the most extreme sex difference that there is: girls spend much of their unstructured time with girls, boys with boys. As we have seen, gender segregation may be influenced by cognitive processes, such that when children become aware of their gender identity, they value members of the same in-group more than members of the out-group. Some preexisting sex differences, influenced by either biology or parenting or both, may also make same-gender companions more appealing. In particular, Maccoby (1990; 1998) has suggested that girls tend to be wary of boys' rough play and to turn away from it. If so, initial differences in children's play styles are then magnified in same-gender peer groups.

> Here is a plausible scenario: Individual boys, each prenatally sensitized (or primed by parents) to respond positively to overtures for rough, arousing play, will choose each other as playmates. . . . And girls, individually sensitized by their parents to others' feelings, or in a state of greater readiness to receive socialization inputs of this kind from their parents, will use (their) attributes to build a new and distinctively female type of interaction with their playmates . . . the whole is greater than the sum of its parts . . . merging individual children . . . into a group, will produce a new form of interaction that is different from what they have experienced with their parents. (Maccoby, 1998, pp. 296–297)

The important point is that within their gendered peer groups children develop interaction styles that are more differentiated than either biology or parenting would predict. In a recent study, Martin and Fabes (2001) observed 3- to 5-year-olds' play-partner choices over a 6-month period. They found that "sex segregation was pervasive" among their 61 study participants. Over 80% of the children had clear same-sex play-partner preferences, even though teachers encouraged gender equity, and the stability of these preferences increased over the 6 months of the study. The results also demonstrated that same-sexed peers seem to have a socializing influence on children, just as Maccoby suggests. Stereotyped sex differences, such as activity level differences, "developed or increased over time." Most interesting was that there was a *social dosage effect:* children who spent more time in same-gender groups showed greater increases in gender-related behaviors even after only a few months.

In adolescence, when boys and girls begin to build cross-gender groups and relationships, their different interaction styles can create difficulties. For example, in studies of mixed-sex problem-solving groups, young women can be at a disadvantage. They tend to express agreement with others more often than young men do, consistent with their gendered discourse style, but unlike their experience in all-female peer groups, they may never get their chance to speak because males do less turn taking and are more domineering. Overall, they tend to have less influence on the outcome (see Maccoby, 1990). Similarly, in heterosexual dyads, males do not offer as much support to their partners as females do for the expression of feelings. As you might expect, males seem less well prepared for the mutuality of intimate relationships, perhaps because of the discourse style they acquire in their larger, less intimate childhood groups (Leaper, 1994b).

Gilligan (e.g., 1993) and Pipher (1994) describe females as "losing their voice" when they reach adolescence because they feel pressure to adapt themselves to what others want them to be. Perhaps, instead, the more cooperative discourse style of females, in the face of the more egoistic male style, makes girls and women less powerful agents when interacting with males than when they are interacting with other females.

A Multidimensional Theory of Sex Differences in Behavior

As we have seen, several different explanations for gender differences in behavior have some empirical support, but all of them have some important limitations as well. Clearly what is needed is a multidimensional theory that takes into account multiple causal influences and that specifies how these influences transact to produce gender differences. A social-cognitive theory proposed by Bussey and Bandura (1999) takes a more complex approach to gender differences than the causal explanations we have considered so far. Bussey and Bandura specify three categories of variables that interact reciprocally to help shape the development of gender role, including gender differences in behavior. These factors include personal influences (cognitive conceptions of gender, affective and biological features of the person), behavioral influences (learning of and execution of activities that are gender linked), and environmental influences (family, peer, and societal). All these influences interact reciprocally to mold the motivational and self-regulatory structures that determine behavior. For example, family and societal influences contribute to children's knowledge base about gender and gender-linked competencies by serving as models and by providing rewards or sanctions for gender-appropriate/inappropriate behavior. In addition, both proximal and distal social forces help shape children's patterns of expectations about how genders behave, their beliefs about how these behaviors will be evaluated by others, and their constructions about their own competence to enact the behaviors in gender-appropriate ways.

Although Bussey and Bandura (1999) specify that affective and biological features of the person are important, in their more detailed analyses of how various causes interact in gender role development they tend to emphasize social (especially parental) and cognitive factors. They suggest that at least initially adult sanctions and direct teaching contribute

Children construct internalized standards for appropriate gender-linked behavior partly based upon adult models and sanctions.

most to the production of behaviors that are considered gender appropriate. As you have seen, research attests to the important role that children's early socialization experiences play in the development of gender-linked behavior. Clearly, there are differences across cultures in the specifics of gender-appropriate behavior, but most cultures do place restrictions on what the genders should and should not do. Yet these behaviors are not shaped just by patterns of external contingencies. Children grow increasingly more adept at monitoring and evaluating themselves according to personal standards and according to the circumstances of the contexts in which they find themselves. Self-regulatory functions become progressively more internalized and direct childrens' behavior in ways that maximize self-satisfaction and minimize self-censure (Bandura, 1986). Children learn to anticipate the consequences of their actions and can thus predict the responses their behaviors will elicit from others. These emerging capacities for self-monitoring and prediction are linked to the development of internalized standards for performance, largely based upon how others in the social world have responded to the behavior, the models that have been observed, and what has been taught directly. Gender-linked behavior is thus maintained by ongoing social influences operating through psychological mechanisms such as motivation, expectancy for success, and self-efficacy. These internal mechanisms have been constructed in the process of interacting with a world in which gender is a highly salient social category.

While Bussey and Bandura (1999) provide an attempt to take into account some of the complexity of interacting causal processes in gender role development, much more work is needed to construct a theory that includes all of the influences that we have seen to be important. Future theorists, for example, need to integrate the recent findings on peers' power to affect the development of gendered behavior. In the next section, we will take a broader look at the whole arena of peer relationships and the place of peers in the lives of children.

PEER RELATIONSHIPS

In 1958, the Primary Mental Health Project, a program for early identification of at-risk students, was initiated in the first grades of several schools in Monroe County, New York. Data from social work interviews with mothers, classroom observations, teacher reports, other school records, and psychological evaluations such as intelligence, personality, and achievement tests were compiled for each of the children in the hope of identifying variables that would predict later adjustment difficulties. Based upon these multiple measures, children were given either a "red" or "non-red" tag. Red-tagged first-graders were those whose behavior, educational achievement, and social-emotional functioning reflected moderate to severe maladaptation. Out of the total of three academic-year samples (1958–1959, 1959–1960, and 1960–1961), approximately one third of the youngsters received red tags (Cowen, Izzo, Miles, Telschow, Trost, & Zax, 1963).

In a separate and fortunate development, the Medical Center of the University of Rochester initiated a county psychiatric registry concurrent with the school-based project. This registry provided an ongoing, longitudinal record of most persons in the county who were diagnosed with mental health problems and who had received treatment. These two unrelated sources of information made it possible to track the histories of the children in the Primary Mental Health Project 11 to 13 years later by means of registry entries (Cowen, Petersen, Babigian, Izzo, & Trost, 1973).

As they moved into early adulthood, individuals who had been "red-tagged" as children showed up in the registry in disproportionate numbers. They represented more than two out of every three individuals on the list of those needing psychiatric care. You already know from reading the previous chapters that there is evidence for continuity of behavioral and emotional problems over time, so this is not too surprising. What is intriguing about this story, however, is what predicted these later problems best. In other words, what kinds of measures separated youth who ended up in the registry from their agemates who did not? If researchers had known the answer to this question, they might have been able to identify and treat children before more serious problems surfaced.

Remember that the researchers administered intelligence, personality, and achievement tests, obtained behavior rating scale data, amassed grade and attendance information, and interviewed parents. They also asked the children themselves to nominate their peers for various hypothetical roles, half positive (e.g., the lead character) and half negative (e.g., the villain) in a "Class Play" exercise (Bower, 1960). Researchers found through retrospective comparison that individuals on the county registry performed slightly less well than their age-mates on most assessment measures, but not significantly so. There was, however, one important exception. The extent to which children were nominated by their grade school peers for negative roles in the class play significantly predicted later membership in the registry. Children far and away outpredicted the adults in recognizing those children destined for later psychological problems. What did these children know?

As we have seen in our discussion of sex role development, peers are a significant force in the lives of children. The story of how effectively grade school children's feelings predicted their peers' later mental health outcomes introduces us to the fascinating world of the peer group, its dynamics in childhood and adolescence, and its relevance to later outcomes. In particular, it implies that peer relationships in childhood are significant predictors of later mental health and social adjustment.

The Peer Group, Social Competence, and Social Skills

What makes for good peer relationships? In order to answer this question, we need to understand something about the nature of peer groups and the distinctions researchers make between social competence and particular social skills. The study of the peer group may be distinguished from the study of simple social interactions or even the study of friendship relationships in ways that are familiar to counselors, given their special training. Group counseling, for example, differs from individual counseling not only because there are more people involved in the process but also because the interrelationships and dynamics become much more complex.

> Groups are more than mere aggregates of relationships; through emergent properties such as norms or shared cultural conventions, groups help define the type and range of relationships and interactions that are likely or permissible. Further, groups have properties and processes, such as hierarchical organization and cohesiveness, that are not relevant to descriptions of children's experiences at lower levels of social complexity. (Rubin, Bukowski, & Parker, 1998, p. 623)

Social competence, a criterion for peer group acceptance, is a broad construct that is not restricted to one set of prescribed behaviors. Affective responses, such as empathy and valuing of relationships, and cognitive processes, such as perspective taking (see Chapter 5) and ability to make mature moral judgments (see Chapter 7), play a part in the repertoire of the socially adept individual. It is impossible to assess the social competence of a child without considering his skill in relating to others at every relationship level. Social but "non-friend" interactions, as well as friendship relationships, are embedded within the larger peer group structure, each influencing and influenced by the other levels of social exchange. Remember, then, that a child's success or lack of success within his peer group

Box 8.1 Prevention

There is a clear connection between developmental knowledge and prevention. Indeed, it is hard to imagine a more compelling reason for studying human growth and development than to be able to use this knowledge to prevent problems from occurring. Thinking developmentally about prevention automatically leads a helper to consider why problems occur, the nature of the forces acting on individuals that lead to certain endpoints, the strengths and weaknesses that are part of personal histories, and the functions addressed by individuals' maladaptive behaviors.

Primary prevention has been a part of community efforts to improve health and human functioning for over a century in this country (Spaulding & Balch, 1983), and counselors, in particular, have been in the business of prevention for a long time (Wrenn, 1962). However, the science of preventing mental health problems has only rather recently been taken seriously. Documented increases in the numbers and kinds of problems affecting children and adolescents over the last several decades (Dryfoos, 1997), combined with advances in our knowledge of effective intervention techniques, have breathed new life into prevention efforts.

The relatively new and evolving discipline of **prevention science,** a multidisciplinary mix of human development, psychopathology, epidemiology, education, and criminology, offers us useful guidelines for understanding what constitutes effective prevention. Coie and his associates (Coie, Watt, et al., 1993) state that the primary objective of this new field is to

> trace the links between generic risk factors and specific clinical disorders and to moderate the pervasive effects of risk factors. If generic risks can be identified and altered in a population, this can have a positive effect on a range of mental health problems, as well as job productivity, and can reduce the need for many health, social, and correctional services. (p. 1014)

The current enthusiasm for the promise of prevention is epitomized by the national interdepartmental initiative Safe Schools/Healthy Students (SS/HS), developed by the Department of Education, Health and Human Services and the Department of Justice for the purpose of funding the implementation and testing of effective programs.

In general, prevention scientists study the origins and early sequences of disorders, such as conduct disorder, depression, or drug abuse. They work on detecting early warning signs of disorders and on developing the most effective ways to disrupt a downward spiral. Their contribution to this effort is not purely theoretical, but rather the result of carefully controlled, well-designed intervention trial studies. The beauty of this discipline is that it has the potential to provide a coherent approach to prevention and intervention that is focused, effective, and developmentally appropriate. For the working counselor who is concerned about best practice, it can provide a sound empirical foundation for intervention strategies. By its very nature as a comprehensive model, it encourages interdisciplinary collaboration in empirically tested programs that address problems at multiple levels.

Within the constellation of disciplines that make up prevention science, developmental psychopathology holds a preeminent place (Institute of Medicine, 1994). This is so because any approach used to prevent the development of problems must obviously be informed by knowledge about how problems arise or remit (see Chapter 4, Box 4.4). A major contribution from developmental psychopathology to prevention science is its focus on risk and protective factors. Good prevention is designed to reduce risk while enhancing those factors that serve protective functions. As we have noted, prevention researchers are engaged in determining the nature of the complicated interplay between risk and resilience.

What might a counselor need to know about effective prevention and the science that supports it? We have attempted to address that question in question-and-answer format. Since the scope of this chapter precludes more comprehensive coverage of this topic, the interested reader is referred to several excellent reviews (see the series entitled *Issues in childrens' and families' lives*, Volumes 1–9, Sage Publications).

Q & A about Prevention

How Is Prevention Defined?

Historically, clinicians interested in community-based mental health programs differentiated between **primary, secondary,** and **tertiary prevention.** *Primary prevention* is an attempt to forestall the development of problems by promoting health and wellness in the general population through group-oriented interventions. Requiring mandatory vaccinations for children or providing developmental guidance activities in schools might constitute primary prevention activities. *Secondary prevention* is an attempt to reduce the incidence of disorders among those who are at high risk or to

Box 8.1   Continued

provide treatment to forestall the development of more serious psychopathology in cases that are already established. Programs developed to identify students at risk for dropping out of school and to provide them with remedial programs might be examples of secondary level prevention. In this case, a selected sample, rather than the general population, receives services. *Tertiary prevention* is directed toward rehabilitating persons with established disorders.

Because of the need to distinguish between the concepts of tertiary prevention and treatment, another way of categorizing types of prevention was suggested by the Institute of Medicine report (1994): **universal, selective,** and **indicated.** These three levels of prevention are clearly distinguished from treatment, which in this model is similar to tertiary prevention. *Universal prevention* is directed to the general population. *Selective prevention* targets individuals at some epidemiological risk, such as low-birth-weight babies. *Indicated prevention* addresses individuals who show subclinical symptoms of disorders, such as children whose behavioral problems are not yet serious enough to warrant a diagnosis of conduct disorder.

What Are Risk and Protective Factors?

Risk factors are those things that compromise healthy development, whereas **protective factors** are those things that moderate the negative effects of risk. Generic risk and protective factors may be internal to the individual, may be part of the individual's developmental history, or may reside in the individual's environment. Examples of risk factors include, but are not limited to, sensory or organic handicaps, low levels of intelligence, academic failure, family conflict, poverty, emotional undercontrol, and peer rejection. Protective factors include positive temperamental characteristics, intelligence, parental support and monitoring, good schools and community environments, and positive relationships with competent adults.

Risk and protective factors seem to have cumulative and interactive effects on development. Negative outcomes are affected by a combination of elements: the number of risk factors present in a person's life, the severity of each, the duration of their effects, and the dearth of protective factors that lessen their ill effects. The presence of several risk factors exponentially increases the probability of a disorder. A good example of this phenomenon was reported by Zagar and his associates in their study of adolescent boys who committed murder (Zagar, Arbit, Sylvies, & Busch, 1991). The risk of committing murder was doubled for boys with the following four risk factors: history of criminal violence in the family, history of being abused, gang membership, and abuse of illegal substances. The chances of committing murder were *three times as great* if these additional risk factors were present as well: prior arrest, possession and use of a weapon, neurological problems affecting cognition and affect, and school difficulties, including truancy.

You may recognize that many of these risks seem to fit together. As Garbarino (1999) points out, many children at risk "fall victim to the unfortunate synchronicity between the demons inhabiting their own internal world and the corrupting influences of modern American culture" (p. 23). So not only do risks gain power as they accumulate, but they also operate in clusters that serve as "correlated constraints" (Cairns & Cairns, 1994). In other words, they reinforce each other by their redundancy and work together to shape the developmental trajectory. Altering one risk factor may not change the overall pattern because the other related risks serve to maintain the status quo.

Certain risks, as well as certain protections, become more important at different points in development. For example, the protection offered by prosocial peers and the risks associated with exposure to deviant ones are particularly powerful as children approach adolescence (Dishion, 1990) but less so in early childhood. On the other hand, some protections, such as authoritative parenting, retain their power thoughout childhood and adolescence. Some risk factors are common to many disorders. As we have noted, deficits in perspective taking or problems with peer relationships may be related to the development of conduct disorder or depression.

How Do Risk and Protective Factors Operate to Produce Developmental Outcomes?

Risk and protective factors are conceptualized as independent, not just opposite ends of a risk-protection continuum. In other words, it is possible to have many risk factors as well as many protective factors operating in a person's life. Researchers are interested in protective factors because they are so closely intertwined with the concept of *resilience,* that quality that permits developmental success for some individuals despite grave setbacks or early adversity.

(continued)

Box 8.1   Continued

It is still unclear how risk and protective factors actually work together, although researchers have hypothesized that protective factors improve life-course outcomes directly by their presence as well as more indirectly by moderating the effects of early vulnerabilities. Jessor and his colleagues (Jessor, Van Den Bos, Vanderryn, Costa, & Turbin, 1995) studied the relationship of protective factors (such as family and other social supports, positive attitudes toward school, self-control, involvement in prosocial behavior, and positive peer models) and risk factors (such as low expectations for success, poor school achievement, deviant peer models, low self-esteem, and greater orientation to peers than to parents) to later problem behaviors. The results of their longitudinal study demonstrated that the presence of protective factors contributed both directly and indirectly to the reduction of later problems. The greater the number of protective factors, the fewer problem behaviors exhibited later. Hauser (1999), reporting on a retrospective analysis of young adults who had experienced severe trauma in adolescence, found that the ones who made the best adjustment had the highest levels of protection despite their early risks. Those who fared less well in adulthood had less support and greater risk. More research is needed, however, to explain these relationships with greater precision.

Does Prevention Really Work?

Based upon a rapidly growing body of research findings, the answer is yes. Prevention scientists have provided evidence that well-designed and well-implemented preventive programs can reduce the incidence of problem behaviors such as aggressiveness, violence, and drug abuse as well as increase positive outcomes, such as academic achievement and social competence.

What Kinds of Prevention Efforts Work Best?

There is an increasing consensus among researchers, practitioners, and policy makers about criteria for successful prevention efforts. First, good prevention is based on developmentally appropriate, empirically valid approaches. Ideally, programs should show evidence that the positive effects have been maintained over a period of time before being implemented widely. Obviously, this implies the need for high-quality program evaluation research as well.

Second, successful programs take a multidimensional approach to problem prevention, enhancing protective factors while reducing risks. They therefore include components directed to many levels of the system. In other words, clinicians, teachers, parents, health-care providers, community leaders, policy makers, and others really need to work together to get the job done. The challenge of combining forces given the spectrum of political, cultural, economic, and social diversity that exists in society is formidable indeed. But it can be done. Programs such as Midwestern Prevention Project (MPP) (Johnson et al., 1990; Pentz et al., 1990) have used school-based, parent, and community efforts to reduce substance abuse in young adolescents. This ambitious project combined in-school social skills training exercises, homework assignments to be completed with parents, community intervention such as TV and radio messages, and community policy changes as part of a comprehensive approach. Results after several years of evaluation indicated lower prevalence of substance use for students exposed to the program.

Third, good programs are sensitive to cultural differences in the application of strategies and in their delivery of messages. Fourth, they focus more on general problem-solving skills rather than on providing didactic information to students, and they are interactive in nature. Fifth, programs are greatly strengthened by the use of peer-oriented strategies, especially for substance abuse prevention (Tobler, 1992). Finally, programs that operate over several years and that are sensitive to the developmental transitions that students experience are more successful than briefer programs.

The failure of prevention programs has been widely attributed to the fact that programs are not fully implemented in accordance with the empirical model or are shortened before they have a chance to work. Commonly observed institutional problems such as lack of funding for services, inadequate training for service providers, lack of effective leadership, and failure to cooperate with "outsiders" who represent various levels or components of the system plague prevention efforts (Gottfredson, Fink, Skroban, Gottfredson, & Weissberg, 1997). Ideally, good prevention should be faithfully executed, be targeted to multiple levels of functioning, have cross-generational linkages, and be kept in place for a sufficient length of time to ease developmental transitions. "To be effective, lifelines that are extended must be kept in place long enough to become opportunities for a lifetime" (Cairns & Cairns, 1994, p. 273).

is not independent of basic interaction skills or the kinds of friendship skills we discussed in Chapter 6.

Good *social skills* are important contributors to socially competent behavior at every level of interaction. They may be defined as discrete, observable behaviors such as making eye contact, using appropriate language, asking appropriate questions, and so forth, which promote effective social interaction and which are part of the broader construct of social competence. Social-skills training approaches grew out of the recognition that students who have peer group problems lack certain essential social skills or behave in ways that are counterproductive to smooth social exchange. Consequently, modeling, coaching, and reinforcement processes are used to teach students how to interact more adaptively in very basic ways.

Both correlational and experimental studies of social skills training programs lend modest support to their usefulness in improving peer acceptance (see Ladd & Asher, 1985; Ladd & Mize, 1983; Michelson, Sugai, Wood, & Kazdin, 1983). One possible reason for their limited effects is the unidirectional approach typically employed in these interventions. In other words, treatment often assumes that the socially troubled individual owns the problem. There is evidence, however, that if children are disliked, peers also process information about them in biased ways. For example, children interpret negative acts as intentionally malicious when committed by disliked children but not when committed by popular children (Dodge, Pettit, McClaskey, & Brown, 1986). Bierman (1986) found that greater success could be achieved by combining social skills training for individual children with attempts to enhance the cooperative nature of these children's peer groups. Thus, addressing the context within which the socially unskilled child functions, along with the transactional nature of his social interactions, allows for more lasting improvements. Social competence, including particular social skills, helps children experience success in friendship relationships. The same holds for children's success in the larger peer context.

Peer groups are complicated webs of social relationships, including friendship *dyads,* *cliques,* and *crowds.* These complex social networks emerge and take on great significance for children as early as middle childhood (Hallinan, 1979). In contrast, the social worlds of preschoolers and early elementary school children are less intricately constructed. By middle childhood, voluntary social or friendship groups of three to nine members, called *cliques,* become more common, although they are still rather informal. At this age the group's structure is flexible, and member turnover is common. The importance of cliques reaches a peak in early adolescence, followed by a general decline in importance over the course of high school (called *degrouping;* see Shrum & Cheek, 1987). Crowds are larger, reputation-based groups, composed of numerous cliques, that become more important in mid-adolescence (Dunphy, 1963). The significance of both cliques and crowds for adolescent development will be discussed in Chapter 10.

The peer group serves many important functions for children and adolescents. It provides opportunities for practice in communication, conflict resolution, joint goal setting, cooperative learning, and shared decision making. Important interpersonal goals, such as the development of empathy, tolerance for others, and a sense of belonging, are met within groups of peers. Skills acquired in activities such as team sports may provide training for certain competitive aspects of adult work roles (Lever, 1978). The peer group is like a real-world laboratory where the skills of living with and getting along with others are tried out and improved.

Zarbatany, Hartmann, and Rankin (1990) explored the function of competitive activities (sports, physical games) and noncompetitive activities (talking on telephone, watching TV) within peer groups of early adolescents. These authors found that the two kinds of activities were important for facilitating different aspects of socioemotional development and social competence. Whereas participation in competitive activities provided opportunities for self-understanding by defining personal strengths and weaknesses, participation in noncompetitive activities enhanced a sense of acceptance and belonging in relationship to others.

Analysis of the World of Peers

Sarah is a sixth-grader who attends middle school in a mid-sized school district. The school is a mix of White, Black, and Asian youngsters whose families live and work in the surrounding communities. Some parents work in the new technology industry developing on the outskirts of the town center. Others are employed in the one manufacturing plant that still operates downtown.

Sarah is a talented member of her school's track team and sings in the concert choir. She is active in her school's student council as well. She has a few close friends whom she has known since early elementary school. Sarah is the one whom they depend on if they need some advice or help. She loves to spend time with her friends, talking on the phone and going to movies.

Recently, Sarah's social life has become more important to her than ever. She spends a great deal of time in consultation with her friends, discussing what to wear and planning social activities. She pays a little less attention to her schoolwork now that she has so many other things to think about in her life. However, she still manages to maintain a B+ average. What can we say about Sarah and her place on the social map of middle school?

The attempt to answer this question presents us with an interesting challenge. We have noted the complexity of peer group structures, so you may have already guessed that there are several levels of analysis. In general, researchers have approached this question from two complementary yet distinct perspectives: analysis of the individual group member's characteristics within the peer group network and analysis of the different groups within the universe of peer groups. The first approach would help us understand Sarah's status within her peer group and would typically depend upon sociometric assessment. The second approach would help us understand the number and nature of the peer groups in Sarah's school and would depend on more ethnographic means of analysis.

Measurement of Individuals within the Peer Group

Sociometry

Before we can understand the kinds of categories that describe children's status within peer groups, we need to appreciate the means by which these differences were first identified. *Sociometry,* the classic way of assessing social competence, had its origins in the work of Moreno (1934), who used children's nomination of their peers to evaluate peer status. Moreno viewed group processes as a mixture of positive forces (attractions), negative forces (repulsions), and indifference (absence of attraction or repulsion). He proposed that the interpersonal relationships within a group could be mapped out on the basis of knowing these social forces. Since this introduction by Moreno, sociometric techniques have diversified and have been applied in a variety of ways. McConnell and Odom (1986) offer the general definition of sociometric measures as "tests in which children make preferential responses to statements about peers in their social group" (p. 217), resulting in a score that defines a child's social status.

Typically, children might be asked to select the classmate or classmates he would most like to play with, work with, or sit next to in class. Although many varieties of analysis have been used in sociometric studies, such as weighting the nominations, the most straightforward approach is to count the number of positive nominations or mentions a child receives. This number, then, reflects the child's **social preference** score. Sociometric techniques are most useful when they also include negative nominations, or children's mention of peers with whom they do not want to work or play. Researchers have found that children who are rejected by peers cannot be identified without the inclusion of negative nominations (Hartup, Glazer, & Charlesworth, 1967). Social preference scores may range from highly positive to highly negative.

A second score, called **social impact,** is computed by adding up the total number of nominations, both positive and negative. This measure indicates the degree to which the child gets noticed within his group.

Sociometric Categories

Based on their scores on the dimensions of social impact and social preference, children can be classified into a variety of sociometric categories. Contemporary researchers most often use the methodology and categories identified by Coie and his associates (Coie, Dodge, & Cappotelli, 1982), which include five subgroups: **popular, average, neglected, rejected,** and **controversial.** *Popular* children receive many positive nominations and few negative nominations from their peers (high preference, high impact). Generally, they are well-liked members of the group and have relatively high visibility among their peers. Remember, however, that the term "popular" refers to a specific sociometric category and has a slightly more forgiving meaning than does the contemporary use of the term. In other words, a student does not have to be the captain of the football team to achieve popular status!

Average children are those who receive an average number of positive and negative nominations (near the mean for the group on preference and impact). *Neglected* children are those who receive few nominations, either positive or negative. This latter group is characterized by its low level of social impact. Students who fall into the *rejected* category receive many negative and few positive nominations. They are typically disliked (low preference) but have generally high visibility (high impact). The final category, called *controversial,* identifies a relatively small group of students who receive many positive and many negative nominations (high impact, average preference). They have been named controversial because they share many of the characterictics of both popular and rejected youngsters. They are seen by some peers as disruptive but as class leaders by others. These categories are presented graphically in Figure 8.3.

Individual Characteristics Related to Sociometric Status

What are the children in these categories like? While it is tempting to think of each group as homogeneous in personality and behavior and thus clearly separable from the others, this kind of simplicity does not fit well with the facts. For example, all rejected children do not behave in aggressive ways. Nor do aggressive rejected children always behave aggressively. Popular children, despite their good qualities, are not perfect. They may also experience peer-related problems from time to time.

In this section, we will describe general identifying characteristics of the groups, with greatest emphasis on popular, rejected, and neglected categories, the three groups most frequently studied. The controversial category has been more difficult to examine because

FIGURE 8.3

Dimensions and Types of Social Statuses

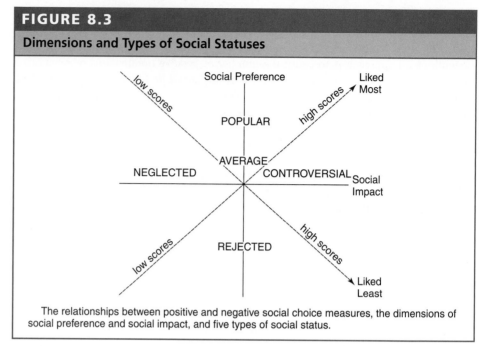

The relationships between positive and negative social choice measures, the dimensions of social preference and social impact, and five types of social status.

Source: Coie, J. D., Dodge, K. A., & Cappotelli, H. (1982). Dimensions and types of social status: A cross-age perspective. *Developmental Psychology, 18,* 557–570. Copyright © 1982 by the American Psychological Association. Adapted with permission.

of its much smaller size and lack of measurement stability. Remember that the categories suggest general tendencies to behave or to process social information in certain ways much, but not all, of the time.

Popular

Popular children are notable for their use of perspective-taking skills. Upon entering a group, these children can adopt the group's frame of reference and join in without calling undue attention to themselves or to their own needs (Putallaz & Wasserman, 1990). They can be assertive, but they are not deliberately antagonistic or disruptive to others (Dodge, Schlundt, Schocken, & Delugach, 1983). In this, they demonstrate high levels of self-regulation and self-control. Popular children also manifest greater cognitive and social problem-solving ability than do children from other groups. Black and Hazan (1990) studied the language patterns of popular preschool children and found them to be particularly adept at communicating clearly with others and following others' conversations. Positive correlations have also been found between popular status and perceived social self-concept (Harter, 1982) and self-efficacy (Ladd & Price, 1986).

In general, popular students tend to be prosocial, cooperative, intelligent, and capable of working well with others. They are likely to enjoy close, dyadic relationships with friends, although the domains of popularity and friendship are not necessarily overlapping. In other words, popularity is not a prerequisite for friendship. Sociometrically average and neglected groups also develop friendships. Peer acceptance and friendship make separate contributions to children's overall adjustment. For example, loneliness in adolescence is more closely associated with lack of friendships than with low peer acceptance (Bukowski & Hoza, 1989).

Certain other attributes, such as physical attractiveness (Langlois & Stephan, 1981) and scholastic competence (Coie & Krehbiehl, 1984), are also associated with popular status. If you think about Sarah, the sixth-grader from our earlier example, you might conclude her sociometric status to be popular.

Rejected

The children who are rejected by their peers have received a great deal of research attention. Rejected children are the least socially skilled of all the groups and also the most heterogeneous category. Originally, researchers took the position that aggression was the primary attribute of children in this social group. In fact, being aggressive is still the most commonly cited behavior associated with being rejected by peers (Rubin, Bukowski, & Parker, 1998). However, it soon became clear that children can be rejected not only because they aggress against their peers (*rejected-aggressive* group) but also because they withdraw from them (*rejected-withdrawn* group).

The characteristics of rejected children contrast sharply with those of the popular group. Instead of modulating negativity, as is the case with popular children, rejected-aggressive youngsters demonstrate high levels of instrumental aggression, verbal negativity, and disruptiveness. You might wonder whether these children are rejected because they are aggressive or act aggressively because they have been rejected. Several longitudinal studies demonstrate a causal link between aggression and subsequent rejection. This evidence is different from most sociometric research findings because it helps to explain what

Both highly aggressive and highly withdrawn children can face rejection by peers. Efforts to enhance peer acceptance may be more effective when they address both rejected children and their peer groups as a whole.

causes a child to be rejected. Over a period of several days, Dodge (1983) observed the interactions of small groups of children who initially did not know each other. After each play session, children were asked to complete a sociometric measure for their group. As the experiment progressed, some children began to take on popular status, while others were rejected. As in other studies of this type (Coie & Kupersmidt, 1983; Kupersmidt, Burchinal, & Patterson, 1995), aggression was the characteristic that best predicted rejection by the other children when all other differences were controlled.

In addition to aggression, rejected youngsters are more likely to demonstrate lower levels of perspective taking, self-control, and positive social interaction skills. Particular deficits in information processing, marked by perceptions of hostile intent or *hostile attribution bias* (see Chapter 7), are significant features of their social cognition. Once rejected, these youngsters are prevented from engaging in the very kinds of social interactions that might help them develop more positive social skills. If you remember Jason, our example from Chapter 7, you might imagine him fitting into the rejected category. Controversial children also demonstrate high levels of aggressive behavior, but they possess correspondingly positive attributes, such as greater sociability and cognitive ability, which buffer their abrasive characteristics and may make them attractive to their peers.

As we indicated earlier, however, aggression is not characteristic of all rejected children. While estimates indicate that approximately 50% are aggressive (Bierman, 1986), another 10% to 20% are extremely withdrawn (Parkhurst & Asher, 1992). Interestingly, social withdrawal begins to elicit the disapproval of peers in middle to late childhood. Whereas isolation in early childhood is not nearly so stigmatizing (Younger, Gentile, & Burgess, 1993), presumably because it is not very important at this age, extreme social withdrawal in middle to late childhood is perceived as deviant and may provoke rejection by the group (Hymel & Rubin, 1985).

Rejected-withdrawn children are more socially anxious than other groups and likely to behave in socially inappropriate ways. Poor perspective-taking skills and general social ineptness may lead these youngsters to behave in ways that are considered odd, infantile, unpredictable, or potentially embarrassing to peers. Consequently, popular peers may ostracize them, just as they ostracize their more aggressive counterparts, for failing to fit in. Both rejected-aggressive and rejected-withdrawn children do have social networks, but their social groups are smaller and are characterized by lower levels of social interaction. Overall, it is important for clinicians to recognize that peer rejection is a heterogeneous category.

Neglected

Neglected children can be distinguished from children in the average group primarily because they have somewhat lower levels of peer interaction. In their meta-analysis of peer relations studies, Newcomb, Bukowski and Pattee (1993) reported some differences between neglected and average groups. Sociometrically neglected children are less aggressive than average children, are less likely to be highly visible within the peer group, and show less sociability, but they are perceived by their peers as relatively likable. These authors conclude that neglected children are simply not choosing to participate very actively within their group of peers. Children in the neglected group are similar to those in the average group in their ability to have friendships. Therefore, even though this group has certain sociometrically distinctive characteristics, neglected children are similar to average children in many respects. Being neglected, as distinct from being in the rejected-withdrawn subgroup, which also incurs high levels of peer neglect, does not seem to be associated with developmental problems (Rubin et al., 1998).

Average

Average children, as you might have guessed, receive an average number of nominations. They are at neither extreme on the impact or preference dimensions. They show lower levels of social competence than popular children and less aggression than rejected-aggressive youngsters. As with the neglected group, no problematic outcomes are associated with this sociometric category.

Gender and Cultural Differences

Differences between boys and girls across sociometric classifications have received relatively little research attention. Those studies that have addressed gender differences report that as children get older, particularly as they approach adolescence, greater intolerance of gender-inconsistent behavior is expressed for males than for females. Boys are more likely to be rejected for behaving in "feminine" ways, whereas girls who behave in "masculine" ways are more likely to be accepted by their peers (Berndt & Heller, 1986).

Only limited information exists on racial and ethnic differences in peer group classifications. Khatri (1995) reported that children defined as popular across a wide variety of cultures are likely to demonstrate sociability, helpfulness, and low levels of disruptive aggression. Interestingly, a certain level of social withdrawal, indexed by cautiousness, self-restraint, and shyness, was considered a feature of popular children in China (Chen, Rubin, & Li, 1995). Similarly, when Yoshida, Kojo, and Kaku (1982) asked Japanese elementary school children to evaluate a hypothetical peer's comments on his or her athletic performance, they found that children viewed the more self-effacing child as more competent, truthful, and likable when compared to the more self-enhancing one. These results suggest that there are some culture-specific differences in behavior, communication, and self-presentational styles preferred in group interactions and in the attributes that constitute popularity across cultures.

Other culturally based differences may give rise to divergent conflict resolution styles among peers. Increasingly, children come to peer group settings from home cultures that differ in what is considered appropriate or valued. Some of these differences may be explained by the specific orientations espoused by diverse groups. Although the frequently mentioned distinction between independence-oriented versus interdependence-oriented cultures can affect the ways peers interact, approach tasks, and solve problems, broad-based differences along this dimension have not been observed. Greenfield and Suzuki (1998) note the following in their review of cultural differences in peer settings:

> It is too simplistic to say that children from collectivist cultures are, on the average, more cooperative than children from individualistic cultures. Instead, children from more collectivistic cultures are more cooperative with in-groups and more competitive with out-groups. Second, the cross-cultural differences are far from absolute. For example, children from more individualistic environments will cooperate when competition is dysfunctional and there are strong cues for cooperating, such as a group reward. (p. 1090)

In other words, in social competence, within-group variability may be greater than between-group variability.

Stability of Categories and Outcomes

Once classified, do children maintain their status in the peer group throughout childhood and adolescence? Many researchers have studied the long-term stability of these sociometric classifications (Asher & Dodge, 1986; Newcomb & Bukowski, 1984) and have found that the most extreme categories (popular and rejected) are also the most stable, at least over short periods of time. Both neglected and controversial status categories show instability even in the short term. Those studies that have looked at the long-term stability of sociometric classifications have produced mixed results. In general, the impact of peer group classification is moderately stable, particularly for the broad-band dimensions of acceptance and rejection, with the category of peer rejection being the most stable of all. Denham and Holt (1993) propose that this stability stems from children's early experience with each other. Once a child's reputation has been formed on the basis of early social interaction, his reputation endures despite evidence to the contrary.

What are the long-term outcomes for children who belong to these different categories? Recently, a number of prospective or follow-up studies have used early peer group designations to predict later performance on various measures of adjustment, much like that of the Rochester Registry. The broad-based categories of early acceptance and rejection have been studied most frequently and provide the most consistent results.

Not surprisingly, peer acceptance has been associated with a myriad of positive outcomes, both psychologically and academically. The outcomes change dramatically, however, for rejected-aggressive children, who often have poorer academic records, are more likely to repeat grades, are absent more frequently, are at greater risk of dropping out, and report more criminal behavior and drug use (see Coie, Terry, Lenox, & Lochman, 1995; Ladd & Burgess, 1999; Olendick et al, 1992; Parker & Asher, 1987; Rutter, Giller, & Hagell, 1998; Wentzel & Asher, 1995). The strongest linkages, by far, have been found between early aggression and peer rejection, on the one hand, and later externalizing problems, on the other (the "early starter model" of antisocial development described in Chapter 7).

Researchers have also investigated outcomes for rejected-withdrawn youngsters and have found more limited evidence for later internalizing problems such as depression, loneliness, and psychological overcontrol (see Hoza, Molina, Bukowski, & Sippola, 1995; Rubin, Chen, McDougall, Bowker, & McKinnon, 1995). A recent prospective study by Ladd and Burgess (1999) followed three groups of children from kindergarten through second grade: aggressive, withdrawn, and those with a comorbid profile of aggression and withdrawal. Consistent with predictions from developmental psychopathology, the children with multiple risks were predisposed to the most severe and enduring outcomes. The children who exhibited aggression *and* withdrawal in kindergarten were the most likely of all the groups to have troubled relationships with teachers and peers in second grade, to report more loneliness and dissatisfaction, and to express greater feelings of victimization.

Measurement of the Peer Group: Another Level of Analysis

Let us turn our attention to peer groups, the cliques and crowds we referred to earlier. These are networks of like-minded individuals who become associated with a specific set of norms, dress, and behaviors, like "jocks" or "brains." When we examine peer processes from this angle, we do not focus on the accepted or rejected status of particular children. It is certainly possible to be a popular member of a group of "jocks" as well as a popular "brain." These peer groups appear to develop more significance in late childhood to early adolescence for the reasons specified in previous sections of this chapter. Moreover, adolescents may be better able to recognize and describe their peer groups effectively because they become increasingly proficient in thinking abstractly about categories as a function of their cognitive development.

B. B. Brown (1990) noted that the term "peer group" has been used rather loosely in the past, often applied to the whole spectrum of peer relationships, from dyadic friendships to membership in large crowds. This lack of clarity compromises our understanding of the role that each type of relationship plays in development. We use the terms "peer group" and "clique" somewhat interchangeably here, consistent with the view that these units are small enough to allow for regular interaction among members and to serve as the center of most peer-related interaction. Crowds, as we noted earlier, are larger collectives, composed of multiple cliques, which serve as social categories for students rather than as actual friendship groups. You might think of crowds as actual peer "cultures" that represent approaches to behavior, attitudes, and values. In Chapter 10, we will take a closer look at crowds. As we noted already, crowds are a more potent force in the lives of middle and late adolescents than for elementary school and early adolescent children.

Peer Group Measurement

Peer group analysis at the level of cliques and crowds can be done in various ways. In general, identification of peer groups or cliques requires students to specify who "hangs around" with whom in their classroom. Based upon this information, maps of the social structure of classrooms or schools can be drawn using sophisticated methodologies such as social network analysis (Cairns, Gariepy, & Kindermann, 1990) or composite social-cognitive mapping (Kindermann, 1993).

Why Do Cliques Form?

Perhaps you are wondering why cliques surface in middle childhood and take on such significance in the first place. Common terms such as "in-group," "clique," "pecking order," and even more pedantic ones like "status hierarchy" make many adults uncomfortable, particularly when these terms are applied to children. This is so because these descriptors imply a set of winners and losers in the game of social relationships. Adults often prefer to believe that children are less critical and more tolerant of each other than these descriptors suggest. But like it or not, there is strong evidence for the existence of stable status groups among children and adolescents.

What motivates the development of distinct cliques? Two major forces are at work: first, the need to establish an identity, and second, needs for acceptance (approval) and belonging. As we shall see in Chapter 10, peers play a central role in the process of identity or self-development. The search for the self rests largely on comparing oneself to and distinguishing oneself from others by means of social comparison processes (see Chapter 6). One's own identity becomes more distinct to the degree that it can be contrasted to that of another. Children who tend to dress, act, or otherwise express themselves in similar ways gravitate to each other. Together, they form a type of social group that provides some identity to its own members and a basis of comparison to, and for, others. A group's identity is based on shared activities, values, clothes, and behaviors (see Fiske & Taylor, 1991, for a review). Recognizing and understanding group characteristics helps early adolescents construct a map of the social world and provides them with a knowledge base about human differences.

Individuals' needs for acceptance and belonging also help to explain the significance of the peer group. Children as well as adults want to be liked by their associates and will typically engage in the kinds of behaviors that result in their friends' praise or approval (Hartup, 1983). In addition to this kind of external social reinforcement, youngsters are also motivated by more internal goals. Berndt and Keefe (1996) point out that children and adolescents are intrinsically motivated to identify with their friends in behavior, dress, and academic achievement, but because they get satisfaction from emulating their friends' characteristics and being part of a group, not because they fear retribution if they fail to conform.

Peer Groups' Influence on Behavior

Our understanding of peer group processes must accommodate the power of both their beneficial as well as their potentially harmful aspects. As a helper, you have undoubtedly read about peer pressure. If you are also the parent of a middle or high school age child, you may have lost some sleep over it. Adults frequently blame early to late adolescent behavior and misbehavior on peer pressure, a notion that almost always has a negative connotation. They may imagine that children and adolescents are forced to conform to peer group standards in order to avoid humiliation or punishment. No one disagrees that peers become increasingly more influential as children mature. However, studies also show that the influence of peers is primarily indirect rather than overtly coercive (Berndt, Miller, & Park, 1989). Furthermore, peers can motivate students to engage in beneficial as well as risky behaviors, such as avoidance of drugs (Steinberg, 1996).

Of course, not all peer group effects are totally benign. The peer group delimits the range of opportunities by its very nature as a group with norms and roles. Within any peer culture, the range of acceptable activities is circumscribed. For example, the peer group determines who may be included as a member, how leisure time is spent, and how the members should dress and behave. In some cases, peer group members may use both indirect (e.g., teasing) and direct (e.g., confrontation) means to promote adherence to these group norms (Eder & Sanford, 1986). Unfortunately, the norms for certain groups may support deviant, antisocial behavior.

Many interventions that address typical developmental problems make the implicit assumption that peer pressure is a *cause* of most early to late adolescent difficulties. Many of these intervention models are built upon "resistance" training, which attempts to prepare children to do battle with dangerous peers. But is this the way it really works? And do these assumptions make sense?

It may be possible to shed some light on this issue and to improve interventions, as well, by reviewing a few principles of peer group dynamics. First, peer groups or cliques are generally homogeneous. There is a well-documented tendency for peer groups to exhibit **homophily,** or a degree of similarity among members on behavioral or attitudinal attributes of importance. This is why you can often identify the members of a group by the way they dress or on the basis of what they do after school. Second, groups are formed based upon processes of **influence** and **selection** (J. M. Cohen, 1977; Kandel, 1978). Basically, influence refers to the fact that the peer group can cause an individual to conform to the norms of the group. For example, if a youngster is part of a peer group that disparages getting good grades, the child presumably reduces his investment in doing homework in order to be accepted by the group. His new behavioral response is motivated by direct pressure as well as by modeling his academically unmotivated peers.

Less attention has been paid to the complementary process, called selection, in which individuals choose to affiliate with others who share similar behaviors or attributes. For example, youngsters who are highly academically motivated are drawn to peers who are similar in this respect. This process is consistent with behavioral genetics theories of "niche picking." You may recall from Chapter 2 that as children mature, they become more able to select the environments that suit them, perhaps influenced by their genetically based predispositions (Scarr & McCartney, 1983).

Contrary to conventional wisdom, which emphasizes the importance of peer influence, many recent studies have found that selection processes are at least as important in the formation of peer groups. For example, Kindermann (1993) investigated how fourth- and fifth-grade students' peer groups affected their academic motivation. He found evidence for an initial selection process, with students selecting a peer context early in the school year that reflected their unique level of motivation. Interestingly, membership in the high- or low-motivation peer groups predicted academic achievement at the end of the year, suggesting that some complementary peer influence processes were at work throughout the year to maintain the levels of motivation.

Ennett and Bauman (1994) looked at this issue as it relates to teenage cigarette smoking. Once again, they found support for both selection and influence processes. Adolescents were drawn to cliques where smoking was the norm if they smoked or viewed smoking as desirable (selection). But it was also the case that nonsmokers in smoking cliques were more likely to begin smoking than were nonsmokers in nonsmoking cliques (influence).

What is important to remember is that both processes contribute to peer group formation and maintenance. Overemphasis on peer influence processes may compromise our understanding of other dynamics, such as motivation to affiliate with similar individuals. Once established, peer groups constitute important social contexts for young people that reinforce certain ways of thinking and behaving. Obviously, peer groups differ in the degree to which they provide a healthy developmental context for children and adolescents, yet their impact can be profound regardless of their benefit or harm. Paxton and her associates (Paxton, Schutz, Weitheim, & Muir, 1999) studied female cliques that varied in their levels of concern about body image and eating. Those girls who showed higher levels of eating-related disorders also inhabited more negative social environments, which appeared to amplify their distorted ideas about body image.

As children mature into adolescents, much more of their time is spent in the company of their peers. The body of research on peer relationships teaches us that we would do well to consider the peer network in our conceptualization of problems and in the structuring of our interventions. A recent study speaks clearly to this final point. Reasoning that some positive modification in environment could alter the course of development for at-risk students, Mahoney (2000) studied the trajectories of 695 boys and girls from elementary school to young adulthood. He specifically focused on the role that participation in

Children's resilience is enhanced when they participate in beneficial activities along with other members of their peer group.

extracurricular activities in school played in ameliorating the difficulties of those participants who were most at-risk. Not too surprisingly, most of the students who participated in extracurricular activities (one or more years of involvement in sixth through tenth grades) graduated from high school and did not become involved in criminal activity as young adults. This result was most obvious for students in the highest risk category.

What was surprising, however, was that this benefit was *limited to* those high-risk students whose peer groups also participated in the activity. There was no appreciable gain from participation unless the youngster's peer group shared in the activity. Participation in positive, highly organized, and supervised activities enriched the adjustment of the whole group, reinforcing more socially adaptive behavior for everyone. It may be that raising the index of positive adaptation for the whole group attracts more adaptive members (selection) while providing a context that promotes healthier activity (influence).

APPLICATIONS

As children mature, they are exposed to influences from many contexts, and the relative power of these contexts shifts with development. Our discussion of gender and peer group development demonstrates the power of these environmental contexts to shape behavior in middle childhood and early adolescence. Indeed, in these years, friendships, peer groups, and other extrafamilial contexts such as school, play greater and greater roles in children's lives. We need to be particularly careful, however, not to interpret these shifts to mean that other influences on behavior, such as the family, become unimportant. This is clearly not the case, as we shall see in Chapter 10.

Because behavior is so multiply determined and so complicated, it is tempting to lay the blame for certain childhood and adolescent outcomes at the feet of one particular cause, such as friends, schools, or parents. Once more, and just as strenuously, we need to avoid the dreaded "either-or" dichotomy. If we do not resist a simplistic stance, we may fall into the trap of attributing causality for certain behaviors to single, "silver-bullet" theories. We have all heard the kind of explanatory reasoning that rests on such beliefs.

For example, a girl's depressed behavior may be attributed solely to her parents' working too many hours, or a boy's involvement in risky behavior may be explained by his association with the wrong set of friends. Certainly these circumstances play a role, maybe even the most significant one, in the development and maintenance of certain problems for certain individuals. However, Zucker (1994) explains why single variable theories are not really useful:

> From a developmental vantage point, the answer is straightforward: Because each factor is, of itself, not sufficient. The individual factors that continue to emerge in the literature (whether they be genetic, psychological, environmental, or macroenvironmental) are only indicators of risk. In order for them to be indicators of disorder they need to cumulate, which requires the operation of time (which is a shorthand for repetitive exposure, or repetitive cycling of process), and the operation of factors (contexts), which continue to hold the individual within the risky situation. Under those circumstances, the end product is more likely to evolve into a crystallized structure with an ongoing momentum. But without such holding on of risk (or continual driving back into risk), cumulation cannot take place. In other words, one needs multiple risks, contextual enhancement, and the operation of internal, self-sustaining processes for a structure to manifest itself. (Gottlieb, 1992, p. 269)

This perspective, while admittedly complicated, offers clinicians multiple opportunities to intervene. If the repeated cycling back into situations that expose youngsters to risk can be disrupted, then the risk may be attenuated. Additionally, if extant protective factors can be bolstered, or new ones introduced, the balance between risk and protection can be favorably altered to shift the trajectory toward more adaptive outcomes.

Let's consider an example. As we have seen, functioning well within a peer group is one of the most significant accomplishments in children's lives. Good peer relationships operate as a powerful protective factor, providing children and adolescents with experiences of friendship, opportunities for social skill development and problem solving, enhancement of perspective taking and empathy. Problematic peer relationships are risks because they elicit or maintain maladaptive behavior and deprive youngsters of the kinds of protective effects mentioned above. The experience of chronic peer problems has consistently been identified as a serious risk factor for later difficulties.

It is helpful to recognize that there is more than one route to peer rejection. In our efforts to conceptualize prevention and treatment, children with two rather different sets of characteristics are likely to elicit peer rejection: those who are aggressive and those who exhibit high levels of social withdrawal (Rubin et al., 1998). In addition, there are multiple pathways to overaggressive behavior and to overly withdrawn behavior in middle childhood and adolescence.

Let's begin with the child who becomes overaggressive. Imagine the parents of a temperamentally irritable or highly active toddler who believe that their parenting efforts are ineffective in changing his difficult behavior because it is biologically determined. Over time, the perception that biology is destiny may lead the parents to feel helpless and to adopt a laissez-faire approach to parenting. They provide their child with none of the countervaling influences that might help curb his out-of-control behavior, behavior that makes the child unacceptable to other children. Or consider the parents of a similarly strong-willed child who believe they need to punish the child harshly, and thereby actually increase this child's aggressiveness over time. He may enter the peer group setting primed to make hostile interpretations and to suffer consequent peer rejection.

Now let's consider possible pathways to highly withdrawn behavior in middle childhood. Infants who are temperamentally hyperarousable or highly reactive to novel, mildly stressful situations might elicit specific kinds of parenting as well. Some parents, when confronted with an anxious child, might take over the situation, micromanage the nature and number of the child's social contacts, or become overprotective or overinvolved. Such a parental response might be engendered by parents' own levels of hypersensitivity and anxiety over their child's social distress or by their impatience with a child whose timidity prevents him from easily negotiating his social world. Either way, high levels of parental overcontrol and overinvolvement have been associated conceptually with children's social withdrawal. Other parents might adopt the "biology is destiny" attitude that we mentioned earlier and fail to protect their child or to intervene in ways that might ease the difficulty of initial social encounters. In either case, social withdrawal in middle childhood is the outcome. And with age, extreme reticence and social anxiety become as great a social handicap as aggression (French, 1988).

Interventions are most successful when they take into account the transactional nature of these problems, considering what elicits the difficulty and what sustains it. For example, Dodge, Coie, Pettit, and Price (1990) note that intervention programs that focus on teaching social skills to unskilled youngsters have met with little success in changing the target child's level of peer acceptance, even when the child's actual level of prosocial behavior has increased. This is so because the child's peers have already developed schemas or constructions for the rejected child that are built on the social reputation of the child as socially unskilled. Interactions with the target child after this schema has been constructed are marked by attention to evidence that confirms the disliked child's antisocial characteristics (called **confirmation bias,** Gurwitz & Dodge, 1977) and discounting of evidence that indicates a departure from his antisocial role. Since these social forces operate to maintain homeostasis, they are quite resistant to change.

Efforts to enhance social competence should target not only the peer-rejected child but also the child's peer group. Peers can be encouraged to initiate more positive interactions with a rejected child through cooperative activities. They may also be taught to clearly communicate that they will not tolerate aggression. The goal should be to try to provide a context wherein the disliked child can behave more prosocially so as to modify the peer group's stereotypical schema.

Although not all vulnerable children have negative outcomes, we know that high-risk behaviors, such as childhood aggression or social withdrawal, are correlated with increasing risk of problems down the line if left untreated (Dryfoos, 1997). We also know that high-risk behaviors come in packages that can be effectively addressed by programs that focus on the multiple determinants of negative outcomes rather than on isolated problems. Complementary prevention efforts at several levels of the system, such as modification of parenting practices, provision of academic supports, enhancement of a culture of cooperation in schools, or increased opportunities to improve quality of life for communities, help to reduce risk and to increase protection for vulnerable youth. Many exemplary prevention programs exist that have demonstrated empirical support. When choosing programs to implement, clinicians should pay particular attention to those that have a successful track record.

Can gender be a risk factor? Some would agree that it is. We have mentioned that there is a greater incidence of depression in females than in males, starting at early adolescence. In Chapter 9, you will see that girls have a greater tendency to engage in passive, ruminative coping and that they feel more threatened than boys by the culture's exacting standards for beauty and behavior. Some recent literature has also focused on the special problems of boys. As you might imagine, they are also related to emotional functioning. If girls' expression of emotions is tolerated, even encouraged, then boys' emotional expression is actively discouraged. You have learned that behaviors considered appropriate according to gender are much more restrictive for boys than for girls and that parents often reinforce different behaviors for their sons and daughters.

Pollack (1998), who provides clinical insights into the particular challenges faced by boys, argues that the "boy code" that is enforced in the masculine socialization process works like a gender straitjacket. Just as girls' voices may be suppressed in certain contexts, Pollack argues that boys also go unheard. The "boy-code" requires learning that feelings of fear, weakness, and vulnerability should be suppressed in order to appear brave and powerful. While we may be primed to notice symptoms of depression in girls, because they fit our conceptions of what depressed behavior looks like, we may miss the cues in boys. Pollack advises adults to avoid shaming boys for expressions of vulnerability and to provide them with the time and safety they need to open up.

Since evidence from so many studies that have examined gender differences in behavior demonstrates that for most characteristics there is actually very little gender difference, we need to remember that girls and boys have many similar qualities and needs. Feelings, either good or bad, should not be "off-limits" because one happens to be a boy or a girl. Counselors can help by examining their own schemas or constructions about what it means to be male and female. That way, we will not selectively attend to information that fits our schema while we discount other important information. For healthy development, both genders need safe spaces in which to exercise their power and to express their vulnerabilities.

Finally, clinicians might do well to take a hard look at their assumptions about peer pressure. It's probably not what you think it is. As we shall discuss in later chapters, children in late childhood and early adolescence spend increasingly greater amounts of time with their peers. They learn and draw support from each other, extracting the rules for newly minted membership in their adolescent cohort along the way. Contemporary writers have come to look at the peer group, once viewed as a pressure cooker, as rather a source of support or a comfort zone (Taffel, 2001). Clinicians are probably well advised to understand the power of the peer context and to use it, when possible, by including peers in intervention and treatment. We'll have more to say about this in Chapter 10.

SUMMARY

Sex Role Development

1. The first step is learning to label oneself as male or female by about $2\frac{1}{2}$. Next comes *gender stability,* by 3 or 4 years, which means realizing that gender doesn't fluctuate over time. Finally comes *gender constancy,* realizing that gender *cannot* change. This may not emerge until 6 or 7, although there is controversy on this issue.

2. Social processes, involving active teaching by others, influence learning one's gender identity. *Gender atypical* children, whose genitalia are either ambiguous or inconsistent with their biological sex, often acquire the identity that is socially assigned even if it is inconsistent with their biological sex.

3. Cognitive development may also influence the acquisition of gender identity. For example, logical thinking may help a child understand gender constancy. Also, being given accurate information about what is and isn't important for gender assignment is helpful.

4. Biological sex may also influence children's gender identity, even when social input is inconsistent with biology. Some gender atypical individuals have eventually rejected their assigned identity, apparently feeling more comfortable adopting an identity that is consistent with their biology.

5. Meta-analyses of many different behaviors, personality characteristics, and preferences have identified some that usually vary between males and females. Some are found across the life span, while others are characteristic of only certain developmental periods. Some have changed historically, such as differences in math problem solving. The average differences are usually quite small.

6. Perhaps more important than the small sex differences in laboratory measures of behavior, is that boys and girls spend their time differently: boys more often with boys, and girls with girls. Gender segregation begins as early as $2\frac{1}{2}$ for girls and 3 for boys and increases with age. In their segregated groups, girls and boys behave differently. For example, boys are more active and engage in more aggressive play when they are with boys than with girls or adults. Girls' play and talk is more cooperative or collaborative, whereas boys' play and talk is more competitive and domineering.

7. Where do sex differences come from? Biology seems to play a role in some traits. For example, girls exposed prenatally to male hormones have stronger male play preferences in childhood than normal girls.

8. Cognitive developmental theories argue that children are motivated to acquire gender-appropriate behavior once they identify themselves as male or female. Gender schema theories also hypothesize that children choose to act in ways that are consistent with their *gender schemas,* that is, their networks of expectations and beliefs about male and female characteristics.

9. Parenting processes are also thought to contribute to gendered behavior. Freud's psychoanalytic theory posits that preschoolers identify with the same-sexed parent in an effort to resolve the *Oedipus complex* (in boys) or the *Electra complex* (in girls).

Identification involves imitation, so girls begin to act like their mothers, and boys begin to act like their fathers. There is little evidence to support this theory. Social learning theorists assume that parents play a more direct role, teaching children to adopt gendered behaviors through the use of rewards and punishments. There are some differences in the ways parents treat girls and boys, and there are differences in the kinds of pressures they place. But there are many similarities as well.

10. Peers appear to play a role in engendering sex-typed behavior. Children spend a great deal of time in their sex-segregated peer groups, and in these groups some preexisting sex differences appear to be magnified. Recent research indicates that the more time preschoolers spend in gendered groups, the more sex-typed their behavior becomes (the *social dosage effect*).

11. Clearly what is needed to explain sex role development is a multidimensional theory that considers all the contributing elements: biology, cognitive processes, and parent and peer socialization pressures.

Peer Relationships

12. In a longitudinal study of children at risk for later mental health problems, one early risk factor stood out as highly predictive of later problems: peer rejection.

13. Evaluating *social competence* involves examining *social skills* at every level of social interaction, both within friendships and outside them. Interventions designed to improve specific children's social skills have moderate success, but they might have more success if both the disliked child *and* the children with whom the target child interacts were included.

14. Peer groups include *dyads, cliques,* and *crowds.* The clique and crowd structures begin to emerge in middle childhood and are crystallized in early adolescence. They play a role in the development of self-understanding, and they provide a sense of acceptance and belonging.

15. In *sociometry,* children's status among their peers is measured. Children in a class are asked to select which children they would most, or least, like to interact with in different contexts. Each child can be categorized on the basis of a *social preference score* (number of positive less negative nominations) and a *social impact score* (total nominations, positive and negative).

16. *Popular children* have high social preference and social impact scores. They have many social skills, tend to be attractive, and are cognitively competent as well.

17. *Rejected children* may be either aggressive or withdrawn, and neither group demonstrates the positive social skills of the popular children. They have low social preference scores but high social impact scores.

18. *Neglected children* have especially low social impact scores but are not perceived negatively by their peers. They may choose not to participate centrally in group activities.

19. *Controversial children* have some of the qualities of popular children and some of the qualities of rejected children. They are seen by some as leaders and by others as disruptive.

20. *Average children* score in the average range on both social preference and social impact. They have less social competence than popular children, more than rejected or neglected children.

21. Preferred qualities in peers seem to differ somewhat across genders and cultures. For example, boys, especially as they approach adolescence, are more likely to be rejected for cross-gendered behavior than girls. In China, shy children are more likely to be popular than in Western cultures.

22. Popular and rejected categories show the most stability over time and have fairly predictable long-term consequences: positive for popular children, negative for rejected children. The strongest links are found between rejected-aggressive status in childhood and later externalizing problems.

23. Cliques play a role in identity development. Kids with similar characteristics form groups that provide some identity and a basis for social comparison. Cliques also serve needs for acceptance and belonging.

24. Peer groups are formed and maintained both through *influence* and through *selection* processes. Influence is largely indirect (e.g., teasing) rather than directly coercive (e.g., confrontation) and can cause an individual to conform. Selection refers to the fact that individuals choose to affiliate with others like themselves.

Case Study

Hyun-Ki's family emigrated from Korea three years ago and now lives in a large city on the West Coast. His parents moved to this location because they had relatives living in the same city, and they wanted the economic and educational opportunities that they believed the United States could afford their family. Both parents immediately found work in their relatives' small business.

The family lives in a modest home in a working-class neighborhood. The daughters, 16-year-old Sun and 17-year-old Cho, attend the local public high school, and they are diligent, academically advanced students. Hyun-Ki, a fifth-grader, is the youngest child. He is quiet and socially reserved. He is also physically slight for his age, shorter than most of the boys and all of the girls in his grade. His heavily accented English is somewhat difficult to understand, and he is sensitive about his speech. Consequently, he does not often volunteer to answer questions in class.

Although there are many ethnic groups represented among the students in his class, Hyun-Ki seems to get the brunt of the teasing, even from other Asian American students. When he enters the classroom, students snicker and deride him. "Look what he has on today!" they call out. They make fun of his speech and his reserved ways. When he walks down the hallway to his locker, he is aware of the disparaging looks he gets from some groups of students. Hyun-Ki has a Korean friend whom he sees every Sunday at church. The two boys enjoy spending time together after the service. Hyun-Ki and his friend share an interest in nature and biking. Hyun-Ki wishes he had a friend like this in his own classroom.

Mrs. Marshall, Hyun-Ki's teacher, has assigned a class project that is to be done by small groups of students. Peter, a boy in Hyun-Ki's group, is an outgoing and popular student who is considered one of the class leaders. He has called Hyun-Ki on the phone several times to discuss the project and is always friendly and pleasant toward him. In school, however, it is a different story. Peter is often part of the group of students who make fun of Hyun-Ki when they pass him in the hall. Hyun-Ki cannot understand why Peter is so nice to him on the phone and so mean to him at school.

Mrs. Marshall observes that Hyun-Ki is not participating very actively in the cooperative group assignment. From the teacher's perspective, Hyun-Ki is "too quiet" and has not contributed sufficiently to get a passing grade for the project. She also notes Hyun-Ki's reluctance to participate in the regular class discussions. She fears that Hyun-Ki's educational needs are not being met in his classroom. Hoping to intervene on the boy's behalf, Mrs. Marshall refers Hyun-Ki to the school's child-study team, whose role is to evaluate the special needs of students in the school.

Discussion Questions

1. How does your knowledge of the topics of sex role development and peer group processes contribute to your understanding of Hyun-Ki's situation?
2. How could you help Hyun-Ki's parents and teachers understand the situation? How would you suggest they help him?
3. What prevention efforts would you like to see initiated in this school?

 Journal Questions

1. Gender-role training can be a "straitjacket" for both girls and boys. Reflect on the gender messages you received as a child and adolescent. Which ones were particularly restrictive? How did these messages affect the decisions you made in your life? Do you think gender-based messages have changed for more recent cohorts of children and adolescents?
2. Identify a gender-related issue that you are personally struggling with at the present time. How are you dealing with it? What resources would be helpful for you in dealing with it?
3. How would you assess your own peer status as an elementary school student? As a middle or junior high school student? As a high school student? What was the most difficult thing you experienced as a child or adolescent in relation to your peers? What could have made the situation better?
4. Give a personal example of an experience you had with "peer pressure" or peer influence. Has the nature of peer pressure changed?

Key Terms

gender identity	gender intensification	selective prevention	social impact
gender stability	hypothesis	indicated prevention	popular
gender constancy	gender schema	risk factors	average
gender atypical	Oedipus complex	protective factors	neglected
congenital adrenal	Electra complex	resilience	rejected
hyperplasia (CAH)	penis envy	social skills	controversial
gender stereotypes	social dosage effect	dyads	rejected-aggressive
meta-analysis	social competence	cliques	rejected-withdrawn
borderwork	prevention science	crowds	homophily
rough and tumble play	primary prevention	degrouping	influence
collaborative discourse	secondary prevention	sociometry	selection
domineering discourse	tertiary prevention	social preference	confirmation bias
tomboyism	universal prevention		

Physical, Cognitive, and Identity Development in Adolescence

9

> I could not prove the Years had feet—
> Yet confident they run
> Am I, from symptoms that are past
> And Series that are done—
> I find my feet have further goals—
> I smile upon the Aims
> That felt so ample—Yesterday—
> Today's—have vaster claims—
> I do not doubt the self I was—
> Was competent to me—
> But something awkward in the fit
> Proves that—outgrown—I see—
> Emily Dickinson (1862)

From Shakespeare's Romeo and Juliet to Salinger's Holden Caulfield to Margaret, the teenager in Judy Blume's novel who poignantly asked, "Are you there, God?" we have enjoyed many memorable literary examples of adolescents' coming of age. In many cultures and throughout many different historical periods, adolescence has evoked a certain fascination. We endow it with meaning and celebrate it as the time when innocent, dependent children are transformed into young adults. However, one reason this life stage is so interesting is that, in reality, it defies easy description. What are the tasks of adolescence, and are they completed by a certain chronological age? Are these tasks the same for all adolescents, or are there some that are culture- or gender-specific? Is adolescence a period of storm and stress or a relatively smooth transition? Should adolescents rebel against convention in order to define their uniqueness, or is rebellion a sign of maladjustment? Is legal adult status a real indicator of adulthood, or should we look to other indicators of cognitive and emotional maturity? These are some of the topics we will discuss in the next two chapters.

Because of its child-to-adult metamorphosis, writers have long recognized the centrality of identity development to the adolescent period. Erik Erikson (1950, 1963, 1968) is possibly best remembered for his writing on the topic of identity. Sometimes, however, his emphasis on the shaping of identity in adolescence, which has been the popular interpretation of Erikson's work, inadvertently suggests that there is no real sense of identity beforehand.

As we consider this important task of adolescence, we should note that Erikson himself was careful to emphasize the epigenetic nature of human development. The human being, like any other growing organism, has a "ground plan" (1968, p. 92) composed of parts that unfold or come into ascendancy at certain times, to eventually become a coherent whole. Success at each new developmental task requires qualities and skills acquired from the work of prior life stages and depends upon relative mastery of earlier tasks as a basis for moving ahead. Thus, far from being divorced from the child's earlier sense of self and self-in-relationship, adolescent identity is a synthesis of earlier elements with new, more cognitively and emotionally mature aspects of the self-system. Erikson makes this point succinctly in the following statement:

> A lasting ego identity, we have said, cannot begin to exist without the trust of the first oral stage; it cannot be completed without a promise of fulfillment which from the dominant image of adulthood reaches down into the baby's beginnings and which, by the tangible evidence of social health, creates at every step of childhood and adolescence, an accruing sense of ego strength. (1963, p. 246)

Let us begin our look at the adolescent period with an exploration of the physical and cognitive changes that mark this time of life. Building on the growth and maturation of these systems, we will then consider how they support the process of adolescent identity development.

PHYSICAL DEVELOPMENT

When we think of physical development and the adolescent years, we are likely to think first of the sometimes startling changes associated with puberty. We will examine these changes first, and then we will take a brief look at other physiological developments, primarily in the brain, that characterize the adolescent period.

Puberty: The Adolescent Metamorphosis

Rebecca recently had her 13th birthday. Her Aunt Cathy, who has just returned from a year abroad, hardly recognizes her. When she saw her last, Rebecca was a cute, pug-nosed pygmy, with a sunny disposition and an easy laugh. Now she is 3 or 4 inches taller. But her rapid growth is not what surprises her aunt; it is the qualitative change in both her appearance and her manner. Her slim, child's body is softening and changing shape. Her breasts are emerging, her hips spreading. And her face is, well, a little weird. Suddenly she has a big nose and a pimply complexion. And although she seems genuinely happy to see her aunt, within the first hour of her reunion with the family she begins interjecting sarcastic remarks into the conversation, and she petulantly rolls her eyes at comments made by other members of her family. Little of what is said escapes her biting criticism. When her mildly exasperated mother gently suggests that she should spend some time studying for tomorrow's test, she suddenly seems near tears, whining, "I always have more to do than anyone else!"

Clearly, Rebecca has entered the land of puberty and has begun her trek across the divide from childhood to adulthood. Strictly speaking, *puberty* is a process of sexual maturation. When it is complete, boys and girls are fertile: males can impregnate females, and females can conceive. But as most of us can recall, puberty is related to a wide range of emotional, behavioral, and social changes as well.

A Glandular Awakening

The process begins when the pituitary gland, located at the base of the brain, is stimulated by the maturing hypothalamus to produce hormones. These hormones stimulate other endocrine glands to increase their hormone production. These glands include the *gonads—testes* in males, *ovaries* in females—which now increase their production of both masculinizing hormones (*androgens,* such as *testosterone*) and feminizing hormones (*estrogen*). Interestingly, both kinds of hormones (as well as *progesterone,* which is involved in the reproductive cycle) are produced in males and in females, but they are produced in different ratios, so that increases in androgen production are much higher in boys than in girls, whereas estrogen production increases much more in girls. In combination with other hormones circulating in the blood, they cause a series of changes in children's bodies that promote the maturing of both *primary sexual characteristics* (those directly involved in reproduction, such as the genitalia) and *secondary sexual characteristics* (physical traits not directly involved in reproduction but indicative of sex, such as enlarged breasts in females and deeper voices in males). Early, outward signs of puberty are usually the appearance of pubic hair in both sexes, the growth of the scrotum and testes in boys, and the budding of breasts in girls. *Menarche* in girls (first menstruation) and *spermarche* in boys (first ejaculation) usually occur near the end of the process and are often treated as important social markers of sexual maturation. But fertility—ovulation in girls and adequate sperm production in boys—may not be achieved for a year or more after these outward manifestations of maturity (Chumlea, 1982; Tanner, 1962, 1990). (See Figure 9.1: *Typical Sequences of Pubertal Change in Males and Females.*)

The timing of puberty appears to be affected by genetic factors: identical twins usually begin and end the process within 2 to 3 months of each other, and mothers' and daughters' ages at menarche are correlated (Brooks-Gunn, 1991; Golub, 1992). But environmental factors are clearly important as well. For example, improvements in nutrition and health care are linked to a downward shift in the average age of menarche in the last century and a half. Today, the average age is just under 13 years, whereas in 1850 it was approximately three years later (Chumlea, 1982; Faust, 1983). Body fat affects the timing of puberty in both girls and boys, such that higher ratios of fat are associated with earlier onsets. Children whose body fat is unusually low, such as those who are malnourished or who are heavily involved in athletics, are likely to begin puberty later than other children (Brooks-Gunn, 1991; Malina, 1983).

The Growth Spurt

Puberty corresponds with the *adolescent growth spurt,* a rapid increase in size accompanied by changes in the shape and proportions of the body. Over about a 4-year span, the average increase in height is about 10 inches for both boys and girls; boys gain about 42 pounds on average and girls about 38 pounds. Different parts of the body grow at different times. Facial features like the nose and ears usually grow before the skull does, accounting in part for Rebecca's strange appearance. It is likely that when her head growth catches up with her features, she will no longer seem to have a big nose. Hands, feet, and limbs usually grow before the torso, which can create awkwardness and adds to the odd look. There can even be asymmetries in growth between the two sides of the body, with one breast or one testicle growing before the other (Hofmann, 1997; Tanner, 1970, 1990).

Some aspects of the growth process play out differently for girls and boys. For girls, the growth spurt begins and ends about two years earlier than for boys. Besides other obvious differences, such as increased breast size and greater pelvic spread in girls and broader shoulders in boys, there are gender differences in internal growth. The size of the heart and lungs increases more in boys, for example, who also develop thicker bones and more muscle tissue than girls. Many of these changes contribute to average differences in physical strength and endurance between the sexes. Adolescent and adult males are typically stronger than females of the same general size. Thus, the adolescent growth spurt increases

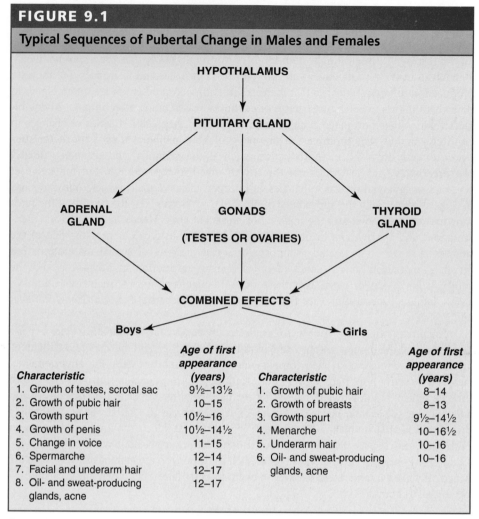

FIGURE 9.1

Typical Sequences of Pubertal Change in Males and Females

HYPOTHALAMUS

PITUITARY GLAND

ADRENAL GLAND

GONADS

(TESTES OR OVARIES)

THYROID GLAND

COMBINED EFFECTS

Boys ← → Girls

Characteristic	Age of first appearance (years)	Characteristic	Age of first appearance (years)
1. Growth of testes, scrotal sac	9½–13½	1. Growth of pubic hair	8–14
2. Growth of pubic hair	10–15	2. Growth of breasts	8–13
3. Growth spurt	10½–16	3. Growth spurt	9½–14½
4. Growth of penis	10½–14½	4. Menarche	10–16½
5. Change in voice	11–15	5. Underarm hair	10–16
6. Spermarche	12–14	6. Oil- and sweat-producing glands, acne	10–16
7. Facial and underarm hair	12–17		
8. Oil- and sweat-producing glands, acne	12–17		

Source: Adapted from *Adolescence and emerging adulthood: A cultural approach* by Arnett, J. J., 2001, and *Adolescence* by Atwater, E., 1996. Reprinted by permission of Pearson Education, Inc., Upper Saddle River, NJ.

both internal and external *sexual dimorphism,* physical differences between the sexes (Chumlea, 1982; Malina, 1990).

Behavioral Changes with Puberty

Part of what surprised her aunt about Rebecca was how moody she had become. Parents whose children have gone through puberty often warn parents of younger children to "Enjoy them while they're young; you don't know what you're in for!" Parents of adolescents often assume that hormones are the underlying cause when their adolescents seem difficult, making comments such as "Her hormones are raging!" Adolescent moodiness—extreme and rapid swings in emotional tone—is indeed notorious. But how extreme is it, really? And how much of it can be attributed directly to the underlying hormonal changes of puberty?

Moodiness is part of a broader set of behavioral tendencies in teens that also includes conflict with parents, negative affect, and risky behavior, such as violating norms and recklessness (Arnett, 1999). G. Stanley Hall, an early developmental researcher, referred to the full complement of difficult behaviors as the "storm and stress" of adolescence (Hall, 1904). Although there is considerable variability in the degree to which adolescents experience storm and stress, with many teens showing few signs of it, a review of research on differences between adolescents and other age groups indicates that teens do indeed experience greater average storm and stress than either younger children or adults (Arnett, 1999). We will look more closely at some features of adolescent storm and stress in the next chapter. Let's consider here adolescent moodiness and negative affect.

Larson and Richards (1994) used a technique called the ***experience sampling method*** to gauge adolescents' moods. Participants in their study wore beepers throughout their waking hours. When they were beeped, they made notes about what they were doing, thinking, and feeling at that moment. In the course of a day, adolescents reported more mood disruptions, more feelings of self-consciousness and embarrassment, more extremes of emotion, and less happiness than younger children or adults. In addition, their emotional reactions to the very same events tended to be more intense than those of other age groups.

Petersen and her colleagues (Petersen, Compas, Brooks-Gunn, Stemmler, Ey, & Grant, 1993) reviewed studies of ***depressed mood,*** defined as a subclinical level of depression, and found that about one third of teens experience depressed mood at any given time.

"Storm and stress" in adolescence, including moodiness, negativity, and intense reactions, can be a trial for parents.

Although clinical depression does not appear to be higher in samples of adolescents than in the general population, rates of clinical depression do increase at adolescence compared to childhood. As we have noted before, both depressed mood and clinical depression occur more often in females than in males, beginning in adolescence.

Moodiness does seem to be more characteristic of adolescents than of other age groups. Do hormones make it happen? As always, when we examine causes for behavior and for developmental changes in behavior, a multidimensional model seems to best fit the available data. Increases in hormone levels early in puberty *are* linked to increases in negative mood (Brooks-Gunn & Warren, 1989) and to young adolescents' volatility (Buchanan, et al., 1992). But hormonal changes are more likely to be predictive of mood if they are combined with negative life events, such as parental divorce or academic problems. In other words, risk factors potentiate each other.

Arnett (1999) provides an interesting example of the potential interaction of biological and social causes of mood disruption in teens. **Delayed phase preference** is a shift in sleep patterns that has been associated with hormonal changes at puberty. Adolescents are more comfortable staying up later in the evening and sleeping later in the morning than younger children (Carskadon, Vieria, & Acebo, 1993). Arnett asks whether requiring adolescents to start school earlier in the morning than younger children, a common practice in many school districts, might contribute to sleep deprivation in teens and by so doing, contribute to emotional volatility.

Moodiness seems to be strongly associated with changes in peer relationships, parent expectations, and self-concept that often accompany sexual maturation. In the next two sections, we will consider how some of these social and psychological repercussions of puberty function to affect mood. First, we'll examine how differently puberty seems to affect mood depending on whether its onset is early or late. Second, we will take a closer look at the gender difference in depressive symptoms that emerges in adolescence and consider how the different social experiences of girls and boys might contribute.

Early Versus Late Maturation.   For girls, early sexual maturation is generally associated with greater storm and stress, including moodiness, than late sexual maturation (Blyth, Simmons, Bulcroft, Felt, VanCleave, & Bush, 1981; Petersen, 1988; Simmons, Blyth, & McKinney, 1983). Thus, even though early and late maturers are subject to the same hormonal influences once puberty begins, early maturers seem to be more affected. The reasons must depend on factors other than hormones. Partly because most girls begin puberty before most boys, an especially early maturing girl is bigger than most of the other children her age. She is also heavier and so is more likely than other girls to be unhappy with her body in a culture such as ours, which prizes slimness in females. Early sexual maturation (e.g., breast development) may make her a target for teasing or innuendo from peers. Also, being physically mature can be a source of outright rejection by less mature girls (Petersen, 1988). Parents of early-maturing girls tend to worry about their daughters being at risk for sexual experiences that they are not ready to handle, and they may limit their daughters' independence in ways that are grating. Parents' concerns may not be exaggerated: early-maturing girls tend to have more behavior problems than other girls, especially if they become involved with older boys (Caspi, Lynam, Moffitt, & Silva, 1993; Ge, Conger, & Elder, 1996).

Early maturation in boys is a different story. Early-maturing boys seem to be *less* moody and *less* likely to exhibit depressed mood than later maturing boys. In fact, it is late-maturing boys who seem more affected by storm and stress. Being larger and stronger than other boys gives early-maturing boys an edge in socially approved male activities, such as athletics, whereas late-maturing boys are at a distinct disadvantage in the same activities. Generally, early-maturing boys are more confident than late-maturing boys, more popular, and more likely to be leaders among their peers. Late-maturing boys are more likely than other boys to be socially awkward, insecure, and variable in mood (Simmons, et al., 1983; Simmons & Blyth, 1987).

Clearly, the storm and stress that accompany the onset of puberty can vary dramatically depending on contextual factors. Overall, these findings suggest that the volatility and negativity of adolescents are largely related to the number of stressors with which they must cope.

Girls' Versus Boys' Susceptibility to Depression. Why should adolescent girls be more susceptible to depression? It is possible that sex differences in circulating hormones directly contribute. But most developmentalists argue that sex differences in social experience are likely to play a bigger role than hormones in the mix of causes. Remember that *both* boys and girls are more subject to depressive moods in adolescence than in the preadolescent period and that each gender experiences increased stress of various kinds (see Chapter 8). But on the whole, it may be that girls face more challenges to their self-esteem and more problems in living in early adolescence than boys do (Petersen, Sarigiani, & Kennedy, 1991). That is, girls must deal with more stressors simultaneously. In comparison to their male counterparts, females report experiencing more stressors from early adolescence onward (Compas, Howell, Phares, Williams, & Giunta, 1989; Wichstrom, 1999). Here are a few:

1. As we saw in the last chapter, by age 11 children are aware that the female gender role is less valued than the male role. They believe that there are greater restrictions on behavior for females and that there is gender-based discrimination (Intons-Peterson, 1988). As they integrate these beliefs into their self-concept, girls may begin to feel less worthwhile than boys, or at least less appreciated. Many studies have found a decline in self-esteem in girls after age 9, whereas boys' self-esteem tends to stabilize (Ruble & Martin, 1998).

2. Although both boys and girls are concerned about **body image** (their concept of, and attitude toward, their physical appearance) (Ferron, 1997), girls also worry more than boys about appearance and weight after puberty (e.g., Mendelson, White, & Mendelson, 1996).

3. Girls more often have lower expectations of success than boys (Ruble, Gruelich, Pomerantz, & Gochberg, 1993).

4. Girls may be more stressed by the burgeoning of their sexuality and their sexual desirability. The traditional **double standard,** by which female sexual behavior is judged more harshly than male sexual behavior, has clearly diminished over the last half century, as the rates and acceptability of premarital sex have increased among teens of both sexes (Astin, Korn, Sax, & Mahoney, 1994). Yet, American college students still consider girls who have multiple sexual partners to be more immoral than boys who do (Robinson, Ziss, Ganza, Katz, & Robinson, 1991), and among adolescents who have intercourse, girls are more likely to judge themselves to be bad or unlovable than boys are to negatively judge themselves (Graber, Brooks-Gunn, & Galen, 1999). Thus, even though girls' acceptance of and experience with sexuality is increasing rapidly, they are still more subject to ambiguous messages about the acceptability of sex and seem to be more uncertain about what is appropriate for them in a world of shifting values. In addition, the physical and social consequences of sexual activity are greater for girls: they are still the ones who get pregnant.

5. After puberty, girls and boys start interacting more in mixed-sex groups and in heterosexual dyads. In these contexts, the differences in their discourse styles may create more stress for girls. You'll recall from Chapter 8 that girls acquire a more cooperative discourse style and boys a more domineering style during childhood. One result is that

when adolescent girls socialize with boys, they are less likely to influence the outcome of a discussion (see Maccoby, 1990). Also, in heterosexual pairs boys do not offer as much support to their partners as girls do (Leaper, 1994b). As a consequence, these relationships may be less affirming and satisfying for girls than for boys (e.g., Pipher, 1994).

6. Because puberty comes earlier for girls, they are more likely than boys to simultaneously face both the changes of puberty and the difficult transition to secondary school (i.e., junior high or middle school) (Petersen, Kennedy, & Sullivan, 1991). (See Chapter 10 for a discussion of this transition.)

Girls may be more subject to depression than boys not only because they face more challenges but because they often adopt a coping style, *rumination,* that increases the risk of depression (Nolen-Hoeksema & Girgus, 1994; Petersen, Compas, et al., 1993). *Rumination* (Morrow & Nolen-Hoeksema, 1990) or self-focused attention (Ingram, Cruet, Johnson, & Wisnicki, 1988) may be defined as a stable, emotion-focused coping style that involves responding to problems by directing attention internally toward negative feelings and thoughts. Ruminating about problems includes both cognitive (self-focused cognitions) and affective (increased emotional reactivity) elements. Ruminative strategies may include isolating oneself to dwell on a problem, writing in a diary about how sad one feels, or talking repetitively about a negative experience with the purpose of gaining increased personal insight. In general, however, ruminative focusing on problems while in a depressed mood may actually make the depression worse.

Experimental studies have found that this type of heightened self-focus increases the duration and intensity of depressive episodes, particularly in adolescent and adult females (Greenberg & Pyszczynski, 1986; Ingram, et al., 1988; Morrow & Nolen-Hoeksema, 1990), who are much more likely to exhibit this style of coping than are males (Butler & Nolen-Hoeksema, 1994). Adolescents and adults who ruminate are more likely to experience depression than those who use *distraction* (Spasjevic & Alloy, 2001; Nolen-Hoeksema, et al., 1993). *Distraction* as a coping style involves deliberate focusing on neutral or pleasant thoughts or engaging in activities that divert attention in more positive directions. Distraction can attenuate depressive episodes (Nolen-Hoeksema, et al., 1993).

To qualify as a gender-linked preexisting risk factor, gender differences in rumination and distraction must be shown to exist prior to adolescence, before the rise in levels of depression. A study of the coping styles of fourth- and fifth-grade children revealed that girls *are* more likely than boys to endorse ruminative coping choices when confronted with academic, family, and peer stressors, even though at these ages girls and boys show no differences in rates of depression (Broderick, 1998). Similar to Nolen-Hoeksema's (1987) finding that older males are more likely to dampen their stress-related negative affect, boys in this study were somewhat more likely to choose distracting or avoidant ways to handle problems than girls were. Girls, on the other hand, were prone to amplifying negative affect by providing responses to stressful situations that were both very negative ("I felt like I was going to die") and persistent ("I'd be in a bad mood all day"). Thus, it appears that when girls at puberty begin to face increased stress, they, more than boys, are more likely to bring to the task a coping style that puts them at greater risk of experiencing depression.

However, gender role also influences how children and early adolescents cope with problems. A ruminative coping style is most pronounced among girls and some boys whose gender roles are stereotypically feminine. These individuals identify themselves as relatively passive and nondominant and are less likely to cope by using active problem solving or distraction. Having a ruminative coping style, or being uncomfortable with or incapable of psychological distraction, may be a particularly heavy burden for feminine-identified boys, for whom such behavior is clearly contrary to the peer group's expectations for appropriate masculine behavior (Broderick & Korteland, 2002).

The Emergence of Sexuality and Sexual Preference

Sexual pleasure is a part of human functioning even in early childhood. Preschoolers and school-aged children may fondle their own genitals for the pleasure of it, and many engage in sex play with others. "Playing doctor," for example, has been known to involve disrobing and/or fondling the genitals of other children (see Shaffer, 1994). However, the strength and urgency of the adult sex drive, emerging as a function of puberty, is a new experience to young adolescents. They are more sensitive to, and interested in, sexually relevant stimuli than younger children. As we have noted, despite having spent most of childhood spontaneously segregating into single-gender groups, young adolescents begin to seek out opportunities to socialize in mixed-gender groups (Maccoby, 1998).

Faced with their increased sexual interest, most adolescents begin to explore their sexuality. Figure 9.2 represents the percentages of the male and female population who engage in masturbation, which begins on average between 11 and 12 years. Table 9.1 presents a typical sequence of sexual experiences during adolescence, and Table 9.2 indicates gender and ethnic differences among American adolescents in the age of first intercourse. It should be noted that as many as 50 percent of young adolescents also have sexual experiences with members of the same sex, primarily displaying and touching genitals, and engaging in mutual masturbation. These activities seem to be partly a function of opportunity, since young adolescents still spend more of their time with same-sex than opposite-sex peers. For most youngsters, these sexual contacts are not indicators of a homosexual orientation (Bell, Weinberg, & Hammersmith, 1981; Ellis, Burke, & Ames, 1987; Leitenberg, Greenwald, & Tarran, 1989; Masters, Johnson, & Kolodny, 1988).

Clearly, sexual maturation is a key determiner of sexual behavior, but just as clearly, many other factors come into play. Adolescents are often moved to engage in sexual behavior out of curiosity or because of pressure to have sex from partners or peer group (e.g., Atwater, 1996; Rodgers & Rowe, 1993). Parents, by monitoring their children's behavior

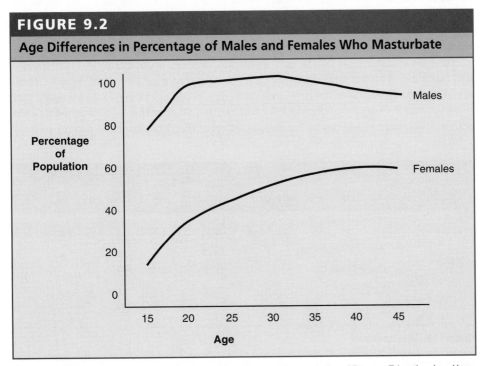

FIGURE 9.2

Age Differences in Percentage of Males and Females Who Masturbate

Source: Adapted from *Adolescence* by Atwater, E., 1996. Reprinted by permission of Pearson Education, Inc., Upper Saddle River, NJ.

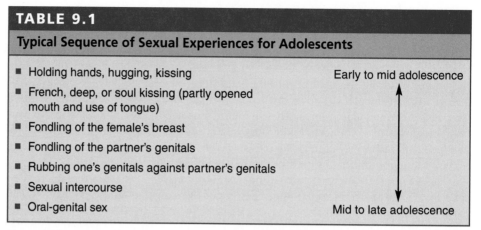

TABLE 9.1

Typical Sequence of Sexual Experiences for Adolescents

- Holding hands, hugging, kissing
- French, deep, or soul kissing (partly opened mouth and use of tongue)
- Fondling of the female's breast
- Fondling of the partner's genitals
- Rubbing one's genitals against partner's genitals
- Sexual intercourse
- Oral-genital sex

Early to mid adolescence

Mid to late adolescence

Source: Adolescence by Atwater, E., 1996. Reprinted by permission of Pearson Education, Inc., Upper Saddle River, NJ.

and by expressing their values, have more influence on the sexual behavior of early adolescents than of late adolescents (Treboux & Busch-Rossnagel, 1991). A myriad of other influences, from social class and ethnicity to religious background, geographic setting (urban versus rural), popular culture (as portrayed in movies, music, teen magazines, and Internet sites), and the quality of sex education in schools, play a part in when and whether adolescents become sexually active (e.g., Crump, Haynie, Aarons, Adair, Woodward, & Simons-Morton, 1999; Day, 1992; Murry, 1992).

A central feature of sexual development in adolescence is the emergence of *sexual orientation,* referring to a preference for sexual partners of one's own sex (*homosexuality*) or the opposite sex (*heterosexuality*) or both (*bisexuality*). A large majority of adolescents eventually identify themselves as heterosexual. In a recent national survey of 18- to 59-year-olds who were assured of anonymity, only about 3% of males and 1½% of females identified themselves as homosexual or bisexual (Dunlap, 1994), although some studies have found the rates to be somewhat higher (e.g., A. Bell, et al., 1981; see LeVay, 1996).

Our understanding of how sexual orientation develops is quite limited. Many theories that postulate environmental causes are clearly wrong. The most famous of these is Freud's account of the Oedipal and Electra complexes (e.g., Freud, 1935/1960). As you will recall from Chapter 8, Freud proposed in his psychoanalytic theory that 3- to 5-year-olds compete with the same-sexed parent for the attentions of the opposite-sexed parent. To avoid

TABLE 9.2

Gender, Race, and Average Age of First Intercourse

Ethnicity and Race	Men	Women
African American	14.3	16.8
Caucasian	16.3	17.4
Latino[a]	15.4	17.8
Mexican-American	16.3	17.6

[a]Except Mexican-American

Source: Adolescence by Atwater, E., 1996. Reprinted by permission of Pearson Education, Inc., Upper Saddle River, NJ.

the punitive consequences of such competition, boys eventually identify with their fathers and girls with mothers, imitating the behaviors and internalizing the values of that parent. According to Freud, this identification process explains why most children eventually adopt a heterosexual orientation. It is just one more way in which the child becomes like the same-sexed parent. Homosexuality or bisexuality results when something goes wrong with the identification process: the Oedipal or Electra complex cannot unfold in the usual way because there is only one parent in the home, or the same-sexed parent is too weak or shows no interest in the child, or the opposite-sexed parent is not nurturing enough to be attractive or is too dominant.

Freud's theory of identification is not supported by the evidence. Adults who are homosexual or bisexual are not more likely than heterosexuals to come from one-parent homes or to have weak fathers or dominant mothers (A. Bell et al., 1981; LeVay, 1996). Another environmental theory, the *seduction hypothesis,* is also wrong. In this view, children or adolescents are seduced into homosexuality by homosexual pedophiles. Yet, survey research indicates that homosexuals often feel inklings of their sexual orientation long before their first sexual experience, and they are no more likely to have had early sexual experiences with predatory adults than are heterosexuals (A. Bell, et al., 1981). These and other theories of parental influence on sexual orientation simply do not work. Even modeling by adults does not seem to affect children's sexual preference. Studies of children raised by homosexual partners indicate that they are no more likely to become homosexual themselves than children raised by heterosexuals (e.g., J. M. Bailey, Bobrow, et al., 1995; Golombok & Tasker, 1996; C. J. Patterson, 1992). It is also interesting to note that children raised by homosexual parents are no more likely to be sexually abused than other children and that they are just as likely to have good relations with peers during childhood (C. J. Patterson, 1992).

There is better evidence for biological influences on sexual orientation. First, prenatal hormones seem likely to play a role. Exposure to masculinizing hormones can affect the sexual orientation of human females. Girls who are exposed to high levels of prenatal androgens (congenital adrenal hyperplasia, or CAH; see Chapter 8) are often found to have a greater frequency of homosexual experiences and fantasies than their non-CAH female relatives (see Collaer & Hines, 1995). For males, delayed exposure to masculinizing hormones during prenatal development has been found to affect sexual behavior in several nonhuman mammalian species. For example, when a male rat fetus is prenatally stressed, effectively delaying its exposure to androgens, the rat in adulthood will show higher frequencies of female sexual posturing and lower frequencies of male sexual behaviors, such as mounting, than nonprenatally stressed males (see Chapter 8, and I. L. Ward, 1992). Whether human males are similarly affected by delayed prenatal exposure to androgens is not yet established, but the generality of the finding among nonhuman mammals makes such an hypothesis plausible.

Heredity seems to have an influence on the development of sexual orientation. When one identical twin is homosexual, the other twin has about a 50% chance of also being homosexual, a much higher concordance rate than we find between less closely related family members (J. M. Bailey & Pillard, 1991; J. M. Bailey, Pillard, Neale, & Agyei (1993). But clearly, sexual orientation cannot be just a function of heredity, or the concordance rates between identical twins would be much higher.

As with most other behavioral phenomena, it seems likely that environmental and hereditary factors interact in complex ways to produce sexual orientation. What the environmental factors might be, however, is not clear. D. J. Bem (1996) has proposed an intriguing alternative to theories that focus on parents or other adults as the primary source of environmental influence. He argues that sexual orientation is strongly affected by peer interactions. In Bem's view, the role of biology is to predispose children to prefer sex-typical activities (and same-sex playmates) or sex-atypical activities (and opposite-sex playmates). "These preferences lead children to feel different from opposite—or same-sex—peers, to perceive them as dissimilar, unfamiliar, and exotic. . . . [Eventually,] the exotic becomes erotic" (p. 320). In other words, Bem proposes that spending one's childhood with same-sexed peers enhances the tendency to perceive members of the opposite sex as mysterious and interesting and contributes to heterosexuality. In this view, if a child spends most of her time in the company of opposite-sexed peers, so that same-sexed peers are intriguing, this promotes the development of homosexuality.

Bem's theory is provocative but is highly speculative and as yet untested. There are some existing data that are consistent with Bem's ideas. For example, children with **gender identity disorder (GID),** who have early preferences for the toys, clothing, and activities of the opposite sex and who show some identity problems (such as wishing to be the other sex), also prefer to spend their time with opposite-sexed peers in middle childhood. According to Bem's theory, their preference for opposite-sexed playmates should eventually result in a homosexual orientation, a preference for same-sexed partners who are less familiar. Indeed, in one sample, 75% of boys with GID became homosexual or bisexual adults (Green, 1987). Thus, young GID boys often do grow up to be gay. Spending their time with opposite-sexed peers in childhood *could* be a causal step in the process, as Bem claims. There are certainly other ways to explain the sexual orientation of GID boys, but these findings are at least compatible with Bem's theory, which provides another outlook on a possible role for the environment in the development of sexual orientation.

Regardless of how biology and environment transact in the determination of sexual preference, it should be noted that most homosexuals, like most heterosexuals, feel that their sexual orientation is not something they have chosen but that it is a part of what they are "naturally" (e.g., Money, 1988). Even so, there are some people who change sexual preference in the course of their adult lives, and for these people personal choice often seems to play a greater role than for others (see Baumrind, 1995; Diamond, 1995; Kitzinger & Wilkinson, 1995; Savin-Williams, 1998).

The Changing Brain

Whereas researchers once believed that brain development is largely complete by the onset of puberty (Siegler, 1998), studies using new technologies, such as magnetic resonance imaging (MRI), are beginning to reveal that many parts of the brain continue to change throughout adolescence. You may recall that in infancy the brain grows through a process of *synaptogenesis,* an increase in the number of synapses (connections) between neurons. By age 2, a *pruning* process has begun: many of these synapses disappear. Pruning seems to be a response to experience, such that synapses that are used are maintained, but synapses that are not used wither (see Chapter 3; Greenough & Black, 1992). Pruning was once thought to be finished by the onset of puberty, but the latest research on brain development indicates otherwise. It now appears that in many parts of the cortex, puberty is correlated with a "growth spurt" in synaptogenesis, followed by a long reprise of the pruning process that lasts, for some parts of the brain, into early adulthood.

Several cortical areas participate in this growth process during adolescence. Current evidence implicates the frontal lobes, which play a role in organization, planning, self-control, judgment, and the regulation of emotion; the parietal lobes, which are involved in integrating information; the temporal lobes, serving language functions and contributing to emotional regulation; and the corpus callosum, the network of fibers connecting the left and right sides of the cortex, aiding in information integration and other higher functions, such as consciousness (e.g., Casey, Giedd, & Thomas, 2000; Sowell, Delis, Stiles, & Jernigan, 2001; Spear, 2000; P. M. Thompson, Giedd, Woods, MacDonald, Evans, & Toga,

2000). Interestingly, when younger teens are shown pictures of faces expressing fear, they exhibit more electrical activity in subcortical structures (such as the amygdala) than in cortical structures, whereas older adolescents and adults show substantial activity in the frontal lobes (Killgore, Oki, & Yurgelun-Todd, 2001). It is tempting to conclude that immaturity of the frontal lobes is partly responsible for extremes in emotional reactivity in early adolescence and that maturing of the frontal lobes helps older teens to achieve better cognitive control over their emotions. It also seems likely that the availability of new synapses in cortical regions contributes to adolescents' increased ability to think logically about abstract contents (see the discussion of cognitive development in adolescence, below).

Another growth process previously thought to end by puberty is *myelination,* the sheathing of axons in a white, fatty substance called myelin, which insulates these neuronal projections and makes transmission of electrical impulses possible. As we noted in Chapter 6, there is now evidence that myelination continues in adolescence, at least in some locations (e.g., Paus, et al., 1999).

In sum, a new wave of brain research indicates that puberty ushers in more than the sexual maturation process. Puberty is coordinated with growth in the highest regions of the brain. The full implications of this growth are far from clear, but one may be that the adolescent period in humans substantially increases our cognitive potential, perhaps dramatically enhancing our capacity for the acquisition and integration of information.

COGNITIVE DEVELOPMENT

When were you first introduced to the mysteries of algebra? When we asked a class of college sophomores that question, a few thought they might have been given a taste of algebra as early as sixth grade (at age 11 or 12). But the majority said it was between seventh and ninth grades (that is, between ages 12 and 15). Recently, the National Council on the Teaching of Mathematics (2000a; 2000b) recommended introducing the more concrete elements of algebra in grades 5 through 8, as a generalization of arithmetic. But the council suggests that the more abstract concepts are better introduced in grades 9 through 12.

Why do curriculum planners wait so long to introduce even the most basic aspects of algebra? Simple equations solving for "x" can be solved using basic mathematical operations such as adding, subtracting, multiplying, and dividing. In a culture known for its desire to do things faster and better, often pushing children along as quickly as possible, why do we wait until fifth or sixth grade to teach them to solve even simple equations? The answer seems to be, "because it does not work if we begin earlier." We make no faster progress if we introduce algebra in second grade than if we wait until later. The juggernaut seems to be that even the simplest algebraic equation involves the use of a symbol for the unknown, the "x." You may recall your first algebra teacher defining those letters that appear in equations as "symbols for unknown numbers," representing "any possible number." When we ask children to use those letters to substitute for unknown numbers, we are asking them to reason logically about an abstraction, something that cannot be represented in concrete terms. "X" can only be defined or exemplified in words or other symbols. There is no concrete example of "an unknown number."

In middle childhood, the period Jean Piaget referred to as the stage of *concrete operational thought,* children clearly can reason logically. They have the capacity to hold several pieces of information in mind at one time and to discover the relations among them. But, as we saw in Chapter 6, they seem to reason most effectively if the information they are working with can be represented readily in the concrete, real world, or at least if parallels can be found in the real world. In early adolescence, we begin to see this limitation of middle childhood recede. More and more, youngsters seem able to leave the ground of reality and to spin a logical tale with abstract contents, contents such as probabilities, hypothetical possibilities, and statements that are contrary to one's belief or even to fact.

Formal Operational Thought

Suppose you have two canisters of hard candy (see Figure 9.3). Your favorite flavor is lemon, the yellow candies. You know the first canister has one green candy and two yellow ones. The second canister has five green and five yellow candies. To get a candy, you must shake one out of a canister, sight unseen. Which canister should you shake to be most certain of getting a yellow candy?

You are faced here with a probability problem. With the first canister, you would get a yellow candy 2 out of 3 times, or 67% of the time. With the second canister, you would get a yellow candy 5 out of 10 times, or 50% of the time. These odds make the first canister your best choice.

An 8-year-old would probably choose to take her chances with the second canister, arguing that it contains more yellow candies. But the absolute number of candies is not important in this case. Rather, the important features to compare are the relative proportions of yellow candies in each canister, which determine the probability of getting a yellow candy. The proportion of yellow candies is an abstraction, one that is difficult for an 8-year-old to reason about when faced with the concrete reality of a larger number of yellow candies in the second canister (see Piaget & Inhelder, 1951/1976).

Even as an adult, you may not have known which canister to choose. Perhaps you got confused about how to calculate the probabilities; perhaps you were momentarily distracted by the concrete reality that is convincing to the 8-year-old—there *are* more yellow in the second canister. But now that you have run through this kind of problem and seen how it works, you are likely to see the importance of the more abstract concepts—the proportion of yellow candies in each canister—as opposed to the actual numbers of candies. Given another problem like this one, you have a good chance of figuring it out correctly. An 8-year-old, however, would not be likely to attack the next problem any differently,

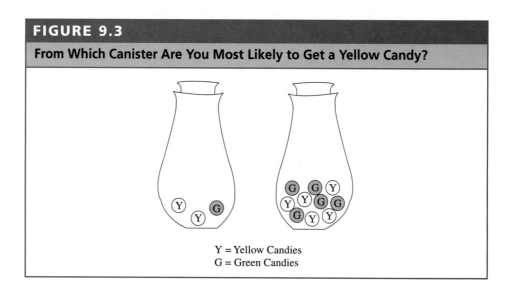

FIGURE 9.3

From Which Canister Are You Most Likely to Get a Yellow Candy?

Y = Yellow Candies
G = Green Candies

even with explanation and training. The 8-year-old's difficulty is not just inexperience with the probability concept; it is a failure to understand and reason effectively about an abstraction.

The problem of the yellow candy illustrates several characteristics of **formal operational thought,** the kind of thinking that Piaget and his colleague, Barbel Inhelder, identified as beginning at about 11 or 12 years (e.g., Inhelder & Piaget, 1955/1958). First, formal thought rises above particular contents and focuses on relationships that govern those contents—that is, on abstractions. In the candy example, the proportion of yellow to green candies, not the number of yellow candies, in each canister is what you had to reason about. Second, formal reasoning involves coordinating multiple relationships. In the candy example, the successful problem solver must discover the relationship between the two proportions, which are *themselves* relationships. Third, formal thought can be difficult even for adults. We all find logical thinking to be easier when the information we must contend with is more concrete. As a result, even adolescents and adults who are capable of formal thought do not always use it effectively (e.g., J. A. Gray, 1990). It helps if we have experience and training in solving a particular kind of problem (e.g., Overton, 1990) or if we have familiarity with the subject matter (the *domain of knowledge*) (e.g., Kuhn, Schauble, & Garcia-Mila, 1992; Schauble, 1996), just as we saw with younger children in Chapter 6. Across a number of studies using a variety of tests of formal operational thinking, researchers report that about 30% of young adolescents (about 13 years old) show *some* tendency to apply formal reasoning in *some* situations, and about 60% of older adolescents or young adults (college students) do so (see P. A. Cowan, 1978, for a summary of early work on this issue; see Kuhn, 1989, and J. A. Gray, 1990, for more recent findings).

As we have seen before, changes in cognitive ability usually occur gradually, not in startling stage-like shifts. The development of formal reasoning is no different, so that we sometimes see glimmerings of formal thought in middle childhood. The kinds of problem-solving strategies that children use at ages 9 or 10 are likely to seem more elaborate than at ages 6 or 7, and they may even involve operating on relatively abstract contents (e.g., Kuhn, Garcia-Mila, Zohar, & Andersen, 1995). But formal thinking is more likely to emerge in adolescence.

Educators have long recognized that more can be expected of adolescents, so that, as with algebra, more abstract subject matter is likely to be introduced to the curriculum after about age 12. In science classes, where younger students may be given laboratory assignments that consist of simple demonstrations, adolescents are often expected to generate and test hypotheses with thorough rigor (see below). In literature, teachers require students to begin to analyze works of fiction at multiple levels, going beyond the sequence of events that creates the story and looking for ironic, satiric, and metaphoric themes. These themes are abstractions, relationships among words on a different plane from the literal meaning. Some of us remember pining for the simpler, easier days when a story was just a story!

The capacity for formal thought can influence many aspects of adolescent life, from the approaches teens take to academic tasks to their views of religion and politics, their self-evaluation, and their relationships with parents and peers. In the following sections, we will look at some examples of these wide-ranging implications.

Scientific Problem Solving

Suppose a high school physics teacher posed the following problem to her class: A pendulum is a swinging object at the end of a length of string. Your job is to determine why some pendulums swing at a faster rate than others. The characteristics of a pendulum you

As teens acquire formal operational thinking skills, the science curriculum makes more demands for careful, abstract thought, such as requiring students to systematically generate and test hypotheses.

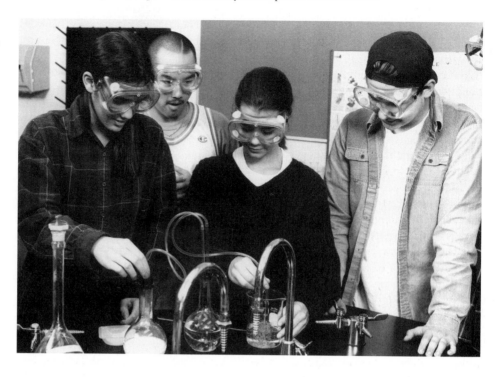

should consider are the weight of the object, the length of the string, the force of the push that starts the swing, and the height of the dropping point" (problem adapted from Inhelder & Piaget, 1955/1958).

One student approaches the problem like this: "I think it could be any of the four characteristics that is important. First, I will try changing the weight of the object; then I'll change the length of the string; then I'll vary the force of the push; then I'll try changing the dropping point." The student makes a change in the weight with no effect on rate of swing. Then she changes the length of the string. Voila! The rate of swing changes. She announces that she has found the solution: length of the string.

Another student approaches the task by changing more than one characteristic at a time. When she changes weight and length together, the rate of swing changes. She concludes that the rate of swing is a result of the combined effects of weight and length.

A third student tests each of the four characteristics and, of course, finds that changing the length affects rate of swing. But she continues her assessment, combining changes in pairs of characteristics: weight plus length, weight plus force of push, weight plus height of dropping point, and so on. Even though each pairing that includes a change of length affects the rate of swing, she continues her tests. She moves on to combine changes in weight plus length plus force of push; then weight plus length plus height of dropping point, and so on until she has tested every combination of three changes, and finally tests a combination of changes in all four characteristics at once. Only combinations in which length of string is changed affect rate of swing—no other combinations make a difference. Finally, she reports her conclusion. Length of string alone is the determining factor.

Only the third student has solved the problem using combinatorial logic, a type of formal operational thought. She has generated every possible hypothesis. Then, she has tested each hypothesis by holding constant all the factors that are not posited to contribute to the rate of swing by that hypothesis, so that by systematic examination of the results of all the tests she can eliminate all but the hypotheses that *must* be correct.

The first and second students provide two examples of concrete operational thinking. There is a degree of systematicity to their generation of hypotheses, but not a complete generation of all possibilities. And their conclusions are too closely tied to concrete outcomes. When the "length of string hypothesis" works for the first student, she stops her testing, even though it remains possible that other characteristics could be involved or that some combination of characteristics could negate the effects of changing the string length. When the combination of weight and length works for the second student, she ends her investigation, drawing the false conclusion that the combination is important.

Adolescents who approach scientific problems by considering every possibility and then carefully testing each one are using formal operational reasoning. The pattern of results among all the tests is what drives the conclusions, not any particular concrete observation.

In effective scientific problem solving, we see another characteristic of people who use formal operational thought. They can generate and think about possibilities. What is *real* is just one of a full set of *possibilities*. These possibilities can be generated only in the realm of thought—they are abstractions, not dependent on observations.

As we noted in Chapter 6, even adults often fail to treat their own theories as just one in a set of possibilities. Even for individuals capable of formal thought, scientific reasoning often runs aground on the shoals of belief, so that evidence is distorted or ignored instead of carefully analyzed for overriding patterns. In other words, our motives and emotional commitments can sidetrack our logical reasoning (e.g., Kuhn, Amsel, & O'Loughlin, 1988; Kuhn, 1989). It appears that those of us who overcome these common difficulties have learned to logically analyze our own thought processes (Kuhn, 1989; Moshman, 1998). When we have favorite theories (e.g., strong beliefs about the value of capital punishment or ideas about the best approach to educating the gifted), we must take our own thinking about those theories as the subject of our formal reasoning, and we must monitor our own thought processes as we evaluate evidence, to assure that we are maintaining logical consistency. As you will see, skill at such self-monitoring clearly advances in adolescence. However, the stronger our emotional commitment to an idea, the harder it is to engage in such self-evaluation effectively and the less likely we are to do it (e.g., Kuhn, 1989). Counselors often struggle to help clients see problematic situations in logical, objective ways in order to facilitate good decision making.

Constructing Ideals

Adolescents who are capable of generating possibilities, without regard for present reality, have acquired a powerful new cognitive tool that can be used to construct **ideals:** logically organized possible systems. As P. A. Cowan (1978) puts it, such individuals are "adept at generating ideas about the world as it *could* be" (p. 291). They might mentally construct an ideal political system, or religion, or school. They might also construct an ideal self, teacher, parent, or friend. Any of these ideal systems will make the real, imperfect forms seem shabby and inadequate by comparison. For some adolescents, this new capacity for constructing ideals leads to a zeal for reform. It may also contribute to a skeptical attitude toward childhood religious beliefs or toward parental politics and values (Cowan, 1978; Piaget, 1964/1968). Family belief systems can become for the adolescent just one of many possibilities. Thus, the capacity to entertain possibilities and to construct ideals appears to contribute to a critical attitude, and to a skepticism about the justifications that others often give for the status quo. Rebecca's critical attitude in conversation with her family may be linked to her ability to construct ideals and her impatience with anything real that does not measure up.

The "cure" for a critical attitude is experience (Cowan, 1978; Piaget, 1964/1968). Ideals, by definition, are not real. They are perfect possibilities. But real systems and people are never perfect. Adolescent idealists are not familiar yet with the enormous complexity of putting ideas into action and with the actual limitations of the concrete world. Until they gain more experience of the difficulties, they are likely to be critical, even unforgiving. In essence, the adolescent's failure to understand the real limits of her ideas is a form of *egocentrism.* Interestingly, this seems to apply to her judgments not only of others but also of herself. The increase in depression in adolescence may in part be affected by a tendency to be discouraged by one's own imperfections: the real self never quite measures up to the ideal. An interesting feature of this new, self-critical attitude is that it is self-generated. Even when an adolescent's appearance or behavior does compare favorably to the standards that others hold, she may judge herself to be inadequate, based on her idealized version of the self. Such misplaced self-criticism can be very frustrating to adults who deal with adolescents and can play a role in some serious disorders, such as anorexia (Vandereycken & Van Deth, 1994).

Advances in Metacognitive Skill: Thinking About Thought

In middle childhood, children gain some *metacognitive* skill, that is, some understanding of their own cognitive processes. They get better and better, for example, at assessing when they have studied a list of words enough to remember them on a test (e.g., Flavell, Friedrichs, et al., 1970). But planful, organized thinking about one's own thought processes involves logical thinking about an abstraction—thought. The capacity for formal operational thinking seems to give this process a strong boost. Adolescents are much more likely than children to "be introspective in an analytic mode, to think critically about themselves and about the way that they think and behave" (Cowan, 1978, p. 289).

On the positive side, improved metacognitive skill seems to benefit scientific thinking, making it possible for some teens to evaluate their theories or beliefs objectively, in the light of evidence, as we noted above (Kuhn, 1989). Such skill also contributes to more careful planning and evaluation of one's activities. For example, once Rebecca sits down to study for her exam, she may test herself to determine what she has learned so far, evaluate the study strategies she has been using for their effectiveness, and allocate her study time planfully, spending the most time on the information she knows least well (e.g., Flavell, Miller, et al., 1993).

On the more negative side, the self-evaluation and self-monitoring that comes with improved metacognitive skill may also contribute to other forms of egocentrism that seem to emerge at adolescence. Elkind (1967), elaborating on some of Piaget's (1964/1968) ideas about adolescence, describes the young teen as intensely self-focused. In a sense, her new capacity for introspection, for evaluating her own mental processes, contributes to an inward focus that is distorting. Although she understands that others have minds of their own and that they have their own concerns, her own fascination with herself, enhanced by the compelling and unpredictable physical changes she is undergoing, leads her to mistakenly assume that others are as intrigued by and concerned about her as she is. Elkind calls this assumption the adolescent's **imaginary audience.** Because she is so sure that others are as interested in her as she is, she feels extremely self-conscious, acutely aware of her looks and her behavior in the presence of others.

Another feature of the adolescent's self-focus is a distorted view of her own importance. Elkind calls this assumption the **personal fable.** Adolescents often seem to feel that their experiences and concerns are unique. The personal fable may also include fantasies of having a special destiny, an important role to play in the lives of others or on the world stage. A feeling of being invulnerable, even immortal, called the **invincibility fable,** can be a part of this fantasy, perhaps accounting for increases in risk taking at adolescence. Adolescents may reason, for example, that others who drive drunk may get hurt in auto accidents or that others who have unprotected sex may get pregnant, but they don't believe that they themselves would suffer these consequences.

The notions of imaginary audience and personal fable are useful, but researchers have raised a number of questions about where they originate and when they recede. Elkind (1967) characterized these egocentric developments as a product of formal operational skill, and he suggested that they diminish in later adolescence as a function of interpersonal experience. Sharing ideas and feelings with others, especially peers, helps an adolescent to do a better job of perspective taking and helps her to recognize that others are focused on themselves and that her experiences are not unique.

Studies indicate that adolescents' self-focused thought is not as closely associated with the emergence of formal operational skills as Elkind suggested (e.g., Lapsley, FitzGerald, Rice, & Jackson, 1989). Lapsley (1993; Lapsley & Murphy, 1985) argues that the social realities of adolescence—the need to separate from parents, to form an adult identity—are at least as important in explaining the egocentrism of the adolescent. He contends that the imaginary audience may be an expression of intense anxiety associated with individuation and that the personal fable may be a useful fantasy for reducing some of that anxiety (see Blos, 1962, for a theoretical discussion of the separation-individuation process).

An adolescent's intense self-focus may contribute to a sense of uniqueness or invulnerability, called the "invincibility fable."

Whatever the cause or causes of adolescent egocentrism, recent research suggests that it is not a phenomenon that belongs exclusively to teens. Several studies have found that elements of the imaginary audience (extreme self-consciousness) and of the personal fable (a sense of invulnerability) continue at least into early adulthood, sometimes not showing much decline even then (e.g., Frankenberger, 2000; Quadrel, Fischhoff, & Davis, 1993). There is little disagreement that these egocentric tendencies begin in adolescence; it may be, however, that some of us are stuck with them far beyond our teen years.

The recent work on adolescent egocentrism reminds us that even if cognitive change contributes to these processes, the adolescent's cognitive abilities do not operate in a vacuum. They are among the many causal elements in a multidimensional mix. Adolescence brings a remarkable confluence of change into a child's life: change in thinking skills, biochemical and brain functioning, physical shape and size, peer and parental expectations, educational structures and requirements. In addition, adult responsibility lurks just around the corner. In the next section, we return to the issue of how the child's self-concept evolves, in the midst of all this change, into an adult identity.

IDENTITY DEVELOPMENT

Some Basic Considerations

Identity, or *ego identity* as Erikson first called it, is a concept that is difficult to define. It incorporates and expands on all the dimensions of self-knowledge that have been discussed in previous chapters. Furthermore, it serves as the foundation for the behavioral, affective, and cognitive commitments to career, relationships, and political and religious belief systems that will be made in adulthood. Erikson himself seemed annoyed by others' attempts to reduce the concept of identity to a flat, mental picture of the self. He described himself as registering

> a certain impatience with the faddish equation, *never suggested by me,* of the term identity with the question "Who am I?" . . . The pertinent question, if it can be put into the first person at all, would be "What do I want to make of myself, and what do I have to work with?" (1968, p. 314)

Note the dynamic, future-oriented quality implied in his statement, which integrates past accomplishments with new directions.

Erikson labeled the process of identity formation in adolescence a "crisis" of "identity versus identity confusion." But his view of the process is more accurately characterized as a specific challenge or task that asserts itself at a particular point in development (see Chapter 1). Erikson himself cautioned against thinking of life stages in terms of either-or propositions. In the case of identity, individuals make choices and have experiences that take them closer to or farther away from a meaningful sense of self until one kind of resolution (e.g., identity achievement) predominates over the other (e.g., identity confusion, also called "diffusion"). Some authors suggest that using the term identity *exploration* instead of identity *crisis* for this stage is more appropriate (Marcia, Waterman, Matteson, Archer, & Orlofsky, 1993). *Exploration* reflects the prolonged effort involved in the discovery process, while *crisis* implies a short-term and possibly traumatic event.

Before we consider the way identity is conceptualized in most research studies, it is important to mention two aspects of Erikson's theory of identity that have generated some discussion: the stability of identity over time and its individualistic emphasis. First, the formation of an identity in adolescence, which is the subject of this section, is not the end of the story. Anyone who has counseled both adolescents and adults will recognize that growth and change of self-representations takes place throughout the life span. What makes this particular period of the life cycle remarkable are the impressive strides young people make during the years of adolescence and young adulthood in developing the essential core of how they will be as adults.

All of our life stories are subject to revision by time, place, and circumstance. However, a core sense of self that "fits," to use the words of the poet at the beginning of this chapter, becomes clearer as the years unfold. Erikson (1968) captures the tension between continuity and change by writing that "ego identity could be said to be characterized by the actually attained but *forever to-be-revised* [italics added] sense of the reality of the Self within social reality" (p. 211).

Second, Erikson's identity theory has been criticized by some for being focused on the realization of the autonomous self at the expense of the collectivist self (Gilligan, 1982; Josselson, 1988). Erikson's theory has also been faulted for its "eurocentric" focus, which "assumes the necessity of individuation operationalized at its extreme" (Root, 1999, p. 69). It is true that classic developmental theories originally incorporated a masculine perspective, as we shall discuss in a later section on gender. However, the idea that identity formation requires valuing extreme individual autonomy may erroneously arise from the very nature of what constitutes identity, namely, the "I-ness" of the construct.

Consider these examples. You might be the type of person who tends to be competitive, who values personal ambition, and who single-mindedly pursues certain goals. Or you might be one who is more highly invested in membership in your social network, who works at being a good partner or friend, and whose values are based less on competition and more on meeting the goals of the whole group. Either way, you possess an identity! What has been overlooked in the individualistic-collectivist discussion is Erikson's primary contribution to theorizing about personality—namely, his emphasis on the power of social contexts to shape development. His writing clearly supports the importance of the cultural milieu as formative to personality development. His view is thus quite consistent with the contemporary notion that those values held in highest regard within one's cultural context strongly affect the nature of one's self-representations, worldviews, and commitments (e.g., Markus & Kitayama, 1991).

Adolescent Identity Development

So much has been written about adolescent identity development over the years that it is indeed a formidable task to summarize this wealth of theoretical and empirical knowledge. The most comprehensive empirical exploration of Erikson's theory is provided by James Marcia and his associates (1966, 1989, 1993), who developed a categorical system for labeling the dimensions or patterns that emerge in the identity development process. We will examine this body of work by focusing on the following questions: What are the categories of identity development? How are these categories assessed? Is there a universal sequence of change? Is the developmental trajectory always the same, or does it vary for different groups?

Identity Status

Individuals at adolescence and beyond may be characterized as belonging to one of four identity status categories: ***diffusion, moratorium, foreclosure,*** or ***achievement.*** These categories borrow from Erikson's conceptualization of identity development as a task involving *exploration* of various possible positions in the world and ultimately making mature *commitments* to certain ones, such as religion, career, political affiliation, and sexual orientation. Therefore, each status category can be defined by the presence or absence of exploration and commitment. Some of the names are similar to those used by Erikson in his writings. However, even though Erikson called the negative outcome associated with failure to achieve identity "identity diffusion," he did not develop the four identity status categories. Marcia and other researchers constructed these categories in their efforts to operationalize aspects of Erikson's ideas.

Let us consider each of the statuses and examine what they mean. *Diffusion* is the state that often characterizes young adolescents as they embark on the identity development process. In this state, they lack both exploration and commitment. Persons in the diffused category are not actively involved in exploring possible life choices, nor have they made any firm commitments to them. While this state of affairs is fairly common in early adolescence, diffusion (or confusion) can be highly problematic later on in adulthood. Persons whose identity is diffused may not trust their ability to find and commit to a meaningful path in life, or they might deny their need to do so. They may lack a sense of optimism about the future and, "many a sick or desperate late adolescent, if faced with continuing conflict, would rather be nobody or somebody totally bad, or, indeed, dead" (Erikson, 1968, p. 176). Alternatively, they may situate themselves within a highly controlling environment that dictates the conditions of their behavior and the nature of their views.

Individuals in *moratorium* also display a lack of commitment, but they are distinguished from the identity diffused by virtue of their exploration. In other words, these adolescents and young adults are straining toward the future, looking for what they might make of themselves. They may demonstrate frequent shifts in goals and changes in behavior, along with the anxiety and exhilaration that accompany active experimentation. Consequently, these exploratory periods may look like "crises" to the observer. Erikson (1950/1963) defined moratorium as the essence of the adolescent mind and in so doing, helped make sense of the transitory, inconsistent, and often incomprehensible nature of many adolescent behaviors. The prize to be gained from this adolescent and early adult trial and error is an identity that has been personally **constructed**. Constructed identity is not based upon a predetermined set of expectations, but represents either a personal redefinition of childhood and early adolescent goals and values or perhaps something very different from them. In moratorium, the future may be perceived as difficult, exciting, or even anxiety producing, but it can be shaped by one's own decision making.

Foreclosure, the third status, describes a category of individuals who make commitments with little or no exploration of alternatives. This status, along with diffusion, may also characterize young people entering adolescence who incorporate the values and goals of significant others, such as their parents, without reflection. Their commitments are, by definition, premature, preordained by family obligation or constrained by circumstance. A very early marriage or settling very early on a career are examples of this. These kinds of decisions are not always problematic, but they may be so. The identity attained by those who are foreclosed is called a **conferred** identity, rather than a constructed one. Foreclosure's perspective on the future involves meeting the expectations of a "prearranged set of ideals, occupational plans, and interpersonal forms" (Marcia, 1993, p. 8). These individuals proceed into the future with the goals and values of early adolescence relatively intact and experience fewer difficulties along the way.

Identity *achievement*, the fourth of Marcia's categories, comprises individuals whose development has been marked by exploration and commitment to certain alternatives. They have decided on a game plan, so to speak, which may be revised as needed. Their identity has been constructed by their own efforts to shape and transform their earlier selves. In theory, at least, they have reached a valued end point. Studies have generally shown positive correlations between identity achievement and psychological well-being

(Meeus, Iedema, Helsen, & Vollebergh, 1999). But is identity, once achieved, really the end of the story? We will discuss this issue in a later section.

Personal and Cognitive Characteristics of Each Identity Status

Researchers have found that personality tends to vary across identity categories. Those in the achieved category have a more internal locus of control as compared to diffused individuals, who are the most external (Dellas & Jernigan, 1987). Anxiety seems to be lowest for foreclosed groups, whereas it is relatively high among diffused groups and highest among those in moratorium (Marcia, 1967; Sterling & Van Horn, 1989). Foreclosed individuals report the highest levels of authoritarianism, conformity, and obedience to authority; those in moratorium report the lowest levels (Marcia, Waterman, Matteson, Archer, & Orlofsky, 1993; Podd, 1972). Autonomy is highest among achieved males and females and foreclosed women, but it is lowest in diffused males and females and foreclosed men (Waterman, 1993; Schenkel & Marcia, 1972).

In a study of the role of adolescent egocentrism in identity formation, B. P. O'Connor (1995) found that more egocentrism is associated with more exploration and, ultimately, with a greater likelihood of identity achievement, especially in males. Degree of exploration is also associated with more early childhood exposure to creative, technical, and cultural activities provided by parents, as demonstrated by Schmitt-Rodermund and Vondracek (1999). Providing children with early exploratory experiences was positively related to a broader range of interests in adolescence, more exploration in these areas, and later identity achievement.

Assessment of Identity Domains

In order to study identity development, it must be translated into something that can be measured. Erikson viewed occupation and ideology, both political and religious, as expressions of one's identity. Marcia (1964) constructed a standardized, semi-structured **Ego Identity Interview** designed to assess these three domains of identity: vocational choice, religious beliefs, and political ideology, using samples of male college students. When his samples were expanded to include women, the domains of work-family conflict (Marcia & Friedman, 1970) and attitudes toward premarital intercourse (Schenkel & Marcia, 1972) were added to the interview schedule. Waterman (1993) distinguishes between the core dimensions that are covered in the majority of studies using the *Ego Identity Interview* and those that are only occasionally included. Core domains include: vocational choice, religious beliefs, political ideology, gender-role attitudes, and beliefs about sexual expression. Supplemental domains include: hobbies, friendships, dating relationships, role of spouse, role of parent, experiences at school, and issues of work-family balance. The interview format consists of general questions such as "Should one believe in God or not?" "What type of work would you like to do?" and "What do you see as the advantages and disadvantages of being single versus being married?" followed up by more specific probes. (See Marcia, et al., 1993, for the complete interview.)

As you reflect on this approach, you may be reminded of the construct of self-concept, which was discussed in Chapters 5 and 7. The construction of ego identity in adolescence and beyond builds on and/or incorporates many of the components of self-concept developed earlier, such as social, academic, and physical self-concept. Identity may be construed as an overarching construct, with each domain representing a more specific aspect. Just as individuals vary in their level of self-esteem across domains, individuals will also show variation in the nature of their identity formation and in the timing of developmental progress. Thus, a person might be foreclosed in the area of religious identity but be in moratorium in the area of vocational choice.

Developmental Sequence in Identity Formation

Based upon the previous discussion, you may think the four statuses have the look of a linear, developmental stage model. Frequently, these statuses are interpreted to be synonymous with stages, and, in fact, Marcia (1967) originally proposed that each resided on a continuum, from diffusion to foreclosure to moratorium to achievement, with achievement representing the desirable end state. More recent research has prompted a rethinking of this perspective. Even though achieved and diffused statuses retain their ultimate significance as positive and negative outcomes, there are no compelling theoretical reasons to position foreclosure and moratorium adjacent to each other on the continuum. In addition, most of the studies done on the topic of identity development have used the categories to classify individuals rather than to follow their developmental progress (Meeus, 1996).

Those studies that have tried to find evidence for a universal, step-by-step sequence of identity development have largely come up short because there are many possible ways to move from category to category over time. The theoretical trajectory advanced in early work using Marcia's categories fails to describe other relatively common pathways. Think of a foreclosed individual who unexpectedly encounters a life event that forces her to rethink her commitments. Plunged back into moratorium, she can move into either achievement or diffusion. Another individual, who has become an identity achiever, may reenter moratorium if the goals she once chose no longer fit. Stephen, Fraser, and Marcia (1992) call the frequently observed cycles of movement from identity achievement to moratorium "MAMA" cycles (moratorium-achievement-moratorium-achievement). The pattern is not as neat as was originally anticipated.

So, are we to assume that the status categories merely provide a descriptive model for all possible states of identity development, or is there also evidence for some common developmental trajectory? In general, longitudinal studies of movement across statuses, or of "progressive developmental shifts" (Waterman, 1993), have been supportive of some developmental trends in identity formation.

Meeus and colleagues (1999), who worked with Dutch adolescents, developed a classificatory system based upon Marcia's, with two main distinctions. First, exploration and commitment are separately measured in Meeus's research to provide a more powerful way to demonstrate developmental trends. Secondly, his classification scheme is based on an individual's current identity development activity without reference to past behavior. For example, diffusion and moratorium categories are similar to Marcia's because the former reflects current disinterest in identity seeking and the latter reflects intense engagement in it. Foreclosure, on the other hand, has been renamed **closed commitment** because it signifies a high level of present commitment with low levels of coexisting exploration. **Achieving commitment** is used instead of achievement because it connotes a dynamic linkage between high levels of commitment and high levels of exploration. Meeus and colleagues explain the differences in approach this way:

> For Marcia, exploration is mainly important in the choice of a commitment, after which it is disregarded, whereas the new statuses are based on the idea that adolescents constantly reconsider their commitments. It is also hypothesized that not only do the commitments become stronger during the course of adolescence, but so too does the exploration of the commitments. A more solid identity structure arises, which is also more carefully considered. (p. 433)

Based on their review of the identity development literature as well as the results of their own large-scale longitudinal studies, the conclusions provided by Meeus et al. (1999) reinforce Waterman's (1993) finding of progressive developmental trends across categories. The number of achievements increases over time, while foreclosures decrease and diffusions decrease or remain the same. The number of moratoriums does not systematically increase or decrease over time. Thus, the categories defined by Marcia do have some directional, developmental significance. Generally, identity development proceeds toward achievement as a goal, with much of the movement accounted for by increases in achievement and decreases in foreclosure. These authors note, however, that a substantial percentage of adolescents remain in one of the other categories in some or all domains. Interestingly, these findings also indicate that individuals in both the achievement category and the foreclosed category experience high levels of psychological well-being. Contrary to earlier theoretical perspectives, this suggests that foreclosure may be an adaptive end point for some individuals.

Identity Crisis: Truth or Fiction?

Research such as this indicates that moratorium should be considered a transitional state that has some elements of an identity crisis. Consider the following situation. If you are in diffusion or foreclosure, you might encounter situations, people, or new information that produces a state of disequilibrium. This exposure causes you to rethink old values and adopt new ideas, albeit after some anxiety and reflection. The physical, cognitive, and emotional changes that accompany adolescence, in addition to the more diversified experiences afforded by larger school settings, provide sufficient disruptions of old patterns to jump-start this process for most adolescents.

Consistent with the notion of constructed and conferred identities, Meeus and his associates (1999) found that individuals tended toward foreclosure in areas over which they had little control (e.g., school or work), which these authors called *closed identity domains.* They speculate that in these domains, adolescents "do not find it so useful to reflect intensively on their commitments because they can assert very little influence on them" (p. 456). Crises in more *open identity domains,* such as those involving personal relationships, were found to be shorter, under more personal control, and more likely to result in achieving commitments.

What influences the outcome of a crisis? Waterman (1993) lists a number of factors which support a positive resolution: successful accomplishment of earlier psychosocial tasks, availability of positive role models with achieved identities, and support for exploration of alternatives. Waterman (1993) and Marcia (1980) report that most of the work of identity development, as measured by transitions into and out of status categories, takes place during early adulthood. This is particularly true for students who attend colleges or universities, settings that facilitate exploratory processes. The results of Meeus's (1996) longitudinal study, however, indicate that the high school years are also a time of active identity formation. He found as many, or more, progressive developmental shifts during this period as in early adulthood.

Identity Development and Diverse Groups

Do individuals differ in their identity development processes because they are members of certain groups? In recent years, there has been intense clinical and research interest in the specific identity development patterns of groups differing in gender, race, ethnicity, and sexual orientation. This body of work developed as an offshoot of more classic identity research for some of the following reasons. First, there has been general interest in understanding the differences that exist among groups of people. Demographic trends that project a growing multicultural citizenry and social movements that emphasize gay, lesbian, and women's rights, as well as pride in one's ethnic heritage, have sparked increased attention to these issues.

Second, there is a growing concern that traditional theories are insufficient to explain development because they are biased in favor of single-culture or single-gender models. Feminist writers (S. L. Archer, 1992; Enns, 1992; J. B. Miller, 1991), for example, point out the need to examine women's identity development separately from men's because of their belief that female and male developmental experiences are fundamentally different. Critical of traditional, monocultural approaches, counselors and other clinicians have also called for recognition and integration of diverse perspectives into practitioner training and therapeutic practice because of the relevance of gender, race, and sexual orientation to personal well-being and to client-counselor interaction (Sue, Arrendondo, & McDavis, 1992).

One of the ways that the message of diversity has been promulgated has been through a burgeoning array of identity development theories that are based on group differences. Developmental schemes have been proposed for identity formation of Blacks (Cross, 1971), Hispanics (Bernal & Knight, 1993), Asian Americans (Sue, Mack, & Sue, 1998), Whites (Helms, 1990), womanists (Parks, Carter, & Gushue, 1996), and lesbians and gays (Cass, 1979). An example of the proliferation of theories can be observed in Eliason's (1996) summary review. She describes eleven different theories of "coming out" or identity development for lesbian, bisexual, and gay individuals published in the social science literature. Similarly, Helms (1990) describes eleven models of Black identity development.

Clearly, scholarly work in this area is long overdue. The effects of race, culture, class, and gender on development are highly significant. To their credit, these identity theories broaden our perspective and encourage a more inclusive look at developmental processes. Yet, how can the practitioner make sense of the plethora of theories? Imagine you are counseling a client who is a 19-year-old lesbian of mixed Jamaican-White heritage. Which of the theories will help you understand her best? Given the diverse names, numbers, and definitions of stages proposed in these theories of identity development, it is easy to imagine clinicians feeling overwhelmed by the complexity and possibly discouraged about their ability to understand the world from their clients' perspectives. In this section, we will try to examine some of the general issues that pertain to the literature on gendered and racial/ethnic identity development and search for some commonalities.

Female Identity Theories

Recent criticism of Erikson's developmental theory has centered on its emphasizing separateness or autonomy, a salient feature of masculine personality, as the desired goal of identity development (Marcia, 1980). Failure to give equal emphasis to the desirability of connectedness to healthy personality development has been viewed as a suppression of women's "voice" (Gilligan, 1982; Josselson, 1973). Consequently, researchers have searched for gender differences in the identity formation process, investigating, for example, whether women's identity development proceeds via a different trajectory than the one traversed by men. Douvan and Adelson (1966) challenged Erikson's view by suggesting that women's successful identity formation depended upon prior resolution of intimacy issues, whereas men's successful resolution of intimacy issues depended first upon achieving identity. Note that in this formulation, the actual developmental progression is assumed to differ by gender, so that the *sequence* of stages and not simply the salient dimensions of identity are transposed.

How well has Erikson's theory fared when applied to women? Two main questions challenge researchers in this area. First, are certain identity domains differentially important to men versus women? Second, does Erikson's sequence of stages apply to males and females equally well? There is some support for the importance of interpersonal domains for women's identity development (Archer, 1992; Josselson, 1988; Kroger, 1983) and for the fact that these relational issues may be *more* important for women's development than for men's (Meeus & Dekovic, 1995). Meeus and Dekovic (1995), reporting on a cross-sectional study of 3,000 Dutch adolescents, found that girls were much more involved than boys in relationship-related activities (exploration) and experienced more personal satisfaction from them (commitment).

Findings such as these, however, do not imply that other domains, such as vocation and religion, are unimportant for women. Nor should they suggest that relational issues are unimportant for men. In fact, Matteson (1993) summarized the large number of studies in this area and found inconsistent gender differences or no differences, depending upon the methodology employed. Similarly, Archer and Waterman (1988) found no differences between genders in levels of self-actualization, internal locus of control, social interdependence, or moral reasoning, suggesting more similarity than difference in identity development and individuation for males and females. It might be useful to interpret the results this way: when studies do identify differences in aspects of self-definition that are more important to one gender or another, it is more likely but not inevitable that women, as a group, will assign interpersonal, communal aspects of themselves a higher priority.

The question of whether the actual pathways are different for males and females is also complicated. Erikson's proposal that a secure identity must be achieved before realizing intimacy has not been fully supported by research on either gender. As we have noted in earlier chapters, a secure sense of self and the ability to relate closely to others are very

Are relationship-related issues a more important part of the self-definition process for girls than for boys?

closely intertwined. The nature and sequence of the linkages await future, more careful studies for their unraveling. At this point, growth in both autonomy and connection appear to be important to the development of males and females alike. Furthermore, while some girls may differ from some boys in their developmental routes, there is no evidence that different trajectories are characteristic of most or all girls versus boys.

It is likely that the achievement of identity and intimacy progress in tandem, with each gender's expression of the outcome looking somewhat different. Cramer (1999) observed that for males and females who have achieved identity, both genders have high levels of self-esteem, adequacy, and assertiveness. But males and females express these aspects of their personalities in different ways. Males are more likely to assert their adequacy in autonomous ways, while females more often do so within the context of social relationships. Overall, Waterman (1993) summarized recent findings by stating that the genders showed more similarities than differences in *processes* of identity formation but that the *content* of their identity choices might differ.

Racial and Ethnic Identity Theories

Distinct theoretical models have also been proposed to explain identity development in different racial and ethnic groups. Researchers have used multiple definitions of "ethnicity" in the studies done on this topic. For our purposes, we will use the term to signify one's sense of belonging to a group and one's beliefs or attitudes concerning group membership (Tajfel, 1981). Despite differences among particular groups, theories of racial/ethnic identity development have certain themes in common. Most describe an initial stage, not unlike diffusion, during which ethnic identity is either unrecognized or considered unimportant. Cross (1994) suggests that this stage may be accompanied by a preference for the dominant culture, although this is not the case for everyone. It may simply be that race/ethnicity is not yet a highly salient feature of one's self-concept. For example, having Mexican heritage may be less important to a young Mexican girl than the fact that she is smart in school, has lots of friends, and is the best soccer player on her team.

In most theories, this period is followed by a moratorium-like stage, typically triggered by some experience that thrusts the importance of one's race/ethnicity to the forefront. This stage is characterized by ambivalence or conflict, as the individual explores and comes to terms with her race or ethnicity. For many young adolescents, it is a time when the racism or cultural oppression that exists in society takes on personal significance. Here is how author Beverly Daniel Tatum (1997) explains the struggle that her 10-year-old son will likely experience:

> When David meets new adults, they don't say, "Gee, you're Black for your age!" If you are saying to yourself, of course they don't, think again. Imagine David, at fifteen, six-foot-two, wearing the adolescent attire of the day, passing adults he doesn't know on the sidewalk. Do the women hold their purses a little tighter, maybe even cross the street to avoid him? Does he hear the sound of the automatic door locks on the cars as he passes by? Is he being followed around by the security guards at the local mall? As he stops in town with his new bicycle, does a police officer hassle him, asking where he got it, implying that it might be stolen? Do strangers assume he plays basketball? Each of these experiences conveys a racial message. At ten, race is not yet salient for David, because it is not yet salient for society. But it will be. (p. 54)

In a "looking-glass" society that sorts people on the basis of race, ethnicity, and appearance and then reflects back to them the measure of their worth, early adolescence is a time when many youngsters such as David, who are members of diverse or marginalized groups, confront the negative stereotypes and discriminatory practices of others head on. Theories suggest that some adolescents may immerse themselves in their racial or cultural groups or even actively reject the dominant culture during this period.

In most theoretical formulations, the highest stage is achieved when the individual, having learned more about her group, affirms her identity as a member (commitment). Phinney (1990) asserts that the resolution is twofold: (1) reconciling the differences that exist between the ethnic minority group and the dominant group and (2) coming to terms with the lower status of one's group within the larger society. She also states, however, that this achievement does not necessarily need to coexist with a high level of involvement in one's own cultural group. The overall pattern of stages is similar to formulations of homosexual identity development as well.

Issues in the Study of Racial/Ethnic and Homosexual Identity Development

Remember the question posed about the true nature of Marcia's categories: do they represent real stage transitions or do they simply classify groups of people? We can respond that evidence is sufficient to demonstrate a directional, developmental trend *toward* achievement and *away from* diffusion, despite the fact that individual trajectories may not follow the same course or sequence in detail. The research that supports this description has been longitudinal in design.

At the present time, most writing in the area of gender, racial/ethnic, and homosexual identity development is theoretical rather than empirical, and those research studies that have been done are primarily cross-sectional in nature. Cross-sectional data do not adequately elucidate the processes underlying development. Consequently, the unique stagewise progressions proposed in many ethnic, racial, and homosexual identity theories have not yet been established as distinct developmental pathways.

Other methodological problems in the existing body of research have been noted as well. Phinney (1990), a respected researcher in the field of ethnic development, puts it this way:

> In published studies of ethnic identity, researchers have generally focused on single groups and have used widely discrepant definitions and measures of ethnic identity, which make generalizations and comparisons across studies difficult and ambiguous. The findings are often inconclusive or contradictory. (p. 2)

As we noted earlier, even terms such as race, ethnicity, and culture are often used by different authors to signify different things, adding to the confusion.

Assuming that members of a race or ethnic group are homogeneous on variables such as ethnic identity is another problem. In a study of Latino adolescents living in the United States, Umana-Taylor and Fine (2002) found evidence for heterogeneity of ethnic identification among Colombian, Guatemalan, Honduran, Mexican, Nicaraguan, Puerto Rican, and Salvadoran participants. These authors concluded that grouping individuals from these Latino cultures into one collective ethnic group masked some real differences. The authors suggest the need to consider generational status, immigration history, and nationality in order to refine our understanding of ethnic identity.

Is whiteness a racial characteristic or a social-cultural one? Whatever stance you take on this issue, it is generally a good idea for people to consider the place of their own race/culture/ethnicity in their self-definition. For members of the dominant White culture, race is often a nonissue in conceptualizations of identity, and many writers have pointed out that Whites are largely unaware of themselves in racial terms. In other words, White people fail to recognize how their being White (i.e., the "in-group") in a society stratified on the basis of race influences their attitudes and behaviors toward themselves and toward members of other racial groups (i.e., the "out-groups") (see Helms, 1990). This myopic and possibly unintentional perspective comes at a price, these authors conclude, because it perpetuates one's point of view as the "real" one, serves as a filter for all information that is race related, and has the effect of maintaining White dominance or privilege. Essentially, it is a failure of perspective taking, with serious consequences for the broader society.

It seems reasonable to interpret the issues of race and ethnicity as content domains that figure prominently in the identities of group members, somewhat like vocation, ideology, and relationship domains. Phinney (2000) noted that for members of ethnic minorities identity development is more complex than it is for persons in the dominant culture, because they have to confront and integrate more aspects of themselves. However, as with gender, the underlying developmental processes of identity formation, such as exploration and commitment, are the same.

APPLICATIONS

Adolescent identity development has been a fruitful area of scholarship. The literature in this area has not only provided us with a general developmental framework for understanding identity processes but has also expanded our knowledge of individual differences in identity development that are shaped by particular biological and social forces. Clearly, there is a real need for clinicians to be sensitive to both the general and the individual aspects of identity development. For adolescents from socially stigmatized or other disadvantaged groups, the process of resolving the challenge posed by Erikson, "What do I want to make of myself, and what do I have to work with?" may be more complicated than for others. The constricted opportunity experienced by some adolescents because of societal discrimination, cultural intolerance, poverty, or lack of support can make the identity domains of relationships, school, and work "closed" domains, accommodating little positive exploration. Prevention and/or intervention in this situation might depend upon opening up opportunities for exploration as well as supporting commitments.

Viewed from another perspective, the plethora of developmental models for identity development may serve to confuse clinicians unless they understand the similarities and differences among them. The goal of many theoretical frameworks of identity development is to promote sensitivity to the unique needs and particular challenges faced by members of specific groups. However, even though external behaviors or outcomes may differ for different groups, underlying developmental processes are similar. Researchers remind us that evidence shows as much or more variability *among* members of the same group as *between* groups (Rowe, Vazsonyi, & Flannery, 1994).

All adolescents face physical, cognitive, and emotional changes during this period of their lives. Understanding the general nature of some of these changes can be very helpful to those who work with young clients. As we have seen, a certain amount of egocentrism appears to go with the adolescent territory. It is often quite a bit easier for parents and other adults to respond authoritatively, with love and limits, to children when they are young. Something in the nature of their open dependence makes adults feel needed, valued, and important. The task often gets harder during the teenage years, at least in cultures and families that value independence and opportunities for personal expression. Being an adult authority figure in an adolescent's life may entail some hard times, when love and patience are put to the test. Sometimes adolescents' self-absorption seems impenetrable. In what may mirror adolescents' own sense of separateness, adults also can feel isolated.

Watching teenagers struggle with the problems of adolescence is painful, particularly when they behave egocentrically, when they are emotionally volatile, when they act as if they do not want or need our help, or when they actively rebel against the limits we have set. In some especially difficult situations, teenagers have managed to convince the adults around them that they are their equals and that they are entitled to wield much of the power. Some adults are inclined to avoid the grueling job of limit setter and enforcer because they may feel worn down, may have their own personal struggles to contend with, or may simply not know what to do. Sometimes parents take their cues, despite their better judgment, from other teenagers' more permissive families. Adults who are responsible for adolescents need to be committed to authoritative practices for the long haul. Despite their protestations, the last thing adolescents need are parents, teachers, or counselors who disengage from them or grant them too much power.

One area of adolescent behavior that can pose long-term risks is that of sexuality. Reports indicate that young people are engaging in sexual practices in greater numbers and at earlier ages than generations before them (Nahom et al., 2001). Yet most adolescents do not have accurate information about the risks associated with these practices. These facts may not be too surprising, given adolescents' egocentrism and their sense of invulnerability, yet the statistics are truly disturbing to anyone concerned with child and adolescent health and well-being. A recent study published by the Washington, DC Urban Institute discovered that most teenagers did not believe that oral or anal sex was "real" sex. Thus, kids concluded, it was safe and had the added benefit of preserving girls' virginity (see Gaiter, 2001).

Fewer than one quarter of teenagers ages 16 to 24 indicate that they have any knowledge at all about HIV/AIDS, according to an MTV survey of 4,140 U.S., Asian, European, and Latin American youth. Approximately one third of the group believed that only drug users who shared needles could get it; 16% believed that only homosexuals contracted the disease. Consider these findings in light of the fact that more than half of new HIV infections are contracted by young people between the ages of 15 and 25 (UNAIDS, 2001). This ignorance exists within a climate of exaggerated and, some say, degrading sexual saturation in movies, music, TV, and Internet, all of which bombard media-savvy teenagers. The messages communicated in these ways undoubtedly contribute to kids' beliefs that sex is a recreational activity that "everyone" is doing, and they also shape kids' views about intimate relationships in general. Gaiter observes,

> Edgy, predatory images of sexuality everywhere in the popular media have left an ugly mark. . . . Such aggression seems to rule the expectations young men bring to relationships and what young women believe are their only options if they want companionship, or something like love. (p. 214)

Caring adults need to address this situation with a combination of information, vigilance, empathy, awareness, and authority. Recently, a TV news reporter asked a panel of teenagers, "If adults . . . knew what was really going on [sexually] in the middle schools and early high-school years, what would they think?" One 14-year-old girl replied, "I think that they would do home schooling." The "head in the sand" technique is of little use to teenagers operating according to their own mental constructions of the real world, influenced by celebrities on TV. Parents need to deal with the realities of teenage sexuality, disturbing as they might be, and provide guidance. Counselors can support parents in this process as well as provide useful information. For example, empirically supported programs that teach teenagers to deal with sexually coercive situations have been used with good effect (Pacifici, Stoolmiller, & Nelson, 2001). Unfortunately, individual families can not fight these negative influences alone. Communities must collectively take a stand against the violent and hypersexualized culture of mass media, which Garbarino (1999) calls part of the "recipe for moral retardation."

Ongoing discussion groups and other kinds of support for parents of adolescents can help educate families about the normative changes of this period. Schools are particularly well positioned to provide adolescents with growth-promoting experiences directed toward career exploration. Adults in many contexts can capitalize on emerging cognitive skills by supporting adolescents' perspective taking, responsible decision making, and critical thinking. It should be noted that universal prevention curricula or other therapeutic activities that encourage identity reflection and that provoke movement from foreclosure to moratorium may elicit resistance from parents who perceive their values to be undermined in the process. Waterman (1994) addresses this ethical concern by suggesting that counselors respect a family's value system and the developmental timetable of students. Pressure to move from foreclosure to active experimentation in certain domains may be counterproductive if the student is not ready or if foreclosure is, for the present, serving an adaptive function.

Some adolescents manage to make the transition to young adulthood in ways that evidence only mild or sporadic periods of upset, while others appear to be on a long roller coaster ride. The temperament and capacities of the adolescent, the contributions of earlier experience, and the fit between the individual and the spheres that influence her will uniquely affect the adolescent experience.

Despite the widely different ways that adolescents engage in the process of exploration, Erikson believed that the reward for the search was the achievement of "fidelity," or something to hold on to:

> The evidence in young lives of the search for something and somebody to be true to can be seen in a variety of pursuits more or less sanctioned by society. It is often hidden in a bewildering combination of shifting devotion and sudden perversity, sometimes more devotedly perverse, sometimes more perversely devoted. Yet in all youth's seeming shiftiness, a seeking after some durability in change can be detected, whether in the accuracy of scientific and technical method or in the sincerity of obedience; in the veracity of historical and fictional accounts or the fairness of the rules of the game, in the authenticity of artistic production, and the high fidelity of reproduction, or in the genuineness of convictions and the reliability of commitments. This search is easily misunderstood, and often it is only dimly perceived by the individual himself, because youth, always set to grasp both diversity in principle and principle in diversity, must often test extremes before settling on a considered course. These extremes, particularly in times of ideological confusion and widespread marginality of identity, may include not only rebellious but also deviant, delinquent, and self-destructive tendencies. However, all this can be in the nature of a moratorium, a period of delay in which to test the rock-bottom of some truth before committing the powers of body and mind to a segment of the existing (or a coming) order. (1968, pp. 235–236)

As Josselson (1994) points out, this search is fundamentally a dialogue that the adolescent does not engage in alone. The success of adolescents' search for fidelity depends upon the community's fidelity to adolescents as they search.

SUMMARY

Physical Development

1. Puberty begins when the *pituitary gland* produces hormones that stimulate hormone production in the *gonads*. These and other circulating hormones promote the maturing of both primary and secondary sexual characteristics. The timing of puberty is affected both by genes and by environmental factors such as nutrition.

2. The adolescent growth spurt parallels puberty and includes large increases in height and weight. Different parts of the body grow at different times, such as the arms and legs before the torso. Gender differences in growth increase both internal and external sexual dimorphism.

3. The "storm and stress" of adolescence includes characteristics such as increased conflict with parents, moodiness, negative affect, and risky behavior. Moodiness and negative affect, including depressed mood, are affected by increases in hormones, but only if they are combined with negative life events. In girls, early maturation usually means greater storm and stress; in boys, later maturation is more problematic. Generally, "storm and stress" seems to depend on the number of stressors children are experiencing.

4. At adolescence, girls are more susceptible to depressed mood than boys are, apparently because of differences in stress and methods of coping with stress. Among the stressors girls experience more than boys are the devaluing of the female role; worries about appearance and weight; fewer expectations of success; the double standard regarding sexuality; the use of a cooperative discourse that makes them less influential in mixed-sex groups; and earlier puberty, which means that girls are more likely to be making school transitions and coping with the onset of puberty simultaneously. Girls are also more likely than boys to deal with stress using a *ruminative coping style,* which increases the risk of depression relative to the *distracting style,* which is more characteristic of boys.

5. Sexual activity and exploration, both with the opposite sex and with the same sex, increases at puberty. Sexual maturation is primarily responsible, but familial, social, and cultural factors are also important.

6. Sexual orientation becomes manifest in adolescence, with up to 97% of males and more than 98% of females becoming heterosexual. The development of sexual orientation is not well understood. Many traditional environmental theories, such as Freud's theory of identification and the *seduction hypothesis,* are not supported by evidence. Even modeling is not a viable explanation: children parented by homosexuals are no more likely than other children to become homosexual. There is some evidence for a strong biological contribution to sexual orientation, through prenatal hormones and heredity. Environment appears to play some role, but the nature of that role is unclear. Bem has proposed that peer processes may be important.

7. Brain growth continues during adolescence, involving *synaptogenesis, pruning,* and continued *myelination.* Several areas of the cortex and the corpus callosum are involved in this development.

Cognitive Development

8. At Piaget's fourth stage in the development of logical thinking, 11- or 12-year-olds begin to be able to think logically about abstract contents, discovering relationships among relationships. Formal thought is difficult even for adults and is easier to apply in domains of knowledge with which we have some expertise.

9. When a formal operational thinker approaches scientific problems, she generates and considers every possible solution, then tests each one. The pattern of results among all the tests determines the conclusions. Generating and evaluating possibilities is a hallmark of formal operational thought.

10. With formal operations comes the ability to construct ideals, such as ideal political systems or ideal people. Young adolescents do not understand, however, that the real always falls short of the ideal. This failure to understand the limits of her ideas is a form of adolescent *egocentrism,* and it contributes to a critical attitude toward anything that is less than perfect, including the self.

11. Other aspects of adolescent egocentrism are derived from a distorting inward focus, which is partially a function of an improved capacity to think about one's own thinking. Self-focus may be a function of other factors as well, such as the need to form an adult identity. The *imaginary audience* and *personal fable* of adolescents are thought to be results.

Identity Development

12. Erikson's notion of an adolescent identity "crisis" is better characterized as an identity exploration, a search for answers to questions such as "What do I want to make of myself, and what do I have to work with?" Identity "attainment" does not imply that

no further change occurs; identity is always to some degree in revision. Identity is also a product of the cultural contexts that shape development.

13. Marcia described four identity status categories. *Diffusion* characterizes adolescents who lack both *exploration* and *commitment*. *Moratorium* describes adolescents who are actively exploring but have made no commitments. Adolescents in *foreclosure* have not experienced exploration but have made commitments. *Achievement* comprises individuals whose development has involved exploration and has reached commitment. Each identity status is associated with certain personal and cognitive characteristics.

14. Assessment of identity status usually involves a semi-structured interview procedure in which status within several domains is assessed. For example, Marcia's original *Ego Identity Interview* assessed status in vocational choice, religious beliefs, and political ideology.

15. There is no fixed sequence of identity statuses, but longitudinal research has found some developmental trends. The number of achievements increases over time, foreclosures decrease, and diffusions decrease or remain the same. The number of moratoriums does not increase or decrease.

16. Both the high school and college years are times of active identity development. Successful accomplishment seems to rest partly on successful accomplishment of earlier psychosocial tasks, availability of positive role models, and support for exploration.

17. There is a proliferation of theories to describe identity development in many diverse groups. Research on gender differences has produced inconsistent results: some studies find gender differences, some do not. When differences are found, women, as a group, are more likely to assign interpersonal, communal aspects of themselves a higher priority. Suggestions that women achieve intimacy before identity are not supported by research. Growth in both autonomy and connection are important for both males and females, and for both, achievements in identity and intimacy issues seem to progress in tandem.

18. Achievement of ethnic identity has been described in different ways for many different groups, but most theories have some sequential aspects in common. Initially, race/ethnicity is not a salient feature of self-concept or one's search for identity. Then a moratorium-like period occurs, when the individual experiences some ambivalence or conflict that makes her ethnicity a personal matter, and she begins to explore its meaning (exploration). The highest stage is achieved when an individual affirms her identity as a group member (commitment). Identity development in homosexuals has been described in a similar way.

19. As yet, little longitudinal research is available to support these theories. At present, it seems reasonable to see race and ethnicity as content domains that figure prominently in the identities of group members, making identity development for minorities more complex than for majority group members.

Case Study

Dean is a White 16-year-old. He is a sophomore at George Washington Carver High School. He lives with his father and his stepmother in a semi-rural community in the South. His father and mother divorced when Dean was 8 years old, and both parents remarried shortly after the breakup. Dean's mother moved to another state, and, although she calls him from time to time, the two have little contact. Dean gets along well with his father and stepmother. He is also a good "older brother" to his 5-year-old stepbrother, Jesse.

Dean's father owns and operates an auto-repair shop in town. His wife works part-time, managing the accounts for the business. She is also an active contributor to many community projects in her neighborhood. She regularly works as a parent volunteer in the elementary school library and is a member of her church's executive council. Both parents try hard to make a good life for their children.

Dean has always been a somewhat lackluster student. His grades fell precipitously during third grade, when his parents divorced. However, things stabilized for Dean over the next few years, and he has been able to maintain a C average. Neither Dean nor his father take his less-than-stellar grades too seriously. In middle school, his father encouraged him to try out for football. He played for a few seasons but dropped out in high school. Dean has a few close friends who like him for his easygoing nature and his sense of humor. Dean's father has told him many times that he can work in the family business after graduation. At his father's urging, Dean is pursuing a course of study in automobile repair at the regional vo-tech school.

Now in his sophomore year, his circle of friends includes mostly other vo-tech students. He doesn't see many of his former friends, who are taking college preparatory courses. Kids in his class are beginning to drive, enabling them to go to places on weekends that had formerly been off-limits. He knows many kids who are having sex and drinking at parties. He has been friendly with several girls over the years, but these relationships have been casual and platonic. Dean wishes he would meet someone with whom he could talk about his feelings and share his thoughts.

Although he is already quite accustomed to the lewd conversations and sexual jokes that circulate around the locker room, he participates only half-heartedly in the banter. He has listened for years to friends who brag about their sexual exploits. He wonders with increasing frequency why he is not attracted to the same things that seem so important to his friends. The thought that he might be gay has crossed his mind, largely because of the scathing comments made by his peers about boys who show no interest in girls. This terrifies him, and he usually manages to distract himself by reasoning that he will develop sexual feeling "when the right girl comes along."

As time passes, however, he becomes more and more morose. His attention is diverted even more from his class work. He finds it more difficult to be around the kids at school. Dean starts to drink heavily and is arrested for driving under the influence of alcohol. He is sentenced to a 6-week drug education program and is assigned community service. His parents are disappointed in him because of this incident, but they believe he has learned his lesson and will not repeat his mistake. Dean's father believes that his son will be fine as soon as he finds a girlfriend to "turn him around."

Discussion Questions

1. What are the issues facing Dean at this point in his development?
2. Enumerate the risks and the protective factors that are present in his life.
3. How would you, as his counselor, assess Dean's situation? What approaches could you take with this adolescent?

 Journal Questions

1. Recount an example of the imaginary audience or the personal fable from your own adolescence. How can this knowledge help you in counseling young people?
2. Were you an early, an on-time, or a late-maturing adolescent? What impact did your physical development have on your adjustment and your peer group relationships?
3. Remember back to the time when you were 18 or 19. Using Marcia's identity categories, assess your own status in the following domains: relationships, career, religious or political ideology, ethnicity, and sexual orientation.

Key Terms

puberty
gonads
testes
ovaries
androgens
testosterone
estrogen
progesterone
primary sexual
   characteristics
secondary sexual
   characteristics
menarche

spermarche
adolescent growth spurt
sexual dimorphism
experience sampling
   method
depressed mood
delayed phase preference
body image
double standard
rumination
distraction
sexual orientation

homosexuality
heterosexuality
bisexuality
seduction hypothesis
gender identity disorder
   (GID)
formal operational
   thought
ideals
imaginary audience
personal fable
invincibility fable

ego identity
diffusion
moratorium
foreclosure
achievement
constructed identity
conferred identity
Ego Identity Interview
closed commitment
achieving commitment
closed identity domains
open identity domains

The Social World in Adolescence

The search for identity is considered the primary developmental task of the adolescent period. In this chapter, you will find that the outcome of an adolescent's search is very much affected by the social world. Peers play a critical role, and so do parents, schools, and neighborhoods. All are in turn influenced by the cultural and historical context in which the adolescent's identity is formed. Counselors and therapists who support adolescents through their explorations and struggles must consider the impact of these multiple, interdependent factors. As we have seen repeatedly, no single factor or influence fully explains any developmental outcome. In this chapter, we present a model of the mechanism for social identity development and explore research on the influence of peers, parents, schools, leisure, work, and culture on that process. We conclude with a discussion of implications for professionals who work with adolescents.

Let's begin with an example: As a balmy October turned into a frigid November, 12-year-old Tamara's mother repeatedly suggested to her daughter that they go shopping to replace Tamara's outgrown winter jacket. Tamara refused. She said she wasn't sure what sort of jacket she wanted, admitting that it depended on what the other girls in her class would be wearing. The key girls had not yet worn jackets to school, despite the cold. They, too, were waiting and watching! Finally, in mid-December, one popular girl in the seventh-grade class capitulated to her mother's demands and made a jacket choice. Tamara and her classmates at last knew what to wear.

Parents and teachers are often perplexed, even dismayed, by the importance of peers to the adolescent. Why would an otherwise sensible young person become so dependent upon the actions and choices of others, and what role do parents and other concerned adults play in an adolescent's life when peers become so important?

Dependence upon peers is a normal and important developmental process for the young adolescent. As you will see, the search for identity (see Chapter 9) that characterizes the adolescent period takes place largely within the world of peers. The adolescent period roughly begins at puberty, although in today's world many of the processes discussed in this chapter are beginning to affect the lives of children even before the onset of puberty.

FRAMEWORKLESSNESS AND AUTONOMY: SELTZER'S MODEL OF ADOLESCENT SOCIAL IDENTITY

Many theorists have noted that one's identity develops within the context of interpersonal interactions (e.g., Cooley, 1902; Mead, 1934; see Chapter 7). Erikson (1968) argued that peers are particularly important in the construction of identity at adolescence. Seltzer (1982) expanded upon Erikson's ideas, specifying how and why the peer group plays such a central role. To understand fully the function of peers, let's look again at what happens when a child enters adolescence. The body changes in appearance, adult sexual needs emerge, hormonal shifts may heighten irritability, the capacity to reflect on the future and on the self expands, maturity demands increase, and so on. These profound changes produce a state of instability and anxiety unique to adolescence, which Seltzer calls **frameworklessness**.

> The adolescent is at sea. Previous boundaries and guideposts are no longer functional. In earlier developmental periods, expansion and growth exist within a context of familiar motion and exercise. The adolescent condition is different, however. The adolescent is possessed of new physical and intellectual capabilities that are both mystical and mystifying. . . . The allure of the adult world calls, and is strong, even as the safety of childhood is close and still beckons. Yet neither fits; the one is outgrown, the other not yet encompassable. (1982, p. 59)

The adolescent's passage to adulthood is in some ways parallel to the infant's passage to childhood status. In order to exercise their developing skills and to explore the beckoning world, infants must give up the security of the caregiver's continual presence and care. Most attachment theorists believe that toddlers manage the stress of this separation by referring to their working model of the other, a kind of mental representation of the caregiver, which provides feelings of security and makes independent exploration possible. For adolescents, the task of establishing adult independence requires separating from

Think about your own experience as a young adolescent. Can you relate to the sense of frameworklessness?

caregivers on a new plane, a process called the "second" individuation (Blos, 1975). Adolescents rework their views of their parents, deidealize them, and loosen, somewhat, their emotional dependency (Steinberg & Belsky, 1991). Thus, the mental representation or concept of the parent becomes more peripheral to the adolescent's self-system. However, a teenager's increasing individuation and sense of autonomy does not come without a price. As adolescents experience a loss in feelings of security, their sense of frameworklessness increases.

The Peer Arena

Paradoxically, as adolescents seek autonomy from their parents, they become more dependent on their peers. Steinberg and Silverberg (1986) asked children ages 10 to 16 questions about their relationships with parents and age-mates. Children between fifth and eighth grades showed a marked increase in agreement on items assessing emotional autonomy, such as, "There are some things about me that my parents don't know" and "There are things that I would do differently from my mother and father when I become a parent." Yet, when the students in this study were asked, "What would you *really* do?" if a friend suggested either some antisocial act such as cheating or some neutral act such as joining a club, they showed a marked decrease between the fifth and ninth grades in their ability to resist peer influence. Roughly between the ages of 11 and 16 it appears that children transfer at least some of their emotional dependency from their parents to their peers. Figure 10.1 illustrates the different trajectories of adolescents' feelings of autonomy from parents versus peers.

Why do peers become so important? Seltzer (1982) proposes that it is because adolescents share in common the unique state of frameworklessness. She describes nine basic characteristics that define this age group in contemporary society. Among them are similar chronological age and educational status and shared coping with feelings of aloneness and the loss of past certainties. Research demonstrates that people under stress tend to affiliate with others perceived as having similar experiences (Schacter, 1959), so that adolescents' shared sense of instability makes the peer group a likely target of affiliation. The sometimes difficult movement toward identity can, at least in part, be shared.

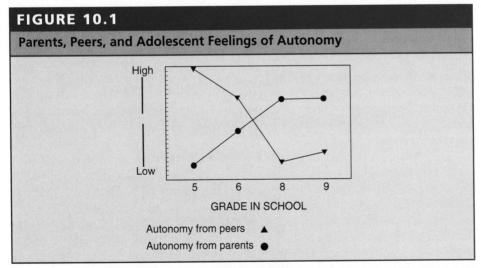

FIGURE 10.1

Parents, Peers, and Adolescent Feelings of Autonomy

GRADE IN SCHOOL

Autonomy from peers ▲
Autonomy from parents ●

Source: Steinberg, L., & Silverberg, S. B. (1986). The vicissitudes of autonomy in early adolescence. *Child Development, 57,* 847. Adapted by permission of Blackwell Publishers, Inc.

Peers are thus a source of support. But Seltzer (1982) argues also that the peer group becomes both the site and the raw material for constructing an identity. There are twin processes at work: the first is social comparison. As we saw in Chapter 7, younger school-age children evaluate themselves in comparison to others. In later chapters we will find that adults continue to use social comparison as a means of self-assessment and self-refinement. But for adolescents, the lack of identity makes this process intense and all consuming.

Second is a process of ***attribute substitution,*** which involves both imitation and identification. Adolescents need to borrow and "try on" various behaviors and attributes that they observe in others, because the state of frameworklessness leaves them without clearly defined ways of behaving and thinking. Peers become an important resource for such borrowing. A formerly quiet boy might imitate the wisecracking style of a friend, a girl may explore the mysteries of Buddhism espoused by a classmate, or a mediocre student might work for hours on a special project, mimicking the approach of a more successful peer. The borrowing goes beyond imitation to partial identification with friends, so that if a boy's friend has a special talent for hockey, the boy might appropriate a sense of accomplishment as a hockey player from his association with the friend. This appropriation of "stand-in elements" provides relief for the adolescent from the anxiety of being without a stable sense of self. The twin processes of social comparison and imitation constitute a type of experimentation that is necessary for mature identity construction. At first, the trying-on process is rapid, intense, and undifferentiated, but toward later adolescence, some features actually become more stable elements that will form the foundation of the young adult's identity. Ideally, the goal of all this effort is the development or construction of a fundamental sense of what fits for the particular adolescent.

In summary, Seltzer (1982) argues that peers in large part provide the arena for identity formation. She also describes the Eriksonian ideal of unrestricted sampling of various "identities" as a normative process, but in reality what adolescents are able to do may be more circumscribed. As we will see in the next section, the structure of the peer culture may constrain the opportunity to try on some characteristics and behaviors.

THE STRUCTURE OF THE PEER NETWORK

As we saw in Chapter 8, by early adolescence a typical youngster is part of a complicated network of peer relationships. He interacts with close friends in dyads, hangs out with a small group or clique, and belongs to a crowd. B. B. Brown (1990) defined adolescent *crowds* as large "reputation-based collectives of similarly stereotyped individuals who may or may not spend much time together" (p. 177). Once a member, a teen's sampling of elements of behavior will be limited to some degree by the crowd to which the teen belongs. Few would be surprised to find that adolescents are strongly influenced by their closest friends. What is striking about the recent data on peer affiliation is how powerful *crowd* membership seems to be.

Support for the impact of crowds on adolescent behavior is provided in a large scale study by Steinberg and his associates (e.g., Lamborn, Mounts, Steinberg, & Dornbusch, 1991; Mounts & Steinberg, 1995; Steinberg, 1996; Steinberg, Fegley, & Dornbusch, 1993; Steinberg, Lamborn, Darling, Mounts, & Dornbusch, 1994; Steinberg, Lamborn, Dornbusch, & Darling, 1992). More than 20,000 adolescents and their families from nine public high schools in Wisconsin and Northern California were studied. Students came from ethnically and socioeconomically diverse communities (more than 40% were ethnic minorities) and from a variety of family structures (intact, divorced, and remarried). Student data were collected over a 3-year period from ninth through twelfth grades. Teens answered questions about their emotional adjustment, academic achievement, and behavior, the parenting practices of their families, and their peer associations.

Just as other researchers have found (see Chapter 8), from these data Steinberg (1996) identified three levels of peer association, which can be described as concentric circles. One or two *best friends,* with whom adolescents spend most of their free time, comprise the innermost circle. A larger *clique* of about 6 to 10 members forms a less intimate second circle, composed of friends who eat lunch or go to class together. The clique's boundaries are somewhat permeable, and the membership may fluctuate. Finally, the third circle is the adolescent's *crowd.* What crowd members share is not necessarily friendship, but similar interests, attitudes, behaviors, and appearance. Crowds tend to be large, and they reflect the individual's social status.

In typical American high schools, one finds a characteristic crowd structure (Barber, Eccles, & Stone, 2001; Steinberg, 1996). Roughly 20% of students belong to popularity-conscious crowds ("populars" and "jocks"), who are moderately achievement oriented and may engage in some illicit behavior, such as drug use. About 20% belong to "alienated" crowds ("druggies" or "burnouts"), who are even less invested in academic success and who may be involved in heavy drug use and delinquent behavior. "Average" crowds, comprising about 30% of students, are not openly hostile to academics but, like the populars, are only moderately concerned about grades. Some crowds are defined primarily by ethnicity (roughly 10% to 15% depending on the school), and academic achievement differences exist among these ethnically defined crowds. Less than 5% of high schoolers belong to crowds characterized by high academic achievement. These students are unlikely to use drugs and may form strong ties with teachers.

How teens find a niche among the available crowds is not well understood (B. B. Brown, 1990). Steinberg (1996) suggests three determining factors: children's personalities and interests as they enter adolescence; the types of crowds available; and the ways that parents attempt to manage their children's peer relationships. We'll take a close look at parents' role in children's crowd membership later in this chapter.

How are adolescents influenced by their crowds? As we noted in Chapter 8, adults frequently attribute the behavior of adolescents to "peer pressure," what we have called the *influence* of peers, which implies that the individual teenager might conform to others' demands despite his or her better judgment. What Seltzer's (1982) theory suggests, and what research findings support, however, is that adolescents operate according to the principles of group dynamics that govern any social group—namely, they *choose* to participate in shared norms, roles, and expectations, a process called *selection.* In other words, teens are willing members of their crowds, influenced by and influencing others. As Seltzer puts it, they are motivated to borrow from others, and they serve as models from whom others borrow.

Steinberg (1996) provides a specific example of the crowd's effects on academic achievement. Recall from the data on teens' distribution among their high school crowds that a relatively small percentage are committed to academic excellence (i.e., are *A* students). Membership in the largest, most appealing, and preferred crowds (populars, jocks, and average) prescribes more modest academic achievement. Most students in these crowds, representing about 50% of high schoolers, earn *B*s on average.

Could it be that these data simply indicate that students who begin with only moderate academic commitments and abilities gravitate toward groups of similar individuals? Several longitudinal studies (e.g., Eccles & Barber, 1999; Steinberg, 1996) suggest otherwise. For example, after tracking students for three years who began with similar academic records and behavior profiles, Steinberg (1996) found that students' crowd affiliation was highly correlated with their later grades and delinquent activities. So, crowd membership made a unique contribution to these outcomes over and above early developmental characteristics.

THE ROLE OF PARENTS

Given that peers become so important to young adolescents, what is the role of adults, especially parents, in adolescents' lives? A brief history of perspectives on adolescent development may be useful here. Early psychoanalytic writers described this period as one of conflict between parents and their teens that is sparked by the reemergence of latent sexual impulses as the child reaches puberty (A. Freud, 1958). The classic interpretation is that the young adolescent's emotional attachments become sexualized and need to be redirected to age-mates. In this view, the child's press for autonomy creates conflict with the parents but is seen as normal and necessary. Neopsychoanalytic views have become more moderate over time (e.g., Blos, 1975), but still assume that the child's cognitive and affective detachment from parents is to be expected in the service of autonomy. Erikson's (1968) view of adolescence as a "normative crisis" supports this as a time of potential upheaval. The early psychoanalytic tradition framed the typical parent-adolescent relationship as a struggle, with teens trying to pull away from parents to the point of rebellion. Prescriptions for appropriate parental behavior often focused on the child's legitimate need to break away and the parents' responsibility to "let go" and allow their adolescents to "be themselves." Parents were advised to back off, because teens must be free to explore with their peers in order to consolidate their identity.

In the 1970s and beyond, studies of adolescence contradicted earlier constructions based on psychoanalytic thought. They indicated that major transformations do occur in family relations as children pass through adolescence but that becoming more independent and personally responsible is not necessarily accompanied by emotional detachment from parents (e.g., Hill & Holmbeck, 1986). Offer (1969) reported that roughly two thirds of teens experienced adolescence as a tranquil period or at least experienced only minor conflicts with parents. Montemayor (1983) reported that in typical families, teens and their parents argued on average twice a week, hardly a matter of great concern. A recent meta-analysis indicates that conflicts with parents occur most frequently in early adolescence. By middle adolescence, they begin to decline in frequency but tend to increase in intensity (Laursen, Coy, & Collins, 1998). Other studies suggested that disagreements with parents tended to center on mundane issues, such as chores and curfews (B. K. Barber, 1994), rather than on differences in beliefs about ethics and values (Rutter, Graham, Chadwick, & Yule, 1976). As a result of such findings, it has been argued that the storminess of relations between parents and adolescents has been overstated (V. Rutter, 1995). Based on this newer view of relative harmony and optimism about long-range outcomes, parenting prescriptions began to include the implicit advice, "Don't worry, things will work out fine." As you might guess, things are not so simple.

Arnett (2000b), for example, raises a word of caution. He suggests that conflicts over relatively minor matters are nonetheless stressful for both parents and children. He further warns that the "mundane" matters that adolescents argue with their parents about may not be as trivial as they seem. Rather, they

> often concern issues such as when adolescents should begin dating and whom they should date, where they should be allowed to go, and how late they should stay out. All of these issues can serve as proxies for arguments over more serious issues such as substance use, automobile driving safety, and sex. (p. 320)

Despite cautions such as Arnett's, the notions that parents should "let go" and that they should "not worry" seem to have permeated contemporary American culture. And yet, paradoxically, warning signals that adolescents today face greater pressures and dangers than at any other time in this century are sounding in both the scientific and popular press. The Carnegie Council on Adolescent Development in 1996 described the risks facing young adolescents: "Altogether, *nearly half* of American adolescents are at high or moderate risk of seriously damaging their life chances. The damage may be near term and vivid, or it may be delayed, like a time bomb set in youth" (p. 2). Increasing risks were identified in physical health, in mental health, and in academic preparedness for children ages 10 to 14. Prevalence indicators from the 1980s and '90s revealed rising rates of death by firearms; more child abuse and victimization; greater use of drugs, alcohol, and cigarettes; higher suicide rates; decreasing age of first intercourse and thus increasing risk of early pregnancy and sexually transmitted diseases, including AIDS; and lower academic achievement, among other worrisome changes. We have all read statistics such as these and often feel a combination of helplessness and desensitization. How can we reconcile our assumptions of what young people need, and what adolescence should be like, with the realities of today? More specifically, how should we parent, how should we educate, how should we counsel and consult to meet the needs of contemporary adolescents?

Research on the family as one supportive context for adolescent development has been growing rapidly. Its theoretical framework rests upon Baumrind's (e.g., 1971, 1978, 1991) studies of parenting styles, in which, you will recall from Chapter 5, she identified two important dimensions of parental behavior, each of which is predictive of a particular constellation of child characteristics. First is parental *warmth* or *responsiveness*. Responsive parents seem to encourage their children's self-acceptance, confidence, and assertiveness by being warm, involved, and accepting of their children's needs and feelings. They take their children's feelings and expressed needs seriously and are willing to explain their own actions, particularly when they impose limits on the child. The second dimension is parental *control* or *demandingness*. Demanding parents apparently foster self-discipline and achievement by making maturity demands on their children. They make and enforce rules, provide consistent supervision or **parental monitoring,** and confront their children when their behavior does not measure up. According to a large body of research by Baumrind and others, the most effective parenting style, *authoritative* parenting, combines high responsiveness and high demandingness. It is as if the key to parenting effectiveness is to blend the listening skills and empathy of a well-trained counselor with the firmness of a watchful vice-principal for discipline.

As we noted in Chapter 5, treating responsiveness and demandingness as two distinct dimensions, three other categories of parenting style can be derived. Besides authoritative, there are *authoritarian, permissive* (also called **indulgent**), and *neglecting* (also called *uninvolved* or **dismissive**) styles (Maccoby & Martin, 1983). Authoritarian parents are low on responsiveness but high on demandingness. Permissive parents are high on responsiveness but low on demandingness, and neglecting or dismissive parents are essentially disengaged, scoring low on both dimensions. Before you read Box 10.1 on how authoritative parenting of adolescents "looks in action," consider the evidence that it can positively influence teen behavior and well-being. Baumrind (e.g., 1991) assessed the behavior of parents and their young adolescents and found that "authoritative parents put out exceptional effort . . . and their adolescents were exceptionally competent (mature, prosocial, high internal locus of control, low internalizing and externalizing problem behavior, low substance use)" (1993, p. 1308). In the large-scale study of 14- to 18-year-olds by Steinberg and his colleagues, parenting style was linked to four aspects of teens' adjustment: psychosocial development, school achievement, internalized distress, and problem behavior. The children of authoritative parents scored best on the majority of

Box 10.1   Authoritative Parenting with Adolescents

Is authoritative parenting for real or some magician's trick? How can a parent, especially the parent of a savvy teenager, be warm, responsive, respectful, and democratic on the one hand but firm, controlling, and watchful on the other?

Imagine that 14-year-old Risa bursts into the house on a Friday after school, literally jumping for joy at a party invitation she has just received. It's from Katy, one of the most popular girls in school, and being at the party will automatically define Risa as one of the popular elite. Risa prattles on about who will be there, and what to wear, and "Oh my god! I've got to start getting ready *now*!" Dad is working at home this afternoon, so he's the P.I.C.—parent in charge. First, he listens with interest and expresses understanding. It is not that difficult in this case. Risa is given to emotional extremes, but when the extreme is ecstasy, Dad has little trouble smiling, nodding, and reflecting ("This party is really something special!") compassionately. But before Risa bolts for the shower, Dad begins to ask questions about who, where, when, and under what circumstances. Risa's joyful prattle turns to impatient disdain: "It doesn't matter, and I don't have time to answer all these questions." Dad continues to try to reflect without being deflected. "I know you're busy, but the answers are very important to me. So let's just take a minute." Risa really does not know the answers, so Dad points out that he can find out more when he calls Katy's parents. "No! You can't! These kids don't even want to know I have parents. If you call I'll be completely humiliated!" Here is the challenge to the authoritative parent: balancing the child's feelings and concerns with the critical monitoring responsibility. Risa's dad stands firm: she is not permitted to attend parties where responsible adults are not present, and the only way to be sure is to speak directly to Katy's parents. Without belittling Risa's concerns, Dad insists on the phone call. He explains, as he has before, why unsupervised parties are not acceptable, and then invites Risa to help problem solve. "I know this is awkward, Risa. Let's try to think of ways to make this go smoothly for everyone. For example, I could call and thank Katy's parents for having the party at their house, and offer to bring over a case of soda." But Risa's idea of reasonable is not consistent with her father's. She has an inkling that the party is not going to be supervised, and in any case she does not want to risk the popular crowd seeing her as a "baby." She attacks her father as "old-fashioned," "overprotective," and "stupid," alternately raging and whining.

At this point, it is difficult for parents to repeat explanations calmly and to hold firm. Sometimes they give up, or lose all patience. Personal assaults from the teenager complicate the parents' role: these attacks are hurtful and demeaning, and they too need to be addressed. In this case, Dad manages to respond, "I know you're upset, but your attacking me hurts my feelings, and it's not going to change my mind. Let's stick to the subject of the party." At another point, he takes a time-out for five minutes to cool down. Rarely do conflicts like these feel happily resolved in the immediate situation. In this case, Risa finally tells her father not to bother to call because she will not go to the party—she will call and make an excuse. She then sulks in her room all night. Both her mother and her father talk to her about it again, giving her an opportunity to vent, to discuss again the pros and cons of the rule about unsupervised parties, and to consider ways of promoting her relationships with her friends, such as having a party herself. Their restrictions on her social life never stop grating on Risa, but her parents hold firm.

These confrontations can be frightening for the most confident parents. On a different occasion, Risa might just walk out rather than sulk in her room. Parents are dependent not only on the quality of the mutual caring that has been established with a child up to the teen years but also on the support that is available in the child's circle of friends. If her friends' parents routinely allow unsupervised parties, Risa's parents are soon going to feel besieged and may have limited success in helping Risa navigate her adolescence safely. On the other hand, if her friends' parents have similar values and are also authoritative, then the impact of her parents' authoritative style will be enhanced: her psychosocial competence, including her self-esteem and self-reliance, will be benefited, and her chances of delinquency, drug abuse, and psychological distress will be reduced (Fletcher, Darling, Steinberg, & Dornbusch, 1995).

these indicators, and those of neglectful parents scored worst (Lamborn, Mounts, et al., 1991). After one year, the adolescents' adjustment status was reassessed. Parenting style was predictive of patterns of change over the year. For example, adolescents from authoritative homes showed increases in self-reliance, while other adolescents showed little change or, if they had neglectful parents, actually declined somewhat (Steinberg, Lamborn, Darling, et al., 1994).

In general, research on parenting styles from as early as the 1940s (e.g., Baldwin, 1948) has produced results that are consistent with the large-scale studies of today, supporting the notion that both responsiveness and demandingness are beneficial. Overall, responsiveness seems more closely tied to adolescents' self-confidence and social competence, and demandingness is more closely associated with "good" behavior and self-control. Recent work indicates that it can be useful to consider responsiveness as comprising separable factors: *acceptance* is being affectionate, praising the child, being involved in the child's life, and showing concern for the child's needs, and it is correlated with children's self-esteem and social adjustment. **Democracy** is the degree to which parents encourage children's psychological autonomy by soliciting their opinions or encouraging self-expression, and it is most closely linked to children's self-reliance, self-confidence, willingness to work hard, and general competence (Steinberg, 1990, 1996). Whether we construe there to be two or three primary dimensions of parenting style, few would deny that the parenting characteristics they comprise are highly desirable. But, relatively speaking, how powerful a role can such parental behaviors actually play by adolescence, when the influence of peers has been found to be so great?

An important key to answering this question is to recall, again, that multiple determinants interact to affect outcomes at every developmental stage. Let's reconsider, for example, school achievement in the teen years. When authoritative parents involve themselves in their adolescents' schooling by attending school programs, helping with course selection, and monitoring student progress, their children are more likely to achieve (Mounts & Steinberg, 1995; Steinberg, Lamborn, Dornbusch, et al., 1992). However, as we have seen, an adolescent's crowd affiliation also impacts school achievement. Steinberg (1996) found that teens who began with similar academic records showed change over time in school performance consistent with their crowd membership, indicating the importance of peer influence despite parental efforts. But parents can affect crowd membership. First, characteristic behaviors of the child are probably important in determining crowd membership, and a child's behaviors are associated with parenting style. Steinberg (1996) describes parenting as "launching" children on a trajectory through adolescence. That launching may *directly* influence what crowd a teenager joins. Mounts and Steinberg (1995) found that specific parenting practices, such as monitoring and encouraging achievement, were correlated with children's choice of more academically oriented peers. Walker-Barnes and Mason (2001) found that urban parents who show high levels of monitoring and involvement have kids who tend to steer clear of joining delinquent groups or gangs.

But the availability of crowds is also important. If, for example, all crowds value high academic achievement, or if none do, the child's trajectory with regard to school performance will be much less affected by authoritative parents who value academic excellence than if there is a diversity of crowds. Here is a clue to other ways in which parenting style may influence behavior. Steinberg proposes that authoritative parents, who are heavily involved in their children's lives, may do things to help structure the child's peer group options and thus indirectly affect achievement by affecting the accessibility of peers. Does the local high school have few, if any, academically oriented students? Parents may arrange for their children to go elsewhere; they might move, or put their children in private schools, or choose to home school. It is not uncommon for parents who live in dangerous environments to send their children to live for brief periods with relatives (Varrett, 1994).

Such behavior, of course, depends on income and on the availability of such options, but it also depends on parental involvement. Authoritative parents are invested parents, often making personal sacrifices to maintain their commitment to their view of good parenting (Greenberger & Goldberg, 1989).

Parents, Peers, and Ethnicity

The complex interplay of parenting style with peer influences stands out in bold relief when we look at teens in different ethnic groups in the United States. Several researchers have found that for minority youngsters, authoritative parenting is not as strongly associated with positive outcomes as it is for White teens (e.g., Baumrind, 1972; Chao, 2001; Dornbusch, Ritter, Leiderman, Roberts, & Fraleigh, 1987; Walker-Barnes & Mason, 2001). (See also Chapter 5 for a discussion of ethnicity and parenting styles.) Steinberg, Dornbusch, and Brown (1992) found ethnic differences in their large survey of adolescents, particularly in the likelihood of academic success: authoritative parenting was not as good a predictor of academic success for teens from Asian American, African American, and Hispanic families as it was for White teens. However, Steinberg, Dornbusch, et al. found some fundamental similarities across all ethnic groups. First, not surprisingly, hard work is linked to academic success regardless of ethnicity; students who put in the most time on homework, for example, are the best school performers. Second, teens across all ethnic groups were equally likely to believe that getting a good education pays off. But the researchers also found some surprising differences in beliefs about the negative consequences of *not* getting a good education. Asian American students were most likely to believe that poor academic preparation could limit their job options later, while African American and Hispanic youngsters were the most optimistic, that is, the least likely to believe that poor academic preparation would hurt their job prospects.

These differences in belief systems were reflected in the degree to which various ethnic peer groups supported academic achievement: Asian crowds were usually highly supportive, whereas African American and Hispanic crowds were not. Unlike White students, minority students often have little choice of which crowd to join; they typically are relegated to one or a few crowds defined primarily by ethnicity. Thus, *regardless* of their parents' support for academics or parenting style, Asian American youngsters are likely to join a crowd that supports academics, whereas African American and Hispanic teens are likely to be part of a crowd that does not. Steinberg, Dornbusch, et al. (1992) found that for all ethnic groups, the most successful students were those whose parents *and* peers supported academics. When peers were at odds with parents, the crowd's support, or lack of it, for homework and hard work was the better predictor of a student's day-to-day school behaviors. Thus, even though Asian American parents were among the least likely to be authoritative or to be actively involved in their children's schooling, their children tended to be academically successful. As Steinberg (1996) noted, even Asian students of disengaged parents are often "saved from academic failure" by their friends' support of academics (p. 157). Yet African American youngsters with authoritative parents often face giving up their academic aspirations to keep their friends, because the crowds they join not only fail to support school effort but may even criticize it as an attempt to "act White" (Fordham & Ogbu, 1986). Indeed, at a very vulnerable age, many Black adolescents are forced to choose low academic standards, greatly limiting their future opportunities, or be ostracized.

The complex interactions between parenting and peer influences can also be seen in the arena of high-risk and deviant behavior. Again, an authoritative approach is the best protection a parent can provide. Lamborn, Dornbusch, and Steinberg (1996) found, for example, that children from permissive or disengaged families were most likely to experiment with alcohol and marijuana, and children from authoritative homes were least likely to do so. But they also found that the peer group had more influence than the parents on whether experimentation would lead to regular use. For example, even the most vulnerable youngsters, those who had experimented with drugs and whose parents were disengaged, were unlikely to become regular users if their peers were not.

As with school achievement, ethnicity and social class are among the predictors of drug use and deviant behavior in America, so that authoritative parenting is less effective for some teens than for others. But interestingly, several recent studies suggest that even among minority teens from poor neighborhoods, one component of authoritative parenting can be a strong force against deviant behavior and drug use: high levels of parental demandingness or control. Parents who closely monitor their children have teens who engage less often in delinquent behavior. These are parents who manage to keep track of their children and to place limits on where they spend their time after school and at night. These parents know with whom their children spend their time and what they spend their time doing. In many studies, even when parents were not particularly warm or democratic, that is, when they were more authoritarian than authoritative, high levels of monitoring helped protect their youngsters from high-risk behavior (e.g., Gorman-Smith, Tolan, Zelli, & Huesmann, 1996; Lamborn, Dornbusch, et al., 1996; Patterson & Stouthamer-Loeber, 1984; Smith & Krohn, 1995; Walker-Barnes & Mason, 2001).

Why are levels of parental monitoring and control so strongly associated with reduced levels of delinquent behavior among Black and other minority teens, even when parents appear to be authoritarian rather than authoritative in their style? As we indicated in Chapter 5, how children construe, or interpret, parenting behaviors may have an influence on how they respond to them. In some ethnic groups, under some environmental circumstances, parents who require absolute obedience to authority without question may be seen by children as operating out of love and concern. For example, if a family lives in a low-income neighborhood where the real dangers of risky behavior may be all too obvious to youngsters, an authoritarian style might be read by a child in just such a way. Interestingly, recent research on Black and White neighborhoods in the United States indicates that Black communities may be more dangerous places for children than White communities even when they are middle class. When Sampson, Morenoff, and Earls (1999) compared middle-class Black versus White communities, they found them to be quite similar internally. But the neighborhoods bordering Black and White communities could be quite different. For White middle-class families the surrounding neighborhoods were often affluent and reasonably safe; but Black middle-class enclaves were more likely to be surrounded by low-income and dangerous neighborhoods. Thus, Black parents, regardless of social class, may more often than White parents perceive a need to monitor and control their children closely to keep them safe. Their children, in turn, may perceive even heavy-handed control as an indicator of affection.

THE ROLE OF SCHOOL

As we have seen, the adolescent experience is strongly influenced by parents and peers. In addition, school plays a major part in the psychosocial, intellectual, and vocational development of adolescents. Teachers, curricula, school activities, and school culture all provide raw material that contributes to the adolescent's growing sense of self and increasing base of knowledge and skill.

Much has been written about the problems with American schools (National Center for Educational Statistics, 2002; National Commission on Excellence in Education, 1983), and it is beyond the scope and purpose of this chapter to articulate all the aspects of the debate about American educational reform. It is important to note, however, that educational institutions have been increasingly challenged to make changes that support the developmental needs of adolescents (Carnegie Council on Adolescent Development, 1996). This movement derives both from the recognition that many contemporary adolescents face a host of social and academic problems that threaten their well-being (National Center for Educational Statistics, 1998) and from the increasing body of evidence that demonstrates a stage-environment mismatch between adolescents and their schools (Eccles, Midgley, Wigfield, et al., 1993).

Many researchers and theorists have noted a decline in academic orientation and motivation starting in the early adolescent years that for some individuals continues throughout high school or culminates in "dropping out" (Harter, 1981; Parsons & Ruble, 1977; Simmons & Blyth, 1987). Instructional practices such as whole-group lectures (Feldlaufer, Midgley, & Eccles, 1988), ability grouping (Oakes, Quartz, Gong, Guiton, & Lipton, 1993) and competitive rather than cooperative activities and assessment (B. A. Ward, Mergendoller, Tikunoff, Rounds, Dadey, & Mitman, 1982) all occur more frequently in middle and junior high schools than in the elementary grades. These practices have been linked to low levels of student motivation and heightened social comparison. For example, just as adolescents become exquisitely sensitive to their place in the peer scene, school-based evaluative policies such as "tracked" academic classes may make differences in ability more noticeable to the adolescent's peers and teachers, leading to decreased status for some (Eccles, Midgley, & Adler, 1984). Compared with elementary schools, junior high schools place a heavier emphasis on discipline and teacher control and provide relatively fewer opportunities for student decision making (Brophy & Evertson, 1976; Midgley, Feldlaufer, & Eccles, 1988). In contrast to this traditional model, longitudinal research by Wentzel (1997) documents the benefits associated with a more personal system of middle and secondary schooling. She found that students who perceived their teachers as caring and supportive were more likely than were students of less nurturant teachers to show greater academic effort and to express more prosocial goals. Interestingly, when students described teachers "who cared," they named characteristics that were quite similar to those of authoritative parents.

The large size of most middle and secondary schools is another factor that detracts from personal, mentoring relationships between students and available adults. Ravitch (1983) writes that the trade-off for bigger, more "efficient" schools means "impersonality, bureaucratization, diminished contact between faculty and students, formalization of relationships among colleagues, a weakening of the bonds of community" (p. 327). Although large school size, per se, has not been correlated with reductions in standardized test scores (Rutter, Maughan, Mortimore, Ouston, & Smith, 1979), smaller schools have been shown to promote prosocial behavior among teenagers (Barker & Gump, 1964) and more community activism among their adult graduates (Lindsay, 1984). Calls for smaller counselor-to-student ratios in secondary schools reflect the fact that critical goals such as curriculum choice and career planning are dependent upon personal knowledge of the student and a trusting relationship (Herr, 1989). Elkind (1984) asserts that the adolescent's identity formation is enhanced by being surrounded by a relatively small group of adults who know the student well and who, over time, are able to support the movement toward responsible autonomy.

The timing and types of transitions involved in the passage from primary to middle to secondary school are also important. These transitions represent turning points that involve a redefinition of social status (e.g., from middle school "top dog" to senior high "bottom dog," Entwisle, 1990) and the experience of several simultaneous stressors. Simmons and Blyth (1987) present evidence for "cumulative stress" theory in a study of the effects of different transition patterns on academic achievement and self-esteem.

Large schools tend to be more impersonal and reduce adolescents' opportunities to be mentored by nurturing adults.

Investigating the school-related outcomes of students who followed a K–8, 9–12 transition model and those who followed a K–6, 7–9, 10–12 model, the researchers found more negative outcomes related to the latter plan. They interpreted these findings as resulting from an interaction between the stresses of puberty (see Chapter 9) and the cumulative stresses inherent in multiple school changes. For students who might be already at risk, the cost of these educational practices could be extremely high. Feldlaufer et al. (1988) found low levels of perceived teacher support were particularly harmful for low-achieving students who enter a less supportive classroom after a school transition.

But providing an emotionally supportive academic climate for young adolescents is not all that is needed to assure their educational progress. Recently, evidence from a study of 23 middle schools demonstrated that the combination of demanding teachers and rigorous curricula was strongly related to increased student achievement in mathematics, whereas warm teacher-student relations and communal classroom organization were not (Phillips, 1997). Perhaps we need to remember that both elements, responsiveness and demandingness, make important contributions to success in schools as well as in homes. In a recent study of middle school students, Wentzel (2002) found that teachers' high expectations for their students was most predictive of students' achievement and motivation to learn. But in addition, negative feedback or criticism from teachers, even in combination with high expectations, was found to be most clearly associated with diminished motivation and poor achievement. This finding applied to all students in her sample, regardless of gender, race, or ethnicity. She points out that "by creating a context free of harsh criticism *and* [italics added] one in which students are expected to do their best, teachers might be better able to convey information clearly and efficiently, encourage student engagement, and focus students' attention on academic tasks" (p. 298).

Finally, the level of involvement by parents in the schooling of adolescents also influences achievement outcomes. Despite scientific and government support of parental involvement as a critical ingredient in school success (e.g., U.S. Department of Education, 1990) particularly for poor and minority children (Comer, 1988), the idea of parents becoming involved in the academic life of the adolescent has been met with serious resistance. Consistent with the "hands-off" philosophy described earlier, many adults tend to leave the business of education to teachers or to the adolescents themselves. Involvement declines sharply at the middle and high school levels (Steinberg, 1996; Stevenson & Stigler, 1992). Steinberg has indicated that approximately one third of the students in his study said their parents were uninformed about their school performance, and another one sixth said that their parents did not care. More than 40% of participants said their parents did not attend any school function or activity. This parental unresponsiveness seems closely tied to the child's age and possibly to parental beliefs about adolescents' right to autonomy. Broderick and Mastrilli (1997) found that parents *and* teachers viewed various dimensions of involvement (for example, monitoring homework and use of time, helping at school, attending meetings and conferences, plus serving as a partner with the school in decision making) as appropriately decreasing once the child has made the transition out of the elementary grades.

LEISURE AND WORK

Outside of school, leisure activities occupy about 40% of adolescents' waking hours (Csikszentmihalyi & Larson, 1984). Estimating conservatively, that represents about 40 to 45 hours per week, in comparison to the average *4 hours per week* that American teenagers spend on homework! Leisure activities can promote skill mastery, such as sports participation, hobbies, and artistic pursuits, or they may be more purely recreational, such as playing video games, watching TV, daydreaming, or hanging out with friends (Fine, Mortimer, & Roberts, 1990). Young people who are involved in extracurricular activities sponsored by their schools and other community organizations—athletics, social service organizations, school newspaper staff, student government, band, and so on—are more likely to be academic achievers and to have other desirable qualities than students who are not involved in sponsored activities (Barber, Eccles, & Stone, 2001; Carnegie Council on Adolescent Development, 1996; Eccles & Barber, 1999; Steinberg, 1996).

While there are general benefits to extracurricular participation, it is becoming clear that the kind of benefit varies somewhat by activity and that not all the outcomes are positive. One longitudinal study followed over 1,000 Michigan young people for 14 years, beginning when they were in the sixth grade and keeping track of, among other things, their extracurricular involvements (Barber, Eccles, & Stone, 2001; Eccles & Barber, 1999). High school participation in either prosocial activities or sports was associated with long-term educational achievements (e.g., going to college). But although kids who participated in prosocial activities were unlikely to use alcohol or other drugs in high school, those who participated in sports were more likely than most other teens to use alcohol in high school. Both personal qualities and peer influences appeared to play a role in shaping these outcomes.

Today's adolescents spend a lot of time doing work for pay. Are there benefits to these early jobs for teens? It seems reasonable to propose some developmental advantages. Having adult responsibilities might help adolescents feel independent and grown up, enhancing self-esteem. Searching for work and being employed might provide training that is hard to come by in any other way, such as learning how to find a job, learning one's own job preferences, and clarifying one's work values (Mortimer, Harley, & Aronson, 1999). Parents often assume that working will help adolescents to learn to manage their money and their time. Mortimer et al. (1999) report that teens who work generally endorse many of these presumed benefits, seeing their jobs as helping them to be more responsible, to manage their time and their money, to establish a work ethic, and to learn social skills. Adolescents also list some negative outcomes, primarily feeling fatigued and having less time for homework and leisure activities, but on balance they see their work in a positive light.

Do adolescents who work need to work—to save for college or even to help ease financial burdens at home? During the Great Depression, economic hardship did send adolescents into the workplace, and working was apparently linked to more responsible use of money and a more "adult" orientation (Elder, 1974). But the culture has changed dramatically since then. Whereas in 1940, only about 3% of 16-year-olds still in school were employed, by 1980 the government estimated that more than 40% were working. Of course, relatively more youngsters complete high school today than in 1940, so that today's students may be more representative of the general population, but there is evidence of a substantial shift in students' priorities as well. Large surveys that depend on students' self-reports rather than government data indicate that in fact about 65% of today's teens are gainfully employed (Fine, Mortimer, & Roberts, 1990). Middle-class teens are more likely to be employed than those from lower socioeconomic groups, and their money is unlikely to be saved or contributed to family expenses. Rather, working teens more frequently spend their money on materialistic pursuits: wardrobes, entertainment, drugs, and alcohol (e.g., Steinberg, Fegley, et al., 1993; Steinberg & Cauffman, 1995).

Cultural change has also affected the kinds of jobs adolescents acquire. In 1940, many teens worked on farms or in manufacturing, in jobs where they were supervised by adults (frequently adults who were family members or were known to their families), and they often received some training that was directly relevant to the jobs they would have after high school. Today, teens are much more likely to work in retail establishments, including restaurants, and to be under the direct supervision of other young people rather than adults. It appears that the work teens do today is often less educational than in 1940 and may have less long-term career value (Aronson, Mortimer, Zierman, & Hacker, 1996).

Although adolescents themselves seem enthusiastic about the value of their part-time work, researchers report that there can be some serious side effects. Note that negative consequences are substantially related to hours of employment—the more hours the more problematic the effects in most cases. The most troublesome finding is that long hours of employment (especially 20 or more hours per week) are associated with increases in problem behaviors like theft (e.g., giving away store products to friends), school misconduct, and alcohol and drug use, including cigarette smoking (e.g., Mihalic & Elliot, 1997; Mortimer et al., 1999; Steinberg & Cauffman, 1995). The effects of work on schooling and school involvement are mixed. Several large-scale studies have found no effects on students' grades but negative effects on total educational attainment: years of schooling tend to be reduced for students who invest long hours in their jobs. Steinberg, Fegley, et al. (1993) point out that negative associations between schooling and long hours of work appear to be bidirectional—for example, teens with less school involvement are more likely to seek jobs, and once they are working substantial hours, teens become even less involved in school. In a review of the literature, Mortimer et al. (1999) conclude that benefits from high school employment, like feelings of self-efficacy and self-esteem, are most likely when work hours are short *and* the quality of the work experience is good. Quality includes opportunities to learn new skills, to use one's skills, to discuss work tasks with supervisors, to be helpful to others, and to have relative freedom from stressors like time pressure, work overload, and responsibility for aspects of the work that are outside the adolescent's control.

The research on adolescent employment helps to illustrate the power of historical and social context to influence the well-being of adolescents. Many of the students who seek part-time work today would not have done so in the first half of this century. The urge to earn is apparently spawned largely by teenagers' wanting the material goods and pleasures so prominently advertised and modeled in today's print media, movies, and television, as we will discuss in the next section. Ironically, the temporary affluence teens experience as a result of working in low-level, part-time jobs actually may, for some, help to diminish their chances of pursuing high-paying, education-dependent careers later in their lives (Steinberg & Cauffman, 1995).

MEDIA AND THE CONSUMER CULTURE

Development is affected by the dynamic interaction between the individual and various other forces that extend beyond the friendship circle, the family, and the school. Peer networks, families, and schools operate, as Bronfenbrenner (1979) pointed out (see Chapter 1) within an even larger context called the *exosystem,* or the level of the culture. The culture's values, laws, politics, customs, and so on directly and indirectly contribute elements and experiences that the adolescent uses to construct a map of the world. Clearly, this influence process is reciprocal and multidirectional. For example, changes in the workplace because of economic forces may put excess demands on parents already suffering from a time deficit. Because they cannot be available to supervise, these parents may then adopt practices that encourage relatively high levels of independent behavior from their adolescents. The economic market may move in to provide goods and services, such as structured tutoring or television programming attractive to teens, to fill their time. Teen preferences and interests then influence the advertising and marketing of goods. (See Hewlett, 1991, or Hochschild, 1997, for a discussion of workplace effects on children.)

It is important for mental health professionals to concern themselves with the effects of cultural forces on adolescent development if they are to take a position that promotes healthy growth and functioning. Jessor (1993) noted that the distal effects of the larger cultural context are rarely taken into consideration when studying development, although "understanding contextual change is as important as understanding individual change" (p. 120). Perhaps the major question to be addressed is: how adolescent-friendly is the society we live in? If family, peers, and teachers are fellow players in the unfolding drama of adolescent identity formation, the culture with its values and broader institutions provides the stage upon which that drama is acted out.

Many writers from diverse fields of study have noted a general loss of community and a focus on individualism and material success evident in American culture at this point in its history (B. R. Barber, 1992; Bellah, Madsen, Sullivan, Swidler, & Tipton, 1985; Hewlett & West, 1998; Lasch, 1991). In their discussion of a culture they call "poisonous," Hewlett and West describe punitive economic forces that undermine family stability and negative media forces that shape attitudes and beliefs. Few adults would deny that the exposure to the realities of the adult world that teens have today has been ratcheted up several levels compared to even recent generations. For example, media exposure to violent, sexualized, and commercial messages occurs at a more intense level and starts at earlier ages.

But how does this kind of media exposure affect children and adolescents and how much of a threat is it? The link between viewing televised violence and behaving aggressively for certain individuals has been well researched and is generally accepted (see Comstock & Scharrer, 1999). Modeling processes (see Chapter 1) are presumed to account for much of this relationship. Recent interest in the role of media (TV, movies, music, and Internet exposure) as a socializer of values expands upon social learning principles to include constructivist conceptions of how individuals make sense of their environments. In other words, people use what they perceive as raw material from which to construct ideas, beliefs, and guiding principles.

Like it or not, teens assimilate views of acceptable behavior from many sources, including TV, movies, popular music, and the Internet.

One area of particular concern for adolescents is the learning of sexual messages and attitudes. Studies using correlational methods have found relationships between frequent viewing of televised portrayals of sexuality with more distorted cognitions, more liberal attitudes about sex, and more tolerance for sexual harassment (Strouse, Goodwin, & Roscoe, 1994). Frequent consumption of sexualized media has also been linked to increased sexual behavior—that is, more sexual partners and earlier sexual initiation than for individuals without such media exposure (Brown & Newcomer, 1991). This may have something to do with the perception that "everybody's doing it." Researchers have found that people's expectations or constructions about what is normative influence what they choose to do. Adolescents who believe that teens in general have frequent sexual experiences engage in riskier and more frequent sexual activity themselves (Whitaker & Miller, 2000).

A recent study by Ward (2002) employed both correlational and experimental methods to study whether television's messages influenced attitudes about sexuality in a multi-ethnic sample of older adolescents. This study confirmed that the three beliefs investigated in this study, that men are driven by sex, that women are sex objects, and that dating is a recreational sport, were very strongly related to heavy TV viewing and to personal involvement with TV. High personal involvement was measured by individuals' goals for TV (entertainment and a way to learn about the world), discussions about TV shows with others, and identification with TV characters, among other things. Outcomes of the experimental part of the study revealed that females more strongly endorsed the stereotypical beliefs after viewing sexual TV clips than did women who saw nonsexual episodes. Interestingly, this pattern was not the same for males. Males' agreement with the three stereotypes was already much higher than women's, so it may not have been realistic for this experimental manipulation to generate higher rates of agreement. Another possibility is that males' attitudes might be differentially influenced by exposure to other types of media, such as music videos.

Certainly not all media use is associated with negative outcomes. Yet it is important to consider the impact of repeated exposure to the violent, sexual, and materialistic images in much of the media adolescents consume. Media messages can provide elements for the construction of identity via the processes we have described in this chapter. Moreover, media images serve as standards for social comparison, molding expectations for normative behavior and amplifying values that may be at odds with those of families and communities. As the report from the Carnegie Council of Adolescent Development (1996) points out, adolescents are careening down the information superhighway, and electronic conduits (TV, videos, cable, computers, movies, and popular music) "have become strong competitors to the traditional societal institutions in shaping young people's attitudes and values" (p. 41).

How do contemporary cultural conditions interact with the adolescent's struggle for autonomy and self-definition? In the next section, we will explore some answers to this question.

RISKY BEHAVIOR AND SOCIAL DEVIANCE

Dane and Andy are talking about drinking to an author who is interviewing them for a book about teenage life. "Another way to get beer is just to go to find a kegger somewhere," Andy says. Dane laughs and says, "Pound it down and get out of there. Go drive around." They realize they've just admitted to drinking and driving. Dane says, "I strongly believe against it, but there are some instances when you just can't help it. And we've done it enough so . . . " Andy adds, "Yes, we're good at it and we know the limit. Driving's kinda habitual anyway. We really don't pay attention to it. We're as responsible as we can be, I guess." Dane admits, "Not really." When asked by the interviewer whether their parents know about this, Dane replies, "My parents are pretty mellow; they're real trusting and stuff. I like my parents pretty well. They're pretty supportive, whatever I do, but they're pretty oblivious to teenage life. Like they say, *We can always tell; you can't get away with this stuff*. And I'm thinking to myself, I've been drinking and smoking for like three years now, so you guys just don't have a clue" (adapted from Pratt and Pryor, 1995).

Are the behaviors Dane and Andy describe normal or deviant? Are they part of a passing phase or predictive of future problems? Should we crack down on these behaviors or look the other way? These questions pose real problems, not only for parents and clinicians but also for social policy makers in fields such as education and criminal justice. These behaviors epitomize a paradox at this stage of development, for rebellion against adult norms, expressed through experimentation with deviant behaviors, has always been part of the adolescent experience and is, in fact, statistically normative (Barnes, Welte, & Dintcheff, 1992; Jessor, Donovan, & Costa, 1991).

Risky behaviors are behaviors that constitute a departure from socially accepted norms or behaviors that pose a threat to the well-being of individuals or groups. Various writers have used different terms to refer to these behaviors, including "reckless," "problem," "deviant," "antisocial," and "delinquent." Here we use the adjectives somewhat interchangeably, although risky and reckless connote slightly more benign behaviors than do deviant, antisocial, or delinquent. Even so, separating these activities into bad and not-so-bad is tricky, because as we shall see, they all pose potential dangers. They vary on a continuum of severity and, when severe, tend to appear in clusters in the lives of teenagers at risk. Some examples of these problem behaviors include drinking and other drug use, smoking, truancy, sexual behavior, high-speed driving, drunk driving, vandalism, and other kinds of delinquency. Society considers some of these behaviors to be not only reckless but illegal as well. Consequently, statistics show that fully four fifths of adolescent males have experienced some police contact for minor infractions during their teenage years (Farrington, 1989). Although most crime statistics indicate that males are disproportionately involved in these offenses, recent evidence points to increasing delinquency among girls (Henggeler, Schoenwald, Borduin, Rowland, & Cunningham, 1998). Risky behaviors escalate sharply during adolescence, peaking around age 17 and then dropping off in early adulthood for most individuals (Moffitt, 1993b). Not all adolescents experiment with reckless behavior, but a high percentage do. Thus, the proportion of adolescents who engage in some variety of reckless or deviant behavior is higher than for groups at any other stage of the life span.

It is hard to get a handle on the actual amount of risky behavior enacted by adolescents. Even though incidence rates of violent crime, including juvenile incidence rates, have fallen since the mid 1990s (U.S. Bureau of Justice Statistics, 2000), the problems associated with risky behavior among teenagers have not disappeared. Consider that approximately two thirds of the 12 million estimated cases of sexually transmitted diseases in the United States each year involve adolescents and young adults (Boyer, Shafer, & Tschann, 1997). Although rates of births to teenage mothers fell somewhat at the end of the 1990s, the number of babies born to teen mothers in the United States is still the highest of all developed countries. Great Britain, whose teenage birth rate is next highest, has only about half the teenage birth rate of the United States (Annie E. Casey Foundation, 1998). By 1997, approximately 30% of children in fourth through sixth grades reported being offered drugs, representing an increase of 47% from 1993 to 1997 (Partnership for a Drug-Free America, 1998). When a national sample of adolescents was surveyed in the early 1990s about *binge drinking* (drinking at least five drinks in a row), 28% of high school seniors and 40% of 20- to 21-year-olds admitted they had binged on alcohol at least once during the previous 2-week period (Johnson, O'Malley, & Bachman, 1994). Results of the same survey in 2000 revealed that 30% of twelfth-graders, 26.2% of tenth-graders, and 14.1% of eighth-graders reported binge drinking in the 2 weeks prior to the survey. The percentage of tenth-grade students who admitted to binge drinking was the highest percentage of tenth-graders in this category since 1991, the first time they were included in the study. In addition, twelfth-graders' perceptions of the risks of drinking one or two alcoholic drinks decreased from 1999 to 2000. This survey also showed that although use of some drugs, such as marijuana, has leveled off or decreased slightly, use of other drugs, such as ecstasy, has increased at all grade levels included in the study (see Monitoring the Future Study, 2000).

Sometimes, clinicians choose to treat the reckless or deviant behaviors of adolescents as separable conditions. When this approach is used, interventions get targeted to specific problems, such as drug use or unsafe sexual practices or drunk driving. However, most problem behaviors come in packages. They frequently coexist on a spectrum of less harmful to dysfunctional. Consider Brianna, a high school sophomore who drinks alcohol at parties, but never to excess, and smokes cigarettes with her friends. She has tried pot now and again, but she thinks she does not want to try anything stronger until she gets older. She is an average student, has a sociable personality, and has stabilizing family and peer supports. Despite this, Brianna and her best friend recently were arrested for shoplifting in the local mall. The girls explained that they did this "on a dare."

Shauna is a freshman who has had academic and behavioral problems since elementary school. Her headstrong, impulsive, and aggressive characteristics have always put her at odds with people in authority. Her boyfriend is part of a gang that steals beer and cigarettes, later selling them to buy harder drugs. The lure of her boyfriend and his lifestyle is stronger than her single mother can overcome. Shauna is now pregnant and will soon drop out of high school. While there are some similar features in both girls' risky behavior, namely, the easy availability of alcohol and drugs, freedom to spend time with peers who may influence risk taking, and the ubiquitous adolescent urge to experiment, there are also some important differences. Consequently, the level of intervention used to address Brianna's problem behaviors would probably be less effective with Shauna (see Box 8.1, in Chapter 8, on prevention issues).

Moffitt (1993b) makes a valuable contribution to understanding these differences by distinguishing between two major developmental trajectories of adolescent antisocial behavior: *life-course-persistent* and *adolescence-limited*. These developmental patterns are also called early-starter and adolescent-onset trajectories. (See Chapter 7 for description.) The life-course-persistent pattern begins in early childhood and continues throughout life. In general, this pattern is associated with early conduct problems, aggressiveness, and academic difficulties, as typified by Shauna. For this particular package of problems, early intervention for children and families is most effective. In contrast, adolescence-limited antisocial behavior, such as Brianna's, develops in adolescence and usually ends shortly thereafter. The prognosis for the latter kind of pathway is generally more favorable.

Is adolescent-limited antisocial behavior the same as reckless behavior in adolescence? The answer may be a matter of degree. Certainly, some teenagers go to more extreme lengths, have more accumulated risk factors and fewer protective ones in their lives, and thus suffer more from the consequences of their behavior than others. But the paradox we introduced earlier seems to apply here. Behaviors traditionally considered deviant are increasingly becoming part of the experimental repertoire of teens who are considered well adjusted. Hersch (1998) closely followed the activities of adolescents in a suburban high school for several years. She got to know the students well, becoming an "insider" in the world of adolescents, and was able to document the escalation of dangerous pursuits as a normal part of contemporary adolescent life. "Behaviors once at the fringe of adolescent rebelliousness have not only permeated the mainstream culture of high school but are seeping into the fabric of middle school" (p. 156). As Jessica, an eighth-grade student interviewed by Hersch said, "This [smoking, using drugs, having sex] is *what you are supposed to do* [italics added]. . . . It's our teenage phase. You are only a kid once" (p. 156). Clinicians who work on the front lines, in middle and high schools or in practices that include adolescents, deal with these problems and attitudes every day. Let us try to examine why reckless behavior is such a part of the adolescent phase in the first place, and then we will consider its benefits and costs to young people.

Setting the Stage for Risk Taking

Arnett (1992) proposes that reckless behavior is a typical feature of adolescence and provides three main reasons why. First, adolescents tend to score higher than other age groups on a dimension called *sensation seeking,* which is defined as "the need for varied, novel, and complex sensation and experiences and the willingness to take physical and social risk for the sake of these experiences" (Zuckerman, 1979, p. 10). Sensation seeking is related to certain physiological processes, including brain arousal and hormone and neurotransmitter levels (Zuckerman, 1994). All of the physiological processes implicated in high levels of sensation seeking are more active in increasing or intensifying stimulation during the period of adolescence than at other periods of life. Second, as we have learned, cognitive limitations such as egocentrism support the fiction that risky behavior is exciting but not potentially catastrophic. Arnett implicates adolescents' weaknesses in reasoning about probability, a kind of formal operational thinking familiar to students of statistics, as particularly important here.

Drawing upon Piaget's ideas, Arnett points out that

> in every judgement of probability, there is a reference, implicit or explicit, to a system of distributions or frequencies. Adolescents' perceptions of these systems are skewed by their desire for sensation and by the personal fable that convinces them of their immunity from disaster. . . . But even if an adolescent were exceptionally proficient at estimating probabilities, on a given

occasion, the likelihood of disaster resulting from drunk driving, or sex without contraception, or illegal drug use, or delinquency/crime is, in fact, statistically small—even when applied to others, and seen through the lens of sensation seeking and egocentrism, the perceived probability fades even further. (p. 350)

Finally, Arnett implicates peer influences in maintaining risky behavior. Peers provide not only role models for deviancy but a kind of **collective egocentrism**. Shauna might reason, for example, that if her boyfriend and his friends aren't worried about getting caught in some illegal scheme, then neither should she worry. Each adolescent's illusion of invincibility strengthens that of the other members of the peer group.

Are these reasons the only explanations for teenage risk taking? Or could reckless behavior possibly serve some beneficial purpose? Chronic, life-course-persistent antisocial behavior exacts an enormous cost from the individual involved, from his family, and from society in general. So it is hard to imagine any redeeming features to this condition. The impact of adolescent-limited antisocial behavior, however, is less clear-cut. In one view, recklessness in adolescents, especially in males, once had a strong fitness value. Nell (2002), for example, argues that in the evolutionary history of the human species, young males who were willing to risk their own safety to fight for territory and for dominance won the most desirable mates. The legacy of this evolutionary history is that, even today, adolescent boys are biochemically prepared to take risks and to engage in aggressive behavior. Another view is that adolescent limited antisocial behavior is adaptive because it promotes individuation and self-determination. Goldstein (1990), for example, suggests that risky behavior is instrumental in relieving the **maturity gap** that afflicts adolescents who are caught in a time warp between physical and social maturity. In order to possess the symbolic trappings of adult status (sexual intimacy, material possessions, autonomy, and respect from parents), adolescents mimic the behavior of more advanced, and often more antisocial, peers, borrowing those elements that elicit respect from others and that affirm personal independence.

Maggs, Almeida, and Galambos (1995) found that increasing levels of engagement in risk-taking behavior across adolescence (disobeying parents, school misconduct, substance abuse, antisocial behavior) were associated with decreased levels of positive self-concept but with increased levels of peer acceptance. In a longitudinal study of youth from preschool through age 18, Shedler and Block (1990) found that adolescents defined as drug "experimenters," as compared with drug users and drug abstainers, had more healthy psychological profiles (characterized by flexibility, openness to new experiences, less over-control yet less impulsivity) than the other two groups. W. J. Wilson (1996) noted that some socially deviant behaviors of disadvantaged inner-city youth represent situationally adaptive means of coping with ghetto life.

Engaging in risk-taking behavior thus represents a paradox that has both positive (status-provision) and negative (social-deviance) aspects. Arnett (1992) theorizes that reckless behavior is a fact of life in cultures with **broad** as opposed to **narrow socialization** practices. Societies with broad socializing practices permit and encourage high levels of individual freedom of expression, have fewer social constraints, expect less community responsibility, and thus tolerate a wider variety of socially deviant behaviors. Cultures with narrow socialization practices, more characteristic of nonindustrialized cultures, exert more control over the expression of behaviors that violate social standards and expect more conformity from young members of the society.

So is reckless behavior among adolescents the price we must pay for living in a society that encourages freedom of expression? What kinds of trade-offs should we be willing to tolerate? Even though adolescent-limited antisocial patterns usually attenuate sometime in early adulthood, when more conventional roles of employee, spouse, or parent are assumed, we should not conclude that this pattern poses no risk at all. To be sure, Moffitt (1993b) notes that risky behavior, while enhancing peer involvement, may also ensnare adolescents in situations that can ultimately prove quite harmful, such as fostering drug dependence or depressing academic achievement.

Society's Role in Adolescent Problem Behavior: Then and Now

Let's reflect again about the continuum of narrow to broad socialization. At which point along the continuum would you place contemporary U.S. culture? While there are certainly regional and ethnic variations, it is likely that you identify contemporary socializing practices as quite broad. Adolescents, and even younger children, seem to have a lot more freedom now than they have had in the past. However, we can also consider this question from a slightly different perspective, focusing not just on freedom but on support. How much support does our contemporary culture provide for young people? How is level of support related to engagement in risky behavior? Has our collective level of responsibility changed in any way from that of the past decades, or is this idea just a nostalgic myth?

Siegel and Scovill (2000) provide a comprehensive look at the approach U.S. society has taken toward young people from the 1920s onward. In the 1920s, society viewed deviant adolescent behavior, as much a problem then as it is now, as an expression of youthful energies gone awry. In addition, social deviancy was considered an alternative pathway that some teenagers used to meet normal developmental goals, such as autonomy and relatedness, when more socially conventional means were unavailable to them. Consequently, it was generally believed that society as a whole was responsible for providing more productive outlets for adolescent energies. Many institutions and organizations were established to encourage teenagers to participate in socially constructive activities, to provide them with structured adult contact, and to facilitate prosocial interactions among youth themselves. Some examples of these organizations, most initiated before the 1920s, include Boy and Girl Scouts, Campfire Girls, Pioneer Youth of America, 4-H Clubs, Junior Achievement, Kiwanis, Order of the Rainbow for Girls, and Optimist International Boys' Work Council. Institutions dedicated to special interests, such as the National Recreation Association, the Girls' Service League of America, and the Sportsmanship Brotherhood, as well as religiously affiliated groups such as the YMCA, the YWCA, the Knights of King Arthur, and the Ladies of Avalon, were also established. All were united in their purpose of providing guidance and character-building activities for youth.

Today, Siegel and Scovill (2000) point out, many of these age-appropriate community support systems have disappeared or have more limited scope. Consequently, the social envelope, which in the past strengthened families and schools and provided a safety net for youth who lacked family support or good educational opportunities, is weak or even absent. Many academic and recreational opportunities, often available free of charge to past generations of children and adolescents as part of their neighborhoods or communities, now come with a price tag. What has happened to cause this shift in attitudes and priorities?

Society's view of the cause of adolescent problem behaviors undoubtedly shapes its attitudes toward responsibility, prevention, and treatment. Contemporary society leans toward perceiving the source of deviancy as something within the individual adolescent rather than within society at large.

> While problem behavior was largely "socialized" through the 1960's, it has become "medicalized" in the 1990's. In an age in which we have been led to believe that there is a "magic scientific bullet" for nearly all physiological and social problems, we have "medicalized" problem

behavior. An unspoken corollary of the "intrapsychic" view is that if the locus of the problem is in the adolescent, then parents and society are off the hook. The genetic or biological perspective provides that out: "There's nothing we could do; our child was born a delinquent." (Siegel & Scovill, 2000, p. 781)

No one should interpret these comments as suggesting that we return to either-or, nature-nurture thinking. As we have seen repeatedly, temperamental influences on behavior are strong, and they contribute significantly to developmental outcomes. What these authors recommend is a serious examination of the personal needs and rationalizations we adults use in interpreting adolescent problem behavior. If, as a society, we emphasize adolescent self-sufficiency and sophistication and deemphasize adolescent needs for adult time, guidance, and connection, then we do them, and us, a great disservice.

Parents, teachers, and other responsible adults who wish to limit adolescents' exposure to antisocial models or who wish to restrict their teens' experimentation are in a position of having to do battle with the culture. In many domains, the best judgment of responsible adults is at odds with information coming from the macrosystem. African American parents, for example, who recognize and support the value of academic achievement, report that music and movies that are made to appeal to their youngsters often explicitly disparage their values (Steinberg, 1996). Sometimes this battle can seem overwhelming. Steinberg estimates from his and other survey research that about 25% of American parents across all ethnic groups are disengaging from the struggle. He aptly describes them as follows:

> [They have] "checked out" of child-rearing. They have disengaged from responsibilities of parental discipline—they do not know how their child is doing in school, have no idea who their child's friends are, and are not aware of how their child spends his or her free time—but they have also disengaged from being accepting and supportive as well. They rarely spend time in activities with their child, and seldom just talk with their adolescent about the day's events. (p. 118)

As we have noted, adolescents whose parents are neglectful experience poorer social and academic outcomes than adolescents from authoritative families.

As Elkind (1994) has suggested, and as we noted earlier, the conceptualization of adolescents typical of the 1950s, '60s, and '70s was that they should be "let go" to experiment and allowed to "be themselves." However, this idea developed within a culture that provided teenagers with a protective "adult envelope" that usually prevented their doing too much harm to themselves. In contemporary society, adolescence is not perceived as an adult apprenticeship but rather as an early pseudo-adulthood. Elkind believes that actively encouraging adolescent experimentation or, at least, looking the other way does not fit with postmodern realities.

With societal attitudes that place the burden of responsibility on the individual adolescent, with more mothers and fathers working longer hours, with larger classrooms and reductions in funding for recreational activities, and with fewer "old heads" around to listen and offer guidance, teens may come to depend more and more on their peers for support and information about life. In the colonized or segregated space Taffel (2001) dubs "Planet Youth," adolescent mimicry of problem behaviors increasingly becomes the norm.

APPLICATIONS

The findings from the research reviewed in this chapter strongly support the general benefits of authoritative parenting, supportive yet challenging schools, prosocial and academically oriented peer groups, and a cultural context that allows for autonomy but also provides guidance and limits. As we have seen in previous chapters, inborn temperamental characteristics affect the developmental trajectory of each individual. For adolescents, genetically affected interests and skills continue to influence personality and social adjustment (e.g., Elkins, McGue, & Iacono, 1997). But social-environmental conditions are critical contributors as well. Consequently, teens who enjoy favorable genetics, temperament, *and* environmental conditions stand the best chance of doing well. Thus, providing strong social supports represents the standard we should strive to achieve if we are to nurture adolescents in their transition to young adulthood.

Not all adolescents have or will have access to all these advantages, and "making it" in adolescence does not necessarily require that all conditions are optimal all of the time. This does not come as a surprise to counselors, whose caseloads can be heavy with at-risk teens. Unfortunately, there are many adolescents who grow up in contexts of poverty, physical danger, and discrimination or who have physical or mental handicaps. These teenagers must confront many serious risks on a daily basis. And if we accept the fact that the broader culture can be hazardous to adolescents' mental and even physical health, then virtually every adolescent today is at some risk. The degree of risk is what is in question.

Since successful negotiation of the adolescent period depends upon the interaction of a number of variables—biology/genetics, social environment, perceived environment, personality, and behavior—a "one size fits all" formula for treatment is not likely to be useful. Moreover, taking an encapsulated perspective on adolescent problems risks ignoring crucial variables that may maintain those problems. Individual counseling, which is often helpful in ameliorating some problems of adolescents, may bring only a temporary resolution to others unless the more systemic roots of the difficulties are also addressed (Cairns & Cairns, 1997). The fact that so many influential systems touch on adolescents' lives and that some systems, such as the peer network, are so resistant to adult intrusion makes it critical to use a wide-angle lens when evaluating and treating teenagers.

One way to put the pieces together comes from the work of prevention researchers who have stressed the need to view successful adolescent development as a function of interrelated risk and protective factors (Jessor, 1993). Protective factors are those "personal, social or institutional resources that can promote successful adolescent development or buffer the risk factors that might otherwise compromise development" (p. 121). The study of the pathways of risk and resilience has helped inform our efforts to conceptualize growth and development from the broadest possible perspective (see Research Network on Successful Adolescent Development in Jessor, 1993). We can infer that enhancing protective factors or building resilience while attempting to address risk factors represents the most comprehensive strategy. This two-pronged approach is central to the traditions of counseling (Van Hesteren & Ivey, 1990).

What are the protective factors that support healthy adolescent development, and how can they be enhanced? In general, advocating for authoritative parenting and providing the information and support parents need to get the job done can have wonderfully beneficial effects on adolescents. Steinberg (1996) asserts that the high rates of parental disengagement in the United States amount to a public health problem that must be remedied by means of parent-education programs in communities and schools and through public-service programming. Encouragement and support should be given to adults who are trying to maintain connections with their adolescents, especially for teenagers at risk. For these parents, "the harrowing balancing act required to lower traditional hierarchical barriers without forfeiting guidance; the anxiety-filled struggle to honor an adolescent's growing autonomy; the sheer fortitude required to resist giving up in the face of repeated setbacks and rejection" (Sandmaier, 1996) can be very challenging.

Steinberg (1994) found that parents of adolescents go through their own perilous transition and that 40% of them experience strong feelings of powerlessness, rejection, and personal regrets when their children become adolescents. Furthermore, while sharing stories of problem behaviors is rather common among parents of younger children, parents of adolescents are often uncomfortable doing so (Sandmaier, 1996). Therefore, in addition to reconnecting adolescents to their families, mental health specialists need to reconnect adults to each other. Parent support or discussion groups, "safe-house" programs, and more informal "phone-tree" arrangements allow parents to communicate with each other. Taffel (1996) describes a group of parents who developed a set of common guidelines for their early adolescents' social lives in order to share in authority and prevent individual teens' being ostracized because of parental restrictions. It should be noted that these strategies are best employed in communities that share similar values. Furstenberg (1992) found in his study of urban Philadelphia communities that social isolation from other families was a strategy that was deliberately chosen by some parents in order to protect their adolescents from the dangers of the neighborhood.

Ways to encourage parental involvement in education should also be strongly promoted. Many parents who have had unpleasant school experiences themselves resist dealing with school personnel despite their concern for their children. Sometimes schools present formidable obstacles, either real or perceived, to parents who wish to obtain help or information. Mental health practitioners can facilitate communication by advocating for parents, by explaining policy and procedures, and by working to develop good relationships with school personnel. Steinberg (1996) found that the most effective parental involvement strategy was to "work the system" on behalf of the student (for example, contacting the school when there is a problem, meeting with teachers or counselors, etc.). When school personnel encourage and facilitate this kind of participation instead of viewing it as an intrusion, it can be very helpful to the adolescents they serve. For difficult teens who are failing in school, coordinating both systems (home and school) creates a powerfully watchful force that signals caring and demandingness. Some schools have created confidential hotlines to allow students to get their friends help if needed. Other implications drawn from the literature include supporting a wide variety of extracurricular activities that provide positive outlets for teens, as well as encouraging some limitations on the number of hours spent in paid employment.

Efforts to change peer networks directly appear less realistic. Peer groups by their very nature represent adolescent attempts to establish independent social networks and to provide a supportive structure that is an alternative to parent and family (Eckert, 1989). Peer society is influenced by so many factors (individual personalities, availability of types, social context, ethnicity, media, and so forth) that proximal interventions are likely to be more difficult. Consequently, calls for changes in the broader societal context and in the more immediate family and school environment are thought to be the best way to exert influence on the chemistry of the peer groups formed. For example, in the matter of achievement, Steinberg (1996) strongly advocates refocusing the American discussion away from the problems of schools to the problem of changing adolescents' and parents' minds (or the collective culture's mind) about what is really important—schooling—and about what is less important—socializing, organized sports, paid employment, and so on.

This is not to suggest that counselors should necessarily leave peer groups alone. Indeed, the school counselor is in a unique position to provide information and a forum for discussion about important topics through developmental guidance programs. Other strategies, such as peer mediation and peer counseling, are useful approaches for teens because they capitalize on the adolescent's dependence upon peers. Findings that indicate a tendency for teens of all ethnic groups to turn to their peers for advice about educational and vocational decisions rather than to professionals in the schools (Mau, 1995) suggest that it may be useful to use peers in the guidance process as well. In counseling sessions, Taffel (1996) suggests using a genogram of the "second family," or the teen's peer group, in order to allow the therapist to gain some sense of this important constellation. Sometimes,

TABLE 10.1

Risk Taking in Adolescence: Examples, Functions, Damaging and Healthy Practices

Examples of Antisocial or Problem Behaviors	Possible Functions of Behavior (i.e., Outcomes Teens May Be Seeking)	Developmental Task
Skipping school, disobeying teachers	Expression of frustration with inability to succeed in school setting	Competence
Engaging in pseudoadult behaviors such as drinking, drug use, and early sexual activity	Means of coping with anxiety, frustration, and fear of inadequacy—seeking to be recognized as competent, capable, respected through mimicry of pseudoadult peers	Transition to adulthood
"Teenage behaviors" (e.g., outrageous clothing, music, use of profanity), violation of minor rules such as curfew, status offenses	Means of making a personal statement (how I'm different, important, angry, etc.) seeking to be recognized as an individual of worth, capable of making a unique contribution	Identity, autonomy, individuation
Joining a gang, involvement with delinquent peers	Means of meeting the need to belong (I want to be part of something)	Intimacy, relationship building
"Acting out" (e.g., causing trouble at school, getting into fights, making threats, theft, running away)	To be heard or understood; to bring attention to perceived inequity of treatment	Identity, competence, industry
Smoking, having sex, drinking, status offenses	Way of asserting/affirming the transition from childhood to adulthood—seeking to be recognized as a person with an opinion that counts; attempting to establish a role for oneself	Transition to adulthood
Speeding, riding on the hoods of cars, "sensation seeking" (Zuckerman, 1979)	Way to avoid boredom and seek excitement—seeking a way to not feel put down, ignored or unimportant	Competence
Playing "chicken" with yourself and others, shoplifting, vandalism	Means of testing personal limits and status—seeking competence, finding something to be "in charge of"	Identity
Violent behavior, law violations, conduct disorder	Expression of opposition to or outrage at adult authority—seeking control and power over disruptive/unsafe environment	Trust vs. mistrust, safety needs

he suggests, peers can be brought into the therapy process. It is also possible for counselors to encourage schoolwide programs that help break down barriers between crowds and cliques and that promote community building (see Chapter 7).

Pipher (1996), a family therapist who has written about the problems today's adolescents face, has taken therapists to task about the myopic focus of many traditional therapeutic practices. She notes that counseling theories, like the great therapists who developed them, are embedded in historical time and place. Ideas such as intrapsychic

TABLE 10.1

Continued

Developmentally Damaging Practices	Developmentally Healthy Alternatives
Large schools, high student to teacher ratios in classrooms, ability grouping	Provide individualized programs where youth with a wide range of skills can be successful
Lack of connectedness with adults created by lack of parental presence at home, few opportunities to develop relationships with adults at school or in the community, little one-on-one time with adults	Teach alternative methods for coping with stress, presence of adult role models, opportunities to learn career skills, involvement in mentoring or apprenticeship programs
Targeting of teens as consumer group by media, lack of opportunities for teens to make a positive contribution to family and society	Allow teens to participate in rule making; allow teens to participate in decision making; increase the types of contributions teens can make to society; increase variety of socially sanctioned clubs at school
Lack of opportunities to meet and interact with prosocial peers, coercive family interactions	Teach relationship enhancement skills, conversations skills, empathy skills; provide alternative niches or ecologies with prosocial peers and adults
Failure to listen to teens, not allowing teens to participate in rule and decision making, doing things "to" teens rather than "with" them	Provide strong adult role models who listen to teens; teach youth to identify and express anger and other emotions (rational self-talk); teach negotiation skills; include teens in decision making
Double standard of behavior for adults and teens	Create more formalized markers to acknowledge transitions; recognize the cost to children/adolescents when adults fail to "walk the way they talk"
Few community centers, clubs, or other environments where adult-monitored youth activities are provided	Develop exciting, adult-monitored activities for adolescents (e.g., midnight basketball)
Few opportunities for teens to succeed and to learn adult skills (e.g., career skills, communication skills) or to make a contribution to society	Create environments where adolescents can gain confidence and excel in something; broaden the scope of what defines success for adolescents beyond academics and sports
Failure to protect children from poverty, child abuse, neglect, mistreatment, physiological disadvantages	(Early childhood intervention has been most successful here; prognosis in adolescence is poor)

Source: Siegel, A. W., and Scovill, L. C. (2000). Problem behavior: The double symptom of adolescence. *Development and Psychopathology, 12,* 787–788. Reprinted with the permission of Cambridge University Press.

causes of distress and even the "dysfunctional family," if emphasized in counseling and diagnosis to the exclusion of culture, history, economics, and politics, ignore critical dimensions affecting adolescents and do a disservice to their already stressed families. She has argued that communities as well as families raise the nation's children and that therapists can do more harm than good by misdiagnosing problems and giving simplistic answers to complicated situations without according due consideration to the effects of the culture. She pointedly notes:

In the past when therapists saw troubled teenagers, they could generally assume that the parents had problems. That's because most teenagers were fine. Troubled teens were an exception and required some explaining. Today most teenagers are not fine. At one time we helped kids differentiate from enmeshed families. Now we need to help families differentiate from the culture. (p. 34)

Pipher (1996) advocates for "protecting" family time by deliberately limiting the encroachment of work and media entertainment and creating family rituals and celebrations to strengthen positive connections. Hewlett and West (1998) have called for a national initiative similar to the American Association of Retired Persons (AARP), called a Parents' Bill of Rights, which would guarantee family-friendly policies such as parenting leave, economic security, help with housing, responsible media, year-round educational programs, and quality schools, to name a few.

To transform the social world of adolescents into a healthier place will take team effort. Neither families nor schools, two of our major socializing institutions, can do this alone. A few general guidelines from A. W. Siegel and Scovill (2000) summarize and reemphasize important points. First, take the social context seriously. Don't rely on intrapsychic interpretations alone when identifying or assessing problems. Adolescents do not engineer all their problems, despite how appealing that argument might appear. Second, consider adolescent problem behavior as a means to an end. Table 10.1 provides some suggestions to help clinicians understand the functions that problem behaviors serve. Third, construct healthy and attractive alternatives to help adolescents meet their developmental needs, including social as well as educational alternatives. Not all adolescents fit into the traditional academic mold for success, yet they want success and they are worthy of it.

SUMMARY

Frameworklessness and Autonomy: Seltzer's Model of Adolescent Social Identity

1. The profound physical, cognitive, and social changes that accompany entry into adolescence create a state of instability and anxiety Seltzer called *frameworklessness*. Establishing adult independence requires separating from caregivers on a psychological level, with the concept of the parent becoming more peripheral to the adolescent's self system, accompanied by a loss in feelings of security. Simultaneously, teens increase their affiliation with and dependency on peers, others who share their state of frameworklessness.

2. Peers are a source of support, of social comparison, and of attribute substitution—imitation and identification. Adolescents borrow from their peers' ways of behaving and thinking, providing some relief from the anxiety of being without a stable sense of self. Thus, peers provide an arena for identity formation.

The Structure of the Peer Network

3. Most adolescents have one or two best friends, who are part of a *clique* of individuals who tend to do things together. Larger groups composed of many cliques comprise *crowds,* whose members may not be friends but share interests, attitudes, behaviors, and appearance.

4. Most American high schools are characterized by fairly similar crowd structures, consisting of "populars" and "jocks," some alienated groups such as "druggies," an "average" crowd, and an academically high-achieving group. Crowd membership is likely to be determined by the child's personality and interests entering adolescence, the types of crowds available, and parents' attempts to manage peer relationships.

5. Crowds *influence* their members, but they are also freely *selected* by their members, who choose to participate in shared norms, roles, and expectations.

6. Parents have often been advised to "let go"—that conflicts with adolescents, and adolescent rebellion, is normal and not something to worry about. But more recent research has focused on whether certain kinds of parenting at adolescence may be more predictive of positive outcomes and have found that both warmth (responsiveness) and control (demandingness, close monitoring) are as important with adolescents as they are with younger children. This kind of authoritative parenting is associated with, among other things, higher achievement, self-confidence, self-esteem, social adjustment, and self-control.

7. But crowd affiliations are also powerful in adolescence and can mitigate parent influences. The complex relationships among peers and parenting are evident across different ethnic groups and social classes. For example, Asian American teens tend to belong to ethnically defined crowds that usually value high achievement. Even if parents are not involved in their children's schooling, these teens are likely to be high achievers because of their crowd affiliation. Conversely, some Black teens are also members of ethnically defined crowds, and these crowds sometimes disparage school achievement as trying to "act White." Even though parents are often quite supportive of school achievement, Black teens may sacrifice high grades, or hide them, to be true to their crowd.

The Role of School

8. Declines in academic orientation and motivation are noted in early adolescence and may be associated with shifting school structures and processes as children enter middle school or junior high school. Larger classes and schools, whole-group lecture, and heavy emphasis on competition are among these practices. Timing of the shift from elementary to secondary schools is also important: later shifts are less stressful than earlier ones. Also, parental involvement declines sharply at secondary school levels, despite evidence that it remains just as important for teens' achievement as for younger children's.

Leisure and Work

9. When teens are involved in school- or community-sponsored out-of-school activities, they tend to be higher achievers and to have other desirable qualities. Many teens work for pay, but spending substantial hours working is associated with lower school achievement, less involvement in school activities, more drug and alcohol use, more delinquency.

Media and the Consumer Culture

10. Adolescents, their peers, families, and schools are affected by the larger culture, and vice versa. Present culture may not be very "adolescent friendly" due to loss of community and a focus on individualism and material success. Negative media forces seem to shape attitudes and beliefs. Teens are increasingly exposed to violence, sex, and commercial messages through the media, affecting what they view as normative and acceptable behavior. Thus, media messages often compete with other, more traditional messages from families and schools, and research demonstrates that media messages do influence teens' beliefs and behaviors.

Risky Behavior and Social Deviance

11. *Risky behavior* increases sharply during adolescence, peaking at about age 17, and rates of risky behavior have increased over the last one or two decades. *Life-course-*

persistent antisocial behavior begins in childhood and continues throughout life, whereas *adolescent-limited* antisocial behavior develops in adolescence and usually ends shortly thereafter. Risky behavior, ranging from mild to severe, may be characteristic of adolescents for several reasons: the need for sensation seeking; egocentric beliefs about one's own invulnerability; modeling of deviant behavior by peers; and the exacerbation of illusions of invulnerability by the collective egocentrism of groups of peers.

12. Risky behavior may also provide some advantages in the teen years, making it, in some cases, adaptive. It can sometimes serve as an indicator of individuation and self-determination and as a source of peer acceptance. Thus, risk taking has both positive and negative aspects. It may be inevitable in cultures with "broad" socialization practices, which encourage high levels of individual freedom.

13. While the United States provides high levels of freedom to adolescents, it may not provide adequate supports to ensure that risk taking is within reasonable limits. In the 1920s, concerns about adolescent risk taking fostered a sense of community responsibility to provide adequate supervision and healthy outlets for young people, and a number of youth-oriented institutions sprang up offering free services to teens. Today such community support systems are often in short supply, and costly when they are available. The current approach seems to be based on a reconceptualization of the issue. Today, risky behavior is seen as a problem of the individual rather than a problem of society as it was seen in the 1920s.

Case Study

Mark Spencer is a White 16-year-old sophomore at a suburban public school. He lives with his mother, father, and older brother in a middle-class community. Mark has attended the local public schools since kindergarten, and until eighth grade he was an above-average student who frequently made honor roll. Mark's father, Doug, commutes to his job at an insurance company and in recent years has increased his hours at the office as his company has downsized and shifted responsibilities to remaining employees. His mother, Joanne, works as a secretary at a local real estate agency. Mark's brother, Dave, is a senior who is also an above-average student and who has been very active in intermural sports, especially soccer and baseball.

During middle school, Mark had a strong interest in scouting and was particularly involved in camping and developing survival skills. Several of Mark's friends in the scout troop left scouting in the seventh grade and began spending more time hanging out with girlfriends and playing sports. Mark continued scouting until eighth grade, but teasing from his friends became unbearable, and he finally gave up. Mark was shy with girls and not particularly interested in sports, so he was left with little in common with his middle school friends. At the same time, his grades began to slip.

When Mark's parents expressed concern about his poor grades, he told them that his teachers were jerks and his classes were boring. Although Doug and Joanne tried to encourage him to study more and to continue scouting or to try sports, Mark would generally react angrily, and his parents would back off so as not to upset him further. By ninth grade he was spending more and more time alone, playing video games and watching television in his room. When Mark turned 16, he begged for a car, and his parents agreed. Because they were so busy, Doug and Joanne felt it would be helpful to give Mark more independence, and they hoped it would increase his social acceptance. Mark was one of the first students in the sophomore class to turn 16, and he found that his old friends' interest in him was piqued when he began driving his new car to school.

Mark began to hang out with his old friends, and began smoking, drinking, and experimenting with drugs. His grades slipped further, although with almost no effort he was able to maintain a *C* average. Once again his parents became concerned about his grades, particularly because college loomed. They even threatened to remove the television from his room, but, as usual, they backed down when confronted by his anger. Doug and Joanne were also loath to rock the boat when Mark finally seemed to be enjoying his social life. He was no longer moping around the house, watching TV, and worrying his parents.

When Mark asked to be allowed to drive his friends to a concert in a nearby city, with plans to spend the weekend at the home of a friend's uncle, his parents disagreed about how to handle his request. Joanne was afraid of giving him so much freedom and worried about the safety of the group. Doug, remembering how restrictive his own parents were, argued that "you're only young once" and that "you have to hope that what you've taught them up to now will stick, because that's all you can do. At 16, kids are really on their own."

The weekend trip was a disaster. After the concert, the group partied at the uncle's home, without adult supervision. Neighbors called the police about the noise. Parents were notified after the police found evidence of underage drinking. Mark persuaded his parents that he did not know the uncle would be away and that he had no control over his friends' drinking. Doug and Joanne gave Mark the benefit of the doubt, but a month later, Joanne found a bottle of vodka hidden in Mark's room. Both parents realized that they needed to seek help.

Discussion Questions

1. Consider the developmental path that Mark has followed. Describe the elements that have been influential in shaping this adolescent's experience.
2. Describe and comment on the parenting style used by Doug and Joanne. Evaluate the parents' approach to Mark throughout his early adolescence and suggest ways they might have responded differently.
3. What role could the school have played in modifying the course of Mark's development?
4. What specific suggestions for treatment might you make for Mark and his family?

 ## Journal Questions

1. Compare and contrast the social world of adolescents today with that of your own adolescence. What similarities and differences do you find?
2. Think of a middle school, junior high school, or high school with which you are familiar. If you could change the school (academically, structurally, or otherwise), what changes would you make, and why?
3. Identify one action step that you could take to improve the lives of adolescents with whom you are in contact.

Key Terms

frameworklessness
attribute substitution
parental monitoring
indulgent parenting
dismissive parenting

acceptance factor
democracy factor
risky behaviors
binge drinking

life-course-persistent
   antisocial pattern
adolescence-limited
   antisocial pattern
sensation seeking

collective egocentrism
maturity gap
broad socialization
narrow socialization

Physical and Cognitive Development in Young Adulthood

Javier, a 19-year-old, is a second-year college student. He enjoys many privileges that could be construed as "adult." He drives a car, votes in elections, and owns a credit card. He shares an apartment near his college campus with two other undergraduates. He drinks alcohol with his friends at parties (albeit illegally) and has regular sexual relations with his girlfriend of 10 months. The couple split up once and subsequently reunited. During the separation, Javier dated another young woman. At this point, Javier and his girlfriend have no plans to marry. He wanted to get a job immediately after high school, but job opportunities in the trade he aspired to went to more experienced workers. He decided to give higher education a try. Javier has little idea of what his ultimate career path will be. Javier's father, who is divorced from Javier's mother, pays for his tuition and housing costs. He has taken out loans to help finance his son's education. Javier's mother provides him with an allowance for food. He works part time for low wages at a clothing store in a local mall, which helps him pay for clothes and entertainment. Javier is very responsible at work, but he is an unenthusiastic college student. His study habits lean toward procrastinating and then trying to make up for lost time by staying up all night to finish assignments by their deadlines. When Javier broke his wrist playing sports, his mother had to take a few days off from her job to accompany him to doctor's visits. Her health insurance covered most of the bills. Yet, despite their financial support, Javier's parents have no legal right to see Javier's college grades.

Is Javier an adult? Scholars are likely to disagree about the answer to this question. Most would agree that the onset of adolescence is marked by the changes of puberty. But there are no easily observed physical changes that signal entry into adulthood. Instead, adulthood is a *social construction*. One or more culturally determined criteria usually must be met before one's maturity is established (Hogan & Astone, 1986), and the criteria vary depending on the observer and the culture.

In the past, sociologists have emphasized the achievement and timing of **marker events** as criteria for adulthood. These have included completing formal education, entering the adult workforce, leaving the family home, getting married, and becoming parents. Around the middle of the last century, a large proportion of the American population achieved these marker events between the ages of 18 and 24 (Rindfuss, 1991). However, if we evaluate our hypothetical student, Javier, according to these traditional marker events, he would not be an adult despite being in the right age range.

From a sociological perspective, it seems to take longer to grow up today than it did at earlier points in history for many reasons. Some of these include the demand for a highly educated work force and the increased cost of this education (Jacobs & Stoner-Eby, 1998), the difficulties inherent in earning enough to support children and in achieving stable employment (Halperin, 1998b), and the frequency of early, nonmarital sexual activity and the availability of contraception (Warner, et al., 1998). All have had profound effects on the timing of life events. On the one hand then, attainment of some traditional measures of adulthood has been considerably delayed. For example, the median age for marriage in 1950 was about 20 for women and 23 for men. By 1993, the median age for marriage had risen to about 25 for women and 27 for men (Arnett & Taber, 1994). On the other hand, other indicators of adulthood, such as the onset of sexual activity, occur much earlier than they did in the past.

Such shifts in the timing of marker events appear to have delayed the onset of adulthood, especially in Western societies, where these shifts have most often occurred. However, even in more traditional, nonindustrialized cultures, the transition to adulthood can be a slow process. For example, after completing the puberty rites that induct boys into the adult ranks of some societies, young males in about 25% of cultures pass through a period of **youth** (Schlegel & Barry, 1991). In these societies, males are seen as needing a period of time to prepare for marriage. Serving as warriors during the transition period, for example, allows boys an opportunity to develop skills and to accumulate the material goods needed to afford a family. Girls enjoy a similar period of youth in 20% of cultures. Thus, even in many non-Western societies, the movement to full adult status takes time.

In past decades, adult status was conferred through the achievement of marker events, such as marriage and parenthood.

In cultures such as that of the United States, the pathways to adulthood are remarkable in their variability, so that specifying when adulthood has been achieved is difficult. Recently, Arnett (1997, 2000; Arnett & Taber, 1994) explored a new way of conceptualizing adulthood. In addition to exploring the timing of marker events, he considered individuals' own conceptions about what makes them adults. The reasoning goes like this: if one's own judgment of adult status were based on criteria other than marker events, we might find more consistency in criteria across cultures or even within the same culture over a period of time. Arnett (2000) asked young people in the United States to rate the importance of criteria in several areas (such as cognitive, behavioral, emotional, biological, and legal criteria, role transitions, and responsibilities) as definitions of adult status. He also asked participants whether they felt they had reached adulthood. A majority of respondents in their late teens and early twenties answered *both* "yes and no." Perhaps Javier would say something similar. As you can see in Figure 11.1, the proportion of young people in Arnett's study who judged themselves to be adults gradually increased with age, with a clear majority of participants in their late twenties and early thirties doing so.

Can this delay in identifying oneself as an adult be attributed to the timing of role transitions? Apparently not. Chronological age and role transitions such as marriage and parenthood, on their own, were not considered significant markers. Arnett's respondents indicated that the two most important qualifications for adulthood are first, accepting responsibility for the consequences of one's actions and second, making independent decisions. Becoming financially independent, a traditional marker event, was third. Consequently, the subjective sense of being an adult may be more important than accomplishment and timing of discrete tasks. There is consensus among many researchers that a broad psychological shift toward increasing independence and autonomy characterizes the subjective experience of what it means to be an adult, at least for members of the American majority culture (Greene & Wheatley, 1992; Scheer, Unger, & Brown, 1994). Moreover, achieving a sense of autonomy is among the identity-related tasks described in Chapter 9. Because the shift to feeling autonomous is a lengthy process for many, Arnett (2000) advocates that the time period roughly between ages 18 and 25 be considered a distinct stage of life called *emerging adulthood.*

FIGURE 11.1

"Do You Feel That You Have Reached Adulthood?"

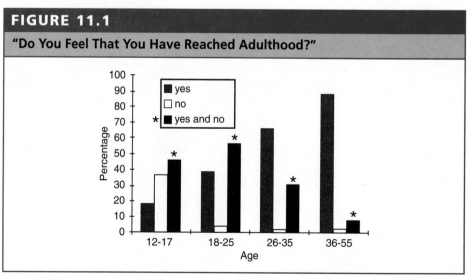

Source: Arnett, J. (2000). Emerging adulthood: A theory of development from the late teens through the twenties. *American Psychologist, 55,* 472. Copyright © 2000 by the American Psychological Association. Reprinted with permission.

Lest we think that very individualistic criteria fully capture the essence of adulthood for young people, we should note that Arnett's respondents also acknowledged the importance of emotional support. As we shall see in the next chapter, strong relationships with others are important in and of themselves and can provide a bulwark for the development of personal autonomy. Encouragement and tolerance for independent action and belief, however, may be greater for young people in the American majority culture than for those in non-Western societies, such as China (Yang, 1988) or in some diverse communities in the United States. Even so, a study of African Americans found that males' perceptions of adulthood resonated with findings from White majority samples. Hunter and Davis (1992) report that Black males defined manhood individualistically, characterized by personal responsibility and self-determination, so the cultural differences were not great. Furstenburg (2000) calls for more research on young people that crosses lines of gender, ethnicity, and social class. Citing the hazards of segregating our research samples into different categories, he concludes that we are left with the impression that "the issues, practices, and identities of youth in different social locations are highly dissimilar, a proposition that calls for further investigation" (p. 900). Much more research is needed to understand the universals and uniqueness of the transition to young adulthood.

In this and the next chapter we will examine some of the key characteristics of life after adolescence, primarily for young people in the United States. We will refer to the period from about 18 to 30 as **young adulthood,** although we acknowledge Arnett's (2000) argument that many 18- to 25-year-olds are better described as "emerging adults." The early years of young adulthood are often an extended period of transition involving exploration of potential adult identities.

In this chapter, we begin by examining the physical characteristics of young adults and then move on to consider the cognitive changes that are likely in this period of life. In Chapter 12, we will explore the complexities of forming intimate, enduring adult attachments, maintaining and/or revamping family relationships, and making vocational commitments. That is, we will look at some of the myriad processes involved in taking one's place as a contributing member of an adult community.

PHYSICAL DEVELOPMENT IN YOUNG ADULTHOOD

Reaching Peak Physical Status

By age 18 to 20, most people have reached their full physical growth. Sometime between 18 and 30, all of our biological systems reach peak potential. For example, we can see, hear, taste, and smell as well as we ever will; our skin is as firm and resilient as it can be; the potential strength of muscle and bone is as great as we will ever experience; and our immune systems provide us with the most effective protection we will ever have from diseases ranging from the common cold to cancer. Not all physical capacities reach their peak simultaneously. Visual acuity, for example, reaches a maximum level at about age 20, with little decline for most people until about age 40. But auditory acuity appears to peak before age 20 and may show some declines soon after (Saxon & Etten, 1987; Whitbourne, 1996).

There are certainly individual differences among us in the achievement of peak physical status—for example, some people reach their full height by age 15, while others may not finish growing until age 18 or 20. There are also substantial differences among different physical skills in the timing of peak performance. Schulz and Curnow (1988) examined athletic performance records for "superathletes" in a wide variety of sports. On the one hand, they found that maximal performance for most sports is reached within the early adult period; on the other hand, they found that the average age of greatest skill (e.g., winning an Olympic gold medal in track or achieving a Number 1 world ranking in tennis) is different from one sport to another, and sometimes depends on which particular skill is examined within a given sport. For example, the average age at which Olympic swimmers win gold medals is 19, while professional golfers typically do not achieve a Number 1 ranking until they are moving out of the early adult period, at about age 34. For a professional baseball player, the average age for "most stolen bases" is 23, but the mean age for "peak batting average" is 28 and for "hitting the most doubles" is 32! (See Table 11.1: *Age of Peak Performance for Some Athletic Skills*.)

The differences in age of peak performance suggest that the relative importance of practice, training, knowledge, experience, and biological capacity varies from one skill to another. Skills that are based on muscle strength, flexibility, and speed of movement and response tend to peak early. Abilities that are heavily dependent on control, arm-hand steadiness, precision, and stamina tend to peak later. Overall, the greater the importance of cognitive factors in performance, factors such as strategy knowledge and use, the later a skill will top out (Schulz & Curnow, 1988).

TABLE 11.1
Age of Peak Performance for Some Athletic Skills

Age	Men	Women
17		swimming
18		
19	swimming	
20		
21		
22		running short distance
23	running short distance	jumping
24	jumping running medium distance tennis	running medium distance tennis
25		
26		
27	running long distance	running long distance
28	baseball	
29		
30		
31	golf	golf
32		
33		
34		

Source: Schulz, R., & Curnow, C. (1988). Peak performance and age among superathletes: Track and field, swimming, baseball, tennis, and golf. *Journal of Gerontology: Psychological Sciences, 43*, P119. Copyright © The Gerontological Society of America. Reproduced by permission of the publisher.

An interesting finding from the research on superathletes is that physical development progresses at different rates for the two sexes. Men reach their peak of performance in many skills approximately one year later than women do (see Table 11.1). No simple explanation is available for the gender differences, but in some instances they appear to be based on earlier skeletal-muscular maturation in women. In other cases, they may depend on the fact that the smaller, more streamlined bodies of young adolescent females confer some speed advantages, as in long-distance swimming.

Superathletes are those whose performance of a skill seems to match their full potential. Most of the rest of us are not concerned about achieving maximal skill, but we usually are motivated to maintain our physical capacities at high levels—including not only performance skills, but sensory abilities, good health, and youthful appearance—during and beyond the early adult period. Clearly, biology plays a role here. For example, regardless of activity level, muscular strength begins to decline somewhat by about age 30. But research supports the importance of lifestyle in this process. There are good habits that help maintain peak or near-peak functioning and appearance, and there are bad habits that can erode functioning (e.g., see Whitbourne, 1996). For example, regular exercise can help both younger and older adults maintain muscle and bone strength and keeps the cardiovascular and respiratory systems functioning well. Smoking, poor diet, and a sedentary lifestyle accelerate loss of peak cardiovascular and respiratory functioning and loss of muscle and bone. Smoking or any excessive drug or alcohol use can diminish functioning in a variety of physiological systems. For example, smoking contributes to more rapid wrinkling of the skin, while alcohol causes damage to the nervous system, the liver, and the urinary tract.

"Eating right" is part of a healthy lifestyle. It means having regularly spaced meals (including breakfast) that are low in fat and that sample a range of food groups, allowing a proper balance of nutrients. Failure to eat right contributes to obesity, to depressed mood, and to many aspects of physical decline. Longitudinal studies that have followed participants for 40 to 50 years have made clear that people who fail to follow healthy lifestyles in their young adult years suffer from poorer health later and that they are less satisfied with their lives in late adulthood when compared to people who do adopt healthy habits in young adulthood (e.g., Belloc & Breslow, 1972; Mussen, Honzik, & Eichorn, 1982).

None of this information is likely to be new to you. Many Americans, including young adults, are aware of the benefits of a healthy lifestyle and of the liabilities that bad living habits pose. Do they heed what they know? We learned in Chapter 10 that adolescents often act in reckless ways that compromise their health and wellness. Often young adults are not much better. Consider their alcohol use. As we have seen, nearly half of college students report that they drink heavily, often *binge drinking* (i.e., having at least five drinks at a time), and many indicate that their drinking has caused them problems, such as having unplanned or unprotected sex, getting hurt, or causing property damage (Johnson, O'Malley, & Bachman, 1994; Presley, Meilman, & Lyerla, 1995). Recent studies of adolescents and young adults indicate that the ongoing development of memory and learning abilities may be inhibited in binge drinkers (Ballie, 2001). In a longitudinal study of 33,000 people, J. Bachman (1997) found that problem drinking and drug use shifts during the young adult period. These problems begin to decline by the mid-twenties. This study also indicates that being in college is a contributing factor to substance abuse in the United States, since college students drink more alcohol and smoke more marijuana than same-aged peers who have never attended college.

The unhealthy, underregulated lifestyles of many young adults are probably an outgrowth of multiple factors: poor application of problem-solving skills to practical problems (see the next section on cognitive development); a continuing sense of invulnerability that began in the adolescent years, which may be exacerbated by the fact that young adults can bounce back from physical stress far more readily than they will in later years; and the stresses of leaving home and facing the social and academic demands of college and/or of the workplace, all steps that create new challenges to one's identity.

The Changing Brain

Study of developmental, age-related changes in the brain has been given a boost in recent years by the emergence of new technologies that allow the mapping of brain tissue and activity without the use of invasive procedures such as surgery. Much of the newer developmental work has focused on infancy and childhood (see Chapter 3), but some researchers have begun to examine systematic brain changes in adolescence and adulthood. As we saw in Chapter 9, it is now clear that major brain developments continue in adolescence and into early adulthood, to the surprise of many researchers. Measures of brain growth (utilizing magnetic resonance imaging, or MRI, procedures) indicate that a resurgent growth of synapses (*synaptogenesis*) occurs around puberty in some parts of the brain, followed by a long period of pruning, which continues into the early adult years (e.g., P. M. Thompson et al., 2000). Such changes may mean an expanded capacity for cognitive advancement.

Hudspeth and Pribram (1992) measured brain activity in children and adults up to 21 years old (using electroencephalography, or EEG, technologies), and they were astonished to find accelerated maturing of electrical activity in the frontal cortex of the 17- to 21-year-olds. Pribram (1997) argues that such acceleration could mean that early adulthood is especially important for the advanced development of frontal lobe functions, such as the ability to organize and reorganize attention, to plan, and to exercise control over one's behavior and emotions. He suggests that the typical timing of a college education may be ideally suited to what he assumes is the heightened flexibility and plasticity of the frontal cortex in young adulthood. A great deal more research needs to be done to determine the degree to which accelerated brain growth is related to the acquisition of cognitive skills and to evaluate the direction of effects. To what extent are observed brain changes the *cause,* as opposed to the *outcome,* of learning and learning opportunities? Clearly, new technologies are making this an exciting time in the study of adult brain development.

COGNITIVE DEVELOPMENT IN YOUNG ADULTHOOD

Each year, millions of young people participate in a rite of passage that marks their entry into young adulthood, the transition to college. Although not all adolescents go on to higher education, statistics indicate the numbers continue to increase. A century ago, fewer than 5% of young adults attended college in the United States; today, over 60% do (Arnett, 2000). So, at least for a sizable subset of American youth, the college experience represents a major influence on their cognitive and social development.

We can all picture the scenes: students piling out of cars driven by their anxious parents, descending upon dorms at the beginning of the semester . . . bustling across campus as fall's first colors begin to tint the foliage, eagerly anticipating the educational challenges that await them in their classes . . . gathered late into the night, talking and laughing with their newfound community of peers, relishing the heady freedom of young adulthood.

If these images remind you of far too many movies you have seen, it may be because they *have* been overly romanticized, due in equal parts to advertising and to nostalgia. Below the attractive exterior these images suggest lies a core set of developmental challenges that await individuals at this time of life. For the most part, these tasks involve continuing the hard work of carving out an identity, now all the more pressing because of one's status as an "adult." Moreover, most of the work takes place outside the protected environments of home and high school, even though continuing attachments to family remain important, as we shall see in the next chapter.

In this section, we will examine the changes in cognitive functioning that appear to characterize many young adults. Most of the research on young adult development has been done on college students and focuses on the kinds of change that one can expect to find among people with the opportunity to continue their education beyond high school, delaying many other adult responsibilities. As we noted earlier, over half of young Americans fall into this category. We know very little about cognitive change in those individuals who move directly from adolescence into the world of work. In the next chapter, we examine some of the special issues that may apply to this segment of our young people.

Unquestionably, early adulthood is a time of great learning. Whether in college or on the job, young people are faced with being the "novices," the "unknowledgeable," or the "inexperienced" when they enter the world of adults, and they spend a great deal of time building their knowledge base and becoming more expert in particular domains of knowledge, such as computer science or philosophy or mechanics. Not surprisingly, at the end of four years of college, students perform better on tests of general knowledge than they do as entering freshmen, and the majority judge themselves to be "much stronger" than they were as freshmen in knowledge of a particular field (Astin, 1993). Comparable change measures are not available for young people who enter the workforce after high school, but it seems reasonable to assume that after four years on the job, some of which may be in job training programs, at least their knowledge of a particular field would have increased.

On the whole, longitudinal research on intellectual change across the life span indicates that many skills (such as spatial orientation abilities and inductive reasoning skills) improve throughout early adulthood, with measures of knowledge acquisition or breadth, such as understanding of verbal meanings, showing the most improvement in this time frame (e.g., Schaie, 1994). As long as opportunities to learn exist, the acquisition of knowledge seems to proceed rapidly during early adulthood. In later chapters, we will look in more detail at the typical progress of specific intellectual abilities throughout adulthood.

Logical Thinking: Is There Qualitative Change?

Is growth of knowledge and skill the only kind of cognitive change that we can expect to find in early adulthood? Or, as in childhood, does the *nature* of one's thinking and problem solving change as well? Piaget's analysis of structural shifts in children's logical thinking skills ends with the description of formal operational thought in the adolescent years (see Chapter 9). Formal operational thinking allows us to think logically about abstract contents. We can discover and understand the implications of relationships among pieces of information that may themselves be abstract relationships—such as proportions, for example. But many theorists have speculated that more advanced forms of rational thought are possible and emerge sometime in adulthood.

Several schemes, many borrowing heavily from Piaget's seminal work, attempt to describe the cognitive shifts that might occur in the adult years. Among these theories are those that propose a stage of adult cognitive thought that has variously been called the *postformal* or *fifth stage,* implying an extension of Piaget's sequence of stages (e.g., Arlin, 1984; Basseches, 1984; Commons & Richards, 1984; Sinnott, 1984, 1998). Some of these theories actually elaborate a number of substages in the movement from formal operations to postformal thought. Two of these—Perry's (1970/1999) and Kitchener's (Kitchener & King, 1981; Kitchener, King, Wood, & Davison, 1989)—we describe in detail in later sections to illustrate the possible processes of change in young adulthood.

In all of these theories, a fifth stage of logical thought is said to evolve as people begin to recognize that logical solutions to problems can come out differently depending on the perspective of the problem solver. In postformal thinking, the problem solver is said to coordinate contradictory formal operational approaches to the same problem. Each approach is logically consistent and leads to a necessary conclusion, and each can be valid. The postformal thinker *both* can understand the logic of each of the contradictory perspectives *and* can integrate the perspectives into a larger whole. Although she will likely make a commitment to one of these for her purposes, she recognizes that more than one can be valid. Thus, postformal thought incorporates formal thinking and goes beyond it. The assumption is that one could not be a postformal thinker without going through Piaget's four stages of thought development.

As you can see, postformal stage theorists have incorporated some features of the Piagetian framework, including stage sequences, into their theories. They assume that there are qualitatively different structural organizations of thought and its contents at each stage. And they have a *constructivist* focus. That is, they assume that what one knows and understands about the world is partly a function of the way one's thought is, or can be, structured but that gradual reorganizations of thought are possible as one confronts and accommodates her thinking to stimuli that cannot be fully assimilated into her current ways of thinking.

Some theorists disagree with the concept of a fifth stage of cognitive development. They often argue that the formal operational system of thinking is powerful enough to address any kind of logical problem. They are more inclined to see qualitative differences in adult problem solving and logical thinking not so much as an indication of a stage beyond formal operations but as a sign that the kinds of problems adults must solve are different from those that children are usually trained and tested on. As a result, adults must adapt their existing problem-solving skills to the new kinds of problems they face in adulthood (e.g., Chandler & Boutilier, 1992; Labouvie-Vief, 1984; Schaie, 1977–1978). Part of what they may learn as they confront adult problems and responsibilities is the limits of their own problem-solving abilities. That is, they may grow in *metacognitive* understanding, recognizing that in some circumstances logical thinking will lead to a clear solution but that in other circumstances they must make decisions based in part on values, needs, and goals (e.g., Chandler, Boyes, & Ball, 1990; Kuhn, Garcia-Mila, et al., 1995; Moshman, 1998).

In sum, theorists disagree about whether adult problem solving represents a fifth stage in the development of logical thinking or is a reflection of the fact that life presents adults with new problems. In the latter view, adults do not achieve a new rational system but learn to recognize the limits of their existing problem-solving systems and to evolve new strategies for applying them. Despite their disagreements, nearly all theorists agree that problem solving takes on a different look and feel in adulthood. In the following sections, we will summarize a few theoretical descriptions of adult logical thinking, and we will examine some of the research demonstrating that indeed, something changes as people face life's grown-up challenges.

Schaie's View of Adults Adjusting to Environmental Pressures

K. Warner Schaie's (1977–1978; Schaie & Willis, 2000) theory emphasizes the importance of new roles, needs, and responsibilities in determining adult intellectual functioning. Schaie does not argue for postformal thought but for shifts in cognitive functioning, or in the use of knowledge and skills, that are straightforward adaptations to the new demands that adults face at different times of life. According to Schaie, we can think of the child and adolescent years as a time when the individual is sheltered from much of life's responsibilities. Schaie calls this the ***acquisition stage*** of cognitive development, when youngsters can learn a skill or a body of knowledge regardless of whether it has any practical goal or social implications. Practical problems and goal setting are monitored by parents and others who take on the responsibility for making decisions that will affect the child's life course. The child has the luxury of learning for learning's sake or problem solving just to sharpen her logical thinking skills. Many of the problems she confronts in this phase are those with preestablished answers.

In young adulthood the protections of childhood rapidly recede and the individual is faced with taking responsibility for her own decisions. The problems she must solve—such as how to maintain good health, what career path to choose, whom to vote for, or whether to marry—usually do not have preestablished answers. Many theorists have described these kinds of problems as ***ill-defined*** or ***ill-structured.*** Not only do they have no preestablished answers, but the "right" answer may be different depending on circumstances and on the perspective of the problem solver. Further, when we solve such problems we often do not have access to all the information that might be helpful.

Young adults are in the ***achieving stage*** of cognitive development, when an individual must apply her intellectual skills to the achievement of long-term goals, carefully attending

Many of the problems that emerging adults face are ill-defined and have no right answers. The ability to deal with complexity is a characteristic of postformal thought.

to the consequences of the problem-solving process. Schaie assumes not that additional thinking skills are emerging beyond formal operational abilities but that previously acquired skills are being sharpened and honed on very different kinds of problems, such that the solution to one problem must be considered and adjusted relative to other life problems and goals. For example, an adult who is contemplating a divorce must contend with a number of issues: her future happiness, her economic status, and the well-being of her children, just to name a few.

According to Schaie, each new stage of adult life brings new kinds of problems, with different skills more likely to play an important role in one stage than in another. In middle adulthood, the *responsible stage,* ill-defined problems are still the norm, but problem solving must take into account not only one's own personal needs and goals but also those of others in one's life who have become one's responsibility: spouse, children, coworkers, members of the community. Schaie suggests that the greater impact of one's problem solutions leads adults to become more flexible in their thinking and to expand their knowledge and expertise and use those qualities more widely than before. For people who take on executive functions at work and in the community, the extended impact of one's problem solving is even greater than for others, and the responsible stage becomes the *executive stage,* requiring that one focus heavily on learning about complex relationships, multiple perspectives, commitment, and conflict resolution. Such individuals must sharpen skills in integrating and hierarchically organizing such relationships.

People's responsibilities usually narrow in early old age as their children grow up and retirement becomes an option. This is the *reorganizational stage,* when flexibility in problem solving is needed to create a satisfying, meaningful environment for the rest of life, but the focus tends to narrow again to a changed set of personal goals and needs. Practical concerns, such as planning and managing one's finances without an income from work, require applying one's knowledge in new ways.

As people move further into their elder years, called the *reintegrative stage,* they need less and less to acquire new domains of knowledge or to figure out new ways of applying what they know, and many are motivated to conserve physical and psychological energy. Schaie suggests that elderly people are often unwilling to waste time on tasks that are meaningless to them, and their cognitive efforts are aimed more and more at solving immediate, practical problems that seem critically important to their daily functioning.

A *legacy-leaving stage* may also characterize people whose minds are sound but whose frailty signals that their lives are ending. Such people often work on establishing a written or oral account of their lives or of the history of their families to pass on to others. Consider Jean, who used her considerable organizational ability to construct a detailed genealogy to pass along to her only son. The activity gave her a sense of satisfaction, purpose, and meaning. Clearly, these goals require substantial use of long-term memory and narrative skill, more than problem-solving skills, but as Schaie points out, such accounts do require decision making, or the use of judgment, about what is important and what is not.

This discussion of Schaie's theory has involved describing cognitive functions beyond early adulthood. We will return to the later stages in Chapters 13 and 14. For now, Schaie's depiction of cognitive functioning as heavily affected by the environmental pressures people face at different times of life should help set the stage for understanding other theories of young adult cognition. Most theories emphasize that advancements or changes in problem solving are embedded in the new experiences faced during adulthood.

Schaie's description of environmental pressures clearly is focused on typical middle-class experiences in Western cultures. He would probably be the first to acknowledge that adults in other cultures, or in some North American cultural groups, might show different shifts in the polishing or use of cognitive skills through life, depending on the unique demands that their environments impose. Arnett and Taber (1994) point out, for example, that in Amish communities within the United States, the importance of mutual responsibility and interdependence is emphasized from childhood through all phases of adulthood. A sense of duty and of the need to sacrifice on behalf of others is central to everyone's life within the culture. Thus, these obligations should be expected to affect cognitive functioning in important ways well before middle adulthood, which is when Schaie considers them to become influential. Keep in mind as you read the following accounts of postformal thought that they are almost entirely based on observations of members of the majority culture in Western societies and that it remains to be seen whether these conceptions adequately characterize adult cognitive development in other cultures.

Postformal Thought

Many theorists argue that the realities of adult experience actually lead to new forms of thought (e.g., Arlin, 1984; Basseches, 1984; Commons & Richards, 1984; Sinnott, 1984, 1998). In many views, the full flower of postformal thinking may not be realized until middle adulthood or even later, but the experiences of young adulthood contribute to the reconstruction of logical thinking. And, as we saw with formal operations, not all individuals will necessarily reach postformal operations. If they do, we can expect them to "skip in and out" of this type of thinking (Sinnott, 1998).

Sinnott (1984, 1998) captures many of the features of postformal thinking described by others. For Sinnott, the essence of postformal thought is that it is *relativistic:* "several truth systems exist describing the reality of the same event, and they appear to be logically equivalent" (1998, p. 25). The knower recognizes both the consistencies and the contradictions among the multiple systems of truth, or systems of formal operations, and depending on her goals and concerns, in many situations she will make a subjective commitment to one; in other situations, she may seek a compromise solution that integrates some of each perspective, but will not lose sight of the inherent contradictions.

For example, advanced study of a science often reveals that more than one theoretical system can account for much of the data, although perhaps not all of it. Let's use Sinnott's example from mathematics to begin our demonstration:

> The knower may be aware that both Euclidean and non-Euclidean geometries exist and that each has contradictory things to say about parallel lines. In Euclidean geometry parallel lines never come together; in non-Euclidean geometry, parallel lines eventually converge. These are two logically contradictory truth systems that are logically consistent within themselves and logically equivalent to one another. A mathematician bent on knowing reality must decide at a given point which system he or she intends to use, and must make a commitment to that system, working within it, knowing all along that the other system is equally valid, though perhaps not equally valid in this particular context. (Sinnott, 1998, p. 25)

In the behavioral sciences and the helping professions, we are quite familiar with the phenomenon of competing truth systems. For example, a counselor may be aware of multiple theories to account for snake phobias. One might be biologically based, another based on assumptions about the symbolic meaning of snakes in a person's life, and another a behavioral theory arguing that irrational fears are classically conditioned. Suppose she understands the logic of each theory and knows that each is supported by a set of evidence. Yet, in a therapeutic situation, she must make a commitment to one of these systems of "truth" for the purposes of developing a therapeutic plan that will achieve relief for her client as quickly as possible. As Sinnott argues, for her purposes that system then becomes her "true description of the world," but if she remains aware of the inherent contradictions among the different systems and realizes that each has some claim on being true, her thinking has postformal characteristics. Truth is relative, but one truth system may be more valid than another, depending on our goals. This example illustrates that descriptions of postformal thinking have parallels in the descriptions of "reflective practice" presented in Chapter 1.

Sinnott's characterization of postformal thought is consistent with what Chandler (1987; Chandler et al., 1990) calls *postrational skepticism,* in which we abandon

> the empty quest for absolute knowledge in favor of what amounts to a search for arguably good reasons for choosing one belief or course of action over another . . . an endorsement of the possibility and practicality of making rational commitments in the face of the clear knowledge that other defensible alternatives to one's views continue to exist. (Chandler et al., 1990, p. 380)

Interestingly, Chandler and his colleagues disagree that postskeptical rationalism actually represents thinking that is more advanced than formal operational thought. They are more inclined to see it as a result of self-reflection, a growing metacognitive awareness that is the product of "an ongoing effort to reflect upon the status of the general knowing process" (p. 380) and to understand its strengths and its limits.

Whether or not relativistic thinking is truly postformal is perhaps less important than when and under what circumstances it emerges. Let's consider in greater detail two descriptions of cognitive change in the college years and the research in which they are grounded. In each of these theories, the final accomplishment is relativistic reasoning like that described by Sinnott. But each draws on data from studies of young adults to specify in detail *how* thinking might be restructured and *why* it is, especially for college students. They each describe a series of stages that we might consider substages in the progression from early formal operational thought to a postformal kind of thinking.

Perry's Theory of Intellectual and Ethical Development in the College Years

William Perry's (1970/1999) theory focuses on the cognitive and moral development of college students. Perry was a professor of education at Harvard and founder of the Harvard Bureau of Study Counsel, a counseling and tutoring center. Using many of Piaget's ideas, Perry proposed a stage-based theory that depicts the typical intellectual and ethical transitions experienced by students in higher education settings, from absolute adherence to authority to beliefs founded on personal commitment. Perry's theory examines the changes that occur over time in the *structure* of young adults' knowledge, or, put another way, the changes in their expectations and assumptions about the world.

Perry's original study involved hundreds of volunteer Harvard and Radcliffe students from 1954 through 1963. The theory was constructed from extensive interviews of students as they moved from freshman through senior year. In general, interview questions were open ended, such as "Why don't you start with whatever stands out for you about the year?" (1970/1999, p. 21), allowing students maximum freedom to talk about their experiences. Initially, Perry considered the differences in students' thinking or worldviews to be a function of their personality differences. It was only after careful reflection on many transcriptions that Perry and his team of raters began to consider the possibility of a developmental sequence. He states, "We gradually came to feel that we could detect behind the individuality of the reports a *common sequence of challenges* to which each student addressed himself in his own particular way" (p. 8). Although Perry acknowledged that specific forms of knowing do vary across domains of knowledge (as we saw in our examinations of cognitive development in childhood), he believed it was possible to identify a dominant position or overarching form of thought for a given individual at a given time.

Perry constructed a sequence of nine "positions," or stages, ranging from extreme dualistic thinking to high levels of personally committed beliefs. What happens in between is the stuff of intellectual growth during the college years. Few students, if any, enter college at the first position, and few leave having achieved the ninth position. Like Piaget's theory, Perry's is a theory of continual movement and transition. Students "rest" for a time at each of the positions, but the dynamic clearly moves forward. From his perspective, the experience of a liberal arts college education accelerates the growth process, particularly in a society that values pluralism, because students are invariably confronted with diversity of thought, values, and beliefs.

In order to understand Perry's ideas, let's consider each of the positions and the three alternatives to growth. (See Table 11.2 for a summary.)

TABLE 11.2

Moving Toward Postformal Thought: Descriptions by Perry and by Kitchener

Perry From Dualism to Relativism	Kitchener Emergence of Reflective Judgment
Dualism	
Position 1: Strict Dualism There is right vs. wrong; authorities know the truth.	**Stage 1** Knowing is limited to single concrete instances.
	Stage 2 Two categories for knowing: right answers and wrong answers.
Position 2: Multiplicity (Prelegitimate) Multiple ideas exist; some authority knows what's right.	**Stage 3** Knowledge is uncertain in some areas and certain in others.
Position 3: Multiplicity (Subordinate), or, Early Multiplicity Multiple perspectives are real and legitimate.	**Stage 4** Given that knowledge is unknown in some cases, knowledge is assumed to be uncertain in general.
Position 4: Late Multiplicity A) *Oppositional Solution*: Either "authority is right" or "no one is right."	
B) *Relative Subordinate Solution*: Some opinions are more legitimate (better supported); outside guidance is needed to learn how to evaluate and to reach this conclusion.	**Stage 5** Knowledge is uncertain and must be understood within a context; can be justified by arguments within those contexts.
Relativism	
Position 5: Contextual Relativism Respectful of differing opinions, but belief that ideas can be evaluated based on evidence.	**Stage 6** Knowledge is uncertain; constructed by comparing and coordinating evidence and opinions.
Position 6: Commitment Foreseen Preference for a worldview begins to emerge despite awareness of legitimacy of other views.	**Stage 7** Knowledge develops probabilistically through inquiry that generalizes across domains.
Positions 7, 8, and 9: Commitment and Resolve (see Text) "Flowering" of commitment; resolve to continue reflecting.	

Source: Adapted from Kitchener et al., 1993, and Perry, 1999.

Position 1: Strict Dualism. *Strict dualism* is really a downward extrapolation of higher stages, given that virtually no one enters college at this level. Strict dualistic thinking implies a rigid adherence to authoritarian views, a childlike division between in-group (the group that includes me, my family, and authorities that have the "right" idea) and out-group (the group who are "wrong" or have no legitimate authority). Individuals in this stage simply never think to question their belief that authority embodies rightness. Since most adolescents have struggled with parents over autonomy issues and have experienced peers and teachers who, at the very least, have exposed them to various viewpoints, it is unlikely that many students would enter college with this extremely simplistic view of the world.

Position 2: Multiplicity (Prelegitimate). *Multiplicity (prelegitimate)* is characterized by the student's first encounters with multiplicity, that is, multiple ideas, answers to life's questions, or points of view. Students now find themselves face-to-face with uncertainty when exposed to a mass of theories, social experiences, and information. Their confusion is exacerbated because they lack the structure to accommodate the sheer volume of ideas. Despite their confusion, however, individuals at this stage maintain the belief that some "authority" possesses the ultimate truth or right answers. It is just up to the individual to find it. It is not uncommon, according to Perry, for students to sort through and organize confusing or contradictory information by creating mental dichotomies. For example, they may distinguish between "factual" courses, such as those in the sciences, and "vague" courses, such as those in the humanities. Students who pursue fields that are relatively clear-cut, at least at the early stages of study, may experience confusion when they later have to confront the multiplicity inherent in advanced levels of study. (Remember our examples of multiple truth systems in advanced sciences.) As one student in Perry's study complained about an instructor,

> "He takes all sort of stuff that, that isn't directly connected with what he's talking about . . . so you get just a sort of huge amorphous mass of junk thrown at you which doesn't really mean much until you actually have some sort of foundation in what the man is talking about." (1970/1999, p. 97)

Position 3: Multiplicity (Subordinate), or Early Multiplicity. In the stage of *multiplicity (subordinate),* the individual grudgingly acknowledges the reality and legitimacy of multiple perspectives. For example, it becomes more difficult to deny that reasonable people can differ in their perspectives on life, and people who hold different views are not so easily dismissed as being wrong. Some of the students' beliefs in a *just world* (M. J. Lerner, 1980), beliefs that the world is fair and that people in it get what they deserve, are now reevaluated. Students realize that working hard on assignments or putting many hours into studying does not necessarily guarantee wished-for results. They may observe other students doing far less work than they do themselves and getting better grades. They may be distressed by their inability to understand "what the professors want." They are nudged toward the sometimes painful realization that even their professors and other authority figures around them don't have all the answers. They may also be distressed by the fact that their teachers continue to evaluate them, despite not having the "right" answers themselves.

Position 4: Late Multiplicity. *Late multiplicity* was the modal position of Harvard and Radcliffe students in the original study in the latter part of their freshman year. Perry's research identified two possible epistemologies or adaptations to the problem of multiplicity at this point in development. In effect, students at this stage now fully realize that even experts differ among themselves in regard to what is true. Students handle the realization in one of two ways. One response, identified as **oppositional,** is characterized by legitimizing multiplicity as one pole of a new kind of dualism. The right-wrong dualism of Position 1 moves to one end of a new continuum, with multiplicity on the other end. Individuals taking this view of the world succeed in maintaining a dualistic either-or structure in their thinking. In other words, *either* "authority is right" *or* "all opinions are equally right." One student in Perry's study captured the essence of this position when commenting to the interviewer about his English course: "I mean if you read them [critics], that's the great thing about a book like Moby Dick. *Nobody* understands it" (1970/1999, p. 108). The viewpoint that nobody possesses the truth, thus rendering all people's opinions equally valid, can provoke students to irritation when they believe their work or the content of their ideas has been evaluated unfairly.

The second alternative, called **relative subordinate** is less oppositional. Students with this perspective begin to understand that some opinions are more legitimate than others, presaging the relativism of Position 5. The value of a perspective is now understood to be related to the supporting arguments and evidence for the position. However, the consideration of alternative points of view is still done primarily under the guidance of authority. A Perry interviewee reported that his first set of grades in a literature course were mediocre because he could not understand the kinds of thinking required.

> "Finally I came to realize, about the middle of the second term, that they were trying to get you to look at something in a complex way and to try to weigh more factors than one, and talk about things in a concrete manner. That is, with words that have some meaning and some relevance to the material you were studying." (1970/1999, p. 112)

Often students receive explicit guidance in helping them weigh opinions or compare and contrast ideas. Instruction such as this fosters the kind of metacognition—awareness of how rational arguments are constructed and weighed—that is the foundation of later relativistic thinking.

Position 5: Contextual Relativism. The move to Position 5, **contextual relativism,** represents a major achievement in intellectual development. The first four positions are variants of a basic dualistic structure. The later positions represent a qualitatively different way of looking at the world. Kneflekamp (1999) reports on a common misunderstanding of Perry's theory, which confuses the "anything goes" quality of late multiplicity with the concept of relativism. He recalls what Perry himself used to say: "Relativism means *relative to what —to something—it implies comparison, criteria, and judgment!* [italics added]" (pp. xix–xx). The individual can no longer accept the fiction that everyone's ideas are as good as everyone else's. While she respects the rights of others to hold diverse views, the student at this stage possesses sufficient detachment to "stand back" on her own and consider ideas and values more objectively than before. In a very real way, the student develops the habit of thinking that relies on some standard of evidence that is appropriate to the domain in question. Students' new analytic abilities allow them to appreciate the merits of diverse perspectives and to find convincing elements in multiple points of view. Thinking relativistically, or thinking about knowledge in context, becomes more habitual.

Authority figures are seen more as colleagues than they were before, as people grappling with the same conflicts that beset students, only with more experience in dealing with those conflicts. They are figures no longer to be opposed but to be respected, as this college junior from the study illustrates:

> "I think when I was younger, when people in general are young, there's so many problems that they feel they don't have to face, and that's why they're indifferent to them. Either it's something that somebody else—the hierarchy, like the family—worries about, or it's something in the

future that isn't any problem yet. And then you, when you mature you begin facing these problems for yourself, and looking at them, and then the family just becomes a help to people . . . with more, with a lot of experience. To help you, and not to take the brunt of the problem or something that's your worry." (Perry, 1970/1999, p. 138)

Position 5 also represents a watershed stage for religious belief, the point of demarcation between belief and the possibility of faith. No longer can an individual's religious belief rest on blind adherence to authority. Real faith, Perry purports, has been tested and affirmed in the context of a relativistic world. This implies that those who hold viewpoints other than one's own may be wrong, but no more wrong than oneself, given that the student now rejects the idea of absolute truth. With some effort, individuals come to respect and tolerate those who hold different viewpoints even while they struggle to clarify their own beliefs.

Position 6: Commitment Foreseen or Anticipation of Commitment. With *commitment foreseen,* we hear echoes of Erikson's discussion of identity development (see Chapter 9). Thinking at this stage incorporates a measure of moral courage, as the individual begins to affirm what it is she believes in, all the while knowing that reason will never provide absolute proof that her ideas or perspectives are right or better than others. Commitments to a set of beliefs, to a field of study or career, to relationships, and so forth, like the constructed commitments we discussed in Chapter 9, can take place "after detachment, doubt, and awareness of alternatives have made the experience of choice a possibility" (Perry, 1970/1999, p. 151). This way of thinking incorporates not only respect for diverse ideas and understanding of their rationales but also emerging, personally chosen, preferences for worldviews. One student captures this element of Position 6:

> "It seems to me that so much of what I've been forced to do here, this taking of two sides at once, just suspends my judgment. There is a value in it, in seeing any perspective, or any one particular facet of, of a problem. But there's also a value in, in being able to articulate one side more than another." (p. 157)

One notices a general trend in thinking toward personal meaning making or reflective thinking.

Positions 7, 8, and 9. Perry discusses Positions 7 (*Initial Commitment*), 8 (*Multiple Commitments*), and 9 (*Resolve*) together. Taken together, they suggest a flowering of the commitments anticipated in Positions 5 and 6. Changes in thinking are more qualitative than structural. According to Perry, 75% of students in the study had a level of commitment at Positions 7 or 8 at graduation. Despite its place at the end of the line, Position 9 does not imply a static resolution of existential conflict. On the contrary, it characterizes a state of courageous resolve to continue the work of reflecting on one's commitments throughout adulthood.

Perry also accounted for individuals who refrain from taking the intellectual challenge necessary for growth through these stages. Fall-back positions include *temporizing, retreat,* and *escape. Temporizing* refers to delaying movement to the next stage. *Escape* characterizes a movement back to relativism when the demands of commitment prove too taxing. *Retreat* occurs when individuals revert to dualistic thinking in times of stress in order to seek the intellectual security of absolute right or wrong, a position that is unavailable at the level of committed relativism.

While Perry's theory has been extremely popular, particularly among student personnel professionals, it has some limitations. The first five positions of the theory emphasize intellectual development, while the last four pertain to moral and identity development. Thus, Perry's scheme incorporates several abstract constructs such as identity, ego development, and cognitive development simultaneously, making it difficult for researchers to agree on definitions and measurement. Some have noted that the lack of uniformity in assessment of stages prevents researchers from making valid comparisons of their findings across studies. Consequently, there is a paucity of recent empirical data on the linkages between Perry's theory and general cognitive processes in adulthood.

Some efforts have been made to address the issue of assessment. Several instruments and questionnaires have been developed to identify stages of reasoning that are less time-consuming to administer than the interview method used in Perry's original work (see Baxter-Magolda & Porterfield, 1985; Moore, 1992; Taylor, 1983). Suggestions for informal assessment of cognitive development for use by residence life professionals have also been proposed (see Stonewater & Stonewater, 1983).

There is some research using Perry's framework to explore the connection between students' beliefs about knowledge and their approach to learning. For example, M. P. Ryan (1984) found that relativists were more successful in their college classes because they tended to use more constructivist approaches to studying course material. They paid attention to context, constructed meaningful interpretations of textual information, and summarized main ideas. Dualists, on the contrary, were more likely to focus on memorization of factual information. These differences were significant even when the effects of scholastic aptitude were eliminated statistically.

Using slightly different conceptual frameworks, other researchers have demonstrated that effective problem solving is related to relativistic thinking (Schommer, Crouse, & Rhodes, 1992) and that relativistic thinkers are more likely than dualistic thinkers to provide legitimate evidence to support their thinking and problem solving (Kuhn, 1992). Wilkinson and Maxwell (1991) found support for the relationship between college students' epistemological style (dualistic, multiplistic, or relativistic) and their approach to problem-solving tasks. Dualists took a rather narrow view of the tasks, breaking them down into unrelated, discrete parts and ignoring some important aspects. Relativists were more likely to consider the whole problem, processing and taking into cognitive account all of its components before attempting a solution.

Gilligan (1977) applied Perry's description of the development of relativistic thinking to an analysis of Kohlberg's scoring of young people's responses to moral dilemmas. She discussed a phenomenon called "late adolescent regression," wherein about one third of Kohlberg's samples actually regressed to lower levels on his scoring criteria. Gilligan argued that this "regression" actually indicates a more contextualized, relativistic stance in response to moral dilemmas, representing a more inclusive form of principled reasoning. As such, so-called regressions should more reasonably be considered advances. Kohlberg's original scoring system has since been revised.

Kitchener's Model of the Development of Reflective Judgment

As we noted earlier, and as counselors know all too well, many problems of adulthood are *ill-defined*. An ill-defined problem has neither one acceptable solution nor one agreed-upon way to solve it (Kitchener, 1983). Should a talented athlete stay in college or accept an attractive job offer? Should a young woman pursue a high-powered career that will leave little room in her life for marriage and child rearing? How can a young adult deal with the pressures of academic and social life? Moreover, how do counselors deal with the messy issues that come to them on a daily basis?

Kitchener and her associates (Kitchener & King, 1981; Kitchener, King, et al., 1989) have proposed a seven-stage theory outlining the development of *reflective judgment,* how people analyze elements of a problem and justify their problem solving (see Table 11.2). They presented individuals with a standard set of ill-structured problems from the social and physical sciences and questioned them about the reasoning they used in coming to conclusions about the problems. Like Perry, these researchers found a predictable, sequential progression that moved from a belief in the existence of absolute, fixed certainty to a kind of contextual relativism.

For Kitchener, different stages of thinking can be differentiated on the basis of three dimensions: *certainty of knowledge, processes used to acquire knowledge,* and *the kind of evidence used to justify one's judgments.* As you can see from Table 11.2, the early stages (1 through 3) are characterized by a belief in the existence of certainties and the use of personal justification ("This is just the way it is") or reliance on authorities for guidance. Individuals in the early stages also tend to use personal observation as evidence of the rightness of their judgments. Individuals in the middle stages (4 and 5), similar to Perry's multiplists, perceive knowledge as uncertain. They believe in the supremacy of personal opinion and tend to make judgments based upon idiosyncratic kinds of reasoning. Those in the later stages (5 through 7) resemble Perry's contextual relativists in that they tend to make judgments based upon a set of rules or logic in combination with personal reflection. For example, one reflective judgment problem concerned whether certain chemicals in foods, such as preservatives, are good or bad for us. The following is a prototypic example of a Stage 5 response to such a problem:

> "I am on the side that chemicals in food cause cancer, but we can never know without a doubt. There is evidence on both sides of the issue. On the one hand there is evidence relating certain chemicals to cancer, and on the other hand there is evidence that certain chemicals in foods prevent things like food poisoning. People look at the evidence differently because of their own perspective, so what they conclude is relative to their perspective." (Kitchener, Lynch, Fischer, & Wood, 1993, p. 896)

Some research demonstrates that reflective judgment is related to level of education (Dunkle, Shraw, & Bendixen, 1993; Kitchener & King, 1981) as well as to the kind of training one has received (Lehman, Lempert, & Nisbett, 1988). Graduate students, for example, reason at higher levels than do college undergraduates, and graduate students in psychology, a discipline that emphasizes statistical reasoning, show higher levels of proficiency on such tasks than do graduate students in chemistry, medicine, or law. Specific kinds of training or support appear to improve skills in reasoning and judgment. In one study, individuals from middle through graduate school were provided with prototypic statements like the one quoted above, with each statement modeling successively higher levels of reflective judgment, and then they were asked to explain the reasoning in the prototypic statement. The results indicated that after such modeling and practice, participants' own levels of reasoning on such problems had advanced.

Another study illustrates that reflective judgment in social and personal issues tends to lag behind problem solving in domains that do not relate to one's own personal concerns (Blanchard-Fields, 1986). In this study, participants ranging in age from 14 to 46 were presented with two accounts of each of three events. One event that had little personal relevance for most people was an account of war (the Livia task) by two opposing parties (see Kuhn, Pennington, & Leadbeater, 1982, for a full description of the task). The remaining two events were characterized as "the visit to the grandparents" and "the pregnancy," and both events were rated by participants as emotionally involving. In the first of these, a teenage boy and his parent each present a story about a time when the boy was required to accompany his parents on a visit to his grandparents. The two stories are inconsistent in emotional tone and in many details. (See Box 11.1: *A Visit to the Grandparents* for the full text of the competing accounts.) In the second emotionally involving event, a woman and a man each take a different stance on the woman's pregnancy, she favoring an abortion, he against an abortion. For each of the three events, study

Box 11.1   A Visit to the Grandparents

Blanchard-Fields (1986, p. 333) presented adolescents and adults with three tasks, each consisting of two discrepant accounts of the same event. Participants were interviewed to assess their reasoning about the events (see the text). The following are the two accounts for the task called "A Visit to the Grandparents."

Adolescent's Perspective

I'd been planning on spending the whole weekend with my friends. Friday, in school, we'd made plans to go to the video game arcade and the school carnival. We were all looking forward to a lot of fun. Saturday morning my parents surprised me by telling me that we were going to visit my grandparents that day. They reminded me that they'd planned this a long time ago. But how am I supposed to remember those things? So, we ended up in one of those big arguments with the typical results; I gave in and went with them. The worst part was when they lectured me on why it was my duty to go without ever once looking at my side of it. When we finally got to my grandparents' I had to do everything they wanted to do. I had to answer silly questions about school, play their games, and see their old slides and movies. It eventually blew up in an argument between me and my parents over the legal age for drinking.

Even though I was being as polite as I could, it was boring. I felt forced into everything. I just can't wait until I am free and out on my own. I was really angry with them. So, on the way home I told them that I wanted to be treated more like an adult; that I wanted more respect from them and I wanted them to take my plans seriously. They seemed to agree with this and decided that I was now old enough to make my own decisions.

Parent's Perspective

Two months had gone by since we had visited the grandparents. We try to visit them at least once a month, but everyone gets so busy that a month slips away very quickly. This time, we planned the visit far enough in advance so that everyone would come. When we tried to get John ready to go with us on Saturday morning, he put up a battle. After all, he hadn't seen his grandparents for a long time. They are getting old and won't be around much longer. We tried reasoning with John, stressing the importance of family unity and obligation as well as consideration of others. Certainly, in the future, he would regret not spending more time with his grandparents after they've gone. Although John was reluctant to go, he finally came with us and actually seemed to really enjoy himself. Since he seemed to be having a good time, we were surprised by how angry he became when we all got into a discussion about the legal age of drinking.

Even though he was reluctant to go with us at first, he seemed to have a good time, to enjoy the family closeness. He showed respect for his grandparents and seemed to understand how good it made them feel to see him. What this means to us is that he's old enough now to enjoy being with adults more and to learn from them. On the way home we agreed that John should take a more active part in discussions about family matters.

---

participants were asked to explain what the conflict was about and what happened. They also responded to probe questions such as "Who was at fault?" and "Could both accounts be right?" The participants' understanding and analysis of the events were scored based on six levels of reasoning, combining features of Perry's (1970/1999) and Kitchener and King's (1981) levels of cognitive maturity. Performance on the Livia task was better at earlier ages than performance on the more emotionally involving tasks. And performance continued to improve on all tasks from adolescence to young adulthood and from young adulthood to middle adulthood.

The following are examples of performance for these three age groups on the emotionally involving "visit to the grandparents" event (from Blanchard-Fields, 1986).

Level 2. This was the average level of response for adolescents on the two emotionally involving events. It is close to an absolutistic conception of reality.

"There's a lot more said by John of what they did and they had an argument and the parents did not say it like—how he talked, and that he wanted to be treated like an adult. It seems more right because I don't like the parent's talk." (Blanchard-Fields, 1986, p. 327)

Box 11.2   Counselor Beware: Decision-Making Pitfalls

Our ability to think our way logically through problems improves and expands throughout childhood and adolescence. As this chapter indicates, problem-solving skill continues to improve in adulthood as well, especially for ill-defined problems. We have also seen in this chapter that using our logical abilities effectively to make decisions can be especially difficult when we deal with social or emotional issues that have personal relevance. Among the many kinds of logical fallacies that commonly ensnare adults are some that may be especially problematic for helping professionals and their clients.

Suppose you want to encourage a client to consider beginning an exercise program. You are concerned that her sedentary lifestyle is contributing both to her depression and to other health problems. When you introduce the idea, however, she counters, "That won't help. I have a neighbor who has run twenty miles a week for all the years I've known her, but she had to be hospitalized last year because she was suicidal." The logical error that your client is making is sometimes called *"the person who" fallacy.* She is refuting a well-documented finding, like the correlation between regular exercise and well-being (both physical and emotional), by calling on knowledge of a person who is an exception. Especially when dealing with psychological and social issues, matters in which most of us have great personal interest, "people tend to forget the fundamental principle that knowledge does not have to be certain to be useful—that even though individual cases cannot be predicted, the ability to accurately forecast group trends is often very informative. The prediction of outcomes based on group characteristics is often called aggregate or *actuarial prediction*" (Stanovich, 1998, p. 149). So, for example, for any individual, a prediction about the effectiveness of a treatment is more likely to be accurate if we base that prediction on general findings for people with that individual's characteristics

than if we base it on one or a few other individuals whom we have known or observed.

Like many logical mistakes, "the person who" fallacy involves failing to step back and consider how well the evidence supports one's theory. Your hypothetical client has a theory that exercise will not relieve her depressive symptoms, perhaps motivated in part by her distaste for exercise. She is aware of one instance in which the prediction of her theory appears to have been correct. She fails to recognize that a single case is an inadequate test of a treatment's effectiveness. One outcome can be influenced by a myriad of factors, many of them unknown. Also, your client completely ignores the evidence *against* her theory: proportionally, more people experience long-term emotional benefits from exercise than not. In other words, probabilistically, regular exercise has a good chance of helping.

Part of the reason that "the person who" fallacy occurs is because of the **vividness effect.** When we are trying to make decisions, some salient or vivid facts are likely to attract our attention regardless of their actual value as evidence. Even when other facts are available, the *vividness* of personal experience or of the personal testimony of other individuals can be greater than that of any other information that we might access. Wilson and Brekke (1994) documented the strength of the vividness effect in a study of consumer behavior. Participants in the study were told they would be given free condoms and that they could choose between two brands. They were also given access to two kinds of information about the condoms to help them choose a brand: one was an extensive analysis of survey data on the performance of condoms from a *Consumer Reports* magazine and the other was a pair of student testimonials. Objectively, the data from the *Consumer Reports* analysis were more useful in this case, but most participants asked for the testimonials as well, and when the testimonials were in conflict with the survey research,

Level 3. This level was about average for young adults in this sample. They recognized that different perspectives appear valid, but they tended to cling to the possibility that there *may* be an absolute truth, even in such ill-defined situations.

> "Yes [they could both be right]. I think you'd have to have a third person not involved emotionally with either party. They'd be able to write without feeling, the facts, just what happened." (Blanchard-Fields, 1986, p. 327)

Note that "just what happened" suggests one correct interpretation of events.

Box 11.2   Continued

about one third of the participants were swayed by the testimonials. Thus, even in a situation where *both* carefully collected group data *and* individual testimony were readily available, the vividness of the less appropriate individual testimony was hard for many participants to resist.

The insidiousness of vividness effects is especially problematic when testimonials are one's source of evidence for the effectiveness of a treatment. When your client's Cousin George swears that his son was relieved of his depression by "Dr. Angelino's oil immersion therapy," the appeal of Cousin George's testimonial may be irresistible to your client, especially when she observes for herself that George's son does indeed appear to be doing quite well. Unfortunately, people can be found to offer testimonials for any therapy or treatment that has ever been offered. One reason for the ready availability of testimonials is, of course, the **placebo effect.** People sometimes improve over time, no matter what the medical or psychological intervention. The actual effectiveness of a treatment can only be determined in careful studies in which some participants are given the treatment and some are given a dummy, or placebo, version of the treatment. Typically in such studies, a substantial percentage of participants given the placebo control will improve, and typically they are convinced that their "treatment" is responsible. Clearly, the actual effectiveness of a treatment approach cannot be determined by testimonials. The only useful indicator of the effectiveness of a treatment is whether or not treatment participants are benefited more than placebo controls.

Counselors, too, often find the vividness effect hard to resist. For example, our own experience with individual cases often looms larger in our decision making about probable treatment outcomes than the actuarial evidence that is available to us from controlled studies of a treatment's effectiveness.

How can we protect ourselves and our clients from making poor decisions based on the "person who" fallacy and the vividness effect? Increased metacognitive awareness—that is, awareness of one's own thinking—seems to be the key. For example, educating clients to see that personal experience or the testimony of others can be limited in its generality, despite its vividness, can help them resist the appeal of such evidence. More generally, we can encourage clients to understand the decision-making process itself. When we try to decide whether a treatment should be pursued, we are actually evaluating the *theory* that a particular treatment alternative will cause improvement. Our task is to specify all the possible theories (treatment options) and to evaluate the evidence for each. When people have a favorite theory, they often do not realize that it is just a theory. As Kuhn (1991) points out, they think *with* their theory, not *about* their theory. In other words, the theory guides their thought and what they pay attention to instead of being an object of thought and evaluation. So, for example, if your client believes that Dr. Angelino's oil immersion therapy works, she will pay more attention to examples that support her theory and may either fail to look for, or will ignore, counterevidence.

Helping clients make better decisions, then, will include encouraging them to recognize that they are working with a theory not a fact. A theory must be justified by evidence, and *all* the available evidence, both pro and con, should be considered. In addition, alternative theories (treatment options) and the evidence for them should be considered. Testimonials or personal experiences are not likely to become less vivid in this process. But when our clients are armed with knowledge about the shortcomings of such data, they may become more cautious about using them as evidence. (Sources: Kuhn, 1991, and Stanovich, 1998.)

Level 4. This level was about average for middle-aged adults. They were not biased toward one side or the other, and the idea that more than one truth might exist was intimated, but there was still a strong sense that one can identify an essential similarity or truth despite the different perspectives.

"I think the accounts, as far as the actual events, are pretty much the same. The important differences are in the presentation . . . the important differences are in their perceptions of what was going on. The actual 'this happened' are the same, but the interpretation of it is different." (Blanchard-Fields, 1986, p. 328)

Level 6. Perhaps you will recognize this relativistic view as one that helping professionals are trained to assume in highly personal matters. There is no hint here that one experience of the event was more valid than the other.

> "They'd have to be able to really share [to resolve this conflict] . . . this way with each other, and even deeper, in terms of getting into some of their fears and some of their angers. They have to be able to accept it in each other, and maybe, they can resolve the conflict, only if they can accept feelings in each other." (Blanchard-Fields, 1986, p. 328)

Only a few participants, all of them middle-aged, responded at such an advanced relativistic level in this study. As Kuhn et al. (1994) point out, "topics in the social sphere both engage people and challenge them. They are easy to think about *but hard to think well about*" (p. 120, italics added). In Box 11.2: *Counselor Beware: Decision-Making Pitfalls*, we consider some of the mistakes in problem solving that researchers have found to be quite common, even among adults. You will notice that these tend to occur in situations that can be very personally involving, so they have particular relevance to helping professionals.

APPLICATIONS

On the cusp of adulthood, individuals in their late teens and twenties confront a number of new developmental milestones. The serious tasks of consolidating an identity, solidifying a career path, and realizing the capacity for intimacy (Erikson, 1968; Keniston, 1971) are both challenging and time-consuming. One competency required for each of these tasks is the ability to make decisions and choices given a wide array of possible alternatives. Counselors are frequently called upon to help clients make decisions, and, to some, this is the quintessential role of the counselor. Decision-making (Krumboltz, 1966; Stewart, Winborn, Johnson, Burks, & Engelkes, 1978) and problem-solving (D'Zurilla, 1986; Egan, 1975) models are widely used among clinicians to help people with personal and career-related issues.

Such models have in common a series of steps, one of which typically advises counselors to take clients' personal values into account during the problem-solving process. For example, a counselor may help a client generate a list of potential solutions or choices and then assist her in evaluating each according to personal values and goals. On its face, this strategy appears to incorporate some aspects of postformal thinking, specifically the relativistic, pro-and-con nature of solutions to fuzzy problems. But it can also suggest, depending on the client, that one's problem is "well defined" and has a correct solution, if only one can figure it out. Although most counselors understand that any solution or decision incorporates some validity and some error, their clients may not.

Given what we know about the importance of belief systems, the counselor might be remiss if she did not consider the client's *epistemology,* or her beliefs about the nature of knowledge, when working on decision making—or other problems, for that matter. In other words, seeing a dilemma through the client's eyes requires an appreciation of the way she views truth, knowledge, and meaning in life.

If a client tends to see the world in absolute terms, she might be confused as to why alternatives are even being considered! Twenty-year-old Hannah recently moved into her boyfriend Mike's apartment near the college campus where both are students. She is upset that Mike wants to spend so much time with his friends, playing basketball and going to bars. Hannah resents the fact that he doesn't spend his free time with her, and, to make matters worse, she believes drinking alcohol is morally wrong. Because the tension between the two is so great, Hannah consults a counselor for advice about how to change Mike's behavior. Hannah becomes indignant when the counselor asks her to consider the advantages of allowing Mike to socialize with his friends and to reflect on her role in the relationship problems. "Mike is the one with the problem," Hannah states emphatically. "I came here to find out how to get him to stop drinking and to spend time with me." Hannah will become frustrated if the counselor presses her to adopt a relativistic stance too quickly, and she may seek out another "authority." She will probably not return to this counselor.

The ability to generate solutions, assess advantages and disadvantages of each, and then integrate aspects of several solutions into one presumes a level of epistemic knowledge that has come to terms with the ambiguity of real-world problems. Yet as Perry and others have demonstrated, this skill develops gradually; it does not necessarily come with a high school diploma. Counselors who are knowledgeable about cognitive development can help clients resolve specific problems and help them acquire more general skills in decision making, such as knowing when and where a strategy is effective.

Based on the evidence that contextual support facilitates progress in reflective judgment, the counselor who recognizes a client's developmental position is in a better place to help her advance cognitively and solve problems more effectively. Stonewater and Stonewater (1984) have proposed a problem-solving model based on Perry's theory that balances a bit of challenge (to introduce disequilibrium) with support and engagement by the counselor. They suggest that individuals who are closer to the dualistic end of the continuum need more carefully controlled exposure to diverse ways of thinking and can benefit from the provision of adequate structure as a framework for incorporating new ideas. For example, students who find the process of career selection overwhelming may be aided by a very specific set of activities that guide them through the exploration process. Students who are at the stages of dualism or early multiplicity may find that knowing what questions to ask or what criteria to investigate allows them to engage in the confusing career decision-making process with a supportive road map. In a process very consistent with Piaget's ideas, individuals will not be able to accommodate new ways of thinking if the complexity of the information is too great and the support is not sufficient. Likewise, individuals will not be motivated to accommodate at all if the challenge is minimal and support is overdone.

The theories of cognitive development described in this chapter make another important contribution to the practicing clinician. They help us understand that certain kinds of thinking, sometimes labeled "irrational," may not be attributes of a dysfunctional personality style but rather the manifestation of a developmental stage. Construing clients' thinking and judgments from this perspective allows us to be more forgiving of their idiosyncracies and more supportive about their potential for growth and change. Sometimes, clients with fairly rigid belief systems may not have been exposed to the kinds of contexts that encourage them to examine beliefs carefully or consider alternative explanations. Or clients who hold less mature perspectives may be retreating from the confusion of too many ideas and too little support. Here the counselor has a good opportunity to assess the person's thinking and provide a balance of support and challenge that facilitates progress from a dualistic, polarized belief system to one that is more cognitively complex (Sanford, 1962).

The exposure to different worldviews, while exciting for some students, can be disturbing to others. Becoming a critical thinker requires that an individual measure up to an existential challenge and move away from modes of thinking with which she is comfortable. Perry added the categories of retreat and escape to illustrate that for many young adults, the road toward mature critical thinking may be personally threatening. For those entering the large and sometimes impersonal environment of the university, the disruptions, losses, and demands of this role transition "all pose a challenge for even the best adjusted student" (Cohler & Taber, 1993, p. 75). Counselors who work with this population need to be sensitive to cognitive as well as emotional aspects of students' struggles. With support, students will become better able to understand the logic of others' positions and clarify their own beliefs as well.

Don't be alarmed if you recognize that some aspects of your own thinking might be dichotomous and authority oriented. Perry noted that new learning in any discipline can evolve in a similar stage-like way. Table 11.3 presents Stoltenberg and Delworth's (1987) model of stages in counselor development. As you can see, Level 1 counselors operate somewhat like dualists. They tend to be dependent upon supervisors to tell them the

TABLE 11.3

Client Conceptualizations at Stages of Counselor Development

Level 1

Self- and Other-Awareness—Emotional and cognitive self-focus. *Indications:* Diagnoses/conceptualizations will be "canned" or stereotypical, trying to fit clients into categories. Incomplete treatment plans will focus on specific skills or interventions, often quite similar across clients. Treatment plans may not reflect diagnoses.

Motivation—High, with strong desire to learn to become effective diagnostician and therapist. *Indications:* Willing student, will seek out additional information from books, colleagues, and other sources.

Autonomy—Dependent. *Indications:* Relies on supervisor for diagnoses and treatment plans. Locus of evaluation rests with supervisor.

Level 2

Self- and Other-Awareness—Emotional and cognitive focus on the client. *Indications:* Realizes treatment plan is necessary and logical extension of diagnosis. May resist "labeling" client into diagnostic classifications. Treatment plans may prove difficult due to lack of objectivity. May reflect various orientations yet lacks integration.

Motivation—Fluctuates depending upon clarity regarding various clients. *Indications:* May be pessimistic, overly optimistic or confident at times.

Autonomy—Dependency-autonomy conflict. *Indications:* May depend upon supervisor for diagnoses and treatment plans for difficult clients, may avoid or resist supervisor suggestions concerning others. Confident with some less-confusing clients. More resistance to perceived unreasonable demands of supervisor, threats to tenuous independence and therapeutic self-esteem.

Level 3

Self- and Other-Awareness—Emotional and cognitive awareness of client and self. *Indications:* Able to "pull back" affectively and cognitively, monitor own reactions to client. The client's perspective and a more objective evaluation will be reflected in conceptualizations. Treatment plans will flow from diagnoses, taking into account client and environmental characteristics. Reflects therapist's own therapeutic orientation.

Motivation—Consistently high, based upon greater understanding of personality-learning theory and self. *Indications:* Not as susceptible to pessimism or undue optimism. Diagnoses and treatment plans consistently thought through and integrated.

Autonomy—Independent functioning. *Indications:* Seeks consultation when necessary. Open to alternative conceptualizations and treatment approaches but retains responsibility for decisions. Makes appropriate referrals.

Source: Stoltenberg, C. D., and Delworth, U. (1987). *Supervising counselors and therapists: A developmental approach.* Copyright © 1987 by Jossey-Bass. This material is used by permission of John Wiley & Sons, Inc.

"right" way to conceptualize cases. Level 1 counselors try to fit clients into categories and often rely on canned strategies. In general, they also tend to attribute too much pathology to their clients because of their own anxiety level. Level 2 counselors vacillate between dependence on supervisors and personal autonomy. Because they have more experience with difficult cases, they may be less optimistic about the possibilities for change in certain circumstances. As with multiplists, exposure to competing theories of human behavior and therapy undermines confidence in the validity of each. Counselors at this level are more skillful yet also more confused about their own efficacy. At Level 3, helping professionals are more independent and also more tolerant of divergent opinions. They come to accept the ambiguity that is inherent in the helping process. They are creative problem solvers and more objective in their assessment of their clients. In the fluid way they utilize the discipline's knowledge base to adjust to the needs of the client, these counselors truly embody the characteristics of reflective practice.

One final point worth mentioning relates to the association between evaluative reasoning, on the one hand, and selection and provision of ethical treatments, on the other hand. Imagine that you make an appointment with Ms. Lovejoy, the only therapist available to you in your small town. You have been feeling depressed and anxious for several months because of problems at your place of work. After much hesitation, you have screwed up the courage to seek help. Ms. Lovejoy, a warm and friendly young woman, interviews you carefully about your current condition. She tells you that she has had great success with clients like you by using her own model of therapy: Person-Focused Astrological Counseling. Being a savvy consumer, you ask her how she knows the approach will be effective with you. Ms. Lovejoy responds that all therapies are pretty much the same. She believes counselors should use approaches that best suit their own particular worldviews.

Certainly you can recognize the ethical problems in this example. Accountability to clients implies selecting treatments that have been carefully evaluated for their effectiveness. Clinicians should avoid the psuedo-relativistic trap of Perry's late multiplicity stage ("All treatments are equally good; one is not necessarily better than another") and aspire to

With experience and supervision, helping professionals develop mature critical thinking.

authentic relativism ("All treatments may have good points, but some have more validity in this particular case as indicated by evidence, despite what I might prefer to do") (see Chambless, 1996). The ethical standards of the American Counseling Association reinforce this position when advising that "Counselors provide information concerning the scientific bases of professional practice" (ACA, 1995, F.2.f).

SUMMARY

1. Specifying exactly when an individual reaches adulthood is surprisingly complex. Sociologists look to *marker events,* such as completing one's education, entering the workforce, leaving the family home, and so on. Young adults themselves tend to emphasize accepting responsibility for their own behavior and making independent decisions. In today's society, the period from about 18 to 25 may be described as a time of *emerging adulthood.*

Physical Development in Young Adulthood

2. Between 18 and 30, all biological systems reach peak potential. There are individual differences in when people reach peak potential, and there are differences among different systems and skills in the timing of peak status. For different skills, these differences reflect differences in the relative importance of practice, training, knowledge, experience, and biological capacity. Males and females also peak at different times.

3. Lifestyle affects the achievement and maintenance of peak or near-peak functioning. Healthy lifestyles include getting regular exercise, eating a healthy diet, and avoiding bad habits such as smoking and drug use. Bad habits in young adulthood are reflected in poorer health later in adulthood, yet many young adults have unhealthy, underregulated lifestyles, probably as a result of poor application of problem-solving skills, continued feelings of invulnerability, the fact that young adults "bounce back" quickly from physical stress, and the many stresses they face.

4. The pruning of synapses continues in young adulthood. The frontal lobes continue to mature, perhaps playing an important role in the young adult's advancing abilities in organization, attention, planning, and self-regulation.

Cognitive Development in Young Adulthood

5. Young adulthood is a time of great learning. We have clear data on the growth of knowledge in the college population (roughly 60% of young adults today), but it seems likely that rapid growth of knowledge characterizes all young adults as they gain training and experience in their vocations and avocations.

6. Logical thinking also appears to change beginning in young adulthood. Theorists and researchers disagree as to the nature of the change. Some propose that a more advanced kind of thinking, *postformal* or *fifth stage thinking,* emerges. Others argue that the formal operational abilities of the adolescent period represent the most advanced form of thinking for humans but that adults learn to apply this kind of thinking to the more *ill-defined* or *ill-structured* problems that adults face. As part of this process, they may also gain better understanding of the limits of their own problem-solving abilities. That is, they may grow in *metacognitive* understanding.

7. Schaie argues against a new kind of adult thinking. Rather, he argues that at different times of adult life people face different kinds of problems, and different skills are brought to bear on those problems. He describes seven stages in adults' intellectual functioning, with each new stage a result of shifts in the challenges people face.

8. Theorists who argue that there is a stage of postformal thought suggest that it may not reach full development until middle adulthood, but its emergence begins in young adulthood. Most theorists, such as Sinnott, describe postformal thought as relativistic. The same reality can be described within several different truth systems, all of which are valid from one perspective or within some context. The postformal thinker recognizes the validity of different truth systems. She may make a subjective commitment to one in some situations or seek a compromise in other situations. Sinnott's description of postformal thought is similar to what Chandler called *postrational skepticism*, although Chandler disagrees that this kind of thinking is more advanced than formal operational thought.

9. Perry's stage theory of intellectual and ethical development in the college years describes a sequence of steps in the movement from more absolutist or dualistic thinking (there is one right answer, other answers are wrong) to relativistic thinking (there is more than one correct way to view the same issue). In addition to Perry's own longitudinal interview study, a number of researchers have provided some evidence for aspects of Perry's theory. For example, students' beliefs about knowledge have been found to relate to their approach to learning, as Perry's theory predicts.

10. Kitchener provides a 7-stage theory of the development of relativistic thinking, calling it *reflective judgment*. Research in which subjects are given ill-defined problems indicates that in the early stages of adult thinking, individuals believe in the existence of certainties. In the middle stages, people perceive knowledge as uncertain. And in the later stages, they base their judgments on a set of rules or logic in combination with personal reflection. Essentially, they are relativistic.

11. Some research indicates that reflective judgment is related to level of education and to the specific kind of training people have received. Graduate students in psychology, for example, tend to show more proficiency than graduate students in other disciplines. Evidence also indicates that people are benefited by modeling of forms of thinking more advanced than their own.

Case Study

Angela, a young Black woman, comes from a close-knit and very religious family who have always taken great pride in her accomplishments. Despite some minor rebelliousness during high school, Angela maintains close ties to her family and considers her parents and younger sister to be her best friends. A solid student all through school and a leader in her church's youth ministry, Angela knew for a long time that she wanted to go to college to be a teacher. Angela's father attended community college for two years, and her mother graduated from high school. Both parents were delighted when Angela became the first member of the family to pursue a baccalaureate degree.

Now a freshman at a state university in the South, she is getting used to college and to life in a dormitory. She enjoys the freedom and the challenge of college but is also experiencing some problems getting along with other students. Her roommate, a young White woman named Jen, poses a particular dilemma for her. It bothers Angela that Jen never goes to church, never prays, frequently spends the night at her boyfriend's apartment, and is an outspoken agnostic. Jen makes various comments about what she has learned in her religion and philosophy classes that trouble Angela, who firmly believes that Jen lacks a proper moral center. Angela has tried to convince Jen about the importance of belief in God and the consequences of her disbelief, but to no avail. Since it is important to Angela to maintain her beliefs, she starts to avoid being in the room when Jen is there and considers finding a new roommate.

During the spring semester, Angela develops a serious infection that confines her to bed and makes her unable to attend classes or to care for herself. She is both surprised and pleased when Jen comes to her assistance. Jen runs errands for her, brings her meals, and does her laundry. Even Jen's boyfriend pitches in to help Angela make up her missed assignments. She is touched by their generosity and confused about how this goodness can coexist with a nonreligious perspective on life. These are the kind of people she had thought were immoral. When the time comes to plan for next year's housing arrangement, Angela is uncertain. Her friends in the ministry counsel her to find a more appropriate roommate. Yet Angela cannot reconcile Jen's kindness toward her with what she believes to be an immoral lifestyle. This disjunction causes her great distress. She decides to seek out a counselor in the University Counseling Center to help her with her decision.

Discussion Questions

1. Discuss Angela's level of development according to the various theories presented in the chapter.
2. How would you respond to her problem as a counselor in a university setting? How would you take her cognitive development into account?

 ## Journal Questions

1. Give examples of your own thinking at one or more points in your life that reflected dualism, multiplicity, and relativism.
2. In what respect and in what areas have you achieved the stage of committed relativism? Discuss this process from your personal experience.
3. Describe your transition to college. What aspects of this adjustment were particularly difficult for you? If you were a counselor working with similar problems, how would you approach them?

Key Terms

marker events	responsible stage	multiplicity (subordinate)	resolve
youth	executive stage	just world	temporizing
emerging adulthood	reorganizational stage	late multiplicity	retreat
young adulthood	reintegrative stage	oppositional	escape
postformal or fifth stage thinking	legacy-leaving stage	relative subordinate	reflective judgment
acquisition stage	relativistic thought	contextual relativism	"the person who" fallacy
ill-defined or ill-structured problems	postrational skepticism	commitment foreseen	actuarial prediction
achieving stage	strict dualism	initial commitment	vividness effect
	multiplicity (prelegitimate)	multiple commitments	placebo effect

Socioemotional and Vocational Development in Young Adulthood

ilar question was simple: "Lieben und arbeiten"—"To love and to work" (Erikson, 1950/1963). For Freud, both love and work are powerful methods by which we "strive to gain happiness and keep suffering away" (1930/1989, p. 732). *Love,* he felt, may bring us closer to the goal of happiness than anything else we do. The disadvantage of love, of course, is that "we are never so defenseless . . . never so helplessly unhappy as when we have lost our loved object or its love" (p. 733). *Work,* from Freud's perspective, not only helps to justify our existence in society, providing the worker with a "secure place . . . in the human community," but it can be a source of special satisfaction if it is "freely chosen—if, that is . . . it makes possible the use of existing inclinations . . . " (p. 732).

For Erikson (e.g., 1950/1963), both *intimacy* (love) and *generativity* (work) are arenas for expressing and developing the self, dominating the concerns of adults in their early and middle years. True intimacy and generativity require achieving an adult identity and are part of its further enrichment and evolution. "Intimacy is a quality of interpersonal relating through which partners share personal thoughts, feelings, and other important aspects of themselves with each other" (McAdams, 2000, p. 118). True intimacy is marked by openness, affection, and trust. Generativity is a *motive or need* that can be filled through one's vocation or avocations, through child rearing, or through community service. It includes productivity and creativity (Erikson, 1950/1963). Generativity is also a *trait* that people can be described as having when they are contributing members of society. "It is about *generating*: creating and producing things, people, and outcomes that are aimed at benefiting, in some sense, the next generation, and even the next" (McAdams, Hart, & Maruna, 1998). For most adults, achieving generativity is central to their belief in the meaningfulness of their lives. Erikson considered young adults to be especially driven by needs for intimacy, middle adults by needs for generativity. Modern research suggests that both are powerful influences on behavior throughout adulthood, although intimacy needs may predominate early and generativity needs later.

More recent conceptions of how adults achieve happiness or mental health or "wellness" are quite consistent with the importance that Freud and Erikson placed on love and work. Close relationships with lovers, friends, and family, as well as the opportunity to make productive use of one's time and talents, figure prominently in nearly all modern theorizing about what people need to be happy and well-adjusted (e.g., R. M. Ryan & Deci, 2000). From a developmental perspective, then, the period of young adulthood should be a time when identity issues are resolved sufficiently to allow a person to make significant progress on two major tasks: the first is establishing and strengthening bonds with people

407

who will accompany him on his life journey, and the second is becoming a productive worker.

"LIEBEN"—TO LOVE

Making connections with others in adulthood—establishing intimacy with a mate, making friends, reworking family ties—has been studied from many perspectives. One promising developmental approach examines the impact of attachment style, which is assumed to have its roots in infancy and childhood, on the formation of adult relationships.

Adult Attachment Theory

Attachment theory has enjoyed a prominent place in the child development literature since the groundbreaking work of John Bowlby and Mary Ainsworth (see Chapter 4). Following an explosion of studies on childhood attachment, researchers began to train their sights on attachment theorists' suggestion that early bonds with caregivers could have a bearing on relationship building throughout the life span (Ainsworth, 1989; Bowlby, 1980a). Today, attachment theory provides a useful framework for conceptualizing adult intimacy. The abundance of research in this area makes it the most empirically grounded theory available for explaining the formation and nature of close interpersonal relationships throughout adulthood.

As we saw in Chapter 4, the process of attaching to a caregiver in infancy is considered species-typical. According to Bowlby (1969/1982; 1973; 1980a), the attachment bonds of infancy serve survival needs. Infant behaviors, such as distress at separation, ensure proximity to the caregiver, who acts as a *secure base* for exploration, a safe haven in case of threat, and a preferred provider of emotional warmth and *affect regulation*.

How the attachment process unfolds is a function of the caregiving relationship. Depending on the caregiver's sensitivity and responsiveness, an infant becomes securely or insecurely attached to that caregiver. To the extent possible, he adapts his behavior to the caregiver's style to get his needs met, and he begins to internalize a working model of how relationships operate.

Despite diminishing demands for physical caretaking as individuals age, adults continue to need the emotional and practical support of significant others. As we have noted, Erikson (1950/1963) identified the achievement of intimacy as the central task of early adulthood. In his view, even though adults are much more independent than children, they still need to establish and maintain intimate connections to people who will provide them with love and care. Although you may never have thought of your adult relationships with significant others, including your bonds to your parents, as attachment relationships, many researchers believe that they are precisely that. Let us look more closely at the various manifestations of attachments in adulthood and consider a framework for organizing the existing research.

Research Traditions in Adult Attachment

Attachment theory has been used to understand relationships as divergent as those between parents and their adult children (Vivona, 2000) and those between romantic partners (Simpson & Rholes, 1998b). It provides a conceptual framework for individual differences in people's responses to bereavement and loss (Rando, 1993), to stress (Mikulincer & Florian, 1998), and to the processing of information about relationships

(Ainsworth, 1989). And, as you will see below, attachment theory predicts intergenerational transmission of attachment classifications (van IJzendoorn, 1995). Among clinicians, attachment theory has been used as a framework for explaining conflict resolution in interpersonal relationships (Cohn & Silver, McInnis, 2001), family dysfunction (Byng-Hall, 1995), and psychopathology (Brennan & Shaver, 1998; Dozier, Stovall, & Albus, 1999), and it provides a basis for therapeutic intervention (Slade & Aber, 1990).

One way to make sense of the multitude of studies on adult attachment is to identify which kind of attachment relationship is being explored. Simpson and Rholes (1998b) offer a useful organizational framework that distinguishes between two major research traditions. First, there is a body of work that examines the outcome of a person's attachment to his primary caregiver in infancy once the person becomes an adult. This has been referred to as the *nuclear family tradition*. Research in this area seeks to understand the degree to which one's earliest attachments to primary caregivers may endure throughout life and how they might affect the quality of the caregiving provided to one's own children. A parallel line of research, called the *peer/romantic partner tradition*, focuses on the peer attachments of adults. Questions about how early attachments impact the quality of romantic and friendship relationships in adulthood form the core of inquiry from this angle. The two bodies of work share conceptual linkages, to be sure. However, they differ in their methodologies and even in their terminology, and they "tend to speak past each other" (Bartholomew and Shaver, 1998, p. 27).

It is sometimes assumed that findings from both traditions should converge into a coherent picture of an adult's attachment status. This has been a difficult goal to achieve, primarily because different domains are studied, different methodologies are used, and different typologies are employed. Despite these problems, there is some correlation between the different kinds of attachment findings in adulthood. As Batholomew and Shaver (1998) note:

> When we step back from the details of specific measures and measure-specific findings, the results produced by attachment researchers are all compatible with the possibility that various forms of adult attachment arise from a continuous but branching tree of attachment experiences, beginning in infancy and developing throughout the life course. (p. 42)

We will continue our discussion of adult attachment by focusing on each approach in turn. First, we will consider how the nuclear family tradition contributes to our understanding of adult caregiving. Then we will present an overview of significant contributions from the peer/romantic partner tradition.

The Nuclear Family Tradition: The Past as Prologue. Does the nature of your attachment to your caregiver predict your behavior in adulthood, influencing the quality of attachment you will form with your own children? This is the intriguing question that is at the heart of the nuclear family line of research. We briefly examined this issue in Chapter 4. Now we'll take a closer look.

You may recall that the primary instrument used to measure the attachment representations of adults vis-à-vis their early caregivers is the *Adult Attachment Interview* (AAI) developed by Main and Goldwyn (1984). It is composed of a series of 18 open-ended questions with follow-up prompts that are transcribed verbatim by a trained interviewer. The questions concern memories of relationships with mother and father, recollections of stressful events such as separations, loss, harsh discipline, or abuse, interpretations of parental behaviors, and evaluation of the effects of these early events on the interviewee's later development.

Main and her colleagues (see Hesse, 1996) hypothesized that the primary task for the interviewee is to resurrect emotionally loaded memories of early childhood experiences while simultaneously presenting them in a coherent fashion to an interviewer. Because the questions deal with very complicated, personal, and often intense issues in a person's early history, they may never have been articulated by the individual prior to this interview experience. The rapidity of questioning, combined with the nature of the items and the interview setting, are thought to elicit material often heretofore unconscious, yet highly descriptive of the adult's state of mind regarding early attachments to primary caregivers.

Interviews are scored according to Grice's (1975) criteria for coherent discourse: truthfulness as supported by evidence, succinctness, relevance to the topic, clarity, and organization of responses. Additional scoring criteria include the coder's assessment of the interviewee's early attachment quality as well as an assessment of the language used in the interview (e.g., angry, passive, derogating). Four qualitatively different classifications, or attachment styles, are then assigned to adults based upon their verbatim transcripts. These are *secure* or *insecure* (which includes 3 subcategories: *dismissing, preoccupied,* and *unresolved*) categories. Different classifications of insecurity are thought to reflect the different strategies and rules of information processing that the person has developed to manage the anxiety of early relationship failure, loss, or trauma. Let us examine each of these categories in turn (see Cassidy and Shaver, 1999, for more detail).

Autonomous (secure) adults provide a transcript that is coherent and collaborative. They answer questions with enough detail to provide sufficient evidence without giving excessive information. For example, incidents of caregiver insensitivity are described matter-of-factly, without embellishment or defensiveness. Secure adults also demonstrate the ability to integrate and monitor their thinking, summarize answers, and return the conversation to the interviewer. They seem to be less egocentric in their presentation than insecure individuals, and they demonstrate good perspective-taking skills. Secure individuals acknowledge the importance of attachment-related experiences in their development. Their memories of the parenting they received match up with the specific instances they present to the interviewer as illustrations.

Can adults be classified as secure if they have had less than favorable experiences as a child? Some individuals do come from circumstances of early adversity but describe their painful backgrounds truthfully and believably, while acknowledging the stressors their own parents faced. This ability to reflect on a difficult past realistically, yet with a certain level of generosity toward parents, results in a special classification called ***earned secure.*** Such adults appear to have come to terms with less than optimal early experiences, quite possibly with the help of a secure spouse or partner. Individuals in both secure categories typically have children who are securely attached to them (see Chapter 4 for a detailed discussion of children's attachment categories).

Dismissing (insecure) individuals provide transcripts that are characterized by markedly low levels of detail and coherence. They are likely to describe parents as very positive or idealized; however, they do not support their evaluations with any specific evidence. Whatever details they do offer may contradict their generally favorable presentation of parental behavior. Dismissive respondents tend to minimize or avoid discussion of attachment-related issues and downplay the importance of close relationships. When discussing nonemotional topics, dismissing individuals generate coherent and comprehensive records and can talk at some length. Responses to attachment themes, in contrast, lack elaboration. Failure to remember is often cited as a reason for the impoverished answers. Adults classified as dismissive tend to have children who are in the avoidant attachment category.

The dismissive style has been linked to early experiences of rejection or other trauma and the development of repressive personality styles. Do these individuals simply hide their distress, or have they managed to actually suppress their attachment needs? Some evidence using an information-processing approach indicates that these individuals, over time, function with the goal of avoiding emotional thoughts and other reminders of unpleasant emotional experiences, such as parental unavailability (Fraley, Davis, & Shaver, 1998). This motivated avoidance may lead to less cognitive elaboration of attachment themes and reduction of behaviors that would encourage intimacy, such as sharing intimate conversation, mutual gazing, cuddling, and so on.

However, it is unlikely that the system has been deactivated completely. Dozier and Kobak (1992) provide interesting evidence that dismissive individuals do react strongly to emotional issues. These researchers interviewed college students using the AAI while measuring their rates of skin conductance. Dismissive subjects, while outwardly appearing unfazed during questioning, had significantly elevated levels of skin conductance, as compared to baseline levels, when asked questions about the emotional availability of their parents and the effects of early attachments on their self-development. This physiological phenomenon suggests that participants were effortfully engaged in diversionary tactics (either idealizing parents or restricting memory) in order to deal with the anxiety generated by the topics. Thus, the early attachment system may never be fully deactivated, but rather just kept at bay. The attachment system responds to emotionally provocative issues when they cannot be avoided.

Individuals in a third group, classified as **preoccupied** (insecure), typically violate the rule of collaboration on the AAI interview. These individuals provide very long, incoherent, egocentric responses that shift from topic to topic. They perform in ways that suggest they are overwhelmed by the emotional memories elicited by the interview questions and are sidetracked from the task of responding succinctly. Such speakers often sound angry, sad, or fearful, as if they have never resolved the painful problems of their childhood. Parents may be remembered as intrusive or egocentric. Their transcripts paint a picture of substantial enmeshment or preoccupation with parents, registered by angry, accusatory language or by conflicted descriptions that connote ambivalence and confusion about early relationships. Linguistic features of their transcripts include run-on sentences, idiosyncratic uses of words, and juxtaposition of past and present tense, as though early problems continue to persist in the present. The children of preoccupied adults often have anxious-ambivalent attachments.

Individuals in the fourth category, called **unresolved** (insecure), produce transcripts characterized by marked lapses in logical thinking, particularly when these individuals discuss loss or other traumatic memories. One example of a lapse in reasoning might be an interviewee's mention of a deceased parent as still living. Hesse and Main (1999) have suggested that these abrupt shifts may be related to temporary changes in consciousness, possibly due to the arousal of unintegrated fear. Individuals in this category may also receive a secondary classification of dismissive or preoccupied. The children of unresolved individuals show a higher frequency of disorganized attachment patterns than other children.

A fifth category, **cannot classify,** is used when protocols do not meet the criteria for other categories. Only a very small number of cases fall into this classification. Data on AAI classifications and psychopathology demonstrate that psychiatric disorders are clearly associated with insecure status and that, in particular, unresolved status is the clearest predictor of emotional disturbance (Dozier, Stovall, et al., 1999).

A number of longitudinal studies have now provided evidence that an infant's attachment behavior, as measured by the strange situation test, reliably predicts the same individual's secure or insecure responses on the AAI in adolescence or adulthood (Beckwith, Cohen, & Hamilton, 1999; C. E. Hamilton, 2000; Waters, Merrick, Treboux, Crowell, & Albersheim, 2000). As we saw in Chapter 4, however, a child's attachment status can become either more or less secure if he has either positive or negative experiences with close relationships after the infant-toddler period. Longitudinal studies in which participants have reached adolescence or young adulthood are finding that people can either "earn" security, as we have already noted, by experiencing later supportive relationships or can develop insecure representations of attachment if they experience negative life events after early childhood. Adults who were secure as children can later demonstrate insecure states of mind because of intervening, highly stressful events such as parental loss, divorce, abuse, illness, or psychiatric disorder. Such findings suggest that deviations from the predicted pathway are most likely explained by lawful rather than random discontinuity (Weinfield, Sroufe, & Egeland, 2000).

In Search of the Working Model

Perhaps you are wondering if the attachment representation categories that are derived from adults' AAI performances could simply be measures of general linguistic style. If so, then interviews would have no particular relevance to attachment, and their predictive value for children's attachment characteristics might be coincidental. Crowell et al. (1996) investigated whether the different linguistic features used to make AAI classifications characterize individuals on other measures of discourse. Using the Employment Experience Interview, he examined a group of adults who had been assigned AAI classifications. The Employment Experience Interview had the same structure as the AAI and was coded using the same criteria. Note that the only difference between the two was in the nature of the questions: about job skills or early attachment relationships. Results showed differences among the transcripts (e.g., vague vs. clear discourse). However, the interesting finding was that respondents' classifications were different on each measure. In other words, an adult who might be judged "secure" on the employment interview could be "insecure" on the AAI. The researchers concluded that there is something unique about the attachment questions. They appear to provide a window into a person's state of mind concerning interpersonal representations.

The power of attachment theory rests upon the concept of the inner working model. The AAI was designed to tap an adult's representation of attachments to primary caregivers. The assumption is that the individual's narrative reflects partly unconscious representations. Results are not considered to be a direct measure of an individual's attachment to any one person, but rather are an indicator of the individual's *state of mind* regarding attachment-related issues. Like an algorithm for our close interpersonal associations, the working model/state of mind is thought to provide rules for processing information about relationships and for behaving in relationships.

Researchers agree that the working model of relationships that one has as an adult cannot simply be a carbon copy of the one that was formed with the primary caregiver in infancy. It is a cognitive structure or schema that must evolve with time and experience, becoming more elaborate, incorporating new elements into the original version in dynamic, qualitatively transformed ways. Like all cognitive schemas, our working models of relationships help us to understand, predict, and act on information that is only fragmentary (Kempson, 1988). The obvious advantage is that they allow us to process information and to respond quickly. The downside is that we may fail to accommodate real differences in present relationships, and we may behave in these relationships in ways that are adapted to quite different circumstances.

For example, consider Sheila, whose mother was depressed and dependent. As a youngster, Sheila felt that her mother's needs always came before her own. Because even the simplest task was a chore for her mother, Sheila began taking on the care of the household and her younger siblings in order to spare her mother. Sheila grew increasingly competent as a caretaker, which, in turn, caused her mother to depend upon her even more. As a young adult, Sheila has difficulty getting close to people. She bristles when any friend or romantic partner, in an attempt to get close to her emotionally, talks about a personal problem. She quickly changes the subject of conversation. Sheila's relationships in adulthood appear to be affected by the legacy of her earlier attachments. She exaggerates other people's reliance on her and fears she will be overcome by their needs, despite any real evidence for this.

Since this is a relatively new area of research, several important questions are yet unanswered. In particular, no one fully understands how the working model of infant-caregiver attachment gets transformed into a working model of attachments in adulthood. Main (1999) suggests that the multiple attachments formed in childhood coalesce into a "classifiable state of mind with respect to attachment in adulthood and that whatever this particular state of mind, it is predictive of a concordant and 'classifiable' form of caregiving" (p. 863). In this description, Main uses the term "state of mind with regard to attachment" instead of "working model," because she wants to avoid the oversimplified assumption that adult states of mind are always derivative of early experiences with parents in straightforward, linear ways. Main notes that insecure children often have multiple, contradictory models of attachment that are harder to integrate than those of secure children, who tend to have more unified models.

As we have seen, adults' attachment representations predict the quality of their attachments to their children (see Chapter 4). This link suggests that attachment representation is a determinant of parental caregiving behavior. Does attachment representation also affect the way that adults interact with other adults? If the working model, in fact, functions like an algorithm for close relationships, individual differences in attachment representations should also affect adults' ability to relate to others in romantic and friendship relationships. This is the subject of our next section.

The Peer/Romantic Relationship Tradition

Any reader of romance novels can testify that the topic of adult love relationships has considerable appeal. In the research community as well, quite a bit of time and energy has been devoted to understanding the formation and development of adult pair-bonds. Researchers have examined specific issues such as mate selection, relationship satisfaction, conflict resolution, relationship dissolution, and so on and have produced a wealth of findings in each of these areas. Studies have also been done that show consistent individual differences in adults' approaches to romantic relationships, sometimes called "love styles" (Lee, 1973). Similarly, there are theories about the elements of love, such as Sternberg's (1986) *passion, intimacy,* and *commitment,* and the ways they function in relationship formation. *Passion* refers to erotic attraction or feelings of being in love. *Intimacy* includes elements of love that promote connection and closeness, while *commitment* refers to making a decision to sustain a relationship with a loved one. We will discuss these elements further in the next chapter.

An early investigation by Shaver and Hazan (1988) contributed significantly to the growing body of knowledge on adult relationships by anchoring the fledgling field within the conceptual framework of attachment theory. These researchers tried to integrate the disparate threads of data into a comprehensive theory of relationships. Today, research conceptualizing adult pair-bonds as attachments represents the second influential offshoot of attachment theory.

Features of Adult Pair-Bonds

Do adult pair-bonds qualify as bona fide attachment relationships? Although there are some dissenting opinions (e.g., McAdams, 2000), many researchers answer yes (see Hazan and Zeifman, 1999). Consider Bowlby's definition of a behavioral system as a set of behaviors that serve the same function or goal. Human beings are equipped with multiple behavioral systems, meeting multiple goals, which interact in coordinated ways. In early childhood, attachment behavior, which includes proximity maintenance, separation distress, and treatment of the caregiver as both a safe haven and a secure base, is the most important behavioral system, because it serves the ultimate goal of survival. When security is felt, other behavioral systems, such as exploration, can be activated. When security is threatened, the attachment system is triggered, and proximity-seeking behaviors increase.

In adulthood, as in childhood, particular behavioral systems are organized to meet specific needs. Attachment (based on the need for felt security) is just one of the adult behavioral systems serving psychosocial needs, which also include caregiving, sexual mating, and exploration. Because of their structure and function, pair-bonds in adults provide an effective way to integrate three of the basic systems: caregiving, attachment (felt security), and sexual mating (Shaver, Hazan, & Bradshaw, 1988). The support provided by the secure base of an attachment relationship also enhances exploration in adults, just as it does in children. Hazan and Zeifman (1999) conclude that adult attachments generally enhance reproductive success (or promotion of the species) as well as provide for the psychological and physical well-being of partners.

Infant-caregiver bonds and adult pair-bonds are notably similar in the kinds of physical contact they involve, such as mutual gazing, kissing, cuddling, and so on, and in the

Adult pair-bonds meet multiple needs, such as attachment needs (especially the need for security), the need for caregiving or nurture, and sexual needs.

goals they serve (support, emotional closeness, etc.). Adult attachments, however, do differ from childhood attachments in the following three ways. First, the attachments adults have with adults are structured more symmetrically than are parent-child bonds. Both partners mutually provide and receive caregiving, whereas the parent is the unilateral source of caregiving for the child. Second, adults rely more than children do on "felt security" rather than on the actual physical presence of the attachment figure (Sroufe & Waters, 1977). Longer periods of separation can be tolerated by adolescents and adults because they understand that attachment figures will be dependable and available when they need contact. Third, adult attachments typically involve a sexual partner or peer rather than a parent figure.

The Process of Relationship Formation in Adulthood

How does the attachment system of early childhood become transformed into the attachments of adulthood? Hazan and Zeifman (1999) chart the progress of attachments by tracing the behaviors that serve the goals of the system. In infancy, as we have stated, all four functions of the attachment system (proximity maintenance, separation distress, secure base, safe haven) depend upon the presence of an attachment figure, and infant behavior toward the caregiver clearly is adapted to meet these goals. As children get older, behaviors toward peers appear to serve some attachment functions as well. For example, children transfer some proximity-seeking behaviors to peers by early childhood. Children begin to spend more time with age-mates and seek them out as preferred playmates (Gottman, 1983). By early adolescence, needs for intimacy and support are often met within the peer group (e.g., Steinberg & Silverberg, 1986), suggesting that needs for a safe haven in times of distress are directed to peers as well as parents (see Chapter 10). By late adolescence and early adulthood, romantic partners may satisfy all the needs of the attachment system.

In order to provide support for this theory, Hazan and Zeifman (1999) asked children and adolescents from 6 to 17 years old a number of questions that tapped attachment needs. Researchers asked the participants whom they preferred to spend time with (proximity maintenance), whom they turned to if they were feeling bad (safe haven), whom they disliked being separated from (separation distress), and whom they could always count on when they needed help (secure base). Results of this study supported shifts away from parents to peers, apparently preparing the way for adult attachment behaviors. The great majority of respondents sought proximity to peers instead of parents at all ages. Between the ages of 8 and 14, participants' responses indicated a shift toward use of peers for safe haven as well. Most children and adolescents identified parents as their secure base and the source of their separation distress. However, among those older participants who had established romantic relationships, all four attachment needs were met in the context of their pair-bonds. See Figure 12.1 for a model of the attachment transfer process across age.

Individual Differences in Adult Attachments

The preceding discussion describes what might be considered normative processes involved in the development of adult attachments. Remember, however, that individuals differ in their states of mind regarding attachment experiences. Do these different "states of mind" predict different approaches to peer or romantic relationships in adulthood? To shed light on this question, we must recall that each tradition of attachment research has its own way of looking at these issues. Even though researchers start from the same premise, namely that adults' attachment styles will resemble Ainsworth's infant attachment typology, the typical measures used are different from those of the nuclear family tradition. Adult romantic relationship research began with self-report or questionnaire measures that were presumed to tap conscious, rather than unconscious, expectations

FIGURE 12.1

Attachment and Close Relationships

DEVELOPMENTAL PHASE	TARGET OF ATTACHMENT BEHAVIORS	
	Parents	**Peers**
Infancy	proximity maintenance safe haven secure base	
Early Childhood	safe haven secure base	proximity maintenance
Late Childhood/ Early Adolescence	secure base	proximity maintenance safe haven
Adulthood		proximity maintenance safe haven secure base

A model of attachment transfer processes. Attachment behaviors gradually shift from parents to peers.

Source: Hazan, C. & Shaver, R. (1994). Attachment as an organizational framework for research on close relationships. *Psychological Inquiry, 5*, pp. 1–22. Reprinted by permission of Lawrence Earlbaum Associates.

about relationships. The sheer volume of work done in the area of measurement prevents a comprehensive discussion of this topic in this chapter. However, we will present an introduction to certain key issues and describe some important instruments. The interested reader is referred to Simpson and Rholes (1998b) for a more thorough presentation.

The first influential measure of adult romantic attachment, developed by Hazan and Shaver (1987), asked adults to identify which of three statements (see Table 12.1) best

TABLE 12.1

Three Attachment Prototypes

Avoidant. I am somewhat uncomfortable being close to others; I find it difficult to trust them completely, difficult to allow myself to depend on them. I am nervous when anyone gets too close, and often, love partners want me to be more intimate than I feel comfortable being.

Anxious–ambivalent. I find that others are reluctant to get as close as I would like. I often worry that my partner doesn't really love me or won't want to stay with me. I want to get very close to my partner, and this sometimes scares people away.

Secure. I find it relatively easy to get close to others and am comfortable depending on them. I don't often worry about being abandoned or about someone getting too close to me.

Source: Hazan, C. & Shaver, P. R. (1987). Romantic love conceptualized as an attachment process. *Journal of Personality and Social Psychology, 52*, 515. Copyright © 1987 by the American Psychological Association. Reprinted with permission.

captured their approach to and beliefs about romantic relationships. Descriptive statements represented avoidant, ambivalent, and secure classifications. As measurement was refined and attempts to integrate the fields of nuclear family and adult peer attachments increased, researchers recognized that the category called "avoidant" from Hazan and Shaver's instrument did not correspond to the "dismissing" category of the AAI. The avoidant person clearly acknowledged anxiety about getting too close to another, while the dismissive individual reported no subjective distress.

Faced with the needs to include both aspects of avoidance, Bartholomew (1990) proposed a new conceptual framework consisting of four categories across two dimensions. Figure 12.2 illustrates her typology. She and her colleagues (Bartholomew and Horowitz, 1991) operationalized Bowlby's (1973) view that working models of the self and of others are interrelated. People are thought to develop expectations about how reliably their significant others will behave in close relationships, as well as expectations about how worthy or unworthy they are of care and support. Four categories of attachment orientation are defined by crossing the working model of self with the working model of others.

In Bartholomew's typology, *secure* individuals have internalized a positive sense of themselves along with positive models of others. In general, they expect others to be available and supportive of their needs in close relationships. They are comfortable with emotional closeness but are also reasonably autonomous. Individuals classified as *preoccupied* hold positive models of others but negative models of themselves. Others are viewed as not valuing the preoccupied person as much as he values them. Preoccupied attachment is marked by emotional demandingness, anxiety about gaining acceptance from others, fear of and hypervigilance to cues of rejection, and excessive preoccupation with relationships.

The *avoidant* category is subdivided into two, based on reports of felt distress. *Dismissing* individuals are characterized by a positive model of the self but a negative

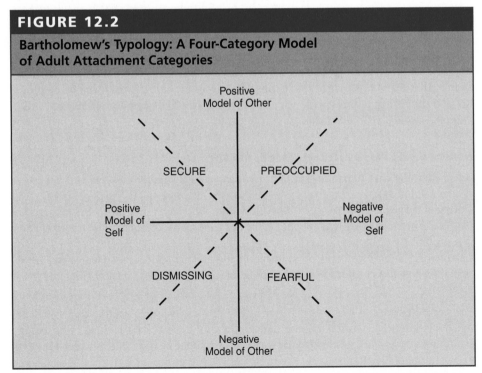

FIGURE 12.2

Bartholomew's Typology: A Four-Category Model of Adult Attachment Categories

Source: Bartholomew, K., & Shaver, P. (1998). Methods of assessing adult attachment: Do they converge? In J. A. Simpson & W. S. Rholes (Eds.), *Attachment theory and close relationships* (pp. 25–45). New York: Guilford Press.

model of the other. Denying the need for close relationships permits these adults to maintain a sense of superiority while devaluing the importance of others to their well-being. Self-sufficiency is preferred, and anxiety about attachment relationships is inhibited. A *fearful* attachment is the product of negative models of both self *and* others. For individuals with this style, attachments are desirable but seen as out of reach. Their desire for close relationships with others is thwarted by fear of rejection, and ultimately they withdraw. A high level of distress surrounds attachment themes.

Several researchers have pointed out that use of categories such as the ones we have just described is intuitively understandable and attractive but poses a number of problems. There is a danger of failing to recognize that individual differences often exist on a continuum, reflecting the *degree* to which a certain tendency is exhibited (e.g., high to low levels of anxiety), as opposed to differences in *kind* (highly anxious vs. not anxious). Therefore, measurements that place people in quadrants will undoubtedly mask the continuity that actually exists along the underlying dimensions. Fraley and Waller (1998) also caution that this kind of categorization actually underestimates the real continuity of attachment patterns from childhood to adulthood and diminishes the strength of associations between attachment research from the parental and romantic traditions. They suggest that attachment status should not be construed as a typology with three or four classifications just because it is convenient. Brennan and colleagues (Brennan, Clark, & Shaver, 1998) expand on these points by demonstrating that most attachment scales are really measuring two continuous dimensions: avoidance and anxiety. The benefit of this dimensional perspective may be that it allows clinicians to think of individuals as operating within a range of possible behaviors. Specific attachment patterns should be viewed as tendencies to perceive and act in certain ways but not as guarantees that individuals will always operate according to type. So clinicians should avoid "typecasting" clients on the basis of attachment categories that are fixed and orthogonal, a practice that can distort clinical judgment by acting as a cognitive bias or stereotype. It may be more helpful to keep in mind that the most basic issues involved in relationships concern a person's level of anxiety about social interaction and his level of approach or avoidance. The prototypical classifications may best represent individuals with very pronounced characteristics at the extremes of the anxiety/avoidance dimensions. It is probably more accurate to think of people having particular attachment styles rather than classifications, which is a less forgiving term. It may also be helpful to keep in mind that there is wide variability in behavioral expression of anxiety and of approach-avoidance in relationships.

Research on Young Adult Dyadic Relationships

Research in the peer/romantic tradition has uncovered a number of interesting aspects of dyadic relationship patterns that are related to attachment style. The focus of most of this work has been the exploration of how individual differences in attachment orientations play out in areas of social interaction. Let us take a brief look at some of the results of these investigations in areas of concern to young adults: partner selection, satisfaction with and stability of relationships, and communication and conflict resolution styles. When appropriate, we will also consider how gender differences mediate these relationships.

Partner Selection.   Attachment theory offers an intuitively reasonable framework for understanding why partners choose one another. First, secure individuals, who neither avoid intimacy nor are desperately in search of it, should be more likely to seek out balanced partners like themselves. Research indicates that secure individuals tend to be paired more often with other secure rather than insecure partners (Senchak & Leonard, 1992).

Mate selection may be influenced by one's adult attachment status: secure individuals are likely to be paired with other secure individuals.

Insecure individuals, according to attachment theory, should also be likely to select partners who confirm their expectations or working models of close relationships. Avoidant partners, who are fearful or dismissing of intimacy, expect partners to cling and overwhelm them with their demandingness. Anxious partners, who crave closeness, may expect rejection and believe that their needs for intimacy will go unmet. Thus, a certain synergy might propel an avoidant individual to pair with an anxious one, fulfilling expectations of both partners.

Several studies have documented the fact that avoidant-avoidant and anxious-anxious pairings are rare. In Kirkpatrick and Davis's (1994) study of 354 heterosexual couples, not a single couple showed either of the above patterns. From the perspective of attachment theory, such symmetrical matches would not make sense because they do not fit the expectations predicted from working models. What is far more likely is the complementary pairing of avoidant with anxious mates, and several studies have found a preponderance of anxious-ambivalent matches among insecure individuals (Collins & Read, 1990; Kirkpatrick and Davis, 1994; Pietromonaco & Carnelley, 1994; Simpson, 1990).

At this point, although the findings match the predictions of attachment theory, it is unclear whether romantic partners actually enter relationships with these complementary attachment styles or whether something in the nature of the relationship alters the attachment style. Although distribution of attachment classification is independent of gender, gender-related stereotypes might be one possible contributor to changes in relationship quality over time. It may be, for example, that once a relationship is established, traditional masculine stereotypes encouraging emotional distance or traditional feminine ones encouraging preoccupation exacerbate preexisting patterns.

Satisfaction and Stability of Relationships. Does attachment style relate to the level of satisfaction people get from their close relationships? That was the question Simpson (1990) addressed in a study of 144 dating couples. Participants' levels of trust, commitment, interdependence, and emotional expression were examined as a function of their attachment style. Attachment was measured using a 13-item scale developed by Hazan and Shaver (1987). Six months after the initial data collection, Simpson contacted each of the couples to inquire about the status of their relationship.

Results showed that different relationship experiences were associated with three attachment patterns. Secure individuals experienced more positive and less negative emotion in relationships than those who were insecure. They also reported more trust, commitment, and interdependence, as attachment theory would predict. Highly avoidant individuals were less interdependent and less committed to their partners than secure individuals; highly anxious people were more likely to report that their relationships lacked trust. In one interesting gender difference, Simpson found that avoidant males experienced the lowest levels of distress when their relationships ended, but no differences in breakup distress were found for categories of women. Perhaps this is due to the commonly held perception that women are primarily responsible for maintenance of personal relationships and are held accountable for their success. Evidence from this study and others (Collins and Read, 1990) also indicates that the attachment status of one partner influences the relationship satisfaction of the other. Both male and female partners reported being less satisfied in relationships when males were avoidant and when females were preoccupied or anxious.

Kirkpatrick and Davis (1994) also studied relationship satisfaction and stability over a three-year period. Security of partners in this study was associated with greater satisfaction with the relationship. As we have seen, the lowest level of satisfaction was reported by couples composed of avoidant men and anxious women. Interestingly, however, when these researchers measured stability at the three-year follow-up, avoidant-anxious matches were *as stable* as the more satisfied secure couples. Couples made up of anxious men and avoidant women were more likely than others to break up over the course of the study. Once again, the authors speculated that this result had something to do with women being the stereotypical tenders of relationships. Avoidant women may be less skilled at accommodating, or less motivated to accommodate, the needs of the more dependent partner. Anxious women, overly concerned with possibilities of abandonment, might be more willing to do what it takes to maintain a relationship with an avoidant partner, hence accounting for the high level of stability in these relationships.

Communication Style and Conflict Resolution. Consider for a moment a problem that you experienced at some time in one of your close relationships. Now reflect on how you dealt with that problem. Was your response typical of the way you usually deal with relationship problems? You undoubtedly know, by virtue of your training, that when faced with a relationship's inevitable glitches, it is a good idea to be open, nondefensive, reasonably assertive, and yet flexible enough to compromise. Keeping a clear head so that problem solving can be effective is another requirement. Easier said than done, you're probably thinking! Why is it often so hard to do this well?

One reason is that conflict and communication in close relationships frequently have one or more subtexts: love, loss, trust, and abandonment, to name a few. In short, conflicts are stressful, they elicit emotions, and, perhaps, they can trigger the patterns of stress management learned in the earliest of attachment relationships. Many studies have documented the advantages of attachment security for interpersonal communication (Keelan, Dion, & Dion, 1998; Mikulincer & Arad, 1999). Secure individuals display more reciprocity and flexibility in communication. Greater self-disclosure characterizes the communication of secure and anxious groups as compared to avoidant ones. Several studies also document the advantages of having a secure orientation when it comes to solving problems (Pistole, 1989). In general, secure individuals are more apt to compromise in ways that are mutually beneficial. Avoidant individuals tend to be more uncompromising, whereas anxious individuals tend to give in.

What actually happens when a couple has to deal with conflict in the relationship? According to attachment theory, the conflict produces stress, which activates the attachment system, makes the working models more accessible, and influences how affect gets regulated. Simpson, Rholes, and Phillips (1996) asked 123 heterosexual couples, who had been dating from six months to two years, to discuss problems in their relationships. Participants were videotaped, and their interactions were rated by observers. Secure individuals were less defensive than insecure ones and held the most favorable views of their partners after discussing a major problem. Avoidant participants kept the greatest emotional distance in the discussion. Presumably uncomfortable with the expression of emotion, they appeared to minimize personal involvement. By the same token, they did not display evidence of anger, distress, or less positive views of their partners. Avoidant men provided less warmth and supportiveness to their partners, consistent with theoretical predictions. In contrast, avoidant women did not display this pattern in this study. The strength of society's mandate that women be relationship caretakers might, in certain circumstances, override avoidant dispositions. But this is not the case in every close relationship. In at least one other study, both men and women with avoidant styles were less likely to give emotional support to close friends (Phillips, Simpson, Lanigan, & Rholes, 1995).

Ambivalent partners in the study by Simpson and colleagues (1996) reacted with the most negative emotion to the discussion of problems, displaying high levels of stress and anxiety during the interaction. They also reported feeling more hostility and anger toward their partners after the session. Ambivalent couples report more disruptions and more shifts in satisfaction in general when compared to other types (Tidwell, Reis, & Shaver, 1996). Consistent with attachment theory, these individuals expect their partners to fail at meeting their needs in stressful situations. Rholes and his colleagues (Rholes, Simpson, & Stevens, 1998) explain the phenomenon in this way:

> Conflict elicits a cascade of unpleasant feelings in ambivalent persons, and it should raise doubts about the quality and viability of their current partner and relationship. Moreover, if fears of abandonment become salient, ambivalent partners ought to derogate the partner and relationship to minimize or "prepare for" potential loss. Persons who are not ambivalent, in contrast, may not experience conflict as aversive, but as an occasion in which open communication and the joint, constructive sharing of feelings can occur. (pp. 181–182)

In general, attachment theory serves as a useful template for conceptualizing the universal human needs served by close, interpersonal relationships as well as the systematic differences individuals display in their personal associations. Clinicians are already very familiar with the notion that certain qualities of family relationships experienced early in life tend to get repeated in later relationships. While not derivative of attachment theory per se, psychoanalytic and some family therapy approaches such as Bowen's (1978) advise clients to examine the nature of conflicted childhood relationships within one's family of origin in an effort to achieve insight and gain the freedom to make more adaptive relationship choices in the present.

"ARBEITEN"—TO WORK

For most young adults, the launching of a vocational life is as important a developmental task as the process of forming or reforming attachments. What are the key elements in a successful launch? A large body of theory and research has addressed this question. The theories share in common a general notion that career success and satisfaction depend heavily on matching the characteristics of an individual and the demands of a job. If this notion is correct, then self-knowledge is a critical element in career decision making. Thus, not only is establishing an occupational role an important part of identity or self-concept development, it is also an emergent property of that process. The stronger our sense of who we are as we become adults, the more likely we are to make good career choices. Two classic theories of career development will illustrate.

Some Theories of the Career Development Process

Holland's Theory of Personality-Environment Types

Holland (e.g., 1966, 1985) suggests that by early adulthood each individual has a ***modal personal orientation:*** a typical and preferred style or approach to dealing with social and environmental tasks. Holland proposed that most people can be categorized as having one of six modal orientations (described in Table 12.2), which can be seen as part of the individual's personality. According to Holland, a job or career typically makes demands on an individual that are compatible with one or more of these interactive types. That is, a job can be construed as creating an environment within which a certain personal orientation will lead to both success and happiness. For example, one of the personal orientation types is "social." A social type is likely to be sociable, friendly, cooperative, kind, tactful, and understanding and is often a good match to occupations that involve working with others to educate, to cure, or to enlighten them—such as counseling or social work. A contrasting type is the "enterprising" individual. He too is likely to be sociable, but more domineering, energetic, ambitious, talkative, and attention getting. He is also likely to be more effective in vocational tasks that involve maneuvering others to achieve goals, such as reaching a certain level of sales, or more efficiently delivering services as a salesperson, for instance, or an executive. Thus, each type of modal personal orientation, such as "social" or "enterprising," is also a type of vocational environment. Usually, neither individuals nor environments fall neatly into only one "type." Holland and his colleagues have developed coding systems for rating both individuals and environments. In these systems, three-letter codes indicate the most characteristic style for the individual (e.g., Holland, Viernstein, Kuo, Karweit, & Blum, 1970) or the environment (e.g., Gottfredson, Holland, & Ogawa, 1982), as well as the second and third most characteristic styles. So, for example, a person (or environment) might be coded "RIS," meaning primarily "realistic (R)," secondarily "investigative (I)," and finally "social (S)." (See Table 12.2 for some characteristics of these types for individuals.)

A number of studies have corroborated the notion that a good fit between modal orientation (also called personal style) and job characteristics is correlated with job satisfaction, performance, and stability, as well as feelings of personal well-being (see Spokane, 1985, for a review). For example, Gottfredson and Holland (1990) studied young adult bank tellers for four months after they were first hired. Congruence between an individual's personal style and job type was clearly correlated with job satisfaction. In two studies of school teachers, Meir (1989) examined several kinds of congruence or fit: between personal style and job type, between personal style and outside activities (avocations), and between the individual's particular skills and opportunities to use those skills on the job. All three kinds of congruence appeared to contribute to the participants' reported feelings of well being. A person's happiness seems to be closely linked to the fit between his personality characteristics and both his work, as Holland predicted, and his leisure pursuits. It appears that creating a good match in one arena can help to compensate for a lack of congruence in another (see also Tinsley, Hinson, Tinsley, & Holt, 1993).

TABLE 12.2

Some Characteristics of Holland's Personality Types

Realistic	Investigative	Artistic
Conforming	Analytical	Complicated
Dogmatic	Cautious	Disorderly
Genuine	Complex	Emotional
Hardheaded	Critical	Expressive
Inflexible	Curious	Idealistic
Materialistic	Independent	Imaginative
Natural	Intellectual	Impractical
Normal	Introverted	Impulsive
Persistent	Pessimistic	Independent
Practical	Precise	Introspective
Realistic	Radical	Intuitive
Reserved	Rational	Nonconforming
Robust	Reserved	Open
Self-effacing	Retiring	Original
Uninsightful	Unassuming	Sensitive

Social	Enterprising	Conventional
Agreeable	Acquisitive	Careful
Cooperative	Adventurous	Conforming
Empathic	Ambitious	Conscientious
Friendly	Assertive	Dogmatic
Generous	Domineering	Efficient
Helpful	Energetic	Inflexible
Idealistic	Enthusiastic	Inhibited
Kind	Excitement seeking	Methodical
Patient	Exhibitionistic	Obedient
Persuasive	Extroverted	Orderly
Responsible	Forceful	Persistent
Sociable	Optimistic	Practical
Tactful	Resourceful	Thorough
Understanding	Self-confident	Thrifty
Warm	Sociable	Unimaginative

Is this a boring job or just a bad match? Classic career development theories emphasize the importance of fitting personal characteristics to the demands of the job. Self-knowledge is seen as critical to making the right career choices.

Super's Developmental Approach

Super (e.g., 1972, 1984, 1990) agrees with Holland's notion that a satisfying work life is most likely when an individual's personal characteristics are well matched to the demands of a job. His theorizing about career development, however, focuses less on specifying personal style or job types and more on describing the developmental processes that determine both the emergence of one's *vocational self-concept* and the multiple factors that influence job choices through the life span. Vocational self-concept is part of one's total identity. It includes ideas about which qualities of the self would (or would not) provide a match to the requirements of an occupation (Super, 1984). Vocational self-concept is a function of two things: first, a person's view of his personal or psychological characteristics, and second, how he assesses his life circumstances, such as the limits or opportunities created by economic conditions; by his socioeconomic status; by his family, friendship network, and community; and so on.

Super described a series of typical life stages in the development of vocational self-concept and experience, beginning in childhood. In the *growth stage* (up to age 14 or so), children are developing many elements of identity that will have a bearing on vocational self-concept, including ideas about their interests, attitudes, skills, and needs. In the *exploratory stage,* which includes adolescence and young adulthood up to about age 24, vocational self-concept is tentatively narrowed down, but often career choices are not finalized. General vocational goals are formulated in the earlier part of this stage (*crystallization*), gradually leading to the identification of more specific vocational preferences (*specification*) and finally to the completion of education along with entry into full-time employment (*implementation*). In the *establishment stage,* from about 25 to 44, work experiences provide the laboratory within which the matching of vocational self-concept and job settings is tried out, sometimes reevaluated, sometimes confirmed, and eventually stabilized (*stabilization*). From about 45 to 64, in the *maintenance stage,* an individual makes ongoing adjustments to improve his work situation, often achieving more advanced status and seniority (***consolidation***). If not, this can also be a time of increasing frustration with work. Finally, in the ***decline stage,*** right before and after 65 for most people, the career winds down, with retirement planning and actual retirement taking precedence over career advancement and consolidation. Note that while these are typical life stages, at least partially verified by longitudinal research (e.g., Super & Overstreet, 1960), an individual can go through additional sequences of crystallization, specification, implementation, and stabilization when life circumstances change. These "mini-cycles" of reevaluation can be initiated by any number of events: disappointment with a career choice, job loss, changes in family life, and so on. Note the similarity to MAMA cycles in identity development described in Chapter 9.

Perhaps Super's most important insight is his recognition that career development is a continuing process. It serves as both a source of and an outgrowth of an individual's overall personal growth. For Super, a career is

> the life course of a person encountering a series of developmental tasks and attempting to handle them in such a way as to become the kind of person he or she wants to become. With a changing self and changing situations, the matching process is never really completed. (1990, pp. 225–226)

Research indicates that many aspects of a job beyond compatibility with one's interests and talents influence how rewarding it is. Quality of supervision, participation in decision making, interaction with others on the job, geographic location, personal health, pay, and a number of other factors are also correlated with job satisfaction (e.g., Decker & Borgen, 1993; Herr & Cramer, 1992; Perry-Jenkins et al., 2000). However, theories and research such as Holland's and Super's make the powerful suggestion that even when all these other factors are acceptable, a person's work responsibilities can be incompatible with his or her personality characteristics. Under these circumstances, although a hard-working individual could succeed in meeting his responsibilities, real satisfaction and the opportunity to truly excel are likely to elude him. We will have more to say about personality characteristics in Chapter 13.

The interdependence of career and self-development is an important focus of some current career counseling approaches. McAuliffe (1993), for example, describes a developmentally oriented career counseling system that has an Eriksonian flavor. He argues that a central role of the counselor is to help clients address the following key question: "Who am I becoming and how shall I express this emerging self?" He points out that many clients may begin counseling with a different, but less helpful, way of conceptualizing their career issues. Some, for example, may be asking themselves, "What does my community, my family, my ethnic or religious group expect of me?" That is, they frame the issue such that their career, and their self-definition, is embedded in interpersonal relationships, not authored from within. Perhaps for this group, career identity represents a closed, rather than a constructed, facet of their identity (see Chapter 9). Other clients, especially those facing some career threat, such as downsizing, may begin with the question, "How do I maintain the current form I am in?" With this conceptual framework the self is embedded in what the person has always done, so that new career paths, expressing other needs or dimensions of the self, are not imaginable. The task for counselors may be to facilitate the development of a new, personally constructed sense of self as worker.

For many clients, then, career counseling may need to begin with help in reframing the way one construes the self. In McAuliffe's words,

> it is the counselor's challenge to assist clients in their transformations of meaning making. . . . For example, for the young adult college student whose seemingly simple dilemma is to choose between pursuing a parent-approved pre-medical track or to consider the internal voice that draws her to the social sciences, counseling would operate on two levels: one to weigh the pros

and cons of various fields of study and the other to support and challenge the person so that the tacit assumptions about "who's in charge" become conscious, so that the dissonant voice that implicitly calls the person to author his or her own career can be considered. (1993, pp. 25–26)

The Realities of Career Development in Young Adulthood

For young adults launching a work life, many variables influence the speed and form of that process. Consider the prospects of two 18-year-olds, Akil and Jarod, who have just graduated from high school. Akil comes from a middle-class family. His parents take great pride in being the first ones in their own families to have graduated from college and to provide their children with a comfortable middle-class life. They expect their children to attend college and to select careers that will help them maintain or even improve upon their socioeconomic status. They have several children to educate, but they are quite savvy about how to finance a college education, having put themselves through college, and they are convinced that college is a necessity for career success. Akil sees college as a necessary step on his way to a professional career, although his future plans are not specific. He expects his college experience to help him figure out what profession to enter.

The expectations that Jarod and his family have are quite different. Jarod's mother earns low wages working for a janitorial service, and she often puts in overtime to help make ends meet. Neither she nor Jarod's father (from whom she is estranged) completed high school, and both are quite proud that Jarod has. However, they have never even considered the possibility of college for Jarod. As they see it, he has completed his education and should now be able to earn a living. His mother expects him to find his own apartment to relieve the crowding in her small place. Jarod himself is quite unsure of what he can do in the world of work. He is simply hoping to find a job, any job, one that will give him a start, providing an opportunity to learn a skill and to find a niche.

Even if these two young men happen to have similar interests and personalities, their careers are likely to follow very different trajectories, largely because of the differences in their socioeconomic class, their families' views of education, and the opportunities that they perceive to be available to them. In the following sections, we will consider what the typical course of career development is for individuals like Akil and Jarod. We will specifically examine the characteristics of the process when young people move on to college from high school and when they do not. We will also consider the impact of other major factors on one's early career experiences, factors such as immediate environment, social class, race, and gender.

The College Student

Young adults entering college have many hopes and expectations for the college years. Some of their concerns are incidental to the educational setting and are focused on either maintaining or establishing social networks and/or finding intimate relationships—the pursuit of "lieben." But many of their hopes are relevant to "arbeiten," their vocational lives. Some freshmen expect the college years to be a time of self-development, when they will "construct a philosophy of life" and become more clear about the course their adult lives might take. For most, very practical, work-related issues are among their highest priorities. The majority of entering freshmen indicate that "to get a better job" and "to make more money" are important reasons why they chose to go to college. Figure 12.3 also illustrates that more recent cohorts of college students are even more likely to emphasize these kinds of practical career concerns than students did 20 or 30 years ago (American Council on Education, 1999; Astin, 1993; Myers, 2000).

The first vocationally relevant decision that students make is the choice of a major. Those students who are career oriented tend to decide on an occupation first and then

FIGURE 12.3

What College Students Consider Important Reasons for Attending College

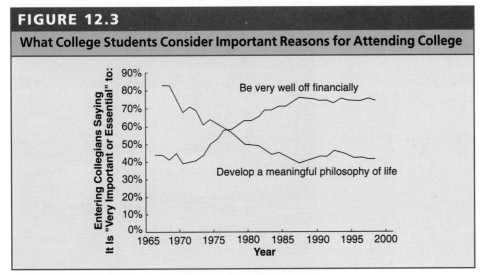

Source: Dey, E. L., Astin, A. W., & Korn, W. S. (1991). *The American freshman: Twenty-five year trends.* Los Angeles: Higher Education Research Institute, University of California. Reprinted by permission.

select a major, whereas students more focused on self-development tend to select a major first and then consider possible occupational choices (Goodson, 1978). A majority of students change their majors at least once during college, although the changes they make are usually among related disciplines (Herr & Cramer, 1992). There are substantial cohort differences regarding which majors and occupations are more popular with students. For example, Astin (1993) compared two large samples of college students who entered college 17 years apart: the first in 1968 and the second in 1985. Members of the 1985 cohort were more likely to want careers in business, law, or medicine and less likely to choose teaching or scientific research than members of the 1968 sample. Surveys of more recent cohorts indicate that the most popular majors today are business, psychology, engineering, education, English literature, and accounting (B. Murray, 1996).

We have seen that theorists such as Holland and Super argue that career choices often are, and should be, based on one's personal characteristics. What other factors, besides self-concept or personal style, might influence the choice of a major in college, and ultimately the choice of a career? First, variations over time in the relative popularity of a major indicate that social and economic changes over time influence choice of major. This might include economic upturns and downturns, change in the kinds of goods and services that are in demand, shifts in population size and composition, advances in technology, and developments in political and legal philosophy, such as in the area of civil rights law.

For example, some of the most interesting changes in majors and occupational choices across recent decades are gender specific and appear to reflect political and social trends in our beliefs about the role of women in society. The Higher Education Research Institute at UCLA reports that the proportion of women currently majoring in traditionally male-dominated fields, such as the biological sciences, the physical sciences, engineering, pre-law, premed, and business, has increased dramatically in just 30 years, as hiring patterns in related fields have become less gender biased than they once were (Dey & Hurtado, 1999).

In addition to the influence of social, civil, and economic change, other more stable factors appear to play a role. As the stories of Akil and Jarod indicate, socioeconomic status (SES) is important in shaping the expectations of young people, heavily influencing the educational choices that they make and the jobs to which they aspire. Research indicates

Reflecting social and political change over recent decades, women often choose occupations traditionally occupied by men.

that other family and environmental factors, such as race and ethnicity, also affect the choice of whether or not to go to college. Individuals from minority and low SES groups are less likely than other groups to make the college choice. If an individual enrolls in college, are a student's career aspirations affected by such variables? Some indicators suggest that the answer is yes. To illustrate, the probability of **retention,** staying in college long enough to graduate, is related to SES (National Center for Education Statistics, 1998). The influence of SES on retention is probably multifaceted. Lower SES students often are not as well prepared academically for the demands of college as higher SES students, although it should be noted that the majority of students who drop out of college are doing adequate work. Lower SES students also have more problems paying for college, and they may experience less support from family and friends to remain in college than higher SES students do (e.g., Ryland, Riordan, & Brack, 1994). Being of minority status is also linked to lower rates of retention. African American students are at particular risk for dropping out, a problem that may be partially a result of the stress of dealing with minority status, such as feeling unwelcome in predominantly white institutions (Newman & Newman, 1999; Sailes, 1993; Zea, Reisen, Beil, Caplan, 1997).

Do factors such as SES affect one's choice of a college major? There is indirect evidence that they can. For example, students attending private universities are more likely to choose premed majors than students attending public four-year colleges, and students at public institutions are more likely to choose school teaching as a career than students at private universities (Astin, 1993). Given that SES has some influence on the choice of private versus public educational facilities, it appears that SES may contribute to these differences.

Other characteristics of the college environment also seem to influence choice of major or career (see Astin, 1993). For example, students are more likely to select college teaching as a career if they attend smaller colleges that provide high levels of student-faculty interaction, opportunities for independent research, and written evaluations of students' work. African American students are more likely to choose premed if they attend a traditionally Black college than if they do not. Membership in a fraternity or sorority is linked to greater tendencies to select business or prelaw as a major. Of course, whether one attends a small college or a Black college, or joins a sorority or fraternity, is probably influenced by preexisting characteristics of the student. For example, extroverts appear to be more attracted to Greek life on campus than introverts (e.g., Sher, Bartholow, & Nanda, 2001). Therefore, it is difficult to say whether such features of college life have a causal influence on students' major or career choices or whether students who favor such environments also tend to prefer certain fields of study. It seems likely that the causal connections work both ways.

One role that the college experience seems to play in choosing a major and ultimately a career is that it provides opportunities to try out different choices with relatively little cost. Some students enter college aspiring to be lawyers or physicians or engineers, for example, only to find that the prelaw, premed, or engineering coursework is not suitable to their interests or abilities. Such majors often lose enrollment as students move through their college years. Other majors tend to draw increasing numbers over the college years. Education and business majors are among these, especially for students who struggle academically and/or have relatively low verbal Scholastic Aptitude Test (SAT) scores. Interestingly, some of the more academically challenging fields also increase their draw somewhat after students get a taste of college, fields like scientific research and college teaching (see Astin, 1993).

Since one's choice of a college major is associated with college success as well as career choice, career counseling in college should begin with advisement on choice of a major. Unfortunately, leaving this task to relatively untrained faculty advisors seems to be insufficient for helping students to make good choices. Herr and Cramer (1992), in their text on career guidance throughout the life span, argue that career guidance professionals at the college level should provide students with assistance in selecting a major. In pursuit of this and other career goals, even freshmen should have help available in self-assessment and self-analysis, as well as in decision making.

It is clear that a college education plays a critical role in occupational opportunity. One's highest educational degree is the single most important predictor of level of job entry, and level of job entry weighs more heavily than IQ or job skill in predicting career advancement. But the value of a college education goes beyond its contribution to career development. For example, being a college graduate means a greater likelihood of being healthy or of having a successful marriage. Some of the effects of higher education are probably due to the income opportunities it creates and so *are* career linked; others may be related to the development of critical thinking skills and flexibility in problem solving that it seems to foster (Pascarella, Bohr, Nora, & Terenzini, 1995; Pascarella & Terenzini, 1991).

"The Forgotten Half"

"The forgotten half" was the name given by the William T. Grant Foundation Commission on Work, Family, and Citizenship (1988) to 18- to 24-year-olds who do not go to college.

These were just under half of the total young adult population in the United States in 1988. They were described as

> the young people who build our homes, drive our buses, repair our automobiles, fix our televisions, maintain and serve our offices, schools and hospitals, and keep the production lines of our mills and factories moving. To a great extent, they determine how well the American family, economy and democracy function. They are also the thousands of young men and women who aspire to work productively but never quite "make it" to that kind of employment. For these members of the Forgotten Half, their lives as adults start in the economic limbo of unemployment, part-time jobs, and poverty wages. Many of them never break free. (1988, as cited in Halperin, 1998a, cover)

Ten years later, The American Youth Policy Forum sponsored a follow-up report on "the forgotten half" (Halperin, 1998a). The good news was that the high school dropout rate had declined since the original report, and the numbers of high school graduates entering 2- or 4-year colleges had increased, so that the proportion of young adults with no post-secondary training had dropped several percentage points. The bad news, however, was that the real income of young adults in the United States had declined, and the most serious losses were experienced by those with the least education. Further, poverty rates had increased for those at every educational level *except* college graduates (see Figure 12.4). "In the 1990's, the wide income gaps correlated with formal educational attainment continued to widen" (Halperin, 1998b, p. 13).

Interestingly, the basic *attitudes* of young adults toward work and family do not differ regardless of whether or not they go to college. Young people usually rank good pay and opportunities for advancement as highly desirable features of a job. They also want their work to make a meaningful contribution to society. As for their social aspirations, young people of all backgrounds generally consider having a good marriage and having children to be important life goals for them (e.g., Hill & Yeung, 1999).

Despite the broad similarities in the goals of college and noncollege youth in the United States, the chances of achieving these goals are substantially reduced for the latter group. As we have already seen, education is a key predictor of employment success, career advancement, and general success in life, so that when a young person chooses to

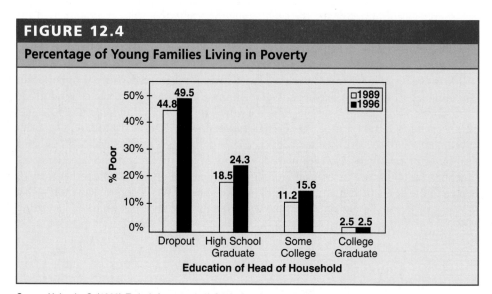

FIGURE 12.4

Percentage of Young Families Living in Poverty

Source: Halperin, S. (1998). Today's forgotten half: Still losing ground. In S. Halperin (Ed.), *The forgotten half revisited: American youth and young families, 1988–2008,* p. 8. Washington, D.C.: American Youth Policy Forum. Reprinted by permission.

end education with high school, he places limits on his options and opportunities. A number of other factors also affect the degree to which a young person's goals are likely to be achieved. These factors include socioeconomic status, as was the case with Jarod. Even when young people fail to attend college, coming from a family of relatively high socioeconomic status provides opportunities and advantages that youth from lower SES families usually do not have. Another important factor is race, which can have profound impact on the probability of employment across all education levels (see Figure 12.5). Finally, a variety of "behavioral obstacles," including having a child early and/or out of wedlock and engaging in criminal behavior, are important determiners of whether or not young adults will make significant strides toward meeting their goals. Among noncollege youth, those most at risk of slipping into poverty, for example, are Blacks with criminal records who come from low-income families (e.g., Halperin, 1998b; Hill & Yeung, 1999). As we have discussed earlier, these outcomes may be the result of histories of accumulating and interlocking risks.

Although many factors can contribute to a slide into poverty, adequate educational preparation is clearly the most effective avenue to *avoiding* poverty and to achieving the typical goals that young people have for work and family. But both the 1988 and 1998 reports on "the forgotten half" argue that the difficulties faced by noncollege youth in America are partly a function of a disorganized and inadequate system for training adolescents and young adults for the kinds of skilled employment that are personally rewarding and that can provide an adequate income to support a family. It is often difficult for young people even to obtain information on *how* to prepare themselves for particular jobs and occupations. Recommendations for improving the lot of noncollege youth begin with ideas for improving basic skill training in public schools, including the teaching of such traditional academic skills as reading, writing, math, and speaking abilities, as well as thinking skills, self-management, and social skills. The particular concern is to improve the quality of secondary education for students who go through general or vocational (non–college preparatory) tracks in high school. These programs are often criticized for having watered down, boring curricula (Bailey & Morest, 1998).

Next, reports on "the forgotten half" encourage providing high school students with better access to extensive vocational counseling and with opportunities for work-based

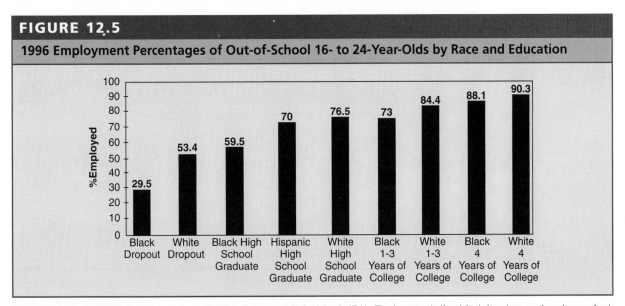

FIGURE 12.5

1996 Employment Percentages of Out-of-School 16- to 24-Year-Olds by Race and Education

Source: Halperin, S. (1998). Today's forgotten half: Still losing ground. In S. Halperin (Ed.), *The forgotten half revisited: American youth and young families, 1988–2008*, p. 14. Washington, D.C.: American Youth Policy Forum. Reprinted by permission.

learning. They also suggest increasing the participation of employers in providing training and apprenticeship programs, using the community college system to create expanded opportunities for technical training, and creating community-based resources to provide young adults with information about pathways into specific occupations (Bailey & Morest, 1998).

Many researchers note that there is a particularly sinister trend that affects mostly young men in "the forgotten half." Arrest and imprisonment for minor crimes (e.g., drug possession) have increased in recent years, in particular for males in minority groups. The number of young men incarcerated in federal and state prisons more than doubled between 1986 and 1995 (Halperin, 1998b; see Table 12.3).

> For some segments of society, crime control policy . . . has regressed to the point that imprisonment is the major governmental intervention in the transition to young adulthood. . . . This means that segments of the population are cut off from voting, employment, and community organizations. This disenfranchisement will further contribute to increased unemployment and undermine family life. (Laub, 1999)

Given that friendships, family ties, and a sense of belonging in a community play a significant role in a young adult's hope for the future and chances for upward mobility, school- and community-based vocational training and counseling seem like a much better alternative than jail for many adolescent and young adult delinquents.

Women Versus Men

Traditionally, gender has been a significant factor in career development. In 1957, Super found that a variety of career patterns characterized adults in the mid-twentieth century in the United States. For men, the "conventional career pattern" included a period or periods of "trial work," that is, trying out possible jobs and then launching into a stable career. The "conventional career pattern" for women, however, involved entry into work as a stopgap after high school or college. Once married, women tended to shift to full-time homemaking. Even in 1957, there were other patterns for both men and women that were common enough not to be considered atypical, but most of the alternative patterns also displayed gender differences. For example, women sometimes followed the "double-track career pattern," first establishing a career and then adding a second career as homemaker. Or they might show the "interrupted career pattern," first establishing a career, then marrying and becoming a full-time homemaker, and then shifting back to a career when home responsibilities were less pressing. Interestingly, none of the patterns Super characterized as typical

TABLE 12.3

Young Men, Ages 18 to 24, Incarcerated in Federal, State, and Local Prisons in 1986 and 1995

Year	Total Population of Young Men	Number in Prisons & Jails	Percent in Prisons & Jails
1986	13,502,061	177,952	1.3
1995	12,904,674	359,419	2.8
Change: 1986 to 1995	−597,387	+181,467	+1.5

Source: Adapted from Halperin, S. (1998). Today's forgotten half: Still losing ground. In S. Halperin (Ed.), *The forgotten half revisited: American youth and young families, 1988–2008* (pp. 1–26). Washington, D.C.: American Youth Policy Forum.

of *men* included "double-track" or any kind of interruption based on family or homemaking concerns.

How important is gender in career development today? As we have already seen, there have certainly been substantial changes relevant to gender in our culture since 1950. These changes have grown out of the civil rights movement, the women's rights movement in particular, and are also linked to technological changes such as the availability of reliable contraceptives and an increase in the use of machines to do heavy labor. Many work-related gender differences have diminished, and some have even disappeared or reversed. For example, women now enter college in larger numbers than men do, whereas up until about 1980, men outnumbered women (U.S. Bureau of the Census, 1999). As we have already noted, women now often choose majors in college that traditionally were the preserve of men, such as premed and business. Women currently earn 40% of the graduate degrees granted, and many of these are in traditionally "masculine" fields such as dentistry and law (Dey & Hurtado, 1999).

But gender differences in career development have by no means disappeared. Women are still more likely than men to select majors in education and the social sciences. Some careers are still overwhelmingly pursued by one gender, such as secretarial work (by women) and firefighting (by men) (e.g., Burgess & Borgida, 1997; Scozzaro & Subich, 1990). Although men and women use most of the same criteria to evaluate potential careers (they try to match their interests, and they carefully consider professional advancement and income opportunities), women are more likely than men to consider relationships with people (opportunity for and kinds of) as an important factor in selecting a career (e.g., Gati, Osipow, & Givon, 1995). These differences are influenced at least in part by gender-role beliefs. Both men and women anticipate that marriage and parenting will be important to their lives, for example, but men give greater priority to their role as breadwinner in the family, and women give greater priority to their role as caregiver (e.g., Gati et al., 1995; Vermeulen & Minor, 1998).

Different role expectations are nowhere more evident than in the typical patterns of career development. There have been several noteworthy changes in career patterns for women, and to some extent for men, but these changes continue to reflect the tendency for women to focus more than men on family and childrearing concerns at every stage of career planning. For example, despite the fact that both men and women have the right to take parental or family leaves in some companies in the United States (a right that is mandated by law in many European countries), it is quite rare for a man to exercise that right. The most dramatic change in women's career patterns since the 1950s has been the great increase in women's choice of a "double-track" pattern. To illustrate the enormity of the change, in 1950, most mothers of children under age 6 were full-time homemakers (88%). In 1990, most mothers of preschoolers were employed (57%), and the percentage of employed mothers continues to rise (e.g., Chadwick & Heaton, 1992). Mothers who work are described as having two careers because they typically take more responsibility for child care and daily household tasks than fathers who work, although there is an increasing tendency for men to share somewhat more equitably in homemaking responsibilities and to make job-related decisions that take into account their parenting role (e.g., J. Glass, 1998; Snarey, 1993). Men have also become more likely to take their wives' careers into account in making other job-related decisions, such as whether to relocate (e.g., Gill & Haurin, 1998).

Despite some improvements, old habits do die hard. Women in general are still overrepresented in lower-level positions, make less money than men, and have less power to make decisions at work than their male counterparts (Stockard & Johnson, 1992; U.S. Bureau of Labor. Women's Bureau, 1998). Organizational structures, possibly constructed and maintained to build in certain privileges for select groups, are slow to change.

Research has demonstrated that women in male-dominated occupations are not viewed as favorably as men, despite comparable skills. Their work is evaluated more negatively than men's, and they face more exclusion from the kinds of informal networks and social activities that often pave the way for advancement in the workplace (see Alban-Metcalfe & West, 1991; Pfost & Fiore, 1990). Clearly, both traditional gender roles and the realities of secular change are influencing career patterns for both women and men. We will revisit the issue of dual careers and parenting in the next chapter.

Work and the Development of Self-Concept

As we have now seen, theorists in the arena of career development see an individual's vocational self-concept as critical for the evolution of a successful, satisfying career. Both Holland and Super specify the importance of self-knowledge in career development: accurate assessment of one's own style, interests, and characteristics. Super also emphasizes that one's vocational self both emerges from his broader sense of identity and contributes to it. Thus, it seems that self-concept is a central force behind career development and is, in turn, a product of it. These ideas have formed the backbone of many career counseling approaches. In the following sections, we will consider how feelings and attitudes toward the self as a worker develop. What do these aspects of identity contribute to work and its role in the life of an adult and vice versa? We begin by recapping Erik Erikson's ideas about how work and self-concept are related in development.

Erikson's Theory of Identity Development

In Erikson's (1950/1963) view of the developing self-concept, children begin to formulate a sense of themselves as workers when they first confront serious work. In both nonindustrial and industrial societies around the world, children are expected to begin to work by the time they are 5 or 6 years old. In nonindustrial societies, they work alongside adults, caring for younger children, doing household tasks, helping with farm animals, working in the fields, or hunting. They are expected both to contribute to the productive efforts of the community and to learn the skills they will need as full-fledged adults. In most industrial societies today, children's work begins in school, where they are expected to achieve competence in basic skills, such as reading and arithmetic, that will serve them in nearly any adult work they might take on. Erikson argued that these early work experiences can provide a child with a feeling of **industry,** which is both a belief in his ability to master the skills and tools needed to be productive and a sense of "the pleasure of work completion by steady attention and persevering diligence" (p. 259). Feelings of industry help the child to be "an eager and absorbed unit of a productive situation" (p. 259). The child can, unfortunately, also slip into feeling inadequate and inferior if he cannot seem to master the skills that are required of him and begins to be discouraged about how effective he can be in contributing to productive work efforts. Feelings of inferiority can also begin at this point if social barriers, such as those experienced by the poor, limit a child's opportunities to try out challenging work, provide substandard educational opportunities, or lead him to question his abilities.

Thus, for Erikson, the elementary school years are a crucial time for establishing a strong sense of industry. In adolescence, teens work on fashioning an adult identity, which includes developing a sense of direction for their vocational lives. This process continues, as we have seen, well into young adulthood. Identity formation is influenced by the attitudes toward self that evolved in childhood. We can expect that young people who bring to this process a strong sense of industry will find the task of vocational self-development less cumbersome than those who are plagued by self-doubt.

As you know, Erikson theorized that in adulthood the process of self-concept development continues. Individuals with a sense of who they are and what they can do are motivated to use their lives and their skills to leave a legacy for the next generation. Erikson called this a need for *generativity* and hypothesized that generativity motives have a strong influence on one's work life as adults move into middle age. Concepts akin to what Erikson called "industry" and "generativity" have been the focus of intensive study in several different research traditions. In the following sections, we will take a closer look at some findings on the importance of these two aspects of self-concept for young adults.

The Importance of Industry. Erikson's ideas about one's sense of industry are similar to what Bandura and his colleagues have called ***self-efficacy beliefs,*** meaning beliefs about our ability to exercise control over events that affect our lives (see Bandura, 1989, for a summary). A positive, optimistic sense of personal efficacy, like a feeling of industry, motivates a person to work hard at a task and to persevere even in the face of obstacles. There is evidence that high levels of achievement usually depend upon "an optimistic sense of personal efficacy" (Bandura, 1989, p. 1176) (e.g., Cervone & Peake, 1986; S. E. Taylor & Brown, 1988).

Closely related to Bandura's work on self-efficacy is research by Dweck and her colleagues who have studied ***mastery orientation*** and ***the helpless pattern*** in school children and in college-age adults (see Dweck, 1999, for a summary). These are two different orientations to failure. Individuals with a mastery orientation move forward optimistically even when they fail, assuming that they can succeed with further effort. They seem to construe failure as a challenge rather than as an obstacle. Individuals with a helpless pattern, however, often begin to denigrate their abilities when they encounter failure and typically stop applying themselves or trying to improve their performance. Dweck emphasizes the importance of one's theories of intelligence or ability in influencing how one deals with failure. She has found that mastery-oriented people are likely to be ***incremental theorists,*** seeing intelligence as a dynamic and malleable quality that can be increased by hard work and instruction. People who show a helpless pattern are more often ***entity theorists,*** who see intelligence or ability as a fixed, concrete thing: "You can only have a certain amount of it, so you'd better show that it's enough and you'd better hide it if it isn't" (p. 20).

When individuals with different orientations to failure move out of work environments where they have been successful into more challenging situations where they encounter more experiences of failure, they show different degrees of progress and different emotional reactions. Mastery-oriented people dig in and try harder and by that very effort make success more likely in the future. Helpless people tend to turn away from the new challenges. They seek tasks where they feel more certain they can succeed, settle for mediocre performance, or give up altogether. They also tend to feel more stress and shame when they find the new work they are faced with difficult. This pattern has been observed in children moving out of elementary school, where teachers often protect children from failure, into the more impersonal and competitive environment of a junior high school (V. Henderson & Dweck, 1992; Sorich & Dweck, 1996). It has also been seen with college students at Berkeley as they moved through four years of challenging college work (R. W. Robins & Pals, 1998). In both kinds of transitions, individuals with entity theories of ability performed less well than those with incremental theories, and they found their experiences in the new situations more emotionally distressing. This was true despite the fact that both groups entered the new environments with equally good credentials.

Findings like these might have particular significance for the patterns of career development observed among women and some minority groups. Gender differences in the choice of a career in male-dominated fields have been linked to lower self-efficacy in women, especially women who perceive themselves as highly feminine. Whereas women in general tend to have lower self-efficacy beliefs for "masculine" occupations requiring quantitative or leadership skills, males have a comparable sense of efficacy for both "masculine" and "feminine" career options (Betz & Hackett, 1981).

As we noted earlier, African American college students are more likely than White students to drop out of college. We also saw that when African American students attend Black colleges, they are more likely to pursue some particularly challenging majors, such as premed, than when they attend predominantly White colleges. Aronson and Fried (1998) posited that African American students are burdened by the stereotype that Blacks are less intelligent than Whites. Being in school with White students may have a tendency to evoke this stereotype and may make some Black students more susceptible to a helpless pattern, interfering with their achievement. Aronson and Fried devised a training program for undergraduates that they hoped would reduce **stereotype threat,** the fear that a stereotype might be true or that one will be judged by that stereotype (see Steele, 1997). The researchers hoped to foster a mastery orientation and thereby help improve achievements. Through film and lecture, citing scientific research, they instructed both Black and White undergraduates at Stanford University on the processes by which intelligence can actually be cultivated and changed. The training emphasized that when people take on new tasks and learn new skills there is neuronal growth so that they literally become smarter. To make sure that students had consolidated the information, participants were required to explain the incremental view of intelligence in letters to elementary school children. By the end of the school year, African American students who had been taught the incremental theory showed significant increases in achievement, reflected in their grade point averages. These students also were enjoying school more and felt more academically oriented than African American students in a control group, who had not been part of the incremental theory training.

There is evidence that many interacting variables in one's development affect the feelings of industry or positive self-efficacy or mastery orientation that people carry into adulthood. Such variables ultimately influence the likelihood of long-term achievement. These variables include parenting styles (e.g., Lamborn, Mounts, et al., 1991), teacher expectations (e.g., Rosenthal & Jacobson, 1968), stimulation and opportunities for personal challenge in one's home environment (e.g., Van Doorninck, Caldwell, Wright, & Frankenberg, 1981), security of attachments (e.g., Jacobsen & Hofmann, 1997), and, as we have just seen, gender and cultural stereotypes.

The Importance of Generativity. How important are generativity needs in career development? As we have seen, Erikson described generativity as most influential in middle adulthood, but some recent work indicates that young adults are also influenced by generativity as they plan and launch their work lives.

Stewart and Vandewater (1998) examined two broad features of generativity—*desire* and *accomplishment*—and found that the desire for generativity is quite strong even in early adulthood and actually declines through middle and late adulthood. *Desire* was defined as expression of generativity goals, such as caring for future generations ("I'm concerned about the planet"), wanting to produce something of lasting value ("I want to write a major piece of nonfiction"), and being concerned about being needed ("It's nice to discover that my kids still come to me for advice and help"). In two cohorts of women who were studied longitudinally, such desires were strong through early adulthood, peaking in the early thirties, and then declining. Generative *accomplishment* peaked later, in middle adulthood. The authors propose that "healthy early adulthood includes the formulation of generativity goals or desires, while healthy midlife includes the subjective experience of the capacity to be generative as well as the beginning of a sense of satisfaction in generative accomplishment" (p. 94). Stewart and Vandewater's results seem consistent with the finding, noted earlier, that even right after high school, young adults from all walks of life are likely to say that they would like their work to make a meaningful contribution (M. S. Hill & Yeung, 1999). We will look again at generativity issues in the next chapter, as we consider the development of adults in midlife.

APPLICATIONS

The search for intimacy in adulthood demonstrates the continuing human need for social connectedness. The deepest aspects of a person's emotional life as an adult are often expressed within the confines of pair-bonds. The importance of these associations is evidenced by the fact that the most common referral problems for counselors are those involving interpersonal relationships (Veroff, Kulka, & Douvan, 1981). As we have seen, early attachment experiences can act as templates for the intimate relationships of adulthood. In particular, they may influence our willingness to rely on others to meet our needs for intimacy and to help us manage stress (approach). They can also affect how trusting we are that others will meet these needs (anxiety). These representations are intimately linked to how we view ourselves.

Attachment theory can provide a very useful way to conceptualize the organizational structure of emotional expression and affect regulation that persons demonstrate within interpersonal contexts. Clinically, it serves as a metaphor for understanding clients' behaviors that are rooted in a very basic human system: the need to give and receive care. In relationships that are marked by lack of perspective taking and conflict, difficulties may be exacerbated by templates that defensively exclude disconfirming evidence about the partner and, thus, resist change. A partner's unavailability or his difficult behavior, the experience of a life crisis or other external stress can activate old patterns and trigger maladaptive responses. On their face, these responses may appear to be saying one thing, but, in reality, they may actually be communicating something very different. If self-awareness predisposes a person to change, it could be helpful for clients to learn the meaning behind their demanding, angry, clingy, hurtful, or aloof behaviors. Beneath the surface, emotional needs may be going unmet.

Clearly, many other factors in addition to attachment style influence the success of our social and close personal relationships. Social skills such as assertiveness, perspective-taking ability, time and opportunity to meet people, and the characteristics of the partner all play a role. Biology is also a factor. High levels of anger and anxiety, the manifestations of poorly managed stress, may have a constitutional basis. A hyper-responsive nervous system or serotonin imbalances have been hypothesized to underlie excessive anxiety and hostility (see R. Williams, 1994, for a review). Obviously, clinicians should avoid overdiagnosing attachment-related problems because there is such wide individual and cultural variation within the range of normal functioning. Some people's relationships appear distant or enmeshed to observers, but they may be perfectly satisfactory to the couple involved. Clinicians should also resist viewing attachment style as a monolithic, trait-like characteristic that resides within a person. Working models of self and relationship are always shaped in context. And even though there has been a surge of interest in attachment-related issues in adulthood, many more questions remain to be answered by researchers (Colin, 1996).

If counselors keep these reservations in mind, attachment theory can also help them understand the meaning in their own patterns of interaction, conflict resolution, and stress management. Dozier, Cue, and Barnett (1994) found that the therapists' level of attachment security was related to countertransference processes. In other words, secure therapists were more likely to respond empathically to the dependency needs of their dismissing/avoidant clients. They were able to see the needs hidden beneath a detached or a rejecting exterior, whereas insecure therapists were more likely to be driven away by the negativity. Secure therapists were also better able to manage clients with ambivalent attachment styles. They were less likely to get trapped into "taking care of" these clients by responding to their obvious needs rather than attending to the more important, underlying ones.

Are working models open to revision? Bowlby believed that working models can change in more positive directions, and recent research supports this. The question that needs much more empirical support concerns how this is accomplished. Bowlby (1988) viewed good therapy somewhat like good parenting. He theorized that in a relationship with an emotionally available therapist, a person is able to reflect on the past, lower defenses, engage in perspective taking, know the experience of "felt security," and, together, co-construct a revision of the internal working model. Lopez and Brennan (2000) make a similar point by suggesting that counseling offers clients a context in which to learn ways of minimizing the negative consequences of insecure attachments (hyperactivation or deactivation) and to find ways of coping more effectively. Although more evidence is needed, some data indicate that attempts to improve social self-efficacy and perspective taking can mediate improvements in working-model representations (Corcoran & Mallinckrodt, 2000).

If working models can be changed, it is probably a slow process. Revising representational models happens by engaging in a curative, therapeutic attachment that takes time, patience, and dedication. Slade (1999) draws our attention to the limitation of certain kinds of short-term, problem-centered therapies that are not well suited to reworking fundamental models of social and emotional relationships.

Finding a place in the world of work is another important challenge at this time of life. Historically, the counseling profession has contributed significantly to the theory and practice of career development. A central tenet of this field is that finding a career is more than a simple choice. This task, like so many others, is a process that requires self-understanding and the ability to use self-knowledge to make informed decisions. Kegan (1982) believed that vocational development is a function of people's levels of self-awareness and the kinds of meaning they attribute to themselves as workers. His theoretical ideas have some things in common with Perry's scheme, which was described in Chapter 11.

According to Kegan, adolescent vocational aspirations are heavily influenced by family and peers. From their foreclosed position, adolescents often construe their early career aspirations as the "right" choice. When confronted with confusing or contradictory feedback about their skills or when given opportunities to pursue other career paths, they may cope by becoming even more rigidly entrenched in the pursuit of their original career goals. They mistake the form of the career (such as medical school) with the underlying functions it serves (such as prestige and service). In other words, vocational identity is construed as a position rather than as an aspect of one's self. Individuals at this stage may resist revising a career goal, even when personal experience or feedback from others challenges its suitability. With maturity, individuals can reflect on this dissonance, integrate the contradictions, and reach a new level of self-understanding and acceptance. They can also identify career goals that are a better fit with their underlying dispositions and goals. Counseling can be particularly helpful for those who need guidance in self-exploration and who may need to reconstruct new meanings about career (McAuliffe, 1993).

Finding productive work enhances our lives, but choosing a career is only one step in the career development process. People also need to adjust to the demands of the workplace. Hershenson's (1996) contextual model proposes that work adjustment is most likely to occur if the ongoing characteristics of the individual (work values, skills, goals, habits, etc.) mesh with the day-to-day demands of the job (behavioral expectations, skill requirements, available rewards and opportunities). For example, an organizational position that is highly structured and requires adherence to routine may be unsatisfying to an individual with high needs for autonomy and little motivation to work in a corporate culture. Helping clients consider the person-environment dimensions of a career can promote more successful adjustment.

Of course, not all problems in the work place are amenable to change. Finding the ideal fit, although a desirable goal, is not always realistic. The work place is harsh and unsatisfying for many people due to job-related threats to health, lack of job security, lack of control over tasks performed, and pressure to increase productivity with limited time and resources (Jones, 1996). In his description of the current state of work in the United States, Reich (2000) points to several significant changes that have had profound effects on workers: the end of steady, dependable work, the obsolescence of loyalty between employers and employees, the ever-widening inequality of wages, and the shrinking time factor. "In 1999, the average middle-income married couple with children worked a combined 3,918 hours—about seven weeks more *than a decade before* [italics added]" (pp. 111–112).

Work stresses can have adverse effects on workers and their families, especially on their dependent children. Jones suggests that counselors help clients consider workplace safety and stability issues when contemplating career choices. In a departure from more traditional ways of viewing career development, he suggests that counselors avoid portraying job success as the primary means of achieving self-esteem. For many people, work may never be particularly meaningful or personally satisfying. The stresses of the contemporary working world should also be factored in when clients come to counseling for other problems, such as problems in relationships or difficulties with children. He also suggests that counselors take an advocacy position on issues related to work, such as government or company policies that support high-quality child care. Given the importance of love and work in adults' lives, understanding and supporting successful adjustment in these two areas is a worthy task for clinicians.

As has been repeatedly noted, achieving a high level of self-efficacy is associated with positive outcomes in many areas of adult functioning. Counselors can be both tutors and coaches in this process, scaffolding the development of a personal sense of control over many of life's important challenges. Since self-efficacy beliefs influence functioning in a whole host of ways, from making decisions (What major shall I select?) to behavioral performance (Shall I ask this person for a date? Or my boss for a raise?), it is a useful target for clinical intervention. Bussey and Bandura (1999) describe four major ways to instill a strong sense of self-efficacy. First, construct and try out graded mastery experiences that are tailored to the individual's level of ability and that maximize the chances of success. Second, discuss or provide models who demonstrate success in an area of difficulty for the client. Successful models encourage individuals to believe in their own capacity for success and provide skills and know-how to the motivated observer. A third way to enhance self-efficacy is to apply social persuasion. This might be done by challenging erroneous beliefs about lack of ability, making attributions for failure to lack of effort (incremental) rather than lack of ability (fixed), and providing support as well as realistic, helpful suggestions for improvement. Finally, attempt to reduce coexisting factors that lower self-efficacy, such as stress, depression, or even features of the environment, when possible.

By means of these processes, clients revise versions of their expectancies, which leads to changes in behavior.

> As they (clients) continue to accumulate more and more of such success experiences, processing this information within the therapy session helps them realign their anticipatory thoughts and feelings with an appropriate self-evaluation of the outcome of their response. Eventually, a new behavior pattern, together with a greater sense of self-efficacy, begins to emerge. (Goldfried, 1995, p. 113)

SUMMARY

1. Freud characterized love (lieben) and work (arbeiten) as the means by which adults strive for happiness. Erikson described *intimacy,* closeness to another that is marked by trust, openness, and affection, as the goal of young adulthood, and *generativity,* creating, producing, and contributing to the human community, as the goal of middle adulthood. Recent conceptions of mental health or "wellness" also emphasize both having close relationships and feeling competent and productive as essential ingredients for happiness.

"Lieben"—To Love

2. Attachment theory provides one framework for conceptualizing adult intimacy. It suggests that early bonds with caregivers could have a bearing on relationship building in adulthood and that intimate adult relationships provide some of the same benefits as infant-adult relationships: a secure base, safe haven, and emotional warmth.

3. Two traditions or lines of inquiry characterize adult attachment research: the *nuclear family tradition,* exploring how early attachments might affect the quality of caregiving that an adult gives his own children, and the *peer/romantic partner tradition,* which focuses on the peer attachments of adults.

4. The *Adult Attachment Interview* (AAI) consists of questions about early memories of relationships with parents. *Autonomous* (secure) adults provide a coherent, collaborative narrative, acknowledging the importance of attachment-related experiences in their development. Individuals described as *earned secure* appear to have come to terms with painful backgrounds. They reflect on their past realistically, acknowledging their parents' perspective. Autonomous adults tend to have securely attached children.

5. *Dismissing* (insecure) adults describe parents positively but provide either no evidence or contradictory evidence. Generally, they downplay the importance of early relationships. Their children tend to form avoidant attachments.

6. *Preoccupied* (insecure) individuals provide long, incoherent, egocentric monologues. They seem overwhelmed by the interview questions and are often angry, sad, or fearful. They seem preoccupied with parents, who are remembered as intrusive or egocentric. Their children often have anxious-ambivalent attachments.

7. *Unresolved* individuals produce narratives with notable lapses in logical thinking. Their children have a tendency to show disorganized attachment patterns. Insecure adults are the most likely to be emotionally disturbed.

8. Longitudinal studies find that an individual's infant attachment status (as measured by the strange situation test) predicts his adult AAI attachment status, although intervening events can shift that status from secure to insecure or vice versa.

9. AAI narratives are different from other interview narratives with the same interviewees, suggesting that the AAI specifically reflects a person's state of mind regarding interpersonal representations. This working model of attachments is assumed to be a schema that has evolved with time and experience and that serves as a guide for understanding, predicting, and acting.

10. Adult pair-bonds integrate three basic behavioral systems: caregiving, attachment, and sexual mating. The attachment system involves proximity seeking and separation distress and serves safe haven and secure base functions. Attachment functions gradually transfer from parents to peers and, eventually, to romantic partners. Proximity seeking begins to shift as early as the preschool years. Between 8 and 14 years, peers also provide safe haven. Eventually attachments to romantic partners involve proximity seeking and separation distress, and they also serve safe haven and secure base functions.

11. The measurement procedures and typologies in the peer/romantic relationship tradition have been different from those in the nuclear family tradition. Several typologies have been proposed, and in the most recent work it is suggested that people may be better characterized as differing along two continuous dimensions, one having to do with their degree of anxiety about close relationships and the other with their approach/avoidance tendencies.

12. Partner selection can be predicted to some degree by the attachment characteristics of the partners. Secure individuals tend to pair with secure partners; anxious and avoidant individuals tend to pair up; but anxious-anxious pairs or avoidant-avoidant pairs are uncommon. Whether individuals actually enter relationships with these characteristics or tend to evolve these styles within their relationships has not been determined.

13. Partnerships between secure individuals seem to involve more positive and less negative emotions than other pairings. Male avoidant individuals show less distress during breakups than other males, but females of all attachment types show similar levels of distress. Ambivalent partners are most stressed by conflict within a relationship.

"Arbeiten"—To Work

14. In Holland's theory of career development, people are categorized as having one of six modal personal orientations, part of their personality. Jobs or careers make demands that are compatible with one or more of these orientations. A good fit between modal orientation and job characteristics benefits job satisfaction and feelings of well-being.

15. In Super's theory, the focus is on the development of a vocational self-concept, part of one's total identity. He describes five stages in its development, from the *growth stage* in early childhood through the *decline stage* in people of retirement age. Super emphasizes that career development is a continuing, lifelong process. Many career counseling approaches emphasize the important relationship between career and self-development, with self-discovery an important ingredient in career satisfaction.

16. College students' first vocationally relevant decision is choice of a major. While personal characteristics and interests influence the choice, so do cultural changes (e.g., economic shifts) and cohort characteristics. Ethnic and socioeconomic differences appear to influence not only who attends college but also the likelihood of college retention and career choices. Career counseling in college should begin with advisement on choice of a major.

17. For the *forgotten half,* those who do not attend college, the chances of achieving career goals shared by all young adults (e.g., good pay, opportunities for advancement, opportunities to make a meaningful contribution to society) are substantially reduced. As with college students, factors such as socioeconomic status and ethnicity affect these chances as well.

18. Career opportunities for noncollege young people could be improved if there were more systematic and effective resources for them, such as basic skill training in public schools, extensive vocational counseling, and opportunities for work-based learning.

19. Traditionally, women with careers have followed different career paths from men. Substantial changes have occurred, such as women outnumbering men in college. But there are still gender differences: some careers are still highly gendered, and women are still more likely to consider the impact of career choices on their relationship opportunities, although men are increasingly attending to such concerns as well.

20. Self-concept and self-understanding are central features of many theories of career development. How do basic feelings and attitudes toward the self as a worker

develop? Erikson describes a sense of *industry,* belief in one's ability to work productively and expectation of satisfaction from work, as beginning in middle childhood, when children have their first work experiences. *Generativity* becomes important in adulthood, as people become motivated to leave a legacy for the next generation.

21. Bandura has studied *self-efficacy beliefs,* beliefs in one's own ability to affect events, as motivating people to work hard and persevere even in the face of failure. Such beliefs are correlated with high levels of achievement.

22. *Mastery orientation* is similar to self-efficacy and to a sense of industry. Mastery-oriented individuals move forward even when they fail, apparently because they are *incremental theorists,* believing that hard work and instruction can affect ability. Conversely, people who show a helplessness pattern, who give up when they fail, tend to be *entity theorists,* seeing ability as fixed.

23. Differences in self-efficacy beliefs, or mastery orientation, may have significant effects on minority groups and women. *Stereotype threat,* the fear that an inferiority stereotype might be true, can influence achievement. In some research, stereotype threat has been reduced and achievement improved when individuals have received intensive training on the scientific evidence for the malleability of intelligence and ability.

Case Study

Tayib, who is 29 years old, works as a paralegal in a public defender's office. His parents came to the United States from India before he was born. Tayib's extended family in India were highly educated people, and his parents encouraged him to get a good education as well. Although he considered going to law school, Tayib never felt confident enough to pursue this goal. In his current place of employment, many coworkers rely on his conscientiousness. He feels that others, including his superiors, often take advantage of him by giving him the most difficult cases to sort out and the shortest deadlines for getting them done. He was recently passed over for a promotion by his boss, who decided to fill the higher-level post by hiring someone from outside the department. He feels unsatisfied in his position, but he thinks that his chances for advancement may be best if he remains in civil service. His parents encourage him to find a position with more prestige and a better income.

Tayib has been dating Rachael, a 27-year-old White woman with a young son, for the past 6 months. Rachael works as a public relations executive in one of the corporate offices in the city. Rachael and her son, Luke, share an apartment with one of Rachael's girlfriends. This has been her living arrangement since the breakup of her relationship with Luke's father, Kevin, 3 years ago. The couple were never married, a factor that led to strained relationships with her own mother and father.

Tayib and Rachael are both interested in finding someone with whom they can have a serious relationship. Lately, however, their relationship has not been going as smoothly as it did in the beginning. As Luke's fourth birthday approached, Rachael wanted to plan a celebration for him. Tayib had already taken Luke and Rachael to an amusement park as a birthday present for the youngster. Rachael decided to have a special birthday dinner for Luke and invited her parents and Tayib. Tayib, in the midst of an important project at work, declined the invitation.

Rachael feels totally rejected by his refusal to attend the dinner. She cannot understand why she and Luke mean so little to Tayib. She believes that she does everything she possibly can in order to keep Tayib interested in her. She prepares meals for him, works on her appearance, listens to him talk about problems at work, calls him to let him know she cares about him, and tries to accommodate her schedule to his. She wonders now if she will ever find someone who wants to make a commitment to her. Tayib can't understand why Rachael is so upset about the dinner. Since she is a working woman with a child to support, he feels that she should understand how important it is to have and keep a job. Tayib begins to wonder if she really understands what is important to him. Although the two do not discuss this incident directly, they both feel tension growing in the relationship.

Discussion Questions

1. What are the issues involved in this case?
2. From an attachment perspective, what inferences can you draw about the relationship styles of Tayib and Rachael?
3. What are the challenges each person faces at this point in his or her development? As a counselor, how would you help them cope with these challenges?

 ## Journal Questions

1. Write a brief relationship autobiography describing how you behaved, thought, and felt about one significant relationship. How would you describe your own attachment style?
2. Describe how you solve conflicts in your closest relationship. How do you deal with stress in this relationship? Explain how these patterns relate to what you experienced in your family of origin.
3. How has your own career history changed since you held your first job? What were the influences (both internal and external) on your career trajectory? How would you evaluate your sense of self-efficacy regarding your career?

Key Terms

intimacy	passion	growth stage	forgotten half
generativity	intimacy	exploratory stage	industry
nuclear family tradition	commitment	crystallization	self-efficacy beliefs
peer/romantic partner tradition	secure	specification	mastery orientation
autonomous	preoccupied	implementation	the helpless pattern
earned secure	avoidant	establishment stage	incremental theorists
dismissing	dismissing	stabilization	entity theorists
preoccupied	fearful	maintenance stage	stereotype threat
unresolved	modal personal orientation	consolidation	generativity desire
cannot classify	vocational self-concept	decline stage	generativity accomplishment
		retention	

CHAPTER 13

Cognitive, Personality, and Social Development in the Middle Years of Adulthood

What is the nature of development at midlife? This is a perplexing question because adult lives are complex and multifaceted. Adults seek out jobs, select them, and sometimes ascend to positions of responsibility in their fields of work. Adults also change employment voluntarily to work in other settings or in other careers. Some adults lose their jobs and may experience unemployment or underemployment. Some work at multiple jobs. Adults take on leadership, executive, or mentoring roles in their communities. Adults move from one location to another, historically now more than ever before. They marry, cohabitate, divorce, date, and often go on to marry again. Some adults have children and grandchildren; others are childless. Adults may have responsibilities for the care of their own aging parents. Those who are parents or stepparents have to deal with the ever-changing developmental needs of their children. Adults are also affected by the close relationships they share with partners or friends. They may experience financial difficulties. They may sustain illness themselves or experience the illness or loss of loved ones. Some adults experience catastrophic events, such as wars, accidents, or natural disasters. Many more deal with chronic adversities such as discrimination of one sort or another, mental problems such as depression, or simply the gradual physical changes involved in the aging process. Moreover, many of these events occur simultaneously.

The complexity of people's experience and functioning is what is most striking about middle adulthood. How are we to make sense of all the variables operating in adult lives? Is there some coherent scheme that helpers can use to understand development in the adult years? In Chapter 1, we examined some of the many theoretical approaches that explain developmental processes, including *stage models,* such as Erikson's or Piaget's, and *incremental models,* such as learning and information processing accounts. As we have seen throughout this book, these approaches to development can be quite helpful in understanding some aspects of psychological functioning, but modern theorists are more and more turning to *multidimensional models,* which are focused on the complexity of interrelated causal processes in development. Recall in Bronfenbrenner's multidimensional model, for example, the description of *proximal processes* in development—reciprocal interactions between an "active, evolving biopsychological human organism and the persons, objects, and symbols in its immediate environment" (Bronfenbrenner & Morris, 1998, p. 996). These proximal processes are modified by more *distal processes,* some within the organism, such as genes, and some outside the organism, such as the family, the workplace, the community, the broader economic and political context, and other aspects of the culture.

Multidimensional theories of adult development, usually called *life span developmental models,* address all the fundamental questions of development, such as the role of heredity versus environment in adulthood and the extent to which adult characteristics are continuous with previous traits and propensities versus how much genuine change there is in adult behavior. Life span developmental models (e.g., Baltes, Lindenberger, & Staudinger, 1998) make one unique assumption in addressing such questions—that from birth to death, adaptation continues. The development of psychological functioning does not end or become fixed when adulthood is reached but goes on until death. The reciprocal interaction of many biological and environmental factors forms an ever-changing "architecture" or scaffolding that supports the development of behavioral and mental functioning (e.g., Baltes, 1997). Thus, middle adulthood is not some kind of holding pattern before the slide into death. An adult's cognitive and socioemotional functioning continues to evolve through her 30s, 40s, 50s, and beyond.

LIFE SPAN DEVELOPMENTAL THEORY

Historically, developmental study in North America focused on children and adolescents. With some rare exceptions, such as Erikson's stage theory, adulthood was given short shrift in most theory and research. Interestingly, in some parts of Europe, such as Germany and Belgium, interest in development over the whole life span was the scientific norm. Baltes et al. (1998) speculate that when developmental psychology became a specialty in this country around 1900, the strong influence of Darwinian theories, which describe growth as a process of maturation, may have helped establish childhood as the primary focus of attention. In contrast, in German-speaking countries, important essays on development began to emerge in the 18th and 19th centuries, before there was much biological science. Early developmental writings were rooted more in philosophy and the humanities, with a special emphasis on concerns about how to optimize human functioning. Thus, there was no special impetus to limit the discussion of development to descriptions of the childhood period.

Around the middle of the 20th century, some American developmentalists began to shift their attention from the growth that characterizes childhood to the declines of aging, and developmental psychology was soon represented by two somewhat independent groups, the child developmentalists and the gerontologists. Even today, textbooks often reflect this disjunction. Chapters on middle adulthood discuss career motivation, stress, marriage, family roles, sexuality, and leisure time, which are all important issues for adults. But there is often a notable absence of an overarching framework for understanding how middle adult life is linked to the childhood years, on the one hand, and to old age, on the other.

Life span developmental theory provides such an organizational framework. It can be construed as a kind of macrotheory under whose umbrella all the processes of *ontogeny,* or the development of organisms, fall into place. This orientation offers a clear benefit to those in the helping professions. First, it provides a way of organizing developmental processes across the life cycle. Think of the multiplicity of challenges and possibilities in adult life, some of which we mentioned at the beginning of this chapter. Rather than viewing them as disconnected parts of a life story, counselors can interpret the choices people make and the ways they adapt as reflecting some degree of lawful continuity. Second, life span developmental theory emphasizes the importance of learning about successful or effective development. Thus, this perspective fits well with therapeutic or psychoeducational goals. Let's now consider some of the elements of life span developmental theory.

Gains and Losses in Development: The Changing Architecture of Biology and Culture

At any point in development, a person brings to proximal processes—the interactive interface with the environment—a set of dispositions and resources (existing abilities, knowledge, skills, and so on) (Bronfenbrenner & Morris, 1998). These are influenced by biological and physical levels of functioning, including the genes, and by the many levels of the environment. Life span developmental theorists such as Baltes describe this web of interacting organismic and environmental influences as the "architecture" of biology and culture. These theorists argue that for children, the biological processes that support development have a long evolutionary history. Natural selection through many generations has created a biological trajectory that tends to optimize development in most typical environments, allowing most individuals to grow up and become fully functioning adults who can contribute to the success of the species by reproducing. Of course, basic cultural supports—adequate parenting, nutrition, education, protection from environmental hazards, and so on—are fundamental for the success of this process as well.

As individuals move through adulthood, the biological supports for life weaken, because the reproductive process is complete, and the selection pressure that the need for reproductive success creates for a species is no longer operative. Thus, biological dysfunctions are more likely. "Evolution and biology are not good friends of old age" (Baltes, 1997, p. 368). During middle adulthood (defined here as ages 30 to 55), people begin to depend more and more on cultural supports for adequate functioning. Indeed, "old age" exists primarily *because* of modern culture. Advances in economics, nutrition, general knowledge, technology, and medicine have compensated for the weakening of the biological supports for life. As a result, from 1900 to 1995, the average life span increased in Western societies from about 45 years to about 75 years! "The older individuals are, the more they are in need of culture-based resources (material, social, economic, psychological) to generate and maintain high levels of functioning" (Baltes et al., 1998, p. 1038).

Viewing development as a life span process makes clear that development or change in functioning with age involves both gains and losses for the individual. Gains are most obvious early in life, losses are more obvious later. But once we are sensitized to the fact that development involves both, we begin to notice that gains and losses characterize change throughout life. Thus, children, not just adults, experience some losses in the normal course of development. One familiar illustration is characteristic of language development. As an infant, you were capable of hearing and producing all of the kinds of sound distinctions that are used across all human languages. But as you learned your native language, you became less adept at discriminating and producing sounds that were not part of that language. If you were introduced to a second language after the preschool years, you probably had trouble producing sounds that were not part of your native tongue, and so you probably speak the second language with a "foreign accent." Another example, suggested by Baltes (1997), is that as adolescents strive for personal autonomy, their relationships with their parents are often strained, as we have seen. The intimacy of the parent-child relationship is diminished for both partners as the adolescent struggles to achieve an adult identity.

Of course, loss is more obvious to us in adulthood as biological declines occur. We saw in Chapter 11, for example, that our biological systems, like our sensory abilities and our immune functions, all reach peak potential between ages 18 and 30. Many of these systems begin to decline soon after (see below). But the increase in losses through adulthood should not mask the fact that the gains also continue. For example, in Chapter 11 we discussed the gains in postformal thinking that seem to characterize some people as they move into middle adulthood. Other examples of gains will become clear throughout this

FIGURE 13.1

The Shifting Relationship Between Gains and Losses Across the Life Span

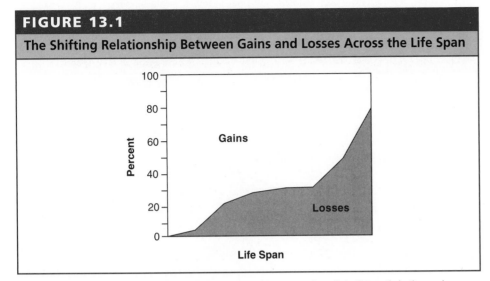

Source: Baltes, P. B. (1997). On the incomplete architecture of human ontology: Selection, optimization, and compensation as foundation of developmental theory. *American Psychologist, 52,* 366–380. Copyright © 1997 by the American Psychological Association. Reprinted with permission.

chapter. However, the relative balance of gains and losses clearly shifts across the life span, until eventually losses outstrip gains for most people in old age (see Figure 13.1). Given this increase in relative losses, how does development proceed in adulthood?

Development as Growth, Maintenance, and Regulation of Loss

Life span developmental theory defines development as a process of adapting to the constant flux of influences on our lives (see Baltes, 1997; Baltes et al., 1998). One kind of adaptation is *growth.* We grow when we add new characteristics, understandings, skills, and so on to our behavioral repertoire. So, for example, an adult might grow by becoming more expert at some task at work, or she might acquire a more balanced and thus empathic perspective on her relationship with her parents. Another kind of adaptive functioning is *maintenance* or *resilience,* finding ways to continue functioning at the same level in the face of challenges or restoring our functioning after suffering some loss. For example, an adult might maintain the concept of herself as a poet despite repeated rejections of her work by persistently revising and resubmitting her work until eventually a piece is published. Or despite the death of a partner, she might eventually reestablish intimacy in her life by returning to social circulation and finding a new partner. A third kind of adaptation is *regulation of loss.* Like maintenance, this form of adaptation involves reorganizing the way we behave. But unlike maintenance, regulation of loss involves adjusting our expectations and accepting a lower level of functioning. Suppose that a woman who prides herself on her ability to remember names, faces, and telephone numbers suffers a reduction in learning ability as she ages. She adapts by using strategies that include writing down essential information that she previously would have recalled. She accepts that she will never have the breadth of information available to her that she had before, but by using her new strategies she assures that she will remember what is really necessary.

According to life span developmental theory, all three adaptive processes—growth, maintenance, and regulation of loss—are part of development from infancy through old age. What changes is the relative probability of each. Growth is much more characteristic of children than it is of the elderly, and regulation of loss is much more characteristic of the

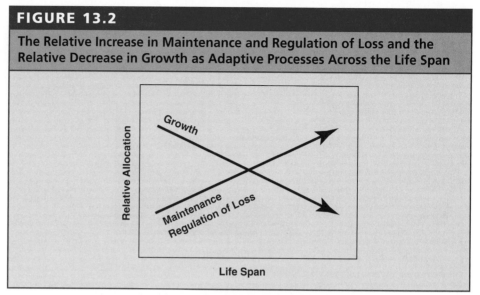

Source: Baltes, P. B. (1997). On the incomplete architecture of human ontology: Selection, optimization, and compensation as foundation of developmental theory. *American Psychologist, 52,* 366–380. Copyright © 1997 by the American Psychological Association. Reprinted with permission.

elderly (see Figure 13.2). The middle adult years appear to be a time when the balance is shifting among the three adaptive processes. It is important to recognize that all three processes occur across the life span. Children experience the need to compensate for loss through maintenance or regulation, and adults of all ages experience growth. However, knowing the relative proportions of each, given a client's stage of life, may provide clinicians with a frame for understanding presenting problems.

Defining Successful Development at Any Age

What counts as successful development? Life span theorists typically describe it as "the relative maximization of gains and the minimization of losses" (Baltes, 1997, p. 367; see also Brandstadter & Wentura, 1995). The adaptation processes we have just described are the means by which successful development is achieved. These processes are made possible both by the physical and psychological resources that individuals bring to the task of adaptation and by the biological and cultural scaffolding that is available. As we have seen, as adulthood proceeds, the more cultural scaffolding there is, the more likely the individual will be able to adapt well.

Consider the nature of developmental success at different times in the life of Emma, now a 91-year-old woman. Emma never married or had children, which she experienced as a loss. In her young adulthood, she compensated for her childlessness by dedicating her considerable talents to teaching poor urban children in public schools. In middle adulthood, she became an administrator, developing innovative programs for young children and mentoring teachers in the public school system. In her early old age, the physical demands of a daily work schedule became too great, so she retired, thereby losing her power to influence the lives of young children in the public schools. But she managed the loss, *maintaining* her view of herself as a child advocate, by serving on the governing boards of nonprofit organizations that provide services for children. Now, Emma suffers from a number of biological losses—near blindness, breathing problems, and general frailty—and she has confined her living space to her small apartment. A good deal of her functioning involves *regulating* her biological losses by living a quiet, sedentary life in her small space

Growth, maintenance, and regulation of loss are part of human adaptation, but their relative proportions change at different points of the life cycle.

and depending on some outside help, which she has the means to pay for as a result of careful financial planning. But she also continues to *grow*: she has learned to use a computer, and she has begun to write for her own enjoyment. She also *maintains* her contacts with friends through e-mail.

At each stage of her life, Emma found ways to manage losses through maintenance or regulation and to continue to grow. The balance of losses and gains in her life has now clearly shifted so that much of her adaptive energy is dedicated to managing losses. With the help of technological supports, such as the computer, Emma has minimized, to the extent possible, the overwhelming losses of her late life and has continued to maximize her gains, to the extent possible. She provides an example of successful development even in old age.

Our description of successful development will sound familiar to most helpers, because it is clearly continuous with what we think of as healthy coping. The life span developmental view helps us to see that healthy coping evolves and changes throughout life. What is adaptive coping at one stage of life may be less adaptive at another. In the following sections, we will consider some relatively stable influences on adult life as well as the sources of change. As we look at these influences, we will begin to identify what resources the mature individual brings to the task of development and which of these resources might most effectively contribute to success.

INFLUENCES ON ADULT DEVELOPMENT: SOURCES OF STABILITY

A popular series of films produced by the British Broadcasting Company (BBC) documents the lives of several men and women at 7-year intervals, from the time they were 7 years old to age 42. The most recently filmed documentaries, which include scenes from earlier films, illuminate the thread of stability that runs through these individual lives. For example, Nick, who at age 7 expressed the desire "to find out all about the moon," is a full professor teaching science at age 42. Sue, who was a vibrant, independent youngster, is now a fun-loving, independent divorced woman. Is this kind of continuity typical of people in general? What are the sources of relative stability in development from childhood through adulthood? Many personality researchers, buoyed by the results of longitudinal studies (e.g., Conley, 1985; Finn, 1986; Costa & McCrae, 1988), have expressed renewed confidence in the stability of personality across the life span. However, how one *defines* personality will make a critical difference in one's perception of personality as stable or changing. Those who espouse personality continuity generally construe personality as a set of traits that may be likened to the temperament characteristics of infants (see Chapter 4). The theory of McCrae and Costa (1999), for example, specifically assumes that traits are biologically based, inherent tendencies that are not influenced by environment.

What are these traits that appear to be so stable? In the 1980s, researchers recognized that the hundreds of words used to express aspects of human personality (called trait adjectives) could be reliably boiled down to five. The *"Big 5,"* as they are called, represent the most basic dimensions of personality: *neuroticism* (N), *extraversion* (E), *openness* (O), *agreeableness* (A), and *conscientiousness* (C). Table 13.1 provides additional detail on these dimensions. Cross-sectional studies of personality traits as measured by questionnaires find evidence of striking similarity across age groups in the degree to which they are characterized by each of these traits, even when different instruments are used. Costa and McCrae (1994) interpret their large body of evidence on the temporal stability of the Big 5 to suggest that personality traits are stable after age 30. Before that time, certain shifts are noted in large cross-sectional samples and among samples from different cultural groups.

For example, college-age students score higher on neuroticism, extraversion, and openness to experience than older adults, and somewhat lower on agreeableness and conscientiousness. This profile reverses in individuals approaching age 30, who show slight

TABLE 13.1

The "Big 5" Personality Traits

Trait	Synonyms
Neuroticism	Tense, touchy, self-pitying, unstable, anxious, worrying
Extraversion	Outgoing, active, assertive, energetic, talkative, enthusiastic
Agreeableness	Warm, sympathetic, generous, forgiving, kind, affectionate
Conscientiousness	Organized, planful, reliable, responsible, careful, efficient
Openness to experience	Creative, artistic, curious, insightful, original, wide-ranging interests

Source: McCrae, R. R., & Johns, O. T. (1992). An introduction to the five-factor model and its applications. *Journal of Personality, 60,* 175–215.

increases in A and C and slight decreases in N, E, and O as compared to younger groups. Little change in basic traits is found after that time (McCrae & Costa, 1990).

Longitudinal and cross-cultural studies have found similar patterns. For example, Watson and Walker (1996) found that negative affect (similar to neuroticism) declined after college, and Mortimer, Finch, and Kumka (1982) found a reduction in reported sociability, similar to extraversion, in their subjects as they moved through their 20s. In addition, some studies have also noted increases in self-control and achievement (similar to C) among participants as they approached middle age (Helson & Klohnen, 1998).

In an impressive cross-sectional study of adults across five different cultures, McCrae, Costa, Pedrosa de Lima, and their colleagues (1999) found highly consistent trends among German, Italian, Portuguese, Croatian, and Korean groups. Despite their differing histori- cal experiences and cultural contexts, older individuals across cultures were slightly higher in agreeableness and conscientiousness and somewhat lower in extraversion and openness to experience than younger adults. The authors suggest that these trends are universal, maturity-dependent, and unrelated to environment. In other words, "persons grow and change, but they do so on the foundation of enduring dispositions" (Costa & McCrae, 1994, p. 36).

The Link to Temperament

Where do these adult traits come from? As we noted, some researchers have looked for links between childhood temperament characteristics and adult personality dispositions, since both are construed to have some basis in biology. Rothbart and her colleagues (Rothbart, Ahadi, & Evans, 2000) call adult personality an outcome of temperament, because it arises from constitutionally based differences in systems such as reactivity (excitability, responsivity) and self-regulation (modulation of activity). A growing literature in the field of developmental psychobiology provides evidence for brain-mediated systems of positive approach, fear, irritability/anger, effortful control, and reactive orienting (Rothbart, Derryberry, & Posner, 1994). As children develop and experience age-related changes, their temperamental characteristics become increasingly more differentiated and integrated into more mature self-systems. So, for example, early manifestations of positive approach, such as smiling and laughing, may be translated into more mature forms, such as social extraversion. When Rothbart and her associates (2000) correlated young adults' temperaments with their Big 5 personality traits, they found evidence for relationships between extraversion and positive approach, between effortful attention and conscien- tiousness, between irritability/anger and neuroticism, and between orienting sensitivity and openness to experience. Additional cross-cultural support is provided by McCrae, Costa, Ostendorf, and their associates (2000) who found modest correlations between the temperamental characteristics of German, British, Turkish, Czech, and Spanish samples with their adult personality traits.

But what if we looked at individual development over time? Would early tempera- mental patterns reliably predict adult personality? Caspi (2000) investigated the continu- ity of temperament in a cohort of New Zealanders from age 3 to age 21. The sample for this study consisted of all children born in Dunedin, New Zealand, between April 1972 and March 1973. Temperamental characteristics were assessed at various points by means of parent report, clinical examiner ratings, and self-report. Data on home environment, school, employment, and social history were also gathered. The assessment measures reflected the typologies, developed by Chess and Thomas, that were available in 1972 (see Chess & Thomas, 1987): undercontrolled or difficult (impulsive, restless, negative), inhibited or slow-to-warm-up (introverted, fearful), and well-adjusted or easy (see Chapter 4).

Results paint a picture of moderate personality stability over time. At age 21, the 10% of children identified at age 3 as undercontrolled were more likely than other groups to be aggressive, sensation-seeking, impulsive, and prone to troubles with the law. They also tended to experience higher levels of interpersonal conflict in family and romantic relationships. Even if the surface features of behavior changed over time, these undercontrolled children were more likely to grow up to be adults whose behavior reflected a similar lack of control and problematic adjustment. The inhibited children (8% of the sample) at 21 were more likely than the other participants to have suffered from depression. As adults, they were more shy, fearful, and nonassertive and less connected to sources of social support.

Several possible explanations might account for trait stability over time. First, genes probably play a role in stability of personality. McCue, Bacon, and Lykken (1993) found that of the roughly 50% consistency in twins' personality traits measured over 10 years, about 80% of that similarity could be attributed to genetics. Remember, however, that we do not inherit trait patterns per se, but rather chemical templates that regulate the building of the nervous system. As multidimensional models of development predict, personality features are also shaped by contextual circumstances. In other words, the transactional interplay between individual and context is what sculpts personality (Buss, 1987).

Viewed from this perspective, personality or trait consistency will be highest if other variables, in addition to biology, provide support or scaffolding for that consistency. For example, the individual's environment should remain consistent. Helson and Roberts's (1994) study of 81 women from Mills College from ages 21 to 52 is illustrative here. Those women whose level of ego development showed no change or whose level of ego development even slightly decreased over the years of the study were the least likely to have experienced disruptive experiences or high levels of responsibility. They seemed to have found comfortable niches for themselves that required little accommodation or change. Personality could remain fairly consistent over time, because these women appeared to have selected environments that suited their personalities in the first place (proactive transactions). Or they may have behaved in ways that communicated their reluctance to change, thus eliciting compliance from others (evocative transactions).

Yet another possible explanation for continuity is that certain kinds of personality styles show more consistency than others. Clausen (1993), for example, suggested that planful competence, a trait found in people who are highly dependable and self-reliant, tends to be consistent across adulthood. Generally, people who possess resilient characteristics tend to be more stable and consistent throughout life. Perhaps any strong, "achieved" identity operates as a cognitive schema or organizer that interprets information and situations in ways that promote consistency with one's personality or reputation (Vandewater, Ostrove, & Stewart, 1997).

INFLUENCES ON ADULT DEVELOPMENT: SOURCES OF CHANGE

Although personality characteristics can be a relatively stable set of influences on the adult's development, there are many changes to which an adult must adapt. Some of these are strongly age determined or *age graded,* such as physical changes that come more or less inevitably with time. Other changes in our life experience are more a function of historical circumstance and are called *history-graded* changes. These include events that we share with our whole cohort, like living through the Great Depression or the Vietnam War.

Finally, there are changes that apply specifically to our own lives. These are **nonnormative changes,** often accidents of fate, like being in a train wreck or winning the lottery.

Age-Graded Changes

We will consider three kinds of age-graded changes. The first two are the physical and cognitive changes that have been documented as a function of aging in adulthood. The last concerns shifts in the relative importance of various life tasks that seem to occur with age. These shifts in life tasks, described by theorists such as Erik Erikson and Daniel Levinson, are generally thought to be a product of one's psychological response to reaching adulthood and facing the typical burdens and challenges that life presents to all of us. All three kinds of change represent challenges to our adaptive functioning as we get older.

Physical Changes in Adulthood

Bodily changes may be the most obvious ones in adult life. By about age 30, as people enter middle adulthood, there begins a shift from **adolescing,** or growing up, to **senescing,** or "growing down" (Levinson, 1986). Although there are physical declines that most people are aware of fairly early in this process, such as some skin wrinkling or hair loss, most declines are much more subtle, such as a decrease in the effectiveness of immune processes or in cardiovascular functioning. For the most part, people continue to feel that they are at peak or near peak levels of physical functioning until they are 40 or older. In their 40s and 50s, most people become more aware of physical losses.

Most sensory systems decline in sensitivity/acuity, although there is considerable variation among the systems and among individuals (see Whitbourne, 1996). Developmental changes in some systems have proven more difficult to study effectively than others. The experience of pain, for example, is caused by the stimulation of free nerve endings in damaged tissue. Some studies indicate that pain detection diminishes with age, and others indicate that pain sensitivity increases with age! The aging of the visual and auditory systems is probably best understood. Visual acuity is maintained at near peak levels until about age 40 and then starts to wane. Individuals who never before wore glasses or contact lenses are likely to need them now, and those who required some visual correction in the past begin to experience more frequent prescription changes, or they now need bifocals or trifocals. Middle adults also begin to notice that they need more light to see well than their younger friends, and they may begin to notice that it takes longer to adapt to lighting changes than it used to. They are most likely to be bothered when there is a sudden change in lighting: coming out of a dark movie theater into daylight or encountering the headlights of an oncoming car on a dark road. Changes in the neurons of the retina, as well as changes in the cornea and lens of the eye, all contribute to these growing problems.

Similar declines in hearing or auditory sensitivity begin in the 30s. Sensitivity to high-frequency (high-pitched) sounds declines earlier and more rapidly, and the losses are usually greater in men than in women. Note that women's voices are therefore more difficult to hear in the later years than are men's, so that men are more likely to have the difficulty than women are. There is much individual variation in the degree and kind of hearing loss, but most individuals find their lives somewhat affected by the end of middle age, in their 60s (Whitbourne, 1996).

Among the functional systems that show developmental changes sometime in middle adulthood is the reproductive system (Whitbourne, 1996). As with the sensory systems, noticeable changes tend to begin in the 40s and 50s. The menstrual cycle usually begins to shorten and becomes somewhat more erratic by the time a woman is in her late 30s. The female **climacteric,** the gradual reduction of reproductive ability, ending in **menopause,** the cessation of menstruation, usually begins in the 40s and continues for at least 10 years. The climacteric is largely a function of a reduction in circulating *estradiol,* a form of the primary female hormone, *estrogen,* produced by the ovaries. Having less estradiol eventually influences many other changes: the thinning and coarsening of pubic hair, the thinning and wrinkling of the labia, and changes in vaginal chemistry that can cause dryness and a greater likelihood of vaginal infections. Despite these changes, and despite a general slowing of sexual response times, sexual functioning and sexual pleasure seem to be affected very little for most women, as long as one key ingredient remains—the availability of sexual partners (see Kellett, 2000, for a review). Many researchers have found only small declines, if any, in the frequency of female sexual activity in middle age (see Table 13.2).

Interestingly, men in the middle years do not produce less *testosterone,* the primary male hormone, than younger men. But reproductive structures, like the testes, do show signs of aging. As a result, by the 40s and 50s, fewer sperm are produced, sperm have less motility, and less seminal fluid is available. These changes cause reduced fertility over time, although most men do not become completely infertile with age as women do. As we noted, testosterone production does not seem to decline in most healthy men, but men who have health problems or who are overweight may produce less testosterone with age. This can lead to changes in secondary sex characteristics: diminished facial and body hair, less muscle growth, changes in the size and appearance of the penis, and so on (Whitbourne, 1996). As with women, while sexual response times begin to increase in middle age, sexual functioning and sexual pleasure can be maintained (see Table 13.2). For a man with an available sexual partner, how sexually active he will be in his older years is closely correlated with how strong his sex drive was in his younger years (see Kellett, 2000).

In today's popular culture, personal worth is linked to physical beauty, defined in part as a youthful, fit appearance. In such a climate, the most problematic physical changes of middle adulthood for some people can be the wrinkling and sagging of the skin and an increase in body fat (e.g., Katchadourian, 1987). Weight gain is not inevitable in middle adulthood, but rather is directly linked to overeating, poor nutrition, and/or inadequate exercise. Unfortunately, the typical habits of many Americans do result in their gaining weight throughout middle adulthood, mostly around the waist and hips, called "middle aged spread" (Whitbourne, 1996). Among the factors contributing to the wrinkling and sagging process are changes in the layers of the skin. For example, *elastin,* a substance in the cells of the dermis, or middle layer of skin, allows the skin to stretch and contract as we move. After age 30, elastin gradually becomes more brittle, reducing skin elasticity. Areas of the body containing fat, such as the arms, legs, torso, and breasts, usually begin to sag by the 40s and 50s.

TABLE 13.2

Frequency of Sexual Activity by Age and Gender

	M	F	M	F	M	F	M	F	M	F
Age	18–26		27–38		39–50		51–54		65+	
N	254	268	353	380	282	295	227	230	212	221
>1/wk	53%	46%	60%	49%	54%	39%	63%	32%	53%	41%
"rarely"	13%	17%	9%	12%	8%	21%	8%	21%	11%	22%

Source: Kellett, J. M. Older adult sexuality. In L. T. Szuchman & F. Muscarella (Eds.) *Psychological perspectives on human sexuality* (p. 357). Copyright © 2000 John Wiley & Sons, Inc. This material is used by permission of John Wiley & Sons, Inc.

Cognitive Changes in Adulthood

Age-graded changes in cognitive functioning are experienced throughout adulthood. An enormous research literature exists on adult cognitive change. We humans, including developmental researchers, seem to worry a great deal about what kinds of intellectual declines we can expect as we get older and how we might avoid them. Early findings, from cross-sectional studies, tended to be a bit discouraging, producing data such as those in Figure 13.3a, reported by Schaie (1994). In such studies, most intellectual skills appear to decline fairly steadily after age 25. But in cross-sectional studies, different ages are represented by people from different cohorts. For example, in Schaie's cross-sectional data

FIGURE 13.3

Cross-Sectional and Longitudinal Findings for Six Intellectual Abilities

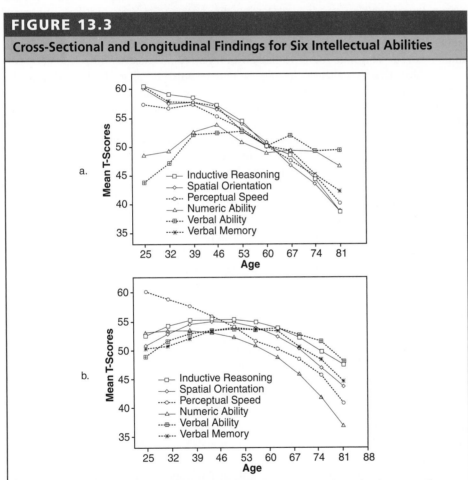

a. An illustration of *cross-sectional* findings for six intellectual abilities. Note that it appears that most skills decline throughout adulthood. An interesting exception are numerical abilities, which appear to increase through the mid-forties. Longitudinal data, however, make it clear that the increases really represent cohort effects. Younger cohorts (more recent generations) have poorer math skills than older cohorts.

b. An illustration of *longitudinal* findings for the same six intellectual abilities. Now you can see that people's numerical skills are best, on average, in early adulthood. However, most skills are maintained or improved until after age 60.

Source: Schaie, K. W. The course of adult intellectual development. *American Psychologist, 49,* 307. Copyright © 1994 by the American Psychological Association. Reprinted with permission.

(collected in 1991), the 81-year-old cohort was born in 1910, and the 25-year-old cohort was born in 1966. Many factors could contribute to what appear to be age effects, because different cohorts are not just different in age. They have also grown up in different eras, such that they may have experienced very different educational, economic, and cultural opportunities. Older cohorts, for example, have, on average, fewer years of postelementary school education than younger cohorts. Their test results may reflect these cohort differences rather than the typical changes in cognitive function that come with age.

A better way to assess cognitive change across the life span is to conduct prospective or longitudinal research, that is, studies that reassess the same individuals periodically as they get older. Figure 13.3b illustrates longitudinal data on the progress of six ability factors, also reported by Schaie (1994). These findings suggest a very different and more complex picture of intellectual change in adulthood. Although some abilities begin to decline early, most cognitive capacities seem to show improvements with age and show only small average declines after age 55 to 60 (Schaie 1994).

One way to make sense of the mixed pattern of improvement and decline through adulthood is to categorize cognitive skills with regard to how heavily they depend on two kinds of underlying intellectual resources. One resource is called *fluid intelligence* by some (e.g., Horn & Cattell, 1966) and is called the **mechanics** of intelligence by others (e.g., Baltes et al., 1998). These terms refer to basic operational characteristics that seem to directly reflect how well the "hardware" of the nervous system is working. Fluid, or mechanical, functions include such things as processing speed and inhibitory mechanisms. They are the most likely kinds of intellectual processes to show declines sometime in middle adulthood. For example, information processing speed may begin to slow down as early as age 30 and declines fairly rapidly after age 40, so that we are slower to take in information as we get older and slower to respond to it (e.g., Kail & Salthouse, 1994). Inhibitory mechanisms show decrements by about age 40, so that in some tasks, older adults are more easily distracted by irrelevant stimulation than younger adults (Hasher & Zacks, 1988; Zacks & Hasher, 1994).

Another intellectual resource is called *crystallized intelligence* (e.g., Horn & Cattell, 1966) or the *pragmatics* of intelligence (e.g, Baltes et al., 1998). It is the compilation of skills and information we have acquired in the course of our lives. Crystallized intelligence, or pragmatics, is a little like the pile of software programs that most of us accumulate for our computers. Our knowledge of language, of how to do a job or to play an instrument, the strategies we have learned for memorizing information or solving problems—all forms of *declarative* and *procedural* knowledge (see Chapter 6)—are included. Crystallized intelligence is less likely than fluid intelligence to show declines with age and, for some individuals, can increase even into old age. For most people in middle adulthood, and for most abilities, declining fluid resources are usually balanced or outweighed by continuing steady increases in crystallized resources (Baltes et al., 1998). It is only after about age 60 that losses in fluid intelligence may be great enough to contribute to overall declines in intellectual functioning.

Changing memory abilities provide a good illustration of the interactive influences of mechanics and pragmatics in overall functioning. Some forms of memory show losses in middle and late adulthood, and some do not. *Working memory,* for example, seems most disrupted by age. You'll remember from Chapter 6 that working memory stores information that we are thinking about or working with at the present moment. This is the part of the information processing system with which we solve problems, make inferences, or transfer information to long-term storage. Working memory has a limited capacity, so that only a restricted number of information units can be retained there at one time, and usually only for 15 to 30 seconds, unless we actually keep working with it—that is, unless we make an effort to pay attention to the information. To put it a different way, working memory is the active, attentive part of the mind, where we solve problems and learn new information. In late middle adulthood, working memory capacity seems to decline. Fewer pieces of information can be attended to at one time, and either problem solving or learning or both can be somewhat affected as a result. For example, imagine a situation in which you look up and dial a 10-digit phone number, and then you immediately attempt to redial the number. Suppose that at age 30, you could remember about 6 of the digits when you redialed. At age 50, given the same kind of memory task, you would probably remember only 5 of the digits. Clearly, what we are describing here are not catastrophic losses. The modest change is more a nuisance factor than anything else. Most people, by about age 50, notice that they have a little more difficulty than they used to recalling the name of a new acquaintance or solving a complex problem that requires attending to several pieces of information at once. Declines in fluid intelligence seem to make the difference. Slower processing speed may make it harder to keep as many pieces of information in mind simultaneously as we once could and/or make it difficult to work our way through to the end of a problem before some of the information that we need has disappeared from short-term storage (Salthouse, 1996). Reduced inhibitory control might also be important. For example, we might experience at times "a kind of 'mental clutter' in which extraneous thoughts and plans can interfere with, and possibly crowd out, goal-relevant thoughts and plans" (Zacks, Hasher, & Li, 2000, p. 297).

The decline of working memory affects problem solving most when either the information that is relevant to the solution or the problem-solving situation is new. But when middle adults are solving familiar, everyday problems or problems in areas of their own expertise, the crystallized resources at their disposal often help them to be more effective than younger adults (e.g., Willis, 1996).

Although the limitations of working memory make it more difficult to get new information into *long-term memory,* we nonetheless do continue to learn in middle and late adulthood, storing new information from our experiences despite our reduced efficiency. Thus, both younger and older adults add new information to *episodic memory*—memory for personal experiences—but younger subjects typically learn more with greater ease (e.g., Zelinski, Gilewski, & Schaie, 1993). To put it differently, we are somewhat less likely, as we get older, to remember specific daily experiences, such as where we parked the car this morning. However, information already learned appears to be maintained as well as in our younger years. In fact, an older person's *semantic memory,* her store of factual information, seems to have a richer network of interrelationships as a result of her greater experience, allowing her to retrieve information through many more routes than a younger person can (e.g., Laver & Burke, 1993; MacKay & Abrams, 1996). As Whitbourne (1996), suggested, you might be well advised to choose an older partner the next time you play a memory game like Trivial Pursuit!

Charness and Bosman (1990) provide an interesting example of the differential effects of age changes in fluid and crystallized intelligence on performance in adulthood. They describe two kinds of chess competitions. In *tournament chess,* participants make their moves quickly, after deliberating for about three minutes. In *correspondence chess,* the participants can have three days to make a move. Clearly, tournament chess makes greater demands on processing speed, whereas correspondence chess seems to draw much more completely on one's knowledge and experience. Not surprisingly, then, top performers win their first world championship in tournament chess at much younger ages, about age 30 on average, than they do in correspondence chess, where the average first-time champion is 46! It is not unusual for middle-aged chess devotees to adapt to declines in fluid intelligence by shifting their focus from tournament chess to correspondence chess as they get older.

In the next chapter we will look more closely at cognitive changes in late adulthood, focusing especially on how older adults compensate for losses in fluid intelligence and on the debate over the growth of wisdom.

Life-Task or Life-Course Changes in Adulthood

People experience another kind of age-graded change as they move through adulthood. Life-course changes, brought on by shifts in the life tasks that seem most important to us at different times of our lives, have been described by many different theorists. While each of these theorists tends to emphasize somewhat different aspects of the life experience, you will see commonalities in their observations as we briefly summarize a sampling of these descriptions.

You may recall that Schaie (1977–1978; Schaie & Willis, 2000; see Chapter 11) proposed a series of stages in adult life, each of which requires the development of new ways to apply and use one's intellectual resources. These changes are directly related to shifts in family roles and in the life tasks that we face as we grow older. In the *achieving stage* of young adulthood, the individual must learn to use logical thinking skills to plan the achievement of long-term goals. In the *responsible stage* of middle adulthood, one must learn to use her problem-solving skills not only to achieve her own goals but to help coordinate her needs with those of others for whom she is responsible at home, at work, and in the community. In the *reorganizational stage* of one's elder years, one's focus narrows again to reaching personal, practical, day-to-day goals as an adult devotes her thinking skills to managing her losses. Finally, in late adulthood, people move into the *reintegrative stage,* when their goals are primarily to conserve energy, and perhaps into a *legacy-leaving stage,* when they use their cognitive resources to help them leave behind a written or oral account of their experience or wisdom.

Schaie emphasizes the shifting allocation of intellectual skills across adulthood, as people confront different kinds of problems related to their age and stage of life. Most other theorists emphasize changes in personality. They do not focus on personality traits, which, as we have seen, are relatively stable in middle adulthood and beyond, but rather they describe structural changes in self-concept and in self-expression.

Perhaps the best-known theory of life-course changes in self-concept is Erik Erikson's, by now quite familiar to you. Erikson (e.g., 1950/1963) describes three stages in self-development in adulthood, based on the kinds of life tasks that become most important to people as they find themselves fully matured and facing the fact that this is the one life that they have to live. Very briefly, in young adulthood, *intimacy* (versus *isolation*) is one's quest; finding a way to validate and expand her own sense of self by committing to a shared life with others. In middle adulthood, *generativity* (versus *stagnation*) becomes most important, giving one's own life purpose by producing and building for the next generation, through work, community service, and/or child rearing. By old age, establishing **ego integrity** (versus **despair**) becomes life's task. Ideally, a process of life review helps the elderly adult to develop a sense that one's own life is "something that had to be," that she has lived a life that has order, meaning, and dignity (see Chapter 1, especially Table 1.1).

Erikson argued that different concerns reach ascendancy in different age periods. Vaillant (1977; Vaillant & Koury, 1994) suggested that two more adult life stages should be added to Erikson's scheme, reflecting that forming deep bonds, becoming productive, and finding meaning in one's life are recurring themes throughout adulthood. In one's mid-twenties, **career consolidation** (vs. **self-absorption**) is a key focus of self-development. In this phase of life, in addition to ongoing intimacy concerns, making a commitment to work that brings personal satisfaction, regardless of its other rewards, rather than just having a job, becomes important. The most positive development for this period is that such a commitment emerges as an important part of one's identity.

Vaillant also described a stage that comes near the end of Erikson's generativity stage, in late middle adulthood. This he called the **keeper of meaning** (vs. **rigidity**) stage, when the adult expands her generative concerns beyond just making a productive contribution, in order to actually preserve something that is part of the culture. In this sense, adults seek ways to establish the meaningfulness of the work or contributions they have made. For example, Tien, a woman who served on the parent advisory board of her children's day care center, might move on after her own children are no longer young to join a child care advocacy group in her community, hoping to assure that future generations of children in her region will have access to the high-quality child care she was able to provide her own children.

As we saw in Chapter 12, research indicates that both intimacy and generativity are central to the lives of young adults. Later in this chapter we will discuss research on how these concerns tend to play out in the arenas of marriage, family life, parenting, and work during the middle years of adulthood.

Several other theorists have proposed stages in adult personality development that repeat many of the themes that we see in Erikson's work. They all emphasize that people have fundamental concerns or needs that shift in importance from one adult stage to another. We will briefly describe Levinson's theory here; some additional theories (e.g., Gould, 1978; Loevinger, 1976) are included in schematic comparison in Table 13.3.

In Levinson's account (e.g., Levinson, 1986; Levinson & Levinson, 1996; Levinson, Darrow, Klein, Levinson, & McKee, 1978), a person's life has structure at any given time.

TABLE 13.3

Adult Life Stages: Some Theories of Self-Development

Approximate Age Period	Erikson	Vaillant	Loevinger	Gould
Adolescence	Identity (vs. Identity Diffusion)	(like Erikson)	Conscientious–Conformist	Separating from parents: becoming independent
Young Adulthood	Intimacy (vs. Isolation)	"	Individualistic	"Nobody's baby"; becoming a competent, self-maintaining adult
Middle Adulthood (Early)	Generativity (vs. Stagnation)	Generativity–Career consolidation (vs. Self-Absorption); producing	Autonomous	Opening up: exploring inner consciousness, coming to deeper understanding of self and needs
Middle Adulthood (Late)		Generativity–Keeper of Meaning (vs. Rigidity); giving, mentoring		Midlife: finding the courage and resourcefulness to act on deeper feelings; awareness of pressure of time
Late Adulthood	Ego Integration (vs. Despair)		Integrated	Beyond midlife: establishing true autonomy; becoming inner-directed rather than governed by roles; "I own myself"

One's *life structure* is a pattern of relationships between the self and the external world, such as relationships to one's "spouse, lover, family, occupation, religion, leisure, and so on" (Levinson, 1986). There may be many components to the life structure, but Levinson found that at any one time there are usually only one or two really significant, defining components for the self, usually marriage-family and/or occupational components. Levinson identified three major adult stages, or eras: early, middle, and late adulthood. Each of these eras begins with a 5-year transitional period and is marked by a smaller mid-era transition, when the life structure's effectiveness for serving the person's goals is reexamined and may be altered.

Whereas Erikson and Vaillant suggest that certain life tasks occur in relatively predictable sequence (e.g., first intimacy needs are greater, then generativity needs), Levinson (1986) argues that life events unfold in many ways depending on a particular individual's life circumstances, gender, and culture and that specific concerns are not necessarily more important in one era than in another. What is predictable, he argues, is the sequence of age periods for building and changing first one life structure and then another. The experience of life changes from one era to the next. Put a different way, what is inevitable in adulthood is that a person will establish and then revise her life structure at particular times as she ages. Figure 13.4 presents the age and sequence of the eras Levinson describes and his view of the general character of the life structure changes in each era.

In sum, many theorists have identified life-course changes affecting self-concept or self-expression during adulthood. There is by no means complete agreement among these theorists on the character of these changes. For example, following Jung (1963), Levinson (e.g., 1986) and Gould (1978) describe the midlife transition as an often tumultuous time, a period of major upheaval and self-evaluation, not unlike adolescence. You may have heard it referred to as a "midlife crisis." Their research, consisting of longitudinal interview studies of relatively small and somewhat selective samples of adults, tends to support these claims (e.g., Gould, 1978; Levinson et al., 1978, 1996). But in much larger interview and questionnaire studies, many researchers have found little evidence of widespread midlife distress, although they have found indications of shifting concerns at midlife (e.g., McCrae & Costa, 1990; Vaillant, 1977; Whitbourne, 1996).

Regardless of such disagreements, there is some similarity among the theoretical descriptions of adult life-course changes. The available empirical work supports the general idea of such change. Despite the enormous variation in the immediate details of adult lives—from culture to culture, from cohort to cohort, from family to family, and from individual to individual—there appear to be some life changes that are widely experienced. These changes lead each of us to reformulate, or at least reevaluate, our selves and our lives periodically. Much more research is needed to establish the specifics of these changes and whom they do and do not affect.

For counselors, awareness of potential stage changes can help enrich our understanding of clients. For example, suppose a woman at 45 comes to a counselor looking for help with marital problems she has tolerated for 20 years. We might be inclined to wonder, why now, and, how likely is it that change can be effected after so many years of entrenched behavior patterns? The answers to both questions may be partly a function of life stage. Many theorists see the 40s as a time when reassessment of one's life structure is very likely and when willingness to act on the basis of one's individual propensities, rather than strictly in adherence with social expectations, increases (see Table 13.3). Vaillant suggests that generativity needs are likely to reorganize, so that direct caregiving to one's spouse or children is less likely to meet one's needs than opportunities to seek broader meaning in one's life by finding ways to preserve the culture. Thus, not only is it a likely time for this woman to reassess her life, it may also be a time when she will be open to trying new ways of meeting her needs.

FIGURE 13.4

Levinson's Conception of the Early and Middle Adult Eras and Transitions

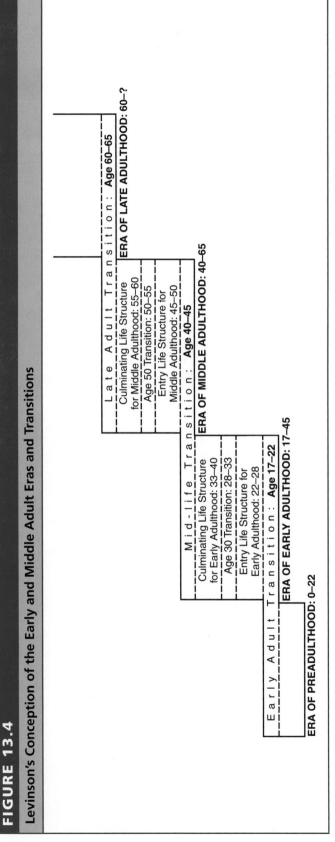

Source: From *The seasons of a man's life* by Daniel Levinson, copyright © 1978 by Daniel J. Levinson. Used by permission of Alfred A. Knopf, a division of Random House, Inc.

History-Graded Changes

The historical events that affect our whole cohort are another source of change in adult lives. People are partly a product of the historical context in which they develop. Imagine that you were a young adult parent trying to support your children during the years of the Great Depression. You would take a job wherever you found one, no matter how difficult the work, and you would probably be grateful for it. What effect might years of deprivation and struggle have on your tendency toward conscientiousness? Or think about moving through early adulthood during the social upheavals and sexual revolution of the 1960s. Do you think this experience might have some effect on your openness to experience? *History-graded events,* also called **cohort effects,** provide a context for development and also influence it directly.

The year of your birth marks your entry into a *cohort* of peers who accompany you through age-graded developmental changes (toddlerhood, puberty, and so on) within the context of a specific set of historical events (wars, technological shifts, and so on). The effect of history is particularly linked to a person's age and stage of life. In addition to age-graded and history-graded changes, we also progress through stages of the family life cycle as child, parent, grandparent, and so on. Researchers who take a **life-course perspective** remind us that development is influenced by the intersection of chronological age (*life time*), family-related roles (*family time*), and membership in a birth cohort (*historical time*) (Elder, 1994). If society experiences an economic recession that results in a lengthy period of corporate downsizing, a young father who has just completed a training program in computer repair might see his chances of getting a well-paying job shrink. He may have to

What do you think might be the nonnormative and cohort effects of the events of September 11, 2001, on your life?

wait to buy a first house, ultimately limiting the lifetime equity he can accrue. Because his family must continue to reside in a low-cost apartment, his preschool son might also be affected because of missed educational opportunities that would have been available with a move to a more advantaged school district. Note that despite the important implications of the economic downturn for this young parent's life, his own grandparents, who are retired and receiving a fixed pension, would not be much affected.

Twenge (2000) provides a recent example of how sociocultural and historical context influences the personality development of cohorts of individuals. She reviewed published reports of child and adolescent anxiety from 1952 to 1993 to see if levels had changed over these years. Her distressing finding showed that the average child in America during the 1980s scored higher on anxiety than child psychiatric patients from the 1950s. Further analysis allowed her to demonstrate that these increases were associated with the breakdown of social connections and with increases in physical and psychological threats. Economic recessions were not related to the increase in anxiety. Twenge's results imply that recent cohorts are living in a world that is less favorable to their positive development than the world in which their own parents grew up. A context that provides for fewer or weaker social bonds at the same time that threats are expanding heightens the sense of vulnerability for these young people, who are truly growing up in an "age of anxiety."

Nonnormative Changes

Just as history-graded changes can significantly affect the development of a whole cohort, individual lives are also changed by unexpected events. These events are called *nonnormative* events, "bolt from the blue" experiences that we don't anticipate, yet that can have powerful developmental effects. Crises such as traumatic illnesses, accidents, imprisonment, the untimely death of a loved one, or even positive events such as winning a lottery can be considered nonnormative. They create new sets of circumstances for people, and these have the potential to alter developmental trajectories (Datan & Ginsburg, 1975).

Imagine a woman at age 45 who has worked hard as a parent and homemaker and looks forward to seeing each of her children move into adult independence. A car accident suddenly leaves her 19-year-old son a quadraplegic. The financial resources she and her husband had carefully saved for their retirement and their children's college years are soon gone, and the mother's dreams of opening a small craft shop are dashed. She is a somewhat introverted woman, but the special needs of her son create circumstances that move her to take initiative with lawyers, insurance companies, and government agencies. Literally, her personality and the whole course of her life begin to move in a new direction. So middle age, like the "ages" before it, is both continuous and changing. Stable personality traits are influenced by age, life stage, history, and unplanned events as people continue to adapt to life.

KEY DEVELOPMENTAL TASKS OF MIDLIFE: THE CONTINUING PURSUIT OF INTIMACY AND GENERATIVITY

In middle adulthood, as in young adulthood, loving relationships and productive, meaningful work continue to be critical elements in the construction of a satisfying life. As you know, Erikson saw *intimacy,* broadly defined as sharing oneself with another, as a more prominent concern in young adulthood and *generativity,* defined as the need to create and produce, as a more central focus of middle adulthood. However, it is clear from available research that while the relative balance between these two concerns may shift (see Chapter 12), both remain important in middle adulthood and beyond. In the following sections we will further explore intimacy issues by examining how marital relationships form, develop, and sometimes fail during adulthood. We will continue our discussion of generativity by considering the parental role from the adult's perspective, and we will touch on other generativity issues in the middle years, having to do with work and community.

Intimacy: Marriage and Other Primary Relationships

One of the most valuable adaptations we humans can make is to establish and maintain close interpersonal relationships. In adulthood, close ties take on a variety of forms, and the number and diversity of forms is increasing. Marriage has provided the traditional structure within which such relationships exist. Approximately 52% of the U.S. population were married, according to 2000 census data, a figure down from 60% in 1980. One quarter of all households in the United States were single-person households. Cohabitation was also on the rise. Although there has been a steep rise in the number of people living alone or as unmarried partners, this condition might be temporary for some. According to 1990 data, only 8.4% of men and 7.1% of women have *never* wed by the time they reach age 45 to 54. Thus, estimates of the marriage rate for people over their lifetimes predict that approximately 90% of the population will have been married at least one time.

The definition of "family" has indeed become more inclusive in the twenty-first century and refers to more than the traditional nuclear family with its own biological children. Particularly since the social changes initiated in the 1960s, people have felt freer to meet their needs for intimacy and connection in a variety of ways. Extended, multigenerational families, adoptive and foster families, same-sex unions, remarried or blended families, single-parent families, and "families" composed of several people living together without legal ties are all examples of new trends in family formation. Some individuals will be part of several different kinds of families as they progress through their lives.

Clearly, psychological wellness does not depend upon any one specific relationship configuration. Kaslow (2001) encourages clinicians to expand their definition of family and to work toward ways of promoting optimal functioning for each of these forms. Yet despite greater social acceptance of alternative family styles, researchers have discovered that good marriages or primary relationships confer a number of physical and psychological benefits that other states may not provide (Horwitz & White, 1998; Ross, 1995). For example, married people report generally higher levels of happiness than unmarried people. They have lower rates of mental illness, drug and alcohol abuse, and physical illness than their unmarried counterparts. They report higher levels of sexual and emotional satisfaction (Waite & Joyner, 2001). Research has even documented that married partners tend to live longer (Freidman et al., 1995)! Perhaps the day-to-day economic and social support that accrues to married couples over the years helps to account for some of these effects. Married couples may also receive more social approval and less social rejection than individuals in other situations, although tolerance for alternative family arrangements is growing. More research is needed to understand whether the same benefits are conferred by alternative relationship forms as well.

While we use marriage as the prototypical vehicle to illustrate the development of intimacy over the adult life span, we acknowledge that this is not the only road, nor even the best one, for many people. We do not underestimate the importance of friendships nor devalue single status in adulthood. However, as you have seen, demographics show that the majority of people will marry or participate in some kind of committed relationship, such as between gay and lesbian couples, for at least some period of time in their life. In some Latin American cultures, there is an historical acceptance of long-term consensual unions (Landale & Fennelly, 1992) even though couples are not formally wed. After divorce, rates of remarriage are still very high. Approximately 80% remarry within 3 years after divorce (Glick & Lin, 1986). So while the traditional marital and family life cycle may not be the best descriptive fit for everyone, there are aspects of its stages that can help us understand many kinds of close adult relationships. The nature of intimate relationships, inside or outside of marriage, is defined by mutual sharing of joys and sorrows, reaching compromises and working out problems, and developing a sense of "we-ness."

The Family Life Cycle

Marriages (and other primary relationships) change as partners age and the demands of family life ebb and flow. The *family life cycle,* a normative, stage-like sequence of traditional family development in intact marriages, has been described in several ways. A well-known early example proposed by Duvall (1971) is depicted in Figure 13.5. Duvall emphasized the time spent in each of the stages of family life as partners become parents, rear and launch their children, become "empty-nesters," and subsequently face old age. B. Carter and McGoldrick (1999) developed a similar model that incorporates the tasks that accompany each stage (see Table 13.4). In the next section, we borrow from this latter model to highlight some important transitions and challenges facing families. Then we take a closer look at marriage itself and address theories of marital satisfaction and dysfunction.

Stages of the Family Life Cycle

Finding a mate is a task that typically involves a relatively lengthy period of experimentation, given that people in the United States marry at later ages than they did in previous

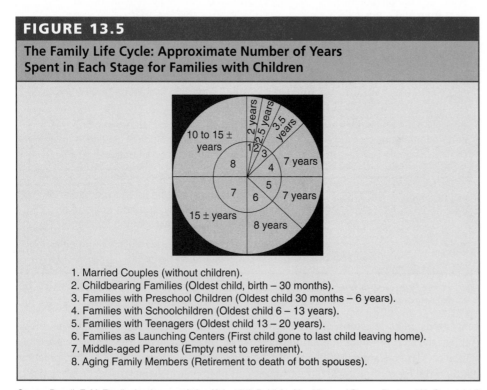

FIGURE 13.5

The Family Life Cycle: Approximate Number of Years Spent in Each Stage for Families with Children

1. Married Couples (without children).
2. Childbearing Families (Oldest child, birth – 30 months).
3. Families with Preschool Children (Oldest child 30 months – 6 years).
4. Families with Schoolchildren (Oldest child 6 – 13 years).
5. Families with Teenagers (Oldest child 13 – 20 years).
6. Families as Launching Centers (First child gone to last child leaving home).
7. Middle-aged Parents (Empty nest to retirement).
8. Aging Family Members (Retirement to death of both spouses).

Source: Duvall, E. M. Family development (4th ed.) (p. 121). Published by Allyn and Bacon, Boston, MA. Copyright © 1971 by Pearson Education. Reprinted by permission of the publisher.

TABLE 13.4

Family Life Cycle Stages, Transitions, and Tasks

Family Life Cycle Stage	Emotional Process of Transition: Key Principles	Second-Order Changes in Family Status Required to Proceed Developmentally
Leaving home: single young adults	Accepting emotional and financial responsibility for self	a. Differentiation of self in relation to family of origin b. Development of intimate peer relationships c. Establishment of self in respect to work and financial independence
The joining of families through marriage: the new couple	Commitment to new system	a. Formation of marital system b. Realignment of relationships with extended families and friends to include spouse
Families with young children	Accepting new members into the system	a. Adjusting marital system to make space for children b. Joining in child rearing, financial and household tasks c. Realignment of relationships with extended family to include parenting and grandparenting roles
Families with adolescents	Increasing flexibility of family boundaries to permit children's independence and grandparents' frailties	a. Shifting of parent/child relationships to permit adolescent to move into and out of system b. Refocus on midlife marital and career issues c. Beginning shift toward caring for older generation
Launching children and moving on	Accepting a multitude of exits from and entries into the family system	a. Renegotiation of marital system as a dyad b. Development of adult-to-adult relationships between grown children and their parents c. Realignment of relationships to include in-laws and grandchildren d. Dealing with disabilities and death of parents (grandparents)
Families in later life	Accepting the shifting generational roles	a. Maintaining own and/or couple functioning and interests in face of physiological decline: exploration of new familial and social role options b. Support for more central role of middle generation c. Making room in the system for the wisdom and experience of the elderly, supporting the older generation without overfunctioning for them d. Dealing with loss of spouse, siblings, and other peers and preparation for death

Source: From Carter & McGoldrick, *Expanded family life cycle: Individual family and social perspectives,* 3/e. Published by Allyn and Bacon, Boston, MA. Copyright © 1999 by Pearson Education. Reprinted by permission of the publisher.

generations. Mate-selection has been compared to a "filtering process" by which people go through the step-by-step elimination of ineligible candidates until they settle on a partner (Janda & Klenke-Hamel, 1980). According to this theory, people initially select potential dates on the basis of physical attractiveness and personality characteristics from a pool of available, eligible candidates. Further sorting or filtering out follows on the basis of *homogomy,* or similarity to oneself in religion, SES, race, education, and so on, as well as on personality *compatibility* (Diamond, 1986). A trial period, such as an engagement or a period of cohabitation, represents the final step in the decision-making or filtering process.

If homogamy and compatibility are the actual standards for mate selection, what about love? In the United States, most people believe that love is the most important consideration when choosing a mate. You might be surprised to learn that this belief is not universal. People from other cultures consider other factors to be more important. Males in South Africa, for example, consider a mate's maturity and ability to keep house as more significant than love in choosing a partner. Chinese women value emotional stability and the desire for a family as important criteria for mate selection (see Buss, 1989).

Sternberg's (1986) view of love, composed of the three elements of *passion, intimacy,* and *commitment,* which were introduced in Chapter 12, may help us understand these differences. The romantic ideal of love portrayed in many movies and songs embodies the element of *passion.* This is the aspect of love most closely associated with sexuality and romance. Love that includes passion without intimacy or commitment is called infatuation. *Intimacy* refers to feelings of attachment or emotional closeness. It characterizes one's willingness to trust another, to value her support, and to care about her well-being. (Note that Sternberg defines "intimacy" differently from Erikson, who defines it more broadly.) According to Sternberg, when intimacy is present in a relationship without the other elements, a state of liking exists, which is similar to friendship.

The third element, *commitment,* is present when partners agree to love each other and/or make a commitment to sustain that love. Maintaining a commitment without intimacy or passion results in the state of "empty love." Sternberg proposed that any of the three elements can be either present or absent in a relationship, accounting for eight different kinds of love (see Table 13.5). He has recently expanded on these ideas by suggesting that people hold implicit narratives for love or "love stories," which direct their choice of a mate and the course of their relationships (Beall & Sternberg, 1995; Sternberg, 1998). Sternberg posits that those who have matching scripts, or similar implicit narratives, stand the best chance of having a compatible relationship. Each script emphasizes certain elements, such as emotional maturity or the commitment factor, as more important than others, and "love scripts" are heavily influenced by cultural values.

TABLE 13.5

Sternberg's Eight Kinds of Love

Kinds of Love	Elements*		
	Intimacy	Passion	Decision/Commitment
Nonlove	−	−	−
Liking	+	−	−
Infatuation	−	+	−
Empty Love	−	−	+
Romantic Love	+	+	−
Companionate Love	+	−	+
Fatuous Love	−	+	+
Consummate Love	+	+	+

*Element present (+) or absent (−)

Source: Sternberg, R. J. A triangular theory of love. *Psychological Review, 93,* 123. Copyright © 1986 by the American Psychological Association. Adapted with permission.

In contemporary U.S. culture, elements of romance and sexual passion are typically central to the definition of love and are considered very important for relationship satisfaction and mate selection. These authors conclude that love is a social construction and that we are strongly influenced by the conceptions of love that are taught by our culture.

Once the members of a couple make a commitment to each other, they begin to develop a new marital or relationship system that is a creative synthesis of the couple's original family systems. Marriages, then, are more than the joining of two individuals. The couple must develop a sense of "we-ness" that is not so rigid that it isolates them from their original family systems nor so weak that it dissolves under pressure from them.

With time, the couple may become parents, creating a new rung on the generational ladder and reaching a new stage in the family life cycle. Caretaking responsibilities then must be integrated into the marital relationship, and each partner needs to adjust to the new parental role. As children move through the adolescent period, the family needs to adapt to children's increasing demands for independence. They must learn how to provide the stability and flexibility that characterize authoritative parenting for adolescents.

Next, a couple must deal with the transition of launching their children and renegotiating the marital relationship. Adult children need to balance the attachments they have with parents with those they form outside the family. Parents need to strive for acceptance of their adult children's extrafamilial attachments as well as of their careers and other personal choices. Overall, all generations need to work toward two goals: tolerance of independence and maintenance of connections. Among families in later life, the transitions involved in grandparenthood, loss of spouse, and physical decline produce further challenges that must be dealt with flexibly.

Marriage and Its Discontents

Recall that the great majority of individuals marry at least once during their lifetimes. Clearly, many of these unions do not last "till death do them part." People still divorce in record numbers despite a modest decline in the divorce rate since 1979. According to the U.S. Bureau of the Census (1997), 50% of first marriages and 60% of remarriages end in divorce. These rates do not account for the number of unions that break up without benefit of legal divorce, considering that the average cost of divorce is $15,000 and the average length of time it takes to finalize is one year.

Women typically experience a 45% drop in standard of living following a divorce. Each year approximately one million children witness the dissolution of their parents' marriages and subsequently often share in their mothers' reduced circumstances. Yet divorce wreaks more than financial hardship for children. Researchers have documented increased emotional and behavioral problems, such as underachievement, antisocial behavior, and depression (Amato, 1993; McLanahan & Sandefur, 1994; Parke & Buriel, 1998) in children and adolescents after divorce. One longitudinal study of children of divorce found enduring problems with establishing intimacy 25 years after the divorce of the participants' parents (Wallerstein, Lewis, & Blakeslee, 2000). Given that divorce is sometimes the best or the only alternative to a troubled marriage and that not every child of divorce suffers dire consequences, we should nonetheless consider how to help prevent what is so often a powerfully negative event in people's lives.

What Makes a Marriage Fail?

Consider two final statistics from the 1997 census data: 4.2% of all divorces were attributed to financial problems, while 80% were attributed to *irreconcilable differences* (U.S. Bureau of the Census, 1998). What makes a difference *irreconcilable*? How do some people manage to reconcile their conflicts while others do not? Are the differences due to the nature of the conflicts or to something about the individuals themselves? These are some of the questions that marital and family researchers have attempted to answer. Increasingly, researchers have relied upon longitudinal studies to describe the course of marriage and to help them identify predictors of distress and divorce as they develop over time. On a more fine-grained level, they have also explored the nature of distressed and nondistressed couples' interaction so that therapeutic recommendations can be made. We will focus on some important research findings in both of these areas to give clinicians a framework for understanding the life of a marriage, the behaviors that lead to successful outcomes, and the behaviors that may foreshadow divorce.

Research done in the 1970s indicated consistent U-shaped patterns for quality of marriage. Couples' satisfaction declined shortly after the marriage, reached a low point when children were adolescents, and recovered initial levels of satisfaction when children were launched (Burr, 1970; Rollins & Feldman, 1970). The problem with this portrayal is that these early studies were cross-sectional rather than longitudinal. The high level of satisfaction reported by long-married couples could have been due to the fact that these marriages were happy enough to have survived, long after less satisfied unions had dissolved. Vaillant and Vaillant (1993) collected assessments of marital satisfaction both prospectively (in a longitudinal study) and retrospectively (in which couples reported what they could remember of their marriages over the past 40 years). Results were different depending on how the data were collected. While retrospective accounts resembled the U-shaped curve found in previous research, prospective ratings showed gradual declines in satisfaction over the entire course of the marriage for both partners, with somewhat greater declines in women's ratings. It appears that fluctuations in the family life cycle did not predict changes in marital satisfaction but were an artifact of the cross-sectional design.

If life cycle changes do not influence satisfaction, then what does? And why, at least for some, does marital satisfaction persistently decline? Let us consider three contemporary hypotheses about marital success and breakdown for some possible answers. Imagine three hypothetical newlywed couples, the Grays, the Whites, and the Greens. Mr. and Mrs. Gray are very much in love. Even when they are in the presence of other people, they behave as if they see only each other. They are highly affectionate and romantic, and their courtship was a whirlwind of exciting events. The Grays believe that they are one another's soul mates, possessing few, if any, negative characteristics. They have no doubts about the happiness that awaits them in marriage.

The Whites are also an affectionate couple. Their view of each other, however, is not quite as rosy as that of the Grays. Their engagement period was a long one because both husband and wife worked to save up enough money to buy a house. Shortly after the wedding, Mrs. White noticed that her husband was becoming less willing to part with any of his income for furniture or other items for the house that she considered important. This has already become a source of tension in the marriage.

The Greens met each other through a dating service that they employed because each was having difficulty meeting eligible romantic partners. Mrs. Green was very insecure in social situations and worried constantly that she would never find a husband. Mr. Green did not want to get married so soon, but he consented because he was afraid that he might lose his chance. Their courtship was a rocky one from the start.

As you read about each of these couples, did you think one or more of them would be more likely to divorce than another? If so, why? Your answers might be illustrative of popular hypotheses about why marriages succeed or fail. Those who espouse the ***disillusionment model*** might choose the hypothetical Grays as the couple most likely to experience marital breakdown. This view posits that overly romantic idealizations of marriage and blissfully optimistic views of one's partner set people up for eventual disappointment. Such fantasies cannot coexist for long with the reality of married life (R. S. Miller,

1997; Waller, 1938). The rise in divorce rates and incidence of cohabitation might be partially attributable to the fact that young adults in the 1990s have high expectations for marriage. Barich and Bielby (1996) reported that contemporary young adults had higher expectations than their 1960s counterparts that marriage would satisfy their needs for emotional security, personality development, and companionship. Disappointment in these areas might be seen as a reason to abandon the relationship.

However, another possibility is that the Grays are not especially likely candidates for divorce because they will work hard to maintain their favorable beliefs about each other, despite the inevitable challenges of marriage. Their positive illusions are supportive of the relationship; thus they may be reluctant to abandon them in order to face reality. This perspective is called the **maintenance hypothesis** (Karney & Bradbury, 1997; Murray, Holmes, & Griffin, 1996).

Perhaps you thought that the Whites were the most likely couple to divorce because of the growing tension in the marriage. Another perspective on marital breakdown, built on **social exchange and behavioral theories,** proposes that increasing problems and mounting conflicts gradually escalate to overwhelm the originally positive perceptions spouses held for each other. Over time, couples who experience chronic conflict and who fail to negotiate it adequately may "fall out of love" with each other once they perceive that the costs of the relationship outweigh its benefits. In truth, no marriage escapes conflict. Approximately half of all divorces occur within the first 7 years of marriage (Cherlin, 1981), suggesting that satisfaction makes its steepest slide during the early period. At this point in development, couples must adjust to each other, work out routines for household tasks, pool resources, and if they have children, take care of them. Several studies have implicated the transition to parenthood as the culprit in the loss of marital satisfaction. For example, Belsky and his colleagues found that many new parents experience a sharp drop in positive interactions and a dramatic increase in conflict following the birth of the first child (Belsky & Kelly, 1994; Belsky, Spanier, & Rovine, 1983). But even couples who remain childless report similar declines in satisfaction. Several prospective studies of young couples' marriages have found much higher rates of divorce among childless couples than among those with children (Cowan & Cowan, 1992; Shapiro, Gottman, & Carrere, 2000). Thus, the existence of conflict in a marriage is simply not a good predictor of its prognosis, but the way couples handle it may be, as we will see later on.

Finally, let's consider the Greens. You may have predicted this couple's marital demise, because they seem to bring more personal problems into the marriage in the first place. **Intrapersonal models,** which draw on theories of attachment or personality, emphasize the contribution of one's personal history or temperament to the success or failure of relationships. One particularly robust finding from many investigations of marriages is that neuroticism is moderately related to lower levels of marital satisfaction and higher levels of relationship dissolution (Karney & Bradbury, 1995; Kelly & Conley, 1987; Kurdek, 1993). Also, people who have higher levels of negative affect tend to view life as more stressful (Marco & Suls, 1993). These individuals may be more easily overwhelmed by the conflicts that are inherent in family life and, therefore, more prone to marital distress.

In an empirical test of this hypothesis, Karney and Bradbury (1997) measured the level of marital satisfaction of 60 newlywed couples at 6-month intervals over a period of 4 years. A measure of neuroticism was obtained for each participant at each of the first two data collections. Questions examined things such as tendency to worry and moodiness. Measures of initial satisfaction and observations of problem-solving interactions were also collected.

The researchers found that marital satisfaction declined, on average, for all participants over the 4 years, replicating many earlier findings. However, the drop in satisfaction was several times greater for couples who divorced than for those who remained together.

Spouses' levels of neuroticism, a presumably stable variable, were related primarily to how satisfied they were at the beginning of the marriage and less so to rates of change in satisfaction. The way couples solved problems was also strongly related to the rates of decline in satisfaction. In other words, both intrapersonal and interpersonal variables made independent contributions to the health of the relationship but in different ways and at different points in time.

Keeping Love Alive

While the models we have described all may contribute something to our understanding of marriage, each by itself is inadequate to explain its complexity. The marital trajectory seems to be affected by intrapersonal (traits, expectations), interpersonal (problem-solving skills), situational (life stresses, environmental conditions), and developmental (transitions, role change) factors. A comprehensive, multidimensional theory of marriage or other committed relationships has yet to be developed. Nevertheless, we can learn a great deal from the research that has been done, particularly during the last decade, to help us improve the relationships of our clients.

Some of the most therapist-friendly information comes from the "love-lab" of John Gottman, who has a unique approach to the study of marital dynamics. Gottman and his colleagues have spent years observing and videotaping couples interacting with each other in order to understand, from the inside out, what makes marriages work or fail. Gottman (1999) has used this descriptive approach as a step toward building a theory of marriage that can be closely tied to clinical application.

Three fundamental ideas are important in understanding Gottman's research. First, he conceptualizes marriage or any primary relationship as a new system that represents a synthesis of the preexisting elements of each partner's personal history and temperament. Second, he draws upon systems theory to describe marriage as a relational system that seeks a stable or **homeostatic steady state** (von Bertalanffy, 1968). This steady state is maintained over time by the couple's unique balance of positive and negative elements in

Research on marital communication styles has helped clinicians understand more about the elements of successful relationships.

areas of *interactive behavior, perception,* and *physiology.* Behavior refers here to a couple's interactions and accompanying affect; perception refers to self-perceptions and attributions directed to partners; and physiology refers to the autonomic, endocrine, and immune system functioning of the partners. Third, he premises his approach on research done in the last few decades, which consistently documents a ratio of high negative to low positive behaviors in distressed/divorcing couples as opposed to nondistressed/stable couples.

Thinking about a marital relationship as a ratio of positive and negative factors is somewhat like considering the relationship to have a typical kind of "weather," for example, sunny, calm, cloudy, stormy, and so forth. The marital climate or stable steady state is made up of *uninfluenced* (intrapersonal elements like neuroticism) and *influenced* (couple's interaction) elements. From a systems perspective, a marital union tends toward stability in its positivity to negativity ratio over time. Obviously, contextual features and crises also play a part in the nature of relationships, but these factors are not emphasized because they are less predictable.

Gottman and his colleagues developed ways to measure levels of positivity and negativity in couples' behavioral interactions, in their perceptions of each other, and in their physiological states, such as arousal or calmness, using observational coding systems, measures of physiological responding, and questionnaire and interview data. Over several extensive longitudinal studies, they set out to predict which couples would divorce and which would remain together. Moreover, they sought to determine whether particular elements were associated with marital breakup or success (see Gottman, 1994; Gottman & Levenson, 2000).

In general, making this kind of marital "weather report" has surprising predictive ability. Assessments done at the beginning of a marriage, including those made from videotapes of the first three minutes of a newlywed marital conflict discussion, predicted later outcomes with a high degree of accuracy (Carrere & Gottman, 1999; Carrere, Buehlman, Gottman, Coan, & Ruckstuhl, 2000; Gottman & Levenson, 2000). What turns out to predict marital dissolution best? A high level of **negative affect reciprocity** is a distinguishing feature. This construct refers to the likelihood that negative emotions in one partner will follow from the other partner's negativity. You may think of it as the likelihood that partners will bring out the worst in each other. This is accomplished through the combined influences of information processing biases (e.g., seeing the other's qualities as negative), heightened physiological arousal (e.g., interpreting arousal as anger), and negative behavioral interactions (e.g., being critical and defensive).

But a number of fine points bear mentioning. As it turns out, conflict and angry feelings are part of *all* intimate relationships, so simply trying to avoid conflict won't help. Furthermore, not all negative affect is equally deleterious to relationships. Anger can play a constructive function when it is a justifiable reaction to a partner's behavior or reflects airing of grievances (Gottman, 1994). The trick is to distinguish between functional and dysfunctional types of negativity. Other researchers have drawn similar distinctions (e.g. Markman, Stanley, & Blumberg, 1994), but, for the sake of simplicity, we will present Gottman's definitions here.

The four kinds of negativity that do the most damage to relationships and that are highly predictive of divorce are *criticism, defensiveness, contempt,* and *stonewalling* (see Table 13.6). The presence of these *"four horsemen of the apocalypse,"* particularly contempt, can be very destructive. But suppose you recognize some of these elements in your own close relationship? Does this forecast an inevitable breakup? You may be somewhat relieved to know that Gottman found criticism, defensiveness, and stonewalling even in happy marriages. In couples headed toward divorce, however, these three behaviors were more frequent, contempt was also present, and there was much less positive affect in the relationship overall. Most importantly, the distressed couples he observed were not skilled

TABLE 13.6

"Four Horsemen of the Apocalypse"

1. *Criticism*:
   A statement that implies that the partner has some global deficit that is an enduring feature of personality: "You always . . . ; You never . . . "

2. *Defensiveness*:
   A statement that serves to defend against the criticism and that implies denying any responsibility for the problem: "Who me? . . . I do not!"

3. *Contempt*:
   A statement or nonverbal behavior that serves to put down the partner while elevating the speaker to a higher level (such as insulting, using hostile humor, or mocking the partner).

4. *Stonewalling*:
   Withdrawal of a partner from verbal interaction, leaving, or nonverbal behaviors that communicate impassiveness (looking away, looking bored).

Source: Based on Gottman, J. M. (1999). *The marriage clinic: A scientifically-based marital therapy.* New York: Norton.

in repairing the relationship after conflict occurred. Instead, prolonged periods of unrelieved distress, accompanied by heightened physiological arousal, fueled negative perceptions of the partner, overwhelmed spouses' positive feelings for each other, and led to a state of isolation and loneliness. Over time, if negativity surpassed positivity, it contributed to the derailment of the relationship.

With the accumulation of stresses and losses that we all experience in adulthood, it makes sense that good coping skills would be an essential component of personal and interpersonal wellness. Therefore, a critical part of marriage maintenance (and probably that of any close relationship) is the capacity to *repair* the frayed relationship after conflict. Gottman observed that the particular type of conflict style that couples demonstrated did not matter as much as the amount of overall positivity in the relationship (humor, interest, affection, and validation) and the couples' ability to soothe hurt or angry feelings. Some couples tended to avoid conflict, others embraced it with gusto, while some discussed their differences with the validating ("I hear what you are saying . . . ") style of counselors. Surprisingly, all three types could be very happily married if the steady state ratios of positivity to negativity in their relationships were 5 to 1. In other words, if a marital climate has substantially more periods of sun than rain, the chances of long-term success are pretty good.

Generativity: Making a Mark at Midlife

Establishing generativity is the primary developmental task of middle adulthood according to Erikson (1950/1963). Generativity has been described as having several components (e.g., McAdams, Hart, et al., 1998; A.J. Stewart & Vandewater, 1998). As we saw in Chapter 12, two primary components are *desire* and *accomplishment* (A.J. Stewart & Vandewater, 1998). Desire refers to *wanting* to be creative, productive, and/or giving, and accomplishment means actually feeling that you *are* creative, productive, and/or giving. Generative desire is more characteristic of young adults, but generative accomplishment is more typical of middle adults.

A core feature of generativity is taking care of or showing concern for the next generation.

The Experience of Child Rearing

For many people, raising children is a significant part of adult life. Not every parent sees child rearing as a generative accomplishment, but people in their middle years often seem to view their parenting role in this light. The nature and quality of the parenting experience, including the parent's feelings of generativity, change substantially as both children and parents grow older.

Each major period or stage of a child's life creates new challenges for a parent, challenges that the parent is more or less prepared to face depending on her age and stage of life, her personality and coping skills, her socioeconomic status, and the available support systems. For example, the gratifications of parenthood and marriage are usually greater for older rather than younger first-time parents. Older parents tend to have a more fully developed self-concept and greater self-esteem, are more advanced in their careers, have more money, and are more likely to find balancing work and family responsibilities easier to negotiate. Older fathers tend to spend more time caring for their children than younger fathers, a factor that not only increases satisfaction with parenting but also improves marital satisfaction for both husbands and wives (Belsky & Hsieh, 1998; Belsky & Rovine, 1990; Levy-Schiff, 1994).

Not surprisingly, very young first-time parents (under 20) are at greater risk than other groups to find that the stress of parenting outweighs its satisfactions. They typically complete fewer years of education than older parents and have lower incomes, they are more likely to divorce than other groups, and their children are more likely to experience developmental problems (e.g., Furstenberg, Brooks-Gunn, & Chase-Lansdale, 1987). The satisfactions of parenting, like all other developmental outcomes, are a function of many interacting risk and protective factors.

The normative experience of parents as they move through each stage of parenting is that the challenges bring *both* intense new stresses and delightful new pleasures (Kach & McGee, 1982; Levy-Schiff, 1994; Levy-Schiff, Goldshmidt, & Har-Even, 1991; B. C. Miller & Sollie, 1980; Ventura, 1987). For example, in the newborn period, first-time parents often feel distressed and overwhelmed (Kach & McGee, 1982; Ventura, 1987). Caring for an infant is far more demanding than most people expect it to be. Distress is linked to insufficient sleep, money worries, anxieties about the baby's dependency and vulnerability, feelings of uncertainty about one's caretaking skill, difficulty balancing the needs of self, spouse, and baby, and disillusionment with the "yucky" side of infant care (such as mounds of laundry, endless spit-up, and baffling crying fits just when it's time for the parents to eat dinner). Simultaneously, however, most parents of newborns report feeling like they have now truly grown up, that their lives have new purpose and meaning, and that they have a strong sense of shared joy.

The parent of the toddler/preschooler must begin to discipline a child who is still very dependent but who is skilled enough to need continuous supervision. Because a toddler is a proficient climber, for example, a parent can no longer put her in a crib to keep her safe while the parent takes a quick shower or talks on the phone. Parents begin to have conflicts with their children as disciplinary efforts are resisted by a child who has little capacity to take the parent's perspective. Also, partners often find themselves in conflict about their children as they negotiate disciplinary styles, time commitments, and divisions of labor. And parents feel physically exhausted as they try to keep up with energetic, active youngsters who have little self-control. Although many parents experience this period as especially stressful, there are new pleasures as well (Crnic & Booth, 1991; Crnic & Greenberg, 1990). Children begin to talk, to participate in organized activities, and to do things on their own, such as feeding themselves. Their temperaments are blossoming into personalities, and a new little self becomes part of the family system. Most parents experience these developments as intriguing and as a source of pride, despite the heavy dose of frustration that these advances can bring.

As children move into middle childhood, the family waters are often somewhat becalmed. If there is a honeymoon period between parents and children, this is it. The child's thinking is more logical, she has a growing capacity to take another's perspective, and she can in many situations keep herself safe, so that supervision can be reduced. At the same time, the child does not yet feel much ambivalence about her dependence on her parents, and parents still enjoy the role of preferred companion. There are plenty of challenges in this period of course. Outside factors—such as peers, teachers, and the media—are increasingly influential. Helping children learn to interpret and negotiate the outside world and to deal with the stress it creates can be difficult (e.g., Compas, Banez, Malcarne, & Worsham, 1991).

Parenting usually becomes more demanding and difficult when children reach adolescence. The child's push for independence, parental worries about the child's risk taking and sexual maturity, and the child's often critical and rejecting attitudes are tough to bear, even when parents are well versed in the needs of adolescents. Many parents reach their 40s and 50s when their children are adolescents, so that they are beginning to confront their own physical aging and perhaps engage in a "midlife review" at the same time. Silverberg and Steinberg (1990) report that adolescent development and parental distress about midlife are interacting factors. For example, parents whose teens are actively dating and involved in mixed-sex activities are more likely to express midlife concerns and to feel less satisfaction with their lives than parents whose teens are not yet dating.

The **launching period,** when emerging adults begin to move away and become more self-sufficient, brings some new challenges. On the whole, by the time adult children are in their 20s parents begin to feel the benefits of fewer parental responsibilities, and their relationships with their children improve (Troll & Fingerman, 1996). We often hear about how sad parents are, especially mothers, when their young adult children depart, leaving an "empty nest." Lewis and Lin (1996) report that although parents often anticipate that the transition will be difficult for them, only about 25% feel very unhappy. Also, fathers usually experience more distress than mothers. They seem to struggle more with the concept of their adult children becoming autonomous, which modifies their role as decision maker and changes the structure of the family (e.g., Lewis & Lin, 1996). Mothers, who typically do more of the day-to-day child rearing, are more struck by the relief they experience from those duties. There is, however, a strong link between both mothers' and fathers' feelings of well-being and generativity, on the one hand, and their children's functioning, on the other. If adult children are seen as personally and socially well-adjusted, parents are likely to experience greater self-acceptance, purpose in life, and feelings of mastery (e.g., Ryff, Lee, Essex, & Schmutte, 1994).

The typical parent is exiting middle age when her children are entering it. Parents whose children are over 30 may find the quality of their relationships changing further, such that they now tend to relate to their children more as equals. Adult children often begin to identify with their parents, appreciating more profoundly what an adult's life is like than they ever could before (Fingerman, 1996, 1997). However, the relationship is still not egalitarian. Assistance and support, such as financial help, are still more likely to be provided by the older generation to the younger one.

As adults move through middle age, they sometimes find themselves in the role of **kinkeeper,** the person in an extended family who helps the generations maintain contact with one another (e.g., Haraven & Adams, 1996). They may also take on new family responsibilities involving care of an ailing parent or another elderly relative. Women are much more likely to play these roles than men in most cultures, although many men take on some kinkeeping or caregiving responsibilities. These tasks can be particularly challenging if they coincide with the adolescence of one's children. People who carry these double responsibilities are described as being in the **sandwich generation** (e.g., Hamill & Goldberg, 1997). Many factors affect how stressful this position is, such as the coping style of the sandwiched individual, educational and cultural factors, and the availability of other family help, especially the support of the spouse. And, as with the challenges of parenting, kinkeeping and elder care often bring emotional rewards as well, such as feelings of mastery and meaningfulness (e.g., Martire, Stephens, & Townsend, 1998).

Work and Community Involvement

Our careers begin in young adulthood, but it is in the middle adult years that people usually feel they are becoming expert in their work. The full fruits of a career are likely to be experienced in this stage of life. Incomes for both men and women tend to reach their peak between ages 45 and 54 (U.S. Bureau of Census, 1997). Top levels of management and professional advancement are most likely to characterize people in this age period as well. Work intensity and time invested in work usually increase in the first half of middle adulthood and then begin to taper off, as many people begin to strike a balance between time spent working and time spent with family and friends and in community service. This shift seems to be motivated for some people by increased confidence in their productivity and their value in the workplace, allowing them to invest more energy and effort into other aspects of their lives. For others, the shift may be motivated by a sense that their work will not bring them the satisfactions they may have once expected or dreamed about (e.g., Levinson, 1986).

This temporal pattern, of course, varies considerably across individuals, and tends to be linked somewhat to gender. Women who continue to work after having children generally give substantial priority to child rearing over career responsibilities (e.g., Gati et al., 1995; Vermeulen & Minor, 1998). Men are less likely to do so, although fathers are more likely to modify the intensity of their work effort if both parents work than if the father is the sole breadwinner. We should note that the degree to which both parents modify their work time and share child care and household duties is a significant factor in determining marital satisfaction, especially for women (e.g., Feeney, Peterson, & Noller, 1994; Schafer & Keith, 1980).

When women interrupt their careers to take on full-time parenting, they may in midlife restart their careers or start new ones, especially after their children reach adolescence. For them, the intensity of work involvement may be greater than it would otherwise be at this stage of their lives, and it can be out of phase with their husbands' work involvement, because they are at an earlier point in career development. Generally though, the opportunity to be productive in another setting seems to provide a buffer against some of the stresses involved in parenting an adolescent (e.g., Larson & Richards, 1994).

Money and promotion are the external markers of achievement for middle adults, but a sense of generative accomplishment appears to be more dependent on how creative and productive we feel. The latter experiences are in turn related to how challenging the work is and to the level of interest and expertise that we bring to the work (see Csikszentmihalyi, 1999; Myers, 1993; Ryan & Deci, 2000). McAdams (1985; Mansfield & McAdams, 1996) explains generativity as constituting both **agency** and **communion.** *Agency* "involves generating, creating, and producing things, ideas, people, events, and so on *as powerful extensions or expressions of the self* [italics added]" (Mansfield & McAdams, 1996, p. 721). Agentic generativity, then, depends on self-knowledge, a sense of identity, and the opportunity to work on tasks that match our interests, values, and skills, all key features of successful career planning, as we saw in Chapter 12. Generativity also involves *communion,* expressed "in the adult's desire to care for the next generation, even to the point of sacrificing his or her own well-being for the good of those who will follow" (pp. 721–722). Behaviors involving giving, offering, and contributing are aspects of communion. Research indicates that adults who are identified by others as "generative" do tend to combine both agency and communion in the concerns that they express and in their occupational and community behaviors (Mansfield & McAdams, 1996).

McAdams and his colleagues have developed a variety of measures of generativity. For example, on a 20-item questionnaire respondents rate the degree to which statements are true of them, such as, "I have a responsibility to improve the neighborhood in which I live" (McAdams & de St. Aubin, 1992). In a measure of generative goals, respondents are asked to describe ten "personal strivings," and the responses are coded for "generative imagery" (McAdams, de St. Aubin, & Logan, 1993). Using these techniques, people who rate high on generativity are found to be more likely to use authoritative, child-centered parenting styles, are more actively involved in political, religious, and social reform activities, and report higher levels of self-esteem and happiness than people who score low on generativity (see McAdams & Bowman, 2001, for a review).

One of the more interesting differences between midlife adults who score high versus low on generativity measures is in the kind of narrative they produce when asked to tell their life story. McAdams (e.g., 1993) argues that the narratives we construct about our lives are reconstructions that are based on the real events in our lives but that they also indicate our characteristic ways of making sense of things. They contribute to and reflect our identities and our sense of well-being. Generative adults, for example, tend to tell life stories with "redemption" themes (McAdams & Bowman, 2001). That is, even though the individual may describe many serious difficulties, her story often progresses from describing an emotionally negative event or bad scene to an emotionally positive or good outcome. Conversely, adults low on generativity tend to include more "contamination" sequences in their life stories. These are descriptions that go from good or positive experiences to negative outcomes.

Generative adults also are more likely to describe themselves as "sensitized to others' suffering at an early age" and as "guided by a clear and compelling ideology that remains relatively stable over time" (McAdams & Bowman, 2001, p. 14). Overall, there is a progressive structure to the generative adult's life story that suggests a reasonably coherent sense of a self who is moving in a positive direction and who feels able and willing to make a difference. In particular, such individuals seem to be able to move on despite sometimes serious setbacks. People low in generativity by midlife, however, seem to be stuck, "unable to grow." McAdams and Bowman (2001) describe one woman who, at 41, is still setting goals that are markedly like those she set as a young woman—"to graduate from high school" and to be "better able to take care of myself." She tells the interviewer that she is "desperately seeking myself." Unfortunately, her persistent expectation that what appears to be good will turn out bad—reflected in the many contamination sequences she includes in her life story narrative—seems to make her quest overwhelming.

Generativity seems to be foreshadowed in the personality characteristics that emerge in adolescence and young adulthood. Peterson and Stewart (1994) found that individuals who as adolescents already had strong power and achievement needs, combined with strong needs for affiliation, were most likely to demonstrate generativity when they reached middle adulthood. The Big 5 personality traits can play a role as well. For example, de St. Aubin and McAdams (1995) found that higher scores on extraversion (which is somewhat agentic) and agreeableness (which is strongly communal) were moderately correlated with generativity in a sample of adults. Finally, as we pointed out above, identity development contributes to generativity. For example, self-knowledge can help a person make choices, such as choices of career and community activities, that provide a good match to her skills and interests, so that she can maintain her intrinsic motivation to produce and create.

APPLICATIONS

The middle years are a challenging period of life. Adults have to contend with jobs, children, partners, and themselves, as well as the unexpected crises that occur. They bring very different experiences, values, and dreams into adulthood. It is impossible to establish a life-stage trajectory that could take into account all this diversity with any level of precision. However, there do seem to be powerful themes, such as the quest for intimacy and generativity, that characterize most adult lives.

We have seen that many theorists (e.g., Erikson, 1950/1963; Levinson, 1986; Vaillant, 1977; and so on) have attempted to specify these themes and their typical progress, though they all seem to recognize that we cannot expect every life story to unfold in some inevitable sequence of events or experiences. These same theorists have also described psychological requirements for healthy functioning as people move through adulthood. One consistent message that these authors communicate in various ways is this: adults have to grow up. Growing up is not always easy and often not much fun, particularly in an age and in a society that heavily invests in the notion of personal satisfaction, youth, and freedom of choice. However, the very nature of the life cycle makes certain changes inevitable, and once those changes are accepted, they can be the source of great personal satisfaction and pride.

Furthermore, people often have to contend with the realization that events or accomplishments that they once wished for have not been achieved. Individuals of all ages may feel distressed by a sense that they did not meet their developmental goals or expectations "on-time." Feeling "off-time," as it relates to such things as getting married, having children, reaching career goals, or other normative achievements, reflects the fact that we all have a set of age-related expectations for the appropriate timing of major life events. This phenomenon is called the **social clock.** Clinicians should be sensitive to this particular source of distress in the lives of their clients so as to help them cope more effectively.

Becoming generative can be viewed as a way of growing up, by taking and accepting responsibility for oneself and for dependents, by forgiving past generations for what they may have done, and by working to leave a legacy. As we have learned, flexibility and adaptability in the face of life's demands support this process. One developmental task involves the shift in expectations that may occur gradually over this time from adolescent idealism to mature acceptance of reality (Gould, 1978).

> Adulthood means getting far enough outside oneself to do as Margaret Mead urged: "to cherish the life of the world," that is, to connect with life itself rather than just with oneself, to overcome the narcissism of our youth and make give-and-take connections from which we can feel the pain and pleasure of others rather than crouching selfishly and alone in our own protective skins. . . . The maturing function of psychotherapy is to get people past a narcissistic state where they notice only what other people do and how it makes them feel, and move them into a mature state where they notice what they do and how it makes other people feel. (p. 257)

Certainly clinicians can support client strivings to find outlets for generative needs. Even the strains of caring for children or older relatives can be reframed as valuable contributions. For clients without such responsibilities, other outlets can be explored.

The need to come to terms with the reality of human nature and relationships is also a theme of Gottman's approach to marital therapy. He has made the interesting observation, based upon his studies of marital interaction, that the content of couples' problem discussions remains remarkably stable over time. Fully 69% of the time, couples' arguments are about a problem that has existed in the relationship for a long time (1999). These "perpetual problems," which have to do with partners' personalities, may be expressed in the partners' different behavioral styles or ways of approaching issues such as money, sex, or in-laws. As we have learned, there is evidence for continuity in many temperamental characteristics, and they constitute relatively stable features of individuals' behavior and cognition throughout their life span. Certainly, many behaviors and cognitions can be modified, but a strict problem-solving emphasis in marital counseling may be misguided.

Based on his work, Gottman (1999) suggests that therapists

> encourage couples to think of these relationship problems as inevitable, much the way we learn to deal with chronic physical ailments as we get older. The chronic back pain, the trick knee and tennis elbow or irritable bowel do not go away, but we learn to have a dialogue with these problems. We keep trying to make things a little better all the time, but we learn to live with these problems and manage our world so as to minimize them. . . . So it is in all relationships. (p. 57)

Once this fact is recognized, brief problem-focused approaches targeted to specific issues can be useful. Even modest improvements, viewed from a mature, realistic perspective, can promote better relationships and support overall adjustment. In other words, the mature individual knows that life does not have to be perfect to be good.

The distinction between types of coping proposed by Folkman and Lazarus (1986) may be appropriate to consider here as well. This influential paradigm distinguishes between coping efforts designed to change the situation (problem-focused, problem-solving) and those directed to emotion management (emotion-focused, tension-reducing). **Problem-focused** efforts are most successful when the problem is solvable. When aspects of the problem are beyond one's ability to control, then **emotion-focused** coping strategies may be more effective. These involve strategies such as adjusting expectations, using self-soothing techniques such as relaxation, and focusing on positive elements of the situation. Sometimes problem- and emotion-focused efforts may be combined. It should also be noted, however, that some aspects of relationships, such as violence, affairs, and substance abuse, should not be glossed over in the service of keeping the peace but require direct attention.

B. Carter and McGoldrick (1999) emphasize that stress is likely to be most intense during both predictable and unpredictable transition points in the family life cycle (such as divorce, the return of an adult child to the parents' home, and so on). As we all probably know from experience, even predictable kinds of change can produce anxiety. As stress increases, a person or a family may have greater difficulty navigating these transitions and may appear more dysfunctional. Counselors need to understand the relationship between stress and symptom formation and take a contextualized, life-cycle view of their clients' concerns. Helping clients learn to discriminate between problem-focused and emotion-focused ways of coping offers them a way of managing the stressors in their lives more effectively.

SUMMARY

Life Span Developmental Theory

1. The complexity of adult development makes it clear that multidimensional models are needed to adequately understand the processes of change. *Life span developmental models* focus on both hereditary and environmental influences and on the continuities and changes that characterize adults. They emphasize that adaptation continues from birth to death.

2. Baltes describes the "architecture" of biology and culture, a web of interacting organismic and environmental influences on development. During childhood, he argues, optimal development is strongly supported by the processes of natural selection, such that most people reach adulthood and can contribute to the success of the species by reproducing. But biological supports weaken by middle adulthood, as selection pressures decline. Thus, from middle adulthood on, more cultural supports are required to assure optimal development.

3. Throughout the life span, change involves both gains and losses, but the relative balance of gains and losses shifts as people move toward old age. Adaptation throughout life involves *growth, maintenance* or *resilience,* and the *regulation of loss,* but growth is more common in childhood, while regulation of loss is more common in old age. Successful development, or healthy coping, at any age is the relative maximization of gains and the minimization of losses, but coping changes as people age.

Influences on Adult Development: Sources of Stability

4. The Big 5 personality traits—neuroticism, extraversion, openness, agreeableness, and conscientiousness—are relatively stable after approximately age 30, according to cross-sectional, longitudinal, and cross-cultural research.

5. Adult personality traits are somewhat correlated with temperament in childhood. While heredity is implicated in the development and stability of traits, a relatively stable environment is probably equally important.

Influences on Adult Development: Sources of Change

6. *Age-graded change* refers to change that comes as a function of time. Some predictable physical changes in adulthood include declines in sensory ability and in reproductive ability (much more for women than for men). Appearance changes as skin wrinkles and sags, and weight gain is common though not inevitable.

7. Cognitive changes with age are best studied with longitudinal methods. A mixed pattern of improvement and decline occurs, related to differences in *fluid intelligence*

(*mechanics*) versus *crystallized intelligence* (*pragmatics*). Fluid or mechanical processes, such as processing speed and inhibitory mechanisms, begin to show declines in middle adulthood. Crystallized resources, including all forms of declarative and procedural knowledge, are not as likely to decline, and for many people they increase throughout middle and even old age. Only after about age 60 do losses in fluid intelligence somewhat outweigh crystallized gains for the average individual.

8. The relative losses and gains are illustrated by memory effects. The capacity of working memory declines with age, which can affect problem solving negatively, as fewer pieces of information can be held in mind simultaneously. Semantic memory, however, continues to expand with age, as we learn more and more information, and often older adults solve problems better than younger ones because they are more likely to have expertise they can bring to the task.

9. *Life-task* or *life-course changes* are age-graded changes in the tasks and responsibilities that confront us or seem important as we age. Theorists such as Schaie, Erikson, Vaillant, Levinson, Jung, Gould, and so on have all described stages or phases in life-task change. Despite the significant differences in the lives of individuals, there do seem to be relatively predictable sequences of change in our concerns as we move through adulthood.

10. *History-graded changes* affect the development of a whole cohort. A *life-course perspective* emphasizes that development is influenced by chronological age, family-related roles, and membership in a birth cohort. Thus, the same historical events can have different effects on members of different cohorts. Recent cohorts of children are experiencing a time of increased breakdown in social connections. Apparently as a result, they experience more anxiety than older cohorts did as children.

11. *Nonnormative changes* refer to unexpected events, such as an accident or untimely death of a loved one, that can alter developmental trajectories.

Key Developmental Tasks of Midlife: The Continuing Pursuit of Intimacy and Generativity

12. Adults involved in a primary relationship such as marriage are generally happier than single adults. Other relationships, such as friendships, are also important sources of life satisfaction. Critical features of such relationships involve sharing, working out problems, and developing a sense of "we-ness."

13. The *family life cycle* begins with mate selection, a kind of filtering process based largely on homogomy and compatibility. Love is also seen as important in our culture. Sternberg described three elements: passion, intimacy, and decision/commitment. Once a commitment is established, a blending of family systems is involved, not just a joining of individuals. Other stages in the more typical family life cycle include becoming parents and then the transition of launching and renegotiating the marital relationship.

14. Sixty percent of marriages end in divorce in the United States, often creating financial hardship for the wife and emotional and behavioral difficulties for children. For many people, marital satisfaction persistently declines over the life of a marriage. Theories about the causes of marital harmony and discord include the *disillusionment model* (when romantic notions are dashed, marriages fail), *the maintenance hypothesis* (romantic couples work to maintain their illusions and therefore their marriage), *the social exchange and behavioral theories* (marriages fail when problems and conflict escalate to become overwhelming because of inadequate strategies for coping with conflict). *Intrapersonal models* draw on attachment theory and notions about temperament to explain marital success or failure.

15. Studies of marital dynamics (e.g., Gottman) suggest that marriages are successful or satisfying to the extent that positive factors outweigh negative factors, including interactive behaviors, perceptions, and physiology (e.g., endocrine functioning). High levels of *negative affect reciprocity* (likelihood that negativity in one partner will be followed by negativity from the other) is especially predictive of marital dissolution. The "four horsemen of the apocalypse" are especially problematic: criticism, defensiveness, contempt, and stonewalling.

Generativity: Making a Mark at Midlife

16. Each period of a child's life presents new challenges to parents. A parent's age, SES, personality and coping skills, and support systems all contribute to how satisfying parenting is (e.g., older parents generally find parenting more rewarding than younger parents).

17. Most parents find their task both stressful and rewarding. Infants are far more difficult to care for than most people expect, but they also bring joy to most parents. Toddlers, combining new skills with poor self-control or understanding, need very close supervision, so they are time and energy consuming. As their unique "selfhood" begins to blossom, they also become more interesting. In middle childhood, parenting is usually much easier as children become logical thinkers but are still relatively unambivalent about their dependence on their parents. Adolescent children are usually experienced as more demanding and difficult as they push for independence, take more risks, and deidealize their parents. The *launching* period usually is experienced as positive, as parents have fewer responsibilities and their children become more self-sufficient. Parents of middle adults relate to their children more as equals, although assistance and support still tends to flow more from parent to child.

18. Sometimes middle-aged adults find themselves with dual caregiving responsibilities—parents to their children and caretaker for their aging parents. This *sandwiched* position can be very stressful, depending on factors such as the availability of other sources of support.

19. In middle age, people generally feel they have reached the peak of their career in terms of expertise, income, and advancement. Work intensity and time invested increase in the first half of middle adulthood and taper off thereafter, with most people increasing time spent with friends and family. This pattern can vary dramatically across individuals, such as women who enter the workplace after their children are grown.

20. A sense of generative accomplishment depends on how creative and productive adults feel. Two kinds of generativity have been described: *agency* (creating, producing) and *communion* (wishing to care for the next generation). People who score high on measures of generativity report higher levels of self-esteem and happiness than others. A coherent sense of a self moving in a positive direction seems to characterize people who score high on generativity.

Case Study

Lupe is a 45-year-old Mexican American woman. She has two adult children, a son and a daughter, as well as one granddaughter. She lives in a small apartment near her mother, now in her late 60s. Lupe visits her mother several times a week to check on her health and her emotional state. Although she is relatively self-sufficient, Lupe's mother expects this kind of attention from her daughter. Lupe has always been very responsible and concerned about the well-being of her family members. Even though this takes a lot of her time, she faithfully attends to her mother's needs without complaint.

When Lupe's children were young, she and her children's father lived together. He left the family after a few years, however, because he found the stress of family life to be overwhelming. In particular, he felt that he could not make enough money to support two children. Although he and Lupe were never legally married, she considered them to be a "married" couple. Single now for 16 years, she feels that she would like to meet someone with whom she could share her life. This is a new feeling for Lupe. Until recently, she was too distracted with the problems of raising her children to think about herself. Now she feels that she only has a limited amount of time left to pursue some of her own wishes. She can envision herself, like her mother, old and alone, and that prospect disturbs her. She has started to attend social functions at her church and has accepted some social invitations from members of the congregation. Lupe feels comfortable with this approach, because she is very close to the members of her parish community.

Lupe's life has recently become more complicated. Her daughter, Lucia, and her 2-year-old granddaughter, Eva, have moved in with her. Lucia and her boyfriend, Tomas, were living together and were planning to marry. Their relationship deteriorated after the baby's birth, and the couple fought frequently. Lucia accused Tomas of spending too much of his paycheck on frivolous things. Tomas, in response, withdrew even further, spent more time with his friends, and continued to spend money as he pleased. Lucia finally took the baby and threatened not to come back.

In addition to this, Lupe was injured on her job as a practical nurse in a large hospital. She was trying to prevent a patient from falling and hurt her back in the process. She will need to receive physical therapy, which means she will be out of work for a few months. Her physician, noticing her depressed mood, referred her to a counselor at the local mental health clinic.

Discussion Questions

1. What are the developmental stresses (age-related) and contextual stresses (non-normative) in Lupe's life at the present time? Consider her age, family role, and cultural context.
2. What are Lupe's sources of strength? What aspects of her cognitive functioning and her personality might support her resilience in the face of difficulties?
3. What is the potential impact of Lucia's return on her mother? On Eva? On Tomas?
4. What advice might you give to Lupe? To Lucia and Tomas?

Journal Questions

1. If you can, ask your parent or a member of your family to describe you using the Big 5 personality traits. Which of your personality traits have remained stable over time? Which have changed?
2. Do you think people normally go through a "midlife crisis?" Why or why not?
3. Think of a married (or otherwise committed) couple you know well. What are the major challenges of their marriage? What are the benefits? What style of relating best characterizes the couple?
4. What are the normative and nonnormative challenges you are facing now? How are you coping with each? What other coping strategies could you try?

Key Terms

life span developmental
    model
ontogeny
growth
maintenance or resilience
regulation of loss
"Big 5"
neuroticism
extraversion
openness
agreeableness
conscientiousness
age-graded changes
history-graded changes

nonnormative changes
adolescing
senescing
climacteric
menopause
estradiol
estrogen
testosterone
elastin
fluid intelligence
    (mechanics)
crystallized intelligence
    (pragmatics)
ego integrity (vs. despair)

career consolidation (vs.
    self-absorption)
keeper of meaning (vs.
    rigidity)
life structure
cohort effects
life-course perspective
family life cycle
homogomy
compatibility
disillusionment model
maintenance hypothesis
social exchange and
    behavior theories

intrapersonal models
homeostatic steady state
negative affect reciprocity
"four horsemen of the
    apocalypse"
launching period
kinkeeper
sandwich generation
agency
communion
social clock
problem-focused coping
emotion-focused coping

Gains and Losses in Late Adulthood

In the last chapter, we described successful development as "the relative maximization of gains and the minimization of losses" (Baltes, 1997, p. 367). In life span developmental theory, we are developing successfully when we are able to *grow* (acquiring new abilities or skills), when we can *maintain* our previous capacities, perhaps restoring them if they are temporarily lost, or when we find ways to *regulate* losses by accepting them and reorganizing the ways that we function. As people move into old age, in their 60s and 70s, or into old-old age, in their 80s and 90s, both gains and losses continue, but losses may considerably outweigh gains. "Even in young people's lives, not everything goes well. Old age is a genuinely difficult situation with lots of sadness and frustration. Many things do not go well" (Pipher, 1999, p. 26). How can the elderly effectively manage the ever-increasing losses they experience? For example, can their developmental trajectory be a positive one when they experience multiple health problems or find themselves in chronic pain? An important focus of this chapter will be to identify the means by which elderly adults manage their lives and the extent to which they can grow, maintain themselves, and regulate their losses.

Clearly, different people manage their late-life losses with varying degrees of success. But you may be surprised to learn that for a majority of us, successful development is what we can expect for much of our old age. At age 81, Helen still maintains her job in a bookstore. As one of the oldest siblings in a large working-class family, she learned early to value hard work and has always been active and productive. Her job provides her with opportunities to maintain her skills as well as the chance to learn new ones, such as the new computerized system her company uses to inventory material. Helen is fortunate in that her health is good, aside from some problems with arthritis that slow down her movement. She recognizes that she must regulate her activity now more than before, reducing extraneous activities so she can be well rested and prepared for work, thus optimizing her performance there. She is an avid crossword puzzle fan, her recipe for staying mentally active. When she noticed herself becoming more forgetful, she compensated by writing notes to herself and establishing and following set routines. She travels and volunteers less these days, compared to what she did years ago when her husband was alive. Now she chooses to spend more time with her family and has eliminated activities she considers unnecessary. She knows what she can do and what gives her a sense of satisfaction. Helen's adaptation is a good example of how a person can cope successfully with the challenges of aging.

The process of adaptation to increasing loss can be thought of as effective coping. For this reason, investigators often look at mental health and life satisfaction to gauge the degree to which elderly people are successfully developing. The findings are heartening:

"The inherent paradox of aging . . . [is] . . . that despite loss and physical decline, adults enjoy good mental health and positive life satisfaction well into old age" (Carstensen & Charles, 1998).

In what follows, we will first review the nature of the losses and challenges that typically confront people in old age. Then we will look at the ways in which the elderly cope with these challenges, paying special attention to the processes that seem most important for the lifelong experience of psychological well-being.

AGING WELL

Challenge and Loss in Late Adulthood

Physical Change

We saw in Chapter 13 that a gradual decline from peak functioning is characteristic of most physiological systems beginning as early as age 30. By late adulthood, the losses are usually noticeable and have required some adjustment in expectations or lifestyle. A lifelong runner who still entered marathons at age 62 remarked, "At 30, my goal was to win. At 50, I celebrated every race that I finished. Today, I'm delighted to be at the starting line."

Maintaining good health becomes more challenging with age, as the immune system becomes progressively less effective in staving off cancer and infections and as the cardiovascular, respiratory, and organ systems function less adequately. Chronic illness and the need for more vigilant health maintenance therefore increase dramatically with age. Age shifts in the leading causes of death illustrate these changing health concerns. In the United States, accidents are the leading cause of death in adults up to age 45. But at 45, heart disease and cancer take over as the leading causes of death (U.S. Bureau of Census, 1993, 1998). People of any age can suffer from acute or chronic illnesses, such as cancer, heart problems, diabetes, and so on. But the risk of these illnesses climbs dramatically and steadily in our later years (U.S. Department of Health and Human Services, 1998).

Among the continuing declines of old age are two that are common and often especially debilitating. First are the increasing sensory deficits (see Chapter 13). Second is the onset of pain, stiffness, and swelling of joints and surrounding tissues that we call *arthritis,* After 65, about half of all adults experience the most common form, *osteoarthritis,* which involves the thinning, fraying, and cracking of cartilage at the ends of bones. Ordinarily, this cartilage helps protect our joints from the friction of bone to bone contact. As cartilage degenerates and other joint changes occur, such as the growth of bony spurs and modifications in connective tissues, joints may stiffen and swell. The upshot is often pain and reduced movement. Being overweight or overusing a particular joint (for example, the knees in sports such as running and tennis) can contribute to susceptibility, but ordinary degeneration with age is part of the problem. Osteoarthritis can range from being a painful nuisance to being a source of major disability, affecting the performance of simple tasks, such as opening a jar or walking, as well as more complex skills such as playing the piano or swinging a golf club (Whitbourne, 1996).

Cognitive Change

We have already seen that cognitive decline begins in middle adulthood, with gradual decrements in *fluid intelligence,* or in other words, in the *mechanics* of intellectual functioning. Processing speed slows and inhibitory functions decline with age. In middle adulthood, such declines may limit the efficiency of working memory operations, such as learning and problem solving, but these effects seem to be balanced by the maintenance or advancement of crystallized intelligence or pragmatics, so that, for example, semantic memory is enriched with age.

But what happens when people move into their 60s—or into their 90s? Does crystallized intelligence begin to decline along with continuing losses in fluid intelligence? Longitudinal studies suggest that crystallized intelligence, as represented by measures of verbal ability and factual knowledge, for example, does not show average declines until about age 74, and the declines are modest thereafter (Schaie, 1996). Good health is a very important factor in these trends. It appears that the bulk of the average decline in the later decades is attributable to sensory and health problems (Backman, Small, Wahlin, & Larsson, 2000). Many old individuals show no declines, and some who have maintained good health actually continue to improve on crystallized intelligence measures.

Dementia. The importance of health to cognitive functioning in the elderly is revealed in research on *dementia* and on a phenomenon called **terminal drop.** When cognitive functioning is so severely impaired that it affects our ability to relate to others and to manage our own daily activities, we are suffering from *dementia*. Many of us have seen the ravages of dementia in a relative or friend, and we worry that extreme memory loss and disorientation are the inevitable consequences of aging. But they are not. Normal aging does not lead to dementia, although the frequency of illnesses and conditions that cause dementia does increase with age. Among these, for example, are cardiovascular problems that limit the oxygen supply to the brain for some period of time. These include **cerebrovascular accidents,** or **strokes,** in which an artery serving the brain is either clogged or bursts. A single stroke can lead to acute onset of dementia; more typically, many minor strokes (**multi-infarct dementia**) can gradually do sufficient damage to cause dementia (see de la Torre, 1997).

Many diseases that affect the brain may eventually lead to dementia. The most common of these is **Alzheimer's disease (AD).** Its prevalence increases with age such that it affects about 1% of 65-year-olds in the United States and about 20% of 85-year-olds (see Zarit & Zarit, 1998). There appear to be different forms of AD with different onsets and

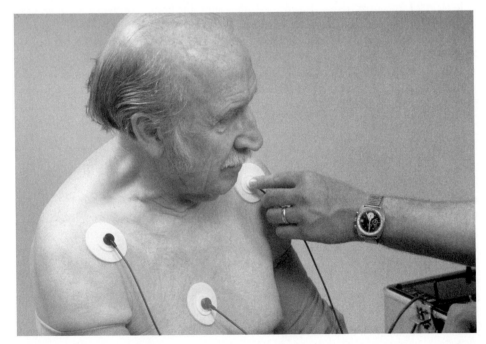

Attention to health maintenance is an important aspect of successful coping in late adulthood.

courses. Early-onset AD strikes 40- to 50-year-olds, ends in death after about 5 years, and clearly has a genetic contribution. Several forms of later-onset AD have been identified, some in which genetic contributions are clearly involved, some in which the environment may play a greater role. Later-onset AD tends to take longer to run its course, about 10 to 15 years. In all forms of AD, extensive brain changes can be identified on autopsy, including the formation of *plaques,* clumps of insoluble protein that are damaging to neurons, and *tangles,* twisted filaments of another protein, which may interfere with communication between neurons and even cause cell death (see Dickson, 1997).

AD is diagnosed primarily by its clinical characteristics and by excluding other possible causes of dementia. In its early stages, it looks like absentmindedness: forgetting where you recently put something or forgetting something that happened in the last few days or the last few hours. More general confusion may follow, especially noticeable in the use of language. Common problems are rambling speech and word substitutions, such as saying "window" when the right word would be "door." People at this stage may be quite distressed by their memory loss, perhaps even paranoid if they frequently cannot remember what they have done or where they've put things, and they also assume that others are responsible. A relative of one of the authors, for example, would insist that people had entered her apartment and had turned on her TV when she wasn't looking. Others may become hostile in their frustration and confusion. In later stages, memory and language problems get worse, disorientation is extreme, and physical coordination is affected. Eventually, Alzheimer's patients, often mute and bedridden, need full-time care and supervision, and death is the eventual outcome (see Whitbourne, 1996).

AD and other forms of dementia are not characteristic of the majority of elderly, although there is some suspicion that the formation of plaques and tangles may occur to some extent in all of us. Some environments seem to enhance or reduce AD rates. For example, lifelong education and intellectual stimulation seem to decrease the risk (Snowdon, 1997).

Terminal drop, or *terminal decline,* is just what it sounds like. As adults approach the end of their lives, between six months and five years prior to death, they may show a substantial decline in intellectual functioning as indicated by scores on intelligence tests (e.g., Berg, 1987; Lieberman, 1965). Figure 14.1 illustrates this finding from one set of longitudinal data. Terminal drop apparently reflects the individual's declining health status, which leads to "lessened ability to cope adequately with environmental demands because of lowered ability to integrate stimuli" (Berg, 1996, p. 326). Interestingly, people often seem to be able to detect in themselves whatever changes in health status are predictive of death. A number of studies have found that when older adults self-rate their health as "poor," they are much more likely to die within the next few years than when they rate their health as "excellent" (e.g., Idler & Kasl, 1991; Wolinsky & Johnson, 1992). Apparently, people often realize when they are going into decline (Berg, 1996).

Autobiographical Memory. One cognitive function that has particular significance for one's sense of self as well as for social interactions throughout the life span is called *autobiographical memory.* This is the remembered self, "representations of who we have been at various points in the past" (Fitzgerald, 1999, p. 143). It draws from several long-term memory systems (see Chapter 6 for an introduction to these systems). When we recall specific experiences in our lives we are calling on *episodic memory;* when we remember that we know some fact we're using our *semantic memory;* and when we remember how to do something we depend on our *procedural memory.* Autobiographical memory has often been treated as synonymous with episodic memory, which is a very important part of it, but our self-recollections are not episodic alone.

Autobiographical memory is important in many ways. It provides us with a "sense of identity in narrative form" (Fitzgerald, 1999, p. 143). It also is a source of information

FIGURE 14.1

The Relationship Between Survival and Scores on an Intelligence Test of Verbal Meaning in a Longitudinal Study

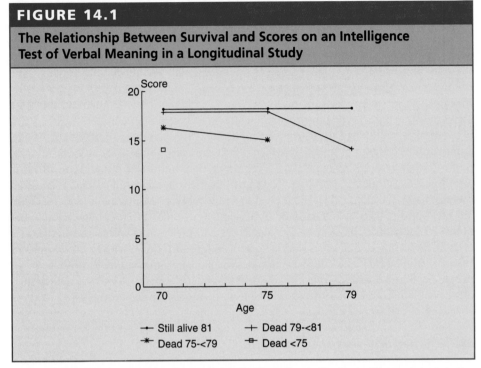

Source: Figure from "Aging, behavior, and terminal decline" by S. Berg in *Handbook of the psychology of aging,* Fourth Edition, edited by James E. Birrens, et al., copyright 1996, Elsevier Science (USA), reproduced by permission of the publisher.

about social interactions that have worked and that have not worked for us in the past. Finally, when we draw on autobiographical memory to tell stories about ourselves to others, it helps us to reveal and share ourselves, to get closer to others, to create impressions, even to teach lessons (Fitzgerald, 1999; Hyman & Faries, 1992).

One stereotype that people often have about the aged is that they remember more about their early lives than about what has happened to them recently. Studies of autobiographical memory indicate that this belief is only partially true. Elderly people actually do remember their more recent experiences better than earlier experiences, although the stories that they tell about themselves are often well-rehearsed experiences from the distant past.

There are two very salient characteristics of self-memories for adults of all ages. One is *recency:* the strength of a memory declines the more time has passed since the memory was formed. That is, we are more likely to remember something that has happened to us recently than something that happened in the more distant past. For example, one way to study autobiographical memory is to say a word, like "dog," and ask a person to report a specific experience in his life that the word calls to mind. Regardless of the age of the respondent, half of all such *cue-prompted memories* will be from the most recent 12 months of his life. Eighty percent are from the most recent decade. "The remembered self is largely a now-self, not a distant-self," even for old people (Fitzgerald, 1999, p. 159).

This may sound a bit confusing, given that adults learn new information less efficiently with age. As we saw in Chapter 13, information in working memory is not as easily transferred to long-term memory at later ages. However, older people nonetheless do continue to learn, and newer memories are more readily retrieved than older memories.

However, a second salient feature of self-memories is a phenomenon that is ignominiously called *"the bump."* Regardless of age, adults' cue-prompted memories of the self from the young adult period (from about ages 18 to 22) are slightly but reliably overproduced. That is, more memories are produced from this era than we would predict on the basis of recency (see Figure 14.2). If we explore autobiographical memory in a different way, by asking adults to tell us about their **flashbulb memories,** nearly all of what they tell us comes from "the bump" era (e.g., Fitzgerald, 1988). *Flashbulb memories* in these studies are defined as recollections that are especially vivid and personally relevant. It appears that when people talk about memories that are intense and important to them, they draw very heavily on experiences from young adulthood, even in their old age. If we ask people to tell stories that they would include in a book about themselves, again, a disproportionate number of the narratives come from "the bump" era (Fitzgerald, 1992). Similar results come from studies in which people are asked to name the most memorable books they have read (Larsen, 2000), the songs they find most desirable to listen to (Holbrook & Schindler, 1989), or the films that help describe their "era" (Schulster, 1996). That is, the elderly refer more often to items from their young adulthood than from any other time of their lives. Fitzgerald (1999) argues that the strength of "the bump" phenomenon for people's most important memories and preferences reveals the significance of late adolescence and young adulthood as a period of intense self-development. However, the recency effect in cue-prompted memory research makes it very clear that people continue to add to their self-stories throughout their adulthood and that healthy older people have their recent past available to them despite some declines in learning efficiency.

Stereotypes and Age Discrimination

Among the challenges that elderly people face are stereotyped attitudes and responses from others based on age category rather than on actual characteristics. An age stereotype can be defined as a set of widely held beliefs about the characteristics of older people. These knowledge structures or schemas can lead to relatively uniform treatment of older people regardless of their own individual characteristics and are thought to account for certain discriminatory or demeaning practices, such as mandatory retirement and patronizing talk (Hummert, 1999).

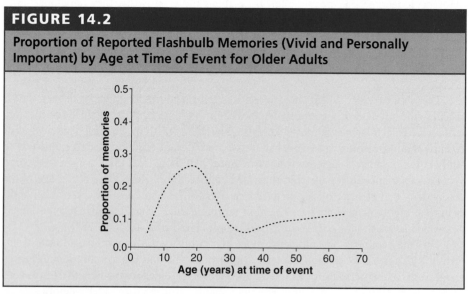

FIGURE 14.2

Proportion of Reported Flashbulb Memories (Vivid and Personally Important) by Age at Time of Event for Older Adults

Source: Figure adapted from "Autobiographical memory and social cognition: Development of the remembered self in adulthood" by J. M. Fitzgerald in *Social cognition and aging,* edited by Thomas M. Hess, copyright 1999, Elsevier Science (USA), reproduced by permission of the publisher.

Recent research on the content of old age schemas in Western cultures has identified seven common stereotypes. Four of these are negative, such as "severely impaired" or "shrew/curmudgeon," but three are more positive, such as "perfect grandparent" (Hummert, Garstka, Shaner, & Strahm, 1994). A description of each is provided in Table 14.1. Facial features associated with aging play a significant role in activating these stereotypes. The older people look, the more likely they are to be described in ways that fit a negative stereotype. In one study, participants were asked to match the photographs of people perceived to be in their 60s, 70s, or 80s with trait sets describing either positive or negative stereotypes (Hummert, Garstka, & Shaner, 1997). The older the appearance of the person in the picture, the more likely participants were to match the picture with a negative stereotype. Sex of the pictured person played a role as well. For example, pictures of unsmiling women were more likely to be matched with a negative stereotype than pictures of unsmiling men.

Because of age stereotypes, the very same behavior in younger versus older individuals is perceived differently. For example, the seriousness and the causes of a memory failure, such as forgetting the name of a new acquaintance, tend to be perceived quite differently depending on whether the failure is ascribed to a 30-year-old or to a 70-year-old. When younger adults forget, the cause is more likely to be seen as transient and external, such as "that's a hard thing to remember." When older people forget, the cause is more likely to be seen as something stable and internal, such as having a poor memory (see Erber & Prager, 1999, for a review of this work).

When age stereotypes are triggered, the quality of social interactions can be affected. For example, people, including clinicians, often use "patronizing talk" when speaking with an elderly person. This kind of conversation has many characteristics: simplified vocabulary and sentence structure, slower pace, careful articulation, an overly familiar or overbearing tone, and disapproving, controlling, or superficial content (e.g., Hummert & Ryan,

TABLE 14.1

Traits Associated with Stereotypes of Older Adults

Stereotype	Traits
Negative	
Severely impaired	Slow-thinking, incompetent, feeble, inarticulate, incoherent, senile
Despondent	Depressed, sad, hopeless, afraid, neglected, lonely
Shrew/curmudgeon	Complaining, ill-tempered, demanding, stubborn, bitter, prejudiced
Recluse	Quiet, timid, naive
Positive	
Golden ager	Active, capable, sociable, independent, happy, interesting
Perfect grandparent	Loving, supportive, understanding, wise, generous, kind
John Wayne conservative	Patriotic, conservative, determined, proud, religious, nostalgic

Source: From "A social cognitive perspective on age stereotypes" by M. L. Hummert in *Social cognition and aging,* edited by Thomas M. Hess, copyright 1999, Elsevier Science (USA), reproduced by permission of the publisher.

1996; Hummert, Shaner, Garstka, & Henry, 1998). Hummert (1999) has argued that such talk is probably grounded in stereotypic ideas about declining memory and hearing abilities in the aged.

It appears, then, that aging brings with it stereotypic reactions and expectations from others, which seem likely to interfere with satisfying social interactions. Some research also indicates that the conversational styles of older people often include features that may cue stereotypes. For example, older people are sometimes prone to making "painful self-disclosures" to relative strangers about illnesses, loss of a loved one, and other personal problems (e.g., Coupland, Coupland, Giles, Henwood, & Wiemann, 1988). For the elderly, self-disclosures may serve self-presentational goals, such as indicating resilience, but for younger listeners they tend to strengthen stereotypes of the elderly as weak or lonely. Thus, misinterpretations of some characteristic behaviors of older adults probably contribute to stereotypic responses from others (Hummert, 1999).

The Shrinking Social Convoy

Aging brings with it the more and more frequent experience of social loss. Friends, partners, and relatives may die or suffer from debilitating disorders such as Alzheimer's disease. In one study of 85-year-olds, 59% of the men and 42% of the women had lost a friend to death in the past year (Johnson & Troll, 1994). But illness and death are not the only sources of social loss. When people retire they lose daily contact with their colleagues at work. If the elderly person is constrained by limited finances or health problems, opportunities to visit others or to be part of club or other social activities may be reduced. Adult children may move to geographically distant locations. The elderly may leave behind neighbors and shopkeepers of long acquaintance if they move from a larger home to an apartment, an adult community, or an assisted-living facility. The shrinking of the social network and the pain of bereavement are problems that increase in late adulthood (Rook, 2000).

In Chapter 10, we noted that adolescents are largely segregated into age-bound communities that share language, interests, and a dress code, among other things. Mary Pipher (1999) proposes that the physical, cognitive, and social changes of late life serve to segregate the old, as well, in ways that are important for helpers to understand. As we have noted, the old often live in circumstances that separate them from their families and their communities, often because poor health makes independent living impossible. While these arrangements may provide the benefit of day-to-day care and companionship, they may also prevent older people from interacting with members of younger generations and deprive them of opportunities for service to others. Thus, some of their own developmental needs may be going unmet. "The old look for their existential place. They ask, 'How did my life matter? Was my time well spent? What did I mean to others?'" (p. 15). Social segregation creates islands of culture that discourage intergenerational bonding and may make older people feel less valued and useful to others.

The elderly are restricted in other, less obvious ways. Older individuals' use of language (e.g., "depression" meaning a period of economic downturn rather than a mental health problem) positions them within a cultural group or cohort that is separated from younger generations. Many elderly people also feel segregated from society because it simply moves too fast. Pipher (1999) recalls the adjustments she needed to make when interviewing her older clients:

> I learned to let the phone ring fifteen times. I learned to wait at doors five minutes after I rang the bell. I had to slow down to work with the old. Their conversation is less linear, and there are pauses and repetitions. Points are made via stories; memories lead to more memories. . . . When I walked the old I walked slowly and held hands at intersections or when sidewalks were

slick. . . . Because their bones break more easily, the old are afraid of falling . . . a broken hip can mean the end of independent living. (p. 27)

In the next section, we will consider how older adults face these and many of the other losses and challenges that we have described. Later in this chapter, we will take a special look at bereavement across the life span, with particular attention to how the elderly cope with the deaths of those close to them and with their own dying process.

Maintaining Well-Being in the Face of Loss: Successful Development

How do aging adults adapt to, or cope with, the increasing losses they face? Baltes and Baltes (e.g., Baltes, 1987; Baltes & Baltes, 1990; Baltes et al., 1998) suggest that three processes are key to successful development at any age, and especially in the later years. The first is *selection.* This is a process of narrowing our goals and limiting the domains in which we expend effort. It is not difficult to see that selection is important at any time in the life cycle. For example, at 20, Len *selected* a career, limiting the possible directions his life could take but also enabling him to achieve high levels of expertise and productivity by focusing his training and practice on career-related skills. At 62, Len *selected* family life instead of career. Because he felt his stamina waning somewhat, and despite the many satisfactions he still gained from his work, he decided to retire earlier than originally planned so that he could give more energy to developing relationships with his young grandchildren.

The second process is *optimization,* finding ways to enhance the achievement of remaining goals or finding environments that are enhancing. Len, for example, traded in his sporty two-door coupé for a larger sedan so that he could take the grandchildren on excursions to movies or museums. He also moved from a small apartment in the city to a place in the suburbs, closer to his children and having amenities such as a yard where he could amuse his grandchildren.

The final process that contributes to successful development is *compensation.* When a loss of some kind prevents the use of one means to an end, we can compensate by finding another means. For example, by age 74, as Len's eyesight began to fail, chauffeuring his grandchildren was no longer possible. He now entertains the youngest ones at his home most of the time, planning special events such as "video marathons" and backyard camping "trips."

Baltes provides the following real-life example of successful development in old age:

> When the concert pianist Arthur Rubinstein, as an 80-year-old, was asked in a television interview how he managed to maintain such a high level of expert piano playing, he hinted at the coordination of three strategies. First, Rubinstein said that he played fewer pieces (*selection*); second, he indicated that he now practiced these pieces more often (*optimization*); and third, he said that to counteract his loss in mechanical speed he now used a kind of impression management such as introducing slower play before fast segments, so to make the latter appear faster (*compensation*). (Baltes et al., 1998, p. 1055)

The three combined processes of successful development are called *selective optimization with compensation* (e.g., Baltes & Baltes, 1990; Marsiske, Lang, Baltes, & Baltes, 1995). Other theorists have described adaptation processes in similar ways and have also attempted to specify the kinds of motivations that might drive such processes. In *self-determination theory,* three basic psychological needs are thought to motivate our adaptation efforts at any age (e.g., Ryan & Deci, 2000; Ryan & LaGuardia, 2000). These needs are *autonomy, competence,* and *relatedness. Autonomy* is defined as being in control of oneself, that is, feeling that one's behavior is congruent with one's "true self," meaning that it is intrinsically motivated. What is especially pertinent here to understanding old age is that autonomy is not the same thing as independence. A person can be dependent on others to meet many of his needs, for example, as a result of poor health or disability, but can still feel autonomous if *he* has set the goals. Several studies of nursing home residents, who are clearly dependent on others for physical care, indicate that residents' vitality, life satisfaction, and psychological adjustment are linked to the extent to which the policies of the home are respectful of the residents' rights to choose their religious practices, daily activities, and approaches to self-care (e.g., Kasser & Ryan, 1999; Vallerand & O'Connor, 1989).

A second basic need, according to self-determination theory, is for *competence,* defined as "feeling effective in one's interactions with the social environment and experiencing opportunities to exercise and express one's capacities" (Ryan & LaGuardia, 2000, p. 150). The feeling of competence comes with finding ways of achieving goals that are self-endorsed. Meeting goals set by others, then, will not satisfy this need. Apparently, feelings of competence depend more on whether one's personally identified goals of the moment are being effectively managed than on whether a person can do all or more than he ever was capable of doing.

Consider Bernard, a retired social studies teacher, who spent his early and middle adulthood working in a small rural town. Always a scholar of history and economics, he was able to share his expertise in these areas with generations of high school students. He is now retired and lives in another part of the country. While he no longer teaches, he has found other outlets for his energies. He expresses his interest in athletics and his commitment to good health in a daily game of golf, although his experience with heart disease and a recent stroke caused him to reduce his exercise regimen for a period of time while he recovered. Bernard also puts his expertise about the stock market, a subject he taught in high school, to good use: he invests wisely and plans to help support his grandchildren's higher education. He also keeps well informed about the state of current affairs, serving as a resource for his family on matters of history. At 82, Bernard has coped well with his losses and physical limitations by identifying and working toward those self-endorsed goals that are meaningful to him.

Finally, *relatedness* is considered a basic need. People need to feel that they are important to others, valued enough to be sensitively and responsively cared for, from infancy onward. In this view, even though social interactions may change greatly over the life span, the processes that create feelings of well-being and security in the earliest attachments do not change with age (Ryan & LaGuardia, 2000). Some research on widowhood seems consistent with this idea. For married adults, relatedness needs have been found to be met in large part by spouses, who serve as supportive confidants and companions (e.g., Connidis & Davies, 1992). Widowed adults are more likely to adjust effectively to their loss if close relatives, especially children, are available to meet their relatedness needs. Friends, including new friends, can eventually meet these needs, but in the initial phases of widowhood there is added value in the care provided by children, perhaps because the newly widowed person feels his relatedness needs so sharply undercut, and his significance in the lives of his children is more certain (see Rook & Schuster, 1996; Stylianos & Vachon, 1993).

The degree to which basic needs for autonomy, competence, and relatedness are met substantially determines a person's sense of well-being and life satisfaction, according to self-determination theory (e.g., Ryan & Deci, 2000). Several theorists argue that whatever challenges we face in meeting our needs, there are two broad types of strategies that people use to control their destinies. Heckhausen (e.g., Heckhausen, 1999; R. Schultz & Heckhausen, 1996) refers to primary and secondary control strategies. When our control efforts are attempts to affect the immediate environment beyond ourselves, we are exerting **primary control.** The growth of competencies of all kinds serves primary control functions and contributes to feelings of mastery and self-esteem. When we choose to develop some competencies and not others (that is, when we engage in *selection,* such as choosing a career) we are using a primary control strategy. From the perspective of self-determination theory, exercising primary control could serve autonomy, competence, and/or relatedness needs. **Secondary control** generally refers to our attempts to change ourselves. We are using secondary control strategies when, for example, we change our aspirations and goals because we cannot do everything we used to do or when we deny or minimize the importance of our needs after failing to achieve some end.

> Both primary and secondary control may involve cognition and action, although primary control is almost always characterized in terms of behavior engaging the external world, whereas secondary control is predominantly characterized in terms of cognitive processes localized within the individual. (R. Schultz & Heckhausen, 1996, p. 708)

When primary control efforts fail or we suffer losses that we cannot overcome, secondary controls are likely to become important. R. Schultz and Heckhausen indicate that our repertoire of both primary and secondary control strategies will increase with age until late midlife but that the sheer weight of late-life declines will make primary control decline as well, so that people are likely to use more secondary control strategies in old age. Heckhausen (1997) found, for example, that adults in their 60s demonstrated more flexibility in adjusting their goals than adults in their 20s.

The concepts of primary and secondary control in development may remind you of the *problem-focused* and *emotion-focused* coping mechanisms described briefly in Chapter 13. Problem-focused mechanisms are aimed at the stressor itself, "trying to alter the aspect of the environment that is producing the challenge . . . [whereas] . . . emotion focused coping strategies are more likely to be used when the problem is inalterable" (Kling, Seltzer, & Ryff, 1997, p. 289). However, secondary control and emotion-focused coping strategies are not identical. Emotion-focused mechanisms have been described as coping processes that are directed internally, such as self-soothing, reframing, ruminating (especially focusing on our own emotions), venting, denying, or giving up. Secondary control strategies may also include behaviors that involve selection and engagement with alternative, compensatory goals that are more attainable than primary goals, so they can be considered problem-focused.

There is some evidence that in late adulthood, people do use more secondary control strategies. For example, when young, middle-aged, and elderly adults were asked to state their five most important goals and plans for the next five years, there was a clear shift in aspirations across age (Heckhausen, 1997). Elderly people had fewer aspirations regarding work, finances, and family and more aspirations related to health, community, and leisure pursuits than young adults. Heckhausen argues that these shifts reflect the fact that older people generally have less primary control potential over work, finances, and family. They therefore shift their goals in a compensatory way to those over which they may be able to take some primary control. This appears to be exactly the kind of coping that helped Bernard, the retired teacher we described earlier, to continue to meet his needs for competence as he became older.

When an elderly person uses the secondary control strategy of redirecting his attention to more manageable goals—goals over which he can effectively exercise some control—there are positive effects. No matter how stressful the problem, being able to address it in some way seems to enhance feelings of happiness and well-being. Thus, for example, Kling, Seltzer, and Ryff (1997) assessed the coping strategies of women with an average age of 70, some of whom were dealing with the difficult task of caring for a disabled adult child. Those who were able to use problem-focused strategies had a greater sense of well-being, despite the difficulties they faced, than the women who used fewer problem-focused strategies. In another study, Heidrich and Ryff (1993) found that good health was associated with measures of well-being in a sample of women ranging in age from 65 to 93 years. However, good health was *only* predictive of feelings of well-being if women felt that they were effective members of their community, that is, if they saw themselves as serving meaningful and valuable roles and doing well relative to others. These findings suggest that what actually contributed to their feelings of well-being was not their good health per se but having some primary control over their lives so that their basic needs could be met.

What about emotion-focused strategies that do *not* help the person cope? Kling, Seltzer, and Ryff (1997) examined the use of emotion-focused strategies such as denial and focusing on one's emotions (ruminating) in their sample of elderly women. These strategies had no impact on some dimensions of well-being, such as feelings of self-esteem or of having a purpose in life. More troubling, however, was that for aged adults with chronic, difficult problems to face, some emotion-focused strategies seemed to interfere with other aspects of well-being, such as feelings of autonomy, environmental mastery, and self-acceptance. The latter finding is consistent with research on happiness and well-being in adults of all ages. People who use certain emotion-focused strategies, such as dwelling on oneself and one's problems, report less happiness and well-being than those who do not (see Lyubomirsky, 2001). This result is also found among bereaved individuals, as we shall see later in this chapter (see also the discussion of rumination at adolescence in Chapter 9).

On the whole, how well do people in old age adapt to the challenges of late life? As we suggested earlier in this chapter, quite well! Ryff and Keyes (1995) analyzed measures of six dimensions of well-being from interviews with 1,108 adults. The responses of young (25 to 29), middle-aged (30 to 64), and old (65 or over) adults were compared, and several measures were found to increase over age. Old adults scored higher on a measure of positive relationships than both younger groups. They scored as well as the middle-aged and higher than the young adults on measures of environmental mastery and autonomy, and they scored as well as both younger groups on self-acceptance. Older adults did score lower than the younger groups on two dimensions of well-being: purpose in life and personal growth. Perhaps as a person leaves behind the arenas in which generativity is most directly expressed—work, parenting, and community service—opportunities to feel useful or to grow seem diminished. This conclusion is consistent with findings that elderly women who continue to care for a disabled adult child report a much greater sense of purpose in life than elderly women who do not have such responsibilities (Kling, Seltzer, et al., 1997). Generativity issues aside, it does appear that, overall, aging and a sense of well-being are often quite compatible and that some aspects of well-being actually improve in old age. Note, however, that longitudinal data are needed to be sure that some of these effects are not attributable to cohort differences.

Are there any specific behavioral characteristics of elderly people that might benefit their general well-being? To put it differently, are there any particular advantages to being old? Let's consider some candidates.

The Role of Wisdom

Wisdom has been defined as "expertise in the fundamental pragmatics of life" (Baltes et al., 1998, p. 1970). We have seen that the practical problems that adults must face do not necessarily have one right answer. These kinds of problems are described as *ill-defined* or *ill-structured*. We saw in Chapter 11 that as young adults gain experience with the complexities of real-life problems, the adolescent expectation that logical, absolute right answers always exist may give way to a more relativistic perspective, acknowledging that there are multiple, contextually embedded truth systems (e.g., Perry, 1970/1999). Some theorists argue that such relativistic thinking represents a new, qualitatively more advanced form of logical thinking, called *postformal* thought. Other theorists regard more

relativistic thinking as a function of reflection and experience, perhaps benefited by advancing metacognitive understanding of the limits of one's own thought processes. In the latter view, relativistic thought does not represent a qualitatively different level of functioning, but the outcome of accumulating knowledge. From either perspective, the result for some, not all, adults, is the achievement of wisdom, which represents "a truly superior level of knowledge, judgment, and advice" addressing "important and difficult questions . . . about the conduct and meaning of life" (Baltes & Staudinger, 2000, p. 123).

Sternberg (2001) describes wise people as both creative and intelligent: "They are perhaps most effective and sought after in positions of leadership because they are likely to balance the need for change (or shaping of the environment) with the need for stability (or adaptation to the environment)" (p. 362). Being able to change, finding new, but effective, solutions to problems, is the creative element; being able to adapt well to existing environments, serving as an agent who will preserve what is valuable, is the intelligent component.

Is wisdom more likely in old age? If it were, it might greatly benefit the older person's ability to manage the problems of decline and loss that aging can bring. In a program of research on wisdom by Staudinger, Baltes, and their colleagues, participants are told about people experiencing difficult real-life problems and are asked to describe and explain what the fictional people should do. One example of such a real-life problem, along with a response that received a low score for wisdom and one that received a high score, is presented in Table 14.2. Scores for wisdom were based on raters' judgments of how rich the respondent's factual and procedural knowledge seemed to be, whether the response took into account the developmental context, the degree to which the response reflected a relativistic view and a recognition of uncertainty, as well as attempts to manage uncertainty (e.g., Staudinger & Baltes, 1996).

Findings from studies using this technique indicate that wisdom, as defined by Staudinger and Baltes (1996), does seem to require experience and thus is somewhat enhanced by age. The years from 15 to 25 appear to be very important for wisdom acquisition (Pasupathi, Staudinger, & Baltes, 1999), but after 25, the proportion of people whose wisdom scores are above average does not change substantially. And after 75, fewer

TABLE 14.2

Wisdom Problem and Abbreviated Responses

Wisdom Problem
A 15-year-old girl wants to get married right away. What should one/she consider and do?

Low Wisdom-Related Score
A 15-year-old girl wants to get married? No, no way, marrying at age 15 would be utterly wrong. One has to tell the girl that marriage is not possible. (After further probing) It would be irresponsible to support such an idea. No, this is just a crazy idea.

High Wisdom-Related Score
Well, on the surface, this seems like an easy problem. On average, marriage for 15-year-old girls is not a good thing. But there are situations where the average case does not fit. Perhaps in this instance, special life circumstances are involved, such that the girl has a terminal illness. Or the girl has just lost her parents. And also, this girl may live in another culture or historical period. Perhaps she was raised with a value system different from ours. In addition, one has to think about adequate ways of talking with the girl and to consider her emotional state.

Source: Baltes, P. B., & Staudinger, O. M. (2000). Wisdom: A metaheuristic (pragmatic) to orchestrate mind and virtue toward excellence. *American Psychologist, 55,* 122–136. Copyright © 2000 by the American Psychological Association. Adapted with permission.

people continue to function at above average levels on measures of wisdom (Baltes & Staudinger, 2000). Studies using somewhat different methods have found a tendency for wisdom to increase well into middle adulthood (e.g., Blanchard-Fields, 1986) but also to decline thereafter (e.g., Labouvie-Vief, Chiodo, Goguen, Diehl, & Orwoll, 1995). There is some indication, though, that very high scores on wisdom are more likely in older than younger people. Baltes and Staudinger (2000) therefore predict that if there were a "world record" for wisdom, it would be likely that someone over 60 would hold it. Thus, for some elderly people at least, wisdom may well be a special asset in the management of their problems.

One interesting finding from the wisdom research is that in addition to age, training and experience in occupations that involve managing and reviewing life's problems seem to promote wisdom. Clinical psychologists, for example, receive higher wisdom scores than people with similar levels of education who are in fields that do not focus on "the fundamental pragmatics of life" (e.g., Smith, Staudinger, & Baltes, 1994). Clinical training itself seems to be important, because even when analyses controlled for the contribution of intelligence and personality differences across professions, clinicians had a wisdom advantage (e.g., Staudinger, Maciel, Smith, & Baltes, 1998).

The Selective Optimization of Social-Emotional Experience

Despite the declines and losses we described earlier in this chapter, there is one domain of experience that often shows significant growth in the second half of life. The socioemotional domain seems to be enhanced and better regulated with age. One reason is that older adults become more selective about the social relationships in which they invest their time. We saw earlier that the social convoy shrinks as we get older, sometimes as a function of the death of loved ones but also because opportunities for casual contacts are reduced. However, recent research indicates that the shrinking of the social convoy is not just a function of *involuntary* changes. Instead, the elderly tend to selectively invest in fewer social relationships, keeping or replacing close, deeply satisfying relationships and eliminating more peripheral ties (Carstensen, 1998; Carstensen & Charles, 1998). Figure 14.3

FIGURE 14.3

Numbers of Very Close Social Partners are Maintained Across Old Age, Whereas More Peripheral Partners Are Reduced in Number

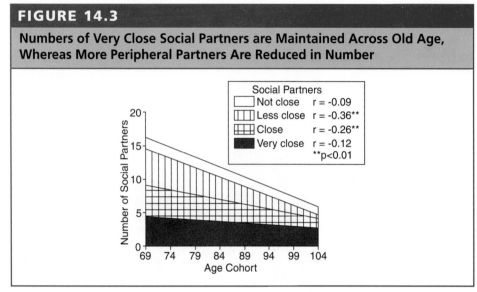

Source: Lang, F. R., & Carstensen, L. L. (1994). Close emotional relationships in late life: Further support for proactive aging in the social domain. *Psychology and Aging, 9,* 315–324. Copyright © 1994 by the American Psychological Association. Reprinted with permission.

demonstrates that in one study the number of very close social partners stayed about the same for people ranging in age from 69 to 104, but the numbers of less close social partners dropped dramatically (Lang & Carstensen, 1994).

Laura Carstensen and her colleagues explain this socioemotional selectivity as a function of people's expectations that the time remaining in their lives is limited (e.g., Carstensen, 1998; Carstensen & Charles, 1998). In both Western and Eastern cultures, they have found that people of any age will become more selective about whom they spend time with if they perceive their remaining time in life to be constrained (e.g., Fredrickson & Carstensen, 1990; Fung, Carstensen, & Lutz, 1999).

Because older people (and others who expect their lives to end soon) pay more attention to their feelings, their emotional experiences are more enhanced and complex (Carstensen, 1998). For example, for older adults emotional characteristics play a greater role than for younger adults in how they categorize potential social partners (Frederickson & Carstensen, 1990). Older adults also remember relatively more emotional information from descriptions of people than younger adults do (Carstensen & Turk-Charles, 1994).

Positive emotional experience is maintained in old age, negative emotional experience is reduced, and the complexity of emotional experience is increased. In an experience-sampling study, participants from 18 to 94 years old wore pagers for a week (Carstensen, Pasupathi, & Mayr, 1998). They were asked to check off the emotion or emotions they were experiencing when they were randomly paged throughout the week. Older adults reported positive emotions as often as younger adults, but they reported significantly fewer negative emotions. They also experienced more mixed emotions. For example, while spending time with an old friend, poignancy might be added to the positive feelings experienced.

Finally, emotion regulation seems to improve in later years. In the experience-sampling study just described, negative emotional states ended more quickly for older participants, but positive states lasted just as long as they did for the younger participants. In a variety of cultures, older adults describe themselves as having greater control over their emotions than younger adults do (Gross, Carstensen, Pasupathi, Tsai, Gotestam Skorpen, & Hsu,

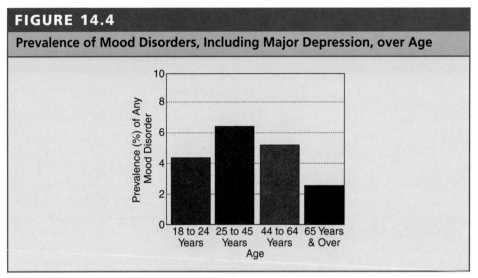

FIGURE 14.4

Prevalence of Mood Disorders, Including Major Depression, over Age

Source: Regier, D. A., Boyd, J. H., Burke, J. D., Rae, D. S., Myers, J. K., Kramer, M., Robins, L. N., George, L. K., Karro, M., & Locke, B. Z. (1988). One-month prevalence of mental disorders in the United States. *Archives of General Psychiatry, 45,* 977–986. Reprinted by permission of the American Medical Association.

1997). And in direct observations of conflict management between spouses, older couples were more skillful than long-married middle-aged couples at interspersing positive, affectionate statements with negative ones and keeping negative expressions to a minimum (e.g., Levenson, Carstensen, & Gottman, 1993, 1994). It appears that older people may be wise in the ways they deal with emotions: don't dwell on sorrow, and make happiness last.

Interestingly, these socioemotional growth patterns occur simultaneously with the tendency for some depressive characteristics to increase in old age. Overall rates of diagnosed mood disorders, including major depression, are lowest in elderly samples (see Figure 14.4), but self-reported depressive *symptoms* increase from middle adulthood into very old age (Gatz, 2000). These depressive symptoms, however, are different from those that younger people are most likely to report, perhaps reflecting the greater emotion regulation of older adults. The elderly are more likely to experience loss of interest and hopelessness rather than self-deprecation or dysphoric mood (Gatz, 2000; Joiner, 2000). Depressive symptoms in old age are also heavily linked to health status. In relatively healthy community samples, depressive symptoms occur in about 15% of the elderly. But 33% of older hospitalized patients and 40% of nursing home residents report depressive symptoms (Blazer, 1994). Fortunately, despite the intractability of many health problems in old age, research on the effectiveness of treatment for depressive symptoms has been encouraging. As with younger clients, elderly people, including nursing home residents, respond positively to a variety of psychotherapeutic interventions, including cognitive, behavioral (e.g., Rybarczyk, Gallagher-Thompson, Rodman, Zeiss, Gantz, & Yesavage, 1992), and brief psychodynamic, interpersonal, and life-review therapies (Scogin & McElreath, 1994).

EXPERIENCING LOSS

Death and Dying

In the expectable rhythm of life, most people begin to take the prospect of their own mortality more seriously during middle adulthood. Illness, the deaths of parents, spouses, siblings, or friends, the experience of watching adult children struggle with problems, and many other bumps in the road grow more frequent, and they signal what has already been lost. At some point, we begin to think of time not as unlimited "time to live" but as "time *left* to live." In old age, the reality of death and loss are inescapable. Even though advances in medicine have extended life and greatly improved its quality for many people, all of us face the certainty of death. And though death can occur at any point in the life cycle, the proportion of individuals who die in late adulthood is much greater than at any other time. Currently, close to 80% of the U.S. population live beyond age 65. Of this group, more than 75% will struggle with heart disease, cancer, stroke, lung disease, or dementia during their last 12 months of life (Lynn, 2000). Despite these statistics, elderly individuals report less anxiety about death and are more realistic about its inevitability than are middle-aged adults (Gesser, Wong, & Reker, 1988).

Clinicians will undoubtedly come face to face with the emotionally challenging issues of death and dying in their work. They may be called on to support children who experience a parent's death, relatives or friends of a suicide victim, families struggling to cope with the aftermath of a fatal accident, or individuals facing their own deaths from illnesses such as cancer or AIDS. Or they may work with the elderly, for whom the prospect of death ever more insistently intrudes into daily life. Death in later life is generally expected. The experience of death for younger persons can be particularly traumatic. While the older person and his family may have time to prepare themselves for the separation, death at earlier ages defies the natural order. Even though we present the issues of death and dying in the context of later life, many of the issues involved in dying and bereavement are similar across the life span. First we will consider the issues involved in dying. Then we will look at the psychological work of bereavement.

Facing Death

Dame Cicely Saunders, founder of the modern hospice movement, recounted a dying patient's words to her: "I thought it so strange. Nobody wants to look at me" (Ewens & Herrington, 1983, p. 5). This remark captures many elements that describe the experience of dying: general reluctance to address the topic of death openly, anxiety about death which informs this reluctance, guilt that emanates from the lack of openness, and the loneliness and isolation of the dying person. If death is a part of every human life, why do many of us avoid discussing it? Death clearly represents unknown territory, and it is difficult to comprehend a more painful or stressful life event than the prospect of dying or of losing a loved one. According to some existential therapists, fear of death is the ultimate source of anxiety and the foundation of most depression and alienation (May, 1979; Yalom, 1980). Some people have also pointed out that the advances of modern medicine, despite their obvious benefits, have encouraged us to think of dying in some of the same ways we conceptualize treatable illnesses (Kane, 1996).

Fortunately, much progress has been made in understanding death and dying relatively recently. Modern U.S. culture is very gradually moving away from one that denies or sanitizes death to one that supports death with dignity. Courageous pioneers such as Elizabeth Kubler-Ross (1969) have directed our collective attention to the issues facing the dying and the bereaved and, in doing so, have shed much-needed light on their needs and concerns. Faced with a growing population of elderly and prompted by advances in research, the field of medicine has taken steps toward more compassionate care of the dying. An emerging consensus among medical specialties regarding ***end-of-life care*** is reflected in the development of a set of core principles for providers (see Table 14.3). These eleven principles list the responsibilities of end-of-life caregivers to patients and their patients' families or support systems. To date, 14 medical specialty societies and the Joint Commission on the Accreditation of Healthcare Organizations have adopted these principles (Cassel & Foley, 1999). In general, the principles support more humanistic

TABLE 14.3

Core Principles for End-of-Life Care

1. Respecting the dignity of both patients and caregivers;

2. Being sensitive and respectful of the patient's and family's wishes;

3. Using the most appropriate measures that are consistent with patient choices;

4. Encompassing alleviation of pain and other physical symptoms;

5. Assessing and managing psychological, social, and spiritual/religious problems;

6. Offering continuity (the patient should be able to continue to be cared for, if so desired, by his/her primary care and specialist providers);

7. Providing access to any therapy that may realistically be expected to improve the patient's quality of life, including alternative and nontraditional treatments;

8. Providing access to palliative care and hospice care;

9. Respecting the right to refuse treatment;

10. Respecting the physician's professional right to discontinue some treatments when appropriate, with consideration for both patient and family preferences;

11. Promoting clinical evidence–based research on providing care at end-of-life.

Source: Cassel, C. K. and Foley, K. M. *Principles for care of patients at the end of life,* p. 2. © 1999 Milbank Memorial Fund. Used by permission.

approaches to end-of-life care, including better pain management, continuity of care, and attention to the psychological dimensions of death and dying. These principles are reflected at the practical level in state initiatives such as Oregon's policies to improve end-of-life care (Wyden, 2000).

What Is a Good Death?

Most people hope for a good death, but what does that really mean? As the poet Robert Frost observed, "Hope does not lie in a way *out,* but in a way *through.*" You might imagine that dying quickly without unnecessary suffering or dying at home surrounded by loved ones would provide good ways through this final passage. But preferences may be different for different people. Steinhauser and her colleagues (Steinhauser, Christakis, Clipp, McNeilly, McIntyre, & Tulsky, 2000) investigated the relative importance of factors that signify a good death in a survey of 2,000 seriously ill patients, physicians, recently bereaved family members, and other care providers. There was general agreement among all respondents that certain attributes were highly important. These included elements of symptom management and care (freedom from pain and anxiety, freedom from shortness of breath, being touched and kept clean), certain practical details (having financial affairs in order, knowing what to expect about one's condition), and patient-professional relationship quality (having caring, trustworthy providers who listen). In addition, specific psychological attributes (maintaining dignity, not dying alone, having the opportunity to resolve unfinished business and say good-bye) were also rated highly by all respondents.

But some differences among respondents were noted as well. In contrast to physicians, patients felt that it was very important for them to remain mentally aware, to have made funeral arrangements, and to feel a sense of completion about their life. African American patients were more likely than their White counterparts to want all available life-sustaining treatments. The entire patient group expressed concern about being burdensome to their families. Somewhat surprisingly, they also viewed being able to help others as an important contribution to their end-of-life quality, suggesting the significance of generativity across the life span. Though many people assume that patients prefer to die at home, this was not the overwhelming preference of this sample. In general, it is important to recognize that there are many ways to define a good death. Some of these preferences may be shaped by cultural and religious perspectives on death. It is incumbent on caregivers not to make assumptions about their clients, but to ask for and listen to individuals' needs.

Despite the importance of these individual differences, many studies have demonstrated that **palliative care** (Hanson, Danis, & Garrett, 1997; Singer, Martin, & Merrijoy, 1999) and the ability to prepare for death (Christakis, 2000; Emanuel & Emanuel, 1998) are two of the most consistently wished-for aspects of end-of-life care reported by patients and families. *Palliative care,* or comfort care, involves services provided by caregivers from several disciplines. It embodies a comprehensive approach to care that addresses pain management, emotional and spiritual care, and psychological support for caregivers and survivors (Billings, 1998).

The philosophy of care embodied in the modern **hospice movement,** which serves people suffering from terminal illness, is a good example of a palliative, patient-centered approach. Considered a hospitable respite for weary travelers in medieval times, hospice is now a place where people on another kind of journey, from life to death, can find peace and comfort. The hospice philosophy of end-of-life care says much about its philosophy of death, primarily about what the dying person needs in order to have a good death (Callanan & Kelley, 1992). Hospice emphasizes the importance of giving patients as much knowledge about their condition as possible so that they maintain some control over their care. The focus is not on curing disease but on managing symptoms and pain by means of palliative (pain-reducing) medicine. Perhaps more difficult to manage are other aspects of dying: the emotional, social, and spiritual sequelae of illness. In this approach to treatment, patients and their families are assisted in coping with the feelings of depression, anxiety, rejection, abandonment, and spiritual discomfort that may arise from the process of dying and losing a loved one.

Some studies have found that hospice patients are more satisfied with their care than conventional hospital patients (Kane, Wales, Bernstein, Leibowitz, & Kaplan, 1984) and that provision of hospice care in nursing homes improves quality of care there (Baer & Hanson, 2000; Wilson, Kovach, & Stearns, 1996). As noted earlier, there are clear worldwide trends toward improving end-of-life care by incorporating palliative care for all patients, regardless of setting (Lynn, 2000). In some areas, coalitions of hospitals, hospices, medical practices, nursing associations, long-term care facilities, social workers, and pastoral and mental health counselors have been formed to provide high-quality, comprehensive services to seriously ill individuals and their families (Mitka, 2000).

Having a good death appears to be related to the person's ability to make informed decisions about treatment, a notion congruent with what has been said about the psychological benefits of control. However, even though the importance of this kind of control has generally been acknowledged by practitioners of palliative care, studies suggest that a significant number of patients, even the most highly educated ones, still misunderstand the treatment options available to them. Silveira and her associates (Silveira, DiPiero, Gerrity, & Feudtner, 2000) examined whether knowledge about end-of-life options such as **refusal of treatment, physician-assisted suicide, active euthanasia,** and **double effect** was improved among patients who had signed **advance directives** or **living wills,** who had experienced previous illness, or who had previously cared for a dying loved one. *Refusal of treatment* refers to patients' refusal of any food, water, or medical treatment that prolongs life. *Physician-assisted suicide* involves prescribing medicine that enables patients to take their own lives. *Active euthanasia* refers to injection of a medication by someone else that causes immediate death. The *double effect* means giving medication intended to relieve pain even though there is a chance that death can result. *Advance directives* or *living wills* are statements, typically in writing, that describe a person's wishes regarding medical treatment in the event of incurable illness.

The results of the study showed that knowledge about end-of life treatment options was generally poor. It was not improved for those who had signed advance directives or who were ill themselves. Knowledge was somewhat more accurate for those who had cared for dying loved ones. In general, caregivers often wait too long to discuss end-of-life preferences. Decisions may be made in haste, when the dying person is too ill or caregivers too distressed to make reflective choices (Gleeson & Wise, 1993). It is important, therefore, to initiate conversations about end-of-life decisions well in advance of the stresses of illness. Table 14.4 presents important legal information about end-of-life care. A sampling of questions that can be used by caregivers to initiate discussions about issues of care is presented in Table 14.5.

The Process of Dying

In the late 1950s, Elizabeth Kubler-Ross (1969), a Swiss-born psychiatrist, began to study the ways that people who were dying faced death. At that time, the dying were largely

TABLE 14.4

Myths and Realities about End-of-Life Care

Myth	Current Status
There must be a law authorizing the termination of life support.	Currently existing law supports the termination of life support in all 50 states for both competent patients and for those who have lost capacity if there is consensus among those who care about the patient that it would be the patient's will or in his/her best interests.
Termination of life support is murder, assisted suicide, or suicide.	Termination of life supports is considered to be freeing the patient from unwanted bodily invasion. Death is legally considered to be a result of the patient's underlying disease. The law clearly distinguishes such acts from suicide, assisted suicide, or euthanasia.
A patient must be terminally ill for life support to be stopped.	The law allows any patient to refuse any treatment that he/she does not want, in the interest of protecting bodily integrity, even if that treatment would be life sustaining and the patient is not terminally ill.
It is permissible to terminate extraordinary treatments, but not ordinary ones.	The distinction between ordinary and extraordinary treatments is not relevant as a matter of law or ethics. The patient has the right to terminate any treatment, potentially life sustaining or not.
It is permissible to withhold treatment, but once started, it must be continued.	Although many clinicians think and feel differently about these types of actions, the law and medical ethics treat the withholding and the cessation of life-sustaining treatment the same.
Stopping artificial nutrition and hydration is legally different from stopping other treatments.	In most states, artificial hydration and nutrition are considered medical treatments like any other.
Termination of life support requires going to court.	The courts generally want clinicians to make these decisions without going to court, provided there is a consensus among those who care about the patient about how to proceed.
Living wills are not legal.	Living wills have legal support in all 50 states, either through legislation or case law.

Source: Meisel, A., Snyder, L., & Quill, T. (2000). Seven legal barriers to end-of-life care: Myths, realities, and grains of truth. *Journal of the American Medical Association, 284,* (p. 2496, table 1). Reprinted by permission.

TABLE 14.5

Questions for End-of-Life Decision Making

Domain	Representative Questions
Goals	Given the severity of your illness, what is most important for you to achieve?
	How do you think about balancing quality of life with length of life in terms of your treatment?
	What are your most important hopes?
	What are your biggest fears?
Values	What makes life most worth living for you?
	Would there be any circumstances under which you would find life not worth living?
	What do you consider your quality of life to be like now?
	Have you seen or been with someone who had a particularly good death or particularly difficult death?
Advance directives	If with future progression of your illness you are not able to speak for yourself, who would be best able to represent your views and values? (health care proxy)
	Have you given any thought to what kinds of treatment you would want (and not want) if you become unable to speak for yourself in the future? (living will)
Do-not-resuscitate order	If you were to die suddenly, that is, you stopped breathing or your heart stopped, we could try to revive you by using cardiopulmonary resuscitation (CPR). Are you familiar with CPR? Have you given thought as to whether you would want it? Given the severity of your illness, CPR would in all likelihood be ineffective. I would recommend that you choose not to have it, but that we continue all potentially effective treatments. What do you think?
Palliative care (pain and other symptoms)	Have you ever heard of hospice (palliative care)? What has been your experience with it?
	Tell me about your pain. Can you rate it on a 10-point scale?
	What is your breathing like when you feel at your best? How about when you are having trouble?
Palliative care ("unfinished business")	If you were to die sooner rather than later, what would be left undone?
	How is your family handling your illness? What are their reactions?
	Has religion been an important part of your life? Are there any spiritual issues you are concerned about at this point?

Source: Quill, T. E. (2000). Initiating end-of-life discussions with seriously ill patients. *Journal of the American Medical Association, 285* (p. 2506, table 3). Reprinted by permission.

invisible among hospital patients, and she encountered a high degree of professional resistance to her work. When she asked her fellow physicians to recommend to her their dying patients so that she could talk to them, she was told that there were no dying patients in her 600-bed hospital (Ewens & Herrington, 1983). But after meeting people who realized that they were dying and after listening carefully to their stories, she described responses to death that appeared to characterize the process: denial, anger, bargaining, depression, and acceptance. Each of these responses represents a type of coping or defense mechanism for dealing with death. Perhaps it was unfortunate that she referred to these processes as "stages" and linked them together in sequence. Although Kubler-Ross herself (1974) emphasized that the stages do not always occur in order and that they can and often do occur simultaneously, the use of a stair-step approach is fraught with the kinds of problems we discussed in Chapter 1. Foremost, perhaps, is that a stage sequence can be irresistible to clinicians who are looking for fixed, clear guidelines for understanding grief.

Criticism of the model has centered on the overall lack of empirical evidence for the existence of stages (Kastenbaum, 1986; Klass, 1982) and the problems that arise when counselors and other caregivers use the stages as a road map by which to evaluate functional versus dysfunctional adjustment to death and dying (Corr, 1993). The belief among caregivers that these five responses are the *only* appropriate ones for the dying represents another limitation of the model as it is applied to practice. Studies of individuals who have received terminal diagnoses do provide some support for the initial manifestation of shock or disbelief as well as for the presence of greater acceptance before death (Kalish, 1985). In general, however, counselors should remember that there is much greater variation in the process than is allowed for by a strict interpretation of these stages. Perhaps the reactions can be viewed as some important ways that people cope with impending loss, but by no means is the sequence fixed nor the range of coping mechanisms exhaustive.

With these caveats in mind, let us consider each of these coping mechanisms in more detail. **Denial** may follow the initial shock that is associated with news of a terminal illness. At best, it temporarily protects the person from the reality of a terrifying situation. Denial is associated with feelings of numbness or disbelief and serves to buffer the person from the full weight of the threat. Considered in this way, some measure of denial can be adaptive. It allows a person to temper the emotional impact, thus rendering it more manageable (Janoff-Bulman, 1993).

Anger is a normal reaction to separation and loss. Anger may be directed toward God ("Why me?"), toward others ("Why didn't you do something to help me?"), or toward the disease itself, which is viewed as an enemy to be battled. Often this is a very difficult response for family members to tolerate from loved ones who are dying. Resentment or hostility toward family members or caregivers who are healthy may reflect the depth of the dying person's pain. Anger can ebb and flow throughout the course of illness, depending upon the individual and the specific circumstances (Rosenblatt, Walsh, & Jackson, 1972).

The essence of **bargaining** is to try to postpone the inevitable by making promises, usually to a divine other. Sometimes individuals will try to delay death until some memorable event, such as an anniversary or a child's marriage, takes place. The individual may offer some prize, such as "a life dedicated to God," if the chance to live longer is granted.

Depression as a reaction to impending death is characterized by sadness and feelings of hopelessness. Kubler-Ross distinguished between reactive depression, or depression that results from loss of functioning or other problems associated with the disease process, and preparatory depression, which is related to prospective loss and separation. **Acceptance** is characterized by a sense of peace and relative tranquility, which suggests that the person has come to terms with his impending death. We stress, however, that this peace is relative. No one should be evaluated on how quickly or completely he accepts death. Remember, too, that these reactions, while important, do not reflect all possible ways of managing the dying process.

Bereavement

Life is death
kept at an arm's length.
Love is grief
dressed in its Sunday best.
And sadness is the tax
assessed on any happiness.
— From: *St. James' Park Epistle*
by Thomas Lynch

Sadness is not the sole province of the dying person. Those who suffer the loss of loved ones are themselves deeply grieved. Grief is a universal reaction to loss or separation, and, as you recall from the discussion of attachment theory, it takes a number of behavioral forms, such as active distress, protest, and searching for the lost attachment figure. Grief has been described with great poignancy from the earliest times by philosophers, poets, and religious leaders. It has been memorialized in song and codified in ritual. Grief is often so unsettling to observe that it elicits from others a desire to give comfort and solace. Many religious and secular customs have grown up around the grieving process in an attempt to help people survive the rigors of suffering and to give meaning to death. Culture also plays a role in determining how grief is expressed, for example, as an emotional versus a physical set of symptoms (Kleinman & Kleinman, 1985). Box 14.1 describes various rituals from different cultures that demonstrate some of the diversity in people's beliefs about, and experiences with, death.

Clinicians are often called upon to offer support to people who have experienced the loss of loved ones. An extensive clinical folklore has developed, primarily about the ways that grief should be expressed and the best ways to help people express it. In the 1980s, a vibrant debate commenced when researchers began to question the lack of empirical support for many of these traditionally accepted assumptions about grief. A number of inconsistencies or "myths" about grieving were uncovered in the process (Wortman & Silver, 1989, 2001), and researchers and clinicians have since continued this important dialogue. What follows is a discussion of some classic approaches to grief, an examination of some of the major tenets of bereavement counseling, and a brief summary of evidence from recent studies.

Classic Approaches to Bereavement

Freud's (1917/1957) theorizing about grief and mourning was very influential in shaping the legacy that came to be known as "grief work." In simple terms, Freud believed that individuals who lose a loved one (or object) must withdraw their emotional attachments or energy (or libido) and detach (or decathect) from the lost object. Loss causes great pain, and bereaved people, Freud believed, inevitably need to struggle with the process of letting go. As manifestations of their mourning, they may lose interest in the world, prefer to isolate themselves from others, dwell on thoughts of the deceased, and suffer from depression. Gradually, the reality of loss is accepted. From Freud's perspective, successful resolution involves *decathecting,* or detaching emotionally, from the former relationship and reinvesting psychic energy into the formation of new attachments.

Freud presented these theoretical ideas on mourning well in advance of some important deaths that were to occur in his own personal life. The loss of his daughter at age 25 and of his grandson at age 4 affected him greatly. He wrote that his life was permanently altered by these enormous losses and that, while acute grief may subside, people "remain unconsolable and will never find a substitute" (1929/1961, p. 239). These words suggest that Freud, in his later years, recognized that one does not necessarily recover from grief nor cut the cords of old attachments. However, his earlier notion that active grieving leads to recovery is one idea that he never formally revised and one that has permeated the canon of grief counseling. Other assumptions, that successful resolution of grief necessitates detachment from lost loved ones and reinvestment in other relationships and that abnormal mourning may follow from conflicted relationships, have also influenced clinical practice.

Bowlby's (1969/1982, 1980) highly influential construction of the bereavement process, based on attachment theory, depicts his view of typical human reactions to the experience of separation from or loss of attachment figures. The theory was initially

Box 14.1 Funeral Rituals in Different Cultures

In virtually every culture, distinct funeral rituals have evolved that are fascinating reflections of people's beliefs about death. Social anthropologists suggest that these rituals serve to bind a culture together by expressing its "collective representations" about fundamental issues such as life, death, and spirituality (Metcalf & Huntington, 1991). To illustrate the diversity of beliefs and the many ways of demonstrating grief, we present a look at funeral practices in four cultures: the Chinese of San Francisco's Chinatown (Crowder, 1999; Hill, 1992), the Luo of Kenya (Nyamongo, 1999), traditional Jewish families (Schindler, 1996), and the San Francisco gay community (Richards, Wrubel, & Folkman, 1999–2000).

For the Chinese, a funeral signifies the important transition from family member to ancestor, that beneficent spirit who will look out for the family's well-being from the spirit world. The connection between living family members and their ancestors is so important that prior to the mid-twentieth century Chinese immigrants living in the United States routinely returned their dead to China to be buried next to other family members. The Chinese community in San Francisco continues to practice elaborate traditional rituals, complete with funeral processions and brass bands. Funerals draw large groups of family members and friends, and they provide an occasion to tell the world about the accomplishments of the deceased. So fundamentally important is this practice that funerals in the Chinese province of Gansu are held *before* the person dies, so that he can be present to hear about the good things he has accomplished in his lifetime (2001, N. Zhang, personal communication).

Chinese funerals in San Francisco may incorporate Christian or Buddhist elements into a ceremony that traditionally consists of five parts: the visit, the service, the procession, the burial, and the dinner. The visit, or wake, allows visitors to view the body of the deceased. Near the body are placed a portrait of the dead person, usually framed with flowers, and items of food, such as chicken, vegetables, rice, and tea, intended to sustain the soul of the person through the journey to the afterlife. Various items such as jewelry, money, and clothing are placed in the coffin for his use as well. The funeral service, usually held the day after the visit, includes prayers and a eulogy. The funeral procession consists of a hearse, the funeral cortege, and a band, which plays hymns and other traditional music. On its way to the cemetery, the procession typically stops at the deceased's home or place of business. The portrait of the dead person is then taken from the hearse and set up facing the building. The mourners bow to pay

Funeral traditions vary dramatically across cultures, reflecting fundamental beliefs about life, death, and spirituality.

Box 14.1   Continued

their respects and may toss "spirit money," pieces of white paper in the shape of bills that are intended to placate malevolent spirits, into the air. Some relatives and friends await the procession at the house and greet the spirit of the ancestor with offerings of food, incense, and candles. At the gravesite, members of the funeral party, males first, followed by females, toss dirt, flowers, coins, or rice into the grave. The ritual is concluded with a formal seven-course meal, because seven is the number for death. At the center of each table is a cup of white rice liquor in honor of the departed.

The Luo live in the western part of Kenya near Lake Victoria. They, like the Chinese, believe that a person who dies becomes transformed from an earthly member of the family into a spiritual one. The funeral ritual is a transformative rite of passage. Death among the Luo is marked by a funeral fire, which is kept burning for approximately one week. The body of a deceased male is prepared by the men of the same clan and lies in state for 4 days, while that of a deceased woman lies in state for 3. After the burial, animals are slaughtered at the site of the funeral fire. Their numbers and kind depend upon the socioeconomic status of the deceased. Relatives and neighbors might contribute some animals for slaughter, knowing that the same will be done for them in their time of bereavement.

During the period of mourning, the sons of the deceased keep company around the fire. Their wives stay together in the house of the deceased, avoiding any sexual contact because of their belief that sexual relations will cause the death of their own sons. The widow of a deceased man is inherited by the dead man's brother, thus transferring her care to another relative and giving him the benefit of an additional laborer.

Traditional Jewish funeral practices emphasize honoring the deceased as well as giving the bereaved time and freedom to grieve. Jewish law is very sensitive to the emotional pain experienced by grieving persons and structures rituals to provide explicit comfort for them. During the funeral service, an emotional eulogy encourages mourners to vent their feelings by crying. A similarly cathartic release is elicited during the recitation of the *Kaddish*, or ritual prayer. Flowers are not customarily given in this cultural tradition because they signify happiness, an emotion that is discordant with the painfulness of death.

Throughout the period of mourning, called *Aninut*, great care is taken to support the bereaved. Jewish law indicates that those who have experienced a loss should be exempt from normal religious obligations, such as studying the scriptures. Customs such as *Kreiah*, or the ritual tearing of garments and the breaking of a shard on the lintel of the deceased's house, provide religious sanctions for outward displays of anger and sadness during the time of mourning. The period of *Shiva*, a 7-day mourning period, is dedicated to visiting and consoling the bereaved. Providing emotional comfort and social support for the survivors is viewed as an important religious obligation that helps to move people beyond the pain of their loss to a state of acceptance. Once the official 12-month grieving period is over, the *Kaddish* prayer is recited again, and excessive outward displays of mourning are expected to cease.

A relatively new culture, that of the gay community in San Francisco, has developed its own ways of dealing with bereavement due to the unfortunate increase in AIDS-related deaths. Since many members of this community die in hospice or home settings, their dying often takes the form of a vigil. Family and friends attend the dying person, keeping him as comfortable as possible while saying their good-byes. After death, rituals such as bathing and dressing the body honor the wishes of the deceased and allow the bereaved to feel connected to the loved one. Photos may be placed around the bedside, and valued objects, such as letters or items of religious significance, are placed near the body. Funeral services may combine elements of formal religious rites with those that signify some personal meaning. For example, planting trees in the loved one's memory, burning incense, playing music, and so forth may be incorporated into the service.

These examples, while certainly not exhaustive, emphasize the healing function of rituals, either traditional ones or those that are newly created. Whatever their type or origin, regardless of their religious or cultural underpinnings, rituals appear to draw people together in their encounter with death. They give voice to fears and to sadness, and they signify love and respect for the persons who have died.

developed to describe the responses of children temporarily separated from their care-givers (see Chapter 4, Box 4.5) and was later adapted to describe permanent separation, or bereavement, in adults. Bowlby's description of various reactions to separation gave rise to popular stage conceptions of dying, such as those of Kubler-Ross (J. Archer, 1999).

Bowlby's description of the grieving process includes four phases. At first, the loss is met by disbelief, a phase Bowlby called **shock.** The grieving person may experience numb-ness or feelings of unreality. Emotions may be blunted, and some individuals may even appear unaffected by the loss. Others may display emotional outbursts or may experience dizziness or other physical symptoms. The sense of disbelief eventually subsides when the reality of loss sets in. A second phase, **protest,** follows. Bereaved individuals may experi-ence periods of obsessive yearning or searching for the lost loved one as well as bouts of restlessness or irritability.

The subsequent period, called **despair,** may be characterized by great sadness; social withdrawal; sleeping, eating, or somatic disturbances; and other symptoms of depression or emotional upset. People may experience flashbacks or intrusive memories of the deceased. They may actively seek support from others by telling and retelling the story of their loss. Yet, as with a child whose attachment figure has left him, the comfort of others cannot replace the presence of the lost loved one. Gradually, the bereaved person begins to adjust to the loss. Bowlby used the term **reorganization** to describe the last phase of griev-ing a permanent separation. Taking a position in opposition to Freud's, Bowlby believed that bereaved individuals do not decathect, or detach, from their lost loved ones. Instead, they discover ways to hold on to the memory of the deceased and integrate that memory into their current life and new attachments. They heal, in part, by drawing comfort from the sense of the deceased person's presence (see Fraley & Shaver, 1999).

Assumptions About Grief Work and Empirical Support

As we have noted, a number of assumptions about bereavement, many derived from clas-sic theories such as these, have been reexamined in the light of new evidence and cross-cultural information. One of the most prevalent myths is that people need to "work though" their loss, by confronting the pain in an active way, for healing to occur. Avoiding the sadness, it is assumed, leads to later emotional problems. The tenets of **grief work** explicitly encourage bereaved individuals to confront and "work through" their feelings about loss in order for recovery to take place (Parkes & Weiss, 1983; Stroebe, 1992). This process, often facilitated by therapeutic intervention, might involve reflecting upon one's relationship to the deceased, expressing anger and other negative emotions related to the death, questioning and trying to construct meaning from the death, and ultimately resign-ing oneself to the loss. Unexpressed grief and unexamined loss, which have not been inte-grated into one's revised view of the world and the self, are thought to place the bereaved person's long-term physical and psychological well-being at risk. Another assumption is that the normal grieving process evolves in a sequence of stages that take a usually brief but arbitrarily determined period of time, such as 6 months to a year, to complete.

Those studies that have investigated the existence of stages in bereavement find little evidence to support the belief that people grieve in a linear, predictable fashion (van der Waal, 1989–1990; Wortman & Silver, 1987). Although many people do report initial shock and, later, some measure of reorganization, the intervening process does not neces-sarily follow in a clear sequence of compartmentalized, independent reactions. There is also a great deal of confusion over how long the manifestations of grief should persist before the grief is judged "abnormal." Diagnostic criteria (see American Psychiatric Association, DSM-IV-TR, 2000, p. 740) indicate that a clinician may consider a diagnosis of major depression if the depressive symptoms attendant to bereavement persist beyond two months. However, it is common for people to show grief symptoms much longer than two months. Several studies report gradual declines in depressive symptoms within the first *two years* after loss (Middleton, Raphael, Burnett, & Martinek, 1997; Stroebe & Stroebe, 1993), but depression may persist even longer (Martinson, Davies, & McClowry, 1991), particularly if the circumstances surrounding the death have been especially traumatic. Such findings have led to newly proposed criteria for use in the diagnosis of complicated or abnormal grief that allow for longer periods of normal grieving (see Horowitz, Siegel, Holen, Bonanno, Milbrath, & Stinson, 1997).

But many other assumptions about what constitutes "normal" and "pathological" (also called chronic, unresolved, or complicated) mourning have also been questioned, and presently there is no widespread consensus about their definitions (Middleton, Raphael, Martinek, & Misso, 1993). Abnormal grief was viewed by Bowlby (1980) as grief that is either excessive and protracted or absent. At one end of the continuum is chronic grief, which, like a preoccupied attachment, is marked by persistent yearning, anxiety, and unremitting distress. This type of mourning serves to immobilize bereaved individuals and to prevent their return to normal functioning. Absence of grieving, on the other end of the continuum, was viewed by Bowlby and others (Deutch, 1937; Parkes, 1965) as a maladaptive defense against the trauma of loss. In this response, characteristic of a highly avoidant attachment pattern, bereaved individuals suppress grief and try to exclude frightening and painful feelings from consciousness. Despite the lack of consistency in empirical support, the concept of abnormal grief has been accepted in clinical practice (Rando, 1993). It is widely assumed that people should demonstrate great distress after a loss and that failure to do so is abnormal, a condition often called the "requirement of mourning" (Wright, 1983).

In general, recent research has failed to find support for the assumption that people need to "work through" loss in the cathartic fashion advised by advocates of grief work in order to adjust successfully. Contrary to what counselors might expect, a certain amount of detachment during the grieving process predicts healthy recovery for many bereaved individuals. Bonanno and Keltner (1997; see also Bonanno & Kaltman, 1999 for a review) provide data demonstrating that minimizing expression of negative emotions can offer some benefit to the bereaved. In this study of individuals whose spouses had died, the remaining partners who manifested a high degree of emotional distress (fear, anger, disgust, and the like) at 6 months after their loss continued to report poorer outcomes after 2 years. Those individuals who had lower initial levels of distress had better health and lower levels of grief after 2 years. Similarly, in a study designed to explore the coping styles of bereaved individuals, Bonanno and his colleagues (Bonanno, Znoj, Siddique, & Horowitz, 1999) reported that detachment or emotional dissociation was not related to the development of later adjustment problems but was, in fact, predictive of positive outcomes. Neimeyer (2000) concludes from an examination of research that the use of grief-focused interventions with individuals who are not highly distressed risks doing them harm.

Other studies of bereaved individuals (Vachon, Rogers, Lyall, Lancee, Sheldon, & Freeman, 1982; Lund, Dimond, Caserta, Johnson, Poulton, & Connelly, 1985–1986), of parents whose babies died from SIDS (Wortman & Silver, 1987), and of individuals who experienced spinal cord injuries (Dinardo, 1971) showed similar results. Those individuals who demonstrated the highest levels of distress initially were also most distressed and less effective in coping with the loss up to several years later. Individuals who showed lower levels of initial distress were generally better adjusted later and were *not* more likely to experience delayed grief reactions. One conceptual explanation for these findings draws on the framework of individual differences in attachment representations. Specifically, adjustment to loss may be less difficult for individuals whose emotional systems can be deactivated more easily (avoidant) than for those who have difficulty suppressing emotions (ambivalent) (see Fraley & Shaver, 1999). Another hypothesis is linked to gender. For example, one study demonstrated that females gave priority to sharing feelings after a loss, while males viewed problem-solving approaches as more important (Hopmeyer & Werk, 1994). Certainly, much more research is needed to understand fully the significance of individual differences in grieving.

Overall, the evidence presented above should not be interpreted to suggest that outward signs of distress are necessarily unhealthy. Either side of an "either-or" argument is problematic. Just as a prescription to demonstrate intense grief is not right for everyone, neither is the advice to remain stoic. What we need to understand are the mechanisms that might explain individual differences in grief reactions, in hopes of constructing a more comprehensive theory of grieving. For those who take the stoic approach, perhaps it is not simply detachment, or the temporary psychic space it provides, but also the restricted focus on loss that makes for better overall adjustment. The traditional advice of grief work, which is to confront pain head-on, may be problematic for some people because of the risk of engaging in excessive yearning or "pining" for the lost loved one. We saw earlier in this chapter that rumination, an emotion-focused style of coping, is correlated with poor adjustment. Excessive preoccupation with the deceased or obsessive dwelling on thoughts of pain and sadness may qualify as rumination.

In a longitudinal study of hundreds of bereaved individuals conducted over 18 months, Nolen-Hoeksema and Larson (1999) found that the use of rumination as a way to cope with loss was highly related to depression at each interview point. In addition, people who ruminated tended to have great difficulty finding meaning in the loss, despite the significant amount of time they spent trying to do so. These findings are consistent with the strong association between ruminative coping and depression in general (Nolen-Hoeksema, 1991).

You might wonder how a bereaved person can make sense of his loss, another assumed measure of successful grieving, if he does not engage in some rumination. Yet, is it really necessary for people to make sense of the loss in order to adapt successfully? C. G. Davis, Lehman, and Wortman (1997) report that not all people who struggle to make sense of deaths, accidents, illnesses, and other tragedies are able to explain these events in satisfactory ways. Many people do not try to do so, preferring to move ahead with their lives without searching for existential or philosophical meaning.

Davis and his associates (C. G. Davis, Wortman, Lehman, & Silver, 2000) reported very consistent findings from several studies that investigated the benefits of meaning-making for later adjustment. In general, individuals who were able to derive meaning from the event relatively early on were least distressed at follow-up interviews. Interestingly, those who were able to find something positive in the experience or who were able to reappraise the loss to extract some benefit from it were the best adjusted. Religious or spiritual beliefs often helped people find meaning in the loss. However, others found that loss precipitated a cascade of doubts about faith because it shattered their views of a just world. Those who did not initiate a search for meaning were also found to have relatively good adjustments. It was the group that struggled for meaning without finding it that suffered most.

Nolen-Hoeksema and Larson (1999) reported significant associations in their bereavement study between the tendency to ruminate and the inability to find meaning in the experience of loss. The highest level of distress at follow-up interviews was demonstrated by the group who struggled continually to make sense of the inexplicable. Certain contextual circumstances may make it more difficult for people to find meaning or benefits from the deaths of loved ones. Among these kinds of deaths are those that occur suddenly (Parkes & Weiss, 1983), deaths of children (Nolen-Hoeksema & Larson, 1999), deaths due to intentional, malicious causes such as homicide (Murphy, 1997), and deaths due to the negligence of others, such as those involving motor vehicle accidents (Wortman, Battle, & Lemkau, 1997). Some measure of restitution made by the perpetrators of these acts can be beneficial in reducing the bereaved families' distress and promoting resolution of grief (Davis, Wortman, et al., 2000).

An Integrated Perspective on Grief

As research in this area increases, more sophisticated models of grieving have been developed (Cook & Oltjenbruns, 1998; Rubin, 1981). One such model that weaves together some of the theoretical and empirical threads described above is the ***dual-process model*** proposed by Stroebe and Schut (1999). This conceptualization depicts an interplay of stressors and coping strategies within a flexible, oscillating framework. Specifically, the authors propose that bereaved individuals simultaneously engage in two kinds of coping mechanisms, approach and avoidance, that wax and wane over the course of grieving.

Approach tendencies are reflected in activities synonymous with grief work: confronting the painful reality of death, expressing sadness, and gradually desensitizing oneself to the reminders of loss. Approach tendencies can be tolerated for only so long. They are ***loss focused*** and can lead to rumination or excessive preoccupation and, often, great distress. According to the dual-process model, the loss-focused work of grieving is balanced by parallel activities that are ***restoration focused.*** This type of coping strategy is directed toward handling the practical tasks that need to be done to carry on with daily life. For example, a widow might experience intense periods of grief during which she focuses on memories of her life with her deceased spouse; however, she might also have dependent children who need care. Attending to their needs serves as a distraction, mitigating the periods of loss-related distress. Both loss and restoration coping strategies are part of the grieving process, and Stroebe and Schut view their dynamic oscillation as a healthy regulatory mechanism. Bereaved individuals go back and forth between emotion-focused (loss-oriented) and problem-focused (restoration-oriented) modes of coping. This approach-avoidance interplay protects bereaved individuals from the exacting extremes of unrelieved distress or rigid mental suppression. In general, there is more loss-oriented coping early in the grieving process and more restoration-oriented coping at later points. Traditional conceptions of abnormal grief can be viewed as "disturbances of oscillation" (Stroebe & Schut, 1999, p. 217), either overly loss oriented or excessively avoidant. Figure 14.5 presents a diagram of the dual-process model of coping.

APPLICATIONS

This chapter presents information about some key ways people change in later life and how they adapt to or cope with those changes. Coping has been defined as a person's "cognitive and behavioral efforts to manage (reduce, minimize, master, or tolerate) the internal and external demands of the person-environment transaction that is appraised as taxing or exceeding the resources of the person" (Folkman, Lazarus, Gruen, & DeLongis, 1986, p. 572). Adaptive coping, or managing the demands of life relatively well, is at the heart of achieving and maintaining optimal health and wellness. This is certainly true at any age, but perhaps even more so in old age, when the threat of overtaxed resources and the need to tolerate limitations becomes inevitable. Life involves gains and losses. It is naïve to assume that everyone can and will maintain a high quality of life right up to their death. But on the other hand, unnecessarily pessimistic views of old age, fueled by negative stereotypes of the elderly, serve to restrict the ways people choose to adapt to aging and limit their sense of control over their lives. Counselors who are knowledgeable about development at this time of life and skilled in understanding coping mechanisms can be

FIGURE 14.5

A Dual-Process Model of Coping with Loss: Pathways

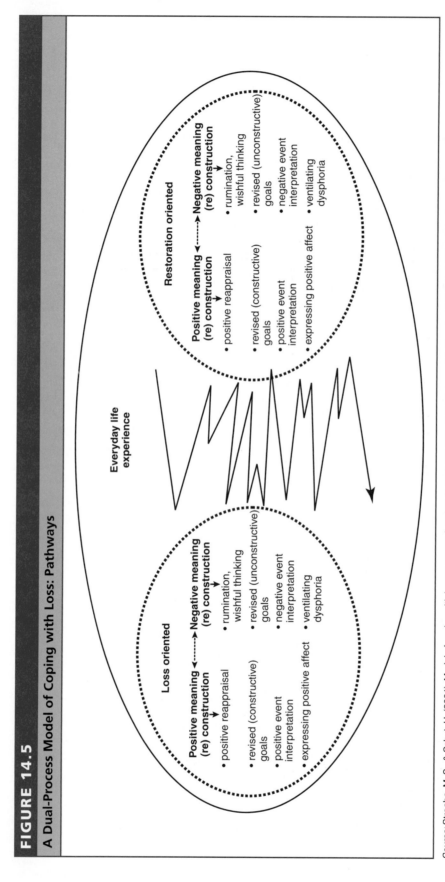

Source: Stroebe, M. S., & Schut, H. (2001). Model of coping with bereavement: A review. In M. S. Stroebe, R. O. Hansson, W. Stroebe, & H. Schut (Eds.). *Handbook of bereavement research: Consequences, coping, and care* (p. 397). Used by permission of the authors.

instrumental in promoting healthy adaptation, regardless of client age (Ponzo, 1992). Sources of concrete information about how to cope with getting old (Skinner & Vaughan, 1983/1997) and how to understand the perspective of elders (Pipher, 1999) can help clinicians build their foundation of knowledge. Whitbourne (1989) summarizes the task:

> The main point that a clinician must keep foremost in mind when working with an aging client is the need to be flexible. The aging process involves multiple physical, psychological, and social demands that can all potentially impact on the individual's ability to function. Clinicians may be called upon to perform advocacy services, environmental interventions, and interdisciplinary consultations, which they would not ordinarily regard as falling within the domain of "psychotherapy." It is only by maintaining an open approach to the multiple needs of the aged client that the clinician can hope to bring about successful change. (p. 168)

The amount of research on aging continues to grow, due, at least in part, to the aging of the U.S. population. The newest wave of research is focused on "successful aging," a perspective that assumes that healthy functioning and even the achievement of certain gains is possible in late life. One such initiative is actually a series of studies called the MacArthur study because of the financial support provided by the John D. and Catherine T. MacArthur Foundation (Rowe & Kahn, 1998). The fruits of 10 years of intensive investigations involving thousands of participants, millions of dollars, and the combined expertise of biologists, neuropsychologists, sociologists, epidemiologists, geneticists, and gerontologists, among others, tell us a great deal about successful aging.

To summarize briefly, enjoying a healthy and productive old age is possible. The more physically and mentally fit older individuals are, the more likely they will age successfully. Clearly, one's lifestyle prior to old age can have a tremendous influence on the quality of later life. A healthy diet and regular exercise, including aerobics and weight training, confers a real physical advantage. Although maintaining healthy habits provides protection from disease and should, ideally, be maintained consistently, the MacArthur study revealed that positive changes in eating and exercise habits, even in old age, can help people live longer and healthier lives.

One of the most interesting findings from the study is that good physical health in old age is strongly related to mental ability and social support. Those who had higher levels of cognitive functioning and higher levels of social support prior to later life were likely to maintain their physical capacities. Continuing to learn, whether it be formal learning or the "just for fun" mental activity of crossword puzzles, provides important environmental stimulation or cognitive "exercise." Surprisingly, the kind of social support that is most important is not instrumental support (for example, providing help in cooking, cleaning, etc.), important as this is, but emotional support (for example, patient listening, cheering up, comforting touch, etc.). Not only is it important for older people to get emotional support from others, but many successful agers say that it is important for them to give it, too.

A sense of being productive appears to be a benchmark of healthy aging as well. Healthy men and women are three times more likely than those with physical or mental health problems to be engaged in paid work or volunteer activities. However, as we have seen, even people with physical limitations often manage, with some creativity, to engage in activities that keep them in touch with the world. Productive engagement with others, in whatever form it takes, is linked to a sense of mastery or personal self-efficacy. A "can-do" attitude contributes enormously to well-being. Counselors can facilitate the development of self-efficacy by fashioning opportunities for older individuals that reflect their self-endorsed goals and that challenge their capacities without overwhelming them. Counselors also need to provide encouragement to old people to engage in these challenges, give confirming feedback for mastery, and help dispel negative stereotypes that lead to passivity and hopelessness.

Older people often meet their need to feel competent and productive by engaging in part-time or volunteer work.

What should we do to help when the losses of later life occur? Based on recent longitudinal studies, several principles appear to be important. Counselors should be aware that grief has many affective, behavioral, and physical manifestations and that there is wide variation in expressions of mourning at the level of the individual and culture. The oversimplified use of stage theories may suggest that there is one correct way to grieve and one circumscribed time frame in which to do so. One can only imagine how discouraging it must be for a bereaved person to be told that he is not grieving correctly. In our fast-paced world, it is often difficult to let people take the time they need to heal. Clinicians should not hold prescriptive rules for how long grief should last, because many people continue to grieve well beyond the limits of several months or even years.

Remember as well that the absence of overt, intense grief is not necessarily problematic. Not everyone who fails to demonstrate great distress or who does not search for meaning in a loss will suffer eventual emotional problems. Furthermore, we often expect people to "recover" from a loss by returning to an earlier level of functioning, despite evidence that this is often impossible.

Difficulties in the grief process may be considered to be an imbalance between too much expression and too little, but even this is mediated by personality, gender, culture, and beliefs. Some interventions that have traditionally been favored by bereavement counselors, such as grief work interventions, may not be useful and may actually be more distressing for individuals given to ruminative tendencies. Even support seeking, a style of coping that involves seeking help from other people, may be a source of stress unless those sought after for help are themselves compassionate and willing to listen (Nolen-Hoeksema & Larson, 1999).

Several sets of tasks have been developed that describe the responsibilities of helpers or other caregivers in times of bereavement (Rando, 1993; Worden, 1982). The following is a brief description of Worden's tasks with evidence-based recommendations derived from the bereavement coping project of Nolen-Hoeksema & Larson (1999). Keep in mind that bereaved individuals differ in their needs, so these recommendations should be considered general guidelines. First, bereaved individuals may need support in order to accept the reality of loss. Providing assistance with funeral arrangements and helping to prepare meals or clean up are all useful ways to be of help. It is important not to "push" the person to accept the loss but to be respectful of the individual's style of coping. Second, helpers and other loved ones should allow bereaved persons to identify and express feelings if they want to do so. Judicious use of open-ended questions and provisional language ("Sometimes people say that they occasionally feel anxious or impatient. I wonder if you ever feel that way?" Nolen-Hoeksema & Larson, 1999, p. 182) can promote feelings of safety and acceptance. Third, bereaved persons need to learn how to live without their lost loved ones. For example, they may need to learn restoration-focused tasks previously handled by the deceased, such as managing finances or cooking for children. The helper can scaffold the development of these skills by anticipating possible needs, helping to break them down into manageable tasks, and providing concrete assistance or information.

The fourth task involves helping survivors find a place in their lives for the deceased. This may take many forms, depending upon the individual, but generally entails finding a way to maintain some emotional connection. For some people, talking about the deceased is easier and more beneficial than talking about themselves. Silverman (2000) noticed in her work with bereaved children that they were much more articulate when asked to talk about the person who died than they were when asked to talk about their own feelings about the death. She called this process "constructing a relationship to the deceased."

The fifth task for helpers requires them to be patient and allow time and a nurturing context for grieving. The sixth task is to help normalize grief for the bereaved. Grieving people often report fears about "going crazy" because of symptoms such as visual or sensory hallucinations, panic attacks, and other signs of intense distress. Learning that these are common occurrences in bereavement that will go away in time is very reassuring. The eighth and ninth tasks require helpers to provide continuing support, as needed, to help survivors weather the trials of grieving and to assist them in examining the effectiveness or ineffectiveness of their coping strategies. Taking notice of strategies that are effective is an empowering exercise because it allows people to recognize that they have some choice. Strategies that are less helpful can be identified, and more useful possibilities can be suggested. Finally, the tenth task for helpers requires them to identify and find other sources of support if they, for whatever reason, cannot provide for the range of needs described above.

Integrity: The Life Cycle Completed

From Erikson's (1950/1963) perspective, people struggle continuously throughout the life cycle with the "hazards of existence" (p. 274) and should not expect to reach a level of achievement in any of the epigenetic stages that is completely impervious to conflict. The negative pole of each developmental task represents its counterpoint, a reminder of each stage's dynamic quality (see Chapter 1, Table 1.1). The period of old age is no exception. Facing old age and death are awesome challenges. Yet over a lifetime, the struggles of earlier stages ideally bear fruit. The resulting *integrity*, that sense of coherence or wholeness that comes from "acceptance of *one's own and only life cycle* [italics added]" (p. 268) is the product of strengths accumulated from each earlier period: drive, self-control, direction, method, devotion, affiliation, and production. Renunciation, the outcome of the final stage according to Erikson, is consummate generativity. It embodies acceptance of the natural order, namely that wisdom which allows us to view death as a stage of life. "Healthy children will not fear life," Erikson wrote, "if their elders have integrity enough not to fear death" (p. 269).

Erikson's view of the life span, then, is less of a straight line and more of a circle, with its final stage a gift of courage and caring for the generations that follow. In his psychosocial view of development, the quality of life from beginning to end is touched by its social intersections. As we are learning, positive relationships keep people well (Ryff & Singer, 2000); they offer long-term protective factors. Nurturing others, so necessary for survival of our species, returns on the investment at the end of life when we receive others' care. As we age, some have suggested the need to reminisce or review life events as a way of integrating the features of one's identity and achieving integrity (Butler, 1963). Part of the benefit of this process, undoubtedly, involves sharing the story with others.

Threaded throughout this book is a review of many aspects of human social functioning: attachments, social networks, marriage and family ties, and their relationships to physical, intellectual, and emotional wellness. There is much left to learn about these interconnections, but the research agendas of the twenty-first century promise to improve even further our working knowledge of mind-body-context connections that can then be applied to practice. Clinicians are in a unique position to use this knowledge to promote positive healthy development and to create and support conditions that foster resilience in the face of life's challenges.

SUMMARY

Aging Well

1. Despite the increasing number of losses older people experience as they move into old age (60s and 70s) or into old-old age (80s and 90s), most older individuals manage to adapt to old age successfully.

2. As people age, they experience declines in many physical systems, including the immune and sensory systems. *Arthritis,* particularly *osteoarthritis,* is especially common.

3. Cognitive declines in fluid intelligence (e.g., processing speed and working memory) may be partially offset by maintenance or even advancements in crystallized intelligence (e.g., verbal ability and factual knowledge). Cognitive functioning in old age is related to overall health, and substantial declines in cognitive functioning, known as *dementia,* are usually due to cardiovascular accidents or disease processes such as *Alzheimer's disease. Terminal drop* refers to a rapid decline in intellectual functioning shortly before death.

4. Studies of autobiographical memory indicate that, contrary to stereotypic notions, older people remember their more recent experiences better than earlier experiences (*recency*), even though older adults learn new information less efficiently than younger adults. However, if adults are asked about *flashbulb memories,* especially vivid and personally relevant recollections, their reports are largely about events in their early adulthood, referred to as "*the bump*" period. That is probably why elderly people often tell stories about their early years.

5. As people age, their network of friends and family members shrinks. Social loss is exacerbated by negative stereotypes about aging that assume all elderly people share certain negative characteristics. These stereotypes can lead to discriminatory or demeaning practices that interfere with positive social interactions.

6. Three processes appear to be important for successful development in old age. *Selection* involves limiting activities to a few that are particularly rewarding. *Optimization* involves finding ways of enhancing achievement of remaining goals. *Compensation* involves finding new means to achieve our ends. Together these processes are called *selective optimization with compensation*.

7. There are other, similar ways of describing adaptation processes. In *self-determination theory*, three needs are said to motivate adaptation at any age: *autonomy, competence,* and *relatedness*.

8. Another description of techniques for facing challenges emphasizes two broad strategies. *Primary-control strategies* are attempts to affect the immediate environment and often increase feelings of mastery and self-esteem. *Secondary-control strategies* are attempts to change ourselves, such as changing goals. If the latter approach allows a person to then take primary control over some stressor, feelings of happiness and well-being are likely to be enhanced.

9. Yet another approach to describing coping efforts refers to *problem-focused* coping (aimed at the stressor itself) and *emotion-focused* coping (such as self-soothing or ruminating). Older people appear to have less problem-focused coping potential in some situations. However, substantial use of some emotion-focused coping strategies can interfere with feelings of autonomy and mastery.

10. On the whole, older people seem to cope well with the challenges of late life. They compare positively with younger adults on some aspects of well-being, such as positive relationships and self-acceptance.

11. Does increased wisdom help the elderly to cope? *Wisdom* involves superior knowledge, judgment, and advice with regard to important questions about life. Research indicates that it is somewhat more likely to characterize older rather than younger adults, although wisdom seems to be as much a quality of the individual person as it is of age.

12. As people age, they pay more attention to their feelings, and their emotions are more enhanced and complex. Positive emotions are as common among the old as the young, but negative emotions occur less often. Also, emotion regulation seems to improve.

Experiencing Loss

13. Elderly people report less anxiety about death than younger people. Dying adults often must deal with others' reluctance to deal with death and may feel lonely and isolated.

14. A "good death" for most people includes symptom management and care (such as freedom from pain, being clean), practical details (such as knowing what to expect), a good patient-professional relationship, and certain psychological attributes (such as maintaining dignity, not dying alone). But many people have very individual needs and desires as well. For example, some people prefer to die at home, but many do not. *Palliative care,* such as that promoted by the *hospice movement,* is important to most people.

15. People who sign living wills or advance directives do not necessarily know more about their end-of-life options, although those who have recently cared for a dying patient are more aware.

16. Kubler-Ross described several reactions to dying that are called stages but that do not necessarily occur for all dying adults and do not occur in any fixed sequence: these are denial, anger, bargaining, depression, and acceptance.

17. Both Freud and Bowlby proposed influential theories of the grief process. Freud originally believed that bereaved individuals needed to withdraw from the lost loved one

and reinvest emotional energy into forming new attachments. Bowlby used attachment theory concepts to describe stages of the grief process: shock, protest, despair, and reorganization. Assumptions derived from these theories have been disputed by contemporary researchers. In particular, the existence of a stage sequence of grief reactions has not been validated. The concept of "abnormal grief" and the need for cathartic "grief work" have been called into question as well.

18. Contemporary models of grieving include diverse ways of coping with loss. The dual-processing model of Stroebe and Schut incorporates both loss-focused (emotion-focused) elements and restoration-focused (active problem-solving) elements within a flexible framework.

Case Study

Isabelle and her husband Victor lived together for 53 years in a small, close-knit Italian-American section of a big city. Victor made a living for the family working as a forklift operator. Isabelle, a stay-at-home mother when her children were young, returned to work as a sales clerk once the youngest two children entered high school. Isabelle enjoyed her years of full-time mothering, but she also loves the social interaction and camaraderie she finds in her job. The family has four grown children, Paul, age 51, Sophia, age 49, and twins Lenore and Joseph, age 45. Paul and his wife own and operate a small restaurant in a nearby suburb. They have two young adult children. Sophia, also married with two children, teaches in a middle school about an hour away from her parents' home. Lenore has recently remarried after a divorce. She lives with her second husband and her three children in the city. Joseph is a salesman who has never married but who lives in another state with his longtime partner, Joanne.

At this time, the family is struggling to come to grips with Victor's recent death. After years of robust health, Victor was diagnosed with pancreatic cancer. During the last 4 months of his life, he was in and out of the hospital as his health demanded. Isabelle tried to care for him as best she could, but it was very difficult. The side effects of Victor's treatment protocol left him feeling ill and in need of constant care. The family members tried to help, but the greatest burden fell to Paul because in this family the oldest child is perceived to have the most responsibility.

As time went on and it became clear that Victor was dying, Isabelle mentioned to her children that their father had not wanted any extraordinary measures to be used to keep him alive in his final illness. Victor had never put this in writing, but Isabelle was sure of his wishes. Victor's family physician, a deeply religious man, Victor's older brother, and Joseph all strongly disagreed with this plan. They believed that every effort should be made to save Victor's life. One night, Victor lapsed into a coma and was having trouble breathing. Joseph prevailed upon his mother to allow the physician to insert a ventilator. Joseph's siblings were very upset about this turn of events, for they believed it caused their father unnecessary suffering. Victor died several days later.

Now 4 months after the death of her husband, Isabelle is grieving the loss of her spouse. She lives alone but is seriously contemplating asking her son Paul to let her move in with his family. She quit her job at the department store because she felt she was unable to concentrate well enough to perform in a satisfactory manner. She has been unable to sleep through the night, and her mind keeps returning to memories of Victor during his illness.

Relationships are strained among the children. Neither daughter speaks to Joseph or Joanne because of their disagreement about Victor's care. Joanne believes that Joseph should "move on" and concentrate on her and their life together. Lenore avoids calling her mother because she does not want to hear her repeat the same troubles over and over again. She uses her hectic schedule as a full-time mother as an excuse. Sophia is somewhat more attentive, but she is also uncomfortable listening to her mother's reminiscences. She wants to believe that her mother is still the same vibrant person she has always known, so she discounts the sadness she hears in Isabelle's voice. Paul is overwhelmed by the responsibility he feels for his family, his business, and his mother. He knows his mother is grieving, but he cannot find a way to make her feel better. For her part, Isabelle feels that she has come to the end of her life as well. She believes that she will end up like many of the other lonely widows she knows in her neighborhood.

Discussion Questions
1. What are the emotional and behavioral responses of each person to Victor's death?
2. Identify the stressors that are operating on this family. Distinguish between those that can be controlled and those that cannot be changed. Develop a list of coping strategies that might be useful in dealing with these problems.
3. As a counselor, how would you begin to work with this family? With Isabelle?

Journal Questions

1. Identify someone you know whom you see as aging successfully. Write a letter to this person (to be given or not) describing how you think the person is dealing with growing old and why you admire the person.
2. What would you do if you had only 6 months to live?
3. What kind of ceremony or funeral ritual would you like to have when you die? Why would you choose this particular type of ritual?

Key Terms

arthritis
osteoarthritis
dementia
terminal drop (terminal decline)
cerebrovascular accidents (strokes)
multi-infarct dementia
Alzheimer's disease (AD)
plaques
tangles
autobiographical memory
recency

"the bump"
flashbulb memories
selection
optimization
compensation
selective optimization with compensation
self-determination theory
autonomy
competence
relatedness
primary control
secondary control

wisdom
end-of-life care
palliative care
hospice movement
refusal of treatment
physician-assisted suicide
active euthanasia
double effect
advance directives (living wills)
denial
anger

bargaining
depression
acceptance
decathecting
shock
protest
despair
reorganization
grief work
dual-process model
loss-focused grief
restoration-focused grief

References

Aboud, F. (1977). Interest in ethnic information: A cross-cultural developmental study. *Canadian Journal of Behavioral Science, 9,* 134–146.

Achenbach, T., & Edelbrock, C. S. (1983). *Manual for the Child Behavior Checklist and Revised Child Behavior Profile.* Burlington: University of Vermont, Department of Psychiatry.

Achenbach, T., & Howell, C. (1993). Are American children's problems getting worse? A 13-year comparison. *Journal of the American Academy of Child and Adolescent Psychiatry, 32,* 1145–1154.

Ackil, J. K., & Zaragoza, M. S. (1995). Developmental differences in eyewitness suggestibility and memory for source. *Journal of Experimental Child Psychology, 60,* 57–83.

Adams, G. R. (1983). Social competence during adolescence: Social sensitivity, locus of control, empathy, and peer popularity. *Journal of Youth and Adolescence, 12,* 203–211.

Ainsworth, M. D. S. (1973). *Infancy in Uganda: Infant care and the growth of love.* Baltimore: Johns Hopkins University Press.

Ainsworth, M. D. S. (1989). Attachments beyond infancy. *American Psychologist, 44,* 709–716.

Ainsworth, M. D. S., Bell, S. M., & Stayton, D. J. (1972). Individual differences in the development of some attachment behaviors. *Merrill-Palmer Quarterly, 18,* 123–143.

Ainsworth, M. D. S., Blehar, M. C., Waters, E., & Wall, S. (1978). *Patterns of attachment.* Hillsdale, NJ: Erlbaum.

Alban-Metcalfe, B., & West, M. A. (1991). Women managers. In J. Firth-Cozens & M. A. West (Eds.), *Women at work: Psychological and organizational perspectives* (pp. 154–171). Milton Keynes, UK: Open University Press.

Allgood-Merten, B., Lewinsohn, P. M., & Hops, R. (1990). Sex differences and adolescent depression. *Journal of Abnormal Psychology, 99,* 55–63.

Amato, P. R. (1993). Children's adjustment to divorce: Theories, hypotheses, and empirical support. *Journal of Marriage and the Family, 55,* 23–38.

American Academy of Pediatrics. (1997). Breastfeeding and the use of human milk. *Pediatrics, 100,* 1035–1039.

American Council on Education. (1999). *The American freshman: National norms for Fall 1999.* Los Angeles: Los Angeles Higher Education Research Institute.

American Counseling Association [ACA] (1995). *American Counseling Association code of ethics and standards of practice.* Alexandria, VA: Author.

American Psychiatric Association. (2000). *Diagnostic and Statistical Manual of Mental Disorders* (4th ed.—text revision). Washington, DC: Author.

American Psychological Association's Board of Educational Affairs. (1995). *Learner-centered psychological principles: A framework for school redesign and reform.* Washington, DC: American Psychological Association.

Anand, B. K., & Brobeck, J. R. (1951). Hypothalamic control of food intake in rats and cats. *Yale Journal of Biology and Medicine, 24,* 123–140.

Anderson, E. (1994, May). The code of the streets. *Atlantic Monthly, 273*(5), 81–94.

Anderson, J. R. (1980). *Cognitive psychology and its implications.* San Francisco: W. H. Freeman.

Anderson, J. R. (1993). Problem solving and learning. *American Psychologist, 48,* 35–44.

Andreasen, N. C., Arndt, S., Swayze, V., Cizadlo, T., Flaum, M., O'Leary, et al. (1994). Thalamic abnormalities in schizophrenia visualized through magnetic resonance image averaging. *Science, 266,* 294–298.

Angoff, W. H. (1988). The nature-nurture debate, aptitudes, and group differences. *American Psychologist, 43,* 713–720.

Annie E. Casey Foundation. (1998). *When teens have sex. Issues and trends: A Kids Count Special Report.* Baltimore: Author.

Antell, S. E., & Keating, D. P. (1983). Perception of numerical invariance in neonates. *Child Development, 54,* 695–701.

Archer, J. (1994). Testosterone and aggression: A theoretical review. *Journal of Offender Rehabilitation, 21,* 2–39.

Archer, J. (1999). *The nature of grief: The evolution and psychology of reactions to loss.* London: Routledge.

Archer, S. L. (1992). A feminist's approach to identity research. In G. R. Adams, R. Montmayor, & T. P. Gullotta (Eds.), *Advances in adolescent development, Vol. 4. Adolescent identity formation* (pp. 25–49). Newbury Park, CA: Sage Publications.

Archer, S. L., & Waterman, A. S. (1988). Psychological individualism: Gender differences or gender neutrality? *Human Development, 31,* 65–81.

Arlin, P. K. (1984). Adolescent and adult thought: A structural interpretation. In M. L. Commons, F. A. Richards, & C. Armon (Eds.), *Beyond formal operations* (pp. 258–271). New York: Praeger.

Arnett, J. J. (1992). Reckless behavior in adolescence: A developmental perspective. *Developmental Review, 12,* 339–373.

Arnett, J. J. (1994). Are college students adults? Their conceptions of the transition to adulthood. *Journal of Adult Development, 1,* 339–373.

Arnett, J. J. (1997). Young people's conceptions of the transition to adulthood. *Youth and Society, 29,* 1–23.

Arnett, J. J. (1999). Adolescent storm and stress, reconsidered. *American Psychologist, 54,* 317–326.

Arnett, J. J. (2000). Emerging adulthood: A theory of development from the late teens through the twenties. *American Psychologist, 55,* 469–480.

Arnett, J. J., & Taber, S. (1994). Adolescence terminable and interminable: When does adolescence end? *Journal of Youth and Adolescence, 23,* 517–523.

Arnold, A. P., & Gorski, R. A. (1984). Gonadal steroid induction of structural sex differences in the central nervous system. *Annual Review of Neuroscience, 7,* 413–442.

Aronson, J., & Fried, C. (1998). *Reducing stereotype threat and boosting academic achievement of African Americans: The role of conceptions of intelligence.* Unpublished manuscript.

Aronson, P. J., Mortimer, J. T., Zierman, C., & Hacker, M. (1996). Generational differences in early work experiences and evaluations. In J. T. Mortimer & M. D. Finch (Eds.), *Adolescents, work, and family: An intergenerational developmental analysis* (pp. 25–62). Newbury Park, CA: Sage.

Asher, S. R., & Dodge, K. A. (1986). Identifying children who are rejected by their peers. *Developmental Psychology, 22,* 444–449.

Astin, A. W. (1993). *What matters in college?: Four critical years revisited.* San Francisco: Jossey-Bass.

Astin, A. W., Korn, W. S., Sax, L. J., & Mahoney, K. M. (1994). *The American freshman: National norms for Fall 1994.* Los Angeles: Higher Education Research Institute, UCLA.

Atwater, E. (1996). *Adolescence.* Upper Saddle River, NJ: Prentice Hall.

Azar, B. (1999, February). Consortium of editors pushes for shift in child research methods. *APA Monitor, 30,* 20–21.

Azmitia, M. (1996). Peer interactive minds. In P. B. Baltes & U. M. Staudinger (Eds.), *Interactive minds.* Cambridge, England: Cambridge University Press.

Azmitia, M., & Hesser, J. (1993). Why siblings are important agents of cognitive development: A comparison of siblings and peers. *Child Development, 64,* 430–444.

Bachman, J. (1997). *Smoking, drinking, and drug use in young adulthood: The impact of new freedoms and responsibilities.* Mahwah, NJ: Erlbaum.

Backman, L., Small, B. J., Wahlin, A., & Larsson, M. (2000). Cognitive functioning in very old age. In F. I. M. Craik & T. A. Salthouse (Eds.), *The handbook of aging and cognition* (pp. 499–558). Hillsdale, NJ: Erlbaum.

Baer, W. M., & Hanson, L. C. (2000). Families' perceptions of the added value of hospice in the nursing home. *Journal of the American Geriatric Society, 48,* 879–882.

Bahrick, L. E., & Pickens, J. N. (1995). Infant memory for object motion across a period of three months: Implications for a four-phase attention function. *Journal of Experimental Child Psychology, 59,* 343–371.

Bailey, J. M., Bobrow, D., Wolfe, M., & Mikach, S. (1995). Sexual orientation of adult sons of gay fathers. *Developmental Psychology, 31,* 124–129.

Bailey, J. M., & Pillard, R. C. (1991). A genetic study of male sexual orientation. *Archives of General Psychiatry, 48,* 1089–1096.

Bailey, J. M., Pillard, R. C., Neale, M. C., & Agyei, Y. (1993). Heritable factors influence sexual orientation in women. *Archives of General Psychiatry, 50,* 217–223.

Bailey, T., & Morest, V. S. (1998). Preparing youth for employment. In S. Halperin (Ed.), *The forgotten half revisited: American youth and young families, 1988–2008* (pp. 115–136). Washington, DC: American Youth Policy Forum.

Baillargeon, R. (1987). Object permanence in 3½- and 4½-month-old infants. *Developmental Psychology, 23,* 655–664.

Baker-Ward, L., Ornstein, P. A., & Holden, D. J. (1984). The expression of memorization in early childhood. *Journal of Experimental Child Psychology, 37,* 555–575.

Baldwin, A. L. (1948). Socialization and the parent-child relationship. *Child Development, 19,* 127–136.

Ballie, R. (2001). Teen drinking more dangerous than previously thought. *Monitor on Psychology, 32,* 12.

Baltes, M. M., & Baltes, P. B. (1990). *The psychology of control and aging.* Hillsdale, NJ: Erlbaum.

Baltes, P. B. (1987). Theoretical propositions of life-span developmental psychology: On the dynamics between growth and decline. *Developmental Psychology, 23,* 611–626.

Baltes, P. B. (1997). On the incomplete architecture of human ontogeny: Selection, optimization, and compensation as foundation of developmental theory. *American Psychologist, 52,* 366–380.

Baltes, P. B., Lindenberger, U., & Staudinger, U. M. (1998). Life-span theory in developmental psychology. In W. Damon (Series Ed.) & R. M. Lerner (Vol. Ed.), *Handbook of child psychology: Vol. 1. Theoretical models of human development* (5th ed., pp. 1029–1143). New York: Wiley.

Baltes, P. B., & Staudinger, U. M. (2000). Wisdom: A meta-heuristic (pragmatic) to orchestrate mind and virtue toward excellence. *American Psychologist, 55,* 122–136.

Bandura, A. (1974). Behavior theory and the models of man. *American Psychologist, 29,* 859–869.

Bandura, A. (1977). *Social learning theory.* Englewood Cliffs, NJ: Prentice Hall.

Bandura, A. (1986). *Social foundations of thought and action: A social cognitive theory.* Englewood Cliffs, NJ: Prentice-Hall.

Bandura, A. (1989). Human agency in social cognitive theory. *American Psychologist, 44,* 1175–1184.

Bandura, A. (1990). Conclusion: Reflections on nonability determinants of competence. In R. J. Sternberg & J. Kolligian, Jr. (Eds.), *Competence considered* (pp. 316–352). New Haven, CT: Yale University Press.

Bandura, A. (1999). Social cognitive theory of personality. In L. Pervin & O. John (Eds.), *Handbook of Personality* (2nd ed., pp. 154–196). New York: Guilford Press.

Banks, W. C. (1976). White preference in blacks: A paradigm in search of a phenomenon. *Psychological Bulletin, 83,* 1179–1186.

Barber, B. K. (1994). Cultural, family and personal contexts of parent-adolescent conflict. *Journal of Marriage and the Family, 56,* 375–386.

Barber, B. L., Eccles, J. S., & Stone, M. R. (2001). Whatever happened to the jock, the brain, and the princess? Young adult pathways linked to adolescent activity involvement and social identity. *Journal of Adolescent Research, 16,* 429–455.

Barber, B. R. (1992). *An aristocracy of everyone: The politics of education and the future of America.* New York: Oxford University Press.

Barich, R. R., & Bielby, D. D. (1996). Rethinking marriage: Change and stability in expectations. *Journal of Family Issues, 17,* 505–525.

Barker, R. G., & Gump, P. V. (1964). *Big school, small school: High school size and student behavior.* Stanford: Stanford University Press.

Barnes, G. M., Welte, J. W., & Dintcheff, B. (1992). Alcohol misuse among college students and other young adults: Findings from a general population study in New York State. *International Journal of the Addictions, 27,* 917–934.

Barr, D. (1997). Friendship and belonging. In R. L. Selman, C. L. Watts, & L. H. Schultz, (Eds.), *Fostering friendship: Pair therapy for treatment and prevention* (pp. 19–30). New York: Aldine de Gruyer.

Barrett, E. E., Radke-Yarrow, M., & Klein, R. E. (1983). Chronic malnutrition and child behavior: Effects of early caloric supplementation on social and emotional functioning at school age. In S. Chess & A. Thomas (Eds.), *Annual progress in child psychology and child development* (pp. 489–492). New York: Brunner/Mazel.

Bartholomew, K., & Horowitz, L. (1991). Attachment styles among young adults: A test of the four category model. *Journal of Personality and Social Psychology, 61,* 226–244.

Bartholomew, K., & Shaver, P. R. (1998). Methods of assessing adult attachment: Do they converge? In J. A. Simpson & W. S. Rholes (Eds.), *Attachment theory and close relationships* (pp. 25–45). New York: Guilford Press.

Basseches, M. (1984). *Dialectical thinking and adult development.* Norwood, NJ: Ablex.

Bates, J. E., Maslin, C. A., & Frankel, K. A. (1995). Attachment security, mother child interaction, and temperament as predictors of behavior-problem ratings at age three years. *Monographs of the Society for Research in Child Development, 50,* 167–193.

Bauer, P. J., & Mandler, J. M. (1989). One thing follows another: Effects of temporal structure on 1- to 2-year-olds' recall of events. *Developmental Psychology, 25,* 197–206.

Bauer, P. J., & Mandler, J. M. (1990). Remembering what happened next: Very young children's recall of event sequences. In R. Fivush & J. A. Hudson (Eds.), *Knowing and remembering in young children.* Cambridge, England: Cambridge University Press.

Baumeister, R. F., & Boden, J. M. (1994). Shrinking the self. In T. M. Brinthaupt & R. P. Lipka (Eds.), *Changing the self: Philosophies, techniques, and experiences.* Albany, NY: SUNY Press.

Baumeister, R. F., Smart, L., & Boden, J. M. (1996). Relation of threatened egotism to violence and aggression: The dark side of high self-esteem. *Psychological Review, 103,* 5–33.

Baumrind, D. (1971). Current patterns of parental authority. *Development Psychology Monographs, Part 2, 4,* 1–103.

Baumrind, D. (1972). An exploratory study of socialization effects on black children: Some black/white comparisons. *Child Development, 43,* 261–267.

Baumrind, D. (1978). Parental disciplinary patterns and social competence in children. *Youth and Society, 9,* 239–276.

Baumrind, D. (1989). Rearing competent children. In W. Damon (Ed.). *Child development today and tomorrow* (pp. 349–378). San Francisco: Jossey-Bass.

Baumrind, D. (1991). Parenting styles and adolescent development. In J. Brooks, R. Lerner, & A. C. Petersen (Eds.), *The encyclopedia of adolescence.* (pp. 758–772). New York: Garland.

Baumrind, D. (1993). The average expectable environment is not good enough: A response to Scarr. *Child Development, 64,* 1299–1317.

Baumrind, D. (1995). Commentary on sexual orientation: Research and social policy implications. *Developmental Psychology, 31,* 130–136.

Baumrind, D. (2001). *Does causally relevant research support a blanket injunction against the use of spanking?* Paper presented at the annual meeting of the American Psychological Association, San Francisco.

Baxter-Magolda, M., & Porterfield, W. D. (1985). A new approach to assessing intellectual development on the Perry Scheme. *Journal of College Student Personnel, 21,* 46–58.

Beall, A. E., & Sternberg, R. J. (1995). The social construction of love. *Journal of Social and Personal Relationships, 12,* 417–438.

Bear, G. G., & Rys, G. S. (1994). Moral reasoning, classroom behavior, and sociometric status among elementary school children. *Developmental Psychology, 30,* 633–638.

Beck, A. T. (1963). *Depression: Causes and treatment.* Philadelphia: University of Pennsylvania Press.

Beckwith, L., Cohen, S. E., & Hamilton, C. E. (1999). Maternal sensitivity during infancy and subsequent life events relate to attachment representations at early adult-hood. *Developmental Psychology, 35,* 693–700.

Beeghly, M., & Cicchetti, D. (1994). Child maltreatment, attachment, and the self-system: Emergence of an internal state lexicon in toddlers at high social risk. *Development and Psychopathology, 6,* 5–30.

Bell, A., Weinberg, M., & Hammersmith, S. (1981). *Sexual preference: Its development in men and women.* Bloomington: Indiana University Press.

Bell, R. Q., & Chapman, M. (1986). Child effects in studies using experimental or brief longitudinal approaches to socialization. *Developmental Psychology, 22,* 595–603.

Bell, R. Q., & Harper, L. V. (Eds.). (1977). *Child effects on adults.* Hillsdale, NJ: Erlbaum.

Bell, T. W. (1971). Stimulus control of parent or caretaker behavior by offspring. *Developmental Psychology, 4,* 63–72.

Bellah, R. N., Madsen, R., Sullivan, W. M., Swidler, A., & Tipton, S. M. (1985). *Habits of the heart: Individualism and commitment in American life.* New York: Harper & Row.

Belloc, N. B., & Breslow, L. (1972). Relationships of physical health status and health practices. *Preventive Medicine, 1,* 409–421.

Belsky, J., Garduque, L., & Hrncir, E. (1984). Assessing performance, competence, and executive capacity in infant play: Relations to home environment and security of attachment. *Developmental Psychology, 20,* 406–417.

Belsky, J., Gilstrap, B., & Rovine, M. (1984). The Pennsylvania infant and family development project: I. Stability and change in mother-infant and father-infant interaction in a family setting at one, three, and nine months. *Child Development, 55,* 692–705.

Belsky, J., & Hsieh, K. H. (1998). Patterns of marital change during the early years: Parent personality, coparenting, and division-of-labor correlates. *Journal of Family Psychology, 12,* 511–528.

Belsky, J., & Kelly, J. (1994). *The transition to parenthood: How a first child changes a marriage. Why some couples grow closer and some grow apart.* New York: Dell.

Belsky, J., & Rovine, M. (1988). Nonmaternal care in the first year of life and the security of infant-parent attachment. *Child Development, 59,* 157–167.

Belsky, J., & Rovine, M. (1990). Patterns of marital change across the transition to parenthood: Pregnancy to three years postpartum. *Journal of Marriage and the Family, 52,* 5–19.

Belsky, J., & Volling, B. L. (1987). Mothering, fathering, and marital interaction in the family triad during infancy: Exploring family system's processes. In P. W. Berman & F. A. Pedersen (Eds.), *Men's transitions to parenthood: Longitudinal studies of early family experience* (pp. 37–63). Hillsdale, NJ: Erlbaum.

Belsky, J., Spanier, G., & Rovine, M. (1983). Stability and change in a marriage across the transition to parenthood. *Journal of Marriage and the Family, 45,* 567–577.

Bem, D. J. (1996). Exotic becomes erotic: A developmental theory of sexual orientation. *Psychological Review, 103,* 320–335.

Bem, S. L. (1981). Gender schema theory: A cognitive account of sex typing. *Psychological Review, 88,* 354–364.

Bem, S. L. (1989). Genital knowledge and gender constancy in preschool children. *Child Development, 60,* 649–662.

Bendersky, M., & Lewis, M. (1998). Arousal modulation in cocaine-exposed infants. *Developmental Psychology, 43,* 555–564.

Benes, F. M. (1994). Developmental changes in stress adaptation in relation to psychopathology. *Development and Psychopathology, 6,* 723–739.

Benninga, J. S., & Wynne, E. A. (1998, February). Keeping in character. A time-tested solution. *Phi Delta Kappan, 79,* 439–445, 448.

Berenbaum, S. A., & Hines, M. (1992). Early androgens are related to childhood sex-typed toy preferences. *Psychological Science, 3,* 203–206.

Berenbaum, S. A., & Snyder, E. (1995). Early hormonal influences on childhood sex-typed activity and playmate preferences: Implications for the development of sexual orientation. *Developmental Psychology, 31,* 31–42.

Berg, S. (1987). Intelligence and terminal decline. In G. L. Maddox & E. W. Busse (Eds.), *Aging: The universal experience* (pp. 414–415). New York: Springer.

Berg, S. (1996). Aging, behavior, and terminal decline. In J. E. Birren & K. W. Schaie (Series Eds.), R. P. Abeles, M. Gatz, & T. A. Salthouse (Vol. Eds.), *Handbook of the psychology of aging* (4th ed., pp. 323–337). San Diego, CA: Academic Press.

Berger, K. S. (2001). *The developing person through the life span.* New York: Worth.

Berk, L. E., & Spuhl, S. (1995). Maternal interaction, private speech, and task performance in preschool children. *Early Childhood Research Quarterly, 10,* 145–169.

Berkowitz, M., & Gibbs, J. C. (1983). Measuring the developmental features of moral discussion. *Merrill-Palmer Quarterly, 29,* 399–410.

Bernal, M. E., & Knight, G. P. (1993). *Ethnic identity: Formation and transmission among Hispanics and other minorities.* Albany: State University of New York Press.

Berndt, Thomas J. (1982). The features and effects of friendship in early adolescence. *Child Development, 53,* 1447–1460.

Berndt, T. J., & Heller, K. A. (1986). Gender stereotypes and social inferences: A developmental study. *Journal of Personality and Social Psychology, 50,* 889–898.

Berndt, T. J., & Keefe, K. (1996). Friends' influence on school adjustment: A motivational analysis. In J. Juvonen & K. R. Wentzel (Eds.), *Social motivation: Understanding children's school adjustment.* New York: Cambridge University Press.

Berndt, T. J., Miller, K. A., & Park, K. (1989). Adolescents' perceptions of friends' and parents' influence on aspects of school adjustment. *Journal of Early Adolescence, 9,* 419–435.

Berninger, V. W., & Hart, T. M. (1992). A developmental neuropsychological perspective for reading and writing acquisition. *Educational Psychologist, 27,* pp. 415–434.

Bernstein, A. C., & Cowan, P. A. (1975). Children's concepts of how people get babies. *Child Development, 46,* 77–91.

Betz, N. E., & Hackett, G. (1981). The relationship of career-related self-efficacy expectations to perceived career options in college women and men. *Journal of Counseling Psychology, 28,* 399–410.

Beuf, A. H. (1977). *Red children in White America.* University Park: Pennsylvania State University Press.

Bidell, T. R., & Fischer, K. W. (1997). Between nature and nurture: The role of human agency in the epigenesis of intelligence. In R. J. Sternberg & E. L. Grigorenko (Eds.), *Intelligence, heredity, and environment* (pp. 193–242). New York: Cambridge University Press.

Bierman, K. (1986). Process of change during social skills training with preadolescents and its relation to treatment outcomes. *Child Development, 55,* 151–162.

Bigler, R. S., & Liben, L. S. (1992). Cognitive mechanisms in children's gender stereotyping: Theoretical and educational implications of a cognitive-based intervention. *Child Development, 63,* 1351–1363.

Billings, J. A. (1998). What is palliative care? *Journal of Palliative Medicine, 1,* 73–81.

Black, B., & Hazan, N. (1990). Social status and patterns of communication in acquainted and unacquainted preschool children. *Developmental Psychology, 26,* 379–387.

Blanchard-Fields, F. (1986). Reasoning on social dilemmas varying in emotional salience: An adult developmental perspective. *Psychology and Aging, 1,* 325–333.

Blazer, D. G. (1994). Epidemiology of late life depression. In L. S. Schneider, C. F. Reynolds III, B. D. Lebowitz, & A. J. Friedhoff (Eds.), *Diagnosis and treatment of depression in late life* (pp. 9–19). Washington, DC: American Psychiatric Press.

Blewitt, P. (1989). Category hierarchies: Levels of knowledge and skill. *Genetic Epistemologist, 17,* 21–30.

Blewitt, P. (1994). Understanding categorical hierarchies: The earliest levels of skill. *Child Development, 65,* 1279–1298.

Block, J. H. (1978). Another look at sex differentiation in the socialization behaviors of mothers and fathers. In J. Sherman & F. L. Denmark (Eds.), *The psychology of women: Future directions of research* (pp. 29–87). New York: Psychological Dimensions.

Blos, P. (1962). *On adolescence: A psychoanalytic interpretation.* New York: Free Press.

Blos, P. (1975). The second individuation process of adolescence. In A. Esman (Ed.), *The psychology of adolescence* (pp. 156–176). New York: International Universities Press, Inc.

Blyth, D. A., Simmons, R. G., Bulcroft, R., Felt, D., VanCleave, E. F., & Bush, D. M. (1981). The effects of physical development on self-image and satisfaction with body-image for early adolescent males. In R. G. Simmons (Ed.), *Research in Community and Mental Health, 2,* 43–73.

Bolotin, S. (1999, February 14). The disciples of discipline. *The New York Times Magazine,* 32–77.

Bonanno, G. A., & Kaltman, S. (1999). Toward an integrative perspective on bereavement. *Psychological Bulletin, 125,* 760–776.

Bonanno, G. A., & Keltner, D. (1997). Facial expression of emotion and the course of conjugal bereavement. *Journal of Abnormal Psychology, 106,* 126–137.

Bonanno, G. A., Znoj, H., Siddique, H. I., & Horowitz, M. J. (1999). Verbal-autonomic dissociation and adaptation to midlife conjugal loss: A follow-up at 25 months. *Cognitive Therapy and Research, 23,* 605–624.

Bornstein, M. H., & Sigman, M. D. (1986). Continuity in mental development from infancy. *Child Development, 57,* 251–274.

Bornstein, M. H., Tal, J., & Tamis-LaMonda, C. S. (1991). Parenting in cross-cultural perspective: The United States, France and Japan. In M. H. Bornstein (Ed.), *Cultural approaches to parenting* (pp. 69–90). Hillsdale, NJ: Erlbaum.

Borod, J. C., Koff, E., & Buck, R. (1986). The neuropsychology of facial expression: Data from normal and brain-damaged adults. In P. Blanck, R. Buck, & R. Rosenthal (Eds.), *Nonverbal communication in the clinical context.* University Park: Penn State Press.

Bouchard, T. J., Lykken, D. T., McGue, M., Segal, N. L., & Tellegen, A. (1990). Sources of human psychological differences: The Minnesota study of twins reared apart. *Science, 250,* 223–228.

Bowen, M. (1978). *Family therapy in clinical practice.* New York: Jason Aronson.

Bower, E. M. (1960). *Early identification of emotionally handicapped children in school.* Springfield, IL: Charles C. Thomas.

Bowlby, J. (1969/1982). *Attachment and loss: Vol. 1. Attachment.* New York: Basic Books.

Bowlby, J. (1973). *Attachment and loss: Vol. 2. Separation.* New York: Basic Books.

Bowlby, J. (1980). *Attachment and loss: Vol. 3. Loss: sadness and depression.* New York: Basic Books.

Bowlby, J. (1988). *A secure base: Parent-child attachment and healthy human development.* New York: Basic Books.

Boyer, C. B., Shafer, M., & Tschann, J. M. (1997). Evaluation of a knowledge and cognitive-behavioral skill-building intervention to prevent STDs and HIV infection in high school students. *Adolescence, 32,* 25–42.

Bradley, S. J., Oliver, G. D., Chernick, A. B., & Zucker, K. J. (1998). Experiment of nurture: Ablatio penis at 2 months, sex reassignment at 7 months, and psychosexual follow-up in young adulthood. *Pediatrics, 102,* 132–133.

Brainerd, C. J. (1996). Piaget: A centennial celebration. *Psychological Science, 7,* 191–195.

Brandstadter, J., & Wentura, D. (1995). Adjustment to shifting possibility frontiers in later life: Complementary adaptive modes. In R. A. Dixon & L. Backman (Eds.), *Psychological compensation: Managing losses and promoting gains* (pp. 83–106). Hillsdale, NJ: Erlbaum.

Brazelton, T. B. (1986). Issues for working parents. *American Journal of Orthopsychiatry, 56,* 14–25.

Brazelton, T. B., Koslowski, B., & Main, M. (1974). The origins of reciprocity: The early mother-infant interaction. In M. Lewis & L. A. Rosenblum (Eds.), *The effect of the infant on its caregiver* (pp. 49–76). New York: Wiley-Interscience.

Brennan, K. A., Clark, C. L., & Shaver, P. R. (1998). Self-report measurement of adult attachment: An integrative interview. In J. A. Simpson & W. S. Rholes (Eds.), *Attachment theory and close relationships* (pp. 46–76). New York: Guilford Press.

Brennan, K. A., & Shaver, P. R. (1998). Attachment styles and personality disorders: Their connections to each other and to parental divorce, parental death, and perceptions of parental caregiving. *Journal of Personality, 66,* 835–878.

Broderick, P. C. (1998). Early adolescent differences in the use of ruminative and distracting coping styles. *Journal of Early Adolescence, 18,* 173–191.

Broderick, P. C., & Korteland, C. (2002). Coping style and depression in early adolescence: Relationships to gender, gender role, and implicit beliefs. *Sex Roles: A Journal of Research.* (In press).

Broderick, P. C., & Mastrilli, T. (1997). Attitudes concerning parental involvement: Parent and teacher perspectives. *Pennsylvania Educational Leadership, 16,* 30–36.

Bronfenbrenner, U. (1979). *The ecology of human development: Experiments by nature and by design.* Cambridge, MA: Harvard University Press.

Bronfenbrenner, U., & Ceci, S. J. (1994). Nature-nurture reconceptualized in developmental perspective: A bioecological model. *Psychological Review, 101,* 568–586.

Bronfenbrenner, U., & Morris, P. A. (1998). The ecology of developmental processes. In W. Damon (Series Ed.) & R. M. Lerner (Vol. Ed.), *Handbook of child psychology: Vol. 1. Theoretical models of human development* (5th ed., pp. 993–1028). New York: Wiley.

Brooks-Gunn, J. (1991). Maturational timing variations in adolescent girls, antecedents of. In R. M. Lerner, A. C. Petersen, & J. Brooks-Gunn (Eds.), *Encyclopedia of adolescence* (Vol. 2) New York: Garland.

Brooks-Gunn, J., & Warren, M. P. (1989). Biological and social contributions to negative affect in young adolescent girls. *Child Development, 60,* 40–55.

Brophy, J. E., & Evertson, C. M. (1976). *Learning from teaching: A developmental perspective.* Boston: Allyn & Bacon.

Brown, B. B. (1990). Peer groups and peer cultures. In S. S. Feldman & G. R. Elliott (Eds.), *At the threshold: The developing adolescent* (pp. 171–196). Cambridge, MA: Harvard University Press.

Brown, J. D., & Newcomer, S. F. (1991). Television viewing and adolescents' sexual behavior. *Journal of Homosexuality, 21,* 77–91.

Brown, L., & Gilligan, C. (1992). *Meeting at the crossroads: Women's psychology and girls' development.* Cambridge, MA: Harvard University Press.

Brown, R., & Hanlon, C. (1970). Derivational complexity and order of acquisition. In J. R. Hayes (Ed.), *Cognition and the development of language* (pp. 11–53). New York: Wiley.

Bruer, J. T. (1999). *The myth of the first three years.* New York: Free Press.

Bryden, M. P. (1988). Does laterality make any difference? Thoughts on the relation between cerebral asymmetry and reading. In D. L. Molfese & S. J. Segalowitz (Eds.), *Brain lateralization in children: Developmental implications* (pp. 509–525). New York: Guilford Press.

Brynner, J. M., O'Malley, P. M., & Bachman, J. C. (1981). Self-esteem and delinquency revisited. *Journal of Youth and Adolescence, 10,* 407–441.

Buchanan, C. M., Eccles, J. S., & Becker, J. B. (1992). Are adolescents the victims of raging hormones? Evidence for activational effects of hormones on moods and behavior at adolescence. *Psychological Bulletin, 111,* 62–107.

Bukowski, W. M., & Hoza, B. (1989). Popularity and friendship: Issues in theory, measurement, and outcome. In T. J. Berndt & G. Ladd (Eds.), *Peer relations in child development* (pp. 15–45). New York: Wiley.

Burgess, D., & Borgida, E. (1997). Sexual harassment: An experimental test of sex-role spillover theory. *Personality and Social Psychology Bulletin, 23,* 63–75.

Burr, W. R. (1970). Satisfaction with various aspects of marriage over the life cycle: A random middle class sample. *Journal of Marriage and the Family, 32,* 29–37.

Buss, D. M. (1987). Selection, evocation and manipulation. *Journal of Personality and Social Psychology, 53,* 1214–1221.

Buss, D. M. (1989). Sex differences in human mate preferences: Evolutionary hypotheses tested in 37 cultures. *Behavioral and Brain Sciences, 12,* 1–49.

Bussey, K., & Bandura, A. (1984). Influence of gender constancy and social power on sex-linked modeling. *Journal of Personality and Social Psychology, 47,* 1292–1302.

Bussey, K., & Bandura, A. (1999). A social cognitive theory of gender development and differentiation. *Psychological Bulletin, 106,* 676–713.

Butler, L. D., & Nolen-Hoeksema, S. (1994). Gender differences in response to depressed mood in a college sample. *Sex Roles, 30,* 331–346.

Butler, R. N. (1963). The life review: An interpretation of reminiscence in the aged. *Psychiatry, 26,* 65–76.

Byng-Hall, J. (1995). *Rewriting family scripts: Improvisation and systems change.* New York: Guilford Press.

Byrne, B. M., & Shavelson, R. J. (1996). On the structure of social self-concept for pre-, early- and late adolescents: A test of the Shavelson, Hubner, and Stanton (1976) model. *Journal of Personality and Social Psychology, 70,* 599–613.

Cacioppo, J. T., & Berntson, G. G. (1992). Social psychological contributions to the decade of the brain: Doctrine of multilevel analysis. *American Psychologist, 47,* 1019–1028.

Cadoret, R. J., Yates, W. R., Troughton, E., Woodsworth, G., & Stewart, M. A. (1995). Genetic-environmental interaction in the genesis of aggressivity and conduct disorders. *Archives of General Psychiatry, 52,* 916–924.

Cairns, R. B. (1991). Multiple metaphors for a singular idea. *Developmental Psychology, 27,* 23–26.

Cairns, R. B., & Cairns, B. D. (1994). *Lifelines and risks: Pathways of youth in our time.* New York: Cambridge University Press.

Cairns, R. B., Gariepy, J. L., & Kindermann, T. A. (1990). *Identifying social clusters in natural settings.* Unpublished manuscript, University of North Carolina at Chapel Hill, Social Development Laboratory.

Callanan, M., & Kelley, P. (1992). *Final gifts: Understanding the special awareness, needs and communications of the dying.* New York: Bantam Books.

Cameron, C. A., & Wang, M. (1999). *Frog, Where Are You?* Children's narrative expression over the telephone. *Discourse Processes, 28,* 217–236.

Campbell, F. A., Pungello, E. P., Miller-Johnson, S., Burchinal, M., & Ramey, C. T. (2001). The development of cognitive and academic abilities: Growth curves from an early childhood educational experiment. *Developmental Psychology, 37,* 231–242.

Campbell, F. A., & Ramey, C. T. (1994). Effects of early intervention on intellectual and academic achievement: A follow-up study of children from low-income families. *Child Development, 65,* 684–698.

Campbell, J. D. (1990). Self-esteem and clarity of the self-concept. *Journal of Personality and Social Psychology, 59,* 538–549.

Campbell, J. D., & Lavallee, L. F. (1993). Who am I? The role of self-concept confusion in understanding the behavior of people with low self-esteem. In R. F. Baumeister (Ed.), *Self-esteem: The puzzle of low self-regard* (pp. 3–20). New York: Plenum.

Campbell, S. B. (1987). Parent-referred problem 3 year-olds: Developmental changes in symptoms. *Journal of Child Psychology and Psychiatry, 28,* 835–845.

Campos, J., Barrett, K., Lamb, M., Goldsmith, H., & Sternberg, C. (1983). Socioemotional development. In P. H. Mussen (Ed.), *Handbook of child psychology: Vol. 2. Infancy and developmental psychology* (pp. 783–915). New York: Wiley.

Campos, J. J., Campos, R. G., & Barrett, K. C. (1989). Emergent themes in the study of emotional development and emotion regulation. *Developmental Psychology, 25,* 394–402.

Carlson, J., & Lewis, J. (1993). Motivation: Building students' feelings of confidence and self-worth. In J. Carlson & J. Lewis (Eds.), *Counseling the adolescent: Individual, family*

and school interventions (2nd ed., pp. 249–270). Denver, CO: Love Publishing.

Carnegie Council on Adolescent Development (1996). *Great Transitions: Preparing adolescents for a new century.* New York: Carnegie Corporation of New York.

Carrere, S., Buelhman, K. T., Gottman, J. M., Coan, J. A., Ruckstuhl, L. (2000). Predicting marital stability in divorced and newlywed couples. *Journal of Family Psychology, 14,* 42–58.

Carrere, S., & Gottman, J. M. (1999). Predicting divorce among newlyweds from the first three minutes of a marital conflict discussion. *Family Process, 38,* 293–301.

Carskadon, M., Vieria, C., & Acebo, C. (1993). Association between puberty and delayed phase preference. *Sleep, 16,* 258–262.

Carstensen, L. L. (1998). A life-span approach to social motivation. In J. Heckhausen & C. S. Dweck (Eds.), *Motivation and self-regulation across the life span* (pp. 341–364). Cambridge, England: Cambridge University Press.

Carstensen, L. L., & Charles, S. T. (1998). Emotion in the second half of life. *Current Directions in Psychological Science, 7,* 144–149.

Carstensen, L. L., Pasupathi, M., & Mayr, U. (1998). *Emotion experience in the daily lives of older and younger adults.* Unpublished manuscript.

Carstensen, L. L., & Turk-Charles, S. (1994). The salience of emotion across the adult life span. *Psychology and Aging, 9,* 259–264.

Carter, B., & McGoldrick, M. (Eds.). (1999). *The expanded family life cycle: Individual, family and social perspectives* (3rd ed.). Boston: Allyn & Bacon.

Carter, R. T. (1999). Is white a race? Expressions of white racial identity. In M. Fine., L. Weis, L. C. Powell, & L. M. Wong (Eds.), *Off-white: Readings on race, power, and society* (pp. 198–209). New York: Routledge.

Cartwright, D. (1950). Emotional dimensions of group life. In M. L. Reymert (Ed.), *Feelings and emotions* (pp. 437–447). New York: McGraw-Hill.

Case, R. (1985). *Intellectual development: Birth to adulthood.* New York: Academic Press.

Case, R. (1991). Stages in the development of the young child's first sense of self. *Developmental Review, 11,* 210–230.

Case, R. (1992). *The mind's staircase: Exploring the conceptual underpinnings of children's thought and knowledge.* Hillsdale, NJ: Erlbaum.

Casey, B. J., Giedd, J. N., & Thomas, K. M. (2000). Structural and functional brain development and its relation to cognitive development. *Biological Psychology, 54,* 241–257.

Caslyn, R. J., & Kenny, D. A. (1977). Self-concept of ability and perceived evaluation of others: Cause or effect of academic achievement? *Journal of Educational Psychology, 69,* 136–145.

Caspi, A. (2000). The child is father of the man: Personality continuities from childhood to adulthood. *Journal of Personality and Social Psychology, 78,* 158–172.

Caspi, A., Lynam, D., Moffitt, T. E., & Silva, P. A. (1993). Unraveling girls' delinquency: Biological, dispositional, and contextual contributions to adolescent misbehavior. *Developmental Psychology, 29,* 19–30.

Cass, V. (1979). Homosexual identity formation: A theoretical model. *Journal of Homosexuality, 4,* 143–167.

Cassel, C. K., & Foley, K. M. (1999). *Principles for care of patients at the end of life: An emerging consensus among the specialities of medicine.* New York: Millbank Memorial Fund.

Cassidy, J., & Shaver, P. R. (Eds.). (1999). *Handbook of attachment: Theory, research, and clinical applications.* New York: Guilford Press.

Caudill, W., & Plath, D. (1966). Who sleeps by whom? Parent-child involvement in urban Japanese families. *Psychiatry, 29,* 344–366.

Ceci, S. J., & Bruck, M. (1995) *Jeopardy in the courtroom: A scientific analysis of children's testimony.* Washington, DC: American Psychological Association.

Ceci, S. J., & Bruck, M. (1998). Children's testimony: Applied and basic issues. In W. Damon (Series Ed.), I. E. Siegel & K. A. Renninger (Vol. Eds.), *Handbook of child psychology: Vol. 4. Child psychology in practice* (5th ed., pp. 713–774). New York: Wiley.

Ceci, S. J., Bruck, M., & Battin, D. B. (2000). The suggestibility of children's testimony. In D. F. Bjorklund (Ed.), *False-memory creation in children and adults: Theory, research, and implications* (pp. 169–201). Mahwah, NJ: Erlbaum.

Ceci, S. J., & Liker, J. (1986). A day at the races: A study of IQ, expertise, and cognitive complexity. *Journal of Experimental Psychology: General, 115,* 255–266.

Ceci, S. J., Loftus, E. W., Leichtman, M., & Bruck, M. (1994). The role of source misattributions in the creation of false beliefs among preschoolers. *International Journal of Clinical and Experimental Hypnosis, 62,* 304–320.

Ceci, S. J., Rosenblum, T., de Bruyn, E., & Lee, D. Y. (1997). A bio-ecological model of intellectual development: Moving beyond h-sup-2. In R. J. Sternberg & E. L. Grigorenko (Eds.), *Intelligence, heredity, and environment* (pp. 303–322). New York: Cambridge University Press.

Centers for Disease Control and Prevention (1998). *Youth risk surveillance: United States, 1997.* Washington, DC: U.S. Department of Health and Human Services.

Cervone, D., & Peake, P. K. (1986). Anchoring, efficacy, and action: The influence of judgmental heuristics on self-efficacy judgments and behavior. *Journal of Personality and Social Psychology, 50,* 492–501.

Chadwick, B. A., & Heaton, T. B. (1992). *Statistical handbook on the American family.* Phoenix: Onyx Press.

Chalmers, J. B., & Townsend, M. A. (1990). The effects of training in social perspective taking on socially malad-justed girls. *Child Development, 61,* 178–179.

Chambless, D. L. (1996). In defense of dissemination of empirically supported psychological interventions. *Clinical Psychology: Science and Practice, 3,* 230–235.

Champion, L. A., Goodall, G. M., & Rutter, M. (1995). Behavioural problems in childhood and stressors in early adult life: A 20-year follow-up of London school children. *Psychological Medicine, 25,* 231–246.

Chandler, M. J. (1973). Egocentrism and antisocial behavior: The assessment and training of social and perspective-taking skills. *Developmental Psychology, 9,* 326–332.

Chandler, M. J. (1987). The Othello effect: Essay on the emergence and eclipse of skeptical doubt. *Human Development, 30,* 137–139.

Chandler, M. J., & Boutilier, R. G. (1992). The development of dynamic system reasoning. *Human Development, 35,* 129–137.

Chandler, M. J., Boyes, M., & Ball, L. (1990). Relativism and stations of epistemic doubt. *Journal of Experimental Child Psychology, 50,* 370–395.

Chao, R. K. (2001). Extending research on the consequences of parenting style for Chinese Americans and European Americans. *Child Development, 72,* 1832–1843.

Character Education Partnership. (1995). *Eleven principles of effective character education.* Washington, DC: Author.

Charmers, J., & Townsend, M. (1990). The effects of training in social perspective taking on socially maladjusted girls. *Child Development, 61,* 178–190.

Charness, N., & Bosman, E. A. (1990). Expertise and aging: Life in the lab. In T. H. Hess (Ed.), *Aging and cognition: Knowledge organization and utilization* (pp. 343–385). Amsterdam: Elsevier.

Charney, D. S., Nestler, E. J., & Bunney, B. S. (1999). *Neurobiology of mental illness.* New York: University Press.

Chase, W. G., & Simon, H. A. (1973). Perception in chess. *Cognitive Psychology, 4,* 55–81.

Chase-Lansdale, P. L., & Brooks-Gunn, J. (1994). Correlates of adolescent pregnancy and parenthood. In C. B. Fisher & R. M. Lerner (Eds.), *Applied developmental psychology* (pp. 207–236). New York: McGraw-Hill.

Chen, X., Rubin, K. H., & Li, Z. (1995). Social functioning and adjustment in Chinese children: A longitudinal study. *Developmental Psychology, 31,* 531–539.

Cherlin, A. (1981). *Marriage, divorce, remarriage.* Cambridge, MA: Harvard University Press.

Chess, S., & Hassibi, M. (1978). *Principles and practice of child psychiatry.* New York: Plenum.

Chess, S., & Thomas, A. (1987). *Origins and evolution of behavior: From infancy to early adult life.* Cambridge, MA: Harvard University Press.

Chi, M. T. H. (1978). Knowledge structures and memory development. In R. S. Siegler (Ed.), *Children's thinking: What develops?* Hillsdale, NJ: Erlbaum.

Chi, M. T. H., Hutchinson, J. E., & Robin, A. F. (1989). How inferences about novel domain-related concepts can be constrained by structured knowledge. *Merrill-Palmer Quarterly, 35,* 27–62.

Chi, M. T. H., & Koeske, R. D. (1983). Network representation of a child's dinosaur knowledge. *Developmental Psychology, 19,* 29–39.

Chisholm, K. (1998). A three-year follow-up of attachment and indiscriminate friendliness in children adopted from Romanian orphanges. *Child Development, 69,* 1092–1106.

Chomsky, N. (1968). *Language and mind.* New York: Harcourt, Brace, World.

Chouros, G. P., & Gold, P. W. (1999). The inhibited child "syndrome": Thoughts on its potential pathogenesis and sequelae. In L. A. Schmidt & J. Schulkin (Eds.), *Extreme fear, shyness, and social phobia: Origins, biological mechanisms, and clinical outcomes* (pp. 193–200). New York: Oxford University Press.

Christakis, N. (2000). *Death foretold: Prophecy and prognosis in medical care.* Chicago: University of Chicago Press.

Chumlea, W. C. (1982). Physical growth in adolescence. In B. J. Wolman (Ed.), *Handbook of developmental psychology* (pp. 471–485). Englewood Cliffs, NJ: Prentice-Hall.

Cicchetti, D. (1984). *Developmental psychopathology.* Chicago: University of Chicago Press.

Cicchetti, D. (1989). How research on child maltreatment has informed the study of child maltreatment: Perspectives from developmental psychopathology. In D. Cicchetti & V. Carlson (Eds.), *Child maltreatment: Theory and research on the causes and consequences of child abuse and neglect* (pp. 377–431). New York: Cambridge University Press.

Cicchetti, D., & Toth, S. L. (Eds.). (1994) *Rochester Symposium on Developmental Psychopathology: Vol. 5. Disorders and dysfunctions of the self.* (pp. 79–148). Rochester, NY: University of Rochester Press.

Cicchetti, D., Toth, S. L., & Lynch, M. (1995). Bowlby's dream comes full circle: The application of attachment theory to risk and psychopathology. *Advances in Clinical Child Psychology, 17,* 1–75.

Cierpal, M. A., & McCarty, R. (1987). Hypertension in SHR rats: Contribution of maternal environment. *American Journal of Physiology, 253,* 980–984.

Clark, M. L. (1982). Racial group concept and self-esteem in black children. *Journal of Black Psychology, 8,* 75–88.

Clark, R., Hyde, J. S., Essex, J. J., & Klein, M. H. (1997). Length of maternity leave and quality of mother-infant interactions. *Child Development, 68,* 364–383.

Clarke-Stewart, K. A. (1989). Infant day care: Maligned or malignant? *American Psychologist, 44,* 266–273.

Clausen, J. A. (1993). *American lives: Looking back at the children of the Great Depression.* New York: Free Press.

Cohen, D., & Strayer, J. (1996). Empathy in conduct disordered and comparison youth. *Developmental Psychology, 32,* 988–998.

Cohen, J. M. (1977). Sources of peer group homogeneity. *Sociology of Education, 50,* 227–241.

Cohler, B., & Taber, S. E. (1993). Residential college as milieu: Person and environment in the transition to young adulthood. In B. Cohler (Ed), *Residential treatment for children and youth* (pp. 69–110). Binghamton, NY: Haworth Press.

Coie, J., Terry, R., Lenox, K., & Lochman, J. (1995). Childhood peer rejection and aggression as predictors of stable patterns of adolescent disorder. *Development & Psychopathology, 7,* 697–713.

Coie, J. D., & Dodge, K. A. (1998). Aggression and antisocial behavior. In W. Damon (Ed.), N. Eisenberg (Volume Ed.), *Handbook of child psychology: Vol. 3. Social, emotional and personality development* (5th ed., pp. 779–862). New York: Wiley.

Coie, J. D., Dodge, K. A., & Coppotelli, H. (1982). Dimensions and types of social status: A cross-age perspective. *Developmental Psychology, 18,* 557–570.

Coie, J. D., Dodge, K. A., & Kupersmidt, J. B. (1990). Peer group behavior and social status. In S. R. Asher & J. D. Coie (Eds.), *Peer rejection in childhood* (pp. 17–59). Cambridge, England: Cambridge University Press.

Coie, J. D., & Krehbiehl, G. (1984). Effects of academic tutoring on the social status of low-achieving, socially rejected children. *Child Development, 55,* 1465–1478.

Coie, J. D., & Kupersmidt, J. (1983). A behavioral analysis of emerging social status in boys' groups. *Child Development, 54,* 1400–1416.

Coie, J. D., Lochman, J. E., Terry, R., & Hyman, C. (1992). Predicting early adolescent disorder from childhood aggression and peer rejection. *Journal of Consulting & Clinical Psychology, 60,* 783–792.

Coie, J. D., Watt, N. F., West, S. G., Hawkins, J. D., Asamow, J. R., Markman, H. J., Ramey, S. L., Shure, M. B., & Long, B. (1993). The science of prevention: A conceptual framework and some directions for a national research program. *American Psychologist, 48,* 1013–1022.

Colapinto, John (1999). *As nature made him: The boy who was raised as a girl.* New York: HarperCollins.

Colby, A., & Damon, W. (1992). *Some do care: Contemporary lives of moral commitment.* New York: Free Press.

Colby, A., & Kohlberg, L. (1987). *The measurement of moral judgment: Vol. 1. Theoretical foundations and research validation; Vol. 2. Standard issue scoring manual.* New York: Cambridge University Press.

Colby, A., Kohlberg, L., Gibbs, J., & Lieberman, M. (1983). A longitudinal study of moral judgment. *Monographs of the Society for Research in Child Development, 48* (1–2, Serial no. 200).

Cole, D. A., Maxwell, S. E., & Martin, J. M. (1997). Reflected self appraisals: Strength and structure of the relation of teacher, peer, and parent ratings to children's self-perceived competencies. *Journal of Educational Psychology, 89,* 55–70.

Cole, M., & Wertsch, J. V. (1996). Beyond the individual-social antinomy in discussions of Piaget and Vygotsky. *Human Development, 39,* 250–256.

Cole, P. M., Barrett, K. C., & Zahn-Waxler, C. (1992). Emotion displays in two-year-olds during mishaps. *Child Development, 63,* 314–324.

Coleman, D. (1995). *Emotional Intelligence.* New York: Bantam Books.

Coleman, D. (1998). *Working with emotional intelligence.* New York: Bantam Books.

Coles, R. (1970). *Erik H. Erikson: The growth of his work.* Boston: Little, Brown.

Colin, V. L. (1996). *Human attachment.* New York: McGraw-Hill.

Collaer, M. L., & Hines, M. (1995). Human behavioral sex differences: A role for gonadal hormones during early development? *Psychological Bulletin, 118,* 55–107.

Collins, N. L., & Read, S. J. (1990). Adult attachment, working models, and relationship quality in dating couples. *Journal of Personality and Social Psychology, 58,* 644–663.

Collins, W. A., Maccoby, E. E., Steinberg, L., Hetherington, E. M., & Bornstein, M. H. (2000). Contemporary research on parenting: The case for nature and nature. *American Psychologist, 55,* 218–232.

Comer, J. P. (1988). Educating poor minority children. *Scientific American, 5,* 42–48.

Commons, M. L., & Richards, F. A. (1984). A general model of stage theory. In M. L. Commons, F. A. Richards, & C. Armon (Eds.). *Beyond formal operations: Late adolescent and adult cognitive development* (pp. 120–140). New York: Praeger.

Compas, B. E., Banez, G. A., Malcarne, V., & Worsham, N. (1991). Perceived control and coping with stress: A developmental perspective. *Journal of Social Issues, 47,* 23–43.

Compas, B. E., Howell, D. C., Phares, V., Williams, R. A., & Giunta, C. (1989). Risk factors for emotional/behavioral problems in young adolescents: A prospective analysis of adolescent and parental stress and symptoms. *Journal of Consulting and Clinical Psychology, 57,* 732–740.

Comstock, G., & Scharrer, E. (1999). *Television: What's on, who's watching, and what it means.* San Diego, CA: Academic Press.

Condon, W. S., & Sander, L. W. (1974). Synchrony demonstrated between movements of the neonate and adult speech. *Child Development, 45,* 1191–1193.

Conley, J. J. (1985). Longitudinal study of personality traits: A multitrait-multimethod-multioccasion analysis. *Journal of Personality and Social Psychology, 49,* 1266–1282.

Connidis, I. A., & Davies, L. (1992). Confidants and companions: Choices in later life. *Journal of Gerontology: Social Sciences, 47,* S115–S122.

Cook, A. S., & Oltjenbruns, K. A. (1998). The bereaved family. In A. S. Cook & K. A. Oltjenbruns (Eds.), *Dying and grieving: Life span and family perspectives* (pp. 91–115). Fort Worth, TX: Harcourt Brace.

Cooley, C. H. (1902). *Human nature and the social order.* New York: Schribner's.

Coon, H., Carey, G., Corley, R., & Fulker, D. W. (1992). Identifying children in Colorado Adoption Project at risk for conduct disorder. *Journal of the American Academy of Child and Adolescent Psychiatry, 31,* 503–511.

Cooper, R. M., & Zubek, J. P. (1958). Effects of enriched and restricted early environments on the learning ability of bright and dull rats. *Canadian Journal of Psychology, 12,* 159–164.

Corcoran, K. O., & Mallinckrodt, B. (2000). Adult attachment, self-efficacy, perspective-taking, and conflict resolution. *Journal of Counseling and Development, 78,* 473–483.

Corr, C. A. (1993). Coping with dying: Lessons that we should and should not learn from the work of Elizabeth Kubler-Ross. *Death Studies, 17,* 69–83.

Costa, P. T., & McCrae, R. R. (1988). Personality in adulthood: A six-year longitudinal study of self-reports and spouse ratings on the NEO Personality Inventory. *Journal of Personality and Social Psychology, 54,* 853–863.

Costa, P. T., & McCrae, R. R. (1994). Set like plaster? Evidence for the stability of adult personality. In T. F. Heatherton & J. L. Weinberger (Eds.), *Can personality change?* (pp. 21–40). Washington, DC: American Psychological Association.

Coupland, N., Coupland, J., Giles, H., Henwood, K., & Wiemann, J. (1988). Elderly self-disclosure: Interactional and intergroup issues. *Language and Communication, 8,* 109–133.

Cowan, C. P., & Cowan, P. A. (1992). *When partners become parents.* New York: Basic Books.

Cowan, P. A. (1978). *Piaget with feeling: Cognitive, social and emotional dimensions.* New York: Holt, Rinehart, & Winston.

Cowan, W. M. (1979). The development of the brain. In Llinas, R. R. (Ed.), *The workings of the brain: Development, memory, and perception.* New York: Freeman.

Cowen, E. L., Izzo, L. D., Miles, H., Telschow, E. F., Trost, M. A., & Zax, M. A. (1963). A mental health program in the school setting: Description and evaluation. *Journal of Psychology, 56,* 307–356.

Cowen, E. L., Petersen, A., Babigian, H., Izzo, L. D., & Trost, M. A. (1973). Long-term follow-up of early detected vulnerable children. *Journal of Consulting and Clinical Psychology, 41,* 438–446.

Cowen, E. L., Hightower, A. D., Pedro-Carroll, J. L., Work, W. C., Wyman, P. A., & Haffey. (1996). *School-based prevention for children at risk: The Primary Mental Health Project.* Washington, D.C.: American Psychological Association.

Crain, W. (1992). *Theories of development: Concepts and applications.* Englewood Cliffs, NJ: Prentice Hall.

Cramer, P. (1999). Development of identity: Gender makes a difference. *Journal of Research in Personality, 34,* 42–72.

Crane, D. A., & Tisak, M. (1995). Mixed-domain events: The influence of moral and conventional components on the development of social reasoning. *Early Education and Development, 6,* 169–180.

Creasey, G., & Hesson-McInnis, M. (2001). Affective responses, cognitive appraisals, and conflict tactics in late adolescent romantic relationships: Associations with attachment orientations. *Journal of Counseling Psychology, 48,* 85–96.

Crews, D. (1994). Animal sexuality. *Scientific American, 270,* 108–114.

Crick, N. R., & Dodge, K. A. (1994). A review and reformation of social information processing mechanisms in children's social adjustment. *Psychological Bulletin, 115,* 74–101.

Crittendon, P. M. (1994). Peering into the black box: An exploratory treatise on the development of self in young children. In D. Cicchetti & S. L. Toth (Eds.), *Rochester Symposium on Developmental Psychopathology: Vol. 5. Disorders and dysfunctions of the self* (pp. 79–148). Rochester, NY: University of Rochester Press.

Crittendon, P. M. (1997). Patterns of attachment and sexual behavior: Risk of dysfunction versus opportunity for creative integration. In L. Atkinson & K. J. Zucker (Eds.), *Attachment and psychopathology* (pp. 47–93). New York: Guilford Press.

Crittendon, P. M., & DiLalla, D. L. (1988). Compulsive compliance: The development of an inhibitory coping strategy in infancy. *Journal of Abnormal Child Psychology, 16,* 585–599.

Crnic, K. A., & Booth, C. L. (1991). Mothers' and fathers' perceptions of daily hassles of parenting across early childhood. *Journal of Marriage and the Family, 53,* 1042–1050.

Crnic, K. A., & Greenberg, M. T. (1990). Minor parenting stresses with young children. *Child Development, 61,* 1628–1637.

Crockenberg, S., & Litman, C. (1991). Effects of maternal employment on maternal and two-year-old child behavior. *Child Development, 62,* 930–953.

Crocker, J., & Major, B. (1989). Social stigma and self-esteem: The self-protective properties of stigma. *Psychological Review, 96,* 608–630.

Crockett, L., Losoff, M., & Petersen, A. C. (1984). Perceptions of the peer group and friendship in early adolescence. *Journal of Early Adolescence, 4,* 155–181.

Cross, W. E. (1971). The Negro to Black conversion experience. *Black World, 20,* 13–17.

Cross, W. E. (1994). Nigrescence theory: Historical and explanatory notes. *Journal of Vocational Behavior, 44,* 119–123.

Crowder, L. S. (1999). Mortuary practices in San Francisco Chinatown. *Chinese America, History & Perspectives,* pp. 33–47.

Crowell, J. A., Waters, E., Treboux, D., O'Connor, E., Colon-Downs, C., Feider, O., Golby, B., & Posada, G. (1996). Discriminant validity of the Adult Attachment Interview. *Child Development, 67,* 2584–2599.

Crowley, K., & Siegler, R. S. (1993). Flexible strategy use in young children's tic-tac-toe. *Cognitive Science, 17,* 531–561.

Crump, A. D., Haynie, D. L., Aarons, S. J., Adair, E., Woodward, K., & Simons-Morton, B. G. (1999). Pregnancy among urban African-American teens: Ambivalence about prevention. *American Journal of Health Behavior, 23,* 32–42.

Csikszentmihalyi, M. (1999). If we are so rich, why aren't we happy? *American Psychologist, 54,* 821–827.

Csikszentmihalyi, M., & Larson, R. (1984). *Being adolescent.* New York: Basic Books.

Cultice, J. C., Somerville, S. C., & Wellman, H. M. (1983). Preschooler's memory monitoring: Feeling-of-knowing judgements. *Child Development, 54,* 1480–1486.

Cunningham, A. E., Stanovich, K. E., & West, R. F. (1994). Literacy environment and the development of children's cognitive skills. In E. Assink (Ed.), *Literacy acquisition and social context.* Wheatsheef, NY: Harvester.

Daley, S. (1991, January 9). Little girls lose their self-esteem on way to adolescence, study finds. *The New York Times,* p. B6.

Damasio, A. R. (1994). *Descartes' error: Emotion, reason, and the human brain.* New York: Grosset/Putnam.

Damon, W. (1988). *The moral child: Nurturing children's natural moral growth.* New York: Free Press.

Damon, W. (1995). *Greater expectations: Overcoming the culture of indulgence in America's homes and schools.* New York: Free Press.

Damon, W., & Hart, D. (1988). *Self-understanding in childhood and adolescence.* New York: Cambridge University Press.

Damon, W., & Hart, D. (1992). Self-understanding and its role in social and moral development. In M. H. Bornstein & M. E. Lamb (Eds.), *Developmental psychology: An advanced textbook* (3rd ed., pp. 421–464). Hillsdale, NJ: Lawrence Erlbaum Associates.

Darling, N., & Steinberg, L. (1993). Parenting style as context: An integrative model. *Psychological Bulletin, 113,* 487–496.

Datan, N., & Ginsberg, L. H. (Eds.). (1975). *Life-span developmental psychology: Normative life crises.* New York: Academic Press.

Davidson, P., Turiel, E., & Black, A. (1983). The effect of stimulus familiarity on the use of criteria and justifications in children's social reasoning. *British Journal of Developmental Psychology, 1,* 49–65.

Davis, C. (1852). *Lecture on the duties and relations of parents, teachers, and pupils as connected with education.* Delivered at the First Session of the Teachers' Institute at the Normal School at Ypsilanti, MI. Free Press Book and Job Office.

Davis, C. G., Lehman, D. R., & Wortman, C. B. (1997). *Finding meaning in loss and trauma: Making sense of the literature.* Unpublished manuscript, University of Michigan.

Davis, C. G., Wortman, C. B., Lehman, D. R., & Silver, R. C. (2000). Searching for meaning in loss: Are clinical assumptions correct? *Death Studies, 24,* 497–540.

Davis, J. (1997). *Mapping the mind: The secrets of the human brain and how it works.* Secaucus, NJ: Birch Lane Press.

Dawson, G., Panagiotides, H., Klinger, L., & Spieker, S. (1997). Infants of depressed and nondepressed mothers exhibit differences in frontal brain electrical activity during the expression of negative emotions. *Developmental Psychology, 33*, 650–656.

Day, R. D. (1992). The transition to first intercourse among racially and culturally diverse youth. *Journal of Marriage and the Family, 54*, 749–762.

DeAngelis, T. (1977). Chromosomes contain clues on schizophrenia. *Monitor of the American Psychological Association, 28*, 26.

DeAngelis, T. (1997). When children don't bond with parents. *Monitor of the American Psychological Association, 28*, 10–12.

Deater-Deckard, K., Dodge, K. A., Bates, J. E., & Pettit, G. S. (1995, March–April). *Risk factors for the development of externalizing behavior problems: Are there ethnic differences in process?* Paper presented at the biennial meeting of the Society of Research in Child Development, Indianapolis, IN.

Deater-Deckard, K., Dodge, K. A., Bates, J. E., & Pettit, G. S. (1996). Physical discipline among African American and European American mothers: Links to children's externalizing behaviors. *Developmental Psychology, 32*, 1065–1072.

Deaux, K. (1993). Commentary: Sorry, wrong number: A reply to Gentile's call. Sex or gender? [Special section]. *Psychological Science, 4*, 125–126.

DeCasper, A. J., & Fifer, W. P. (1980). Of human bonding: Newborns prefer their mothers' voices. *Science, 208*, 1174–1176.

DeCasper, A. J., Lecaneut, J., Busnel, M., Granier-Deferre, C., & Maugeais, R. (1994). Fetal reactions to recurrent maternal speech. *Infant Behavior and Development, 17*, 159–164.

DeCasper, A. J., & Prescott, P. A. (1984). Human newborns' perception of male voices: Preference, discrimination, and reinforcing value. *Developmental Psychobiology, 17*, 481–491.

DeCasper, A. J., & Spence, M. J. (1986). Newborns prefer a familiar story over an unfamiliar one. *Infant Behavior and Development, 9*, 133–150.

de Castro, B. O., Veerman, J. W., Koops, W., Bosche, J. D., & Monshouwer, H. J. (2002). Hostile attribution, intent, and aggressive behavior: A meta-analysis. *Child Development, 73*, 916–934.

DeCatanzaro, D. A. (1999). *Motivation and emotion: Evolutionary, physiological, developmental, and social perspectives.* Upper Saddle River, NJ: Prentice-Hall.

Decker, P. J., & Borgen, F. H. (1993). Dimensions of work appraisal: Stress, strain, coping, job satisfaction, and negative affectivity. *Journal of Counseling Psychology, 40*, 470–478.

de la Torre, J. C. (1997). Cerebrovascular changes in the aging brain. In P. S. Timiras, E. E. Bittar (Series Eds.), M. P. Mattson, & J. W. Geddes (Guest Eds.), *Advances in cell aging and gerontology* (Vol. 2, pp. 77–107). Greenwich, CT: JAI Press.

DeLisi, R., & Gallagher, A. M. (1991). Understanding of gender stability and constancy in Argentinean children. *Merrill-Palmer Quarterly, 37*, 483–502.

Dellas, M., & Jernigan, L. P. (1987). Affective personality characteristics associated with undergraduate ego identity formation. *Journal of Adolescent Research, 3*, 306–324.

DeLoache, J. S. (1987). Rapid change in the symbolic functioning of very young children. *Science, 238*, 1556–1557.

DeLoache, J. S. (1999, April). *Becoming symbol minded.* Paper presented at the biennial meetings of the Society for Research in Child Development, Albuquerque, NM.

DeLoache, J. S., Miller, K. F., & Pierroutsakos, S. L. (1998). Reasoning and problem solving. In W. Damon (Series Ed.), D. Kuhn, & R. S. Siegler (Vol. Eds.), *Handbook of child psychology: Vol. 2. Cognition, perception, and language* (5th ed., pp. 801–850). New York: Wiley.

DeLoache, J. S., Miller, K. F., & Rosengren, K. (1997). The credible shrinking room: Very young children's performance in symbolic and non-symbolic tasks. *Psychological Science, 8*, 308–313.

Dempster, F. N. (1981). Memory span: Sources of individual and developmental differences. *Psychological Bulletin, 89*, 63–100.

Denham, S. A., & Holt, R. W. (1993). Preschoolers' likability as cause or consequence of their social behavior. *Developmental Psychology, 29*, 271–275.

de St. Aubin, E., & McAdams, D. P. (1995). The relations of generative concern and generative action to personality traits, satisfaction/happiness with life, and ego development. *Journal of Adult Development, 2*, 99–112.

Deutch, H. (1937). Absence of grief. *Psychoanalytic Quarterly, 6*, 12–22.

Developmental Studies Center. (1996). *Child development project.* Oakland, CA: Developmental Studies Center.

Dewey, J. (1933/1998). *How we think: A restatement of the relation of reflective thinking to the educative process.* Boston: Houghton-Mifflin.

de Wolf, M. S., & van IJzendoorn, M. H. (1997). Sensitivity and attachment: A meta-analysis on parental antecedents of infant attachment. *Child Development, 68*, 571–591.

Dey, E. L., & Hurtado, S. (1999). Students, colleges, and society: Considering the interconnections. In P. G. Altbach, R. O. Berndahl, & P. J. Gumport (Eds.), *American higher education in the twenty-first century: Social, political, and economic challenges* (pp. 298–322). Baltimore: Johns Hopkins University Press.

Diamond, J. (1986). I want a girl, just like the girl . . . *Discover, 7*, 65–68.

Diamond, L. M. (1998). Development of sexual orientation among adolescent and young adult women. *Developmental Psychology, 34,* 1085–1095.

Diamond, M., & Sigmundson, K. (1997). Sex reassignment at birth: Long-term review and clinical implications. *Archives of Pediatric Adolescent Medicine, 151,* 298–304.

Dickson, D. W. (1997). Structural changes in the aged brain. In P. S. Timiras, E. E. Bittar (Series Eds.), M. P. Mattson, & J. W. Geddes (Guest Eds.), *Advances in cell aging and gerontology* (Vol. 2, pp. 51–76). Greenwich, CT: JAI Press.

Dinardo, Q. (1971). *Psychological adjustment to spinal cord injury.* Unpublished doctoral dissertation, University of Houston, Houston, TX.

Dion, K. K., Berscheid, E., & Walster, E. (1972). What is beautiful is good. *Journal of Personality and Social Psychology, 24,* 285–290.

Dishion, T. J. (1990). The peer context of troublesome behavior in children and adolescents. In P. Leone (Ed.), *Understanding troubled and troublesome youth* (pp. 128–153). Beverly Hills, CA: Sage.

Dix, T. (1991). The affective organization of parenting: Adaptive and maladaptive processes. *Psychological Bulletin, 110,* 3–25.

Dixon, J. A., & Moore, C. F. (1990). The development of perspective taking: Understanding differences in information and weighting. *Child Development, 61,* 1502–1513.

Dodge, K. A. (1983). Behavioral antecedents of peer social status. *Child Development, 54,* 1386–1399.

Dodge, K. A., Bates, J. E., & Petit, G. S. (1990). Mechanisms in the cycle of violence. *Science, 250,* 1678–1683.

Dodge, K. A., Coie, J. D., Pettit, G. S., & Price, J. M. (1990). Peer status and aggression in boys' groups: Developmental and contextual analyses. *Child Development, 61,* 1289–1309.

Dodge, K. A., Pettit, J. M., McClaskey, C. L., & Brown, M. M. (1986). Social competence in children. *Monographs of the Society for Research in Child Development, 51,* 1–80.

Dodge, K. A., Schlundt, D. G., Schocken, I., & Delugach, J. D. (1983). Social competence and children's social status: The role of peer group entry strategies. *Merrill-Palmer Quarterly, 29,* 309–336.

Donovan, W. L., Leavitt, L. A., & Walsh, R. (1990). Maternal self-efficacy: Illusory control and its effect on susceptibility to learned helplessness. *Child Development, 61,* 1638–1647.

Dornbusch, S. M., Ritter, P. L., Leiderman, P. H., Roberts, D. F., & Fraleigh, M. J. (1987). The relation of parenting style to adolescent school performance. *Child Development, 58,* 1244–1257.

Douvan, E., & Adelson, J. (1966). *The adolescent experience.* New York: Wiley.

Dozier, M., Cue, K., & Barnett, L. (1994). Clinicians as caregivers: Role of attachment organization in treatment. *Journal of Consulting and Clinical Psychology, 62,* 793–800.

Dozier, M., & Kobak, R. R. (1992). Psychophysiology in attachment interviews: Converging evidence for deactivating strategies. *Child Development, 63,* 1473–1480.

Dozier, M., Stovall, K. C., & Albus, K. E. (1999). Attachment and psychopathology in adulthood. In J. Cassidy & P. R. Shaver (Eds.), *Handbook of attachment: Theory, research, and clinical applications* (pp. 497–519). New York: Guilford Press.

Dozier, M., & Tyrell, C. (1998). The role of attachment in therapeutic relationships. In J. A. Simpson & W. S. Rholes (Eds.), *Attachment theory and close relationships* (pp. 221–248). New York: Guilford Press.

Dryfoos, J. G. (1997). The prevalence of problem behaviors: Implications for programs. In R. P. Weissberg, T. P. Gullotta, R. L. Hampton, B. A. Ryan, & G. R. Adams, (Eds.), *Enhancing children's wellness* (Vol. 8, pp. 17–46). Thousand Oaks, CA: Sage Publications.

Dryfoos, J. G. (1990). *Adolescents at risk: Prevalence and prevention.* New York: Oxford University Press.

Dunkle, M. F., Schraw, G., & Bendixen, L. (1993, April). *The relationship between epistemological beliefs, causal attributions, and reflective judgement.* Paper presented at the Annual Meeting of the American Educational Research Association, Atlanta, GA.

Dunlap, D. W. (1994, October 18). Gay survey raises a new question. *The New York Times,* p. B8.

Dunn, J., Bretherton, I., & Munn, P. (1987). Conversations about feeling states between mothers and their young children. *Developmental Psychology, 23,* 132–139.

Dunn, S., & Morgan, V. (1987). Nursery and infant school play patterns: Sex-related differences. *British Educational Research Journal, 13,* 271–281.

Dunphy, D. C. (1963). The social structure of urban adolescent peer groups. *Sociometry, 26,* 230–246.

DuPont, R. L. (1997). *The selfish brain: Learning from addiction.* Washington, DC: American Psychiatric Press.

Duran, R. T., & Gauvain, M. (1993). The role of age versus expertise in peer collaboration during joint planning. *Journal of Experimental Child Psychology, 55,* 227–242.

Durlak, J. A., Fuhrman, T., & Lampman, C. (1991). Effectiveness of cognitive-behaviour therapy for maladapting children: A meta-analysis. *Psychological Bulletin, 11,* 204–214.

Duvall, E. M. (1971). *Family Development* (4th ed.). Philadelphia: J. B. Lippincott.

Dweck, C. S. (1999). *Self-theories: Their role in motivation, personality, and development.* Philadelphia: Taylor & Francis.

D'Zurilla, T. J. (1986). *Problem-solving therapy: A social competence approach to clinical intervention.* New York: Springer.

Easterbrooks, M. A., & Goldberg, W. A. (1990). Security of toddler-parent attachment: Relation to children's socio-personality functioning during kindergarten. In M. T. Greenberg, D. Cicchetti, & E. M. Cumings (Eds.),

Attachment in the preschool years (pp. 221–244). Chicago: University of Chicago Press.

Eaton, W. O., & Enns, L. R. (1986). Sex differences in human motor activity level. *Psychological Bulletin, 100,* 19–28.

Eccles, J. S., & Barber, B. L. (1999). Student council, volunteering, basketball, or marching band: What kind of extracurricular involvement matters? *Journal of Adolescent Research, 14,* 10–43.

Eccles, J., Midgley, C., & Adler, T. (1984). Grade-related changes in the school environment: Effects on achievement motivation. In J. J. Nicholls (Ed.), *Advances in motivation and achievement.* (Vol. 3, pp. 283–331). Greenwich, CT.: JAI Press.

Eccles, J. S., Midgley, C., Wigfield, A., Buchanan, C. M., Reuman, D., Flanagan, C., & MacIver, D. (1993). Development during adolescence: The impact of stage-environment fit on young adolescents' experiences in schools and in families. *American Psychologist, 48,* 90–101.

Eckert, P. (1989). *Jocks and burnouts: Social categories and identity in the high school.* New York: Teachers College Press.

Edelman, G. M. (1987). *Neural Darwinism: The theory of neuronal group selection.* New York: Basic Books.

Eder, D., & Sanford, S. (1986). The development and maintenance of interactional norms among early adolescents. *Sociological Studies of Child Development, 1,* 283–300.

Egan, G. (1975). *The skilled helper: A model for systemic helping and interpersonal relating.* Monterey, CA: Brooks/Cole.

Eisenberg, N., Cialdini, R., McCreath, H., & Shell, R. (1987). Consistency-based compliance: When and why do children become vulnerable? *Journal of Personality and Social Psychology, 52,* 1174–1181.

Eisenberg, N., Fabes, R. A., Karbon, M., Murphy, B. C., Wosinski, M., Polazzi, L., Carlo, G., & Juhnke, C. (1996). The relations of children's dispositional prosocial behavior to emotionality, regulation, and social functioning. *Child Development, 67,* 974–992.

Eisenberg, N., & Fabes, R. A. (1998). Prosocial development. In W. Damon (Ed.) & N. Eisenberg (Vol. Ed.), *Handbook of child psychology: Vol. 3. Social, emotional and personality development* (5th ed., pp. 701–778). New York: Wiley.

Eisenberg, N., Lennon, R., & Roth, K. (1983). Prosocial development: A longitudinal study. *Developmental Psychology, 19,* 846–855.

Eisenberg, N., Pasternack, J. F., Cameron, E., & Tryon, K. (1984). The relation of quality and mode of prosocial behavior to moral cognitions and social style. *Child Development, 155,* 1479–1485.

Eisenberg, N., Shell, R., Pasternack, J., Lennon, R., Beller, R., & Mathy, R. M. (1987). Prosocial development in middle childhood: A longitudinal study. *Developmental Psychology, 24,* 712–718.

Ekman, P. (1992). Are there basic emotions? *Psychological Review, 99,* 550–553.

Ekman, P. (1994). Strong evidence for universals in facial expression: A reply to Russell's mistaken critique. *Psychological Bulletin, 115,* 268–276.

Ekman, P., & Friesen, W. V. (1969). The repertoire of nonverbal behavior: Categories, origins, uses, and coding. *Semiotica, 1,* 49–98.

Ekman, P., & Friesen, W. V. (1971). Constants across cultures in the face and emotion. *Journal of Personality and Social Psychology, 17,* 124–129.

Ekman, P., & Oster, H. (1979). Facial expression of emotion. *Annual Review of Psychology, 30,* 527–554.

Elder, G. (1974). *Children of the great depression.* Chicago: University of Chicago Press.

Elder, G. H., Jr. (1994). Time, human agency, and social change: Perspectives on the life course. *Social Psychology Quarterly, 57,* 4–15.

Eliason, M. J. (1996). Identity formation for lesbian, bisexual and gay persons: Beyond a "minoritizing" view. *Journal of Homosexuality, 30,* 31–58.

Elkind, D. (1967). Egocentrism in adolescence. *Child Development, 38,* 1025–1031.

Elkind, D. (1968, May 26). Giant in the nursery—Jean Piaget. *The New York Times Magazine.* NY: New York Times Company.

Elkind, D. (1981). *Children and adolescents.* New York: Oxford University Press.

Elkind, D. (1984). *All grown up and no place to go: Teenagers in crisis.* Reading, MA: Addison-Wesley.

Elkind, D. (1994). *Ties that Stress: The New Family Imbalance.* Cambridge, MA: Harvard University Press.

Elkins, I. J., McGue, M., & Iacono, W. G. (1997). Genetic and environmental influences on parent-son relationships: Evidence for increasing genetic influence during adolescence. *Developmental Psychology, 33,* 351–363.

Ellis, L., Burke, D., & Ames, M. A. (1987). Sexual orientation as a continuous variable: A comparison between the sexes. *Archives of Sexual Behavior, 16,* 523–529.

Ellis, S., Klahr, D., & Siegler, R. S. (1993, March). *Effects of feedback and collaboration on changes in children's use of mathematical rules.* Paper presented at the meeting of the Society for Research in Child Development, New Orleans, LA.

Ellis, S., & Rogoff, B. (1986). Problem solving in children's management of instruction. In E. Mueller & C. Cooper (Eds.), *Process and outcome in peer relationships* (pp. 301–325). Orlando, FL: Academic.

Emanuel, E., & Emanuel, L. (1998). The promise of a good death. *The Lancet, 251,* 21–29.

Emde, R. N., Biringen, Z., Clyman, R. B., & Oppenheim, D. (1991). The moral self of infancy: Affective core and procedural knowledge. *Developmental Review, 11,* 251–270.

Emde, R. N., & Buchsbaum, H. (1990). "Didn't you hear my mommy?" Autonomy with connectedness in moral self-emergence. In D. Cicchetti & M. Beeghly (Eds.), *The self in transition: Infancy to adulthood* (pp. 35–60). Chicago: University of Chicago Press.

Emde, R. N., Johnson, W., & Easterbrooks, M. (1987). The do's and don'ts of early moral development: Psychoanalytic tradition and current research. In J. Kagan & S. Lamb (Eds.), *The emergence of morality in young children* (pp. 245–276). Chicago: University of Chicago Press.

Ennett, S. T., & Bauman, K. E. (1994). The contribution of influence and selection to adolescent peer group homogeneity: The case of adolescent cigarette smoking. *Journal of Personality & Social Psychology, 67,* 653–663.

Enns, C. Z. (1992). Toward integrating feminist psychotherapy and feminist philosophy. *Professional Psychology: Research and Practice, 23,* 453–466.

Entwisle, D. R. (1990). Schools and the adolescent. In S. S. Feldman & G. R. Elliott (Eds.), *At the threshold: The developing adolescent* (pp. 197–224). Cambridge, MA: Harvard University Press.

Erber, J. T., & Prager, I. G. (1999). Age and memory: Perceptions of forgetful young and older adults. In T. M. Hess & F. Blanchard-Fields (Eds.), *Social cognition and aging* (pp. 197–217). San Diego: Academic Press.

Erhardt, A. A., Epstein, R., & Money, J. (1968). Fetal androgens and female gender identity in the early-treated adrenogenital syndrome. *Johns Hopkins Medical Journal, 122,* 160–167.

Erhardt, A. A., & Baker, S. W. (1974). Fetal androgens, human central nervous system, differentiation, and behavior sex differences. In R. C. Friedman, R. M. Richart & R. L. Van de Wiele (Eds.), *Sex differences in behavior* (pp. 33–51). New York: Wiley.

Erhardt, A. A., & Money, J. (1967). Progestin-induced hermaphroditism: IQ and psychosexual identity in a study of ten girls. *Journal of Sex Research, 3,* 83–100.

Erickson, M. F., Sroufe, L. A., & Egeland, B. (1985). The relationship between quality of attachment and behavior problems in preschool in a high-risk sample. In I. Bretherton & E. Waters (Eds.), Growing points of attachment theory and research. *Monographs of the Society for Research in Child Development, 50* (Serial No. 209), 147–166.

Erikson, E. (1975). The problem of ego identity. In Asman, A. H. (Ed.), *The psychology of adolescence: Essential readings* (pp. 318–346). New York: International Universities Press.

Erikson, E. H. (1950/1963). *Childhood and Society* (2nd ed.). New York: Norton.

Erikson, E. H. (1968). *Identity, youth, and crisis.* New York: Norton.

Erwin, P. (1985). Similarity of attitudes and constructs in children's friendships. *Journal of Experimental Child Psychology, 40,* 470–485.

Etzioni, A. (1998, February). How not to discuss character education. *Phi Delta Kappan, 79,* 446–448.

Ewens, J., & Herrington, P. (1983). *Hospice.* Santa Fe, NM: Bear & Co.

Eysenck, H. J., & Schoenthaler, S. J. (1997). Raising IQ level by vitamin and mineral supplementation. In R. J. Steinberg & E. Grigorenko (Eds.), *Intelligence, heredity, and environment* (pp. 362–393). Cambridge: Cambridge University Press.

Ezzo, G., & Bucknam, R. (1995). *On becoming babywise: Vol. 2: Parenting Your Pretoddler.* Sisters, OR: Multnomah Books.

Ezzo, G., & Bucknam, R. (1999). *On becoming childwise: Parenting your child from three to seven years.* Sisters, OR: Multnomah Books.

Fagan, J. F. (1990). The paired-comparison paradigm and infant intelligence. In A. Diamond (Ed.), *The developmental and neural bases of higher cognitive functions. Annals of the New York Academy of Sciences, 608,* 337–364.

Fagot, B. I. (1984). The consequences of problem behavior in toddler children. *Journal of Abnormal Child Psychology, 12,* 385–397.

Fagot, B. I. (1985). Changes in thinking about early sex-role development. *Developmental Review, 5,* 83–98.

Fagot, B. I., & Leinbach, M. D. (1989). The young child's gender schema: Environmental input, internal organization. *Child Development, 60,* 663–672.

Fankenberger, K. D. (2000). Adolescent egocentrism: A comparison among adolescents and adults. *Journal of Adolescence, 23,* 343–357.

Farrington, D. P. (1989). Self-reported and official offending from adolescence to adulthood. In M. W. Klein (Ed.), *Cross-national research in self-reported crime and delinquency.* Boston: Kluwer Academic Publishers.

Farrington, D. P., Ohlin, L., & Wilson, J. Q. (1986). *Understanding and controlling crime.* New York: Springer-Verlag.

Faust, M. S. (1983). Alternative constructions of adolescence and growth. In J. Brooks-Gunn & A. C. Petersen (Eds.), *Girls at puberty: Biological, psychological, and social perspectives* (pp. 105–125). New York: Plenum.

Feagans, L., & Farran, D. C. (1981). How demonstrated comprehension can get muddled in production. *Developmental Psychology, 17,* 718–727.

Feeney, J., Peterson, C., & Noller, P. (1994). Equity and marital satisfaction over the family life cycle. *Personality Relationships, 1,* 83–99.

Feingold, A. (1988). Cognitive gender differences are disappearing. *American Psychologist, 43,* 95–103.

Feinman, S., & Entwhistle, D. R. (1976). Children's ability to recognize other children's faces. *Child Development, 47,* 506–510.

Feldlaufer, H., Midgley, C., & Eccles, J. S. (1988). Student, teacher, and observer perceptions of the classroom environment before and after the transition to junior high school. *Journal of Early Adolescence, 8,* 133–156.

Ferron, C. (1997). Body image in adolescence: Cross-cultural research. *Adolescence, 32,* 735–745.

Feschbach, N. D., & Feschbach, S. (1982). Empathy training and the regulation of aggression: Potentialities and limitations. *Academic Psychology Bulletin, 4,* 399–413.

Festinger, L. (1954). A theory of social comparison. *Human Relations, 7,* 117–140.

Field, T. (1989). Maternal depression effects on infant interaction and attachment behavior. In D. Cicchetti (Ed.), *Rochester symposium on developmental psychology: Vol. 1. The emergence of a discipline* (pp. 139–163).

Field, T. (1998). Massage therapy effects. *American Psychologist, 53,* 1270–1281.

Field, T., Fox, N., Pickens, J., & Nawrocki, T. (1995). Relative right frontal activation in 3- to 6-month-old infants of depressed mothers. *Developmental Psychology, 31,* 358–363.

Field, T. M., Healy, B., Goldstein, S., Perry, S., Bendell, D., Schnaberg, S., Zimmerman, E. A., & Kuhn, C. (1988). Infants of depressed mothers show "depressed" behavior even with nondepressed adults. *Child Development, 59,* 1569–1579.

Finch, A. J., Nelson, W. M., & Ott, E. S. (1993). *Cognitive-behavioral procedures with children and adolescents.* Boston: Allyn & Bacon.

Fine, G. A., Mortimer, J. T., & Roberts, D. F. (1990). Leisure, work, and the mass media. In S. S. Feldman & G. R. Elliott, *At the threshold: The developing adolescent* (pp. 225–253). Cambridge, MA: Harvard University Press.

Fingerman, K. L. (1996). Sources of tension in the aging mother and adult daughter relationship. *Psychology and Aging, 11,* 591–606.

Fingerman, K. L. (1997). Being more than a daughter: Middle-aged women's conceptions of their mothers. *Journal of Women and Aging, 9,* 55–72.

Finn, S. E. (1986). Stability of personality self-ratings over 30 years: Evidence for an age-cohort interaction. *Journal of Personality and Social Psychology, 50,* 813–818.

Fischer, K. (1987). Relations between brain and cognitive development. *Child Development, 58,* 623–632.

Fischer, K. W. (1980). A theory of cognitive development: The control and construction of hierarchies of skills. *Psychological Review, 87,* 477–531.

Fischer, K. W., Hand, H. H., Watson, M. W., Van Parys, M., & Tucker, J. (1984). Putting the child into socialization: The development of social categories in preschool children. In L. Katz (Ed.), *Current topics in early childhood education* (vol. 5, pp. 27–72). Norwood, NJ: Ablex.

Fisher, C. B., & Lerner, R. M. (1994). *Applied developmental psychology.* New York: McGraw-Hill.

Fiske, S. T., & Taylor, S. E. (1991). *Social cognition* (2nd ed.). New York: McGraw-Hill.

Fitzgerald, J. M. (1988). Vivid memories and the reminiscence phenomenon: The role of a self narrative. *Human Development, 31,* 261–273.

Fitzgerald, J. M. (1992). Autobiographical memory and conceptualizations of the self. In M. A. Conway, D. C. Rubin, H. Spinnler, & W. A. Wagenaar (Eds.), *Theoretical perspectives on autobiographical memory* (pp. 99–114). Boston: Kluwer.

Fitzgerald, J. M. (1999). Autobiographical memory and social cognition: Development of the remembered self in adulthood. In T. M. Hess & F. Blanchard-Fields (Eds.), *Social cognition and aging* (pp. 145–171). San Diego: Academic Press.

Fitzgerald, J. M., & Lawrence, R. (1984). Autobiographical memory across the life-span. *Journal of Gerontology, 39,* 692–699.

Flannery, K. A., & Watson, M. W. (1993). Are individual differences in fantasy play related to peer acceptance levels? *Journal of Genetic Psychology, 154,* 407–416.

Flavell, J. H. (1963). *The developmental psychology of Jean Piaget.* New York: Van Nostrand.

Flavell, J. H., Botkin, P., Fry, C. L., Wright, J. & Jarvis, P. (1968). *The development of role-taking and communication skills in children.* New York: Wiley.

Flavell, J. H., Friedrichs, A. G., & Hoyt, J. D. (1970). Developmental changes in memorization processes. *Cognitive Psychology, 1,* 324–340.

Flavell, J. H., & Miller, P. H. (1998). Social cognition. In W. Damon (Series Ed.), D. Kuhn, & R. S. Siegler (Vol. Eds.), *Handbook of child psychology: Vol. 2. Cognition, perception, and language* (5th ed., pp. 851–898). New York: Wiley.

Flavell, J. H., Miller, P. H., & Miller, S. A. (1993). *Cognitive development* (3rd ed). Englewood Cliffs, NJ: Prentice Hall.

Flavell, J. H., Mumme, D. L., Green, F. L., & Flavell, E. R. (1992). Young children's understanding of different types of beliefs. *Child Development, 63,* 960–977.

Fleming, A. S., Ruble, D. L., Flett, G. L., & Schaul, D. L. (1988). Postpartum adjustment in first-time mothers: Relations between mood, maternal attitudes, and mother-infant interactions. *Developmental Psychology, 24,* 71–81.

Fletcher, A. C., Darling, N. E., Steinberg, L., & Dornbusch, S. M. (1995). The company they keep: Relationships of adolescents' adjustment and behavior to their friends' perceptions of authoritative parenting in the social network. *Developmental Psychology, 31,* 300–310.

Foley, M. A., Harris, J., & Hermann, S. (1994). Developmental comparison of the ability to discriminate between memories for symbolic play enactment. *Developmental Psychology, 30,* 206–217.

Folkman, S., & Lazarus, R. S. (1986). Stress processes and depressive symptomatology. *Journal of Abnormal Psychology, 95,* 107–113.

Folkman, S., Lazarus, R. S., Gruen, R. J., & DeLongis, A. (1986). Appraisal, coping, health status, and psychological symptoms. *Journal of Personality and Social Psychology, 50,* 571–579.

Fordham, S., & Ogbu, J. U. (1986). Black students' school success: Coping with the burden of "acting White." *Urban Review, 18,* 176–206.

Fox, N. A., Kimmerly, N. L., & Schafer, W. D. (1991). Attachment to mother/attachment to father: A meta-analysis. *Child Development, 62,* 210–225.

Fraley, R. C., Davis, K. E., & Shaver, P. R. (1998). Dismissing-avoidance and the defensive organization of emotion, cognition, and behavior. In J. A. Simpson & W. S. Rholes (Eds.), *Attachment theory and close relationships* (pp. 249–279). New York: Guilford Press.

Fraley, R. C., & Shaver, P. R. (1999). Loss and Bereavement: Attachment theory and recent controversies concerning "Grief Work" and the nature of detachment. In J. Cassidy & P. R. Shaver (Eds.), *Handbook of attachment: Theory, research and clinical applications* (pp. 735–759). New York: Guilford Press.

Fraley, R. C., & Waller, N. G. (1998). Adult attachment patterns: A test of the typological model. In J. A. Simpson & W. S. Rholes (Eds.), *Attachment theory and close relationships* (pp. 77–114). New York: Guilford Press.

Frankenberger, K. D. (2000). Adolescent egocentrism: A comparison among adolescents and adults. *Journal of Adolescence, 23,* 343–347.

Fredrickson, B. L., & Carstensen, L. L. (1990). Choosing social partners: How old age and anticipated endings make us more selective. *Psychology and Aging, 5,* 335–347.

French, D. C. (1988). Heterogeneity of peer-rejected boys: Aggressive and nonaggressive subtypes. *Child Development, 59,* 976–985.

Freud, A. (1958). Child observation and prediction of development. In *Psychoanalytic study of the child, Vol. 13,* (pp. 92–116). New York: International Universities Press.

Freud, S. (1905/1989). Three essays on the theory of sexuality. In P. Gay (Ed.), *The Freud reader.* New York: Norton.

Freud, S. (1917/1957). Mourning and melancholia. In J. Strachey (Ed.), *Standard edition of the complete works of Sigmund Freud.* London: Hogarth Press.

Freud, S. (1929/1961). [letter] To Ludwig Binswanger. In E. L. Freud (ed.), *Letters of Sigmund Freud 1873–1939,* trans. T. & J. Stern. London: Hogarth Press.

Freud, S. (1930/1989). Civilization and its discontents. In P. Gay (Ed.), *The Freud Reader* (pp. 722–772). New York: Norton.

Freud, S. (1935/1960). *A general introduction to psychoanalysis.* New York: Washington Square Press.

Freud, S. (1949/1969). *An outline of psychoanalysis.* New York: Norton.

Freud, S. (1956). *Delusion and dream: An interpretation in the light of psychoanalysis of Gravida, a novel, by Wilhelm Jensen.* Boston: Beacon Press.

Frey, K. S., & Ruble, D. N. (1992). Gender constancy and the "cost" of sex-typed behavior: A test of the conflict hypothesis. *Developmental Psychology, 28,* 714–721.

Friedman, H. S., Tucker, J. S., Schwartz, J. E., Tomlinson-Keasey, C., Martin, L. R., Wingard, D. L., & Criqui, M. H. (1995). Psychosocial and behavioral predictors of longevity: The aging and death of the "Termites." *American Psychologist, 50,* 69–78.

Fullard, W., & Reiling, A. M. (1976). An investigation of Lorenz's "babyness." *Child Development, 47,* 1191–1193.

Fung, H., Carstensen, L. L., & Lutz, A. (1999). The role of time perspective in age differences in social preferences. *Psychology and Aging, 14,* 595–604.

Furstenberg, F. E. (2000). The socialization of adolescence and youth in the 1990's: A critical commentary. *Journal of Marriage and the Family, 62,* 896–911.

Furstenberg, F. F., Brooks-Gunn, J., & Chase-Lansdale, L. (1987). *Adolescent mothers in later life.* New York: Cambridge University Press.

Furstenberg, F. F., Brooks-Gunn, J., & Chase-Lansdale, L. (1989). Teenaged pregnancy and childbearing. *American Psychologist, 44,* 313–320.

Furstenburg, F. F., Jr. (1992, March). *Adapting to difficult environments: Neighborhood characteristics and family strategies.* Paper presented at the meeting of the Society for Research on Adolescence, Washington, DC.

Fuson, K. C., & Kwon, Y. (1992). Effects on children's addition and subtraction of the system of number words and other cultural tools. In J. Bideaud, C. Meljac, & J. P. Fischer (Eds.), *Pathways to number: Children's developing numerical abilities* (pp. 283–306). Hillsdale, NJ: Erlbaum.

Gaiter, J. M. (2001). Let's talk about sex and health. *Essence, 32,* 214.

Galambos, N. L., & Leadbeater, B. J. (2000). Trends in adolescent research for the new millenium. *International Journal of Behavioral Development, 24,* 289–294.

Garbarino, J. (1999). *Lost boys: Why our sons turn violent and how we can save them.* New York: Free Press.

Garcia, J. L. (1995). Freud's psychosexual stage conception: A developmental metaphor for counselors. *Journal of Counseling and Development, 73,* 498–502.

Gardner, H. (1991). *The unschooled mind: How children think, how schools should teach.* New York: Basic Books.

Gardner, H. (1983). *Frames of mind: The theory of multiple intelligences.* New York: Basic Books.

Garmezy, N., & Masten, A. (1994). Chronic adversities. In M. Rutter, L. Hersov, & E. Taylor (Eds.), *Child and adolescent psychiatry* (3rd ed. pp. 191–208). Oxford: Blackwell.

Garrod, A., & Beal, C. (1993). Voices of care and justice in children's responses to fable dilemmas. In A. Garrod (Ed.), *Approaches to moral development: New research and emerging themes* (pp. 59–71). New York: Teachers College Press.

Gati, I., Osipow, S. H., & Givon, M. (1995). Gender differences in career decision making: The content and structure of preferences. *Journal of Counseling Psychology, 42,* 204–216.

Gatz, M. (2000). Variations on depression in later life. In S. H. Qualls & N. Abeles (Eds.), *Psychology and the aging revolution: How we adapt to longer life* (pp. 239–254). Washington, DC: American Psychological Association.

Gauvain, M. (1992). Social influences on the development of planning in advance and during action. *International Journal of Behavioral Development, 15,* 377–398.

Gauvain, M., & Rogoff, B. (1989). Collaborative problem solving and children's planning skills. *Developmental Psychology, 25,* 139–151.

Ge, X., Conger, R. D., & Elder, G. H., Jr., (1996). Coming of age too early: Pubertal influences on girls' vulnerability to psychological distress. *Child Development, 67,* 3386–3400.

Gelehrter, T. D., & Collins, F. S. (1990). *Principles of medical genetics.* Baltimore: Williams & Wilkins.

Gelman, R. (1982). Basic numerical abilities. In R. J. Sternberg (Ed.), *Advances in the psychology of human intelligence* (Vol. 1). Hillsdale, NJ: Erlbaum.

Gelman, R., & Gallistel, C. R. (1978). *The child's understanding of number.* Cambridge, MA: Harvard University Press.

Gelman, R., & Williams, E. M. (1998). Enabling constraints for cognitive development and learning: Domain specificity and epigenesis. In W. Damon (Series Ed.), D. Kuhn, & R. S. Siegler (Vol. Eds.), *Handbook of child psychology: Vol. 2. Cognition, perception, and language* (5th ed., pp. 575–630). New York: Wiley.

Gergen, K. J. (1971). *The concept of self.* New York: Holt, Rinehart & Winston.

Gerth, H., & Mills, C. W. (1953). *Character and social structure: The psychology of social institutions.* New York: Harcourt Brace.

Geschwind, N. (1990). Specializations of the human brain. In Llinas, R. R. *The workings of the brain: Development, memory, and perception* (pp. 105–120). New York: Freeman.

Gesser, G., Wong, P. T., & Reker, G. T. (1988). Death attitudes across the life span: The development and validation of the Death Attitude Profile (DAP). *Omega: Journal of Death and Dying, 18,* 113–128.

Gewirtz, J. L., & Boyd, E. F. (1977). Does maternal responding imply reduced infant crying? A critique of the 1972 Bell and Ainsworth report. *Child Development, 48,* 1200–1207.

Gibbs, J. (1987). Social processes in delinquency: The need to facilitate empathy as well as sociomoral reasoning. In W. Kurtines and J. Gewirtz (Eds.), *Moral development through social interaction.* New York: Wiley.

Gill, H. L., & Haurin, D. R. (1998). Wherever he may go: How wives affect their husband's career decisions. *Social Science Research, 29,* 264–279.

Gilligan, C. (1977). In a different voice: Women's conceptions of self and of morality. *Harvard Educational Review, 47,* 481–517.

Gilligan, C. (1982). *In a different voice.* Cambridge, MA: Harvard University Press.

Gilligan, C. (1993). Adolescent development reconsidered. In A. Garrod (Ed.), *Approaches to moral development: New research and emerging themes.* New York: Teachers College Press.

Gilligan, C., & Attanucci, J. (1988). Two moral orientations: Gender differences and similarities. *Merrill Palmer Quarterly, 23,* 77–104.

Ginsburg, H. P. (1989). *Children's arithmetic: How they learn it and how you teach it* (2nd ed.). Austin, TX: Pro-Ed.

Ginsburg, H. P., Klein, A., & Starkey, P. (1998). The development of children's mathematical thinking: Connecting research with practice. In W. Damon (Series Ed.), I. E. Sigel, & K. A. Renninger (Vol. Eds.), *Handbook of child psychology: Vol. 4. Child psychology in practice* (5th ed., pp. 401–478). New York: Wiley.

Glanzer, P. L. (1998, February). The character to seek justice: Showing fairness to diverse visions of character education. *Phi Delta Kappan,* pp. 434–438, 448.

Glass, G. (1976). Primary, secondary and meta-analysis of research. *Educational Research, 5,* 3–8.

Glass, J. (1998). Gender liberation, economic squeeze, or fear of strangers: Why fathers provide infant care in dual-earner families. *Journal of Marriage and the Family, 60,* 821–834.

Gleeson, K., & Wise, S. (1993). The do-not resuscitate order. Still too late. *Archives of Internal Medicine, 153,* 1999–2003.

Gleitman, H. (1996). *Basic psychology.* New York: Norton.

Glick, P. C., & Lin, S. (1986). Recent changes in divorce and remarriage. *Journal of Marriage and the Family, 48,* 737–747.

Goldfried, M. R. (1995). *From cognitive-behavior therapy to psychotherapy integration.* New York: Springer.

Goldstein, A. P. (1990). *Delinquents on delinquency.* Champaign, IL: Research Press.

Goldstein, A. P. (1992, May 4). *School violence: Its community context and potential solutions.* Testimony presented to the Subcommittee on Elementary, Secondary, and Vocational Education of the Committee on Education and Labor of the United States House of Representatives.

Golinkoff, R. M. (1983). The preverbal negotiation of failed messages: Insights into the transition period. In R. M. Golinkoff (Ed.), *The transition from prelinguistic to linguistic communication.* Hillsdale, NJ: Erlbaum.

Golombok, S., & Tasker, F. (1996). Do parents influence the sexual orientation of their children? Findings from a longitudinal study of lesbian families. *Developmental Psychology, 32,* 3–11.

Golub, S. (1992). *Periods: From menarche to menopause.* Newbury Park, CA: Sage.

Gondolf, E. W. (1985). *Men who batter.* Holmes Beach, FL: Learning Publications.

Goodman, G. S., & Clarke-Stewart, A. (1991). Suggestibility in children's testimony: Implications for child sexual abuse investigations. In J. L. Doris (Ed.), *The suggestibility of children's recollections* (pp. 92–105). Washington, DC: American Psychological Association.

Goodson, W. D. (1978). Which do college students choose first—their major or their occupation? *Vocational Guidance Quarterly, 30,* 230–235.

Goodstein, R., & Ponterotto, J. G. (1997). Racial and ethnic identity: Their relationship to and their contribution to self-esteem. *Journal of Black Psychology, 23,* 275–292.

Goossens, F. A., & Van Ijzendoorn, M. H. (1990). Quality of infants; attachments to professional caregivers: Relation to infant-parent attachment and day-care characteristics. *Child Development, 61,* 832–837.

Gopnik, A., & Astington, J. W. (1988). Children's understanding of representational change and its relation to the understanding of false belief and the appearance-reality distinction. *Child Development, 59,* 26–37.

Gorbman, A., Dickoff, W. W., Vigna, S. R., Clark, N. B., & Ralph, C. L. (1983). *Comparative endocrinology.* New York: Wiley.

Gordon, B., Ornstein, P. A., Clubb, P. A., Nida, R. E., & Baker-Ward, L. E. (1991). *Visiting the pediatrician: Long term retention and forgetting.* Paper presented at the annual meeting of the Psychonomic Society, San Francisco, CA.

Gordon, E. W., & Lemons, M. P. (1997). An interactionist perspective on the genesis of intelligence. In R. J. Steinberg & E. Grigorenko (Eds.), *Intelligence, heredity, and environment* (pp. 323–342). Cambridge: Cambridge University Press.

Gorman-Smith, D., Tolan, P. H., Zelli, A., & Huesmann, L. R. (1996). The relation of family functioning to violence among inner city youths. *Journal of Family Psychology, 10,* 115–129.

Gottfredson, D. C., Fink, C. M., Skroban, S., Gottfredson, G. D., & Weissberg, R. P. (1997). Making prevention work. In R. P. Weissberg, T. P. Gullotta, R. L. Hampton, B. A. Ryan, & G. R. Adams (Eds.), *Healthy children 2010: Establishing preventive services* (pp. 219–252). Thousand Oaks, CA: Sage Publications.

Gottfredson, G. D., & Holland, J. L. (1990). A longitudinal test of the influence of congruence: Job satisfaction, competency utilization, and counterproductive behavior. *Journal of Counseling Psychology, 37,* 389–398.

Gottfredson, G. D., Holland, J. L., & Ogawa, D. K. (1982). *Dictionary of Holland occupational codes.* Palo Alto, CA: Consulting Psychologists Press.

Gottlieb, G. (1970). Conceptions of prenatal development. In L. R. Aronson, E. Tobach, D. S. Lehrman, & J. S. Rosenblatt, (Eds.), *Development and evolution of behavior* (pp. 111–137). San Francisco: Freeman.

Gottlieb, G. (1991). Experiential canalization of behavioral development: Theory. *Developmental Psychology, 27,* 4–13.

Gottlieb, G. (1992). *Individual development and evolution: The genesis of novel behavior.* New York: Oxford University Press.

Gottman, J. M. (1983). How children become friends. *Monographs of the Society for Research in Child Development, 48*(3, Serial No. 201).

Gottman, J. M. (1994). *What predicts divorce?* Hillsdale, NJ: Erlbaum.

Gottman, J. M. (1999). *The marriage clinic: A scientifically-based marital therapy.* New York: Norton.

Gottman, J. M., & Levenson, R. W. (2000). The timing of divorce: Predicting when a couple will divorce over a 14-year period. *Journal of Marriage and the Family, 62,* 737–745.

Gould, R. L. (1978). *Transformations: Growth and change in adult life.* New York: Simon & Schuster.

Graber, J. A., Brooks-Gunn, J., & Galen, B. R. (1999). Betwixt and between: Sexuality in the context of adolescent transitions. In R. Jessor (Ed.), *New perspectives on adolecent risk behavior* (pp. 270–318). New York: Cambridge University Press.

Grammer, K. (1993). 5-a-androst-16en-3a-on: A male pheromone? *Ethology and Sociobiology, 14,* 201–207.

Gray, J. A. (1990). Brain systems that mediate both emotion and cognition. *Cognition and Emotion, 4,* 270–288.

Gray, W. M. (1990). Formal operation thought. In W. F. Overton (Ed.), *Reasoning, necessity, and logic: Developmental perspectives* (pp. 227–254). Hillsdale, NJ: Erlbaum.

Gray-Little, B., & Hafdahl, A. R. (2000). Factors influencing racial comparisons of self-esteem: A quantitative review. *Psychological Bulletin, 126,* 26–54.

Green, R. (1987). *The "sissy boy syndrome" and the development of homosexuality.* New Haven, CT: Yale University Press.

Greenberg, J., & Pyszczynski, T. (1986). Persistent high self-focus after a failure and low self-focus after success: The depressive self-focusing style. *Journal of Personality and Social Psychology, 55,* 1039–1044.

Greenberg, L. S., & Safran, J. D. (1989). Emotion in psychotherapy. *American Psychologist, 44,* 19–29.

Greenberg, M. T., & Speltz, M. L. (1988). Attachment and the ontogeny of conduct problems. In J. Belsky & T. Nezworski (Eds.), *Clinical implications of attachment* (pp. 177–218). Hillsdale, NJ: Lawrence Erlbaum Associates.

Greenberger, E., & Goldberg, W. (1989). Work, parenting, and the socialization of children. *Developmental Psychology, 25,* 22–35.

Greene, A. L., & Wheatley, S. M. (1992). "I've got a lot to do and I don't think I'll have the time": Gender differences in late adolescents' narratives of the future. *Journal of Youth and Adolescence, 21,* 667–685.

Greenfield, P. M. (1994). Independence and interdependence as developmental scripts: Implications for theory, research, and practice. In P. M. Greenfield & R. R. Cocking (Eds.), *Cross-cultural roots of minority child development* (pp. 1–40). Hillsdale, NJ: Erlbaum.

Greenfield, P. M., & Juvonen, J. (1999, July/August). A developmental look at Columbine. *Monitor: American Psychological Association.*

Greenfield, P. M., & Suzuki, L. K. (1998). Culture and human development: Implications for parenting, education, pediatrics, and mental health. In W. Damon (Series Ed.), I. E. Siegel, & K. A. Renninger (Vol. Eds.), *Handbook of child psychology: Vol. 4. Child psychology in practice* (5th ed., pp. 1059–1109). New York: Wiley.

Greeno, K. (1989). *Gender differences in children's proximity to adults*. Ph.D. dissertation, Stanford University.

Greenough, W. T., & Black, J. E. (1992). Induction of brain structure by experience: Substrates for cognitive development. In M. R. Gunnar & C. A. Nelson (Eds.), *Minnesota Symposium on Child Psychology*: Vol. 24. *Developmental behavioral neuroscience* (pp. 155–200).

Greenspan, S. I., & Weider, S. (1997). An integrated developmental approach to interventions for young children with severe difficulties in relating and communicating. *Zero to three, 17*(5), 279–306.

Grice, P. (1975). Logic and conversation. In P. Cole & J. L. Moran (Eds.), *Syntax and semantics: Vol. 3. Speech acts* (pp. 41–58). New York: Academic Press.

Grodin, M. A., & Laurie, G. T. (2000). Susceptibility genes and neurological disorders: Learning the right lessons from the Human Genome Project. *Archives of Neurology, 57*, 1569–1574.

Gross, J., Carstensen, L. L., Pasupathi, M., Tsai, J., Gotestam Skorpen, C., & Hsu, A. (1997). Emotion and aging: Experience, expression and control. *Psychology and Aging, 12*, 590–599.

Grossmann, K. E., Grossmann, K., Huber, F., & Wartner, U. (1981). German children's behavior towards their mothers at 12 months and their fathers at 18 months in Ainsworth's Strange Situation. *International Journal of Behavioral Development, 4*, 157–181.

Gurwitz, S. B., & Dodge, K. A. (1977). Effects of confirmations and disconfirmations on stereotype-based attributions. *Journal of Personality and Social Psychology, 35*, 495–500.

Guterman, J. T. (1994). A social constructionist position for mental health counseling. *Journal of Mental Health Counseling, 16*, 226–244.

Haith, M. M., & Benson, J. B. (1998). Infant cognition. In W. Damon (Series Ed.), D. Kuhn, & R. S. Siegler (Vol. Eds.), *Handbook of child psychology: Vol. 2. Cognition, perception, and language* (5th ed., pp. 199–254). New York: Wiley.

Haley, J. (1976). *Problem-solving therapy*. San Francisco: Jossey-Bass.

Halford, G. S. (1993). *Children's understanding: The development of mental models*. Hillsdale, NJ: Erlbaum.

Hall, G. S. (1904). *Adolescence: Its psychology and its relation to physiology, anthropology, sociology, sex, crime, religion, and education*. (Vols. 1 & 2). Englewood Cliffs, NJ: Prentice-Hall.

Hallinan, M. T. (1979). Structural effects on children's friendships and cliques. *Social Psychology Quarterly, 42*, 43–54.

Halperin, S. (Ed.). (1998a). *The forgotten half revisited: American youth and young families, 1988–2008*. Washington, D.C.: American Youth Policy Forum.

Halperin, S. (1998b). Today's forgotten half: Still losing ground. In S. Halperin (Ed.), *The forgotten half revisited: American youth and young families, 1988–2008* (pp. 1–26). Washington, D.C: American Youth Policy Forum.

Halpern, D. F. (1992). *Sex differences in cognitive abilities* (2nd ed.). Hillsdale, NJ: Erlbaum.

Hamer, D., & Copeland, P. (1998) *Living with our genes: Why they matter more than you think*. New York: Doubleday.

Hamill, S. B., & Goldberg, W. A. (1997). Between adolescents and aging grandparents: Midlife concerns of adults in the sandwich generation. *Journal of Adult Development, 4*, 135–147.

Hamilton, C. E. (2000). Continuity and discontinuity of attachment from infancy through adolescence. *Child Development, 71*, 690–694.

Hamilton, J. E. (1993, June). Smart ways to use time-out. *Parents Magazine*, pp. 110–112.

Hanson, L., Danis, M., & Garrett, J. (1997). What is wrong with end-of-life care? Opinions of bereaved family members. *Journal of the American Geriatric Society, 45*, 1339–1344.

Haraven, T. K., & Adams, K. (1996). The generation in the middle: Cohort comparisons in assistance to aging parents in an American community. In T. K. Haraven (Ed.), *Aging and generational relations: Life course and cross-cultural perspectives* (pp. 3–29). New York: Aldine de Gruyter.

Hare-Mustin, R. T., & Maracek, J. (1988). The meaning of difference: Gender theory, postmodernism, and psychology. *American Psychologist, 43*, 455–464.

Harris, J. R. (1998). *The nurture assumption: Why children turn out the way they do*. New York: Free Press.

Harris, P. L. (1983). What children know about situations that provoke emotions. In M. Lewis & C. Saarni (Eds.), *The socialization of affect* (pp. 117–130). New York: Plenum Press.

Hart, B., & Risley, T. R. (1992). American parenting of language-learning children: Persisting difference in family-child interactions observed in natural home environment. *Developmental Psychology, 28*, 1096–1105.

Hart, B., & Risley, T. R. (1999). *Meaningful differences in the everyday experience of young American children*. Baltimore, MD: Brookes.

Hart, N. (1993). Famine, maternal nutrition and infant mortality: A re-examination of Dutch hunger winter. *Population Studies, 47*, 27–46.

Harter, S. (1981). A new self-report scale of intrinsic versus extrinsic orientation in the classroom: Motivational and informational components. *Developmental Psychology, 17*, 300–312.

Harter, S. (1985). *The self-perception profile for children*. Unpublished manual, University of Denver, CO.

Harter, S. (1988). *The self-perception profile for adolescents*. Unpublished manual, University of Denver, CO.

Harter, S. (1990). Causes, correlates, and the functional role of global self-worth: A life-span perspective. In R. Sternberg & J. Kolligian, Jr., (Eds.), *Competence considered* (pp. 67–98). New Haven, CT: Yale University Press.

Harter, S. (1993). Causes and consequences of low self-esteem in children and adolescents. In Baumeister, R. F. (Ed.). *Self-esteem: The puzzle of low self-regard* (pp. 3–20). New York: Plenum Press.

Harter, S. (1998). The development of self-representations. In W. Damon (Ed.) & N. Eisenberg (Vol. Ed.), *Handbook of child psychology: Vol. 3. Social, emotional and personality development* (5th ed., pp. 553–618). New York: Wiley.

Harter, S. (1999). *The construction of the self: A developmental perspective.* New York: Guilford Press.

Harter, S., & Pike, R. (1984). The pictorial scale of perceived competence and social acceptance for young children. *Child Development, 55,* 1969–1982.

Hartshorne, H., & May, M. A. (1928–1930). *Studies in the nature of character: Vols. 1–3).* New York: Macmillan.

Hartup, W. W. (1983). Peer relations. In P. H. Mussen (Series Ed.) & E. M. Hetherington (Vol. Ed.), *Handbook of child psychology: Vol. 4. Socialization, personality, and social development* (pp. 103–196). New York: Wiley.

Hartup, W. W., Glazer, J., & Charlesworth, R. (1967). Peer reinforcement and sociometric status. *Child Development, 38,* 1017–1024.

Harwood, R. L., Schoelmerich, A., Schulze, P. A., & Gonzalez, Z. (1999). Cultural differences in maternal beliefs and behaviors: A study of middle-class Anglo and Puerto Rican mother-infant pairs in four everyday situations. *Child Development, 70,* 1005–1016.

Hasher, L., & Zacks, R. T. (1988). Working memory, comprehension, and aging: A review and a new view. *The Psychology of Learning and Motivations, 22,* 193–225.

Hastings, P. D., & Grusec, J. E. (1998). Parenting goals as organizers of responses to parent-child disagreement. *Developmental Psychology, 34,* 465–479.

Hatano, G. (1994). Introduction: Conceptual change—Japanese perspectives. *Human Development, 37,* 189–197.

Hatfield, E., & Sprecher, S. (1986). Measuring passionate love in intimate relationships. *Journal of Adolescence, 9,* 383–410.

Hattie, J. (1992). *Self-concept.* New York: Erlbaum.

Hauser, S. T. (1999). Understanding resilient outcomes: Adolescent lives across time and generations. *Journal of Research on Adolescence, 9,* 1–24.

Hawkins, J. (1987, April). *Collaboration and dissent.* Paper presented at the meetings of the Society for Research in Child Development, Baltimore.

Hayes, C. D. (Ed.). (1987). *Risking the future: Adolescent sexuality, pregnancy, and childbearing* (Vol. 1). Washington, DC: National Academy Press.

Hayes, R. L. (1994). The legacy of Lawrence Kohlberg: Implications for counseling and human development. *Journal of Counseling and Development, 72,* 498–502.

Hazan, C., & Shaver, P. (1987). Romantic love conceptualized as an attachment process. *Journal of Personality and Social Psychology, 52,* 511–524.

Hazan, C., & Shaver, P. R. (1994). Attachment as an organizational framework for research on close relationships. *Psychological Inquiry, 5,* 1–22.

Hazan, C., & Zeifman, D. (1999). Pair bonds as attachments. In J. Cassidy & P. R. Shaver, (Eds.), *Handbook of attachment: Theory, research, and clinical applications* (pp. 336–377). New York: Guilford Press.

Heath, A. C., Bucholz, K. K., Madden, P. A. F., Dinwiddie, S. H., Slutske, W. S., Bierut, L. J., Statham, D. J., Dunne, M. P., Whitfield, J. B., & Martin, N. G. (1997). Genetic and environmental contributions to alcohol dependence risk in a national twin sample: Consistency of findings in women and men. *Psychological Medicine, 27,* 1381–1396.

Heckhausen, J. (1997). Developmental regulation across adulthood: Primary and secondary control of age-related challenges. *American Psychologist, 33,* 176–187.

Heckhausen, J. (1999). *Developmental regulation in adulthood: Age-normative and sociostructural constraints as adaptive challenges.* New York: Cambridge University Press.

Heidrich, S. M., & Ryff, C. D. (1993). Physical and mental health in later life: The self-system as mediator. *Psychology and Aging, 8,* 327–338.

Helms, J. E. (1990). An overview of Black racial identity theory. In Helms, J. E. (Ed.), *Black and White racial identity: Theory, research and practice* (pp. 9–32). New York: Greenwood Press.

Helmuth, L. (2001). Brain calls dibs on many genes. *Science, 291,* 1188.

Helson, R., & Klohnen, E. C. (1998). Affective coloring of personality from young adulthood to midlife. *Personality and Social Psychology Bulletin, 24,* 241–252.

Helson, R., & Roberts, B. W. (1994). Ego development and personality change in adulthood. *Journal of Personality and Social Psychology, 66,* 911–920.

Henderson, N. D. (1972). Relative effects of early rearing environment and genotype on discrimination learning in house mice. *Journal of Comparative and Physiological Psychology, 79,* 243–253.

Henderson, V., & Dweck, C. S. (1992). Achievement and motivation in adolescence: A new model and data. In S. Feldman and G. Elliott (Eds.), *At the threshold: The developing adolescent.* Cambridge MA: Harvard University Press.

Henggler, S. W., Schoenwald, S. K., Borduin, C. M., Rowland, M. D., & Cunningham, P. B. (1998). *Multisystemic treatment of antisocial behavior in children and adolescents.* New York: Guilford Press.

Herold, E., Goodwin, M., & Lero, D. (1979). Self-esteem, locus of control, and adolescent contraception. *Journal of Psychology, 101,* 83–88.

Herr, E. L. (1989). *Counseling in a dynamic society: Opportunities and challenges.* Alexandria, VA: American Counseling Association.

Herr, E. L., & Cramer, S. H. (1992). *Career guidance and counseling through the life span: Systematic approaches* (4th ed.). New York: HarperCollins.

Hersch, P. (1998). *A tribe apart: A journey into the heart of American adolescence.* New York: Fawcett Columbine.

Herschenson, D. B. (1996). Work adjustment: A neglected area in career counseling. *Journal of Counseling and Development, 74,* 442–446.

Hesse, E. (1996). Discourse, memory, and the Adult Attachment Interview: A note with emphasis on the emerging cannot classify category. *Infant Mental Health Journal, 17,* 4–11.

Hesse, E., & Main, M. (1999). Frightened behavior in traumatizing but non-maltreating parents: Previously unexamined risk factor for offspring. In D. Diamond & S. J. Blatt (Eds.), *Psychoanalytic theory and attachment research I: Theoretical considerations. Psychoanalytic Inquiry, 19.*

Hetherington, E. M. (1998). Relevant issues in developmental science. *American Psychologist, 53,* 93–94.

Hetherington, E. M., Reiss, D., & Plomin, R. (Eds.). (1994). *Separate social worlds of siblings.* Hillsdale, NJ: Erlbaum.

Hewlett, S. A. (1991). *When the bough breaks: The cost of neglecting our children.* New York: Basic Books.

Hewlett, S. A., & West, C. (1998). *The war against parents: What we can do for America's beleaguered moms and dads.* Boston: Houghton-Mifflin.

Higgins, E. T. (1991). Development of self-regulatory and self-evaluative processes: Costs, benefits, and tradeoffs. In M. R. Gunnar & L. A. Sroufe (Eds.), *Minnesota Symposium on Child Development: Vol. 23. Self processes and development* (pp. 125–166). Hillsdale, NJ: Erlbaum.

Hill, A. M. (1992). Chinese funerals and Chinese ethnicity in Chiang Mai, Thailand. *Ethnology, 31,* 315–330.

Hill, J., & Holmbeck, G. (1986). Attachment and autonomy during adolescence. In G. Whitehurst (Ed.), *Annals of child development.* Greenwich, CT: JAI Press.

Hill, J. P., & Lynch, M. E. (1983). The intensification of gender-related role expectations during early adolescence. In J. Brooks-Gunn & A. C. Petersen (Eds.), *Girls at puberty: Biological and psychosocial perspectives* (pp. 201–228). New York: Plenum.

Hill, M. S., & Yeung, W. J. (1999). How has the changing structure of opportunities affected transitions to adulthood? In A. Booth, A. C. Crouter, & M. J. Shanahan (Eds.), *Transitions to adulthood in a changing economy: No work, no family, no future?* (pp. 3–39). Westport, CT: Praeger.

Hinshaw, S. P. (1987). On the distinction between attentional deficits/hyperactivity and conduct problems/aggression in child psychopathology. *Psychological Bulletin, 101,* 443–463.

Hochschild, A. R. (1997). *The time bind: When work becomes home and home becomes work.* New York: Metropolitan Books.

Hoffman, M. L. (1970). Moral development. In P. H. Mussen (Ed.), M. M. Haith, & J. J. Campos (Vol. Eds.), *Handbook of Child Psychology: Vol. 2. Infancy and developmental psychobiology* (pp. 261–354). New York: Wiley.

Hoffman, M. L. (1975). Altruistic behavior and the parent-child relationship. *Journal of Personality and Social Psychology, 31,* 937–943.

Hoffman, M. L. (1982). Development of prosocial motivation: Empathy and guilt. In N. Eisenberg (Ed.), *The development of prosocial behavior* (pp. 281–313). New York: Academic Press.

Hoffman, M. L. (1983). Affective and cognitive processes in moral internalization. In E. T. Higgins, D. Ruble, & W. Hartup (Eds.), *Social cognition and social development: A sociocultural perspective* (pp. 236–274). New York: Cambridge University Press.

Hofmann, A. D. (1997). Adolescent growth and development. In A. D. Hofmann & D. E. Greydanus (Eds.), *Adolescent medicine* (3rd ed.). Stamford, CT: Appleton and Lange.

Hogan, D. P., & Astone, N. M. (1986). The transition to adulthood. *American Sociological Review, 12,* 109–130.

Holbrook, M., & Schindler, R. M. (1989). Some exploratory findings on the development of musical taste. *Journal of Consumer Research, 16,* 119–124.

Holland, J. L. (1966). *The psychology of vocational choice.* Waltham, MA: Blaisdell.

Holland, J. L. (1985). *Making vocational choices. A theory of vocational personalities and work environments* (2nd ed.). Englewood Cliffs, NJ: Prentice-Hall.

Holland, J. L., Viernstein, M. C., Kuo, H. M., Karweit, N. L., & Blum, S. D. (1970). *A psychological classification of occupations* (Report No. 90). Baltimore, MD: Johns Hopkins University, Center for the Study of Social Organization of Schools.

Homer, B. D., Brockmeier, J., Kamawar, D., & Olson, D. R. (2001). Between realism and nominalism: Learning to think about names and words. *Genetic, Social, and General Psychology Monographs, 127,* 5–25.

Hopmeyer, E., & Werk, A. (1994). A comparative study of family bereavement groups. *Death Studies, 18,* 243–256.

Horn, J. L., & Cattell, R. B. (1966). Refinement and test of the theory of fluid and crystallized intelligence. *Journal of Educational Psychology, 57,* 253–270.

Horney, K. (1950). *Neurosis and human growth.* New York: Norton.

Horowitz, M. J., Siegel, B., Holen, A., Bonanno, G. A., Milbrath, C., & Stinson, C. H. (1997). Diagnostic criteria for complicated grief disorder. *American Journal of Psychiatry, 154,* 904–910.

Horwitz, A. B., & White, H. R. (1998). The relationship of cohabitation and mental health: A study of a young adult cohort. *Journal of Marriage and the Family, 60,* 505–514.

Hoshman, L. T., & Polkinghorne, D. E. (1992). Redefining the science-practice relationship and professional training. *American Psychologist, 47,* 55–66.

Hoza, B., Molina, B. S., Bukowski, W. M., Sippola, L. K. (1995). Peer variables as predictors of later childhood adjustment. *Development & Psychopathology, 7,* 787–802.

Hudspeth, W. J., & Pribram, K. H. (1992). Psychophysiological indices of cognitive maturation. *International Journal of Psychophysiology, 12,* 19–29.

Hughes, C., & Dunn, J. (1998). Understanding mind and emotion: Longitudinal associations with mental-state talk between young friends. *Developmental Psychology, 34,* 1026–1037.

Hummert, M. L. (1999). A social cognitive perspective on age stereotypes. In T. M. Hess & F. Blanchard-Fields (Eds.), *Social cognition and aging* (pp. 176–196). San Diego: Academic Press.

Hummert, M. L., Garstka, T. A., & Shaner, J. L. (1997). Stereotyping of older adults: The role of target facial cues and perceiver characteristics. *Psychology and Aging, 12,* 107–114.

Hummert, M. L., Garstka, T. A., Shaner, J. L., & Strahm, S. (1994). Stereotypes of the elderly held by young, middle-aged, and elderly adults. *Journal of Gerontology: Psychological Sciences, 49,* P240–P249.

Hummert, M. L., Shaner, J. L., Garstka, T. A., & Henry, C. (1998). Communication with older adults: The influence of age stereotypes, context, and communicator age. *Human Communication Research, 25,* 124–151.

Hummert, M. L., & Ryan, E. B. (1996). Toward understanding variations in patronizing talk addressed to older adults: Psycholinguistic features of care and control. *International Journal of Psycholinguistics, 12,* 149–169.

Hunter, A. G., & Davis, J. E. (1992). Constructing gender: An exploration of Afro-American men's conceptualization of manhood. *American Sociological Review, 12,* 109–130.

Huston, A. C. (1983). Sex-typing. In E. M. Hetherington (Ed.), *Handbook of child psychology: Vol. 4. Socialization, personality, and social development* (pp. 388–467). New York: Wiley.

Huttenlocher, J., & Smiley, P. (1990). Emerging notions of persons. In N. L. Stein, B. Leventhal, & T. Trabasso (Eds.), *Psychological and biological approaches to emotion* (pp. 283–295). Chicago: University of Chicago.

Huttenlocher, P. (1994). Synaptogenesis, synapse elimination, and neural plasticity in human cerebral cortex. In C. A. Nelson, (Ed.), *Minnesota Symposium on Child Psychology: Vol: 27. Threats to optimal development: Integrating biological, psychological, and social risk factors* (pp. 35–54).

Hyde, J. S. (1984). How large are gender differences in aggression? A developmental meta-analysis. *Developmental Psychology, 20,* 722–736.

Hyde, J. S., Fennema, E., & Lamon, S. J. (1990). Gender differences in mathematics performance: A meta-analysis. *Psychological Bulletin, 107,* 139–155.

Hyman, I. E., & Faries, J. M. (1992). The function of autobiographical memory. In M. A. Conway, D. C. Rubin, H. Spinnler, & W. A. Wagenaar (Eds.), *Theoretical perspectives on autobiographical memory* (pp. 207–221). Boston: Kluwer.

Hymel, S., & Rubin, K. H. (1985). Children with peer relationship and social skills problems: Conceptual, methodological, and developmental issues. In G. J. Whitehurst (Ed.), *Annals of child development* (Vol. 2, pp. 254–297). Greenwich, CT: JAI Press.

Idler, E. L., & Kasl, S. (1991). Health perceptions and survival: Do global evaluations of health status really predict mortality? *Journal of Gerontology: Social Sciences, 46,* S55–S65.

Imperato-McGinley, J., Peterson, R. E., Gautier, T., & Sturla, E. (1979). Androgyns and the evolution of male gender identity among male pseudo-hermaphrodites with 5a-reductase deficiency. *New England Journal of Medicine, 300,* 1233–1237.

Ingram, R. E., Cruet, D., Johnson, B., & Wisnicki, K. (1988). Self-focused attention, gender, gender-role, and vulnerability to negative affect. *Journal of Personality and Social Psychology, 55,* 1039–1044.

Inhelder, B., & Piaget, J. (1955/1958). *The growth of logical thinking from childhood to adolescence.* New York: Basic Books.

Inhelder, B., & Piaget, P. (1964). *The early growth of logic in the child.* New York: Harper & Row.

Institute of Medicine. (1994). *Reducing risks for mental disorders: Frontiers for preventive intervention research.* Washington, DC: National Academy Press.

International Human Genome Sequencing Consortium (2001). Initial sequencing and analysis of the human genome. *Nature, 409,* 860–921.

Intons-Peterson, M. J. (1988). *Gender concepts of Swedish and American youth.* Hillsdale, NJ: Erlbaum.

Ivey, A. E. (1986). *Developmental therapy: Theory into practice.* San Francisco: Jossey-Bass.

Izard, C. (1991). *The psychology of emotion.* New York: Plenum Press.

Izard, C. E. (1979). *The maximally discriminative facial movement coding system (Max).* Newark: University of Delaware, Information Technologies and University Media Services.

Izard, C. E. (1991). *The psychology of emotions.* New York: Plenum Press.

Izard, C. E. (1992). Basic emotions, relations among emotions, and emotion-cognition relations. *Psychological Review, 99,* 561–565.

Izard, C. E., Dougherty, L. M., & Hembree, E. A. (1983). *A system for identifying affect expression by holistic judgments (Affex).* Newark: University of Delaware, Computer Network Services and University Media Services.

Izard, C. E., & Malatesta, C. Z. (1987). Perspectives on emotional development I: Differential emotions theory of early emotional development. In J. D. Osofsky (Ed.), *Handbook of infant development* (2nd ed., pp. 494–554). New York: Wiley.

Jacobs, J. A., & Stoner-Eby, S. (1998). Adult enrollment in higher education and cumulative educational attainment, 1970–1990. *The Annals of the Academy of Political and Social Science, 559,* 91–108.

Jacobsen, T., & Hofmann, V. (1997). Children's attachment representations: Longitudinal relations to school behavior and academic competency in middle childhood and adolescence. *Developmental Psychology, 33,* 703–710.

James, W. (1890). *Principles of psychology.* Chicago: Encyclopedia Britannica.

Janda, L. H., & Klenke-Hamel, K. E. (1980). *Human sexuality.* New York: Van Nostrand.

Janoff-Bulman, R. (1993). *Shattered assumptions: Toward a new psychology of trauma.* New York: Free Press.

Janowsky, J. S., & Carper, R. (1996). Is there a neural basis for cognitive transitions in school age children? In A. J. Sameroff & M. M. Haith (Eds.), *The five to seven shift: The age of reason and responsibility* (pp. 33–60). Chicago: University of Chicago Press.

Jarrett, R. L. (1994). Living poor: Family life among single parent, African-American women. *Social Problems, 41,* 30–49.

Jessor, R. (1993). Successful adolescent development among youth in high-risk settings. *American Psychologist, 48,* 117–126.

Jessor, R., Donovan, J. E., & Costa, F. M. (1991). *Beyond adolescence: Problem behavior and young adult development.* New York: Cambridge University Press.

Jessor, R., Van Den Bos, J., Vanderryn, J., Costa, F. M., & Turbin, M. S. (1995). Protective factors in adolescent problem behavior: Moderator effects and developmental change. *Developmental Psychology, 31,* 923–933.

Johnson, A., & Ames, E. (1994). The influence of gender labelling on preschoolers' gender constancy judgements. *British Journal of Developmental Psychology, 12,* 241–249.

Johnson, C. A., Pentz, M. A., Weber, M. D., Dwyer, J. H., Baer, N., MacKinnon, D. R., Hansen, W. B., & Flay, B. R. (1990). Relative effectiveness of comprehensive community programming for drug abuse prevention with high-risk and low-risk adolescents. *Journal of Consulting & Clinical Psychology, 58,* 447–456.

Johnson, C. L., & Troll, L. (1994). Constraints and facilitators to friendships in late late life. *The Gerontologist, 34,* 79–87.

Johnson, L. D., O'Malley, P. M., & Bachman, J. G. (1994). *National survey results on drug use from the Monitoring the Future Study: 1975–1993.* Rockville, MD: National Institute on Drug Abuse.

Johnson, M. H. (1998). The neural basis of cognitive development. In *Handbook of Child Psychology Vol. 2,* 1–49. New York: Plenum.

Johnson, T. H. (1960). *The complete poems of Emily Dickinson.* Boston: Little, Brown.

Joiner, T. E., Jr. (2000). Depression: Current developments and controversies. In S. H. Qualls & N. Abeles (Eds.), *Psychology and the aging revolution: How we adapt to longer life* (pp. 223–237). Washington, DC: American Psychological Association.

Jones, L. K. (1996). A harsh and challenging world of work: Implications for counselors. *Journal of Counseling and Development, 74,* 453–459.

Jordan, N. C., Huttenlocher, J., & Levine, S. C. (1994). Assessing early arithmetic abilities: Effects of verbal and nonverbal response types on the calculation performance of middle- and low-income children. *Learning and Individual Differences, 6,* 413–432.

Josselson, R. L. (1973). Psychodynamic aspects of identity formation in college women. *Journal of Youth and Adolescence, 2,* 3–15.

Josselson, R. L. (1988). *Finding herself: Pathways of identity development in women.* New York: Jossey-Bass.

Josselson, R. L. (1994). The theory of identity development and the question of intervention: An introduction. In S. Archer, (Ed.), *Interventions for adolescent identity development* (pp. 12–25). Thousand Oaks, CA: Sage.

Judd, C. M., Park, B., Ryan, C. S., Bauer, M., & Kraus, S. (1995). Stereotypes and ethnocentrism: Diverging interethnic perceptions of African American and White American youth. *Journal of Personality and Social Psychology, 69,* 460–481.

Jung, C. G. (1928). *Two essays on analytical psychology.* New York: Dodd, Mead.

Jung, C. G. (1963). *Memories, dreams, reflections.* New York: Random House.

Kach, J. A., & McGee, P. E. (1982). Adjustment of early parenthood. *Journal of Family Issues, 3,* 375–388.

Kagan, J. (1981). *The second year: The emergence of self-awareness.* Cambridge, MA: Harvard University Press.

Kagan, J. (1984). *The nature of the child.* New York: Basic Books.

Kagan, J. (1994). Yesterday's premises: Tomorrow's promises. In R. D. Parke, R. A. Ornstein, J. J. Rieser, & C. Sahn-Waxler (Eds.), *A century of developmental psychology* (pp. 551–568). Washington, DC: American Psychological Association.

Kagan, J. (1997). Temperament and the reactions to unfamiliarity. *Child Development, 68,* 139–143.

Kagan, J. (1998). Biology and the child. In W. Damon (Series Ed.) & N. Eisenberg (Vol. Ed.), *Handbook of child psychology: Vol. 3, Social, emotional and personality development* (5th ed., pp. 177–236).

Kagan, J., Arcus, D., Snidman, N., & Rimm, S. E. (1995). Assymmetry of forehead temperature and cardiac activity. *Neuropsychology, 9,* 1–5.

Kagan, J., Arcus, D., Snidman, N., Yufeng, W., Hendler, J., & Greene, S. (1994). Reactivity in infants: A cross-national comparison. *Developmental Psychology, 30,* 342–345.

Kagan, J., Kearsley, R., & Zelazo, P. (1978). *Infancy: Its place in human development.* Cambridge, MA: Harvard University Press.

Kail, R. (1991). Developmental changes in speed of processing during childhood and adolescence. *Psychological Bulletin, 109,* 490–501.

Kail, R., & Salthouse, T. (1994). Processing speed as a mental capacity. *Acta Psychologica, 86,* 199–225.

Kalish, R. A. (1985). The social context of death and dying. In R. H. Binstock, & E. Shanas (Eds.), *Handbook of aging and the social sciences* (2nd ed., pp. 147–170). New York: Van Nostrand Reinhold.

Kamii, C. (1986). Place value: An explanation of its difficulty and educational implications for the primary grades. *Journal of Research in Childhood Education, 1,* 75–86.

Kamii, M. (1990). Why Big Bird can't teach calculus: The case of place value and cognitive development in the middle years. In N. Lauter-Klatell (Ed.), *Readings in child development.* Mountain View, CA: Mayfield (pp. 101–104 & 170).

Kandel, D. B. (1978). Homophily, selection, and socialization in adolescent friendships. *American Journal of Sociology, 84,* 427–436.

Kane, R. S. (1996). The defeat of aging versus the importance of death. *Journal of the American Geriatric Society, 44,* 321–325.

Kane, R., Wales, J., Bernstein, L., Leibowitz, A., & Kaplan, S. (1984). A randomized controlled trial of hospice care. *The Lancet, 302,* 890–894.

Kaplan, H. B. (1980). *Deviant behavior in defense of self.* New York: Academic Press.

Karen, R. (1998). *Becoming attached: First relationships and how they shape our capacity to love.* New York: Oxford University Press.

Karmiloff-Smith, A. (1992). *Beyond modularity: A developmental perspective on cognitive science.* Cambridge, MA: MIT Press.

Karmiloff-Smith, A. (2000). Why babies' brains are not Swiss army knives. In H. Rose, & S. Rose (Eds.), *Alas, poor Darwin* (pp. 173–187). New York: Harmony Books.

Karney, B. R., & Bradbury, T. N. (1995). The longitudinal course of marital quality and stability: A review of theory, method, and research. *Psychological Bulletin, 118,* 3–34.

Karney, B. R., & Bradbury, T. N. (1997). Neuroticism, marital interaction, and the trajectory of marital satisfaction. *Journal of Personality and Social Psychology, 72,* 1075–1092.

Kaslow, F. W. (2001). Families and family psychology at the millennium. *American Psychologist, 56,* 37–46.

Kasser, T., & Ryan, R. M. (1999). The relation of psychological needs for autonomy and relatedness to vitality, well-being, mortality in a nursing home. *Journal of Applied Social Psychology, 29,* 935–954.

Kastenbaum, R. (1986). *Death, society, and human experience* (3rd Ed.). Columbus, OH: Merrill.

Katchadourian, H. A. (1987). *Fifty: Midlife in perspective.* New York: Freeman.

Katz, L. C., & Shatz, C. J. (1996). Synaptic activity and the construction of cortical circuits. *Science, 274,* 1133–1138.

Katz, P., & Zalk, S. (1974). Doll preferences: An index of racial attitudes? *Journal of Educational Psychology, 66,* 663–668.

Kazdin, A. (1988). *Child psychotherapy: Developing and identifying effective treatments.* New York: Pergamon Press.

Keelan, J. P. R., Dion, K. K., & Dion, K. L. (1998). Attachment style and relationship satisfaction: Test of a self-disclosure explanation. *Canadian Journal of Behavioural Science, 30,* 24–35.

Keenan, K., & Shaw, D. (1997). Developmental and social influences on young girls' early problem behavior. *Psychological Bulletin, 121,* 95–113.

Kegan, R. (1982). *The evolving self.* Cambridge, MA: Harvard University Press.

Kellett, J. M. (2000). Older adult sexuality. In L. T. Szuchman, & F. Muscarella (Eds.), *Psychological perspectives on human sexuality* (pp. 355–379). New York: Wiley.

Kelly, E. L., & Conley, J. J. (1987). Personality and compatibility: An analysis of marital stability and marital satisfaction. *Journal of Personality and Social Psychology, 52,* 27–40.

Kempermann, G., & Gage, F. H. (1999). New nerve cells for the adult brain. *Scientific American, 280,* 48–53.

Kempson, R. M. (1988). *Mental representations: The interface between language and reality.* Cambrige, MA: Cambridge University Press.

Kendall, P. C. (1993). Cognitive-behavioral therapies with youth: Guiding theory, current status, and emerging developments. *Journal of Consulting and Clinical Psychology, 61,* 235–247.

Kendall, P. C., & Wilcox, L. E. (1980). Cognitive-behavioral treatment for impulsivity: Concrete versus conceptual training in non-self-controlled problem children. *Journal of Consulting and Clinical Psychology, 48,* 80–91.

Keniston, K. (1971). *Youth in dissent: The rise of a new opposition.* New York: Harcourt Brace Jovanovich.

Kerig, P. K., Cowan, P. A., & Cowan, C. P. (1993). Marital quality and gender differences in parent–child interaction. *Developmental Psychology, 29,* 931–939.

Kernberg, O. (1976). *Object relations theory and clinical psychoanalysis.* New York: Aronson.

Khatri, P. (1995, March). *Behavioral and academic correlates of sociometric status among rural Indian children.* Paper presented at the biennial meeting of the Society for Research in Child Development, Indianapolis, IN.

Kikuchi, J. (1988, Fall). Rhode Island develops successful intervention program for adolescents. *National Coalition Against Sexual Assault Newsletter.*

Killgore, W. D. S., Oki, M., & Yurgelun-Todd, D. A. (2001). Sex-specific developmental changes in amygdala responses to affective faces. *Neuroreport: For Rapid Communication of Neuroscience Research, 12,* 427–433.

Kilmartin, C. T. (1994). *The masculine self.* New York: Macmillan.

Kindermann, T. A. (1993). Natural peer groups as contexts for individual development: The case of children's motivation in school. *Developmental Psychology, 29,* 970–977.

Kirkpatrick, L. A., & Davis, K. E. (1994). Attachment style, gender, and relationship stability: A longitudinal analysis. *Journal of Personality and Social Psychology, 66,* 502–512.

Kirschner, D. (1992). Understanding adoptees who kill: Dissociation, patricide, and the psychodynamics of adoption. *International Journal of Offender Therapy and Comparative Criminology, 36,* 323–333.

Kitchener, K. S. (1983). Cognition, metacognition, and epistemic cognition: A three-level model of cognitive processing. *Human Development, 4,* 222–232.

Kitchener, K. S., & King, P. M. (1981). Reflective judgment: Concepts of justification and their relationship to age and education. *Journal of Applied Developmental Psychology, 2,* 89–116.

Kitchener, K. S., King, P. M., Wood, P. K., and Davison, M. L. (1989). Sequentiality and consistency in the development of reflective judgment: A six-year longitudinal study. *Journal of Applied Developmental Psychology, 10,* 73–95.

Kitchener, K. S., Lynch, C. L., Fischer, K. W., & Wood, P. K. (1993). Developmental range of reflective judgment: The effect of contextual support and practice on developmental stage. *Developmental Psychology, 29,* 893–906.

Kitzinger, C., & Wilkinson, S. (1995). Transitions from heterosexuality to lesbianism: The discursive production of lesbian identities. *Developmental Psychology, 31,* 95–104.

Klass, D. (1982). Elisabeth Kubler-Ross and the tradition of the private sphere: An analysis of symbols. *Omega, 16,* 241–261.

Klein, A., & Starkey, P. (1995). *Preparing for the transition to school mathematics: The Head Start Family Math project.* Paper presented at the meeting of the Society for Research in Child Development, Indianapolis, IN.

Klein, M. (1921–1945). *Contributions to psychoanalysis.* London: Hogarth.

Kleinman, A., & Kleinman, J. (1985). Somatization: The interconnections in Chinese society among culture, depressive experiences, and the meanings of pain. In A. Kleinman and B. Good (Eds.), *Culture and depression: Studies in the anthropology and cross-cultural psychiatry of affect and disorder* (pp. 429–490). Berkley: University of California Press.

Kling, K. C., Hyde, J. S., Showers, C. J., & Buswell, B. N. (1999). Gender differences in self-esteem: A meta-analysis. *Psychological Bulletin, 125,* 470–500.

Kling, K. C., Seltzer, M. M., & Ryff, C. D. (1997). Distinctive late-life challenges: Implications for coping and well-being. *Psychology and Aging, 12,* 288–295.

Klinnert, M. (1984). The regulation of infant behavior by maternal facial expression. *Infant Behavior and Development, 7,* 447–465.

Kneflekamp, L. L. (1999). Introduction. In W. G. Perry, *Forms of ethical development in the college years: A scheme* (p. xix). San Francisco: Jossey-Bass.

Kochanska, G. (1993). Toward a synthesis of parental socialization and child temperament in early development of conscience. *Child Development, 64,* 325–347.

Kochanska, G. (1995). Children's temperament, mothers' discipline, and security of attachment: Multiple pathways to emerging internalization. *Child Development, 66,* 597–615.

Kochanska, G. (1998). Mother-child relationship, child fearfulness, and emerging attachment: A short-term longitudinal study. *Developmental Psychology, 34,* 480–490.

Kochanska, G., Aksan, N., & Koenig, A. L. (1995). A longitudinal study of the roots of preschoolers' conscience: Committed compliance and emerging internalization. *Child Development, 66,* 1752–1769.

Kochanska, G., Casey, R. J., & Fukumoto, A. (1995). Toddlers' sensitivity to standard violations. *Child Development, 66,* 643–656.

Kochanska, G., & Murray, K. T. (2000). Mother-child mutually responsive orientation and conscience development: From toddler to early school age. *Child Development, 71,* 417–431.

Kochanska, G., Tjebkes, T. L., & Forman, D. R. (1998). Children's emerging regulation of conduct: Restraint, compliance, and internalization from infancy to the second year. *Child Development, 69,* 1378–1389.

Kohlberg, L. (1966). Moral education in the school. *School Review, 74,* 1–30.

Kohlberg, L. (1976). Moral stages and moralization: The cognitive developmental approach. In T. Lickona (Ed.), *Moral development and behavior: Theory, research and social issues* (pp. 31–53). New York: Holt, Rinehart and Winston.

Kohlberg, L. (1984). *Essays on moral development: The psychology of moral development.* San Francisco: Harper & Row.

Kohlberg, L. A. (1966). A cognitive-developmental analysis of children's sex role concepts and attitudes. In E. E. Maccoby (Ed.), *The development of sex differences* (pp. 82–173). Stanford, CA: Stanford University Press.

Kohn, A. (1997, February). How not to teach values: A critical look at character education. *Phi Delta Kappan,* pp. 428–439.

Konner, M. J., & Worthman, C. (1980). Nursing frequency, gonadal function and birth-spacing among !Kung hunters and gatherers. *Science, 207,* 788–791.

Kopp, C. B. (1982). Antecedents of self-regulation: A developmental perspective. *Developmental Psychology, 18,* 199–214.

Kopp, C. B., & Wyer, N. (1994). Self-regulation in normal and atypical development. In D. Cicchetti & S. L. Toth (Eds.), *Rochester symposium on developmental psychopathology: Vol. 5. Disorders and dysfunctions of the self* (pp. 31–56). Rochester, NY: University of Rochester Press.

Kotch, J. B., Blakely, C. H., Brown, S. S., & Wong, F. Y. (Eds.). (1992). *A pound of prevention: The case for universal maternity care in the US.* Washington, DC: American Public Health Association.

Kreutzer, M. A., Leonard, C., & Flavell, J. H. (1975). An interview study of children's knowledge about memory. *Monographs of the Society for Research in Child Development, 40* (Serial No. 159).

Kroger, J. (1983). A developmental study of identity formation among late adolescent and adult women. *Psychological Documents, 13* (Ms. No. 2537).

Kruger, A. C. (1992). The effect of peer and adult-child transductive discussions on moral reasoning. *Merrill-Palmer Quarterly, 38,* 191–211.

Kruger, A. C., & Tomasello, M. (1986). Transactive discussions with peers and adults. *Developmental Psychology, 22,* 681–685.

Krumboltz, J. D. (1966). Behavioral goals for counseling. *Journal of Counseling Psychology, 13,* 153–159.

Kubler-Ross, E. (1969). *On death and dying.* New York: Macmillan.

Kubler-Ross, E. (1974). *Questions and answers on death and dying.* New York: Macmillan.

Kuczynski, L. (1984). Socialization goals and mother-child interaction: Strategies for long-term and short-term compliance. *Developmental Psychology, 20,* 1061–1073.

Kuhl, P. K., Williams, K. A., Lacerda, F., Stevens, K. N., & Lindblom, B. (1992). Linguistic experience alters phonetic perception in infants by 6 months of age. *Science, 255,* 606–608.

Kuhn, D. (1989). Children and adults as intuitive scientists. *Psychological Review, 96,* 674–689.

Kuhn, D. (1991). *The skills of argument.* Cambridge: Cambridge University Press.

Kuhn, D. (1992). Thinking as argument. *Harvard Educational Review, 62,* 155–178.

Kuhn, D. (2000). Does memory development belong on an endangered topic list? *Child Development, 71,* 21–25.

Kuhn, D., Amsel, E., & O'Loughlin, M. (1988). *The development of scientific reasoning skills.* New York: Academic Press.

Kuhn, D., Garcia-Mila, M., Zohar, A., & Andersen, C. (1995). Strategies of knowledge acquisition. *Monographs of the Society for Research in Child Development, 60* (Serial No. 245).

Kuhn, D., Pennington, N., & Leadbeater, B. (1982). Adult thinking in developmental perspective. In P. B. Baltes & O. Brim (Eds.), *Life span development and behavior* (pp. 157–195). New York: Academic Press.

Kuhn, D., Schauble, L., & Garcia-Mila, M. (1992). Cross-domain development of scientific reasoning. *Cognition and Instruction, 9,* 285–327.

Kupersmidt, J. B., Burchinal, M., & Patterson, C. J. (1995). Developmental patterns of childhood peer relations as predictors of externalizing problems in adolescence. *Child Development, 61,* 1350–1362.

Kurdek, L. A. (1993). Predicting marital dissolution: A 5-year prospective longitudinal study of newlywed couples. *Journal of Personality and Social Psychology, 64,* 221–242.

Kurtz, B. E., Scheider, W., Carr, M., Borkowski, J. G., & Rellinger, E. (1990). Strategy instruction and attributional beliefs in West Germany and the United States: Do teachers foster metacognitive development? *Contemporary Educational Psychology, 15,* 268–283.

Labouvie-Vief, G. (1984). Logic and self regulation from youth to maturity: A model. In M. L. Commons, F. A. Richards, & C. Armon (Eds.), *Beyond formal operations: Late adolescent and adult cognitive development* (pp. 158–179). New York: Praeger.

Labouvie-Vief, G., Chiodo, L. M., Goguen, L. A., Diehl, M., & Orwoll, L. (1995). Representations of self across the life span. *Psychology and Aging, 10,* 404–415.

Lacasa, P., & Villuendas, D. (1990). Adult-child and peer relationship: Action, representation, and learning process. *Learning and Instruction, 2,* 75–93.

Ladd, G. W., & Asher, S. R. (1985). Social skills training and children's peer relations. In L. L'Abate & M. Milan (Eds.), *Handbook of social skills training and research* (pp. 219–244). New York: Wiley.

Ladd, G. W., & Burgess, K. B. (1999). Charting the relationship trajectories of aggressive, withdrawn, and aggressive/withdrawn children during early grade school. *Child Development, 70,* 910–929.

Ladd, G. W., & Ladd, B. K. (1998). Parenting behaviors and parent-child relationships: Correlates of peer victimization in kindergarten? *Developmental Psychology, 34,* 1450–1458.

Ladd, G. W., & Mize, J. (1983). A cognitive-social learning model of social skills training. *Psychological Review, 90,* 127–157.

La Freniere, P., Stayer, F. F., and Gauthier, R. (1984). The emergence of same-sex affiliative preferences among preschool peers: A developmental/ethological perspective. *Child Development, 55,* 1958–1965.

Lahey, B., Loeber, R., Quay, H. C., Frick, P. J., & Grimm, J. (1992). Oppositional defiant and conduct disorders: Issues to be resolved for DSM-IV. *Journal of the American Academy of Child and Adolescent Psychiatry, 31,* 539–546.

Lamb, M. E., & Sternberg, K. J. (1990). Do we really know how day care affects children? *Journal of Applied Developmental Psychology, 11,* 352–379.

Lamborn, S. D., Dornbusch, S. M., & Steinberg, L. (1996). Ethnicity and community context as moderators of the relations between family decision making and adolescent adjustment. *Child Development, 67,* 283–301.

Lamborn, S. D., Mounts, N. S., Steinberg, L., & Dornbusch, S. M. (1991). Patterns of competence and adjustment among adolescents from authoritative, authoritarian, indulgent, and neglectful families. *Child Development, 62,* 1049–1065.

Landale, N. S., & Fennelly, K. (1992). Informal unions among mainland Puerto Ricans: Cohabitation or an alternative to legal marriage? *Journal of Marriage and the Family, 54,* 269–280.

Lang, F. R., & Carstensen, L. L. (1994). Close emotional relationships in late life: Further support for proactive aging in the social domain. *Psychology and Aging, 9,* 315–324.

Langlois, J. H., Ritter, J. M., Casey, R. J., & Savin, D. B. (1995). Infant attractiveness predicts maternal behaviors and attitudes. *Developmental Psychology, 31,* 164–172.

Langlois, J. H., & Stephan, C. W. (1981). Beauty and the beast: The role of physical attraction in peer relationships and social behavior. In S. S. Brehm, S. M. Kassin, & S. X.

Gibbans (Eds.), *Developmental social psychology: Theory and research* (pp. 152–168). New York: Oxford University Press.

Lapsley, D. K. (1993). Toward an integrated theory of adolescent ego development: The "new look" at adolescent egocentrism. *American Journal of Orthopsychiatry, 63,* 562–571.

Lapsley, D. K., FitzGerald, D. P., Rice, K. G., & Jackson, S. (1989). Separation-individuation and the "new look" at the imaginary audience and personal fable: A test of an integrative model. *Journal of Adolescent Research, 4,* 483–505.

Lapsley, D. K., & Murphy, M. N. (1985). Another look at the theoretical assumptions of adolescent egocentrism. *Developmental Review, 5,* 201–217.

Larrieu, J. A., & Mussen, P. (1986). Some personality and motivational correlates of children's prosocial behavior. *Journal of Genetic Psychology, 147,* 529–542.

Larsen, S. F. (2000). Memorable books: Recall of reading in its personal context. In M. S. MacNealey & R. Kreuz (Eds.), *Empirical approaches to literature and aesthetics: Advances in discourse processes: Vol. 52* (pp. 583–599). Norwood, NJ: Ablex.

Larson, R., & Richards, M. H. (1994). *Divergent realities: The emotional lives of mothers, fathers, and adolescents.* New York: Basic Books.

Lasch, C. (1991). *The true and only heaven: Progress and its critics.* New York: Norton.

Laub, J. H. (1999). Alterations in the opportunity structure: A criminological perspective. In A. Booth, A. C. Crouter, & M. J. Shanahan (Eds.), *Transitions to adulthood in a changing economy: No work, no family, no future?* (pp. 48–55). Westport, CT: Praeger.

Laursen, B. M., Coy, K. C., & Collins, W. A. (1998). Reconsidering changes in parent-child conflict across adolescence: A meta-analysis. *Child Development, 69,* 817–832.

Laver, G. D., & Burke, D. M. (1993). Why do semantic priming effects increase in old age? A meta-analysis. *Psychology and Aging, 8,* 34–43.

Lay, K. L., Waters, E., & Parke, K. A. (1989). Maternal responsiveness and child compliance: The role of mood as a mediator. *Child Development, 60,* 1405–1411.

Leaper, C. (1991). Influence and involvement in children's discourse: Age, gender, and partner effects. *Child Development, 62,* 797–811.

Leaper, C. (1994a). Exploring the consequences of gender segregation on social relationships. In C. Leaper (Ed.), *Childhood gender segregation: Causes and consequences.* (pp. 67–68). San Francisco: Jossey-Bass.

Leaper, C. (1994b). Exploring the correlates and consequences of gender segregation: Social relationships in childhood, adolescence, and adulthood. In B. Damon (Series Ed.) & C. Leaper (Vol. Ed.), *New directions for child development. The development of gender relationships.* San Francisco: Jossey-Bass.

Leaper, C., Anderson, K. J., & Sanders, P. (1998). Moderators of gender effects on parents' talk to their children. *Developmental Psychology, 34,* 3–27.

L'Ecuyer, R. (1992). An experimental-developmental framework and methodology to study the transformations of the self-concept from infancy to old age. In T. M. Brinthaupt & R. P. Lipka (Eds.), *The self: Definitional and methodological issues* (pp. 96–136). Albany State University of New York Press.

Lederman, R. P. (1996). Relationship of anxiety, stress, and psychosocial development to reproductive health. *Behavioral Medicine, 21,* 101–112.

LeDoux, J. (1996). *The emotional brain: The mysterious underpinnings of emotional life.* New York: Simon & Schuster.

LeDoux, J. E. (1995). Emotion: Clues from the brain. *Annual Review of Psychology, 46,* 209–236.

LeDoux, J. E. (2002). *Synaptic self: How our brains become who we are.* New York: Viking.

Lee, J. A. (1973). *The colors of love: An exploration of the ways of loving.* Don Mills, Ontario, Canada: New Press.

Lehman, D. R., Lempert, R. O., & Nisbett, R. E. (1988). The effects of graduate training on reasoning. *American Psychologist, 43,* 431–442.

Leibowitz, S. F., Hammer, N. J. & Chang, K. (1981). Hypothalamic paraventricular nucleus lesions produce overeating and obesity in the rat. *Physiology and Behavior, 27,* 1031–1040.

Leichtman, M. D., & Ceci, S. J. (1995). The effects of stereotypes and suggestions on preschoolers' reports. *Developmental Psychology, 31,* 568–578.

Leinbach, M. D., & Fagot, B. I. (1986). Acquisition of gender labeling: A test for toddlers. *Sex Roles, 15,* 655–666.

Leinbach, M. D., & Fagot, B. I. (1993). Categorical habituation to male and female faces: Gender schematic processing in infancy. *Infant Behavior and Development, 16,* 317–332.

Leitenberg, H., Greenwald, E., & Tarran, M. J. (1989). The relation between sexual activity among children during preadolescence and in early adolescence and sexual behavior and sexual adjustment in young adulthood. *Archives of Sexual Behavior, 18,* 299–313.

Leming, J. S. (1986). Kohlbergian programs in moral education: A practical review and assessment. In S. Modgil & C. Modgil (Eds.), *Lawrence Kohlberg: Consensus and controversy* (pp. 245–262, 275–276). Philadelphia: Falmer Press.

Leming, J. S. (1997). Whither goes character education? Objectives, pedagogy, and research in education programs. *Journal of Education, 179,* 11–34.

Leonard, S. P., & Archer, J. (1989). A naturalistic investigation of gender constancy in three- and four-year-old children. *British Journal of Developmental Psychology, 7,* 341–346.

Lepore, S. J., & Sesco, B. (1994). Distorting children's reports and interpretations of events through suggestion. *Applied Psychology, 79,* 108–120.

Lerner, M. J. (1980). *The belief in a just world: A fundamental delusion*. New York: Plenum.

Lerner, R. M. (1996). Relative plasticity, integration, temporality, and diversity in human development: A developmental contextual perspective about theory, process, and method. *Developmental Psychology, 32*, 781–786.

Lerner, R. M. (1998). Theories of human development: Contemporary perspectives. In W. Damon (Series Ed.) & R. M. Lerner (Vol. Ed.), *Handbook of child psychology: Vol. 1. Theoretical models of human development* (5th ed., pp. 1–24). New York: Wiley.

Lester, B. M., Freier, K., & LaGasse, L. (1995). Prenatal cocaine exposure and child outcome: What do we really know? In M. Lewis & M. Bendersky (Eds.), *Mothers, babies, and cocaine: The role of toxins in development* (pp. 19–39). Hillsdale, NJ: Erlbaum.

Leukowicz, D. J. (1988). Sensory dominance in infants. 1. Six-month-old infant's response to auditory-visual compounds. *Developmental Psychology, 54*, 155–171.

LeVay, S. (1991). A difference in hypothalamic structure between heterosexual and homosexual men. *Science, 253*, 1034–1037.

LeVay, S. (1996). *Queer Science: The use and abuse of research into homosexuality*. Cambridge, MA: MIT Press.

Levenson, R. W., Carstensen, L. L., & Gottman, J. M. (1993). Long-term marriage: Age, gender, and satisfaction. *Psychology and Aging, 8*, 301–313.

Levenson, R. W., Carstensen, L. L., & Gottman, J. M. (1994). Marital interaction in old and middle-age long-term marriages: Physiology, affect, and their interrelations. *Journal of Personality and Social Psychology, 67*, 56–68.

Lever, J. (1978). Sex differences in the complexity of children's play and games. *American Sociological Review, 43*, 471–483.

Levin, J. & McDevitt, J. (1993). *Hate crimes: The rising tide of bigotry*. New York: Plenum Press.

Levine, S. (1969). Infantile stimulation: A perspective. In A. Ambrose (Ed.), *Stimulation in early infancy* (pp. 3–19). N. Y.: Academic Press.

Levinson, D. J. (1986). A conception of adult development. *American Psychologist, 41*, 3–13.

Levinson, D. J., & Levinson, J. D. (1996). *The seasons of a woman's life*. New York: Knopf.

Levinson, D. J., Darrow, C. N., Klein, E. B., Levinson, M. H., & McKee, B. (1978). *The seasons of a man's life*. New York: Knopf.

Levy, S. R., Stoessner, S. J., & Dweck, C. S. (1998). Stereotype formation and endorsement: The role of implicit theories. *Journal of Personality and Social Psychology, 74*, 1421–1436.

Levy-Shiff, R. (1994). Individual and contextual correlates of marital change across the transition to parenthood. *Developmental Psychology, 30*, 591–601.

Levy-Shiff, R., Goldshmidt, I., & Har-Even, D. (1991). Transition to parenthood in adoptive families. *Developmental Psychology, 27*, 131–140.

Lewis, M. (1993). The emergence of human emotions. In M. Lewis & J. Haviland (Eds.), *Handbook of emotions*, (pp. 563–573). New York: Guilford Press.

Lewis, M. (1994). Myself and me. In S. T. Parker, R. W. Mitchell, & M. L. Boccia (Eds.), *Self-awareness in animals and humans: Developmental perspectives* (pp. 20–34). New York: Cambridge University Press.

Lewis, M., & Brooks-Gunn, J. (1979). *Social cognition and the acquisition of the self*. New York: Plenum.

Lewis, M., & Michalson, L. (1983). *Children's emotions and moods: Developmental theory and measurement*. New York: Plenum Press.

Lewis, R. A., & Lin, L. W. (1996). Adults and their midlife parents. In N. Vanzetti & S. Duck (Eds.), *A lifetime of relationships* (pp. 364–382). Pacific Grove, CA: Brooks/Cole.

Lewkowicz, D. J., & Turkewitz, G. (1980). Cross-modal equivalence in early infancy: Auditory-visual intensity matching. *Developmental Psychology, 16*, 597–607.

Lewkowicz, D. J., & Turkewitz, G. (1981). Intersensory interaction in newborns: Modification of visual preferences following exposure to sound. *Child Development, 52*, 827–832.

Liben, L. S., & Signorella, M. L. (1980). Gender-related schemata and constructive memory in children. *Child Development, 57*, 11–18.

Liben, L. S., & Signorella, M. L. (1993). Gender-schematic processing in children: The role of initial interpretations of stimuli. *Developmental Psychology, 29*, 141–149.

Liben, L. S., Bigler, R. S., & Krogh, H. R. (2002). Language at work: Children's gendered interpretations of occupational titles. *Child Development, 73*, 810–828.

Lickona, T. (1998, February). A more complex analysis is needed. *Phi Delta Kappan, 79*, 449–454.

Lieberman, M. A. (1965). Psychological correlates of impending death: Some preliminary observations. *Journal of Gerontology, 20*, 181–190.

Light, P., Littleton, K., Messer, D., & Joiner, R. (1994). Social and communicative processes in computer based problem solving. *European Journal of Psychology of Education, 9*, 93–109.

Lincoln, Y. S., & Guba, E. G. (1985). *Naturalistic inquiry*. Beverly Hills: Sage.

Lindsay, P. (1984). High school size, participation in activities, and young adult social participation: Some enduring effects of schooling. *Educational Evaluation and Policy Analysis, 6*, 73–83.

Locke, J. L. (1993). *The child's path to spoken language*. Cambridge, MA: Harvard University Press.

Loeber, R., Wung, P., Keenan, K., Giroux, B., Stouthamer-Loeber, M., VanKammen, W. B., & Maugham, B. (1993). Developmental pathways in disruptive child behavior. *Developmental Psychopathology, 5*, 103–133.

Loevinger, J. (1976). *Ego development: Conception and theory*. San Francisco: Jossey-Bass.

Loftus, E. F. (1979). *Eyewitness testimony*. Cambridge, MA: Harvard University Press.

Lomax, E. M. R., Kagan, J., & Rosenkrantz, B. G. (1978). *Science and patterns of child care*. San Francisco: Freeman.

Looft, W. R. (1972). Egocentrism and social interaction across the lifespan. *Psychological Bulletin, 78,* 73–92.

Lopez, F. G., & Brennan, K. A. (2000). Dynamic processes underlying adult attachment organization: Toward an attachment theoretical perspective on the healthy and effective self. *Journal of Counseling Psychology, 47,* 283–300.

Lund, D. A., Dimond, M. F., Caserta, M. S., Johnson, R. J., Poulton, J. L., & Connelly, J. R. (1985–1986). Identifying elderly with coping difficulties after two years of bereavement. *Omega, 16,* 213–224.

Lyddon, W. J. (1990). First- and second-order change: Implications for rationalist and constructivist cognitive therapies. *Journal of Counseling and Development, 69,* 122–127.

Lyddon, W. J. (1995). Forms and facts of constructivism. In R. A. Neimeyer & M. J. Neimeyer (Eds.), *Constructivism in psychotherapy* (pp. 69–92). Washington, DC: American Psychological Association.

Lynch, T. (1998). *Still life in Milford*. New York: Norton.

Lynn, J. (2000). Learning to care for people with chronic illness facing the end of life. *Journal of the American Medical Association, 284,* 2508–2513.

Lyons, M., True, W. R., Eisen, S. A., Goldberg, J., Meyer, J. M., Faraone, S. V., Eaves, L. J., & Tsuang, M. T. (1995). Differential heritability of adult and juvenile antisocial traits. *Archives of General Psychiatry, 52,* 906–915.

Lyons-Ruth, K., Connell, D. B., Grunebaum, H. U., & Botein, S. (1990). Infants at social risk: Maternal depression and family support services as mediators of infant development and security of attachment. *Child Development, 61,* 85–98.

Lyons-Ruth, K., Repacholi, B., McLeod, S., & Silva, E. (1991). Disorganized attachment behavior in infancy: Short-term stability, maternal and infant correlates, and risk-related subtypes. *Development and Psychopathology, 3,* 377–396.

Lytton, H. (1990). Child and parent effects in boys' conduct disorder: A reinterpretation. *Developmental Psychology, 26,* 683–697.

Lytton, H., & Romney, D. M. (1991). Parents' differential socialization of boys and girls: A meta-analysis. *Psychological Bulletin, 109,* 267–296.

Lyubomirsky, S. (2001). Why are some people happier than others? The role of cognitive and motivational processes in well-being. *American Psychologist, 56,* 239–249.

Maccoby, E. E. (1990). Gender and relationships: A developmental account. *American Psychologist, 45,* 513–520.

Maccoby, E. E. (1994). The role of parents in the socialization of children: An historical overview. In R. Parke, P. Ornstein, J. Rieser, & C. Zahn-Waxler (Eds.), *A century of developmental psychology* (pp. 589–615). Washington, DC: American Psychological Association.

Maccoby, E. E. (1998). *The two sexes: Growing up apart, coming together*. Cambridge, MA: Belknap Press of Harvard University Press.

Maccoby, E. E., & Jacklin, C. N. (1974). *The psychology of sex differences*. Stanford, CA: Stanford University Press.

Maccoby, E. E., & Jacklin, C. N. (1987). Gender segregation in childhood. In H. Reese (Ed.), *Advances in child behavior and development* (pp. 239–288). New York: Academic Press.

Maccoby, E. E., & Martin, J. A. (1983). Socialization in the context of the family: Parent-child interaction. In P. H. Mussen (Series Ed.) & E. M. Hetherington (Vol. Ed.), *Handbook of child psychology: Vol. 4. Socialization, personality and social development* (4th ed., pp. 1–101). New York: Wiley.

MacDonald, K. B., & Parke, R. D. (1986). Parent-child physical play: The effects of sex and age of children and parents. *Sex Roles, 7–8,* 367–379.

MacKay, D. G., & Abrams, L. (1996). Language, memory, and aging: Distributed deficits and the structure of new-versus-old connections. In J. E. Birren & K. W. Schaie (Series Eds.), R. P. Abeles, M. Gatz, & T. A. Salthouse (Vol. Eds.), *Handbook of the psychology of aging* (4th ed., pp. 287–307). San Diego, CA: Academic Press.

MacLean, P. D. (1952). Some psychiatric implications of the physiological studies on the frontotemporal portion of the limbic system. *Electroencephalography and Clinical Neurophysiology, 4,* 407–418.

MacLean, P. D. (1970). The triune brain, emotion, and scientific basis. In F. O. Schmidt (Ed.), *The Neurosciences: Second study program* (pp. 336–349). New York: Rockefeller University Press.

Maggs, J. L., Almeida, D. M., & Galambos, N. L. (1995). Risky business: The paradoxical meaning of problem behavior for young adolescents. *Journal of Early Adolescence, 15,* 344–362.

Mahler, M. S., Pine, F., & Bergman, A. (1975). *The psychological birth of the human infant: Symbiosis and individuation*. New York: Basic Books.

Mahoney, J. L. (2000). School extracurricular activity participation as a moderator in the development of antisocial patterns. *Child Development, 71,* 502–516.

Mahoney, M. J. (1993). Introduction to special section: Theoretical development in the cognitive psychotherapies. *Journal of Consulting and Clinical Psychology, 61,* 187–193.

Mahoney, M. J. (Ed.). (1995). *Cognitive and constructive psychotherapies*. New York: Springer.

Main, M. (1996). Overview of the field of attachment. *Journal of Consulting and Clinical Psychology, 64,* 237–243.

Main, M. (1999). Epilogue: Attachment theory: Eighteen points with suggestions for future studies. In J. Cassidy & P. R. Shaver (Eds.), *Handbook of attachment: Theory, research, and clinical applications* (pp. 845–887). New York: Guilford Press.

Main, M., & George, C. (1985). Responses of abused and disadvantaged toddlers to distress in agemates: A study in the day care setting. *Developmental Psychology, 21,* 407–412.

Main, M., & Goldwyn, R. (1984). Predicting rejection of her infant from mother's representation of her own experience: Implications for the abused-abusing intergenerational cycle. *International Journal of Child Abuse and Neglect, 8,* 203–217.

Main, M., & Goldwyn, R. (1985–1994). *Adult attachment classification system.* Unpublished manuscript, University of California Berkeley.

Main, M., & Hesse, E. (1990). Parents' unresolved traumatic experiences are related to infant disorganized attachment status: Is frightened and/or frightening parental behavior the linking mechanism? In M. Greenberg, D. Cicchetti, E. M. Cummings (Eds.), *Attachment in the preschool years* (pp. 161–182). Chicago: University of Chicago Press.

Main, M., Kaplan, N., & Cassidy, J. (1985). Security in infancy, childhood, and adulthood: A move to the level of representation. In I. Bretherton & E. Waters (Eds.), Growing points of attachment theory and research. *Monographs of the Society for Research in Child Development, 50,* (Serial No. 209), 55–104.

Main, M., & Soloman, J. (1990). Procedures for identifying infants as disorganized/disoriented during the Ainsworth Strange Situation. In M. Greenberg, D. Cicchetti, & E. M. Cummings (Eds.), *Attachment in the preschool years: Theory, research, and intervention* (pp. 121–160). Chicago: University of Chicago Press.

Malina, R. M. (1983). Menarche in athletes: A synthesis and hypothesis. *Annals of Human Biology, 10,* 1–24.

Malina, R. M. (1990). Physical growth and performance during the transitional years (9–16). In R. Montemayer, G. R. Adams, & T. P. Gullotta (Eds.), *From childhood to adolescence: A transitional period?* (pp. 41–62). Newbury Park, CA: Sage.

Mandler, J. M. (1998). Representation. In W. Damon (Series Ed.), D. Kuhn, & R. S. Siegler (Vol. Eds.), *Handbook of child psychology: Vol. 2. Cognition, perception, and language* (5th ed., pp. 255–308). New York: Wiley.

Mangelsdorf, S., Gunnar, M., Kestenbaum, R., Lang, S., & Andreas, D. (1990). Infant proneness-to-distress temperament, maternal personality, and mother-infant attachment: Associations and goodness of fit. *Child Development, 61,* 820–831.

Mansfield, E. D., & McAdams, D. P. (1996). Generativity and themes of agency and communion in adult autobiography. *Personality and Social Psychology Bulletin, 22,* 721–731.

Marcia, J. E. (1964). *Determination and construct validity of ego identity status.* Unpublished doctoral dissertation, University of California at Davis, CA.

Marcia, J. E. (1966). Development and validation of ego identity status. *Journal of Personality and Social Psychology, 3,* 551–558.

Marcia, J. E. (1967). Ego identity status: Relationship to change in self-esteem, "general maladjustment," and authoritarianism. *Journal of Personality, 35,* 118–133.

Marcia, J. E. (1980). Identity in adolescence. In J. Adelson (Ed.), *Handbook of Adolescent Psychology* (pp. 159–187). New York: Wiley.

Marcia, J. E. (1989). Identity and intervention. *Journal of Intervention, 12,* 401–410.

Marcia, J. E. (1993). The status of the statuses: Research review. In J. E. Marcia, A. S. Waterman, D. R. Matteson, S. L. Archer, & J. L. Orlofsky, (Eds.). *Ego identity: A handbook for psychosocial research* (pp. 22–41). New York: Springer-Verlag.

Marcia, J. E., & Friedman, M. L. (1970). Ego identity status in college women. *Journal of Personality, 38,* 249–263.

Marcia, J. E., Waterman, A. S., Matteson, D. R., Archer, S. L., & Orlofsky, J. L. (1993). *Ego identity: A handbook for psychosocial research.* New York: Springer-Verlag.

Marco, C. A., & Suls, J. (1993). Daily stress and the trajectory of mood: Spillover, response assimilation contrast, and negative affectivity. *Journal of Personality and Social Psychology, 64,* 1053–1063.

Marcus, R. F. (1975). The child as elicitor of parental sanctions for independent and dependent behavior: A simulation of parent-child interaction. *Developmental Psychology, 11,* 443–452.

Marcus, R. F. (1976). The effects of children's emotional and instrumental dependent behavior on parental response. *Journal of Psychology, 92,* 57–63.

Markman, H. J., Stanley, S., & Blumberg, S. L. (1994). *Fighting for your marriage: Positive steps for preventing divorce and preserving a lasting love.* San Francisco: Jossey-Bass.

Markus, H. (1977). Self-schemata and processing information about the self. *Journal of Personality and Social Psychology, 35,* 63–78.

Markus, H., Crane, M., Bernstein, S., & Siladi, M. (1982). Self-schemas and gender. *Journal of Personality and Social Psychology, 42,* 38–50.

Markus, H., & Kitayama, S. (1991). Culture and the self: Implications for cognition, emotion, and motivation. *Psychological Review, 98,* 224–253.

Markus, H., & Kitayama, S. (1991). Culture and the self: Implications for cognition, emotion, and motivation. *Psychological Review, 41,* 954–969.

Markus, H., & Nurius, P. (1986). Possible selves. *American Psychologist, 41,* 954–969.

Marsh, H. W. (1990). The structure of academic self-concept: The Marsh/Shavelson model. *Journal of Educational Psychology, 82,* 623–636.

Marsh, H. W. (1994). Using the National Longitudinal Study of 1988 to evaluate theoretical models of self-concept: The Self-Description Questionnaire. *Journal of Educational Psychology, 86,* 107–116.

Marsh, H. W., & Hattie, J. (1996). Theoretical perspectives on the structure of the self-concept. In B. A. Bracken (Ed.), *Handbook of self-concept* (pp. 38–90). New York: Wiley.

Marsh, H. W., & Roche, L. A. (1996). Structure of artistic self-concepts for performing arts and non-performing arts students in a performing arts high school: "Setting the stage" with multigroup confirmatory factor analysis. *Journal of Educational Psychology, 88,* 461–477.

Marsh, H. W., & Shavelson, R. (1985). Self-concept: Its multi-faceted, hierarchical structure. *Educational Psychologist, 20,* 107–123.

Marsiskei, M., Lang, F. R., Baltes, M. M., & Baltes, P. B. (1995). Selective optimization with compensation: Life-span perspectives on successful human development. In R. A. Dixon & L. Backman (Eds.), *Compensation for psychological defects and declines: Managing losses and promoting gains* (pp. 35–79). Hillsdale, NJ: Erlbaum.

Martel, J. G. (1974). *Smashed potatoes: A kid's-eye view of the kitchen.* Boston, MA: Houghton Mifflin.

Martin, C. L., & Fabes, R. A. (2001). The stability and consequences of young children's same-sex peer interactions. *Developmental Psychology, 37,* 431–446.

Martin, C. L., & Little, J. K. (1990). The relation of gender understanding to children's sex-typed preferences and gender stereotypes. *Child Development, 61,* 1427–1439.

Martinson, I. M., Davies, B., & McClowry, S. (1991). Parental depression following death of a child. *Death Studies, 15,* 259–267.

Martire, L. M., Stephens, M. A. P., & Townsend, A. L. (1998). Emotional support and well-being of midlife women: Role-specific mastery as a mediational mechanism. *Psychology and Aging, 13,* 196–404.

Marx, K., & Engels, F. (1972). The German ideology. In R. C. Tucker, (Ed.), *The Marx-Engels reader.* New York: Norton. (Original work published 1846)

Masangkay, Z. S., McCluskey, K. A., McIntyre, C. W., Sims-Knight, J., Vaughn, B. E., & Flavell, J. H. (1974). The early development of inferences about the visual percepts of others. *Child Development, 45,* 237–246.

Maslow, A. H. (1954). *Motivation and personality.* New York: Harper & Row.

Masters, W. H., Johnson, V. E., & Kolodny, R. C. (1988). *Human sexuality.* (3rd ed.). Boston: Little Brown.

Matteson, D. R. (1993). Differences within and between genders: A challenge to the theory. In J. E. Marcia, A. S. Waterman, D. R. Matteson, S. L. Archer, & J. L. Orlofsky, (Eds.), *Ego identity: A handbook for psychosocial research* (pp. 69–110). New York: Springer-Verlag.

Mattson, S. N., Riley, E. P., Gramling, L., Delis, D. C., & Jones, K. L. (1998). Neuropsychological comparison of alcohol-exposed children with or without physical features of fetal-alcohol syndrome. *Neuropsychology, 12,* 146–153.

Mau, W. (1995). Educational planning and academic achievement of middle school students: A racial and cultural comparison. *Journal of Counseling & Development, 73,* 518–526.

May, R. (1979). *Psychology and the human dilemma.* New York: Norton.

Mayer, J. D., & Cobb, C. D. (2000). Educational policy on emotional intelligence. Does it make sense? *Educational Psychology Review, 12,* 163–183.

McAdams, D. P. (1985). *Power, intimacy, and the life story: Personalogical inquiries into identity.* New York: Guilford.

McAdams, D. P. (1993). *The stories we live by: Personal myths and the making of the self.* New York: Morrow.

McAdams, D. P. (2000). Attachment, intimacy, and generativity. *Psychological Inquiry, 11,* 117–120.

McAdams, D. P., & Bowman, P. J. (2001). Narrating life's turning points: Redemption and contamination. In D. P. McAdams, R. Josselson, & A. Lieblich (Eds.), *Turns in the road: Narrative studies of lives in transition* (pp. 3–34). Washington, DC: American Psychological Association.

McAdams, D. P., & de St. Aubin, E. (1992). A theory of generativity and its assessment through self-report, behavioral acts, and narrative themes in autobiography. *Journal of Personality and Social Psychology, 62,* 1003–1015.

McAdams, D. P., de St. Aubin, E., & Logan, R. L. (1993). Generativity among young, midlife, and older adults. *Psychology and Aging, 8,* 221–230.

McAdams, D. P., Hart, H. M., & Maruna, S. (1998). The anatomy of generativity. In D. P. McAdams & E. de St. Aubin (Eds.), *Generativity and adult development: How and why we care for the next generation* (pp. 7–44). Washington, DC: American Psychological Association.

McAuliffe, G. J. (1993). Constructive development and career transition: Implications for counseling. *Journal of Counseling & Development, 72,* 23–28.

McBride, S. L., & DiCero, K. (1990). Separation: Maternal and child perspectives. In N. Lauter-Klatell (Ed.) *Readings in child development.* Mountain View, CA: Mayfield Publishing Company.

McClellan, B. E. (1992). *Schools and the shaping of character: Moral education in America, 1607–present.* Bloomington, IN: ERIC Clearinghouse for Social Studies/Social Science Education and the Social Studies Development Center.

McConnell, S. R., & Odom, S. L. (1986). Sociometrics: Peer-referenced measures and the assessment of social competence. In P. S. Strain, M. J. Guralnick, & H. M. Walker (Eds.), *Children's social behavior: Development, assessment, and modification* (pp. 215–284). New York: Academic Press.

McCrae, R. R., & Costa, P. T. (1990). *Personality in adulthood.* New York: Guilford Press.

McCrae, R. R., & Costa, P. T. (1999). A five-factor theory of personality. In L. Pervin & O. P. John (Eds.), *Handbook of Personality* (2nd ed., pp. 139–153). New York: Guilford Press.

McCrae, R. R., Costa, P. T., Ostendorf, F., Angleitner, A., Hrebickova, M., Avia, J., Sanchez-Bernardos, M., Kusdil, M. E., Woodfield, R., Saunders, P. R., & Smith, P. B. (2000). Nature over nurture: Temperament, personality and life span development. *Journal of Personality and Social Psychology, 78,* 173–186.

McCrae, R. R., Costa, P. T., Pedroso de Lima, M., Simoes, A., Ostendorf, F., Angleitner, A., Marusic, I., Bratko, D., Caprara, G., Bararanelli, C., Chae, J., & Piedmont, R. L. (1999). Age differences in personality across the adult life span: Parallels in five cultures. *Developmental Psychology, 35,* 466–477.

McCrae, R. R., & John, O. T. (1992). An introduction to the five-factor model and its applications. *Journal of Personality, 60,* 175–215.

McCue, M. (1994). Why developmental psychology should find room for behavioral genetics. In C. A. Nelson (Ed.), *Minnesota Symposium on Child Psychology: Vol. 27. Threats to optimal development: Integrating biological, psychological, and social risk factors* (pp. 105–119). Hillsdale, NJ: Erlbaum.

McCue, M., Bacon, S., & Lykken, D. T. (1993). Personality stability and change in early adulthood: A behavioral genetic analysis. *Developmental Psychology, 29,* 96–109.

McEwen, B. S., & Sapolsky, R. M. (1995). Stress and cognitive function. *Current Opinion in Neurobiology, 5,* 205–216.

McGuffin, P., Riley, B., & Plomin, R. (2001). Toward behavioral genomics. *Science, 291,* 1232–1233.

McLanahan, S. S., & Sandefur, G. (1994). *Growing up with a single parent: What hurts, what helps.* Cambridge, MA: Harvard University Press.

McLane, J. B. (1987). Interaction, context, and the zone of proximal development. In M. Hickmann (Ed.), *Social and functional approaches to language and thought* (pp. 267–285). Orlando, FL: Academic Press.

McLoyd, V. C. (1990). The impact of economic hardship on black families and children: Psychological distress, parenting, and socioemotional development. *Child Development, 61,* 311–436.

Mead, G. H. (1934). *Mind, self, and society.* Chicago: University of Chicago Press.

Means, M., & Voss, J. (1985). Star wars: A developmental study of expert and novice knowledge structures. *Memory and Language, 24,* 746–757.

Meeus, W. (1996). Studies on identity development in adolescence: An overview of research and some new data. *Journal of Youth and Adolescence, 25,* 569–597.

Meeus, W., & Dekovic, M. (1995). Identity development, parental and peer support in adolescence: Results of a national Dutch study. *Adolescence, 30,* 931–944.

Meeus, W., Iedema, J., Helsen, M., & Vollebergh, W. (1999). Patterns of adolescent identity development: Review of literature and longitudinal analysis. *Developmental Review, 19,* 419–461.

Meichenbaum, D. (1986). Cognitive behavior modification. In F. Kanfer & A. Goldstein (Eds.), *Helping people change: A textbook of methods* (3rd ed., pp. 346–380). New York: Pergamon.

Meichenbaum, D. H., & Goodman, J. (1971). Training impulsive children to talk to themselves: A means for self-control. *Journal of Abnormal Psychology, 77,* 115–126.

Meir, E. I. (1989). Integrative elaboration of the congruence theory. *Journal of Vocational Behavior, 35,* 219–230.

Meisel, A., Snyder, L., & Quill, T. (2000). Seven legal barriers to end-of-life care: Myths, realities, and grains of truth.

Journal of the American Medical Association, 284, 2495–2501.

Meltzoff, A. N. (1988). Infant imitation and memory: Nine-month-old infants in immediate and deferred tests. *Child Development, 59,* 217–225.

Meltzoff, A. N. (1990). Foundations for developing a concept of self: The role of imitation in relating self to other and the value of social mirroring, social modeling, and self practice in infancy. In D. Cicchetti & M. Beeghly (Eds.), *The self in transition: Infancy to childhood* (pp. 139–164). Chicago: University of Chicago Press.

Meltzoff, A. N., & Borton, R. W. (1979). Intermodal matching by human neonates. *Nature, 282,* 403–404.

Mendelson, B. K., White, D. R., & Mendelson, M. J. (1996). Self-esteem and body esteem: Effects of gender, age, and weight. *Journal of Applied Developmental Psychology, 17,* 321–346.

Merewood, A. (1991, April). Sperm under seige. *Health,* pp. 53–57, 76–77.

Metcalf, P., & Huntington, R. (1991). *Celebrations of death: The anthology of mortuary ritual* (2nd ed.). New York: Cambridge University Press.

Meyer, E. E., Chrousos, G. P., & Gold, P. (2001). Major depression and the stress system: A life-span perspective. *Development and Psychopathology, 13,* 565–580.

Michel, G. F., & Moore, C. L. (1995). *Developmental psychobiology: An interdisciplinary science.* Cambridge, MA: MIT Press.

Michelson, L., Sugai, D., Wood, R., & Kazdin, A. E. (1983). *Social skills assessment and training with children: An empirical handbook.* New York: Plenum.

Middleton, W., Raphael, B., Burnett, P. & Martinek, N. (1997). Psychological distress and bereavement. *Journal of Nervous and Mental Diseases, 185,* 447–453.

Middleton, W., Raphael, B., Martinek, N., & Misso, V. (1993). Pathological grief reactions. In M. Stroebe, W. Stroebe, & R. O. Hansson (Eds.), *Handbook of bereavement: Theory, research and intervention* (pp. 44–61). New York: Cambridge University Press.

Midgley, C., Fedlaufer, H., & Eccles, J. S. (1988). The transition to junior high school: Beliefs of pre- and post-transition teachers. *Journal of Youth and Adolescence, 17,* 543–562.

Mihalic, S. W., & Elliot, D. (1997). Short- and long-term consequences of adolescent work. *Youth and Society, 28,* 464–498.

Mikulincer, M. (1997). Adult attachment style and information processing: Individual differences in curiosity and cognitive closure. *Journal of Personality and Social Psychology, 72,* 1217–1230.

Mikulincer, M., & Arad, D. (1999). Attachment working models and cognitive openness in close relationships: A test of chronic and temporary accessibility effects. *Journal of Personality and Social Psychology, 77,* 710–725.

Mikulincer, M., & Florian, V. (1996). Emotional reactions to interpersonal losses over the lifespan: An attachment theory perspective. In C. Magai & S. H. McFadden (Eds.), *Handbook of emotion, adult development and aging* (pp. 269–285). San Diego: Academic Press.

Mikulincer, M., & Florian, V. (1998). The relationship between adult attachment styles and emotional and cognitive reactions to stressful events. In J. A. Simpson & W. S. Rholes (Eds.), *Attachment theory and close relationships* (pp. 143–165). New York: Guilford Press.

Miller, A. (1981). *The drama of the gifted child.* New York: Basic Books.

Miller, B. C., & Sollie, D. L. (1980). Normal stresses during the transition to parenthood. *Family Relations, 29,* 459–465.

Miller, D. L. (1983). Developmental changes in male/female voice classification by infants. *Infant Behavior and Development, 6,* 313–330.

Miller, J. B. (1991). The development of women's sense of self. In J. V. Jordan, A. G. Kaplan, J. B. Miller, I. P. Stiver & J. L. Surrey (Eds.), *Women's growth in connection* (pp. 11–26). New York: Guilford Press.

Miller, K. F., & Stigler, J. W. (1987). Counting in Chinese: Cultural variation in a basic cognitive skill. *Cognitive Development, 2,* 279–305.

Miller, P. A., & Eisenberg, N. (1988). The relation of empathy to aggression and externalizing/antisocial behavior. *Psychological Bulletin, 103,* 324–344.

Miller, P. A., Eisenberg, N., Fabes, R. A., & Shell, R. (1996). Relations of moral reasoning and vicarious emotion to young children's prosocial behavior toward peers and adults. *Developmental Psychology, 32,* 210–219.

Miller, P. H. (1994). Individual differences in children's strategic behavior: Utilization deficiencies. *Learning and Individual Differences, 6,* 285–307.

Miller, R. S. (1997). We always hurt the ones we love: Aversive interactions in close relationships. In R. M. Kowalski, (Ed.), *Aversive interpersonal behaviors* (pp. 11–29). New York: Plenum.

Mitka, M. (2000). Suggestions for help when the end is near. *Journal of the American Medical Association, 284,* 2441–2444.

Miura, I. T., Okamoto, Y., Kim, C. C., Steere, M., & Fayol, M. (1993). First graders' cognitive representation of number and understanding of place value: Cross-national comparisons—France, Japan, Korea, Sweden, and the United States. *Journal of Educational Psychology, 85,* 24–30.

Moffitt, T. E. (1993a). The neuropsychology of conduct disorder. *Development and Psychopathology, 5,* 135–151.

Moffitt, T. E. (1993b). Adolescence-limited and life-course persistent antisocial behavior: A developmental taxonomy. *Psychological Bulletin, 100,* 674–701.

Moffitt, T. E., & Lynam, D. R. (1994). The neuropsychology of conduct disorder and delinquency: Implications for understanding antisocial behavior. In D. C. Fowles, P. Sutker, & S. H. Goodman (Eds.), *Progress in experimental personality and psychopathology research* (pp. 233–262). New York: Springer-Verlag.

Mohanty, A. K., & Perregaux, C. (1997). Language acquisition and bilingualism. In J. W. Perry, P. R. Dasen, & T. S. Saraswathi (Eds.), *Handbook of cross-cultural psychology: Vol. 2. Basic processes and human development* (pp. 217–254). Boston, MA: Allyn & Bacon.

Molfese, D. (1990). Auditory evoked responses recorded from 16-month-old human infants to words they did and did not know. *Brain and Language, 38,* 345–363.

Money, J. (1988). *Gay, straight, and in-between: The sexology of erotic orientation.* New York: Oxford University Press.

Money, J., & Dalery, J. (1977). Hyperadrenocortical 46, XX hermaphroditism with penile urethra: Psychological studies in seven cases, three reared as boys, four as girls. In P. A. Lee, L. P. Plotnick, A. A. Kowarski, & C. J. Migeon (Eds.), *Congenital adrenal hyperplasia* (pp. 433–446). Baltimore: University Park Press.

Money, J., & Ehrhardt, A. (1972). *Man and woman, boy and girl.* Baltimore: Johns Hopkins University Press.

Money, J., & Tucker, P. (1975). *Sexual signatures: On being a man or a woman.* Boston: Little, Brown.

Monitoring the Future Survey. (2000). Retrieved April 5, 2002, from http://www.drugabuse.gov/

Montemayor, R. (1983). Parents and adolescents in conflict: All families some of the time and some families all of the time. *Journal of Early Adolescence, 3,* 83–103.

Moore, K. L., & Persaud, T. V. N. (1993). *Before we are born: Essentials of embryology and birth defects* (4th ed.). Philadelphia: Saunders.

Moore, W. (1982). *The Measure of Intellectual Development: A brief review.* Baltimore, MD: University of Maryland Center for Application of Developmental Instruction.

Morell, V. (1993). The puzzle of the triple repeats. *Science, 260,* 1422–1423.

Morelli, G. A., Rogoff, B., Oppenheim, D., & Goldsmith, D. (1992). Cultural variations in infants' sleeping arrangements. Questions of independence. *Developmental Psychology, 28,* 604–613.

Moreno, J. L. (1934). *Who shall survive? A new approach to the problem of human interrelations.* Washington, DC: Nervous and Mental Disease Publishing Co.

Morgane, P. J., Austin-LaFrance, R., Bronzino, J., Tonkiss, J., Diaz-Cintra, S., Cintra, L., Kemper, T., & Galler, J. R. (1993). Prenatal malnutrition and development of the brain. *Neuroscience and Biobehavioral Reviews, 17,* 91–128.

Morrison, F. J., Holmes, D. L., & Haith, M. M. (1974). A developmental study of the effects of familiarity on short-term visual memory. *Journal of Experimental Child Psychology, 18,* 412–425.

Morrow, J., & Nolen-Hoeksema, S. (1990). Effects of responses to depression on the remediation of depressive affect. *Journal of Personality and Social Psychology, 58,* 519–527.

Mortimer, J. T., Finch, M. D., & Kumka, D. (1982). Persistence and change in development: The multidimensional self-concept. In P. B. Baltes & O. G. Brim, Jr. (Eds.), *Life-span development and behavior* (Vol. 4, pp. 264–315). New York: Academic Press.

Mortimer, J. T., Harley, C., & Aronson, P. J. (1999). How do prior experiences in the workplace set the stage for transitions to adulthood? A. Booth, A. C. Crouter, & M. J. Shanahan (Eds.), *Transitions to adulthood in a changing economy: No work, no family, no future?* New York: Praeger.

Mosher, R. L. (1995). Educational and psychological applications of theories of human development: A brief overview. *Journal of Education, 177,* 1–15.

Moshman, D. (1982). Exogenous, endogenous, and dialectical constructivism, *Developmental Review, 2,* 371–384.

Moshman, D. (1998). Cognitive development beyond childhood. In W. Damon (Series Ed.), D. Kuhn, & R. S. Siegler (Vol. Eds.), *Handbook of child psychology: Vol. 2. Cognition, perception and language* (5th ed., pp. 947–978). New York: Wiley.

Mounts, N. S., & Steinberg, L. (1995). An ecological analysis of peer influence on adolescent grade point average and drug use. *Developmental Psychology, 31,* 915–922.

Mpofu, E., & Crystal, R. (2001). Conduct disorder in children: Challenges and prospective cognitive behavioural treatments. *Counselling Psychology Quarterly, 14,* 21–33.

Murphy, S. A. (1997). A bereavement intervention for parents following the sudden, violent deaths of their 12–28-year-old children: Descriptions and applications to clinical practice. *Canadian Journal of Nursing Research, 29,* 51–72.

Murray, B. (1996, February). Psychology remains top college major. *APA Monitor,* p. 1.

Murray, S. L., Holmes, J. G., & Griffin, D. W. (1996). The benefits of positive illusions: Idealization and the construction of satisfaction in close relationships. *Journal of Personality and Social Psychology, 70,* 79–98.

Murry, V. M. (1992). Sexual career paths of Black adolescent females. *Journal of Adolescent Research, 7,* 4–27.

Mussen, P. H., Honzik, M., & Eichorn, D. (1982). Early adult antecedents of life satisfaction at age 70. *Journal of Gerontology, 37,* 316–322.

Myers, D. G. (1993). *The pursuit of happiness.* New York: Avon.

Myers, D. G. (2000). The funds, friends, and faith of happy people. *American Psychologist, 55,* 56–57.

Nahom, D., Wells, E., Gillmore, M. R., Hoppe, M., Morrison, D. M., Archibald, M., Murowchick, E., Wilsdon, A., & Graham, L. (2001). Differences by gender and sexual experience in adolescent sexual behavior: Implications for education and HIV prevention. *Journal of School Health, 71,* 153–159.

Nathan, P. (1969). *The nervous system.* Philadelphia, PA: Lippincott.

Nathanielz, P. W. (1992). *Life before birth: The challenges of fetal development.* New York: Freeman.

National Campaign to Prevent Teen Pregnancy. (1999). *Teenpregnancy.org.* Retrieved April 5, 2002, from http:/www.teenpregnancy.org/

National Center for Education Statistics. (2002). *The condition of education, 2002.* Washington, DC: U.S. Department of Education.

National Center for Education Statistics. (1998). *America's children: Key national indicators of well-being.* Washington, D.C.: U.S. Department of Education.

National Commission on Excellence in Education. (1983). *A Nation at Risk: The imperative for educational reform.* Washington, DC: U.S. Government Printing Office.

National Council on the Teaching of Mathematics (2000a). *Principles and standards for school mathematics: Grades 5–8: Standard 9–Algebra.* Available: http:/www.standards.nctm.org/previous/currevstds/5–8s9.htm.

National Council on the Teaching of Mathematics (2000b). *Principles and standards for school mathematics: Grades 9–12: Standard 5–Algebra.* Available: http:/www.standards.nctm.org/previous/currevstds/9–12s5.htm.

National Institute of Child Health & Human Development, [NICHD], Early Child Care Research Network (1997). The effects of infant child care on infant-mother attachment security: Results of the NICHD study of early child care. *Child Development, 68,* 860–879.

National Institute of Child Health & Human Development, [NICHD], Early Child Care Research Network. (1998). Early child care and self-control, compliance, and problem behavior at twenty-four and thirty-six months. *Child Development, 69,* 1145–1170.

Neimeyer, R. A. (2000). Searching for the meaning of meaning: Grief therapy and the process of reconstruction. *Death Studies, 24,* 541–558.

Neisser, U. (1967). *Cognitive psychology.* New York: Appleton-Century-Crofts.

Neisser, U. (1993). *The perceived self: Ecological and interpersonal sources of self-knowledge.* New York: Cambridge University Press.

Nell, V. (2002). Why young men drive dangerously: Implications for injury prevention. *Current Directions in Psychological Science, 11,* 75–79.

Nelson, K. (1993a). Events, narratives, memory: What develops? In C. A. Nelson (Ed.), *Minnesota Symposium on Child Psychology: Vol. 26. Memory and affect* (pp. 1–24). Erlbaum.

Nelson, K. (1993b). The psychological and social origins of autobiographical memory. *Psychological Science, 4,* 7–14.

Nelson, K. (1996). Memory development from 4 to 7 years. In A. J. Sameroff & M. M. Haith (Eds.), *The 5 to 7 shift* (pp. 141–160). Chicago: University of Chicago Press.

Nelson, M. L., & Neufelt, S. A. (1998). The pedagogy of counseling: A critical examination. *Counselor Education and Supervision, 38,* 70–88.

Nelson, S. A. (1980). Factors influencing young children's use of motives and outcomes as moral criteria. *Child Development, 51,* 823–829.

Newcomb, A. F., & Bukowski, W. M. (1984). A longitudinal study of the utility of social preference and social impact sociometric classification schemes. *Child Development, 55,* 1434–1447.

Newcomb, A. F., Bukowski, W. M., & Pattee, L. (1993). Children's peer relations: A meta-analytic review of popular, rejected, neglected, and average sociometric status. *Psychological Bulletin, 113,* 99–128.

Newman, P. R., & Newman, B. M. (1999). What does it take to have a positive impact on minority students' college retention? *Adolescence, 34,* 483–492.

Nix, R. L., Pinderhughes, E. E., Dodge, K. A., Bates, J. E., Pettit, G. S., & McFayden-Ketchum, S. A. (1999). The relation between mothers' hostile attribution tendencies and children's externalizing behavior problems: The mediating role of mothers' harsh discipline practices. *Child Development, 70,* 896–909.

Noam, G. G. (1992). Development as the aim of clinical intervention. *Development and Psychopathology, 4,* 679–696.

Noam, G. G. (1998). Clinical-developmental psychology: Toward developmentally differentiated interventions. In W. Damon (Series Ed.), I. E. Sigel, & K. A. Renninger (Vol. Eds.), *Handbook of child psychology: Vol 4:* (5th ed., pp. 585–634). New York: Wiley.

Noam, G. G., & Fischer, K. W. (Eds.), (1996). *Development and vulnerability in close relationships.* Mahwah, NJ: Erlbaum.

Nolen-Hoeksema, S. (1987). Sex differences in unipolar depression: Evidence and theory. *Psychological Bulletin, 101,* 259–282.

Nolen-Hoeksema, S. (1991). Responses to depression and their effects on the duration of depressive episodes. *Journal of Abnormal Psychology, 100,* 569–582.

Nolen-Hoeksema, S., & Girgus, J. S. (1994). The emergence of gender differences in depression during adolescence. *Psychological Bulletin, 115,* 424–443.

Nolen-Hoeksema, S., & Larson, J. (1999). *Coping with loss.* Mahwah, NJ: Erlbaum.

Nolen-Hoeksema, S., Morrow, J., & Fredrickson, B. L. (1993). Response styles and the duration of episodes of depressed moods. *Journal of Abnormal Psychology, 102,* 20–28.

Northcutt, R. G., & Kaas, J. H. (1995). The emergence and evolution of mammalian neocortex. *Trends in Neuroscience, 18,* 373–379.

Nyamongo, I. K. (1999). Burying the dead, culture, and economics: An assessment of two Kenyan cases. *International Social Science Journal, 51,* 255–262.

Oakes, J., & Lipton, M. (1994). Tracking and ability grouping: A structural barrier to access and achievement. In J. I. Goodlad & P. Keating (Eds.), *Access to knowledge: The continuing agenda for our nation's schools.* New York: College Board.

Oakes, J., Quartz, K. H., Gong, J., Guiton, G., & Lipton, M. (1993). Creating Middle Schools: Technical, normative, and political considerations. *The Elementary School Journal, 93,* 461–480.

O'Connor, B. P. (1995). Identity development and perceived parental behavior as sources of adolescent egocentrism. *Journal of Youth and Adolescence, 24,* 204–227.

O'Connor, T. G., Deater-Deckard, K., Fulker, D., Rutter, M., & Plomin, R. (1998). Genetic-environment correlations in later childhood and early adolescence: Antisocial behavioral problems and coercive parenting. *Developmental Psychology, 34,* 970–981.

Offer, D. (1969). *The psychological world of the teenager.* New York: Basic Books.

O'Leary, D. D. M. (1989). Do cortical areas emerge from a protocortex? *Trends in Neuroscience, 12,* 400–406.

O'Leary, D. D. M., & Stanfield, B. B. (1989). Selective elimination of axons extended by developing cortical neurons is dependent on regional locale: Experiments utilizing fetal cortical transplants. *Journal of Neuroscience, 9,* 2230–2246.

Oliner, S. P., & Oliner, P. M. (1988). *The altruistic personality: Rescuers of Jews in Nazi Europe.* New York: Free Press.

Omark, D. R., Omark, M., and Edelman, M. (1973). Formation of dominance hierarchies in young children. In T. R. Williams (Ed.), *Psychological anthropology.* The Hague, Netherlands: Mouton.

Orcutt, H. (1874). *The parent's manual or home and school training.* Boston, MA: Thompson, Brown.

Ornstein, P. (1994). *School girls: Young women, self-esteem, and the confidence gap.* New York: Anchor Books, Doubleday.

Ornstein, R., & Thompson, R. F. (1984). *The amazing brain.* Boston: Houghton Mifflin.

Ortony, A. & Turner, T. T. (1992). Basic emotions: Can conflicting criteria converge? *Psychological Bulletin, 99,* 566–571.

Osherson, D. N., & Markman, E. M. (1975). Language and the ability to evaluate contradictions and tautologies. *Cognition, 2,* 213–226.

Osofsky, H. J., & Osofsky, J. D. (2001). Violent and aggressive behaviors in youth: A mental health and prevention perspective. *Psychiatry: Interpersonal & Biological Processes, 64,* 285–295.

Overton, W. F. (1990). Competence and procedures: Constraints on the development of logical reasoning. In W. F. Overton (Ed.), *Reasoning, necessity, and logic: Developmental perspectives* (pp. 1–32). Hillsdale, NJ: Erlbaum.

Overton, W. F. (1998). Developmental psychology: Philosophy, concepts, and methodology. In W. Damon (Series Ed.) & R. M. Lerner (Vol. Ed.), *Handbook of child psychology: Vol. 1. Theoretical models of human development* (5th ed., pp. 107–188). New York: Wiley.

Oyserman, D., Coon, H. M., & Kemmelmeier, M. (2002). Rethinking individualism and collectivism: Evaluation of theoretical assumptions and meta-analyses. *Psychological Bulletin, 128,* 3–72.

Pacifici, C., Stoolmiller, M., & Nelson, C. (2001). Evaluating a prevention program for teenagers on sexual coercion: A differential effectiveness approach. *Journal of Consulting and Clinical Psychology, 69,* 552–559.

Panksepp, J. (1982). Toward a general psychobiological theory of emotions. *The Behavioral and Brain Sciences, 5,* 407–467.

Panksepp, J. (1992). A critical role for "affective neuroscience" in resolving what is basic about basic emotions. *Psychological Review, 99,* 554–560.

Panksepp, J., Herman, B., Conner, R., Bishop, P., & Scott, J. P. (1978). The biology of social attachments: Opiates alleviate separation distress. *Biological Psychiatry, 13,* 607–618.

Papez, J. W. (1937). A proposed mechanism of emotion. *Archives of Neurology and Psychiatry, 79,* 217–224.

Paris, S. G., Newman, R. S., & McVey, K. A. (1982). Learning the functional significance of mnemonic actions: A microgenetic study of strategy acquisition. *Journal of Experimental Child Psychology, 34,* 490–509.

Parke, R. D., & Buriel, R. (1998). Socialization in the family: Ethnic and ethological perspectives. In W. Damon (Series Ed.) & N. Eisenberg (Vol. Ed.), *Handbook of child psychology: Vol. 3. Social, emotional, and personality development* (5th ed., pp. 463–552). New York: Wiley.

Parker, J. (1995). Age differences in source monitoring of performed and imagined actions on immediate and delayed tests. *Journal of Experimental Child Psychology, 60,* 84–101.

Parker, J. G., & Asher, S. R. (1987). Peer relations and later personal adjustment: Are low-accepted children at risk? *Psychological Bulletin, 102,* 357–389.

Parker, S. T., & Gibson, K. R. (1979). A developmental model for the evolution of language and intelligence in early hominids. *Behavioral and Brain Sciences, 2,* 367–408.

Parkes, C. M. (1965). Bereavement and mental illness. *British Journal of Medical Psychology, 38,* 388–397.

Parkes, C. M., & Weiss, R. S. (1983). *Recovery from bereavement.* New York: Basic Books.

Parks, E. E., Carter, R. T., & Gushue, G. V. (1996). At the crossroads: Racial and womanist identity development in Black and White women. *Journal of Counseling & Development, 74,* 624–631.

Parkurst, J. T., & Asher, S. R. (1992). Peer rejection in middle school: Subgroup differences in behavior, loneliness, and interpersonal concerns. *Developmental Psychology, 28,* 231–241.

Parsons, J. E., & Ruble, D. N. (1977). The development of achievement-related expectancies. *Child Development, 48,* 1975–1979.

Partnership for a Drug-Free America. (1998). *The boomer-rang: Baby boomers seriously underestimate the presence of drugs in their children's lives.* Retrieved March 28, 2002, from http://www.drugfreeamerica.org

Pascarella, E., Bohr, L., Nora, A., & Terenzini, P. (1995). Cognitive effects of 2-year and 4-year colleges: New evidence. *Educational Evaluation and Policy Analysis, 17,* 83–96.

Pascarella, E., & Terenzini, P. (1991). *How college affects students: Findings and insights from twenty years of research.* New York: Wiley and Sons.

Pasupathi, M., Staudinger, U. M., & Baltes, P. B. (1999) *The emergence of wisdom-related knowledge and judgment during adolescence.* Berlin: Max Planck Institute for Human Development.

Patterson, C. J. (1992). Children of lesbian and gay parents. *Child Development, 63,* 1025–1042.

Patterson, G. R. (1982). *Coercive family process.* Eugene, OR: Castalia Press.

Patterson, G. R., & Stouthamer-Loeber, M. (1984). The correlation of family management practices and delinquency. *Child Development, 55,* 1299–1307.

Paus, T., Zijdenbos, A., Worsley, K., Collins, D. L., Blumenthal, J., Giedd, J. N., Rapoport, J. L., & Evans, A. C. (1999). Structural maturation of neural pathways in children and adolescents: In vivo study. *Science, 283,* 1908–1911.

Paxton, S. J., Schutz, H. K., Weitheim, E. H., & Muir, S. L. (1999). Friendship clique and peer influences on body image concerns, dietary restraint, extreme weight-loss behaviors, and binge-eating in adolescent girls. *Journal of Abnormal Psychology, 108,* 255–266.

Pecheux, M. G., & Labrell, F. (1994). Parent-infant interactions and early cognitive development. In A. Vyt, H. Bloch, & M. H. Bornstein (Eds). *Early child development in the French tradition: Contributions from current research.* Hillsdale, NJ: Erlbaum.

Peery, J. C. (1979). Popular, amiable, isolated, rejected: A reconceptualization of sociometric status in preschool children. *Child Development, 50,* 1231–1234.

Peltonen, L., & McKusick, V. A. (2001). Dissecting human disease in the postgenomic era. *Science, 291,* 1224–1229.

Pentz, M. A., Trebow, E. A., Hansen, W. B., MacKinnon, D. P., Dwyer, J. H., Johnson, C. A., Flay, B. R., Daniels, M. S., & Cormack, C. C. (1990). Effects of program implementation on adolescent drug use behavior: The Midwestern Prevention Project (MPP). *Evaluation Review, 14,* 264–289.

Perry, W. G. (1970/1999). *Forms of ethical and intellectual development in the college years: A scheme.* San Francisco: Jossey-Bass.

Perry-Jenkins, M., Repetti, R. L., & Crouter, A. C. (2000). Work and family in the 1990s. *Journal of Marriage and the Family, 62,* 981–998.

Petersen, A. C. (1988). Adolescent development. *Annual Review of Psychology, 39,* 583–608.

Petersen, A. C., Compas, B. E., Brooks-Gunn, J., Stemmler, M., Ey, S., & Grant, K. E. (1993). Depression in adolescence. *American Psychologist, 48,* 155–168.

Petersen, A. C., Kennedy, R. E., & Sullivan, P. (1991). Coping with adolescence. In M. E. Colten & S. Gore (Eds.), *Adolescent stress: Causes and consequences* (pp. 93–110). New York: Aldine de Gruyter.

Petersen, A. C., Sarigiani, P. A., & Kennedy, R. E. (1991). Adolescent depression: Why more girls? *Journal of Youth and Adolescence, 10,* 247–271.

Petersen, B. E., & Steward, A. J. (1996). Antecedents and contexts of generativity motivation at midlife. *Psychology and Aging, 11,* 21–33.

Peterson, C., Maier, S. & Seligman, M. (1993). *Learned helplessness.* New York: Oxford.

Pettit, F., Fegan, M., & Howie, P. (1990, September). *Interviewer effects on children's testimony.* Paper presented at the International Congress on Child Abuse and Neglect, Hamburg, Germany.

Pfeiffer, S. (2001). Emotional intelligence: Popular but elusive construct. *Roeper Review, 23,* 138–142.

Pfost, K. S. & Fiore, M. (1990). Pursuit of nontraditional occupations: Fear of success or fear of not being chosen? *Sex Roles, 23,* 15–24.

Philips, D., Simpson, J. A., Lanigan, L., & Rholes, S. W. (1995). *Providing social support: A study of adult attachment styles.* Paper presented at the joint meeting of the European Association of Social Psychology and the Society of Experimental Social Psychology, Washington, DC.

Phillips, M. (1997). What makes schools effective? A comparison of the relationships of communitarian climate and academic achievement and attendance during middle school. *American Educational Research Journal, 34,* 633–662.

Phinney, J. S. (1990). Ethnic identity in adolescents and adults: Review of research. *Psychological Bulletin, 108,* 499–514.

Phinney, J. S. (2000). Identity formation across cultures: The interaction of personal, societal, and historical change. *Human Development, 43,* 27–31.

Piaget, J. (1926). *The language and thought of the child.* New York: Harcourt Brace.

Piaget, J. (1928). *Judgment and reasoning in the child.* New York: Harcourt Brace.

Piaget, J. (1932/1965). *The moral judgment of the child.* New York: Free Press.

Piaget, J. (1952). *The origins of intelligence in children.* New York: International Universities Press.

Piaget, J. (1954). *The construction of reality in the child.* New York: Basic Books.

Piaget, J. (1962). *Play, dreams, and imitation in childhood.* New York: Norton.

Piaget, J. (1964/1968). *Six psychological studies.* New York: Random House.

Piaget, J. (1970). *Science of education and the psychology of the child.* New York: Orion Press.

Piaget, J. (1975/1985). *The equilibration of cognitive structures.* Chicago: University of Chicago Press.

Piaget, J. (1977). *The development of thought. Equilibration of cognitive structures.* New York: Viking.

Piaget, J. (1995). In L. Smith, (Ed.), *Sociological studies.* London/New York: Routledge & Kegan Paul. (Original work published 1977)

Piaget, J., & Inhelder, B. (1951/1976). *The origin of the idea of chance in children.* New York: Norton.

Piaget, J., & Inhelder, B. (1956). *The child's conception of space.* New York: Norton.

Piaget, J., & Inhelder, B. (1973). *Memory and intelligence.* New York: Basic Books.

Pietromonaco, P. R., & Carnelley, K. B. (1994). Gender and working models of attachment: Consequences for self and romantic relationships. *Personal Relationships, 1,* 63–82.

Pinker, S. (1994). *The language instinct.* New York: Morrow.

Pintrich, P. R. (2000). Multiple goals, multiple pathways: The role of goal orientation in learning and achievement. *Journal of Educational Psychology, 92,* 544–555.

Pintrich, P., & Schunk, D. (1996). *Motivation in education: Theory, research, and application.* Upper Saddle River, NJ: Prentice Hall.

Pipher, M. (1994). *Reviving Ophelia: Saving the selves of adolescent girls.* New York: Ballantine Books.

Pipher, M. (1996). *The shelter of each other: Rebuilding our families.* New York: Ballantine Books.

Pipher, M. (1999). *Another country: Navigating the emotional terrain of our elders.* New York: Riverhead Books.

Pistole, M. C. (1989). Attachment in adult romantic relationships: Style of conflict resolution and relationship satisfaction. *Journal of Social and Personal Relationships, 6,* 505–510.

Pittman, F. (1998). *Grow up! How taking responsibility can make you a happy adult.* New York: St. Martin's Press.

Plomin, R. (1986). *Development, genetics, and psychology.* Hillsdale, NJ: Erlbaum.

Plomin, R., & Rutter, M. (1998). Child development, molecular genetics, and what to do with genetics once they are found. *Child Development, 69,* 1223–1242.

Plomin, R., Corley, R., DeFries, J. C., & Fulker, D. W. (1990). Individual differences in television viewing in early childhood: Nature as well as nurture. *Psychological Science, 1,* 371–377.

Plomin, R., DeFries, J., Craig, I. W., & McGuffin, P. (2003). *Behavioral genetics in the postgenomic era.* Washington, DC: American Psychological Association.

Plomin, R., Fulker, D. W., Corley, R., & DeFries, J. C. (1997). Nature, nurture, and cognitive development from 1 to 16 years: A parent-offspring adoption study. *Psychological Science, 8,* 442–447.

Plomin, R., Owen, M. J., & McGuffin, P. (1994). The genetic basis of complex human behaviors. *Science, 264,* 1733–1739.

Podd, M. H. (1972). Ego identity status and morality: The relationship between two developmental constructs. *Developmental Psychology, 6,* 497–507.

Pollack, W. (1998). *Real boys: Rescuing our sons from the myths of boyhood.* New York: Henry Holt.

Pollitt, E., Golub, D., Gorman, K., Grantham-McGregor, S., Levitsky, D., Schurch, B., Strupp, B., & Wachs, T. (1996). *A reconceptualization of the effects of undernutrition on children's psychological, psychosocial, and behavioral development* (Social Policy Report, Vol. 10, No. 5). Ann Arbor, MI: Society for Research in Child Development.

Pollitt, E., Gorman, K. S., Engle, P. L., Martorell, R., & Rivera, J. (1993). Early supplementary feeding and cognition. *Monographs of the Society for Research in Child Development, 58*(Serial No. 235).

Ponzo, Z. (1992). Promoting successful aging: Problems, opportunities, and counseling guidelines. *Journal of Counseling and Development, 71,* 210–213.

Poulin-Dubois, D., Serbin, L. A., Kenyon, B., & Derbyshire, A. (1994). Infants' intermodal knowledge about gender. *Developmental Psychology, 30,* 436–442.

Powell, G. J. (1985). Self-concepts among African-Americans in racially isolated minority schools: Some regional differences. *Journal of the American Academy of Child Psychiatry, 24,* 142–149.

Pratt, J., & Pryor, K. (1995). *For real: The uncensored truth about America's teenagers.* New York: Hyperion.

Presley, C. A., Meilman, P., & Lyerla, R. (1995). *Alcohol and drugs on American college campuses.* Carbondale: Southern Illinois University Press.

Pribram, K. H. (1997). The work in working memory: Implications for development. In N. A. Krasnegor, G. R. Lyon, & P. S. Goldman-Rakic (Eds.), *Development of the prefrontal cortex: Evolution, neurobiology, and behavior* (pp. 359–378). Baltimore: Brookes.

Price, J. M., & Dodge, K. A. (1989). Peers' contributions to children's social maladjustment: Description and intervention. In *Peer Relationships in Child Development* pp. 341–370. San Francisco: Jossey-Bass.

Putallaz, M., & Wasserman, A. (1990). Children's entry behaviors. In S. P. Asher & J. D. Coie (Eds.), *Peer rejection in childhood.* New York: Cambridge University Press.

Pyszczynski, T., Greenberg, J., & LaPrelle, J. (1985). Social comparison after success and failure: Biased search for information consistent with a self-servicing conclusion. *Journal of Experimental Social Psychology, 21,* 129–138.

Quadrel, M. J., Fischhoff, B., & Davis, W. (1993). Adolescent (in)vulnerability. *American Psychologist, 48,* 102–116.

Quill, T. E. (2000). Initiating end-of-life discussions with seriously ill patients. *Journal of the American Medical Association, 285,* 2502–2507.

Quinton, D., Pickles, A., Maughan, B., & Rutter, M. (1993). Partners, peers, and pathways: Assortative pairing and continuities in conduct disorder. *Development and Psychopathology, 5,* 763–783.

Rakic, P. (1988). Specification of cerebral cortical areas. *Science, 241,* 170–176.

Ramsey, P. G., & Myers, L. C. (1990). Young children's responses to racial differences: Relations among cognitive, affective, and behavioral dimensions. *Journal of Applied Developmental Psychology, 11,* 49–67.

Rando, T. A. (1993). *Treatment of complicated mourning.* Champaign, IL: Research Press.

Raths, L., Harmin, M., & Simon, S. (1966). *Values and teaching.* Columbus, OH: Merrill.

Ravitch, D. (1983). *The troubled crusade: American education, 1945–1980.* New York: Basic Books.

Reese, E., & Fivush, R. (1993). Parental styles of talking about the past. *Developmental Psychology, 29,* 596–606.

Reich, R. B. (2000). *The future of success.* New York: Knopf.

Reid, J. B., Patterson, G. R., & Snyder, J. J. (2002). Antisocial behavior in children and adolescents: A developmental analysis and the Oregon model for intervention. Washington, DC: American Psychological Association.

Reiss, D., & Neiderhiser, J. M. (2000). The interplay of genetic influences and social processes in developmental theory: Specific mechanisms are coming into view. *Development and Psychopathology, 12,* 357–372.

Reiss, D., Neiderhiser, J. M., Hetherington, E. M., & Plomin, R. (2000). *The relationship code: Deciphering genetic and social influences on adolescent development.* Cambridge, MA: Harvard University Press.

Renner, M. J., & Rosenzweig, M. R. (1987). *Enriched and impoverished environments.* New York: Springer.

Rheingold, H. L. (1956). The modification of social responsiveness in institutional babies. *Monographs of the Society for Research in Child Development, 21* (2, Serial No. 63).

Rholes, W. S., Simpson, J. A., & Stevens, J. G. (1998). Attachment orientations, social support, and conflict resolution in close relationships. In J. A. Simpson & W. S. Rholes (Eds.), *Attachment theory and close relationships* (pp. 166–188). New York: Guilford Press.

Richards, T. A., Wrubel, J., & Folkman, S. (1999–2000). Death rites in the San Francisco gay community: Cultural developments of the AIDS epidemic. *Omega, 40,* 335–350.

Rindfuss, R. R. (1991). The young adult years: Diversity, structural change, and fertility. *Demography, 28,* 493–512.

Roberts, D. F. (1993). Adolescents and the mass media: From "Leave it to Beaver" to Beverly Hills 90210." *Teachers College Record, 94,* 629–644.

Roberts, T., & Kraft, R. (1987). Reading comprehension performance and laterality: Evidence for concurrent validity of dichotic, haptic, and EEG laterality measures. *Neuropsychologia, 25,* 817–828.

Roberts, W., & Strayer, J. (1996). Empathy, emotional expressiveness, and prosocial behavior. *Child Development, 67,* 449–470.

Robertson, J., & Robertson, J. (1989). *Separation and the very young.* London: Free Association Books.

Robins, L. N. (1978). Sturdy childhood predictors of adult antisocial behavior: Replications from longitudinal studies. *Psychological Medicine, 8,* 611–622.

Robins, R. W., & Pals, J. (1998). *Implicit self-theories of ability in the academic domain: A test of Dweck's model.* Unpublished manuscript.

Robinson, I., Ziss, K., Ganza, B., Katz, S., & Robinson, E. (1991). Twenty years of sexual revolution, 1965–1985: An update. *Journal of Marriage and the Family, 53,* 216–220.

Robinson, J. L., Zahn-Waxler, C., & Emde, R. N. (1994). Patterns of development in early empathic behavior: Environmental and child constitutional influences. *Social Development, 3,* 125–145.

Rodgers, J., & Rowe, D. (1993). Social contagion and adolescent sexual behavior: A developmental EMOSA model. *Psychological Review, 100,* 479–510.

Rogan, W. J., & Gladen, B. C. (1993). Breast-feeding and cognitive development. *Early Human Development, 31,* 181–193.

Rogers, C. R. (1951). *Client-centered therapy.* Boston: Houghton-Mifflin.

Rogoff, B. (1998). In W. Damon (Series Ed.) & R. S. Siegler (Vol. Ed.), *Handbook of child psychology: Vol. 2. Cognition, perception and language* (5th ed., pp. 679–744). New York: Wiley.

Rogoff, B., & Gauvain, M. (1986). A method for the analysis of patterns illustrated with data on mother-child instructional interaction. In J. Valsiner (Ed.), *The individual subject and scientific psychology* (pp. 261–290). New York: Plenum Press.

Rolf, J., Masten, A., Cicchetti, D., Neuchterlein, K., & Weintraub, S. (Eds.). (1990). *Risk and protective factors in the development of psychopathology*. New York: Cambridge University Press.

Rollins, B. C., & Feldman, H. (1970). Marital satisfaction over the family life cycle. *Journal of Marriage and the Family, 32,* 20–28.

Rook, K. S. (2000). The evolution of social relationships in later adulthood. In S. H. Qualls & N. Abeles (Eds.), *Psychology and the aging revolution: How we adapt to longer life* (pp. 173–191). Washington, DC: American Psychological Association.

Rook, K. S., & Schuster, T. L. (1996). Compensatory processes in the social networks of older adults. In G. Pierce, B. R. Sarason, & I. G. Sarason (Eds.), *The handbook of social support and family relationships* (pp. 219–248). New York: Plenum Press.

Root, M. P. P. (1999). The biracial baby boom: Understanding ecological constructions of racial identity in the 21st century. In R. H. Sheets & E. R. Hollins (Eds.), *Racial and ethnic identity in school practices* (pp. 67–89). Mahwah, NJ: Erlbaum.

Rosemond, J. K. (1991). *Parent power: A common sense approach to parenting in the 90's and beyond*. Kansas City, MO: Andrews McMeel.

Rosenblatt, P. C., Walsh, R., & Jackson, D. A. (1972). Coping with anger and aggression in mourning. *Omega, 3,* 271–284.

Rosenthal, R., & Jacobson, L. (1968). *Pygmalion in the classroom*. New York: Holt.

Ross, C. E. (1995). Reconceptualizing marital status as a continuum of social attachment. *Journal of Marriage and the Family, 57,* 129–140.

Ross, H., Tesla, C., Kenyon, B., & Lollis, S. (1990). Maternal intervention in toddler peer conflict: The socialization of principles of justice. *Developmental Psychology, 26,* 994–1003.

Rothbart, M. K., Ahadi, S. A., & Evans, D. E. (2000). Temperament and personality: Origins and outcomes. *Journal of Personality and Social Psychology, 78,* 122–135.

Rothbart, M. K., & Bates, J. E. (1998). Temperament. In W. Damon (Series Ed.) & N. Eisenberg (Vol. Ed.), *Handbook of child psychology: Vol. 3. Social, emotional and personality development* (5th ed., pp. 105–176).

Rothbart, M. K., Derryberry, D., & Posner, M. I. (1994). A psychobiological approach to the development of temperament. In J. E. Bates & T. D. Wachs (Eds.), *Temperament: Individual differences at the interface of biology and behavior* (pp. 83–116). Washington, DC: American Psychological Association.

Rourke, B. P., & Conway, J. (1997). Disabilities of arithmetic and mathematical reasoning: Perspectives from neurology and neuropsychology. *Journal of Learning Disabilities, 30,* 34–46.

Rovee-Collier, C. K. (1990). The "memory system" of prelinguistic infants. In A. Diamond (Ed.), *The development and neural bases of higher cognitivie functions*. New York: New York Academy of Sciences.

Rowe, J. W., & Kahn, R. L. (1998). *Successful aging*. New York: Pantheon Books.

Rowe, D. C., Vazsonyi, A. T., & Flannery, D. J. (1994). No more than skin deep: Ethnic and racial similarity in developmental process. *Psychological Review, 101,* 396–413.

Rubin, K. H., Bukowski, W., & Parker, J. G. (1998). Peer interactions, relationships, and groups. In W. Damon (Series Ed.), N. Eisenberg (Vol. Ed.), *Handbook of child psychology, 5th Edition: Vol. 3. Social, emotional, and personality development* (pp. 619–700). New York: Wiley.

Rubin, K. H., Chen, J. S., McDougall, P., Bowker, A., & McKinnon, J. (1995). The Waterloo Longitudinal Project: Predicting internalizing and externalizing problems in adolescence. *Development and Psychopathology, 7,* 751–764.

Rubin, K. H., & Coplan, R. J. (1992). Peer relationships in childhood. In M. H. Bornstein & M. E. Lamb (Eds.), *Developmental psychology: An advanced textbook* (3rd ed., pp. 519–578). Hillsdale, NJ: Lawrence Erlbaum.

Rubin, K. H., Hastings, P., Chen, X., Stewart, S., & McNichol, K. (1998). Intrapersonal and maternal correlates of aggression, conflict, and externalizing problems in toddlers. *Child Development, 69,* 1614–1629.

Rubin, S. (1981). A two-track model of bereavement: Theory and application in research. *American Journal of Orthopsychiatry, 51,* 101–109.

Ruble, D. N., Gruelich, F., Pomerantz, E. M., & Gochberg, G. (1993). The role of gender-related processes in the development of sex differences in self-evaluation and depression. *Journal of Affective Disorders, 29,* 97–128.

Ruble, D. N., & Martin, C. L. (1998). Gender development. In W. Damon (Series Ed.) & N. Eisenberg (Vol. Ed.), *Handbook of child psychology: Vol. 3. Social, emotional and personality development* (5th ed., pp. 933–1016).

Ruffman, T., Slade, L., & Crowe, E. (2002). The relation between children's and mother's mental state language and theory-of-mind understanding. *Child Development, 73,* 734–751.

Rush, D., Stein, Z., & Susser, M. (Eds.). (1980). *Diet in pregnancy: A randomized controlled trial of nutritional supplements*. New York: Liss.

Rutter, M. (1997). Nature-nurture integration: The example of antisocial behavior. *American Psychologist, 52,* 390–398.

Rutter, M., & Giller, H. (1983). *Juvenile delinquency: Trends and perspectives*. Harmondsworth, England: Penguin Books.

Rutter, M., Graham, P., Chadwick, O. F., & Yule, W. (1976). Adolescent turmoil: Fact or fiction? *Journal of Child Psychology & Psychiatry & Allied Disciplines, 17,* 35–56.

Rutter, M., Maughan, B., Mortimore, P., Ouston, J., & Smith, A. (1979). *Fifteen thousand hours: Secondary schools and their effects on children.* Cambridge, MA: Harvard University Press.

Rutter, V. (1995, January/February). Adolescence: Whose hell is it? *Psychology Today,* pp. 54–60, 62, 64, 66, 68.

Ryan, M. P. (1984). Monitoring text comprehension: Individual differences in epistemological standards. *Journal of Educational Psychology, 76,* 248–258.

Ryan, R. M., & Deci, E. L. (2000). Self-determination theory and the facilitation of intrinsic motivation, social development, and well-being. *American Psychologist, 55,* 68–78.

Ryan, R. M., & LaGuardia, J. G. (2000). What is being optimized?: Self-determination theory and basic psychological needs. In S. H. Qualls & N. Abeles (Eds.), *Psychology and the aging revolution: How we adapt to longer life* (pp. 145–172). Washington, DC: American Psychological Association.

Rybarczyk, B., Gallagher-Thompson, D., Rodman, J., Zeiss, A., Gantz, F. E., & Yesavage, J. (1992). Applying cognitive-behavioral psychotherapy to the chronically ill elderly: Treatment issues and case illustration. *International Psychogeriatrics, 4,* 127–140.

Ryff, C. D., & Keyes, C. L. M. (1995). The structure of psychological well-being revisited. *Journal of Personality and Social Psychology, 69,* 719–727.

Ryff, C. D., Lee, Y. H., Essex, M. J., & Schmutte, P. S. (1994). My children and me: Mid-life evaluations of grown children and of self. *Psychology and Aging, 9,* 195–205.

Ryff, C. D., & Singer, B. (2000). Interpersonal flourishing: A positive health agenda for the new millennium. *Personality and Social Psychology Review, 4,* 30–44.

Ryland, E. B., Riordan, R. J., & Brack, G. (1994). Selected characteristics of high-risk students and their enrollment persistence. *Journal of College Student Development, 35,* 54–58.

Sachs, J. (1987). Preschool boys' and girls' language use in pretend play. In S. U. Phillips, S. Steele, and C. Tanz (Eds.), *Language, gender, and sex in comparative perspective* (pp. 178–188). Cambridge: Cambridge University Press.

Sadker, M. P., & Sadker, D. M. (1991). *Teachers, schools, and society* (2nd ed). New York: Random House.

Sagi, A., Lamb, M. E., Lewkowicz, K. S., Shoham, R., Dvir, R., & Estes, D. (1985). Security of infant-mother, -father, and -metapelet attachments among kibbutz-reared Israeli children. In I. Bretherton & E. Waters (Eds.), Growing points of attachment theory and research. *Monographs of the Society for Research in Child Development, 50*(Serial No. 209), 257–275.

Sagi, A., van IJzendoorn, M. H., Aviezer, O., Donnell, F., Koren-Karie, N., Joels, T., & Harel, Y. (1995). Attachments in a multiple-caregiver and multiple-infant environment: The case of the Israeli kibbutzim. In

E. Waters, B. E. Vaughn, G. Posada, & K. Kondo-Ikemura (Eds.), Caregiving, cultural and cognitive perspectives on secure-base behavior and working models: New growing points in attachment theory and research. *Monographs of the Society for Research in Child Development, 60*(Serial No. 244), 71–91.

Sailes, G. A. (1993). An investigation of Black student attrition at a large, predominantly White, midwestern university. *Western Journal of Black Studies, 17,* 179–182.

Salovey, P., & Mayer, J. D. (1990). Emotional intelligence. *Imagination, Cognition, and Personality, 9,* 185–211.

Salthouse, T. A. (1996). The processing-speed theory of adult age differences in cognition. *Psychological Review, 103,* 403–428.

Sameroff, A. (1989). General systems and the regulation of development. In M. Gunner & E. Thelen (Eds.), *Systems and development.* Hillsdale, NJ: Erlbaum.

Sameroff, A., & Chandler, M. J. (1975). Reproductive risk and the continuum of caretaking casualty. In F. D. Horowitz, M. Hetherington, S. Scarr-Salapatek, & G. Siegel (Eds.), *Review of child development research* (Vol. 4, pp. 187–244). Chicago: University of Chicago Press.

Sampson, R. J., Morenoff, J. D., & Earls, F. (1999). Beyond social capital: Spatial dynamics of collective efficacy for children. *American Sociological Review, 64,* 633–660.

Sandmaier, M. (1996, May/June). More than love. *Family Therapy Networker,* pp. 21–33.

Sandnabba, N. K., & Alhberg, C. (1999). Parents' attitudes and expectations about children's cross-gender behavior. *Sex Roles, 40,* 249–264.

Sanford, N. (1962). *The American college: A psychological and social interpretation of higher learning.* New York: Wiley.

Savin-Williams, R. C. (1998). *And then I became gay: Young men's stories.* New York: Routledge.

Saxe, G. B. (1991). *Culture and cognitive development: Studies in mathematical understanding.* Hillsdale, NJ: Erlbaum.

Saxe, G. B., Guberman, S. R., & Gearhart, M. (1987). Social processes in early number development. *Monographs of the Society for Research in Child Development, 52*(Serial No. 216).

Saxon, S. V., & Etten, M. J. (1987). *Physical change and aging: A guide for the helping professions.* New York: Tiresias Press.

Scarr, S. (1992). Developmental theories for the 1990's: Development and individual differences. *Child Development, 63,* 1–19.

Scarr, S. (1993). Biological and cultural diversity: The legacy of Darwin for development. *Child Development, 64,* 1333–1353.

Scarr, S. (1997). Behavior-genetic and socialization theories of intelligence: Truce and reconciliation. In R. J. Sternberg & E. L. Girgorenko (Eds.), *Intelligence, heredity, and environment* (pp. 3–41). Cambridge, England: Cambridge University Press.

Scarr, S. (1998). American child care today. *American Psychologist, 53,* 95–108.

Scarr, S., & McCartney, K. (1983). How people make their own environments: A theory of genotype-environment effects. *Child Development, 54,* 424–435.

Scarr-Salapatek, S. (1976). Genetic determinants of infant behavior: An overstated case. In L. Lipsitt (Ed.), *Developmental psychobiology: The significance of infancy* (pp. 59–79). Hillsdale, NJ: Erlbaum.

Schacter, S. (1959). *The psychology of affiliation.* Stanford, CA: Stanford University Press.

Schacter, S., & Singer, J. E. (1962). Cognitive, social, and physiological determinants of emotional state. *Psychological Review, 69,* 379–399.

Schafer, R. B., & Keith, P. M. (1980). Equity and depression among married couples. *Social Psychology Quarterly, 43,* 430–435.

Schaffer, H. R., & Emerson, P. E. (1964). The development of social attachments in infancy. *Monographs of the Society for Research in Child Development, 29* (3, Serial No. 94).

Schaie, K. W. (1977–1978). Toward a stage theory of adult cognitive development. *Journal of Aging and Human Development, 8,* 129–139.

Schaie, K. W. (1994). The course of adult intellectual development. *American Psychologist, 49,* 304–313.

Schaie, K. W. (1996). *Intellectual development in adulthood: The Seattle Longitudinal Study.* New York: Cambridge University Press.

Schaie, K. W., & Willis, S. L. (2000). A stage theory model of adult cognitive development revisited. In R. L. Rubinstein, M. Moss, & M. H. Kleban (Eds.), *The many dimensions of aging* (pp. 175–193). New York: Springer.

Schauble, L. (1991). Belief revision in children: The role of prior knowledge and strategies for generating evidence. *Journal of Experimental Child Psychology, 49,* 31–57.

Schauble, L. (1996). The development of scientific reasoning in knowledge-rich contexts. *Developmental Psychology, 32,* 102–119.

Scheer, S. D., Unger, D. G., & Brown, M. (1994, February). *Adolescents becoming adults: Attributes for adulthood.* Poster presented at the biennial meeting of the Society for Research on Adolescence, San Diego, CA.

Schenkel, S., & Marcia, J. E. (1972). Attitudes toward premarital intercourse in determining ego identity status in college women. *Journal of Personality, 3,* 472–482.

Schindler, R. (1996). Mourning and bereavement among Jewish religious families: A time for reflection and recovery. *Omega, 33,* 121–129.

Schlegel, A., & Barry, H. III. (1991). *Adolescence: An anthropological inquiry.* New York: Free Press.

Schmitt-Rodermund, E., & Vondracek, F. W. (1999). Breadth of interests, exploration, and identity development in adolescence. *Journal of Vocational Behavior, 55,* 298–317.

Schneider, W. (1993). Acquiring expertise: Determinant of exceptional performance. In K. A. Heller, F. J. Monks, & A. H. Passow (Eds.), *International handbook of research and development of giftedness and talent.* Oxford, England: Pergamon Press.

Schneider, W., & Bjorklund, B. F. (1998). Memory. In W. Damon (Series Ed.) & R. S. Siegler (Vol. Ed.). *Handbook of child psychology: Vol. 2. Cognition, perception and language* (5th ed., pp. 467–522). New York: Wiley.

Schneider, W., & Pressley, M. (1997). *Memory development between 2 and 20* (2nd Ed.). New York: Springer.

Schneider-Rosen, K., Braunwald, K. G., Carlson, V., & Cicchetti, D. (1985). Current perspectives in attachment theory: Illustration from the study of maltreated infants. In I. Bretherton & E. Waters (Eds.), Growing points of attachment theory and research. *Monographs of the Society for Research in Child Development, 50*(Serial No. 209), 194–210.

Schneider-Rosen, K., & Cicchetti, D. (1984). The relationship between affect and cognition in maltreated infants: Quality of attachment and visual self-recognition. *Child Development, 55,* 648–658.

Schneider-Rosen, K., & Cicchetti, D. (1991). Early self-knowledge and emotional development: Visual self-recognition and affective reactions to mirror self-image in maltreated and non-maltreated toddlers. *Developmental Psychology, 27,* 481–488.

Schoenthaler, S., Doraz, W., & Wakefield, J. (1986). The impact of a low food additive and sucrose diet on academic performance in 803 New York City public schools. *The International Journal of Biosocial Research, 7,* 189–195.

Schommer, M., Crouse, A., & Rhodes, N. (1992). Epistemological beliefs and mathematical text comprehension: Believing it is simple does not make it so. *Journal of Educational Psychology, 84,* 435–443.

Schon, D. (1987). *Educating the reflective practitioner: Toward a new design for teaching and learning in the professions.* San Francisco: Jossey-Bass.

Schore, A. N. (1994). *Affect regulation and the origin of the self: The neurobiology of affective development.* Hillsdale, NJ: Erlbaum.

Schraw, G., & Moshman, D. (1995). Metacognitive theories. *Educational Psychology Review, 7,* 351–371.

Schubert, J. B., Bradley-Johnson, S., & Nuttal, J. (1980). Mother-infant communication and maternal employment. *Child Development, 51,* 246–249.

Schulster, J. R. (1996). In my era: Evidence for the perception of a special period of the past. *Memory, 4,* 145–158.

Schultz, L. H., Barr, D. J., & Selman, R. L. (2000). *The value of a developmental approach to evaluating character education programs: An outcome study of Facing History and Ourselves.* Manuscript submitted for publication.

Schultz, R., & Heckhausen, R. (1996). The life span model of successful aging. *American Psychologist, 51,* 702–713.

Schulz, R., & Curnow, C. (1988). Peak performance and age among superathletes: Track and field, swimming, baseball, tennis, and golf. *Journal of Gerontology, 43,* 113–120.

Scogin, F., & McElreath, L. (1994). Efficacy of psychosocial treatments for geriatric depression: A quantitative review. *Journal of Consulting and Clinical Psychology, 62,* 69–74.

Scott, C. G., Murray, G. C., Mertens, C., & Dustin, E. R. (1996). Student self-esteem and the school system: Perceptions and implications. *Journal of Educational Research, 89,* 286–293.

Scozarro, P. P., & Subich, L. M. (1990). Gender and occupational sex-type differences in job outcome factor perceptions. *Journal of Vocational Behavior, 36,* 109–119.

Sears, R., Maccoby, E., & Levin, H. (1957). *Patterns of child rearing.* Evanston, IL: Row, Peterson.

Seligman, M. E. P. (1993). *What you can change and what you can't.* New York: Ballantine Books.

Seligman, M. E. P. (1995). *The optimistic child.* Boston, MA: Houghton-Mifflin.

Selman, R. L. (1980). *The growth of interpersonal understanding: Developmental and clinical analysis.* Orlando, FL: Academic Press.

Selman, R. L., & Schultz, L. H. (1990). *Making a friend in youth: Developmental theory and pair therapy.* Chicago: University of Chicago Press.

Selman, R. L., Levitt, M. Z., & Schultz, L. H. (1997) The friendship framework: Tools for the assessment of psychosocial development. In R. L. Selman, C. L. Watts, & L. H. Schultz, (Eds.). (1997). *Fostering friendship: Pair therapy for treatment and prevention* (pp. 31–52). New York: Aldine de Gruyer.

Selman, R. L., Watts, C. L., & Schultz, L. H. (Eds.). (1997). *Fostering friendship: Pair therapy for treatment and prevention.* New York: Aldine de Gruyer.

Seltzer, V. C. (1982). *Adolescent social development: Dynamic functional interaction.* Lexington, MA: Heath.

Selye, H. (1980). The stress concept today. In I. L. Kutash, L. B. Schlesinger, & Assoc. (Eds.). *Handbook on stress and anxiety* (pp. 127–143). San Francisco: Jossey-Bass.

Senchak, M., & Leonard, K. E. (1992). Attachment styles and marital adjustment among newlywed couples. *Journal of Personality and Social Psychology, 9,* 51–64.

Shaffer, D. R. (1994). *Social and personality development* (3rd ed.). Pacific Grove, CA: Brooks/Cole.

Shaffer, D. R. (2000). *Social and personality development.* Belmont, CA: Wadsworth/Thomson.

Shapiro, A. F., Gottman, J. M., & Carrere, S. (2000). The baby and the marriage: Identifying factors that buffer against decline in marital satisfaction after the first baby arrives. *Journal of Family Psychology, 14,* 59–70.

Shavelson, R. J., Hubner, J. J., & Stanton, G. C. (1976). Validation of construct interpretations. *Review of Educational Research, 46,* 407–441.

Shaver, P. R., & Hazan, C. (1988). A biased overview of the study of love. *Journal of Personal and Social Relationships, 5,* 473–501.

Shaver, P. R., Hazan, C., & Bradshaw, D. (1988). Love as attachment: The integration of three behavioral systems. In R. J. Sternberg & M. L. Barnes (Eds.), *The psychology of love* (pp. 68–99). New Haven, CT: Yale University Press.

Shedler, J., & Block, J. (1990). Adolescent drug use and psychological health: A longitudinal inquiry. *American Psychologist, 45,* 612–630.

Sher, K. J., Bartholow, B. D., & Nanda, S. (2001). Short- and long-term effects of fraternity and sorority membership on heavy drinking: A social norms perspective. *Psychology of Addictive Behaviors, 15,* 42–51.

Shettles, L. B. (1961). Conception and birth ratios. *Obstetrics and Gynecology, 18,* 122–130.

Shiloh, S. (1996). Genetic counseling: a developing area of interest for psychologists. *Professional Psychology: Research and Practice, 27,* 475–486.

Shrum, W., & Cheek, N. H. (1987). Social structure during the school years: Onset of the degrouping process. *American Sociological Review, 52,* 218–223.

Siegel, A. W., & Scovill, L. C. (2000). Problem behavior: The double symptom of adolescence. *Development and Psychopathology, 12,* 763–793.

Siegel, M. (1987). Are sons and daughters treated more differently by fathers than mothers? *Developmental Review, 7,* 183–209.

Siegel, M., & Peterson, C. C. (1998). Preschoolers' understanding of lies and innocent and negligent mistakes. *Developmental Psychology, 34,* 332–341.

Siegler, R. S. (1987). Strategy choices in subtraction. In J. A. Sloboda & D. Rogers (Eds.), *Cognitive processes in mathematics* (pp. 81–106).

Siegler, R. S. (1996). *Emerging minds: The process of change in children's thinking.* New York: Oxford University Press.

Siegler, R. S. (1998). *Children's thinking* (3rd ed.). Upper Saddle River, NJ: Prentice Hall.

Siegler, R. S., & Shrager, J. (1984). Strategy choices in addition and subtraction: How do children know what to do? In C. Sophian (Ed.), *The origins of cognitive skills.* Hillsdale, NJ: Erlbaum.

Sigelman, C., & Mansfield, K. (1992). Knowledge of and receptivity to psychological treatment in childhood and adolescence. *Journal of Clinical Child Psychology, 21,* 2–9.

Signorella, M. L., & Liben, L. S. (1984). Recall and reconstruction of gender-related pictures: Effects of attitude, task difficulty, and age. *Child Development, 55,* 393–405.

Signorella, M. L., Bigler, R. S., & Liben, L. S. (1993). Developmental differences in children's gender schemata about others: A meta-analytic review. *Developmental Review, 13,* 147–183.

Silberg, J., Meyer, J., Pickles, A., Simonoff, E., Eaves, L., Hewitt, J., Maes, H., & Rutter, M. (1996). Heterogeneity among juvenile antisocial behaviors: Findings from the Virginia Twin Study of Adolescent Behavioural Development. In G. R. Bock & J. A. Goode (Eds.), *Genetics of criminal and antisocial behaviour* (pp. 76–86). Chichester, England: Wiley.

Silveira, M., DiPiero, A., Gerrity, M. S., & Feudtner, C. (2000). Patients' knowledge of options at the end of life. *Journal of the American Medical Association, 284,* 2483–2488.

Silverberg, S. B., & Steinberg, L. (1990). Psychological well-being of parents with early adolescent children. *Developmental Psychology, 26,* 658–666.

Silverman, P. (2000). Research, clinical practice, and the human experience: Putting the pieces together. *Death Studies, 24,* 469–478.

Simmons, R. G., & Blyth, D. A. (1987). *Moving into adolescence: The impact of pubertal change and school context.* Hawthorne, NY: Aldine de Gruyter.

Simmons, R. G., Blyth, D. A., & McKinney, K. L. (1983). The social and psychological effects of puberty on white females. In J. Brooks-Gunn & A. C. Petersen (Eds.), *Girls at puberty: Biological and psychological perspectives* (pp. 229–272). New York: Plenum.

Simpson, J. A. (1990). Influence of attachment styles on romantic relationships. *Journal of Personality and Social Psychology, 59,* 971–980.

Simpson, J. A., & Rholes, W. S. (1998a). Attachment in adulthood. In J. A. Simpson & W. S. Rholes (Eds). *Attachment theory and close relationships* (pp. 3–21). New York: Guilford Press.

Simpson, J. A., & Rholes, W. S. (1998b). *Attachment theory and close relationships.* New York: Guilford Press.

Simpson, J. A., Rholes, W. S., & Phillips, D. (1996). Conflict in close relationships: An attachment perspective. *Journal of Personality and Social Psychology, 71,* 899–914.

Singer, P., Martin, D., & Merrijoy, K. Quality of end-of-life care. *Journal of the American Medical Association, 281,* 163–168.

Sinnott, J. D. (1984). Postformal reasoning: The relativistic stage. In M. L. Commons, F. A. Richards, & C. Armon (Eds.), *Beyond formal operations: Late adolescent and adult cognitive development* (pp. 298–325). New York: Praeger.

Sinnott, J. D. (1998). *The development of logic in adulthood: Postformal thought and its applications.* New York: Plenum.

Skinner, B. F., & Vaughan, M. E. (1983/1997). *Enjoy old age: A practical guide.* New York: Norton.

Skodak, M., & Skeels, H. M. (1949). A final follow-up study of children in adoptive homes. *Journal of Genetic Psychology, 75,* 85–125.

Skogan, W. G. (1989). Social change and the future of violent crime. In T. R. Gurr (Ed.), *Violence in America: Vol. 1. The history of crime.* Newbury Park, CA: Sage.

Slaby, R. G., & Frey, K. S. (1975). Development of gender constancy and selective attention to same-sex models. *Child Development, 52,* 849–856.

Slade, A. (1999). Attachment theory and research: Implications for the theory and practice of individual psychotherapy with adults. In J. Cassidy & P. R. Shaver (Eds.), *Handbook of attachment: Theory, research, and clinical applications* (pp. 575–594). New York: Guilford Press.

Slavin, R. E. (1995). *Cooperative learning: Theory, research, and practice* (2nd ed.). Boston: Allyn & Bacon.

Slomkowski, C., & Dunn, J. (1996). Young children's understanding of other people's beliefs and feelings and their connected communication with friends. *Developmental Psychology, 32,* 442–447.

Smetana, J. G. (1988). Adolescents' and parents' conceptions of parental authority. *Child Development, 59,* 321–335.

Smetana, J. G. (1989). Toddlers' social interactions in the context of moral and conventional transgressions in the home. *Developmental Psychology, 25,* 499–508.

Smetana, J. G., & Asquith, P. (1994). Adolescents' and parents' conceptions of parental authority and adolescent autonomy. *Child Development, 65,* 1147–1162.

Smetana, J. G., & Braeges, J. L. (1990). The development of toddler's moral and conventional judgments. *Merrill-Palmer Quarterly, 36,* 329–346.

Smetana, J. G., Schlagman, N., & Adams, P. W. (1993). Preschool children's judgements about hypothetical and actual transgressions. *Child Development, 64,* 204–214.

Smith, C. L. (1979). Children's understanding of natural language hierarchies. *Journal of Experimental Child Psychology, 27,* 437–458.

Smith, C., & Krohn, M. D. (1955). Delinquency and family life among male adolescents: The role of ethnicity. *Journal of Youth and Adolescence, 24,* 69–93.

Smith, J., Staudinger, U. M., & Baltes, P. B. (1994). Occupational settings facilitating wisdom-related knowledge: The sample case of clinical psychologists. *Journal of Counseling and Clinical Psychology, 62,* 989–999.

Smith, R. E., & Smoll, F. L. (1990). Self-esteem and children's enhancement to youth coaching behaviors: A field study of self-enhancement processes. *Developmental Psychology, 26,* 987–993.

Snarey, J. R. (1993). *How fathers care for the next generation: A four-decade study.* Cambridge, MA: Harvard University Press.

Snowdon, D. A. (1997). Aging and Alzheimer's disease: Lessons from the Nun Study. *Gerontologist, 37,* 150–156.

Snyder, J. J., & Patterson, G. R. (1995). Individual differences in social aggression: A test of a reinforcement model of socialization info-processing mechanisms in children's social adjustment. *Behavior Therapy, 26,* 371–391.

Socha, T. J., & Socha, D. M. (1994). Children's task-group communication. In L. R. Frey (Ed.), *Group communication in context: Studies of natural groups* (pp. 227–246). Hillsdale, NJ: Erlbaum.

Sonderegger, T. B. (Ed.). (1992). *Perinatal substance abuse: Research findings and clinical implications.* Baltimore: John Hopkins University Press.

Sorich, L., & Dweck, C. S. (1996). Mastery-oriented thinking. In C. R. Snyder (Ed.), *Coping.* New York: Oxford University Press.

Sowell, E. R., Delis, D., Stiles, J., & Jernigan, T. L. (2001). Improved memory functioning and frontal lobe maturation between childhood and adolescence: A structural MRI study. *Journal of the International Neuropsychological Society, 7,* 312–322.

Spangler, G., & Grossmann, K. E. (1993). Biobehavioral organization in securely and insecurely attached infants. *Child Development, 64,* 1439–1450.

Spasjevic, J., & Alloy, L. B. (2001). Rumination as a common mechanism relating depressive risk factors to depression. *Emotion, 1,* 25–37.

Spaulding, J., & Balch, P. (1983). A brief history of primary prevention in the twentieth century: 1908 to 1980. *American Journal of Community Psychology, 11,* 59–80.

Spear, L. P. (2000). Neurobehavioral changes in adolescence. *Current Directions in Psychological Science, 9,* 111–114.

Spencer, M. B. (1982). Preschool children's social cognition and cultural cognition: A cognitive developmental interpretation of race dissonance findings. *Journal of Psychology, 112,* 275–286.

Spencer, M. B., & Markstrom-Adams, C. (1990). Identity processes among racial and ethnic minority children in America. *Child Development, 61,* 290–310.

Spenser, J. T. (1970). *The effects of systematic and token reinforcement on the modification of racial and color-concept attitudes in preschool-age children.* Unpublished master's thesis, University of Kansas.

Sperry, R. W. (1964). The great cerebral commissure. *Scientific American, 201,* 42–52.

Spokane, A. (1985). A review of research on person-environment congruence in Holland's theory of careers. *Journal of Vocational Behavior, 26,* 306–343.

Sroufe, L. A. (1989). Pathways to adaptation and maladaptation: Psychopathology as developmental deviation: The roots of maladaptation and competence. In D. Cicchetti (Ed.), *Rochester Symposium on Developmental Psychopathology: Vol. 1. The emergence of a discipline* (pp. 13–40). Hillsdale, NJ: Erlbaum.

Sroufe, L. A. (1996). *Emotional development: The organization of emotional life in the early years.* New York: Cambridge University Press.

Sroufe, L. A., Bennett, C., Englund, M., Urban, J., and Shulman, S. (1993). The significance of gender boundaries in preadolescence: Contemporary correlates and antecedents of boundary violation and maintenance. *Child Development, 64,* 455–466.

Sroufe, L. A., Fox, N. E., & Pancake, V. R. (1983). Attachment and dependency in developmental perspective. *Child Development, 54,* 1615–1627.

Sroufe, L. A., & Rutter, M. (1984). The domain of developmental psychopathology. *Child Development, 55,* 17–29.

Sroufe, L. A., & Waters, E. (1977). Attachment as an organizational construct. *Child Development, 48,* 1184–1199.

Stanhope, L., Bell, R. Q., & Parker-Cohen, N. Y. (1987). Temperament and helping behavior in preschool children. *Developmental Psychology, 23,* 347–353.

Stanovich, K. E. (1998). *How to think straight about psychology.* New York: Addison Wesley Longman.

Staudinger, U. M., & Baltes, P. B. (1996). Interactive minds: A facilitative setting for wisdom-related performance? *Journal of Personality and Social Psychology, 71,* 746–762.

Staudinger, U. M., Maciel, A. G., Smith, J., & Baltes, P. B. (1998). What predicts wisdom-related performance? A first look at personality, intelligence, and facilitative experiential contexts. *European Journal of Personality, 12,* 1–17.

Steele, C. (1997). A threat in the air: How stereotypes shape intellectual identity and performance. *American Psychologist, 52,* 613–629.

Steenbarger, B. N. (1991). All the world is not a stage: Emerging contextualist themes in counseling and development. *Journal of Counseling and Development, 70,* 288–296.

Stein, Z., Susser, M., Saenger, G., & Marolla, F. (1975). *Famine and human development: The Dutch hunger winter of 1944/45.* New York: Oxford University Press.

Steinberg, L. (1988). Reciprocal relation between parent-child distance and pubertal maturation. *Developmental Psychology, 24,* 122–128.

Steinberg, L. (1990). Interdependency in the family: Autonomy, conflict, and harmony. In S. Feldman & G. Elliot (Eds.), *At the threshold: The developing adolescent* (pp. 255–276). Cambridge, MA: Harvard University Press.

Steinberg, L. (1994). *Crossing paths: How your child's adolescence triggers your own crisis.* New York: Simon & Schuster.

Steinberg, L. (1996). *Beyond the classroom: Why school reform has failed and what parents need to do.* New York: Simon & Schuster.

Steinberg, L., & Avenevoli, S. (2000). The role of context in the development of psychopathology: A conceptual framework and some speculative propositions. *Child Development, 71,* 66–74.

Steinberg, L., & Belsky, J. (1991). *Infancy, childhood, and adolescence: Development in context.* New York: McGraw-Hill.

Steinberg, L., & Cauffman, E. (1995). The impact of employment on adolescent development. In R. Vasta (Ed.), *Annals of child development* (Vol. 11, pp. 131–166). London: Kingsley.

Steinberg, L., Dornbusch, S. M., & Brown, B. B. (1992). Ethnic differences in adolescent achievement: An ecological perspective. *American Psychologist, 47,* 723–729.

Steinberg, L., Fegley, S., & Dornbusch, S. M. (1993). The negative impact of part-time work on adolescent adjustment: Evidence from a longitudinal study. *Developmental Psychology, 29,* 171–180.

Steinberg, L., Lamborn, S. D., Darling, N., Mounts, N. S., & Dornbusch, S. M. (1994). Overtime changes in adjustment and competence among adolescents from authoritative, authoritarian, indulgent and neglectful families. *Child Development, 65,* 754–770.

Steinberg, L., Lamborn, S. D., Dornbusch, S. M., & Darling, N. (1992). Impact of parenting practices on adolescent achievement: Authoritative parenting, school involvement and encouragement to succeed. *Child Development, 63,* 1266–1281.

Steinberg, L., & Silverberg, S. B. (1986). The vicissitudes of autonomy in early adolescence. *Child Development, 57,* 841–851.

Steinhauser, K. E., Christakis, N. A., Clipp, E. C., McNeilly, M., McIntyre, L., & Tulsky, J. A. (2000). Factors considered important at the end of life by patients, family, physicians, and other care providers. *Journal of the American Medical Association, 284,* 2476–2482.

Stephen, J., Fraser, E., & Marcia, J. E. (1992). Moratorium-achievement (MAMA) cycles in lifespan identity development: Value orientations and reasoning system. *Journal of Adolescence, 15,* 283–300.

Sterling, C. M. & Van Horn, K. R. (1989). Identity and death anxiety. *Adolescence, 24,* 321–326.

Stern, D. (1985). *The interpersonal world of the infant.* New York: Basic Books.

Sternberg, R. J. (1985). *Beyond IQ: A triarchic theory of human intelligence.* New York: Cambridge University Press.

Sternberg, R. J. (1986). A triangular theory of love. *Psychological Review, 93,* 119–135.

Sternberg, R. J. (1998). *Love is a story.* New York: Oxford University Press.

Sternberg, R. J. (2001). What is the common thread of creativity: Its dialectical relation to intelligence and wisdom. *American Psychologist, 56,* 360–362.

Sternberg, R. J., & Grigorenko, E. L. (1999). *Our labeled children.* Reading, MA: Perseus Books.

Stevens-Long, J. (1973). The effect of behavioral context on some aspects of adult disciplinary practice and affect. *Child Development, 44,* 476–484.

Stevenson, H. W., Chen, C., & Lee, S. (1993). Mathematics achievement of Chinese, Japanese, and American children: Ten years later. *Science, 159,* 53–59.

Stevenson, H. W., & Stigler, J. W. (1992). *The learning gap: Why our schools are failing and what we can learn from Chinese and Japanese education.* New York: Simon & Schuster.

Stevenson-Hinde, J., & Marshall, P. J. (1999). Behavioral inhibition, heart period, and respiratory sinus arrhythmia: An attachment perspective. *Child Development, 70,* 805–816.

Stewart, A. J., & Vandewater, E. A. (1998). The course of generativity. In D. P. McAdams & E. de St. Aubin (Eds.), *Generativity and adult development: How and why we care for the next generation* (pp. 45–74). Washington, DC: American Psychological Association.

Stewart, N., Winborn, B., Johnson, R., Burks, H., & Engelkes, J. (1978). *Systematic counseling.* Englewood Cliffs, NJ: Prentice-Hall.

Stipek, D. J., Gralinski, J. H., & Kopp, C. B. (1990). Self-concept development in the toddler years. *Developmental Psychology, 26,* 972–977.

Stipek, D., Recchia, A., & McClintic, S. (1992). Self-evaluation in young children. *Monographs of the Society for Research in Child Development, 57*(1, Serial No. 226).

Stockard, J., & Johnson, M. M. (1992). *Sex and gender in society.* Englewood Cliffs, NJ: Prentice Hall.

Stoltenberg, C. D., & Delworth, U. (1987). *Supervising counselors and therapists: A developmental approach.* San Francisco: Jossey-Bass.

Stonewater, B. B., & Stonewater, J. K. (1983). Developmental clues: An aid for the practitioner. *NASPA Journal, 21,* 52–59.

Stonewater, B. B., & Stonewater, J. K. (1984). Teaching problem-solving: Implications from cognitive development research. *AAHE Bulletin, 36,* 7–10. Washington, DC: American Association for Higher Education.

Strachan, T., & Read, A. P. (2000). *Human molecular genetics* (2nd ed.). New York: Wiley & Sons.

Strassberg, Z., Pettit, K. A., Gregory, S., & Bates, J. E. (1994). Spanking in the home and children's subsequent aggression toward their peers. *Development and Psychopathology, 6,* 445–462.

Stratton, K., Howe, C., & Battaglia, F. (1996). *Fetal alcohol syndrome: Diagnosis, epidemiology, prevention, and treatment.* Washington, DC: National Academy Press.

Straus, M. A., & Gelles, R. J. (1990). *Physical violence in American families: Risk factors and adaptation to violence in 841 families.* New Brunswick, NJ: Transaction Books.

Straus, M. A., & Yodanis, C. L. (1996). Corporal punishment in adolescence and physical assault on spouses in later life: What accounts for the link? *Journal of Marriage and the Family, 58,* 825–841.

Strauss, A., & Corbin, J. (1990). *Basics of qualitative research: Grounded theory, procedures, and techniques.* Newbury Park: Sage.

Streissguth, A. P., & Dehaene, P. (1993). Fetal alcohol syndrome in twins of alcoholic mothers: Concordance of diagnosis and IQ. *American Journal of Medical Genetics, 47,* 857–861.

Strickberger, M. W. (1985). *Genetics* (3rd ed.). New York: Macmillan.

Stroebe, M. (1992). Coping with bereavement: A review of the grief work hypothesis. *Omega, 26,* 19–42.

Stroebe, M., & Schut, H. (1999). The dual process model of coping with bereavement: Rationale and description. *Death Studies, 23,* 197–224.

Stroebe, M. S., & Schut, H. (2001). Models of coping with bereavement: A review. In M. S. Stroebe, R. O. Hansson, W. Stroebe, & H. Schut (Eds.), *Handbook of bereavement research: Consequences, coping, and care* (pp. 375–403). Washington, DC: American Psychological Association.

Stroebe, M., & Stroebe, W. (1993). Determinants of adjustment to bereavement among younger widows and widowers. In M. Stroebe, W. Stroebe, & R. O. Hansson (Eds.), *Handbook of bereavement: Theory, research, and intervention* (pp. 208–226). New York: Cambridge University Press.

Strouse, J., Goodwin, M. P., & Roscoe, B. (1994). Correlates of attitudes toward sexual harassment among early adolescents. *Sex Roles, 31,* 559–577.

Strupp, H. H. (1988). What is therapeutic change? *Journal of Cognitive Psychotherapy, 2,* 75–82.

Stylianos, S. K., & Vachon, M. L. S. (1993). The role of social support in bereavement. In M. S. Stroebe, W. Stroebe, & R. O. Hansson (Eds.), *Handbook of bereavement: Theory, research, and intervention* (pp. 397–410). New York: Cambridge University Press.

Suda, W., & Fouts, G. (1980). Effects of peer presence on helping in introverted children. *Child Development, 51,* 1272–1275.

Sue, D., Mack, W. S., & Sue, D. W. (1998). Ethnic identity. In L.C. Lee & N. W. S. Zane (Eds.), *Handbook of Asian American Psychology* (pp. 289–323). Thousand Oaks, CA: Sage.

Sue, D. W., Arrendondo, P., & McDavis, R. J. (1992). Multicultural counseling competencies and standards: A call to the profession. *Journal of Counseling and Development, 70,* 477–486.

Suess, G. J., Grossmann, K. E., & Sroufe, L. A. (1992). Effects of infant attachment to mother and father on quality of adaptation in preschool: From dyadic to individual organization of self. *International Journal of Behavioral Development, 15,* 43–65.

Sullivan, H. S. (1953). *The interpersonal theory of psychiatry.* New York: Norton.

Suls, J. M., & Miller, R. L. (1977). *Social comparison processes: Theoretical and empirical perspectives.* Washington, DC: Hemisphere.

Super, D. E. (1957). *The psychology of careers.* New York: Harper & Row.

Super, D. E. (1972). Vocational development theory: Persons, positions, and processes. In J. M. Whiteley & A. Resnikoff (Eds.), *Perspectives on vocational development.* (pp. 13–33). Washington, DC: American Personnel and Guidance Association.

Super, D. E. (1984). Career and life development. In D. Brown & L. Brooks (Eds.), *Career choice and development* (pp. 192–234). San Francisco: Jossey-Bass.

Super, D. E. (1990). A life-span, life-space approach to career development. In D. Brown & I. Brooks (Eds.), *Career choice and development: Applying contemporary theories to practice* (pp. 197–261). San Francisco: Jossey-Bass.

Super, D. E., & Overstreet, P. L. (1960). *The vocational maturity of ninth-grade boys.* New York: Teachers College, Columbia University.

Taffel, R. (1996, May/June). The second family. *Family Therapy Networker,* 36–45.

Taffel, R. (2001). *The second family: How adolescent power is challenging the American family.* New York: St. Martin's Press.

Tajfel, H. (1981). *Human groups and social categories.* Cambridge, England: Cambridge University Press.

Takahashi, K. (1986). Examining the strange-situation procedure with Japanese mothers and 12-month-old infants. *Developmental Psychology, 22,* 265–270.

Takahashi, K. (1990). Are the key assumptions of the "Strange Situation" procedure universal? A view from Japanese research. *Human Development, 33,* 223–30.

Tannen, D. (1999). *The argument culture: Stopping America's war of words.* New York: Ballantine.

Tanner, J. M. (1962). *Growth at adolescence.* Oxford, England: Blackwell Scientific Publications.

Tanner, J. M. (1970). Physical growth. In P. H. Mussen (Ed.), *Carmichael's manual of child psychology* (3rd ed.) (Vol. 2, pp. 77–156). New York: Wiley.

Tanner, J. M. (1990) *Fetus into man: Physical growth from conception to maturity* (2nd ed.). Cambridge: Harvard University Press.

Tatum, B. D. (1997). *"Why are all the Black kids sitting together in the cafeteria?" and other conversations about race.* New York: Basic Books.

Tavris, C. (1998). A grain of salt: Some annotations to "Lessons of the new genetics." *Family Therapy Networker, 42,* 109.

Taylor, M. B. (1983). The development of the Measure of Epistemological Reflection. *Dissertation Abstracts International, 44,* 1065A (University Microfilms No. DA83–18, 441).

Taylor, M. S., Locke, E. A., Lee, C., & Gist, M. E. (1984). Type A behavior and faculty research productivity: What are the mechanisms? *Organizational Behavior and Human Performance, 34,* 402–418.

Taylor, S. E., & Brown, J. D. (1988). Illusion and well-being: A social-psychological perspective on mental health. *Psychological Bulletin, 103,* 193–210.

Teasley, S. D. (1995). The role of talk in children's peer collaborations. *Developmental Psychology, 31,* 207–220.

Tessler, M., & Nelson, K. (1994). Making memories: The influence of joint encoding on later recall by young children. *Consciousness and Cognition, 3,* 307–326.

Tesson, G., Lewko, J. H., & Bigelow, B. J. (1987). The social rules that children use in their interpersonal relations. *Contributions of Human Development, 18,* 36–57.

Teti, D. M., & Gelfand, D. M. (1991). Behavioral competence among mothers of infants in the first year: The mediational role of maternal self-efficacy. *Child Development, 62,* 918–929.

Tharp, R. G., & Gallimore, R. (1988). *Rousing minds to life: Teaching, learning, and schooling in social context.* New York: Cambridge University Press.

Thelen, E., & Smith, L. B. (1998). Dynamic systems theories. In W. Damon (Series Ed.) & R. M. Lerner (Vol. Ed.), *Handbook of child psychology: Vol. 1. Theoretical models of human development* (5th ed., pp. 563–634). New York: Wiley.

Thomas, A., & Chess, S. (1977). *Temperament and development.* New York: Brunner/Mazel.

Thompson, P. M., Giedd, J. N., Woods, R. P., MacDonald, D., Evans, A. C., & Toga, A. W. (2000). Growth patterns in the developing brain detected by using continuum mechanical tensor maps. *Nature, 404,* 190–193.

Thompson, R. A. (1998). Early sociopersonality development. In W. Damon (Series Ed.) & N. Eisenberg (Vol. Ed.), *Handbook of child psychology: Vol. 3. Social, emotional and personality development* (5th ed., pp. 25–104). New York: Wiley.

Thompson, R. A., & Leger, D. W. (1999). From squalls to calls: The cry as a developing socioemotional signal. In

B. Lester, J. Newman, & F. Pedersen (Eds.), *Biological and social aspects of infant crying.* New York: Plenum Press.

Thorne, B. (1986). Girls and boys together, but mostly apart: Gender arrangements in elementary schools. In W. W. Jartup and Z. Rubin (Ed.). *Relationships and development.* Hillsdale, NJ: Erlbaum.

Thorne, B. (1994). *Gender play: Girls and boys in school.* New Brunswick, NJ: Rutgers University Press.

Tidwell, M. O., Reis, H. T., & Shaver, P. R. (1996). Attachment, attractiveness, and social interaction: A diary study. *Journal of Personality and Social Psychology, 71,* 729–745.

Tinsley, H. E. A., Hinson, J. A., Tinsley, D. J., & Holt, M. S. (1993). Attributes of leisure and work experiences. *Journal of Counseling Psychology, 40,* 447–455.

Tisak, M. S. (1993). Preschool children's judgments of moral and personal events involving physical harm and property damage. *Merrill-Palmer Quarterly, 39,* 375–390.

Tobler, N. S. (1992). Drug prevention programs can work: Research findings. *Journal of addictive diseases, 11,* 1–28.

Toma, C. (1991a, April). *Speech genre of school in U.S. and Japan.* Paper presented at the meeting of the American Education Research Association, Chicago.

Toma, C. (1991b, October). *Explicit use of others' voices for constructing arguments in Japanese classroom discourse: An analysis of the use of reported speech.* Paper presented at the Boston University Conference on Language Development, Boston.

Tomlinson-Keasey, C., & Keasey, C. B. (1974). The mediating role of cognitive development in moral judgment. *Child Development, 45,* 291–298.

Townsend, J. W., Klein, R. E., Irwin, M. H., Owens, W., Yarbrough, C., & Engle, P. L. (1982). Nutrition and preschool mental development. In D. A. Wagner & H. W. Stevenson (Eds.), *Cross-cultural perspectives on child development.* San Francisco: Freeman.

Treboux, D. A., & Busch-Rossnagel, N. A. (1991). Sexual behavior, sexual attitudes, and contraceptive use, age differences in adolescence. In R. M. Lerner, A. C. Petersen, & J. Brooks-Gunn (Eds.), *Encyclopedia of adolescence* (Vol. 2). New York: Garland.

Trevarthen, C. (1988). Universal co-operative motives: How infants begin to know the language and culture of their parents. In G. Jahoda & I. M. Lewis (Eds.), *Acquiring culture: Cross-cultural studies in child development* (pp. 232–259). Lincoln: Nebraska University Press.

Troll, L. E., & Fingerman, K. L. (1996). Connections between parents and their adult children. In C. Magai & S. H. McFadden (Eds.), *Handbook of emotion, adult development, and aging* (pp. 185–205). San Diego: Academic Press.

Tronick, E. (1989). Emotions and emotional communication in infants. *American Psychologist, 44,* 112–119.

Tronick, E. Z., Als, H., & Brazleton, T. B. (1980). Monadic phase: A structural descriptive analysis of the infant-mother face to face interaction. *Merrill-Palmer Quarterly, 26,* 3–24.

Troseth, G. L., & DeLoache, J. S. (1996, April). *The medium can obscure the message: Understanding the relation between video and reality.* Poster presented at the biennial meeting of the International Conference on Infant Studies, Providence, RI.

Tucker, D. M. (1986). Neural control of emotional communication. In P. Blanck, R. Buck, & R. Rosenthal (Eds.), *Nonverbal communication in the clinical context.* University Park, PA: Penn State Press.

Tulving, E. (1985). How many memory systems are there? *American Psychologist, 40,* 385–398.

Turiel, E. (1978). Social regulation and domains of social concepts. In W. Damon (Ed.), *Social cognition: New directions for child development* (pp. 45–74). San Francisco: Jossey-Bass.

Turiel, E. (1998). The development of morality. In W. Damon (Ed.) & N. Eisenberg (Vol. Ed.), *Handbook of child psychology: Vol. 3. Social, emotional and personality development* (5th ed., pp. 863–932). New York: Wiley.

Turner, F. J. (1986). *Social work treatment: Interlocking theoretical approaches* (3rd Ed.). New York: Free Press.

Uba, L., & Huang, K. (1999). *Psychology.* New York: Longman.

Uccelli, P., Hemphill, L., Pan, B. A., & Snow, C. E. (1999). Telling two kinds of stories: Sources of narrative skill. In L. Batter & C. S. Tamis-LeMonda (Eds.), *Child psychology: A handbook of contemporary issues* (pp. 215–233). Philadelphia: Psychology Press.

Umana-Taylor, A. & Fine, M. A. (2001). Methodological implications of grouping Latino adolescents into one collective ethnic group. *Hispanic Journal of Behavioral Sciences, 23,* 347–362.

UNAIDS. (March, 2001). UNAIDS reports. *Curriculum Review, 40*(7), 3.

UNICEF. (1995). *The state of the world's children. 1995.* New York: United Nations.

United Nations Educational, Scientific, and Cultural Organization [UNESCO]. (1950/1978). Statement on race. Reprinted in *Man, 220,* 138–139.

U.S. Bureau of the Census. (1993). *Statistical abstract of the United States: 1993* (113th ed.). Washington, DC: U.S. Government Printing Office.

U.S. Bureau of the Census. (1997). *Current Population Reports, P60–200, Money Income in the United States: 1997 (with separate data on valuation of noncash benefits).* Washington, DC: U.S. Government Printing Office.

U.S. Bureau of the Census. (1998). *Statistical abstract of the United States: 1998* (118th ed.). Washington, DC: U.S. Government Printing Office.

U.S. Bureau of the Census. (1999). *Statistical abstract of the United States.* Washington, DC: U.S. Government Printing Office.

U.S. Bureau of Justice Statistics. (2000). *Violent crime rate trends.* Washington, DC: Author.

U.S. Bureau of Labor. Women's Bureau (1998). *The median wages of women as a proportion of the wages that men receive.* Washington D.C.: U.S. Bureau of Labor.

U.S. Department of Education. (1990). *National goals for education*. Washington, DC: U.S. Government Printing Office.

U.S. Department of Health and Human Services. (1998). *Health United States 1997* (DHHS Publication No. PHS 90–1232). Washington, DC: U.S. Government Printing Office.

University of Michigan. (1998). *Monitoring the future study*. Ann Arbor: Institute for Social Research.

Vachon, M. L., Rogers, J., Lyall, W. A., Lancee, W. J., Sheldon, A. R., & Freeman, S. J. J. (1982). Predictors and correlates of adaptation to conjugal bereavement. *American Journal of Psychiatry, 139,* 998–1002.

Vaillant, C. O., & Vaillant, G. E. (1993). Is the U-curve of marital satisfaction an illusion? A 40-year study of marriage. *Journal of Marriage and the Family, 55,* 230–239.

Vaillant, G. E. (1977). *Adaptation to life*. Boston: Little, Brown.

Vaillant, G. E. (1993). *The wisdom of the ego*. Cambridge, MA: Harvard University Press

Vaillant, G. E., & Koury, S. H. (1994). Late midlife development. In G. H. Pollock & S. I. Greenspan (Eds.), *The course of life*. Madison, CT: International Universities Press.

Vallerand, R. J., & O'Conner, B. P. (1989). Motivation in the elderly: A theoretical framework and some promising findings. *Canadian Psychology, 30,* 538–550.

van den Boom, D. C. (1994). The influence of temperament and mothering on attachment and exploration: An experimental manipulation of sensitive responsiveness among lower-class mothers with irritable infants. *Child Development, 65,* 1457–1477.

Vandereycken, W., & Van Deth, R. (1994). *From fasting saints to anorexic girls: The history of self-starvation*. New York: New York University Press.

van der Veer, R. (1996). Vygotsky and Piaget: A collective monologue. *Human Development, 39,* 237–242.

van der Veer, R., & Valsiner, J. (1994). *The Vygotsky reader*. Cambridge, MA: Blackwell.

van der Waal, J. (1989–1990). The aftermath of suicide: A review of empirical evidence. *Omega: Journal of Death and Dying, 20,* 149–171.

Vandewater, E. A., Ostrove, J. M., & Stewart, A. J. (1997). Predicting women's well-being in midlife: The importance of personality development and social role involvements. *Journal of Personality and Social Psychology, 72,* 1147–1160.

van Doorninck, W. J., Caldwell, B. M., Wright, C., & Frankenberg, W. K. (1981). The relationship between twelve-month home stimulation and school achievement. *Child Development, 52,* 1080–1083.

van Geert, P. (1998). A dynamic systems model of basic developmental mechanisms: Piaget, Vygotsky and beyond. *Psychological Review, 105,* 634–677.

Van Hesteren, F., & Ivey, A. E. (1990). Counseling and development: Toward a new identity for a profession in transition. *Journal of Counseling and Development, 68,* 524–528.

van IJzendoorn, M. H. (1993). The association between adult attachment representations and infant attachment, parental responsiveness, and clinical status: A meta-analysis on the predictive validity of the Adult Attachment Interview. *Psychological Bulletin, 113,* 404–410.

van IJzendoorn, M. H. (1995). Adult attachment representations, parental responsiveness, and infant attachment: A meta-analysis on the predictive validity of the Adult Attachment Interview. *Psychological Bulletin, 117,* 387–403.

van IJzendoorn, M. H., & Bakermans-Kranenburg, M. J. (1997). Intergenerational transmission of attachment: A move to the contextual level. In L. Atkinson & K. Zucker (Eds.), *Attachment and psychopathology*. New York: Guilford Press.

Vaughn, B. E., Egeland, B., Sroufe, L. A., & Waters, E. (1979). Individual differences in infant-mother attachment at twelve and eighteen months: Stability and change in families under stress. *Child Development, 50,* 971–975.

Ventura, J. N. (1987). The stresses of parenthood reexamined. *Family Relations, 36,* 26–29.

Vermeulen, M. E., & Minor, C. W. (1998). Context of career decisions: Women reared in a rural community. *The Career Development Quarterly, 46,* 230–245.

Veroff, J., Kulka, R. A., & Douvan, E. (1981). *Mental health in America: Patterns of help-seeking from 1957 to 1976*. New York: Basic Books.

Vispoel, W. P. (1995). Self-concept in the arts: An extension of the Shavelson, Hubner, and Stanton (1976) model. *Educational and Psychological Measurement, 53,* 1023– 1033.

Vivona, J. M. (2000). Parental attachment style of late adolescents: Qualities of attachment relationships and consequences for adjustment. *Journal of Counseling Psychology, 47,* 316–329.

von Bertalanffy, L. (1968). *General systems theory: Foundations, development, applications*. New York: Brazilles.

Vosniadou, S., & Brewer, W. F. (1992). Mental models of the earth: A study of conceptual change in childhood. *Cognitive Psychology, 24,* 535–585.

Vygotsky, L. S. (1931). Development of higher mental functions. In *Psychological research in the USSR*. Moscow: Progress Publishers.

Vygotsky, L. S. (1934). *Thought and language*. Cambridge, MA: MIT Press.

Vygotsky, L. S. (1978). *Mind and society*. Cambridge, MA: MIT Press.

Vygotsky, L. S., & Luria, A. R. (1930). The function and fate of egocentric speech. In Cattell, J. M. (Ed.), *Ninth international congress of psychology. Procedings and papers* (pp. 464–465). Princeton, NJ: Psychological Review Company.

Waddington, C. H. (1942). Canalization of development and the inheritance of acquired characters. *Nature, 150,* 563–564.

Waddington, C. H. (1957). *The strategy of the genes*. London: Allen & Unwin.

Wahlstein, D., & Gottlieb, G. (1997). The invalid separation of effects of nature and nurture: Lessons from animal experimentation. In R. J. Sternberg & E. L. Grigorenko (Eds.), *Intelligence, heredity, and environment* (pp. 303–322). New York: Cambridge University Press.

Waite, L. J., & Joyner, K. (2001). Emotional satisfaction and physical pleasure in sexual unions: Time horizon, sexual behavior, and sexual exclusivity. *Journal of Marriage and the Family, 63,* 247–264.

Walker, L. J. (1980). Cognitive and perspective-taking prerequisites for moral development. *Child Development, 51,* 131–139.

Walker, L. J. (1984). Sex differences in the development of moral reasoning: A critical review. *Child Development, 55,* 677–691.

Walker, L. J. (1995). Sexism in Kohlberg's moral psychology? In W. M. Kurtines & J. L. Gewirtz (Eds.), *Moral development: An introduction* (pp. 83–107). Boston: Allyn & Bacon.

Walker, L. J., & Pitts, R. C. (1998). Naturalistic conceptions of moral maturity. *Developmental Psychology, 34,* 403–419.

Walker, L. J., & Taylor, J. H. (1991). Family interactions and the development of moral reasoning. *Child Development, 62,* 264–283.

Walker-Barnes, C. J., & Mason, C. A. (2001). Ethnic differences in the effect of parenting on gang involvement and gang delinquency: a longitudinal; hierarchical linear modeling perspective. *Child Development, 72,* 1814–1831.

Waller, W. (1938). *The family: A dynamic interpretation.* New York: Cordon.

Wallerstein, J. S., Lewis, J. M., & Blakeslee, S. (2000). *The unexpected legacy of divorce: A 25-year landmark study.* New York: Hyperion.

Walters, K. L., & Simoni, J. M. (1993). Lesbian and gay male group identity attitudes and self-esteem: Implications for counseling. *Journal of Counseling Psychology, 40,* 94–99.

Ward, B. A., Mergendoller, J. R., Tikunoff, W. J., Rounds, T. S., Dadey, G. J., Mitman, A. L. (1982). *Junior high school transition study: Executive summary.* San Franciso: Far West Laboratory.

Ward, I. L. (1992). Sexual behavior: The product of perinatal hormonal and prepuberal social factors. In A. A. Gerall, H. Moltz, & I. L. Ward (Eds.), *Handbook of behavioral neurobiology: Vol. 11. Sexual differentiation* (pp. 157–180). New York: Plenum.

Ward, I. L., & Stehm, K. E. (1991). Prenatal stress feminizes juvenile play patterns in male rats. *Physiology and Behavior, 50,* 601–605.

Ward, L. M. (2002). Does television exposure affect emerging adults' attitudes and assumptions about sexual relationships? Correlational and experimental confirmation. *Journal of Youth and Adolescence, 31,* 1–15.

Wark, G. R., & Krebs, D. L. (1996). Gender and dilemma differences in real-life moral judgments. *Developmental Psychology, 32,* 220–230.

Warner, C. W., Santelli, J. S., Everett, S. A., Kann, L., Collins, J. L., Cassell, C., Morris, L., & Kolbe, L. J. (1998). Sexual behavior among U.S. high school students, 1990–1995. *Family Planning Perspectives, 30,* 170–172, 200.

Waterman, A. S. (1993). Developmental perspectives on identity formation. In J. E. Marcia, A. S. Waterman, D. R. Matteson, S. L. Archer, & J. L. Orlofsky (Eds.), *Ego identity: A handbook for psychosocial research* (pp. 42–68). New York: Springer-Verlag.

Waterman, A. S. (1994). Ethical considerations in interventions to promote identity development. In S. Archer (Ed.), *Interventions for adolescent identity development* (pp. 231–244). Thousand Oaks, CA: Sage.

Waters, E., Merrick, S., Treboux, D., Crowell, J., & Albersheim, L. (2000). Attachment security in infancy and early adulthood: A twenty-year longitudinal study. *Child Development, 71,* 684–689.

Watson, D., & Walker, L. M. (1996). The long-term stability and predictive validity of trait measures of affect. *Journal of Personality and Social Psychology, 70,* 567–577.

Watts, C. L., Nakkula, M. J., & Barr, D. (1997). Person-in-pairs, pairs-in-program: Pair therapy in different institutional contexts. In R. J. Selman, C. L. Watts, & L. H. Schultz (Eds.), *Fostering friendship: Pair therapy for treatment and prevention* (pp. 167–184). New York: Aldine de Gruyter.

Weinfield, N. S., Sroufe, L. A., & Egeland, B. (2000). Attachment from infancy to early adulthood in a high-risk sample: Continuity, discontinuity and their correlates. *Child Development, 71,* 695–702.

Weinraub, M., Clemens, L. P., Sockloff, A., Ethridge, R., Gracely, E., & Myers, B. (1984). The development of sex role stereotypes in the third year: Relationships to gender labeling, gender identity, sex-typed toy preferences, and family characteristics. *Child Development, 55,* 1493–1503.

Weizman, Z. O., & Snow, C. E. (2001). Lexical input as related to children's vocabulary acquisition: Effects of sophisticated exposure and support for meaning. *Developmental Psychology, 37,* 265–279.

Welch-Ross, M. K., & Schmidt, E. R. (1996). Gender-schema development and children's constructive story memory: Evidence for a developmental model. *Child Development, 67,* 820–835.

Wellman, H. M. (1990). *The child's theory of mind.* Cambridge, MA: MIT Press.

Wellman, H. M., Cross, D., & Watson, J. (2001). Meta-analysis of theory of mind development: The truth about false belief. *Child Development, 72,* 655–684.

Wentzel, K. (2002). Are effective teachers like good parents? Teaching styles and student adjustment in early adolescence. *Child Development, 73,* 287–301.

Wentzel, K. R. (1997). Student motivation in middle school: The role of perceived pedagogical caring. *Journal of Educational Psychology, 89,* 411–419.

Wentzel, K. R., & Asher, S. R. (1995). The academic lives of neglected, rejected, popular, and controversial children. *Child Development, 66,* 754–763.

Werner, H. (1948/1973). *The comparative psychology of mental development.* New York: International Universities Press.

Wertsch, J. V. (1991). *Voices of the mind: A sociocultural approach to mediated action.* Cambridge, MA: Harvard University Press.

Whitaker, D., & Miller, K. (2000). Parent-adolescent discussions about sex and condoms: Impact on peer influences of sexual risk behavior. *Journal of Adolescent Research, 15,* 251–273.

Whitbourne, S. K. (1989). Psychological treatment of the aging individual. *Journal of Integrative and Eclectic Psychotherapy, 8,* 161–173.

Whitbourne, S. K. (1996). *The aging individual: Physical and psychological perspectives.* New York: Springer.

Whiteley, J. M. (Ed.). (1984). Counseling psychology: A historical perspective. *The Counseling Psychologist, 12,* 1–26.

Whiting, B. B., & Edwards, C. P. (1988). *Children of different worlds: The formation of social behavior.* Cambridge, MA: Harvard University Press.

Wichstrom, L. (1999). The emergence of gender differences in depressed mood during adolescence: The role of intensified gender socialization. *Developmental Psychology, 35,* 232–245.

Wiesel, T. N., & Hubel, D. H. (1965). Comparison of the effects of unilateral and bilateral eye closure on cortical response in kittens. *Journal of Neurophysiology, 26,* 1029–1040.

Wilkinson, W. K., & Maxwell, S. (1991). The influence of college students' epistemological style on selected problem-solving processes. *Research in Higher Education, 32,* 333–350.

Willatts, P. (1989). Development of problem-solving in infancy. In A. Slater & G. Bremner (Eds.), *Infant development.* Hove, England: Erlbaum.

William T. Grant Foundation Commission on Work, Family, and Citizenship. (1988). *The forgotten half: Noncollege-bound youth in America.* New York: William T. Grant Foundation.

Williams, C. D. (1933). A nutritional disease of childhood associated with a maize diet. *Archives of Disease in Childhood, 8,* 423–433.

Williams, R., Jr. (1994). Basic biological mechanism. In A. Siegman & T. Smith (Eds.), *Anger, hostility, and the heart* (pp. 117–125). Hillsdale, NJ: Erlbaum.

Willis, S. L. (1996). Everyday problem solving. In J. E. Birren & K. W. Schaie (Series Eds.), R. P. Abeles, M. Gatz, & T. A. Salthouse (Vol. Eds.), *Handbook of the psychology of aging* (4th ed, pp. 287–307). San Diego, CA: Academic Press.

Wilson, J. G. (1973). *Environment and birth defects.* New York: Academic Press.

Wilson, S. A., Kovach, C. R., & Stearns, S. A. (1996). Hospice concepts in the care for end-stage dementia. *Geriatric Nursing, 17,* 6–10.

Wilson, T. D., & Brekke, N. (1994). Mental contamination and mental correction: Unwanted influences on judgments and evaluations. *Psychological Bulletin, 116,* 117–142.

Wilson, W. J. (1996). *When work disappears: The world of the new urban poor.* New York: Random House.

Wimmer, H., & Perner, J. (1983). Beliefs about beliefs: Representation and constraining function of wrong beliefs in young children's understanding of deception. *Cognition, 13,* 103–128.

Winnicott, D. W. (1965). *The maturational processes and the facilitating environment.* New York: International University Press.

Wolinsky, F. D., & Johnson, R. D. (1992). Perceived health status and mortality among older men and women. *Journal of Gerontology: Social Sciences, 47,* S304–S312.

Wood, D., Bruner, J. A., & Ross, G. (1976). The role of tutoring in problem solving. *Journal of Child Psychology and Psychiatry, 17,* 89–100.

Woodward, A. L. (1998). Infants selectively encode the goal object of an actor's reach. *Cognition, 69,* 1–34.

Worden, J. W. (1982). *Grief counseling and grief therapy: A handbook for the mental health practitioner.* New York: Springer.

Wortman, C. B., Battle, E. S., & Lemkau, J. P. (1997). Coming to terms with sudden, traumatic death of a spouse or child. In R. C. Davis & A. J. Lurigio (Eds.), *Victims of crime* (pp. 108–133). Thousand Oaks, CA: Sage.

Wortman, C. B., & Silver, R. C. (1987). Coping with irrevocable loss. In G. R. Vanden Bos & B. K. Bryant (Eds.), *Cataclysms, crises, and catastrophes: Psychology in action* (pp. 189–235). Washington, DC: American Psychological Association.

Wortman, C. B., & Silver, R. C. (1989). The myths of coping with loss. *Journal of Consulting and Clinical Psychology, 57,* 349–357.

Wortman, C. B., & Silver, R. C. (2001). The myths of coping with loss revisited. In M. S. Stroebe, R. O. Hansson, W. Stroebe, & H. Schut (Eds.), *Handbook of bereavement research: Consequences, coping and, care* (pp. 405–429). Washington, DC: American Psychological Association.

Wrenn, C. G. (1962). *The counselor in a changing world.* Washington, DC: American Personnel and Guidance Association.

Wright, B. A. (1983). *Physical disability: A psychosocial approach.* New York: Harper & Row.

Wyden, R. (2000). Steps to improve the quality of life for people who are dying. *Psychology, Public Policy, and Law, 6,* 575–581.

Xu, K., Shi, Z. M., Veeck, L. L., Hughes, M. R., & Rosewaks, Z. (1999). First unaffected pregnancy using preimplantation genetic diagnosis for sickle cell anemia. *Journal of the American Medical Association, 281,* 1701–1706.

Yager, S., Johnson, R. T., Johnson, D. W., & Snider, B. (1986). The impact of group processing on achievement in cooperative learning groups. *Journal of Social Psychology, 126,* 389–397.

Yalom, I. (1980). *Existential psychotherapy.* New York: Basic Books.

Yang, K. S. (1988). Will societal modernization eventually eliminate cross-cultural psychological differences? In M. H. Bond (Ed.), *The cross-cultural challenge to social psychology* (pp. 67–85). Newbury Park, CA: Sage.

Yates, M., & Youniss, J. (1996). A developmental perspective on community service in adolescence. *Social Development, 5,* 85–111.

Yatkin, U. S., & McClaren, D. S. (1970). The behavioral development of infants recovering from severe malnutrition. *Journal of Mental Deficiency Research, 14,* 25–32.

Yoon, J., Yoon, C., Lim, H., Huang, Q., Kang, Y., Pryn, K., Hirasawa, K., Sherwin, R., & Jun, H. (1999). Control of autoimmune diabetes in NOD mice by GAD expression or suppression in Beta cells. *Science, 284,* 1183.

Yoshida, T., Kojo, K., & Kaku, H. (1982). A study on the development of self-presentation in children. *Japanese Journal of Educational Psychology, 30,* 120–127.

Yoshinaga, K., & Mori, T. (Eds.). (1989). *Development of preimplantation embryos and their environment.* New York: Wiley-Liss.

Youngblade, L. M., & Belsky, J. (1992). Parent-child antecedents of 5-year-olds' close friendships: A longitudinal analysis. *Developmental Psychology, 28,* 700–713.

Younger, A. J., Gentile, C., & Burgess, K. (1993). Children's perceptions of withdrawal: Changes across age. In K. H. Rubin & J. Asendorpf (Eds.), *Social withdrawal, inhibition, and shyness in childhood* (pp. 215–236). Hillsdale, NJ: Erlbaum.

Zacks, R. T., & Hasher, L. (1994). Directed ignoring: Inhibitory regulation of working memory. In D. Dagenbach & T. H. Carr (Eds.), *Inhibitory mechanisms in attention, memory, and language* (pp. 241–264). San Diego, CA: Academic Press.

Zacks, R. T., Hasher, L., & Li, K. Z. H. (2000). Human memory. In F. I. M. Craik & T. A. Salthouse (Eds.), *The handbook of aging and cognition* (2nd ed., pp. 293–357). Mahwah, NJ: Erlbaum.

Zagar, R., Arbit, J., Sylvies, R., & Busch, K. G. (1991). Homicidal adolescents: A replication. *Psychological Reports, 67,* 1235–1242.

Zahn-Waxler, C., Cole, P. M., Welsh, J. D., & Fox, N. A. (1995). Psychophysiological correlates of empathy and prosocial behaviors in preschool children with problem behaviors. *Development and Psychopathology, 7,* 27–48.

Zahn-Waxler, C., Iannotti, R. J., Cummings, E. M., & Denham, S. (1990). Antecedents of problem behaviors in children of depressed mothers. *Development and Psychopathology, 2,* 349–366.

Zahn-Waxler, C., & Kochanska, G. (1990). The origins of guilt. In R. Thompson (Ed.), *The 36th Annual Nebraska Symposium on Motivation: Socioemotional development* (pp. 183–258). Lincoln: University of Nebraska Press.

Zahn-Waxler, C., & Radke-Yarrow, M. (1982). The development of altruism: Alternative research strategies. In N. Eisenberg (Ed.), *The Development of prosocial behavior* (pp. 109–137). New York: Academic Press.

Zahn-Waxler, C., Radke-Yarrow, M., Wagner, E., & Chapman, M. (1992). Development of concern for others. *Developmental Psychology, 28,* 126–136.

Zahn-Waxler, C., Robinson, J., & Emde, R. N. (1992). The development of empathy in twins. *Developmental Psychology, 28,* 1038–1047.

Zarbatany, L., Hartmann, D. P., & Rankin, D. B. (1990). The psychological functions of preadolescent peer activities. *Child Development, 61,* 1067–1080.

Zarit, S. H., & Zarit, J. M. (1998). *Mental disorders in older adults: Fundamentals of assessment and treatment.* New York: Guilford.

Zaslow, M. J., & Hayes, C. D. (1986). Sex differences in children's responses to psychosocial stress: Toward a cross-context analysis. In M. E. Lamb, A. L. Brown, & B. Rogoff (Eds.), *Advances in developmental psychology* (Vol. 4). Hillside, NJ: Erlbaum.

Zea, M. C., Reisen, C. A., Beil, C., & Caplan, R. D. (1997). Predicting intention to remain in college among ethnic minority and nonminority students. *Journal of Social Psychology, 137,* 149–160.

Zelazo, P. D., Helwig, C. C., & Lau, A. (1996). Intention, act, and outcome in behavioral prediction and moral judgment. *Child Development, 67,* 2478–2492.

Zelinski, E. M., Gilewski, M., & Schaie, K. W. (1993). Individual differences in cross-sectional and 3-year longitudinal memory performance across the adult life span. *Psychology and Aging, 8,* 176–186.

Zigler, E. (1994). Reshaping early childhood intervention to be a more effective weapon against poverty. *American Journal of Community Psychology, 22,* 894–906.

Zigler, E., & Styfco, S. J. (1994). Head Start: Criticisms in a constructive context. *American Psychologist, 49,* 127–132.

Zucker, R. A. (1994). Pathways to alcohol problems and alcoholism: A development account of the evidence for multiple alcoholisms and for contextual contributions to risk. In U.S. Department of Health and Human Services. The development of alcohol problems: Exploring the biopsychosocial matrix of risk. *NIHHS Research Monograph, 26,* 255–289). Washington, DC: DHHS.

Zuckerman, M. (1979). *Sensation seeking: Beyond the optimal level of arousal.* Hillsdale, NJ: Erlbaum.

Zuckerman, M. (1994). *Behavioral expressions and bisocial bases of sensation seeking.* Cambridge, England: Cambridge University Press.

Author Index

Subject Index